FOURTH EDITION

ACCOUNTING INFORMATION SYSTEMS AND BUSINESS ORGANIZATIONS

FOURTH EDITION

ACCOUNTING INFORMATION SYSTEMS AND BUSINESS ORGANIZATIONS

Barry E. Cushing
The Pennsylvania State University

Marshall B. Romney
Brigham Young University

Addison-Wesley Publishing Company
Reading, Massachusetts ▪ Menlo Park, California ▪ Don Mills, Ontario
▪ Wokingham, England ▪ Amsterdam ▪ Sydney ▪ Singapore ▪ Tokyo
▪ Madrid ▪ Bogotá ▪ Santiago ▪ San Juan

Sponsoring Editor: Frank Burns
Copy Editor: Susan Badger
Text Designer: Catherine L. Dorin
Cover Designer: Marshall Henrichs
Art Editor: Richard Morton
Illustrator: Dixie Clark Production
Permissions Editor: Mary Dyer
Manufacturing Supervisor: Hugh Crawford

Materials from Uniform CPA Examination Questions and Unofficial Answers, copyright ©
1956, 1958, 1961, 1962, 1963, 1964, 1965, 1969, 1971, 1972, 1973, 1974, 1975, 1978, 1979, 1980,
1983, 1984 by the American Institute of Certified Public Accountants, Inc., are reprinted or
adapted with permission.

Materials from the Certificate in Management Accounting Examinations, copyright © 1973,
1974, 1975, 1976, 1977, 1978, 1979, 1980, 1981, 1982, 1983 by the National Association of Accountants, are reprinted or adapted with permission.

Materials from the Certified Internal Auditor Examination Questions and Unofficial Answers,
copyright © 1974, 1976, 1977, 1978, 1979, 1980, 1983 by The Institute of Internal Auditors,
Inc., are reprinted or adapted with permission.

Materials from the Society of Management Accountants of Canada Examinations, copyright ©
1976, 1979, 1981, 1982, 1983 by the Society of Management Accountants of Canada, are reprinted or adapted with permission.

Library of Congress Cataloging-in-Publication Data

Cushing, Barry E.
   Accounting information systems and business organizations.

   Includes bibliographies and index.
   1. Accounting—Data processing.   2. Information
storage and retrieval systems—Accounting.   3. Management
information systems.   I. Romney, Marshall B.   II. Title.
HF5679.C84 1987   657'.028'5   86-17301
ISBN 0-201-10317-6

Reprinted with corrections June, 1987

DEFGHIJ-DO-898

Preface

Today's professional accountant performs in a world that is dynamic and complex. Progress in information technology is being made at an increasing rate. Patterns of organizational behavior are evolving rapidly. Economic and legal considerations are having a much greater impact upon the work of accountants. All of these environmental trends require the accounting student of today to be better prepared than ever before to enter the accounting profession.

A central feature of accounting work in today's business world is the interaction of accounting professionals with computer-based information systems. As the major users of information systems in organizations, accountants must participate in their design and understand their operation. Accounting managers must measure and evaluate the performance of information systems. Internal and external auditors must assess the quality of information processing and evaluate the accuracy of information output. The major share of the work of accounting consultants is in the design, implementation, and evaluation of information systems.

To be adequately prepared for a career in the accounting profession, today's accounting student must acquire a basic knowledge of computer-based information systems and their role in the performance of the accounting function in contemporary business organizations. Fundamental to this basic knowledge are: (1) an understanding of the patterns of flow of accounting data and information in business; (2) a familiarity with the tools of accounting systems work, such as flowcharting; (3) an understanding of the use of computer technology in information processing; and (4) a thorough knowledge of the principles of internal control and their application in various organizational contexts. The objective of this book is to provide students with these essential elements of preparation for an accounting career, to help build a foundation for the development of today's accounting students into tomorrow's users, auditors, and managers of computer-based information systems.

This book is intended for use in a one-semester course in accounting information systems at the advanced undergraduate or graduate level. Introductory financial and managerial accounting courses are necessary prerequisites, and an introductory course in data processing that covers a computer language is helpful. The book could also be used as the main text in graduate or advanced undergraduate courses in management information systems.

Organization

The fourth edition has the same basic structure as the first three editions. Part One, consisting of four chapters, reviews several underlying concepts that are basic to an understanding of any kind of accounting information system—regardless of the technology employed. These concepts include principles and practices of business organization, responsibility accounting, forms design, information coding, accounting information processing cycles, and internal control concepts and techniques.

Part Two, which contains five chapters, examines contemporary information technology from an accounting perspective. The first three of these chapters introduce basic hardware and software concepts for both large computers and microcomputers. The important techniques of systems and program flowcharting are introduced here. The last two chapters of Part Two review the more advanced topics of data communications systems and data base management systems.

Part Three, which encompasses six chapters, explores a variety of issues relating to the management of information technology, including systems planning, management involvement in systems activities, and systems selection and acquisition. Also covered in Part Three are numerous techniques of systems work, including document flowcharting, work measurement, structure charts, feasibility studies, point scoring, PERT, and various control and audit techniques.

Part Four, which consists of five chapters, integrates the first three parts by providing a detailed look at applications of accounting information systems in a typical business organization. This section discusses the information needs of the marketing, purchasing, production, personnel, and finance functions in business and explains the accounting processes and data bases that help to fulfill those needs. Within each application area, manual, computerized batch processing, and real-time systems are described and contrasted.

Changes in the Fourth Edition

One new chapter has been added to this edition, and five chapters have been substantially rewritten and condensed into four chapters. Significant changes have been made to several of the other fifteen chapters. Learning objectives and a chapter outline now appear at the beginning of each chapter, and a brief chapter summary has been added to the end of each chapter. Many new photographs and illustrations have been incorporated. A comprehensive 25-page glossary has been added and appears immediately following the final chapter of the text. Finally, many new problems and cases have been added, while many others have been revised to reflect changes made in the text.

The following list summarizes by chapter the major changes that have been made in the text.

1. Chapter 1 contains an expanded discussion of information system resources that compares and contrasts manual systems, small computer systems, and large-scale computer systems.

2. Chapter 3 has been substantially rewritten. The section on File Processing has been replaced by a section on Elements of Accounting Cycles that contains expanded coverage of file processing concepts and their accounting applications.

3. Chapter 4 now contains a discussion of management control and its relationship to internal control. Also, an expanded discussion of the use of batch totals in locating numerical data processing errors has been added to Chapter 4.

4. Chapters 5 and 6 of the third edition were replaced by a newly written Chapter 5 that provides an up-to-date summary of hardware concepts. It contains a review of the major components of a computerized information system, including the central processing unit, storage devices and media, input/output devices, and systems flow charts.

5. Chapter 6 is a substantially revised version of Chapter 7 of the third edition. It contains a review of software concepts, including topics such as the levels of computer languages, systems software, applications software, writing computer programs, and programming and documentation tools.

6. Chapter 7 is a new chapter covering microcomputer hardware and software and the uses of microcomputers in accounting and auditing.

7. Chapter 8 is a substantially rewritten version of Chapter 9 of the third edition. Its focus is data communications systems. Topics include data communications hardware and software, communications channels, data communications networks, and data communications applications.

8. Chapter 9 covers data base and file-oriented systems, and replaces Chapter 8 of the third edition. It includes a discussion of the file and data base approaches to data storage, the logical and physical view of data, data base management systems, both file and data base organization and access, and file and data base design considerations.

9. Chapter 10 contains expanded discussions of the organizational location of the systems function, the impact of microcomputers and communications networks on the degree of centralization of the information systems function, and the use of information technology assessment in systems planning.

10. In Chapter 11 the presentation of document flowcharting has been revised to be consistent with contemporary approaches to the subject. Descriptions of prototyping and structure (HIPO) charts have also been added to this chapter.

11. Chapter 12 contains a significantly revised discussion of the costs and benefits of computer acquisition.

12. In Chapter 13 the description of PERT has been significantly revised to improve its understandability.

13. Chapter 14 has been revised to reflect recent AICPA literature on internal control, and also contains an expanded discussion of online access controls.

14. All document flowcharts in Chapters 16–20 have been revised to be consistent with the modernized treatment of the subject presented in Chapter 11.

15. Chapter 17 now contains a discussion of just-in-time systems of inventory and production management, and an expanded discussion of real-time systems for purchasing and inventory management.

16. Chapter 18 now includes a discussion of factory automation, including such topics as CAD/CAM, numerical control, robotics, and flexible manufacturing systems.

17. Chapter 20 contains a substantially revised discussion of real-time financial information systems.

Teaching Aids

From the very beginning, the guiding objective in preparing this textbook has been to simplify the teaching of accounting information systems by freeing the instructor from the burden of locating, assembling, and distributing materials, thus enabling him or her to concentrate on classroom presentation and discussion. We view this book and the related materials available from Addison-Wesley as not just a textbook but as a teaching system. The major elements of this teaching system are described below.

1. Over 220 figures containing photographs and diagrams illustrating major concepts are contained in the book.

2. Over 320 discussion questions and problems and cases suitable for assignment to students appear in the book. These include selected items from professional examinations, such as the CPA, CMA, CIA, and SMAC examinations, for those instructors who wish to expose their students to them.

3. A bibliography is included at the back of each chapter, and footnotes have been used liberally within the text. This should help those instructors who wish to locate background material or additional readings for assignment to their students.

4. An Instructor's Resource Guide is available to instructors who consider adopting the book. For each chapter this guide contains: (a) a one-page outline of major topics, suitable for reproduction in transparency form; (b) transparency masters of many of the tables and charts in the chapter; (c) a brief discussion of the content and objectives of each problem in the text; (d) guidelines for leading a discussion of each discussion question; and (e) suggested solutions for each of the problems and cases. Further-

more, the solutions to the problems and cases have been paginated in a modular fashion in order to facilitate the preparation of transparencies of the solutions.

5. A Test Bank containing numerous multiple choice questions and solutions, organized by text chapter, appears at the back of the Instructor's Resource Guide.

6. The book *Accounting Information Systems: A Book of Readings with Cases,* by James R. Davis and Barry E. Cushing (Addison-Wesley, 1987), is being published simultaneously with the publication of this textbook. It is intended to supplement this book with outside readings organized according to the same topical outline, and with more complex and comprehensive cases.

By incorporating these features we have attempted to develop a comprehensive teaching package that will render the teaching of accounting systems courses an enjoyable experience rather than an unwelcome burden.

Acknowledgments We are indebted to numerous faculty members throughout the world who have adopted the earlier editions and who have been generous with their suggestions for improvement, and to those who participated in reviewing the fourth edition as it was being developed. Among those who have been most helpful are A. Faye Borthick of the University of Tennessee, Walter Campbell of Millsaps College, Eric Denna of Michigan State University, Edward J. Gurry of Boston University, Lynn J. McKell of Brigham Young University, Denise Nitterhouse of DePaul University, Richard S. Savich of the University of Southern California, James H. Scheiner of the University of Tennessee, and Charles W. Stanley of Baylor University.

We are grateful for permission received from four professional accounting organizations to use problems and unofficial solutions from their past professional examinations in this book. Thanks are extended to the American Institute of Certified Public Accountants for use of CPA Examination materials, to the Institute of Certified Management Accountants of the National Association of Accountants for use of CMA Examination materials, to the Institute of Internal Auditors for use of CIA Examination materials, and to the Society of Management Accountants of Canada for use of SMAC Examination materials.

Special thanks are extended to Jim Stegall, Darv Whipple, and Steve Allen, Masters candidates at Brigham Young University, for their assistance in preparing problems, problem solutions, and the glossary for this edition, and for other helpful suggestions.

Suggestions and comments from users on the text and the related materials are welcome.

University Park, Pennsylvania   Barry E. Cushing
Provo, Utah   Marshall B. Romney
January 1987

Contents

3

Accounting Information Processing: Elements and Procedures   62

4

Control and Accounting Information Systems   98

PART TWO

THE TECHNOLOGY OF INFORMATION SYSTEMS

5

A Review of Mainframe Computer Hardware   133

6
A Review of Software Concepts   190

7
Microcomputers and Accounting Information Systems   240

8
Data Communications and Advanced Systems   288

9

Data Base and File Oriented Systems   340

PART THREE

SYSTEMS MANAGEMENT

10

Basic Issues of Systems Management   397

CONCEPTUAL FOUNDATIONS OF ACCOUNTING INFORMATION SYSTEMS

C H A P T E R   1

Accounting Information Systems: An Overview

LEARNING OBJECTIVES

Careful study of this chapter should enable students to:

- ☐ Describe the role of information systems in organizations.
- ☐ Describe the basic features of accounting information systems.
- ☐ Explain why the study of accounting

information systems is an important part of their educational program.

- ☐ Outline the major steps in the information systems life cycle.

CHAPTER OUTLINE

Accounting information is essential to the efficient management of economic affairs. Within a business organization, accounting information is produced by a system. Most readers are probably familiar with many of the elements of such systems. These elements include journals, ledgers, and other records, as well as the people who carry out the procedures necessary to the operation of the system. And increasingly they include machines designed to relieve people of the burden of routine and repetitive tasks. The purpose of this book is to develop an understanding of these accounting information systems—the elements they contain, the ways in which they are designed, and the role they play in supplying information to those requiring it, both within the business organization and outside it.

Why Study Accounting Information Systems?

Accounting students often ask why a course in accounting information systems is a necessary part of the accounting curriculum. Such a course is quite different in structure and content from other accounting courses, which leads students to question its relevance. However, there are several reasons why the student's knowledge of accounting is not complete without an understanding of accounting information systems.

In most other accounting courses, the student is placed in the role of an information user. It is assumed that certain information is available to the student, who will address such questions as (1) how to account for the information; (2) how to report the information to managers, stockholders, taxing authorities, or other government bodies; or (3) how to audit the information. These questions are certainly relevant, but by focusing only on these, most accounting courses virtually ignore another very relevant question—Where did the information come from?

The answer is, of course, that the information used by accountants, managers, auditors, etc., is produced by an information system. This raises a number of other questions: (1) Who decides what information is relevant for a particular purpose? (2) How do they make that decision? (3) What steps are required in order to obtain the relevant information and make it available? (4) What resources (people, machines, money, etc.) are consumed in obtaining the information and making it available? (5) What is the most cost-effective way of coordinating the necessary resources to perform the required steps? (6) Is the value of the information worth the cost of producing it? (7) How can it be ensured that the information is available on a timely basis? (8) How can it be ensured that the information is accurate and reliable? These are the kinds of questions that are addressed by a course in accounting information systems. Virtually all organizations must find answers to these questions—and in most organizations the accountant plays a central role (often a dominant role) in finding these answers.

The accounting student of today may tomorrow become an auditor, accountant, manager, or management consultant. Each of these positions requires a close involvement with the information system. For example, one of the auditor's main objectives is to evaluate the accuracy of information, and one of the most common approaches used by auditors for this purpose is a detailed assessment of the reliability of the information system. The accountant—whether in industry, government, or nonprofit organizations—is likely to have a major responsibility for the evaluation of existing information systems and the design of new ones. Accountants at the managerial level are often directly responsible for the management of the information systems department. Finally, many accountants become management consultants because of the opportunity to employ more effectively their expertise in the design, evaluation, and management of information systems.

Within the past several years, an ongoing revolution in information technology has continued to exert a profound effect on accounting information systems (as well as all other types of information systems). The driving force behind this revolution is, of course, the computer. In virtually all large organizations, and in many smaller ones as well, the computer is responsible for processing accounting transactions and preparing accounting reports. As computers become smaller, faster, more reliable, easier to use, and less expensive, this trend toward the computerization of accounting work will continue. This development makes it even more essential for the accounting student to understand accounting information systems and especially the role of the computer in these systems. The organization of the future that does not use a computer to do its accounting work will be a rare exception. Therefore a course in accounting information systems that emphasizes the role of the computer is an essential element of a student's preparation for a career in accounting.

This belief is widely shared by accounting educators as well as professional accountants. For example, the following statement was issued by a joint task force of the American Accounting Association (representing accounting educators) and the American Institute of Certified Public Accountants.

> The accounting graduate will very likely be involved in the use of the computer. Corporations are expanding their data processing applications, and CPA [certified public accountant] firms are also increasingly using computer systems in-house. (The availability of lower cost and easier to use computing equipment has accelerated this trend.)
>
> The accounting graduate should not start a career in awe—or fear—of a computerized accounting system. Rather, the graduate should have a good appreciation of the benefits and drawbacks of a computer system as well as a general understanding of its operation.[1]

It is true that most undergraduate accounting and business curricula have incorporated computer education for many years. However, many prominent

---

[1]Committee on Accounting Education, American Accounting Association, and Computer Education Subcommittee, American Institute of Certified Public Accountants, "Inclusion of EDP in an Undergraduate Auditing Curriculum: Some Possible Approaches," *The Accounting Review* **49** (October 1974): 863.

practicing accountants feel that the emphasis in such education has been mis-placed. For example, one describes the educational deficiencies of newly hired staff auditors as follows.

> The first [deficiency] involves computer applications in business. Their [students] experience with computers has been in a problem-solving mode, using canned packages or programming rather simple mathematical problems. They seem to have very little feel for accounting transaction processing: the concepts of files, transaction updates, editing, reporting, and so forth. The second common deficiency was in flowcharting analysis and documentation, not strictly limited to computers, but emphasizing computers.[2]

Although general course work dealing with computers and electronic data processing is important and useful, many accounting students are still left with a gap in their knowledge of how modern information technology relates to accounting. This book is written with the intention of closing this gap and providing a more solid foundation of knowledge for future accounting grad-uates who will participate in the evaluation, design, audit, and management of accounting information systems.

The Role of the Accounting Information System

Virtually all organizations—from businesses and government agencies to hos-pitals, educational institutions, and churches—have an accounting informa-tion system. Among these groups, the accounting information systems of busi-ness organizations tend to be the most highly developed and innovative and, for this reason, will be the primary focus of this book. However, many of the same concepts, techniques, and principles are equally applicable to account-ing information systems in other kinds of organizations.

The modern business organization served by the accounting information system is a very complex institution. Such an organization may employ thou-sands of people in tasks ranging from the development and engineering of new products to the management of a large sales force. The activities of prom-inent companies are of interest to many segments of society—customers, sup-pliers, employees, lenders, stockholders, and the various governments under whose jurisdiction they operate.

How can the modern business organization plan, coordinate, and control the multitude of activities that it undertakes? How can it supply information to the many people and institutions that are interested in its activities? The accounting information system plays a vital role in accomplishing these tasks. Figure 1.1 shows the relationship of the accounting information system to the business organization and to the environment (indicated by the large E-shaped structure to the left) of which the business organization is a part. Several as-pects of this diagram will be referred to at various points in this section.

---

[2]Michael R. Moore, "Undergraduate Computer Curriculum Requirements for Entering Staff in Accounting and Auditing," in *Education for Expanding Computer Curriculums,* ed. Daniel L. Sweeney (New York: American Institute of Certified Public Accountants, 1976), p. 7.

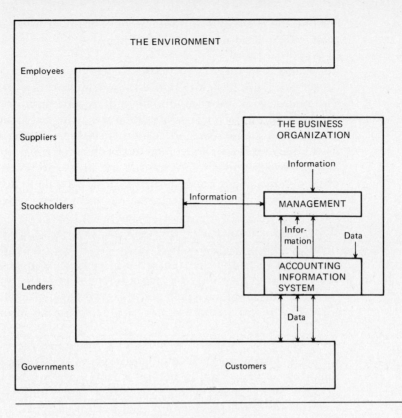

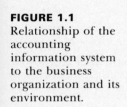

FIGURE 1.1
Relationship of the accounting information system to the business organization and its environment.

It is useful to examine accounting information systems from the viewpoint of users who utilize accounting information as a basis for making decisions. There are two basic categories of such users—those external to the business organization and those internal (management). External users are many and varied. Their needs are met to some extent by the publication of general purpose financial statements, such as the income statement and balance sheet. The subset of accounting that is concerned with the information needs of external users is known as *financial accounting*.

Internal users are also many and varied, but their needs for information do reflect a common objective—to maximize the economic well-being of the business organization in society. *Management accounting* is the subset of accounting concerned with internal information needs and how such information should be put to use. The accounting information system serves both external and internal users of information.

External information requirements

The six major external interest groups that receive information from the business organization are indicated in Fig. 1.1. The information each group receives includes both information for decision making and routine data concerning the execution of transactions. The six groups and some examples of their information needs are as follows.

Customers. In this era of market orientation, the customers of a business organization are perhaps the most important of the external interest groups. The requirements of customers include receiving information regarding the products of the business: prices, features, where and how they can be purchased, and guarantees and related servicing arrangements. These requirements are met through a combination of advertising, publication of catalogs and price lists, and communications by sales representatives. Customers may often obtain some product information, such as the reputation of the product for reliability and quality performance, from sources external to the business itself.

Routine information required by the customers of a business organization includes billing data, which is typically included on the document of sale prepared as a record of the transaction. Credit customers also require periodic information concerning the status of their accounts, including the amount owed, the discount available, and the date payment is due. These routine information requirements are met by the accounting information system.

Suppliers. The typical business entity purchases its inventories of raw materials or salable goods from a large variety of sources. If the business entity makes its purchases on credit (and most do), its suppliers require information concerning its reliability, credit standing, and ability to pay. A supplier typically obtains such information partly from external sources, such as credit rating agencies, and partly from the accounting information system of the business entity itself.

In the exchange between a business entity and its supplier, the supplier also requires certain routine transaction documents. One of these is the purchase order, which indicates the items, quantities, and special features required by the business placing the order. If the goods are not acceptable to the business entity, information must be exchanged concerning possible adjustments in sale terms or the return of the goods. When the business entity pays for the goods, its payment will be accompanied by supporting transaction documents. Much of this routine transaction data is furnished by the accounting information system.

Stockholders. A company's stockholders are vitally interested in all phases of its operations. They wish to evaluate past and predict future performance. The publication of annual financial statements is perhaps the single most important means of meeting these requirements. Quarterly financial reports are also becoming an increasingly important form of management reporting to stockholders. Providing such reports to stockholders is often referred to as the *stewardship function* and has traditionally been the responsibility of the accounting information system. Stockholders often obtain additional information regarding the business entity from external sources, such as securities analysts and financial publications. Also required by stockholders is certain routine information concerning the execution of their stock transactions and the receipt of dividend payments. These routine information requirements are generally met by the accounting information system.

Employees. As a group, employees are interested in certain general information regarding the business entity. This includes financial information, such as average wage levels, fringe benefit costs, and profits, as well as nonfinancial information such as levels of employment and productivity. Labor unions often represent the employee group in obtaining this information. Much of this information is provided by the accounting information system.

As individuals, employees expect periodic receipt of wages and salaries, accompanied by detailed information concerning deductions for income taxes, social security, insurance, union dues, etc. In the day-to-day performance of their job, employees often must refer to manuals to obtain information on company policy in a particular situation or on how a certain aspect of their job should be performed. The accounting information system is usually responsible for providing much of this routine information.

Lenders. Financial institutions that supply the business entity with capital for investment or expansion are very much interested in such factors as the reputation and ability of the company's management, its ability to meet its financial obligations, and its prospects for future success. A company's financial statements are an important source of information in this regard. Perhaps more so than other groups, lenders will also rely on outside sources for their information. The need of lenders for routine information concerning lending transactions requires an interchange of information with the accounting information system of the borrowing entity.

Governments. Many agencies of federal, state, and local governments require information concerning the business entity. The Internal Revenue Service (IRS) requires information concerning the company's profits and the amount of taxes that the company owes to the government. The IRS also requires information about the amount of employee taxes withheld. The Social Security Administration requires information concerning the amount of wages earned and social security taxes withheld. If the company is in a regulated industry, such as railroads or insurance, one or more federal or state agencies is likely to desire information about its operations. If the company has international operations, many foreign governments may desire information about its activities in their countries. The requirements of governments are perhaps the most varied of all external reporting requirements faced by the business organization. The accounting information system plays an important role in satisfying such requirements.

Many other groups also desire information about the business entity. These may include (1) credit agencies, such as Dun & Bradstreet, which publish information about a company's credit standing; (2) industry and trade associations, which publish information about a particular industry; (3) competitors, interested, of course, in a company's pricing policies, marketing strategies, product development plans, and profitability; (4) the community of which the business organization is a part; (5) financial analysts, who advise clients interested in making investments; or (6) private citizens who are simply interested in some aspect of the company's activities.

For the most part the information supplied to external users is either "mandatory" or "essential." Examples of mandatory information include reports to governments on taxable income and tax withholdings, and financial statements, which must be issued to stockholders by all publicly traded corporations. Examples of essential information include product information and billings to customers, and credit capacity information to lenders. The necessity for reporting information of this type places certain constraints upon accounting information systems, which will be discussed later in this chapter.

As shown in Fig. 1.1, much of the routine data provided to external parties by the business organization is channeled through the accounting information system. In turn, the accounting information system also receives much routine data from these exchanges. However, note that the information for decision making that is provided to external parties is shown to be provided directly by management rather than by the accounting information system. This reflects the fact that the ultimate responsibility for the fairness and accuracy of any information reported by the business upon which external parties base their decisions rests with management. This is true even though the accounting information system may serve as the actual channel for reporting this information.

Internal information requirements

In sharp contrast to external information is internal, or "discretionary," information. This means that choices must be made regarding information: what should be made available, to whom, how frequently, and so forth. Primarily because of this fact the area of internal information presents a much greater challenge to those who design accounting information systems than the external reporting area. In meeting mandatory and essential information requirements, the primary consideration is to minimize costs while meeting minimum standards of reliability and usefulness. When the reporting of information is discretionary, the primary consideration is that the benefit obtained from each report exceed the cost of supplying it. Much of the challenge in designing an information system is due to the fact that it is often very difficult to measure the benefit derived from reporting a given set of information.

All the various levels of management in a business organization—from the executive management responsible for achieving overall company goals to the operating management responsible for achieving the specific objectives of a single department—require information in the performance of their duties. As indicated in Fig. 1.1, the accounting information system is a major, but not the only, source of information to management. The general business environment provides information on such matters as economic conditions, new technologies, legal constraints, and market standing. Other sources within the organization provide information on the success of research and development projects, the morale of employees, the level of worker productivity, and other company matters.

Although the accounting information system is the primary "formal" information system in most organizations, there are many other formal, as well as "informal," channels of information. A formal information system is one to which an explicit responsibility for information production has been assigned. In contrast, an informal information system is one that simply arises out of a need unsatisfied by a formal channel and operates without a formal assignment of responsibility. The "grapevine" is a familiar example of an informal channel of information common to all organizations. As organizations grow in size, it is natural for some informal channels to become formalized.

As shown in Fig. 1.1, the accounting information system receives data not only from sources outside the business but also from internal sources. For example, product cost information in a manufacturing firm is generated from data on materials usage, labor usage, etc., that are collected within the factory. The accounting information system prepares information for management by performing certain operations on all the source data it receives. The management of the business organization receives this information and utilizes it as a basis for decision making. Management decisions in turn affect the internal operation of the business organization, including the accounting information system, and also affect the relationship of the business organization with its environment.

Two major roles of accounting information in management decision making can be identified. First, accounting information often provides a stimulus for management decision making by indicating the existence of a situation requiring management action. For example, a cost report that indicates a large variance of actual costs over budgeted costs might stimulate management to take corrective action. Second, accounting information often provides a basis for choice among possible alternative actions. For example, accounting information is often used as a basis for setting prices or for choosing which capital assets to purchase. The importance of accounting information in this latter role is due to its contribution to the reduction of uncertainty regarding the merits of various alternatives.

Designers of accounting information systems must determine what the information requirements of management are and respond quickly to changes in those requirements. The accounting system must be designed to meet these needs effectively. If management does not receive enough information, or receives poor information, its performance will not be as effective as it potentially could be. This could have an adverse effect on the entire organization. Thus the accounting information system plays an important role in contributing to the effectiveness of the business organization.

Analysis of the Accounting Information System

Thus far the accounting information system has been examined as a "black box"—that is, its role in the business organization has been discussed, but the way in which it operates internally to perform that role has not. In this section the lid of the black box is lifted in order that its contents and the operations performed within it may be analyzed. The objective is to formulate a precise definition of what is meant by the term *accounting information system.*

Many readers may already be more or less familiar with the concept of the management information system. Accounting information systems are closely related to management information systems, both conceptually and in the real world. It is worthwhile to define and explore the concept of management information systems as a prelude to developing an understanding of accounting information systems.

Management information systems

The term *management information system* has been defined in many different ways.[3] However, for our purposes, it will be defined as the set of human and capital resources within an organization that is responsible for the collection and processing of data to produce information that is useful to all levels of management in planning and controlling the activities of the organization. To many people, the term implies a computer-based system, but the term encompasses noncomputer systems as well. All business organizations have a management information system, but such systems vary greatly in their level of sophistication.

A fuller understanding of the concept of a management information system can be obtained from a careful analysis of the definition above. Several of the concepts referred to in the definition will now be examined in greater depth.

Management planning and control. The major purpose of management information systems is to facilitate the management of an organization. As used here, the term management encompasses all levels of administration in an organization, from top management responsible for the overall success or failure of the organization to operating management responsible for the day-to-day operation of a single department. Depending on the size of the organization, there may be one to several layers of management between these two extremes.

The basic functions of management are planning and control. Planning includes such activities as setting objectives, establishing policies, choosing

---

[3]For example, seventeen different definitions are listed in Raymond J. Coleman and M. J. Riley, *MIS: Management Dimensions* (San Francisco: Holden-Day, Inc., 1973), pp. 4–7.

subordinate managers, deciding on capital expenditures, and making decisions on products and their promotion. Control involves implementing policies, evaluating the performance of subordinates, and taking action to correct substandard performance. Information of various kinds is required in the performance of all these functions.

Data vs. information. As implied in the definition, a distinction is generally drawn between data and information. *Data* can be thought of as comprising any set of characters that is accepted as input to an information system and is stored and processed. *Information* refers to an output of data processing that is organized and meaningful to the person who receives it. For example, data concerning a sale may indicate who the salesperson was. When a large number of such data elements is organized and analyzed, it may provide important information to marketing directors attempting to evaluate their sales forces. The term data processing system is often used interchangeably with information system.

The major categories of information that can be distinguished in a business organization are (1) financial information, which concerns the flow of financial resources through the organization; (2) logistics information, which concerns the physical flow of inventories and resources within and through the organization; (3) personnel information, which concerns the people who work for the organization; and (4) marketing information, which concerns the markets for the organization's products and the means of serving those markets. Much information within a business organization overlaps into more than one of these categories.

The data processing cycle. Much of the study of information systems involves the operations that are performed on data in order to generate meaningful and relevant information. A useful method of classifying these operations is the concept of the data processing cycle. As shown in Figure 1.2, the data processing cycle may be perceived as having five stages: collection, refinement, processing, maintenance, and output.

The collection stage includes two fundamental activities. The first is *observation* of the data generating environment, usually by a human observer, though sometimes a machine may perform this function. The second is the *recording* of data, generally in the form of written source documents, though

FIGURE 1.2
The data processing cycle.

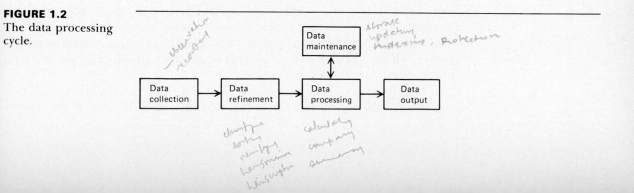

again it is possible that data may be recorded in a nonwritten, machine-readable form.

The data refinement stage includes a number of operations performed on data in order to facilitate subsequent processing steps: (1) *classifying* of data, which involves the assignment of identification codes (account number, department number, etc.) to data records based on a predetermined system of classification, such as a chart of accounts; (2) *batching* of data, which involves the accumulation of similar input records to be processed as a group; (3) *verification* of data, which involves a variety of procedures for checking the accuracy of data prior to submitting it for processing; (4) *sorting* of data, which involves the arrangement of a batch of input records into some desired numerical or alphabetical sequence; (5) *transmission* of data from one location to another; and (6) *transcription* of data from one form to another, such as from handwriting to typing or from documents to punched cards. Data refinement activities of some kind are performed in virtually all types of information systems, but they generally take on greater significance in more automated systems.

The processing stage of the cycle also includes a variety of activities. *Calculating* encompasses any form of mathematical manipulation. *Comparing* involves the simultaneous examination of two or more items of data, such as an "inventory balance on hand" and "reorder point," as a basis for subsequent action. *Summarizing* is a very important processing activity involving the aggregation of bits of data into meaningful totals or condensations. A related activity is *filtration,* which is the screening out of extraneous data from subsequent processing. Still another processing activity is *retrieval,* which is the fetching of data items from storage for use in processing or for output purposes.

There are several activities in the data maintenance stage, the most prominent being the *storage* of data for future reference. Other maintenance activities include the *updating* of stored data to reflect more recent events; the *indexing* of data, which involves cataloging of reference information pertaining to a body of stored data (such as in a library card catalog) in order to facilitate retrieval of specific items of data upon request; and the *protection* of stored data, which encompasses a variety of procedures and techniques for preventing its destruction or unauthorized disclosure.

The output stage represents the ultimate objective of the data processing cycle. Data output may be in one of two general forms—documents or reports. The term *issuance* may be used to refer to the preparation of output documents, such as checks, invoices, and purchase orders. Such documents may be returned to the information system for use in other data processing activities, or they may be provided to external users. The other major output activity is *reporting,* which is the formal presentation and distribution of processed data (information), usually in summary form.

It is important to note that most data do not have all these activities performed upon them, and some data may not even pass through all five stages.

For example, data from a transaction may be simply recorded and stored, perhaps never reaching the output stage. On the other hand, data on the plans of competitors may be collected and immediately reported to management without passing through any processing steps. Since such cases are generally the exception rather than the rule, the study of information systems must focus on all stages of the data processing cycle.

Information system resources. A management information system utilizes both human and capital resources, the latter consisting primarily of data processing equipment. With reference to the relative utilization of these two types of resources, two basic categories of data processing systems can be distinguished: (1) manual data processing systems, in which the major share of the data processing load is carried by people; and (2) automated data processing (ADP) systems, in which the major share of the data processing load is carried by machines. Several levels of sophistication are possible within these two categories.

The lowest level of sophistication in data processing systems is a completely manual system in which people perform all data processing functions. Such systems are common in small, local businesses, in which the data processing functions may be a secondary part of the responsibilities of several persons rather than the primary responsibility of a single individual. The major advantages of people as data processors are their flexibility, or ability to perform all the various functions of a data processing system, and their judgment, or ability to adapt to unfamiliar situations. The major disadvantages are their lack of reliability and speed.

Most manual data processing systems utilize one or more forms of special-purpose business machines. The most common types of these machines include (1) typewriters, which increase recording speed and legibility; (2) calculating machines, which increase speed and accuracy of calculation; (3) cash registers, which record, classify, and provide control over cash receipts; (4) duplicators, which conserve time in the making of duplicate copies of documents or reports; and (5) cassette tape recorders, which record, store, and play back voice data. This is by no means a complete list of available types of business machines. In general, machines of this sort increase the speed and reliability of data processing in manual systems. They require constant interaction with people and so do not undermine the advantages of people as data processors, but neither do they completely eliminate the disadvantages of people.

Historically, the earliest form of automated data processing system was the *punched card system*. Such a system, which has been made obsolete in recent years by the computer, consisted of several different machines. Using the punched card as a data medium, each machine was capable of performing one or a limited number of data processing functions that included recording (punching), sorting, collating, calculating, duplicating, and printing. Human intervention was required at the beginning and end of each processing step but was minimal in between. For many years prior to the advent of computer systems, punched card systems represented the highest level of automation in office equipment. At the present time, some organizations still use one or more punched card machines as auxiliary equipment within a computer system.

A vastly more sophisticated level than the punched card system is *electronic data processing* (EDP), or computer systems. Because of their ability to store and execute a set of instructions (called a *program*), computers can perform many processing steps in a series with no human intervention. Computer systems are much faster and more accurate than punched card systems because of their use of electronic, rather than electromechanical, components. However, computer systems also tend to be less flexible and adaptable than manual systems, and the extent of the initial design effort is often enormous.

Available computer facilities have a wide range of capabilities and features, including differences in speed and storage capacity. In recent years a distinction has evolved between large-scale computer systems and small-scale systems consisting of many personal computers distributed among multiple users. Large-scale systems have a larger storage capacity and can process higher volumes of data, whereas small systems are easier to use and provide programs that are more readily adaptable to solving the problems of computer users. Large-scale systems are typically operated and managed at a centralized location within the organization by computer specialists; small systems are operated and managed by end-users and located at various end-user sites spread throughout the organization. In many business organizations, both large-scale and small computer systems are utilized, each for those applications to which they are best suited.

The scale of automation required by an information system increases in direct proportion to the volume of data processing that the system must accomplish. It is useful to compare data processing systems conceptually in terms of the relationship between processing costs and the volume of data items processed. In a manual system, most data processing costs are variable relative to volume. Therefore as processing volume increases, total processing costs increase proportionately and cost per item processed stays relatively constant.

On the other hand, fixed costs of facilities represent a significant portion of the cost of a large-scale computer system. Therefore as processing volume increases, total processing costs in an automated system do not increase in the same proportion, and cost per item processed actually declines.

Finally, a system of small computers will incur a combination of fixed and variable costs somewhat in between a manual system and a large-scale computer system. These concepts are illustrated graphically in Figure 1.3. The curves shown represent relative values rather than actual figures. These graphs help to explain why manual systems are suited to low-volume operations, small computer systems to moderate-volume operations, and large-scale computer systems to high-volume operations. In a growing organization the increasing volume of data processing work represents one of the major pressures toward

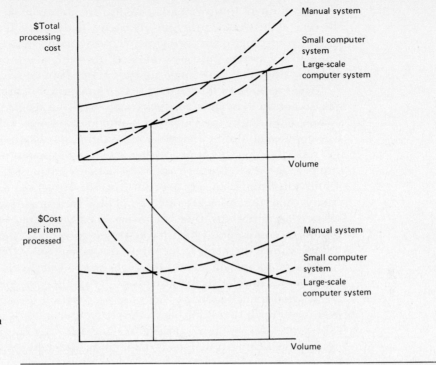

FIGURE 1.3
Relationship of
processing costs to
processing volume in
manual and
automated data
processing systems.

converting from a manual to an automated system. The vertical lines connecting the two graphs represent break-even points between, first, manual and small computer systems, and second, small and large-scale computer systems.

System.   The final aspect of the definition of management information system to be discussed here is the concept of *system,* a word having many diverse meanings and implications. In its broadest and most abstract sense, a system is an entity consisting of two or more components or subsystems that interact to achieve a goal. Used in this sense, the term could be applied to a community, a family unit, or a business organization. In a more specific sense, the term is used by specialists in the computer field to refer to either the equipment and programs making up a complete computer installation, or a set of programs and related procedures for performing a single task or set of related tasks on a computer.

Closely related to this notion is the process known as *systems analysis,* which also has both abstract and specific meanings. In its most abstract sense, systems analysis refers to a rigorous and systematic approach to decision making, characterized by a comprehensive definition of available alternatives and an exhaustive analysis of the merits of each alternative as a basis for choice. The approach often involves attempts to quantify factors that would otherwise be considered on an intuitive basis and also frequently makes use of computers. The central theoretical principle of systems analysis is referred to as the *systems concept.* According to this principle, choices among alternative courses of action within a system must be evaluated from the standpoint of the system as a whole rather than any single subsystem or set of subsystems.

When applied to information systems in complex organizations, one major effect of the systems concept has been to encourage *integration,* which refers to the combining of previously separated subsystems. Integration has made data processing more efficient by eliminating duplication of recording, storage, reporting, and other processing activities within an organization. For example, where it was formerly common in many businesses for the preparation of bills and maintenance of accounts receivable records to be performed separately, these functions are often combined in a single operation in modern business organizations. Integration has been facilitated by the increased utilization of computers, which have tended to replace specialized clerks and thereby reduce the need for separate specialized subsystems.

In a more specific sense, the term *systems analysis* is used by computer professionals to refer to the process of designing computer applications. It is the step that immediately precedes the preparation of computer programs. A meaning of the term dating back to precomputer times is that systems analysis is the process of designing procedures and selecting equipment for performing data processing functions in manual or punched card systems.

Accounting information systems—A definition

Accounting information systems possess all the characteristics of management information systems. They utilize the same kinds of resources and have a data processing cycle that produces information for management planning and control. The major difference is one of scope. The management information system encompasses all data entering the organization, all processing activities within the organization, and all information used by persons in the organization. The accounting information system is concerned only with certain types of data and information. Thus the accounting information system is actually a subsystem of the management information system within an organization.

It is possible to identify two types of management information with which accounting information systems are primarily involved: (1) financial information and (2) information generated from the processing of transaction data. Although much management information actually falls into both of these categories, there is also much that fits only one or the other description. For example, unit inventory or unit sales information is not financial but is often produced from transaction processing. Similarly, budgets and capital investment analyses are representative of the kinds of financial information that are not generated directly from transaction processing. Figure 1.4 illustrates that these two types of information are subsets of management information, that they do overlap, but that neither is a complete subset of the other.

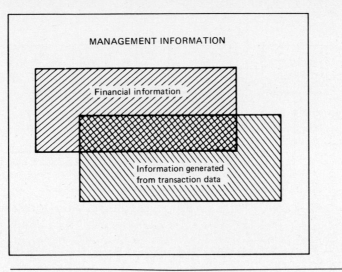

FIGURE 1.4
Relationship of management information, financial information, and information generated from transaction data.

The accounting information system is the most pervasive and often the largest of the information subsystems in business organizations. It is pervasive in the sense that all members of the organization participate in some way in the generation of transaction data, and all managers utilize financial information to some extent. In many organizations, the accounting information system is the only formally designated information system and is thus in effect the management information system. In most organizations that do have a formally designated management information system, accountants play a key role in its administration and operation. Thus an understanding of accounting information systems is essential to the study of management information systems, and vice versa.

To summarize, the term *accounting information system* is defined as the set of human and capital resources within an organization that is responsible for the preparation of financial information and also of the information obtained from the collection and processing of transaction data. This information is then made available for use by all levels of management in planning and controlling an organization's activities. Functions of transaction processing and financial information preparation will now be examined in greater detail.

Transaction processing

The processing of transaction data in accounting utilizes its own version of the data processing cycle, which is illustrated in Fig. 1.5. The portion of this process that begins with source documents and ends with financial statements is often called the double entry accounting process. Many other reports and analyses containing both financial and nonfinancial information may be generated as a by-product of the double entry accounting process.

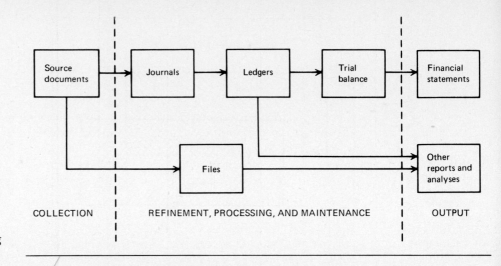

FIGURE 1.5
The data processing
cycle in accounting.

It is helpful to use the terminology of the data processing cycle when examining the accounting process. Input data are observed and recorded on source documents, such as sales invoices or time cards. These data may then be verified for accuracy, classified and batched by type of transaction, sorted into sequence by document number or account number, transcribed from source documents to journals, and perhaps at some point transmitted to a different location, such as a central accounting or data processing office.

Steps in the data processing stage of the accounting cycle include calculation of payrolls, invoice totals, taxes, and numerous other totals and percentages. Various comparisons of these figures to each other and to stored data may be made as a matter of routine during processing. The preparation of the trial balance is an important summarizing step, whereas the balancing of the trial balance is a useful means of verifying the accuracy of the entire accounting cycle. Retrieval of accounting information in response to inquiries from customers or management occurs frequently. Filtration is represented by ignoring data irrelevant to the accounting process, such as a customer's telephone number or an employee's height and weight (though such data may be relevant for other purposes).

The storage activity is represented by the saving of accounting data in ledgers and other files. A *file* is defined as a set of logically related records, such as the payroll records of all employees. A *record* is defined as a set of logically related data items, such as all payroll data relating to a single employee. The updating activity is represented by the posting of transactions from journals and source documents to ledgers and files. Indexing occurs when each record is assigned one or more identifying codes, such as account number, product stock number, or department number, for reference purposes. Protection of stored data may involve such simple techniques as locking of filing cabinets.

The reporting step in the output phase of the double entry process is exemplified by the financial statements of the organization, which are perhaps the most important single summary of the organization's activities. Numerous other reports may also be prepared as a by-product of accounting data processing. In addition, documents such as customer statements and employee paychecks are issued by the accounting system.

A typical business entity will engage in a large volume of transactions, which may also be greatly varied. However, designers of accounting information systems can be thankful that a great majority of transactions fall into one of a few basic categories. This fact allows the system to achieve a greater degree of efficiency in processing. At this point a few basic categories of business transactions will be reviewed.

Purchasing of assets and services.   The purchase of inventories, fixed assets, services, and supplies is one of the most basic business transactions of all business entities. This transaction could be considered the starting point of the entire business process. The transaction is represented by the following journal entry.

Purchases	XXX	
Fixed assets	XXX	
Expenses (various accounts)	XXX	
Accounts payable		XXX

The purchases account represents either the raw material inventory of a manufacturing concern or the merchandise inventory of a retail or wholesale firm. The accounts involved in this transaction are summary accounts, so such an entry usually represents a large volume of transactions. Individual inventory purchases may be recorded in a detailed inventory ledger by item number, individual fixed asset purchases may be recorded in a fixed asset ledger, and expenses may be recorded in various expense ledgers. Each accounts payable entry would be posted to the appropriate vendor record in an accounts payable ledger. These detailed ledgers and transaction data may be used to generate many useful reports and analyses of expenses, inventories, vendor activity, and so forth.

Payroll.   The payment of wages and salaries is another type of transaction that is very basic in most business entities. It is represented by the following journal entry.

Payroll	XXX	
Taxes payable (various accounts)		XXX
Other deductions		XXX
Cash		XXX

This entry is a summarization of tens, hundreds, or perhaps thousands of individual transactions with employees. Detailed records must be kept for each employee, primarily to fulfill tax requirements. The amount in the payroll account is distributed to various expenses and inventory accounts. The payroll account is also frequently analyzed to prepare various detailed cost reports used for decision-making purposes.

Sale of products and services.   The sale of a product or service is perhaps the most essential of the basic business transactions. It is represented by the following journal entry.

        Accounts receivable   XXX
            Sales   XXX

If the sale is of a product, another journal entry is also made to reflect the cost of the product inventory transferred to the customer.

        Cost of goods sold   XXX
            Inventory   XXX

Once again, these entries represent several detailed sets of records. A detailed accounts receivable ledger contains a record of the account of each individual customer, whereas a detailed inventory ledger contains a record of each type of inventory item. Cost of goods sold may be analyzed in detail by inventory categories as a basis for planning the composition of future inventories. Sales may be analyzed according to salesperson or territory as a basis for evaluating the effectiveness of marketing effort.

Cash receipt and disbursement.   Transactions involving the receipt and disbursement of cash are very important to all business entities. Receipt of cash usually initiates the following journal entry.

        Cash   XXX
            Accounts receivable   XXX

Disbursement of cash is reflected by the following entry.

        Accounts payable   XXX
            Cash   XXX

Such entries affect the detailed accounts receivable and accounts payable ledger records as well as the cash account. These detailed ledgers, and the transaction details underlying these entries, may be used to generate many different reports, including cash flow analysis and projections, and cash budgets.

Flow of inventory through production.   This process is represented by two basic transactions, the first of which reflects the accumulation of all production costs.

Work-in-process inventory	XXX	
Raw materials inventory		XXX
Payroll		XXX
Manufacturing overhead		XXX

The second reflects the completion of production.

Finished goods inventory	XXX	
Work-in-process inventory		XXX

These transactions are, of course, peculiar to a special type of business organization—one that is engaged in manufacturing. They are also distinguished from those mentioned previously in that they are "internal" rather than "external" transactions, meaning that there is no outside party involved. These transactions reflect several detailed sets of inventory and production records, and the data underlying the entries are used in the preparation of a large number of various "cost accounting" reports.

The transactions outlined above represent the vast majority of all business transactions in terms of volume. Each of the entries summarizes hundreds, or perhaps thousands, of typical, individual transactions. Of course, there are many other types of transactions with which an accounting system must cope, but none that are as basic in terms of volume. A major concern in the study of accounting information systems is the design of systems to perform these high-volume tasks efficiently and reliably.

Preparation of financial information

The design of accounting information systems must also concern itself with the preparation of financial information for management. As mentioned previously, much financial information is generated directly as a by-product of transaction processing. However, it is dangerous for management to rely solely on by-product information. In most businesses of medium to large size, management's needs for financial information go well beyond that which is generated from transaction processing.

For example, consider the planning function. Since transaction-generated information necessarily involves only the past, it is not by itself relevant in planning for the future. The budget is an important financial planning tool, as is capital expenditure analysis. Both of these techniques use transaction data to some extent but must also rely upon financial forecasts. Financial information relating to the environment of the business firm is also important for planning purposes. Examples include price level and national income information as well as information on the prices and profitability of the products of competitors.

As business organizations grow in size, the number and variety of financial reports necessary also multiply. This is confirmed by considering the number of ways in which reports may be categorized. For example, reports may be categorized according to scope (from firmwide to departmental), time horizon (from historical summaries to long-range forecasts), format (narrative, numeric, tabular, graphical, oral), user (operating employees, managers, governmental agencies), timing (issued weekly or monthly, or by request only, or according to circumstances), and purpose (stewardship, planning, control, motivation).[4] These and other factors are important considerations in the design of effective financial reports.

An example of an accounting information system

At this point it may be helpful to illustrate the concepts discussed thus far by describing briefly the main components of an accounting information system for a typical small business. Let us consider a retail home-appliance dealer whose product line includes refrigerators, freezers, electric ranges, washers, dryers, television sets, radios, stereo and hi-fi equipment, air conditioners, vacuum cleaners, and other household appliances. Such a dealer would probably employ from ten to fifteen persons—two or three office personnel, two or three in delivery, two or three in service and repair, and four to six in sales.

Our dealer's most important management decisions relate to inventories—determining what is on hand, what should be purchased and when, what prices should be charged, what trade-in allowances should be provided, and so forth. The dealer also needs to be able to assess the relative profitability of the various product lines. Other significant management concerns include advertising and promotion, credit and collection of receivables, and supervising of personnel. The accounting system should provide information useful for making many of these decisions.

It is helpful to consider the most significant categories of accounting transactions engaged in by the dealer: (1) sales, including cash sales, credit card sales, installment sales, sales of trade-ins, and sales of parts and service; (2) purchases of inventory; (3) payroll; (4) expenses such as utilities, advertising, supplies, insurance, taxes; (5) cash receipts on account; and (6) cash disbursements.

As is the case in most retail business, the typical home-appliance dealer uses a manual data processing system, augmented by a few small business machines such as a cash register, typewriter, and calculator. Accounting personnel might include a bookkeeper, credit manager, and secretary. The owner is very likely to be involved in numerous procedures and activities related directly to the accounting function.

An important component of any accounting system consists of the documents used to record input data. In a retail home-appliance store, two of the more important of these are the sale document and the service work order. The sale document is filled out at the point of sale and includes data pertaining to the customer, terms of sale, items and quantities sold, prices and

---

[4]For further elaboration on such categorizations, see Joseph W. Wilkinson, "Effective Reporting Structures," *Journal of Systems Management* (November 1976): 38–42.

total charges, and delivery information. The multiple copies that are prepared include one for the customer, one for delivery, and one for accounting. The service work order, which is also prepared in multiple copies, contains data relating to the customer, product, work performed, parts sold, and amount collected.

The files and records maintained by the store's accounting system reflect the information requirements of its owner-manager. The two most important files are the inventory ledger and the accounts receivable ledger. The inventory ledger contains one record for each type of inventory item carried. This record contains data on the cost, list price, quantity on hand, quantity on order, and pattern of past sales of an inventory item. It must be updated when sales are made and when purchase orders are placed or delivered. The accounts receivable ledger includes one record for each installment sale; this record contains data on the amount due and payments received. New installment sales and customer payments are posted to these records. Other significant accounting files include an accounts payable file, a payroll file, and the general ledger, whose records are the balance sheet and income statement accounts.

A significant part of any accounting system consists of the procedures followed in processing accounting data. One procedure is a daily comparison of the cash in the register against the cash register tape and the sales documents. A similar comparison is made of cash received for parts and services against the service work orders. Service workers and delivery people are required to have the customer sign one copy of a work order to acknowledge receipt of goods or services. To provide control over customer payments on account, the owner opens all mail and totals all checks received. The owner also signs all outgoing checks and prepares a monthly bank reconciliation. A periodic review of accounts receivable records is made in order to detect customers who are behind in their payments; these customers are sent letters encouraging them to keep their accounts current. Inventory stocks and ledger records are also reviewed periodically to determine what items should be ordered. At the end of each month various procedures are performed: journal entries are posted from the general journal to the general ledger; detailed ledgers are totaled and reconciled to their general ledger control account balance; accrual and adjusting entries are made; a trial balance is prepared and balanced; closing entries are made; and finally, a balance sheet and income statement for the month are prepared.

This has been only a very brief description of a small business accounting information system, the main components of which are summarized in Fig. 1.6. This example is intended to provide a preliminary idea of the nature of accounting information systems. Later, the book provides many other examples of accounting information systems in greater detail. However, all such systems contain the same basic set of components—people, equipment, transactions, files and records, documents, and procedures.

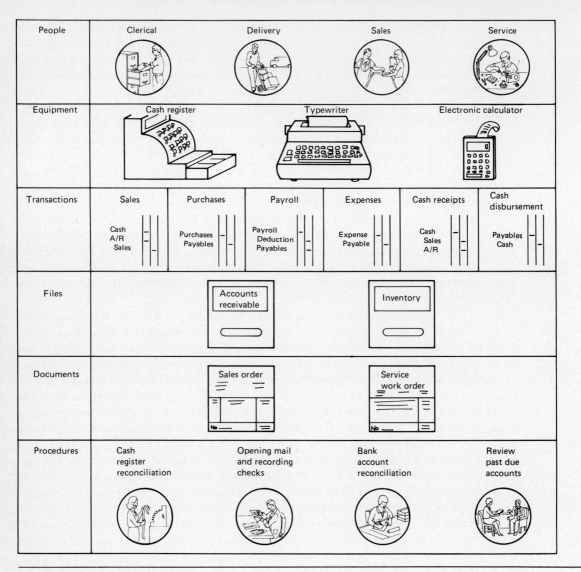

FIGURE 1.6
Components of an
accounting
information system
for a home-appliance
dealer.

The Evolution of Accounting Information Systems

The system life cycle

In a growing business organization, an information system undergoes a limited life cycle, from the point at which it is born to meet needs not satisfied by its predecessor system, to the point at which it is replaced because it fails to meet the new needs of the business. Two factors have tended to shorten the life cycles of business and accounting systems in recent years: the rapid growth of business organizations, and rapid changes in information processing technology. The life cycle of information systems is examined here in three separate stages, namely, (1) analysis and design, (2) implementation, and (3) operation.

Analysis and design. The analysis and design stage is equivalent to the gestation period of an information system. It begins with the recognition that the continuing growth of the organization is raising problems with which the old system may be unable to cope. This initiates an extensive survey of the existing system and of current and future information processing needs. An analysis of the facts obtained in the survey may delineate the major problem areas in the existing system. If the old system is a manual one, the feasibility of automation may be considered.

One of the most important steps in this phase is the survey of information requirements. In accounting information systems, much of the data processing and information preparation is either mandatory or essential, particularly that done for external users. These mandatory and essential requirements are thus fixed and given to the designer of an accounting information system. The designer faces the problem of determining the remaining information needs, primarily internal, that the system should fulfill. The next step is to determine the extent to which these internal information needs may be satisfied by information prepared as a by-product of the processing of mandatory and essential information. Any remaining information needs must be met with discretionary information, which will involve the systems designer in comparing the value of the information with the cost of enlarging the accounting information system to enable the information to be prepared.

Following the survey and analysis is a period of *synthesis,* in which a program of corrective action is developed. Such a program may entail only minor modification of the existing system, or it may entail complete replacement of the system. Throughout this period each alternative is rigorously evaluated in terms of its costs and benefits to the organization. If the program recommended in the synthesis is approved by management, work proceeds on the detailed systems design.

All aspects of the new system are considered in the detailed systems design, including personnel, hardware, procedures, and data flows. Almost any major systems project will involve some personnel problems—such as employee displacement, relocation, hiring, and retraining—which must be planned for. Also common are problems associated with equipment acquisition, such as selecting desired features, arranging for maintenance service, and financing the purchase. Procedures must be designed to ensure efficiency and reliability of processing. In EDP systems, many procedures must be programmed. Data flow problems include deciding on the content and arrangement of data on source documents, designing record layouts, establishing the content and organization of files, and determining the appropriate content, format, and distribution of reports.

Implementation.   Once the detailed systems design is completed, the new system must be successfully implemented. If the new system is a major revision or replacement of the old, the first important step in this stage will be to plan and coordinate properly the various implementation activities. Another step in implementation is to hire and train new employees and to relocate existing employees if necessary. In addition, new processing procedures must be tested and perhaps modified. New equipment must be installed and tested. Standards and controls for the new system must be established. Complete system *documentation,* consisting of descriptions of procedures, charts, instructions for employees, and other descriptive material, must be developed. When the new system is ready to begin functioning, it may be operated simultaneously with the old system for a brief period, with the output of the two systems being compared to ensure that the new system has no major defects. The final step in this phase is the dismantling of the old system and complete conversion to the new.

Operation.   After the new system has been operating on its own for a short while, follow-up studies are usually conducted to detect and correct the inevitable minor, and sometimes major, design deficiencies that were not apparent at the point of conversion. Throughout its lifetime the system will be subject to periodic review. Minor modifications may be made as problems arise or as new needs become evident. Eventually the reviews will indicate that major modification or replacement should be considered, and the process will begin all over again.

The accountant's role in systems change

In most business organizations, accountants will play a key role in this process of systems change. As mentioned previously, the accounting and information systems functions are one and the same in some firms, and accountants are thus directly responsible for performing systems work. In other firms, accountants are at least one of the primary users of the information system and so are vitally interested in how the system operates. It is always important for the users of an information system to become involved in its design.

In many smaller companies the expertise necessary to analyze and design information systems may not be present within the company, and as a result, reliance may have to be placed upon outside consultants. One of the main sources of such consultants is the public accounting profession. Many public accounting firms, particularly the larger ones, employ specialists in systems work in their "management advisory services" departments. Other major sources of consulting in the systems area are business machine manufacturers and management consultants not associated with public accounting.

Future Challenges to Accounting Information Systems

Change is inevitable in society, and the pace of change in today's society seems to be accelerating. Such change will bring new problems and new challenges to designers of accounting information systems. It is possible to predict some of the major challenges of the future by looking at the trends visible in society today.

Social responsibility in business

A major trend of the present era is the demand by society that business organizations become more socially responsible. This trend is evident in several respects, including the consumer protection movement, legislation encouraging the hiring and training of members of socially disadvantaged groups, and perhaps more dramatically, the movement to save the environment. The business world is beginning to respond to these demands. Accounting information systems have a definite contribution to make here. They can estimate the costs and benefits of proposed projects designed to improve the well-being of society and thus assist business management in deciding which projects are worthwhile. While such projects are in operation, there is a need for information systems to process data on them and to provide business management with information that is useful in evaluating existing projects and planning future ones. Business organizations are increasingly required to report to government agencies on their compliance with social or environmental goals established by regulation or legislation—and business executives look to their accounting information systems to meet these demands.

Accounting for human assets

Another major trend is the growing importance of human knowledge and skill as a valuable economic resource. The initial development of modern accounting information systems took place early in the twentieth century. During this period, the most important assets were physical assets, such as cash, inventories, buildings, and machinery. The vast majority of the labor force was unskilled. Physical assets were thus the primary concern of accounting information systems.

In modern business organizations, human knowledge and skill are usually primary factors in their success or failure. Yet the accounting information systems of the present day do not reflect this fact. They continue to treat physical assets as being of primary importance, and all but ignore human assets.

The effective management of human assets requires information. The function of accounting information systems is to provide such information. Management must develop new methods of recording, classifying, and processing data concerning human resources. Systems designers must revise methods of reporting information to management to incorporate the human factor and give it adequate consideration in management decisions. Systems of internal control for human assets are needed. These needs clearly call for innovative thinking and action on the part of designers of accounting information systems.

Scientific approaches to management

Another major trend is the movement toward more scientific approaches to management. The last three decades have seen the development of an entirely new discipline, commonly referred to as *management science* or *operations research*. This discipline approaches management decision making by attempting to construct mathematical models of real decision problems. Solutions to such models are then used in making the actual decisions. Practitioners of this discipline make liberal use of computers in building and solving mathematical models. The field is often considered to be a branch of systems analysis.

Among the most important variables that operations researchers require in building models of business decision problems are measures of cost and benefit. However, when they attempt to obtain such measures from accounting information systems, they are often frustrated to find that the information is not in the form they require because accounting systems have never before had to provide inputs to operations research models.

The operations research approach has tremendous potential for generating better management decisions. The full realization of this potential requires that accounting information systems be structured to provide relevant and reliable inputs to operations research models. Designers of accounting information systems must study the common forms of operations research models in order to develop an understanding of the type of information that is needed. Changes in patterns of recording, classifying, and processing will be required.

Inflation accounting

In recent years price inflation has become an increasingly significant phenomenon of modern industrial society. Inflation causes a significant distortion of accounting information, which affects financial statements and other accounting system outputs. This has been recognized by those organizations that regulate financial reporting, including the Financial Accounting Standards Board and the Securities and Exchange Commission in this country and their counterparts in numerous other countries. These groups have issued proposals and requirements for financial reporting that reflects the impact of inflation. One of the most important of these was Statement 33 of the Financial Accounting Standards Board, issued in September 1979, that required all public companies meeting certain criteria of size to prepare inflation accounting information and disclose it in their annual reports to stockholders.[5]

---

[5]As of December, 1986, supplemental disclosure of inflation accounting information in annual reports is voluntary rather than required.

Inflation accounting has a significant impact upon accounting information systems. There is a need to collect, process, and maintain data on price levels, replacement costs, current values, and so forth. Systems of accounting for inventories, fixed assets, and other financial items must be revised. Systems of reporting to stockholders and other external parties must be modified to meet the requirements imposed by regulatory groups. Perhaps even more important is the need to revise internal management reports to eliminate inflationary distortions that might lead to bad management decisions. Implementation of the systems required for these purposes has been accomplished in many large companies. If price inflation remains a significant feature of our economy, many other companies are likely to implement such systems in the future.

A look ahead

The problems discussed in this section represent only a few of the major challenges in the field of accounting information systems today. Before students can fully appreciate and respond to these future challenges, they must first develop an understanding of the present state of the art in accounting information systems. This book will help them to achieve this end. Part 2 discusses the processing equipment and systems available to designers of accounting information systems, with particular emphasis on computer systems. Part 3 covers the major issues involved in the analysis, design, implementation, management, and control of information systems. Part 4 develops an understanding of the primary uses to which accounting information is put in the management of the marketing, logistics, personnel, and finance functions in the modern business organization.

As has been discussed, accounting information systems may be completely manual, partially mechanized, or fully automated. However, there are certain concepts, principles, and techniques common to all of them regardless of their degree of mechanization or other differences. One example is the concept of the accounting cycle discussed in this chapter. In the remainder of Part 1, several other fundamental topics are covered. The topic of business organization is examined in Chapter 2, which focuses on the impact of business organization upon the collection and processing of accounting data and the reporting of accounting information, and on the internal organization of the accounting function. In Chapter 3 the general concepts of file processing and records management are introduced and explained. In Chapter 4 the basic concepts and principles of control in a business organization are discussed. Note that these topics are closely interrelated. Together they provide a strong general understanding of accounting information systems useful in exploring the more specific topics of information technology, systems management, and business applications of systems.

Summary

Accounting information systems in business organizations provide information useful to business management as well as to parties external to the business, including customers, suppliers, stockholders, employees, lenders, and government agencies. This information is produced from a series of steps known as the data processing cycle, which includes the collection, refinement, processing, maintenance, and output phases.

The accounting information system in an organization is a subset of the management information system. A management information system is the set of human and capital resources within an organization that is responsible for the collection and processing of data to produce information useful to all levels of management in planning and controlling the activities of the organization. An accounting information system deals with two specific types of information: (1) financial information and (2) information obtained from the collection and processing of transaction data. The latter includes information produced as a by-product of the processing of familiar accounting transactions such as purchases, sales, payroll, inventory, and cash receipts and disbursements.

Because of the central role of information systems in modern business organizations, the study of information systems is an important part of student preparation for careers in accounting or business.

Review Questions

1. Define the following terms.

financial accounting	systems analysis (three meanings)
management accounting	systems concept
stewardship function	integration
management information system	accounting information system
data	file
information	record
punched card system	synthesis
electronic data processing	documentation
program	management science
system (three meanings)	operations research

2. Explain why the study of accounting information systems is important for today's accounting students.

3. What are two major categories of users of accounting information? What are the major user groups within each category, and what is the nature of their information needs?

4. From what sources other than the accounting information system does management receive information?

5. Distinguish between "mandatory," "essential," and "discretionary" reporting of information and give an example of each.

6. Distinguish between "formal" and "informal" information systems and give an example of each.

7. Identify two major roles of accounting information in management decision making.

8. The two basic management functions are assumed to be planning and control. What are some of the specific activities involved in each of these functions?

9. Identify and describe four major categories of information in a business organization.

10. Identify the five major stages of the data processing cycle and indicate the major activities in each stage. Relate the data processing cycle to the double entry accounting process.

11. Identify two basic categories of data processing systems. Within each category describe the various levels of sophistication in data processing facilities that are available to the information systems designer.

12. What are the advantages and disadvantages of people as data processors? As a data processing system becomes more automated, what effect is there on these factors?

13. What are some of the common types of special-purpose business machines?

14. Compare manual and automated data processing systems in terms of the relationship between processing costs and the volume of data items processed. What are the implications of this comparison for an accounting system in which processing volume is growing?

15. What are the advantages of integration of accounting systems? Describe an example of integration.

16. How are accounting information systems distinguished from management information systems?

17. What are some of the basic transactions of a business organization? Can you give the journal entries for these transactions?

18. Why is it dangerous for management to rely solely on information generated as a by-product of transaction processing in meeting its needs for financial information? What are some examples of financial information that is not generated from transaction processing?

19. Describe some of the ways in which financial reports may be classified.

20. Describe the components—people, equipment, transactions, files and records, documents, procedures, etc.—that you might expect to find in the accounting information system of a typical retail home-appliance store.

21. What are the three major stages in the life cycle of an information system? What activities are performed in each stage?

22. What are four contemporary social trends that present challenges to the designers of accounting information systems?

Discussion Questions

23. Should an accounting information system be structured to meet the needs of external or internal users? To what extent are these two categories of needs similar, and to what extent do they differ?

24. How do the information systems of nonprofit organizations or governments differ from those of business organizations? In what ways are they similar?

25. How do general-purpose financial statements meet the needs for information about the business organization of (a) customers, (b) suppliers, (c) stockholders, (d) employees, (e) lenders, (f) governments?

26. When a business undertakes projects to improve the well-being of society, how can it measure the benefits of such projects in order to evaluate their relative worth?

27. Suppose a business wished to record its human assets on its balance sheet. How could it assign asset values to them?

Problems and Cases

28. In this chapter, several of the highest volume transactions of a typical manufacturing company were discussed, and corresponding accounting journal entries were illustrated.
    a) List several of the highest volume transactions of a typical life insurance company and give the corresponding journal entries.
    b) List several of the highest volume transactions of a typical banking institution and give the corresponding journal entries.
    c) List several of the highest volume transactions of a typical management consulting or similar service organization and give the corresponding journal entries.

29. You are a payroll clerk responsible for the manual preparation of the weekly employee payroll for a small firm having about 150 employees. Every Monday, you receive from all department heads or supervisors a list of the hours worked by each employee in their departments for the previous week. You must determine the gross pay, net pay, and payroll deductions for each employee. You utilize a series of tax withholding tables to help determine the amount of social security and income tax withholding. You also utilize, and update each week, a payroll master file containing for each employee such data as identification number, pay rate, the number of tax exemptions claimed, and year-to-date totals of gross pay, net pay, and all deductions. You must prepare all paychecks and also

a report listing for each employee the hours worked, gross pay, net pay, and deductions for the week. Consider the activities in the data processing cycle described in this chapter. For each of these activities, give an example from the process described above.

30. List in the appropriate order the journal entries reflecting the movement of inventory through a manufacturing firm.
    a) Which of these entries represent internal transactions and which represent external transactions?
    b) Which of the accounts included in your journal entries would normally be summary accounts representing a large number of subsidiary ledger records?

31. Katie Kimball has decided to go into the florist business under the name of Katie's Flower Shop. She has made arrangements to lease a downtown store and to purchase a delivery truck. One full-time employee has been hired to help Katie prepare floral arrangements, wait on customers, keep records, and so forth. Katie expects to hire two part-time delivery boys.

    There are three wholesale florists in the area that Katie expects to use as a source of supply. In the florist business, a wide variety of flowers and plants must be kept in stock, but the product is perishable. Intelligent buying and inventory control is a major factor in the success of a florist. Knowledge of seasonal trends is very important.

    Katie expects that the majority of her sales will be made over the telephone and will be on account rather than for cash. Collection of accounts is thus likely to be a significant problem.

    Katie has come to you for assistance in designing an accounting information system for her business.

REQUIRED
    a) Design a document for the recording of sale transactions. How many copies of this document should be prepared, and for what purposes?
    b) Design a set of records, procedures, and reports to enable Katie to obtain up-to-date information on unpaid customer accounts.
    c) Design a set of records, procedures, and reports to provide Katie with the information she needs to manage her inventories properly.
    d) Design a set of records and procedures to enable Katie to maintain control of cash receipts and disbursements and to prepare monthly financial statements.

32. The McCann brothers have decided to open an auto repair shop. John will be in charge of machine work, stocking of parts and supplies, and accounting. Ted will be the head mechanic and supervise the auto repair work. Arrangements have been made to lease a suitable building, and three other qualified auto mechanics have been hired.

    The shop will maintain an inventory of the most commonly used parts and accessories. Other parts and accessories can be obtained as needed from local parts wholesalers. A separate room within the shop has been equipped with shelving to serve as a parts storeroom. The McCanns wish to minimize their investment in inventories as much as possible but also hope to avoid the need for frequent trips to buy unstocked parts.

As customers bring their autos into the shop for repairs, a service work order detailing the work to be done will be prepared. At this time, many customers will ask for an estimate of the repair cost and when the work will be completed. As the work is performed the cost of parts and labor will be recorded on the service work order. When the customer returns to pick up the repaired vehicle, a copy of the service work order will serve as a bill. Customers may pay their bill by cash, check, or credit card. The McCanns intend to guarantee their work for thirty days.

The McCanns have asked you for assistance in designing an accounting information system for their business.

REQUIRED

a) Design a format for the service work order document. How many copies of this document should be prepared, and for what purposes?

b) What type of records and procedures should the McCanns utilize to help them make inventory decisions?

c) What type of records and procedures should the McCanns utilize to help in making estimates of repair costs?

d) What type of records and procedures should the McCanns utilize to control cash receipts and disbursements and enable the preparation of monthly financial statements?

References

Berliner, Robert W., and Dale L. Gerboth. "FASB Statement No. 33 'The Great Experiment.'" *Journal of Accountancy* (May 1980): 48–54.

Churchman, C. West. *The Systems Approach.* New York: Dell, 1968.

Coleman, Raymond H., and M. J. Riley. *MIS: Management Dimensions.* San Francisco: Holden-Day, Inc., 1973.

Committee on Accounting Education, American Accounting Association, and Computer Education Subcommittee, American Institute of Certified Public Accountants. "Inclusion of EDP in an Undergraduate Auditing Curriculum: Some Possible Approaches." *The Accounting Review* **49** (October 1974): 859–864.

Committee on Management Information Systems, American Accounting Association. "Report of the Committee." *The Accounting Review,* Supplement to Vol. **49** (1974): 140–155.

Davis, Gordon B. "Computer Curriculum for Accountants and Auditors—Present and Prospective." In *Education for Expanding Computer Curriculums,* edited by Daniel L. Sweeney, pp. 12–21. New York: American Institute of Certified Public Accountants, 1976.

Firmin, Peter A. "The Potential of Accounting as a Management Information System." *Management International Review* (February 1966): 45–55.

Gorry, G. Anthony, and Michael S. Scott Morton. "A Framework for Management Information Systems." *Sloan Management Review* (Fall 1971): 55–70.

Hodge, Bartow; Robert A. Fleck, Jr.; and C. Brian Honess. *Management Information Systems.* Reston, Va.: Reston Publishing Company, Inc., 1984.

Johnstone, Anthony Gordon. "The Systems Accountant: How? Where? When? Who?" *Internal Auditor* (February 1979): 23–28.

Lynch, David. "MIS: Conceptual Framework, Criticisms, and Major Requirements for Success." *Journal of Business Communication* (Winter 1984): 19–31.

MacVeagh, Charles. "MIS: Building a Structure that Works." *Price Waterhouse Review* **22** (2) (1977): 42–49.

Moore, Michael R. "Undergraduate Computer Curriculum Requirements for Entering Staff in Accounting and Auditing." In *Education for Expanding Computer Curriculums,* edited by Daniel L. Sweeney, pp. 6–9. New York: American Institute of Certified Public Accountants, 1976.

Wilkinson, Joseph W. "Effective Reporting Structures." *Journal of Systems Management* (November 1976): 38–42.

C H A P T E R   2

Organization and Accounting Information Systems

The distribution of authority and responsibility within an entity is indicated by its organizational structure. An understanding of the patterns of authority and responsibility distribution is essential to the assessment of information needs within an organization. In turn, information needs define the required structure of data collection and processing activities within the accounting information system. Therefore the structure of data collection, processing, and reporting activities within an accounting information system must closely parallel the organizational structure of the entity it serves. An understanding of the concepts of organization thus provides part of the foundation for the study of accounting information systems.

Introduction to Concepts of Organization

Organization may be defined as the way in which the activities of people are coordinated to achieve a goal. In large, complex organizations the goal is usually divided into several subgoals, each of which is assigned to various subunits of the organization. Each subgoal may be further subdivided into still smaller subgoals, and so on, down to the lowest levels of the organizational structure. This pattern of subdividing organizational goals and tasks into a graded series of lower-level goals and tasks is called a *hierarchical* structure of organization.

A simple example of an organizational hierarchy is illustrated in Fig. 2.1. Each circle represents an organizational unit having a goal or subgoal and a manager responsible for achieving the goal or subgoal, and the lines between the circles represent relationships between subordinate managers and their superiors. These relationships reflect the assignment of subgoals to subordinates by their superiors. The superiors must also delegate to their subordinates the authority to direct the operations of lower-level units toward the accomplishment of assigned subgoals. Acceptance of this authority creates for the subordinates a responsibility to manage operations in a manner that will result in the achievement of assigned subgoals. This is accompanied by a responsibility to report results to superiors. Subordinates may divide assigned subgoals into still smaller subgoals and delegate the authority for achieving these to other persons, who then become responsible to them. However, managers cannot delegate their responsibility—that is, they do not escape responsibility for achievement of assigned subgoals even though they may delegate a portion of their authority.

An organization is partially described by its number of *levels of supervision* and average *span of control*. The number of levels of supervision is simply the number of ranks between the highest- and lowest-level units of the organization. Span of control refers to the number of subordinates reporting to a superior. For example, in Fig. 2.1, there are four levels of supervision, and the average span of control of each manager is two.

An organization can also be described in terms of the degree of centralization or decentralization of authority among its management levels. In a highly centralized organization, authority is concentrated at the higher man-

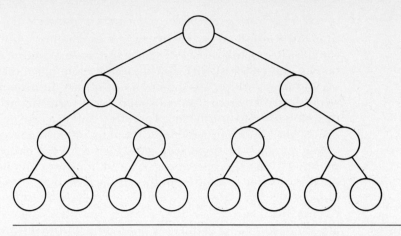

FIGURE 2.1
A hierarchical
structure.

agement levels, with lower levels possessing a minimum of decision-making power. In a highly decentralized organization, a significant amount of decision-making authority may be delegated to lower levels. The concept is relative, and most organizations fall well within the two extremes. Even within the same organization, authority may be highly centralized in one functional area, such as production, and highly decentralized in other functional areas.

In Chapter 1 the two basic functions of management in an organization are defined as planning and control. These two functions are performed through the medium of organizational structure. An overall plan for the business organization is subdivided into more specific plans for lower-level organizational units. At each level, plans are subdivided into lower-level plans with the objective of providing effective coordination among all organizational units at that level. Control in the sense of implementing plans is carried out within organizational units at the lowest levels, under the supervision of managers acting in accordance with plans. Middle-level and higher-level managers reinforce this control by monitoring the performance of the organizational units whose managers report to them relative to the plan. When actual performance does not compare favorably with the plan, control action is initiated by the managers responsible for the organizational unit in which the deviation took place. Organizational structure is therefore clearly essential to the effective performance of the management functions of planning and control in large organizations.

**Problems of modern
organizations**

According to Whisler,[1] the four most prominent problems of modern organizations that have implications for information systems are (1) rigidity, (2) information failures, (3) suboptimization, and (4) individual motivation.

[1]Thomas L. Whisler, *Information Technology and Organizational Change* (Belmont, Calif.: Wadsworth, 1970), pp. 20–23.

Rigidity refers to a tendency within organizations to resist change. This problem has definite implications for information systems in particular. In the past several years improvements in information technology have accelerated. Organizations have been, and continue to be, faced with the problems of adopting these new technologies in a manner that obtains the maximum advantage from their expanded capabilities. Rigidity has tended to aggravate the organizational problems of transition to new information technologies.

Information failures refers to failures in communication between organizational units because of their physical separation and specialization of functions. Messages may be lost in transit, inaccurate or distorted, or vague or unclear. Information channels may become overloaded, causing delay or loss of information. This set of related problems has direct implications for the design of information systems. As organizations grow and functions become more separated and specialized, systems designers must identify problems of information failure as they arise and design information systems in a manner that minimizes these problems.

The problem of *suboptimization* occurs when an organizational subunit, by attempting to optimize in the accomplishment of its assigned subgoal, makes it more difficult for the organization as a whole to optimally achieve its collective goals. This situation may be caused by the ineffective decomposition of goals into subgoals, but it is primarily a problem of coordination of operations among the various units within an organization. Because the accurate and timely reporting of information is essential to coordination, it is obvious that the problem of suboptimization also has direct implications for designers of information systems. Modern computer systems, if properly implemented, have great potential for improving the degree of coordination within large organizations, thus reducing the magnitude of the problem of suboptimization.

The problem of individual motivation refers to the areas of conflict between individual goals and organizational goals. This problem is often aggravated by attempts to implement new information technologies. Designers of information systems may be able to relieve this problem to some extent by incorporating motivational factors into their designs.

Business Organization

Thus far the discussion of organizational concepts has been general, applying to all types of organizations. We will now turn to business entities and attempt to relate general organizational concepts to the specific problems and practices of business organizations.

Most business organizations define their primary goal as the maximization of long-run profits. There are two commonly used patterns of division of this overall goal into subgoals through organization. The first is the *functional organization structure,* under which employees with the same or similar occupational specialties, such as marketing, production, and accounting, are grouped together within organizational subunits of the business. The second pattern is the *divisional organization structure,* under which the organization consists of several divisions, each of which is relatively independent of the others and operates almost as a separate smaller company.

For example, in a manufacturing business organized along functional lines, the overall goal of profit maximization may be divided into subgoals through the use of the following organizational subunits: (1) marketing, with the goal of maximizing sales revenue; (2) production, with the goal of minimizing the production cost per unit; (3) finance, with the goal of providing the resources required for operation of the business at a minimum of expense; and (4) accounting, with the goal of measuring the success of the organization in achieving its goals. These goals may be broken down still further into additional sets of subgoals, assigned to lower-level units, and so on. For example, the finance function could be further divided into the subunits of (a) investor relations, with the goal of maintaining good relations with the firm's sources of long-term debt and equity funds; (b) credit and collections, with the goal of establishing and enforcing credit policies that will maximize the excess of sales revenue over bad debt losses; and perhaps (c) insurance, with the goal of optimum management of the risk of loss of resources by the firm. This is an example of how the efficiencies of specialization may be achieved by means of the hierarchical structure of organizations.

A familiar means of illustrating patterns of authority delegation is the organization chart. A partial organization chart for a typical single-plant manufacturing company organized along functional lines appears in Fig. 2.2.[2] Many of the general concepts discussed thus far are reflected in this chart. Each box represents an organizational unit supervised by a manager. Each line connecting a manager to a lower-level manager represents the delegation of authority to a subordinate and the corresponding responsibility of the subordinate to report to the superior. A manager is responsible for all the activities that appear under that manager's span of control on the chart—that is, for the performance of all managers to whom a portion of that manager's authority has been delegated. The hierarchical structure of the organization is clearly apparent.

The chart illustrates organizational relationships within the production department in detail but provides no detail with regard to the other major functional areas. A more detailed breakdown of the controllership function is provided in the next section of this chapter, whereas the other major functions are discussed in greater detail in later chapters. The chart omits reference to the information systems function, but it must be pointed out that in many modern organizations this function has achieved status as a major department on the same level as production, marketing, and accounting. The information systems function is also discussed in greater detail in subsequent chapters.

---

[2]This figure is adapted with some revision from John. A. Higgins, "Responsibility Accounting," *Arthur Andersen Chronicle* **12** (2) (April 1952): 1–17.

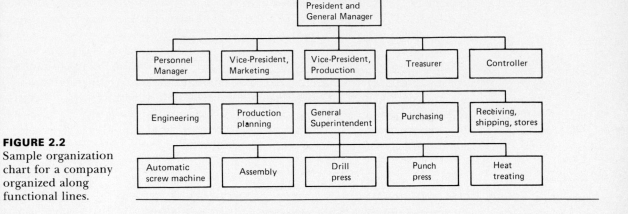

FIGURE 2.2
Sample organization
chart for a company
organized along
functional lines.

The functional organization structure provides the advantages of greater functional effectiveness due to specialization, centralized control, and economies of scale. However, as a business organization grows by adding new product lines, or new plants, or even by diversifying into other lines of business, the pure functional organization structure may prove ineffective in coordinating and motivating employees to achieve the overall goal. Under the divisional organization structure, each division has virtually the same primary goal—that is, maximization of long-run profits—as the organization as a whole. An example of a business organization using a divisional structure appears in Fig. 2.3. Note that even when the divisional structure is used at the higher levels of the organization, the functional structure is still likely to be used at the lower levels, as shown in the figure. Furthermore, some vestiges of the functional structure may also appear at the top of the organization in the office of the Executive Vice-President for Administrative Services, which coordinates such functions as personnel, accounting, finance, and systems.

If an organization can divide its overall goal into subgoals in such a way that all employees working to achieve their assigned subgoals are also contributing to the optimal achievement of the overall goal, the situation is referred to as one of *goal congruence.* The larger the organization becomes, the more difficult it is to achieve goal congruence, and the more likely it is that situations of *goal conflict* will arise in which a decision or action consistent with one subgoal is at variance with a decision or action dictated by another subgoal. This is true regardless of the form of organization chosen. For example, in a business organized along functional lines, the marketing subgoal of maximizing sales revenue may suggest offering a highly diverse product line, whereas the production subgoal of minimizing per unit production costs suggests offering a limited product line. In a divisionalized company, goal conflict may be present when two divisions compete with each other in the same market. Goal conflict also occurs frequently in divisionalized companies when a raw material or component produced by one division is used as input

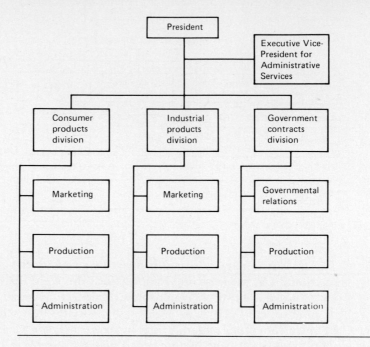

FIGURE 2.3
Sample organization
chart for a company
organized along
divisional lines.

by another division. The producing division may maximize its profits by selling to the consuming division at a specified price, whereas the consuming
division may be able to maximize its profits by buying the input from another
source at a lower price.

Variations of the functional and divisional forms of organization include
the use of project groups, the use of product line groups, and the matrix
organization structure. Project groups are temporary organizational units
consisting of employees drawn from several functional specialties and assigned to a particular task, such as building a new plant, introducing a new
product line, or implementing a new information system. Product line groups
also consist of employees from different functional specialties, but their assignment involves a somewhat more permanent responsibility for all aspects
of a particular product line. In a *matrix organization structure,* both functional
departments and project or product groups are present, and many employees
have a dual responsibility to both a functional department and a particular
project or product line.

A business organization's choice of its organization structure has significant implications for its accounting information system. A major responsibility of the accounting information system is to provide financial information to each organizational unit to assist in planning and controlling its
operations. Thus the information required by any particular organizational
unit is a function of its assigned subgoal. Planning information must assist
the unit's manager in making decisions and taking actions to achieve its

subgoals. This becomes especially difficult when the manager's span of control encompasses several departments among which a goal conflict exists. Control information includes measures of financial performance relative to goals. In order to provide the most relevant set of financial information for planning and control purposes, the designer of the accounting information system must understand (1) the structure of the organization, (2) the way in which the overall goal has been divided into subgoals, (3) the kinds of decisions and actions necessary to achieve the various subgoals, and (4) the information that is most useful in making those decisions and taking those actions.

Another relevant organizational issue in large businesses is the problem of establishing the degree of centralization of decision-making authority within the organization as a whole. If decision making is highly centralized, an organization will, theoretically, be better able to coordinate and control its activities in order to achieve optimal results with respect to its overall goal. However, it is generally believed that decentralization of decision-making authority to the divisional level results in divisional managers being more highly motivated to achieve maximum levels of performance. Furthermore, information failures may occur in the reporting of information from the divisions to a central location, and these failures could cause centralized decision makers to receive bad information and make poor decisions. Modern information technology permits accounting information systems to minimize the problem of information failures and therefore encourages a strategy of centralization. However, the motivational factor continues to be a strong influence in favor of a strategy of decentralization. Whichever of these strategies is adopted by a business organization, the accounting information system must be designed to provide the necessary planning and control information to the appropriate managers on a timely basis.

According to a prominent organizational concept known as the *contingency theory,* the best way for a particular business enterprise to structure its organization is contingent upon a number of factors, including its size, the diversity and complexity of its products and production processes, and the degree of variability of its environment. For each business enterprise, some ways of organizing are likely to be better than others. However, there is no general method of organization that is superior for all types of businesses. A corollary of this theory must be that there is no general design for an accounting information system that is superior for all types of businesses. Thus the accounting information system must be designed to match the unique needs and characteristics of the business organization of which it is a part.

Organization of the accounting department

The way in which the accounting and information processing functions are organized may have a significant influence on the effectiveness of an accounting information system. Therefore recommendations concerning the organization of these particular functions are a legitimate concern of the accounting systems designer. Figure 2.4 provides one example of how the accounting

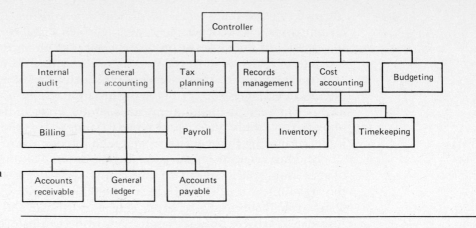

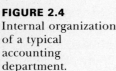

FIGURE 2.4
Internal organization
of a typical
accounting
department.

function in a typical manufacturing company might be organized. It should be understood that the illustration does not represent a prescription for all organizations but merely serves as an example reflecting patterns of organization that are somewhat common in practice.

The chief accounting executive is commonly referred to as the *controller,* a top-level executive in most business organizations, ranked on the same level with—or one level below—the executive vice-presidents. As such, the controller is a participant in top-level decision making affecting the entire organization.

Reporting to the controller are the staff functions of budgeting, records management, tax planning, and internal audit. The budgeting function involves the preparation of operating budgets, capital expenditure budgets, and related forecasts and analyses to assist management in planning and controlling the operations of the organization. Records management involves the design of business forms and the establishment of policies and procedures governing the retention and retrieval of business records. The tax planning function involves the administration of tax-reporting activities and the planning of transactions having significant tax effects in order to minimize the total long-run tax liability of the organization. The internal audit function is described more fully in the paragraph below. In large business organizations, there are likely to be several additional staff departments reporting to the controller, whereas in small- or medium-sized companies the controller alone, or together with a single assistant, may perform all these functions. Also reporting to the controller are a general accounting manager, whose responsibility is to supervise the routine operating functions of the accounting department, and a cost accounting manager, who supervises those accounting activities directly relating to factory operations.

An active internal audit department plays an important role in a well-managed business. The responsibilities of this function typically include (1) independent appraisal of the performance of various levels of management with regard to efficiency and adherence to company policies; (2) continuous review and recommendation of improvements in the system of internal checks and protective measures in the organization; (3) periodic assessment of the reliability of financial records and the effectiveness of processing methods; and (4) the execution of certain miscellaneous control functions that must be performed independently of other operating units. Examples of the last function include the preparation of bank reconciliations and the control of cash register tapes. Because of the necessity for independence and objectivity in this function, many companies require that the internal audit executive report to the president or board of directors instead of, or in addition to, the controller.

The distribution of general accounting functions shown in Fig. 2.4 is in accordance with major transaction account categories and is fairly typical. The payroll function maintains employee payroll records and prepares paychecks. The accounts payable department authorizes and disburses payments to short-term creditors for goods and services and maintains records of these accounts. The general ledger department maintains the ledger of all balance sheet and income statement accounts. The billing function is distinguished from accounts receivable in that billing is responsible for sending out invoices at the time of sales, whereas accounts receivable is responsible for maintaining records of customer accounts and for sending out periodic statements of account.

The relative significance of the cost accounting function depends on the type of company and its industry. In a manufacturing company the cost function is an important one and includes the keeping of inventory records for raw materials, work in process, finished goods, and perhaps the timekeeping function for factory employees whose wages are charged to work in process.

Two functions closely related to accounting—cashier, and credit and collections—are not shown in Fig. 2.4 because in most organizations they are the responsibility of the treasurer. The cashier is responsible for maintaining a record of cash receipts, endorsing and depositing checks, and reviewing and/ or signing checks disbursing company funds. The credit-and-collections function involves the establishment of credit policies, the granting of credit to customers, and in some cases the administration of mailroom procedures relative to the receipt of customer payments through the mail. In some companies, either function, or both, may be performed within the accounting department itself.

In the sample organization chart, the clerical functions within the accounting department have been detailed to a considerable degree. In all but very large single-plant operations, each clerical function shown reporting to the accounting manager would probably be performed by one or two persons, rather than by completely separate departments. Furthermore, in organizations using a computer system, some of these clerical functions—particularly billing, payroll, and inventory—might well be replaced completely by the computer. Note that the primary purpose of the sample chart is to illustrate common patterns of distribution of functions within accounting departments. It bears repeating that the chart is *not* intended to be a model of how manufacturing companies *should* be organized, and that each company must adopt that structure best suited to its own particular needs and characteristics.

Responsibility Accounting

Responsibility accounting is a term describing the reporting of financial results in accordance with the assignment of managerial responsibilities within an organization. There are three major factors in a responsibility accounting system: (1) initial assignment of managerial responsibilities, which is reflected in the organization chart; (2) translation of these responsibilities into a formal set of goals, expressed in financial terms; and (3) reports showing how actual performance compares with the established goals. Responsibility accounting, particularly as it relates to the second and third of these factors, is one of the more vital functions of the accounting information system.

It can be said that a responsibility accounting system mirrors the organization structure, a point that is stressed throughout this section, which focuses on formal goal setting and performance reporting.

When a formal statement of the goals or plans of an organization is expressed in financial terms, it is called a *budget*. Business organizations commonly use several types of budgets, including operating budgets, capital budgets, and cash budgets. An *operating budget* is an estimate of an organization's revenues and expenses for normal operations; it generally covers a period of either one month or one year. A *capital budget* represents an appropriation of funds for acquisition of major capital assets and investment in significant long-term projects. A *cash budget* is simply a forecast of cash inflows and outflows for the short-term future. Because operating budgets are the ones most commonly associated with responsibility accounting, the remainder of this section will be limited to them.

The preparation of budgets for a business organization is a function of the controller's staff, but this process also requires the participation of personnel from production, marketing, and other operating departments. The budget of a business organization has a structure that corresponds to the organization structure; that is, the overall budget of the entity is made up of a hierarchy of smaller budgets, each representing the financial plan of a division, department, or other unit of the organization structure.

The process of preparing the annual budget for a business organization begins with the sales forecast. Detailed predictions of the quantities of each individual product to be sold during the budget period are prepared at the lowest level of the marketing organization. These predictions are aggregated, adjusted, and approved by each field manager, who then submits them to an immediate superior for approval. The process is continued until a complete sales budget for the organization is developed. This budget not only summarizes total predicted sales for each of the products in the organization as a whole but also provides a breakdown of these totals for every organizational unit within the sales organization.

The sales budget must then be disaggregated to provide an estimate of the level of activity for every organizational unit in the firm during the budgeted period. For example, if the sales budget estimates total sales of 45,000 units of product X, this total may be disaggregated by assigning Plant A to produce 25,000 units and Plant B to produce 20,000 units. These production goals in turn provide a basis for estimating the level of activity required within individual departments of the two plants. A forecast of the expenditures required for each department is prepared from this. These expenditures may be categorized according to the important types of activities engaged in by the department. The result is the department budget—an explicit statement in financial terms of the subgoals for which the department is responsible.

Whereas the budget is the primary vehicle of financial planning in a business organization, the *performance report* is the primary vehicle of financial control. A performance report is a summary of actual, as opposed to planned, results achieved by a particular manager. Of primary concern here is the financial performance report, which typically includes an itemized list of budgeted revenues, costs or expenses, the corresponding actual dollar amounts, and the *variances,* which are the differences between budgeted and actual dollar amounts for each item.

Note that the budget is not simply an exercise in estimating the future; it is in addition an important instrument of management control. The budget represents a standard of performance established by management for the achievement of the organization's goals. All managers, aware that their job performance will be evaluated relative to the budget, are motivated to attain and perhaps exceed the budgeted results. To the extent that the budget accurately reflects the organization's goals, managers are motivated to direct their activities toward the achievement of those goals. Therefore the budget and the financial performance report, which are the cornerstones of a responsibility accounting system, are also vital elements of management control within the business organization.

The effective responsibility accounting system incorporates two additional concepts, flexible budgeting and controllability of performance criteria. *Flexible budgeting* involves adjusting the budgeted elements of the performance report for differences between the forecasted level of activity and the actual level of activity. This means that all cost and expense items must be classified either as fixed or variable. *Fixed costs* remain constant as the level of activity (sales or production volume) increases or decreases, whereas *variable costs* rise or fall in proportion to increases or decreases in the level of activity. If the actual level of activity varies from the forecast level of activity upon which the budget was based, then flexible budgeting requires that the variable cost elements of the budget be adjusted to reflect the actual level of activity. This places the budgeted costs and actual costs in the performance report on a comparable basis, which makes the report a more equitable measure of performance.

To illustrate the concept of flexible budgeting, suppose that the monthly cost of repair and rework in an assembly department (see Fig. 2.2) is deemed to be partially fixed and partially variable, with the fixed portion estimated as $300 and the variable portion as $5 per unit on the average. If the budget for a particular month is based upon *estimated* production of 100 units, then the amount budgeted for repair and rework will be $300 + $5(100) = $800. However, if the *actual* production volume is 120 units, then $800 is no longer an equitable performance standard. A flexible budgeting system would adjust the budgeted amount on the performance report to $300 + $5(120) = $900.

The concept of controllability means that a manager's performance should be evaluated in terms of only those factors for which that manager has responsibility and authority. Thus *controllable costs* are those over which managers, through the exercise of their delegated authority, have some influence. To the foreman of a production department who has no influence over the purchase of assets, depreciation on that department's machinery is not controllable. To the same foreman, however, materials usage and labor usage represent controllable costs. A performance report should focus on controllable costs in its comparison of budgeted and actual costs.

Since the performance report is essentially an extension of the budget, the performance reporting system within a business organization will, like the budgeting system, possess a hierarchical structure. This point is illustrated in Fig. 2.5,[3] which shows performance reports for managers at each of the four levels of Fig. 2.2. Note that each report shows actual costs and variances (the amount budgeted is not shown) for the current month and the year to date, but only for those items that are controllable at that level. The hierarchical nature of performance reporting is evident in that the total cost of each department below the top level becomes a single-line item on the performance report of the manager at the next higher level. Thus the hierarchy of cost aggregation and reporting in a responsibility accounting system corresponds almost exactly to the hierarchy of authority delegation as reflected in the organization chart. This is an important example of how the accounting information system is influenced by organization structure.

In a responsibility accounting system, each organizational unit may be designated as either a cost center, a profit center, or an investment center. A *cost center* is an organizational unit whose assigned objective is to achieve its operational function at a minimum cost. Reports on a cost center thus focus on variances from actual costs that are controllable within the center. The reports in Fig. 2.5 are illustrative of this type of reporting. The organizational units most commonly treated as cost centers are operating departments and project groups. A *profit center* is a department or division whose assigned objective is to maximize net profit. Reports on a profit center must therefore include both the costs and revenues assignable to it. Product line groups within a division are often treated as profit centers. An *investment center* is a depart-

---

[3] *Ibid.*

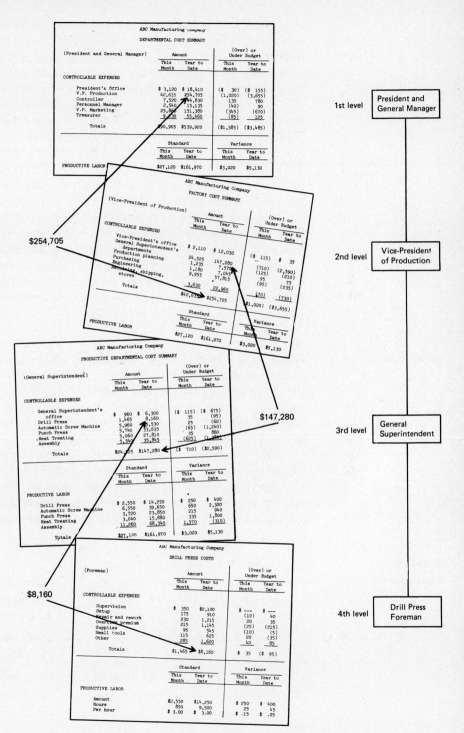

FIGURE 2.5
The hierarchy of performance reports.

ment or division whose assigned objective is to maximize return on investment (net profit divided by total assets). Investment center performance reports thus include costs, revenues, and assets identifiable with its operation.
Business organizations using the divisional form of organization structure
generally treat their divisions as investment centers.

Another important concept closely related to responsibility accounting is
the principle of *management by exception.* If the performance report shows actual
costs of less than, or only slightly greater than, budgeted figures, a manager
can assume that the item is under control. On the other hand, if actual costs
are significantly higher than budgeted costs, management is made aware of
an item of cost that may be out of control. The exception triggers a study of
the situation and, where needed, action to correct the problem.

In general terms, the position and responsibilities of managers in a business organization provide useful insight into their needs for information.
Knowledge of the organizational structure and the division of authority and
responsibility within an entity is thus essential to a designer of accounting
information systems. Once the nature of the desired output of the system is
known, the system designer can concentrate upon structuring the system to
produce that output most effectively.

Summary

Organization is defined as the way in which the activities of people are coordinated to achieve a goal. In a large organization the goal is generally subdivided into subgoals that are assigned in a hierarchical pattern to individuals
or groups within the organization. Goal congruence exists when persons who
accomplish their assigned subgoals are contributing to the optimal achievement of the overall organizational goal.

The effective reporting and utilization of information by persons in the
organization is critical to the process of coordinating organizational activities
to achieve goal congruence. A central part of this process is a responsibility
accounting system, which reports financial results associated with the responsibilities assigned to managers and employees within the organization.

Review Questions

1. Define the following terms.

organization	operating budget
hierarchical	capital budget
levels of supervision	cash budget
span of control	performance report
suboptimization	variance
functional organization structure	flexible budgeting
divisional organization structure	fixed costs
goal congruence	variable costs

goal conflict   controllable costs
matrix organization structure   cost center
contingency theory   profit center
controller   investment center
responsibility accounting   management by exception
budget

2. Why is an understanding of concepts and practices of organization important to the study of accounting information systems?

3. Can responsibility be delegated? What is the relationship of responsibility to authority delegation?

4. Explain the concepts of centralization and decentralization of authority.

5. Explain how organizational structure contributes to the effective performance of the management functions of planning and control.

6. Identify and briefly explain four prominent problems of modern organizations and their implications for information systems.

7. What is the commonly accepted goal of business organizations? In what way does organizational structure contribute to the achievement of that goal?

8. What are the relative advantages and disadvantages of the functional and divisional forms of organization structure? Which form is best?

9. Describe some examples of goal conflict in a business organization.

10. Describe three forms of organization structure other than the functional and divisional forms.

11. How does the organization structure of a business affect the design of its accounting information system?

12. What are the relative merits of centralization and decentralization of authority within a business organization?

13. What are some examples of staff functions reporting to the controller in a typical business organization?

14. What are the responsibilities of the internal audit function in business? What are the issues in the question of to whom the internal audit executive should report?

15. What distinction is there between the billing function and the accounts receivable function in a business?

16. Explain the three major factors in a responsibility accounting system.

17. Explain how the responsibility accounting system mirrors the organization structure.

18. Identify three different kinds of budgets commonly used in business organizations.

19. Describe the steps in the process of preparing the annual operating budget in a business organization.

20. Explain the relationship of a performance report to a budget.

21. How does management by exception enter into the process of budgetary control?

Discussion Questions

22. What contribution can the accounting information system make to the resolution of goal conflict within a business organization? (It may be useful to refer to the examples of goal conflict presented in the chapter.)

23. It is stated in this chapter that "business organizations generally interpret their primary goal to be the maximization of long-run profits." Is this goal in conflict with social goals such as a clean environment and a lasting world peace? How can the accounting profession contribute to the resolution of such conflicts of business and social goals?

24. Discuss the similarities and differences between the organization structure of a business and of a university. What is the nature of the role played by an accounting information system within a university?

Problems and Cases

25. Prepare a simple illustration of an organizational hierarchy. Using a set of descriptive labels, identify one example within your illustration of each of the following.
    a) a manager
    b) an organizational unit
    c) the goal of the organization
    d) a subgoal
    e) delegation of authority
    f) reporting responsibility
    g) span of control

26. Mr. John Newman is president of the New Manufacturing Company. His three sons are vice-presidents: Robert is in charge of the Production Department, David is responsible for the Marketing Department, and Steven heads the Accounting Department.

    Within the Production Department are four departments, each headed by a supervisor who reports to Robert Newman. These are Personnel (with two employees in addition to the supervisor), Purchasing (with four additional employees), Engineering (with two additional employees), and the Factory. There are three departments within the Factory, each with a boss who reports to the factory supervisor. These are Shipping and Receiving (with three employees in addition to the boss), Assembly (with six additional employees), and Finishing (with six additional employees).

Within the Marketing Department are three departments, each headed by a manager who reports to David Newman. These are Advertising (with two additional employees), Credit (with two additional employees), and the Sales Manager (who supervises six field salespersons).

Within the Accounting Department are three departments, each headed by a manager who reports to Steven Newman. These are General Accounting (with four additional employees), Data Processing (with three additional employees), and the Treasurer (with two additional employees).

REQUIRED

a) Prepare an organization chart for the New Manufacturing Company.
b) How many levels of supervision are there within the company?
c) What is the average span of control within the company?
d) Identify the major differences in allocation of responsibilities between the New Manufacturing Company and the company whose chart is shown in Fig. 2.2. Do these differences imply that the New Manufacturing Company has a problem with its organization structure? Comment.

27. Bill Werner is the boss of a factory department in a small manufacturing company. The company recently began to prepare financial performance reports to assist in evaluating its bosses. However, Bill feels that his performance report for the most recent month was an unfair measure of his managerial performance.

There are two principles of performance reporting that, if not followed, could have caused the problem in evaluating Bill's performance. Identify these two principles and explain how they should be incorporated into a performance reporting system.

28. Several years ago, Dr. Grey formed the Grey Corporation to perform research in the energy field. The company has grown dramatically but continues to operate as it was originally organized. Grey still tries to personally supervise all major projects and support functions, although he now finds it virtually impossible to do so. Nevertheless, he hesitates to relinquish operating control, fearing that quality might deteriorate. The present staff of seventy researchers requires the support of three financial, ten technical, twelve clerical, and two custodial employees. Grey Corporation may have as many as twenty-five research projects under way at any given time.

REQUIRED

a) State an important organizational principle that Grey is violating.

b) Give three recommendations that would improve Grey Corporation's current organizational structure. (CIA Examination)

29. A partial organization chart for the Ohio Manufacturing Company is shown in Fig. 2.6.

Draw another chart showing how the organization might be structured if it were to adopt a divisional rather than a functional organization structure.

30. General Hardware Industries (GHI) is a large manufacturer of hardware for home and industrial use. GHI is organized along divisional lines, each of its three major plants being a separate division. These are the Power Tools Division (St. Louis), the Hand Tools Division (Omaha), and the Specialty Tools Division (Kansas City). A partial organization chart for GHI is shown in Fig. 2.7.

GHI has recently completed the acquisition of Kimball's Lawn Management, Inc. (KLM), a manufacturer of lawn and garden equipment, and chemical sprays and fertilizers. KLM has five major plants located in the Midwest and specializing in the following product lines.

Chicago plant (company headquarters)—fertilizers

Springfield plant—weed and bug sprays

St. Paul plant—garden tools (hoes, rakes, shovels, etc.)

Sioux Falls plant—sprinkler systems

Milwaukee plant—power mowers, tillers, spreaders, etc.

FIGURE 2.6
Ohio Manufacturing Company organization chart.

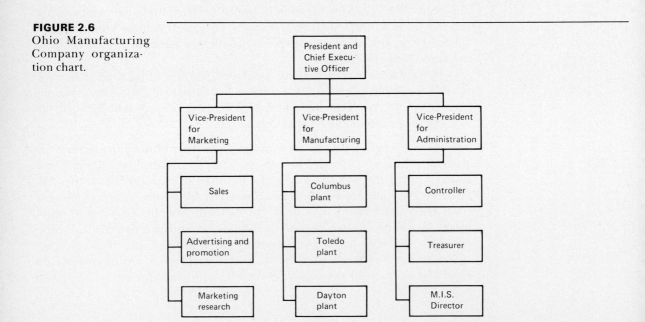

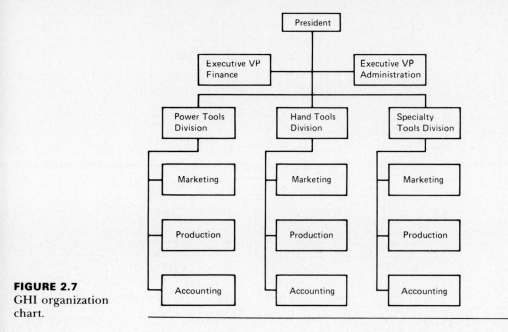

FIGURE 2.7
GHI organization chart.

REQUIRED

KLM is organized along functional lines, as shown in Fig. 2.8.

a) Discuss whether the newly merged company should be organized along functional or divisional lines.

b) If the new organization structure is to be functional, draw an organization chart indicating how it might be formed.

c) If the new organization structure is to be divisional, draw an organization chart indicating how it might be formed.

d) Assuming that the company will use the divisional form of organization, identify some organizational units that could be treated as investment centers, profit centers, and cost centers.

e) If the company changes its name to GHIJKLM, Inc., what will the *J* stand for?

31. The Argon County Hospital is located in the county seat. Argon County is a well-known summer resort area. The county population doubles during the vacation months (May-August), and hospital activity more than doubles during these months. The hospital is organized into several departments. Although it is a relatively small hospital, its pleasant surroundings have attracted a well-trained and competent medical staff.

An administrator was hired a year ago to improve the business activities of the hospital. Among the new ideas he has introduced is responsibility accounting. This program was announced along with quarterly cost reports supplied to department heads. Previously, cost data were presented to department heads infrequently. Excerpts from the announce-

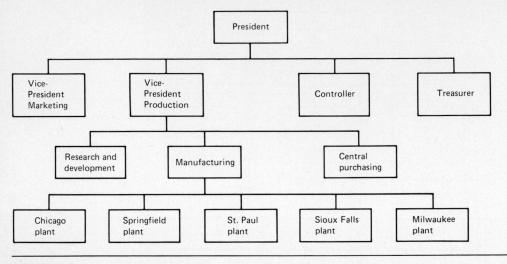

FIGURE 2.8
KLM organization
chart.

ment and the report received by the laundry supervisor are presented below.

The hospital has adopted a 'responsibility accounting system.' From now on you will receive quarterly reports comparing the costs of operating your department with budgeted costs. The reports will highlight the differences (variations) so you can zero in on the departure from budgeted costs. (This is called 'management by exception'.) Responsibility accounting means you are accountable for keeping the costs in your department within the budget. The variations from the budget will help you identify what costs are out of line and the size of the variation will indicate which ones are the most important. Your first such report accompanies this announcement. [See Fig. 2.9]

The annual budget for 1973 was constructed by the new administrator. Quarterly budgets were computed as one fourth of the annual budget. The administrator compiled the budget from analysis of the prior three years' costs. The analysis showed that all costs increased each year, with more rapid increases between the second and third year. He considered establishing the budget at an average of the prior three years' costs, hoping that the installation of the system would reduce costs to this level. However, in view of the rapidly increasing prices, he finally chose 1972 costs less three percent for the 1973 budget. The activity level measured by patient days and pounds of laundry processed was set at 1972 volume, which was approximately equal to the volume of each of the past three years.

REQUIRED

a) Comment on the method used to construct the budget.
b) What information should be communicated by variations from budgets?

Argon County Hospital
Performance Report—Laundry Department
July-September 1973

	BUDGET	ACTUAL	(OVER) UNDER BUDGET	PERCENT (OVER) UNDER BUDGET
Patient days	9,500	11,900	(2,400)	(25)
Pounds processed—laundry	125,000	156,000	(31,000)	(25)
Costs				
Laundry labor	$ 9,000	$12,500	$(3,500)	(39)
Supplies	1,100	1,875	(775)	(70)
Water, water heating and softening	1,700	2,500	(800)	(47)
Maintenance	1,400	2,200	(800)	(57)
Supervisor's salary	3,150	3,750	(600)	(19)
Allocated administration costs	4,000	5,000	(1,000)	(25)
Equipment depreciation	1,200	1,250	(50)	(4)
	$21,550	$29,075	$(7,525)	(35)

Administrator's Comments: Costs are significantly above budget for the quarter. Particular attention needs to be paid to labor, supplies, and maintenance.

FIGURE 2.9

c) Does the report effectively communicate the level of efficiency of this department? Give reasons for your answer. (CMA Examination)

32. In the Carlton Manufacturing Company, the supervisors of three production departments (Machining, Assembly, Finishing) and one service department (Maintenance) report to the plant manager. Among the plant manager's other responsibilities are the making of recommendations concerning salary increments for these subordinates as well as his own staff and the making of recommendations concerning equipment purchases for the departments under his span of control.

The following summary of costs for the Assembly Department for the month of May 1985 was compiled for use in inventory costing.

COST	BUDGET	ACTUAL
Direct labor	$10,500	$12,000
Materials spoilage	600	630
Overtime premium	1,500	1,740
Reassembly	1,200	1,170

(cont.)

COST	BUDGET	ACTUAL
Supplies and small tools	900	930
Supervisor's salary	1,950	1,950
Allocation of depreciation on building	300	300
Allocation of depreciation on equipment	300	360
Allocation of plant manager's salary	600	600
Allocation of salaries of plant manager's staff	750	780
Allocation of maintenance department costs	3,200	3,290
Total	$21,800	$23,750

ADDITIONAL
INFORMATION

☐ Budgeted costs are based upon budgeted activity of 1000 units of production. Actual number of units of production was equal to 1100.

☐ All other departments also exceeded their budgeted activity level by exactly ten percent.

☐ Maintenance Department costs are allocated in three equal amounts to the three production departments.

☐ All other allocations are made in four equal amounts to the four departments under the plant manager.

☐ Budgeted and actual salaries for the four department supervisors total $7500, including $1950 for the maintenance supervisor.

☐ Depreciation is computed on a straight-line basis. Equipment has been purchased during 1981 that was not included in the initial budget for the year.

REQUIRED

a) Categorize each cost in the above list according to whether it is (1) controllable by Assembly Department supervisor, (2) controllable by plant manager, or (3) controllable by neither.

b) Categorize each cost in the above list according to whether it is (1) fixed or (2) variable with the level of activity.

c) Prepare a performance report for the month of May for the Assembly Department supervisor. Use a three-column format, with the first column listing budget amounts, the second listing actual amounts, and the third listing variances. Assume that it is company policy for performance reports to include only controllable costs and to use the principle of flexible budgeting.

d) The total actual cost from the performance reports for the Machining and Finishing departments and the total budgeted cost for these departments according to the budgeted (rather than the actual) activity level are as follows.

DEPARTMENT	BUDGET	ACTUAL
Machining	$7500	$8400
Finishing	6000	6300

Using the same format and company policies described in part (c), prepare a performance report for the plant manager.

References

Anstine, Patricia A., and Michael E. Scott. "ARCO Establishes Responsibility Accounting at Prudhoe Bay." *Management Accounting* (March 1980): 13–20.

Bridge, Ronald E. "The Plant Controller—A Member of the Management Team." *Financial Executive* (September 1979): 26–30.

Clancy, Donald K. "The Management Control Problems of Responsibility Accounting." *Management Accounting* (March 1978): 35–39.

Daft, Richard L. *Organization Theory and Design.* St. Paul: West Publishing Company, 1980.

Duncan, Robert. "What Is the Right Organization Structure?" *Organizational Dynamics* (Winter 1979): 59–80.

Emery, James C. *Organizational Planning and Control Systems.* New York: Macmillan, 1969.

Galbraith, Jay. *Organization Design.* Reading, Mass.: Addison-Wesley, 1977.

Hernandez, William H. "Is the Controller an Endangered Species?" *Management Accounting* (August 1978): 48–52.

Higgins, John A. "Responsibility Accounting." *Arthur Andersen Chronicle* **12** (2) (April 1952): 1–17.

Horngren, Charles T. *Cost Accounting: A Managerial Emphasis.* 5th ed. Englewood Cliffs, N.J.: Prentice-Hall, 1982.

Jackson, John H., and Cyril P. Morgan. *Organization Theory: A Macro Perspective for Management.* Englewood Cliffs, N.J.: Prentice-Hall, 1978.

Krueger, Donald A. "Responsibility Accounting in Perspective." *Arthur Andersen Chronicle* (December 1966): 1–14.

March, James G., and Herbert A. Simon. *Organizations.* New York: Wiley, 1958.

Osborn, Richard N.; James G. Hunt; and Lawrence R. Jauch. *Organization Theory: An Integrated Approach.* New York: Wiley, 1980.

Reece, James S., and William R. Cool. "Measuring Investment Center Performance." *Harvard Business Review* (May/June 1978): 28–46, 174–176.

Simon, Herbert A. "On the Concept of Organizational Goal." *Administrative Science Quarterly* (June 1964): 1–22.

Todd, John. "Management Control Systems: A Key Link Between Strategy, Structure, and Employee." *Organizational Dynamics* (Spring 1977): 65–78.

Toy, James H. "Responsibility Accounting: A Practical Application." *Management Accounting* (January 1978): 23–26.

Vancil, Richard F. "Managing the Decentralized Firm." *Financial Executive* (March 1980): 34–43.

Whisler, Thomas L. *Information Technology and Organizational Change.* Belmont, Calif.: Wadsworth, 1970.

C H A P T E R　　3

Accounting Information Processing: Elements and Procedures

LEARNING OBJECTIVES

Careful study of this chapter should enable students to:

- ☐ Describe and give examples of the primary elements of accounting transaction cycles.
- ☐ Explain the steps necessary for updating accounting records.
- ☐ Design business forms in accordance with the principles of good forms design.
- ☐ Design coding systems for simple data processing applications.

CHAPTER OUTLINE

Elements of Accounting Cycles
    Transaction files, master files, and file maintenance
    General characteristics of files and records
    Modes of file maintenance
    Other types of files
    Other file characteristics
    Record retention policies
    Records management
    Information output
    Examples of accounting cycle elements

Principles of Forms Design

Coding Techniques
    Basic coding concepts
    The chart of accounts
    Organizational codes
    Other examples of coding
    Coding design considerations

Summary

Review Questions

Discussion Questions

Problems and Cases

References

In Chapter 1 the concept of the data processing cycle is introduced and discussed in the context of processing transaction data in accounting (see Fig. 1.5). That chapter points out that accounting transactions generally fall into a few major categories, five of which are briefly described: (1) purchasing of assets and services, (2) payroll, (3) sale of products and services, (4) cash receipt and disbursement, and (5) flow of inventory through production. The data processing cycles that deal with accounting transactions such as these are often called *accounting cycles* or *transaction processing cycles*. This chapter examines the elements and procedures of accounting cycles in greater detail.

Accounting cycles are at the heart of accounting information systems. The five major accounting cycles represented by the transactions listed above are the subject of the five chapters in the concluding section (Part 4) of this book. These are the revenue cycle (Chapter 16), the procurement cycle (Chapter 17), the production cycle (Chapter 18), the personnel/payroll cycle (Chapter 19), and the finance cycle (Chapter 20). As their names suggest, each of the cycles corresponds with a major functional activity of a typical business organization. Each accounting cycle consists of the accounting activities corresponding to the related business cycle functions.

The first section of this chapter focuses on the elements of accounting cycles, which include transactions, records, files, and outputs, and on the procedures used to deal with these elements. The two remaining sections of the chapter deal with the more specialized topics of forms design and coding techniques.

The principles and procedures described in this chapter are applicable to both manual and computerized data processing systems; to the accounting function as well as to the marketing, personnel, and production functions in business organizations; and to governmental agencies, educational institutions, charitable organizations, and many other types of nonbusiness organizations. The material in this chapter thus provides an important foundation for later chapters dealing with computerized data processing, with the analysis and design of accounting systems, and with specific accounting cycles associated with the major functional areas of business organizations.

Elements of Accounting Cycles

The primary elements of accounting cycles and their relationship to the stages of the data processing cycle (from Chapter 1) are illustrated in Fig. 3.1. As shown, accounting cycles begin with the occurrence of *transactions,* which are formal or informal agreements between two entities to exchange goods or services having an economic value. *External transactions* are those that take place between the business organization and an external party such as a customer or a supplier. *Internal transactions* take place between separate departments or divisions of the same business entity, as, for example, when one department transfers goods to another or performs services for another.

While most business transactions occur at the same time as the associated

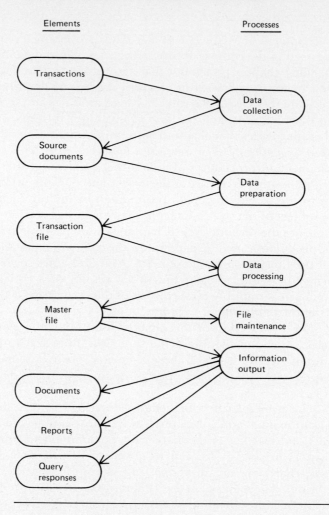

FIGURE 3.1
Elements and
processes of
accounting cycles.

exchange of value, some occur prior to the actual time of exchange. An example of this prospective type of transaction is the signing of a contract that commits the business entity to deliver goods or provide services to a customer at some future date.

The five processes listed on the right side of Fig. 3.1 correspond to the five stages of the data processing cycle described in Chapter 1. The data collection stage involves the observation of transaction data and the preparation of an initial record of that transaction data called a *source document.* Source documents are usually recorded on preprinted forms. The nature and design of business forms is described in the next section of this chapter. Examples of typical business source documents include sales invoices, purchase requisitions, and employee time cards.

Transaction files, master files, and file maintenance

Following data preparation steps such as verification, batching, and sorting (see Chapter 1), all source documents of a particular type are compiled to form a set of records called a *transaction file*. Recall from Chapter 1 that a file is defined as a set of logically related records, whereas a record is a set of logically related data items. Those data items that appear on a source document are "logically related" in the sense that they all pertain to a particular transaction. Generally, the transaction file will contain one record for each source document. Examples of typical business transaction files include a file of inventory issue and receipt transactions, a file of product sales transactions, or a file of employee timekeeping records.

In a manual data processing system, a transaction file generally consists of a batch of source documents. However, in a computerized system the source document data are usually transcribed onto a machine-readable medium such as magnetic tape or punched cards. These and other examples of machine-readable media are described in Chapter 5.

Even in a computerized system, most transaction data are originally recorded on source documents prior to being transcribed onto machine-readable media. However, some devices exist that collect data directly in machine-readable form at the time and place of their origin. This technique is called *source data automation*. Familiar examples of such devices include the automatic teller machines used by banks, and the optical scanners used in grocery and other retail stores.

Whereas a transaction file is generally a temporary file that reflects current business activity of a particular type (such as sales or purchases), a *master file* is a permanent file of records that reflect the current or nearly current status of items relevant to the business, such as inventory, employees, or customer accounts. The current status of such things changes as a result of transactions, and so transaction files are periodically processed against master files to update the master file records or make them current for the most recent transactions. A master file is permanent in that it will exist indefinitely, even though individual records within it may frequently be inserted, deleted, or changed. In contrast, a transaction file is temporary in the sense that its retention is not essential once it has been processed to update the master file (although transaction files may be retained for a certain length of time for backup and reference purposes or to satisfy legal or tax requirements).

Transactions may be classified into four general types according to their impact upon the master file—record additions, record deletions, record updates, and record changes. Record additions refer to insertions of entire new records into the file, whereas record deletions refer to extracting entire records from the file. Record updates involve revising a current master file balance, generally by adding or subtracting an amount from a transaction record. Record changes involve such things as corrections of balances, revisions to credit ratings, or changes of address.

The periodic processing of transaction files against master files to make current the master file records is referred to as *file maintenance*. File mainte-

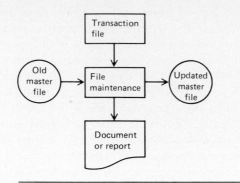

FIGURE 3.2
File maintenance.

nance is the most common task performed in virtually all data processing systems. A general diagram of the file maintenance process appears in Fig. 3.2.

A distinction is sometimes made between file maintenance and *file processing*. According to this distinction, the alteration of a master file for transactions involving record additions, record deletions, and record changes is file maintenance, whereas the alteration of a master file for transactions involving record updates is file processing. In practice, all four of these general types of transactions are often processed together. Thus the distinction is artificial, and it will not be adhered to in this book. Throughout this book the term file maintenance is used to refer to the alteration of a master file for all four of the general types of transactions described above.

The double entry accounting process may be viewed as a special case of file maintenance. The transaction files used in double entry accounting are called *journals*, and accounting master files are called *ledgers*. The process of updating accounting ledgers to reflect the transactions recorded in journals is called *posting*.

A more specific example of a file maintenance application in accounting is shown in Fig. 3.3. This simple illustration shows the updating of an accounts receivable master file record for a sales transaction. Note that even for this very simple example involving only one general type of transaction (an update), the process contains several steps.

**General
characteristics of
files and records**

Speaking in very general terms, we may say that file records contain data concerning the attributes of various entities. We may define an *entity* as an item about which information is stored in a record. Examples would thus include employees, inventory items, and customer accounts. An *attribute* is a property of an entity, such as the pay rate of an employee or the address of a customer. Generally all entities of the same type possess the same set of attributes. For example, all employees possess an employee number, a pay rate, a home address, and so on. However, the specific data values for those attributes will

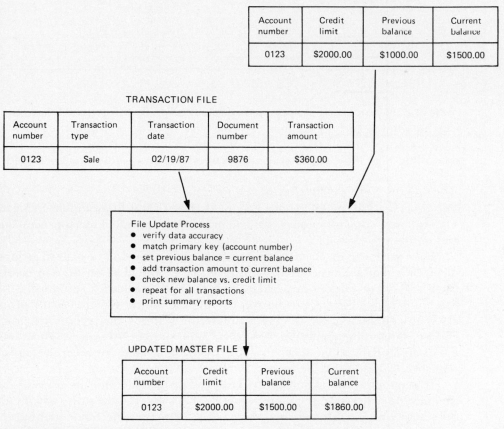

PREVIOUS MASTER FILE

Account number	Credit limit	Previous balance	Current balance
0123	$2000.00	$1000.00	$1500.00

TRANSACTION FILE

Account number	Transaction type	Transaction date	Document number	Transaction amount
0123	Sale	02/19/87	9876	$360.00

File Update Process
- verify data accuracy
- match primary key (account number)
- set previous balance = current balance
- add transaction amount to current balance
- check new balance vs. credit limit
- repeat for all transactions
- print summary reports

UPDATED MASTER FILE

Account number	Credit limit	Previous balance	Current balance
0123	$2000.00	$1500.00	$1860.00

FIGURE 3.3
Example of accounting file maintenance.

differ among entities—for example, one employee's pay rate might be $4.00, whereas another's is $4.25. Using this terminology, we may say that a record is a collection of data values for the attributes of an entity, and that a file is a group of records for all entities of a particular type.

Within a particular file, each record will have a format similar or identical to the format of every other record. This format will generally consist of a series of *fields,* with each field designated to contain a data value for a particular attribute. For example, the first field in all accounts receivable records may be reserved for the customer account number, the second field for the customer's credit limit, and so on (refer to Fig. 3.3).

The relationship between these concepts and terms is illustrated in Fig. 3.4. Whereas entity group, entity, attribute, and attribute value are very general terms, file, record, field, and data value represent their specific counter-

General Terminology	Specific Terminology	Specific Example
Entity group	File	General ledger
Entity	Record	Account
Attribute	Field	Balance
Attribute value	Data value	$150.00

FIGURE 3.4
Relationship between
processing concepts.

parts in data processing. A specific example is given by the general ledger file, which contains various account records, such as cash or prepaid expenses. Each account contains several fields, one of which is the account balance. The data value $150.00 is one that could occur within the account balance field.

Modes of file maintenance

The process of file maintenance may be accomplished in a number of ways. The two most common modes of file maintenance are called batch processing and online processing.

Batch processing involves the accumulation of transaction records in groups or batches that are processed against the master file at given time intervals (such as daily or weekly) or perhaps after the batch reaches a certain size. In batch processing the transaction records and the master file are usually processed in sequential order. In most business applications, the records are processed in numeric sequence, such as by account number. In some applications either an alphabetic sequence (usually involving a name) or a chronological sequence (by date) may be used.

In sequential file maintenance, both the master file and the transaction file must be ordered in the same sequence. This generally requires sorting of the transaction file into the same sequence as the master file. Subsequent processing involves the matching of each transaction file record with its master file counterpart according to the sequence number. Matches result in the posting of the transaction to the master file record. Unmatched master records imply no activity relating to that entity and are therefore skipped over in processing. Unmatched transaction records may have an incorrect sequence number or may be additions for insertion into the file.

An alternative means of assembling transactions for batch processing is called *remote batch processing*. This approach involves accumulating transaction records for batch processing at locations geographically separated from the central processing site. Usually, such records are recorded on a machine-readable medium and transmitted to the central processing site electronically.

Online processing refers to the processing of individual transactions through a system as they occur and from their point of origin, as opposed to accumulating them to be processed in batches. As each individual transaction is processed to update the master file record or records to which it pertains, each master file record must be directly accessed and updated. To be accomplished efficiently, this requires online data entry terminals and direct access file storage media; the nature of these forms of information systems technology is explained in Part 2 of this book.

Online processing usually entails two forms of processing, online updating and inquiry processing. *Online updating* is a form of file maintenance in which individual transactions are processed as they occur to update a master file. In *inquiry processing,* the computer system receives queries from users about information in the master file or files and searches the files for information to be compiled into an appropriate response to each query.

Online updating of master files provides the advantage that all records are up-to-date at all times. Any user can therefore obtain up-to-date information in response to a query. Such a capability is very useful in dealing with customers, in monitoring production processes, or in general managerial decision making. With batch processing, on the other hand, files are up-to-date only immediately after the processing of a batch of transactions, which may be once a day, once a week, or even once a month. Another advantage of online updating is that it minimizes or eliminates the need for data preparation activities such as sorting, batching, and transcription.

Other types of files
While transaction files and master files are the most common types of files maintained in accounting and business information systems, there are also several other types of files that are commonly used in such systems. A number of these are described here.

A *table file* is a master file of reference data, generally numeric, that is retrieved during data processing to facilitate calculations or other tasks. An example would be a payroll tax withholding table, which is entered according to marital status, number of deductions, and gross pay and provides the correct amount of income tax withholdings. Other examples include sales tax tables, freight rate tables, and statistical tables.

An *index file* is a master file of record identifiers and corresponding storage locations. A familiar example is the card catalog in a library. An index file generally uses a field such as name or account number as the record identifier. Such files are common in data processing systems that use advanced file storage technology.

A *history file* contains records of past transactions that have already been processed to update appropriate master files but are nonetheless retained for reference purposes. Examples would be a sales history file containing a record of each past sales transaction for a particular time period, and a vendor history file containing records of past transactions with vendors of products and services. History files are often a source of useful management information; for example, a sales history file may be analyzed to provide useful summary and trend information on total sales by region, by salesperson, by customer, by product, and so forth. History files are generally voluminous and so are often stored in condensed or summary form.

A *backup file* is a duplicate copy of a current master or other file. Backup copies of current files are continuously maintained in well-managed systems in order to protect the organization from the consequences of partial or complete loss of a current file. To provide maximum protection, at least one set of backup files should be stored at a location separate from the main data processing and file storage site.

A *suspense file* contains records that have been identified as erroneous or of uncertain status. Examples of the latter would be missing inventory items or accounts of uncertain collectibility. The use of a suspense file enables such records to be temporarily removed from regular processing and focuses attention on the need to investigate the errors or status problems in order to rectify them in a timely manner.

A *report file* is a temporary file generated as an intermediate step in the preparation of a report. Information may be extracted from one or more other files and recorded on a report file. This information may then be rearranged, summarized, and formatted to prepare one or more management reports.

A *data base* is a collection of integrated data from a number of related files that is stored in such a way as to facilitate both efficient online updating of the data and effective user access to the data. The nature of data bases and their related information systems is explored in Chapter 9.

Other file characteristics

Files have numerous other characteristics that are relevant from the standpoint of data processing. One is the medium upon which the file data are stored. The most common and well known of such media is the paper used in documents and forms. However, advances in information technology have brought forth a variety of other data media. Among these are magnetic tape, magnetic disk, punched cards, and microfilm. On magnetic media such as tape and disk, data are represented by means of patterns of magnetization, or demagnetization, of magnetic bits, which can be interpreted by computer input devices. On punched cards, data are represented by patterns of hole punches, also interpretable by computer input equipment. With microfilm, document records are simply reduced drastically in size by photographic means but can be enlarged by microfilm equipment for visual display. Subsequent chapters provide more extensive discussion of these and other file storage media and their related equipment.

Other concepts relevant to the design of files and file processing procedures include the activity ratio, volatility, and accessibility. The *activity ratio* is a measure applied to the file maintenance process to indicate the proportion of master file records referenced by transaction records during the process.

$$\text{Activity ratio} = \frac{\text{Number of master file records}}{\text{Total number of master file records}}$$

For example, a payroll file generally has a very high activity ratio, whereas a customer file often has a relatively low activity ratio. Knowledge of this ratio may be useful in designing systems for file maintenance. For example, a file with a very high activity ratio is generally maintained more efficiently using sequential batch processing, whereas a file with a low activity ratio may best be maintained using online updating.

Volatility is a measure of the relative frequency of additions, deletions, and other transactions requiring reference to a particular master file during a specified time period.

$$\text{File volatility} = \frac{\substack{\text{Total number of transactions} \\ \text{relating to the file}}}{\text{Standard unit of time (day, week, etc.)}}$$

For example, an airline reservation file has very high volatility, whereas a sales history file has very low volatility. This is also a useful measure for systems design purposes, as explained below.

Accessibility refers to the ease with which records can be retrieved, and is a function of the storage medium and equipment used, the coding system used, the availability of indexes, and the extent of cross-referencing between records. The need for maximum accessibility becomes more important as the volatility of a file increases. That is, a highly volatile file should be stored so that its records are quickly and easily accessible for reference and update. The need for accessibility is also a key factor in the establishment of record retention policies, which are discussed in the next section.

Record retention policies

Virtually all business records experience a relatively short period of active use followed by a much longer period of inactivity. Retention of records during this inactive period may be important—the records may be needed for occasional reference, or they may be used to satisfy legal and tax requirements. Eventually, most records reach a point when they are no longer needed for any purpose and can be destroyed.

A systematic approach to the management of business records requires the establishment of a record retention schedule. Such a schedule identifies all the types of records stored throughout the organization and indicates (1) the period of time after which each type of record can be transferred from active to inactive status and (2) the period of time after which each type of record can be safely destroyed. Inactive records should be stored in inexpensive bulk storage equipment located in a record storage center, out of the way of regular data processing activity but nonetheless accessible when needed.

Organizations that have established a formal record retention program of this kind have generally experienced substantial cost savings by significantly reducing the volume of records stored in active files. The need for expensive filing equipment is reduced, which also brings about a savings in office space. Furthermore, office employees can work more efficiently with smaller files that are not clogged with inactive records. Further savings can be achieved by utilizing less expensive file storage media for inactive records.

Records management

Because the processing of business records and files is such a key element of the operations of business organizations, many companies have established a records management function within a separate department (see Fig. 2.4). Records management involves a systematic approach to all phases of the life cycle of business records, including (1) the creation of business forms to serve as a medium for the collection and storage of record data; (2) the period of active processing, storing, and retrieving of the records themselves; (3) the period of retention of inactive records; and (4) the point of discarding obsolete records.

Some of the functions that are commonly the responsibility of a records management department include the analysis and design of forms, the selection of filing systems and equipment, the administration of a printing and copy center, the establishment and staffing of a record retention center for bulk storage of inactive records, and the administration of mail handling and distribution services. Other related functions include typing and secretarial services, telecommunications services, and the design of office work methods and procedures. In some companies many or all these functions are grouped together organizationally in a department of "office services" or "office administration."

Information output

The final elements of accounting cycles as diagrammed in Fig. 3.1 are various forms of output from the information system. Information outputs are generally compiled from information stored in master files, although this may often be combined with information from other types of files within the system. Three categories of information output identified in Fig. 3.1 are documents, reports, and query responses.

Documents that are to be utilized as transaction records are an essential form of information system output. Examples include purchase orders, customer statements, and employee paychecks and earnings statements. Documents such as these that are generated as a result of transaction processing activities are sometimes called *operational documents* in order to distinguish them from the source documents that arise at the beginning of transaction processing.

A *turnaround document* is a document that is generated as an output of transaction processing; it is used as a record of an external process or transaction and then returns to the system as a source document for that external process or transaction. An example is the machine-readable card that many utilities send out as a bill, requesting that customers return the card with their payment. Turnaround documents are generally prepared in a form that can be automatically read by a machine, such as an optical scanner, in order to facilitate their subsequent processing as input records.

Reports and query responses are used by employees to effectively control the operational activities of the business organization and by managers to make decisions and design strategies for the business. As explained in Chapter

1, there are many different types of reports, and this is apparent from the fact that reports may be categorized according to scope, time horizon, format, user, timing, and purpose. Report design considerations are discussed further in Chapter 11.

A query response is the product of inquiry processing, which in turn entails searching appropriate files for information relevant to the query, retrieving and summarizing the information in a format suitable for the person submitting the query, and then communicating the response. Some advanced information systems are designed for very fast response to queries and other online processing requirements. Systems in which the fast-response feature is important in facilitating the operation of an external process or the execution of a transaction with an external party are called *real-time systems*. Examples are airline reservation systems and online bank teller systems.

Examples of accounting cycle elements

The opening paragraphs of this chapter list five primary accounting cycles. Fig. 3.1 shows seven major elements of any accounting cycle. The discussion of accounting cycles to this point has provided several examples of these elements. To provide a more comprehensive set of examples and introduce the reader to the basic features of all five primary accounting cycles, Fig. 3.5 provides one example of each of the seven cycle elements within each of the five primary cycles. A more detailed description of these and other accounting cycle elements is provided in Part 4 of this book.

FIGURE 3.5
Examples of elements
of primary
accounting cycles.

CYCLE ELEMENTS	MANUFACTURING COMPANY TRANSACTION PROCESSING CYCLES				
	Revenue	Procurement	Production	Personnel	Financial
Transaction	Sale	Purchase	Assembly	Employee services rendered	Cash receipts and disbursements
Source document	Invoice	Purchase requisition	Production order	Employee clock card	Journal voucher
Transaction file	Sales journal	Purchases journal	Job time records	Payroll transactions	General journal
Master file	Accounts receivable	Inventory ledger	Work-in-process file	Payroll file	General ledger
Report	Sales analysis	Vendor performance	Production cost summary	Payroll register	Trial balance
Output document	Customer statement	Purchase order	Quality inspection record	Employee paycheck	Disbursement check
Query response	Customer balance	Order status	Production job status	Employee qualifications	Account status

**Principles of
Forms Design**

Many source documents and other business records are initially recorded on business forms. A *form* is a document preprinted with headings and spaces for the insertion of data. The preprinted data on a form are referred to as *constant data,* whereas the items to be filled in are referred to as *variable data.* Once the variable data have been filled in, the form becomes a record. Figure 3.6, a sample credit memorandum form, illustrates many of the principles of forms design discussed in this section.

Most forms consist of four major elements: (1) the introduction, (2) instructions, (3) the main body, and (4) the conclusion. The introduction generally should appear at the top of the form and should contain the title of the form, the form number, and if the form is to be distributed to outside parties, the name and address of the organization sending the form. Each of these elements is present in the sample form in Fig. 3.6.

Instructions are generally of two types: (1) how to fill out the form and (2) what to do with the form after filling it out. In simple forms such as the sample credit memo, the preprinted data that indicate what information is to be recorded on the form usually serve as the instructions on how to complete the form. Specialized forms that are infrequently used or that deal with technical information may require more specific written instructions on the body of the form or occasionally on the reverse side. Instructions on what to do with the form should indicate, when applicable, the sequence of departments to which the form is to be routed, or the appropriate distribution of completed copies of the form, as illustrated in the sample credit memo.

In the main body of the form, the primary design objective is to make the form as simple as possible to use. Logically related information should be grouped together on the form, with box and columnar arrangements used as much as possible to set off spaces for recording data. Care should be taken to provide ample room for recording the data required by each space. In addition, the sequence in which the data item spaces appear on the form should be consistent with the sequence in which the data itself will be initially recorded on the form, and/or the sequence in which the data items will be transcribed from the form to some other medium. The latter point is especially critical when the form is to be used as a source document for keying the data into an automated data processing system. Each of these principles is evident in the design of the form in Fig. 3.6.

A useful technique that minimizes the extent to which users are required to write explanations or other lengthy statements on a form is to preprint the most commonly used of such explanations or statements on the face of the form. The user then decides which of the preprinted items is applicable and simply records the code number associated with it or checks off a box next to it. To provide for unusual cases not encompassed by the preprinted list, an "other" category may be provided, along with sufficient space to record a written explanation. The application of this technique is illustrated by the "reason for return codes" in the sample credit memo. It is clear that this technique will significantly reduce the time required to fill out a form.

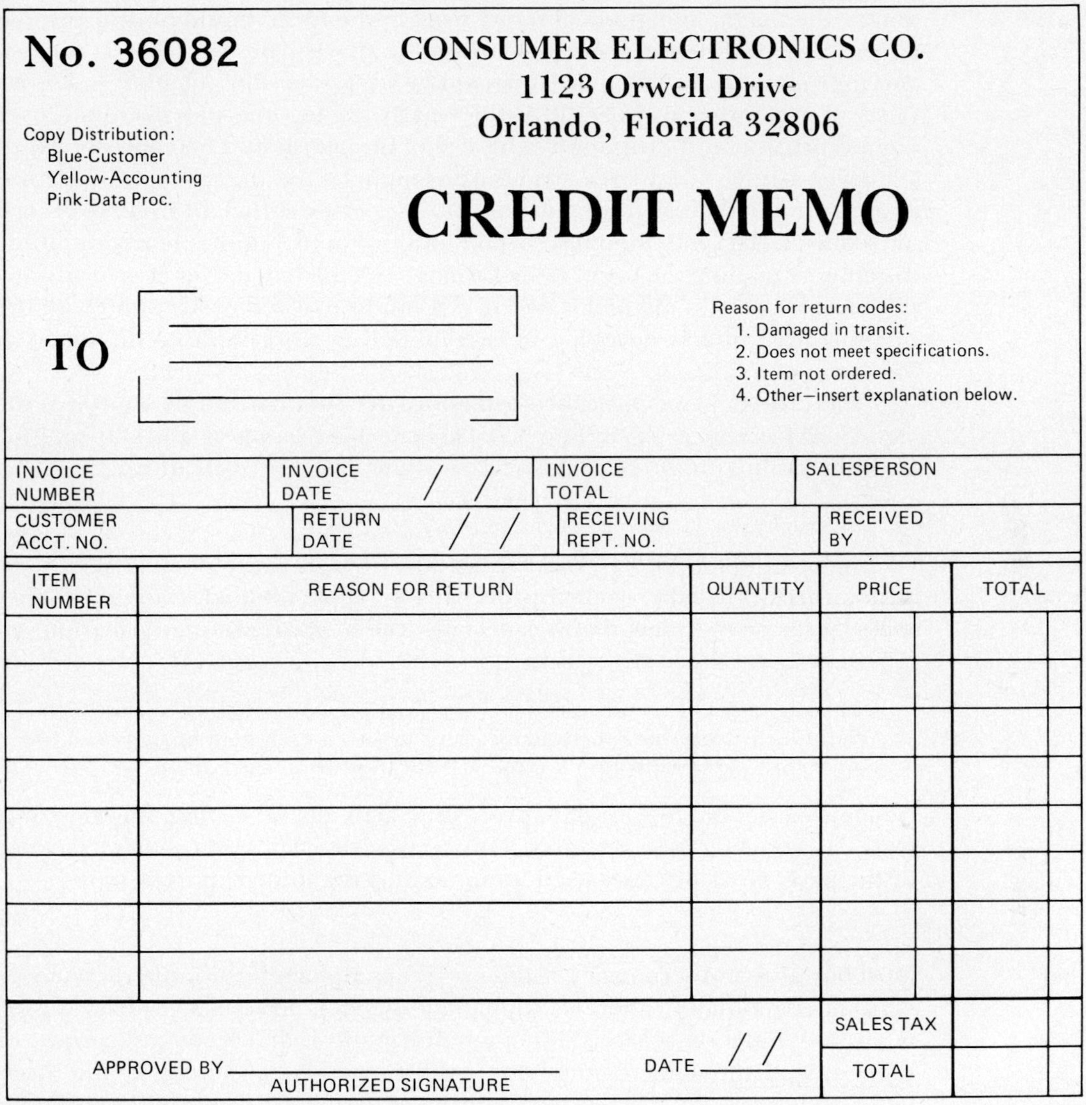

No. 36082

CONSUMER ELECTRONICS CO.
1123 Orwell Drive
Orlando, Florida 32806

Copy Distribution:
Blue-Customer
Yellow-Accounting
Pink-Data Proc.

CREDIT MEMO

TO

Reason for return codes:
1. Damaged in transit.
2. Does not meet specifications.
3. Item not ordered.
4. Other—insert explanation below.

INVOICE NUMBER	INVOICE DATE / /	INVOICE TOTAL	SALESPERSON	
CUSTOMER ACCT. NO.	RETURN DATE / /	RECEIVING REPT. NO.	RECEIVED BY	

ITEM NUMBER	REASON FOR RETURN	QUANTITY	PRICE	TOTAL	
			SALES TAX		
APPROVED BY _____ AUTHORIZED SIGNATURE		DATE ___ / / ___	TOTAL		

FIGURE 3.6
Sample credit
memorandum form.

The concluding portion invariably appears at the bottom of the form. This portion should allow space to record information concerning the final disposition and/or final approval of the transaction recorded on the form, including an approval signature and date. If the form concerns a financial transaction, a dollar total will also appear here. Once again, these elements are illustrated in the sample credit memo in Fig. 3.6.

There are also certain principles that apply to the form itself. For example, the weight and grade of paper used in the form should be appropriate to its usage and retention requirements. Boldface type, extra thick rulings, varying colors, and shaded areas should be used liberally to highlight key aspects of the form, to separate distinct parts, or to otherwise facilitate user comprehension and utilization. The size of a form should be consistent with whatever standardized sizes are used throughout the organization. The size chosen for a particular form must of course provide sufficient room to record all required data but should also take into account requirements for filing, binding, or mailing the form. If the form is to be mailed, the name and address of the addressee should be located in a position that will correspond with the opening in a window envelope, as exemplified by the sample credit memo in Fig. 3.6.

The various principles discussed above are summarized in the forms design checklist appearing in Fig. 3.7. This checklist serves as a useful tool for both the evaluation of existing forms and the design of new ones.

Coding Techniques

Coding techniques are an essential aspect of the design and control of business records. Virtually all data processing systems, whether manual or automated, use codes—a fact that is especially true of accounting information systems. *Coding* has been defined as

> the assignment of numbers, letters, or other symbols according to a systematic plan for distinguishing the classifications to which each item belongs and for distinguishing items within a given classification from each other.[1]

Codes are essential to such data processing activities as sorting, summarizing, storage, reporting, and retrieval. This section describes and illustrates some of the basic types of codes used in an accounting information system.

Basic coding concepts

Most business and accounting codes use either alphabetic or numeric symbols, or some combination thereof. Alphabetic symbols have two primary advantages over numeric symbols. First, an alphabetic code can be mnemonic, or suggestive of the name of the item it represents. For example, in the three-letter code used by airline companies to identify airports, DFW represents Dallas–Fort Worth, and JFK stands for New York's Kennedy airport. The second advantage is that a single position in an alphabetic code can represent up to twenty-six different possible categories, as opposed to only ten for a numeric code. Thus alphabetical codes are potentially more economical in terms of the number of code positions used.

Despite these factors, numeric codes have long been more common in business and accounting. It has been found that numeric codes are less error

---

[1]National Association of Accountants, *Classification and Coding Techniques to Facilitate Accounting Operations,* Research Report 34 (New York: National Association of Accountants, 1959), p. 3.

FORMS DESIGN CHECKLIST

General Considerations

1. Are preprinted data used to the maximum extent feasible?
2. Is the weight and grade of paper appropriate for planned usage?
3. Are bold type, double-thick rulings, varying colors, and shaded areas appropriately used?
4. Is the form of a standard size?
5. Is the form large enough for its intended purpose?
6. Is the size of the form consistent with requirements for filing, binding, or mailing?
7. Does the design of the form enable its use in a window envelope?

Introductory Section

8. Does the name of the form appear in bold type?
9. Are copies of the form consecutively prenumbered?
10. If the form is externally distributed, is the company's name and address preprinted on it?
11. Do all introductory data appear at the top of the form?

Instructions

12. Is it clear how the form is to be filled out?
13. Is the routing of the form indicated?
14. Is the distribution of completed copies indicated?

Main Body

15. Is logically related information grouped together?
16. Are box and columnar arrangements appropriately used?
17. Is there sufficient room to record each data item?
18. Is the ordering of the data items consistent with the sequence in which they are recorded or transcribed?
19. Are standardized explanations preprinted to enable codes or checkoffs to replace written user entries?

Conclusion

20. Is space provided to record data concerning final disposition of the form?
21. Is space provided for a signature or signatures indicating final approval?
22. Is space provided to record the date of final disposition or approval?
23. Is space provided for a dollar or other numeric total?
24. Do all concluding data appear at the bottom of the form?

FIGURE 3.7
Forms design
checklist.

prone and more easily remembered when the length of the code is more than just a few positions. Furthermore, numeric codes are more amenable to machine processing.

Perhaps the most common application of coding in data processing is the assignment of a unique identification number to each data record within the system. This number is referred to as a *key* or, more specifically, a *primary key*. Figure 3.8 lists some of the common types of data records in a business organization and identifies the key most commonly used for each. The basic purpose of the key is to fix the location of each record within a large file of similar records. The key is therefore essential to such data processing activities as retrieval of specific records from a file, storing of records, and updating of records to reflect the occurrence of transactions.

Records are generally maintained in sequence according to their primary key. However, records may at times be sorted into sequence on a different

Record Type	Primary Key
Payroll	Employee Number
Customer	Account Number
Parts Inventory	Stock Number
Work-in-Process	Job Number
Finished Goods	Product Code
General Ledger	Account Code
Fixed Assets	Asset Number
Accounts Payable	Vendor Code

FIGURE 3.8
Examples of record keys for typical business records.

key field for some other purpose. For example, payroll records may normally be sequenced by employee code number but may be sorted by social security number prior to preparation of tax reports. The term *secondary key* refers to such fields. At times a secondary key is used as a secondary determinant of file sequence when many records have the same primary key. For example, a bank that maintains its customer transactions file in sequence according to the primary key of account number may also use the secondary key of date processed to order transactions within each customer account. Secondary keys are also used frequently in index files for cross-referencing purposes.

Many of the codes used in business and accounting applications are *sequence codes*. In this coding system, items are numbered consecutively, and each new item is assigned a number one higher than the last to ensure that there will be no gaps in the sequence. The basic advantage of this technique is that it enables the user to account for all the items because any missing items will cause a gap in the numerical sequence. Applications of this technique in business and accounting systems include the numbering of checks, invoices, purchase orders, job orders, and many other documents. In most cases these documents are prenumbered to further facilitate control.

Another commonly used coding technique is the *block code*. This involves reserving blocks of numbers within a numerical sequence, with each block corresponding to a category having meaning to the user. For example, consider a manufacturer of home appliances with four basic product lines—electric ranges, refrigerators, washers, and dryers. Within each product line, there may be a wide variety of models, varying in size, style, color, year of manufacture, and so forth. If a seven-digit product code is used, block coding can be applied by reserving a specific range of code numbers for each of the four major product categories, as illustrated in the following example.

PRODUCT CODE	PRODUCT TYPE
1000000–2999999	Electric range
3000000–5999999	Refrigerator
6000000–7999999	Washer
8000000–9999999	Dryer

Under this scheme, a user familiar with the code can readily identify the type of item by code number alone. In addition to product code numbers, this technique can be applied to ledger account numbers (blocked by account type), employee numbers (blocked by department), customer numbers (blocked by region), and several other codes used in business and accounting.

Still another technique, often used in conjunction with the block code, is the *group code*. Under this scheme, there are two or more subgroups of digits within the code number, and each subgroup is used to code the item. If the seven-digit product code number is used as an example, the group-coding technique may be applied as follows.

DIGIT POSITION	MEANING
1–2	Product line, size, style
3	Color
4–5	Year of manufacture
6–7	Optional features

Thus there are four subcodes within the product code, with a different meaning conveyed by each subcode. Given the actual code number of a particular product, a user who decodes the number can learn a significant amount about the item itself. Furthermore, this type of code enables sorting, summarizing, and retrieval of information based upon one or more of the subcodes. This technique is often applied to general ledger account numbers and has several other possible applications in business data processing.

The chart of accounts

The *chart of accounts* is a list of codes for all balance sheet and income statement accounts of a business. The codes are account numbers, and they represent the key field for the general ledger records. There are few other areas in which coding techniques are more highly developed or widely applied than in the development of a chart of accounts. This fact reflects the importance of the chart of accounts in the processing and reporting of information by the accounting information system.

Most charts of accounts use numeric codes with a combination of group coding and block coding techniques. An example of a group coding scheme for account numbers is the following.

DIGIT POSITION	CLASSIFICATION
1–2	Division, plant, or office
3–4	Department
5–7	Major account
8–9	Subaccount

The first two digits indicate the division, plant, or office location to which the transaction relates, and the second two digits indicate the specific department within that division, plant, or office. The major account code identifies broad account classifications, such as cash or selling expenses. Finally, the subaccount code identifies the account according to more detailed categories, such as cash in bank or sales commissions.

Block coding is usually applied to the major account codes and often to the divisional and departmental codes as well. One possible block coding scheme for a chart of accounts appears below.

MAJOR ACCOUNT CODE	MAJOR ACCOUNT TYPE
100–199	Current assets
200–299	Noncurrent assets
300–399	Liabilities
400–499	Capital
500–599	Revenue
600–699	Cost of goods sold
700–799	Selling expenses
800–899	General and administrative expenses
900–999	Nonoperating income and expenses

A simplified chart of balance sheet accounts consistent with this block coding scheme appears in Fig. 3.9. A corresponding chart of income statement accounts appears in Fig. 3.10. These charts are "simplified" in that many of the accounts represent general categories that can include a number of more detailed accounts. For example, categories within the cash account may include cash on hand, petty cash funds, demand deposits, savings accounts, and certificates of deposit. The degree of detail required will vary with the size of the organization and its needs. For example, the level of detail shown in the figures might be adequate for a very small company, whereas a large company might require hundreds of separate accounts.

The chart of accounts is an extremely useful tool for processing of accounting data in organizations of all types and sizes. It facilitates the recording and posting of transactions, and it simplifies the preparation of financial statements and a variety of other summary reports. The account codes are suitably concise to be used for cross-referencing purposes. A well-designed chart of accounts is easily adapted to automated methods of data processing. Even a very small single-location business can obtain substantial benefits from the use of a chart of accounts.

Organizational codes

In a medium-size to large company, it is generally very useful for the chart of accounts to incorporate subcodes indicating the division or branch responsible for the transaction, and also the department within that division or branch. In the group coding scheme for accounts shown earlier, the first two

Account Code	Account Name	Account Code	Account Name
100–199	Current Assets	300–399	Liabilities
100	Cash	300	Accounts Payable
110	Marketable Securities	310	Accrued Wages and Salaries
120	Accounts Receivable	320	Accrued Taxes
125	Allowance for Doubtful Accounts	330	Accrued Interest
130	Notes Receivable	340	Dividends Payable
140	Inventory—Raw Materials	350	Notes Payable
150	Inventory—Work in Process	360	Bonds Payable
160	Inventory—Finished Goods	370	Other Liabilities
170	Prepaid Expenses		
200–299	Noncurrent Assets	400–499	Capital Accounts
200	Land	400	Capital Stock
210	Buildings	410	Preferred Stock
215	Allowance for Depreciation—Buildings	420	Paid-in Surplus
220	Equipment	430	Retained Earnings
225	Allowance for Depreciation—Equipment		
230	Office Fixtures		
235	Allowance for Depreciation—Office Fixtures		
240	Long-Term Investments		
250	Intangible Assets		
260	Other Assets		

FIGURE 3.9
Simplified balance
sheet chart of
accounts.

digits represent the division, and the third and fourth digits represent the department. The importance of these codes is quite simple: They greatly facilitate the accumulation, analysis, summarization, and reporting of accounting information according to responsibilities. In other words, such codes are an essential part of a responsibility accounting system, as described in Chapter 2.

An example of a two-digit departmental coding scheme is shown in Fig. 3.11. The organization structure reflected in this illustration is consistent with, but somewhat more detailed than, the organization chart shown in Fig. 2.4.

The following sample transactions illustrate how these departmental codes might be used in conjunction with the account codes in recording accounting data: an expenditure for indirect labor within the Drill Press Department; a requisition of raw materials from Stores by the Assembly Department; a sale on account within Sales District 43; the purchase of office fixtures for use in the Controller's Office; and a consultant's fee incurred by the Marketing Department.

The indirect labor expenditure would be debited to account number 23–631, where "23" refers to the Drill Press Department, and "631" refers to the Indirect Labor account. The account credited would be 00–800, where "800" refers to the Payroll Control account. The "00" is used as the departmental code to indicate that the Payroll account is a general account not applicable to any particular organizational unit.

Account Code	Account Name	Account Code	Account Name
500–599	Operating Revenues	700–799	Selling Expenses
500	Sales Revenue	700	Sales Commissions
510	Sales Discounts	710	Advertising
520	Sales Returns and Allowances	720	Entertainment
530	Miscellaneous Revenue	730	Delivery
		740	Warrantee
		750	Other Selling Expenses
600–699	Cost of Goods Sold		
600	Cost of Goods Sold		
610	Direct Materials	800–899	General and Administrative Expenses
620	Direct Labor	800	Payroll Control
630	Factory Overhead Control	810	Wages and Salaries
631	Indirect Labor	820	Legal and Consulting
632	Supplies and Small Tools	830	Travel
633	Supervision	840	Depreciation—Office Fixtures
634	Depreciation—Plant	850	Stationery and Supplies
635	Depreciation—Equipment	860	Postage
636	Heat, Light, and Power	870	Communications
637	Taxes and Insurance	880	Interest
640	Applied Factory Overhead	890	Taxes
		895	Other Administrative

FIGURE 3.10
Simplified income
statement chart of
accounts.

FIGURE 3.11
Sample departmental
codes for chart of
accounts.

Code	Department	Code	Department
00	General Accounts	50–59	Finance Department
01	President's Office	50	Treasurer
10–29	Production Department	51	Credit and Collections
10	Vice-President, Production	52	Cashier
11	Engineering	53	Insurance
12	Production Planning	60–69	Accounting Department
13	Purchasing	60	Controller
14	Receiving, Shipping, Stores	61	Budgeting
20	General Superintendent	62	Tax Planning
21	Automatic Screw Machine	63	Internal Audit
22	Assembly	64	Cost Accounting
23	Drill Press	70	Accounting Manager
24	Punch Press	71	Billing
25	Heat Treating	72	Accounts Receivable
30–49	Marketing Department	73	Accounts Payable
30	Vice-President, Marketing	74	General Ledger
31	Advertising and Promotion	75	Payroll
32	Product Planning	80–89	Personnel Department
33	Customer Service	80	Personnel Manager
34	Marketing Research	81	Employment Office
40	Sales Manager	82	Education and Training
41–49	District Sales Managers	83	Welfare and Safety

The materials requisition would result in a debit to an account coded 22–610, where "22" indicates that the Assembly Department accepted responsibility for the materials, and "610" represents the account code for Direct Materials (alternatively, the debit might be made directly to "150," the Work-in-Process Inventory account). The credit for this transaction would be made to an account coded 14–140, where "14" indicates that the Stores Department relinquished its responsibility for the materials, and "140" indicates the account code for Raw Materials Inventory.

The sale transaction would be debited to account 00–120 (General–Accounts Receivable) and credited to account 43–500 (District 43 Sales Revenue). Note that only the sales district is reflected by the account number. An indication of the salesperson, the product, and the customer would have to be obtained from codes other than those in the chart of accounts.

The purchase of office fixtures for the Controller's Office would be debited to account 60–230 (Controller–Office Fixtures). The credit would normally be to account 00–300 (General–Accounts Payable).

The account code used to charge the consultant's fee would depend upon which manager within the Marketing Department had received the consulting services. For example, if the services had been performed for the Marketing Research Department, the correct departmental code for the debit portion of the entry would be "34." If the services had been performed for the Vice-President of Marketing, "30" would be the appropriate departmental code. The journal account code for the debit portion would in either case be "820," Legal and Consulting Expenses. The credit portion of the entry would be made to account 00–300 (General–Accounts Payable).

In general, all costs and expenses incurred by the organization should be charged to an account coded to indicate the department for which the cost or expense is controllable. All sales should be coded to reflect the regional department that generated the sale. Asset accounts such as Inventories or Fixed Assets may be coded to indicate the department having custodial responsibility for the asset. Most other accounts are general or control accounts, such as Cash, Accounts Payable, or Payroll, and need not contain any specific departmental code.

The organizational codes facilitate several data processing activities related to responsibility accounting. For example, cost and expense data may be sorted by department code and then summarized for each department to generate reports of controllable costs for all departments. Budgeted data would be similarly coded and processed to enable the preparation of performance reports indicating budget variances. The codes are used to perform the function of filtration in preparing these reports, meaning that for each department uncontrollable costs are filtered out and not included in the performance summary. The organizational codes serve as a partial index to store cost and expense data, thus simplifying the retrieval of such data for purposes of comparing and analyzing past trends within and among departments.

Other examples of coding

The coding concepts discussed above may be applied within a business organization to a wide variety of items in addition to accounts—items such as raw materials and parts, customers, employees, vendors, job orders, fixed assets, sales transactions, and salespeople. This section contains a brief description of two such coding systems, one for employees and the other for sales transactions.

Employee number serves as a key field for the payroll and personnel files. An example of a group code for employee numbers is as follows.

DIGIT POSITION	MEANING
1–2	Division
3–4	Department
5	Pay code (salaries, wages, etc.)
6–10	Unique employee number

Numerous data processing activities can make use of this code. For example, pay records would likely be batched to pay code, and perhaps also by department number, prior to preparation of paychecks. Since payroll processing is generally sequential, pay records would be sorted by employee number prior to processing. The employee code could serve as a basis for summarizing, reporting, retrieval, and analysis of personnel or payroll information by division, by department, and/or by pay code for numerous purposes.

The analysis of sales transactions is an important management activity that is facilitated by a good coding system for sales transactions. An example of such a code is as follows.

DIGIT POSITION	MEANING
1–2	Geographical area
3–5	Type of product
6–10	Salesperson number
11	Type of customer
12	Customer's credit rating
13–17	Customer's identification number

In this type of coding system, sales may be sorted, summarized, and reported in a variety of ways useful to management. For example, a summary report of sales by geographic area indicates which regions are making the best contributions to sales and provides a guide to future allocation of marketing resources among regions. A summary report by type of product is useful for making product-line decisions. A summary report by salesperson would be useful in evaluating the performance of salespeople. Finally, summary reports by type of customer and customer number are useful in assessing the significance of various classes of customers and identifying the most important individual customers.

Coding design considerations

The most obvious consideration in the design of a coding system is that the codes be chosen in a manner consistent with their intended usage. This implies that the code designer must determine the types of system outputs desired by users prior to selecting the code. For example, a responsibility accounting system certainly requires that accounting transactions be coded by organizational unit. Similarly, if sales analyses according to salesperson are important to the evaluation of sales performance, then sales transactions should include the salesperson code.

There are numerous other considerations in code design. One is that the designer should allow sufficient latitude in the code for likely growth in the number of items to be coded. For example, a three-digit employee code is probably inadequate for an organization with 950 employees. Another consideration is that the coding system be as simple as possible in order to minimize costs, facilitate memorization and interpretation of coding categories, and ensure employee acceptance. The likely use of mechanized processing should also be taken into account, even though the data processing system may not yet be mechanized. Finally, it is important that the coding systems selected in different areas of an organization be consistent in order to facilitate subsequent integration of data processing activities across functional lines. For example, the group coding system given earlier for account numbers is consistent across the first four positions with the employee number codes given in the previous section. Also, the appearance of the salesperson number in positions 6–10 of the sales transaction code shown above is consistent with the corresponding digit positions of the employee number code.

Summary

Accounting cycles involve the collection, processing, and maintenance of accounting transaction data. A key task in any accounting cycle is file maintenance, or the updating of an accounting ledger or master file to reflect recent transaction activity. Batch processing and online processing are the two common modes of file maintenance.

Many source documents and other business records are initially recorded on business forms. Therefore designers of business information systems should understand the principles underlying the design of a good business form.

Coding of records and files is a central feature of business information systems. All records have a primary key, which serves as a unique record identifier, and they may also have secondary keys, which facilitate processing and retrieval. The chart of accounts commonly used in accounting is a highly developed example of a business coding system. The design of coding systems that facilitate efficient processing and reporting of business data is an important skill for information systems specialists.

Review Questions

1. Define the following terms.

accounting cycle	index file
transaction processing cycle	history file
transaction	backup file
external transaction	suspense file
internal transaction	report file
source document	data base
transaction file	activity ratio
source data automation	volatility
master file	operational document
file maintenance	turnaround document
file processing	real-time system
journal	form
ledger	constant data
posting	variable data
entity	coding
attribute	key
field	primary key
batch processing	secondary key
remote batch processing	sequence code
online processing	block code
online updating	group code
inquiry processing	chart of accounts
table file	

2. What are the five major accounting cycles?

3. Identify the seven primary elements of accounting cycles and explain how they are associated with the five stages of the data processing cycle.

4. Identify some examples of (a) typical business transaction files and (b) typical business master files.

5. Identify and describe the four major categories of transactions.

6. Explain how double entry accounting may be viewed as a special case of file maintenance.

7. Explain the relationship between the concepts of entities and attributes, on one hand, and the concepts of files, records, fields, and data, on the other.

8. Compare and contrast the two most common modes of file maintenance.

9. Identify, describe, and give examples of several different types of files.

10. Identify several media upon which file records may be stored.

11. Give an example of a file that has (a) a high activity ratio; (b) a low activity ratio.

12. Give an example of a file that has (a) high volatility; (b) low volatility.

13. Explain how knowledge of a file's (a) activity ratio and (b) volatility might be useful in designing an information system.

14. Explain the concept of record accessibility.

15. Explain the purpose of a record retention schedule.

16. How can cost savings be achieved by a formal record retention program?

17. What is records management? What phases of the record life cycle does it encompass?

18. List several functions commonly performed by a records management department.

19. Identify examples of accounting cycle elements within each of the five primary accounting cycles.

20. When does a form become a record?

21. List the four major elements of a form and describe what each of these should contain.

22. What is the primary design objective in the main body of a form? Describe several principles that can help to achieve this objective.

23. Which activities in the data processing cycle rely heavily on the use of codes?

24. Describe the advantages and disadvantages of alphabetic codes relative to numeric codes in data processing.

25. Identify the likely primary key for several types of business records.

26. Explain three ways in which secondary keys may be used.

27. What is the basic advantage of the sequence code? Give some examples of the use of this type of code.

28. Give some business examples of the use of block codes.

29. Give some business examples of the use of group codes.

30. Describe and illustrate the use of both block codes and group codes in the chart of accounts.

31. Explain some of the benefits of using a chart of accounts in processing accounting data.

32. Describe the use of organizational codes in accounting data processing. Explain the advantages of using these codes.

33. Explain several considerations relevant to the design of a coding system.

Discussion Questions

34. Examples of files and file processing given in this chapter related primarily to retail or manufacturing companies. Identify some of the types of files and file processing procedures you would be likely to encounter in the following organizations:
    a) a university
    b) a hospital
    c) a bank
    d) an insurance company
    e) a stockbrokerage
    f) an advertising agency

35. For each type of organization listed in the previous question, select one of the major files and discuss the type of coding system that would be appropriate for records in that file.

36. In theory, a business organization should not use any procedure or technique unless its benefits exceed its costs. Discuss the benefits and costs of a chart of accounts.

37. The BMI Manufacturing Company has recently merged with another company and substantially expanded its product line. As a result, marketing executives have decided to redesign the company's coding system for products. Discuss the role that the accounting department should (or should not) play in this redesign process.

Problems and Cases

38. Computer data processing is based upon the logical organization of data into files, records, and data-items. For each of the following, state whether it is a file, a record, or a data-item (field).
    a) all information on one customer
    b) accounts receivable subsidiary ledger
    c) employee number
    d) amount owed a particular vendor
    e) general ledger
    f) accounts payable subsidiary ledger
    g) information on a particular vendor
    h) the name of one vendor
    i) all information on one inventory item

39. For each of the following data processing applications, indicate whether (a) batch processing or (b) online processing would be the more appropriate mode of processing. Explain each answer.

    a) weekly processing of employee time cards to prepare paychecks

    b) processing of customer reservation requests by a motel chain

    c) processing of credit checks by a retail credit bureau

    d) preparation of monthly customer bills by a utility company

    e) processing of customer transactions occurring at teller windows by a bank

    f) scheduling of material and labor activity in an automated factory

    g) preparation of monthly financial statements

    h) processing of cash receipts on account from customers

    i) reordering of merchandise inventory in a high-volume retail store

40. Prepare a diagram representing file maintenance of an accounts receivable file. Use a format similar to Fig. 3.2, except label each of the peripheral symbols according to their specific content (i.e., specific to accounts receivable processing).

41. In five recently completed file maintenance jobs, the Dalton Department Store processed the following numbers and types of transactions.

☐ three fixed asset acquisitions

☐ two fixed asset retirements

☐ 150 credit journal entries

☐ 5400 credit sales on account

☐ 650 debit journal entries

☐ 18,000 items of merchandise sold

☐ 300 payment authorizations

☐ 270 payments on account to suppliers

☐ 30 purchase returns

☐ 1800 receipts of payment on account

☐ 870 receipts of merchandise from suppliers

☐ 100 sales returns

The five master files being maintained, together with the number of records within each file, are

☐ accounts payable, 2000 records

☐ accounts receivable, 8800 records

☐ fixed asset ledger, 250 records

☐ general ledger, 100 accounts

☐ inventory, 7600 records

During file maintenance, some of the master file records updated will have only one related transaction, whereas others may have several transactions posted to them at once. For each of the master files mentioned above, the average number of transactions pertaining to each master file record referenced (i.e., excluding those master records having no transactions) is

☐ accounts payable, 1.5

☐ accounts receivable, 2

☐ fixed asset ledger, 1

☐ general ledger, 8

☐ inventory, 5

Compute the activity ratio for each of the five files given above. [**Hint:** First compute the total number of master file records referenced during the file maintenance for each file.]

42. Prepare a diagram representing file maintenance of a raw materials and parts inventory file, using a format similar to that shown in Fig. 3.2. Label each of the peripheral symbols according to their specific content (i.e., content specific to inventory processing).

43. As controller of the Easy Insurance Company, you have recently authorized a study by a records management consultant on the feasibility of establishing a formal record retention program that would include the installation of a bulk record storage center. The consultant has prepared the following estimates.

☐ There are approximately 500,000 documents now stored in Easy's office files.

☐ If a formal record retention program is established, three fourths of Easy's documents can be moved out of active storage. Of these, two thirds can be destroyed, and the remaining one third can be stored in the record storage center.

☐ The cost per year of storing a document in the active office files will be $0.02, which includes the cost of equipment, labor, supplies, and overhead.

☐ The cost per year of storing a document in the record storage center will be $0.002.

☐ Retrieval of a document from the record storage center will cost an additional $3.00. There will be an estimated 200 such retrievals per year.

☐ The initial cost of starting up the program and establishing the record storage center will be $10,000.

a) Compute the estimated annual cost savings if the proposed record retention program is established.

b) Should you authorize establishment of the record retention program? Discuss.

44. Consider the sales document form you designed for Katie's Flower Shop (Chapter 1, Problem 31). Evaluate your form using the forms design checklist in Fig. 3.7.

45. Consider the service work order form you designed for McCann's Auto

Repair Shop (Chapter 1, Problem 32). Evaluate your form using the forms design checklist in Fig. 3.7.

46. The Wong Lee Restaurant uses customer checks with prenumbered sequence codes. A waitress prepares the customer's check, which the customer then presents to the cashier. Waitresses are told not to destroy any checks and, if a mistake is made, to void the check and prepare another. All voided checks are given to the manager daily.

REQUIRED

Explain the role of sequence codes in controlling cash receipts in this situation.

47. Refer to the discussion in Chapter 1 of the accounting information system of a retail home-appliance dealer. Design a form to be used as a sales document by a company of this type.

48. As an accountant for Radiotronics Corporation, a manufacturer and distributor of radios, you have been asked to design a sales analysis code. Some facts relevant to this task follow.

☐ The company has four major product lines: portable radios, table radios, digital clock radios, and citizen's band radios. The number of styles available within each product line are twelve, four, ten, and five, respectively.

☐ The company has divided its sales area (that covers most of the United States and part of Canada) into nine regions. Each region is divided into six to twelve districts, each of which is assigned to a salesperson.

☐ The company sells to seven major categories of customers and has approximately 1500 separate customer accounts.

REQUIRED

Design a group coding system for assignment of sales analysis codes to sales transactions. Indicate the meaning and usefulness of each digit position or group of digit positions within the code.

49. Using the codes from the sample charts of accounts in Figs. 3.9 and 3.10 and the organizational codes in Fig. 3.11, assign a five-digit transaction code to both the debit and credit entries for the following accounting transactions.

a) sale of a used punch press for cash equal to its book value

b) authorization to pay a bill for a national advertising campaign

c) accrual of salary and sales commission for a salesperson in District 48

d) approval of an allowance for damaged merchandise requested by a customer in District 46

e) authorization to pay a bill for travel expenses incurred by the President

50. Properly designed and utilized forms facilitate adherence to prescribed

internal accounting control policies and procedures. One such form might be a multicopy purchase order, with one copy intended to be mailed to the vendor. The remaining copies would ordinarily be distributed to the stores, purchasing, receiving, and accounting departments.

The purchase order shown as Fig. 3.12 is currently being used by National Industrial Corporation.

REQUIRED

In addition to the name of the company, what other necessary information would you recommend be included in the illustrative purchase order? (CPA Examination)

FIGURE 3.12

PURCHASE ORDER
SEND INVOICE ONLY TO:

297 HARDINGTEN DR., BX., NY 10461

TO _____   SHIP TO _____

DATE TO BE SHIPPED	SHIP VIA	DISC. TERMS	FREIGHT TERMS	ADV. ALLOWANCE	SPECIAL ALLOWANCE
QUANTITY		**DESCRIPTION**			

PURCHASE CONDITIONS

1. Supplier will be responsible for extra freight cost on partial shipment, unless prior permission is obtained.

2. Please acknowledge this order.

3. Please notify us immediately if you are unable to complete order.

4. All items must be individually packed.

51. Forward Corporation is a progressive and fast-growing company. The company's executive committee consists of the president and the four vice-presidents who report to the president—marketing, manufacturing, finance, and systems.

The company has ordered a new computer for use in processing its financial information. Because the computer acquisition required a substantial investment, the president wants to make certain that the computer is employed effectively.

The new computer will enable Forward to revise its financial information system so that the several departments will get more useful information. This should be helpful especially in marketing because its personnel are distributed widely throughout the country.

The marketing department is organized into nine territories and twenty-five sales offices. The vice-president of marketing wants the monthly reports to reflect those items for which the department is responsible and can control. The marketing department also wants information which identifies the most profitable products; this information is used to establish a discount policy which will enable the company to meet competition effectively. Monthly reports showing performance by territory and sales office also would be useful.

The vice-president of finance has recommended that the accounting system be revised so that reports would be prepared on a contribution margin basis. Further, only those cost items which are controlled by the respective departments would appear on their reports. The monthly report for the manufacturing department would compare actual production costs with a budget containing the standard costs for the actual volume of production. The marketing department would be provided with the standard variable manufacturing cost for each product so it could calculate the variable contribution margin of each product. The monthly reports to the marketing department would reflect the variable contribution approach; the reports would present the net contribution of the department calculated by deducting standard variable manufacturing costs and marketing expenses (both variable and fixed) from sales.

A portion of Forward Corporation's chart of accounts is shown below.

ACCOUNT NUMBER	DESCRIPTION
2000	Sales
2500	Cost of sales
3000	Manufacturing expenses
4000	Engineering expenses
5000	Marketing expenses
6000	Administrative expenses

The company wants to retain the basic structure of the chart of accounts to minimize the number of changes in the system. However, the numbering system will have to be expanded in order to provide the additional information that is desired.

REQUIRED

The coding structure now in effect must be modified to satisfy the needs of Forward Corporation's management. Using the marketing areas as the example, devise an account number coding system which will permit the preparation of the contribution reports for the marketing department. In the presentation of the account number coding system

1. add additional accounts to the chart of accounts as needed.

2. provide flexibility in the coding structure so that it would not have to be revised completely should Forward Corporation expand or restructure its sales area.

3. explain and justify the coding structure presented. (CMA Examination)

52. Universal Floor Covering is a manufacturer and distributor of carpet and vinyl floor coverings. The home office is located in Charlotte, North Carolina. Carpet mills are located in Dalton, Georgia, and Greenville, South Carolina; a floor covering manufacturing plant is in High Point, North Carolina. Total sales last year were just over $250 million.

The company manufactures over 200 different varieties of carpet. The carpet is classified as being for commercial or residential purposes and is sold under five brand names with up to five lines under each brand. The lines indicate the different grades of quality; grades are measured by type of tuft and number of tufts per square inch. Each line of carpet can have up to fifteen different color styles.

Just under 200 varieties of vinyl floor covering are manufactured. The floor covering is also classified as being for commercial or residential use. There are four separate brand names (largely distinguished by the type of finish), up to eight different patterns for each brand, and up to eight color styles for each pattern.

Ten different grades of padding are manufactured. The padding is usually differentiated by intended use (commercial or residential) in addition to thickness and composition of materials.

Universal serves over 2000 regular wholesale customers. Retail showrooms are the primary customers. Many major corporations are direct buyers of Universal's products. Large construction companies have contracts with Universal to purchase carpet and floor covering at reduced rates for use in newly constructed homes and commercial buildings. In addition, Universal produces a line of residential carpet for a large national retail chain. Sales to these customers range from $10,000 to $1,000,000 annually.

There is a company-owned retail outlet at each plant. The outlets carry overruns, seconds, and discontinued items. This is Universal's only retail sales function.

The company has divided the sales market into seven territories, with the majority of concentration on the East Coast. The market segments are New England, New York, Mid-Atlantic, Carolinas, South, Midwest, and West. Each sales territory is divided into five to ten districts, with a salesperson assigned to each district.

The current accounting system has been adequate for monitoring the sales by product. However, there are limitations to the system because specific information is sometimes not available. A detailed analysis of operations is necessary for planning and control purposes and would be valuable for decision-making purposes. The accounting systems department has been asked to design a sales analysis code. The code should permit Universal to prepare a sales analysis that would reflect the characteristics of the company's business.

REQUIRED

a) Account coding systems are based upon various coding concepts. Briefly define and give an example of the following coding concepts:
  1. sequence coding
  2. block coding
  3. group coding

b) Identify and describe factors which must be considered before a coding system can be designed and implemented for an organization.

c) Develop a coding system for Universal Floor Covering which would assign sales analysis codes to sales transactions. For each portion of the code:
  1. explain the meaning and purpose of the position.
  2. identify and justify the number of digits required. (CMA Examination)

53. Ollie Mace has recently been appointed controller of a family-owned manufacturing enterprise. The firm, S. Dilley & Co., was founded by Mr. Dilley about twenty years ago, is seventy-eight percent owned by Mr. Dilley, and has served the major automotive companies as a parts supplier. The firm's major operating divisions are heat treating, extruding, small parts stamping, and specialized machining. Sales last year from the several divisions ranged from $150,000 to over $3,000,000. The divisions are physically and managerially independent except for Mr. Dilley's constant surveillance. The accounting system for each division has evolved according to the division's own needs and to the abilities of individual accountants or bookkeepers. Mr. Mace is the first controller in the firm's history to have responsibility for overall financial management. Mr. Dilley expects to retire within six years and has hired Mr. Mace to improve the firm's financial system.

Mr. Mace soon decides that he will need to design a new financial reporting system that will:

1. Give managers uniform, timely, and accurate reports on business activity. Monthly divisional reports should be uniform and available by the tenth of the following month. Companywide financial reports also should be prepared by the tenth.

2. Provide a basis for measuring return on investment by division. Divisional reports should show assets assigned each division and revenue and expense measurement in each division.

3. Generate meaningful budget data for planning and decision-making purposes. The accounting system should provide for the preparation of budgets which recognize managerial responsibility, controllability of costs, and major product groups.

4. Allow for a uniform basis of evaluating performance and quick access to underlying data. Cost center variances should be measured and reported for operating and nonoperating units including headquarters. Also questions about levels of specific cost factors or product costs should be answerable quickly.

A new chart of accounts, as it appears to Mr. Mace, is essential to getting started on other critical financial problems. The present account codes used by divisions are not standard.

Mr. Mace sees a need to divide asset accounts into six major categories, i.e., current assets, plant and equipment, etc. Within each of these categories, he sees a need for no more than ten control accounts. Based on his observations to date, 100 subsidiary accounts are more than adequate for each control account.

No division now has more than five major product groups. The maximum number of cost centers Mr. Mace foresees within any product group is six, including operating and nonoperating groups. He views general divisional costs as a non–revenue-producing product group. Altogether, Mr. Mace estimates that about forty-four natural expense accounts plus about twelve specific variance accounts would be adequate.

Mr. Mace is planning to implement the new chart of accounts in an environment that at present includes manual records systems and one division which is using an EDP system. Mr. Mace expects that in the near future most accounting and reporting for all units will be automated. Therefore the chart of accounts should facilitate the processing of transactions manually or by machine. Efforts should be made, he believes, to restrict the length of the code for economy in processing and convenience in use.

REQUIRED

a) Design a chart of accounts coding system that will meet Mr. Mace's requirements. Your answer should begin with a digital layout of the coding system. You should explain the coding method you have chosen and the reason for the size of your code elements. Explain your code as it would apply to asset and expense accounts.

b) Use your chart of accounts coding system to illustrate the code needed for the following data:

1. In the small parts stamping division, $100 was spent by foreman Bill Shaw in the polishing department of the Door Lever Group on cleaning supplies. Code the expense item using the code you developed above.

2. A new motorized sweeper has been purchased for the maintenance department of the extruding division for $3450. Code this asset item using the code you developed above. (CMA Examination)

References

Caldwell, Don L. "Managing Information Resources." *Information and Records Management* (April 1980): 14–22.

Diamond, Susan Z. *Records Management: A Practical Guide.* New York: American Management Association, 1983.

Gildersleeve, Thomas R. *Design of Sequential File Systems.* New York: Wiley-Interscience, 1971.

Hatfield, Jack D. "How to Establish an Effective Records Retention Program." *Management Accounting* (March 1980): 55–57.

Johnson, Mina M., and Norman F. Kallaus. *Records Management.* Cincinnati: South-Western Publishing Co., 1982.

National Association of Accountants. *Classification and Coding Techniques to Facilitate Accounting Operations.* Research Report 34. New York: National Association of Accountants, 1959.

Martin, James. *Computer Data-Base Organization.* 2d ed. Englewood Cliffs, N.J.: Prentice-Hall, 1977.

Place, Irene, and Estelle L. Popham. *Filing and Records Management.* Englewood Cliffs, N.J.: Prentice-Hall, 1966.

Terry, George R. *Office Management and Control.* 7th ed. Homewood, Ill.: Irwin, 1975.

Thomas, Violet S., and Dexter R. Schubert. *Records Management: Systems and Administration.* Silver Spring, Maryland: Association for Information & Image Management, 1983.

Control and Accounting Information Systems

LEARNING OBJECTIVES

Careful study of this chapter should enable students to:

☐ Explain the basic principles of control in business organizations.

☐ Evaluate a system of internal accounting control, identify its deficiencies, and prescribe modifications that will remove those deficiencies.

CHAPTER OUTLINE

In an abstract sense, control is the process of exercising a restraining or directive influence over the activities of an object, organism, or system. Assisting management in the control of business organizations is one of the primary functions of accounting information systems.

Accountants often use the term *internal control* as a synonym for control within business organizations. A brief history of the concept of internal control is of interest. The term was first defined in 1949 by a committee of the American Institute of Accountants (now named the American Institute of Certified Public Accountants, or AICPA) as follows.

> Internal control comprises the plan of organization and all of the coordinate methods and measures adopted within a business to safeguard its assets, check the accuracy and reliability of its accounting data, promote operational efficiency, and encourage adherence to prescribed managerial policies.[1]

This definition still appears in AICPA professional literature, although they have several times published extensions or clarifications of it. For example, a 1958 pronouncement drew the following distinction between *accounting controls* and *administrative controls*.

> Accounting controls comprise the plan of organization and all methods and procedures that are concerned mainly with, and relate directly to, the safeguarding of assets and the reliability of the financial records. . . . Administrative controls comprise the plan of organization and all methods and procedures that are concerned mainly with operational efficiency and adherence to managerial policies.[2]

In 1972, an AICPA pronouncement provided the following clarifications of these definitions.

> Administrative control includes, but is not limited to, the plan of organization and the procedures and records that are concerned with the decision processes leading to management's authorization of transactions. Such authorization is a management function directly associated with the responsibility for achieving the objectives of the organization and is the starting point for establishing accounting control of transactions.
>
> Accounting control comprises the plan of organization and the procedures and records that are concerned with the safeguarding of assets and the

---

[1]Committee on Auditing Procedure, American Institute of Accountants, *Internal Control* (New York: American Institute of Certified Public Accountants, 1949), p. 6. Copyright © 1949 by the American Institute of Certified Public Accountants, Inc., and reprinted with permission.

[2]Committee on Auditing Procedure, American Institute of Certified Public Accountants, *Statement on Auditing Procedure No. 29* (New York: American Institute of Certified Public Accountants, 1958), pp. 36–37. Copyright © 1958 by the American Institute of Certified Public Accountants, Inc., and reprinted with permission.

reliability of financial records and consequently are designed to provide reasonable assurance that

a) Transactions are executed in accordance with management's general or specific authorization.

b) Transactions are recorded as necessary (1) to permit preparation of financial statements in conformity with generally accepted accounting principles or any other criteria applicable to such statements and (2) to maintain accountability for assets.

c) Access to assets is permitted only in accordance with management's authorization.

d) The recorded accountability for assets is compared with the existing assets at reasonable intervals and appropriate action is taken with respect to any differences.[3]

According to the AICPA, the primary concern of the independent auditor is accounting controls. However, the internal accountant responsible for the design of accounting information systems is concerned with all aspects of internal control.

In 1977, shock waves were sent through the accounting profession when the United States Congress incorporated certain language from the AICPA's 1972 pronouncement into the Foreign Corrupt Practices Act. Specifically, all publicly owned corporations subject to the Securities Exchange Act of 1934 are now legally required to

(A) make and keep books, records, and accounts, which, in reasonable detail, accurately and fairly reflect the transactions and dispositions of the assets of the issuer; and (B) devise and maintain a system of internal accounting controls sufficient to provide reasonable assurances that—

(i) transactions are executed in accordance with management's general or specific authorization;

(ii) transactions are recorded as necessary (I) to permit preparation of financial statements in conformity with generally accepted accounting principles or any other criteria applicable to such statements, and (II) to maintain accountability for assets;

(iii) access to assets is permitted only in accordance with management's general or specific authorization; and

(iv) the recorded accountability for assets is compared with the existing assets at reasonable intervals and appropriate action is taken with respect to any differences.[4]

---

[3]Committee on Auditing Procedure, American Institute of Certified Public Accountants, *Statement on Auditing Procedure No. 54* (New York: American Institute of Certified Public Accountants, 1972), pp. 239–240. Copyright © 1972 by the American Institute of Certified Public Accountants, Inc., and reprinted with permission.

[4]*Foreign Corrupt Practices Act of 1977, U.S. Code,* 1976 edition, Supplement II, Volume One. Washington, D.C.: United States Government Printing Office, 1979, p. 862.

In essence, corporations are now required by law to maintain good systems of internal accounting control! Needless to say, this requirement has in recent years generated tremendous interest among managements, accountants, and auditors in the design and evaluation of internal control systems.

Another way to view control concepts in business organizations is from the standpoint of management. According to Mautz and Winjum, corporate managers view control more broadly than it is viewed in the accounting literature as "a means of motivating, encouraging, and assisting officers and employees to achieve corporate goals and to observe corporate policies."[5] They refer to this concept as *management control* and conclude that it has three essential features. First, they view management control as an integral part of management responsibilities associated with the goals and purposes established for the organization by management. Second, management control is broader than internal accounting control in that it encompasses both measures to reduce errors and irregularities *and* positive activities directed toward the achievement of organizational goals. Third, management control is personnel-oriented; that is, it seeks to facilitate the success of the organization's employees in attaining the organization's goals within the constraints of organizational policy.[6]

From a theoretical perspective, control systems may be classified into three general types—feedback control systems, feedforward control systems, and preventive control systems. *Feedback* is defined as the informational output of a process that returns as input to the process, in the sense that it initiates the action necessary for process control. *Feedback controls* operate by measuring some aspect of the process being controlled and adjusting the process when the measure indicates that the process is deviating from plan.

In contrast to this detection and correction mode of operation, both feedforward and preventive controls attempt to stop errors and deviations from occurring. However, they approach this task in quite different ways. *Feedforward controls* monitor both process operations and inputs in an attempt to predict potential deviations, in order that adjustments can be made to avert problems before they occur. *Preventive controls* operate from within the process by placing restrictions on and requiring documentation of employee activities in such a way that the occurrence of errors and deviations is retarded. Because preventive controls operate from "within" the process being controlled, they are perhaps the type of control most consistent with the original meaning of the term *internal* control.

One way to reconcile these various control concepts is to assume that preventive controls correspond to what the AICPA labeled accounting con-

---

[5]R. K. Mautz and James Winjum, *Criteria for Management Control Systems.* (New York: Financial Executives Research Foundation, 1981), p. 2.

[6]*Ibid*, p. 4.

trols, that feedback and feedforward controls correspond to the AICPA's administrative controls, and that management control encompasses all of these other control concepts. Because the Foreign Corrupt Practices Act refers only to "internal accounting controls," its focus is seen to be primarily on preventive controls. This interpretation is consistent with the primary intent of the act, which was to "prevent" bribes and other corrupt practices.

Regardless of what the law requires, all forms of control are important to business organizations. Furthermore, the accounting information system plays a central role in implementing each form of control. The remainder of this chapter describes control using the theoretical distinction between feedback, feedforward, and preventive controls as a frame of reference. A general description of each of these three types of control systems is provided, together with numerous examples of each that are typically found in business and accounting information systems.

Feedback Control Systems

Fundamental characteristics

A feedback control system contains five fundamental components. In general terms, these are (1) an operating process, which converts an input into an output; (2) a characteristic of the process, which is the subject of control; (3) a measurement system, which assesses the state of the characteristic; (4) a set of standards or criteria against which the measured state of the process is evaluated; and (5) a regulator, whose functions are to compare measures of the process characteristic to the standards and to take action to adjust the process if the comparison reveals that the process is deviating from plan. The relationships of these components are illustrated graphically in Fig. 4.1.

Incorporating feedback control into a process creates a dynamic, self-regulating system. In such a system, the process is expected to deviate from equilibrium occasionally. However, the ability both to restore the process to equilibrium and to know when such restoration is needed is built into the system itself. Thus it can operate for long periods of time, performing its necessary functions and correcting itself when necessary, without the need for external direction. The theoretical study of feedback control systems is referred to as *cybernetics*.

A commonly cited example of a feedback control system is the thermostat.

FIGURE 4.1
A feedback control system.

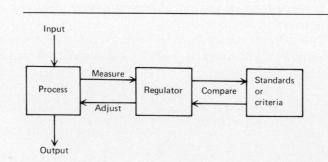

This control system operates by measuring the temperature of an object or process and triggering a heating (or cooling) device when the temperature deviates from a specified level of coldness (or warmth).

Feedback control systems are common within business organizations. The production of goods and the operation of a department are processes requiring control. Characteristics of such processes that are controlled might be quality of output, cost of operation, or speed of operation. Measurement systems are frequently component parts of the accounting information system. Standards or criteria for evaluating the process are established by management policy. Finally, the regulator is a manager, or person responsible for the satisfactory operation of the process.

Although it is instructive to apply the concept of a feedback control system to various processes within business organizations, it should be noted that business organizations cannot operate as precisely and automatically as, say, a thermostat. This is true because of the complexity of business operations and because of the limitations in perception and memory of people generally. However, the concept is useful as a theoretical ideal for control systems in business.

Essentials of proper functioning

The successful application of feedback control systems in a business organization requires that certain general principles be observed. First, it is essential that a control have a benefit value at least as great as the cost of administering it. Deciding whether a given control meets this criterion will usually be a matter of subjective judgment. The cost of a control may not be too difficult to estimate, but its benefit might be expressed only in vague terms, such as "increased efficiency" or "better customer service." Ability to make this judgment with a fair degree of success is one factor that separates good managers from inferior ones. Satisfaction of this principle is essential not only to feedback control systems but also to preventive control and to all activities of a business.

A second essential principle in a feedback control system is that its measurement component report deviations from standards on a timely basis, so that corrective action can restore the process to its desired state as quickly as possible. This principle has direct implications for accounting information systems, which, as noted, often provide the measurement function in a feedback control system. A common criticism of accounting reports is that they are not timely, which indicates that perhaps more attention should be given to this factor by designers of accounting information systems.

The third basic principle is that feedback reports be simple and easy to understand and that they highlight important relationships or factors requiring the attention of the manager to whom the report is directed. This principle also has implications for accounting systems design. Accounting reports are sometimes criticized for not containing enough information, or for not emphasizing the most important aspects of the process upon which they are reporting. On the other hand, some accounting systems, particularly those that are computerized, may be criticized for providing too much information. Managers who receive a forty- or fifty-page report or printout may have difficulty in determining exactly what has been communicated to them. It is thus important that control reports be easy to comprehend and tailored to the purpose of the control system.

The fourth basic principle is that feedback control systems be integrated with the organizational structure of which they are part. The boundaries of each process subject to control must be within the span of control of a single manager. That manager must be the one who receives control reports on the process and who has the authority to direct the operations of, and implement necessary changes in, the process. Being the one who perhaps best understands the process, that manager should participate in the formation of the standards against which its performance will be evaluated.

The functions of a feedback control system in business correspond roughly to the internal control objectives of promoting operational efficiency and encouraging adherence to prescribed managerial policies. These functions are effectively accomplished by means of a reporting system adhering to the general principles outlined above. Feedback reports promote operational efficiency by highlighting inefficient operations requiring management's attention. Furthermore, such reports encourage adherence to managerial policies through the knowledge that deviations from such policies and standards are promptly reported.

Feedback control systems in business

Discussion of the principles of feedback control systems underscores the importance to accounting information systems of the concepts of organization and control. To further clarify these relationships, some examples of feedback control systems in business will be presented.

Responsibility accounting systems.   As discussed in Chapter 2, an information system that reports financial results in accordance with the assignment of responsibilities within an organization is called a responsibility accounting system. This is a prime example of a feedback control system.

Each of the five components of a feedback control system is exemplified in a responsibility accounting system. The process being controlled is the operation of the department or other organizational unit. The characteristic being controlled may be either cost, profit, or return on investment. The measurement system is the accounting information system, which collects and processes data and reports information in accordance with the organizational considerations discussed in Chapter 2. The regulator of the system is the manager under whose authority the department operates. Finally, the set of standards is represented by the budgets, quotas, and/or prior performance levels against which actual performance is compared.

Standard cost systems. Standard cost systems are a close relative of responsibility accounting systems. According to its most common usage, the term *standard cost* refers to the cost that should be incurred in producing a unit of product under efficient operating conditions. The total standard cost per unit of product may be broken down into costs of material components, labor, and overhead elements, and by departments or other cost centers. In the latter case, standard costs may serve as the basis for budgeted amounts on performance reports in a responsibility accounting system.

In a standard cost system, actual costs are compiled on a per unit basis and compared with standards to obtain standard cost variances. Two general types of standard cost variances are rate variances and usage variances. A *rate variance* indicates that portion of a total variance attributable to a deviation from a standard rate or price, such as a labor rate or a material price. A *usage variance* indicates that portion of a total variance attributable to a deviation from some standard amount of usage of, for example, labor hours or material quantities.[7] Standard cost variances of this sort provide a good indication of the corrective action necessary to restore the production process to a satisfactory state.

Credit control. The credit control system governs the relationship between a business organization and customers who have purchased from it on credit. The characteristic of this process that is the subject of control is the loss from bad debts. The accounting information system can provide two measures of success for this process. The first of these is an aging of accounts receivable balances, which indicates those customers who have become delinquent in paying their accounts. When such delinquencies reach a prescribed level, the credit manager can act to refuse additional credit to the customer and perhaps initiate special procedures to collect the amount of the existing past due balance. The second measure provided by the accounting system is the total of bad debts written off as uncollectable during a given period. If this total rises beyond an acceptable level, the credit manager may act to tighten policies governing the initial extension of credit.

Internal audit. The internal audit function was discussed in Chapter 2. Two aspects of this function provide feedback for management control. First, the function of independent appraisal of the performance of various levels of management provides feedback to top management on the effectiveness of subordinate managers. Second, the function of reviewing and assessing the system of preventive controls within an organization provides feedback to accounting executives on the effectiveness of that system. In both cases, there are no precise standards or measures of effectiveness, no formula or sum that

---

[7]For a detailed treatment of standard cost accounting, see Charles T. Horngren, *Cost Accounting, A Managerial Emphasis,* 5th ed. (Englewood Cliffs, N.J.: Prentice-Hall, 1982), chapters 6 and 7.

can easily be determined. Therefore this type of feedback control system is perhaps more difficult to administer successfully than those described previously.

Examples of the kinds of control problems that the internal audit function is often able to uncover include failure to pay on account in time to earn discounts, excess overtime, underused assets, obsolete inventory, conservative budgets and quotas, failure to adhere to prescribed policies and procedures, poorly justified capital expenditures, and production bottlenecks. Feedback on the existence and nature of such problems is very useful to management in maintaining effective control of an organization.

Production control. The production control process is concerned primarily with maintaining efficiency and avoiding delays in the production process. Thus the characteristic being controlled is time, and the standard used is the production schedule. The regulator consists of the production planning or production control department and the expeditors it employs to monitor production in the factory.

Feedforward Control Systems

Feedback control systems are essential in many areas of management control. However, their basic disadvantage is that they do not signal a deviation until after it has become significant. As a result, costly deviations may persist or worsen before corrective action becomes effective. Feedforward control systems aim directly at this problem by attempting to prevent such deviations before they occur.

Fundamental characteristics

The components of a feedforward control system are similar to those of a feedback system. They include (1) an operating process, which converts input into output; (2) a characteristic of the process, which is the subject of control; (3) a measurement and prediction system, which assesses the state of the process and its inputs and attempts to predict its outputs; (4) a set of standards or criteria against which the predicted state of the process is evaluated; and (5) a regulator, which compares predictions of process output to the standards and takes corrective action when this comparison indicates a likely future deviation. The relationship of these components is diagramed in Fig. 4.2.

As indicated by this description and the diagram, a distinguishing feature of feedforward control systems is the monitoring of process inputs. Therefore in order for a feedforward control system to be effective, there must be a reasonably predictable relationship between process inputs and process outputs. As in the case of feedback systems, business applications of the feedforward control concept should not be expected to operate as precisely and automatically as their engineering counterparts. Nevertheless, there are some management control systems whose essential features parallel the basic feedforward model.

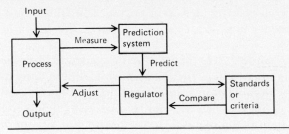

FIGURE 4.2
A feedforward
control system.

Feedforward control systems in business

Koontz and Bradspies describe three examples of feedforward systems in a business context.[8] Each of these is described briefly here.

Cash planning. The objective of a cash planning system is to maintain the organization's cash balance at some desired level. The process being controlled encompasses all aspects of the organization's activities and decisions that impact upon the level of cash. Among the input variables that must be monitored in a typical business organization are the level of sales, receipts on account, purchases and payments on account, wages and salaries, selling, administrative and other expenses, tax payments, capital expenditures, borrowing and loan repayments, investments, and dividends.

The process characteristic subject to control in a cash planning system is simply the cash balance. The control standard is generally a desired range within which the cash balance should fall, which in turn may be based upon a desired relationship between the cash balance and the balance of other current asset or current liability accounts. The measurement and prediction system is the accounting information system, which measures cash flows via the traditional accounting process and predicts future cash flows and cash balances via a budgeting system.

The regulator in the cash planning process is the executive responsible for cash management, who may be the treasurer or financial vice-president. Actions available to this person to adjust or correct the cash balance include investing excess funds, borrowing short-term, and delaying capital expenditures.

Note the inadequacies of feedback control in the cash planning situation. If feedback indicates that the cash balance is higher than the desired level, then the investment of the excess cash in interest-bearing securities has already been delayed. Similarly, if feedback indicates an abnormally low cash balance, the opportunity to avoid costly borrowing by delaying expenditures or making other adjustments may be lost. Thus the application of the feed-

---

[8]Harold Koontz and Robert W. Bradspies, "Managing through Feedforward Control," *Business Horizons* **15** (June 1972): 25–36.

forward concept provides an important contribution to the efficiency of cash management.

Inventory control.   The process being controlled by an inventory control system is the operation of ordering, storing, and making available when needed within the organization various items of raw materials, parts and supplies, and finished goods inventories. The characteristic being controlled is the balance of each item of inventory. The measurement system is the set of inventory records maintained by the accounting information system. The regulator may be either an inventory clerk or a computer.

The most significant input variable to an inventory feedforward control system is either the expected rate of sales (for a retail or wholesale company) or the planned usage requirements (for a manufacturing company). Other input variables include the amount of inventory purchases, purchase returns, sales returns, spoilage, and shrinkage. Order and shipping times are also important considerations. These variables are used to predict the future inventory level in order to determine the best time to reorder. In many systems the criterion established to decide when to reorder is the *reorder point,* or the level to which the inventory balance of an item must fall before an order to replenish the stock is initiated. The reorder point for each inventory item is established to minimize the sum of holding costs and costs of being out of stock. Thus placing an order to replenish the stock of inventory represents the corrective or regulative action in the system.

In another sense the characteristic being controlled in an inventory system is the sum of the costs of holding and ordering inventory and of stockouts. The input variables that must be measured in order to achieve this objective include the expected demand or usage of each inventory item, the *lead time* (the time between order and receipt for each item), the holding cost rate of each item, the cost of placing an order for a batch of each item, and the cost of a stockout of each item. The standards that must be established should include not only the optimal reorder point for each item but also the *economic order quantity* (EOQ), which is the order quantity of an item that minimizes the sum of holding costs and ordering costs for that item. A simple formula for economic order quantity is

$$EOQ = \sqrt{\frac{(2)(C_2)(D)}{C_1}}$$

where C_1 is the carrying cost per unit per year, C_2 is the cost of placing a single order, and D is the demand per year.

New product development.   The goal of a new product development program is to introduce a successful new product while making efficient use of time, cost, and other resources. Such a project requires close coordination among a variety of activities including product research and development, market research, production engineering, capital expenditure planning, sales and distribution planning, packaging design, and advertising and promotion. Such coordination of multiple activities may be provided by a management control plan based upon the feedforward concept.

In this process the primary characteristics subject to control are the timing of related activities and the quality of the results. The standard against which success is measured is the product development plan. The measurement system consists of periodic progress reports and meetings between project staff. Input variables to be monitored include the activities, findings, and conclusions of those people playing a key role in the process. The regulator is represented by the project manager, marketing vice-president, or other executive in charge.

The importance of the feedforward concept in this process is related to the future-oriented nature of project control. Results obtained and conclusions reached are evaluated primarily in terms of their impact upon the ultimate success of the project, rather than in terms of past expectations. For example, if the engineering department concludes that the product cost will be substantially higher than previous estimates, or if the marketing research department estimates that product demand will be lower than expected, an attempt is made to predict the resulting impact upon the product's success and to adjust plans for subsequent stages of the development process accordingly. It is entirely possible that this process will result in the termination of the product development process in many cases. The feedforward concept therefore plays a very important role in the success or failure of new product development.

Preventive Control Systems

Both feedback and feedforward controls function externally to the process being controlled, monitoring its operations and intervening to make corrective adjustments where necessary. In contrast, preventive controls are policies and procedures that are actually a part of the process itself. As such, they are often more effective than either feedback or feedforward controls, but they are more costly. In this section, the generally accepted principles and practices of preventive control systems are explained, and several examples from the field of accounting are described.

Functions of a preventive control system

The AICPA definition of internal control cited previously provides a useful way of classifying the functions of a preventive control system. Of the four functions cited in that definition, the first two—safeguarding of assets, and checking the accuracy and reliability of its accounting data—are most consistent with the concept of preventive control. This section elaborates on the nature of these two functions.

Safeguarding assets.   According to the AICPA, safeguarding of assets refers to their "protection against loss arising from intentional and unintentional errors in processing transactions and handling the related assets."[9] Examples of unintentional errors include such things as "understatement of sales through failure to prepare invoices or through incorrect pricing or computation; overpayments to vendors or employees arising from inaccuracies in quantities of materials or services, prices or rates, or computations; and physical loss of assets such as cash, securities, or inventory."[10] "Intentional errors" is a reference to *embezzlement,* which is the fraudulent appropriation of business property by an employee to whom it has been entrusted, often accompanied by falsification of records. Safeguarding of assets also encompasses protection against theft of assets by shoplifters, burglars, etc.

Embezzlement results in substantial loss to business firms each year. The United States Fidelity and Guaranty Co., a major bonding company, cites estimates that place the annual loss in the neighborhood of $4 billion. In addition, they estimate that more than 30 percent of all bankruptcies are caused by employee dishonesty.[11] Such losses are costly not only in financial terms but also in terms of the loss of a productive human resource to the firm and to society. Many embezzlers would never commit a crime if it were not for the weak control system that encourages the act.

Embezzlement is committed in a large variety of ways. The study cited above describes forty different cases of embezzlement.[12] An article by Elmer I. Ellentuck describes twenty methods of employee fraud and presents a checklist containing a large number of suggested control procedures for preventing such frauds.[13] An article by E. J. Gurry lists eighteen methods of embezzlement and describes internal control remedies for each of them.[14]

The accounting information system contributes quite effectively to the safeguarding of assets by means of keeping a record of the assets. Discrepancies between the records and the actual quantity on hand can be investigated to discover their source. With respect to cash, the accounting records and the quantity on hand may be compared and brought into agreement weekly or monthly by means of a bank reconciliation. Each individual discrepancy is resolved in this process. In the case of inventories, such a reconciliation typically takes place once annually, when a physical inventory is taken.

---

[9]Committee on Auditing Procedure, American Institute of Certified Public Accountants, *Statement on Auditing Standards No. 1* (New York: American Institute of Certified Public Accountants, 1973), p. 17.

[10]*Ibid.*

[11]United States Fidelity and Guaranty Co., *The Forty Thieves* (Baltimore: USF&G, 1970), pp. 2–3.

[12]*Ibid.,* pp. 9–50.

[13]Elmer I. Ellentuck, "How to Minimize Employee Fraud: A Checklist," *Practical Accountant* **5** (March/April 1972): 30–37.

[14]E. J. Gurry, "Locating Potential Irregularities," *Journal of Accountancy* **140** (September 1975): 111–114.

In most cases, tracing of individual differences between inventory records and quantities on hand is impossible, and so trends in the total discrepancy may be used as the basis for relaxing or tightening overall control policies.

Safeguarding of assets is also accomplished by close supervision of asset-handling operations and physical protective measures such as plant security forces and limited access to storage areas. These are not strictly accounting functions, although they may be under the authority of the accounting executive in some businesses. However, the accounting system provides information that is useful in evaluating the effectiveness of such controls. The accounting information system thus plays a central role in safeguarding assets in business as well as nonbusiness organizations.

Internal check.   The function of checking the accuracy and reliability of accounting data in a system is referred to as *internal check*. This function is obviously compatible with the functions of recording and processing data. Internal check is a form of verification and is often accomplished through utilization of the maxim of the double entry accounting system that debits must equal credits. Payroll processing provides a good example of this form of internal check. Debits in a payroll entry are allocated to numerous inventory and/or expense accounts. Credits are allocated to several liability accounts for taxes, insurance, and union dues as well as the liability to employees. At the end of this complex operation, the comparison of total debits to total credits provides a powerful check on the accuracy of the process. Any error will create a discrepancy, which will initiate action to discover and correct the error.

In the processing of data in batches, internal check is accomplished by means of *batch totals,* or *control totals,* which are sums of a numerical item accumulated from all documents in a batch. Batch totals are typically established at the point of initial formation of a batch and then checked at various stages in processing to control against loss of records or errors in data transcription.

If a batch total check identifies a discrepancy between a batch total and a previously computed batch total, the numerical difference between the two batch totals is often helpful in locating some of the more commonly made errors in processing groups of numerical data. For example, the difference may be exactly equal to the amount of one of the transactions in the batch, which indicates that that amount may have been omitted from the computation of one of the batch totals. A difference divisible by nine with no remainder may indicate the existence of a *transposition error,* in which the column positions of two adjacent digits are inadvertently exchanged (for example, 46 instead of 64). If the difference is an amount having only one digit other than zero (such as 5000, 200, 10, or .08), it is likely that one digit has been transcribed incorrectly during processing (for example, if a "4" in the tens column is transcribed as a "9," this will cause an error of 50 in the amount). If none of these conditions is present, divide the difference by 2 and look for a transaction amount equal to the quotient; this may identify a transaction amount that was incorrectly debited instead of credited, or subtracted instead of added. Of course, if more than one error is made in processing the batch of data, these shortcuts may not be very helpful in locating the specific errors.

Errors in accounting data can have harmful effects upon the relationship of a business to all the major external parties with which it deals. Such errors may also damage the effectiveness of internal management, which relies upon accounting information as a basis for decision making. Finally, errors in the accounting records of a publicly held corporation could indicate a lack of compliance with the Foreign Corrupt Practices Act. In many respects the maintenance of accurate and reliable records is closely related to the safe-guarding of assets because the former will contribute significantly to the latter. The remainder of this section discusses the essential elements of preventive control systems and describes some common examples, then explains the steps corporate managers can take to demonstrate compliance with the Foreign Corrupt Practices Act.

Essential elements of preventive control systems

Sound organizational practices.   Reference to the "plan of organization" in the definition of internal control underscores the importance of sound organizational practices. Of particular importance is the separation of assigned duties and responsibilities in such a way that no single employee can both perpetrate and conceal errors or irregularities. This separation of functions is often referred to as *organizational independence.*

Three general categories of functions must be separated in order to maintain effective organizational independence. These are (1) functions involving custody of assets, such as writing checks or handling cash or other assets; (2) recording functions, such as maintaining the disbursements journal or preparing the bank reconciliation; and (3) performance of line operating functions, especially those involving the authorization of transactions. Separation of custodial and recording functions prevents an employee from falsifying records in order to conceal the theft of assets entrusted to that employee's custody. Separation of custodial and operating functions prevents an employee from authorizing a fictitious or inaccurate transaction as a means of concealing theft. Finally, separation of recording and operating functions prevents operating employees or managers from falsifying records in order to conceal substandard operating performance. Figure 4.3 illustrates some of the primary examples of custodial, recording, and operating functions that should be separated.

In a system that incorporates an effective separation of duties among employees, it should be almost impossible for any single employee to commit embezzlement successfully. In such a system, *collusion,* or conspiracy of two or more persons to commit fraud, may still be possible, but a well-designed system can minimize the chances of successful collusion.

Sound personnel practices.   The safety of assets and the reliability of accounting records are both affected by an organization's personnel policies. The

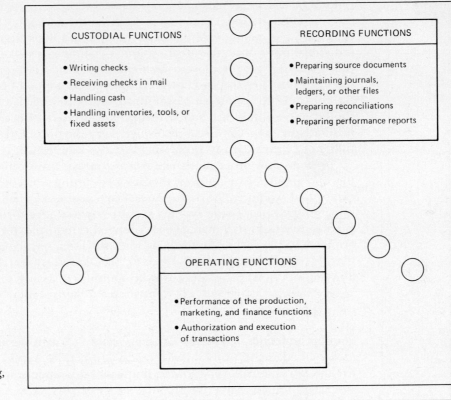

FIGURE 4.3
Separation of
custodial, recording,
and operating
functions.

qualifications established for each job designation in a company should reflect the degree of responsibility associated with the position. Qualifications for responsible positions may include a level of experience, intelligence, character, dedication, and capacity for leadership. Training programs should be planned carefully to familiarize new employees with their responsibilities. Policies with respect to working conditions, raises in salary, and promotion are very important and can be a powerful force in encouraging efficiency and loyal service. For employees in positions involving direct access to property, fidelity bond coverage is important. A *fidelity bond* is a contract with an insurance company that provides a financial guarantee of the honesty of a named individual.

Another very important personnel practice is that all employees holding key positions with respect to recording or custody of assets should be required to take an annual vacation, during which time their functions are performed by someone else. Many of the employee frauds that have been discovered were revealed when the embezzler was suddenly forced by illness or accident to take time off. Periodic rotation of duties among key employees is another policy that may achieve the same results.

Written guides to policies and procedures. Closely related to sound organizational and personnel practices is the need for manuals of policies and procedures. Such manuals should describe in detail the responsibilities of each individual position in the organization, a feature that makes the manuals useful in training new employees. The manuals should also give an overview of the functioning of the system with respect to each type of transaction, so that the relationship of one employee function to another is clear. The manuals should also contain a detailed listing of the chart of accounts, in order to facilitate the accurate initial recording of transactions. Other instructions for filling out forms used in processing are also important.

Systems and procedures manuals encourage uniformity in data processing and financial operations, thereby preventing the confusion and inefficiency that would result from unnecessary inconsistencies. For example, automated data processing systems require input whose form and content are rigidly specified. If a manual describing the required form and content is available to the various individuals who provide a particular type of input to the system (perhaps the sales force or production workers), the problems of jumbled or incomplete input can be minimized. Using the manuals in employee training programs also contributes to consistency of practices within the organization.

Physical protection of assets. An important factor in the safeguarding of assets is an adequate program of physical protection. Access to cash should be limited to responsible employees. Important documents or records should be stored in limited-access file cabinets or perhaps a safe. Access to inventory storage areas should be limited. Plant facilities should be protected during nonoperating hours by means of security police, burglar alarms, and other safeguards.

An important factor in the physical protection of cash in retail businesses is the cash register and its numerous control features. For example, the bell that sounds when a cash sale is rung up and the totals that appear in the display window facilitate supervision of sales clerks. The display window total and customer receipt provide the opportunity for the customer to notice a discrepancy between the amount paid and the amount recorded, which discourages any deliberate errors. Once a sale is recorded, a record of it is printed on a paper tape locked inside the register to prevent subsequent alteration. At the end of a day, this internally accumulated total should check with the amount of cash accumulated in the cash drawer. Other available features of cash registers that provide increased control are multiple cash drawers, so that each sales clerk can be made responsible for an individual cash drawer, and an attachment that dispenses the exact amount of coin change due to a customer.

Well-designed documents. Documents that are designed carefully and used effectively can contribute greatly both to the safeguarding of assets and to the accuracy of records. Source transaction documents should be designed to facilitate the collection of all necessary information with respect to the transaction. Documents that initiate a transaction should contain a space for the authorization of the person or persons charged with that responsibility. Transfer of responsibility for assets from one department to another should be recorded in order to enable the pinpointing of responsibility for any subsequent shortages. Document design should also be simple so that processing can be as efficient as possible. The document format should facilitate review and verification.

An important practice with respect to the design of any document used for control purposes is the sequential prenumbering of all documents. This practice makes it possible to account for and review every document used in a process. Any missing documents would create a missing number in the sequence. This practice reduces the likelihood of fraudulent use of documents by dishonest employees.

The record-keeping system throughout a business organization should be well coordinated in order to facilitate the tracing of individual transactions through the system. The path that a transaction traces through a data processing system, from source document to summary reports and account balances, is referred to as the *audit trail* or *transaction trail*. The audit trail consists of such things as reference numbers, codes, dates, and other forms of cross-reference data that are recorded in files, ledgers, and journals to facilitate the tracing of these records to source documents or to records in other files. Good audit trails facilitate the correction of errors and the verification of output information in a system.

Supervision. The availability of supervisory assistance contributes to the accuracy of records by reducing the possibility that employees engaged in data processing activities will err in recording situations with which they are unfamiliar. Surveillance of employees who have direct access to assets provides an additional safeguard over such assets. Supervision is especially important as a means of safeguarding assets in businesses that are too small to fully achieve organizational independence.

Examples of preventive control systems

Preventive control systems in business generally are integrated with transaction processing subsystems, each of which is concerned with processing a particular class of accounting transactions. These subsystems are often referred to as transaction processing cycles. An example of the partitioning of the accounting information system into transaction processing cycles is provided by the delineation in Chapter 1 of five basic categories of business transactions—purchasing, production, payroll, sales, and cash receipts and disbursements. In this section some of the most important control features within these cycles are reviewed. The emphasis here is on manual rather than automated systems, but the basic control concepts in both systems are similar. Each of the processing and control systems discussed in this section is described in greater detail in Part 4 of this text.

Purchasing of inventory.   The basic function of controls in the purchasing function is to ensure purchase of all needed inventory items while preventing losses of inventory. To ensure that only items that are needed are actually purchased, initiation of a purchase order should result from the preparation of a formal requisition by a responsible employee in the stores-keeping or production departments. Copies of the purchase order should be furnished by the purchasing department to both the accounts payable department and the receiving department. The receiving department should be responsible for preparing a report listing the quantity of each item received. This report should be signed by an employee of stores to acknowledge the transfer of goods from receiving to stores.

The accounts payable department performs the most significant control function in a purchasing system through its procedure for authorizing payment of vendor invoices. Such authorization is granted only after a review of the purchase order, to ensure that the goods were actually ordered, and of the receiving report, to ensure that they were received and have been properly transferred to the stores-keeping department. Organizational independence in this process is achieved by separation of the operating functions (purchasing and authorization of accounts payable) from the custodial functions (the receiving and stores-keeping departments) and from the recording functions (record keeping for accounts payable and inventories).

Flow of inventory through production.   The primary functions of controls in a production accounting system are to ensure production of only those items that are needed and to prevent loss of inventories. The production planning department decides what items will be produced. A reliable system of reporting on sales trends and finished goods inventory balances is essential to this function.

Control over goods in production begins with the transfer of raw materials from stores-keeping to the factory. This is controlled by documents initiated by the production planning department authorizing the transfer. The production planning or cost accounting department must keep strict documentary control over each batch of work in process as it moves through the factory. Maintaining a record of quantities involved in each transfer of goods from one department to another enables the tracing of any shortage to a single department. The final step in the production process is the transfer of goods to the finished goods storeroom, which is evidenced by a document signed by the finished goods custodian acknowledging receipt of the goods.

Organizational independence with respect to production work in process is achieved by separation of the custodial functions (raw material stores, factory departments, and finished goods stores) from the recording function (cost accounting) and from the authorization function (production planning). Although the factory departments are operating departments that also perform custodial and recording functions, their operating activities in this case do not extend to the authorization of transactions, and their recording functions are effectively controlled by the signed acknowledgment required for every transfer of goods from one department to another. In addition, control over production is also provided by effective supervision on the part of factory supervisors and by a program to maintain the physical security of the factory premises.

Payroll.   The primary purpose of controls in a payroll processing system is to ensure that wages and salaries are paid in appropriate amounts for services properly rendered. In a typical manufacturing company, a record of hours worked for each factory employee is obtained both in the form of clock cards, showing when employees punch in and out, and in the form of job tickets, which are verified by supervisors and show the time an employee spent at a particular job. These two input records should be reconciled as an initial step in payroll processing. Job-time tickets form the basis for distribution of labor costs to the various inventory accounts representing work in process. Clock cards are used as a basis for the calculation of gross pay, net pay, and various deductions, and for the preparation of paychecks. When these two processes are completed, the total amount of payroll computed in one should be compared with the other as a check on the accuracy of both.

In processing payrolls for office employees or in a nonmanufacturing company, the supervisor's function is even more significant in providing input to payroll processing. Often the only such input will be a written form prepared by a supervisor listing time worked for each employee, although time clocks may also be used in some cases. For salaried employees, the weekly or monthly salary is constant, and so control over input data is not needed unless extra pay is provided for overtime work.

Records of employment, rates, and authorized deductions for each employee should be maintained by the personnel department as well as the department responsible for preparing checks. All changes in these records, including hirings and terminations as well as rate changes, should be authorized through the personnel department. Organizational independence in payroll processing is achieved by separation of the operating function (the personnel department) from the custodial functions (preparation and distribution of paychecks) and from the recording functions (timekeeping, payroll record keeping, and cost accounting). A separate bank account for payroll only is also a desirable control feature because it facilitates the subsequent preparation of bank reconciliations.

Sale of products.   Nearly all transactions between companies are on account, and so problems of handling cash do not arise. The primary functions of controls in a sales order processing, billing, and accounts receivable system are to ensure that all sales of finished goods are properly recorded, to prevent loss of finished goods inventories, and to facilitate the collection of accounts. Toward these ends, shipments of goods are not approved until the credit of the customer has been approved. Transfer of goods from the finished goods storeroom to the shipping department must be authorized by documents evidencing a sale. The shipping department must acknowledge receipt of the goods and notify the billing department once the shipment is made. The billing department then prepares the invoice from the original sales order and the documentation supplied by the shipping department. After the invoices are prepared and copies are mailed to the customer, they are posted in batches to the accounts receivable ledger, with batch totals being used to control the accuracy of posting. The accounts receivable department may prepare and send to each customer a periodic statement of his or her account.

Cash receipt and disbursement.   The basic purpose of controls in systems for processing cash receipts and disbursements is to prevent loss of cash. With respect to sales of merchandise for cash by a retail store, the primary controls are good supervision and the proper use of a cash register. Another control is the use of prenumbered sales slips, which enables each department to account for all sales slips. At the end of each day, an internal check on cash sales may be performed by comparing the total of all cash sales slips with the total recorded on the cash register tape.

With respect to receipt of payments on account, it has been noted that nearly all such payments are made by check. Control over these receipts typically begins in the mail room where they are opened, recorded, and batched. If customers are requested to return a copy of the invoice or other document indicating the amount of the payment enclosed, an independently prepared record of each payment is obtained. Close supervision provides additional control over the mail-opening function.

The cashier's department is responsible for endorsing and depositing checks. The accounts receivable department posts the records of payment to individual accounts. The batch total established in the mail room provides a control over both of these processes. Additional control is provided by the preparation of a bank reconciliation by the internal audit department. Organizational independence is achieved by separation of the functions of opening incoming mail, posting to customer accounts, endorsing and depositing checks in the bank, and preparing a bank reconciliation.

One form of embezzlement involving cash receipts is called *lapping*. To do this, an employee would have to be responsible for both depositing checks and maintaining the record of accounts receivable. Lapping involves concealing a cash shortage by means of a series of delays in posting collections of accounts. The employee would cash a check received from a customer and keep the cash, neglecting to make the entry debiting cash and crediting accounts receivable. Since the customer's account balance cannot be left in error for too long, the employee credits the balance of the first customer upon receiving a check from a second customer. This corrects the first customer's balance but leaves the second in error. This process of falsifying one customer's account to correct that of another must be continued indefinitely if the shortage is to be concealed.

In companies that are too small to establish a separation of functions, lapping can be prevented by an agreement with the bank that all checks made out to the company will be deposited directly into the company's account. A bank can also help to provide control over a company's cash receipts in other ways. For example, many firms use a "lockbox" collection system in which customers are requested to mail payments on account to a post office box. The bank empties the post office box daily, deposits the payments received in the customer's account, and provides the customer with a record of the receipts. Although not appropriate for all firms because of its cost, such a system not only provides a good control over receipts but also provides faster deposit of collections and faster notification of checks drawn on insufficient funds.

With respect to cash disbursements, it is essential that the function of authorizing payment and recording accounts payable be separated from the function of writing checks. Many firms use a system in which the assembly of documents supporting a disbursement is followed by the preparation of a *voucher,* which summarizes the data relating to the disbursement and represents final authorization of payment. The person writing checks should examine the voucher and other supporting documents provided by the payables clerk prior to making the check and should stamp "paid" or some other notation on the supporting documents to prevent them from being used more than once. Further control is provided by having a second person examine the supporting documents and sign the checks. The function of preparing the bank reconciliation should also be performed independently of authorizing payment and signing checks.

In many organizations it is convenient to be able to make some small disbursements in cash in order to avoid the delay and inconvenience of the voucher and check preparation procedure. In such cases it is often appropriate to establish a petty cash fund from which small disbursements of cash may be made. For control purposes it is best to limit the size of disbursements that may be made from the fund and to require its custodian to obtain a receipt for every disbursement made. The total amount of the fund should be maintained at a constant sum in order that the total of all receipts and cash on hand is equal to the fund total at all times. Responsibility for the fund should be assigned to one person only and not separated. Checks to replenish the fund should pass through the regular voucher procedure, and supporting documentation in the form of all petty cash receipts should be required for such checks.

Compliance with the foreign corrupt practices act

As mentioned previously, the Foreign Corrupt Practices Act of 1977 requires all publicly held corporations to maintain good systems of internal accounting control. However, most if not all companies would contend that their systems of internal accounting control were already good prior to the Act. Despite such contentions, wise executives should take positive steps to demonstrate that their companies are complying with the Act.

The first step in a compliance program is to document the company's existing internal control systems. This requires the development of narrative descriptions of control objectives and procedures, flowcharts of data and information flows, and organization charts and other descriptions of assigned responsibilities. Many authorities suggest that this process can be facilitated by considering the internal accounting control system as a series of transaction processing cycles, as described in the previous section.[15] Each cycle then becomes the focal point of a separate analysis and documentation effort.

The second step in a compliance program is to evaluate the quality of the internal accounting control system. To do this requires an understanding of the risks to which a company is exposed in the absence of good control, such as loss of assets, inaccurate records, poor management decisions, fraud and embezzlement, and excessive operating costs. With respect to each of these risks, a measure of the potential magnitude in dollars may be multiplied by the estimated frequency of occurrence, or probability, to obtain a measure of the expected loss for a specified period of time, such as a year. This measure may be referred to as the *exposure*. Those risks for which the exposure is too high represent control weaknesses that should be evaluated further.

The third step is to evaluate the costs and benefits of instituting controls that deal with the control weakness. Costs include direct expenditures to implement control procedures, plus possible indirect effects such as reductions in employee morale or delays in transaction processing. Benefits include direct savings measured by the amount of reduction of exposure, plus possible indirect effects such as increased management confidence in the system. The exposure may be reduced by reducing its magnitude, its expected frequency of occurrence, or both. Although the direct costs and benefits may be relatively easy to quantify, the indirect costs and benefits often cannot be accurately measured and must be evaluated subjectively.

The final step is to weigh the costs and benefits. If the benefits of a control procedure (both quantitative and subjective) outweigh the related costs, then that control procedure should be implemented.[16]

Compliance with the internal control requirements of the Foreign Corrupt Practices Act is a continuous process—not simply a one-year project—of reviewing and evaluating control systems. The primary responsibility for this process rests with management, who in turn rely on the assistance of accounting systems designers and internal and external auditors. The corpo-

---

[15]See, for example, Arthur Andersen and Co., *A Guide for Studying and Evaluating Internal Accounting Controls* (Chicago: Arthur Andersen, 1978); or American Institute of Certified Public Accountants, *Report of the Special Advisory Committee on Internal Accounting Control* (New York: American Institute of Certified Public Accountants, 1979).

[16]This evaluation procedure is described in greater detail in Price Waterhouse & Co., *Guide to Accounting Controls: Establishing, Evaluating and Monitoring Control Systems* (New York: Price Waterhouse & Co., 1979), pp. 24–48.

ration's board of directors and its audit committee are also responsible for ensuring that management is adopting the necessary policies and processes involved in compliance. Many corporations have discovered that, regardless of the legal requirements, a compliance program that continuously monitors the effectiveness of internal accounting controls also makes good business sense.

A Perspective on Control Concepts

Each of the three types of control systems discussed in this chapter has its advantages and disadvantages. Feedback systems are generally less costly and easier to implement and are effective in restoring a process that goes out of control. Their basic disadvantage is that they may permit costly errors or deviations from plan to persist for too long before they are detected and corrected. Feedforward systems may overcome this deficiency, but they are generally the least effective and most difficult (or even impossible) to implement, owing to uncertainty in predicting future process outputs.

Preventive systems are also quite effective in avoiding costly errors and deviations. They are generally easy to implement but tend to be more costly because of the necessity for separation of functions, additional documentation, and other requirements. In addition, preventive controls are not self-regulatory; that is, once an error or irregularity occurs and avoids detection by preventive controls, there is no mechanism that will ensure subsequent review, discovery, and correction of the problem. In contrast, both feedback and feedforward systems have regulatory mechanisms in the form of periodic reviews that activate an automatic corrective action when problems are disclosed.

Figure 4.4. summarizes this discussion by indicating in tabular form the most significant advantages of each type of control system relative to the others.

As this discussion suggests, these control concepts are most effective when they are used to complement one another. Few, if any, processes can operate efficiently for long periods of time using only one type of control. In some processes, all three types of control may be useful. For example, credit control

FIGURE 4.4
Comparative summary of advantages of the three primary types of control system.

Control system advantages	Characteristic of:		
	Feedback	Feedforward	Preventive
Low cost	✓		
Ease of implementation	✓		✓
Effectiveness	✓		✓
Minimal time delays		✓	✓
Self-regulation	✓	✓	

makes use of feedback concerning bad debt losses and customer payment records, as discussed earlier. However, feedforward control in the form of analysis of the financial statements and credit ratings of potential customers is also an important policy of credit control. In addition, the requirement that the shipping department obtain shipment authorizations from the credit department is a form of preventive control over this process. Therefore credit control policies often integrate all three of the control concepts discussed in this chapter. There are probably several other business processes for which this is true.

All three types of control systems bear a close relationship to the accounting information system. Preventive controls are an integral part of virtually all accounting data processing, and much of the information generated by the accounting system is used for preventive control purposes; examples of the latter include control totals, the bank reconciliation, and the trial balance. In feedback control systems, accounting often performs the functions of standard setting, measurement of performance, and reporting on results of process operations. In feedforward control systems, accounting may also be involved in standard setting, as well as in the monitoring of process inputs and operations and in the prediction of process outputs. Thus it is true that control and accounting are inexorably intertwined. Indeed it might be said that control is the central concept and purpose of accounting, and that accounting is the primary vehicle of control in business organizations.

Summary

Assisting management in the control of business organizations is one of the primary functions of accounting information systems. The reporting of accounting information plays a central role in the regulation of business operations that use the principles of feedback or feedforward control systems. The design of policies and procedures for accounting data processing also incorporates preventive controls designed to safeguard assets and to ensure the accuracy and reliability of accounting information.

The essential elements of preventive control systems include sound organizational practices, including separation of responsibility for recording, custodial and authorization functions, sound personnel practices, written guides to policies and procedures, physical protection of assets, well-designed documents, and effective supervision. The importance of such practices is underscored by the Foreign Corrupt Practices Act of 1977, which requires publicly owned U.S. corporations to maintain systems of internal accounting control that meet certain minimum standards.

Review Questions

1. Define the following terms.

internal control	embezzlement
accounting controls	internal check
administrative controls	batch totals

management control	control totals
feedback	transposition error
feedback control	organizational independence
feedforward control	collusion
preventive control	fidelity bond
cybernetics	audit trail
standard cost	transaction trail
rate variance	lapping
usage variance	voucher
reorder point	exposure
lead time	
economic order quantity	

2. Describe the legal requirements of the Foreign Corrupt Practices Act with respect to internal controls. To what type of company does this law apply?

3. Identify three general types of control systems. What are their distinguishing features?

4. Relate the distinction between feedback, feedforward, and preventive control systems to AICPA's distinction between accounting and administrative controls.

5. What are the five fundamental components of a feedback control system and how are they related?

6. In what respect is a feedback control system a self-regulating system?

7. How do feedback control systems in business operations differ from mechanical feedback control systems such as the thermostat?

8. What are four essential factors in the successful operation of feedback control systems in business? Which of these have direct implications for accounting systems?

9. How do feedback control systems in business operate to promote operational efficiency and encourage adherence to managerial policies?

10. What are five examples of feedback control systems in business? Describe the operation of each.

11. List several examples of control problems that the internal audit function should discover.

12. Describe the five fundamental components of a feedforward control system and explain the relationships between them.

13. What condition must exist in order for a feedforward control system to be effective?

14. Identify three examples of feedforward control systems in business and explain the operation of each.

15. Explain in general terms how an accounting system uses preventive controls to contribute to the safeguarding of assets.

16. The loss to society from embezzlement may be looked at in different ways. Describe some of them.

17. Describe two examples of preventive control through internal check.

18. Describe six essential elements of preventive control systems in accounting processes.

19. Identify three general classes of functions that should be separated in order to maintain effective organizational independence. Give some examples of each.

20. Explain why it may be important for an organization to have a policy requiring certain key employees to take annual vacations.

21. Explain several ways in which the cash register contributes to the physical control of cash receipts in a retail enterprise.

22. Explain how sequential prenumbering of documents adds to control.

23. Describe the nature of preventive control systems in business relating to the following functions.
    a) purchasing of inventory
    b) flow of inventory through production
    c) payroll
    d) sale of products
    e) cash receipts
    f) cash disbursements

    Indicate the basic purpose or purposes of the control system in each case and, where relevant, describe applications of the principles of organizational independence, control by recorded documentation, batching, physical protection, and supervision.

24. Describe the steps that a corporation might take in order to effectively demonstrate compliance with the Foreign Corrupt Practices Act.

25. Describe the relative advantages and disadvantages of preventive, feedback, and feedforward control systems.

26. Explain how preventive, feedback, and feedforward control systems are related to accounting information systems.

Discussion Questions

27. Organizational independence is sometimes difficult to achieve in small companies. What other elements of control take on more importance in such situations?

28. Some people feel that controls in business organizations are dysfunctional in that they create resentment and loss of morale without producing much benefit. Discuss this position.

29. For each of the control activities listed below, discuss whether the activity contains elements of a preventive control, a feedback control, and/or a feedforward control. (Note: Some may contain elements of two or all three.)
   a) audit of a governmental agency by the General Accounting Office
   b) tabulation and review of customer complaints by a manager
   c) review of sales statistics indicating the impact of various advertising techniques on consumer buying behavior
   d) review of trends in the number of passengers on various routes by an airline
   e) analysis of résumés of potential employees by a manager responsible for hiring
   f) reporting of student grades in a university
   g) analysis of accident statistics in a factory

30. You are an executive with a corporation that has in recent years received from its external auditors clean opinions on its financial statements and favorable evaluations of its internal control systems. Discuss whether it is necessary for your corporation to take any further action to comply with the Foreign Corrupt Practices Act.

Problems and Cases

31. You are employed as the internal auditor for the Easy Manufacturing Corporation. Prior to your recent appointment, the company had not employed anyone in this position. To familiarize yourself with the company, you have investigated several clerical operations and have discovered the following.
   a) The person who opens incoming mail prepares a list of receipts of payments on account, which is then supplied to the accounts receivable clerk. The mail opener is also responsible for endorsing checks and preparing the bank deposit.
   b) A third individual receives invoices from suppliers, files them by due date, and writes checks to pay the invoices on the due date.
   c) A fourth employee is responsible for the timekeeping function and each week supplies a record of hours worked by each factory employee to a fifth employee, who prepares paychecks. The former is also responsible for maintaining personnel records and for distributing paychecks to employees.
   d) Only one bank account is used, and no bank reconciliation is prepared.

   Which of the above employees could possibly embezzle company funds? How? What changes would you recommend to strengthen the system of accounting controls?

32. Prudence Honeyfeather is responsible for maintaining the accounts receivable ledger for the Perfect Controls Corporation. Twice daily she receives a batch of invoices from billing and posts them as debits to customer accounts. One day she mistakenly posted the amount of $1007.67 to a customer account, when the proper amount was actually $1070.67. At the next step in processing, the existence of an error was discovered, and a comparison of invoices with amounts posted quickly revealed the account in which the error occurred, and it was corrected.

     What procedure or control probably resulted in the discovery that an error existed?

33. The Y Company, a client of your firm, has come to you with the following problem: It has three clerical employees who must perform the following functions.

    a) maintain general ledger
    b) maintain accounts payable ledger
    c) maintain accounts receivable ledger
    d) prepare checks for signature
    e) maintain disbursements journal
    f) issue credits on returns and allowances
    g) reconcile the bank account
    h) handle and deposit cash receipts

    Assuming that there is no problem as to the ability of any of the employees, the company requests that you assign the above functions to the three employees in such a manner as to achieve the highest degree of internal control. It may be assumed that these employees will perform no other accounting functions than the ones listed, and that any accounting functions not listed will be performed by persons other than these three employees.

    a) State how you would distribute the above functions among the three employees. Assume that, with the exception of the nominal jobs of the bank reconciliation and the issuance of credits on returns and allowances, all functions require an equal amount of time.
    b) List four possible unsatisfactory pairings of the functions listed above. (CPA Examination)

34. The Wise Wholesale Company wishes to establish an inventory control system for Widgets, its best-selling item. The demand rate for Widgets is a constant 10 units per day, or 3600 per year. The cost of placing an order for Widgets is $50. The lead time is a constant two days, and the holding cost rate is $1.00 per unit per year.

REQUIRED

    a) Determine the appropriate standards for an inventory control system that will minimize the sum of the costs of holding and ordering inventories and of stockouts.
    b) Identify the five fundamental components of a feedforward control system in the above situation.

   c) If demand and lead time were variable instead of constant, what additional problems would exist in the system?

35. McClain's lumberyard uses the following procedures in selling lumber to customers:

   a) The customer informs a clerk in the office of the sizes and quantities of lumber to be purchased.

   b) The clerk records the items on a sales document, calculates the total cost, and collects payment from the customer.

   c) A yard worker obtains the lumber from the yard and assists in loading it onto the customer's car or truck; or if the purchase is large and the customer wishes, McClain's will deliver the order.

REQUIRED

Explain several aspects of the design and usage of the sales document that will facilitate control of cash receipts and inventories by McClain's.

36. Below, in the margin, is a list of amounts from source documents that have been summed to obtain a batch total. You may assume that these amounts, and the batch total, are correct.

    Columns *a–d* are four batch totals computed from the same amounts after these source documents were processed in a subsequent processing step. In each of these four cases, one processing error was made. In each case, you are to (1) compute the difference between the batch total obtained after processing and the correct batch total shown in the margin, (2) explain specifically how this difference is helpful in discovering the processing error, and (3) identify the processing error.

	(a)	*(b)*	*(c)*	*(d)*
$3,630.62	$3,630.62	$3,630.62	$3,630.62	$3,630.62
1,484.86	1,484.86	1,484.86	1,484.86	1,484.86
2,164.67	2,164.67	2,164.67	2,164.67	2,164.67
946.43	946.43	946.43	946.43	946.43
2,626.28	−2,626.28	2,626.28	2,626.28	2,626.28
969.97	969.97	969.97	969.97	969.97
2,772.42	2,772.42	2,772.42	3,772.42	2,772.42
934.25	934.25	934.25	934.25	934.25
1,620.94	1,620.94	1,620.94	1,620.94	1,620.94
4,566.86	4,566.86	4,656.86	4,566.86	4,566.86
1,249.32	1,249.32	1,249.32	1,249.32	1,249.32
1,070.27	1,070.27	1,070.27	1,070.27	1,070.27
2,668.51	2,668.51	2,668.51	2,668.51	2,668.51
1,762.62	1,762.62	1,762.62	1,762.62	873.26
873.26	873.26	873.26	873.26	$27,578.66
$29,341.28	$24,088.72	$29,431.28	$30,341.28	

37. The Future Corporation is a small manufacturing concern in Aggie, Texas. It operates one plant and employs fifty workers in its manufacturing facility. Employees are paid weekly. Each week the department supervisors supply the payroll clerk with signed time sheets and also with a list of any employees hired or terminated by the supervisor. The payroll clerk compares the time sheets with the time cards and prepares and signs payroll checks. The paychecks are then given in sealed envelopes to the supervisors, who in turn give them to the respective employees.

REQUIRED   Identify several weaknesses in internal control over Future's payroll system; and for each weakness, describe how internal control could be improved.

38. The following is a list of duties performed by Ms. C. Nation for the Quick and Easy Corporation.
   a) Credit sales for the day are totaled and reported to the general bookkeeper.
   b) Collections on accounts receivable for the day are totaled. The checks and an adding machine tape of receipts are turned over to the cashier.
   c) Sales and cash collections are posted daily to the accounts receivable ledger.
   d) A trial balance of the receivable ledger is prepared monthly, and the total is compared with the total shown by the general control account.
   e) Statements are prepared and mailed on each account monthly. Accounts not paid by the tenth of the month are followed up with a series of collection notices and letters.
   f) Accounts determined to be uncollectable are reported to the general bookkeeper for write-off of the amount included in the control account.

   The company is considering hiring another person to help Ms. Nation with her numerous duties. Cite at least two forms of manipulation that could possibly be accomplished by Ms. Nation as her duties are presently defined. What division of duties between Ms. Nation and a new employee would you recommend to prevent such manipulation?

39. The cashier of the Easy Company intercepted Customer A's check payable to the company in the amount of $500 and deposited it in a bank account which was part of the company petty cash fund, of which he was custodian. He then drew a $500 check on the petty cash fund bank account payable to himself, signed it, and cashed it. At the end of the month while processing the monthly statements to customers, he was able to change the statement to Customer A so as to show that A had received credit for the $500 check that had been intercepted. Ten days later he made an entry in the cash-received book which purported to record receipt of a remittance of $500 from Customer A, thus restoring A's account to its proper balance but overstating the cash in bank. He covered the overstatement

by omitting from the list of outstanding checks in the bank reconcilement two checks, the aggregate amount of which was $500.

List what you regard as five important deficiencies in the system of internal control in the above situation and state the proper remedy for each deficiency. (CPA Examination)

40. In the XYZ Company, when supplier invoices are received they go to the cashier, who reviews supporting documentation and prepares a payment voucher authorizing a disbursement. The vouchers, with the invoices attached, are then provided to the assistant controller, who records them in a vouchers payable ledger and files them by due date. Each day the batch of vouchers due for payment is provided to the cashier, who prepares and signs checks and stamps the vouchers "PAID." The assistant controller then records all disbursements in the cash disbursements journal and files all the paid vouchers. The checks go to the treasurer for mailing to the suppliers.

REQUIRED   Identify (a) a form of embezzlement that could be perpetrated by one of these persons and (b) the deficiencies in the internal control system that make this possible.

41. What principle of feedback control systems is probably being violated in each of the following cases?

   a) A monthly report to the credit manager of the Morgan Company indicated that one of the firm's customers, Shylock Corporation, owed Morgan a large sum of money on account, which was over ninety days past due. Morgan's policy is to refuse to sell on account to a customer whose account is ninety days or more past due. However, on the day before the monthly report was received, a large order by Shylock was approved by the credit manager.

   b) Each month, the Morgan Company provides its factory supervisors with a performance report indicating budgeted and actual costs for each supervisor's department. Each report contains an analysis of material, labor, and overhead costs. Among the overhead costs are proportionate allocations of the salary of the plant manager and staff and of depreciation for the plant and equipment. The performance reports are considered to be the single most important tool for evaluating the performance of factory supervisors.

   c) A special study indicated that lax control over office supplies in the Morgan Company had resulted in waste totaling from $100 to $300 per month. As a result a room was set aside to be a supplies storeroom, a clerk was hired to manage the storeroom, and a control system designed around a supplies requisition document was implemented.

   d) Each week, the purchasing agent of the Morgan Company is provided with a computer listing of the parts inventory ledger. The purchasing agent determines which parts must be ordered by comparing the quantity on hand with the reorder point on the report for each item. For those items that must be reordered, the agent refers to catalogs listing which vendors sell the part, selects a vendor, and then prepares the purchase order. Delays in this process have often resulted in stock-outs of parts needed in production.

42. Explain how the principle of organizational independence is being violated in each of the following situations.

a) A payroll employee recorded a forty-hour workweek for an employee who had quit the previous week. He then prepared a paycheck for this employee, cashed it by forging the signature, and kept the cash.

b) While opening the mail, the cashier set aside two checks payable to the company on account and later cashed these checks and pocketed the cash.

c) The cashier prepared a fictitious invoice from a company having the name of his brother-in-law and wrote a check in payment of the invoice, which the brother-in-law later cashed.

d) An employee of the finishing department walked off with several parts from the storeroom and recorded the items in the inventory ledger as being issued to the assembly department.

e) The cashier cashed a check from a customer in payment of an account receivable, pocketed the cash, and concealed the theft by properly posting the receipt to the customer's account in the accounts receivable ledger.

43. It has been said that internal auditors are not responsible for detecting defalcation, embezzlement, or fraud. Yet, when a fraud is uncovered, the question is usually asked, "Where were the auditors?"

While it is obvious that an internal auditor cannot be expected to guarantee that there is no fraud, there are a number of indicators that an alert auditor might spot and investigate as a deterrent to fraud or as an early disclosure of possible fraud.

REQUIRED

Discuss the following six indicators or danger signs, including the potential fraud that could be involved, and the initial approach you would take in each case.

a) employees living beyond their apparent means
b) reluctance by a key employee to take a vacation
c) unreasonable association with supplier's personnel by members of the Purchasing Department
d) erasures, changes, or manually inserted times on time cards
e) date of deposits per cash book significantly different from date of deposits on bank statements
f) lack of cooperation in relinquishing records for audit. (CIA Examination)

References

American Institute of Certified Public Accountants. *Report of the Special Advisory Committee on Internal Accounting Control.* New York: American Institute of Certified Public Accountants, 1979.

American Institute of Certified Public Accountants. *Statement on Auditing Standards No. 1–49.* New York: American Institute of Certified Public Accountants, 1974. (Note: This statement codifies and incorporates all the material contained in *Statements on Auditing Procedure* referred to in this chapter.)

Arthur Andersen and Co. *A Guide for Studying and Evaluating Internal Accounting Controls.* Chicago: Arthur Andersen, 1978.

Baggett, Walter O. "Internal Control: Insight from a General Systems Theory Perspective." *Journal of Accounting, Auditing & Finance* (Spring 1983): 227–233.

Benjamin, James J.; Paul E. Dascher; and Robert G. Morgan. "How Corporate Controllers View the Foreign Corrupt Practices Act." *Management Accounting* (June 1979): 43–45.

Carmichael, Douglas R. "Internal Accounting Control—It's the Law." *Journal of Accountancy* (May 1980): 70–76.

Cook, J. Michael, and Thomas P. Kelley. "Internal Accounting Control: A Matter of Law." *Journal of Accountancy* (January 1979): 56–64.

Cushing, Barry E. "A Further Note on the Mathematical Approach to Internal Control." *The Accounting Review* **50** (January 1975): 151–155.

Ellentuck, Elmer I. "How to Minimize Employee Fraud: A Checklist." *Practical Accountant* **5** (March/April 1972): 30–37.

Elliott, Robert K., and John J. Willingham. *Management Fraud: Detection and Deterrence.* United States: Petrocelli Books, 1980.

Foreign Corrupt Practices Act of 1977. U.S. Code, 1976 edition, Supplement II, Title 15, Selection 78. Washington, D.C.: United States Government Printing Office, 1979.

Grollman, William K., and Robert W. Colby. "Internal Control for Small Businesses." *Journal of Accountancy* (December 1978): 64–67.

Gurry, E. J. "Locating Potential Irregularities." *Journal of Accountancy* **140** (September 1975): 111–114.

Horngren, Charles T. *Cost Accounting, A Managerial Emphasis.* 5th ed. Englewood Cliffs, N.J.: Prentice-Hall, 1982.

Koontz, Harold, and Robert W. Bradspies. "Managing through Feedforward Control." *Business Horizons* **15** (June 1972): 25–36.

Loebbecke, James K., and George R. Zuber. "Evaluating Internal Control." *Journal of Accountancy* (February 1980): 49–56.

MacKay, A. E. "Management Control in a Changing Environment." *Financial Executive* (March 1979): 25–36.

McQueary, Glenn M., II., and Michael P. Risdon. "How We Comply with the Foreign Corrupt Practices Act." *Management Accounting* (November 1979): 39–43.

Mautz, Robert K.; Walter G. Kell; Michael W. Maher; Alan G. Merten; Raymond R. Reilly; Dennis G. Severance; and Bernard J. White. *Internal Control in U.S. Corporations: The State of the Art.* New York: Financial Executives Research Foundation, 1980.

Mautz, Robert K., and Bernard J. White. "Internal Control—A Management View." *Financial Executive* (June 1979): 12–18.

Mautz, R. K., and James Winjum. *Criteria for Management Control Systems.* New York: Financial Executives Research Foundation, 1981.

Passage, Howard D., and Donald A. Fleming. "An Integrated Approach to Internal Control Review." *Management Accounting* (February 1980): 29–35.

Price Waterhouse & Co. *Guide to Accounting Controls: Establishing, Evaluating and Monitoring Control Systems.* New York: Price Waterhouse & Co., 1979.

Sherwin, Douglas S. "The Meaning of Control." *Dun's Review* (January 1956): 45–46, 83–84.

Touche Ross and Co. *The New Management Imperative: Compliance with the Accounting Requirements of the Foreign Corrupt Practices Act.* New York: Touche Ross, 1978.

United States Fidelity and Guaranty Co. *The Forty Thieves.* Baltimore: USF&G, 1970.

PART TWO

THE TECHNOLOGY OF INFORMATION SYSTEMS

CHAPTER 5

A Review of Mainframe Computer Hardware

LEARNING OBJECTIVES

Careful study of this chapter should enable students to:

☐ Identify the major components of an information system.

☐ Explain how the three components of a CPU function and how data is represented in a computer.

☐ Compare and contrast the secondary storage devices used in computer systems.

☐ Compare and contrast the input and output devices used in computer systems.

☐ Explain why business computer systems are input/output bound and how system throughput can be improved.

☐ Draw system flowcharts that show how the various components of an information system are related.

Most accountants and businesspeople need to have a basic understanding of computer technology. While few need to be technical experts, most need to understand what computers are, what they are composed of, how they operate, how they store and process data, and so forth. This understanding helps them to design, manage, and operate their information systems. Chapters 5 through 9 provide students with this understanding. Chapter 5 examines the hardware devices that are most likely to be found in traditional, large-computer-oriented data processing shops. Chapter 6 reviews software concepts and helps students understand how computers are given instructions and how they operate. Chapter 7 delves into the microcomputer hardware and software concepts that have had a significant impact on accounting information systems, and Chapter 8 discusses data communications and advanced systems. Finally, Chapter 9 explores file and data base management and storage concepts.

Components of an Information System

An information system, in order to transform data into usable information, embodies at least five basic elements:

1. Data, or input, to be processed by the system,
2. A data processor (human or machine),
3. A means of storing data for future use,
4. An output medium to communicate the information, and
5. Instructions or procedures for processing the data.

This process can be depicted pictorially, as shown in Fig. 5.1. Notice that the other four elements either flow into or out of the data processor, making this

FIGURE 5.1
Basic elements of an
information system.

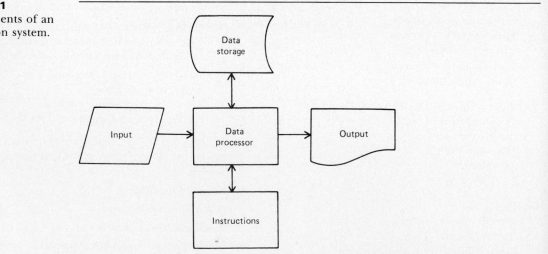

the central, pivotal function. As explained in Chapter 1, a number of data processing activities relate to each of these five elements.

Both manual and computer information systems have these five basic elements. In a manual inventory management system a person (possibly aided by an adding machine, calculator, etc.) is usually the processor. The input is the inventory transactions that are collected and captured on purchase orders, invoices, cash registers, etc. The output is inventory management reports. Inventory records are maintained in a journal or ledger and are usually stored in file cabinets. The instructions are the rules and procedures used to operate the inventory system.

Computer system components

In a computer system the essential information system elements can be divided into four categories: hardware, software, personnel, and data base. *Computer hardware* comprises all the physical equipment necessary to carry out the electronic data processing (EDP) tasks, and includes input and output devices, storage devices, and the processor of the information—the computer. It usually includes data preparation devices that prepare data for input into the computer. It might also include telecommunications devices that are used to transmit input, output, and stored data from one location to another. For reasons of convenience, as many of these hardware devices as possible are usually housed together in what is called the computer room or the *data processing center*. Since the other hardware surrounds the *central processing unit* (CPU) and is attached to it, these devices are referred to as peripherals. Fig. 5.2 is an expansion of Fig. 5.1 and shows the hardware devices that are used for data preparation, input, processing, storage, data communications, and output.

The computer system shown in Fig. 5.3 is representative of some of the devices commonly used by large organizations. The cables that connect the peripherals to the computer are concealed by the raised floors common to computer rooms. Devices connected to the CPU by cables, telephone lines, etc., are called *online devices*. They are referred to as "online" because they can directly access the CPU and carry out input/output processes as needed. *Offline equipment*, on the other hand, is not connected directly to the CPU and is usually used to prepare data for input into the system or to prepare output for distribution. Examples of online devices are cathode-ray tube (CRT) terminals, disk drives, and tape drives. Examples of offline equipment are keypunch/verification machines and key-to-tape (or disk) encoders. These devices are discussed later in the chapter.

Software includes the programs that give instructions to the CPU, the programming languages, and the documentation of the system. Both hardware and software are necessary for an EDP system to operate; neither can operate alone. Hardware without software is like an airplane without a pilot. Computer personnel are those individuals who use, design, operate, control, and manage an EDP system. Computer personnel (including accountants) is not

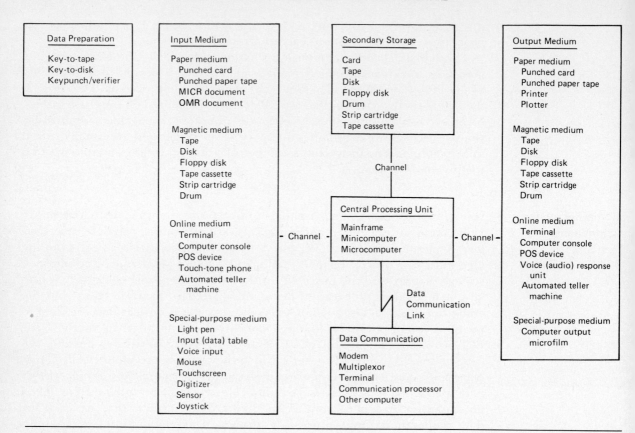

FIGURE 5.2
Computer hardware.

the topic of a specific chapter. Instead, the people involved with the system are discussed throughout the entire text. A data base contains all the data stored and maintained by the system in order to meet the organization's information needs.

The human vs. the electronic data processor

The human and the computer have significant strengths and weaknesses as data processors. Humans are flexible and can think, perceive unusual items, and deal with unexpected events or problems. They can interact with others and gather the information necessary to reason through problems and develop satisfactory solutions. Computers can only do what humans have instructed them to do, and the data they receive must be structured in a specific way. Not only would it be difficult for humans to anticipate and then program every possible problem and solution, but it would not be economically or technically feasible to even attempt it.

Humans are slow and error prone, they get tired and they sometimes do not follow instructions very well. They usually cannot process high volumes of

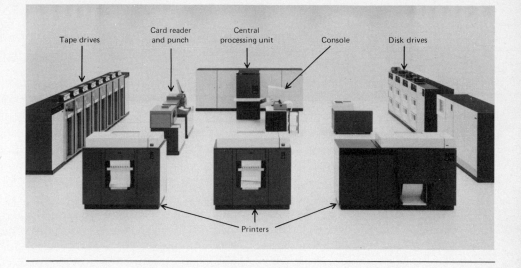

Tape drives Card reader and punch Central processing unit Console Disk drives

Printers

FIGURE 5.3
A computer system.
(Courtesy of IBM
Corporation.)

data or easily handle highly complex calculations and manipulations of data. Computers are uniquely adapted to handle these problems. They are extremely fast and can store massive quantities of data. They are very accurate, follow instructions exactly, and can operate around the clock. They do not become tired, bored, emotional, or dissatisfied with their job. They can handle complex transactions and quickly manipulate large quantities of data.

Most accounting and business organizations need the human's ability to think and reason and the computer's speed, reliability, accuracy, and reduced cost. As a result the most efficient information systems are usually a man-machine combination. The two complement each other as they produce the information needed to make effective business decisions.

Central Processing Unit

For a data processor to fulfill its function it must be able to:

a. Perform logic and make arithmetic calculations.

b. Store data, instructions, and calculations made by the system.

c. Control the process—a "traffic cop" is needed to interpret instructions, locate and route data, and perform arithmetic and logic functions.

The processing functions mentioned above are performed by the CPU. The CPU has three main components: (1) the arithmetic-logic unit, (2) the memory, and (3) the control unit. The *arithmetic-logic unit* carries out all the arithmetic calculations and logical comparisons (such as comparing the values of two data items). All the data and instructions used by the system are stored in the *memory unit*. The *control unit* interprets program instructions and controls and coordinates input, output, and storage devices in the system. The relationship of these components to each other, and to computer input, output, and storage, is illustrated in Fig. 5.4. Note that all components, both internal and external to the CPU, interact with and through memory.

Computer generations

The electronic circuitry of a CPU has been used to classify computers into several distinct generations. The "first generation" of computers was developed in the late 1940s and early 1950s; they were used in scientific applications at government and university sites. Computers were first made commercially available in the early 1950s, and businesses soon began using them for data processing tasks. In the late 1950s, transistors and printed circuitry replaced the vacuum tubes used in early computers. This led to computers that were not only much smaller in size but also much faster and more reliable. This development was so significant that the new computers were referred to as "second generation" computers.

In the early 1960s, computers with microelectronic circuitry (also called integrated circuits, or ICs) were introduced. These ICs were much smaller and faster than anything that preceded them. They greatly improved the computer's ability to handle data communications from remote locations and to execute several different jobs simultaneously. So significant were these improvements that a "third generation" of computers was hailed.

Computers entered into a "fourth generation" when several new types of circuitry were introduced. These include monolithic systems technology (MST), large-scale integration (LSI) or very large-scale integration (VLSI) semiconductor circuits, and metal oxide silicon field effect transfer (MOSFET) circuitry. Computer designers are currently busy working on developments that

FIGURE 5.4
Interaction of main components of a computer.

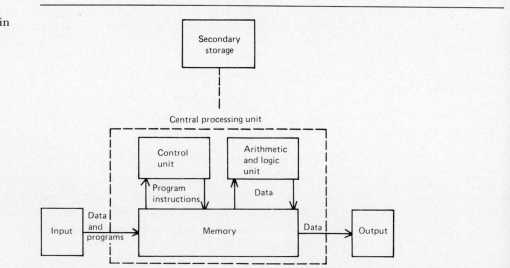

will one day introduce a "fifth generation" of electronic computing devices. In all likelihood, these computers will be able to see, listen, talk, and think. In fact, the Japanese have publicly stated that they hope to have this fifth generation on the market by the early 1990s.

How the CPU functions

Before a computer program is executed, both the program instructions and the data to be processed are transferred into the CPU's memory. Each instruction and data value is stored in a separate memory location. The CPU can keep track of the location of any particular instruction or data value because each storage location in the CPU's memory has an address that uniquely identifies that specific memory location. This is analogous to every house on every street in a city having its own address. Computer instructions are transferred one at a time to the control unit where they are interpreted. The control unit then initiates the detailed set of electronic operations called for by that instruction.

If an instruction involves input or output, the control unit activates the appropriate device, and data are either read from an input device into the CPU's memory or written from the CPU's memory to an output device. If the instruction involves logic operations or arithmetic calculations, the control unit transfers the appropriate data values to the arithmetic-logic unit, which performs the necessary operations and returns the result.

As instructions and data are transferred from memory to the control or arithmetic-logic unit, they are stored in high-speed temporary storage locations called registers. Registers are classified according to their function: instruction registers hold an instruction code, address registers hold a memory address of another instruction or data value, and accumulators hold the results of arithmetic operations. When the control unit finishes with an instruction, it checks the appropriate address register to locate the next instruction. It then reads that instruction into an instruction register for interpretation and execution.

Computer operators interact with large computer systems using a *control console*. In the system illustrated in Fig. 5.3, the console consists of a panel containing various lights and switches, a monitor, a keyboard, and a printer. The console panel enables the operator to monitor certain aspects of the CPU's operations, whereas the console keyboard, monitor, and printer provide limited input-output capability. In smaller systems, the user controls the system with a keyboard and a monitor.

Internal memory

Certain elementary computer operations and programs, called *microcode*, are permanently stored in the computer. Microcode is stored in *read only memory* (ROM) to prevent its being accidentally changed or altered. The contents of ROM may be read but usually may not be altered by other program instructions. However, some types of ROM are erasable and reprogrammable using special techniques or software not available to the normal user. The computer industry has used the term *firmware* to describe the computer software that has been permanently installed inside the computer. If present trends are maintained, more and more software will be stored inside the hardware as firmware.

Computers temporarily store programs, data, and instructions in their internal *random access memory* (RAM). Any memory location in RAM can be directly accessed by the computer, and RAM can be erased and reused as needed. A *semiconductor*, which is a tiny silicon chip upon which is inscribed a number of miniature circuits, is the most common form of RAM. Figure 5.5 shows a semiconductor chip lying on a magnetic core plane. Magnetic core storage was the predominant form of primary storage in the CPU through the 1960s and early 1970s. The primary memory of most modern computers consists of large-scale integration (LSI) or very large-scale integration (VLSI) RAM cir-

FIGURE 5.5
Semiconductor memory chip with magnetic core plane in background. (Courtesy of IBM Corporation.)

cuits. These semiconductor memory chips are small, inexpensive, and very fast.

Bubble memory, a recent innovation in memory storage, has more than ten times the storage capacity of today's most powerful integrated circuit semiconductor chips. Bubble memory consists of a chip covered with a thin magnetic film that forms a bubble when a magnetic field is applied. Although not as fast and not yet competitive in price with semiconductors, bubble memory should play a significant role when it becomes price competitive with other types of memory.

Computer manufacturers express memory capacity in terms of a *kilobyte*, which is abbreviated to K or KB. Although 1K actually represents 1024 characters, it is usually expressed in terms of 1000 characters of memory. Therefore 64K represents approximately 64,000 characters of storage. Memory is also expressed in terms of megabytes (M), a million characters of data; gigabytes, a billion characters; and terabytes, a trillion bytes of storage. On the small end of the scale, microcomputers typically have internal memory ranging from 16K to 4M. On the large end of the scale, large mainframes have internal memory capacities that go up to 40M or more.

Measuring time in a CPU

Time in computers is measured in the following fractions of a second.

TIME TERMINOLOGY	FRACTION OF A SECOND	USED TO MEASURE TIME OF
Millisecond	Thousandth	First generation computers
Microsecond	Millionth	Second generation computers
Nanosecond	Billionth	Third generation computers
Picosecond	Trillionth	Fourth generation computers
Femtosecond	Quadrillionth	Fifth generation computers

To illustrate the magnitude of these speeds, consider that if a person took one step a nanosecond, as many large computers do, a person could circle the earth twenty times in one second. To illustrate how small a femtosecond is, consider that there are as many femtoseconds in one second as there are seconds in thirty million years.

When comparing one computer with another, some of the more important measures of CPU performance include access time and execution time. Access time refers to the time required to retrieve data from memory. Execution time refers to the time required to perform a computer instruction, such as add, multiply, or compare.

Data representation

Computers store data in what are called *bits* (short for "binary digit"). A bit is a storage location capable of assuming one of two possible states ("on" or "off," "0" or "1," etc.). Computer users, however, want a coding system capable of representing, at a minimum, the twenty-six letters of the alphabet, ten decimal digits, and special characters such as "$" and "+". To represent all these characters, a group of bits, called a *byte*, is used. Two coding schemes, or grouping of bits, are used. The 6-bit coding system is called the binary-coded decimal (BCD). The more common coding system is EBCDIC (pronounced eb-see-dick), an acronym for extended binary-coded decimal interchange code. It is an 8-bit code providing for 256 (2^8) possible characters.

Generally, a character of data is stored in each byte, the exception being numeric data stored in *packed decimal* form. Since only 4 bits are required to store a single numeric digit, it is possible to "pack" two numeric digits into an 8-bit byte. Since much of the data used in an accounting information system is numeric data, packing can provide a considerable savings in storage requirements.

Computers move data internally using a group of bytes that is referred to as a *word*. Generally, a computer moves one word at a time to and from its storage locations. Although word sizes vary among computers, the most common word size in large computers is 32 bits. Most microcomputers now use 16-bit words, although there are a few with 8- or 32-bit words. The word size depends upon the capacity of the registers used in the CPU and the width of the data path or data bus used to move data and instructions through the CPU's circuitry. Some computers, for example, may have 32-bit registers but only have a 16-bit data bus. These 16/32-bit computers are not as fast as the 32/32-bit systems since only 16 (rather than 32) bits can be transferred at a time. Word size also determines the number of instructions that can be executed by the system, the precision of arithmetic calculations, and the amount of directly addressable memory.

A *page* is anywhere from 2K to 4K bytes. In a *virtual memory* system, online secondary storage is considered to be an extension of primary memory. The operating system is continually switching pages (or blocks of memory) back and forth between primary and secondary memory. This process, called paging, makes the system appear to have virtually an unlimited amount of primary memory. The virtual memory technique increases the number of programs that the system is able to process at one time, thereby increasing the efficiency of the system.

Secondary Storage Devices and Media

Internal (or primary) memory is expensive in comparison with secondary storage. In addition, it is difficult for computer manufacturers to place enough primary memory in a system to meet users' storage needs. As a result, computer systems make extensive use of *secondary storage*, which is storage media such as tapes and disks that store data not currently needed by the system. Because many of these storage media are separate from the devices that read them (i.e., disk drives, tape drives), the user has at his or her disposal an almost unlimited amount of storage space.

There are two basic categories of secondary storage: sequential access storage and direct access (often called random access) storage. With *sequential access*, a stored record may be accessed only after reading all other records that precede it. Magnetic tape is the most frequently used sequential access media. Sequential access files are generally stored offline when they are not being processed. All records in a sequential file must be maintained in numeric or alphabetic order according to an identifying number or name, called the primary key, that is stored in the same field within each record.

With *direct access*, records in a file may be accessed directly without reading any other records. Each secondary storage location has an address, just like internal storage locations. Once the computer determines the address of the desired record, it can directly access that record. A record stored on a direct access device must have a primary key and may also have one or more secondary keys. Records accessed directly may or may not be ordered sequentially. Direct access files can be maintained online or stored offline. There are a variety of direct access secondary storage media, but magnetic disk and floppy diskettes are the most common. Other direct access secondary storage media include magnetic drums, magnetic strips (also called data cells), magnetic cards, magnetic cores, magnetic bubbles, laser disks, and charge-coupled devices.

Punched cards

Figure 5.6 illustrates the standard eighty-column punched card, showing the hole pattern for numeric, alphabetic, and selected special characters. A smaller card having ninety-six columns and utilizing a different coding system is less widely used. It is less than half the size of the eighty-column card, and yet it holds twenty percent more data.

FIGURE 5.6
Standard eighty-column punched card (Courtesy of IBM Corporation.)

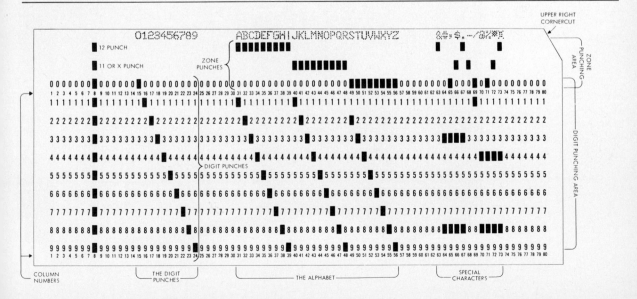

Punched cards are read by a card reader that senses the pattern of holes in each card. Output is punched onto cards by a card punch. As shown in Fig. 5.7, a *multifunction card machine* combines the read and punch functions into a single device. Card readers operate at an average speed of about 600 cards per minute and card punches at about 300 per minute.

Magnetic tape

A reel of *magnetic tape* is typically $\frac{1}{2}$ inch in width, $10\frac{1}{2}$ inches in diameter, and up to 2400 feet long. Magnetic tape generally has seven or nine horizontal rows, called tracks, into which data are recorded in the form of magnetic bits. In the more common nine-bit system, each unique character is represented by some combination of magnetized and nonmagnetized bits. In Fig. 5.8, each column represents a character of data, with the numbers 1 through 9 being displayed. The coding system uses eight bits (a byte) to represent each character. The ninth bit, called a *check* or *parity bit,* is used to check the accuracy of each recorded character when the tape is read. In an even parity system, the check bit is magnetized only if an odd number of the other eight bits is magnetized. In this way, the total number of magnetized bits in any column is always even. If a bit is lost, the check would be violated and the erroneous data would be discovered. It is also possible to have odd parity, where every

FIGURE 5.7
Multifunction card machine. (Courtesy of IBM Corporation.)

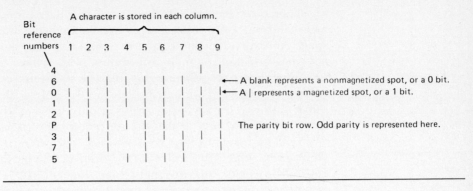

FIGURE 5.8
Nine-track tape.

column contains an odd number of magnetized bits. Data are very tightly packed on magnetic tape. In the past the most common recording density has been 1600 bytes per inch, but densities as high as 38,000 bytes per inch are also in use.

As explained in Chapter 3, characters (bytes) are aggregated into fields, fields into records, and records into files. For example, the characters "123 Elm" can be stored in a field named Address. The Name, Address, and Amount fields might constitute the Accounts Receivable record, and all Accounts Receivable records are stored together in an Accounts Receivable file. A computer file usually contains two special records in addition to the data records. The *header record,* which is the first record on the file, and the *trailer record,* which is the last record on the file, contain descriptive data about the file. Examples of the data stored in these records are file name, file destruction date, and control totals.

Records are stored on magnetic tape in blocks of several records, with a gap called the *interblock gap* between each pair of blocks. Figure 5.9 illustrates a section of magnetic tape upon which records are stored in blocks of four. The interblock gaps provide room for the tape drive to slow down and stop after reading a block, then start up again and reach peak speed before reading the next block of data. Depending on the speed with which the computer is actually processing the data, this space for stopping and starting may be required at some times, whereas at other times the tape drive is able to pass the interblock gap at peak speed without stopping and starting. Blocking of records obviously reduces the effective data storage capacity of magnetic tape because no data are stored in the interblock gaps. Even so, a reel of magnetic tape can hold up to as many as 200 million characters of data.

FIGURE 5.9
Blocking of records.

Interblock gap	Record #21	Record #22	Record #23	Record #24	Interblock gap	Record #25	Record #26	Record #27	Record #28	Interblock gap

There are several advantages to storing data on magnetic tape. Magnetic tape can hold a lot of data, tapes are inexpensive and take up little storage space, and records on the tape may be of varying lengths. The biggest disadvantage of tapes is their inflexibility. Tapes have to be read sequentially (meaning direct access is not possible). In addition, records cannot be added, deleted, or updated without processing the entire file. Because of the flexibility problem, usually tapes are used only for data that are not needed frequently by the system or that do not require direct access.

Data on magnetic tape are read into the central processing unit by means of magnetic tape drive units. A tape drive is also used to write data from the central processor onto magnetic tape. Figure 5.10 is a picture of a typical magnetic tape drive unit. Typical peak operating speeds of available tape drive units range from 15,000 to 3 million characters per second.

Magnetic disks

Magnetic disks are the dominant direct access storage device because they provide the optimum trade-off among such factors as cost, access time, storage capacity, and flexibility. A magnetic disk storage unit contains one or more magnetic disks and a mechanism for reading and writing data on the disks. Figure 5.11 illustrates several characteristics of a typical disk unit. Note that the disks in the unit are similar in appearance to a stack of phonograph records except that there is space between each adjoining pair of disks. Data are recorded on both the upper and lower surfaces of each disk. The unit shown has one read/write head for each surface. Data are stored in each of several concentric circular tracks (somewhat analogous to the grooves on a phonograph record) on each recording surface. Data are accessed by moving the head in or out to the appropriate track while the disk revolves to the appropriate segment of the track. Disks typically rotate at speeds of 2400 to 3600 revolutions per minute and can read at speeds up to over 3 million characters of data per second.

Disk units vary widely in storage capacity and cost. The capacity depends on the number of bytes per track, the number of tracks per surface, and the number of surfaces. Although tracks on the outer surface are usually larger than those on the inner track, manufacturers usually create disks that store the same amount of data on the inner as on the outer tracks. A typical small disk has 7294 bytes per track, 200 tracks per surface, and twenty surfaces, for a total capacity of almost 30 million bytes. A typical large disk has 13,030 bytes per track, 808 tracks per surface, and nineteen surfaces for data storage, providing a total capacity of 200 million bytes. Some of the larger disks can store over 5 billion characters of data.

A fixed disk is one in which the disks are permanently attached to the disk drive unit and cannot be removed. A removable disk is one in which the set of disks, called a disk pack, may be physically removed from the disk drive unit and replaced by another disk pack. With a removable disk system, users have an almost unlimited amount of secondary memory available to meet their

FIGURE 5.10
Magnetic tape drive
unit. (Courtesy of
IBM Corporation.)

needs. A fixed-head disk is a unit in which there is a separate read/write head
for each track, which enables data to be accessed without moving the read/
write heads. In contrast, movable-head disks have one or a few heads per surface, so that the heads must move in order to access the appropriate track.
The unit shown in Fig. 5.11 is a movable-head disk.

The biggest advantage of disks is their direct access capability. Unlike tape
storage, the computer does not have to read an entire file to find the record
desired. Instead, because each segment of the disk has a unique address, the
system can readily locate the record needed and access it directly. This means
that record accessing, deleting, and updating can be quickly and easily accom-

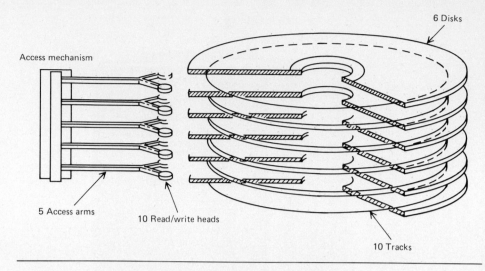

FIGURE 5.11
Magnetic disk storage features.

plished. In addition, disks have faster transfer rates than do tapes. This combination of direct and faster access makes disks the most popular secondary storage medium.

The disadvantages of disks are their cost and their bulkiness. Disk packs can cost up to as much as eighty or ninety times the cost of a reel of tape. Even though more data can be stored on disks than can be stored on tape, disk storage is still three to six times what it is for tape storage. Disk packs also take up as much as ten to fifteen times more space than do tapes.

Diskettes

A *diskette,* or *floppy disk,* is a round piece of flexible magnetic film that is enclosed in a protective cover. As an input medium it has been employed by many firms to replace punched cards or punched paper tape. As a storage medium, its relatively modest storage capacity makes it popular among small organizations whose file sizes are compatible with diskette limitations. Its greatest advantages are its compactness as a storage medium and its relatively low cost. Diskettes have a much smaller storage capacity and a slower access time than do magnetic disk packs. As a result the diskette is commonly used for secondary storage only in smaller computer systems and otherwise is primarily used as a data entry medium. Floppy disks are discussed in greater detail in Chapter 7.

Optical disks

A recent innovation in secondary storage is the *optical disk*. Lasers are used to burn microscopic holes in a recording surface that fits between two transparent twelve-inch disks. Laser beams also read the stored information. Until recently, once written upon, they could not be erased. Erasable disks, however, have recently been developed and should be commercially available by the time this description is read. Laser optical disks are currently used predominantly to record historical, or archival, information and for engineering applications with large storage requirements. Their usage should significantly expand as erasable disks are made available, as the technology is refined, and as they become a commercially reliable product.

There are significant advantages to these laser optical disks. First, they can contain up to ten times more data than can magnetic disks of similar size. For example, Groliers has published its twenty-one-volume Academic American Encyclopedia on a single optical disk. Second, laser disks can be removed from their drives, allowing the disk unit to read or write to an almost unlimited number of disks. Third, recorded disks can be mass-produced easily and inexpensively. As with all other storage media, they have some disadvantages, one of which is access time. The access time for these disks is much slower than for magnetic disks.

Input Devices

There are several different approaches to entering data into the system. In the more traditional information systems, input is usually a multistep process. In many instances the data are originally captured on some sort of paper document like a sales or purchase order. The documents are batched into small groups and data entry people convert the data into a machine-readable form such as cards, tape, or disk. The data are often edited and otherwise checked for accuracy owing to the possibility of human error. In some instances the data have to be sorted before they can be entered into the system. The data are then ready for input. Unfortunately, there are a number of significant disadvantages to this approach. It is time-consuming, costly, and error prone, and it requires several distinct steps involving several people. It also utilizes several different forms of data media (paper, then cards or tape, etc.).

A second approach is to key the data directly into the computer via an online terminal. However, this still requires a significant effort in keying in all the data and still may require that the data be captured on paper before they are keyed into the system. A third approach, involving devices that automate the data capture and entry process, was developed in order to decrease the time, effort, and errors of the first two approaches.

No organization is likely to use just one form of data entry for all its input transactions. Instead, most organizations utilize several different forms. This enables them to choose the method best suited to each of their data entry applications. The devices used in these three approaches are discussed below.

Data preparation devices

Data entry operations often constitute a major portion of the cost of data processing. The hardware, personnel, and supplies required for data entry may consume up to forty percent of the total data processing budget. This is because data entry is usually the only major function in an automated system that makes extensive use of human labor, with its speed and reliability limitations. Once data have been successfully entered into a computer system, subsequent processing steps usually proceed rapidly and accurately with a minimum of human intervention.

Keypunch and key verification devices.   The machine used to record data on punched cards is called a *keypunch*. Many have a small electronic memory where the data for a card are stored temporarily. If a keying error is made, the operator can backspace and enter the correct character instead of having to repunch the entire card. Modern keypunch machines may also be "programmed" to perform certain functions automatically, such as automatic punching of data and skipping blank spaces within fields.

Another function keypunches can perform is *keyverification*. When the machine is in the verify mode, the operator keys the same data that were originally used in keypunching the cards. This time, instead of punching holes, the machine checks the holes in each card to verify that the correct data were punched. Keyverification is an expensive form of data verification because every field that is to be keyverified must be keyed twice. As a result, keyverification is generally only applied to critical input fields. Names, inventory item descriptions, and other noncritical data are often not keyverified. Data on punched cards are often transcribed onto magnetic tape or disk before reading them into the computer.

Key encoders.   A *key-to-tape encoder* is similar to the keypunch except that the data are recorded on tape instead of punched cards. In a *key-to-disk-to-tape* system, several keying stations are linked to a minicomputer that has an attached disk memory. Data may be entered simultaneously from each of the several keystations and pooled on the disk file. The computer edits the data when all the records have been entered and then writes the data from the disk file onto a magnetic tape file for subsequent processing on the main computer. Key encoders have several significant benefits: keying errors can be corrected immediately; they can be programmed to edit input for accuracy, completeness, and reasonableness; and they are quieter, faster, and more reliable than keypunch machines. Their major drawback is that they are relatively expensive.

Terminals and other on-line entry devices

A *terminal* is an input/output device that can enter data directly into the computer or receive output directly from the computer. The CRT (also known as a VDT, or visual display terminal) is the most frequently used terminal. As shown in Fig. 5.12, it uses a keyboard for input, and the output is displayed visually on a TV-like screen or monitor. Some CRT terminals also have a printer attached. CRT output speeds range from 250 to 10,000 characters per second. The push-button telephone, which sometimes incorporates the picture phone screen as a device for displaying input and output, can also be used as a data input device.

FIGURE 5.12
CRT terminal.
(Courtesy of IBM
Corporation.)

Terminals can be classified by the function they perform. A teleprinter, or printing terminal, produces a typed paper copy of the input or output. Graphics terminals allow the user to transfer numeric data into a variety of graphic forms, including line, bar, and pie charts. The more sophisticated terminals can produce three-dimensional graphs of almost anything, including maps and detailed peeks inside the human body. They are also used in engineering and architecture for computer-assisted design (CAD) and computer-assisted manufacturing (CAM). These CAD/CAM computers have helped to automate the design and manufacturing of a wide variety of products. The terminals also allow the user to zoom in and out (make the item on the screen larger or smaller) and to rotate the item in different directions to better view or analyze it.

The last few years have seen the development of what are called smart or *intelligent terminals*. These terminals have a limited amount of storage capacity and processing capability. As a result, they can edit data, prepare data for submission to the mainframe computer, and perform a limited number of similar input validation and data processing tasks. They can also operate off-line while preparing input and then switch to online to effect the data transfer. A recent trend is to combine microcomputer and terminal technology. The result is a machine that can act as a terminal when desired and as a microcomputer at other times.

The use of online terminals as a means of data entry has at least two significant advantages. First, editing transaction data for accuracy is greatly facilitated because the computer can perform various logic and reasonableness tests on each data item. The computer can also notify the terminal operator of any errors, thereby enabling the operator to correct the errors before they are entered into the system. Second, terminals can be placed in remote locations, which enables transaction data to be entered into the system from their place of origin as they occur. This arrangement, which is usually for the user's convenience, requires the use of telephone lines or special cables to transmit data and messages between the terminal and the central processor.

Source data automation devices

For a number of years organizations have been moving toward devices that collect input in machine-readable form at the time and place the data originate. This data collection approach is referred to as *source data automation* (SDA). Among the more familiar SDA devices are embossed-card imprinters (used for credit card sales), factory data collection devices, automated bank teller machines (ATMs), and point-of-sale (POS) recorders (used as cash registers). Each of these SDA devices are designed to meet the needs of a particular type of data entry application.

SDA devices have a number of important advantages. Capturing data in a machine-readable format often significantly decreases human involvement in the collection and input process. For example, it eliminates many of the data preparation steps such as batching, sorting, and keying in the records. This results in considerable time and dollar savings and avoids the bottlenecks that often occur with slower input media. It is also much more accurate since there are fewer opportunities for humans to make transcription errors. Since data are captured at the time they originate, SDA also results in more timely data input. Because it is usually faster, easier, and more timely, SDA is the preferred method of data capture and entry when its use is possible.

Magnetic ink character recognition. *Magnetic ink character recognition* (MICR) involves the use of characters encoded on documents in a special magnetic ink. The most significant use of MICR is in the banking industry, where it is used to encode account numbers and amounts on customers' checks and deposit tickets. If you examine a blank check, you will see the bank number, account number, and check number encoded on the lower-left portion of the check. If you examine a check that has been processed and returned by the bank, you will notice that the check amount has also been inscribed on it in the lower-right portion. The original encoding of magnetic ink characters on a document is performed by special inscribers. Other necessary equipment in an MICR installation, which is often combined in one machine, includes a reader and an electromechanical sorter. Typical MICR devices read about 1200 to 2000 documents per minute.

Optical character recognition. *Optical character recognition* (OCR) devices read documents containing typewritten, computer-printed, or in some cases, hand-printed characters. Unlike an MICR device, an OCR device does not require characters printed in a special magnetized ink. Instead, an OCR recognizes a limited number of specific patterns or character fonts. A font is a complete character set (digits, letters, and special symbols) in which the size, style, and shape of each character is rigidly specified. OCR is commonly used on documents such as credit card statements, insurance company premium notices, and utility company billings. These documents are printed by a computer and, when returned to the company, are read by an OCR reader. Thus significant human participation in the data entry process is necessary only when a customer does not pay the full amount of the bill, or when the OCR reader rejects a document as unreadable. Because OCR equipment is relatively expensive, it is best suited for high-volume applications. A typical OCR speed is about 500 documents per minute, although some read as many as 1800 per minute.

Optical mark readers. An *optical mark reader* (OMR) automatically reads pencil marks made in specific locations on preprinted cards or forms. An example usage is machine grading of multiple-choice and true-false exam questions. A common application in business involves documents in a factory environment. A card or form may be prepunched with the part number, operation number, and department number for a particular factory operation. The worker marks the quantity completed, time required, and employee number at designated locations on the card. The cards then become input to a computerized production cost accounting system.

Point-of-sale equipment. A *point-of-sale* (POS) recorder is an electronic cash register that can also be used as an online data terminal. Functionally, it consists of a keyboard for entering transaction data, a display window in which transaction data are displayed as they are entered, and a printer for printing customer receipts. It also usually has a communications link to a centralized computer and its data files. Many POS recorders utilize devices that read price or product code data. One example is the OCR tag reader that reads data from price tags printed in an OCR font. Another example is the optical scanner commonly used in grocery stores to read the Universal Product Code (UPC) that is now standard on many products. These devices electronically collect sales data at the time a sale is made and transmit it directly to the computer. The transmitted data can be checked for accuracy, reasonableness, and completeness. If correct, the data can then be stored for later use. A POS recorder can perform other functions that are beyond the capability of the conventional cash register. For example, when the UPC is read, the system can access a product file to retrieve the current price and to update the quantity sold and the inventory balance stored in the file. For credit sales it is also possible to enter the customer's account number, have the system check the customer's credit, and update the accounts receivable record. The automatic performance of these and similar functions greatly enhances the productivity of retail sales clerks. A typical POS recorder and a UPC are both pictured in Fig. 5.13.

Voice input.   A source data automation approach that has made great strides in recent years is *voice input*. However, developers are still only on the frontier of this technology since most of the systems in use are lacking in sophistication. At a minimum a voice input system would need a voice recognition unit, a microphone, and a terminal to display the recorded input. Some of the systems have vocabularies of over 5000 words. However, the user usually must "train" the computer to recognize his or her voice by repeating words several times to "program" the voice pattern into the system. The systems are expensive (from $1200 to $5000) and can become confused by background noises. There are a number of systems currently in use. The airline and parcel delivery industries, for example, use voice input systems to route packages. It is estimated that by 1990 there will be over one million units in use.

Computer data entry and accounting

Accountants within an organization must be concerned about computer data entry for at least two reasons. First, in most organizations a large volume of accounting data are entered into the computer for processing, and the accountant is concerned about the accuracy, timeliness, and security of this operation. Second, in many organizations accountants, in their role of controller or internal auditor, are responsible for evaluating the efficiency and effectiveness of data entry personnel and operations. In this section, each of these two concerns is discussed briefly.

Accuracy, timeliness, and security.   Computerized accounting applications are usually typified by high volumes of input; a need to document activities for purposes of reference, control, and audit; an emphasis on reliability and accuracy; and a need for timely data entry in order to keep the master files current. Cost considerations are also very important in the choice of data entry alternatives. However, accounting applications differ to such an extent that no single method of data entry is likely to be appropriate for all accounting uses.

Computer applications with large volumes of input require a method of data entry (1) that minimizes the amount of manual keying or other data preparation work, (2) that utilizes a compact recording medium, and (3) that utilizes a high-speed computer input device. Unfortunately, no single approach meets all these criteria. The use of *turnaround documents* is ideal from the standpoint of minimal data preparation. A turnaround document is a machine-readable form of output that is used in an external process and then returned to the system as an input record. Turnaround documents can take one of several forms: punched card, a document read by an OCR, or a magnetic me-

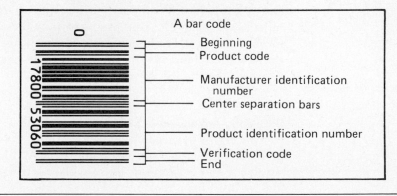

A bar code

- Beginning
- Product code

- Manufacturer identification number
- Center separation bars

- Product identification number

- Verification code
- End

FIGURE 5.13
Point-of-sale recorder
(Courtesy of NCR
Corporation) and
universal product
code.

dium. An example is the card that utility companies send out as a bill with the request that the card be returned with the payment. Since turnaround documents are produced by the system, their use reduces the input preparation work load and the possibility of input errors. However, not all accounting applications are by nature suitable for the use of turnaround documents. In addition, computer input devices for these media are relatively slow. Magnetic tape and diskette input devices are very fast, but extensive keying operations are required to initially record the data on these media. A good compromise for high-volume applications is to use turnaround documents but to transcribe the input data from the documents to magnetic tape prior to updating the master files.

The use of data terminals is appropriate for those accounting applications in which timeliness in entering transaction data is important in order that master files are as current as possible. If special-purpose terminals are available to match the task, they should be considered in preference to general-purpose terminals because their user-oriented design generally facilitates the data entry process.

The need for accuracy and reliability exists both at the input preparation stage and at the point of data entry. Turnaround documents have a high degree of accuracy because they are prepared automatically as an output from the computer. However, turnaround documents may be lost or mutilated, and card, mark, and OCR readers are not 100 percent accurate. Magnetic tape, especially if prepared on a shared processor key-to-disk system, measures high in both data preparation accuracy and reading accuracy. Online data terminals also provide a high degree of accuracy because they reduce the number of steps in the data entry process to one, and because the computer can be programmed to detect many data entry errors and request immediate reentry of the suspect data.

It is difficult to generalize about the cost of data entry alternatives because cost is a function of volume. For low-volume data entry, cards, diskettes, terminals, and magnetic tape prepared by stand-alone key-to-tape encoders are most economical. For high-volume applications, cost factors tend to favor SDA devices, special-purpose terminals, OCR, or magnetic tape prepared by shared processor key-to-disk systems.

Data entry effectiveness and efficiency. The second major computer data entry concern of the accountant is the efficient and effective performance of the data entry function. One useful approach to this concern is performance measurement and evaluation. This involves setting a standard performance rate and establishing a data entry work schedule, with each application scheduled to consume a total time estimated on the basis of the standard. Data preparation department performance may then be evaluated in terms of whether it meets its schedule. The performance of individual operators may also be measured and evaluated in terms of the standard, with raises and promotions being based on superior performance.

Data preparation efficiency may be improved by properly designing the formats of source documents and input transaction records. Transaction record formats should correspond to source document formats in terms of the sequencing of data. This helps ensure that data entry personnel can read the source document easily while keying, without having to shift their eyes from side to side or top to bottom and back again. Another method of improving data entry efficiency is for constant data, such as date or transaction code, to be entered into all records automatically.

Computer Output Devices

To a large extent the choice of output devices in a computer system determines the choice of data entry devices and media. Many output devices also prepare input for computer users. Examples of these devices are the multifunction card machine and the CRT display terminal. This section describes four output devices that are not directly related to any specific form of computer data entry: printers, plotters, voice response units, and computer output microfilm. These devices accept data from the computer and convert it into a form that users can understand.

The printer

The *printer* is the most common output device and is connected to the CPU by means of a cable. Printers can be characterized in three ways.

- [ ] *Serial*. Prints one character at a time, and speed is measured in characters per second.
- [ ] *Line*. Prints one line at a time, and speed is measured in characters per second.
- [ ] *Page*. Prints one page at a time, and speed is measured in lines per minute or pages per minute.

Mainframe printer speeds generally range between 100 and 3000 lines per minute, although for high-volume applications there are models available that can print over 20,000 lines per minute. A typical printer appears in Fig. 5.14.

In addition to printing reports on regular computer paper, printers may be used to print data on accounting documents such as invoices, purchase orders, and paychecks. For this purpose, special forms are often used that have been preprinted with constant data, a document format, and a sequential document number. In either case, blank paper or the special forms are usually fed into the printer in a continuous stack. Each page or form is separated from the preceding page or form by means of a folded perforation. After a set of documents has been printed, the individual pages or forms may be automatically separated from each other using an outline device called a burster. Printers are discussed further in Chapter 7.

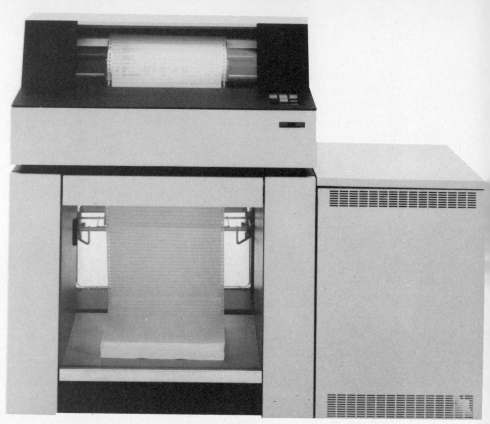

FIGURE 5.14
Printer. (Courtesy of
IBM Corporation.)

The plotter

A *plotter* produces a graphical output on paper by moving a writing arm across a paper surface. Modern plotters can produce three-dimensional and multicolored drawings. Plotters are used extensively in architectural and engineering design applications. The growing interest in computer graphics as a tool for management decision making has led to an increased use of plotters for preparing management reports. Dot-matrix printers are also used to produce graphic output.

**Voice response
units**

Audio response units generate "voice" responses from a computer. They are most useful when the desired response is relatively short and when no documentation is necessary. Accounting examples include checking a customer's credit by a sales clerk and inquiries about a customer's bank balance. Other examples include the response received when calling to get the time and temperature or to obtain telephone directory assistance. A typical voice response unit contains a collection of recorded words and phrases representing its vocabulary. Each word or phrase has an address. The computer determines the sequence of addresses necessary to respond to an inquiry, accesses the sounds needed to generate the necessary message, and transmits the message to the user.

Computer output microfilm devices

Computer output microfilm (COM) devices use a photographic process to place computer output on microfilm. COM is an extremely fast output technique, with output speeds ranging from 20,000 to 50,000 lines per minute. COM recorders may be operated either online to the computer or offline with input from magnetic tape. They produce a roll of film containing up to three thousand $8\frac{1}{2}$-by-11-inch documents. Microfilm may be stored in roll form or in microfiche form, in which a set of related documents are included on a single sheet of film.

The advantages of microfilm include reduced storage space requirements (by ninety-five to ninety-nine percent), a less expensive storage medium than paper, and faster document retrieval. The primary disadvantage is the cost of the COM recorder and other required equipment. The cost factor often limits its application primarily to high-volume situations. Microfilm is not an appropriate storage medium for records that must be frequently updated. Instead, microfilm is used by businesses to store their noncurrent accounting records and copies of company documents. Examples of common applications include the retention of copies of depositors' checks by banks, and the retention of documents by retail or industrial firms.

Increasing System Throughput

Business data processing systems face a unique design problem in that they are characterized by high volumes of input and output and relatively simple computations. However, input and output device speeds are much less than those of central processors. CPU speeds are measured in nanoseconds or picoseconds, whereas input and output device speeds are stated in terms of characters per second or lines per minute. As a result of this mismatch in speeds, business systems are often referred to as being *input/output bound* since the system's processing capabilities are limited by the speed of input and output devices.

Throughput is the total amount of useful work performed by a computer system during a given period of time. This concept encompasses resource scheduling as well as input, output, and processing concerns. One of the simplest and easiest approaches to increasing throughput is to carefully schedule processing jobs so that valuable system time is not lost or wasted. Other than scheduling, most approaches to increasing throughput must focus upon circumventing the basic mismatch of CPU and input/output speeds. Several approaches to this problem are discussed here.

CPU advances that increase throughput

Overlap is the capability of the computer system to use peripheral devices to execute input/output operations while the CPU continues processing data. In early computers, the CPU would remain idle while the input or output device completed the tasks assigned to it. However, in today's larger computer systems, input/output instructions are performed by *channels,* which are hardware devices that act as communication interfaces between the CPU and all input/output devices. A channel is like a tiny computer that specializes strictly in input and output functions. The CPU instructs a channel to perform input/output tasks, and while the channel is carrying out this instruction, the CPU continues processing. When the channel completes its input/output task, it is free to perform other tasks assigned it by the CPU. The number of input and output operations that may be overlapped with CPU processing is a function of the number of channels in the system. Linked to each channel are one or more controllers that translate signals for use by input or output devices. The overlap capability does not eliminate the basic mismatch of CPU speeds and input/output speeds, but it at least ensures that the CPU does not remain idle while waiting for input and output operations to be performed.

The larger computers in use today also permit *multiprogramming*. Modern CPUs are so fast that they can switch back and forth among a number of different programs fast enough to keep the input and output devices for all the programs working at peak speed. Although the CPU is working on only one program at any one instant, the computer system as a whole is executing several programs at the same time. For example, one program might be reading a tape and transferring its contents to disk while simultaneously a second program is reading a second disk and writing its contents on a printer and a third program is handling terminal inquiries relating to a third disk file. In general the larger the internal memory, the greater the multiprogramming capability and increased throughput.

Multiprocessing is the simultaneous execution of two or more tasks, usually by two or more processing units that are part of the same system. Each processing unit shares access to its main memory with the other processors. This type of multiprocessing requires that each central processor possess additional control and interfacing capabilities.

Note the distinction between multiprocessing, which involves multiple computers functioning simultaneously, and multiprogramming, which generally involves one computer that is rapidly switching back and forth among several jobs. In both multiprogramming and multiprocessing systems, the CPU should have special features that facilitate the allocation of memory for various purposes and that keep track of committed and uncommitted memory blocks. Special features for memory protection are also essential to prevent the transfer of data into a memory area that is already in use. Many of the large central processing units are capable of performing parallel operations, where calculations and other operations are actually performed at the same time within a single CPU. This means that the CPU can actually process more than one set of instructions and data at the same time.

Designing systems for increased throughput

While overlap, multiprogramming, and multiprocessing capabilities come with the system itself, several avenues to increased throughput are available to the system designer. When *exception reporting* is used, the output reports from a system include only that information that might affect a user's decision or cause him or her to take action. For example, a report concerning credit customers should perhaps include data on only those customers whose accounts are past due, rather than contain data on all customers. This approach not only improves throughput in an information system but increases the usefulness of system output as well.

To increase throughput, additional input and output devices can be used, or high-speed input and output devices can be substituted for slower ones. The result is a more efficient use of CPU time. This is one of the reasons why most organizations have switched from keypunching source data onto punched cards to using key-to-tape (or disk) encoders. Furthermore, even organizations that use OCR forms or turnaround documents often transfer source data onto magnetic tape prior to processing them against the master files. On the output side, reports or documents prepared during file processing may first be written onto magnetic tape for later conversion to printed form. When multiple input or output devices are used simultaneously, it is called *spooling* (SPOOL is an acronym for simultaneous peripheral operations online).

Storage of master file records on a direct access storage medium such as magnetic disk also increases throughput. It allows a single program to post transactions to more than one master file. This eliminates the need for a separate program to update each master file and for intermediate sorting steps to resequence the transactions according to the primary key of each successive master file. Throughput can also be increased by using data base technology. This eliminates most of the need for multiple file updates. Finally, records stored on disk may be updated from online terminals, which eliminates time-consuming data preparation, record transcription, and record-sorting processes.

A final approach to increasing throughput is to replace existing hardware with one or more systems that are smaller, faster, more efficient, and less costly. Alternatively, these smaller systems could be used to augment the existing system. These micro- and minicomputers can be easily adapted to a variety of processing tasks. They are especially useful when dedicated to specific tasks such as inventory or production control.

Systems Flowcharts: A Pictorial View

Thus far the chapter has discussed the hardware used in data processing systems. It would be nice to have some way to diagram, or pictorially represent, the hardware devices used by an organization. Likewise, it would also be desirable to represent an organization's data processing operations in the same way. This is possible using flowcharts.

A flowchart is a diagrammatical representation of the flow of information and/or the sequence of operations in a process or system. Since a flowchart is a pictorial representation of what happens in a system, it is easy to understand and to use. With respect to flowcharts, there is truth to the saying that a picture is worth a thousand words. Because of their clarity of presentation, they have become very popular both as a system design and as a documentation tool. Flowcharts are used in a number of ways, and among the most popular are the following.

1. To portray existing company procedures. These flowcharts help systems analysts and auditors to understand the system and to identify system strengths and weaknesses during systems analysis and during audits.

2. To portray the new information system created during the design phase. The flowcharts can then be critically evaluated to see if the system will be complete, accurate, and free of design flaws.

3. To document the system. The flowcharts help the designer and other users or developers to understand how the system operates.

4. To help train new employees.

5. To help implement the system.

Types of flowcharts   There are several different types of flowcharts, and each has its own specialized set of symbols. In this book, flowcharts are classified into three major categories:

1. *Systems flowcharts*, which show the flow of data through a series of operations in an automated data processing system. They show how data are captured and/or input into the system, the processes that operate on the input to produce information, and system outputs. They are also used to represent the hardware configuration used by an organization. The essential elements of a systems flowchart are shown in Fig. 5.15. Systems flowcharts are discussed in more depth later in the chapter.

2. *Program flowcharts*, which show the logic processes used in computer programs. Each of the data processing steps shown in the systems flowcharts is usually performed by a computer program and is therefore often supported by a program flowchart. The program flowchart shows the comparisons, calculations, and data manipulations used to read the input and create the output and storage records needed by the system. Program flowcharts are discussed in more detail in Chapter 6.

3. *Document (procedural) flowcharts*, which show the movement of documents through the different departments and functions of an organization. They trace the flow of a document from its creation to its destruction or permanent storage location. For example, a document flowchart would show a sales order being created in the sales order department. It would then trace the sales order through the credit, shipping, billing, and accounting departments. The flowchart would show what happens to the document

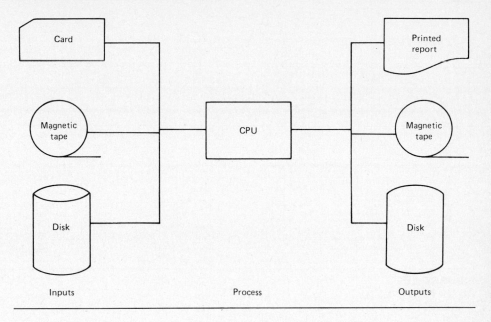

FIGURE 5.15
Essential systems
flowchart
components: inputs,
processes, outputs.

and how it affects other documents as it flows through the system. Document flowcharts are discussed in more detail in Chapter 11.

Systems flowcharting symbols

A different set of symbols is used for each type of flowchart. As each type of flowchart is explained, the appropriate set of symbols for that type of flowchart will be shown and explained. Most of the symbols shown are very easy to draw or trace if a *flowcharting template*, such as the one shown in Fig. 5.16, is used. The template is a rectangular sheet of plastic out of which the flowcharting symbols have been cut.

Systems flowcharts consist of a sequence of processing steps, each having one or more related input and output symbols. A systems flowchart begins by identifying the inputs to a particular process. The input "layer" is followed by a process layer. The third layer is an output layer. In many instances, the output from one process becomes an input to another process, and the layers repeat themselves. This pattern is clearly evident in the systems flowcharts shown later in the chapter.

The symbols used in a systems flowchart, shown in Fig. 5.17, can be divided into three categories: input/output, processing, and data flow and storage symbols. Input/output symbols represent either devices or media that provide input to, or record output from, processing operations. Note that the use of these symbols in a flowchart will be indicative of the operations performed, the hardware devices used, and the input, output, and storage media employed. Input can be entered on cards; magnetic tape, disk, or diskette; man-

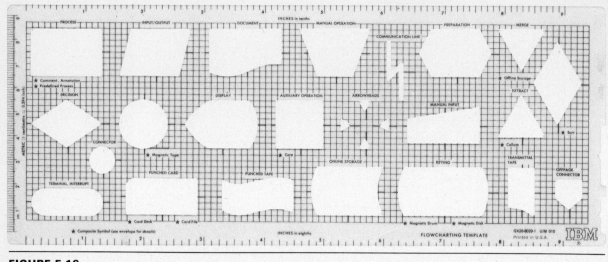

FIGURE 5.16
An IBM flowcharting
template.

ually by using an online device; or by using punched tape. The input may also need to be controlled using batch control total transmittal tapes.

There are four processing symbols shown in Fig. 5.17. These are (1) major processing functions, which encompass any operations performed by the CPU; (2) manual operations performed with no machine assistance; (3) auxiliary machine operations performed automatically by a machine not connected to the main computer, such as a key-to-tape encoder; and (4) keying operations performed manually at a keyboard not connected to the main computer, such as a keypunch, key-to-diskette, or typewriter keyboard.

When a systems flowchart is prepared, a label is inserted into each symbol describing the data or operations represented by that symbol. If there is insufficient room for the necessary label, the annotation symbol may be used to provide a more complete explanation. Straight lines with arrows attached indicate the flow of information and the sequence of operations. If there is insufficient room on one page for a complete flowchart, the off-page connector is used to show the links between separate pages. The communications link symbol is used when data are transmitted over data communication lines. Data that are stored until they are ready to be entered into the system are typically stored in an offline file.

Systems flowcharts employing these symbols are used as a tool to explain and illustrate data processing systems and operations explained in this chapter and in the remainder of this book. They must also be used to complete many of the problems and cases appearing at the back of this and subsequent chapters. To illustrate these symbols and how they are used, several sample systems flowcharts are presented below.

FIGURE 5.17 System flowcharting symbols.

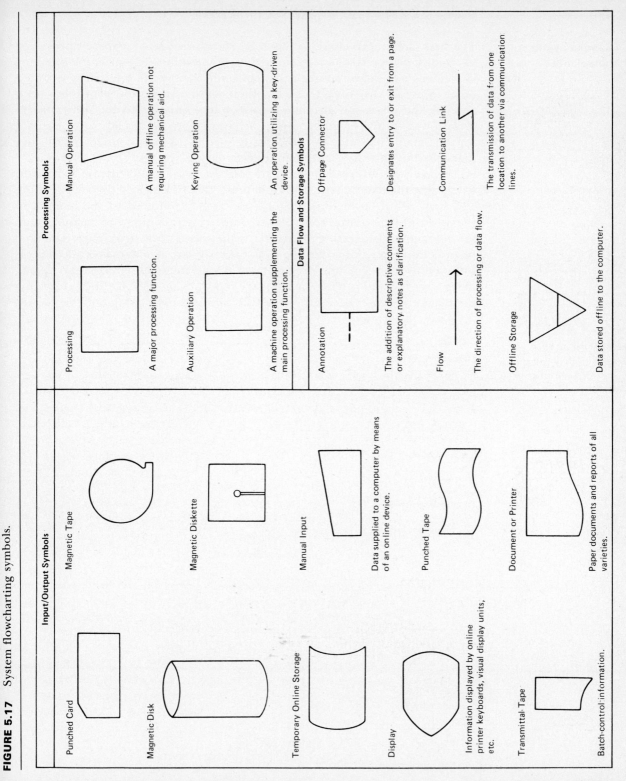

Input/Output Symbols

Punched Card

Magnetic Disk

Temporary Online Storage

Display

Information displayed by online printer keyboards, visual display units, etc.

Transmittal Tape

Batch-control information.

Magnetic Tape

Magnetic Diskette

Manual Input

Data supplied to a computer by means of an online device.

Punched Tape

Document or Printer

Paper documents and reports of all varieties.

Processing Symbols

Processing

A major processing function.

Auxiliary Operation

A machine operation supplementing the main processing function.

Manual Operation

A manual offline operation not requiring mechanical aid.

Keying Operation

An operation utilizing a key-driven device.

Data Flow and Storage Symbols

Annotation

The addition of descriptive comments or explanatory notes as clarification.

Flow

The direction of processing or data flow.

Offline Storage

Data stored offline to the computer.

Offpage Connector

Designates entry to or exit from a page.

Communication Link

The transmission of data from one location to another via communication lines.

165

**Sample systems
flowcharts**

The first sample flowchart, in Fig. 5.18, shows the use of a shared processor key-to-disk-to-tape system for source data preparation. The machine operator keys the data found on source documents into the system, where it is recorded on a temporary disk file. Once a complete set of transaction records has been entered, the processor sorts the records into sequential order and transfers their contents onto magnetic tape. The records are then ready to be entered into the main computer for processing, but the off-page connector indicates that this step appears on a separate page.

Figure 5.19 illustrates the preparation of source data using punched cards, converting the data to tape, and updating a file. In Fig. 5.19 the keypunching and keyverification of source data onto cards is followed by the reading of the cards into the central computer to transfer their contents to magnetic tape for subsequent processing. The CPU is then used to sort the magnetic tape records into sequence according to the primary key of the master file. This is followed by the sequential processing of the magnetic tape records to update the master file and generate a summary report. Note that the line connecting the magnetic disk master file to the CPU shows arrows going both ways. This

FIGURE 5.18
Key-to-disk-to-tape
processing of source
data.

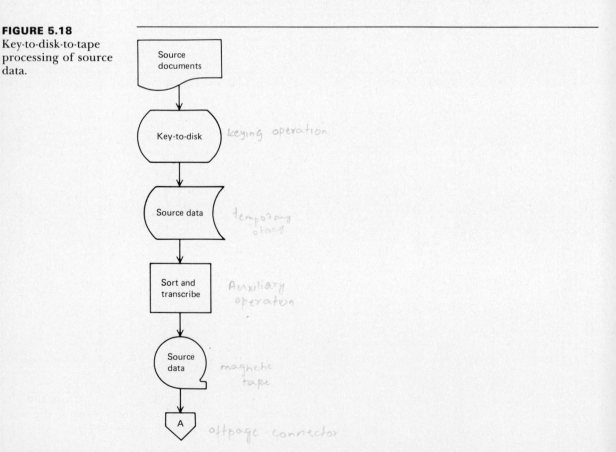

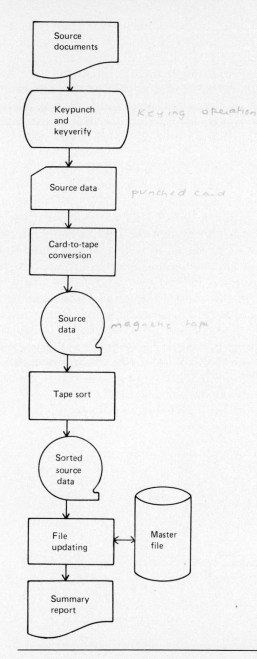

FIGURE 5.19
Source data preparation using cards, card-to-tape conversion, tape sorting, and file updating.

is necessary because the updating of disk records consists of reading the old record from the disk into the CPU, updating it, and then writing the new record back onto the disk unit into the same location from which the old record was read.

Figure 5.20 illustrates a manual batching and filing procedure. In this case the source documents are vendor invoices that have been approved for payment. The manual operation symbol is used to represent the sorting of these invoices by hand according to their payment due date. Batch totals of amount due by due date are prepared as part of this process. The chronologically sorted invoices are then filed in separate batches. The annotation symbol is used to provide an extended description of the procedure followed at certain points in the flowcharted process—in this case, at the point of filing the invoices.

Flowcharting symbols may be used to represent an equipment configuration as well as a data processing operation. For example, Fig. 5.21 illustrates a small configuration consisting of a teleprinter terminal, a remote CRT terminal, a CPU, and a magnetic disk file. Note that the communication link symbol is used to indicate that the CRT is geographically remote from the central processor, connected to it through a telephone hookup. In contrast, the ordinary line connecting the teleprinter to the central processor indicates that the teleprinter is located on the same site as the processor. A second factor of note in this illustration is the use of combinations of symbols to represent the terminals. There is no single flowcharting symbol with which to represent either a teleprinter terminal or a CRT display terminal. However, because a teleprinter consists of a keyboard and printer, it can be represented by a combination of the online keyboard and document or report symbols. Similarly, a CRT terminal can be represented by a combination of the online keyboard and information display symbols.

A more typical business data processing equipment configuration is shown

FIGURE 5.20
Manual batching and filing procedure.

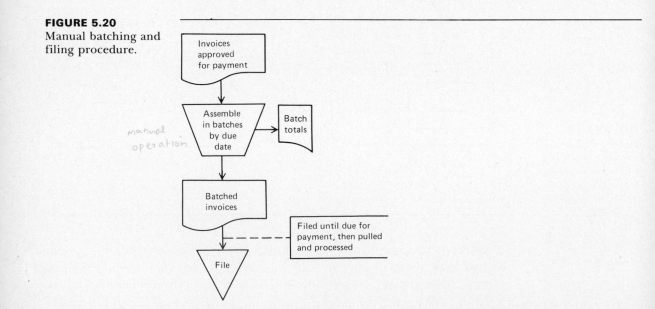

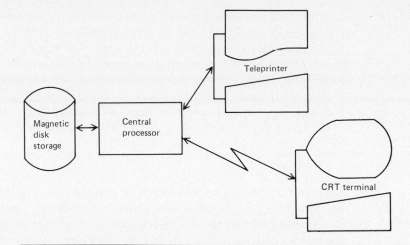

FIGURE 5.21
Computer system
with teleprinter and
remote CRT.

in Fig. 5.22. This illustrates a computer system that includes four tape drives, two disk drives, a multifunction card machine for punched card input and output, a printer, and a CPU with an online console keyboard. Note that the four tape drives are connected to the CPU through a single line; this line may be interpreted as representing the channel that is shared among all the tape drives. The console keyboard, card machines, and printer share a second channel, and the two disk drives share a third channel.

Although our primary purpose here is to use systems flowcharting to il-

FIGURE 5.22
Business-oriented
computer system.

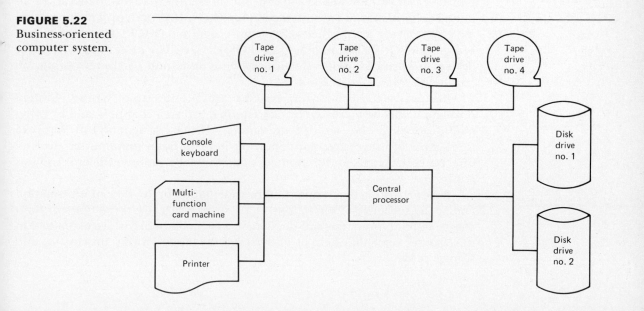

lustrate data processing concepts, it should be pointed out that systems flow-charts are an important tool of systems analysis. They play a key role in the evaluation of existing systems, the design of new systems, and the documentation of systems. Using a template makes systems flowcharts relatively easy to prepare. They are universally employed in systems work and therefore provide a ready form of communication among systems personnel. The flow-charts presented in this section have included at least one example of most of the symbols included in Fig. 5.17. Additional systems flowcharts using these symbols are included in subsequent chapters.

Summary

An information system, whether it be manual or computerized, contains five essential elements: input, a data processor, a storage medium, an output medium, and instructions or procedures. A computer system is composed of hardware, software, a data base, and people to operate the system. The best information system is usually a man-machine combination.

A CPU has three main sections: a control unit, an arithmetic-logic unit, and memory. Memory can be either read only (ROM) or random access (RAM). Memory is most frequently expressed in terms of thousands of characters, called a kilobyte (K), or a million characters, called a megabyte (M). The computer stores data in binary form, called bits. Bits are aggregated into even larger groups called bytes and words.

Secondary storage devices are either sequential or direct access in nature. The most common sequential mediums are punched cards and magnetic tape. The most common direct access devices are magnetic disks and diskettes. Data are prepared for input into the system using data preparation devices (key-punch/keyverification and key-to-disk encoders). Alternatively, data can be input using terminals or source data automation (SDA) devices. The most common SDA devices are magnetic character recognition (MICR), optical character recognition (OCR), and point-of-sale (POS) devices. The most common output devices are printers, plotters, voice response units, and computer output microfilm (COM).

Business data processing systems are input/output bound. System throughput can be increased by overlapping, by using channels, and by using multiprocessing and multiprogramming. System designers can improve throughput by using exception reporting, more or faster input/output devices, direct access storage, and computers that are smaller, more efficient, and less costly.

A flowchart is a diagrammatical representation of the flow of information and/or the sequence of operations in a system. There are three types of flow-charts: systems, program, and document. Systems flowcharts are explained in this chapter since they help us understand the input, output, processing, and storage of data.

Appendix: Disk, Tape, and Card Storage and Speeds

This appendix discusses the storage capacities and speed of the two most common storage mediums: magnetic disks and magnetic tape. The information discussed in this appendix is used by those who design systems to determine how much storage space files will occupy and the amount of time it will take to read the file.

Disk speeds and storage

The time required to read a record from a disk file is the sum of the access time and the data transfer time. Access time is the sum of the time required for the access arm to move the read/write head to the appropriate track and the time required for the disk to rotate to the necessary location within the track. Both of these times will vary, depending on the initial location of the read/write head relative to the location of the desired record, so it is only possible to speak in terms of average times. The data transfer time is determined by dividing the number of characters in the record by the device's transfer rate.

For example, consider the average time required to read a 156-character record stored in a disk file that has an average head movement time of 60 milliseconds, a rotation speed of 2400 revolutions per minute, and a transfer rate of 312,000 bytes per second. First convert the rotation speed into revolutions per second (2400 revolutions per minute ÷ 60 seconds per minute = 40 revolutions per second). Then the rotation time required for one revolution may be determined (1 second ÷ 40 revolutions = .025 seconds per revolution, or 25 milliseconds per revolution). The average rotational delay is one half of the rotation time, or 12.5 milliseconds (25 milliseconds ÷ 2). The average access time is the sum of the average head movement time of 60 milliseconds and the average rotational delay of 12.5 milliseconds, or 72.5 milliseconds. Next, assuming no packing, 156 bytes will be required to store 156 characters, and the data transfer time may be computed as 156 bytes ÷ 312,000 bytes per second = .0005 seconds, or 0.5 milliseconds. Finally, the average read time is the sum of the average access time of 72.5 milliseconds and the data transfer time of 0.5 milliseconds, or a total of 73 milliseconds.

If records on a disk file are being accessed sequentially, then the access time will be zero. This is because when the read/write heads are finished reading one record, they are already positioned to read the next one, thus eliminating both the head movement time and the rotation time. If records are being accessed randomly on a fixed-head disk, the head movement time is zero because the existence of one read/write head for each track eliminates the need for head movement.

Tape speeds and storage

Records are stored on magnetic tape in blocks of several records, with a gap called the interblock gap between each consecutive pair of blocks. Blocking of records obviously reduces the effective data storage capacity of magnetic tape because no data are stored in the interblock gaps. For example, suppose that records of 320 characters each are being stored on a magnetic tape having a density of 1600 bytes per inch. Assume that 1 byte is used to store 1 character. If there were no blocking, then the tape capacity would be 5 records per inch (1600 characters per inch ÷ 320 characters per record). To determine the effect of blocking, it is necessary to know the size of the interblock gaps and the number of records per block. Assume that the interblock gaps are each 0.6 inch in width (a common size) and that 7 records are to be stored in one block. Then the number of characters per block is equal to 2240 (320 characters per record × 7 records per block). The number of inches required for these 7 records is therefore equal to 1.4 (2240 characters per block ÷ 1600 characters per inch). However, for each and every block of 7 records, there is also an interblock gap 0.6 inch in width, so that 2 inches (1.4 + 0.6) are required for every 7 records. In this case, blocking reduces the tape capacity from 5 records per inch to 3.5 records per inch.

Blocking also reduces the effective reading speed of records stored on magnetic tape. For example, assume that tape records are being read on a tape drive that operates at 120,000 bytes per second. It is useful to convert this figure into inches per second by dividing by the tape recording density: 120,000 bytes per second ÷ 1600 bytes per inch = 75 inches per second. In the case above, if there were no blocking, the reading speed would be 375 records per second (75 inches per second × 5 records per inch). Blocking reduces the effective reading speed to 262.5 records per second (75 inches per second × 3.5 records per inch). The actual reading speed may be even less than this if the tape drive is required to stop and start between blocks.

Card speeds and storage

This example may be extended to provide a comparison of the effective reading speeds of punched cards and magnetic tape. Suppose that a file of 63,000 records is to be read. At the rate of 262.5 records per second, 240 seconds, or 4 minutes, would be required to accomplish this task. If this file were on punched cards, four eighty-column cards would be required to hold each 320-character record. Thus a total of 252,000 cards would be needed for the 63,000 records. Using a relatively fast card reader operating at 2,400 cards per minute, 105 minutes would be required to read the data into the computer. Thus, in this case, the input speed for tape records is roughly twenty-six times as fast as for card records.

Review Questions

1. Define the following terms:

   computer hardware   online and offline devices

   data processing center   software

   central processing unit   arithmetic-logic unit

memory unit

control unit

control console

microcode

read only memory

firmware

random access memory

semiconductor

kilobyte

bit

byte

packed decimal

word

page

virtual memory

secondary storage

sequential access

direct access

multifunction card
machine

magnetic tape

check or parity bit

header record

trailer record

interblock gap

magnetic disk

diskette, floppy disk

optical disk

keypunch

keyverification

key-to-tape encoder

key-to-tape-to-disk encoder

terminal/CRT

intelligent terminal

source data automation

magnetic ink character recognition

optical character recognition

optical mark reader

point-of-sale recorder

voice input

turnaround document

printer

plotter

audio response unit

computer output microfilm

input/output bound

throughput

overlap

channel

multiprogramming

multiprocessing

exception reporting

spooling

systems flowchart

program flowchart

document (procedural) flowchart

flowcharting template

2. Identify and briefly describe the five basic elements involved in transforming data into information.

3. Identify and describe the four basic elements of a computer information system.

4. Compare and contrast the human processor and the electronic data processor.

5. Identify the three basic components of a central processing unit and explain how they interact with each other and with computer input and output.

6. Describe the major developments in the evolution of the computer from a "first generation" to a "fourth generation" machine.

7. Compare and contrast RAM and ROM.

8. What is firmware and how does it differ from hardware and software?

9. How are the following terms related: word, bit, record, byte, field, file?

10. Explain what paging is and how it is related to virtual memory.

11. What is the difference between "primary" and "secondary" storage in a computer system? Identify some examples of secondary storage media and hardware.

12. Identify several types of direct access secondary storage devices. Which are the most commonly used today? Give some examples of accounting applications for which direct access file storage may be useful.

13. Discuss the characteristics of both sequential and random access files. Which would be more useful when frequent updates are made? Which would be more useful when doing batch processing? Why?

14. What is the difference between fixed-head and movable-head disk drives?

15. Discuss the advantages and disadvantages of magnetic disks, magnetic tapes, and punched cards for memory storage. What significant difference exists between the way a magnetic tape file is updated and the way a magnetic disk file is updated?

16. Explain the difference between online and offline equipment. In online processing, what means of input and what type of file storage are generally used? What kinds of accounting applications are best suited to online processing? Describe an example.

17. What are the pros and cons of optical disk technology?

18. Why is data preparation often such a significant portion of the cost of business data processing? How can data entry efficiency be improved?

19. How does source data automation improve the timeliness and reliability of data input?

20. Identify the industry(s) and application(s) most likely to use the following types of source data automation devices.
    a. MICR
    b. POS
    c. OCR
    d. optical scanner
    e. OMR
    f. voice input

21. What are two reasons why accountants within an organization must be concerned about computer data entry?

22. Explain how turnaround documents are prepared, used, and interpreted. Explain the advantages of turnaround documents and give an example of their use.

23. Distinguish between serial, line, and page printers. Between printers and plotters. What are the advantages and disadvantages or each?

24. What are some of the most popular uses of flowcharts in an information system? List the three categories of flowcharts discussed in this chapter and briefly describe each.

25. Explain why systems flowcharts are useful in the study of information systems and in systems design.

Discussion Questions

26. Each new generation of computers has revolutionized the computer industry. These revolutions have changed our society. What effects do you believe the "fifth generation" of computers will have on the computer industry, and more important, what effect do you see it having on our society?

27. Since computers are becoming more prevalent in the business world, they are of great interest to the accountant and the auditor. Computers are also more accurate and consistent than are humans. In light of this, can the accountant put more reliance on a computerized accounting system than a manual system? What problems, if any, do you see the computer posing to the auditor?

28. Source data automation devices are increasing in popularity. Some futurists envision a day when a person will not use any cash, checks, or credit cards. Rather, a person will use a card on which his or her personal identification number is inscribed. Do you believe this system will be an advantage or a disadvantage to the individual and to the ease of conducting business transactions? What are the advantages and disadvantages of moving the data entry process closer to the point at which data enter the organization?

29. Volume of processing is an important consideration in the design of a data processing system. Explain how volume of processing would be taken into consideration in selecting the best equipment configuration for a computer system.

30. Computers are highly reliable. Would you expect that a computer system would therefore have little need for accounting controls to check the accuracy of processing and to safeguard assets? Discuss.

**Problems
and Cases**

31. For each of the following situations, identify which input, output, or storage medium or device is most appropriate

   a) A large plumbing parts manufacturer uses two clerks to enter supplier invoices into the system. The first clerk inputs the data, and the second clerk uses a similar device to make sure the data were entered correctly.

   b) Many modern department stores use this device to ring up a customer's sale and to post the information from that sale directly to accounts receivable and inventory records.

   c) When making a professional graphics presentation, a high-level manager would want to use this device to produce the highest quality hardcopy output.

   d) A large university would store its payroll information on this medium and then use the medium, in batch processing mode, to update the payroll file and print employee paychecks.

   e) Joe needs $20 to buy gas and to go to the movies, but his bank is closed. How can he get the money?

   f) Credit unions use this device to read the checks written by their members so that the amount can be deducted from their account.

   g) When making reservations, airline personnel use this device extensively to access the computer system and get information about the status of a specific flight.

   h) This storage device is used by stock exchanges so that a record can be accessed immediately, without having to process any other records.

   i) This humanly readable storage medium was widely used during the early years of computers. However, it is not used as much now, owing to its bulkiness and the slow reading speed.

   j) This storage device represents recently developed technology and is used to store historical and other permanent information. Only very recently has it been made an erasable medium.

   k) Large insurance companies use this device to prepare form letters and hard copies of any other computer-generated document.

   l) This device is used by utility companies to read the turnaround documents that it receives from its customers.

   m) This device is used by universities in grading true-false and multiple-choice exams.

   n) This device is used by modern grocery stores to read the UPC of food items. Based upon the UPC, the system can extract the price of the product from the computer's memory.

   o) This device is used by the parcel industry to route packages to their appropriate destination.

   p) This device is used by large industrial corporations to condense historical data by up to ninety-nine percent or more for storage purposes.

q) This device is used by telephone companies to give a person the telephone number they are seeking when they dial directory assistance.

r) Some universities use this device to prepare the time cards that are distributed to employees.

s) The computer operator at ABC Computer Systems uses this device to tell the computer that a tape has been mounted on the tape drive.

32. When the Sunnydale Electronics Company receives invoices from its suppliers requesting payment for merchandise purchased, it provides them in batches of fifty to data entry personnel for keying onto 100-character magnetic tape records. These are subsequently entered into its computerized accounts payable system. When the due date for each invoice arrives, the computer automatically issues a check to the vendor for the net invoice amount. Characteristics of the data items on each vendor invoice record are as follows.

- ☐ Batch number, two characters
- ☐ Discount rate code, one character
- ☐ Gross invoice amount, never exceeds $20,000
- ☐ Invoice due date, six characters
- ☐ Purchase order number, six characters
- ☐ Transaction-type code, one character
- ☐ Vendor invoice number, eight characters
- ☐ Vendor code number, six characters
- ☐ Vendor name, twenty-one characters
- ☐ Vendor street address, twenty-one characters
- ☐ Vendor city, state, and zip code, twenty-one characters

a) Assuming that the data entry device may be programmed to automatically enter constant data values into each record, which of the data items listed above could be entered in this way?

b) Design a format for the magnetic tape input record that indicates the sequence in which these items are to be keyed. Explain the reasons for your choice of format.

c) Assume that keyverification is the only available means of checking the accuracy of the keyed data before they are entered into the main computer system. Which of the data items listed above should be keyverified, and which should not? Explain.

d) Assume that there is a volume of 500 invoices per day, that the keying rate is 6000 keystrokes per hour, and that twenty characters per record must be verified. How many hours of keying are required to complete the entry and verification of these records each day?

e) Which of the data items listed above could generally be stored within the computer system so that they would not have to be rekeyed for each and every invoice? Assuming that this is done, determine the effect that it would have on your answer to part (d).

33. The Western Oil Company began issuing credit cards several years ago. The volume of its credit card business has increased rapidly in recent years. At present the company's data processing center must process an average of 8500 charge sales documents per business day. This has resulted in a decision to replace the company's keypunch machines, which are presently used to enter data from charge sales documents. The two alternatives being considered are an optical character recognition (OCR) system and a shared-processor key-to-disk system.

The OCR system rents for $1500 per month. It would require an operator who would receive a monthly salary of $1800. It could be expected to read sucessfully between ninety-seven and ninety-nine percent of all charge sales documents. For those documents it rejects, the operator would manually enter the correct data from a console. Even considering the time required to deal with rejected documents, this system would have more than enough capacity to handle Western's current and projected volume of charge sales.

If the key-to-disk system is acquired, the shared processor would rent for $1000 per month, and each keystation required would rent for $120 per month. Each keystation would be operated by a data entry clerk who would receive a monthly salary of $1600. These operators could be expected to achieve a net productivity rate of 9600 keystrokes per hour. During each eight-hour day, they would spend approximately six hours and forty minutes working at the keyboard. Each charge sale document has fifteen characters that must be keyed.

REQUIRED

a) If the key-to-disk system is acquired, how many keystations and operators will be required, assuming all work is done on the day shift?

b) From an economic standpoint, which of the two alternatives is most attractive? Show computations.

c) Can you identify any additional factors that should be considered in deciding between the two alternatives?

34. You are a systems analyst employed by the New Acme Manufacturing Company. You have been asked to design a computer system application that will control the company's raw materials and parts inventories. A master file will be maintained and updated twice weekly for purchases, production usage, and other transactions. The average size of each master record will be 400 characters, and there will be about 20,000 records in the master file.

a) Assume that you have a choice of designing this system so that the master file is stored on either magnetic disk or magnetic tape. All the equipment required for either approach is available. Explain the arguments that could be advanced in favor of *both* approaches.

b) Consider each of the following items of additional information independently and explain whether or not it would affect the choice between tape and disk and, if so, how.

    i) The activity ratio for each update run will be close to 100 percent.

    ii) The activity ratio for each update run will be close to 1 percent.

    iii) Production planners will require frequent access to the information in the file.

    iv) The size of the file is expected to double within five years.

35. Pinta Company is a regional discount department store chain headquartered in Salt Lake City, Utah. Its stores are scattered throughout the Southeast and sell general merchandise. The firm is thinking about buying a point-of-sale (POS) system for its stores. There are a number of POS systems available, but the president believes that the type using a light pen to scan the universal product code on merchandise is the most suitable. However, it is quite expensive, so the president of the company asks the systems staff to prepare a report answering the following questions.

REQUIRED

Prepare a report that:
a) Explains the functions and operation of a POS system, including its use in credit checking and electronic transfers of funds.
b) Identifies the advantages and disadvantages of the POS system described in part a, above.
c) Identifies the special control and security problems that the POS system described in part a could present. Also identify suitable controls and security measures that should effectively counteract these problems. (CMA Examination adapted)

36. The Fleming Furniture Company (FFC) in High Point, North Carolina, uses a medium-sized computer to process sales orders. FFC is one of the largest wholesale distributors of furniture in the nation. It has purchasing agreements with all the furniture manufacturers in North Carolina. It sells furniture by mailing out catalogs showing the furniture it sells and by displaying its merchandise at quarterly furniture fairs across the country. Its sales force uses WATS lines to contact its customers and writes up the orders on company order forms.

    Periodically during the day, order forms are picked up from the sales people and taken to the data entry department. There, they are batched and entered using a key-to-disk-to-tape system linked to a minicomputer. At the end of the day, the orders that have been entered and stored on the disk are sorted and transferred to tape. The tape is then used as input into the order processing program. The output is a sales order containing the data on the order form.

    The firm is investigating the possibility of placing terminals on each salesperson's desk and having them enter the sales order directly into the computer. A local company has proposed a hardware configuration that costs $13,000 per month. The proposed system includes all the hardware (terminals, CPU, printer, etc.) needed to process the orders. In order to determine whether or not to switch, FFC has asked you, their accountant, to calculate the cost of the current system. You have gathered the following information.

1. There are an average of twenty working days in each month.
2. An average of 900 sales orders are processed each day, except after the quarterly furniture fair when the number of orders processed increases.
3. Each sales order contains an average of 125 characters of data.
4. Each preprinted, multicopy sales order costs twenty cents. The order forms cost ten cents each.
5. According to the internal pricing mechanism used by the company, costs for the medium-sized computer are allocated at $250 per hour. This includes the cost of the CPU, the peripherals, and the operator.
6. The multiple station key-to-disk-to-tape encoder is rented from a local company for $35 per operator hour. It is used to enter data for several different functions, including order entry.
7. The data entry clerks who operate the encoder work 7.5-hour days and are paid $1050 a month.
8. Data entry clerks can enter an average of three order forms every two minutes.
9. The tape drive reads 60,000 characters per minute.
10. It takes the computer fifteen minutes per day to read the 900 sales orders and generate the sales orders.
11. It takes the encoder six minutes per day to sort the records.

REQUIRED

a) Compute the monthly costs of the old system according to the following categories:

1. Equipment
2. Labor
3. Materials
4. Total cost

b) Should the company rent the new system or stay with the old system? What factors should the company consider other than cost?

37. Visit a local business or university, tour their computer facilities, and interview one or more of the organization's computer personnel. The facility toured should use a minicomputer or mainframe, and should not be a micro-based system. Write a report summarizing:

a. The hardware devices used by the company for input, output, processing, storage, and data communication (if applicable). Include in your report items such as the speed of the devices used, storage capacities, equipment, and prices.
b. The software used by the organization. (Refer to Chapter 6 if you need to.)
c. Your overall impression of the facility, the personnel who operate and manage it, and the controls used to safeguard the system.

d. Your views as to how the visit has helped you get a better grasp of the material covered in the chapter.

38. For each of the following situations:
   a) Determine what type of hardware the company will need.
   b) Draw a systems flowchart of the system described.

   1) U-Bag-M Groceries maintains an electronic inventory system and has computerized the receipt, sales, and ordering of merchandise. When a shipment is received, the cases are run along specialized conveyer belts. A scanner that is attached to the store's central computer is located on each side of the conveyer. The scanner reads the Universal Product Code on each package as it passes and updates the inventory records for the items received. When merchandise is sold, the customer's purchase is scanned as it passes through the check stand. Customer payments are received and the inventory levels are credited for the sales that take place. When the on-hand quantity of a stock item falls below the reorder point, the computer system prints a copy of the order form. All receiving and sales transactions that cannot be handled by the scanners are entered manually.

   2) Higher Education University has a computerized registration system. Prior to the beginning of classes, students can register twenty-four hours a day from anywhere in the country using a touch-tone phone. Once classes begin, the telephone registration is shut down, and any adding or dropping of a class is handled by registration employees who process registration queries and requests through an online terminal. Prior to the beginning of class, the computer generates a class confirmation form that is mailed to the student. A report for each class section is also prepared and distributed to the professors who are teaching the class.

   3) Quick Snack Incorporated distributes its snack food items through grocery stores and vending machines. Route personnel deliver, stock the shelves, and collect out-of-date products for client stores. The route personnel use small lap-size computers to help them record the sales and the out-of-date pulls made at each store. The route personnel also provide the store managers with printed bills and receipts. At the end of the day, the data stored in the lap-top are transferred to the company's centralized computer. To stock the vending machines, the company's computer prepares a card on each machine to be serviced on a given day. The vendor then services the machine and records the stock information on the card. He then returns the card to the main office, where the cards are processed nightly by the computer. Management can access the corporate data through online queries and by using the periodic, scheduled reports prepared by the computer.

4) U-Dial Phone Company maintains community offices as well as a corporate office. Owing to the large number of customers, U-Dial staggers both monthly billing dates and payment deadline dates. When a customer billing date comes, an itemized bill (including a payment form) is prepared by the computer and mailed to the customer. A customer can either mail the payment to the corporate office, or he or she can personally pay the bill at the community office. When a customer mails in the payment, it is supposed to be accompanied by the payment form. Each day, the preprinted forms are read and transferred onto a tape that is used to update the customer master file stored on disk. If a customer pays in person, a teller updates the customer's files online.

39. Prepare systems flowcharting segments for each of the operations described below.

a) Processing of transactions on punched cards on the computer to update a master file stored on magnetic tape.

b) Processing of transactions on punched cards on the computer to update a master file stored on a magnetic disk unit.

c) Conversion of source data from OCR documents to magnetic tape using an offline OCR reader/converter.

d) Online processing of OCR documents to update a master file on magnetic tape.

e) Reading of data on paper tape into the computer to be listed on a printed report.

f) Keying of data from source documents to magnetic tape using an offline key-to-tape encoder.

g) Manual sorting and filing of invoices.

h) Online processing of source data using a CRT terminal from a remote location to a central computer system for updating a magnetic disk master file and also for recording the source data on a magnetic tape file.

40. The independent auditor must evaluate a client's system of internal control to determine the extent to which various auditing procedures must be employed. A client who uses a computer should provide the CPA with a flowchart of the information processing system so the CPA can evaluate the control features in the system. Shown below is a simplified flowchart, such as a client might provide. Unfortunately the client had only partially completed the flowchart when it was requested by you. (CMA Examination adapted)

REQUIRED

a) Complete the flowchart shown in Fig. 5.23.

b) Describe what each item in the flowchart indicates. When complete, your description should provide an explanation of the processing of the data involved. Your description should be in the following order.

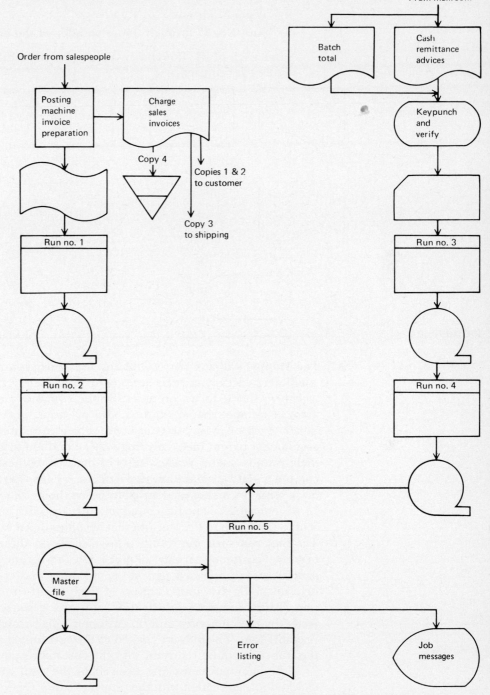

Order from salespeople

Posting machine invoice preparation

Charge sales invoices

Copy 4

Copies 1 & 2 to customer

Copy 3 to shipping

Run no. 1

Run no. 2

From mailroom

Batch total

Cash remittance advices

Keypunch and verify

Run no. 3

Run no. 4

Run no. 5

Master file

Error listing

Job messages

FIGURE 5.23

    i) "Orders from Salespeople" to "Run No. 5."

    ii) "From Mailroom" to "Run No. 5."

    iii) "Run No. 5" through the remainder of the chart.

c) Name each of the flowchart symbols shown in Fig. 5.24 and describe what each represents.

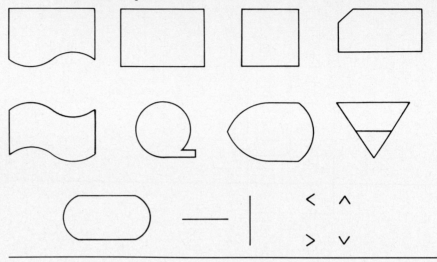

FIGURE 5.24

41. The Happy Valley Utility Company uses turnaround documents in its computerized customer accounting system. Meter readers are provided with preprinted forms prepared by the computer, each containing the account number, name, address, and previous meter readings of a customer. Each of these forms also contains a formatted area in which the customer's current meter reading may be marked in pencil. After making their rounds, meter readers turn in batches of these documents to the computer data preparation department, where they are processed by a mark-sense document reader that transfers their contents to magnetic tape.

The magnetic tape file containing the customer meter readings is then sent to the computer center where it becomes input to two computer runs. The first run sorts the transactions records on the tape into sequential order by customer account number. On the second run, the sort transaction tape is processed against the customer master file, which is stored on a magnetic disk unit. Outputs of this second run are (1) a printed report listing summary information and any erroneous transactions detected by the computer and (2) customer bills printed in a special OCR-readable font. The bills are mailed to the customers, with the request that the stub portion be returned with the customer's payment.

Customer payments are received in the mail room, where they are checked for agreement with the returned stubs. Customer checks are then sent to the cashier's office. The mail room provides the data preparation department with three sets of records: (1) stubs for which the amount received agrees with the stub amount, (2) stubs for which the amount received differs from the stub amount, and (3) a list of amounts received from customers who did not return their stubs. For the latter two types of records, data preparation personnel use a special typewriter to prepare corrected stubs. All the stubs are then processed by an OCR document reader that transfers their contents onto magnetic tape.

The magnetic tape containing the payment records is then sent to the computer center where it is (1) sorted on the computer into sequential order by customer account number and (2) processed against the customer master file to post the payment amounts. Two printed outputs from this second process are (1) a report listing erroneous transactions and summary information and (2) a report listing past-due customer balances.

a) Draw a systems flowchart of the billing operations, commencing with the computer preparation of the meter reading forms and ending with the mailing of bills to customers.

b) Draw a systems flowchart of the processing of customer payments, starting with the mail room operations and ending with the computer run that posts the payment amounts to the customer master file.

c) Prepare a list of the equipment in the company's hardware configuration that is required at a minimum to accomplish all the operations described.

42. The Dewey Construction Company processes its payroll transactions to update both its payroll master file and its work-in-process master file in the same computer run. The payroll master file is maintained on magnetic tape and accessed sequentially, whereas the work-in-process master is maintained on disk and accessed randomly.

Input to this system is keypunched and verified from job time tickets. The cards are then read into the computer to transfer their contents to magnetic tape. The tape is then processed by a tape sorting routine on the computer to sort the records into sequence by employee number. The sorted tape is then processed to update the files. This run also produces a payroll register on magnetic tape, employee paychecks and earnings statements, and a printed report listing error transactions and summary information.

Prepare a systems flowchart of the process described above.

43. Peabock Co. is a wholesaler of softgoods. The inventory is composed of approximately 3500 different items. The company employs a computerized batch processing system to maintain its perpetual inventory records. The system is run each weekend so that the inventory reports are available on Monday morning for management use. The system has been functioning satisfactorily for the past 15 months, providing the company with accurate records and timely reports.

The preparation of purchase orders has been automatic as a part of the inventory system to insure that the company will maintain enough inventory to meet customer demand. When an item of inventory falls below a predetermined level, a record of the inventory item is written. This record is used in conjunction with the vendor file to prepare the purchase orders.

Exception reports are prepared during the update of the inventory and the preparation of the purchase orders. These reports identify any errors or exceptions identified during the processing. In addition, the system provides for management approval of all purchase orders exceeding a specified amount. Any exceptions or items requiring management approval are handled by supplemental runs on Monday morning and are combined with the weekend results.

A system flow chart of Peabock Co.'s inventory and purchase order procedure appears in Fig. 5.25.

REQUIRED

a) The illustrated system flow chart of Peabock Co.'s inventory and purchase order system was prepared before the system was fully operational. Several steps which are important to the successful operations of the system were inadvertently omitted from the chart. Now that the system is operating effectively, management wants the system documentation complete and would like the flow chart corrected. Describe the steps which have been omitted and indicate where the omissions have occurred. **The flow chart does not need to be redrawn.**

b) In order for Peabock's inventory/purchase order system to function properly, control procedures need to be included in the system. Describe the type of control procedures Peabock Co. would use in their system to assure proper functioning and indicate where these procedures would be placed in the system. [Note: you may not be able to do part (b) if you have not read Chapter 14.] CMA Examination adapted)

Problems and Cases for Appendix

1. You wish to store employee payroll records on a reel of magnetic tape 2400 feet long with a density of 1600 bytes per inch and with interblock gaps measuring 0.6 inch. Each record contains 400 characters, and there are 1600 bytes of storage available in the central processor for storing a block of input records.

a) How many employee payroll records may be stored on one reel of magnetic tape?

b) Assume that the magnetic tape has nine tracks and that, by storing data in packed form, the equivalent of eighty percent of the data in each record can be stored at two characters per byte. Compute the effect of this change in assumptions on your answer to part (a).

FIGURE 5.25

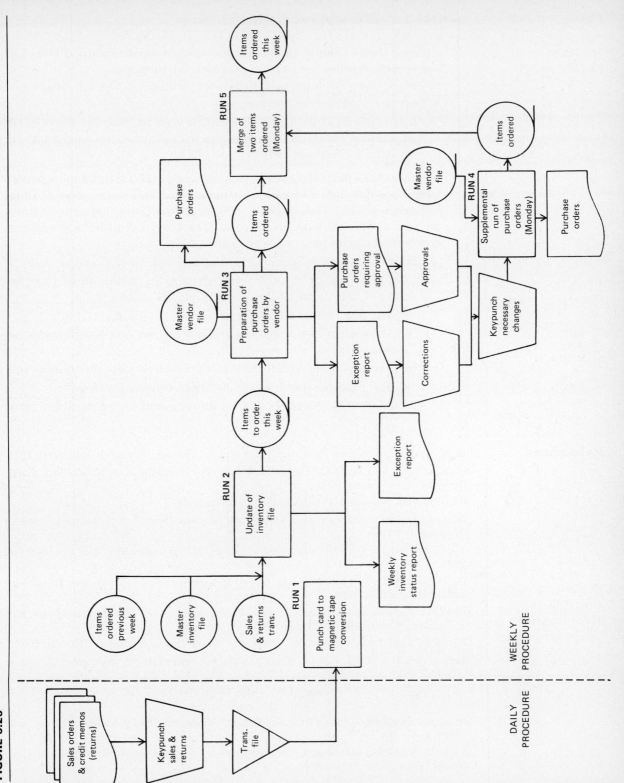

2. Suppose that a company's accounts receivable records contain 200 characters each, seventy-five percent of which are numeric.

   a) If a six-bit code such as BCD is used to store the records, how many bits are required for each record?

   b) If an eight-bit code such as EBCDIC is used to store the records, but all numeric characters are stored in packed form, how many bits are required for each record?

3. Suppose that a payroll record having 538 characters is stored in unpacked form on a disk file. The disk unit has a head movement time of thirty milliseconds, a rotation speed of 3600 revolutions per minute, and a transfer rate of 806,000 bytes per second. The record is to be accessed randomly in response to a management inquiry.

   a) How much time is required for the disk unit to read the record?

   b) Consider each of the following changes in assumptions independently of the others and compute a revised answer to (a).

      i) The disk unit is a fixed-head disk.

      ii) The record is accessed sequentially as part of a batch processing run.

      iii) The bit storage density is doubled, which doubles the transfer rate.

      iv) The rotation speed is only 3125 revolutions per minute.

      v) Of the 538 characters, 324 are numeric and stored in packed form.

References

Bohl, Marilyn. *Information Processing*. 3d ed. Chicago: Science Research Associates, 1980.

Capron, H. L., and Brian K. Williams. *Computers and Data Processing*. Menlo Park, Calif.: Benjamin/Cummings, 1982.

Chapin, Ned. *Flowcharts*. Princeton, N.J.: Auerbach, 1971.

Datapro Research Corporation. *Datapro EDP Solutions*. Delran, N.J.: Datapro Research Corporation, 1986.

————. *Datapro 70: The EDP Buyer's Bible*. Delran, N.J.: Datapro Research Corporation, 1986.

Davis, Gordon B., and Margrethe H. Olsen. *Management Information Systems*. 2d ed. New York: McGraw-Hill, 1985.

Dock, V. Thomas, and Edward L. Essick. *Principles of Business Data Processing with MIS. . . . including BASIC*. 4th ed. Chicago: Science Research Associates, 1981.

Feingold, Carl. *Introduction to Data Processing*. 3d ed. Dubuque: Wm. C. Brown, 1980.

Kelley, Neil D. "Micrographics: A Role in the Paperless Office." *Infosystems* (February 1980): 52–80.

————."Point of Sale Systems: More Than Meets the Eye." *Infosystems* (March 1980): 72–80.

Krasan, Victor J. "Enter the Electronic Editor." *Management Focus* (November/December 1980): 2–8.

Lines, M. Vardell, and Boeing Computer Services Company. *Minicomputer Systems*. Cambridge, Mass.: Winthrop, 1980.

Moscove, Stephen A., and Mark G. Simkin. *Accounting Information Systems*. 2d ed. New York: John Wiley & Sons, 1984.

O'Brian, James A. *Computers in Business Management*. Homewood, Ill.: Richard D. Irwin, 1985.

Paddock, Harold E. "Voice Input a Reality." *Internal Auditor* (December 1983): 23–26.

Rockart, J. F., and M. S. Scott-Morton. "Implications of Changes in Information Technology for Corporate Strategy." *Interfaces* (January/February 1984): 84–95.

White, Robert M. "Disk-Storage Technology." *Scientific American* (August 1980): 138–148.

Wieselman, Irving L. "Technology Profile: Non-Impact Printing in the 1980s." *Mini-Micro Systems* (January 1980): 93–100.

C H A P T E R 6

A Review of Software Concepts

LEARNING OBJECTIVES

Careful study of this chapter should enable students to:

☐ Compare and contrast the different levels of computer languages.

☐ Compare and contrast the different third and fourth generation computer languages.

☐ Identify the functions and purposes of the different types of systems software.

☐ Compare and contrast the custom, canned, and modified canned approaches to application software development and acquisition.

☐ Describe the life cycle that is used to develop computer programs and the program design considerations that should be followed.

☐ Construct program flowcharts and decision tables.

The nonhardware elements of a computer system are referred to as *software* and can be divided into two categories: computer programs and documentation. A *computer program* is a set of detailed instructions that tells a computer what to do. These instructions tell the computer what data to access, how to manipulate those data, and what to do with the data once processed. Documentation encompasses all nonprogram elements of software and includes such items as operating manuals and program descriptions.

There are several reasons why accountants need to understand the software concepts mentioned in this chapter. One significant reason is the important role software plays in an accounting information system. Software is certainly as essential as hardware because without appropriate software, computers are of no practical use. And in some cases, having the wrong software may even be worse than having no software.

A second reason is the accountant's role in systems design. As an information user in an organization that is either developing or purchasing software, an understanding of software concepts helps the accountant specify his or her requirements. This helps the individuals who are designing or purchasing the software to get the software that best meets the accountant's needs. In many instances the accountant is a member of the team that is charged with software design or development. In this capacity the accountant needs to understand software concepts in order to design a system that will efficiently meet the user's needs. One of the most important responsibilities of an accountant acting in this capacity is to make sure that adequate controls are written into the program (or contained in the purchased software) to ensure the accuracy, completeness, and security of the data.

A third reason relates to the accountants' role as information system evaluators. Both internal and external auditors are called upon to evaluate the strengths and weaknesses of information systems. In doing so, they must evaluate software for things such as the adequacy of internal controls, the effectiveness and usefulness of the system, how well user's needs are met, and the timeliness with which the information is being provided.

A fourth reason is the role accountants play as end-users of the system. As technology advances and as hardware costs fall, more and more people (or end-users) in an organization have access to the power of computers. End-users are increasingly being provided with personal computers or terminals and powerful and easy-to-use software. Many have taken advantage of this power and ease of use to access corporate data, write their own programs, and develop sophisticated models. As a result, end-users are able to satisfy their own needs on a timely basis, without having to wait for the assistance of their programming staff. This has allowed the programming staff to concentrate on the complex, multiuser information systems that are needed by most large organizations but that are difficult and time-consuming to develop. It has also put computer power within the reach of those who do not have access to programming staffs. This "taking computer power to the people" has resulted in an explosive growth in the area of microcomputers and personal productivity tools (discussed in the next chapter). The growth of end-user computing has caused a shift in the role of corporate data processing staffs. There has been a move away from centralized control and development of information to supporting users who develop and operate their own information systems.

To accomplish these tasks, accountants need to be well versed in the software concepts presented in this chapter. This does not necessarily mean that accountants should have a detailed knowledge of programming. However, familiarity with at least one programming language does provide a useful perspective. Several common programming languages are discussed in the appendix to this chapter.

Levels of Computer Languages

To carry out an information or transaction processing task, an instruction set must be created that tells the computer what to do. This instruction set, or computer program, may be written in 1 of the over 200 programming languages in active use. The programming languages range from very simple to very complex and from being easy to learn to being difficult to learn. Each has its own unique vocabulary, grammar, and use. They are often classified in terms of being high-level languages or low-level languages. The closer the language is to the language used by the computer, the lower the level of the language. Generally speaking, the closer they are to English, the higher the level of the language. This segment of the chapter briefly addresses four levels of languages (from the lowest to the highest level): machine language, symbolic (or assembly-level) languages, procedure-oriented languages, and fourth generation languages. Some people refer to these languages as first, second, third, and fourth generation languages, respectively. These programming language generations are similar to the hardware generations discussed in Chapter 5. Figure 6.1 shows an example of the code, or program statements, that could be used in each of the four language levels to give instructions to the computer.

Machine-level languages

Each make of computer has its own *machine language,* which is a binary code (a string of zeros and ones) that can be interpreted by the internal circuitry of the computer. A typical machine language instruction might consist of (1) an operation code, (2) an operand (the data items upon which the operation is performed), (3) the address where the result of the operation is to be stored, and (4) the address of the next instruction to be performed. Programming in machine language is very difficult and confusing. The binary instruction codes are complex, and the programmer must keep track of the addresses of each instruction and data item used in the program. Since this is a time-consuming, error-prone process, programming in machine language is very uncommon.

LANGUAGE	INSTRUCTION
Machine language	010110000010000000001000011110000 010110100010000000001000011110001 010100000010000000001000011110010
Symbolic assembly language	L 2,A A 2,B ST 2,C
Procedure-oriented language	ADD SALARY, COMMISSION, GIVING TOTALPAY
Fourth generation language	COMPUTE THE TOTALPAY OF ALL EMPLOYEES BY ADDING THEIR SALARY AND COMMISSION.

FIGURE 6.1
Typical instructions in the four levels of programming languages.

Symbolic or assembler languages

A more English-like and understandable alternative to machine language is the *assembler language.* In an assembler, or *symbolic language,* each machine instruction is represented by symbols that bear some relation to the instruction. For example, the symbols "A," "CP," and "MV" might represent the "ADD," "COMPARE," and "MOVE" instructions, respectively. Furthermore, each data item used in the program is given a name, and the computer keeps track of the storage address where each item of data is stored.

Before it can be used by the computer, a symbolic language program must be converted to machine language by a special program called an *assembler.* Each unique machine has a somewhat different assembler, depending on the computer's architecture. In this conversion process, the symbolic language program, called the *source program,* and the assembler are input to the CPU. The machine language program, called the *object program,* is the output.

Although assembler programs are easier and faster to write and correct than machine language programs, they are by no means easy for most people to learn or use. In addition, they are *machine dependent;* that is, the programs written in assembler language only work on a specific machine and with its unique assembler program. Except for operating system programs and some applications that require very efficient use of primary memory, assembler languages are not commonly used for business data processing.

High-level languages

The use of *macroinstructions*—instructions that are translated into multiple machine language instructions—is one reason more advanced languages were initially referred to as high-level languages. High-level languages are usually classified as being either procedure oriented or problem solving. In *procedure-oriented languages,* the programmer specifies the procedures, or logic, necessary to accomplish a specific data processing task. Some procedure-oriented languages, like COBOL, are designed for use in business data processing. Others, like FORTRAN, are designed to solve scientific applications.

Problem-solving languages are designed to help the programmer solve specific types of problems. With problem-solving languages, the programmer need only specify the input to be used, the output desired, and the parameters of the problem. The procedures used to solve the problem need not be specified since these are embedded within the problem-solving language. These problem-solving languages, which can be classified as query languages, report generators, program generators, and analysis and modeling languages, are defined and discussed later in the chapter.

Procedure-oriented languages are *machine independent.* The same language can be used on many makes of computers, although minor differences may exist between different machines. *Compilers* are used to convert procedure-oriented languages into machine language. Since each procedure-oriented language is different, a different compiler is needed for each. In other words a FORTRAN compiler would be needed to translate a FORTRAN program, a COBOL compiler for a COBOL program, etc. Source and object program have the same meaning as they do in assembler programs.

A systems flowchart showing the process of compiling and executing a procedure-oriented program appears in Fig. 6.2. As the flowchart shows, the compiler and the source program are input into the system. The compiler translates the source program into a machine language object program that is written onto a disk file. Two other outputs are possible: a report listing the source program and diagnostic messages. *Diagnostic messages* inform the programmer of *syntax errors,* which are errors in the use of the language rather than logic, or programming, errors. Syntax errors occur when the language is used improperly—that is, when the compiler is given an instruction that it cannot understand. Logic errors occur when the instructions given to the computer do not accomplish the desired objective. If there are significant syntax errors, the program will not compile and the user must correct the errors and resubmit the program. If there are no significant syntax errors, the machine language object program and the input are read into the computer. The program is executed and a printed report and a data file are written out.

An alternative translation program, called an *interpreter,* is used in some procedure-oriented languages. For example, the BASIC language used in microcomputers is usually an interpreted language. An interpreter takes each programming instruction and, one at a time, checks it for syntax errors, translates it into machine language, and executes it. In contrast, a compiler translates all instructions into machine language and then executes them. In some instances, each program statement can be interpreted and checked for syntax errors as it is entered. The computer informs the programmer of any errors so they can be corrected immediately. This is known as *interactive debugging.* Since the interpreter translates and executes instructions one at a time, neither object programs nor diagnostics are produced.

Procedure-oriented languages are generally easier to learn and use, and are thus less error prone, than symbolic languages. Because they are machine independent, they are not as likely to become obsolete when a new computer is installed, and programs can also be shared with other users. However, symbolic language programs are likely to be more efficient because there is more

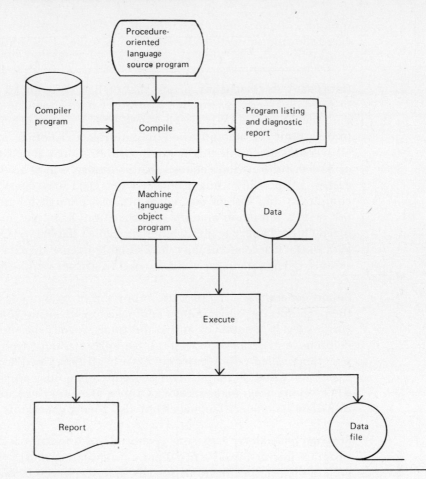

FIGURE 6.2
Compiling and
executing a
procedure-oriented
language program.

of a one-to-one correspondence between symbolic language instructions and machine language instructions. A programmer writing in symbolic language can take maximum advantage of his or her expertise in designing an efficient program. It is difficult to design a compiler program that is as skillful as an expert programmer.

Fourth generation languages

As computers have become more accessible to nonprogrammers the trend has been toward languages that are easy to learn and that do not require the user to understand the technical details of the computer. This trend has led to *fourth generation languages* (also known as very high level, application-oriented, and user-oriented languages). There are significant advantages to these fourth generation languages. Some so closely resemble English (or other languages) that they are referred to as natural languages. Most were designed with ease of use and learning in mind and are end-user (or nonprogrammer) oriented. Since most are used with microcomputers and online terminals, users can interact with the system to get immediate responses to their information needs. The following subsections briefly discuss some of the fourth generation languages.

Data base query languages. Information users often need to produce reports or need quick responses to questions they have about the contents of certain data files. An example is a savings and loan accessing a person's loan records to determine the amount owed on a mortgage. Another example is selecting all accounts receivable that are both sixty or more days past due and in excess of $1000. Information requests of this nature, which are often called *ad hoc queries,* are possible using *query languages.* Data base query languages vary in complexity and ease of use. Some are easy enough for nonprogrammers to use, with a minimum amount of instruction. Examples include IBM's Structured Query Language (SQL) and Pansophic's Easytrieve. Others such as Mark IV and Datatrieve are usually only suitable for use by data processing professionals. Query languages are discussed in greater depth in Chapter 9.

Report generators. To produce reports, a programmer must place titles on the page, specify page numbers and page breaks, group similar data, calculate various levels of subtotals and grand totals, specify the number and width of columns, etc. Because these steps are fairly standard from report to report, programs called *report generators* have been developed to make the process easier and faster. Perhaps the most frequently used report generator is called RPG (report program generator). Others, like Easytrieve and Mark IV, are not only data base query languages but also report generators.

Program generators. *Program generators* are software packages that generate program instructions. To use them a programmer must provide the program generator with specifications such as what the screen layouts should look like and what processing procedures need to be performed. The remainder of the information needed is entered in an interactive mode. That is, the programmer answers questions asked by the system. Martin has published some interesting examples of the power and time-saving benefits of program generators.[1] He states that IBM claims to have achieved a 27:1 improvement in productivity when ADF, its report generating program, was used to write programs instead of COBOL or IDS (a data base program). At another company, it took six months to write a management reporting system. That same program was created in half a day using a program generator called FOCUS.

Statistical and problem solving. Most statistical and problem-solving applications in business are used to facilitate management decision making. Of importance are statistical applications involving correlation and regression,

---

[1] James Martin, *Application Development without Programmers* (Englewood Cliffs, N.J.: Prentice-Hall, 1982) p. 30.

analysis of variance, statistical sampling, or time-series analysis. Also significant are applications utilizing operations research models, linear programming, inventory or queuing models, PERT and critical path analysis, cash flow
discounting, forecasting, and cost-volume-profit analysis. Most "data crunch-
ing" performed by these packages is based on standard formulas. Therefore
the only input needed are the data and input parameters describing the data
and the procedures to be performed. Some of the most frequently used statistical and problem-solving packages are SPSS (Statistical Package for the Social Sciences), BMDP (BioMedical Data Analysis Package), and SAS (Statistical
Analysis System).

Modeling or decision support.   Modeling and *decision support systems (DSS) software* are available for all levels of computers, including microcomputers, minicomputers, and large mainframes. The most popular software for the microcomputer are packages like Lotus 1–2–3, Symphony, Framework, Multiplan,
and Supercalc. These user-friendly microcomputer packages are also known
as electronic spreadsheets and are discussed in Chapter 7 in more detail.
Mainframe DSS software is typically more sophisticated than that available
for microcomputers. It uses simple, English-like statements to define the input
and output and to define the variables and elements to be used in the model.
Common abilities of DSS software include:

☐ "What-if" capabilities. What effect would changing the variables in the
   model have on the system's output?

☐ Goal seeking. What would have to be done to achieve a specified goal?
   For example, what sales and expense levels would have to be met to reach
   a certain net income goal?

☐ Simulation. These packages use different probabilities, expectations, etc.,
   to simulate a particular situation.

Some of the most popular DSSs available for large systems are IFPS, EX-
PRESS, and SYSTEM W.

Expert systems and artificial intelligence.   A comparatively recent innovation in
computer software is artificial intelligence. *Artificial intelligence* (AI) is software
that can use its accummulated knowledge to reason and, in some instances,
learn from experience and thereby modify its subsequent reasoning. There are
several types of AI, including natural language, visual recognition, robotic,
voice recognition, and expert systems. Except for expert systems, AI has yet to
have much impact on accounting information systems.

An *expert system* is a computerized information system that allows nonexperts to make decisions about a particular problem that are comparable to
those of an expert in the area. In designing an expert system, a process known
as knowledge engineering is used to develop a knowledge base. This knowledge base represents the data, knowledge, rules-of-thumb, and decision rules

that experts use to make decisions. Alternatively, the knowledge base can contain the facts and results of many similar cases. The software allows the nonexpert user to interact with the knowledge base and make the same decision that an expert would make. Expert systems usually apply to a narrow, specific subject area and are typically most beneficial for complex or ill-structured tasks that require experience and specialized knowledge. Expert systems typically contain the following components:

1. *Knowledge data base.* The data, knowledge, rules-of-thumb, and decision rules used by experts to solve a particular type of problem.

2. *Database management system.* The software that manages the knowledge data base.

3. *Inference engine.* The program containing the logic and reasoning mechanisms that simulate the logic process of the expert. The inference engine uses data obtained from the knowledge data base and from the user to draw conclusions.

4. *User interface.* The program that allows the user to communicate with the expert system.

5. *Knowledge acquisition facility (or development engine).* The program used to gather data and decision rules from the human expert and enter it into the system.

Expert systems provide several gradations of expertise. Some function as assistants or aides. They perform routine analysis and call the user's attention to the tasks that require human expertise. Other expert systems function as colleagues or peers. The user "discusses" a problem with such a system until they both agree on a common solution. When a user can accept the system's solution without question, the expert system can be referred to as a true expert. Developers of expert systems are still striving to create a true expert; meanwhile, most current systems function at the assistant or colleague level.

Expert systems can be classified according to the type of inference engine used. In an example-based system, the developer enters the facts and results of a large number of cases. Through induction, the expert system converts the examples to a decision tree. The system uses the decision tree to match the case at hand with those previously entered in the knowledge base. Rule-based systems are created by obtaining the data and decision rules used by experts and expressing them in the form of complex conditional logic expressed in terms of if-then rules. The system operates by asking the user a series of questions and applying the if-then rules to the answers in order to draw conclusions and make recommendations. Rule-based systems are appropriate when a history of cases is unavailable or when a body of knowledge can be structured in a set of if-then rules. In a frame-based system, all the information (data, descriptions, rules, etc.) about a topic is organized into logical units called frames. These frames are similar to records in data files. The frames are linked together using software "pointers." Rules are then established as to how the frames are assembled or interrelated to meet the user's needs.

Expert systems offer the following benefits to nonexpert users:

☐ They can provide a cost-effective alternative to human experts.

☐ They enable users to produce better quality and more consistent decisions. Users can identify potential problems with their decisions and increase the probability of making correct decisions.

☐ They can greatly increase the speed with which an "expert" decision is made.

☐ Possibly the greatest benefit is that they can increase productivity. For example, Westinghouse claims to have increased the volume of their business by more than ten million dollars per year using an expert system. Likewise, Texas Instruments has achieved a 10 percent increase in semiconductor production using an expert system.

Although expert systems have many advantages and great promise, they also have a number of significant problems that currently limit their use.

☐ They are costly and time consuming to develop. Some large experimental systems have required up to 15 years to develop and have cost millions of dollars.

☐ It is difficult and costly to obtain the knowledge needed for the system from expert users. Experts often have difficulty in specifying exactly how they make decisions.

☐ Unfortunately, it has not been possible to program common sense into current systems. As a result, rule-bound systems tend to break down when presented with a situation they are not programmed to handle.

☐ Until just recently, developers have encountered a somewhat skeptical market. This was partly due to the poor quality of expert systems produced and partly due to human reactions to machine-made decisions. Some humans find it distasteful to think that a machine could produce a better decision than they can and are distrustful of expert systems and reluctant to use them.

As technology advances most of these problems will be overcome and expert systems will play an increasingly important role in accounting information systems in the future. Some of the most popular expert systems currently used by accountants are Expert Ease, TI Personal Consultant, Rule Master, AUDITOR, TICOM, TAXMAN, and TAX ADVISOR.

Systems Software

For discussion purposes, software programs can be divided into two separate categories: application software and systems software. *Application software* is written to accomplish specific information or transaction processing needs.

Examples include programs to keep the accounts receivable, payable, inventory, and payroll records up to date. *Systems software* is the interface between the hardware and the application program. It interprets the application program instructions and tells the hardware how to execute them. Because of the vital role that accountants have in an EDP system, it is essential that they understand the importance of systems software, what it does, and how it is used. Systems software performs at least four major functions.

- [ ] It controls the use of the hardware, the application software, and other system resources used in executing data processing tasks.
- [ ] It supports these processing tasks by performing common tasks like merging and sorting.
- [ ] It monitors and records system performance.
- [ ] It prepares user programs for execution by translating them into machine language. It can also help develop application programs.

Systems software can be classified as operating systems, data base management systems, utility or service programs, language translators, and communications software. These five categories (and related subcategories) are shown in Fig. 6.3. Computer users usually purchase, rather than develop, the needed systems software. Most is purchased from the hardware manufacturer; in fact, much of it is included as part of the total purchase price of the hardware. However, some, like data base management system software, can also be purchased from independent software houses.

Operating Systems

An operating system is the most important and indispensable systems software package. It is a group of related programs that manage the processing operations and the input, output, and storage functions of the computer system. It resides in main memory or in an online storage device readily accessible to main memory. Each make of computer has an operating system written for it by the computer manufacturer.

The principal objective of an operating system is to manage system resources in order to maximize the effectiveness and efficiency of a computer system. It does this by minimizing human interventions and by simplifying the job of computer programmers. Among other things, the operating system performs administrative functions such as scheduling of jobs, allocation of primary memory space, maintenance of operating statistics, communication with equipment operators, and coordination of input/output operations. Prior to the advent of multiprogramming, operating systems were relatively simple. However in a multiprogrammed system several jobs are being processed on the computer at the same time, and the operating system must be very sophisticated in order to successfully manage all the programs, data, and peripheral devices that are simultaneously under its control.

Some of the primary component programs of an operating system include the job-control program, the scheduling program, the library manager, the

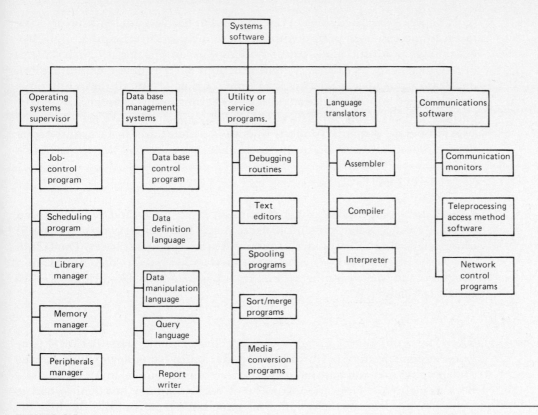

FIGURE 6.3
Five different categories of systems software.

memory manager, the peripherals manager, and the supervisor. The job-control program reads and interprets instructions written in *job-control language* (JCL), which is the language used to instruct the operating system. JCL also identifies the physical equipment needed for the job, initiates the processing and terminating of each job, and communicates with the computer operator. The scheduling program establishes priorities for all jobs being processed or waiting to be processed on the system. It also schedules and directs the flow of jobs through the system. The library manager keeps track of the storage locations of all language translators, application programs, utility routines, and other system programs so that these programs may be retrieved and read into primary memory when they are called upon. The memory manager assigns primary memory space to programs and data, maintains a record of the status of all available areas of primary memory, and protects the areas reserved for one program from being used by other programs. The peripherals manager controls the assignment of input and output devices to jobs in process. The supervisor program is the "chief executive officer" among all the programs in the system. It directs the operations of all the other programs and is called upon to resolve conflicts in job scheduling or resource management in the most efficient manner for the system as a whole.

Chapter 5 discussed some of the approaches hardware manufacturers have taken to increase system throughput. These included overlapping, multiprogramming, multiprocessing, parallel operations, and paging (or virtual memory). Other chapters discuss systems functions such as data communication, data base management systems, and time sharing. When all these functions are combined with the functions discussed earlier in this chapter, it is apparent that it takes a very sophisticated operating system to make the computer system operate properly. Modern operating systems are, in fact, quite complex; however, a discussion of those complexities is beyond the scope of this text.

Data base management systems

A computerized data base is a collection of related files and records stored together and accessible to multiple users. A *data base management system* (DBMS) is a specialized set of computer programs that manages data bases. The DBMS acts as the interface between the data in a data base, the related application programs, and the operating system. Data bases and DBMS software are discussed in Chapter 9.

Utility or service programs

There are a number of common file and data handling tasks that most computer systems have to perform on a regular basis. Examples include sorting and merging files and transferring data from one medium to another. It would be a tremendous duplication of effort if each computer installation had to write its own programs to accomplish these tasks. To avoid this duplication, computer manufacturers and independent software houses have written *utility programs.* These utility programs handle a wide variety of housekeeping chores and are sufficiently generalized that they can be tailored to a wide variety of applications. They are made available to all users of a computer system and are generally easy to use, efficient to operate, and inexpensive to acquire.

There are many types of utility packages. Sort/merge programs either sort a file into a specific order or merge two or more sorted files into one file. Media conversion programs transfer data from one medium to another (cards to tape, tape to disk, etc.). Program debugging aids help a user correct programs. A memory dump program prints memory contents to help the programmer locate programming errors. A trace routine prints data values and diagnostic information after specific instructions in a program are executed. Text editors allow online terminal users to modify the contents of data files and computer programs. There are programs that allow the user to create backup copies of files and analyze disks for defective tracks.

Language translators

Language translators are software programs that convert programming language instructions into the computer's machine language. Because the electrical design and architectural structure of most computers differ, language translators are written by the hardware manufacturer for each specific machine it sells. Most language translators are called either assemblers, compilers, or interpreters. Assemblers and compilers translate all program instructions (called source code), and then the computer executes the machine language program (called the object code). Interpreters translate and execute each program statement one at a time. A summary of these translators is presented in Fig. 6.4.

Communications software

More and more EDP users are moving to distributed processing or to other forms of transmitting data electronically over communication lines. They transmit data between computers, and between terminals and computers, and they access large data bases to extract information. To operate efficiently, data communications systems require control programs called communications monitors, teleprocessing access methods (TPAM), and network control programs (NCP). These programs control and support the data communications activity occurring in a communications network. They connect and disconnect communication links and terminals, automatically poll terminals or other computers for input/output activity, prioritize communication requests, and detect and correct data transmission errors. Communications software is discussed in more depth in Chapter 8.

FIGURE 6.4
Language translators.

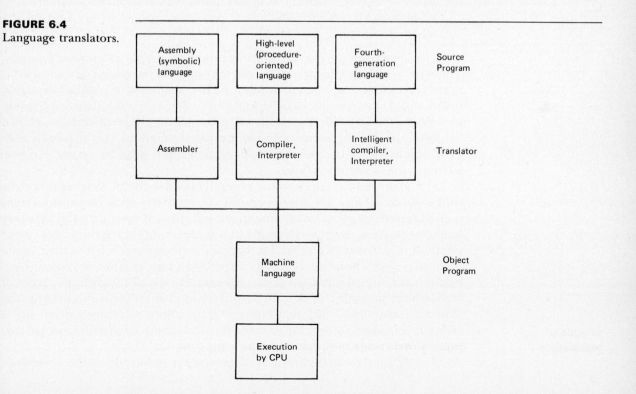

Application software

Application programs perform the specific data or information processing tasks required by a company. Since there are hundreds of different types of businesses, each with a number of unique processing needs, there are thousands of different application programs in use. These application programs can be divided into at least five different categories.

1. Business. These programs update files and support the various business functions of a company. They include accounting, marketing, production, finance, personnel, and operations production and management. Chapters 16 through 20 cover these topics.

2. General-purpose, or "generic." These programs facilitate the handling of tasks common to many users. They include word processing, spreadsheets, graphics, and data bases. These topics are covered in greater depth in Chapter 7.

3. Scientific. These programs carry out the scientific research and development tasks needed by such disciplines as mathematics, the sciences, and engineering. These programs are beyond the scope of this book.

4. Intelligent. These applications focus on expanding the role of the computer beyond the traditional data processing functions. Examples include decision support software, expert systems, and artificial intelligence. These programs were briefly discussed earlier in this chapter.

5. Other. This is a "catch-all" category and includes applications in arts, entertainment, medicine, education, etc. These programs are beyond the scope of this book.

The most common data processing programs are *file maintenance programs*. These programs update master files, so they include the effects of transactions as they take place. Examples of accounting files that must be regularly updated include payroll, accounts payable and receivable, general ledger, and inventory. As explained in Chapter 3, file maintenance may be performed in a batch or online processing mode. File maintenance programs also generally perform certain other functions, such as editing input data for errors and preparing reports and documents.

File maintenance applications generally involve the processing of a wide range of file activity. On the one hand are regularly recurring transactions such as the sale of goods on account or the purchase of inventory. On the other hand, there are many different types of nonrecurring transactions such as the addition or deletion of a record, a change in an employee's pay rate or in the price of an inventory item, or the correction of an erroneous record. Generally, it is more efficient to update a master file for all the different types of transactions that affect it in a single processing run, using a single program. When the number of different kinds of transactions affecting a given file is large, as is commonly the case in many business applications, one can see that the file maintenance program can be very complex.

Many of the early applications of computers in business were devoted to processing accounting data. Several programming languages have been created to accommodate the characteristics of data processing applications in accounting, such as complex input and output data structures and a need for control. In addition, some of the major accounting firms have developed their own higher-level languages to assist in audit work. Such languages have commands that are peculiar to audit work, and programs written using these commands must first be translated into a procedure-oriented language. For example, the command to FOOT must be translated into a procedure-oriented language routine that adds a column of numbers.

Application software can be obtained in one of three ways: (1) by developing it or writing it, (2) by buying a "canned" or "off-the-shelf" software package, or (3) by buying a canned package and modifying it. Application program purchase costs range from $250 to several thousand dollars and 20 to 100 times that to develop. The advantages and disadvantages of each of these approaches are discussed below.

Custom software

In the early days of computers, almost all organizations designed and wrote their own application software. In some cases, this was done because the company had no other alternative. Often, only a few programs were available for purchase, and they typically did not adequately meet the organization's needs. Even though more canned software is now available, some organizations feel that their needs are too unique to be met by a package sold on the open market. Other organizations are so large and their needs so complex that the only way their needs can be met is to develop their own *custom software*.

Custom programming is usually accomplished in one of the following ways.

1. Have the programs developed and written in-house. This topic is addressed later in the chapter and throughout the analysis and design life cycle chapters.

2. Engage an outside programmer/analyst or software company to custom write an application package.

3. Engage a software company to "assemble" a customized package from their inventory of program modules, or components.

Developing custom software is a difficult, error-prone, and time-consuming process. For example, consider the translation that must occur between the end-user who defines his or her requirements and the programmers and analysts who must interpret these requirements and fashion them into a structure of programs, data files, inputs, and outputs. The programmer/analyst, together with the users, must decide the exact format of all output reports and terminal screen formats. They must identify all system inputs and the specific data elements required for each input and the data to be retained in the files. The programmer/analyst must also develop detailed descriptions of all the internal processing logic necessary to produce the desired system output. Due to the many and varied tasks that must be accomplished, the entire process requires a significant amount of discipline and management supervision.

Supervision of program development.   Because of the discipline required, a company should control the development process properly, especially when contracted from external personnel. In such cases a company should ensure, inasmuch as possible, that

- ☐ An informed and well-researched decision as to who should develop the software is made.
- ☐ The contract places responsibility for meeting the company's requirements on the developer.
- ☐ All aspects of the software project are designed in painstaking detail.
- ☐ The relationship between the company and the developer is rigorously defined.
- ☐ There is regular and frequent communication between users and developers.
- ☐ There are frequent checkpoints for monitoring the project.
- ☐ Cash outflows are minimized until project completion and acceptance.
- ☐ There is an opportunity to discontinue the project at any time.
- ☐ Costs are controlled tightly.
- ☐ Disciplined effort and continuity of service from development personnel is achieved.

The role of the software developers.   Much of the custom software development work for smaller systems is done by software houses who package and sell both the hardware and the software necessary for a particular job. These software houses are responsible for current programming, support of future programming, and systems implementation. They often specialize in one or more industries and can often provide an excellent system at a good price.

For the software developer to operate successfully, he or she must have an in-depth understanding of the way a company conducts business. Detailed system requirements and specifications are normally documented as an early step in the traditional system development. However, detailed specifications are not always completed by a proposing developer until after a contract is obtained, due to the time and cost involved in developing them. In such cases the software cost estimates are usually based on standard criteria, such as the number of reports, screens, program modules, and files required. Developers are able to estimate, within an acceptable tolerance, the effort required to meet a customer's requirements due to prior experience, the use of very high level programming languages, and programming modules that they keep in their "inventory." In many of the development efforts, the developer does not write a completely new program. Instead, inventory modules are adapted, added to, combined, and organized to form a customized product that meets a company's specific needs.

Canned software

Canned software is written by computer manufacturers or software development companies for sale on the open market to a broad range of users with similar needs. Some developers combine their software with hardware and sell them as a package. These combinations are called *turnkey systems* because the vendor installs the entire system and the user only has to "turn on the key" (at least theoretically) to get the system to function. Among the most popular software packages that are "bundled" and sold with hardware are accounting packages. The most popular of these accounting packages might be referred to as the "Big Six." They are general ledger, accounts receivable, accounts payable, inventory, payroll, and asset management.

Historically, software was twenty percent of the cost of computerized systems and hardware was eighty percent. However, there have been dramatic decreases in hardware costs and increases in people, or labor, costs. As a result the eighty percent hardware, twenty percent software proportion has been reversed, at least in regard to custom software. Since custom software is becoming so expensive, more and more people are turning to the much less costly prepackaged, or canned, software. They see no reason to continually "reinvent the wheel" by writing programs from scratch when they can be purchased commercially. In fact, some estimates show that as much as seventy percent of today's computer installation base is either using or considering canned software packages. As time passes, more and better packages should become available. It is likely that in the years ahead application systems will be developed in-house only by very large organizations and organizations that have very unique requirements. Organizations will, instead, subscribe to the philosophy of "leave the programming to them."

Modified canned software

Some people feel that the best of the canned and custom worlds can be achieved by customizing a canned package to meet a user's specific needs—that is, by creating *modified canned software*. These modifications can be made by the creator of the software through an extracost contract or on an hourly fee basis, by internal programmers, by a third party software vendor, or by other users of the same package.

Which approach is best?

Because situations and conditions differ, there is no definitive answer as to which approach is best. Each situation must be handled on an individual basis. The advantages and disadvantages of each approach, as shown in Fig. 6.5, must be considered in making the decision. As a general rule, however, canned software is usually the best approach when a package can be located that ad-

ADVANTAGE	DISADVANTAGE

Custom software approach

1. The program can be tailored to meet the company's exact needs.
2. This approach allows the company to operate the way it wants to, rather than be constrained by limitations imposed by an off-the-shelf program.

1. It is very costly. Even the smallest application may cost thousands of dollars.
2. It usually takes months, or even years, to develop application programs.
3. Few (if any) custom programs are bug free when first put into use.
4. In-house development requires significant cost, management time, and stringent controls. Standards for programming, development, and documentation must be developed. There are many people concerns: salary, promotion, supervision, etc.
5. The process can be frustrating to users and management: analyze needs, develop system, revise system, test system, debug, revise, etc.
6. It requires significant user and developer interaction to make sure exact needs are met. The quality of the package partly depends on how well users can specify their needs and how well those needs are understood by developers.
7. External development requires careful selection of a developer to avoid inexperienced, poorly qualified, undercapitalized companies.

Canned software approach

1. The cost is much less than other approaches because development and maintenance costs are spread over many users.
2. There is little, if any, waiting. Packages are sitting on the shelf ready to run. A company can implement a computerized system in a much shorter time.
3. A buyer can reduce risk by "test driving" the software before purchasing it and talking to other users.
4. Users can match their requirements against available packages and select the ones that best meet their needs.
5. Programs are more likely to be bug free since they are usually field-tested at customer sites.
6. A supplier will keep canned software up-to-date at a fraction of the cost for the purchaser to update software.
7. Experts often can produce highly specialized packages that are difficult or expensive to duplicate.

1. Available packages may not "fit" the company's needs very well. In order to use the packages, the company may have to change schedules, do away with special practices, revise forms, do without certain reports, or otherwise modify the way it does business. These changes may not be acceptable to the company or in its best interests.
2. The evaluation of available packages can be time-consuming and costly, raising the overall cost of the package selected.
3. Programs that are generalized enough for many users are often not as efficient as custom or modified software.
4. There may not be anyone in-house capable of solving hardware and software problems.

FIGURE 6.5
Advantages and disadvantages to three application software approaches.

ADVANTAGE	DISADVANTAGE
8. User documentation is often better.	
9. A user does not need any (or as many) expensive analysts and programmers to design and maintain software.	
Modified software approach	
1. The end result should meet or at least more closely meet the company's needs and preferences than canned software.	1. It is sometimes hard to locate quality programmers since modification is often more difficult than initial programming.
2. It allows the company to operate the way it wants to, rather than be constrained by limitations imposed by an off-the-shelf program.	2. Many vendors do not allow their programs to be modified. Unauthorized modification may not be supported or updated.
3. It may be less costly and time-consuming and take less time to implement than a custom program.	3. Documentation of changes may not be made or may be incomplete.
	4. Significant modifications may cost as much as a custom-written program.
	5. Modification may introduce program logic errors, control problems, or other unanticipated results.

equately meets an organization's needs. This is especially true for smaller systems and where company needs are not overly complex. As the size and complexity of the system or its requirements rises, there is less likelihood that software can be found that will meet the company's needs. Many people believe that a company should never attempt to write custom software unless they have in-house, experienced programming personnel and the job cannot be done more cheaply on the outside. In the final analysis, an organization will have to look at its specific needs and the software available on the market and decide what is best.

Writing Computer Programs

This section introduces the program life cycle, the process that analysts and programmers use to develop their programs. It also introduces three principles of program design that lead to efficient and effective programs.

The computer program life cycle

Although accountants usually need not be experienced computer programmers, they should understand the programming process and programming concepts. In addition, they should understand the development cycle that is typically used in creating a computer program. The time required for program preparation may range from a few days to a few years, depending on the complexity of the program. The steps in the program life cycle are shown in Fig. 6.6.

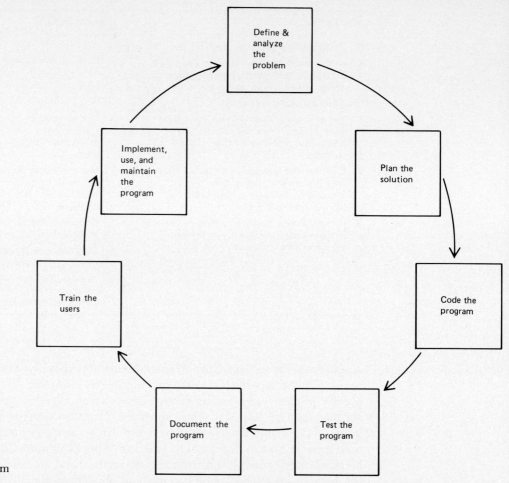

FIGURE 6.6
Computer program
life cycle.

Define and analyze the problem.   There are many reasons why an organization begins the program development process. Examples include new information needs, users noting a problem with the system, or newly imposed governmental requirements. After a need for program development becomes
apparent, users must gain authorization for the project. This usually requires
a statement of objectives and a preliminary analysis of costs and benefits as
justification for the program. Once permission is obtained, a systems analyst
studies the situation to determine user needs and to verify that a change to
the current system is indeed necessary. This study usually means that output
requirements and input sources must be determined and the contents of files
must be specified. A flowchart is often prepared to illustrate the preliminary
design of program data flows. The end result should be an agreement with the
users as to the detailed requirements to be met by the new software.

Plan the solution.   Once the problem has been defined and requirements specified, the next step is to plan how to meet the program requirements. This plan is a step-by-step approach to achieving the desired objectives. There are a number of programming tools that are available to the system analyst. These tools, which are explained later in the chapter, include program flowcharts and decision tables. Systems flowcharts, which were explained in Chapter 5, and HIPO charts, which are explained in Chapter 11, are also used.

Code the program.   Once the program has been planned, the next step in program preparation is to write the program instructions in a computer language, which is referred to as *coding*. The program can usually be coded relatively easily by using the program flowchart or decision table as a reference. However, care should be exercised to ensure that all programming language rules are followed. Once the coding is complete, the source program is keyed onto an input medium such as cards, tape, or disk.

In some organizations, there is a formalized review process called *structured walkthrough*. It consists of one or more programmers "walking through" the design logic of another programmer's code to detect weaknesses and errors in program design. Structured walkthroughs most often come at the conclusion of the design phase but also sometimes come at the end of the coding phase. The walkthrough can be accomplished in one of two ways. The first is that the program designer can make a presentation to all those who are to review the program design. Alternatively, those who are doing the reviewing can take copies of the program design and review it individually. The advantage of the group walkthrough is the interaction that is achieved. The disadvantage is that there might not be time for an in-depth analysis. Of course, the advantages of both approaches are achieved by allowing for individual study of the program prior to the group walkthrough. There are a number of benefits of the walkthrough beyond more error-free and effective programs. When programmers know others are going to review their programs, they tend to make them more readable and to make the documentation clearer and complete it sooner. Programmers also learn from each other by participating in the walkthrough.

Testing the program.   There are three different levels, or phases, that programmers use to test the programs they write. The first phase is called desk checking, which is a visual and mental review of the program to discover keying or programming errors. Desk checking is sometimes more effective if performed by someone other than the original programmer. After correcting any errors discovered during desk checking, the second test phase, involving program compilation, is attempted. If syntax errors have been made in writing the program, it will not compile. Any errors identified during program compilation must be investigated and corrected before the program can be run.

Once the program has been successfully compiled, the next step is to test the program for logic errors. Program testing often utilizes test data that simulate all possible real processing situations or input data combinations to which the program may be exposed. This would include all valid transactions and all possible error conditions. The response of the program to each test case is observed, and an improper response indicates that the program contains some flaw, or bug. An improper response would be the program's failing to process a valid transaction properly or failing to detect an error condition.

Programs are often tested in three phases. In the first phase, each individual program module is tested for internal consistency and correctness. In the second phase, program modules are linked together and tested to see that they interface properly. The error detection process is simplified if modules are linked one at a time or a few at a time. This minimizes the places that the error could be occurring and is more efficient than linking all modules together at once. The third phase is testing the program together with any other programs it must interface with. In other words, the program, as a part of the entire system, is tested.

Debugging is the process of discovering an error in a program and eliminating it once its existence is known. Once all the bugs have been removed, the program is ready for final compilation and utilization.

Document the program.   There are a number of reasons for documenting the system. One is to describe how the program works so others will know how to use the system. Another is to supplant human memory by helping the programmer and anyone that follows to understand what the computer does so the program can be modified or errors can be corrected. Attention should be given to this step throughout the program preparation process. For example, during the program coding, descriptive remarks should be inserted into the program where appropriate. Systems flowcharts, record layouts, program flowcharts, decision tables, and related items used in program preparation should be prepared according to prescribed standards and retained as part of the program documentation. When the program is finished, the program documentation should also be complete and ready to be organized into a meaningful documentation manual.

Train the users.   Before the program can be implemented, those who are to use the system must be trained. Training may take place during the latter portion of the test phase. The program documentation is often the material used to train the user.

Implement, use, and maintain the program.   The program is now ready to be used. It must be installed on the system and used as intended. During the time it is being used, any number of factors may require program revisions. This process is referred to as *program maintenance*. Examples of factors that may necessitate a specific change include requests from managers for new reports or for revisions in old reports; changes in program input or file content; changes in values, such as tax rates, that are part of the program; correction of a previously undiscovered bug; or modification to convert to new system hardware.

The utilization period of a business data processing program varies widely but usually is not longer than six or seven years. A program may be made obsolete (1) by business growth or a change in information needs within the business or (2) perhaps by changes in system hardware or software. At this point its life cycle has come to an end, and the program is discarded, replaced, or substantially revised.

Program design considerations

The fact that a single program may be used for several years underscores the importance of careful program design. Three basic principles of program design are discussed.

Modular or structured programs. This principle dictates that programs be composed of *modules,* which are small, relatively well defined segments or subroutines within a program. Program complexity is reduced and reliability and modifiability increased by having each of these modules perform a separate logical function. For example, in a file maintenance program that processes several different types of transactions, there could be a separate module for each transaction type. Each module should have only one entry point and one exit point to facilitate testing and changing individual modules. Generally, these modules should have no interaction with each other, interacting primarily, if not exclusively, with the program's control module or central logic section. The control module would be responsible for determining the type of each transaction, directing program control to the appropriate module, and passing data between modules. This modular approach to programming is generally referred to as *structured programming.* It is also referred to as "GOTO-less" programming because the modular design of the programs makes GOTO statements unnecessary.

Modularity should begin in the program design phase. A popular approach to designing a complex program is to determine the overall approach that the program should take. Once the approach has been determined and related program steps have been identified, each program step can be planned in greater detail. This process of designing a program from the top level down to the detail level is often referred to as *hierarchical program design.*

Modularity facilitates program design and utilization in several respects. Program preparation is made easier in many ways: program logic design is simplified; coding is made easier and may be split, with different programmers working on different program modules; documentation is made easier; and debugging is facilitated because errors requiring the correction of a module should not affect any other module. Modularity also makes a program easier to review and understand because the control module provides a capsule summary of the entire program. Program maintenance is also easier to accomplish.

Generality.   Programs should be designed for general usage, not for just a single specific task or set of requirements. This means that a program must be able to accommodate different sets of circumstances and changes in requirements. A general program is not as likely to generate unexpected errors and therefore will probably require less program maintenance. The key to applying the principle of generality is program planning and testing. Use of decision tables in program planning helps to ensure program generality, for a decision table may reveal unusual logical relationships that would not otherwise be planned for.

Maintainability.   Extra care in program design is justified if a program is made easier to maintain because program maintenance will be necessary over a period of several years. As mentioned above, program maintenance is simplified with programs that are modular and general. Good documentation is also an essential factor in easily maintained programs.

Programming and Documentation Tools

Program documentation should include a narrative description of the objectives, functions, and cost justification of the application. It should also contain systems flowcharts; an indication of the equipment configuration used; and *record layouts,* which illustrate the arrangement of items of data in input, output, and file records. Program flowcharts and decision tables, program listings, program change descriptions and authorizations, and instructions to the operator for running the programs should also be included. Additional items to include are a list of the recipients of each output report and a summary of the control features used in the system. Good application documentation of this type is essential to program development and system control.

Program flowcharts

A *program flowchart* illustrates the sequence of logical operations performed by a computer in executing a program. Like the systems flowchart, it uses a set of symbols with specialized meanings. The symbols used in program flowcharts and their meanings are shown in Fig. 6.7. Once designed and approved, the program flowchart serves as the blueprint for coding the computer program. The program flowchart represents the detailed steps performed within the process symbol of the systems flowchart.

A simple illustration of a program flowchart appears in Fig. 6.8. The flow direction line connects the other symbols and indicates the sequence in which logical operations are performed. In the absence of an arrowhead or other directional indicator, the sequence of operations is assumed to proceed from top to bottom and from left to right. The processing symbol represents a data movement or arithmetic operation, such as the assignment of a value to a variable or the performance of a calculation. The input/output symbol represents either the reading of input or the writing of output. The decision symbol represents a comparison of one or more variables and the transfer of flow

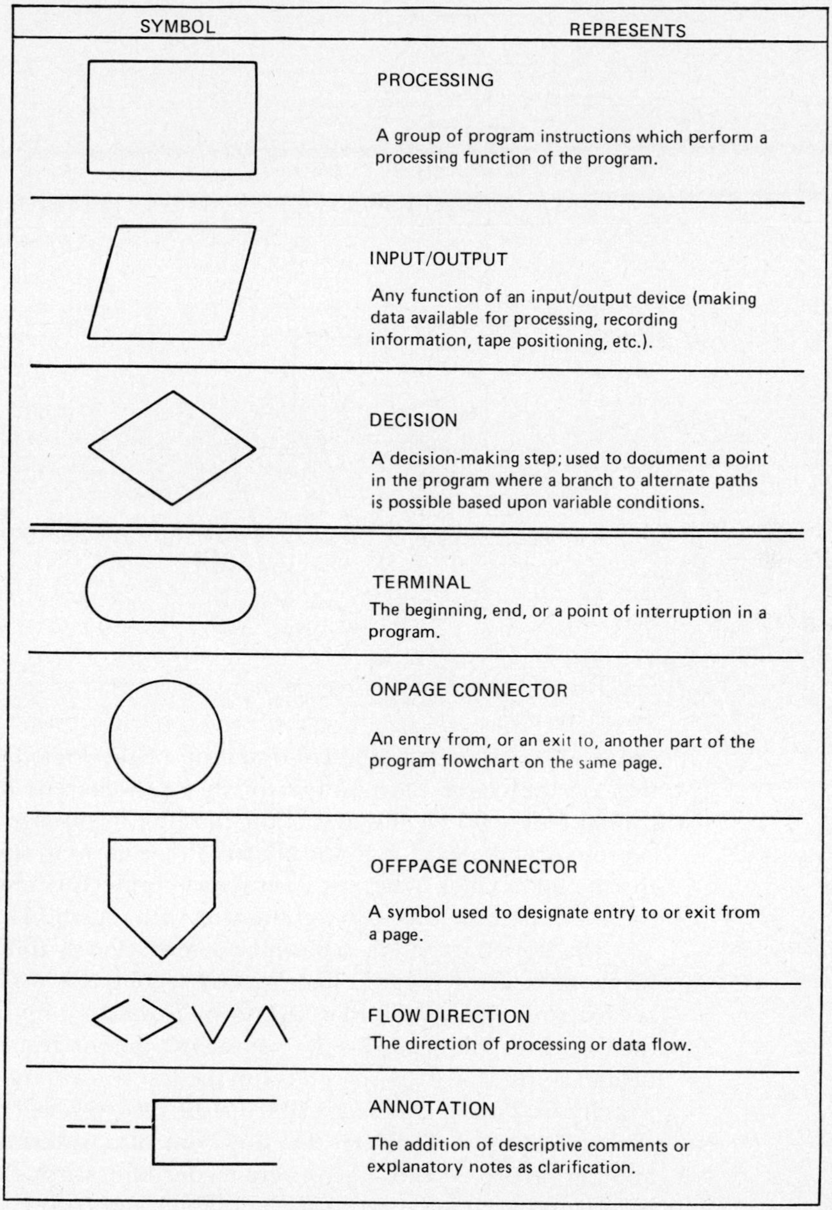

SYMBOL	REPRESENTS
	PROCESSING A group of program instructions which perform a processing function of the program.
	INPUT/OUTPUT Any function of an input/output device (making data available for processing, recording information, tape positioning, etc.).
	DECISION A decision-making step; used to document a point in the program where a branch to alternate paths is possible based upon variable conditions.
	TERMINAL The beginning, end, or a point of interruption in a program.
	ONPAGE CONNECTOR An entry from, or an exit to, another part of the program flowchart on the same page.
	OFFPAGE CONNECTOR A symbol used to designate entry to or exit from a page.
<> V ∧	**FLOW DIRECTION** The direction of processing or data flow.
	ANNOTATION The addition of descriptive comments or explanatory notes as clarification.

FIGURE 6.7
Program flowchart
symbols.

to one of two or more alternative locations, depending on the results of the comparison. All points in a program flowchart at which the flow begins, ends, or is interrupted are represented by the terminal symbol. The onpage and offpage connectors are not logic symbols but merely provide a convenient

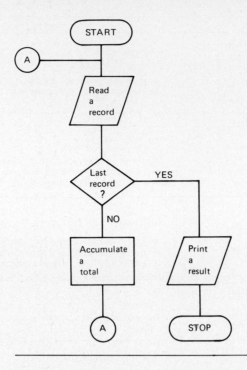

FIGURE 6.8
A simple program flowchart.

means of representing the continuation of the logic flow at a different location on the chart. Each connector in a flowchart is labeled with a digit or capital letter. When the logic flow reaches an onpage or offpage connector representing an exit, it continues from that point at the entry connector having the same label. Whereas several exit connectors may have the same label, there can be only one entry connector with a given label.

The flowchart in Fig. 6.8 can be interpreted as follows. After starting, the program reads a record. The next step compares one of the values in the record with a number that is known to occur only in the last record on the file. If yes, the record is the last record, the program branches to print a total and stops. If no, the record is not the last record, the next step accumulates a total based upon the data read from the record. The connector following this accumulation step indicates that flow control transfers back to the point where another record is read. The program continues through this loop of reading a record and accumulating a total until the last record is recognized.

Sequential file update flowchart.   A more complex example of a program flowchart, illustrating a generalized, sequential file update, appears in Fig. 6.9. There are two sets of inputs to this file maintenance program, a master file and an activity file. Both files are ordered in the same sequence. Each master file record contains an identifying number and a balance, and each activity record contains an identifying number and a positive or negative amount to

FIGURE 6.9

A generalized file maintenance program flowchart.

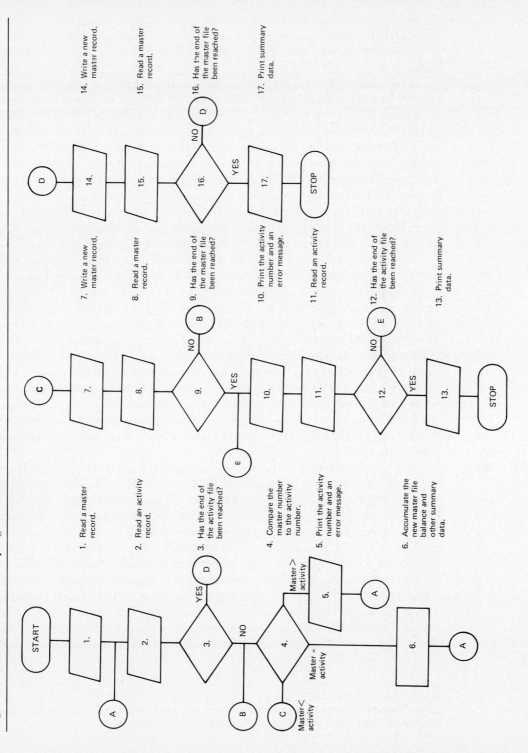

1. Read a master record.

2. Read an activity record.

3. Has the end of the activity file been reached?

4. Compare the master number to the activity number.

5. Print the activity number and an error message.

6. Accumulate the new master file balance and other summary data.

7. Write a new master record.

8. Read a master record.

9. Has the end of the master file been reached?

10. Print the activity number and an error message.

11. Read an activity record.

12. Has the end of the activity file been reached?

13. Print summary data.

14. Write a new master record.

15. Read a master record.

16. Has the end of the master file been reached?

17. Print summary data.

be used in updating the master record. There may be one, several, or no activity records pertaining to each master record. Output produced by the program consists of an updated master file and a printout of errors and summary data.

After reading both a master record and an activity record (steps 1 and 2), the file maintenance program determines if the end of the activity file has been reached (step 3). If it has, processing continues at step 14, through connector D. If the end of the file has not been reached, the program compares the master and activity identifying numbers (step 4). If a comparison of identifying numbers reveals that the master number is greater than the activity number, this indicates that the activity record was not matched with a master record. This is an error condition because a master record should be present for every activity record.[2] If this condition arises, the program prints an appropriate error message identifying the number of the activity record (step 5) and proceeds to read another activity record (step 2).

If the master file number and activity number are equal, a match exists and the program posts the activity amount to the master balance (step 6) and reads another record (step 2). This loop is continued until an activity record with a number higher than the master record is read. At that point, program control is shifted to the sequence headed by connector C, which writes the new master record (step 7). The fact that the identifying number of the activity is greater than the identifying number of the master indicates that there is no more activity pertaining to that master record, which is why the new master record is written at this point. The next step is to read the next master record (step 8) and then test to see if the end of the master file has been reached (step 9). If it has not, program flow, through connector B, returns the program to where the master file identifying number can be compared with that of the previously read activity record (step 4).

If in step 9 the end of the master file has been reached, steps 10 through 13 in the flowchart will be executed. These steps will not be executed in most runs of the program, but they are necessary in the unlikely event that the end of the master file is reached prior to the end of the activity file. In such an instance the activity record being processed and all subsequent activity records are in error, because they cannot match with a master record. Thus if the end of the master file is reached prior to the end of the activity file (step 9), an error message is printed indicating that there is no master record for the activity record in process (step 10) and another activity record is read (step 11). If the end-of-file check (step 12) indicates that this next record is not the end-of-file indicator, the program loops back to again print the error message (step 10) and read another activity record (step 11). When the end-of-file in-

---

[2]One other possibility (not provided for in this program) is that instead of being a regular transaction, this could be a new master record to be added to the master file. An additional set of program steps would be required to deal with this possibility.

dicator is read, the program prints out the summary data for the run (step 13) and stops execution.

When the end of the activity file is reached (step 3) the program writes the previously read or updated master record (step 14). Then, since there may be one or more master records that have not yet been processed, the program reads another master record (step 15) and checks for the end of the master file (step 16). If the record is a master record and not the end-of-file indicator, the program loops back up and writes the record on the new master file (step 14) and reads another master (step 15). This loop is continued until the end-of-file indicator is reached, at which point the program prints whatever summary data it may have accumulated as part of step 6 and stops execution. Note that the reading and writing of master records in this loop can continue without the need to check for activity because it is known before this loop is entered that there are no remaining activity records.

Decision tables

A *decision table* is a tabular representation of program logic that indicates the possible combinations of alternative logic conditions in the program and the corresponding courses of action taken by the program for each condition. Decision tables may be prepared as an alternative or as a supplement to program flowcharts. They differ in that program flowcharts emphasize the sequence of logical operations, whereas decision tables emphasize alternative logic relationships among the data being processed.

The general form of the decision table is illustrated in Fig. 6.10. The upper half of the decision table is concerned with the various logic conditions tested for in the input data. The lower half is concerned with the action steps

FIGURE 6.10
General form of a decision table.

STUB	ENTRY								
	Condition Rule Number								
Condition	1	2	3	4	5	6	7	8	9
(Specific									
conditions)									
	Action Rule Number								
Action	1	2	3	4	5	6	7	8	9
(Specific									
actions)									

taken by the program for each set of conditions. The condition portion of the table consists of a number of horizontal rows, each of which represents one condition test within the program. The action portion of the table also consists of a number of horizontal rows, each representing an action taken within the program. The conditions or actions are written out in the left half, or stub portion, of the table. The right half, or entry portion, of the table consists of a set of vertical columns, each representing one possible combination of logical relationships. Each such column is called a decision rule. Each entry in a cell of the upper-right quarter, or condition entry portion, of the table indicates the result of the condition test in that row. Each entry in a cell of the lower-right quarter, or action entry portion, of the table indicates whether or not the action in that row is executed if the decision rule in that column is met. These concepts are illustrated in the sample decision table of Fig. 6.11, which represents the file maintenance program flowcharted in Fig. 6.9.

The condition entries in a decision table may be in one of two forms. In the limited entry form, the condition test result may be either yes or no. An example is the condition test for end of activity in Fig. 6.11. In the extended entry form, more than two condition test results are possible, and the exact specifications of each result are indicated in the entry. As an example, consider the file maintenance program. In the comparison of master record and activity record account numbers, three results are possible. The master record account number may be (1) less than, (2) equal to, or (3) greater than the activity record account number. These conditions are entered in the condi-

FIGURE 6.11
Sample decision table
for generalized file
maintenance
program.

End of activity	No	No	No	Yes	No	Yes
End of master	No	No	No	No	Yes	Yes
Compare account number: Master vs. activity	M<A	M=A	M>A	——	——	——
Print activity number and error message				X	X	
Update new master and summary data		X				
Write new master record	X			X		
Read an activity record		X	X		X	
Read a master record	X			X		
Print summary data						X
Stop processing						X
Repeat this table	X	X	X	X	X	

tion entry portion of the decision table as $M < A$, $M = A$, and $M > A$, as shown in Fig. 6.11.

The remaining condition entry illustrated in the table is the dash, or "don't-care" entry. This indicates that the result of the condition test in that row makes no difference with respect to the decision rule of that column. For example, when the end of the activity file or the master file is reached in the sample program, a comparison of account numbers is no longer relevant. The don't-care entry may appear in either an extended entry row or a limited entry row.

The entry in each cell of the action entry portion of the table may be either an X or a blank. An X indicates that the action described in that row is performed if the input data meet all the condition tests specified in that column. A blank indicates that the action is not performed. Using the first column of Fig. 6.11 as an illustration, we see that if the input data represent the end of neither the activity file nor the master file, and if the account number of the master record is less than that of the activity record, the program writes a new master record, reads a master record, and repeats the condition tests in the table.

Several observations regarding the construction of decision tables are important. First, note that the decision rules in a table must be mutually exclusive. This means that no decision rules should be repeated in the table. Second, the set of decision rules should be logically complete. This means that there should be one decision rule for every possible combination of logical relationships among the input data. Fig. 6.12 shows how the completeness of limited entry decision tables can be verified. Third, to the extent possible, the conditions listed in the condition stub portion of the table should be sequenced in the order in which the conditions are to be tested in the program. In addition, the actions listed in the action stub should be sequenced in the order in which the actions are to be performed following the condition tests. This rule was followed in the decision table in Fig. 6.11 but cannot always be followed precisely. Finally, note that, for completeness, a decision table should include the action "repeat this table" if the program is designed to operate on more than one input record.

As a program planning tool, decision tables provide both advantages and disadvantages relative to program flowcharts. The primary advantage is that a decision table indicates clearly all the possible logical relationships existing among the input data. As a result the program can be prepared to recognize and respond properly to each possible decision rule. The primary disadvantage of decision tables relative to program flowcharts is that decision tables do not reflect the sequence in which operations are to be performed within the program. Another disadvantage of decision tables is that they may become unmanageably large if the program is quite complex. Since each approach has advantages and each approach mitigates the disadvantages of the other approach, both program flowcharts and decision tables are prepared by many programmers.

The following decision table for filling inventory orders is used to explain how the completeness of limited entry decision tables can be verified.

	a	b	c	d
Credit approved	N	Y	Y	Y
Order ≤ inventory on hand	—	N	Y	Y
Order > 500 units	—	—	N	Y
Reject order	X			
Back order		X		
Fill order			X	X
Give 20% discount				X

Completeness check: $\quad\quad 2^2 \quad\; 2^1 \quad 1 \quad\; 1$

$\quad\quad\quad\quad\quad\quad\quad\quad\quad\quad\quad 4 \;+\; 2 \;+\; 1 \;+\; 1 = 8 \text{ possible rules.}$

Total Possible Number of Rules

1. Total possible number of decision rules = 2^n,

2. Where n = number of conditional entries in a limited entry decision table.

3. Since there are three condition entries, there are 2^3, or 8, possible decision rules.

Completeness Check

1. Each column without a dash (don't-care) entry represents an independent decision rule.

2. Each don't-care entry represents two possible entries (a yes or a no, but it does not matter which).

3. To calculate the completeness check, examine each decision rule column.

   a) Those columns without don't-care entries are assigned a value of 1 (see columns c and d).

   b) Those columns with don't-care entries are assigned a value of 2^n, where n represents the number of don't-care entries. See column a— 2^2; also column b—2^1.

4. If the total number calculated in this manner equals the total possible, as is the case in this example (8 = 8), the decision table is complete.

FIGURE 6.12
Determining the completeness of limited entry decision tables.

Summary

Software languages have progressed through several different language generations: machine-level, symbolic (assembler), high-level (procedure), and fourth generation. Each succeeding generation has been more English-like and easier to learn and use.

Software programs can be divided into two separate categories: systems software and application software. Systems software controls the system and tells the computer how to operate or perform common routine tasks like sorting records or printing reports. Systems software consists of operating systems, data base management systems, utility or service programs, language translators, and communications software. Application software is written to accomplish specific information or transaction processing needs. Application software can be obtained in one of three ways: having it custom written, buying a "canned" or "off-the-shelf" software package, and buying an off-the-shelf package and modifying it.

There is a computer program life cycle that should be followed in developing software programs. The following steps should be followed: (1) define and analyze the problem, (2) plan the solution, (3) code the program (the solution), (4) test the program, (5) document the program, (6) train the users, and (7) implement, use, and maintain the program.

There are a number of programming and documentation tools that can improve the development and documentation process. This chapter discussed two of these—program flowcharts and decision tables.

Appendix: Procedure-Oriented Programming Languages

In this appendix a brief overview of some of the most common procedure-oriented languages is presented. This section is not intended to help the student develop a working knowledge of those languages but instead to provide a general knowledge of their basic characteristics. Its primary purpose is to develop a perspective on the nature of procedure-oriented languages and fourth generation languages and to establish a basis for discussion of the relative merits of these languages, particularly FORTRAN, COBOL, and BASIC.

The FORTRAN Language

FORTRAN was the first procedure-oriented language to be widely used and accepted. The name FORTRAN is an acronym for *FOR*mula *TRAN*slator. Development of the language was begun in 1955, and it has evolved through a number of versions. It is still one of the most popular computer languages, and most companies with a large computer have a FORTRAN compiler available.

The FORTRAN language is oriented toward scientific data processing problems that can be expressed in terms of mathematical formulas. It can also be applied to other kinds of problems, including business data processing. However, FORTRAN lacks many of the features that are desirable in a computer language for business and accounting applications. This is especially true with respect to the maintenance of files and the processing of complex data structures.

Despite its lack of business data processing orientation, FORTRAN should not be completely ruled out for all business applications. FORTRAN would be most appropriate for the application of mathematical modeling techniques to the solution of business problems. It is also appropriate for any situation in which there are a significant number of computations and the input and output processes are relatively straightforward. For installations that have only limited requirements for file processing, the lack of programmers skilled in more business-oriented languages may make it more appropriate to use FORTRAN even for file maintenance programs.

Figure A6.1 illustrates the FORTRAN language. The tasks that the program performs are (1) reading the records of utility customers, each of which contains the customer number, previous utility meter reading, and current reading; (2) calculating the amount of each customer's utility bill; and (3) printing out a report containing this information. A FORTRAN program consists of a series of statements, some of which are numbered because they are referred to elsewhere in the program. The statements in a FORTRAN pro-

```
        PROGRAM UTILITY
1       FORMAT(I4,2F6.0)
2       FORMAT(1X,I4,5X,F4.0,8X,F6.2,5X,F6.2,8X,F6.2)
3       FORMAT(1H1,13X,23HCUSTOMER BILLING REPORT)
4       FORMAT(2X,49HCUST      UTILITY     AMOUNT      AMOUNT      TOT AMT)
5       FORMAT(2X,49HNO        USAGE       RATE-1      RATE-2      CHARGED)
        OPEN (UNIT=6,ACCESS='SEQINOUT',DEVICE='PTR')
        OPEN (UNIT=5,ACCESS='SEQINOUT',DEVICE='RDR')
15      NTCR=0
        WRITE(6,3)
        WRITE(6,4)
        WRITE(6,5)
23      READ(5,1)NO,RD1,RD2
        IF(NO-9999)27,70,27
27      USE=RD2-RD1
        IF (USE-500.)31,31,35
31      AMT1=USE*.025
        AMT2=0.
        GO TO 40
35      AMT1=500.*.025
        AMT2=(USE-500.)*.03
40      TOT=AMT1+AMT2
        WRITE(6,2)NO,USE,AMT1,AMT2,TOT
        NTCR=NTCR+1
        IF (NTCR-30)23,15,15
70      STOP
        END
```

FIGURE A6.1
Sample FORTRAN
language program.

gram can be classified into three basic types—input/output, control, and arithmetic.

Both input and output operations in FORTRAN must utilize the FORMAT statement, which specifies the format in which the input data and output reports will appear. The READ statement, labeled number 23, performs the input operation in conjunction with the FORMAT statement labeled number 1. Output is accomplished by the use of the WRITE statement in conjunction with the FORMAT statement. The first three WRITE statements in the program result in the printing of headings for the output report, which are specified in FORMAT statements, numbers 3, 4, and 5. The WRITE statement near the bottom of the program, together with FORMAT statement number 2, performs the printing of output data for each customer.

Control statements regulate the sequence in which FORTRAN statements are executed. In the absence of control statements, the FORTRAN statements would be executed one at a time from top to bottom (except for FORMAT statements, which are not executed separately). The IF statement is one of the control statements in FORTRAN. An IF statement is executed by evaluating the expression that appears in parentheses following the IF. If the value of the expression is negative, control is transferred to the first statement number appearing after the closing parenthesis. If the value is zero, control transfers to the second statement number, and if the value is positive, to the third statement number. The GO TO statement directly transfers program control to the statement number indicated. Another common FORTRAN control statement that does not appear in the illustration is the DO statement. The DO statement establishes a loop in which a set of statements is executed over and over for a specified number of times. Another control statement is the STOP statement, which terminates the execution of the program.

Arithmetic statements accomplish the calculations in a FORTRAN program. All arithmetic statements appear in the form of an equation. A single variable name is to the left of the equal sign, and one or more variables or numbers appear on the right together with an indication of the operations (addition, multiplication, etc.) to be performed. The statement is executed by performing the operations on the right side and setting the left-side variable equal to the resulting value.

The COBOL language

COBOL is an acronym for *CO*mmon *B*usiness-*O*riented *L*anguage. As the acronym suggests, the language was designed specifically for business applications involving large amounts of records processing and file updating. The language was developed in 1960 and 1961 by a committee containing representatives of computer manufacturers and large users, including the federal government. This development group was called CODASYL, an acronym for *CO*nference on *DA*ta *SY*stems *L*anguages. COBOL is one of the most common procedure-oriented languages used for business data processing.

There are several reasons why COBOL is a superior language for writing file maintenance and related programs. One of the major factors is the self-documenting nature of the language. Instruction verbs and related syntax in COBOL describe the items they represent. This makes it much easier for a person other than the original programmer to understand what a given program is intended to accomplish. The superior documentation provided by COBOL also (1) facilitates communication among several programmers working on a single large project, (2) contributes to easier program testing and debugging, and (3) simplifies program maintenance over the life cycle of a program.

As will be explained in more depth in a later chapter, the additional documentation provided by COBOL is also a significant factor in the accounting control of a computer system. Such audit functions as program review, monitoring of program changes, tracing of audit trails, and the preparation of test decks are facilitated by good documentation. Some additional features of COBOL that serve to protect files from unintentional destruction include the provisions for assigning files to equipment and for automatic checking of file labels to guard against loading the wrong file for a job.

A sample COBOL program appears in Fig. A6.2. This program is designed to accomplish the same task as the FORTRAN program in Fig. A6.1. Every COBOL program consists of four major divisions—the IDENTIFICATION, ENVIRONMENT, DATA, and PROCEDURE DIVISIONS, which must always appear in that order. The IDENTIFICATION DIVISION is used only for documentation purposes and may contain only a program name. The ENVIRON-

```
IDENTIFICATION DIVISION.
PROGRAM-ID.  UTILITY BILLING
REMARKS.   PROGRAM COMPUTES A MONTHLY UTILITY BILL AND FORMATS A
           CUSTOMER BILLING REPORT.
ENVIRONMENT DIVISION.

CONFIGURATION SECTION.
SOURCE-COMPUTER.  DECSYSTEM-20.
OBJECT-COMPUTER.  DECSYSTEM-20.
SPECIAL-NAMES. PRINTER  IS PRTR.

INPUT-OUTPUT SECTION.
FILE-CONTROL.   SELECT USAGE-FILE ASSIGN TO CARD-READER.
                SELECT PRINT-FILE ASSIGN TO PRINTER.

DATA DIVISION.
FILE SECTION.
FD USAGE-FILE
        LABEL RECORD IS OMITTED
        RECORD CONTAINS 80 CHARACTERS.
01 USAGE-CARD.
        02 CUST-NO             PICTURE X(4).
        02 READ-1              PICTURE 9(6).
        02 READ-2              PICTURE 9(6).
        02 FILLER              PICTURE X(64).
FD PRINT-FILE
        LABEL RECORD IS OMITTED
        RECORD CONTAINS 136 CHARACTERS.
01 PRINT-LINE.
        02 FILLER              PICTURE X.
        02 CUST-NO-OUT         PICTURE X(4).
        02 FILLER              PICTURE X(5).
        02 USAGE-OUT           PICTURE 9(4).
        02 FILLER              PICTURE X(5).
        02 AMT-RATE-1          PICTURE ZZZ9.99.
        02 FILLER              PICTURE X(5).
        02 AMT-RATE-2          PICTURE ZZZ9.99.
        02 FILLER              PICTURE X(5).
        02 TOT-AMT-OUT         PICTURE ZZZ9.99.
        02 FILLER              PICTURE X(86).

WORKING-STORAGE SECTION.
        77 CTR                 PICTURE 99.
        77 NET                 PICTURE 9(6).
        77 AMT-R1              PICTURE 9999V99.
        77 AMT-R2              PICTURE 9999V99.
        77 NET-USAGE           PICTURE 9(6).
        77 TOT-AMT             PICTURE 9999V99.

PROCEDURE DIVISION.
START.   OPEN INPUT USAGE-FILE, OUTPUT PRINT-FILE.
HEAD-PROCEDURE.  MOVE 0 TO CTR.
        DISPLAY "1            CUSTOMER BILLING REPORT" UPON PRTR.
        DISPLAY " CUST      UTILITY      AMOUNT       AMOUNT      TOT AMT"
           UPON PRTR.
        DISPLAY " NO         USAGE       RATE-1       RATE-2      CHARGED"
           UPON PRTR.

READ-USAGE.   READ USAGE-FILE INTO USAGE-CARD AT END GO TO FINISHED.

COMPUTE-LOGIC.
        SUBTRACT READ-1 FROM READ-2 GIVING NET-USAGE.
        IF NET-USAGE IS GREATER THAN 500 PERFORM DISCOUNT
          ELSE PERFORM REG.
        ADD AMT-R1, AMT-R2 GIVING TOT-AMT, GO TO PRINTT.

DISCOUNT.
        MULTIPLY 500 BY .025 GIVING AMT-R1.
        SUBTRACT 500 FROM NET-USAGE GIVING NET.
        MULTIPLY NET BY .03 GIVING AMT-R2.

REG.
        MULTIPLY NET-USAGE BY .025 GIVING AMT-R1.
        MOVE 0 TO AMT-R2.

PRINTT.
        MOVE SPACES TO PRINT-LINE, MOVE NET-USAGE TO USAGE-OUT.
        MOVE TOT-AMT TO TOT-AMT-OUT.   MOVE AMT-R1 TO AMT-RATE-1.
        MOVE AMT-R2 TO AMT-RATE-2, MOVE CUST-NO TO CUST-NO-OUT.
        WRITE PRINT-LINE  ADD 1 TO CTR.
        IF CTR EQUALS 30 GO TO HEAD-PROCEDURE ELSE GO TO READ-USAGE.

FINISHED.  CLOSE USAGE-FILE, PRINT-FILE.  STOP RUN.
```

FIGURE A6.2
Sample COBOL
language program.

MENT DIVISION describes the equipment configuration on which the program will be run. The description includes the computer that will compile the program (the source computer) and the computer that will execute the program (the object computer). It also includes the devices that will be responsible for each input and output file.

The DATA DIVISION specifies the format of each input and output file and of each variable used in the program. The DATA DIVISION enables the establishment of a complex hierarchical file structure in which each record contains several fields, each field may contain several smaller fields, and so forth. Data editing provisions in COBOL facilitate the design of output reports having a very neat appearance, with dollar signs, debit and credit notation, commas, etc., inserted where appropriate. In the sample program the four lines under 01 USAGE-CARD describe the content of an input record to the program. The several lines under 01 PRINT-LINE describe the format of the output report. The lines under WORKING-STORAGE SECTION indicate the specifications for all variables used in the program but not contained in either an input or an output file.

The PROCEDURE DIVISION contains the actual instructions for processing. In the COBOL language these instructions are in the form of English language words. One can, therefore, fairly easily understand what the program does by reading the PROCEDURE DIVISION. COBOL PROCEDURE DIVISION statements perform the same set of functions as do FORTRAN statements. Input is accomplished in COBOL through the READ statement, and output through either the WRITE or DISPLAY statement. Control statements in COBOL include the IF and GO TO statements, which execute in a manner quite similar to their counterparts in FORTRAN. Arithmetic operations in COBOL are performed by statements such as those beginning with ADD, SUBTRACT, or MULTIPLY.

The BASIC language

BASIC is an acronym for *B*eginner's *A*ll-purpose *S*ymbolic *I*nstruction *C*ode. As the acronym implies, the language was designed to be very simple to learn so that nonprogrammers could easily use it. It bears a close resemblance to FORTRAN, although it is simpler and easier to learn than FORTRAN. BASIC is the language most commonly used both by small personal computer systems and by online time-sharing services.

A sample BASIC program appears in Fig. A6.3. Once again, this is a program written to accomplish the same task as those in Figs. A6.1 and A6.2. Note that all statements in BASIC must be numbered, and they are arranged in numerical order, which is not true of FORTRAN. READ statements together with DATA statements are one primary means of data input, and the PRINT statement is used for output. The IF and GO TO statements perform control functions as in FORTRAN. Very few conventions have to be learned to obtain a working knowledge of BASIC, but the language is lacking in some of the advanced features of FORTRAN.

```
00100 LET N=0
00110 PRINT '              CUSTOMER BILLING REPORT'
00120 PRINT
00130 PRINT 'CUSTOMER ','UTILITY','AMOUNT','AMOUNT','TOT AMT'
00140 PRINT ' NUMBER',' USAGE'.'RATE-1','RATE-2','CHARGED'
00150 READ N1,R1,R2
00160 IF N1=9999 THEN 290
00170 LET U =R2-R1
00180 IF U>500 THEN 220
00190 LET A1=U*0.025
00200 LET A2=0
00210 GO TO 240
00220 LET A1=500*.025
00230 LET A2=(U-500)*0.03
00240 LET T=A1+A2
00250 PRINT N1,U,'$';A1,'$';A2,'$';T
00260 LET N=N+1
00270 IF N=30 THEN 100
00280 GO TO 150
00290 STOP
00300 DATA 123,4700,5500,124,6300,6650,9999,0,0
00310 END
```

FIGURE A6.3
Sample BASIC
language program.

One of the special characteristics of BASIC is the INPUT verb (not shown in Fig. A6.3) that enables conversational programs to be written. Such programs interact with a user at a remote terminal by printing questions for him or her to type answers to, or by printing requests for specific data. The INPUT statement stops program execution until a response is received. After the user responds, the program continues its execution in accordance with the responses and may subsequently print output and/or ask for more input from the user.

Most online versions of BASIC are implemented using an interpreter rather than a compiler. This means that if the programmer makes an error in entering a line of BASIC code, the system will immediately respond with an error message. As a result, many kinds of programming errors can be detected and corrected prior to actually running the program.

The BASIC language, like FORTRAN, is not as effective or efficient as COBOL for file maintenance applications. It is not designed to handle large data processing chores, nor does it have the self-documenting features found in COBOL. However, it has many potential applications to mathematical problem solving in accounting. In fact, its simplicity gives it a significant advantage over FORTRAN for this purpose, since most accountants will not use such a language enough to justify an extensive learning effort. A common use of BASIC in accounting involves the programming of financial planning models, which simulate the financial aspects of a firm's operations for one or more years into the future. The interactive capability of the language enables such programs to be easily used by nontechnical persons, such as top management executives. Other areas of accounting in which BASIC is useful include tax planning and cost analysis.

Other languages

There are over 200 procedure-oriented languages. To give the reader an indication of some of the languages that are available, a few of them will be briefly mentioned here.

One very popular scientific and mathematical language is ALGOL (*ALGO*rithmic *L*anguage). It is an international algebraic language that is very popular in Europe. PASCAL, an increasingly popular language for both large and small computers, offers a powerful data structuring and data manipulation feature. It is an excellent language for instructional purposes because it requires the user to develop certain elements of good programming style. It was designed specifically to incorporate structured programming concepts and to facilitate top-down design. A language that is common in small installations with business applications is RPG (*R*eport *P*rogram *G*enerator). A language designed by IBM to incorporate features and advantages of both COBOL and FORTRAN is PL/1 (*P*rogramming *L*anguage *1*). It is a highly flexible, modular language that is oriented toward applications that require a significant number of computations and the processing of large amounts of data records. A language offered by IBM for time-sharing is APL (*A P*rogramming *L*anguage). It is especially useful in making vector and matrix computations. Several languages designed specifically for simulation problems include SIMSCRIPT, DYNAMO, and GPSS (*G*eneral-*P*urpose *S*ystems *S*imulator).

Generally, each computer language is designed to perform certain tasks well. This inevitably means that there are other tasks that the language does not perform well. It is probably not possible to design a universal language that will do a good job of satisfying the needs of all users. Therefore the present situation in which different languages are appropriate for different purposes may be expected to continue for the foreseeable future.

Review Questions

1. Define the following:

software	diagnostic message
computer program	syntax error
machine language	interpreter
assembler or symbolic language	interactive debugging
assembler	fourth generation languages
source program	ad hoc queries
object program	query languages
machine-dependent language	report generators
macroinstruction	program generators
procedure-oriented language	decision support systems software
problem-solving language	artificial intelligence
machine independent	expert system
compiler	application software

systems software
operating system
job-control language
data base management
   system
utility program
language translators
application programs
file maintenance programs
custom software
canned software
turnkey system

modified canned software
coding
structured walkthrough
debugging
program maintenance
modules
structured programming
hierarchical program design
record layout
program flowchart
decision table

2. List the three ways that computer software can be developed.

3. What are some of the reasons why accountants should be familiar with software? How do the reasons relate to the duties of an accountant?

4. Describe the process of converting a procedure-oriented source program into machine-language object code and then executing the program. Include a discussion on the outputs produced at the different steps in the conversion process.

5. Distinguish between a compiler and an interpreter. How is the translation different, and what is the difference in execution?

6. Identify and explain the classifications of problem-solving languages.

7. What are the advantages of fourth generation languages?

8. What are the major functions of systems software?

9. What has caused operating systems to change from simple to complex? Explain.

10. Identify and briefly describe some examples of utility routines.

11. What are the different types of language translators? Who provides them? Are they interchangeable from one type of machine to the next?

12. Distinguish between file maintenance and program maintenance and give an example of each.

13. What should a company do to properly control the development of software when it has contracted with an outside party for its development?

14. Describe how software houses "assemble" customized software packages for their clients.

15. Why is canned software usually less expensive than customized software?

16. What should determine which type of software (customized, canned, or modified) a company should acquire?

17. Outline the steps in computer program development.

18. Identify and explain the basic principles of program design.

19. Identify the symbols used in program flowcharting, indicate the meaning of each, and describe or give an example of the usage of each.

20. Explain why it is important to use structured programming concepts when developing a computer program.

21. In all batch processing file maintenance programs, one essential step is a comparison of the identifying number of the master record with that of the activity record. What are the three possible outcomes of this comparison? Explain one possible meaning of each outcome.

22. Describe the format of a decision table. What two forms can the condition entries in a decision table take? Explain both.

23. Describe the primary advantages and disadvantages of decision tables relative to program flowcharts as a tool of program preparation.

24. Why is COBOL a superior language for file maintenance and related programs?

25. What are the four major divisions of a COBOL program and what does each do?

26. What are the advantages and disadvantages of the BASIC language?

Discussion Questions

27. If the definition of computer software were to be restricted to programs, would you consider programming languages to be a form of software? Why or why not?

28. Is it necessary for an accountant in a firm that uses computers extensively in data processing to have either (a) some knowledge or (b) an expert's knowledge of programming in a language such as COBOL? Is it necessary for an auditor working for a public accounting firm to have either (a) some knowledge or (b) an expert's knowledge of programming in a language such as COBOL? Discuss both of these.

29. Programs can be custom-made or purchased off the shelf, or purchased programs can be modified. All three of these alternatives have advantages and disadvantages. In this age of increasing computer importance, which do you feel will become most predominant? Do you feel that any of the methods will be phased out? Does your response vary depending on the type and size of the user organization being considered?

30. Accountants in all the specialty areas are experiencing increased exposure to the computer. The accountant uses computers both in his or her work at the office and at the client's location. Also, the accountant's clients are increasing their use of computers. Discuss how an accountant in each of the functional areas of tax, audit, and MAS (Management Advisory Services) uses computers and what he or she needs to be aware of when exposed to the client's computer system.

Problems and Cases

31. The Hi-Lo Manufacturing Company utilizes a medium-sized computer system for data processing. Compilers for both the FORTRAN and COBOL languages are available, as are programmers who specialize in each language.

The company has decided to write a computer program to analyze its monthly financial statements. Input to the program would consist of detailed balance sheets and income statements for the current and preceding months. The program would calculate various ratios, percentages, growth rates, etc., and print out an analysis in the form of several schedules. The program would, of course, be run once monthly.

REQUIRED

a) What arguments could be made favoring the use of COBOL in writing this program? Of FORTRAN? Explain.
b) What arguments could be made for buying a canned software package?
c) What arguments could be made for buying and modifying a canned software package?
d) What would you have to know before you could decide which of these three approaches is best?

32. Don Otno is confused. He has been looking into software for several months and has narrowed his software selection decision to three alternatives. He can't decide between the three alternatives and has come to you for help.

Computers Made Easy (CME), a computer store located in Otno's office complex, was where Otno started his search. He almost wished he hadn't looked any further. Steve Young, the manager of CME, appeared to be very knowledgeable and listened attentively as Otno explained his problems, needs, and concerns. The manager had asked Otno a list of hard questions, a number of which he couldn't answer. At the end of that first visit, Steve had asked Otno to find out the answers to the questions he couldn't answer and to return the next day. Steve felt he had the solution to Otno's problem.

The next day, Otno went back with the answers, and after discussing them, Steve stated that he had a series of prepackaged software packages that would, with a few exceptions, come fairly close to meeting Otno's needs. The packages run on one of two high-powered microcomputers that

Steve carried. He could fix Otno up with a complete package, and Don could start implementing the package almost immediately. The price for the whole system was unexpectedly reasonable.

Otno was impressed but cautious. He had heard too many stories about bad vendor choices when the buyer didn't shop around. His next visit was to Custom Designed Software (CDS), who sold hardware and wrote customized software for their clients. This time Otno was prepared for all their questions and after three hours left convinced that CDS could produce a program that was exactly what he needed. Cost and time estimates hadn't been established, but CDS assured him that the cost would be reasonable and that the programs would only take a few months to complete.

Seeking a third opinion, Otno called a friend who had computerized several years ago. The friend recommended he visit Modified Software Unlimited (MSU). The MSU representative was very persuasive. She said customized packages were very good but expensive. Packaged software was inexpensive, she said, but rarely met all your needs. The best of both worlds could be obtained by MSU modifying the package that came closest to meeting Don's needs. The resultant software would, like the custom software, meet Otno's needs better than the packaged software but would be cheaper than the custom software.

On his way back to his office, Don stopped by CME and tactfully asked Steve's opinion of customized software and modified packages. Steve expressed enough concerns about both types that Otno came full circle: thinking that packaged software was best.

Late that night at dinner he realized that he really wasn't qualified to make the decision. He would be swayed by whichever vendor he was talking to at the time. The next morning he called you for help.

Recognizing the opportunity to render an important service, you agreed to counsel him on the subject. At Otno's request, you agreed to conduct a study and submit a report showing the advantages and disadvantages of each of the three vendor's approaches. The report is to be concluded by your recommending a course of action to Otno.

REQUIRED

a) Outline the report contents by identifying the advantages and disadvantages to each approach.

b) Recommend a course of action that you feel would be best for Otno and support your decision.

33. The following was adapted from an article that appeared in an issue of *Computerworld*,[3] a weekly magazine dealing with the computer industry.

WASHINGTON, D.C.—One unhappy federal agency recently spent almost $1 million on a software development contract that produced no

---

[3]Jake Kirchner, "GAO Tells a $970,000 Horror Story," reprinted from *Computerworld*, December 3, 1979, p. 12. Copyright 1979 by CW Communications/Inc., Framingham, MA 01701.

usable software, the General Accounting Office (GAO) reported. The million-dollar boondoggle resulted from an agency contract to design an integrated personnel/payroll system originally contracted out for $445,158 and 15 months. The agency terminated the contract after 28 months with nothing to show for an expenditure of $970,000.

When it issued the request for proposals for the software, the agency was still in the initial stages of system development. It had not fully developed user requirements or system specifications for any of the proposed software. The agency awarded a fixed-price contract requiring phased software development, but did not require agency approval of a completed phase before work continued. The contract did not contain acceptance testing procedures and did not identify quality criteria for documentation. Delivery dates, the scope of work, and costs were revised several times. The contractor complained of extensive changes requested and inexcusable delays caused by the agency. Agency officials acknowledged that some of the changes requested were not clearly identified in the contract and that others were obviously outside the scope of the work.

The contractor further maintained that the agency took too much time to review products submitted for approval. The agency admitted the delays, but blamed those delays on the poor quality of the documentation under review. The contractor did not clearly understand the software systems the agency desired because the contract did not specify system requirements or performance criteria. Both agency and contractor staff agreed that the contract was not specific, that the terminology was vague and that many systems requirements were not clearly identified. The contractor did not wait for approval of completed phases before proceeding. When the agency rejected the general system design, the contractor had to scrap work already done on detailed system work.

User requirements were never adequately defined and frozen, and changes delayed completion schedules, increased contract costs, and caused the agency and the contractor to disagree about whether the new requirements were included in the original scope of work. The contract was amended 13 times to provide for additional work to be done to add or delete requirements and to reimburse the contractor for the extra costs resulting from agency-caused delays. The amendments were to increase the cost of the contract to $1,037,448.

The agency eventually became convinced that the contractor could not deliver at an acceptable time and cost, canceled the contract, and tried to withhold payment for poor performance. A negotiated settlement price of $970,000 was agreed upon. None of the software was ever used by the agency.

REQUIRED

a) What went wrong in this particular case? Whose fault is it?
b) How could the agency have done a better job of managing the systems development project? The contractor?
c) Can we generalize from this case that organizations and agencies should not try to have custom software written for them?

34. A city in the Midwest, with a population of 45,000, purchased a mini-computer from a major mainframe vendor and set about the task of developing applications programs with an in-house staff of programmers. Four years later, an analysis of the system showed that only one new major applications system had been programmed in four years. Further analysis showed that the one program was neither complete nor functioning properly. Moreover, none of the applications software running on the system fully met the minimum requirements of users. The system, both the hardware and the applications software, frequently failed. The annual DP personnel budget was in excess of $100,000.

    The analysis also showed that purchase of a similarly configured system, fully programmed with packaged software, would have saved the city nearly half a million dollars. What is more, the city's annual DP costs exceed the annual costs of a brand-new turnkey system with packaged software.

REQUIRED
    a) Why would the city have been better off purchasing canned software?
    b) Do you think the city would have been able to find software to adequately meet its needs?
    c) Why do you think the city was unable to produce quality, workable systems?

35. This exercise involves tracing the operations performed on a hypothetical set of master and activity records through the program flowchart of Fig. 6.9. Assume that the master file and activity file are composed of the record numbers shown below in the sequence given.
    Master: 011, 013, 014, 015, 016, 017, 018, 019, EOF
    Activity: 011, 012, 014, 014, 016, 018, EOF

REQUIRED
    a) Construct a table containing five columns with headings as follows: Read Master, Read Activity, Match, Write Master, Write Error. Begin tracing the records above through the program. Each time a record is read, a match is found between a master and activity record, or a record is written, write down the identifying number of the record in the appropriate column of the table. Number each item that you write in the table in sequence beginning with one. Continue until you have traced all records through the program.
    b) Assume that there had been an activity record with the number 020 after record number 018 and in front of the end-of-file record. Beginning at the point at which this change would first have made a difference, trace the records through the program to the finish, recording in your table as described above.

36. You are to modify the generalized file maintenance program flowchart (Fig. 6.9) and the related decision table (Fig. 6.11) to provide for the possibility that some of the activity records may be newly created master records that are to be added to the file. To simplify this problem, you may

assume that there should not be any regular activity records that update the newly created master records.

REQUIRED
a) Prepare the revised decision table.
b) Prepare the revised program flowchart. Note that the rightmost module of the flowchart (steps 14–17) is not affected by the required modification and need not be redrawn.
c) Suppose that we drop the simplifying assumption and allow regular activity records that update the newly created master records. Briefly discuss the additional complexities that this would introduce into the program.

37. Prepare a program flowchart and a decision table for the following program.

Input to the program consists of an accounts receivable file containing (among other things) the amount due, due date, and credit limit for each customer. The program checks the due date of each customer record against the current date and prepares an aging schedule. Each customer's record is listed on a separate line of the aging schedule, with the amount due printed in one of three columns: (1) less than 60 days past due, (2) 61–180 days past due, and (3) over 180 days past due.

The program next compares the amount due with the customer's credit limit. Customer records that are both over 180 days past due and have an amount due in excess of the credit limit are printed on a "Bad Debts Report" for possible writeoff by the credit manager. Other accounts that have an amount due in excess of the credit limit are printed on a "Credit Review Report" that goes to the Treasurer.

After the last record in the accounts receivable file is processed, the program is halted.

38. Prepare a program flowchart and a decision table for the program described below.

Input to the program consists of records in an inventory file, each of which contains the item number, quantity on hand, price, and total cost of an inventory item. At the beginning of processing, and after every fifty lines of output, the program prints a set of report headings.

For each input record, the program calculates the product of price and quantity on hand and then compares this product with the total cost. If the product and total cost do not agree, the item number and an error message are printed out on one line. If the product and total cost do agree, the four items of data in each record are printed out, along with a message, on one line of the report. The message field contains blank spaces if the total cost of the item is less than $1000; otherwise, the message is used to place the label "high-value item" beside the item.

When the end of the inventory file is reached, processing is halted.

39. The Andy Dandy Co. is a retailer, in the business of buying goods from wholesalers and reselling these goods to the public. The company wishes to make its purchases from the most reliable wholesaler. The following information was compiled and is now available to the computer:

☐ A quality rating from 1 to 4 for each wholesaler (1 is considered the highest).

☐ Percentage of times each wholesaler has been late in delivering each Andy Dandy Co. order.

☐ If each wholesaler's prices have been stable or unstable.

☐ If each wholesaler is in an economically rich area or a depressed area.

☐ Whether or not each vendor has suggested new products from time to time.

Purchasing personnel have established the following criteria to be used in wholesaler selection.

☐ If the quality rating is 1, award the wholesaler with 20% of the business.

☐ If the quality rating is 2, and the wholesaler is not more than 10% late, award him with 15% of the business.

☐ If the quality rating is 2 and the wholesaler is more than 25% late, reject him.

☐ If the quality rating is 2 and the wholesaler is between 10% and 25% late, award him with 10% of the business, but only if prices have been stable.

☐ If the quality rating is 3 and the wholesaler is not more than 5% late, award him with 10% of the business, but only if he is in a depressed area and if he has been good at suggesting new products.

☐ If the quality rating is 4, reject the wholesaler.

REQUIRED

Prepare a decision table to show the computer logic that is needed to write a program for vendor selection for the Andy Dandy Co. (SMAC Examination adapted)

References

Aron, Joel D. *The Program Development Process.* Reading, Mass.: Addison-Wesley, 1974.

Bohl, Marilyn. *Information Processing.* 3d ed. Chicago: Science Research Associates, 1980.

Boillot, Michel H.; Gary M. Gleason; and L. Wayne Horn. *Essentials of Flowcharting.* Dubuque: Wm. C. Brown, 1975.

Capron, H. L., and Brian K. Williams. *Computers and Data Processing.* Menlo Park, Calif.: Benjamin/Cummings, 1982.

Chapin, Ned. *Flowcharts.* Princeton, N.J.: Auerbach, 1971.

Datapro Research Corporation. *Datapro 70: The EDP Buyer's Bible.* Delran, N.J.: Datapro Research Corporation, 1986.

———. *Datapro Applications Software Solutions.* Delran, N.J.: Datapro Research Corporation, 1986.

————. *Datapro Directory of Software.* Delran, N.J.: Datapro Research Corporation, 1986.

Davis, Gordon B., and Margrethe H. Olsen. *Management Information Systems.* 2d ed. New York: McGraw-Hill, 1985.

Enockson, Paul G. *A Guide for Selecting Computers and Software for Small Business.* Reston, Va: Reston Publishing, 1983.

Kirchner, Jake "GAO Tells a $970,000 Horror Story." *Computerworld,* December 3, 1979, p. 12.

Martin, James. *Application Development without Programmers.* Englewood Cliffs, N.J.: Prentice-Hall, 1982.

Morris, Robert A. "Comparison of Some High-Level Languages." *BYTE* (February 1980): 128–139.

Moscove, Stephen A., and Mark G. Simkin. *Accounting Information Systems.* 2d ed. New York: John Wiley & Sons, 1984.

Murach, Mike. *Structured COBOL.* Chicago: Science Research Associates, 1980.

O'Brian, James A. *Computers in Business Management.* Homewood, Ill.: Richard D. Irwin, 1985.

Ogdin, Carol Anne. "The Many Choices in Development Languages." *Mini-Micro Systems* (August 1980): 81–84.

Reifer, Donald J., and Stephen Trattner. "A Glossary of Software Tools and Techniques." *Computer* (July 1977): 52–60.

Shneiderman, Ben. *Software Psychology.* Cambridge, Mass.: Winthrop, 1980.

Stair, Ralph M. *Principles of Data Processing.* Homewood, Ill.: Richard D. Irwin, 1984.

Zelkowitz, Marvin V. "Perspectives on Software Engineering." *Computing Surveys* (June 1978): 197–216.

C H A P T E R 7

Microcomputers and Accounting Information Systems

LEARNING OBJECTIVES

Careful study of this chapter should enable students to:

- ☐ Explain why accountants need to be able to understand and use microcomputer technology.

- ☐ Explain the risks and benefits associated with microcomputer technology.

- ☐ Identify and describe the features, benefits, and uses of the hardware components used in microcomputer systems.

- ☐ Identify and describe the capabilities, benefits, and uses of the different types of microcomputer software.

Through the 1960s, mainframe computers cost so much that their purchase could only be justified in large organizations. When smaller and less powerful computers, called minicomputers, were introduced in the 1970s, only medium-sized organizations or departments in large organizations could afford them. In the early 1970s technological advances made possible the production of integrated circuits that contained all CPU logic on a single chip. This development paved the way for the birth of microcomputers. Today, microcomputers, or desktop computers, are so inexpensive that organizations of any size and even individuals can easily afford them. Not only is it now financially feasible for most individual workers to have their own personal computers, but they are easy enough to use that they are referred to as "user-friendly." This means that people with little or no technical background can use them with a minimal amount of training.

An Introduction to Microcomputers

The first microcomputers were produced in the mid-1970s in the form of a $400 kit for electronic hobbyists. In the late 1970s the Apple II was introduced, and microcomputers were available to the general public. When IBM entered the market in late 1981, the microcomputer market was then estimated at several hundred thousand units per year. Those estimates proved to be very pessimistic. It is estimated that fourteen million microcomputers were shipped in 1986, and that sales will increase by twenty-five to fifty percent a year through the 1980s.

In the mid-1980's ads in computer magazines stated that if the automobile industry had made the same progress that the computer industry had, a Mercedes-Benz would cost $2.50 and get two million miles per gallon. In a similar vein, if the aircraft industry had evolved as spectacularly as the computer industry, a Boeing 767 would cost $500 and would circle the globe in twenty minutes on five gallons of fuel.[1] These performances are analogous to the reduction in cost, the increase in speed, and the decrease in energy consumption of computers. The result is a personal computer that for less than $5000 is as powerful as the large mainframe computers of the 1970s and the minicomputers of the early 1980s. They come in all shapes and sizes, ranging from those that occupy much of a desktop to those that fit inside a briefcase. Enormous sums are spent on research and development, and new products with improved technology are announced regularly. Apple, for example, has spent as much as $75 million a year on research and development.

There are over 200 microcomputer manufacturers. Thousands of other companies provide support by developing software, by manufacturing peripheral devices, by selling system components, and by providing training,

---

[1] Hoo-Min D. Tong and Amar Gupta, "The Personal Computer," *Scientific American* (September 1982): 87.

FIGURE 7.1
The IBM Personal
Computer AT (Model
339), with monitor,
Enhanced Personal
Computer Keyboard,
a 1.2 megabyte
diskette drive, a 30
megabyte fixed disk
drive, and a 512
kilobyte memory
expandable to 10.5
megabytes. (Courtesy
of IBM Corporation)

service, maintenance, consulting services, and a myriad of other products and services. In a few short years, microcomputers have become one of the fastest growing areas of the computer industry, sparking what some are calling a "second computer revolution." So great has been their impact that some people claim that micros will eventually have a greater impact than the Industrial Revolution. While that may or may not be true, microcomputers have certainly become one of the most common, yet important, personal and professional productivity tools. Figure 7.1 is a picture of the IBM Personal Computer AT, one of the best-selling larger microcomputers.

Accountants are becoming heavy users of microcomputers. Accordingly, accounting graduates must have an understanding of microcomputer hardware and software and must understand how to use them. A recent study shows what the employers of some accounting graduates considered necessary to function in their organizations.[2] Figure 7.2 shows that the majority of the companies surveyed want new hires to have either an in-depth or a working knowledge of operating systems, electronic spreadsheets, data base management systems, word processing, and methods of transferring data between programs.

---

[2]Thomas C. Waller and Rebecca A. Gallun, "Microcomputer Literacy Requirements in the Accounting Industry," *Journal of Accounting Education* **3** (Fall 1985): 31–40.

	NON–BIG EIGHT CPA FIRMS (%)	BIG EIGHT CPA FIRMS (%)	INDUSTRY (%)
Operating systems			
In-depth or working knowledge	73	62	46
Overview	27	38	38
No knowledge	0	0	16
Electronic spreadsheets			
In-depth or working knowledge	100	100	92
Overview	0	0	8
No knowledge	0	0	0
Data base management			
In-depth or working knowledge	53	62	62
Overview	47	38	38
No knowledge	0	0	0
Word processing			
In-depth or working knowledge	33	50	70
Overview	53	50	8
No knowledge	14	0	22
General ledger			
In-depth or working knowledge	60	12	54
Overview	20	88	31
No knowledge	20	0	15
Programming (BASIC)			
In-depth or working knowledge	33	37	53
Overview	20	38	31
No knowledge	47	25	16
Graphics			
In-depth or working knowledge	13	50	54
Overview	67	38	38
No knowledge	20	12	8
Modems and networks			
In-depth or working knowledge	20	50	16
Overview	67	50	76
No knowledge	13	0	8
File transfer			
In-depth or working knowledge	60	43	77
Overview	33	43	23
No knowledge	7	14	0
Downloading from mainframe			
In-depth or working knowledge	13	37	77
Overview	73	63	23
No knowledge	14	0	0

FIGURE 7.2
Depth of microcomputer knowledge desired of new accountants.

Programming languages—BASIC programming in particular—was the only topic where more than just a few of the respondents felt that no knowledge was required. Many of these firms also make computer literacy a requirement for promotion. As time passes, microcomputer competence as a condition of employment and advancement will increase.

Benefits and risks of microcomputer usage

There are a number of reasons why microcomputer usage has increased so significantly. Most relate to the ability of users to create, control, and implement their own information systems. This is known as *end-user computing*. In traditional program design, the users must specify what they need, and a systems analyst translates those needs into a series of specifications that the programmer uses to write the program. In end-user computing, users identify the problem, specify what information must be produced, and create an application that meets their needs. The information is usually produced on a timely basis, and the information produced can usually be easily changed as requirements change. These systems almost always meet the users' needs. There is no scheduling of meetings between all the involved parties, no waiting for time on the mainframe computer, and less waiting on others. Users can create the system at their convenience, and if the micro is transportable, this creation can be done at home, on a plane, at work, or anywhere the microcomputer can be set up. The benefits and risks of microcomputer usage are summarized in Fig. 7.3.

There are, however, some significant drawbacks to end-user computing and to eliminating analyst/programmer involvement in systems creation. Perhaps the problems inherent in user-created applications can best be illustrated with an example.

> Let me tell you a true story from the oil and gas industry. One of the O&G majors was looking at a proposed acquisition last spring. One member of the hush-hush team analyzing the deal was a spreadsheet whiz who built a lot of very sophisticated-looking models, using 1–2–3.
>
> When the group had finished its work, which showed that the company should go ahead with the acquisition, a couple of people from the firm's Big Eight CPA firm were brought in to examine and bless the results. The CPAs plugged copies of the working group's data disks into their own PCs, played their own "what if" games and decided the data looked good.
>
> Back at the company, the leader of the working group and a high-level aide to the company's chief financial officer were assigned the job of pitching the acquisition to the board of directors. The aide, wanting to be ready for tough questions from the directors, played his own "what if" games with the data disks the day before the special meeting of the board. Trying to understand the underlying logic in the formulas, he suddenly discovered that something was very, very wrong with the numbers. A panicky afternoon and evening followed. The working group was hastily reassembled. The accounting firm's local managing partner was called; he came over with the two partners who'd approved the work. They called for a half-dozen colleagues.

Benefits of Microcomputer and End-User Computing

□ *User creation, control, and implementation.* Users can identify and meet many of their needs without having to use a systems analyst or programmer.

□ *Faster development.* With user-created applications, much of the delay inherent in the traditional system development process is avoided.

□ *Ease of use.* Compared with other computer systems, micros are easy to learn, use, and operate. This is evidenced by the number of people currently using micros and the fact that many micro users previously knew virtually nothing about computers.

□ *Affordability.* For a few thousand dollars, an individual can have a CPU, a keyboard, two diskette drives, a printer, a monitor, and a modem.

□ *Versatility.* Micros are versatile enough to handle most information processing needs using word processors; spreadsheets; data bases; and data communications, accounting, financial modeling, and decision support packages.

□ *Increases in productivity.* Microcomputers can improve the quality of users' work; handle complex tasks; eliminate or reduce time-consuming, repetitive tasks; and free users for more creative, thought-oriented activities and for planning and control functions.

Risks of Microcomputers and End-User Computing

□ *Logic errors.* Mary user-created systems are developed by inexperienced users who are more likely to err and less likely to recognize that an error has been made.

□ *Inadequate testing.* Users are not as likely to rigorously test their applications either because they are not cognizant of the need or because of the difficulty or time-consuming nature of the testing process.

□ *Poorly designed systems.* User-created systems are more likely to be poorly designed because of inadequate problem definition or system requirements.

□ *Inefficient systems.* Inexperienced users often take longer to develop a system that often does not operate as efficiently as one developed by a professional.

□ *Poor control.* User-created systems often fail to include any type of input, output, processing, security, or backup and recovery controls.

□ *Poor documentation.* User-created systems are often poorly documented.

□ *Inability to solve problems.* Because others are rarely involved in the analysis, design, and implementation of end-user systems, the user generally must be the one to fix the application when something goes wrong. If the user is unable to resolve the problem, it may not get resolved. It often takes too long for someone else to become acquainted with the purpose and design of the system.

FIGURE 7.3
Benefits and risks of microcomputer systems.

There was no pitch to the board. The deal would have been a disaster. A very few sloppy formulas in the spreadsheets had skewed the projection of what could be gotten from spinning off properties, what a restatement of reserves would mean and what would happen when a consolidated balance sheet was prepared for the combined entities. The spreadsheet jock was fired. That Big Eight accounting firm no longer does any special work for the company and won't have the O&G company as an audit client much longer.

I shudder to think how common are mistakes like that now that so many of the assumptions we make in preparing pro formas and other complex analyses on our micros are hidden behind the calculated values that appear in our worksheets. I was telling this story to a group of accountants recently. One protested that it sounded pretty unlikely to him. He was almost hooted out of the room by his colleagues. They thought it rang perfectly true and said that they worried about the problem a lot. It turned out later that the graybeard who was skeptical didn't use a micro himself at all and simply didn't understand how electronic spreadsheets work.[3]

Although the example deals with spreadsheet software, similar problems are possible with other microcomputer software. As the complexity and sophistication of the system and the quantity of data processed by the application increase, the greater the likelihood of a problem. Many of the risks summarized in Fig. 7.3 are common to all information systems. However, they are more likely to occur in user-created systems because of the lack of system analyst involvement and the inexperience of the users developing the system. Although the risks are real, they have to be put into perspective and viewed in light of the benefits to be achieved. Most organizations want the benefits of user-created systems and do not want to curb their development. At the same time, however, they want to minimize their risks. This can be done by providing systems analysts as advisers and reviewers and by requiring that user-created systems be reviewed and documented before they are used. In addition, users can be trained in the systems analysis process so they can identify and adequately meet their needs and so they can review the work of other users.

Microcomputer Hardware

Microprocessors, memory, and the CPU

The central processing unit (CPU) in a microcomputer is a *microprocessor*. A microprocessor is a large-scale integrated circuit on a silicon chip. Other silicon chips constitute the computer's primary memory, where both instructions and data are stored. Still other chips govern the input and output of data and carry out control operations.

Microcomputer chips are often given a number for a name. For example, some of the recent chips are known as the 6502, Z80, 68000, 8080, 8088, 8086, 80286, and 80386 chips. At the time this book was written, the Intel 80386 was the newest chip on the market, and many micro manufacturers were designing new machines based on the chip. Many feel this chip will finally lead to mainframe power in a desktop computer. An in-depth discussion of these chips and which machines use which chips is beyond the scope of this text. Even if it were not, there would almost certainly be new and enhanced chips on the market by the time this book was printed. For example, as this is written, developers are working on a multifunction chip that will combine the functions of many current chips onto a single chip. This should lead to a significant reduction in the size and cost of microcomputers.

The chips are mounted on a heavy plastic circuit board called the main circuit board, or *"motherboard."* Communications between the computer's electrical components, in the form of digital electronic pulses, travel along an

---

[3]Jim Seymour, "Left Unchecked, Spreadsheets Can Be a What-If Disaster," reprinted from *PC Week* (August 21, 1984): 37. Copyright © 1984, Ziff Communications Company.

electrical connector, called a *data bus,* that connects the various components of the microcomputer. The electrical pulses are synchronized and controlled to keep them from interfering with each other. Many of the more recent personal computers have more than one bus to speed up operations. Figure 7.4 shows a data bus and a diagram of how the hardware components of a microcomputer system are hooked to it.

Most personal computers have *expansion slots* on the motherboard that allow the user to increase the memory capacity of the computer. They also allow other functions such as a battery-operated clock/calendar, modems, and additional communication ports to be added. Separate boards can be inserted for each of these functions, but that uses too many expansion slots. To conserve slots, *multifunction boards* were created. They combine additional memory and several of the more desirable functions on one board.

There are three important measures of the speed and computational power of a microprocessor. The first is the *word size,* or the number of bits processed at one time. The second is the frequency of the processor's electronic clock, or how many steps a computer can execute per second. The third is the bus size, or the number of bits that can, at one time, be transmitted from one location in the computer to another. The trend is toward a larger word and bus size and a higher frequency. As the word and bus sizes increase, an operation can be completed or transferred in fewer machine cycles. As the frequency of the internal clock increases, and there are more cycles per second, computer operations can be completed faster. Microcomputer clock frequency speeds have improved from one *megahertz* (one million cycles per second) a number of years ago to over ten megahertz.

FIGURE 7.4
Hardware diagram of
a microcomputer
system.

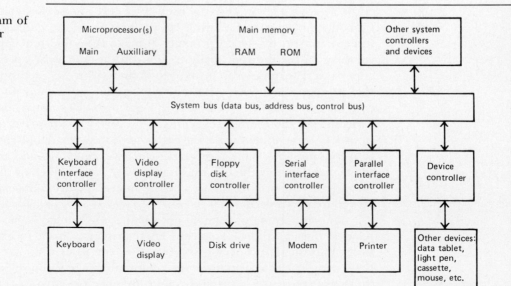

Microcomputers are often categorized by their bus and word size. The first generation of micros (Apple, Radio Shack, Atari, Osborne, etc.) had 4- or 8-bit microprocessors. The second generation was built with 16-bit chips (IBM PC, Compaq, etc.). Now, 32-bit microprocessor chips are available, and as improved technology lowers costs, more micros will have 32-bit processors. Many of the recent microcomputers contain several processors. For example, an arithmetic processor, called a *coprocessor,* can be used to complete calculations up to 200 times faster than the main processor.

Business applications typically require a minimum of 256K of random access memory (RAM). However, memory requirements are rising, and 512K is usually needed. Memory expandability is much more important than how much memory a system currently has. Microcomputers purchased for business purposes should be expandable up to at least 640K—and preferably much beyond. Read-only memory (ROM) contains information that is permanently stored in the micro. ROM usually contains at least the most fundamental of the system programs, including all or part of the operating system and the language translator. It might also include the program that initializes the computer (gets it going when it is turned on), interprets keystrokes, and prints data. As the cost of ROM drops, more system programs will be stored in ROM.

Data entry devices

Most data are initially entered in micros using a *keyboard.* If the keyboard that comes with a particular micro is unsatisfactory, replacement keyboards are available. They offer alternative key layouts, features not found on standard keyboards, different physical characteristics, or some combination of these items.

A *mouse* is a small device that is connected to a computer, usually by a cord. To issue a command, the user moves the mouse. System software interprets the movement of a device on the bottom of the mouse and causes the screen's cursor, or screen pointer, to make the same movement. When the cursor is in the desired position, keys on the mouse are pressed to issue a command. The mouse can be used to point to icons, or pictures, on the screen that represent activities. Alternatively, "pull-down" *menus,* or lists of microcomputer commands, can be used to perform tasks not readily represented by icons. The mouse reduces typing, is relatively inexpensive, and is very easy to use. Its friendliness makes it easier for computer neophytes to learn how to use computers. Many input tasks can be speeded up and simplified using the mouse. Possibly the biggest disadvantage is that much of the popular software does not support the use of the mouse. Figure 7.5 shows a mouse attached to an Apple IIc.

Light pens are pencil-shaped devices that use photoelectric circuitry to enter data through the CRT screen. Their principal use is in graphics applications. With the appropriate software, they can draw, fill, or color shapes on the screen. They can also move the cursor and make menu selections. A *joystick* looks like a gearshift lever and is used to move the cursor on the screen. Joy-

FIGURE 7.5
Apple IIc with a
mouse attached.
(Courtesy of Apple
Computer, Inc.)

sticks are especially popular for controlling video games and are used in computer-assisted design. *Touch-sensitive screens* allow users to enter data or select menu items by touching the surface of a sensitized video display screen with their finger or a special pointer. Voice input and audio response, as described in Chapter 5, are also available.

Secondary storage for microcomputers

Several secondary storage devices are used in microcomputer systems. The following are discussed here: floppy and microfloppy disks, hard disks, cassette tapes, and optical disks.

Floppy disks. *Floppy disks* were developed by IBM in the early 1970s to transport new programs and insert them into large mainframes. Microcomputer manufacturers capitalized on the idea and used them as mass-storage devices. Floppy disks, or diskettes, use the same data storage techniques and access methods as magnetic disks. They come in various sizes, and the most common has been the $5\frac{1}{4}$-inch diskette. However, the $3\frac{1}{2}$-inch *microfloppy* is quickly gaining ground on the $5\frac{1}{4}$-inch disk and will soon replace it as the industry standard. Diskettes come in single, double (where twice as much information is packed into the same space), or quad (four times) density. Data can be recorded on one (single-sided) or both (double-sided) sides of the disk, and storage capacity varies. Most micros can determine the density of the disk and whether it is single- or double-sided and store and retrieve data accordingly. A single diskette can hold up to 3.5 million characters of data.

Figure 7.6 is an illustration of a $5\frac{1}{4}$-inch floppy. It is a circular piece of flexible film, coated with magnetic oxide, and inserted in a plastic protective cover. The diskette has a large hole in its center that fits over the disk drive spindle that rotates the disk. A small circular hole in the plastic cover allows the drive to locate the sectors, or storage locations, on the disk. There is an oval opening on both sides of the diskette's protective cover. The read/write mechanism of the disk drive uses the opening to write to and to read from the disk. A small square notch on the side of the protective cover is used to protect the contents of the disk. When the notch is covered, the drive can only read from the disk; it cannot write to it. On the outside edge of the disk, and on either side of the read/write opening, are two notches used to help position the disk inside the disk drive.

The $3\frac{1}{2}$-inch microfloppy eliminates some of the weak points in $5\frac{1}{4}$-inch disks. The slots on the $3\frac{1}{2}$-inch disk are covered by an aluminum shutter that opens only when the disk is inserted in a drive. This protects the disk from dust, moisture, and fingerprints. The $3\frac{1}{2}$-inch disk has a sturdier metal hub in the center of the disk that connects magnetically to a drive shaft when the disk is inserted into the disk drive. The hard-plastic jacket of the $3\frac{1}{2}$-inch disk offers much more protection to the disk. The case can be written on, mailed, or otherwise handled without fear of damaging the disk. The disks have a built-in write protector in the form of a plastic tab that slides over the re-

FIGURE 7.6
Floppy disk.

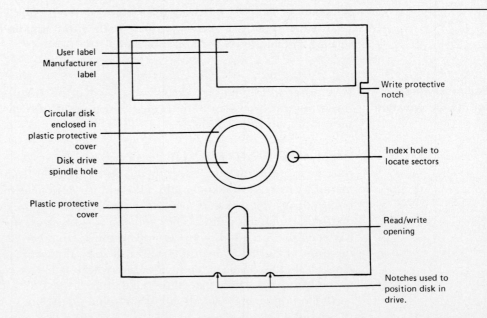

User label
Manufacturer label

Write protective notch

Circular disk enclosed in plastic protective cover

Disk drive spindle hole

Index hole to locate sectors

Plastic protective cover

Read/write opening

Notches used to position disk in drive.

cording notch, preventing unintentional recording of data. Microfloppy drives take about one quarter the volume of the $5\frac{1}{4}$-inch drive and thus require less space. They are lightweight, use less power, and are quite reliable. Microfloppies slip easily into a shirt pocket and can store more than two million characters, with even higher capacity diskettes under development.

Floppy disk drives vary in cost, but most run between $100 and $600. Some drives are stand-alone units, and some are built into the microcomputer unit. Many are full-sized, but manufacturers also use half-size units. These half-size units occupy half the space of a regular disk drive and, because of space limitations, are very popular on portable computers.

Hard disks.   The small capacity of floppy disks, which have to be endlessly cataloged, filed, inserted, and removed from the disk drive, can impair the efficiency of microcomputers. One solution to "storage-bound" floppy systems is a *hard disk* patterned after mainframe disks but designed especially for micros. They are easy to use, consume little power, need little maintenance, and have several advantages over floppy disk systems. Read/write functions are much faster since a hard disk rotates as much as ten times faster than a floppy disk. The read/write head rides on the floppy disk's surface while reading or writing, thereby reducing the diskette's speed. Hard disks avoid this time loss and the wear and tear on the disk by floating the read/write head on a cushion of air a fraction of a centimeter above the disk's surface.

Floppy disks are made of Mylar, a plastic material that expands and contracts with changes in temperature and humidity. The tracks on these disks must be relatively far apart to allow for these changes in dimension. Hard disks are made of aluminum, which does not expand or contract in response to changes in atmospheric conditions. This means that hard disks can hold more tracks, since they can be placed closer together. The most commonly used floppy disks store only about 360,000 bytes (although some of the newer diskettes hold more). Common hard disks store 10, 20, and 40 million bytes. Larger hard disks (up to 500 megabytes) are also available.

Hard disks operate in a clean, airtight environment. This eliminates the major causes of disk failure: surface and head contamination. As shown in Fig. 7.7, particles on the surface of the disk can have disastrous effects since the read/write head is only a fraction of a centimeter above the disk's surface.

FIGURE 7.7
Disk contaminants, and their size relative to a read/write head.

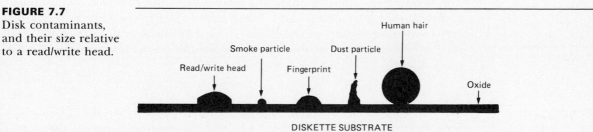

DISKETTE SUBSTRATE

Floppies are susceptible to damage from frequent handling and require periodic cleaning. Hard disks, on the other hand, require little or no handling or cleaning and are usually more reliable and have a longer life than do diskettes.

Cassette tape.   A simpler, less expensive secondary storage medium is the *cassette tape.* A cassette can store about as much information as a relatively low-capacity floppy disk, but the access time is much slower because it is accessed sequentially. The most popular use of cassette tapes is as backup media for hard disks.

Optical disks.   Optical disks, which were discussed in Chapter 6, are also available for micro-based systems. When erasable optical disks are developed, they will probably represent the storage medium of the future. It is entirely possible that within a few years this laser-based storage medium, where light is used to write and read disks, will have standard storage capacities of one billion characters.

Monitors

The most popular microcomputer monitor is a CRT, a device that displays phosphorus characters on the screen. In recent years a flat-panel display that uses liquid-crystal or gas-discharge technology has also been used, particularly for small, portable systems. Prices of computer monitors vary from $150 to $1200, depending on quality, color requirements, and the manufacturer. The more expensive ones usually have the highest quality color monitors, are faster, and have better resolution. *Resolution* refers to how small a particle of information (called a *pixel*) one can put on the screen. The more pixels per square inch, the higher the resolution. This means that the screen will be sharper, diagonal lines will be straighter, filled-in areas will be darker, and graphics will be clearer.

Monitors can be classified as monochrome or color. With *monochrome monitors,* there are three color choices: amber, white, and green. The amber and green screens are preferable because they cause less eyestrain. Some monochrome monitors cannot produce graphics on the screen. However, a graphics board can be installed in one of the expansion slots that makes it possible for the monitor to display graphics. If graphs or data need to be displayed in several different colors, then a *color monitor,* rather than a monochrome monitor, is required. There are basically two kinds of color monitors—composite and RGB (red, green, and blue). These terms refer to the kind of signal that arrives at the monitor, not to the way the monitor generates its color. RGB monitors are more expensive than composite monitors because they provide the best color clarity and graphics resolution.

Printers

Printers vary widely in terms of print quality, speed, paper size, graphics capabilities, and cost. The first four of these characteristics have a direct relationship to cost. That is, the better the quality, the higher the speed, etc., the greater the cost of the printer.

Printers can be classified as impact or nonimpact. Impact printers, which have been the most common, print by striking an embossed character against an inked ribbon positioned next to the paper. Nonimpact printers transfer images without actually striking the paper. Nonimpact printer speeds can be up to 20,000 lines per minute as compared with 3,000 lines per minute with the fastest impact printers. Nonimpact printers are generally more reliable than impact printers that contain pieces of metal that move and strike at a very high speed. However, impact printers have two primary advantages over nonimpact printers. First, impact printers have historically been less expensive. Second, impact printers can produce multiple printed copies of reports or documents using carbons or similar duplication methods, whereas nonimpact printers can usually produce only one copy at a time of each printed output. Printers can also be classified as *letter-quality* (characters that are fully formed) or *dot-matrix* (characters made up of small dots).

Dot-matrix printers.   There are several types of printers that form characters using dots. In dot-matrix printers the characters are formed by the way a group of small wires force the ribbon against the paper. Two approaches have been taken to make dot-matrix characters look more fully formed: (1) using more dots in forming the characters so that the image is denser and (2) using multiple printhead "passes," with the dots printed in a slightly different location than on the prior pass. Dot-matrix printers are well suited for computer graphics. By printing individual dots, they can produce pictures that are much more detailed than those produced by character printers. The cost of dot-matrix printers range from $200 to almost $6000 for near letter-quality printers. They print at speeds from 100 to over 1000 characters per second.

Electrostatic-discharge printers form characters on aluminized paper by discharging a voltage that removes a dot of the aluminum coating. They are very fast, but many people object to the glare of the silver paper. Ink-jet printers spray ink through an electronic field to form a dot-matrix character. The printhead in thermal dot-matrix printers is heated and discolors heat-sensitive paper to form characters. Thermal printers are quiet and do not have fast-moving parts that slam into hard objects.

Letter-quality printers.   There are several different types of letter-quality printers. Both daisy wheel and thimble printers rotate a print element between a ribbon and a print hammer. As the appropriate character comes into printing position, the print element strikes the ribbon and prints the character. Both have print elements that are interchangeable and come in a variety of character fonts and type styles. Both are comparatively slow (twelve to ninety characters per second) and noisy but have good print quality.

In laser printers, laser beams are reflected off a rotating disk that contains the available print characters. The reflected laser beam is projected onto the paper where it forms an electrostatic image. The paper is then passed through a toner to produce high-quality images. Xerographic printers transfer printed images to a special surface to which ink is applied. Then electrically charged paper is passed over the surface, and dry ink is attracted, forming the printed image.

Letter quality printers cost anywhere from $200 to over $10,000 for the highest-quality laser printer. Automatic paper-feeding devices, which feed $8\frac{1}{2}$-by-11-inch paper into the printer, can further increase the cost. Many organizations have more than one printer. High-speed dot-matrix printers are used for all draft copies. The slower, letter-quality printers, which print nicer-looking output, are used for final drafts.

Printer characteristics.   Printers typically come in two page widths: 80 columns and 132 columns (at ten characters per inch). Printers have three main paper-feed mechanisms: friction, pin feed, or tractor feed. Friction feed, the method typewriters use, can allow the paper to become misaligned, which means the print lines will be inappropriately spaced. Pin or tractor feeds keep this from happening by using pins to pull the paper through the printer. Pin feed uses pins that are in fixed positions and only accept one width, or a limited number of widths, of paper. Tractor feed is similar to pin feed except that it has movable pin assemblies that allow a greater variety of paper widths to be accommodated. If lots of draft-quality printing is required, a printer should have pin or tractor feed.

Color printing is available but at significant additional cost. Color printers work by combining inks of the primary colors to generate the desired color. Printers with color capabilities are usually either impact dot-matrix types that use multicolored ribbons or ink-jet printers that squirt the ink on the page.

Printers can be speeded up with bidirectional printing. When a bidirectional printer gets to the end of a line, it prints the next line in reverse order—from right to left. With short lines, however, it is faster to print the following line from left to right. A logic-seeking printer will decide whether to print a line backward or return and print the line from left to right.

Printers are connected to computers by means of a cable, or wire, or by a data communication line. The signals that determine what is to be printed are generated by the computer and must be conveyed to the printer. Devices that do this, called *printer interfaces,* are either serial or parallel. If the computer sends the data needed to generate a character along a single wire one bit at a time, the printer needs a serial interface. If the computer sends the bits needed to generate a character simultaneously along parallel wires, the printer must have a parallel interface. Serial transmission is slower but can be used over longer distances. Serial transmission is also used whenever the computer and the printer must communicate over a telephone line.

Modems and I/O ports

Business communications is currently one of the fastest-growing segments of the microcomputer market. To illustrate business communications uses, consider the following examples.

☐ The president of a manufacturing company uses a micro tied into an electronic data base called Dow Jones News/Retrieval to monitor changes in the firm's stock price. Meanwhile, a vice-president is using a micro to compose the strategy memo he plans to relay to all manufacturing sites via the firm's electronic mail system.

☐ Late at night, when phone rates are lowest, micros in the offices of mortgage brokers nationwide exchange data with a mainframe in Chicago. The micros receive data on additions or changes to available loan products, whereas the mainframe receives data on new loan applications and changes in existing applications.

☐ An auditor working in a client's office wants to double-check a recent accounting pronouncement. Rather than going back to her office, she uses her micro to query a data base maintained in New York. Within minutes the pronouncement and the firm interpretation are stored electronically in her microcomputer files.

These activities depend on fast, reliable data transmissions between geographically separated points. *Modems* (or *m*odulators/*dem*odulators) convert (modulate) the computer's digital signals to analog (telephone line) signals and then demodulate the signal at the destination. A modem, combined with the appropriate software, makes these and other telecommunications tasks possible.

The *baud rate* is the speed at which a modem transmits and/or receives data. As a general rule the higher the baud rate, the less expensive the transmission costs but the higher the modem cost. There are currently three common speeds to choose from: 300, 1200, and 2400 baud. About 300 to 350 words per minute can be transmitted at 300 baud; approximately four times that at 1200 baud, etc. Speeds lower than 300 baud are unacceptable, and speeds faster than 2400 baud (that is, 4800, 9600 baud) until recently were not very common. Many users prefer the flexibility of modems that can transmit at several different speeds.

Modems can be classified as internal (mounted on an expansion board within the micro) or external (a free-standing unit that connects to the micro by way of a serial card or port). Internal modems are often easier to use, since the manufacturer usually "bundles," or includes, the communications software with the modem. Software is usually not bundled with external modems. External modems can be used with more than one type of computer, whereas internal ones can only be used for a specific machine. This results in greater flexibility, since a new modem does not have to be purchased for each computer.

The duplex feature of the modem is important. Half duplex allows the operator to send or receive data—but not both at the same time. Full duplex is faster because data can be transmitted in both directions at the same time. A full duplex modem allows faster transmission but is usually more expensive. Modems that allow both are even more expensive, but for many users, they are often the best choice. There are advanced features that many users find

□ *Autodialing/answer.* The modem automatically dials a number and connects the user to another system or automatically answers a call without the user tending the machine.

□ *True dial tone connection.* The modem listens for a dial tone, rather than just expecting a dial tone to be there after a short wait.

□ *Software disconnection.* The modem automatically hangs up the phone when data transmission is completed.

□ *Self-tests.* The modem performs routines that automatically establish protocol (the rules computers use to communicate with each other) and compatibility and detect transmission errors.

□ *Compression of data.* Data are compressed as much as possible for maximum efficiency of transmission.

□ *Internal clocks.* The modem can be programmed to place calls when data transmission costs are lowest.

□ *Indicator lights.* They show a modem's current status, indicate when a successful connection has been made, and detect when another computer is trying to make contact.

□ *Modem speakers.* They allow the operator to hear what is happening on the phone line.

FIGURE 7.8
Advanced features of modems.

useful. These features, which allow for unattended, interactive communication, are summarized in Fig. 7.8.

Microcomputer Software

In 1978 a Harvard Business School student and a programmer friend introduced an electronic spreadsheet named VisiCalc for use on the Apple II computer. It quickly became one of the most popular software products in history, and thousands of people bought the Apple computer just to be able to use the spreadsheet. The introduction and overwhelming success of VisiCalc demonstrated the market for prepackaged microcomputer software. The years following 1978 have witnessed a steady flow of new microcomputer software products. Currently, there are thousands of software products for a wide variety of home, educational, and business uses.

As explained in Chapter 6, software can be classified as systems software or as application software. This chapter briefly explains the systems software available for microcomputers. Two types of application software are also briefly described: (1) specialized application software (accounts receivables, inventory, etc.) and (2) general-purpose software (spreadsheets, word processors, data bases, etc.). This section concludes with a discussion of some of the more popular general-purpose software.

Systems software for microcomputers

The operating system manages a computer, coordinates system hardware and software, and serves as an interface for the user. The operating system is provided by the computer manufacturer and usually comes stored on a diskette. The diskette is placed in the primary disk drive (if there is more than one). With the use of a "bootstrap" program stored in the micro's permanent memory, the operating system is loaded into memory. Once the operating system has been loaded, application programs can be loaded into memory and executed.

At present, there are several different microcomputer operating systems, including CP/M (Control Program/Monitor), MS/DOS (Microsoft/Disk Operating System), UNIX, XENIX, APPLE-DOS, and TRS-DOS. Since most are not compatible with each other, it is very important that there is compatibility among the software packages selected for use, the operating system, and the hardware. When CP/M was developed in 1975, it was the first disk-based eight-bit operating system and became an early "defacto" standard for operating systems. MS/DOS is the sixteen-bit processor operating system used by IBM personal computers. Since the IBM machines and their compatibles are the most popular personal computers, it has become the leading operating system. UNIX is a flexible and widely used operating system for sixteen-bit machines. XENIX was designed to allow multiple users and to allow a user to run several programs at the same time. APPLE-DOS and TRS-DOS are the operating systems used by Apple and Tandy (Radio Shack) computers, respectively.

The English-like, higher-level languages used in microcomputers vary in terms of ease of use and capabilities. Some of the most popular microcomputer languages are BASIC, C, PASCAL, FORTH, LOGO, COBOL, and FORTRAN. Other types of microcomputer system software include communications control programs, application development software, and utilities. Communications control programs allow the microcomputer to be used as an intelligent terminal to communicate with other computers tied into a data communications network. Application development systems help users develop their own application programs. Utilities are programs written to handle common disk and file management tasks like formatting disks, copying or comparing disks and files, checking the status of disk and main memory, and sorting records.

Application programs

Application programs are used to accomplish specific data processing tasks, such as updating accounts receivable or payable records. Good application software is so important that some microcomputer owners will eventually invest more in software than in hardware. The investment can be made either by buying programs or by spending the substantial amount of time and money needed to write them. The number of applications supported by a system and the number of different programs available for each application should be significant considerations in the selection of hardware.

Software for accounting applications has been available for micros since shortly after micros were introduced. The problem with the early accounting packages was that they were not fully integrated. For example, entries in an Accounts Receivable package were not summarized and passed along to the General Ledger or to other accounting functions. This lack of interface among accounting functions limited the usefulness of these stand-alone accounting packages and made them awkward to use. Recently, integrated accounting software packages have been introduced that rival the power and capability of those available for mainframes a decade ago. The most popular accounting packages are General Ledger, Accounts Receivable, Accounts Payable, Inventory, Fixed Assets, and Order Processing. These packages are especially popular and useful in smaller organizations since they have allowed companies to computerize their manual systems and to provide better and more prompt information. In addition, there are programs for generating a federal income tax return, real estate analysis and management, mortgage loan analysis, investment portfolio analysis, and many more too numerous to mention.

There are a large number of general-purpose or "generic" software packages that meet a wide variety of needs. These include electronic spreadsheets, data base management packages, word processing, and business graphics. Other classifications include financial modeling/forecasting, personal finance, mailing list management, telecommunications packages, desk organizers, and project management. Many business users initially buy a micro to be able to use a spreadsheet package, a data base package, or a word processor. As they begin using the system, they realize a number of other ways the system can help them. Soon they add graphics, modeling packages, accounting, and other general business packages.

Integrated spreadsheets

Electronic spreadsheets have played a major role in the personal computer revolution. For many businesses, they have eliminated the need for paper, pencil, eraser, and calculator in the production of worksheets and reports. Their use is widespread in a variety of functional areas in businesses of all sizes.

An *electronic spreadsheet* is a matrix of columns and rows containing blank "cells." Many spreadsheets have more than 8000 rows and 250 columns, which is more than two million cells. Since all cells cannot be viewed at the same time, only a small section of the matrix, called a window, is displayed on the screen at any one time. Directional (arrow) keys are used to scroll through the worksheet, viewing a different portion of the matrix as it is scrolled. The screen can also be split into two or more windows so that different parts of the screen can be viewed at the same time. For example, one window could display the top, or beginning, of a worksheet, and a second window could display the bottom, or end, of the worksheet.

Cells can hold alphabetic or numeric data, formulas, and references to other cells. Cells are referred to by their column letter and row number. For example, cell S3 is the cell where column S and row 3 intersect. An electronic spreadsheet is used the same way that a regular worksheet is except that the computer does all the calculating. Labels can be put along the top, down the side, or wherever they are desired. For example, a company's income statement could be set up as shown in Fig. 7.9. Column A contains the trial balance

	A	B	C	D	E	F	G
			Trial Balance		Adjustments		Ending Balance	
1	Account							
2		DR	CR	DR	CR	DR	CR
3							
4	Sales		XX	XX	XX		+C4−D4+E4
5	Cost of Goods Sold						
6	Beginning Inventory	XX		XX	XX	+B6+D6−E6	
7	Purchases	XX		XX	XX	+B7+D7−E7	
8	Goods Available	+B6−B7				+F6+F7	
9	Ending Inventory	XX		XX	XX	+B9+D9−E9	
10	Cost of Goods Sold	+B8−B9				+F8−F9	
11	Operating Expenses	XX		XX	XX	+B11+D11−E11	
12							
13	Net Income		+C4−B10−B11				+G4−F10−F11

XX = Input data.

FIGURE 7.9
Spreadsheet setup for
Income Statement.

account names, and columns B through G contain the trial balance, the adjustments, and the postadjustment balances. The cells can contain a number (XX) or a formula that takes the contents of the cells indicated and calculates a value. Cell G4, for example, will show the result of the formula C4 − D4 + E4. Figure 7.10 shows what the screen would look like after numbers were entered in the various cells that contain an XX in Fig. 7.9. The cells containing a formula automatically calculate the values shown based on the formula in the cell.

The most impressive feature of an electronic spreadsheet is the ability to ask "what-if" questions. Data can be changed, added, or deleted, and the effect of these changes will quickly be calculated. In Fig. 7.10, for example, if sales were entered in cell C4 as $210,000, instead of $200,000, each affected cell would be immediately recalculated, and the results would appear on the screen as shown in Fig. 7.11 (see cell C4, G4, and G13 to note the $10,000 difference). This immediate, automatic recalculation provides a what-if feature that has made spreadsheets an essential tool for many business applications.

Electronic spreadsheets are extremely diverse in that almost anything involving mathematical relationships can be done quickly and accurately on them. The features that make spreadsheets powerful and useful include speed, memory capacity, worksheet space, command capabilities, and user-friendliness. Some of the more important features that a user should consider when selecting a spreadsheet are listed in Fig. 7.12. Some of the more popular and powerful spreadsheets on the market are 1-2-3, Symphony, Framework, Multiplan, SuperCalc, KnowledgeMan, and Enable.

	A	B	C	D	E	F	G
		Trial Balance		Adjustments		Ending Balance	
1	Account	DR	CR	DR	CR	DR	CR
2							
3							
4	Sales		200,000	5,000			195,000
5	Cost of Goods Sold						
6	Beginning Inventory	20,000				20,000	
7	Purchases	140,000				140,000	
8	Goods Available	160,000				160,000	
9	Ending Inventory	30,000		3,000		33,000	
10	Cost of Goods Sold	130,000				127,000	
11	Operating Expenses	40,000		2,000		42,000	
12							
13	Net Income		30,000				26,000

FIGURE 7.10
Sample results.

	A	B	C	D	E	F	G
		Trial Balance		Adjustments		Ending Balance	
1	Account	DR	CR	DR	CR	DR	CR
2							
3							
4	Sales		210,000	5,000			205,000
5	Cost of Goods Sold						
6	Beginning Inventory	20,000				20,000	
7	Purchases	140,000				140,000	
8	Goods Available	160,000				160,000	
9	Ending Inventory	30,000		3,000		33,000	
10	Cost of Goods Sold	130,000				127,000	
11	Operating Expenses	40,000		2,000		42,000	
12							
13	Net Income		40,000				36,000

FIGURE 7.11
Sample results after
change in sales
figure.

Once a particular spreadsheet has been created with appropriate headings, formulas, and functions, the spreadsheet logic can be saved and reused. This becomes what is known as a *template*. For example, a template could be created for analyzing the purchase of real estate. It could then be used over and over again to analyze various properties. The reusable nature of the spreadsheet and its what-if capability make the spreadsheet a simple but important decision support system. It helps managers select the best decision alternative by interacting with a computerized model that compares alternative solutions to the problem.

- [ ] User-oriented menus, prompts, and other ease-of-use features.
- [ ] Copying (replicating) and moving commands, which allow formulas, numbers, and text to be copied and moved from one location to another.
- [ ] Formatting features that specify the number of decimal places and allow a cell's contents to be displayed using dollar signs, negatives, percent signs, commas, etc. A global formatting feature, which specifies the format for all spreadsheet cells, is also desirable.
- [ ] The ability to specify the width of any worksheet column.
- [ ] The ability to insert and delete rows and columns.
- [ ] Protection of cells so the accidental alteration or erasure of information in a cell is avoided.
- [ ] Split windows so that different parts of the spreadsheet can be seen at the same time. Also desirable is a synchronization feature that allows the windows to move together or independently.
- [ ] The ability to freeze titles so they do not move off the screen as the user moves or scrolls to other spreadsheet locations.
- [ ] Mathematical functions that calculate present value, trigonomic functions, totals, subtotals, averages, standard deviation, etc.
- [ ] Calendar functions that perform mathematical calculations using dates.
- [ ] The ability to sort rows and columns in ascending or descending order.
- [ ] Editing features that allow the user to change any portion of a cell's contents without having to reenter the entire contents of the cell.
- [ ] The ability to center or to right or left justify cell contents.
- [ ] Logical functions such as greater than, less than, equal to, etc.
- [ ] "Error" or "not available" messages when a cell formula does not have adequate reference input.
- [ ] The ability to select cell values by referring to an internal table.
- [ ] The ability to consolidate separate spreadsheets with similar formats.
- [ ] The ability to utilize spreadsheet data to produce graphs directly within the software package.
- [ ] The ability to perform data base functions (find, extract, etc.) on spreadsheet data directly within the software packages.
- [ ] A tutorial to familiarize the user with the software.
- [ ] A spreadsheet capacity (in terms of rows, columns, dimensions, and memory) that is sufficient to meet user's needs.
- [ ] Macrolevel programming so the user can "save" a series of keystrokes, create his or her own menus, or use other programming commands.
- [ ] The ability to drive a large variety of printers, especially those the user is most likely to use.
- [ ] The ability to make use of hard disk technology.
- [ ] Adequate program support (frequent updates, hot line, newsletter, etc.).
- [ ] Well-written, comprehensive documentation to help users get started, learn the program's advanced features, and answer their questions.
- [ ] The type of hardware and the amount of memory required to operate the software.
- [ ] The ability to communicate with data bases, word processors, etc.

FIGURE 7.12
Some important considerations in selecting an electronic spreadsheet.

Most spreadsheets provide a *macro command* capability. Macros allow the user to store a series of keystrokes that can be easily activated each time the keystrokes must be repeated. Most spreadsheets also provide a number of macro programming commands that allow the user to actually write programs. The nature and power of the available commands vary depending upon the package in use. Most macro functions also allow users to create their own menus so that they can customize their templates. An entirely new programming industry has arisen that uses these macros and the other capabilities of the spreadsheets. These programmers develop and sell specialized templates to a wide variety of unsophisticated users. This allows these unsophisticated users to have access to all the power of the spreadsheets without having to learn all the sophisticated commands and functions.

If you add to the spreadsheet functions some combination of a graphics, word processing, data base, or telecommunications capability, the result is a very powerful *integrated software* package. In an integrated package, the user can easily switch back and forth between these general-purpose applications or transfer data from one application to the other. By dividing the screen into two or more windows, the user can actually view displays from several of the applications at the same time. The advantage of an integrated package is that only one software program is needed rather than several. That means that data only have to be entered into one package, rather than into each separate stand-alone package. A disadvantage of the integrated package is that some of the components are often not as powerful, fast, or flexible as single-function packages.

Data bases

In data bases, which are discussed in detail in Chapter 9, data are organized and stored electronically in such a way that the data can be easily located, updated, and retrieved. A powerful software program, called a *data base management system* (DBMS), is required to manipulate and store the data. Only a few short years ago these sophisticated software products were only available on mainframe computers and cost up to $100,000. Today, however, there is a wide variety of quality data base software for micros that cost less than $500.

Data bases differ in their capabilities and range from simple to very complex. However, most quality micro-based data base management systems allow the user to perform a number of basic functions. They allow the user to create, update, and delete records in a file and to sort the data base according to one or more key fields. They facilitate searching the data base for specific records or records containing certain data. They provide for the printing of reports, which are usually formatted according to user needs. Finally, they perform mathematical and logic operations, and they make use of prewritten business and scientific functions to calculate totals, averages, etc. Some of the more important considerations in selecting a data base are listed in Fig. 7.13. Some of the more popular DBMS packages on the market are listed in Fig. 9.13.

- ☐ User-oriented menus, prompts, and other ease-of-use features.
- ☐ Multiple sort criteria so the user can sort on more than one field.
- ☐ Ad hoc (one-time) query capabilities.
- ☐ Program access and data sort times fast enough to meet user needs.
- ☐ Adequate capacity limits. For example, How many characters can be placed in a field and a record? How many fields in a record? How many records in a file? How many disks can be used to store a file?
- ☐ Maximum report width (number of characters that fit on a line).
- ☐ Ability to support page breaks, control breaks, titles on each page, etc.
- ☐ Flexible report writing features so that fields can be printed anywhere on a page and on more than one line.
- ☐ Mathematical functions, including present value functions, trigonomic functions, totals, subtotals, averages, maximum, minimum, standard deviation, etc.
- ☐ The ability to merge a name and address list with text to produce personalized mass correspondence.
- ☐ The ability to generate mailing labels.
- ☐ Password protection to restrict access to stored information.
- ☐ The ability to identify records by specifying conditions to be met by multiple fields (one condition per field) or multiple conditions for one field (more than one condition per field).
- ☐ The ability to test and reject input data at the time of entry.
- ☐ The ability to modify an existing data file by creating a new file.
- ☐ The ability to add selected information from other files to the data base.
- ☐ A programming language and a macro capability.
- ☐ Well-written, comprehensive documentation to help users get started, learn the program's advanced features, and answer their questions.
- ☐ The type of hardware and the amount of memory required to operate the software.
- ☐ A tutorial to familiarize the user with the software.
- ☐ The ability to drive a large variety of printers, especially those the user is most likely to use.
- ☐ The ability to make use of hard disk technology.
- ☐ The ability to communicate with spreadsheets, word processors, etc.
- ☐ Adequate program support (frequent updates, hot line, newsletter, etc.).

FIGURE 7.13
Some important considerations in selecting a data base package.

Word processing

Word processing is the computer-assisted creation, editing, and printing of documents that contain word and text data. Textual data are usually entered using a keyboard, stored in internal memory, and displayed on the computer's video screen. Data that are entered can be checked for accuracy, and any errors can be easily corrected. Textual data can be easily inserted, deleted, or moved around inside the document. The data can also be formatted (indented, bolded, centered, etc.) as needed. All corrections and changes are immediately stored in internal memory and displayed on the screen. The document can be stored on a diskette for later use, printed out on paper, or both. The stored document can be retrieved from the disk at a later date, and the editing, changing, storing, and printing of the data can be repeated as often as desired.

Because of their flexibility, word processing packages have become one of the most popular microcomputer software packages. They have made the writing, editing, correcting, and printing of documents much easier and much less time-consuming. In a typical accounting function, there are a wide variety of potential applications for word processing, including the typing of letters, memos, proposals, reports, manuals, product catalogs, price lists, brochures and sales literature, newsletters, billings, and financial statements.

Word processors are usually either screen- or command-oriented. Screen-oriented packages display text on the screen almost exactly as it will appear when printed. The screen will have the same indentation, line widths, underlining, bolding, page breaks, etc., as will appear on the printed document. Command-oriented programs display special commands within the body of the text in order to indicate indentation, underlining, and so on. Since these special characters take up space on the screen, yet do not appear on the printed page, it is hard to tell what the printed page will look like until it is printed. As a result, screen-oriented packages are easier to use and are more popular. Some of the functions that increase the power and usefulness of word processing packages are shown in Fig. 7.14. There are quite a few word processors on the market. Some of the most popular are Word Perfect, WordStar, Bank Street Writer, EasyWriter, Volkswriter, Microsoft Word, and Perfect Writer.

Word processing systems are the primary component of *office automation systems* that use computer and data communications technology to automate most information processing tasks in business organizations. These office automation systems provide for automated and computerized typing, copying, filing, and routing of documents through a telecommunications network. For example, some word processors can be equipped to operate as terminals on-line to a central computer system. Some have a data communications capability that enables them to be linked by telecommunications lines to other word processors located in other parts of the country. This enables a multi-location organization to send its internal mail by means of a word processing network rather than by means of the post office. Some word processors can be equipped with an OCR wand that can read text typed in specified type fonts into the processor's memory. For larger offices it is possible to obtain a shared-processor word processing system in which several word processing stations share the processing capabilities, memory, and input/output capabilities of a small central computer.

Graphics software

It is said that a picture is worth a thousand words. In computer terms, one might say that a graph is worth a thousand spreadsheet cells. The concept in both thoughts is the same: It is much easier to understand data presented in graphic or pictorial form than data presented in text or numerical form.

The graphs produced on microcomputers can be divided into two categories: information graphics and presentation graphics. *Information graphics*

□ User-oriented menus, prompts, and other ease-of-use features.

□ A memory swap feature that places part of a file on a disk when its length exceeds internal memory capability.

□ The ability to insert data from one file into another and to transfer files to other software programs (spreadsheets, data bases, etc.).

□ A macro capability that allows frequently used text or command sequences to be assigned to a few keystrokes.

□ Well-written, comprehensive documentation to help users get started, learn the program's advanced features, and answer their questions.

□ Automatic creation of backup files.

□ Insertion and deletion by character, word, line, block, and page.

□ Easy and fast cursor movement by word, line, screen, and page and to the beginning and end of the document.

□ ''Cut-and-paste'' features that allow the insertion, movement, and deletion of data.

□ A search feature so that specific character strings can be found and a search-and-replace feature that allows the user to replace a specific character string with a replacement string.

□ Text control features such as multiple columns per page; the ability to move entire columns; and variable column widths, page lengths, and margin settings. Underlining, italicizing, boldfacing, super- or subscript features, automatic printing of headings, footings, and page numbers are also important. Also important are conditional page breaks, which specify that a page break should occur if lines are not available on the current page.

□ Index, outline, and table of contents generators.

□ The ability to perform mathematical operations within the text.

□ Spooling so that the printer works independently of the word processing package.

□ The ''feel'' of the program, as determined by a ''test drive'' of the system to determine its quirks and special features.

□ The ability to produce printouts with centered or with even right- or left-hand margins through interword or intercharacter spacing.

□ Global default margins and specific margins within text.

□ The ability to establish tab markers within text, including the ability to line up numbers by decimal points, rather than just by the first character.

□ The ability to correctly renumber pages after the text has been edited.

□ System will wrap around any word not fitting on a line, and hyphenation that must be accomplished by manual override.

□ The ability to merge a name and address list with text to produce personalized mass correspondence.

□ The ability to insert any data field information from a separately maintained list into identified locations of the text.

□ Spelling checkers, which proofread text by having the system identify words that do not exist in its dictionary. A user-definable spelling checker allows the user to add to, or change words in, the dictionary.

□ The ability to drive a large variety of printers, especially those the user is most likely to use.

□ The ability to make use of hard disk technology.

□ Adequate program support (frequent updates, hot line, newsletter, etc.).

□ The type of hardware and the amount of memory required to operate the software.

□ A tutorial to familiarize the user with the software.

□ A command that lets the user abort the last command issued. The system stores the last command in memory and lets the user back out of that command. For example, this allows a user to replace the paragraph he or she just deleted.

□ The ability to edit multiple files on the screen.

□ Running footnotes, where a footnote moves anytime the text it references is moved.

FIGURE 7.14
Some important considerations in selecting a word processing package.

are typically produced by people for their own use or for the use of their colleagues in solving a particular problem. The graphs are sometimes displayed only on the computer's screen and when printed are usually produced on a dot-matrix printer or inexpensive plotter. The software most frequently used to produce these graphs are integrated software packages that contain graphics capability. These packages are used to analyze the data, and a graph is an extension of that analysis.

Presentation graphics are usually produced for formal presentations and are often displayed on the screen or presented on color transparencies, color slides, or some other high-resolution color medium. Before quality presentation graphics programs were available, the data to be graphed had to be sent to a graphics artist for preparation. Unfortunately, this was a time-consuming, error-prone, and costly process. With the introduction of presentation graphics packages and flexible input devices like the mouse and the light wand, graphics capabilities are now available for the microcomputer for a few thousand dollars. These same capabilities were previously available only in dedicated graphics packages that cost as much as $100,000. Placing these packages in the hands of the user has several distinct advantages. First, the users get exactly what they need because they are producing it. This eliminates the problem that exists when users try to explain their needs to a graphics artist. Second, they save time since users can produce the graphics when desired and without having to explain their needs to someone else. Finally, if many graphs are to be prepared these packages cost much less than it would cost to hire graphics artists to do them.

Microcomputer users have discovered graphics packages in the last few years. The sales of graphics packages is expected to skyrocket during the late 1980s. This tremendous growth rate is due in large part to the following benefits of presentation graphics.

☐ Graphics presentations are more persuasive than verbal presentations.

☐ Graphics presentations shorten meetings. The same information can be presented in less time using graphics.

☐ Graphics aid decision making and shorten the decision-making process. They help managers spot trends, problems, and opportunities earlier, and they help in analyzing and interpreting data.

☐ Graphics make a good impression. People using graphics are perceived as being better prepared, as being able to make clearer and more interesting presentations, and as being more effective, credible, and professional.

What-if analysis, which is so popular with spreadsheets, is also possible with graphics packages. What-if graphing makes it possible for the user to view, in graph form, the effects of various alternatives. This improves users' productivity and improves the quality of their analysis and decision making. Packages where the screen can be divided into more than one window allow graphs to be viewed at the same time as text or spreadsheet data. This means users can change data in the spreadsheet and see the results of those changes graphically. Figure 7.15 presents some of the important features users should consider in selecting a graphics package. Some of the more popular graphics packages are PC Draw, CHART-MASTER, PC Paintbrush, and BPS Business Graphics.

Decision support systems

A *decision support system* (DSS) helps managers make decisions in unstructured and semistructured problem situations. These decisions require that judgment, experience, and intuition be used when there may not be a "correct" answer.

FIGURE 7.15
Some important considerations in selecting a graphics package.

___

☐ User-oriented menus, prompts, and other ease-of-use features.

☐ Automatic sizing and scaling of all graphs, with the option of setting these scaling operations manually.

☐ The variety of graph types (point, line, bar, stacked-bar, clustered bar, overlapping bar, pie, expanding pie, three-dimensional, organization charts, flow charts, Gantt charts, bubble charts, etc.).

☐ The number of data ranges displayed simultaneously on the screen.

☐ The ability to generate labels for titling the X and Y axes.

☐ Labels and legends that "float"—that is, the user can decide where they are placed, rather than being restricted to prescribed locations.

☐ The variety of colors, font sizes, and styles.

☐ The ability to draw lines of varying sizes (thick, thin, etc.).

☐ The type of hardware and the amount of memory required to operate the software.

☐ Statistical features such as regression analysis, etc.

☐ Whether the package has free-hand drawing or animation capabilities.

☐ The ability to enter data using light pens, digitizers, or a mouse.

☐ Whether the package has a picture library that contains things like geometrical designs, maps, pictures, fancy designs, etc.

☐ The ability to specify the length, width, and rotation of a graph to be transferred to an output device.

☐ The ability to recall graphs and modify ranges, features, and labeling, without reconstructing the graph from scratch.

☐ The ability to generate multiple data sets (lines, bars) on one graph using different colors or shading.

☐ The ability to direct graphics output to various devices to generate paper copies, transparencies, photographic slides, or saved diskette copies.

☐ The ability to accept data interactively from stored files, a separate application program, or an integrated application program.

☐ A tutorial to familiarize the user with the software.

☐ The ability to drive a large variety of printers, especially those the user is most likely to use.

☐ The ability to make use of hard disk technology.

☐ Adequate program support (frequent updates, hot line, newsletter, etc.).

☐ Well-written, comprehensive documentation to help users get started, learn the program's advanced features, and answer their questions.

A computer-based DSS, by using decision models and the decision maker's knowledge and experience, helps users formulate problems and channel their thinking so that the best possible decision can be made.

Historically, DSSs were available only on large computers. However, in the past several years a number of excellent DSS packages have been introduced for microcomputers. Software has also recently been introduced that makes it easy for the micro to electronically access data contained in other systems and transfer, or download, it to microcomputer-based files. These two advancements have allowed DSSs to become micro-based. As micro hardware expands in size and capacity and as the DSS software for micros improves, micro-based DSSs will become even more powerful and widely used. There are dozens of micro-based DSSs currently on the market, including IFPS, Encore!, Expert Choice, and MicroPROPHIT.

Expert systems

An *expert system* is a computer application used to make, or help make, decisions that require experience and specialized knowledge. Some are able to replace knowledgeable people who used to make these decisions. By capturing and storing an expert's knowledge and decision rules, organizations have been able to save humans from having to perform repetitive analyses. By using an expert system to apply expert knowledge and predefined decision rules, organizations are able to ensure consistent results and improve productivity. Many organizations currently use micro-based expert systems. For example, the Infomart exhibition center in Dallas uses expert systems to help novice computer buyers select computer hardware and software.

Use of Micros in Accounting and Auditing

Microcomputers are revolutionizing the world of accounting and auditing by significantly increasing the productivity of those who use them. Accountants in industry have found a multitude of uses for micros. These uses range from running their entire accounting system to accessing the company's mainframe and downloading data to their microcomputer files to making simple calculations. There are thousands of uses in between these extremes.

The what-if capabilities of the micro significantly improve a tax accountant's ability to view the consequences of different tax planning strategies. The micro can also be used to enter, process, and prepare individual and corporate tax returns in a matter of minutes. Since the early years of micros, tax accountants have been among the heaviest users of microcomputers. Management consultants use the micros for decision support. The micro helps them help a client to decide whether to build, buy, or lease a building; manufacture a product; acquire another company; divest themselves of a line of business; or make any number of other important decisions.

Auditors use micros in a number of different ways to automate the audit process. One of the first applications to be computerized was the working trial balance. This allows auditors to input working trial balance numbers, handle all types of adjusting and reclassification entries, and compute the adjusted trial balance. It also facilitates the completion of the financial statements and footnotes to those statements. Going one step further, many or all of the working papers that support the numbers in the financial statements can be automated and tied to the trial balance. Time-consuming clerical processes like keeping track of confirmations, writing memos and reports, preparing budgets and time reports, and developing and managing audit programs can also be automated. Evidence-gathering procedures like accessing data in the client's files and ratio and trend analysis are also possible. Auditors can also use the micro as an automated decision support system to help them make decisions as the audit progresses. It can help with decisions such as the scope of the audit and the nature and timing of evidence collection.

Most organizations need someone who is experienced in the field of microcomputers and who understands their business, their information system, and the way they operate. They want someone who can communicate with corporate management and who can determine their business needs, translate them into "computerese," and communicate them to the computer industry. To provide the needed assistance, CPA and consulting firms have organized special groups in their consulting or audit staffs, and large organizations have set up microcomputer support staffs. As microcomputer usage continues to grow, the need for microcomputer consultants will also grow. As this field grows in importance, it should offer a viable career path to students familiar with accounting and with microcomputers.

Summary

The use of microcomputers by accountants has skyrocketed in the last few years, and usage will continue to grow in the future. Usage has grown so significantly because of the tremendous benefits of end-user computing, such as (1) user creation and control of programs and (2) ease of use. The risks of microcomputers include logic errors, inefficient systems, and poor control over the programs developed.

The hardware components and devices used in microcomputer systems include microprocessor CPUs, internal memory, data entry devices, secondary storage mediums (diskettes, hard disks, tapes, and optical disks), printers, and modems. The software used in microcomputer systems includes system software, such as operating systems and computer languages, and application software, such as accounting packages. It also includes general-purpose programs such as integrated spreadsheets, word processors, data bases, graphics, decision support systems, and expert systems.

Review Questions

1. Define the following:

   end-user computing   data bus
   microprocessor   expansion slots
   motherboard   multifunction boards

word size	letter-quality printer
megahertz	dot-matrix printer
coprocessor	printer interfaces
keyboard	modem
mouse	baud rate
menu	electronic spreadsheets
light pen	template
joystick	macro commands
touch-sensitive screens	integrated software
floppy disks	data base management system
microfloppy	word processing
hard disk	office automation systems
cassette tape	information graphics
resolution	presentation graphics
pixel	decision support system
monochrome monitor	expert system
color monitor	

2. Why has the use of microcomputers grown so rapidly? How rapidly has microcomputer technology advanced?

3. What type of computer knowledge do employers of new accounting graduates want their recruits to have?

4. What is an end-user system? Explain the benefits and risks of end-user–developed systems.

5. Explain the relationships between microprocessors, main circuit boards, and the data bus. Describe how each functions.

6. Identify the three important measures of a computer's speed and computational power. Explain how increases in each improves speed and computational power.

7. How much RAM should business-oriented machines have? What is more important: the amount of memory that is initially installed in the machine or how much the memory can be expanded?

8. What types of data entry devices are available for micros? Describe how each operates.

9. How does the $5\frac{1}{4}$-inch floppy disk differ from the $3\frac{1}{2}$-inch microfloppy disk?

10. Identify and explain the advantages and disadvantages of floppy disks. Of microfloppies. Of hard disks. What advantages do hard disks have over floppy disks?

11. Explain the methods used to make dot-matrix characters look more fully formed.

12. Explain how the following printers form their characters:
    a) electrostatic-discharge printer
    b) daisy wheel printer
    c) thimble printer
    d) thermal dot-matrix
    e) laser printer
    f) xerographic printer
    g) ink-jet printer

13. Identify and explain the three types of paper-feed mechanisms used by most printers.

14. Distinguish between serial and parallel printer interfaces.

15. Compare the advantages and disadvantages of internally and externally mounted modems. Explain the advantages of the following modem features:
    a) autodialing/answer
    b) true dial tone connection
    c) software disconnection
    d) self-tests
    e) compression
    f) internal clocks
    g) indicator lights
    h) modem speakers

16. Which was the first disk-based operating system? Which operating system is the most popular today?

17. Describe the use of the following:
    a) utilities
    b) communications control programs
    c) application development systems

18. What makes electronic spreadsheets so powerful? Explain the popularity of spreadsheet programs. How do macro commands increase this popularity?

19. What are the basic functions found in quality data base systems? Electronic spreadsheets? Graphics packages? Word processors?

20. Why have word processors become so popular in the business world? What type of accounting applications can the word processor be used for?

21. What are the advantages of making presentation graphics packages available to the user?

22. What are decision support systems and expert systems and how are they used?

23. Employers of newly graduated accountants want their new employees to have a good working knowledge of business-related computer applications. However, many of the employers do not feel that a knowledge of computer programming is as important. Explain what you feel the reasons are for the differences in emphasis.

24. The textbook lists important features of various software packages. Examine each of the features listed in Figs. 7.12 through 7.15. Then select the six features from each list that you feel are the most important. Why do you think they are the most important?

25. More and more companies are automating their offices. Experts predict that in the near future business offices will be totally automated and integrated. What advantages do you see in this automation? What disadvantages do you see coming from office automation?

26. Owing to your persuasive arguments, the chief executive officer (CEO) of your manufacturing firm has authorized you to acquire and install a computerized system. It will be your duty to obtain both the hardware and software for the new system. You feel there are two selection strategies available to you. You can select the hardware configuration and then find the software to adapt to the hardware, or you can select the software and then find the hardware that will run the software. Which approach do you think is the most appropriate? Why? Also enumerate the arguments you could have used to persuade the CEO to acquire a computerized system.

27. Microcomputers have emerged as an efficient source of data processing. However, the uncontrolled proliferation of microcomputers throughout an organization may create problems such as increased maintenance cost and nonstandard documentation. Briefly state three additional problems that may occur if microcomputers are allowed to proliferate throughout an organization. In addition, briefly describe three steps that an organization can take to control the proliferation of microcomputers and their effects. (CIA Examination adapted)

28. To operate an automobile, you only need to know how to drive. How much do you think microcomputer users need to know about computers? For example, do they need to know how to operate it, repair it, how all its components work, etc.? Do you think this will change in the future?

29. If you were the owner of a business that was considering buying a microcomputer, what resources might you draw upon to determine whether or not to acquire a microcomputer? To determine what your micro-based

system should accomplish? To determine which model would best meet your needs?

30. A wide variety of companies are now using microcomputers. For the following types of firms, identify several specific ways they could use microcomputers.
    a) The banking industry
    b) Manufacturing companies
    c) Retail firms
    d) Governmental units
    e) Universities and colleges
    f) Service firms (CPAs, attorneys, etc.)

Problems and Cases

31. Larsen & Larsen is a local CPA firm with about 500 small clients. The firm's winter work consists of doing individual, partnership, estate, trust, and small corporate tax returns. During the summers and the rest of the year, the firm does tax planning, prepares quarterly financial statements and tax returns for their clients, and does write-up and consulting work. The firm consists of two partners and two staff accountants as well as two secretaries.

REQUIRED

Propose a computer system that would serve Larsen & Larsen's needs. Include in your proposal the following.
    a) How a microcomputer system could benefit Larsen & Larsen.
    b) Some of the drawbacks of a microcomputer system.
    c) The software that Larsen & Larsen would most likely need.
    d) The hardware needed to make the system effective.

32. The U-Fix-It auto parts company sells foreign and domestic auto parts in Pasadena, California. Sam Turner started the company six years ago with his son working as a sales clerk. The company has since blossomed into one of the larger auto parts stores in Pasadena. Sam is now semiretired, Bob has been promoted to general manager, and the company employs a total of fifty people.

Company sales exceeded $1.5 million last year. Of the sales, thirty percent are at wholesale prices to local garages and mechanics who have the option of purchasing on credit. When a credit sale takes place, a three-part invoice is prepared. One copy is sent to the customer. A second is used to update the company's inventory records. The third copy is used to help the company keep track of the accounts receivable records of its 500 credit customers. The remaining sales (seventy percent) are made at retail to customers who pay either with cash or with bank cards.

Since Sam disliked computers, no computer system has been used by the company. Bob does not share his father's views about computers; in fact, he feels computers are necessary if U-Fix-It is to remain competitive. Bob is looking for a computer system that will meet the company's present as well as future needs.

Bob would like the system to keep track of the company's inventory of 20,000 parts. He would like to store information such as part description, quantity on hand, economic order point, retail price, supplier information, and part cost. U-Fix-It purchases its inventory on credit from about a dozen suppliers.

When a customer comes in or calls the company to purchase a part, the sales clerk should be able to access the inventory status and sales information on the part. If the customer is buying on credit, the system should produce a sales invoice.

Bob also wants to be able to use the computer to spot sales trends and to make sales and cash flow projections. He would like to have reports dealing with sales, accounts receivable, and accounts payable. He also feels that if data can be represented graphically, it will help him make better decisions. Finally, Bob wants the system to process the company's correspondence.

REQUIRED

a) How would a microcomputer system benefit U-Fix-It? What disadvantages might a microcomputer have for U-Fix-It?
b) List the application software that will be required to meet U-Fix-It's needs. Also, describe the system software that will be needed.
c) List the microcomputer hardware that will be needed for the system Bob has in mind.
d) Diagram the hardware chosen in part (c) and label the various parts of the configuration.

33. The Registry Corporation is in the process of purchasing a data base package for its microcomputer-based system. The Registry Corporation is a mail-order house that deals in nationally advertised cookware. Customers place their orders by calling a toll-free number and giving their bankcard number as payment. Upon receipt of an order, the operators will record the orders in the data base. Each morning, shipping personnel will access the data base to ship the orders received the previous day.

Every morning, a detailed report of all orders received the prior day is prepared on one of the company's five printers. Once a week, summary reports are generated that show weekly sales and shipments, comparisons to prior periods, etc. The company would also like to periodically produce special reports that do things like analyze the effectiveness of their marketing programs, analyze their customer base and their characteristics, and analyze the geographical location of its customers. Reports of this type should prove very useful to company officials as they try to better understand their customers and determine who is most likely to buy their product.

Registry considered a number of data bases and has narrowed the field down to two packages: Easy File and Merge All. As shown in the following table, your assistant has prepared a schedule of the characteristics of each package.

CHARACTERISTIC	EASY FILE	MERGE ALL
User-oriented menus	Yes	Yes
Online tutorial, help functions	Yes	No
Mailing labels and mass correspondence	Yes	Yes
Report titles and page breaks	Yes	Yes
Report subtitles	No	Yes
Password controls	No	Yes
Ability to transfer data between data base files	No	Yes
Ability to select records based on criteria in more than one field	Yes	Yes
Ability to change the data base structure without loosing data	Yes	No
Hard disk compatibility	No	Yes
Number of fields the program can sort on	5	2
Record types per data base file	5	20
Maximum fields per record	32	400
Maximum records per data base file	60,000	Unlimited
Number of company printers that can be driven by the data base	4	2
Number of record selection conditions per field	3	2
Number of print fonts possible	4	1
Rating of data base capabilities on a scale of 1 (poor) to 10 (excellent)		
Quality of documentation	4	3
Quality of mathematical functions	8	8
Quality of reports	3	9
Quality of query language	7	6
Quality of macros	9	4
Ease of use	8	9

REQUIRED

a) What advantages and disadvantages do the two packages have in common?

b) In addition to those mentioned in part (a), what are the advantages and disadvantages of the Easy File package? Of the Merge All package?

c) Which data base appears to best meet the needs of the Registry Corporation? Why? Would you recommend this package to Registry?

34. International Conglomerate (IC) is looking for a word processor and is trying to choose between the ExecWrite and GoodWriter packages. The

personnel in the word processing department can be divided into two basic groups. One group has extensive training, are versatile in word processors, and understand IC's report formats. The second group are new employees, have limited training on word processors, and are not familiar with IC's unique report formats. Some executives have their own secretary, whereas others use the secretarial pool. Jobs within the pool are transferred frequently.

Typed documents range from simple memos to formal letters and lengthy, detailed reports. Certain documents follow standard formats where the only unique characteristics are the name and address. In other documents the majority of the text is unique, with words and phrases being repeated within the document. Formal reports often contain financial data and charts.

As shown in the following table, your assistant has conducted a preliminary evaluation of the two word processors being considered.

CHARACTERISTIC	EXECWRITE	GOODWRITER
Menu-driven	Yes	Yes
Automatic file backup	No	Yes
Text appears on the screen the same as it does on the printed output	No	Yes
Page breaks displayed	Yes	No
Ability to create and print footnotes	Yes	Yes
Memory swap feature	No	Yes
Single character, line, and block insertion and deletion	Yes	Yes
Printer spooling	No	Yes
Ability to merge name and address lists with text	Yes	Yes
String searches and replacements	Yes	Yes
Automatic indexing and table of contents generation	No	Yes
Ability to perform mathematical operations within the text	Yes	No
Ability to export text to other applications and files	Yes	Yes
Ability to merge two or more files	Yes	Yes
Ability to import files from other applications	Yes	No
On-line tutorial and help functions	No	Yes
Ability to run on a hard disk	Yes	No
Number of print fonts	4	6
Rating of program capabilities on a scale of 1 (poor) to 10 (excellent)		
Ease of command use	5	6
Quality of macros	9	No macros
Quality of documentation	6	8
Quality of text control features	8	9
Quality of program support	5	8

a) What advantages and disadvantages do the word processors have in common?

b) What are the advantages and disadvantages of the ExecWrite word processor? Of the GoodWriter word processor?

c) Which word processor appears to best meet IC's needs? Why? Would you recommend it to International Conglomerate?

35. The Gritts Food distributor is a small food broker serving independent grocery stores in the Denver, Colorado, area. The company must maintain a large amount of information and be able to access that information quickly. It has been a few years since Gritts purchased its microcomputer-based system and has decided to upgrade its outdated system.

John Glade, the company's president, has listed the components he would like the new microcomputer system to have. They are as follows.

1. Large internal memory (for rapid processing of large amounts of data) and large external memory (for storage of data).
2. Expandability of internal memory (anticipating future growth).
3. A 20MB (or larger) hard disk.
4. Two floppy disks.
5. A modem to communicate with its suppliers in Los Angeles, New York, Chicago, etc.
6. A printer that will allow for high volume and quick data output.

Two computers, the Banana and the Centennial, are being considered. Information on each is given below.

FEATURE	BANANA	CENTENNIAL
ROM	128KB	64KB
RAM	1MB	256KB
Internal memory expansion capacity	3MB	4MB
Internal disk drive(s) (quantity; capacity)	1; 800KB	2; 320KB
Monitor	Monochrome	Color
Pixels (graphics mode)	320 × 200	640 × 320
Computer cost	$2600	$3500
External disk drive (cost; capacity)	$350; 800 KB	N/A
Hard disk drive capacity	20MB	20MB
Hard disk cost	$1200	$1500
Modem cost	$320	$200
Expansion slots	7	8
Graphics card cost	Not needed	$150
Printer cost	$400	$250
Printer speed	1 text page/min.	3 text pages/min.
Software availability and support	Limited	Extensive
Service	Good	Good

a) For each of the two computers, compute the cost of the total system desired by Gritts Food distribution.
b) For each system, compute the cost, per K, of the memory available to the user.
c) Based on cost, which system would you recommend for Gritts Food?
d) What other factors besides cost might influence your decision?

36. Master's Clothier operates a chain of men's clothing stores in the Seattle, Washington, area. The store offers its own credit card to preferred customers. The store's accounts receivable department is located at corporate headquarters in downtown Seattle. The accounts receivable department is a manual system that is staffed by a supervisor and five employees. Three of the employees are full-time (forty hours a week), and the other two employees are part-time (twenty hours a week). The supervisor is paid $25,000 a year, full-time employees are paid $5.50 per hour, and part-time employees are paid $4.00 per hour.

The company has been studying the feasibility of computerizing the accounts receivable department. If computerized, the computer system will consist of two microcomputers, two 40MB hard disks, two printers, and all the software needed by the company. This system will provide thirty percent excess capacity on each machine.

The system would reduce the number of employees needed in the department. With the computerized system, there would be a supervisor, two full-time employees, and two part-time employees for fifteen hours a week. Owing to the increased skills needed, salaries for the hourly employees would increase to $7.50 an hour for full-time and $4.50 an hour for part-time employees. The supervisor is a salaried employee, and her salary would not be affected.

The cost for the hardware, which has an estimated useful life of four years, and for the software is as follows.

Computer	$3600 each
40MB hard disk	1500 each
Printer	550 each
Software	950 each
	$6600 each

Yearly expenses for the computerized system would also be incurred. Yearly expenses include maintenance contracts of $200 for each computer and $50 for each hard disk. Software updates will cost $250 per year per machine. Office supplies under the old system are $1500 per year. With the new system, office supplies are estimated to be $1100 per year. Money is worth ten percent a year to Master's Clothier.

a) Compare the net present value of the yearly savings generated by the proposed computer system with the purchase price of the proposed system. Ignore the tax benefits of the purchase in making your calculations. Show your computations.

    b) What factors besides the costs shown above would influence the computer acquisition decision?

    c) Would you recommend the purchase of the computer system to Master's Clothier? Would your answer change if the system had a three-year useful life?

37. Tom Rasmussen is a senior with a medium-sized CPA firm. His most important client is Highfees, Unlimited. Tom is about to begin his audit of Highfees and went to lunch with Charlie Client, the company's controller. During lunch, the following conversation took place.

CC: Tom, I've been talking to some of my customers and they say Ajax Manufacturing, my biggest competitor, is buying a small business computer (SBC) and will be able to give them better service than I can. I'm worried. Do you think I need an SBC also?

TR: Oh, sure you do. You have to keep up with the competition. Why, their having an SBC could put you at a serious disadvantage.

CC: Yeah, I agree I need one, but I'm just not sure which SBC I need. What do you think? Which SBC do you think I should buy?

TR: I'm not really sure it matters. I kind of like the one Bill Cosby advertised on TV—though, at the moment, the name escapes me. Or, how about the Charlie Chaplin ad—that seems to be a nice computer. I remember that one—it's IBM, and anything IBM produces has got to be good.

CC: I've seen those ads, and I also like both of them. I'm also impressed with the ads for some of the other SBC's. Do you think the Apple, the IBM, the AT&T, or one of the foreign imports would be best to monitor employee performance, do some complicated job costing, and keep all my accounting records?

TR: I think you are best protected by going with the largest, most secure supplier. I think I'd go with IBM if I were you. Like I said before, you can't go wrong by buying from IBM. They aren't really very expensive—I've seen them advertised in *The Wall Street Journal* for $1695.

CC: One of the things I want to do with the SBC I buy is spreadsheet analysis with a program like 1-2-3. That IBM PC you mentioned comes with 64K. Do you think that will be enough, or should I get more memory?

TR: I think sixty-four million bytes should be plenty. Most micros only have 64K, and they run spreadsheet packages just fine.

CC: I was thinking about using prepackaged software, but I've heard that you have a hard time finding a package that fits your needs just right. The vendor I talked to said I could learn to program in just a few weeks. He said that after just a few weeks of experience, I would be able to write whatever software was needed to exactly meet my needs. What do you think I should do?

TR: I certainly wouldn't try and use prepackaged software. Besides, it takes a lot of time to find the package that comes closest to your needs. By that time, you could have learned to program. In the same amount of time, you could have picked up a new skill, and with a little more time, you could have exactly what you want, rather than some approximation of your needs.

CC: You know, another thing I need is a printer. For what I want to do, I'll have to print a lot of reports. I'm not sure whether I should get a dot-matrix printer or a letter-quality one.

TR: Is a dot-matrix printer the one that prints those characters that look a lot like a bunch of dots?

CC: Yes.

TR: Gee, I think those characters look terrible. The character quality is really poor. I'd go with a letter-quality.

CC: How about secondary storage? Should I get a floppy disk drive and one of those new hard disk drives, or should I get two floppy disk drives?

TR: Hard drives are really expensive. I'd stick with two floppy drives. Floppies are only a few dollars each, and you can use as many as you want.

CC: Well, you have been very helpful. I think I'll buy the IBM system you recommended and install it. I should have everything up and running by the time you want to start the audit next month.

TR: You should be okay now. Selecting the SBC and writing the software is the hard part. From there it is all downhill.

REQUIRED

a) Identify and explain any problems or inaccuracies you noted in Tom's comments. Is Tom very knowledgeable about small business computer systems?

b) What can you learn from this conversation?

38. Rent-A-Fridge (RAF) is a two-year-old company located in Boulder, Colorado. It is owned by two enterprising accounting students who realized that there was a need for a company that rented refrigerators to students during the school year. While the owners started by renting refrigerators, they have now expanded to renting stereos, televisions, telephones, VCRs, and microwaves. The company employs three full-time people and a dozen part-time people who work mostly at the beginning and ending of the school year. The owners plan to expand their business to other college towns when they graduate.

As accounting students, the owners understand the importance of an efficient and effective information system. To produce the information they need, they have decided to buy a microcomputer. They feel the computer will allow them to process their transactions promptly, keep their files up to date, produce correspondence, assist in planning, and allow them to easily and quickly retrieve the large quantities of information they need.

REQUIRED
   a) Draw and label the hardware configuration diagram that you feel will be most suitable for RAF.

   b) List several applications that you feel would be most suited for RAF's microcomputer system.

   c) Briefly describe the system software that would likely be suitable for use by RAF's microcomputer system.

   d) Suppose that RAF grows to four stores and sixty employees. Will a single microcomputer system be sufficient for their needs? If not, what alternative systems might RAF consider?

39. Visit two or more of the larger microcomputer stores in your area and do the following.

   a) Make a list of

      1. the microcomputers that are available for sale,

      2. the microcomputer peripheral devices (printers, modems, etc.) that are available for sale, and

      3. the different types of software (word processing, spreadsheets, etc.) that are available for sale.

   b) Using a business that you are familiar with as a frame of reference, refer to the material contained in the chapter and develop a list of criteria that you can use to select a microcomputer, peripheral equipment, and two different software packages. After you have developed the criteria, you should make your selection based upon what you feel would best meet this company's needs.

40. This assignment requires you to research one of the topics discussed in the chapter. The technology discussed in the chapter is changing and expanding at a dramatic rate. This assignment will help you and your classmates keep abreast of these technological developments.

REQUIRED
   a) Select one of the following topics (or one of your choice approved by your instructor):

     ☐ Microcomputer literacy requirements (for a vocation of your choice, i.e., corporate accounting, auditing, tax, etc.)

     ☐ Microprocessors

     ☐ Microcomputer memory

     ☐ Data entry devices

     ☐ Secondary storage devices

     ☐ Monitors

     ☐ Printers

     ☐ Modems

     ☐ Systems software

☐ Accounting packages

☐ Spreadsheet programs

☐ Data bases

☐ Word processing

☐ Graphics software

☐ Decision support systems

☐ Expert systems

b) Research the topic to determine what advancements or developments have taken place since the textbook was written. There are a number of ways to research the topic, including visiting computer stores and reading current computer literature (like *PC Week, Personal Computing,* etc.).

c) Write up a report that covers your findings. Alternatively (or in addition), your instructor may ask you to present your findings to the class.

Case Study: Selecting a Small, Business-Oriented Computer

Jim Daniels had just returned home to Seattle from the annual Retail Hardware Business National Convention. The session that had impressed him most was the Thursday afternoon Small Computers for Business display. The displays were truly mind-boggling; he had seen systems do things that he hadn't even dreamed of doing in his three hardware stores. The cost of the convention was clearly worth the knowledge that he had gained of the power of computers to outperform humans on almost every job.

Jim spent the plane ride home thinking about how he could use a computer in his company. Tops on his list was an inventory application. Jim carried about 4200 different inventory items from over fifty vendors. The information he needed to store for each inventory item consisted of about 480 characters of data, each identified by a twelve-digit product code. Inventory had been troubling him for some time, and he knew if he didn't get control of that crisis, he might eventually go bankrupt because of his high carrying costs and the large quantities of slow-moving items that he carried. Not only could a computer be the solution to all his problems, but it would be much better at spotting all the unusual inventory balances or transactions that so often seemed to crop up in the 500 transactions that he records daily.

Jim knew that he didn't have the necessary computer skills or the time to learn them, so his first morning back at work Jim called in Steve Lindsley, his bright young accountant. Steve had been out of school for two years and was a perfect choice for the job of selecting the computer since he seemed to have a special knack with electronic devices and even had his own small home and game computer. He was confident that Steve could handle the selection and operation of the new system, and if Steve needed any help, Jim would make himself available whenever possible.

The hardware

Steve was elated with the new assignment. As soon as he was able to train his replacement to take over his duties in accounts payable and payroll, he paid a visit to a close friend, Dennis Larsen, who had just opened a large computer store in town. Over lunch Steve quizzed Dennis at length regarding what Dennis thought was the most appropriate computer for his needs. Dennis impressed him not only with his knowledge but with his recent successes and experience in the field. Dennis had spent two and a half years on the audit staff of a national Big 8 CPA firm and had become intrigued with computers. The impending explosion in the mini and micro market had convinced him to borrow $20,000 and open his new store. Dennis was aware of the importance of training and had spent a fairly large sum of money to attend a four-week intensive school to learn all about the three lines of small, business-oriented computers he carried in the store.

In the next two weeks, Steve paid several more visits to Dennis and asked him every question he could think of. Dennis knew all the answers, and so one Friday afternoon Steve made an appointment to talk about the financial terms of a sale. Steve and Dennis were able to work out a deal that was mutually advantageous for both. In consideration for a reduction in the hardware price, Steve agreed to allow Dennis to use his computer system as a showcase of Dennis's ability to help clients computerize their businesses. Dennis also agreed to do a free feasibility study to determine just exactly what Steve's needs were in terms of software. Steve also got a break on the price because the computer itself was on sale. The particular model he bought was very reliable; in the four years it had been manufactured Dennis said it had a very impressive record. Dennis explained that a new model was expected shortly to replace the model he was buying, but some manufacturers had recently had problems with new models, and he advised Steve against the new model since it normally took six months to work out all the bugs in the hardware. Steve was aware that a common mistake most first-time buyers make is to over- or underbuy and was pleased that the computer he purchased, which was the top of its line, could be expanded an additional twenty percent to meet future growth needs.

The installation

Steve was able to get $12,500 worth of equipment for only $8,400, and Jim was pleased with Steve's progress. There wouldn't be any wait for the computer since Dennis had one in stock. Dennis would deliver it early the next week, and Jim was anxious to plug it in and start solving his problems.

When the computer arrived on Wednesday, Jim wrote out a check for the $8400 and had Dennis install the computer along the wall next to his office. The company's data files, stored on floppy disks, would be stored in the desk adjacent to the computer. It was a happy day for Jim, and the next day he invited a number of his friends in to show them his new powerful desktop computer. He explained to his friends that he had 256K of internal memory, two floppy disk drives that could hold 360,000 characters of data on each floppy, and a dot-matrix printer capable of printing 40 characters per second, which was *much* faster than any typist. In addition, the CPU was reported to be very reliable, and this greatly reduced the need for the service and support agreements Dennis had tried to sell him.

The software

A couple of days after the computer was installed Steve set out either to find someone to develop his software or to find prepackaged software. Dennis gave him some names of people who had offered to contract out as programmers. Since Dennis didn't have any inventory software, he also gave Steve the names of some other stores in the area that had a wider selection of software. Steve interviewed the programmers and decided against hiring any of them since they were either too inexperienced or too expensive. Dennis had given him a general idea of the cost of packaged programs, and he knew the good programmers would cost significantly more than the packages.

After several days of visiting the stores on the list Dennis had given him, Steve narrowed his search to the vendor who seemed most likely to be responsive to the hardware store's needs. The vendor, Sophisticated Organizational Software (SOS), had indicated its willingness to provide, at no additional fee, virtually unlimited support for a software package after it was purchased. Johnny Walker, the SOS salesman, demonstrated SOS's accounts payable package using a demonstration computer, a hard disk, and a top-of-the-line dot-matrix printer. The payables package was very fast and responsive, and Steve spent the better part of the day at SOS experimenting with the software packages they offered. He left confident that the SOS packages were responsive, fast, and of high quality. The inventory package Steve wanted was not yet completed, but programming was scheduled to be completed in two weeks. Another week or two would be required for testing the package and producing diskettes. Steve was assured that he would have one of the first copies. The documentation on the package would take a week or two longer, but in the meantime, Steve could get his inventory application up and running. The package was quite versatile, allowing for a ten-digit product number, a twenty-digit name, a thirty-five-digit address, and plenty of fields for special codes and balances. If it didn't meet all of Steve's needs, it could easily be modified. The software program code would occupy 180K of memory and could be operated using a hard disk or two floppies. The package would be capable of handling over 400 inventory transactions a day. Steve paid the relatively modest price of $1000 for the package and signed the vendor's purchase and maintenance contract. Steve made sure that the vendor guaranteed him three weeks of free training at the company's school located at their main headquarters in South Carolina. Additional training at the school was available at a very nominal fee.

The next day when Steve reported his progress, Jim asked him to check out a word processing application. He called SOS from Jim's office, and for another $500, they bought a word processing package to handle their correspondence. Including the software maintenance, for just over $10,000 they had a complete inventory and word processing package. In addition, they had the ability in the future to expand and at a minimal cost add other applications. To top it all off, Steve could now handle all the inventory-related items by himself, freeing up several other people to take on additional tasks. As the system expanded to include all the other applications, even fewer people would be needed to handle the accounting chores.

Jim and Steve were pleased with their progress to date and were looking forward to next week when the software would be ready. Installation and start-up should take a day or two, and then the reports that Jim had designed and that were so badly needed would start coming out of the computer. Steve had done such a good job that Jim decided to give him a raise out of all the money the company would now save by using a computer.

REQUIRED

Identify and briefly discuss the weaknesses, errors, misconceptions, or mistakes you think Jim or Steve may have made in selecting a computer.

References

Alesandrini, Kathryn. "Graphics That Dress for Success." *PC Magazine* (January 8, 1985): 164–175.

Allen, Robert J. "Electronic Spreadsheets: A Next Step." *Modern Office Technology* (December 1984): 56–64.

Backes, Robert W., and Robert J. Glowacki. "Microcomputers: Successful Management and Control." *Management Accounting* (September 1983): 48–51.

Benjamin, R. I. "Information Technology in the 1990s: A Long Range Planning Scenario." *MIS Quarterly* (June 1982): 11–31.

Benke, Ralph L., Jr. "Computers in Accounting." *New Accountant* (November 1985): 4–8, 46.

Bonner, Paul, and James Keogh. "Connected! A Buyer's Guide to Modems." *Personal Computing* (April 1984): 122–128, 171.

Capron, H. L., and Brian K. Williams. *Computers and Data Processing.* Menlo Park, Calif.: Benjamin/Cummings, 1982.

Connors, Suzanne. "NAA Research—Microcomputer Use High Among NAA Members." *Management Accounting* (December 1983): 62–63.

Connors, Suzanne. "NAA Research—Microcomputer Software: Who Uses What?" *Management Accounting* (November 1984): 16, 65.

Coon, Jennifer, L. "Documenting Microcomputer Systems." *EDPACS* (October 1983): 1–8.

Cooper, Michael S. "Micro-Based Business Graphics." *Datamation* (May 1984): 99–105.

Daney, Charles. "A Micro-Mainframe Primer." *PC Magazine* (January 22, 1985): 115–130.

Datapro Research Corporation. *Datapro 70: The EDP Buyer's Bible.* Delran, N.J.: Datapro Research Corporation, 1986.

———. *Datapro Directory of Microcomputer Software.* Delran, N.J.: Datapro Research Corporation, 1986.

———. *Datapro Directory of On-Line Services.* Delran, N.J.: Datapro Research Corporation, 1986.

———. *Datapro Directory of Small Computers.* Delran, N.J.: Datapro Research Corporation, 1986.

———. *Datapro Reports on Word Processing.* Delran, N.J.: Datapro Research Corporation, 1986.

———. *Management of Small Computer Systems.* Delran, N.J.: Datapro Research Corporation, 1986.

Davis, Gordon B., and Margrethe H. Olsen. *Management Information Systems.* 2d ed. New York: McGraw-Hill, 1985.

Edwards, Chris. "Developing Microcomputer-Based Business Systems." *Journal of Systems Management* (April 1983): 36–38.

Enockson, Paul G. *A Guide for Selecting Computers and Software for Small Business.* Reston, Va.: Reston, 1983.

Frotman, Alan. "AICPA 1985 EDP Survey: Hardware." *Journal of Accountancy* (October 1985): 136–138.

———. "AICPA 1985 EDP Survey: Software." *Journal of Accountancy* (November 1985): 128–134.

King, Martin J. "Microcomputers—The Central Support Approach." *EDPACS* (December 1983): 1–4.

Mansfield, Mark D. "Plugging the DP Gap: Small Computers for Big Business." *Management Accounting* (September 1983): 58–62.

Merritt, John. "MODEMS. You Can 'Reach Out and Touch Someone' From Your PC." *PC Week* (August 24, 1984): 47–55.

O'Brian, James A. *Computers in Business Management.* Homewood, Ill.: Richard D. Irwin, 1985.

Parker, Christopher. "The Micro and the CPA." *New Accountant* (November 1985): 18–20, 50.

Person, Stanley. "A Microcomputer in a Small CPA Firm." *CPA Journal* (March 1984): 20–25.

Rockart, J., and L. Flannery. "The Management of End-User Computing." *Communications of the ACM* (October 1983): 776–784.

Romney, Marshall B., and James V. Hansen. *An Introduction to Microcomputers and Their Controls.* Altamonte Springs, Fl.: The Institute of Internal Auditors, 1985.

Romney, Marshall B., and Kevin D. Stocks. "Microcomputer Controls." *Internal Auditor* (June 1985): 18–22.

———. "How to Buy a Small Computer System." *Journal of Accountancy* (July 1985): 46–60.

Roussey, Robert S. "Microcomputers and the Auditor." *Journal of Accountancy* (December 1983): 106–108.

Ruby, Daniel. "The Spread Sheet Race: Keeping Up with Lotus." *PC Week* (March 20, 1984): 28–34.

Ruby, Daniel, and Chris Shipley. "Graphics Software." *PC Week* (August 7, 1984): 41–69.

St. Clair, Linda. "Security for Small Computer Systems." *EDPACS* (November 1983): 1–10.

Seymour, Jim. "Left Unchecked, Spreadsheets Can Be a What-If Disaster." *PC Week* (August 21, 1984): 37.

Stair, Ralph M. *Principles of Data Processing.* Homewood, Ill.: Richard D. Irwin, 1984.

Tong, Hoo-Min D., and Amar Gupta. "The Personal Computer." *Scientific American* (September 1982): 87–105.

Waller, Thomas C., and Rebecca A. Gallun. "Microcomputer Literacy Requirements in the Accounting Industry." *Journal of Accounting Education* **3** (Fall 1985): 31–40.

White, Clinton E. "The Microcomputer as an Audit Tool." *Journal of Accountancy* (December 1983): 116–120.

Wilkinson, Joseph W. *Accounting and Information Systems.* 2d ed. New York: John Wiley & Sons, 1986.

Wood, Donald R. "The Personal Computer: How It Can Increase Management Productivity." *Financial Executive* (February 1984): 15–19.

C H A P T E R 8

Data Communications and Advanced Systems

LEARNING OBJECTIVES

Careful study of this chapter should enable students to:

☐ Explain the fundamental concepts upon which data communications systems are built.

☐ Identify the hardware and software typically found in data communications systems and explain how they operate.

☐ Compare and contrast alternative communications channels, communications channel configurations, and data communications carriers.

☐ Compare and contrast the following data communications networks: centralized, distributed processing, local area, and public data.

☐ Describe a number of common data communications applications and explain how the data communications model elements are combined to meet the user's needs.

CHAPTER OUTLINE

In the world in which we live, businesses require quick and efficient decisions based upon timely and accurate information. As businesses become more complex and geographically dispersed, the problems of data collection, processing, and communication increase, and the need for information intensifies. Many organizations are finding that communication by letter or even by telephone no longer meets their needs. Instead, they are using computers and communications technology to form *telecommunications systems*. These systems make it possible to bridge geographical distances so authorized users can have immediate access to a company's computerized data.

Data communications is the transmission of data from a point of origin to a point of destination. Data communications systems, which typically transmit data over communications lines or by satellite, have gradually evolved. In the early days of computers, control, efficiency, and personnel considerations, as well as economies of scale, led many organizations to consolidate their systems into one large *centralized data processing system*. As organizations became larger and more diversified, this centralization often proved inconvenient. It required data to be transported to the data center, entered into the system and processed, and the output returned to the user. To overcome this problem, *teleprocessing systems* (a combination of the words "telecommunications" and "data processing") were introduced. These systems use computer terminals to connect users with the central computer. The terminal is used to input data and to receive output, and the centralized computer continues to do all the data processing. While this solved some of the input/output problems, teleprocessing systems were still unable to meet all the needs of geographically dispersed users.

When minicomputers were introduced, they were placed in remote locations within an organization and linked to a centralized computer to form a *distributed data processing* (DDP) system. DDP systems provide organizations with a great deal of flexibility. The remote computers can (1) act as a terminal, or input device, in a teleprocessing system; (2) meet the specific processing needs of the remote location and communicate summary results to the centralized (host) system; or (3) be a self-contained system. Microcomputers have further fueled the trend toward DDP systems. They have also resulted in local area networks (LANs) and micro-to-mainframe links (MMLs). These data communications systems are discussed later in the chapter.

Data communications technology is important in the development and operation of accounting information systems. The number and importance of data communications systems are sure to grow as advances in data communications technology are made and as businesses expand and grow. Accountants must understand data communications fundamentals and concepts, such as the hardware and software used, the types of data communications systems, and how these systems are being used. This knowledge is becoming increasingly important as accountants use, audit, and help select data communications systems. This chapter provides a basic understanding of these topics.

Fundamental Data Communications Concepts

Before specific data communications configurations, approaches, and uses can be discussed, certain communications concepts must be understood. This section introduces these concepts.

A data communications system model

As shown in Fig. 8.1, a data communications system consists of five major components: the sending device, the communications interface device, the communications channel, the receiving device, and communications software. The figure also lists some common devices and communications channels.

A data communications system transmits data from one location (the source) to another (the receiver). For example, a remote terminal transmits data to a centralized computer for processing. The data to be transmitted, called the *message,* are entered into the sending terminal and stored. When the terminal is ready to transmit the data, a communications interface device such as a modem converts the input data to signals that can be transmitted over a communications channel such as a telephone line. At its destination another communications interface device converts the data back into internal computer code and forwards the message to the receiving computer. When the receiving unit sends a message back to the source to verify that the message is received, the communications process is reversed. Communications software controls the system and manages all communications tasks. The capacity and speed of data transmission are measured by how many *bits per second* (bps) are transferred.

FIGURE 8.1
The five components of a data communications system.

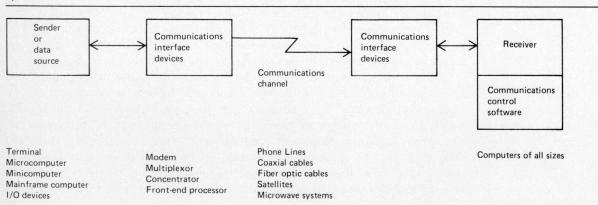

Terminal
Microcomputer
Minicomputer
Mainframe computer
I/O devices

Modem
Multiplexor
Concentrator
Front-end processor

Phone Lines
Coaxial cables
Fiber optic cables
Satellites
Microwave systems

Computers of all sizes

Transmission concepts

Messages can be transmitted in a number of ways. Depending upon the hardware and the data communications system configuration in use, transmission signals may be analog or digital; serial or parallel; asynchronous or synchronous; or simplex, half-duplex, or full-duplex. The choice the user makes between these alternatives has a direct impact upon the speed, cost, and reliability of data transmission.

Computers store data internally in discrete, or *digital,* form as the presence or absence of an electronic pulse. The communications channels in most frequent use, like ordinary telephone lines, send signals in *analog* (or wave) form. As explained in Chapter 7, data transmitted over telephone lines must often be converted into analog signals using a modem. However, data can also be transmitted in digital form. Transmitting data in digital form (as distinct electronic pulses) has a number of advantages. Digital transmission is faster and more efficient, it is less error prone, and it does not require a modem since the modulation/demodulation process is unnecessary. However, digital transmission has a number of problems that limit its use. Digital data transmission is often more expensive and more difficult because the signals drop in intensity because of the physical resistance offered by the lines. Digital transmission equipment is not as available as analog equipment because it has only recently come into accepted use. Although some lines accept digital transmissions directly, most lines in use were designed for analog signals. Because of these drawbacks, analog transmission is more common than digital transmission. A comparison of analog and digital signals is shown in Fig. 8.2.

Data transmission can be either serial or parallel, depending on the hardware and the communications channel used. With *serial transmission,* bits are transferred one at a time. With *parallel transmission,* two or more bits are transferred at the same time over separate communications channels. Transferring an eight-bit byte serially is like eight cars traveling on a single-lane highway. Transferring them eight at a time is like all eight cars traveling abreast down an eight-lane highway. Parallel transmission is used when the increased speed is more important than the added cost of parallel transmission. Figure 8.3 illustrates serial and parallel transmission.

FIGURE 8.2
Analog and digital signals contrasted.

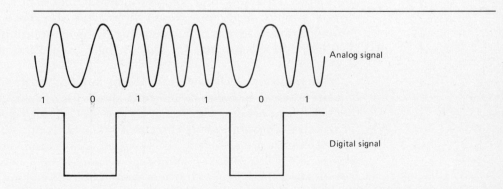

Analog signal

1   0   1   1   0   1

Digital signal

Parallel Transmission

Serial Transmission

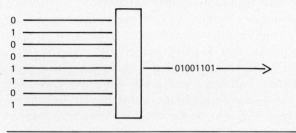

FIGURE 8.3
Parallel and serial
transmission of an
eight-bit byte.

When electronic signals are sent over a communications channel, both the sending and receiving unit must be in synchronization so the signals can be interpreted properly. With *asynchronous transmission* (or start/stop transmission), each character is transmitted separately and is preceded by a start bit and followed by a stop bit. With *synchronous transmission,* a block of characters is transmitted, with start and stop bits required only at the beginning and end of each group of characters. The beginning and end of each character are determined by the timing mechanisms of the sending and receiving units. Since the timing mechanisms of both devices are "in sync" during the entire transmission, the receiving device knows when each new character begins and ends. The decision as to which method to use usually involves a trade-off between speed, efficiency, and cost. Asynchronous transmission is inexpensive and simple and allows for irregular transmission of data. Synchronous transmission is much faster and more efficient but also more expensive. Asynchronous transmission is usually used for low-speed transmissions of less than 2000 bps, and synchronous is used for high-speed transmissions exceeding 2000 bps.

Communications channels provide for three different directions of transmission options. A *simplex channel* only allows for one-direction communication—that is, to send or receive signals but not both. *Half-duplex channels* allow for data transmission in both directions but in only one direction at a time. These channels are sufficient for low-speed data transmission, for telephone service, or for use where an immediate response is not necessary. *Full-duplex channels* allow the system to transmit data in both directions at the same time.

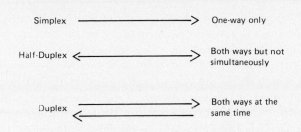

FIGURE 8.4
Simplex, half-duplex, and full-duplex data transmission.

They are used for high-speed data transmission between computers or when real-time processing (immediate responses to data inquiries) is necessary. Figure 8.4 illustrates the three directional transmissions.

Data Communications Hardware

Data input devices

There are a number of hardware devices that can be attached to a communications channel and used to send data or to receive data from a computer. These include dumb and intelligent terminals; micro-, mini-, and mainframe computers; and source data automation devices. These devices have all been discussed in Chapters 5 and 7. Another data communications device is the *terminal emulator*. A terminal emulator is a microcomputer that uses communications software to emulate a dedicated terminal. When not in use as a terminal, the micro can be used as a personal productivity tool.

Communications interface devices

Slow-speed devices, such as terminals, typically do not use the full capacity of medium- or high-speed transmission lines. To take advantage of these more expensive lines, a *multiplexor* can be used to combine signals from several sources. These combined signals are then transmitted over the communications channel, and a multiplexor on the other end separates the signal back out into the individual messages. The process is reversed when data are sent back out to the individual devices. Some multiplexors are able to do so many things that they are called intelligent multiplexors. These multiplexors are able to monitor errors, provide a variety of data handling and manipulation tasks, temporarily store data, and interface with satellites and other advanced communications networks.

A *concentrator* performs multiplexing tasks as well as a variety of data validation, data formatting, and backup tasks. It uses microprocessor intelligence, storage, and stored programs to store, merge, and control messages from a variety of input devices. Concentrators are generally more powerful and expensive than multiplexors. In addition, they generally store signals until they are complete and then forward them over the high-speed line rather than transmit bits and pieces of messages as multiplexors do.

The principal advantage of multiplexors and concentrators is that transmission speeds are increased, which reduces the time the central processor and the terminals would have to sit idle waiting for messages to be received. Costs are usually reduced because there is less waiting and because only one communications channel is needed for several terminals. This is illustrated in Fig. 8.5, which shows a data communications system without multiplexing, and Fig. 8.6, which shows the system with multiplexing. Without multiplexing, each terminal needs a modem at each end of the system and an individual communications channel between them. With multiplexing, only one modem is needed on each end and only one channel in between. Cost reductions come from using fewer modems and communications channels. These cost savings, however, may be partially or completely offset by the cost of the multiplexors and the more expensive communications channels needed for multiplexing.

When the volume of data transmission surpasses a certain level, a programmable minicomputer called a *front-end processor* (FEP) or *communications processor* is useful. An FEP can connect a large CPU to hundreds of communications channels. It can also handle communications tasks, such as handling messages and assigning them priorities, restricting access to authorized users,

FIGURE 8.5
Data communications system without multiplexing.

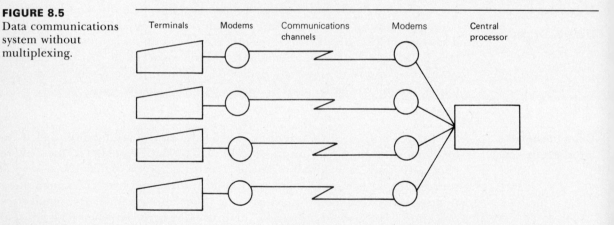

FIGURE 8.6
Data communications system with multiplexing.

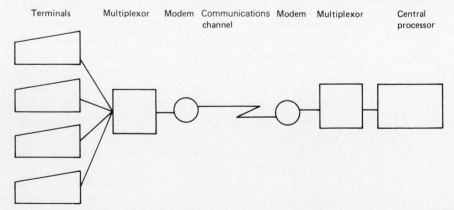

and controlling the interaction between terminals and the CPU more economically than the CPU. It can edit data, detect and correct errors, and keep a log of all messages sent and received and all errors detected. It can also poll terminals to determine if they are ready to send or receive data, store data until called for by the CPU, validate transmitted data, and preprocess data prior to transmitting to the central computer. In summary, a front-end processor relieves the CPU of time-consuming data communications coordination and control functions and helps it to make more efficient use of its resources.

An FEP provides several advantages, one of the most important of which is the increased effectiveness of the CPU (up to thirty-five percent more effective). Its main disadvantages are extra cost and the increased system complexity that results. The data communications system shown in Fig. 8.6 is redrawn in Fig. 8.7 to show a communications processor. Note that the multiplexor on the CPU end of the system is replaced by the communications processor.

Data Communications Software

Data communications system software is usually more complex than conventional system software because requests for service arrive in unpredictable patterns from many terminals. To cope with the problem, special *communications control programs* manage the data communications activity and interact with the various terminals. The control programs may be executed either by the main computer or by a programmable front-end processor. The communications control programs free the operating system from the task of managing data communications, thereby enabling it to more efficiently perform its overall supervisory functions. Figure 8.8 is a listing of some of the many procedures and tasks accomplished by this software.

However, users are no longer content with using terminals (or micros that emulate terminals) to access the data base. They want to be able to interactively search for the data they need, download it into their micro, manipulate

FIGURE 8.7
Data communications system with a communications processor.

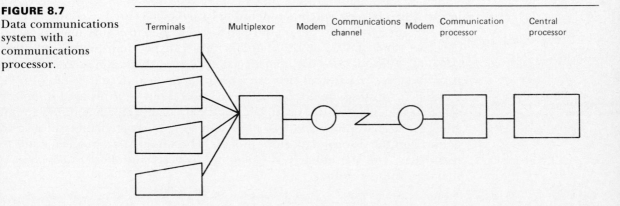

Terminals   Multiplexor   Modem   Communications channel   Modem   Communication processor   Central processor

Data communications software performs the tasks necessary to link two devices and transfer data from one to the other. The following is a listing of some of the tasks the software may perform.

☐ Control data transmissions features such as baud rate and duplexing.

☐ Connect and disconnect communications links by automatically dialing, redialing, answering, and disconnecting. To accomplish this, the system must usually store commonly used phone numbers.

☐ Poll terminals in the system to see if they are ready to send/receive data.

☐ Queue the input entries awaiting processing and the output messages waiting to be sent.

☐ Execute tasks according to user-assigned priorities.

☐ Route messages in the system to their proper destination.

☐ Detect and correct system errors.

☐ Log statistics of errors and other system activity.

☐ Provide for system security and privacy by means of passwords, encryption, etc.

☐ Temporarily store data that have been received or are to be sent.

☐ Format messages for forwarding to the central processor or a terminal.

☐ Transfer files from one computer to another.

☐ Create macros to simplify data communications tasks, such as logging on to an external system.

☐ Edit data in a file. In more sophisticated packages, the user can create, delete, edit, and copy files without leaving the communications program.

FIGURE 8.8
Tasks performed by data communications software.

the data to meet their needs, and when necessary, upload the data back into the corporate data base. To do this, special software, called a *micro-to-mainframe link* (MML), is needed. There are two parts to this MML software—the software resident in the mainframe and the software used by the micro. Current MML software costs anywhere from $150 to over $100,000. The wide variance is due to whether just one or both of the two software components is purchased, how many micros will be linked to the mainframe, and how many modules of the mainframe software are needed.

An MML requires a number of control strategies. Only authorized people should be able to download or upload data. Passwords (with varying clearance levels or hierarchies) and other identifiers are typically used to control access. The content of the data files should also be controlled to ensure that uploaded data are valid and accurate. The data files can be controlled by creating "shadow" files to store the uploaded data. These shadow files are separate from the "live" data bases that are stored on the mainframe. It can also be controlled by using the normal data entry and input controls used in online real-time systems. A third way to control the upload problem is simply to not allow the upload process to take place and to require all changes in data to go through the normal data entry process. The whole MML process is still in its infancy, and the industry is struggling to determine how to best operationalize and control it.

Software conventions, or protocols

For two computer systems to communicate successfully, the hardware devices and the communications channel must conform to a mutually acceptable set of conventions, called the *protocol*. The protocol is the set of rules governing the exchange of data between the two systems. These rules establish how the systems identify themselves, how data are to be transferred, when the transfer should start and stop, what devices should be involved, how errors should be handled, etc. Key elements of a protocol are the format of the data, the codes to be used, the type of signal, control information for coordination and error management, matching the speed of systems devices, and the proper sequencing of data.

Communications Channels

A *communications channel* is the line, or link, that connects the sender and the receiver in the data communications network. This connection can be a line that physically connects the two devices like a coaxial cable, a standard telephone line, or a fiber optics cable. The connection can also be made by terrestrial microwave systems, by satellite microwaves, or by cellular radio. This section discusses the various types of channels, channel capacities and speeds, and the companies that market communications links.

Alternative communications channels

The communications channel choice can have a significant impact upon system reliability, cost, and security. Therefore it is important that the accountant understand the various channels that are available and their characteristics, advantages, and disadvantages. This section provides the perspective needed by those managing or designing a data communications system.

Standard telephone lines.   Most telephone lines consist of two insulated copper wires, called twisted pairs, that are arranged in a spiral pattern. Large numbers of these pairs are bundled together in large cables wrapped in protective sheaths. Although used primarily for voice, twisted pairs can be used to transmit both analog and digital signals. For analog signals, amplifiers are needed on the line at frequent intervals to boost the signal. For digital signals, repeaters are needed at even more frequent intervals to recover the original pattern of on-off pulses and retransmit a new signal. Telephone lines are the most convenient communications channel because large numbers of them are already installed.

Coaxial cable.   A *coaxial cable* is a group of copper and aluminum wires that are wrapped and insulated to minimize interference and signal distortion. These cables are usually buried underground or placed on the ocean floor. Coaxial cable is used in long-distance telephone networks, and a single cable can carry as many as 15,000 calls simultaneously. Local area networks use coaxial cable because it can support a large number of devices having a variety of data and traffic types. Coaxial cable is also used for short-range connectors between computing devices. Coaxial cable can transmit both analog and digital signals. It can be used at higher frequencies and data rates than twisted pairs and is less susceptible to interference and cross talk. For long-distance transmission of analog and digital signals, amplifiers or repeaters are needed every few kilometers. Data rates as high as 800 million bps have been achieved with digital signals.

Fiber optics.   A *fiber optics cable* consists of thousands of very tiny filaments of glass or plastic that transmit data using light waves. The light waves, which are generated by lasers, are very concentrated and of high frequency. There are many advantages to fiber optics. They are much faster, smaller, lighter, and less expensive than coaxial cables. Speeds up to several billion bits per second are possible. A transmission that takes an hour on copper wires can be accomplished in less than a second using fiber optics. A fiber optics cable can contain up to ten times more channels and weigh up to ten times less than a coaxial cable of the same size. Fiber optics cables do not require messages to be amplified or rebroadcast nearly as frequently. Optical fibers are practically immune to electrically generated noise and cross talk and therefore have a lower error rate. Fiber optics cables have a very high resistance to wire taps and offer much higher levels of security. They operate at temperatures that would melt copper cables. Notwithstanding its many advantages, fiber optics are not likely to surpass telephone lines and coaxial cables as the most frequently used transmission medium since there are currently just too many copper wires in use. However, it is estimated that by the early 1990s fiber optics cables will be carrying thirty-five percent or more of the traffic now carried on telephone and coaxial cables.

Terrestrial microwave systems.   *Terrestrial microwave* is a frequently used medium for long-distance data or voice transmission. It does not require the laying or the expense of cable because long-distance dish or horn antennas with microwave repeater stations are placed approximately twenty-five to thirty miles apart. Each transmitter station receives a signal, amplifies it, and retransmits it to the next station. All the transmitters and receivers must be in a straight line because the signal cannot bend around the curvature of the earth. Both analog and digital signals can be transmitted over microwave at speeds of up to 500,000 bps.

Communications satellites.   *Satellite microwave* is similar to terrestrial microwave transmission except that instead of transmitting to another nearby microwave dish antenna, the signal is transmitted to a satellite in space. This satellite acts as a relay station and sends the transmission back to any of the earth stations that care to pick up the signal. A satellite that is placed in orbit approximately 22,000 miles above the earth maintains a fixed position as the earth rotates. This "stationary" satellite is therefore able to send and receive signals from almost fifty percent of the earth's surface. The other fifty percent of the world can be reached by transmitting to a satellite on that side of the world. There are several dozen of these communications satellites currently in use. They are powered by solar panels, weigh several thousand pounds, and are able to transmit microwave signals at a rate of several hundred million bits per second. Unlike most other media, the cost of satellite transmissions is independent of the distance the message must be transmitted.

Cellular radio. Using *cellular radio,* companies can take greater advantage of the number of radio frequencies available. Instead of having a single powerful transmitter for a large area, the area is divided into small sections called cells. There is a transmitter for each cell, and this allows each frequency to be used by different companies in each cell. This allows the radio frequencies to be put to greater use (up to twenty-five times more people using the frequencies). A powerful central computer and sophisticated interface equipment coordinate and control the transmission between cells.

Channel capacity and speed

Communications channels are graded or classified into three categories, or bandwidths, according to their information carrying capacity or data transfer rate. *Narrowband,* or subvoice-grade *lines* operate at speeds of up to 300 bps. They are limited to low-volume applications using devices like teletypewriters and low-speed printing terminals. They are not suitable for transmitting audible or voicelike signals. *Voiceband* channels can be used for voice or data communications. They are typically telephone lines and operate at speeds from 300 to 9600 bps. Voiceband lines are commonly used to communicate with microcomputers, CRT terminals, and medium-sized printers. *Wideband* or *broadband* channels transmit at rates up to fifty million bps. Their primary use is for high-speed data transmission between computer systems. Coaxial and fiber optics cables, terrestrial microwave systems, and satellites are usually used because of their greater reliability and fewer interferences. The higher the bandwidth selected, the greater the volume of data that can be transmitted and the higher the cost.

Voiceband line options

Three types of voice-grade telephone line services are available for data communications. These are *leased lines, switched lines* (dial-up service using public lines), and *Wide Area Telephone Service* (WATS). Leased lines are devoted exclusively to the use of a single customer. The cost is fixed and is determined by the line length. Advantages of leased lines relative to the alternatives include lower error rates, faster rates of data transmission, and increased privacy. Leased lines also provide a line that is always connected, which eliminates the fifteen- to twenty-second connection time needed with the other options.

Both switched lines and WATS lines use the long-distance telephone service available to the general public. The difference between them lies in the rate structure. The cost of switched line service varies in proportion to the amount of time the lines are used. With a WATS line, the user pays a fixed charge to use the line and then pays an additional charge that varies directly with the amount of extra usage. Switched lines are more flexible than leased or WATS lines because any telephone may be used for data transmission. A further advantage of WATS and switched lines is that more than one computer system may be accessed from a single terminal.

A primary consideration in choosing among leased, switched, and WATS lines is cost, which in turn is dependent upon both volume of usage and distance between transmission points. At very low volumes of usage, switched line service is usually most economical. At very high volumes of usage, leased lines are usually most economical. A WATS line is usually most economical at intermediate levels of usage. As the distance between transmission points increases, switched lines and WATS lines are less costly than leased lines. Few users depend entirely upon one alternative. When leased lines are used, for example, switched lines are often used for backup purposes.

An example should clarify the economic factors affecting the choice among these three alternatives. Consider a company that wishes to connect a remote terminal in Salt Lake City to a processing center 922 miles away in Kansas City. Using Bell System rates in effect in January 1986, cost estimates for the three alternative forms of service are determined as follows.

1. *Leased voice-grade analog line.* There is a fixed line charge of $557.16 plus $0.35 a mile ($322.70) for a total of $879.86 per month. This line can transmit 4800 bps very reliably. For another $105 per month the line can be conditioned to carry 9600 bps.

2. *Switched line.* The weekday rate for each direct-dialed call is $0.55 for the first minute and $0.38 for each additional minute. Assuming an average of four minutes per call, this works out to an average of $0.4225 per minute, or $25.35 per hour.

3. *WATS line.* It costs $57.65 to connect these two points and $19.26 per hour for the first fifteen hours, $17.14 from fifteen to forty hours, $15.04 between forty and eighty hours, and $12.72 for every hour over eighty.

Figure 8.9 graphs the total monthly cost under each of these three alternatives as a function of the number of hours of usage. The graph indicates that switched lines are most economical up to a usage volume of approximately 9.5 hours per month. WATS lines are most economical for usage volumes ranging between approximately 9.5 and 47 hours per month, and leased lines are most economical for usage volumes in excess of approximately 47 hours per month. Note that the specific break-even points will vary depending on the distance between the two points but that the general shape of each of the three cost functions will be as shown in Fig. 8.9. However, the closer one gets to the break-even points, the more important other factors become. For

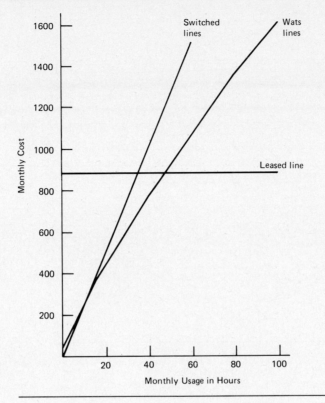

FIGURE 8.9
Sample economic
comparison of leased
lines, switched lines,
and WATS lines.

example, since leased lines are much more reliable, less time is needed for retransmission of erroneous data and for error determination and investigation, and less manpower is required to monitor the data.

Communications channel configurations

The communications channels that connect the various points in a data communications system may be configured in a number of ways. The three basic configurations are point-to-point, multidrop, and line-sharing. To illustrate these configurations, assume a central computer that is to have several terminals attached. The simplest configuration uses *point-to-point lines,* or one line from each terminal to the central processor, as illustrated in Fig. 8.10. *Multidrop lines,* illustrated in Fig. 8.11, link the terminals to each other, with only one or a few terminals linked directly to the CPU. All other terminals are indirectly linked to the CPU by means of lines that connect through other terminal locations. The use of a *line-sharing device,* in which data from (or to) several terminals are combined for transmission on a single line, is illustrated in Fig. 8.12. In all three figures, the terminals are located in the same place, and therefore the distance between the terminals and the central computer are the same.

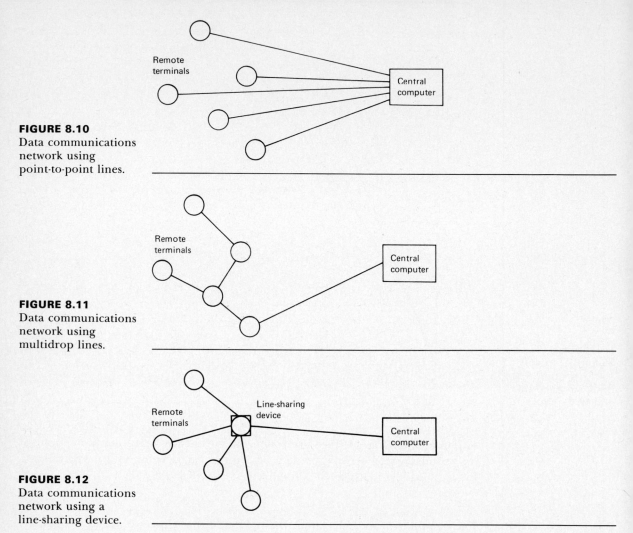

FIGURE 8.10
Data communications network using point-to-point lines.

FIGURE 8.11
Data communications network using multidrop lines.

FIGURE 8.12
Data communications network using a line-sharing device.

Point-to-point lines. In a system using point-to-point lines, either leased lines, WATS lines, or switched lines may be used, whichever is most economical. It is even possible to have a combination of different types of lines within the same network. The primary advantages of the point-to-point configuration are its simplicity in terms of hardware requirements; its increased availability to users, who are rarely required to wait on others who have tied up the lines; and its reliability in the sense that if a line fails, only one user is affected. The primary disadvantage of this configuration is that it maximizes total line mileage in the network. Since most data communications costs are directly related to line mileage, point-to-point lines are frequently more costly than alternative configurations.

Multidrop lines. A visual comparison of Fig. 8.10 with Fig. 8.11 indicates the potential for reduction in line mileage and data communications costs from the use of multidrop lines. However, the multidrop configuration does have some disadvantages. First, only one terminal at a time can transmit data, which means that line conflicts must be controlled. Using the *polling approach*, the computer asks each terminal on the multidrop line if it has a message to send and then lets each, in turn, transmit data. The *contention approach* has the terminal "listen" to the line to see if it is in use. If the line is free, the message is transmitted. If it is busy, the terminal waits a predetermined time and then tries again. Polling is frequently used because the central computer can control transmission and keep terminals from monopolizing the line. A second disadvantage is that all terminals down the line from the point where a line fails are cut off from the central computer. Finally, multidrop lines are the least flexible of the three basic configurations. Usually, all the lines must be leased, whereas switched or WATS lines may be used for some or all connections under the other two alternatives.

Line-sharing device. Line-sharing devices, such as multiplexors and concentrators, combine two or more incoming data signals from low-speed lines into one signal and transmit them simultaneously on a single high-speed line. This eliminates or substantially reduces the wait time experienced by users of multidrop lines. A comparison of Fig. 8.10 with Fig. 8.12 shows that line-sharing devices can also reduce the line mileage required in a point-to-point system. However, the cost savings that result will be partially or wholly offset by the cost of the line-sharing equipment and the more expensive high-speed line that is generally required to connect the line-sharing device to the central computer. System reliability may be a problem in that a failure in the shared line will cause all users to be cut off from the system. Line-sharing systems offer the flexibility of choice among leased, switched, or WATS lines to connect each remote terminal to the line-sharing device. However, the shared line itself must be leased.

A large data communications network often contains a combination of all three approaches. The network designer does not simply choose one of the three approaches for the entire network. Instead, the relative advantages and disadvantages of each configuration are evaluated, and the best approach for each individual terminal connection is chosen. Figure 8.13 illustrates a network in which all three approaches are represented. This figure also demonstrates the relationships that exist among the various hardware elements within a data communications network.

Data communications carriers

Data communications carriers are organizations authorized by the Federal Communications System or state agencies to provide public communications services. Common carriers, such as AT&T, Western Union, MCI, and General Telephone and Electric, offer a wide range and variety of communications

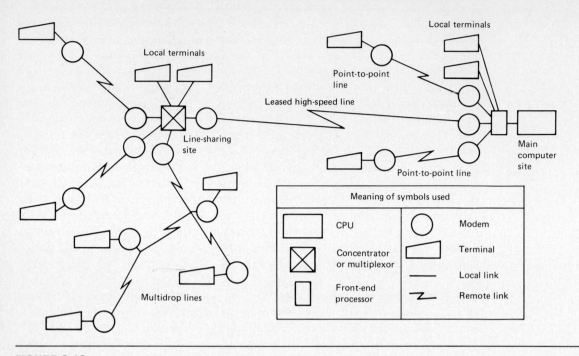

FIGURE 8.13
A data communications network.

services. Specialized carriers sell high-speed voice and data communications services in selected high-density areas of the country. Value-added carriers lease communications facilities from the common carriers and combine messages from customers into groupings called packets, which are then transmitted. They offer specialized hardware, software, and data handling techniques that are not ordinarily available with traditional data communications services. In this way, they are able to "add value" to the transmission by improving transmission effectiveness and decreasing costs. Some firms are large enough, or localized enough, that they are able to establish their own private data communications networks.

Communications Networks

An information system may consist of a "standalone" computer that does not need to communicate with other computers. However, most information systems consist of one or more computers, a number of other hardware devices, and communications channels linking the devices together to form a *communications network*. The network can take so many forms that most networks in use today are unique. This section of the chapter explains some of the more popular approaches to networks.

There are a large number of suppliers of data communications components, each with its own interface approach. The absence of interface standards has made it difficult for users to develop simple, unified data communications systems. It has also resulted in increased cost and complexity and reduced efficiency and effectiveness. To overcome this problem, manufacturers and computer organizations have banded together to develop standards. Their goal is to develop a *standard network architecture,* complete with standard protocols, and standardized hardware, software, and communications channel interfaces.

Centralized network   In a *centralized network,* data processing is done at a large, centralized processing center using sophisticated software. User terminals and other computers are linked to the host computer by point-to-point lines, multidropped lines, or multiplexed communications channels. Local terminals are usually directly, or "hard-wire," connected using coaxial cables. User interface may be by terminals, microcomputers emulating a terminal, or any of a number of remote or local source data automation devices. Terminals may be structured to provide online, online real-time, or remote job entry (batch processing) access. Highly trained personnel operate and manage the system. Data are stored in large, integrated data bases. There are smaller centralized systems that require less complexity, but the data processing approach remains the same.

Varying degrees of complexity are possible in the basic hardware configuration. The simplest configuration is illustrated in Fig. 8.14. In this configuration several input/output terminals are linked directly to a central processor. A system of this type is called a *simplex system* because there is only one central processor. A simplex system cannot be available for use at all times because of preventive maintenance requirements and equipment malfunctions. Provisions for a manual backup system are thus necessary. To offset these disadvantages, however, the simplex system offers the advantage of real-time capability at the lowest possible cost and with a minimum of complexity in hardware and software system design.

Centralized configurations often utilize more than one CPU to maximize system availability and reliability. The *duplex system* illustrated in Fig. 8.15 uses two central processors. The second CPU takes over for the first during its

FIGURE 8.14
Simplex system.

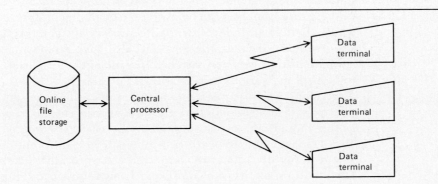

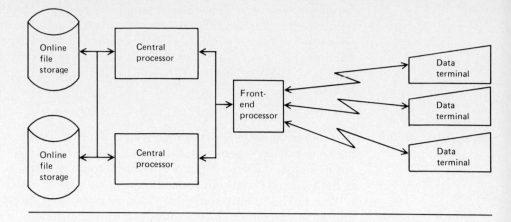

FIGURE 8.15
Duplex system.

scheduled maintenance or during an equipment failure. When the second
computer is not substituting for the first, it generally performs batch processing or other jobs. The advantage of the duplex system is that it greatly
increases system availability. Major disadvantages are increased system cost
and the increased complexity of the software system required to switch operations from one computer to the other.

Centralized networks provide a number of significant advantages. Among
them are economies of scale, better control, more experienced personnel, and
elimination of duplicate functions. Among the significant disadvantages are
greater complexity, higher communications costs, and less flexibility. The advantages and disadvantages of centralized processing are summarized in Fig.
8.16.

**Distributed data
processing
networks**

A problem with centralized processing is that one system is trying to meet the
needs of a large number of users, many of whom have unique needs. The
larger the system, the greater the likelihood that the users feel the centralized
system is not meeting their needs. The busier the system, the greater the likelihood of the system being overloaded, making access difficult and slow. Some
of these disadvantages can be overcome by implementing a *decentralized system,*
where there is an independent CPU and a data processing manager at each
site. However, decentralized systems also have disadvantages such as lack of
communication between systems, insufficient information, and the inability
to control the various organizational entities.

An approach that achieves many of the advantages and eliminates many
of the disadvantages of both centralized and decentralized processing is known
as distributed data processing (DDP). In a DDP system, data processing and
data management tasks are distributed to the different company locations.
The different locations are connected electronically to form a DDP network.
Each location has its own computer, its own storage and input/output devices,

Advantages of Centralized Processing

☐ Economies of scale may result from using a large mainframe rather than several smaller computers. Similar economies of scale apply to software and personnel costs.

☐ Processing is often easier to control since all significant processing is handled in one location.

☐ It may be easier to attract and retain more highly skilled technical, professional, and managerial personnel because of more varied experiences, greater career opportunities, etc.

☐ Centralization of administrative functions such as billing, payroll, and purchasing may lead to cost savings and fewer coordination problems.

☐ It may be easier to develop and enforce standardized procedures and documentation, which facilitates communication, coordination, and control.

☐ It may be easier to structure, update, and control data, since the use of integrated data bases is facilitated. Also central processing may provide greater accessibility to data, which makes it easier to meet management needs.

Disadvantages of Centralized Processing

☐ Larger computers are usually more complex, which often requires increased managerial supervision and better-trained and more experienced computer personnel.

☐ Its use may involve higher communications costs than distributed processing.

☐ If there is only one central computer and it goes down, all processing stops.

☐ Centralized processing may not allow adequate or timely access to system resources if there are many users all competing for time on the system.

☐ Operating systems are more costly and complex, requiring more system overhead.

☐ There is a greater tendency for the system to be rigid and inflexible. As a result, it is not as likely to meet a specific user's needs.

FIGURE 8.16
Advantages and disadvantages of centralized processing.

and often its own data. Each local system is capable of processing its own data, and this provides it with most of the advantages of decentralized processing. However, since each local system is part of a network of interconnected processors, data can be transferred electronically between locations. Often, a large computer serves as the host computer, and local systems pass data to the host for summarizations and for preparing top management reports. This gives the company many of the benefits of centralized processing. The result is a user-oriented (decentralized) as well as a top management-oriented (centralized) architecture.

DDP systems were introduced in the early 1970s, but their growth did not skyrocket until the microcomputer became a factor in the early 1980s. Since micros are as powerful as many of the mainframes of the early 1970s, they can handle much of the processing burden once borne by the centralized mainframes. Moreover, their processing power-to-cost ratio makes them very attractive ways to reduce the burden on centralized systems and spread the processing capabilities out to those who really need it—the users. As the power and capabilities of micros increase and as technological advances make data communications easier to use, the impact of DDP systems is bound to grow. A growth rate of thirty to forty percent a year is forecast for the next decade.

There are a number of significant advantages to DDP systems. Computing power is placed in the hands of the user, and there is a great deal of flexibility built into the approach. Each local system can be treated as a module of the entire system that can easily be added, upgraded, or deleted from the system. There are also a number of important disadvantages to a DDP system. The system may be more expensive than a centralized system. In addition, it is more difficult to coordinate the system and maintain hardware, software, and data consistency as each location tries to meet its own unique needs. The advantages and disadvantages of DDP systems as compared with centralized systems are summarized in Fig. 8.17.

DDP systems design.   DDP systems can be organized in many different ways, and there are a number of system components that can be distributed. System designers can distribute the processing capability (the hardware and software) to each location. Some locations may have their own computers and software, others may only have data preparation and data entry equipment, and still other locations may have some combination of processing capability between these two extremes. The data base can also be distributed by dividing the data base and partitioning it out to the individual locations. Alternatively, the data base could be stored at a central location, and copies of the data needed by each location could be maintained locally. The partitioning approach avoids data redundancy but requires more complex data communications to permit other locations to find and access the data they need. The replication (or copy) approach has the advantage of a centralized data base, built-in backup files, and simpler data communications. However, it does result in data redundancy. In practice, both approaches are used frequently, and large organizations often use a combination of approaches. That is, some data bases may be distributed, whereas others are not. In addition, some of the distributed data bases may use partitioning, whereas others use replication.

System functions can be distributed. One location may process receivables, another payables, another payroll, etc. While functional distribution works well in some organizations, it is not a workable distribution in many organizations. Control and authority can also be distributed. This is not the norm, however, as it makes it more difficult for the company to make sure that the data and security needs of the company are adequately met.

In designing and implementing a DDP system, there are several important things to keep in mind. Since most DDP systems are complex, the system should be designed to ensure reliability. The more complex the system, the more things that can go wrong and therefore the greater the need for reliability. The system should be easy to use. The more difficult the system is to use, the less likely people are to use it. The system should be properly controlled to ensure data integrity and security. The system should be responsive to the user. If the system is slow and cumbersome, it will not be able to respond to users in a timely fashion and therefore will not be used. The system should also be flexible. It should be capable of handling a wide range of tasks

Advantages of DDP Systems

☐ Users have control over the local system, plus access to a more powerful system as needed.

☐ It often meets users' needs better because processing is done at or closer to local level. Users can tailor a system to their needs and improve the quality of the information generated.

☐ There is increased system availability and faster system response time.

☐ Network computers can provide backup for each other, and there is less risk of catastrophic loss since DP resources are in multiple locations.

☐ Smaller systems are often less complex, which requires less managerial supervision and less experienced and well-trained operators.

☐ Communications costs are often less, since most processing is done at local levels.

☐ The processing burden of the host computer is reduced.

☐ Local processing usually provides faster response since communication delays are eliminated, and there is usually less competition for system resources.

☐ Increased throughput is possible by assigning tasks to specialized processors.

☐ Divisional managers are often more motivated to seek out profitable computer applications and participate in their development.

☐ Optimal usage of system resources occurs. For example, smaller systems can call on centralized systems (or the computer in the network) if a job is too large or if it is temporarily overloaded. This allows the work load to be better balanced and peaks in processing to be smoothed out.

☐ Processing locations can easily be added, upgraded, or deleted from the network as needed.

☐ During peak processing times, processing tasks can be forwarded to other systems in the network.

Disadvantages of DDP Systems

☐ There may be significant data duplication owing to multiple locations, each with a data base.

☐ Hardware costs may be higher owing to the resources needed at each location.

☐ It may be more difficult to document and control since authority and responsibility are also distributed.

☐ Multiple locations and communications channels make it harder to have adequate security controls. Also, relatively unsophisticated operating systems of smaller computers in the network make elaborate security features and controls difficult.

☐ Localized processing can make separation of duties more difficult.

☐ There is less on-site expertise since the expertise possible with a centralized system cannot be duplicated at each site.

☐ Local computers usually do not have the capacity, power, or sophistication of a centralized computer.

☐ It may be difficult to maintain hardware, software, and data consistency as locations meet their specific needs.

☐ It may be more difficult to transfer data between system components.

☐ It may be more difficult to control hardware acquisitions, resulting in incompatible equipment.

FIGURE 8.17
Advantages and disadvantages of DDP systems.

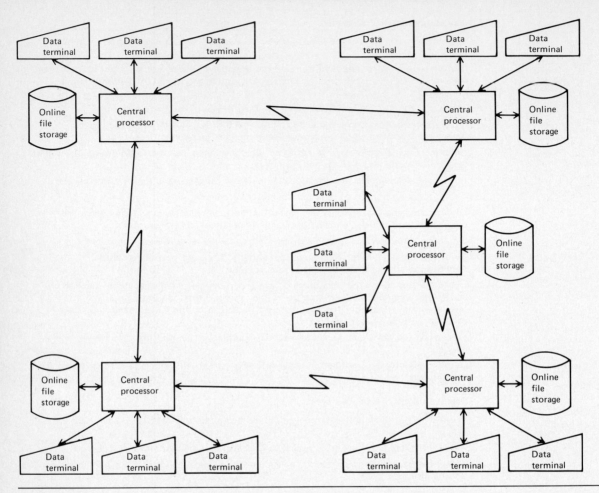

FIGURE 8.18
A distributed
processing network—
the ring
configuration.

and of efficiently meeting the varied needs of users. The system should probably not be installed unless it will pay for itself through cost savings or increased revenues.

Configurations.   In a distributed network, there are several ways the network
devices can be linked together. Figure 8.18 illustrates a *ring network* in which
the data communications channels form a loop or circular pattern as they link
the local processors together. Each computer communicates with its neighbor
and passes any message not intended for it around the ring to the appropriate
computer. Communications processors are often used to handle communications activities at each location.

   At the opposite extreme is the *star network,* which is illustrated in Fig. 8.19.
In a star network, there is a real-time central computer system to which all

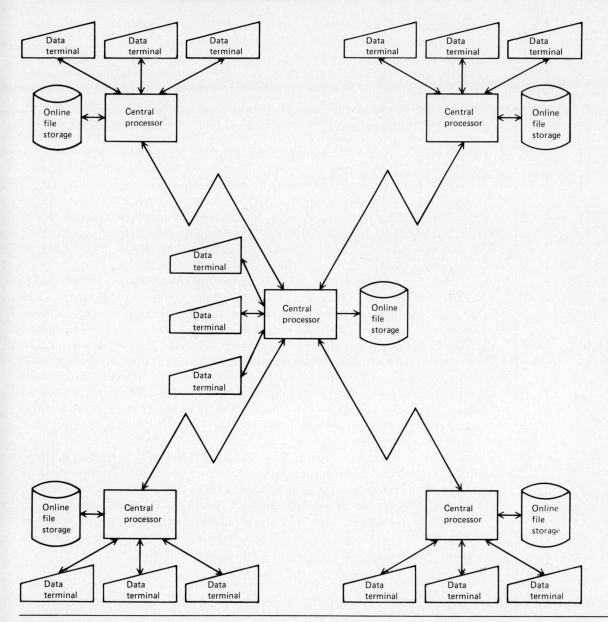

FIGURE 8.19
A distributed
processing network—
the star
configuration.

other computer systems in the network are linked. Each distributed computer routes all data and messages through the central computer, which forwards it to the proper location (this process is called *network switching*). A star network has the same configuration as a point-to-point centralized processing system. This centralized system can be changed to a DDP system by substituting microcomputers or minicomputers for the remote terminals and shifting some of the processing to the micros or minis.

Between these two extremes, there are *hybrid networks* containing both ring and star patterns. For example, several large systems could be linked together in a ring configuration while each also serves as the center of a star configuration consisting of smaller systems. A *hierarchical network* is a variation of the star network. It is so named because it looks and acts like a hierarchical organization chart. It consists of several levels of computers, all tied to a central or host computer. For example, the company might have a large computer to service the central office and top management needs. It can be connected to medium-sized computers at each regional office, each of which in turn is linked to small computers in each branch location. Each level processes its own data and passes upward the summary level data needed at the higher level. In addition, any job that is too large to be handled at the current level is passed upward. Data are likewise transferred from the top level down to lower levels. Figure 8.20 is an illustration of a hierarchical network.

The ring configuration allows "adjacent" computers to communicate directly. However, a message sent to a nonadjacent computer will have to pass through one or more other computers in the ring. If there is much communication within the system, each distributed system may need sophisticated control hardware and software. For this reason, many systems requiring a lot of internal communication use a star network so only one set of hardware and software is needed to route messages. However, a star network is less reliable since all messages must go through one unit. If the central computer goes down, the entire system goes down. In a ring network, there is an alternative route (around the ring in the other direction) if one of the computers or communications channels goes down.

Because of these conflicting factors, there is no simple answer as to which approach is best. That decision is usually based upon the distance between the points in the network, the amount of data to be transmitted, how quickly the message must be communicated, and the ability of each location in the network to handle messages. The decision also depends upon the organization's needs and the specific circumstances of the situation. In practice, most organizations use some combination of the approaches.

Local area networks   Many organizations would like to improve their communications systems by allowing equipment located in the same geographical area to communicate with each other or to share hardware devices. This reduces the investment required in hardware since everyone, for instance, would not have to have a high-quality printer. It would also allow users to conduct many of their communications tasks electronically. This communication is possible using a *local area network* (LAN). A LAN can link together microcomputers, word processors, disk drives, printers, modems, computer terminals, and a variety of other

FIGURE 8.20

Hierarchically distributed processing network.

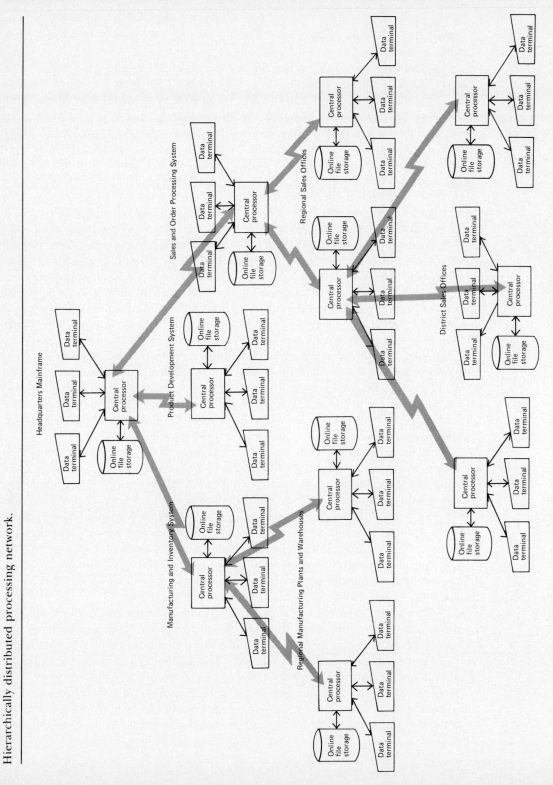

office and data processing equipment located in a limited geographical area, such as a building.

LANs are composed of several major components. The first is the hardware, such as micros, printers, and disk drives. The second is the wiring, or the cable that connects the hardware. In a cable LAN, coaxial or fiber optics cable is used to connect the network devices. If the cable is very long, electronic devices are used to boost signals so they remain strong and clear. In newer buildings, this cable is strung during construction so that the hardware devices can be plugged into the cable in the wall, just like telephones are now hooked up. As a result, these new buildings have electrical outlets, telephone outlets, and data or information outlets.

A third component is the LAN interface. Each hardware device that is to be connected to the network cable needs an interface device that manages the attachment and transmission process. A fourth component is the network master controller, which is the brain of the LAN. It is either a chip on an expansion card, a hard disk drive, or a dedicated computer. It is the intelligence of the LAN and acts as a traffic manager to route data between the hardware and to prevent and detect data "collisions." A fifth component is the network server. It is usually a hard disk drive containing the software (or protocols) that run the LAN and the programs that are available to network users. A sixth component is a communications interface device called a gateway. The gateway allows the LAN to be connected to external or wide-area networks and to communicate with external mainframes and data bases. This allows the network devices to communicate with computers almost anywhere in the world and to draw upon the greater computing power and storage capacity of larger systems. An example LAN configuration is shown in Fig. 8.21.

When a device is ready to send a message over the LAN, it breaks the messages down into packets of data. Each packet usually contains 1024 characters of data. Each packet is assigned a code that identifies the sending and the destination location. The sending station then "listens" to the line, and when it is free the message is placed on the line. The message is carried along the LAN line to its destination. Each station listens for packets addressed to it and removes them as they arrive. When transmission is completed and the message has been removed from the line, the receiving station sends an acknowledgment back to the sending station. Data transmission in a LAN is very fast—up to ten million bits (500 pages of text) per second.

There are a number of companies that have developed LAN systems. The most popular are Ethernet (by Xerox Corporation), Omninet (Corvus Systems), WangNet (Wang), Decnet (Digital Equipment), and NetWare (Novell).

Most LAN systems are quite flexible. Hardware devices can easily be added and deleted, and breakdowns in devices have no effect on other system devices. They offer enormous potential for improving communication in organizations. The major deterrents to the system are the lack of quality software for the LAN systems and the lack of protocol standards. As better software is

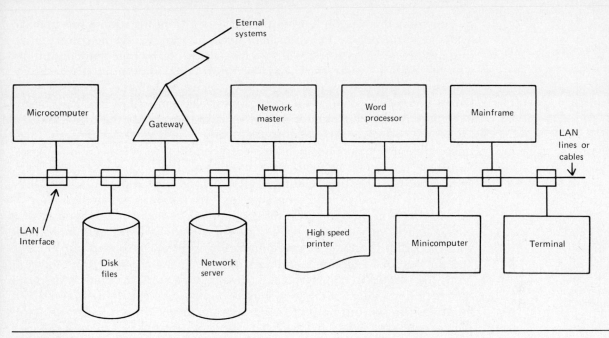

FIGURE 8.21
Local area network
configuration.

developed and as protocols are standardized, LAN systems will become a major force in bringing to pass the automated office of the future.

**Public data
networks**

Most organizations cannot afford their own private data communications systems to gather and maintain all the data they might need to make decisions.
Public data networks provide a viable alternative for these organizations. These
networks are large, privately owned organizations that sell computing services
and information to the public for a fee.

One service that public data networks make available is *time-sharing.* A
time-sharing system sells users small slices of time on large mainframes. A
company can rent hardware time, software programs, or both. Users can send
data to the service electronically, have it processed, and then have it returned
to them. Public data networks can also be used for teleconferencing, electronic mail, sending and retrieving messages, and electronic funds transfer
(EFT). The public data networks can be used for sending high-resolution
graphics and for generating voice responses. The services can also be used to
share a centralized data base with remote users or connect otherwise incompatible machines together.

One of the most important services that is offered is access to public data
bases. These public data bases are electronic libraries that contain millions of
items of data that can be reviewed, retrieved, analyzed, saved, etc. They con-

tain anything that a publisher or other provider of information wants to make available to the public. The information can be supplied by the company setting up these data base retrieval systems (DBRSs) or by independent authors who are paid a royalty each time the information they supply is accessed. Almost any information that a user might need is available, including some that is not even in print. As a result, these "electronic libraries" have begun to replace regular libraries for those who know how to use the DBRS and can afford the cost. Over 300 vendors supply more than 2000 data bases to over thirty million people who spend almost $3 million to access the data bases. Some of the most popular data bases are Dow Jones News/Retrieval, CompuServe, The Source, Quotron, TRW Inc., and Mead Data Central. These services are the most popular because they are the most comprehensive.

All that is needed to access these data bases is a personal computer or a terminal, a modem, communications software, a telephone, and an account with the DBRS vendor. The communications software is loaded into the PC, and the vendor's telephone number is dialed. The communications software helps the two devices interface, and the vendor's software sends a menu to the computer. Using a series of menus, the user selects the desired service and identifies the tasks to be performed and any criteria the software needs to perform the task. When finished, the communications software logs the user off the system. Search costs run from $5 to $300 an hour and vary depending on the time of day. In addition to the search charge, there are communications network charges and local telephone charges. A typical data base search takes from eight to eighteen minutes and, depending upon the data base searched, costs between $5 and $20.

The major advantage of such a system is obvious: instant access to a large amount of data. The main disadvantage is the difficulty in learning how to access the different DBRS services and to search them effectively. The costs of the searches are very reasonable given the information retrieved. It would often take hours of painstaking research to find the same information in a nonelectronic library.

Videotex, a new class of service, has become available in the last few years. Videotex services use a telephone, a television, and a special decoder. Modems and personal computers are not required. Using videotex, the user can access data bases and retrieve both text and graphic images. Users pay a fee for each page or screen of data accessed. Among the potential applications are electronic shopping, electronic banking, and electronic newspaper delivery. Shoppers of the future, for example, may be able to see models displaying the latest clothing lines while someone either by voice or printed text extols the virtues of the particular clothing.

Data Communications Applications

Although data communications systems are generally more costly and complex than conventional data processing systems, their utilization has increased sharply in recent years. This reflects their high potential as a profitable management tool. This section discusses just a few of the many uses for data communications systems in today's businesses.

Sales order processing

Many companies gain a significant competitive advantage from using a system that shortens the time between the receipt of customer orders and their delivery. Such a system could maintain its finished goods inventory file online and could have data terminals or microcomputers distributed throughout its sales territory. Salespeople could call orders in to a regional center at which the terminals or computers are located, or alternatively, each salesperson might be equipped with a small portable terminal or computer with which he or she could enter orders directly from the customer's plant or office. The system would access the finished goods inventory file to confirm the availability and quantity of each item ordered, and this information would be relayed to the salesperson immediately. The finished goods inventory file would be updated as the orders were placed. All appropriate journal entries would be made immediately in the general ledger, and the invoice could be immediately posted to an online accounts receivable ledger. If inventories were stored in a network of warehouses, delivery could be initiated by electronically transmitting a shipping order to the warehouse closest to the point of delivery.

In addition to speeding up the sales-order delivery cycle, the system could also have several other useful features. With the accounts receivable file online, a salesperson could answer customer inquiries about the status of the customer's account. The credit checking process could also be accomplished online as part of the order entry process. In addition, a sales analysis master file could be updated as orders were placed. This file could be used by marketing executives to provide up-to-date information on sales trends, thus facilitating management control of the sales function. Furthermore, as the finished goods inventory balances were updated, the updated balance of each item could be checked to determine if reordering or additional production were necessary to replenish the stock.

In addition to confirming sales orders in real time, the system is also significant from the standpoint of the complete integration of the accounting function. One entry of data results in the updating of all accounting records affected by the data and initiates the preparation of all documents necessary for processing the transaction. A more extensive discussion of such a system is provided in Chapter 16; in particular, see the systems flowchart in Fig. 16.11.

Transportation and travel reservations

Firms in the travel industry, notably the airline companies and major motel chains, were among the first to implement data communications systems. Applications involve processing and confirming customer reservations and are actually quite similar to processing sales orders. Data terminals or microcomputers are located at each reservations counter or motel lobby. Online file storage devices contain a record of the availability of services, such as available seats on airline flights or rooms at all motels in a chain. A customer may request a reservation in person or by phone. The reservation is entered into the system, and if the requested seat, room, or other service is available, the file record is updated and the reservation is immediately confirmed to the customer.

In an airline reservations system, several functions may be performed in addition to maintaining records of seat availability and processing reservations. These include calculating fares, updating sales and accounts receivable records, responding to customer requests for reconfirmation, and processing passenger check-ins. In a motel room reservations system, functions such as calculation of room charges, guest check-in and check-out, and revenue accounting are generally performed at each local unit rather than by the data communications system.

Banking systems

Banks were also among the first institutions to use data communications systems. In a banking system, various customer functions are performed at teller windows and automated teller machines (ATMs). A primary function is checking a customer's account to determine whether the balance is large enough for a withdrawal being made by the waiting customer. In addition, deposits and withdrawals may be posted to customer accounts through the system. Hardware requirements include a data terminal for each teller window, ATMs at various locations, and online file storage to maintain a record of each customer's account.

The banking system makes an up-to-date record of each customer's account available to every teller and ATM, even those located at a distance from the main bank. Such systems enable banks to provide faster and more convenient service to customers, which allows a reduction in the number of tellers required to wait on customers and reduces the amount of time each customer must wait for service.

Many banks have since expanded their applications into other areas, such as mortgages, commercial loans, consumer loans, and credit files. In recent years the concept of one gigantic data communications system to handle all banking transactions has emerged. Retail merchants would be tied into the banking network through point-of-sale terminals and microcomputers, and sales transactions would be immediately charged to the consumer's bank account and simultaneously credited to the merchant's account. Transactions among corporations and other institutions would be handled electronically rather than by check. Deposit of paychecks to the bank accounts of employees by their employers would also be done electronically. Individuals, using microcomputers and modems, could access the bank's system and pay all their bills electronically. This concept has become known as *electronic funds transfer* (EFT).

The ATM provides bank customers with twenty-four–hour banking. All they have to do is find an ATM, insert their specially coded plastic bankcard, and punch in a PIN (personal identification number). The PIN is a confidential code known only to the bank's customer and the computer. Using the bank's data communications network, the ATM checks the PIN to see if it matches the account number on the bankcard. If it does, the user can withdraw or deposit funds. With the proper ATM and data communications links, the user can also purchase a variety of other items, such as stamps, airline tickets, and movie and play tickets.

Retail sales

Many retail organizations utilize data communications systems to collect and summarize sales data and to perform credit checking and inventory control functions. Electronic cash registers and point-of-sale recorders serve as data terminals for these applications. They capture, at the point of sale, such things as the item sold, the quantity, and the price. In such applications a customer's credit standing may be checked at the time a credit transaction is initiated. The credit is checked by forwarding the credit card number to their bank's computer where it electronically determines the credit standing and amount of credit that can be granted. If the credit sale is authorized, or if the sale is for cash, the inventory file is accessed and updated for the specific merchandise sold. Since this enables an up-to-date record of all inventory items to be maintained, the system can originate inventory reordering as needed. Up-to-date sales and inventory totals are available to management through online data base queries. The system can also maintain the price of the item purchased and automatically ring up the amount. Many systems use audio response units to inform the customer of the amount.

Computer-based message systems

Data communications systems are used to electronically transmit a wide variety of items, including documents, memos, pictures, graphics, mail, and voice messages. A number of word processing systems are configured in such a way that they can communicate directly with other word processing systems. As a result, documents can be easily forwarded between the connecting word processing systems. *Facsimile transmission* allows not only documents but also pictures, graphics, signatures, etc., to be sent over a data communications system. A facsimile machine at the sending station translates the different shades of light and dark on a page into signals that can be sent over the communications links. A similar machine on the receiving end translates the item back to the proper images and reproduces them on a piece of paper. The disadvantage of facsimile transmission is the high cost of the hardware and the slow transmission times.

Electronic mail systems allow a person to send, receive, or forward a message to or from anyone else on the system who has a "mailbox," or electronic storage location, in the system. The system can be used to send messages internally or to units external to the organization. These systems can at least partially replace written memos, the telephone, and the regular mail system. Users can set up predefined distribution lists to avoid having to reenter names each time a message is sent to the same group.

Voice mail, or a voice store-and-forward system, is a flexible means of sending a spoken message to someone even when they are not at their remote terminal (telephone). These systems convert a spoken message into a computer-storable digital message that is stored in the receiver's electronic mailbox. Voice mail can be distributed in the same way that text messages are except that hard (printed) copies cannot be produced.

Teleconferencing is another means of communicating electronically. AT&T, for example, is setting up teleconferencing rooms where conferees can gather and use closed-circuit TV to conduct a conference with multiple users at multiple locations. Personal computers are also being used for teleconferencing. All communication is written, but multiple users in different locations can all be linked together. Teleconferencing is expected to grow rapidly in the late 1980s and early 1990s.

Computer-based messages have a number of important advantages. The messages can be distributed very quickly, and the sender does not have to worry about busy signals or unanswered phones. In addition, since most systems are capable of informing the sender that the message was placed in the receiver's mailbox, the sender has fewer worries about whether a message was received. The cost of the communication is quite reasonable. A further advantage is that the user and receiver can send or read their mail at any time simply by accessing the system.

These computer-based message systems are the foundation of the widely heralded *automated office* or office of the future. In these offices, all workers are connected electronically and pass messages, files, worksheets, etc., to each other over the LAN that connects their *multifunction workstations*. These workstations will usually be high-powered microcomputers that share common resources and are capable of both data and word processing.

Summary

A data communications system consists of five major components: the sending device, the communications interface device, the communications channel, the receiving device, and communications software. Signals in a data communications system may be analog or digital; serial or parallel; asynchronous or synchronous; simple, half-duplex, or full-duplex.

There are a number of hardware devices that can be attached to a communications channel and used to send data to or receive data from a computer. These include dumb and intelligent terminals; micro-, mini-, and mainframe computers; and source data automation devices. Communications interface devices, such as multiplexors, concentrators, and front-end processors, make it possible for slow-speed data communications devices to take advantage of high-speed transmission lines.

Data communications system software is usually more complex than conventional system software. Special communications control programs manage the data communications activity and interact with the various terminals. The control programs may be executed either by the main computer or by a programmable front-end processor.

A communications channel connects the sender and receiver in a data communications network. This connection can be accomplished by utilizing a coaxial cable, a standard telephone line, or a fiber optics cable or by using terrestrial microwave, satellite, or cellular radio. Communications channels are classified according to their information carrying capacity: narrowband, voiceband, and wideband. Three voice-grade telephone line services are available: leased lines, switched lines, and WATS lines. Communications channels may be configured in three basic ways: point-to-point, multidrop, and line-sharing. Communications channels link a variety of hardware devices together to form a communications network. The networks can take one of the following forms: centralized, decentralized, distributed data processing, local area, and public data.

There are a wide variety of data communications systems, including sales order processing, transportation and travel reservations, banking, retail sales, and computer-based message systems.

Review Questions

1. Define the following:

telecommunications system	communications control program
data communications	micro-to-mainframe link
centralized data processing system	protocol
teleprocessing system	communications channel
distributed data processing	coaxial cable
message	fiber optics cable
bits per second	terrestrial microwave
digital data	satellite microwave
analog data	cellular radio
serial transmission	narrowband line
parallel transmission	voiceband line
asynchronous transmission	wideband (or broadband) line
synchronous transmission	leased line
simplex channel	switched line
half-duplex channel	Wide Area Telephone Service (WATS)
full-duplex channel	
terminal emulator	point-to-point line
multiplexor	multidrop line
concentrator	line-sharing device
communications (or front-end) processor	polling approach
	contention approach

communications networks   local area network
standard network architecture   time-sharing
centralized network   videotex
simplex system   electronic funds transfer
duplex system   facsimile transmission
decentralized system   electronic mail system
ring network   voice mail
star network   teleconferencing
network switching   automated office
hybrid network   multifunctional workstation
hierarchical network

2. Distinguish between a centralized data processing system, a teleprocessing system, and a distributed data processing system. Which is the most widely used today?

3. List the five major components of a data processing system.

4. Describe analog and digital transmission. Which is most frequently used? Why?

5. Describe both serial and parallel transmission. When is parallel transmission used instead of serial transmission?

6. What problems can arise in electronic communications if the electronic signals are not synchronized? What methods are used to keep the signals in sync?

7. List some of the more popular interface devices.

8. How do concentrators differ from multiplexors? What are the principal advantages of multiplexors and concentrators? What causes these advantages?

9. How can a communications processor make a mainframe computer more efficient? What disadvantages are associated with the communications processor?

10. List some of the tasks performed by data communications software.

11. What are the parts of a micro-to-mainframe link? Why are controls in a micro-to-mainframe link important? What are some of the controls that can be used?

12. List the different types of communications channels and give the characteristics of each.

13. Why do fiber optics show so much promise over copper wire? While fiber optics has many advantages, what are some of its disadvantages?

14. How are communications channels classified? List these categories and give their use in data transmission.

15. Give the advantages and disadvantages of
    a) leased lines,
    b) switched lines, and
    c) WATS lines.

16. What are the basic configurations for a communications network?

17. Give the primary advantages and disadvantages of the following configurations:
    a) point-to-point
    b) multidrop
    c) line-sharing

18. Distinguish between common, specialized, and value-added communications carriers.

19. Why has it been difficult for users to develop simple, unified data communications networks?

20. Distinguish between a simplex system and a duplex system. Which is more reliable and at what cost is this increased reliability obtained?

21. Which system—centralized, decentralized, or distributed—has a user-oriented as well as a top-management oriented architecture? Discuss the strengths and weaknesses of centralized, decentralized, and distributed systems.

22. List the portions of a DDP system that may either be centralized or distributed.

23. What factors control the type of configuration that should be used in a distributed network?

24. What are the major components of a local area network?

25. Describe the use of data communications systems in the following areas.
    a) sales order processing
    b) transportation and travel reservations
    c) banking
    d) retail sales
    e) message systems

Discussion Questions

26. At some future date, it is conceivable that all households and merchants will possess a microcomputer that serves as an online terminal to a communitywide data communications system. Discuss some of the ways in which

members of a household might use such a system. How could they use the microcomputer on a stand-alone basis?

27. Do you feel that data communications systems are useful to top management executives in the performance of the management function? Do you feel that it would be worthwhile for each top executive in a large, multidivisional company to have in his or her office a computer terminal linked to the company's central computer system? Describe circumstances in which it would (a) definitely be worthwhile or (b) definitely not be worthwhile.

28. Communication is vital to any organization. It is especially vital to a multidivisional company that is spread over a wide geographic area. Corporate structure is often aligned along communication lines. Discuss the organizational structure that might conform to the star, ring, or hybrid network configuration. Could organizational difficulties arise if an improper configuration is chosen?

29. Data base retrieval systems are increasing in popularity. They are used by doctors, lawyers, accountants, and other professional and private groups. Data base systems are changing the way people think about information. Some people feel that data bases will eventually replace books and libraries. Discuss the extent to which you feel data base retrieval systems will replace traditional information gathering techniques. Also, discuss the implications of rapid information retrieval.

30. Discuss how a data communications system might be usefully applied within
    a) a university,
    b) a life insurance company,
    c) a hospital, and
    d) a construction company.

Problems and Cases

REQUIRED

31. The management of Cross Country Company is currently considering a change from centralized data processing to either decentralized or distributed data processing.
    a) Briefly define *each* of the following:
       1. centralized data processing
       2. decentralized data processing
       3. distributed data processing
    b) Each of these data processing approaches has advantages and disadvantages as compared with one or both of the other two approaches. Match the advantages and disadvantages in column 2 with the processing approaches shown in column 1. The items in column 2 may be used more than once. (CIA Examination adapted)

COLUMN 1	COLUMN 2
Processing Approaches	Advantages or Disadvantages
1. Centralized 2. Decentralized 3. Distributed	a) Reduces the risk of loss or destruction to hardware and critical data. b) No opportunity for distributed network. c) Dependence on one computer. d) Permits the use of the data base approach and minimizes the duplication of common data. e) Most difficult to maintain the overall security of data. f) No method for coordinating or exchanging data during processing.

32. The directors of Colorgraph Printing are reviewing a proposal to acquire Puball Publishers. Puball's operations are located in an urban area about 300 miles from Colorgraph's headquarters. Colorgraph's success in recent years, according to its management, has been attributed in large part to its computerized management information system. Puball, however, has used a computer only for financial accounting applications such as payroll and inventory records.

   In considering the acquisition, Colorgraph's board of directors focused on two options for developing a computerized management information system that would include Puball: (1) a centralized system or (2) a distributed system.

REQUIRED

   a) Indicate whether computer terminals having programmed intelligence limited to collecting, editing, transmitting, and receiving data may be used with a centralized system, a distributed system, or with both types of systems.

   b) Compare the degree of detail likely to be transmitted from a site location to headquarters in a centralized system and in a distributed system.

   c) Explain briefly why Puball's management would be more likely to be involved in and concerned with data processing in a distributed system than in a centralized system. Assume Puball would be organized as a separate profit center.

   d) Explain briefly why a distributed system would be less subject to a complete system breakdown. (CIA Examination adapted)

33. The Widget Manufacturing Company is planning to install a data terminal at its San Francisco regional sales office that would be online to its computer center in Los Angeles 400 miles away. One decision that must be made is whether to lease a line, obtain a WATS line, or use switched pub-

lic lines. The monthly cost of a leased line would include a service charge of $83.50 plus mileage charges based upon the following rates.[1]

Mileage	0–100	101–250	251–300	Over 300
Rate/mile	$2.82	$1.48	$0.79	$0.26

The charge for a WATS line would be a $30.50 per month service charge plus an $18 per hour monthly usage charge. Public telephone rates are $0.57 for the first minute and $0.34 for each additional minute. It is estimated that the time required to enter a transaction over the terminal will average two minutes.

REQUIRED

a) Compute the monthly cost of the leased line.
b) At what average monthly volume of transactions would the total cost of the leased line be equal to the cost of using (1) the WATS line and (2) switched public lines? (Make each computation separately.)
c) Assume that an average volume of 810 transactions per month is expected. Which of the three alternatives would be least expensive? Show all supporting calculations.
d) Assume that the transactions would be entered in groups of three so that the extra rate for the first minute would be avoided for two thirds of all transactions if switched public lines were used. How would this affect your answer to part (c)?

34. The Zion Company utilizes a real-time computer system for inventory control. Leased voice-grade data communications lines connect the main warehouse and computer center in Chicago directly with warehouses in Cleveland, Cincinnati, Detroit, and Pittsburgh. There is a monthly access fee of $166.26 per line. In addition, the monthly rates for these lines are:

Mileage	1–15	16–25	26–100	101–250	Over 250
Rate/mile	$2.47	$1.92	$1.31	$0.79	$0.67

(**Note:** For an explanation of how these rates are used, see footnote 1.)

Distances from Chicago to the other four cities are:

From Chicago to	Cleveland	Cincinnati	Detroit	Pittsburgh
Distance in miles	350	302	298	472

---

[1]In computing total monthly mileage charges using these rates, a separate calculation is needed for each individual mileage segment, with the results then added to obtain a total cost. For example, a line of 300 miles would include a fixed cost of $83.50 plus mileage charges of $2.82 (100) + $1.48 (150) + $0.79 (50), for a total of $627.00 per month.

The company is considering obtaining a multiplexor to be installed in its Cleveland warehouse. The voice-grade lines from Chicago to Cincinnati, Detroit, and Pittsburgh would then be replaced by leased voice-grade lines from Cleveland to Cincinnati, Detroit, and Pittsburgh. Distances from Cleveland to those cities are:

From Cleveland to	Cincinnati	Detroit	Pittsburgh
Distance in miles	238	172	128

In addition, the line from Chicago to Cleveland would be conditioned to allow higher transmission speeds, and this would cost $50 per month. The multiplexor would cost $100 per month.

REQUIRED Calculate the amount that the Zion Company would save per month by obtaining the multiplexor.

35. The Illinois Wholesale Liquor Corporation utilizes a real-time invoicing, inventory, and accounts receivable system. All sales orders are received in a central sales order department where they are entered into the system by clerks utilizing CRT terminals. The system immediately transmits a shipping order to one of several warehouses, each of which has a teleprinter online to the system to receive these orders. It also prepares six copies of a customer invoice for each order and updates accounts receivable and finished goods master files. The firm's financial vice-president utilizes a CRT terminal for an occasional inquiry into the system. Periodic reports generated by the system include an inventory reorder report (daily) and an accounts receivable aging schedule (monthly).

REQUIRED Prepare a systems flowchart of the system.

36. The Texas Machinery Distributing Company is a wholesaler of a variety of machinery products that has its headquarters and a central warehouse in Houston, Texas. Sales offices are located in Dallas, Waco, Austin, San Antonio, Corpus Christi, Abilene, and Laredo, Texas. The company has decided to install a real-time data communications system for processing sales orders. The computer center is located in Houston, and one or more microcomputers that will also function as terminals will be located in each sales office.

A major concern of the company in the design of a real-time system has been the cost of the data communications network. The company is considering four alternative configurations:

1. Seven voice-grade leased lines, from Houston to each sales office;
2. A wideband line from Houston to Austin and a communications processor in Austin to service six voice-grade leased lines from the other six sales offices;
3. Dial-up service from each sales office to Houston; and
4. A wideband line from Houston to Austin and a communications processor in Austin to service dial-up lines from the other six sales offices.

Monthly cost figures for voice-grade and wideband leased lines are as follows.

Voice-grade	Mileage	0–50	51–150	Over 150
	Rate/mile	$2.20	$1.40	$1.05

There is a monthly charge of $98.50 for each voice-grade line.

Wideband	Mileage	0–50	51–150	Over 150
	Rate/mile	$2.40	$1.60	$1.20

In addition, there is a $165.20 monthly charge for each wideband line. (**Note:** For an explanation of how these rates are used, see footnote 1.)

The following table shows the distance in miles from Houston to the seven sales offices, and from Austin to the other six sales offices.

	Waco	Austin	Dallas	San Antonio	Laredo	Corpus Christi	Abilene
Houston	181	164	244	195	312	208	349
Austin	106	—	198	79	233	194	217

The table below shows the cost of a two-minute long-distance call from Houston to the seven sales offices, and from Austin to the other six sales offices.

	Waco	Austin	Dallas	San Antonio	Laredo	Corpus Christi	Abilene
Houston	0.88	0.85	0.91	0.88	0.94	0.88	0.94
Austin	0.82	—	0.88	0.76	0.91	0.88	0.91

It is assumed that each call will consume approximately two minutes. The table below shows the expected average monthly volume of calls from each of the seven sales offices.

Office	Waco	Austin	Dallas	San Antonio	Laredo	Corpus Christi	Abilene
Monthly volume	200	450	650	500	150	350	200

If either alternative (2) or (4) is chosen, the communications processor will cost $500 per month.

REQUIRED

Determine the total monthly cost of the data communications network under each of the four alternatives. Based on cost, which alternative should the company select?

37. Shown below is a map illustrating the relative relationship of six major plants operated by the Gardiner Manufacturing Company.

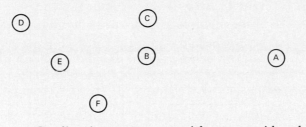

   Gardiner's management wishes to provide a data communications link between its main computer center at point A and data terminals at the other five locations. The alternative network configurations have been narrowed down to three: (1) use multidrop lines, (2) locate a multiplexor at point B, lease a line to connect the multiplexor to the central computer, and lease four lines to connect the other four points to the multiplexor; (3) same as (2) except use switched lines to connect points C, D, E, and F to the multiplexor. Additional information follows.

☐ The distances between each point and the other five points are indicated in the following table.

Distance from \ to	A	B	C	D	E	F
A		200	220	370	300	280
B			50	180	100	100
C				160	130	150
D					80	140
E						60
F						

☐ Leased lines that provide digital data transmission service will be used. Rates for these lines are as follows.

Mileage	1	2–15	16–25	26–100	Over 100
Rate/mile	$56.36	$1.99	$1.66	$1.24	$0.73

(**Note:** For an explanation of how these rates are used, see footnote 1.)

☐ Under alternative (1), there will be an additional service charge of $93.45 per month for each of the six points serviced.

☐ Under alternative (2), the monthly service charge is $311 each for points A and B, and $93.45 each for points C, D, E, and F.

☐ Under alternative (3), the monthly service charge is $311 each for points A and B only.

☐ Separate mileage charges must be computed for each separate link in a multidrop line.

☐ If multidrop lines are used, several "dumb" terminals would have to be replaced with "smart" terminals, which would raise equipment rental costs by $500 per month.

☐ If the multiplexor is used, its monthly rental is $100.

☐ If switched lines are used, the cost per minute for a long-distance hookup between point B and the other four points is as follows:

Point B to	C	D	E	F
Rate/minute	$0.25	$0.30	$0.29	$0.29

☐ The estimated volume of usage in terms of hookup hours per month for locations C, D, E, and F is as follows:

Location	C	D	E	F
Hours/month	20	10	15	12

☐ The use of switched lines would require four modems at location B and one at each of locations C, D, E, and F. Their monthly cost is $25 each.

REQUIRED　　Compute the total monthly cost of data communications under each of the three specified alternatives.

38. The Establishment Manufacturing Corporation (EMC) has its headquarters and central data processing facility in Boston, and four regional data processing centers located in Hartford, New York City, Philadelphia, and Washington, D.C. EMC plans to establish a distributed data processing network by linking these centers together using data communications. Two plans are under consideration: (1) a star network in which separate lines would link Boston to each of the other four centers and (2) a ring network that would include links from Boston to Hartford, Boston to New York City, Hartford to Philadelphia, New York City to Washington, and Philadelphia to Washington.

One of the factors affecting the choice among these alternatives is the cost of data communications. Leased wideband lines would be used because of the high volume of data transmission expected. The rates that have been quoted are as follows.

Mileage	1–250	251–500	Over 500
Rate/mile	$15.75	$11.05	$7.90

(**Note:** For an explanation of how these rates are used, see footnote 1.)

The following table shows the distance in miles between each of the pairs of cities. In addition to the line charges, another element of cost is modems. Two high-speed modems are required for each link between a pair of cities. The monthly lease cost for each modem is $215.

Distance from \ to	Boston	Hartford	New York City	Philadelphia	Washington
Boston		93	204	302	440
Hartford			114	211	347
New York City				100	238
Philadelphia					142
Washington, D.C.					

REQUIRED

Compute the total monthly data communications cost under each of the two alternatives under consideration.

39. Classy Videos is a chain of eight video rental stores located in Chicago, Illinois. Classy rents video cassettes of the most popular movies and VCRs. Each store has between 2000 and 3000 videos in stock as well as 200 to 400 video machines. Last year, the chain had its best year ever with rental revenue in excess of $3 million.

Classy Videos only rents to members of the Classy Video Rental Club. A person can become a member by filling out an application and by paying a $100 deposit. The company needs the application information and deposit since the company has experienced problems with cassettes and machines being stolen by customers. Once a customer has rented items and promptly returned them six times, the $100 deposit is returned.

Each cassette and VCR has its own identification number and checkout card. When club members want to check out a movie or VCR, they select its checkout card from the rental catalog and give the card to a clerk on duty. The clerk then pulls the customer's file and enters the rental information. A club member may also reserve a movie or machine by calling the store and having the clerk pull the identification card. If a store does not have the desired movie in stock, the movie can be acquired on loan from another of its stores.

When Classy Videos consisted of a few stores, the system described above was adequate. Now, however, problems exist. Some of the problems have been lost identification cards and lengthy lines of customers waiting for service—especially during peak hours. Additional problems include an inability to determine which movies and VCRs are available for rental and which have been rented, movies and VCRs being checked out to the wrong customers, members finding out that the movie they reserved has been checked out to someone else, and problems with keeping track of transferred inventory.

Classy is in the process of reviewing computer systems that will help solve some of the problems mentioned as well as provide for future expansion. The company is trying to choose between (1) stores connected by dumb terminals to a minicomputer at a central store, (2) microcomputers at each store that can communicate with each other on demand, and (3) microcomputers at each store and a minicomputer at a control store.

REQUIRED

a) Identify the hardware needed for each approach and explain the advantages and disadvantages of each of the three alternatives.

b) Select the configuration you feel will best meet Classy's needs and support your decision.

c) Irrespective of your decision in part (b), draw and label configuration (3).

d) Describe the files that Classy will need to maintain to store the information it needs.

e) Would a computer system solve all of Classy Video's problems? Explain why or why not.

40. Kozbosco is a manufacturing firm with four offices located in Alphaville, Beta City, Gamma Heights, and Sigma Flats. The firm has its headquarters in Sigma Flats. The company wants to computerize the flow of information from the outlying offices to the firm's headquarters. The diagram shown below illustrates the relative location of the cities and also indicates the distance between the cities.

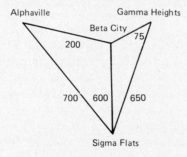

The following costs apply.

1. The monthly lease cost for the hardware switching equipment needed with multidrop lines is $400.

2. Long-distance phone calls from Sigma Flats to Alphaville, Beta City, and Gamma Heights are $0.60, $0.50, and $0.55 per minute, respectively.

3. Long-distance daytime phone charges are $0.30 per minute from Beta City to Alphaville and $0.20 per minute from Beta City to Gamma Heights.

4. The amount of time each city expects to spend in communications activities per month are as follows: sixty hours for Alphaville, fifty for Beta City, and forty-five for Gamma Heights.

5. The cost of leased lines is $4.00 per mile for the first 50 miles, $3.50 per mile for the next 50 miles, $3.00 per mile for the next 100 miles, and $2.00 per mile for every mile over 200 miles.

a) Compute the monthly cost of the communications system if

1. A point-to-point configuration with switched lines is used to connect Sigma Flats to the other three cities,
2. A point-to-point configuration with leased lines is used to connect Sigma Flats to the other three cities,
3. A multidrop approach is used and a leased line connects Sigma Flats to Beta City and switched lines are used to connect Alphaville and Gamma Heights to Beta City, or
4. A multidrop configuration over totally leased lines is used.

b) Based on price, which configuration alternative should Kozbosco select?

41. The Savings Bank of California (SBC) is a large bank headquartered in Los Angeles. A strong selling point for the bank is a customer's ability to conduct his or her banking at offices throughout the state. SBC has regional offices in San Diego, Orange County, southern Los Angeles, northern Los Angeles, and San Francisco. Each region consists of between five to eight local banks.

SBC has established its own statewide real-time computer system. Each regional office maintains a data base for its local savings, checking, and loan customers. This data base is accessed by the banks in that particular region, by other regional offices, and by the corporate headquarters. Each local bank has four to twelve terminals that tie into a minicomputer. The minicomputers at each local bank are linked directly to computers located at SBC's regional offices. The lines between the local banks and the regional offices have fairly heavy usage because of the number of transactions handled each day by the banks. Each regional computer is tied to two other regional computers so that if one computer goes down, information can be rerouted around the computer that is down. In addition to being tied to two other regional computers, each regional computer is tied directly to a mainframe computer at corporate headquarters.

Both the regional computers and the headquarters mainframe use front-end processors to help manage the data communications process. The regional computers are used during the day to process checks, bankcard payments, and other transactions to customer accounts. Periodically during the day, the regional computers update the mainframe data bases for the transactions processed during the day. The mainframe computer at corporate headquarters coordinates the activities of the regional computers and maintains SBC's companywide records. The headquarters mainframe also handles all funds transfers with the bank's office in New York. Communications between corporate headquarters and the New York office is through microwave transmission.

When a customer goes to a local bank, the teller, through a terminal, uses the local bank's minicomputer to access the regional computer data base. If the customer is a member of the region, his or her account is updated for the transaction. If the customer's account is not maintained by the local region, the correct regional data base is accessed and updated. Funds from the local region are then transferred from or to the accessed region to cover the transaction.

REQUIRED

a) What type of communications network is SBC using: centralized, decentralized, DDP, LAN, or public data network? Explain your answer and state why the other networks are not what SBC is using.

b) Draw the communications network configuration used by SBC. Is this network a star, ring, hybrid, or hierarchical network?

c) What kinds of communications channels can SBC use in its data communications system?

d) The communications channels that connect the local banks and the regional offices can be either point-to-point, multidropped, or line-shared. When is each most appropriate and what are the advantages and drawbacks of each?

e) Should the channels that connect the local banks and the regional centers be narrowband, voiceband, or wideband?

42. The corporate office of Chancy's, Inc., located in Portland, Oregon, handles the billings, collections, accounting, and projections for the company. Currently, all computer processing is done on the company's mainframe computer using dumb terminals. Because of the heavy demands placed on the system, it is often overtaxed. Users sometimes have to wait in long queues to gain access. Once the system is accessed, response time is often slow due to the number of jobs being run on the mainframe. This overloading causes the system to periodically malfunction. The malfunctions and poor response time have had a negative effect on company productivity; for example, billings are often late and the collection process is very slow.

The company has purchased a number of microcomputers in the last few years in an attempt to improve productivity. The micros have allowed Chancy's people to significantly increase the quality of their projections, forecasts, and other planning tools. The company is currently thinking about installing micro-to-mainframe link (MML) software that would allow corporate users to access Chancy's corporate mainframe data base using their personal computers.

a) What would be the advantage to Chancy of installing the MML?

b) What risks is the company taking by installing the MML?

c) What controls should Chancy implement to minimize its risk?

43. The Simplex Corporation, a large distributor of electronic equipment, recently moved their corporate headquarters into a new office building

designed to meet their unique needs. Among the needs was a state-of-the-art computer system that had the ability to link together all computer hardware devices within the building. In addition, the system had to have the ability to communicate with systems other than the one in the head-quarters building.

The company has six main functions that are computerized. These functions are accounts payable, accounts receivable, payroll, inventory routing, accounting, and support (mostly word processing). The company also uses spreadsheet and data base software for planning, for making projections, and for analyzing costs. These items are passed back and forth between corporate personnel using the company's new local area network (LAN) system.

The system consists of thirty microcomputers, one of which serves as the master controller, at $1995 a piece. The system has seven hard disk drives, as $1200 each. Six of the hard disks serve as data base storage, whereas the seventh is host to the system's programs. There are ten high-speed dot-matrix printers at $1500 and four laser printers at $3500 each. All the computer devices are linked through LAN interfaces that cost $595 each. The LAN is linked to the company's mainframe computer and to external data bases using a gateway that costs $5530. One of four modems, at a cost of $450 each, is used to access data bases external to corporate headquarters.

REQUIRED

a) What is a local area network? Include in your answer a description of the major components of the local area network and an explanation of what each does.

b) Draw the hardware configuration described in the problem. You only need to sketch one micro, printer, hard disk, etc.

c) Calculate the total hardware cost of the local area network as described in the problem.

44. For each of the cases described below, (i) diagram the configuration described and (ii) determine

☐ Whether the configuration is a centralized, decentralized, or distributed processing system,

☐ Whether a star, ring, hierarchical, or hybrid configuration is used, and

☐ Whether the lines used in the configuration are point-to-point, multidrop, or line-shared.

a) Mountain West Milk Producers process milk and milk products for consumers in Utah. The association's headquarters are in downtown Salt Lake City. Milk is processed at a plant ten miles west of down-town. Ice cream is made thirty miles south of Salt Lake, and cheese is cured sixty miles north of Salt Lake City.

Each morning, drivers collect raw milk from the association's milk producers and transport the milk to storage tanks at the processing plant. Information on the amount of milk collected and the amount of fat content is keyed into the processing plant's microcomputer. The type of products produced, their cost, sales data, and transfers are also kept on the micro. The processing plant prints out daily reports to meet its information needs. Similar information is also collected from the ice cream and cheese processing plants.

The information from the three locations is transferred by modem to a front-end processor linked to the mainframe computer at company headquarters. The information gathered is stored on disk and used by headquarters to prepare payroll, invoices, payment checks to milk producers, and financial statements.

b) The Nevada Department of Motor Vehicles (DMV) has an office at the state capital and offices in each major city in the state to register motor vehicles and license drivers. The capital office has a number of terminal emulators that are linked to a front-end processor. Upon receipt of a registration form in the mail, processing clerks at the state office use the vehicle's serial number to update the vehicle record in the DMV's data base. As people come in to the local offices to be licensed or to register their vehicles, the clerks use the terminals to update the local division data base. At the end of each working day, the capital's mainframe pulls the day's update information from the division minicomputers and updates the state's data bases. Receipts are printed at both the local and state offices and given to or mailed to the appropriate people.

Besides being linked to the capital mainframe, the local minicomputers are linked to the computers of two other divisions. As a result, all the division minis are linked together to provide quicker access to local information as well as to provide system backup. Computerization of the system has helped state, county, and local police to quickly obtain drivers license and registration information. These agencies are tied by modem to the local and state data bases.

c) Rollo Community Bank in Rollo, North Dakota, is an independently held and operated bank. The bank makes business, car, farm, and mortgage loans. Due to its close proximity to the Canadian border, the bank handles currency exchanges for a small fee. The bank employs three officers and seven tellers. The tellers operate five terminals that are tied to a minicomputer. The tellers handle all monies coming into or going out of the bank. The three officers have access to the minicomputer through the terminals but do not have the authorization to conduct transactions. When the loan officer approves a loan, the debtor presents the loan papers to a teller who issues a check for the loan amount. The bank also uses the minicomputer to communicate with a currency exchange data base in New York. Up-to-date exchange rate information is vital, especially in times of rapid currency rate fluctuation.

d) Luxury Cars International is a worldwide manufacturer and distributor of automobiles whose headquarters are in Kansas City. Its U.S. operations include four production plants, twenty regional warehouses, and 300 franchise distributors. The company's production efforts are driven by demand, so accurate distribution information is vital to ensure proper inventory levels.

The franchise dealerships keep their inventory records on a microcomputer. Car orders are generated in two ways: (1) a customer makes a special order for an automobile that the dealer does not have in stock, or (2) the dealer estimates the demand for makes and models, compares this demand with inventory levels, and generates orders as needed. The dealerships are tied, by modem, to a minicomputer at a regional warehouse. When the dealer has a special order, the microcomputer is used to access the regional data base. This data base stores the warehouse inventory, as well as the inventory levels of dealerships in the same region. If the desired car is not in the regional data base, an order is sent to a minicomputer in St. Louis that controls inventory for the entire company. This computer polls the other regional computers to try to find the car desired. If the desired car is found, the computer decides whether it is better to have the car transferred to the desired location or to special order the car. If the decision is made to transfer, the appropriate regional warehouse is notified.

If a special order is to be placed, the computer in St. Louis calls a minicomputer in Chicago that controls production for the company. The production computer then forwards the order to the plant that makes the desired car, and the order is processed. Each of the four plants makes a different line of automobiles. The plants use a mainframe computer to process the order requests and to control the production process. The ordering process for a regular order (nonspecial order) is processed in the same fashion except that the other dealerships in the region and the other regions are not scanned to help fill the orders.

The franchises periodically forward summary data to the regional minicomputer where it is summarized and regional reports are produced. The various regions pass summary-level information to the St. Louis minicomputer that coordinates the company's inventory. There the data are summarized, and corporate-level sales and inventory reports are produced. The production plant computers produce information to help production plant management. They also send summary-level information to the computer in Chicago where the data are summarized and corporate-level production reports are produced. The Chicago and St. Louis computers pass information to the headquarters computer in Kansas City where corporate financial statements are prepared.

45. Luana's Clothing Distribution, Inc., has recently installed a mainframe computer at their headquarters building. All twelve branch offices will be linked to the mainframe and will have access to the company's online data base. The diagram below shows the various branch locations with respect to the corporate headquarters. The headquarters mainframe is marked by *HQB* in the diagram. Branch locations are marked by *BR* and the branch number.

```
BR1
        BR4

BR2
            BR5
                                            BR9
                                                            BR12
                            HQB
                                            BR11
        BR6
                                    BR10
                        BR8
BR3

        BR7
```

REQUIRED

a) Join the various branch locations to form a centralized computer network according to the following configurations. Assume that the branch locations are using terminals.
   1. Point-to-point
   2. Multidrop
   3. Multiplexed or line-shared

b) Assume that one of the branches in each of the three clusters has a minicomputer and that the other locations have a microcomputer. Each cluster will have its own distributed processing system. Draw this distributed processing system using the following configurations.
   1. Star
   2. Ring
   3. Hybrid

References

Buchanan, Jack R., and Richard G. Linowes. "Understanding Distributed Data Processing." *Harvard Business Review* (July/August 1980): 65–76.

Canning, Richard G. "An Update on Corporate EFT." *EDP Analyzer* (May 1980): 1–13.

Capron, H. L., and Brian K. Williams. *Computers and Data Processing.* Menlo Park, Calif.: Benjamin/Cummings, 1982.

Caruso, Robert L. "Paying Bills the Electronic Way." *Management Accounting* (April 1984): 24–27.

Cerullo, Michael J. "Data Communications: Opportunity for Accountants." *CPA Journal* (April 1984): 40–47.

Cushing, Barry E., and David H. Dial. "Cost-Performance Trade-offs in Real-Time Systems Design." *Management Advisor* (November/December 1973): 29–38.

Daney, Charles. "A Micro-Mainframe Primer." *PC Magazine* (January 22, 1985): 115–130.

Datapro Research Corporation. *Datapro Communications Solutions.* Delran, N.J.: Datapro Research Corporation, 1986.

———. *Datapro Directory of On-Line Services.* Delran, N.J.: Datapro Research Corporation, 1986.

———. *Datapro Reports on Data Communications.* Delran, N.J.: Datapro Research Corporation, 1986.

———. *Datapro 70: The EDP Buyer's Bible.* Delran, N.J.: Datapro Research Corporation, 1986.

Davis, Gordon B., and Margrethe H. Olsen. *Management Information Systems.* 2d ed. New York: McGraw-Hill, 1985.

Evans, Roger L. "Basic Data Communication Techniques." *Mini-Micro Systems* (March 1980): 97–104.

———. "Reducing Communication Line Costs with Multiplexors." *Mini-Micro Systems* (April 1980): 114–120.

Hessinger, Paul R. "Distributed Systems and Data Management." *Datamation* (November 1981): 179–182.

Kiechel, Walter. "Everything You Always Wanted to Know May Soon Be On-Line." *Fortune* (May 5, 1980): 226–240.

Kneer, Dan C., and James C. Lampe. "Distributed Data Processing: Internal Control Issues and Safeguards." *EDPACS* (June 1983): 1–14.

Lowenthal, Eugene. "Database Systems for Local Nets." *Datamation* (August 1982): 97–106.

McCauley, Herbert N. "Developing a Corporate Private Network." *MIS Quarterly* (December 1983): 19–33.

O'Brian, James A. *Computers in Business Management.* Homewood, Ill.: Richard D. Irwin, 1985.

Romney, Marshall B., and James V. Hansen. *An Introduction to Microcomputers and Their Controls.* Altamonte Springs, Fla.: Institute of Internal Auditors, 1985.

Sobol, Michael L. "Data Communications Primer for Auditors." *EDPACS* (March 1984): 1–5.

Stallings, William. "Beyond Local Networks." *Datamation* (August 1983): 167–176.

———. *Data and Computer Communications.* New York: Macmillan, 1985.

Stiefel, Malcolm L. "A Primer on Modems." *Mini-Micro Systems* (March 1980): 111–122.

Vanecek, Michael T.; Robert F. Zant; and Carl Stephen Guynes. "Distributed Data Processing: A New 'Tool' for Accountants." *Journal of Accountancy* (October 1980): 75–83.

C H A P T E R 9

Data Base and File-Oriented Systems

An accounting information system is designed to produce information for a wide variety of users. These users need the information for record keeping, planning and evaluation, and decision making. To produce this information, an organization must process and store records of the events, activities, and transactions that occur. If these data were not stored, the company would not be able to meet its information needs. As a result management and storage of data is one of the most critical functions of an accounting information system.

Accountants have a significant involvement in the data management and storage process. For example, they must interact with systems analysts to help the organization answer questions such as these.

☐ What data should be stored by the organization and who should have access to it?

☐ Which data storage approach should be used: manual, file-based, or data base?

☐ How should the data be organized, updated, stored, accessed, and retrieved?

☐ How can both scheduled and unanticipated information needs be met?

To answer these questions and others like them, accountants must understand the data management and storage concepts explained in this chapter. The first section of the chapter discusses data storage concepts and the file and data base approaches to data storage. The second section examines the differences between the way users view the data and the way it is actually stored in the computer. The third section looks at the software that makes the data base approach possible and the people who typically use data base systems. The next two sections explore file and data base organization and access approaches. Finally, the last two sections discuss the involvement of accountants in data base design and the implications of data base systems for accounting.

The File and Data Base Approaches to Data Storage

There are certain fundamental concepts and definitions that must be mastered in order to understand how data are stored and retrieved. These concepts, as well as the file and data base approaches to storing data, are discussed in this section of the chapter.

Fundamental data storage concepts and definitions

Imagine how hard it would be to read a textbook if it was not organized into chapters, headings and subheadings, paragraphs, and sentences. Also imagine how hard it would be for an organization to find anything if its data were randomly dumped into file cabinets. Fortunately, most books and company files are organized in such a way that information can be easily retrieved and used. Likewise, most data in EDP systems can be organized such that it can be efficiently stored and retrieved. This section of the chapter reviews and expands the basic data storage concepts and definitions introduced in Chapter 3 using accounts receivable information as an example.

As explained in Chapter 3, an entity is an item about which information is stored. Each entity has attributes, or characteristics of interest, that need to be stored. For the various entities, each attribute has a data value. For example, P.O. Box 7 is the data value of the address (the attribute) for XYZ Company (the entity). A *relationship* is a correspondence or association between entities. For example, a customer is an entity and a sales transaction is an entity and there is a relationship between the two entities.

Data in EDP systems are stored by organizing smaller units of data into larger and more meaningful units of data. This data hierarchy, beginning with characters (the smallest element), and moving to data bases (the largest), is shown in Fig. 9.1. A *character* is a number or letter and is the smallest element of data that is meaningful to a user. Characters are combined to form *data values* (such as P.O. Box 7). Data values are stored in fields, which are grouped together to form records. Thus a record represents a collection of data values that describes specified attributes of an entity. In Fig. 9.2, for example, each row represents a different record, and each column represents an attribute.

FIGURE 9.1
Hierarchy of data
elements.

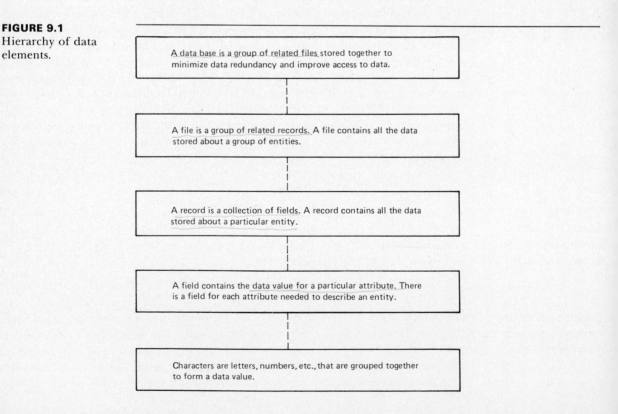

A data base is a group of related files stored together to minimize data redundancy and improve access to data.

A file is a group of related records. A file contains all the data stored about a group of entities.

A record is a collection of fields. A record contains all the data stored about a particular entity.

A field contains the data value for a particular attribute. There is a field for each attribute needed to describe an entity.

Characters are letters, numbers, etc., that are grouped together to form a data value.

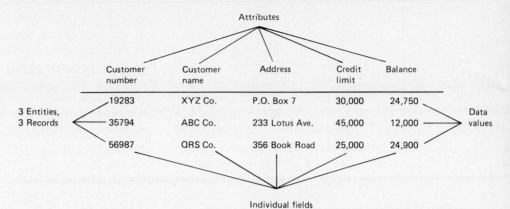

This accounts receivable file stores information about three separate entities: XYZ Co., ABC Co., and QRS Co. As a result, there are three records in the file. Five separate attributes are used to describe each customer: customer number, customer name, address, credit limit, and balance. There are, therefore, five separate fields in each record. Each field contains a data value that describes an attribute for a particular entity (customer). For example, the data value 19283 is the customer number for the XYZ Co.

FIGURE 9.2
Accounts receivable file.

The intersection of each row and column is a field. Each field contains a data value that describes the particular attribute and record to which it pertains.

A field may be characterized by its format—that is, the type of data stored in it. A numeric field contains only numeric data such as a dollar amount. Fields that can contain only alphabetic data, such as a name, are alphabetic fields. Alphanumeric fields contain both alphabetic and numeric characters, such as street addresses or inventory item descriptions. Monetary fields contain data such as wage rates and account balances. The characters stored in a date field are always interpreted by the system to represent a specific month, day, year, or some combination thereof.

A record is similar in concept to an individual folder in a manual file. In a manual system, all the information about a particular customer may be stored in an individual file folder. Likewise, in an EDP system all the data about a customer is stored in a record. Records can be of fixed or variable length. *Fixed-length records* contain the same number of fields in each record and are used when each record is to contain the same number of fields. *Variable-length records* differ in length and are used when the number of fields to be stored per record differs. Suppose, for example, that the invoice numbers of the sales documents that make up the receivables balance are to be stored in the accounts receivable record. There may be one or dozens of invoices that make up the balance. Using variable-length records to store the invoice numbers is more space efficient than designing fixed-length records that contain fields for all possible invoice numbers (assuming that the maximum number could be identified).

Similar records are grouped together to form a *file* (or data set). For example, all receivable records are stored together in an accounts receivable file. The different types of files used in business organizations are described in Chapter 3. In recent years, files containing related data have been combined to form what are called data bases. For example, the accounts receivable file might be combined with the customer, sales analysis, and other similar files to form a customer data base. The use of files and data bases has led to the two alternative approaches to computer-based data management that are now available. The use of files as the primary structure for storing data is referred to by a variety of names, including the *file-oriented approach,* the traditional approach, and the application approach. The use of data bases as the primary data storage structure is referred to as the *data base approach,* or the data base management system approach.

The file-oriented approach

Organizations that have used computers in data processing for several years have typically experienced a proliferation of computer applications. Accompanying this proliferation has been a corresponding growth in the number of computer files needed to support the data storage needs of each new application. Thus many companies have developed their information systems on a piecemeal basis by adding new applications as the need arises. These new application programs have been designed to meet the specialized needs of a limited number of users. The end result is an approach that focused on the individual application. The data needed by each of these independent applications are organized, processed, and stored in one or more independent master files. The set of data thus stored "belongs" to, and is managed by, the department or organizational entity that creates it, and each set of files is independent of every other set.

However, problems arise when users need information contained in two or more files. If an application program does not already exist to provide the information needed, it can be very costly and time-consuming to satisfy the information request. The inability to meet even the simplest requests for information in such situations can be frustrating to management and other users. Additional problems of the file-oriented approach are data redundancy, data inconsistencies, and inefficiencies due to the large number of data files that must be updated and processed. Figure 9.3 contains a more complete explanation of the disadvantages of file-oriented systems.

Even though it has disadvantages, the file-oriented approach is still widely used and, in many situations, serves its users very well.

The data base approach

As the number of applications and data files increased, organizations recognized a need for a data storage approach that was more oriented toward the organization as a whole. This led to the data base approach, which came into being during the 1960s to solve many of the problems of file-oriented systems.

The file-oriented approach has the following disadvantages.

□ *Data redundancy.* The same item of data often is included in more than one file. This is costly and inefficient, and requires that multiple files be updated each time duplicated data change. This requires that the separate file maintenance programs be coordinated to ensure that each file is properly updated.

□ *Data inconsistencies.* Where duplicate data are stored on separate files, data inconsistencies can arise. Long-term inconsistencies arise when an item is not updated or changed on all files. Temporary inconsistencies occur when there is a time lag between the updating or changing of the duplicate data items.

□ *Costly development of new applications.* New applications development may be costly because of the need to create new files, redesign existing files, or develop interfaces between existing data.

□ *Lack of data integration.* Most file-oriented systems are limited to predetermined information requests. Because data are spread over different files, it often is difficult to respond to unanticipated information requests. Responding to the information requests is usually very costly and requires that a new computer program be written. The information can rarely be produced on a timely basis. By the time the information has been produced, it is often either no longer required or no longer useful.

□ *Large number of data files.* Each requires periodic updates, file backups, cataloging, etc. Data organization and management often becomes time-consuming and expensive.

□ *Program/data dependence.* File-oriented programs typically contain references to the specific format and location of data stored on files. Changes to the data on the file usually require that changes be made to all the programs that use the files. In organizations that use thousands of programs to process hundreds of files, it becomes very difficult to keep track of what data fields are used by which programs. Thus program maintenance can consume a significant amount of time in file-oriented systems.

□ *Lack of data compatibility.* Because each application file is independent, there usually is little standardization of field names or lengths, attribute values, data representation, etc. For example, the product description field might be called P_DESC on one file and Prod_D on another. One file might allow twenty spaces for the description, whereas another allows thirty.

□ *Lack of data sharing.* This results when the "owner" of data is either unwilling to share the data or when an entity developing a new application is not aware of the data's existence elsewhere in the organization.

FIGURE 9.3
Disadvantages of the file-oriented approach.

The data base philosophy is that data are an organizational resource that should be used by and managed for the entire organization, not just the creating department or function. To accomplish this task efficiently, it makes sense that related application files be combined into larger "pools" of data called data bases, which can then be accessed by many different application programs. For example, creation of an employee data base consolidates data formerly segregated in separate files such as a payroll file, a personnel file, a job skills file, etc.

A *data base* is a set of interrelated, centrally coordinated data files. The data stored in the data base are independent of both the computer programs using them and the secondary storage devices on which they are stored. The specialized computer program that manages and controls the data and interfaces between the data and the application programs is the *data base management system* (DBMS). The combination of the data base, the DBMS, and the application programs that access the data base through the DBMS is the *data base system.* The person responsible for the creation, updating, maintenance, and control of the data base is the *data base administrator* (DBA). Data base management systems and the data base administrator are explained in greater depth later in the chapter.

Advantages of the data base approach.   Figure 9.4 illustrates the differences between the file-oriented approach to data processing and the data base approach. Note that the redundancy of data items B and E shown under the file-oriented approach does not exist under the data base approach. Further note that the data base approach provides *data independence,* which is not present in the file-oriented approach. In the file-oriented approach each program has its own fixed data file, whereas in the data base approach, the data exist separately, or independently, from the programs.

In file-oriented systems, a manager's ability to obtain information from data files is often constrained by the limitations of the system. For example, generating special-purpose reports involving data from two or more separate applications could require substantial effort and might take so long to complete that the report is not timely enough to be useful. Data base systems can substantially reduce these limitations. For example, on short notice a manager may need to know "Which parts are supplied by GHI Corp.?" or "Which deliveries are past due?" Using a data base such questions may be quickly answered. A data base can also be used to identify entities possessing more than one specified attribute. Questions such as "Which employees in the Engineering Department speak Spanish?" or "Which parts used in the Claven product line are supplied by GHI Corp.?" fall into this category.

The reporting capabilities of a data processing system are substantially enhanced by data base capabilities. Report formats can be easily revised in response to managerial needs. Reports may be generated on an "as needed" basis instead of, or in addition to, using a regular weekly or monthly schedule. By using the interactive capability of a data base system, a manager can "browse" through the data base to search for causes underlying the problems highlighted on an exception report, or to obtain detailed information underlying a summary report. The interactive feature of the system also enables the manager to formulate new questions based upon the system's response to previous questions.

Data base systems support "cross-functional" data analysis much more readily than do file-oriented systems. Cross-functional refers to the analysis of data relating to different functional areas of the business, such as marketing and accounting. Many data relationships exist that are cross-functional in nature, such as the association between dollar sales and marketing regions, or between selling costs and promotional campaigns. A file-oriented system is typically capable of maintaining only a few such relationships among data elements. In a data base system, most or all such relationships may be explicitly defined and used in the preparation of management reports. A greater variety of reports in terms of content and format is thus possible. Further, the

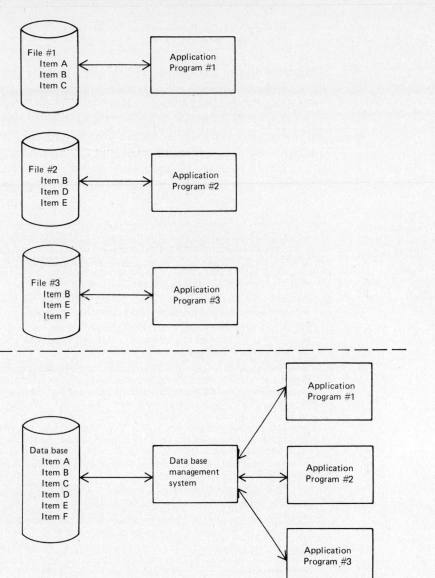

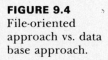

FIGURE 9.4
File-oriented
approach vs. data
base approach.

system is more capable of responding to managerial requests of an unusual
nature that arise on short notice and may not have been foreseen.

By combining related files, records, and data elements into a data base,
data redundancy can be eliminated or minimized and data inconsistencies
avoided. The data base approach can also help standardize operations and
data names, synchronize file updates, reduce the duplication of processing,

and increase the availability of data. These and other advantages of data base systems are summarized in Fig. 9.5.

Disadvantages of the data base approach.   While data bases have a number of significant advantages over file-oriented systems, they are not always the best way to organize and access data. Data bases have a number of disadvantages that make their use inappropriate in certain situations. Possibly the most important disadvantage is cost. Mainframe data base systems may require both more hardware and software and more expensive hardware and software than file-oriented systems. The data base package itself is often expensive to lease, purchase, or develop. Some mainframe data bases cost over $100,000. In ad-

FIGURE 9.5
Advantages of the data base approach.

The data base approach has the following advantages.

☐ *Minimal data redundancy.* "Pooling" multiple files means each data item need be stored only once unless duplication is necessary to enhance system performance. This usually reduces the amount of storage space needed for the data.

☐ *No data inconsistencies.* Since only one copy of each item is stored, the data inconsistency found in file-oriented systems is eliminated.

☐ *No duplicate processing.* With data stored only once, updates are more efficient since data only need to be entered once and updated once. This eliminates inconsistencies between data inputs and improves data integrity.

☐ *Data independence.* In a data base system, the physical organization of data is not tied directly to specific applications. Instead, data are stored independently of the programs that use them and DBMS software interfaces between the data and the application program. The application programs need not specify the structure or format of the data or be aware of any of the other physical details of storage, since the DBMS manages the data storage and retrieval tasks. This frees the user from the mechanical aspects of file handling and allows the user to concentrate on the use of the data. Because the data are independent, the application program need not be changed when changes are made to the data base. This allows the data base to evolve as application usage and information query needs change.

☐ *Standardized data.* Without duplicate data, there is no problem with different data names, field lengths, formats, etc.

☐ *Lack of data ownership.* When the organization owns the data, no group has special rights over it. It can be shared by all authorized users.

☐ *Central management of data.* A data base administrator is typically responsible for coordinating, controlling, and managing data as a firmwide resource. As a result, data management and coordination usually are more efficient.

☐ *Integration of related items.* With related data stored together, data elements can be more easily related to each other. This increases a company's ability to quickly and efficiently meet unusual requests for information.

☐ *Increased accessibility and flexibility.* When data are pooled and closely interrelated, and data management is centralized, the data are more fully, easily, and quickly accessed. This makes it much easier to meet users' information demands.

☐ *User-oriented inquiry/response capability.* With a DBMS, users can easily query a data base to retrieve information on an as-needed basis.

☐ *Security.* Many DBMS software packages have built-in controls that help ensure data integrity. For example, passwords can be used to limit access to authorized users. Security is often better because data bases typically have a data base administrator, one of whose main duties is to ensure the security of the data base.

dition, a data base usually requires more highly trained (and therefore more costly) personnel to install, operate, and maintain the system. The highly trained people are necessary because of the complexity of a DBMS. This complexity, along with the newness and unfamiliarity of DBMS technology, can create complications and undesirable behavioral reactions among the users of the system. These resistances can increase system costs, reduce the efficiency of the system, and lead to delays in implementing the system.

A DBMS adds an additional layer of system software. This increases storage requirements and may add to the total time it takes to execute a data processing task. Data base systems are also difficult to design and implement. Another possible disadvantage is that some DBMS are machine dependent, which means that they can only run on certain types of computers. Two final disadvantages of a DBMS are its vulnerability and its sensitivity to incorrect data. Since a DBMS is so highly integrated and concentrated, it is more vulnerable to hardware and software failures. In the file-oriented approach, the loss of a file only affects a few application programs. In a DBMS, loss of the data base renders inoperable all the applications using the data base. Likewise, in a file-oriented system an erroneous update affects only a few programs. In a DBMS, it will affect all applications using the data item erroneously updated.

Despite these weaknesses and shortcomings, the use of data bases is growing. More and more organizations are implementing data base technology and reaping the rewards they offer. So many companies are implementing the technology that it is estimated that by the end of the 1980s over eighty-five percent of all mainframe computer sites will be using data base technology. As explained in Chapter 7, data base usage is also growing rapidly in microcomputer systems.

Logical and Physical View of Data

Most file-oriented data storage techniques require the programmer to know the actual physical location and layout of the data records used in the application program. To illustrate this, refer to Fig. 9.6, which shows a record layout of the accounts receivable file introduced in Fig. 9.2. Suppose that a programmer needs to produce a credit report showing the customer number, credit limit, and current balance. To write the program, the programmer would usually need to understand the technical characteristics of the hardware, how the data are stored, the location of the fields needed for the report (i.e., record position 1 through 10 for customer number), the length of each field, the format of each field (alphanumeric or numeric), and so forth. The process becomes more complex if the programmer needs to access several files to obtain the data needed for the report.

Data base systems overcome this problem by separating the storage of data elements from the use of those data elements. In other words, the data base provides two separate views of the data. These are referred to as the physical and the logical view of the data. Figure 9.7 shows the accounts receivable data and the two views of those data.

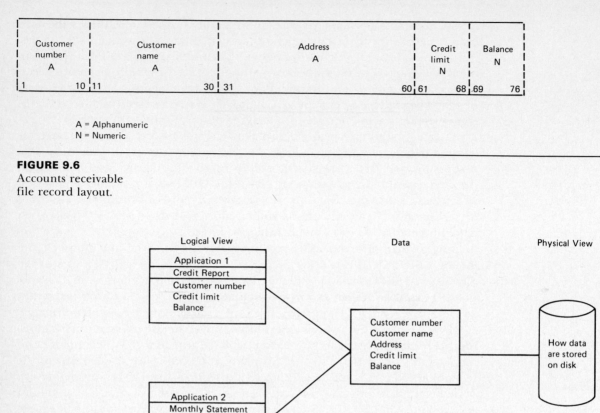

A = Alphanumeric
N = Numeric

FIGURE 9.6
Accounts receivable
file record layout.

FIGURE 9.7
Logical and physical
views of data in a
customer data base.

Logical view

The *logical view* is how users conceptually organize, view, and understand the relationships between data items. Because of the logical view, users can access, make queries of, or update the data stored in the customer data base without reference to how or where the data are stored. Using the data base approach, the monthly statement in Fig. 9.7 could be produced without understanding the details of how the data on the report are physically stored on disks, tapes, etc. The user or analyst is responsible for defining the logical data requirements of their application.

Separating how data are used from how they are stored and accessed means that users can change their logical view (the data items needed) without having to make changes in the physical view (or the physical storage of the data). Likewise, the data base administrator can change the physical storage of the data without the user having to change the application programs.

A model of the overall logical organization of a data base is referred to as the conceptual *schema* (plural: schemata). The schema describes the types of data elements that are in the data base (fields, records, files, etc.), the relationships between the data elements, and the structure or overall logical model used to organize and describe the data. A subset of the schema that includes only those data items used in a particular application program or by a particular user is referred to as a *subschema* (or *user schema* or *view*). The subschema, however, is more than just the data items used in an application. It is also the way the user defines the data and the data relationships. It is, therefore, a part of the conceptual schema that defines the entire data base.

In Fig. 9.7, for example, the schema consists of all the data: the customer number, name, address, credit limit, and balance. The subschema, or user view, for Application 1 consists of customer number, credit limit, and balance. The subschema for Application 2 is the customer name, address, and balance. From a given schema, several subschemata may be derived—in fact, one subschema for each of the programs that access the data base.

Physical view

The *physical view* is bits- and bytes-oriented and refers to how and where data are physically arranged and stored on disks, tapes, etc. EDP personnel use this view to make efficient use of storage and processing resources. Programmers and users, however, generally have no need for this information since they are only interested in using the data, regardless of how it is stored. The person responsible for the data base, called the data base administrator, is responsible for physically storing the data in a way that will allow the logical requirements to be met.

Data Base Management Systems

What is the difference between the file-oriented approach and the data base approach? How can the file-oriented approach be data dependent, whereas the data base approach provides data independence? How are the logical and physical views coordinated in the data base approach? The answer to these questions is a complex software package—the DBMS.

While each user may have his or her own separate logical view of the data, the system stores the data in only one way. DBMS software provides the link between the actual organization of the data on file storage media and the various logical views of the data in the minds of the users. In some cases the physical data organization that optimizes data storage factors such as access time and capacity utilization may differ from the logical data organization best suited to the needs of data users. As a result, data items such as customer account balance, name, address, and credit history may be stored in separate locations, or even a separate device, even though users perceive a close logical relationship between them. It is the responsibility of the DBMS to manage the data base in such a way that a user may work effectively with a logical set of data items, without being aware of the possible complexities involved in the physical organization of that set of data items. Ideally, the system should appear to each user to behave as if the data were physically stored in exactly the way in which that user logically views them.

One of the most significant differences between the processing of traditional files and the processing of data bases is that traditional files are processed only by a small number of programs, each doing its work at a separate time, whereas data bases are processed by several programs, some of which may be working on the same data base concurrently. In this situation, there is a danger that errors may be introduced into the data base when different programs attempt to use or modify the same data items simultaneously. Data base management systems must include capabilities for dealing with these multiple concurrent updates.

DBMS languages and interfaces

Most DBMS packages contain a number of different languages and interfaces. Each package is different, but this section describes some of the more common components of a DBMS. Just as the operating system is the "master" program that controls all other systems software, the *data base control system* controls the various components of the DBMS. The *data definition language* (DDL) ties the logical and physical views of the data together. It is used to initialize or create the data base and to describe the schema and each individual subschema. It is also used to describe all the records and fields in the data base. The DDL is also used to specify any security limitations or constraints that are imposed upon records or fields in the data base.

The *data manipulation language* (DML) is used to update, replace, store, retrieve, insert, delete, sort, and otherwise manipulate the records and data items in the data base. Because of the DML, these manipulations can be accomplished by using data names rather than by referring to the physical storage location of the items. The DML also provides the interface to the programming languages used by the applications programmers.

The *data query language* (DQL) is a high-level language that is used to interrogate the data base. Most contain a fairly powerful set of commands that are easy to use and yet provide a great deal of flexibility. They make it possible for users to answer many of their information needs without having to involve an applications programmer. An example of a DQL is Structured Query Language (SQL), a package produced by IBM. Figure 9.8 illustrates the SQL language.

The query language is typically available to all users. For control purposes, the data base definition language and the programming language are often confined to use by the data base administrator and the applications programmer, respectively. Restricting these languages to their respective users helps maintain proper control.

Report writers are similar to data query languages. All users need to do is specify the data elements to be printed and the desired output. The report writer searches the data base, extracts the desired items, and prints them out in the user-specified format.

Structured Query Language (SQL) Query:

SELECT	NAME,EXPERIENCE
FROM	PER.RECORDS
WHERE	DEPT = DP AND EXPERIENCE > 9
	AND LANGUAGE = SPANISH
ORDER BY	EXPERIENCE,DESC

Sample Output

NAME	EXPERIENCE
Carter, V.	30
Sheide, G.	23
Nielson, G.	21
Wilson, M.	19
McMahon, J.	17
Young, S.	15
Bosco, R.	13
Covey, S.	10

FIGURE 9.8
Examples of a data query language.

This query selects (the SELECT command) the fields named Name and Experience for all records in the file PER.RECORDS (the FROM command) that meet specified criteria (the WHERE command). The stated criteria are that they work in the data processing department, that they have more than 9 years of experience, and that they speak Spanish. The selected fields from the records are printed out in descending order (the ORDER BY and the DESC commands) based upon their number of years of experience.

DBMS functions and users

The functions of a DBMS may be divided into three broad categories: creation, maintenance, and interrogation. Data base creation is the defining, organizing, creating, and revising of the content, relationships, and structure of the data needed to build a data base. Data base maintenance involves the adding, deleting, updating, changing, and controlling of the data in the data base. Data base interrogation is querying the data base in order to access the data needed to support information retrieval and report generation. The three DBMS functions are reflected in the three different types of users who typically interact with the data base. The three DBMS functions and the three types of users are illustrated in Fig. 9.9.

Data base administrator. The DBA is responsible for coordinating, controlling, and managing the data in the data base. The DBA can be thought of as the human equivalent of the DBMS. That is, the DBA must not only be aware of users and their data requirements; the DBA must also understand how the DBMS operates and how data are stored and processed. In other words, the

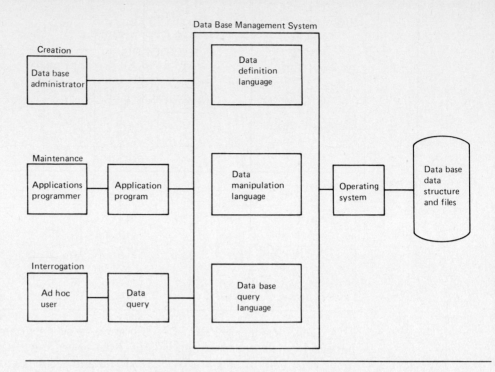

FIGURE 9.9
Data base users and
how they interface
with the data base
system.

DBA must understand both the users and the technical data storage side of
the system so that he or she can coordinate the two functions. This concept
is illustrated in Fig. 9.10.

The DBA typically has the following major responsibilities:

☐ To help establish the data models that describe the relationships among
the data used in the organization.

☐ To establish data standards and specifications.

☐ To specify the content, relationships, and structures of the data base.

☐ To provide for creating, updating, adding to, deleting from, changing,
and otherwise maintaining the data base. This would include approving
changes to the data base so that one user could not change data to the
detriment of others who use the same data.

☐ To develop retrieval methods to meet the needs of the data base users.

☐ To specify and maintain the physical structure of the data base.

☐ To maintain a data dictionary (discussed later in the chapter).

☐ To provide for adequate security and control over the data base. This
would include edit, security, backup and recovery, authorization, and
other such controls. The DBA function is itself a control since the responsibility for data is taken from users and programmers and entrusted
to the DBA.

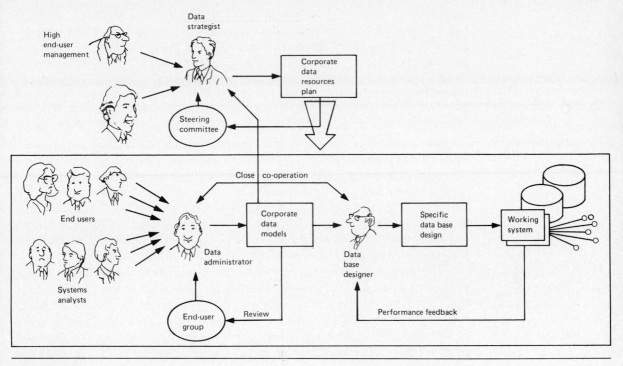

FIGURE 9.10
Responsibilities of the data base administrator. (James Martin, *An End-User's Guide to Data Base,* © 1981, p. 33. Reprinted by permission of Prentice-Hall, Inc., Englewood Cliffs, N.J.)

Applications programmers. The programs that process the data stored in the data base are developed by *applications programmers.* Applications programmers formulate a logical model, or user view, of the data to be processed. Then they write an application program, using a programming language. The application programs are sent to the DBMS, which refers to the appropriate subschema to determine the internal physical schema of the data requested. The DBMS requests the operating system to retrieve the required data, and the DBMS then turns it over to the application program for processing. When processing is completed, the data are turned back to the DBMS, which instructs the operating system to store it.

DBMS software has greatly expanded the ability of applications programmers to handle complex data structures. It has also simplified the tasks of the applications programmers and the ad hoc users. As a result, a broader range of timely reports can be produced for users with a smaller investment in programming time and with less difficulty.

Users. Those who use data base information are referred to as users. Users can receive periodic, scheduled reports, or they can query the data base as desired. Users who make unscheduled, as-needed inquiries of the data base are often referred to as *ad hoc users.* Ad hoc users can receive an immediate response to their query in the form of a screen display or a printed report formatted to meet their specific needs. The ease and speed with which users can produce reports has had a significant impact on organizations with data bases. Only a few short statements are needed to answer questions about company operations. As a result, organizations with data base systems are less dependent upon periodic, scheduled reports than are organizations with only file-oriented systems.

The data dictionary

A data base system cannot be successfully implemented in an organization unless the implementers have a thorough understanding of the data elements used within the organization, where they come from, and how and by whom they are used. This is why taking an inventory of data elements is one of the very first steps in the process of implementing a data base system. The information collected during the inventory is recorded in a special file called a *data dictionary*. The information stored in the data dictionary contains both the types of data and the uses of data, as shown in Fig. 9.11.

The data dictionary is a centralized source of data about data. For each data element used in the organization, there is a record in the data dictionary that contains data about that data element. For example, each data dictionary record might contain the name of the data element, its description, the name of the record(s) in which it is contained, the name of the source document from which it originates, its size or field length, and its field type (numeric, alphanumeric, etc.). It might also contain the names of all programs that use it, the names of all output reports in which it is used, the names of people (programmers, managers, etc.) who are authorized to use it, and any data names from other files or systems that are applied to the same data element. Figure 9.12 provides an example of what a data dictionary might contain.

The data dictionary is usually automatically maintained by the DBMS. In

FIGURE 9.11
The information in a data dictionary. ("The British Computer Society Data Dictionary Systems Working Party Report," *Data Base* **9** [Fall 1977]:5.)

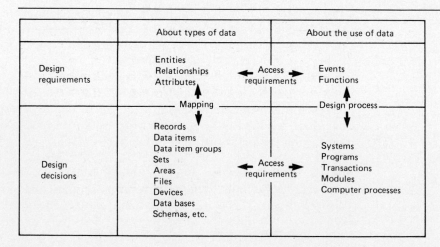

		About types of data		About the use of data
Design requirements		Entities Relationships Attributes	← Access requirements →	Events Functions
		——— Mapping ———		——— Design process ———
Design decisions		Records Data items Data item groups Sets Areas Files Devices Data bases Schemas, etc.	← Access requirements	Systems Programs Transactions Modules Computer processes

FIGURE 9.12

An example of a data dictionary.

DATA DICTIONARY

DATA ELEMENT NAME	DESCRIPTION	RECORDS IN WHICH CONTAINED	SOURCE	FIELD LENGTH	FIELD TYPE	PROGRAMS USED IN	OUTPUTS CONTAINED IN	AUTHORIZED USERS	OTHER DATA NAMES
Customer number	Unique identifier of each customer	A/R record, customer record, sales analysis record	Customer number listing	10	Alpha-numeric	A/R update, customer file update, sales analysis update, credit analysis	A/R aging report, customer status report, sales analysis report, credit report	No restrictions	None
Customer name	Complete name of customer	Customer record	Initial customer order	20	Alpha-numeric	Customer file update, statement processing	Customer status report, monthly statement	No restrictions	None
Address	Street, city, state, and zip code	Customer record	Credit application	30	Alpha-numeric	Customer file update, statement processing	Customer status report, monthly statement	No restrictions	None
Credit limit	Maximum credit that can be extended to the customer	Customer record, A/R record	Credit application	8	Numeric	Customer file update, A/R update, credit analysis	Customer status report, A/R aging report, credit report	R. Drummond W. Francom H. Heaton	CR_limit
Balance	Balance due from customer on credit purchases	A/R record, sales analysis record	Various sales and payment transactions	8	Numeric	A/R update, sales analysis update, statement processing, credit analysis	A/R aging report, sales analysis report, monthly statements, credit report	O. Cherrington J. Hansen K. Stocks	Cust_bal

357

fact, this is often one of the first applications of a newly implemented data base system. Inputs to the data dictionary include records of any new or deleted data elements, as well as changes in names, descriptions, or uses of existing data elements. Outputs include a variety of reports useful to programmers, data base designers, and users of the information system. Sample reports include a list of all programs in which a data item is used, a list of all synonyms for the data elements in a particular file, a list of all data elements used by a particular user, or a list of all output reports in which a data element is used. Reports of this type are extremely useful to the design and implementation of a data base system, as documentation of the system, and as an audit trail.

In a business organization, the accountant has a very good understanding of the data elements that exist in the organization, where they originate, and where they are used. This knowledge is a result of the accountant's role in the design of information systems and in the processing of financial data. Therefore an experienced accountant should play a key role in the development of the data dictionary.

Commercially available DBMS packages

Few organizations attempt to write their own DBMS software because the complex and sophisticated programming involved makes it cost ineffective. Instead, they purchase or lease one of the commercially available data base packages. Although data base packages are available for most models and makes of computers, the available packages can be divided into two categories: mainframe and microcomputer packages. These packages sell for as little as $200 for the microcomputer data bases to over $100,000 for the mainframe data bases. In general, the larger the computer and the more sophisticated and expensive the package, the more powerful, flexible, and versatile the package. Figure 9.13 lists a few of the more popular packages in these two categories, along with the companies who sell the packages. As with any other software, users who are selecting a data base package should carefully evaluate the available packages to ensure that they select the package that best meets their needs.

File Organization and Access

All computer systems must have some formalized means of organizing and accessing their data. Users need conceptual models of the data and their interrelationships. In addition, the data must be organized and stored on the physical devices such that they can be easily and efficiently accessed. It is not necessary for accountants to understand the technical details of the storage process. However, for the following reasons it is important that they understand how files and data bases are organized and accessed.

☐ During systems design, accountants typically play a significant role in developing the logical representations of an organization's data. They need to understand the constraints that may be imposed on the logical representation by organization and access methods.

Mainframe Data Bases	
PACKAGE	VENDOR
ADABAS	Software AG
DATACOM DB	Applied Data Research
IDMS	Cullinet Corp.
IDS	Honeywell
IMS	IBM Corp.
Model 204	Computer Corp. of America
Oracle	Relational Software, Inc.
RAMIS II	Mathematic Products Group
Systems 2000	Intel Corp.
TOTAL	Cincom Systems, Inc.
FOCUS	Information Builders, Inc.

Microcomputer Data Bases	
PACKAGE	VENDOR
Condor III	Condor
Data Star	Micropro
dBase II, III	Ashton-Tate
Knowledgeman	Micro-Data Base System
MDBS	International Software Enterprises, Inc.
R:Base	MICRORIM
Revelation	Cosmos
Selector V	Micro AP
PC/FOCUS	Information Builders, Inc.

FIGURE 9.13
Commonly used
DBMS software.

☑ A system should be designed to meet the needs of the users, and accountants should understand file organization and access methods well enough to select the approach that best meets those needs.

☑ Organization and access methods significantly impact the efficiency and speed with which records can be created, retrieved, updated, added or deleted, and otherwise maintained. Each file organization and access method is more efficient at some of these functions than are others. Since systems and file design involves a series of trade-offs, the accountant needs to understand the organization and access approaches in order to make the proper trade-off choices.

File organization refers to the way data are stored on the physical storage media. The data may be stored in sequential order or randomly (without sequential order). These are referred to as *sequential* and *direct* (or random, nonsequential or relative) *file organization,* respectively. *File access* refers to the way the computer finds, or retrieves, each record it has stored. If accessed sequentially, the records are read, one by one, in the sequential order in which they are stored. If accessed directly, the computer must have some means of locating the desired record without having to search each record in the file. Several approaches are commonly used to locate the records: individual keys, pointers, indexes, and randomized calculations. These methods are explained later in the chapter.

File access methods are a way of logically organizing the records in a file and are referred to as methods of logical file organization. Four file access methods are discussed in this portion of the chapter: (1) sequential access, and three direct methods, (2) indexing, (3) hashing, and (4) multikey (multiattribute) retrieval. Methods of logical data base organization are discussed later in the chapter.

Sequential file organization

Records in sequential files are stored in numeric or alphabetical order according to the record key (i.e., customer numbers from 00001 to 99999). The sequence of the records in the file can be changed by sorting the file according to a new key (i.e., by customer name rather than customer number). To access a sequential file record, the system must start at the beginning of the file and read each record. As each record is read, its key is compared with the key of the desired record. This process continues until the desired record is located. Unfortunately, the entire file would have to be read to find the items stored at the end of the file.

Sequential file organization is common for a number of reasons. It can be used both on the less expensive sequential mediums like magnetic tapes and on the more versatile and flexible random access devices like disks. Its usage is consistent with periodic business reporting processes such as weekly payroll, monthly billing, and so on. In addition, it is very efficient for batch processing operations. The approach also has disadvantages like inefficient retrieval of individual records and unavailability of up-to-date records. These and other advantages and disadvantages of sequential file organization are further explained in Fig. 9.14.

Random (direct) access organizations

With a random access storage medium, transactions can be processed as they occur, rather than accumulating them in batches prior to processing. When a transaction or other event affecting the master file occurs, the system searches the file for the desired master record. When found, it is read into the computer and updated. It is then written back out to its original physical location on the direct access storage medium. Since the "new" (updated) record is written over the "old" record, the old record is lost unless it is written to a separate file.

Random access methods are used when it is not practical or possible to anticipate the sequence in which records will be processed or queried, or when

Advantages of the Sequential File Organization

☐ Much accounting data lend themselves to ascending sequential order.

☐ It is a simple, fast, and efficient method of file organization when a large volume and a reasonably high percentage of records are processed on a periodic basis (batch processing).

☐ Since the records are generally stored in the order they would be printed, it facilitates applications that require frequent printouts or screen displays of all or most of the file.

☐ It makes efficient use of storage space since records are stored sequentially with no gaps (except as needed to read the data) between them.

☐ It makes efficient usage of less expensive storage media such as tapes.

Disadvantages of the Sequential File Organization

☐ It is impractical for applications that require immediate access to records because the search process is inefficient. On average, one half of the records must be searched to locate a record.

☐ Records are up-to-date only immediately after the update process takes place. That is, transactions that occur between updates are not reflected in the file.

☐ It requires that both master and transaction files be sorted in the same order.

☐ It requires that the whole file be searched in order to add, delete, or modify a data record.

☐ When a sequential storage medium is used, it requires that a new file be created each time a change is made to the file.

FIGURE 9.14
Advantages and disadvantages of sequential file organization.

other advantages of the approach are desired. While it has significant advantages, the major difficulty of the random access approach is determining the storage location of the record. To determine the storage location, a relationship between the storage location and the record key must be established. Three methods of doing this are hashed file, indexed file, and multiattribute search file organization.

Hashed file organization. For some records, it may be possible to establish an equivalence between record keys and machine addresses. For example, invoices 0001 to 9999 may be stored at storage addresses 0001 to 9999. This method, called *direct addressing,* is the fastest form of record addressing. However, it is not feasible for the coding systems upon which most sets of record keys are based because there is no one-to-one correspondence between the coding system and the storage addresses. An alternative, called *hashing, key transformation,* or *randomizing,* is to perform an arithmetic calculation on the key to convert it into a near-random number. This number is then converted into the address where the record is to be stored or from which it is to be retrieved.

One common form of hashing is the division remainder method. Using this method, record addresses are found by dividing the record key by a prime number approximately equal to the total number of storage addresses required for the file. The quotient is discarded, and the remainder is used as the record address. For example, suppose 2400 employee records are to be stored in blocks of 5 in 500 storage addresses numbering from 000 to 499. When the key (social security number) is divided by 499, the prime number closest to 500, a remainder ranging from 0 to 498 will result. Ideally, each of the 499 possible remainders will be obtained approximately five times. This minimizes the number of unused storage locations and the number of over-flow locations used to store additional records (called *synonyms*) with the same physical storage address. There are several ways to handle overflow, such as using an adjacent storage location, using a separate overflow area, or using a pointer to indicate the location of the synonym.

The advantages of hashing are its flexibility, its speed in storing and re-trieving records, and its ability to find a record without having to conduct a sequential search. In addition, records can be added or deleted without know-ing about physical sequencing. Disadvantages are unused storage locations, too many records for a particular location, and the need to provide for overflow storage locations. Another potential disadvantage is its inability to handle large volumes of transactions efficiently.

Indexed file organization.   A second way to access records directly is to use an index or directory. The indexed file organization makes use of two different files: the file containing the data records and an index file. The *index file* stores record identifiers and the physical address of the records in the data file.

An index file is used in the same way a card catalog in a library is used. To find a book in the library, you could examine each book on each shelf in some predetermined sequence. However, this sequential examination would be extremely time-consuming. Instead, you go to the card catalog, determine the approximate physical location of the book, proceed to the shelf that holds the book, and search that shelf for the book. In a similar fashion, an index file can be used to find a record in the data file. The following steps are fol-lowed:

1. The user requests a specific record by specifying its key.
2. The index is read into primary memory, if necessary, and accessed.
3. The index is searched to find the desired key. This search may be time-consuming, especially if the index is large. To shorten these search times, an index to the index is sometimes used to help zero in on the key being sought.
4. Once the key is located in the index and the corresponding address is obtained, the block of records comprising the contents of that address are read into primary memory.
5. Finally, the records in that block are searched to find the specific record desired.

Files can be fully or partially indexed. In a fully indexed file, there is an entry in the index file for every record in the data file. In a partially indexed file, the index contains one entry for every nth key, where *n* is the number of records that fit in each storage location. Fully indexed files are much larger than partially indexed files and require more storage space and a greater access time.

The most popular indexing approach is the *indexed-sequential access method* (ISAM). With this approach, records are stored in the sequential order of their primary key on a direct access storage device. Because records are stored sequentially, the file can be used as any other sequential file. However, an index file is also created and used with the file. This means that the file can also be accessed randomly. In other words, an ISAM file has the advantages of both the sequential and the random file organization. Either file processing method can be chosen, depending upon the specific business needs.

The ISAM approach does have drawbacks, however. It is slower than direct organization and takes more storage space, due to the index. In addition, it can be costly to create, store, and maintain the indexes. Finally, large quantities of new records cannot be added easily to the file. To help solve the problem of additions and deletions, the file can be reorganized periodically.

Figure 9.15 is an example of an indexed-sequential file. In this example, twenty-five customer records numbered from 1478 to 1502 are stored in blocks of five in five storage addresses numbered from 4061 to 4065. The index contains five entries—one for each address. Each index entry contains the key of the last customer record in the block and the address of that block.

Multiattribute search file organization.   The three file organizations previously described allow the file to be accessed by the primary key, but they do not facilitate the access of data records based upon one or more secondary keys. Access is possible through secondary keys, however, when a multiattribute search file organization is used. Two such methods are discussed here: linked lists and inverted lists (also called inverted files).

Linked Lists. In a *linked list,* each data record contains a pointer field containing the address of the next logical record in the list. Thus all logically related records are linked together by pointers. A group of records "connected" by pointers is referred to as a list or a *chain.*

Figure 9.16 illustrates the use of embedded *pointers* to chain together parts records having the same secondary keys. Each record is assumed to reside in a storage location coded with a two-digit machine address. For each of the secondary keys, supplier and product line, there are four different chains—one for each of the four possible values that each secondary key might assume. The links in each chain are pointers contained in the fields labeled "Next S" and "Next PL." Each of these fields "points to" the storage address of the next record having the same value for supplier and product line, respectively. For example, the chain for all parts supplied by ABC Co. may be traced through the records at machine addresses 11, 16, 17, 21, and 30.

A linked list may be connected by means of a forward pointer, which starts with the first record, or head of the list, and proceeds to the end of the chain. Records may also include backward pointers, which point to the prior record

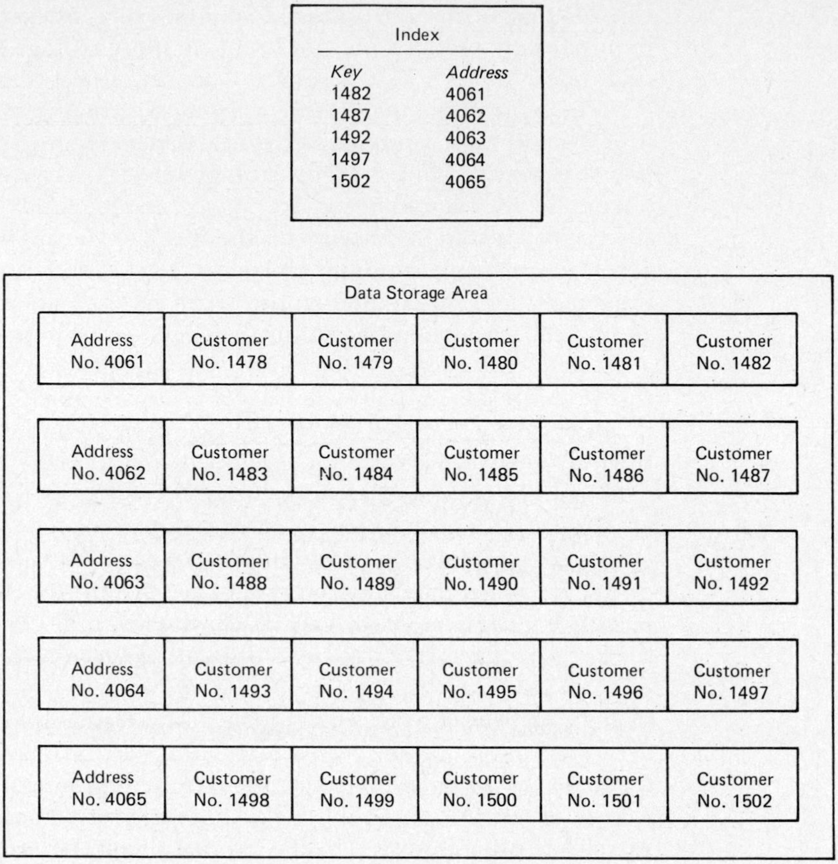

Index

Key	Address
1482	4061
1487	4062
1492	4063
1497	4064
1502	4065

Data Storage Area

Address No. 4061	Customer No. 1478	Customer No. 1479	Customer No. 1480	Customer No. 1481	Customer No. 1482
Address No. 4062	Customer No. 1483	Customer No. 1484	Customer No. 1485	Customer No. 1486	Customer No. 1487
Address No. 4063	Customer No. 1488	Customer No. 1489	Customer No. 1490	Customer No. 1491	Customer No. 1492
Address No. 4064	Customer No. 1493	Customer No. 1494	Customer No. 1495	Customer No. 1496	Customer No. 1497
Address No. 4065	Customer No. 1498	Customer No. 1499	Customer No. 1500	Customer No. 1501	Customer No. 1502

FIGURE 9.15
An indexed-sequential file.

FIGURE 9.16
Parts records chained on two secondary keys using embedded pointers.

Address	Part No.	Supplier	Next S	Product Line	Next PL
11	125	ABC Co.	16	Widget	17
12	164	XYZ Inc.	14	Doodad	16
13	189	GHI Corp.	18	Clavet	15
14	205	XYZ Inc.	24	Lodix	18
15	271	RST Mfg.	19	Clavet	22
16	293	ABC Co.	17	Doodad	20
17	316	ABC Co.	21	Widget	23
18	348	GHI Corp.	20	Lodix	19
19	377	RST Mfg.	22	Lodix	21
20	383	GHI Corp.	23	Doodad	24
21	451	ABC Co.	30	Lodix	25
22	465	RST Mfg.	25	Clavet	27
23	498	GHI Corp.	26	Widget	*
24	521	XYZ Inc.	28	Doodad	26
25	572	RST Mfg.	*	Lodix	28
26	586	GHI Corp.	27	Doodad	29
27	603	GHI Corp.	29	Clavet	*
28	647	XYZ Inc.	*	Lodix	30
29	653	GHI Corp.	*	Doodad	*
30	719	ABC Co.	*	Lodix	*

in the list, and parent pointers, which point to the head of the list. The use of backward and parent pointers facilitates recovery from damage or loss of pointers due to a system malfunction of some kind.

There are many uses for linked lists and pointers. A common use in accounting systems is linking a set of detail records to a master record. For example, an accounts receivable record may have associated with it a number of transaction records, which could be connected to it by means of linked lists. Similarly, an invoice or purchase order record could have line-item records connected to it using pointers. Another example of the use of chains is to link together all records in a file that meet a particular criterion, such as all accounts past due. Chains may also be used to link together all records in a file that have the same secondary key, such as all employees who work in the same department.

Linked lists have several advantages. They reduce record redundancy because a record that is physically stored only once may be a member of several lists. If the records are chained together in a particular sequence, then it may not be necessary to perform a time-consuming sort operation when they must be processed in that sequence. Linked lists also facilitate the retrieval of records whenever their physical sequence does not correspond to the desired logical sequence. For example, employee records may be in sequence by employee number, but a user may wish to retrieve only those for a particular department.

Linked lists have some significant disadvantages, as well. First, additional storage space is required for the pointers. Second, and more significantly, lists must be updated as new records are added, old records are deleted, and linked data within current records are modified. This adds considerably to the complexity of the file updating process.

Inverted Lists. While linked lists use pointers embedded within the records, inverted lists use pointers stored within an index. An *inverted file* is one in which inverted lists are maintained for some of the attributes. Such a file is fully inverted if there are inverted lists for every one of its attributes. A partially inverted file is one for which inverted lists are maintained for some but not all attributes.

Using the sample data records from Fig. 9.16, inverted lists for the secondary keys supplier and product line are shown in Fig. 9.17. There is one list for each value of each attribute, and each list contains the machine addresses of all records having that value. Using these inverted lists, any or all records containing a particular supplier or product line can be easily and quickly accessed.

Multiple indexes can also be compared so that records with the same attributes can be located. For example, a search routine could examine the following three indexes of the personnel file: foreign language, experience, and department. All records with the common attributes Spanish, ten years or more, and data processing could then be selected. This would help the company find the employees that speak Spanish, have ten years or more of ex-

Supplier	Addresses		Product Line	Addresses
ABC Co.	11, 16, 17, 21, 30		Clavet	13, 15, 22, 27
GHI Corp.	13, 18, 20, 23, 26, 27, 29		Doodad	12, 16, 20, 24, 26, 29
RST Mfg.	15, 19, 22, 25		Lodix	14, 18, 19, 21, 25, 28, 30
XYZ Inc.	12, 14, 24, 28		Widget	11, 17, 23

FIGURE 9.17
Inverted lists for the secondary keys of Fig. 9.16.

perience, and are in data processing. This information could then be used to help the company fill a foreign assignment. Since the index, rather than the file, is searched for the attribute values, it is a very efficient information retrieval approach.

The basic advantage of inverted files is that they facilitate the retrieval of information. The disadvantages of inverted files are that the indexes often require a substantial amount of storage space and that the indexes must be continually updated as the data records are updated.

Data Base Organization and Access

Most modern data bases contain records and files that are interrelated. These relationships fall into three different categories called *logical data structures* or *models*. The logical model selected by users depends upon their conceptual view of the data and what they want to accomplish. The three logical models are tree (or hierarchical), network, and relational. Although a flat file is theoretically a physical implementation of data, it is frequently used and is also discussed in this section. This section of the chapter explains these four data models.

Flat file structure

A file structure in which each record is identical to every other record in terms of attributes and field lengths may be termed a *flat file*. A simple example of a flat inventory file appears in Fig. 9.18. Note that each and every record maintains data on an identical set of attributes—stock number, description, color, vendor, on-hand quantity, and price. Further, the field size available for each attribute is identical for each record. These characteristics are typical of many accounting files.

FIGURE 9.18
A flat file.

Stock Number	Description	Color	Vendor	On Hand	Price
1036	Refrigerator	White	Gibman	12	$349.99
1038	Refrigerator	Yellow	Gibman	07	$359.99
1039	Refrigerator	Copper	Gibman	05	$379.99
2061	Range	White	Hotspot	06	$489.99
2063	Range	Copper	Hotspot	05	$499.99
3541	Washer	White	Whirlaway	15	$349.99
3544	Washer	Yellow	Whirlaway	10	$359.99
3785	Dryer	White	Whirlaway	12	$249.99
3787	Dryer	Yellow	Whirlaway	08	$259.99

A significant advantage of a flat file is that it can be viewed as a table where the rows are records and the columns are attributes. Records can easily be selected by establishing selection criteria for one or more attributes (columns). Flat files are frequently used as the basic physical implementation approach for the relational model discussed later in this chapter.

Tree (hierarchical) data base structure

A *tree* is a data structure, or a logical data model, in which relationships between data items may be expressed in the form of a hierarchical structure (see Fig. 2.1). A customer file in which data relationships are represented in the form of a tree structure appears in Fig. 9.19. This tree consists of four *nodes,* which are the record types: customer data, credit transactions, invoices, and invoice line-items. The upper-most record type, which in this case contains the customer data, is referred to as the *root* of the tree. One characteristic of a tree is that each node other than the root is related to one and only one other node at a higher level, which is called its *parent.* However, each node may have one or more nodes related to it at a lower level, and these are called its *children.* The tree structure is implemented and controlled using pointers and chains.

The arrows in Fig. 9.19 have important implications for the data relationships. In the diagram, each line between a parent and child has one arrow pointing to the parent and two arrows pointing to the child. This indicates that each is a *one-to-many* (1:M) relationship. This means that each child has only one parent, but each parent may have several children. For example, each invoice is associated with only one customer, but each customer may have several invoices. Also, each line-item belongs to a single invoice, but a given invoice may have several line-items. In a one-to-many relationship, the child record is referred to as a *repeating group.* Such relationships are very common in accounting records. For example, a company can have several sales offices, each sales office can have several salespeople, each salesperson can have sev-

FIGURE 9.19
Customer accounts data in a tree structure.

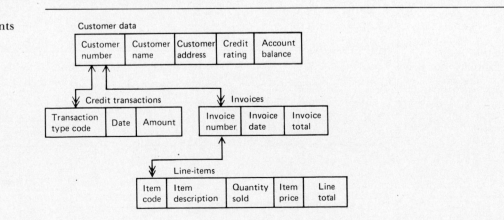

eral customers, each customer can make several purchases, and each purchase can include several items.

Network data base structure

In traditional business systems, virtually all files are either flat files or trees. For example, a manual system might consist of a separate file folder for each customer containing an account ledger card and copies of invoices, remittance advices, and credit memos. When such records are computerized, they would undoubtedly continue to be structured in the form of a tree, as shown in Fig. 9.19.

More complex relationships than those that can be expressed in trees or flat files often exist among data items or groups of items. Refer again to the sample data structure in Fig. 9.19. This company probably also maintains a separate file of general ledger accounts in which invoices sent to customers and credits to customers are entered as transactions. Furthermore, the organization may also have an inventory file in which sales to customers are recorded as reductions in the quantity on hand. In flat file and tree structures, such relationships among data in separate files are not recognized explicitly. However, it becomes possible to explicitly recognize data relationships across files in a data structure known as a network.

A *network* may be defined as a data structure involving relationships among multiple record types such that (1) each parent may have more than one child record type (as in a tree), and (2) each child may have more than one parent record type (not possible in a tree). For example, if we add the record types "general ledger account" and "inventory records" to the data structure of Fig. 9.19, and incorporate the relationships mentioned in the preceding paragraph, we obtain the network data structure illustrated in Fig. 9.20. Note that, in accordance with the definition of a network, the child record type "credit transactions" has more than one parent record type—both "general ledger accounts" and "customer data." The record type "invoices" has the same two parents. Also, both "invoices" and "inventory records" are parents of "line-items."

FIGURE 9.20
Accounting data files in a network structure.

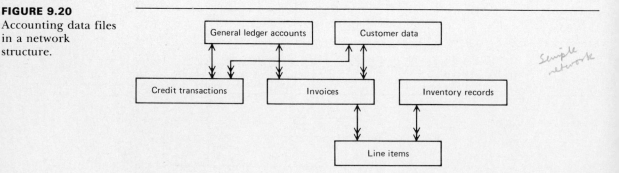

A fundamental characteristic of business records is that records in one file tend to be related to records in one or more other files. This means that virtually all business records can be structured as a network. This is done by allowing the data base user to define a schema with a network structure. Figure 9.20 is one example of such a schema. Separate users may then define separate subschemata in either a flat file, tree, or network structure. The tree structure in Fig. 9.19 is an example of one subschema that could be derived from the schema in Fig. 9.20.

Each of the data relationships represented in Fig. 9.20 is a one-to-many relationship. One additional characteristic distinguishing network structures from tree structures is that a network structure may contain one or more *many-to-many* (M:M) relationships. These are distinguished from one-to-many relationships in that a particular occurrence of a child record type may be owned by one or more occurrences of its parent record type. For example, consider the relationship between production parts, subassemblies, and finished products as diagramed in Fig. 9.21. A subassembly may consist of several parts, and a product may consist of several subassemblies and parts, which is consistent with a one-to-many relationship. In addition, however, a given part may be included in several different subassemblies or products. Therefore each of the three relationships shown in the schema is a many-to-many relationship; this is represented in the diagram by the double arrows going in both directions for each relationship.

A network in which all the data relationships are one-to-many, as in Fig. 9.20, is referred to as a *simple network*. One in which some or all the relationships are many-to-many, as in Fig. 9.21, is referred to as a *complex network*.

The advantage of networks is that many tree structure limitations can be avoided. More complex logical relationships between records can be represented by allowing many-to-many relationships. The disadvantages are the complexity and the difficulty of use. In most network systems, the user must have specialized training in data processing (including a detailed knowledge of the relationships represented in the network and the physical storage structure used) in order to query or update the network. Networks seem to be best suited for applications that are recurring and voluminous and for which there

FIGURE 9.21
A network structure involving many-to-many relationships.

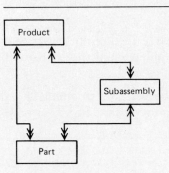

are relatively few user queries. Correspondingly, a network structure is least useful for applications where users frequently query the data base.

Relational data base structure

The *relational data base* model was developed as a way of simplifying the complex data relationships used in tree and network structures. The data structures discussed previously require that all data relationships be planned and defined in advance. However, often there are relationships that are not anticipated when a data base is organized. Tree and network structures afford little additional processing flexibility when these relationships are needed. Instead, the entire data base may need to be redesigned. The ability to handle unanticipated, or ad hoc, data relationships is partially solved using the relational model.

In the relational model, all data elements within the data base are logically viewed as being stored in the form of two-dimensional tables called *relations*. These tables are, in effect, flat files in which each row (called a *tuple*) is a record that represents a unique occurrence of an entity. Each column (called a *domain*) represents a field where the record's attributes are stored.

A relational data base can therefore be viewed as a collection of tables where the relationships among the data have been reduced to their simplest forms. The tables serve as the building blocks from which more complex relationships can be created. In other words, updates and queries are accomplished by using a DBMS to select or combine data elements from one or more tables. Since the data can be selected and combined in a variety of ways, the relational model provides a very powerful access capability.

Three fundamental operators are used to process the tables:

☐ PROJECT selects specified columns from a table to create a new table. Any rows that are exact duplicates of each other are deleted.

☐ SELECT   creates a new table by selecting rows, or records, that meet specified conditions.

☐ JOIN   creates a new table by selecting rows or columns that meet specified conditions in two or more tables. Join is used frequently since a single relation often does not contain all the data necessary to satisfy a user inquiry.

Relational data bases are stored on direct access devices using a complex addressing scheme that the user need not be aware of or understand. Physical implementation, which is hidden from the user, often involves indexes, inverted lists, and pointers.

Relational vs. network data bases. Smith and Mufti[1] developed an example that clearly shows the difference between a network-based data base and a

---

[1]This example is adapted, with permission, from James F. Smith and Amer Mufti, "Using the Relational Database," *Management Accounting* (October 1985): 43–54.

relational data base. They used an inventory record to compare a network data base (Fig. 9.22) with a relational data base (Fig. 9.23). The upper-left-hand corner of Fig. 9.22 shows a list of item numbers used to identify various inventory items. For each item, the data base stores data regarding the quantity on hand, the minimum and maximum quantities allowed, and the item classification (lower-left corner). In addition, a list of inventory suppliers is maintained by vendor number (upper-right corner) and is supported by data regarding vendor names, addresses, and telephone numbers (lower-right corner).

Finally, the center of the figure depicts a table of authorized suppliers for each inventory item. The arrows represent but a few of the many relationships between the various data. For example, the relationships represented by the solid arrows labeled A1 and A2 would be used by the computer to obtain quantity and classification data for Item #1. Similarly, the computer would use the relationships represented by the solid arrows labeled A3, A4, and A5 to determine which vendors are authorized to supply Item #1, and the rela-

FIGURE 9.22
Network data base design for inventory record.

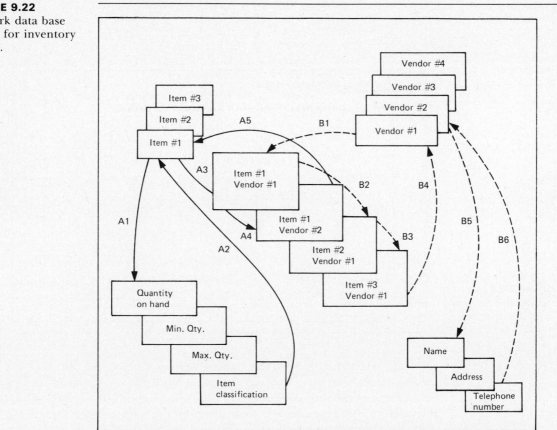

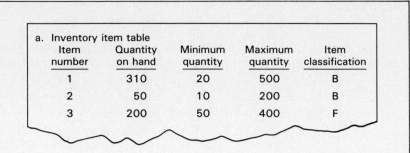

a. Inventory item table

Item number	Quantity on hand	Minimum quantity	Maximum quantity	Item classification
1	310	20	500	B
2	50	10	200	B
3	200	50	400	F

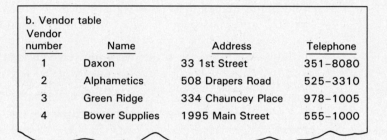

b. Vendor table

Vendor number	Name	Address	Telephone
1	Daxon	33 1st Street	351–8080
2	Alphametics	508 Drapers Road	525–3310
3	Green Ridge	334 Chauncey Place	978–1005
4	Bower Supplies	1995 Main Street	555–1000

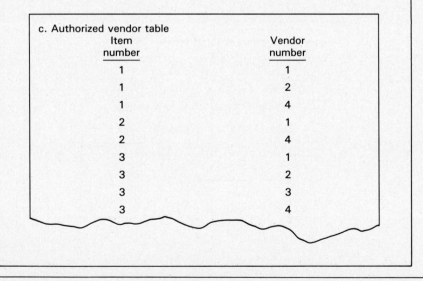

c. Authorized vendor table

Item number	Vendor number
1	1
1	2
1	4
2	1
2	4
3	1
3	2
3	3
3	4

FIGURE 9.23
Relational data base design for inventory record.

tionships represented by the broken arrows labeled B1, B2, B3, and B4 to determine those inventory items that Vendor #1 is authorized to supply.

Figure 9.23 shows the identical inventory record in a relational data base. Notice how much easier it is to understand the nature of the data being stored in the tabular structure of the relational model. In addition, access to the data is facilitated since the data base can be accessed directly with simpler and more easily understood instructions.

Suppose, for example, that we want to order inventory items classified as B in Fig. 9.23a. To do that, we need a list of the names and addresses of all vendors authorized to supply these items. To generate such a list using either model requires us to integrate the separate data files on the inventory items, the vendors, and the authorized vendor table. To perform such an integration using the network model requires considerable programming skills, including proficiency in a computer language such as COBOL. It also requires a knowledge of the relationships contained in the data base, such as those presented in Fig. 9.22. For most accountants, this process would require the assistance of a computer specialist. However, to generate a printed list of vendors using a relational DBMS would require a set of simple, readily understandable instructions such as the following.

PRINT ITEM NUMBER FROM INVENTORY ITEM TABLE
AND NAME AND ADDRESS FROM VENDOR TABLE
WHERE ITEM CLASSIFICATION IS B IN INVENTORY ITEM TABLE

Once those simple commands are issued, we need only wait while the data base system: (1) extracts from the Inventory Item Table (Fig. 9.23a) the item numbers for all inventory items having a B classification, (2) uses those item numbers to find in the Authorized Vendor Table (Fig. 9.23c) the vendor numbers for all vendors authorized to supply those items, and (3) uses these vendor numbers to retrieve from the Vendor Table (Fig. 9.23b) all the appropriate vendor names and addresses. Figure 9.24 is an example of how these data might be presented on a printed report.

Advantages and disadvantages of the relational data base. From the above example it is apparent that a relational DBMS can provide users with direct,

FIGURE 9.24
Information from DBMS based on a user request.

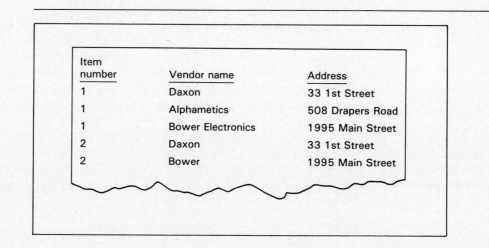

Item number	Vendor name	Address
1	Daxon	33 1st Street
1	Alphametics	508 Drapers Road
1	Bower Electronics	1995 Main Street
2	Daxon	33 1st Street
2	Bower	1995 Main Street

Advantages of the Relational Data Base Model

☐ It often is the most flexible and useful approach for unplanned, ad hoc queries. In a relational data base, access paths are not predetermined; instead, creating new relations simply requires joining tables. In contrast, in a tree or network approach new connections and access paths must be established if a new relationship is to be added.

☐ The DDL and DML are usually simple and user-oriented, and maintenance and physical storage are fairly simple. In contrast, the preestablished relationships of the tree and network structures usually require a more complex DDL and DML, and maintenance often is more difficult.

☐ It provides a clear and conceptually simple design and view of complex data relationships but at the same time offers a set of powerful data manipulation capabilities.

☐ The data base is very flexible since each relation within the data base can serve as a point of entry.

☐ Data can be easily added, deleted, or modified.

☐ Data are maintained in table form, which is more consistent with the human mental process and is very familiar to business-oriented users. This makes it easier for unsophisticated computer users to master and use.

Disadvantages of the Relational Data Base Model

☐ Current relational data bases are often less efficient than a nonrelational DBMS. They can occupy more memory, take longer to update, and be slower in retrieving data. This usually makes them less effective for high-volume data bases that are frequently accessed.

☐ The indexes used in the relational model, which must be created and maintained along with the records themselves, can be very large and cumbersome.

FIGURE 9.25
Advantages and disadvantages of the relational data base model.

easy, and immediate access to a readily understandable data base. Advocates of the relational data base believe that this approach provides data bases that are easier to work with, more flexible, and more easily modified than any other type of data base. The essence of a well-designed relational data base is that it can provide users with the particular information that they want, when they want it.

Specific advantages and disadvantages of the relational data base model are shown in Fig. 9.25. Since the advantages greatly outweigh the disadvantages for many applications, the relational approach has experienced rapid growth. This growth means that the relational model is, or soon will be, the dominant data base approach. That means that accountants should understand the model, how it works, and its advantages and disadvantages.

File and Data Base Design Considerations

When an organization decides to implement a data base, there are a number of important steps that must be taken. Among the most significant are: (1) taking an inventory of data elements used in the organization; (2) designing schemata for initial data base applications; (3) surveying available DBMS software and selecting a package that best meets the organization's requirements; (4) defining subschemata for specific applications; (5) writing new applications programs or modifying existing ones; (6) loading the data into the data base; (7) processing transaction data to update the data base; and (8) maintaining the schemata, subschemata, and applications programs. These tasks can be categorized into four different phases: requirements definition, conceptual design, physical design, and implementation and operation.

Requirements definition

In the first phase, the data requirements, or logical views, of the individual users and applications are determined. There are at least two different types of system requirements: those arising from processing and recording transactions and events, and those arising from user's information needs.

There are several different strategies for developing system requirements. One is to organize existing applications and files into a data base and then let the data base evolve as new applications are needed and new queries arise. This approach works well for data bases that are not expected to change very much or very often. Another approach is to do a detailed study of all current applications. The data requirements for each application are determined and then combined to form the data base. A third approach, often referred to as *conceptual data modeling,* tries to identify all current and anticipated needs. It is based on the argument that data and the relationships between the data are the foundation of an information system. This approach calls for developing a conceptual model of an organization and its components (people, resources, events). By modeling all entities within the organization and the relationships between those entities, present and future data requirements can be determined. A data base built upon this model can then meet an organization's information needs as long as users do not change the way they view the data entities and the relationships between those entities.

No matter which approach is used, the end result should be a listing of the data that are required in an organization's data base. Determining data requirements is covered in greater depth in Chapter 11.

Conceptual design

In designing a data base system, certain data base design objectives should be kept in mind. These objectives are summarized in Fig 9.26. Unfortunately, all of these objectives cannot be maximized. As in all areas of systems design, certain trade-offs are required. For example, cost-effectiveness is usually at odds with other objectives like flexibility, efficiency, accessibility, integrity, and security. The key is to achieve the best possible trade-off so that each objective is maximized, given the restraints imposed by the other objectives.

Designing network and tree data base schemata. A critical step in implementing a data base is the design of data base schemata. Most organizations use separate data bases for major functional areas, rather than a single comprehensive data base for the entire organization. Thus the first step in schema

Completeness	The data base should contain all the data (and the relationships between the data) needed by its various users. There should be a proper integration and coordination between all users and suppliers of data. The data contained in the data base are recorded in the data dictionary.
Relevance	Data should not be captured and stored unless they are relevant and useful.
Accessibility	Stored data should be accessible to all authorized users on a timely basis.
Up-to-Date	Stored data should be kept current and up-to-date.
Flexibility	The data base should be flexible enough that a wide variety of users can satisfy their information needs.
Efficiency	Data storage should be accomplished as efficiently as possible. As few resources as possible should be used to store the data. Data base update, retrieval, and maintenance time should be minimized.
Cost-Effectiveness	Data should be stored such that desired system benefits can be achieved at the lowest possible cost.
Integrity	The data base should be free from errors and irregularities.
Security	The data base should be protected from loss, destruction, and unauthorized access. Backup and recovery procedures should be in place so that the data base can be reconstructed if needed.

FIGURE 9.26
Data base design
objectives.

design is to determine which data elements to include in which schema. To resolve this problem, it is necessary to identify "clusters" of files and programs closely related to each other in terms of processing and usage but not closely related to files and programs in other clusters.

Once the data elements to be included within a particular schema have been identified, it is necessary to specify the relationships that exist between them. Those data elements having a one-to-one relationship with each other are candidates to be included within the same record. Each entity within a schema may be related to one or more other entities, and each such relationship may be either a one-to-many or many-to-many relationship. All relationships that are relevant, either to the processing of transactions against the data base or to the retrieval of information from the data base in response to specific user needs, should be explicitly recognized in the data base schema.

Another important aspect of schema design is designating the data elements that will serve as keys. The appropriate primary key for each record is generally obvious. However, the choice of secondary keys is also significant because they can enhance data base processing efficiency and facilitate information retrieval. The most appropriate secondary keys generally are those data elements that identify certain properties held in common by groups of records. Examples include invoice due date, employee department number, and inventory location code.

An important objective in the design of a data base schema is the simplification of the data structure. The reason for this is that complicated data

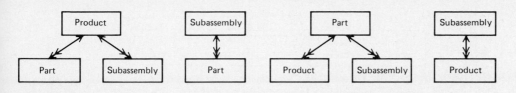

FIGURE 9.27
Representation of a network data structure by means of a series of tree structures.

structures such as networks (especially complex networks) are more difficult for DBMS software packages to work with than are simpler data structures such as trees and flat files. In fact, the schema definition techniques used by some DBMS software packages do not allow network data structures to be specified explicitly.

By introducing limited redundancy into a data base schema, a network data structure can be represented as a series of tree structures. For example, consider the network structure in Fig. 9.21. As shown in Fig. 9.27, this complex network can be represented by four tree structures. Although there is redundancy in the record types appearing in this schema, this does not necessarily mean that there will be redundancy in the physical data stored in this data base. The links shown in Fig. 9.27 can be represented by pointers without having to store redundant data records.

Designing relational data bases. Many data base specialists feel that it is desirable to simplify schemata further by reducing all data base files to two-dimensional tables, or flat files. As explained earlier, this type of data base is called a relational data base. Any type of data base structure can be reduced to a relational form. Figure 9.28 illustrates the tree data structure from Fig. 9.19 converted to relational form.[2] Note that each of the three relations represented by arrows in Fig. 9.19 is represented in Fig. 9.28 by pairs of data elements that are contained within the same record. For example, the link between customer and invoice records is established in Fig. 9.28 by including both the customer number and the invoice number within the invoice records.

A complete explanation of how to design relational data bases is beyond the scope of this text. However, two important guidelines to be followed will be presented here to provide a background in relational data base design.[3] The first guideline is that a separate data table should be used for each conceptual relationship of interest. That is, no table should incorporate more than one conceptual relationship. In Fig. 9.23a, for example, the Inventory Item Table contains only information about inventory items—the quantity on

[2]The process of converting a conventional data base to relational form is beyond the scope of this book. A good treatment of this topic may be found in James Martin, *Computer Data Base Organization,* 2d ed. (Englewood Cliffs, N.J.: Prentice-Hall, 1977), Chapters 13 and 14.

[3]These guidelines and the example are adapted from Smith and Mufti, "Using a Relational Database."

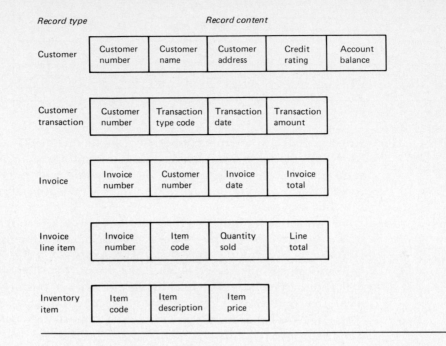

Record type   *Record content*

Customer

Customer number	Customer name	Customer address	Credit rating	Account balance

Customer transaction

Customer number	Transaction type code	Transaction date	Transaction amount

Invoice

Invoice number	Customer number	Invoice date	Invoice total

Invoice line item

Invoice number	Item code	Quantity sold	Line total

Inventory item

Item code	Item description	Item price

FIGURE 9.28
A relational data base.

hand, the minimum and maximum quantities, and the classification of each inventory item. Similarly, the Vendor Table (Fig. 9.23b) contains only information relating specifically to each vendor (i.e., name, address, and telephone number), organized by vendor number.

If these two tables were combined, as shown in Fig. 9.29, the resulting table would contain information regarding two separate objects of interest: inventory items and vendors. This combined table would also result in data redundancy. Note in Fig. 9.29 that Item Number 3 has to be stored four times since there are four vendors for that item. Likewise, Vendor Number 1 would have to be stored more than once since it supplies more than one item. Because each vendor may supply hundreds or even thousands of inventory items, the vendor information may be repeated an inordinate number of times. This redundancy could cause file maintenance to be unnecessarily time-consuming and highly susceptible to errors.

A second weakness of the combined table is that vendor data are not maintained independently of inventory item data. If, for example, a vendor is not currently supplying any inventory items to the firm, its name, address, and telephone number will not be included in the data base even though we may wish to maintain this vendor information for future reference.

A second guideline is that each table should be designed so that every row in the table is unique. This can be accomplished by ensuring that at least one column, referred to as the *table key,* contains a different value for each row. For example, the key to Fig. 9.23a is the Item Number column. In this instance,

FIGURE 9.29

Data table containing two distinct concepts.

INVENTORY TABLE

ITEM NUMBER	QUANTITY ON HAND	MINIMUM QUANTITY	MAXIMUM QUANTITY	ITEM CLASSIFICATION	VENDOR NUMBER	VENDOR NAME	VENDOR ADDRESS	TELEPHONE
1	310	20	500	B	1	Daxon	33 1st Street	351-8080
1	310	20	500	B	2	Alphametics	508 Drapers Road	525-3310
1	310	20	500	B	4	Bower Supplies	1995 Main St.	555-1000
2	50	10	200	B	1	Daxon	33 1st Street	351-8080
2	50	10	200	B	4	Bower Supplies	1995 Main St.	555-1000
3	200	50	400	F	1	Daxon	33 1st Street	351-8080
3	200	50	400	F	2	Alphametics	508 Drapers Road	525-3310
3	200	50	400	F	3	Green Ridge	334 Chauncey Pl.	978-1005
3	200	50	400	F	4	Bower Supplies	1995 Main St.	555-1000

each item number, which uniquely identifies each item of inventory, also uniquely identifies a row in the table. Thus each row contains information pertaining to a specific item of inventory. In Fig. 9.23c, there is no single column that contains unique row values. In this instance the two columns, taken together, constitute a key. That is, the combined values in the two columns, which uniquely identify a relationship between inventory items and vendors authorized to supply those items, also uniquely identify each row.

The accountant should play a key role in the design of data base schemata. The accountant's basic familiarity with record content and data relationships endows him or her with the perspective necessary to ensure that schema designs adequately satisfy all user requirements. It is also important that other management personnel be involved in the design of those schemata that relate specifically to their areas of responsibility.

Physical design and implementation

Physical design consists of taking the conceptual design and converting it into physical storage structures. Physical data base design is seldom of concern to accountants and is therefore beyond the scope of this book.

The implementation phase consists of converting the current system to the data base approach and getting it up and running properly. Implementation concerns are covered in Chapter 13.

Implications of Data Base Systems for Accounting

Accounting data within many large organizations are now stored in data base systems. This has some interesting implications for accounting. One of these—the need for accountants to be involved in the process of designing and implementing data base systems—has already been examined. At the organizational level, another significant issue involves the impact of data base systems on internal control. The centralization of data storage and the integration of data processing brought about by data base systems require that an emphasis be placed upon matters such as the accuracy of input data, the preservation of audit trails, the control of access to the data, and the maintenance of backup copies of data files. In essence, the organization's data base is an asset that must be safeguarded just like cash, inventories, and equipment.

At a more general level, data base technology may have a profound impact on the fundamental nature of accounting. For example, the accounting process traditionally begins with recording transactions from source documents onto journals. This is followed by posting from the journals to ledgers, balancing ledger accounts, and ultimately generating financial statements. If the accounting system is converted to a data base, all the accountant needs to do is enter source document data into the data base. Because of predefined data linkages within the accounting data base, the posting and balancing steps are accomplished automatically and immediately as the source data are entered. Financial statements or other accounting reports may then be generated at any time in response to a user request.

Even more important, data base technology could conceivably lead to the abandonment of the double entry accounting model. The basic philosophy of the double entry model is the use of redundancy to provide a check on the accuracy of data processing. Every transaction generates equal debit and credit entries, and the equality of debits and credits is checked and rechecked at numerous points in the accounting process. However, data redundancy is the antithesis of the data base concept. If the amounts associated with a transaction are entered into a data base system correctly, it is necessary to store them only once, not twice. Computer data processing is sufficiently accurate to ensure that the elaborate system of checks and double checks, which characterizes the double entry accounting model, is unnecessary. Thus data base technology could conceivably do away with the need for the double entry model. This has not happened yet because alternative accounting models that are more consistent with data base concepts are not widely used. Furthermore, the double entry model is so firmly entrenched in accounting that it may never change—rather, it may just be implemented on data base systems with little or no modification, in spite of the apparent inconsistencies.

Summary

There are two principal approaches to data storage: file-oriented and data base. The file-oriented approach works well in many situations but has a number of significant disadvantages, including data redundancy, lack of data independence, and inability to meet many types of information requests. The data base approach overcomes many of these disadvantages.

In the data base approach, there are two data views: logical and physical. The logical view is how users perceive the data to be organized. The physical view is how data are actually stored on disks, tapes, etc. Separating the two views, called data independence, is one of the reasons why data base technology is so powerful.

The data base management system is a sophisticated software program that handles the translation between the two data views. It consists of a number of different languages, including data definition, data manipulation, and data query languages. There are three types of DBMS users: data base administrators, applications programmers, and users. Data elements stored in the data base are recorded in a data dictionary.

There are a number of file organization and access methods. These include: sequential, random, hashed, indexed, linked list, and inverted list. Likewise there are a number of data base organizations and access methods. These include flat file, tree, network, and relational. The relational data base is regarded as the most intuitive.

Data base design consists of four phases: requirements definition, conceptual design, physical design, and implementation. This chapter discusses the first two phases, and Chapter 13 discusses the last phase. The third, physical design, is typically of little concern to accountants. Since accountants are among those who are most familiar with their organization's data, they should assume a significant role in data base design. To fulfill that role, they must understand and be able to apply the concepts explained in this chapter.

Review Questions

1. Define the following terms.

relationship	direct addressing
character	hashing (randomizing)
data value	synonyms
fixed-length record	index file
variable-length record	indexed-sequential access method
file	linked list
file-oriented approach	chain
data base approach	pointer
data base	inverted file
data base management system	logical data structures
	flat file
data base system	tree
data base administrator	node
data independence	root
data redundancy	parent
logical view	children
schema	one-to-many
subschema (user view)	repeating group
physical view	network
data base control system	many-to-many
data definition language	simple network
data manipulation language	complex network
data query language	relational data base
report writer	relations
applications programmer	tuple
ad hoc user	domain
data dictionary	conceptual data modeling
file organization	table key
sequential file organization	
direct file organization	
file access	

2. Explain the relationship between characters, fields, records, files, and data bases.

3. Describe the advantages and disadvantages of the file-oriented approach to data processing.

4. Discuss the advantages and disadvantages of the data base approach to data processing.

5. Compare and contrast the file-oriented approach and the data base approach.

6. What is the importance of data independence and data redundancy and how do they relate to the file-oriented and data base approach?

7. Compare the physical view of data to the logical view of data in a data base system. What is the importance of each?

8. What is DBMS software and why is it so important to the data base approach?

9. Describe the four major DBMS languages and interfaces. List the major uses and users of each.

10. Discuss the three main functions of a DBMS and how they relate to the three types of system users.

11. List the major elements of a data dictionary and explain the use of the data dictionary in a data base management system.

12. Identify some of the major DBMS packages on the market. Have you had any exposure to any of these packages?

13. Identify three important reasons why an accountant should understand how files are organized and accessed.

14. Explain the concept of sequential file organization along with its advantages and disadvantages.

15. Explain the concept of direct access file organization and discuss its advantages and disadvantages.

16. Briefly describe the different methods of hashing and their advantages and disadvantages.

17. Explain the concept of indexed file organization and describe the process of locating a record in a file. Discuss the advantages and disadvantages of the indexed sequential access method.

18. Discuss the advantages and disadvantages of linked lists and inverted files and explain how they work.

19. List the advantages and disadvantages of a flat file.

20. Describe the tree data base structure and explain how it works.

21. Explain the network data base approach and how it is used in data base systems.

22. Discuss how the relational data base approach has simplified complex data relationships and why the approach is becoming so popular.

23. List the most important steps in designing a data base and discuss the first two phases of data base design.

24. Discuss how network and tree data base schemata should be designed.

25. Identify and discuss two important guidelines that should be followed in designing relational data bases.

Discussion Questions

26. What would be the advantages and disadvantages of integrating all of an organization's data into a single comprehensive data base? Would you favor such an approach? Explain.

27. Does an auditor working for a public accounting firm need to have any knowledge of data base systems? Explain.

28. Discuss the potential impact of data base technology on the fundamental nature of accounting. Do you believe that this potential impact will ever be realized? Why or why not?

29. What are the advantages and disadvantages of the relational data base approach? How is this approach changing the type of computer users?

30. How has the data base concept changed the nature of computer use by companies? In what circumstances would you justify using the file-oriented approach instead of the data base approach?

Problems and Cases

REQUIRED

31. The need for a more coordinated approach to the management of data has resulted in the development of data base management systems.

Describe briefly each of the following aspects of data base management systems:
  a) Advantages of using data base management systems.
  b) Problem areas when data base management systems are in use. (CIA Examination Adapted)

32. Changes in the design and development of computer-based accounting information systems have been impressive in the last two decades. Traditionally, computer-based data processing systems were arranged by departments and applications. Computers were applied to single, large volume applications such as inventory control or customer billing. Other applications were added once the first applications were operating smoothly.

As more applications were added, problems in data management developed. Businesses looked for ways to integrate the data processing systems to make them more comprehensive and to have shorter response times. As a consequence, the data base system was composed of the data base itself, the data base management system, and the individual application programs.

a) Explain the differences between the traditional (file-oriented) approach to data processing and the use of the data base system in terms of:
   - ☐ File structure.
   - ☐ Processing of the data.

b) Many practitioners have asserted that security in a data base system is of greater importance than in traditional systems.
   - ☐ Explain the importance of security and the problems which may arise in implementing security in a data base system.
   - ☐ Identify special control features a company should consider incorporating in its data base system.

c) Identify and discuss the favorable and unfavorable issues other than security which a company should consider before implementing a data base system. (CMA Examination Adapted)

33. Using inventory record keeping as an illustration, give an example of an entity, an attribute, a record, a data item, a repeating group, a primary key, and a secondary key.

34. Consider the following data items composing an accounts receivable record which is to be incorporated into a data base system.
   - ☐ Customer account number (primary key)
   - ☐ Customer name
   - ☐ Customer address
   - ☐ Location code
   - ☐ Credit rating code
   - ☐ Credit limit
   - ☐ Beginning account balance
   - ☐ Current transactions (repeating group)
     Transaction type
     Document number
     Transaction date
     Amount
   - ☐ Current balance

Identify the data items within this record that are good potential candidates to be designated as secondary keys. Explain each of your choices.

35. The following schema was developed for a personnel data base that is used in the QRS Manufacturing Company. This data is to be accessed by a number of corporate users. Identify three potential users and design a subschema for each.

Employee number
Employee name
Job title
Department number
Department name
Salary
Social Security tax withheld
Federal tax withheld
State tax withheld
Pay period

36. Refer to the inverted lists in Fig. 9.17. Describe the process the system would follow to answer the question "Which parts supplied by RST Mfg. are used in the Lodix product line?" Retrieve the appropriate part numbers from Fig. 9.16.

37. Refer to the set of hypothetical inventory records in Fig. 9.18. Assume that these are stored sequentially at machine addresses numbered from 1 to 9, and that we wish to use embedded pointers to chain together all items having the same color.

    REQUIRED

    a) Prepare a table with column headings "machine address," "stock number," "color," and "next C" (for the pointer to the next item of the same color). Fill in this table according to the specifications described above.
    b) Using an index, invert this file on the secondary key "color."

38. The HFO organization has decided to store its data files on a random access storage medium using a hashed file organization. The organization has decided to use a form of hashing called the division remainder method. Assume that 1900 accounts receivable records are to be stored in blocks of four at 500 storage addresses numbered from 1000 to 1499. Determine the storage address for each of the accounts receivable records whose primary keys are listed below. *Hints:* (1) the prime number closest to 500 is 499, (2) once you obtain a remainder, you must add a constant to it to obtain the machine address.

Key	Address
a) 11021	1043
b) 17185	1219
c) 22458	1003
d) 33982	1050
e) 54499	1108

39. The MASI Corporation has decided to store its records using the indexing approach known as ISAM. Assume that 50 records with key values numbered sequentially from 500 to 549 are stored in blocks of five at ten machine addresses numbered sequentially from 200 to 209. Each entry in the index contains the key of the last record in a block, and the address of that block.

a) Prepare an index for this file segment.

b) Assuming an indexed-sequential file organization, explain how the system would access record number 522.

40. Using *Company* and *Agent* as secondary keys, chain together the following independent insurance broker records. Set up a pointer field for each secondary key that contains the address of the next logical record in the list. (*Hint:* See Fig. 9.16.)

Address	Policy No.	Insured	Company	Agent
50	999	Joseph	ABCDE	Kathy
51	888	Elizabeth	FGHIJ	Kevin
52	777	Peter	KLMNO	Jeri
53	666	Heidi	ABCDE	Dee
54	555	Paul	QRSTU	Kevin
55	444	Julie	KLMNO	Kathy
56	333	James	FGHIJ	Jeri
57	222	Teresa	QRSTU	Kevin
58	111	John	ABCDE	Jeri
59	100	Carolyn	KLMNO	Dee
60	90	Mark	FGHIJ	Kathy
61	80	Anna	QRSTU	Dee

41. Using the information in problem 40, prepare an inverted list for the secondary keys. (*Hint:* See Fig. 9.17)

42. Use table A to satisfy relational data base user inquiries. (*Hint:* See Fig. 9.8)

TABLE A

Company No.	Company Name	Commission Rate	Revenue
10000	SNIOZ CORP	25%	$10,000
20000	TSRIF CORP	35%	$100,000
30000	SEOJ CORP	75%	$230,000
40000	ASERET CORP	20%	$481,000
50000	LLAM CORP	68%	$23,000
60000	OIDAR CORP	19%	$770,000
70000	POTA CORP	55%	$999,000
80000	OISAC CORP	13%	$99,999
90000	MBI CORP	92%	$38,000

a) What records would be displayed in response to the following inquiry:

SELECT	COMPANY NAME, REVENUE
FROM	TABLE A
WHERE	REVENUE > $200,000
ORDER BY	REVENUE, DESC

b) What records would be displayed in response to the following inquiry:

SELECT	COMPANY NAME, COMMISSION RATE, REVENUE
FROM	TABLE A
WHERE	COMMISSION RATE > 30% AND REVENUE < $100,000
ORDER BY	COMMISSION RATE, DESC

c) Design a relational data base query similar to those above that selects all companies that have commission rates less than 50 percent and where revenues exceed $250,000. Have the records displayed in ascending (ASC) order of commission rate. Show the records that will be displayed in response to this query.

43. You are a systems analyst for the Consumer Electronics Co. The company has just acquired a data base management system, and one of the first applications of it will be to customer accounting. A credit memo form identical to that shown in Fig. 3.6 is used. You have been assigned to diagram the data structure of the credit memo as a first step in the application design. Use a format similar to that in Fig. 3.6. Note that the data base is to contain only the variable data on the form, not the constant data.

44. You are to design a schema for a purchasing data base. This data base will encompass the data in five records that are presently maintained on magnetic disk files. These records, and their data content, are as follows.

(1) supplier record—supplier number, supplier name, supplier address, shipment terms, billing terms
(2) purchase order record—order number, supplier number, order date, buyer name
(3) purchase order line-item record—part number, part description, quantity ordered, quantity received, price, line total, requested delivery date
(4) parts inventory record—part number, part description, standard cost, quantity on hand, quantity on order
(5) part quotation record—part number, supplier number, quoted price

REQUIRED

a) Prepare a schema diagram. Use a format similar to that of Fig. 9.19. For each relationship between a pair of records, indicate by means of arrowheads whether it is a one-to-one, one-to-many, or many-to-many relationship.

b) Prepare a diagram (using the Fig. 9.19 format) showing the subschema that would be used by a program that adds new purchase order records to the data base.

c) Prepare a diagram (using the Fig. 9.19 format) showing the subschema that would be used by a program that enters records of receipts of parts on order into the data base.

d) Prepare a diagram (using the Fig. 9.19 format) showing the subschema that would be used by a program designed to generate a report that shows quotations and related supplier information for a specified part.

45. The Paradise Hotel is a 1000-room, fifty story resort hotel in San Diego, California. The hotel is very popular with tourists and with business conventions. A convention center was built next to the hotel to meet the needs of the business clientele.

Room rentals at Paradise fluctuate because of seasonal cycles, business convention schedules, and special promotions offered by the competition. Business is heaviest during the tourist season, when reservations must be booked several months in advance to assure room preferences and availability. Even though most business conventions are held during the off season, advance notice of nearly a year must be made for business conventions in order to have a large enough block of rooms available. In the off season, more rooms are available and reservations are not as important for nonconvention guests.

If Paradise Hotel kept a constant room rate for the entire year, the hotel would be empty during the off season and overcrowded during the tourist season. In order to control demand, low rates are charged during the off season, premium rates are charged during the peak tourist season, and regular rates are charged the rest of the year. When people making reservations identify themselves as members of an approved convention, they are extended a special rate. A group reserving a large block of rooms is extended an even lower rate. In addition to varying in price due to season, convention, or group, room prices vary according to floor and size.

Staffing and managing a complex as large as the Paradise Hotel and convention center is a formidable task. The work force must be kept low in the off season, and additional help must be hired for the peak season. These employees must be assigned to departments and scheduled so that adequate help is always on hand. Meal planning and preparation vary according to how many guests are anticipated. Smaller conventions need to be planned around the large conventions and all convention participants must be given adequate information. Throughout the entire process, adequate information must be kept for the accounting function.

Since most of the hotel's clientele come through travel agencies, the hotel works closely with them. The travel agencies make their reservations by calling the hotel's toll-free number where service representatives record the reservations.

    a) How can Paradise use a data base to improve the effectiveness and efficiency of their operation?

    b) What other types of computer applications do you foresee Paradise as having? Discuss their importance to Paradise.

46. Visit a local business, university, or governmental entity that uses a data base system. Write a report covering your visit. Include in your report information such as:

☐ The name of the data base.

☐ The way the data base is used.

☐ How the data base is controlled.

☐ Resources needed to implement, operate, and maintain the data base.

☐ Any problems encountered in using the data base.

☐ Advantages to the company from using the data base.

47. Wekender Corporation owns and operates fifteen large departmentalized retail hardware stores. The stores carry a wide variety of merchandise but the major thrust is toward the weekend "do-it-yourselfer." The company has been successful in this field, and the number of stores in the chain has almost doubled since 1980.

    Each retail store acquires its merchandise from the company's centrally located warehouse. Consequently, the warehouse must maintain an up-to-date and well-stocked inventory to meet the demands of the individual stores.

    The company wishes to maintain its competitive position with similar type stores. Therefore, Wekender Corporation must improve its purchasing and inventory procedures. The company's stores must have the proper goods to meet customer demand, and the warehouse in turn must have the necessary goods available. The number of company stores, the number of inventory items carried, and the volume of business all are providing pressure to change from a manual data processing system to a computerized data processing system. Recently, the company has been investigating two different approaches to computerization—a computer with batch processing or a computer with online real-time processing. No decision has been reached on the approach to be followed.

    Top management has determined that the following items should have high priority in the new system.

    a) Rapid ordering to replenish warehouse inventory stocks with as little delay as possible. (Wekender buys from over 1500 vendors.)

    b) Quick filling and shipping of merchandise to the stores. (This involves determining whether sufficient stock exists.)

    c) Some indication of inventory activity. (Over 800 purchase orders are prepared each week.)

    d) Perpetual records in order to determine inventory level by item number quickly. (Wekender sells over 7500 separate items.)

A description of the current warehousing and purchasing procedures is given below.

Stock is stored in bins and is located by an inventory number. The numbers generally are listed sequentially on the bins to facilitate locating items for shipment; frequently this system is not followed, and as a result, some items are difficult to locate.

Whenever a store needs merchandise, a three-part merchandise request form is completed—one copy is kept by the store and two copies are mailed to the warehouse. If the merchandise requested is on hand, the goods are delivered to the store together with the third copy of the request. The second copy is filed at the warehouse.

If the quantity of goods on hand is not sufficient to fill the order, the warehouse sends the quantity available and notes the quantity shipped on the request form. Then a purchase memorandum for the shortage is prepared by the warehouse. At the end of each day all the memos are sent to the purchasing department.

When ordered goods are received, they are checked at the receiving area and a receiving report is prepared. One copy of the receiving report is retained at the receiving area, one is forwarded to Accounts Payable, and one is filed at the warehouse with the purchase memorandum.

When the purchase memoranda are received from the warehouse, purchase orders are prepared. Vendor catalogs are used to select the best source for the requested goods, and the purchase order is prepared and mailed. Copies of the order are sent to Accounts Payable and the receiving area; one copy is retained in the purchasing department.

When the receiving report arrives in the purchasing department, it is compared with the purchase order on file. Both documents are compared with the invoice before forwarding the invoice to Accounts Payable for payment.

The purchasing department strives periodically to evaluate vendors for financial soundness, reliability, and trade relationships. However, because the volume of requests received from the warehouse is so great, this activity currently does not have a high priority.

Each week a report of the open purchase orders is prepared to determine if any action should be taken on overdue deliveries. This report is prepared manually from scanning the file of outstanding purchase orders.

REQUIRED

a) Wekender is considering a batch processing system and an online real-time computer system. Which system would best meet the needs of Wekender Corporation? Explain your answer.

b) Briefly describe the hardware components Wekender needs for the system recommended in part (a). Sketch a configuration of this system.

c) Identify the data files that would be necessary, and briefly indicate the type of information that would be contained in each file.

d) Specify how each of the files identified in part (c) should be organized and accessed.

e) How might Wekender benefit by using a data base rather than a file-oriented approach?

f) Which data base organization and access method would you recommend to Wekender? Why?

g) Regardless of your answer to part (f), design a relational data base table for vendor data.

References

Barnhardt, Robert S. "Implementing Relational Data Bases." *Datamation* (October 1980): 161–172.

Burch, John G., Jr., and Gary Grudnitski. *Information Systems: Theory and Practice.* 4th ed. New York: Wiley, 1986.

Canning Publications. "Relational Data Systems Are Here!" *EDP Analyzer,* October 1982.

Claybrooke, Billy. *File Management Techniques.* New York: John Wiley, 1983.

Curtis, Robert M., and Paul E. Jones, Jr. "Data Base: The Bedrock of Business." *Datamation* **30** (June 1984): 163–166.

Datapro Research Corporation. "A Buyer's Guide to Data Base Management Systems." In *Datapro 70: The EDP Buyer's Bible.* Delran, N.J.: Datapro Research Corporation, 1980.

Date, C. J. *An Introduction to Data Base Systems.* 4th ed. Reading, Mass.: Addison-Wesley, 1986.

———. *Relational Database: Selected Writings.* Reading, Mass.: Addison-Wesley, 1986.

Everest, G. C. *Database Management: Objectives, System Functions, and Administration.* New York: McGraw-Hill, 1985.

French, Robert L. "Making Decisions Faster with Data Base Management Systems." *Business Horizons* **23** (October 1980): 33–46.

Howe, D. R. *Data Analysis for Data Base Design.* London: Edward Arnold Publishers, Ltd., 1983.

Martin, James. *Principles of Data Base Management.* Englewood Cliffs, N.J.: Prentice-Hall, 1976.

———. *Computer Data-Base Organization.* (2d ed.) Englewood Cliffs, N.J.: Prentice-Hall, 1977.

McCarthy, William E. "An Entity-Relationship View of Accounting Models." *Accounting Review* **54** (October 1979): 667–686.

———. "The REA Accounting Model: A Generalized Framework for Accounting Systems in a Shared Data Environment." *Accounting Review* **57** (July 1982): 554–578.

Nolan, Richard L. "Computer Data Bases: The Future Is Now." *Harvard Business Review* (September/October 1973): 98–114.

Nusbaum, Edward E.; Andrew D. Bailey, Jr.; and Andrew B. Whinston. "Data-Base Management, Accounting, and Accountants." *Management Accounting* (May 1978): 35–38.

Rolfe, Michael, and Frank Kowalkowski. "How Successful Is Data Base Management?" *Infosystems* (March 1980): 56–64.

Romney, Marshall B. "Should Management Jump on the Data Base Wagon?" *Financial Executive* (May 1979): 24–30.

Smith, James F., and Amer Mufti. "Using the Relational Database." *Management Accounting* (October 1985): 43–54.

Stoeller, Willem. "Panacea or Pitfall? The Impact of Relational Databases on Your Environment." *Proceedings of the 1983 National Computer Conference.* Arlington, Va. AFIPS Press, 1983, pp. 309–315.

Sweet, Frank. "What, If Anything, Is a Relational Database?" *Datamation* **30** (July 1984): 118–124.

Walsh, Myles E. "Rational Data Bases." *Journal of Systems Management* (June 1980): 11–15.

PART THREE

SYSTEMS MANAGEMENT

C H A P T E R   1 0

Basic Issues of Systems Management

LEARNING OBJECTIVES ───────────────────────────────

Careful study of this chapter should enable students to:

☐ Discuss key organizational issues associated with the information systems function.

☐ Explain the nature and importance of long-range planning for information systems.

☐ Describe the objectives and techniques of pricing computer services to users within business organizations.

☐ Discuss strategies for obtaining effective management involvement in the information systems function.

The information systems function is a relatively new administrative unit in modern organizations. Management of this function has proved to be a difficult and complex task. This is because the information systems function is unique—it is based on a rapidly changing technology, the use of which cuts across traditional organizational lines in a very fundamental way. Further, the application of this technology continues to expand and shows no signs of reaching a peak.

In this environment, there have understandably been many failures in systems management. Some of these, such as massive cost overruns, computer frauds, and system malfunctions, have been well publicized. However, within the past few years, there has gradually developed a body of knowledge relating to the successful management of the systems function. This body of knowledge represents a combination of the basic principles of management and an understanding of the unique issues raised by systems technology and its application. In Part 3 of this book (Chapters 10 through 15) this body of knowledge is reviewed and discussed.

In this chapter some of the most important issues associated with the management of the information systems function are identified, and the related management policies and methods are discussed. The first such topic covered involves the allocation of organizational responsibilities necessary to provide effective direction and administration for the information systems activity. Next, the important subject of long-range planning for information systems is explained. Other topics covered include internal pricing systems for computer services, obtaining the involvement of line managers in systems activities relating to their functions, and the institutional impact of automation.

In the remaining chapters of Part 3, various other topics relating to management of the information systems function are covered. Chapter 11 explains and illustrates some of the techniques of systems analysis and design and discusses strategies relevant to the management of systems change. Chapter 12 discusses techniques and problems peculiar to the selection and acquisition of new systems of hardware or software. Chapter 13 covers the process of implementing a major systems change and describes related techniques of project management and control. Chapter 14 examines the problems of data security, data integrity, and internal control in computer-based information systems and explains a variety of related policies, procedures, and techniques. Chapter 15 deals with the concepts and techniques of auditing of computer-based information systems.

Part 3 is written primarily from the broad perspective of management rather than from the more limited perspective of the accountant. This perspective encompasses the role of top management relative to information systems, as well as the functions of management within the information systems department. However, much of this material is relevant to the role played by accountants in modern organizations. For example, in many organizations the management of information systems is a direct responsibility of the accounting department. Even when this is not true, the accounting department is still likely to have some responsibility for such matters as long-range systems planning, internal pricing of computer services, cost analysis of systems, data security and integrity, and internal control of information systems. Furthermore, the accounting department is inevitably involved in systems activities because of its role as a primary user of information systems.

Organizing for the Systems Function

A critical factor in the success of information systems is the manner in which responsibilities for directing and administering the systems function are allocated within the organization. A major issue here is the appropriate organizational location of the systems function. Another important issue involves the composition and role of an information systems steering committee. In large, multidivisional organizations, the question of whether the systems function should be centrally located and controlled or decentralized becomes important. These and related issues are discussed in this section.

Organizational location of the systems function

The introduction of information technology has had a profound effect upon the structure of many organizations. The installation of a computer system in an organization creates a completely new department, with new responsibilities, a new set of employees, and new problems. Since computers began to be applied on a major scale in business in the 1950s, a wide variety of patterns of locating the computer activity in the organization has evolved. According to various surveys, the most common arrangement is for the top computer executive to report to the controller or financial vice-president. Another common approach consists of the top computer executive's serving as a vice-president having equal status with the controller, treasurer, and other vice-presidents. A somewhat less common pattern, which exists when one of the major departments in a company has a special need for a computer unique to the company or industry, is for the computer activity to be located within a particular department, such as manufacturing or marketing. Still another possibility is for the information systems function to be combined with other administrative departments such as accounting and finance under the authority of a Vice-President for Administration, as illustrated in Fig. 10.1.

FIGURE 10.1
Organization of the accounting, finance, and information systems functions under a Vice-President for Administration.

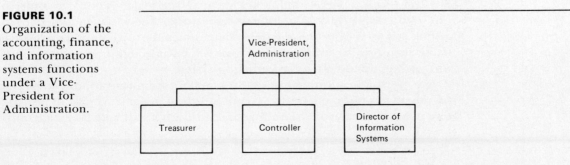

One factor that helps to explain the frequency with which the computer activity is located under the controller or financial executive is that early computer applications were primarily to accounting operations, such as payroll, billing, or inventory. These applications have been among the first to be automated because of their routine nature, which makes them relatively simple to program. Those who support the location of the computer function within the accounting department argue that it is only logical for the computer to be located within the department responsible for the majority of the data processing work load. They further argue that the major reorganization necessary to create a computer department separate from the accounting department is quite costly in terms of disruption of familiar organizational relationships. They cite the traditional role of the accounting department in supplying information to managers in all other functional areas and argue that the separation of responsibility for information preparation between two major departments makes very little sense.

Those who oppose the location of the computer activity within the accounting department argue that the nature of computer applications has evolved to the extent that most or all departments in an organization are likely to be interested in applying the computer to their own individual needs or problems. They feel that accountants naturally possess certain biases that limit their capacity to manage the computer activity in a manner that encourages the profitable application of computers throughout the organization. For example, systems personnel responsible to a controller may have a tendency to favor the development of financially oriented applications. Similarly, computer operations personnel may feel obligated to give top priority in processing schedules to accounting work. They further argue that the narrow perspective of accountants leads to premature rejection of applications whose benefits cannot be tangibly measured in dollars, and that systems designs prepared by accountants tend to emphasize processing efficiency rather than analysis of the information needs of users.

Those who favor the location of the computer activity in a separate department reporting to a top-level executive argue that this separation is necessary to free the computer facility from the biases of accounting management. They argue that specialists in accounting or any other functional area are generally not sufficiently well qualified to manage the computer activity. They feel that a top-level computer executive can make important contributions to top-management planning and control for the organization. They argue that this arrangement is the only one in which the top computer executive obtains the organizational status necessary to bring about integration of functions leading toward a total information system.

Creation of the position of Vice-President for Administration is advocated not only as a compromise in the computer location controversy but also as a more effective means of controlling administrative staff activities generally.[1]

---

[1]See John Dearden, "MIS is a Mirage," *Harvard Business Review* (January/February 1972): 98.

It reduces the potential for lack of objectivity on the part of the executive responsible for the computer system because the Vice-President for Administration is presumably a neutral officer. It also appeals to those who do not believe that a top computer executive is generally qualified to serve in a top-management position with vice-presidential status.

The best organizational location of the computer function may depend to a great extent on the nature of the organization's primary business activities and the extent to which information technology is critical to the success of those activities. For some companies, information technology is a key element in providing products and services to customers. In many of these companies, innovativeness in applying information technology in the development of new products and services is critical to the company's competitive success. Mc-Farlan cites banks, insurance companies, retailers, aerospace companies, and stockbrokerages as examples of companies in this situation.[2] In such cases the top computer executive should be a key member of the top management team and therefore should have a high status in the organizational hierarchy. On the other hand, where information technology plays primarily a supporting role, rather than a strategic role, it may be quite appropriate to locate the systems function within the accounting department or the administrative services group.

Several trends in recent years have tended to reduce the significance of the computer location controversy in many organizations. One such trend is the development of participatory approaches to managing the systems function that increase the involvement of all users of computer services in determining the direction of information systems activities. These include systems steering committees, long-range planning procedures, and policies that enable users to "buy" computer services via a transfer pricing mechanism established by the organization. Such policies and procedures have tended to reduce the basis for conflict over decisions regarding the use of computer resources. Each of these is considered in greater depth later in this chapter.

A second trend is technological in origin—a movement toward small computers, computer terminals from which larger systems are accessible, simple programming languages, and "packaged" application programs. This makes computer resources more readily available to personnel throughout an organization, rather than completely concentrated under the control of a single department. This also tends to lead to a reduction of conflict over the use of systems development and data processing resources.

In summary, the issue of organizational location of the computer facility is an unresolved one, both generally and in many specific organizations. In many organizations, recent technological and managerial trends have reduced the importance of this issue. However, in some companies, competitive pressures may dictate that the top computer executive report at a high level. One

---

[2]F. Warren McFarlan, "Information Technology Changes the Way You Compete," *Harvard Business Review* (May/June 1984): 98–103.

certainty is that each organization is unique, and each therefore must search for a means of organization best suited to its own individual circumstances.

The information systems steering committee

In recent years many organizations have found it useful to establish executive-level steering committees or advisory boards to oversee the information systems function.[3] Such committees should typically consist of the top computer executive and one or more other managers from the systems function, the controller, the financial vice-president, and all other functional vice-presidents or division heads whose areas of responsibility are significantly affected by the activities of the information systems function.

As an executive-level committee, the information systems steering committee should concern itself with broad policies and plans and not get overly involved in technical details or administration of specific projects. It should meet only when necessary to carry out its functions. A key function of the committee is establishing objectives for the organization's computer usage and linking these objectives to the organization's overall strategy. Other functions include review of proposals for major systems projects, review of long-range systems plans, monitoring of progress on major systems projects, approval of systems selection and acquisition decisions, review of the performance of the systems department, and consideration of organizational and key personnel changes relating to the systems department.

Effective use of an information systems steering committee provides several advantages. First, it provides a vehicle for productive top management involvement in the information systems function, a factor that has been found to correlate very highly with successful use of computers.[4] Second, it facilitates coordination and integration among departments and functions with respect to information systems activities. Third, it tends to reduce the conflict (mentioned earlier) over the best organizational placement of the systems function. Finally, it should lead to more effective management control over the allocation of resources in a manner that best reflects organizational goals.

Centralization vs. decentralization of information systems

In a large multidivisional organization, one important issue that must be resolved involves the degree of centralization most appropriate for the information systems function. At one extreme is the highly centralized approach, under which there is a central data processing facility responsible for all aspects of the organization's data processing, including hardware selection and operation, software development and maintenance, data base design and

---

[3]See, for example, Richard L. Nolan, "Managing Information Systems by Committee," *Harvard Business Review* (July/August 1982): 72–79; and D. H. Drury, "An Evaluation of Data Processing Steering Committees," *MIS Quarterly* (December 1984): 257–265.

[4]William J. Doll, "Avenues for Top Management Involvement in Successful MIS Development," *MIS Quarterly* (March 1985): 17–35.

administration, and planning and control of information systems resources. At the other extreme is the highly decentralized approach, under which each division operates its own independent data processing facility with little or no firmwide coordination or control. There is a wide variety of approaches that fall somewhere between these two extreme points. While most companies lean toward one or the other of these approaches, in practice there are few if any companies at either of the two extremes.

A highly centralized information systems function offers several advantages. One of these is the economies of scale provided by large computer systems; that is, the work load capacity per dollar spent on a computer increases substantially with the size of the computer.[5] Similar economies of scale apply to software, programming, and personnel costs. In addition, a larger computer facility may be more able to attract and retain more highly skilled technical, professional, and managerial personnel than would a smaller facility. Further, a common computer facility provides the opportunity for centralization of some administrative functions, such as billing, payroll, and purchasing, that can lead to substantial cost savings. Finally, a centralized systems function can develop and enforce standardized procedures and documentation, which facilitates communication, coordination, and control on an organizationwide basis.

A decentralized approach to the systems function also has advantages. Foremost among these is that there is closer proximity of the systems function to system users. As a result systems personnel generally have a better understanding of user needs and are more able and willing to respond to those needs. Also, divisional managers and personnel are more motivated to seek out profitable computer applications and participate in their development. In addition, decentralized computer facilities provide diffusion of the risk of system failure; that is, a system failure would affect only one division rather than the entire organization. Finally, expenditures for data transmission and other forms of communication are much smaller when separate divisional systems are used than when a central facility is set up to process data for the divisions.

Recent technological trends have caused many companies to be confronted abruptly by the centralization-decentralization issue. A common scenario involves a division or department that is dissatisfied with the service it receives from the central data processing facility and decides to acquire its own mini- or microcomputer. Such temptations have been magnified in recent years by the declining size and cost of computer hardware and the increasing sophistication of computer users. However, it is not in the long-run best interests of a company to permit the proliferation of small computers to

[5]One rule of thumb that has been found to be accurate is that the rate of increase in computer power is proportional to the square of the rate of increase in computer cost. This is known as *Grosch's Law.* See Phillip Ein-Dor, "Grosch's Law Re-Revisited: CPU Power and the Cost of Computation," *Communications of the ACM* (February 1985): 142–151.

continue unchecked. Some form of coordination is desirable, but it must be accomplished without stifling the initiative of computer users.

An approach to coordinating the acquisition of small computers that has proved effective in many organizations is to charge the information systems department with providing guidance and support to user departments that wish to acquire their own computers. Guidance takes the form of identifying hardware and software that is compatible with the organization's existing computer facilities and effective in performing the desired tasks. Support takes the form of providing links to central computer facilities and data bases, providing user training and consulting, furnishing assistance in hardware and software implementation, and maintaining the equipment. This form of cooperation between users and systems personnel promises to promote better understanding and cooperation between these two groups while at the same time facilitating the inevitable transition to a future environment in which small computers play a more important role in meeting the organization's computing requirements.

A related technological development that has had a significant impact on this issue is the development of communications networks. Such networks link central mainframe computers with other mainframes, minicomputers, and microcomputers at user locations. Linkage enables each user to decide whether to utilize central or local facilities, depending upon which is better suited to the specific application. In this environment it is possible to exercise centralized control over the hardware configuration and technical support staff while each location performs its own systems analysis and design and data processing. Thus the organization can achieve some of the advantages of both centralization and decentralization.

More generally, it is coming to be recognized that the choice between centralization and decentralization of the information systems function is not one-dimensional. That is, the systems function encompasses a wide variety of tasks, some of which may be best performed on a centralized basis, whereas others are best performed at the divisional level. For example, Withington suggests that a central authority should be responsible for hardware and software selection, design of data communications networks, and data base administration, whereas such functions as systems analysis and programming should be distributed among divisional or functional users of systems resources.[6] Others such as King[7] and Buchanan and Linowes[8] argue that each company must design its own hybrid organization for data processing, with each function centralized or decentralized as appropriate. One thing is clear:

---

[6]Frederic G. Withington, "Coping with Computer Proliferation," *Harvard Business Review* (May/June 1980): 152–164.

[7]John Leslie King, "Centralized versus Decentralized Computing: Organizational Considerations and Management Options," *Computing Surveys* (December 1983): 319–349.

[8]Jack R. Buchanan and Richard G. Linowes, "Understanding Distributed Data Processing," *Harvard Business Review* (July/August 1980): 143–153; and *idem,* "Making Distributed Data Processing Work," *Harvard Business Review* (September/October, 1980): 143–161.

The way in which this problem is dealt with by today's organizations is going to have a significant impact upon the structure of information systems for many years to come.

Long-range Planning for Information Systems

Managerial planning for information systems involves decisions about the most advantageous utilization of systems resources in the future. These decisions, in turn, affect the requirements of the system for additional hardware, personnel, and financial resources. The need for an effective system of long-range planning is especially critical in large computerized information systems.

The basic building block of information systems planning is the project development plan. Each such plan is a proposal to develop a particular application for the computer system. One project plan might call for the development of a production cost reporting system, whereas another proposes an online order entry system. Responsibility for the identification, selection, and implementation of new computer applications within an organization rests jointly with the systems development staff of analysts and programmers and the systems user groups. At any given time, there may be several projects in the process of implementation or in the proposal stage.

The most important single decision made by an organization's management with respect to its information system is the assignment of priorities to the various systems projects under development. This decision defines the future direction of the information system and determines its ultimate success or failure as a profitable tool of management. This decision is becoming even more critical for the growing number of companies that employ information technology as a central element of their products, services, and operations. The great significance of this decision dictates that it must be made at the top management level and that it should not be left to computer specialists. The costs and benefits of each project proposal should be thoroughly analyzed to provide management with a basis for assigning priorities among competing projects. The priority assignment establishes which of these projects deserve a share of the organization's currently available systems development resources.

This section begins with a description of the appropriate content of each project development plan, then explains how the overall long-range systems plan is derived on the basis of the various individual project development plans. After a brief discussion of commonly observed patterns of evolution of the information systems function in modern business organizations, the section concludes with a discussion of the payoffs of systems planning.

Content of a project development plan

Each project development plan is basically an analysis of the requirements and expectations for a proposed computer application. Requirements are broken down into two categories, developmental and operational. Developmental requirements include all resources necessary to implement the new application. Operational requirements include all resources consumed by regular utilization of the new system subsequent to its implementation.

The resources required for development of a new computer application consist primarily of personnel work-hours. Each new application is really a software system that includes a set of programs and system documentation. The development of such a software system will consume the time of programmers, systems analysts, supervisors, and user group representatives. For each project the number of work-hours required of personnel within each job classification should be estimated. A timetable should be established that indicates the number of weeks required to complete each step in the development process and the number of work-hours required for each step. Network planning techniques such as PERT (Program Evaluation and Review Technique; see Chapter 13) are often used for this purpose.

In addition to personnel work-hours, each development project will also consume some hardware resources. Computer time will be required to test and debug individual programs as they are written. As the project nears completion the system as a whole must be tested and operators trained in its usage. If the system is to replace an existing system, parallel operation will be necessary. The computer time requirements for all these activities should be specified with respect to the amount of time required and the timetable for utilizing that time.

An estimate of the financial resources needed for development of each application can be derived from the analysis of personnel, hardware, and other miscellaneous requirements such as supplies. These will consist primarily of personnel salaries and hardware utilization costs. All cost outflows should be classified into time periods to produce a project budget. The total of all these costs, discounted if the time factor is significant, represents the total financial investment in the project.

The operational requirements of a computer application include the hardware time required for processing, the time of machine operators required to prepare input data and monitor the operation of the computer and other equipment, the time of programmers and analysts required to maintain the software system, and the supervisory time required for all these activities. The project development plan should include a conversion of these requirements into financial terms. The operating cost estimate should be stated on a per week or per month basis.

Finally, each project development plan should include an analysis of the expected economic benefits of the new application. This analysis is essential to management's determination of priorities for proposed projects, as well as to the establishment of responsibility for the success of the project. Few general guidelines can be specified for this analysis, but one essential rule is that the users who will receive the benefits of a computer application must be involved in the estimation of its economic utility.

The overall systems plan

The individual project development plans form the basis for the overall long-range systems plan of an organization. For purposes of combining individual project plans in preparing an overall plan, the planned requirements for each individual project plan should be summarized in a form similar to that shown in Fig. 10.2. The requirements of all individual project plans (for those projects that have been accepted) may then be summed together to determine total resource requirements per month for all projects by category of resource. In addition, operational requirements for presently operating applications should be estimated from projections of growth in their current resource usage and added to the total resource requirements. The result, as shown in Fig. 10.3, is a summary projection of total systems resource requirements for the future. This diagram illustrates the three dimensions of long-range systems planning: requirements, time (months), and applications (development projects and current operations). Projections obtained from this process form the heart of the long-range systems plan.

From a planning perspective the resource requirement totals shown on the right in Fig. 10.3 are extremely valuable. In essence they show how much of each resource will be required during each future month in order to carry out the systems plan. Comparing these totals with currently available resources enables management to schedule the acquisition of any needed additional resources in an orderly manner. For example, once it is known when additional analysts, programmers, operators, etc., will be needed, the personnel department can make arrangements for interviewing, hiring, and training new employees and promoting and reassigning existing employees, in order

FIGURE 10.2
Summary content of a computer project development plan.

REQUIREMENTS	DEVELOPMENT PHASE					OPERATION (per month)
	Month 1	2	3	4	etc.	
Personnel Man Hours						
Systems analysis						
Programming						
Operations						
Data preparation						
Other						
Hardware						
CPU time						
Disk storage						
Tape input/output						
Card input						
Print output						
Terminals						
Other						
Financial						
Salaries						
Hardware/Software						
Other						

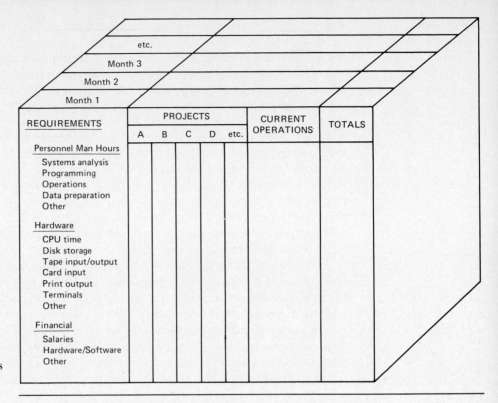

FIGURE 10.3
The three dimensions
of a long-range
systems plan.

that positions are filled as they become available. This is a tremendous improvement on the haphazard approach to personnel management so often found in the data processing field.

The same point can be made with respect to computer hardware. There have been many cases in which an organization has waited until the capacity of its computer system is strained before realizing the need to obtain additional capacity. However, computer acquisition is a long and complex process—and one that should be undertaken in an orderly manner. The hardware requirement totals provided by the systems plan provide the information needed for this purpose. Once the appropriate time for adding new capacity or upgrading to a new system has been pinpointed, plans can be made to begin the process with sufficient lead time to enable an orderly transition.

In addition to project plans and resource requirement projections, a systems plan usually contains some narrative information as well. This might include a summary of the objectives of the information systems function and an explanation of how they relate to organizational goals. Related to this would be a description of criteria for assigning project priorities. Another important element of such narrative information would be a description of the relationship between the systems plan and the organization's overall strategic plan, which identifies the systems requirements that are most critical to the organization's success.

In today's environment of rapidly improving information technology, an increasingly important element of a systems plan is an information technology assessment program. Such a program consists of an ongoing attempt to forecast future trends in information technology and its application in business environments, with particular emphasis on the economics of alternative forms of information technology. Extrapolated from this are projections concerning the organization's future utilization of emerging information technology and the implications for systems staffing, organization structure, investment requirements, and corporate strategy. An excellent example of information technology assessment as performed at Xerox is provided by Robert Benjamin.[9]

A planning horizon of approximately five years is reasonable for the long-range systems plan. Projections should be reasonably firm for the first year of the plan and moderately firm for the second year in the future. For the third and subsequent years, projections will be much rougher and plans will be stated in more general terms. The plan should be updated at least once each year.

The "stage hypothesis" of data processing growth

According to Richard L. Nolan, a prominent author and consultant in the information systems field, systems planning is greatly facilitated by the recognition that the data processing function in most business organizations evolves through six stages of growth.[10] These stages, together with a brief explanation of their characteristics, follow.

1. *Initiation.* Computer technology is introduced and applied to high-volume accounting applications for which cost savings are greatest.

2. *Contagion.* Computer applications proliferate in functional areas throughout the organization.

3. *Control.* New computer applications are restricted, and the emphasis shifts to documenting and restructuring existing applications and the development of formalized systems for planning and controlling the computer resource.

4. *Integration.* Data base technology is introduced, and existing applications are modified to utilize this new technology. There is a shift in emphasis from managing the computer to managing the company's data resources.

---

[9]Robert I. Benjamin, "Information Technology in the 1990s: A Long Range Planning Scenario," *MIS Quarterly* (June 1982): 11–31.

[10]See Richard L. Nolan's "Managing the Crises in Data Processing," *Harvard Business Review* (March/April 1979): 115–126. In an earlier article coauthored with Cyrus F. Gibson, Nolan had identified and described the first four stages. See "Managing the Four Stages of EDP Growth," *Harvard Business Review* (January/February 1974): 76–88.

5. *Data administration.* Data base technology is used to integrate existing applications on an increasingly wider scale, and the data resource management concept is implemented throughout the organization.

6. *Maturity.* The applications portfolio is complete, and its structure mirrors the organization and information flows in the company.

Nolan indicates that many large organizations have undergone the transition from stage 3 to stage 4 in recent years, and that this transition is characterized by explosive growth in data processing expenditures.

Nolan recommends that companies identify the stage their data processing is in so that they may better understand their past problems and gain insight into their most promising future strategies. Benchmarks indicating which stage a company is in include the growth rate of the data processing budget, the extent of use of data base technology, the nature of data processing applications, the type of organization structure for data processing, the focus of data processing planning and control, and the depth of user involvement. Nolan stresses the importance of a formal data processing growth plan to smooth the evolutionary process. He also emphasizes the need to monitor new developments in information technology, and the importance of an effective senior-management data processing steering committee to establish priorities and formulate growth strategies. Finally, he suggests that companies must recognize and prepare for the fundamental organizational transition from computer management to data resource management, because this will have a profound impact upon the way in which new applications are structured and the way in which systems for planning and controlling data processing are designed.

Advantages of systems planning

An effective program of long-range planning for its computer-based information systems pays dividends to an organization in several ways. The ability to approach hardware acquisition and personnel planning in a more systematic way has already been mentioned. Another important advantage is that the systems planning process provides a sound basis for selection of new computer applications. The alternative to long-range planning is to decide upon each proposal as it is made, independently of other proposals. Since all development projects consume the limited financial and personnel resources of the organization, it is essential that each of the potentially profitable computer applications be subjected to comparative scrutiny for identification and ranking according to their expected profitability, rather than be considered separately. Only in this way can management maximize the return on its investment in computer systems.

Another advantage of systems planning is that it enables an organization's computer effort to be coordinated with its overall long-range planning program. This is important because the information system competes with many other functions, projects, and departments for a share of the available resources within the organization. The systems plan provides a better basis for deciding what portion of available organizational resources should be allocated to the information systems function. Projected financial requirements from the plan can be incorporated into the organization's budgeting system. Furthermore, if the organization revises its long-range goals and strategies, the systems plan provides a sound basis for appropriately revising project priorities and reassigning resources in an orderly fashion.

Long-range systems planning also enables better coordination among the various information subsystems within the total system. It also permits management to plan for the most effective utilization of new technological developments. Finally, the overall plan and the individual project plans provide standards for evaluating the performance of information systems managers and project development teams. In summary, the long-range systems plan is an essential cornerstone of good management of the information systems function.

Internal Pricing of Computer Services[11]

An important consideration relating to the management of the information systems function in all organizations is the extent to which users of computer services are charged for such services. A system of charging user departments for computer services is analogous to a system of transfer pricing of products exchanged between two divisions of the same company. Even though this system is simply an accounting procedure, it has a significant effect on the management and on the utilization of information systems resources. In this section the objectives of a pricing system for computer services are explained, and several different approaches and techniques used in such systems are described and compared.

Objectives and criteria

Before settling on the details of a pricing system for computer services, it is necessary to consider what should be the most important objectives of the system, and what criteria will be used for selecting among alternative methods.

Among the objectives most often established are (1) equitable allocation of the computer resource to its most worthwhile uses while discouraging frivolous use; (2) motivation of computer management and personnel to provide efficient, high-quality service to users, (3) establishment of an objective basis upon which to evaluate the performance of computer management, and (4) encouragement of user interest and participation in the development and implementation of information systems. The relative importance attached to each of these objectives will vary depending on the specific needs and characteristics of the organization.

---

[11]Portions of this section are reprinted with permission from Barry E. Cushing's "Pricing Internal Computer Services: The Basic Issues," *Management Accounting* (April 1976): 47–50.

Numerous criteria have been proposed for systems of pricing computer services. For example, nearly all authorities agree on the importance of devising a charging system that is understandable to users. This encourages user decision making consistent with the most efficient allocation of the computer resource. Many experts also stress the importance of consistency or stability of charges, which means that the same job processed at two different times under different work-load conditions should be charged the same price. Another important criterion is that charges be equitable in the sense that they are proportional to the amount of computer resources actually consumed by the user application. The charging system should be economical in the sense that the costs associated with the system itself should not be so great as to outweigh the benefits obtained from the system. These criteria may at times conflict so that value judgments may have to be made about which are more important in specific circumstances.

Selecting the allocation base

The allocation base refers to the measure of work performed by the computer system. A base is multiplied by a rate to arrive at a charge. Three different types of allocation bases may be used: a single factor base, a unit pricing base, and a multiple factor base.

Two commonly used single factor bases are wall clock time (WCT) and central processing unit (CPU) time. In both cases a single measure of time usage is multiplied by a single rate to derive the charge. The simplicity of this approach makes it easily understood by users and easily implemented. Relatively minor changes in the operating system software enable the charge to be computed and reported as each job is being processed.

Disadvantages of single factor bases arise in a multiprogramming environment. WCT becomes very inconsistent, varying in accordance with the particular mix of jobs being processed. For example, a job that takes fifteen minutes to complete when it is the only job being run may take thirty minutes when several other jobs are also being run.

Both WCT and CPU time also tend to be inequitable in the sense that charges are not related to the resources used. A job using five input/output devices could consume the same WCT or CPU time as a job using only two input/output devices, but to charge the same amount for the two jobs does not fairly reflect their differences in resource utilization. Once again, this disadvantage relates primarily to the multiprogramming environment in which system components not required in one job may be used by any other job being executed at the same time.

The unit pricing approach seeks to develop a single unit measure of work performed by the system that reflects all the systems components available to the user during execution of the job. For example, the unit measure might be defined as the total amount of work the system can perform in one minute. For a given job, this measure would be derived by counting the various operations performed by the system during execution, such as reading a card or printing a line, then applying a weighting factor to each count and summing the results. This unit measure would then be multiplied by a single rate to compute the charge.

The unit pricing approach has the advantage of producing a reasonably stable charge for a given equipment configuration, and it is reasonably equitable. Furthermore, each user's bill for services is uncomplicated, showing the total units consumed, the rate, and the total charge. A unit pricing system, however, is difficult to design and implement and must be refined each time new equipment is added to the system. In addition, the concepts and techniques underlying the computation of the unit measure may not be easily understood by users.

A multiple factor base involves the use of a separate rate for each of the several system components used during the execution of a job. These components may include CPU time, core storage, cards read, cards punched, lines printed, tape accesses, disk accesses, and so forth. Each measure is multiplied by a separate rate, and the resulting individual component charges are summed to arrive at a total job charge. This is probably the most equitable pricing approach for the user, and in addition, the information generated by this approach may be used by the computer staff to evaluate and improve the efficiency of scheduling of computer operations.

A significant disadvantage of the multiple factor allocation base is that it is difficult and costly to develop and implement. Because of its complexities, it may also be confusing to users. Considerable testing of alternatives may be required before a particular scheme is chosen. Costs common to a number of system components—such as the wages of machine operators—must be allocated in some manner to the rates of the various components.

Setting rates

Rates charged for data processing services may be based upon three methods: full costing, market prices, or flexible pricing. Closely related to this issue is the question of whether the computer department is to be treated as a cost center or as a profit center. Under the full costing method, rates charged for computer services are intended to generate revenues just sufficient to cover the costs of the computer center, which is consistent with the cost center concept. The use of market prices should provide an excess of revenues over costs and is therefore consistent with the profit center concept. Flexible pricing is a technique that may be used in conjunction with either the cost center or profit center approach.

The full costing method (also called average cost pricing) requires that a rate, or rates, be computed on the basis of the actual total costs of the data processing operation. For example, where the single factor of CPU time is used as the allocation base, total cost is divided by total CPU time to derive a rate per hour. The rate is generally recomputed at short intervals, such as at the end of each month.

The full costing approach offers the advantage of simplicity. Charges are easily understood by users and are thus less subject to dispute. Furthermore, the rates may also be used for project costing and economic feasibility analysis of proposed new applications. Charges for computer services under this approach should be relatively low, thus encouraging fuller use of computer resources and stifling any desire by users to patronize outside service bureaus. Also, the use of a cost-based charge should tend to reduce the occurrence and intensity of disputes over the equity of charges. Such disputes are especially common when rates based upon market prices are used.

Full costing has its disadvantages. Since the rates are periodically revised, charges tend to be unstable over time because of changes in usage and total costs. When total use is relatively low, service rates tend to be high, which may discourage desirable increases in demand. On the other hand, when use is high, rates are relatively low, which encourages increased use and aggravates the problem of undercapacity.

Full costing also fails to deal directly with the problem of an uneven work load characterized by periods of slack demand in the evenings and on weekends. Furthermore, it fails to recognize that some jobs deserve higher priority in terms of turnaround time than others. It also provides low motivation for data processing management to minimize costs, since users will be billed for actual costs, whatever they may be.

Market prices generally provide a more stable charging rate for computer services. Furthermore, used in conjunction with the profit center concept, market prices provide a superior means of motivating the management of the computer facility. There is motivation not only to hold costs down but also to provide quality services that will maximize the satisfaction of user needs. The computer center manager becomes market-oriented and seeks to develop and provide new services that take advantage of the best available technology for the benefit of users and the total organization.

The profit center approach also provides a better basis for economic evaluation of the computer facility by top management. Comparison of the return on investment of the computer facility with that of other divisions of the company gives some indication of whether the investment in computer resources is justified relative to alternative uses of corporate funds. If users are willing to pay the rates charged and to use most or all the available capacity, a large profit should be generated to signal the need, as well as to provide justification, for additional investment in computer facilities.

There are also significant disadvantages to the use of market prices. Unless the computer center sells its services commercially, market prices may not be readily available. In such instances, it is difficult to obtain a comparable market price. Therefore costly, time-consuming negotiations between users and data processing management may be necessary. This also raises the issue of whether users should be permitted to use an outside service bureau when internal prices are too high. Finally, market prices do not solve the problems of handling peak demands and providing fast turnaround for high-priority work.

Flexible pricing involves adjusting prices for the purpose of stabilizing the demand for computer services. High rates are charged for services rendered during periods of peak demand and for jobs requiring fast turnaround. In conjunction with a multiple factor allocation base, higher rates may be charged for heavily used system components in order to prevent those components from becoming bottlenecks. When system capacity is substantially increased (as it may be by the acquisition of a new computer), lower rates may be charged for a brief period in order to encourage users to consume the available capacity. Note that under flexible pricing, rates do not necessarily bear any relation to cost. Rates may be established to recover total costs or to recover costs plus a profit.

If properly administered, a flexible pricing scheme may generate significant benefits. Those users whose needs are critical enough to justify fast turnaround and service during peak periods will presumably be willing to pay higher rates, and those users whose needs are less critical will be encouraged to accept slower turnaround or processing during slack periods. Flexible pricing thus seeks to establish a stable and acceptable equilibrium between the supply and demand of computer services.

The use of flexible pricing adds to the complexity and expense of a charging system. In addition, prices may have to be changed frequently to accommodate changes in user behavior. Despite these disadvantages, the need to balance the work load of the computer facility over time is often important enough to justify the use of some form of flexible pricing. In a business data processing environment, flexible pricing for peak and slack period demand and for accommodation of differing turnaround requirements would seem to be the most appropriate forms.

In conclusion, the final choice of the allocation base and the technique of computing rates is a complex issue. A major factor in resolving this issue should be the degree of sophistication of computer management and users. If these groups possess a great deal of experience and expertise, the more complex techniques such as unit pricing, multiple factor bases, market prices, or flexible pricing may be appropriate. Otherwise, the simple approach of full costing using a single factor base may be best.

Selecting new computer applications

When a pricing system for computer services is used, there is merit to the idea that computer users should be free to select among new computer applications. Under this approach computer applications would be selected for development only if a user department is willing to pay the systems development and operating costs out of its departmental budget. Proponents of user freedom to select new applications contend that such freedom makes users feel responsible for the success of the projects they select, thereby ensuring user involvement and motivation to achieve success. They argue further that user managers understand the needs of their own department better than anyone else and are better able to evaluate the subjective benefits of proposed new applications. Thus if the data processing staff can provide a reasonably accurate forecast of cost, the user can evaluate whether the benefits outweigh the costs by a sufficient amount to justify the project.

There are disadvantages to this concept of user freedom to select new computer applications. Because of the relative newness and complexity of computer systems in many organizations, users may not be knowledgeable enough to make responsible choices. Also, the development of integrated systems that cross departmental boundaries is often desirable and is made easier when the selection process is centralized. Furthermore, the centralized approach provides a better basis for long-range systems planning because such plans are not subject to constant change due to new user requests. Finally, there is merit to the idea of comparing all proposed applications at one time and assigning highest priority to those that are most consistent with overall organizational goals.

Resolution of this difficult question will obviously depend to a great extent on management's philosophy with respect to the general issue of centralization vs. decentralization. However, a compromise approach is used in many organizations. Under this approach, users are free to accept computer projects costing less than a certain amount but must seek approval at a higher level of authority for more expensive projects.

Advantages of pricing systems

Organizations that do not charge users for computer services frequently encounter serious problems. Users are motivated to request computer services without regard to cost. On the other hand, a user who is not charged for computer services is less likely to involve himself or herself in the development and implementation of computer applications, and such involvement is often critical to the success of the information system. Another problem is that it is difficult for management to evaluate the economic merits of requests by systems personnel for additional computer resources. If such requests are fulfilled, the computer budget may grow out of control, whereas denial of these requests may limit computer capacity to such an extent that user demand cannot be serviced adequately. Furthermore, the demand for computer services may exceed the supply during peak periods but may be inadequate to provide full utilization of the system during slack periods.

A system of internal pricing for computer services should alleviate many of these problems. Users will request services only when they believe the benefits of such services outweigh the costs charged against their budgets. User managers are more likely to involve themselves in systems development and implementation in order to assure themselves that expected benefits will be realized, and that involvement enhances the likelihood of success. Because the computer function is paying its own way, increases in budget to enlarge system capacity are much easier to justify on an economic basis.

If a charging system includes a flexible pricing scheme to charge higher rates for peak period usage, then the problem of balancing the processing work load between peak and slack periods may be substantially reduced. Furthermore, if users are permitted the freedom to use the services of an outside service bureau in lieu of the internal computer function, a tremendous incentive is provided to the internal computer management to minimize its costs and maximize the quality of its services.

The difficulties in developing an internal pricing system are being reduced as computer manufacturers and software vendors develop packages and algorithms for job costing in multiprogrammed systems. As a result, systems of pricing for computer services are now recognized as an important cornerstone of sound computer management.

Management Involvement in the Systems Function

As mentioned earlier, the degree of management involvement with respect to the systems function has been found to correlate highly with success in the utilization of computer systems. When discussing management involvement in the systems function, it is helpful to distinguish two categories of management—executives at the top level of the organizational hierarchy, and managers of middle-level departments that make significant use of computer services.

The role of top management relative to the systems function encompasses the areas of planning, policy setting, performance review, and decision making. Top management should delineate the overall goals and objectives of the organization and identify what it feels are the key success factors in the organization's operations in order to provide guidance and direction to the systems activity. Top management should review long-range systems plans and strive to integrate such plans with the overall long-range planning effort of the organization. Top management should participate in major decisions relating to the systems function, including hiring of key personnel, acquisition of major equipment, and selection of major systems projects. Review of performance of the systems department, its key management personnel, and its major systems development projects is another important role of top management. The establishment of policies relating to project selection, pricing of computer services, organizational structure, and career paths for systems personnel is also important.

The role of user department managers primarily concerns the identification, selection, design, and development of new computer applications. User managers should participate in the determination of information requirements for their departmental operations. They should cooperate with systems analysts in the estimation of costs and benefits for proposed systems applications. They should be willing to assign key members of their own staff to full-time participation in systems development projects and should themselves be actively involved in directing and monitoring such projects. Furthermore, they must make a financial commitment from their departmental budgets to support the development and operation of new systems.

Strategies for obtaining effective management involvement

It is relatively easy to identify what the roles of management should be with respect to the systems function. However, achieving effective management involvement to fulfill these roles has been one of the most difficult of all the problems of systems management. This section discusses some of the formal steps that can be taken to achieve effective management involvement in the systems function.

Perhaps the most critical barrier to effective management participation in systems activities is the communications gap that exists between operating managers having little or no technical expertise and systems personnel having great technical expertise but little understanding of line operations. This gap can probably never be eliminated, but it must be recognized and dealt with to the greatest extent possible.

The first step toward dealing with this problem is education and training. Large organizations may assign staff employees to the development of in-house training programs for management and systems personnel. Programs for management and systems users should focus on the basic elements of systems technology, its terminology, its applications, its economics, and its evolution. Smaller organizations that cannot afford such in-house programs can make use of similar programs available from a variety of professional organizations such as the Association for Systems Management, the Data Processing Management Association, the American Institute of Certified Public Accountants (CPAs), and the National Association of Accountants. It should be noted that the success of such programs depends in large measure on the encouragement and support of top management, which should urge its subordinates to participate in such programs and should back up its encouragement by taking account of such participation in the evaluation of employee performance.

A second approach to the management involvement issue relates to staffing policies. Too many organizations take the attitude that their systems department is a completely separate entity with respect to career paths of management and staff personnel. Such policies cannot help but widen the communications gap mentioned earlier. A more enlightened approach permits career paths to cross this boundary freely. Staff personnel in operating departments should be considered as candidates for assignment to positions in the systems department, and vice versa. It is particularly important that the systems department not be looked upon as a "dead end" in terms of career advancement but that systems personnel with good administrative skills be given the opportunity to move up the organizational hierarchy, possibly to executive status if merited by performance. This approach is obviously not a short-run solution to the issues of management involvement and the communication gap, but in the long run, it may be the best possible solution.

Two policies whose effect is to enhance management involvement in the systems function have already been discussed in this chapter. One is the use of an information systems steering committee composed of top-level executives and systems personnel. Another is the use of a formal pricing mechanism for computer services. With respect to the latter, line managers are naturally more inclined to take interest in an activity that they are paying for through large allocations of their departmental budgets.

Another common approach is the use of project teams to carry out systems development work involving applications for the operating departments. Such teams include both systems analysts and programmers from the systems department and user department managers and staff from the appropriate operating departments. Some of these personnel may be assigned to the team on a full-time basis, others on a part-time basis. Such teams are formed when a systems development project is formally approved, and they continue to function until the system is implemented. Once again, it is necessary that the organizational reward structure clearly reflect management's desire for effective user department participation in such project teams.

In summary, there are a variety of policies and procedures that can be used to foster management involvement in the systems function. However, nothing is quite so effective as a clear signal from the top level of the organization that such involvement is important and will be rewarded.

Impact of the Computer on Patterns of Organization

Computer and related information technology continue to have a profound impact on organizational patterns within the business world. One example concerning the issue of organizational location of the computer activity has already been discussed. At this point several other related issues of computer impact on organizations are identified and briefly discussed.

Centralization or decentralization of management

Prior to the advent of computers a trend toward decentralization of management functions had existed in business. Large multidivision companies could not effectively make decisions for, and exercise control over, far-flung operating divisions. This was true because accounting, the primary information supplying function, did not have available the technology to provide company headquarters with adequate information on the timely basis that was necessary to make decisions at the operating level.

Some authorities predicted that the increased information processing capability provided by the computer could have the effect of eliminating this trend toward decentralization. The computer enables company headquarters to receive more timely and reliable information in greater quantities from the operating divisions. The use of real-time systems and distributed networks of computers linked by data communications is the ultimate expression of this trend. This would seem to provide top management with the capability to centralize decision making for operating divisions.

To date, no widespread trend toward recentralization of management control has been evident in multidivisional companies. Many companies have centralized certain administrative functions, such as customer accounting, purchasing, or cash management, but the primary motivation for this has been to improve efficiency rather than to centralize management control. At the same time, recent technological trends such as the advent of mini- and microcomputers and distributed processing networks have greatly enhanced the computer capability available to the divisions. Thus the divisions no longer simply provide input to a central computer facility, but they also have their own processing facility as well. In short, modern computer technology can effectively support either a philosophy of centralization or a philosophy of decentralization, and it is up to each company to design a system that best fits its own philosophy and objectives.

Effect on management tasks

Another hotly debated issue has been the effect of information technology on the functions performed by management, especially middle management. Some have suggested that computers would take over the routine decision-making functions of middle management and result in a greater degree of centralization of creative activities within the higher management levels.[12] As middle management was eliminated, the shape of the organization structure would shift from the form of a triangle toward the form of an hourglass. Others suggest that computers will not eliminate middle management but will remove the routine tasks from this group and give it more time to concentrate on the creative aspects of its jobs. No clear pattern has yet emerged with respect to this question.[13]

Examining this question very carefully, Whisler suggests that management functions can be delineated into four basic categories: (1) problem solving, (2) communication, (3) goal setting, and (4) pattern perception, or the recognition of problems and opportunities. He argues that computers possess advantages over human beings with respect to the functions of problem solving and communication of expected results. However, he does not foresee an ability for computers to replace managers with respect to goal setting, pattern perception, or the motivational aspects of communication.[14]

Effect on routine tasks

Still another major issue has been the effect of computer technology on clerical workers, production line employees, and others whose jobs are routine and repetitive in nature. Prominent labor leaders and others have predicted that automation would cause mass unemployment by displacing thousands of clerical and production employees. This argument is countered by those who contend that computer technology enhances worker productivity, enables

---

[12]The classic statement of this position is found in Harold J. Leavitt and Thomas L. Whisler, "Management in the 1980's," *Harvard Business Review* (November/December 1958): 41–48.

[13]For further discussion of this subject, see Rob Kling, "Social Analyses of Computing: Theoretical Perspectives in Recent Empirical Research," *Computing Surveys* (March 1980): 61–110; and Paul Attewell and James Rule, "Computing and Organizations: What We Know and What We Don't Know," *Communications of the ACM* (December 1984): 1184–1192.

[14]Thomas L. Whisler, *Information Technology and Organizational Change* (Belmont, Calif.: Wadsworth, 1970): 24–26, 81–82.

workers to escape from the drudgery of traditional industrial or clerical jobs, and opens up more creative jobs requiring knowledge, judgment, and higher levels of skill.

Has computer technology contributed to greater unemployment in our society? It is difficult to tell because computer technology has not been the only variable affecting employment. The unemployment rate in this country was about the same in 1968 that it was in 1948, but it has risen substantially since then. Employment in the data processing field has been growing rapidly for over thirty years. Other trends such as the increasing participation of women in the work force and changing government policies have also significantly affected the employment marketplace. Thus it is probably impossible to isolate the net effect of computer technology on unemployment rates.

One thing that now seems clear is that the computer's impact on the nature of jobs is not something that is beyond our control. That is, it is possible to design man-machine systems in which the role of the employee involves little more than pushing buttons or reacting to the machine's needs, but it is also possible to design man-machine systems in which the judgment and creativity of the employee complements the speed, memory, and accuracy of the machine. In short, whether or not the new technology can eliminate the drudgery of menial jobs depends on the ingenuity of systems designers to devise systems that fulfill the promise of the computer era.

In summary, the long-range effects of computers on traditional organizational structures and job responsibilities are not entirely clear. The major point of agreement is that the impact will be profound. Much speculation has been offered by experts on this subject, and the Kling, and Attewell and Rule articles cited above provide a good synthesis of some of this literature. The process of change is made less orderly by the seemingly continuous advancements being made in information technology. The future promises to be hectic but interesting.

Summary

An effective information systems function is taking on greater strategic importance for the management of contemporary business organizations. To meet this challenge, management must increase its involvement in the information systems function in order to shape its course in a manner that is most consistent with long-range business strategy. Establishing an effective program of long-range systems planning that incorporates projected resource requirements and information technology assessments is a key element of this process. A system of internal pricing of computer services can also help management to guide the future direction of computer resource utilization within the organization.

Management must also address a number of key organizational issues involving the information systems function. These include the organizational location of the systems function, the level of the top computer executive in the organizational hierarchy, and the extent of centralization or decentralization of various information systems operations. Each organization must find a "best" way to resolve these issues in a manner that is most consistent with the environmental, technological, and human factors that shape its strategies and policies.

Review Questions

1. Explain why the management of the information systems function has proved to be such a difficult and complex task.

2. How is the study of information systems management relevant to the role played by accountants in modern organizations?

3. What are four existing patterns of location of the computer operation within business organizations?

4. What business data processing tasks were among the first to be automated? Why?

5. Describe several arguments both favoring and opposing the location of the computer activity within the accounting department in organizations.

6. What arguments are advanced by those who favor the location of the computer activity in a separate department whose manager is a top-level executive in an organization?

7. What arguments are advanced by those who favor the creation of a position of vice-president for administration to whom the controller, treasurer, and director of information systems would report?

8. Describe some recent trends in the systems field that have tended to reduce the significance of the computer location controversy in organizations.

9. Explain the role of an executive-level information systems steering committee. What should be the composition of such a committee? What advantages can be attained from effective use of such a committee?

10. List several arguments in favor of a centralized approach to the information systems function in a large organization.

11. List several arguments in favor of a decentralized approach to the information systems function in a large organization.

12. Describe some effects of recent technological trends on the issue of centralization vs. decentralization of the information systems function.

13. Explain why the assignment of priorities to proposed new computer applications is a very critical decision for an organization's management.

14. Describe in some detail the content of a systems project development plan.

15. Describe in some detail the content of an overall information systems plan for an organization.

16. What are the six stages of growth in the data processing function in most business organizations, according to Richard Nolan? What implications does this "stage hypothesis" have for systems planning?

17. Explain several advantages of long-range planning for information systems.

18. Explain briefly what a system of internal pricing of computer services is.

19. Explain some of the objectives that are often established for pricing of computer services.

20. Explain some of the criteria most often used in designing a system of pricing computer services.

21. Identify some alternative allocation bases for pricing of computer services and describe their relative advantages and disadvantages.

22. Describe some alternative methods of setting rates for computer services and explain their relative advantages and disadvantages.

23. What effect should the degree of sophistication of computer management and users have upon the selection of a system of pricing computer services?

24. When a system of pricing computer services is being used, what arguments favor permitting users to freely select new computer applications? What arguments oppose such an approach? Is there a possible compromise between these two points of view?

25. Explain several advantages of internal pricing of computer services.

26. Explain the role that top management should play relative to the systems function in an organization.

27. Explain the role that user department managers and personnel should play relative to the systems function in an organization.

28. What has been the most significant barrier to effective management participation in the activities of the systems function in most organizations?

29. Explain several strategies for obtaining effective management involvement in the systems function.

30. Identify and briefly discuss three issues of computer impact upon organizational patterns.

Discussion Questions

31. The approach to long-range information systems planning described in this chapter is obviously important for large organizations having extensive investments in computer facilities. Should small organizations—in which the computer department employs fewer than, say, ten persons—attempt to implement such planning programs? Discuss.

32. Do you believe that it is possible to generalize with respect to the proper organizational location of the computer activity in business? Why or why not? Discuss.

33. If a multidivisional company decides to adopt a decentralized approach to the information systems function, is there a role for long-range information systems planning in that company? Discuss.

34. Discuss the impact of computers and automation on the nature of job responsibilities and on unemployment in our society.

Problems and Cases

35. The Dobson Manufacturing Company has recently decided to replace its small business computer system with a large general-purpose computer system employing online terminals and real-time processing capability. The feasibility study that recommended this step was carried out by the assistant controller, who is also the manager of the current system, and by the assistant vice-president for production, who is an expert in real-time production control systems. One of the first steps in planning for acquisition and implementation of the new system is to decide how the change will affect the company's organization structure. The company is currently organized into five major functional areas: Production, Marketing, Personnel, Finance, and Accounting.

   Some facts from the feasibility study that bear upon the decision are as follows.

   ☐ The budget and staff of the new department will be three times as large as that of the old department.

   ☐ The computer will perform all the basic accounting functions previously performed by the small business computer system.

   ☐ The primary justification for the new computer system is the contribution to profit that will be generated as a result of its immediate application to production planning and control.

   ☐ Estimated usage of computer time by each of the five functional areas is expected to be as follows: Production, thirty percent; Marketing, ten percent; Personnel, five percent; Finance, five percent; Accounting, fifty percent.

   ☐ High potential exists for profitable application of the new computer in Marketing, Personnel, and Finance, and total usage of computer time by these three areas should eventually reach forty percent.

   REQUIRED   Considering all aspects of the situation described, identify and discuss the relative merits of several alternative locations of the new computer facility within the organizational structure of the Dobson Manufacturing Company.

36. The Dooley Company operates its Data Processing Center as a cost center. Each year a budget for the center is developed by the company's con-

troller and the manager of the Data Processing Center. The manager's performance is evaluated on the basis of a comparison of actual costs incurred to budgeted costs.

The manager of the Data Processing Center is responsible for accepting or rejecting proposals from user departments for new applications. User departments are not charged for either programming work or data processing service. Some of the main problems relating to the operation of the center have been as follows.

1. The manager has complained that budget allowances are not sufficient to pay for necessary new equipment and personnel.
2. There is frequent uncertainty and disagreement regarding decisions on whether proposed new applications should be undertaken.
3. The Accounting, Production, and Marketing departments have frequently disputed over whose applications should obtain priority in development and scheduling.

REQUIRED

a) Identify the policy or policies that are the probable cause of each of the problems cited above. Explain.
b) Describe an alternative system of management control that might be appropriate for the Data Processing Center. Explain how this approach would be implemented and how it might contribute to solution of the problems above.

37. The Perry Corporation has four new computer applications under development or scheduled to begin development shortly. The monthly requirements of these development projects for computer time and for system analyst-programmer time over the next two years are indicated below.

| Months | PROJECT A | | PROJECT B | |
	System hours	Analyst-programmer hours	System hours	Analyst-programmer hours
1–6	20	240	30	352
7–12	75	380	30	400
13–18	80	100	100	550
19–24	88	110	150	120

| Months | PROJECT C | | PROJECT D | |
	System hours	Analyst-programmer hours	System hours	Analyst-programmer hours
1–6	25	264	—	—
7–12	30	280	—	120
13–18	30	300	20	380
19–24	100	500	30	410

Operational requirements for the company's existing applications total 400 computer system hours and 200 analyst-programmer hours. These requirements increase by ten percent at the end of each six-month period.

The firm presently employs six analyst-programmers who work 8 hours per day for an average of 22 days each month. There are a total of 720 hours of available computer time per month (30 days × 24 hours per day). However, for each hour of computer time used, an average of only eighty percent is used for productive work, with the other twenty percent used for equipment maintenance, reruns, etc.

a) At what point in time will a significant increase in the capacity of Perry's computer system become necessary? Why?

b) Assume that a new computer system is to be acquired and that the conversion to this new system will be complete as of the first day of month 13. Further assume that one analyst-programmer will devote full-time effort to implementing this conversion during the six months preceding the first day of month 13. How many full-time analyst-programmers must Perry employ during each of the four six-month periods?

c) Assume that (1) the monthly salary of an analyst-programmer is $2000; (2) the monthly hardware rental and all other fixed costs for the present system total $10,000 and will total $15,000 after the new system is implemented; (3) upon implementation the new system will exactly triple throughput (i.e., work formerly taking three hours on the computer will now take one hour); and (4) all variable costs relating to the operation of both the old and new systems, during both productive and nonproductive usage, total $20 per hour. Prepare a financial projection of the monthly total of these costs for each month over the two-year period.

38. The Maxwell Company uses unit pricing to compute charges to user departments for computer services. For each job run on the computer, the number of machine units (MU) is measured according to the following formula.

$$MU = 0.14 \times (0.07C + 0.0002I) \times [13 + 0.3(0.9D + 0.2D^2) + 0.1(T + 0.02T^2) + 0.4(0.01R + 0.0002R^2)],$$

where C = CPU seconds, I = input/output count, D = disk drives used, T = tape drives used, and R = number of units of primary memory.

The charge for each machine unit is $10.

a) What would be the total cost charged for a job that uses (1) 300 CPU seconds, (2) an input/output count of 10,000, (3) two disk drives, (4) four tape drives, and (5) sixty-four units of primary memory?

b) Suppose that you are interested in the incremental cost of various resources used on the job above. For example, the incremental cost of one disk drive would be the difference between the cost computed for part (a) and the cost that would have been computed if one less disk drive were used. Compute the incremental cost of

1) one CPU second
2) 1000 input/output count units
3) one disk drive
4) one tape drive
5) four units of primary memory

39. The Hunter Company uses a system of full costing in charging its computer-using departments for computing services. Operating and cost data for a recent month are as follows.

RESOURCE	TOTAL COST	UNITS USED
Central processor	$180,000	500 hours
Main memory	56,000	280,000 units
Disk/tape I/O	115,000	230,000 units
Card/print I/O	60,000	60,000 units
Total cost	$411,000	

Data on resources used by two jobs recently run on the computer system are as follows.

RESOURCE	ACCOUNTING JOB	ENGINEERING JOB
Central processor	1 hour	2 hours
Main memory	500 units	2000 units
Disk/tape I/O	500 units	100 units
Card/print I/O	500 units	40 units

REQUIRED

a) If the single factor base of CPU hours is used to price computer services, what will be the rate charged? How much would be charged to each of the two jobs described?
b) If a four-factor base is used, what will be the rates for each of the four factors? Under this scheme, how much would be charged to each of the two jobs?
c) Which of these two alternative pricing systems do you think is better? Discuss.

40. Stevens Chemical Company is a manufacturer of a wide variety of chemicals, including cleaning fluids, weed and bug sprays, lubricants, and several industrial chemicals used as raw materials by other firms. The company has total sales of about $300 million and is made up of six operating divisions located in five southern states whose sales range from $30 million to $80 million. The company has always operated under a philosophy of

decentralization, wherein each divisional management has authority to set prices, determine its product mix, and establish other policies. Company headquarters has exercised a loose form of budgetary control, generally approving budget requests submitted by divisions and reviewing divisional performance to the extent necessary to reward division managements for successful performance and to make recommendations for improvement where appropriate. The company has operated profitably under this arrangement for several years, except that in the last two years one division has sustained a loss owing to a combination of downward pressures on prices and large increases in selling and administrative costs.

The company's management has recently made a decision to acquire an advanced computer system that will be installed at company headquarters and will have data communications links to each of the divisions. Mr. Thomas Shockley, a former management consultant with the company's auditors and a specialist in data processing, has been hired as assistant controller to be in charge of the computer facility. Mr. Karl Pearson, formerly a controller at the largest of the company's operating divisions, has been the company's controller for the last ten years. The new computer is due to be installed within three months, and Mr. Shockley is in the process of supervising staff training, system design, and programming activities.

As a result of his work in preparing for installation of the new computer system, Mr. Shockley has proposed that the company adopt a philosophy of greater centralization of decision-making responsibility. He argues that the major reason for decentralization of such responsibility is that timely and relevant information is not available to top management to enable them to make major decisions for the divisions. He believes that the new computer system will make available to corporate headquarters enough relevant information on a timely basis to enable top management to effectively make major decisions for the divisions. Shockley has been authorized to develop a computer-based accounting system that will consolidate accounting functions for all the divisions on the new computer; these functions include general ledger, billing, payroll, production and cost accounting, accounts receivable, accounts payable, inventory, budgeting, and performance reporting. Performance reports on each division, comparing actual with budgeted results, should be available to corporate headquarters each month, within a week from the end of the month, according to Mr. Shockley. A list of the functions that he feels should be centralized instead of performed at the divisional level includes (1) establishing pricing policies, (2) deciding on the product lines, (3) purchasing raw materials, (4) scheduling production, (5) extending credit, (6) deciding on capital expenditures, and (7) deciding on salaries and promotions for divisional management personnel.

In discussions of Mr. Shockley's proposal by the company's top executives, Mr. Pearson has argued in opposition to the idea of centralization. He points to the company's long history of profitability under a philosophy of decentralization. He has expressed doubt that the new computer system will be able to provide company headquarters with information that is as reliable, timely, and complete as that available to the division managers. He feels that the freedom provided to division managers has been a significant factor in motivating them to perform successfully.

In response to Mr. Pearson's arguments, Mr. Shockley points out that the company's decision to acquire a computer system with real-time capability places it at a major crossroads. Top management must decide whether the computer will merely become an expensive form of mechanized bookkeeping or an effective tool contributing to the profitable management of the company. He argues that centralized decision making is necessary because of the increasing lack of coordination of activities of operating divisions, as evidenced by some cases in which two different divisions have marketed competing products. He further argues that the new computer system will make it more efficient to centralize the administration functions than to continue the policy of decentralization. He cites the case of the division that has incurred operating losses as evidence of the need for more centralized financial control.

REQUIRED

a) Examine the list of functions that Mr. Shockley suggests should be centralized. Which of these functions do you feel could be more effectively performed if centralized? Which could be more effectively performed under decentralization? Explain.

b) Mr. Pearson has expressed doubt that the new computer system will be able to provide company headquarters with information that is as reliable, timely, and complete as that available to the divisional managers. Do you agree? Explain.

c) Mr. Shockley defines the issue at one point as "whether the computer will merely become an expensive form of mechanized bookkeeping or an effective tool contributing to the profitable management of the company." Do you feel that this is the relevant issue in the case? Explain.

d) Are there any other alternatives to the strict centralization of decision making advocated by Mr. Shockley and the status quo defended by Mr. Pearson? Explain.

e) What action do you feel should be taken by the management of Stevens Chemical Company with respect to the proposal of Mr. Shockley? Which arguments do you feel are the most compelling and why?

41. The Independent Underwriters Insurance Co. (IUI) established a Systems Department two years ago to implement and operate its own data processing systems. IUI believed that its own system would be more cost-effective than the service bureau it had been using.

IUI's three departments—Claims, Records, and Finance—have different requirements with respect to hardware and other capacity-related resources and operating resources. The system was designed to recognize these differing needs. In addition, the system was designed to meet IUI's long-term capacity needs. The excess capacity designed into the system would be sold to outside users until needed by IUI. The estimated resource requirements used to design and implement the system are shown in the following schedule.

	HARDWARE AND OTHER CAPACITY- RELATED RESOURCES	OPERATING RESOURCES
Records	30%	60%
Claims	50	20
Finance	15	15
Expansion (outside use)	5	5
Total	100%	100%

IUI currently sells the equivalent of its expansion capacity to a few outside clients.

At the time the system became operational, management decided to redistribute total expenses of the Systems Department to the user departments based upon actual computer time used. The actual costs for the first quarter of the current fiscal year were distributed to the user departments as follows.

DEPARTMENT	PERCENTAGE UTILIZATION	AMOUNT
Records	60%	$330,000
Claims	20	110,000
Finance	15	82,500
Outside	5	27,500
Total	100%	$550,000

The three user departments have complained about the cost distribution method since the Systems Department was established. The Records Department's monthly costs have been as much as three times the costs experienced with the service bureau. The Finance Department is concerned about the costs distributed to the outside user category because these allocated costs form the basis for the fees billed to the outside clients.

James Dale, IUI's controller, decided to review the distribution method by which the Systems Department's costs have been allocated for the past two years. The additional information he gathered for his review is reported in Figs. 10.4, 10.5, and 10.6.

| | ANNUAL BUDGET | | FIRST QUARTER | | | |
| | | | BUDGET | | ACTUAL | |
	Hours	Dollars	Hours	Dollars	Hours	Dollars
Hardware and other capacity-related costs	—	$ 600,000	—	$150,000	—	$155,000
Software development	18,750	562,500	4,725	141,750	4,250	130,000
Operations—						
Computer-related	3,750	750,000	945	189,900	920	187,000
Input/output–related	30,000	300,000	7,560	75,600	7,900	78,000
		$2,212,500		$556,350		$550,000

FIGURE 10.4
Systems Department
costs and activity
levels.

| | HARDWARE AND OTHER CAPACITY NEEDS | SOFTWARE DEVELOPMENT | | OPERATIONS | | | |
| | | | | COMPUTER | | INPUT/OUTPUT | |
		Range	Average	Range	Average	Range	Average
Records	30%	0–30%	12%	55–65%	60%	10–30%	20%
Claims	50	15–60	35	10–25	20	60–80	70
Finance	15	25–75	45	10–25	15	3–10	6
Outside	5	0–25	8	3–8	5	3–10	4
	100%		100%		100%		100%

FIGURE 10.5
Historical utilization
by users.

FIGURE 10.6
Utilization of Systems
Department's services
in hours, first
quarter.

| | Software Development | OPERATIONS | |
		Computer-Related	Input/Output
Records	425	552	1,580
Claims	1,700	184	5,530
Finance	1,700	138	395
Outside	425	46	395
Total	4,250	920	7,900

Dale has concluded that the method of cost distribution should be changed to reflect more directly the actual benefits received by the departments. He believes that the hardware and capacity-related costs should be allocated to the user departments in proportion to the planned, long-term needs. Any difference between actual and budgeted hardware costs would not be allocated to the departments but remain with the Systems Department.

The remaining costs for software development and operations would be charged to the user departments based upon actual hours used. A predetermined hourly rate based upon the annual budget data would be used. The hourly rates that would be used for the current fiscal year are as follows.

FUNCTION	HOURLY RATE
Software development	$ 30
Operations	
Computer-related	$200
Input/output–related	$ 10

Dale plans to use first quarter activity and cost data to illustrate his recommendations. The recommendations will be presented to the Systems Department and the user departments for their comments and reactions. He then expects to present his recommendations to management for approval.

REQUIRED

a) Calculate the amount of data processing costs that would be included in the Claims Department's first quarter budget according to the method James Dale has recommended.

b) Prepare a schedule to show how the actual first quarter costs of the Systems Department would be charged to the users if James Dale's recommended method was adopted.

c) Explain whether James Dale's recommended system for charging costs to the user departments will:

1) improve cost control in the Systems Department.
2) improve planning and cost control in the user departments.
3) be a more equitable basis for charging costs to user departments. (CMA Examination)

42. Acme Novelty Co. provides a wholesaling service for some 2000 retailers. Orders are received in person or over the phone and transcribed to input source documents. These identify the retailer and the quantity of goods ordered. The order documents are delivered twice a day to the offices of Sharecomp, a computer utility. At Sharecomp, they are entered through CRTs, edited, checked against a file for credit standing, and stored on a temporary file. A second program, operating at the end of each day, sorts the orders by retailer and creates a sorted order file. Also at the end of

each day, the sorted order file is processed against an inventory file, creating an updated inventory file, a file of charges to customers, and a printout of summarized orders.

Once a month, the accumulated charges to customers are processed against a file of customer records, generating an updated customer record, and invoices to the retailers.

The operation is shown in the systems flowchart in Fig. 10.7.

Average volumes and times are as follows.

☐ Each day 400 documents are processed.

☐ Program 3 requires twenty minutes of CPU time, and six connect hours, per day.

☐ File 4 requires ten tracks per day and 5000 I/O's.

☐ File 5 requires fifty tracks per day and 40,000 I/O's.

☐ Program 6 requires five minutes of CPU time per execution.

☐ File 7 requires fifty tracks per day and 40,000 I/O's.

☐ Program 8 requires twenty minutes of CPU time per day.

☐ File 9 requires 200 tracks per day and 75,000 I/O's, as does File 10.

☐ Printout 11 involves 7000 lines per day.

FIGURE 10.7

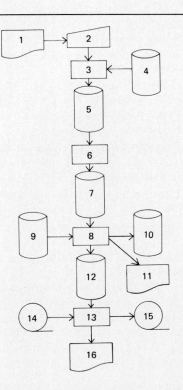

☐ File 12 requires 40,000 I/O's per day. The file size increases over the month, but the average size of File 12 is 1000 tracks per day.

☐ Program 13 requires fifteen minutes of CPU time per execution.

☐ Files 14 and 15 require 20,000 I/O's each time Program 13 is run.

☐ Print output 16 prints 12,000 lines of output.

Sharecomp Charge Schedule:

CPU time	$10.00/minute
Terminal connect	$ 5.00/hour
Document entry	$ 0.10/document
Disk storage	$ 0.05/track/day
Disk I/O's	$ 2.00/thousand
Tape I/O's	$ 2.00/thousand
Printing	$ 1.50/thousand lines
Tape mounts	$ 3.00/mount

REQUIRED

How much do you expect Sharecomp will bill Acme Novelty per month for this service? Show your calculations clearly. Assume twenty working days per month. (SMAC Examination)

References

Attewell, Paul, and James Rule. "Computing and Organizations: What We Know and What We Don't Know." *Communications of the ACM* (December 1984): 1184–1192.

Benjamin, Robert I. "Information Technology in the 1990s: A Long Range Planning Scenario." *MIS Quarterly* (June 1982): 11–31.

Buchanan, Jack R., and Richard G. Linowes. "Understanding Distributed Data Processing." *Harvard Business Review* (July/August 1980): 143–153.

———. "Making Distributed Data Processing Work." *Harvard Business Review* (September/October 1980): 143–161.

Canning, Richard G. "Coping with End User Computing." *EDP Analyzer* (February 1984): 1–12.

———. "Six Top Information Systems Issues." *EDP Analyzer* (January 1985): 1–12.

Cushing, Barry E. "Pricing Internal Computer Services: The Basic Issues." *Management Accounting* (April 1976): 47–50.

Dearden, John. "MIS Is a Mirage." *Harvard Business Review* (January/February 1972): 90–99.

Doll, William J. "Avenues for Top Management Involvement in Successful MIS Development." *MIS Quarterly* (March 1985): 17–35.

Drury, D. H. "An Evaluation of Data Processing Steering Committees." *MIS Quarterly* (December 1984): 257–265.

Ein-Dor, Phillip. "Grosch's Law Re-Revisited: CPU Power and the Cost of Computation." *Communications of the ACM* (February 1985): 142–151.

Gibson, Cyrus F., and Richard L. Nolan. "Managing the Four Stages of EDP Growth." *Harvard Business Review* (January/February 1974): 76–88.

Joy, James J. "Pricing DP Services." *Journal of Systems Management* (November 1977): 36–41.

Kanter, Jerome. "The Role of Senior Management in MIS." *Journal of Systems Management* (April 1986): 10–17.

Keen, Peter G. W., and Lynda A. Woodman. "What to Do with All Those Micros." *Harvard Business Review* (September/October 1984): 142–150.

King, John Leslie. "Centralized versus Decentralized Computing: Organizational Considerations and Management Options." *Computing Surveys* (December 1983): 319–349.

Kling, Rob. "Social Analyses of Computing: Theoretical Perspectives in Recent Empirical Research." *Computing Surveys* (March 1980): 61–110.

Leavitt, Harold J., and Thomas L. Whisler. "Management in the 1980's." *Harvard Business Review* (November/December 1958): 41–48.

McFarlan, F. Warren. "Problems in Planning the Information System." *Harvard Business Review* (March/April 1971): 75–89.

———. "Information Technology Changes the Way You Compete." *Harvard Business Review* (May/June 1984): 98–103.

Miller, William B. "Building an Effective Information Systems Function." *MIS Quarterly* (June 1980): 21–30.

Nolan, Richard L. "Managing the Crises in Data Processing." *Harvard Business Review* (March/April 1979): 115–126.

———. "Managing Information Systems by Committee." *Harvard Business Review* (July/August 1982): 72–79.

Porter, Michael E., and Victor E. Millar. "How Information Gives You Competitive Advantage." *Harvard Business Review* (July/August 1985): 149–160.

Pyburn, Philip J. "Linking the MIS Plan with Corporate Strategy: An Exploratory Study." *MIS Quarterly* (June 1983): 1–14.

Rockart, John F., and Adam D. Crescenzi. "Engaging Top Management in Information Technology." *Sloan Management Review* (Summer 1984): 3–16.

Selig, Gad J. "Approaches to Strategic Planning for Information Resource Management (IRM) in Multinational Corporations." *MIS Quarterly* (June 1982): 33–45.

Sullivan, Cornelius H., Jr. "Systems Planning in the Information Age." *Sloan Management Review* (Winter 1985): 3–12.

Whisler, Thomas L. *Information Technology and Organizational Change.* Belmont, Calif.: Wadsworth, 1970.

Withington, Frederic G. "Coping with Computer Proliferation." *Harvard Business Review* (May/June 1980): 152–164.

C H A P T E R   1 1

Systems Analysis and Design

LEARNING OBJECTIVES

Careful study of this chapter should enable students to:

☐ Describe the steps in the system life cycle.

☐ Discuss key issues and approaches associated with the systems analysis process.

☐ Describe the nature and purposes of several techniques used in the design of information systems.

☐ Prepare and utilize document flowcharts in the design and evaluation of information systems.

CHAPTER OUTLINE

Systems Analysis
    Who performs systems analysis?
    The systems approach
    Defining the objectives of the information system
    Top-down vs. bottom-up approach
    Assessing the information needs of management

Systems Survey
    Human factors in systems survey
    Review of system documentation
    Document flowcharting
    Volume analysis
    Work measurement
    Reliability analysis
    Interviews with personnel
    Use of checklists
    Review of personnel
    Problem analysis

Systems Synthesis

Systems Design
    Output design
    Input and file design
    Prototyping
    Process design
    Work distribution analysis
    Work scheduling
    Comprehensive approaches to systems design

Summary

Review Questions

Discussion Questions

Problems and Cases

References

Two factors create the necessity for frequent change in the information systems of business organizations. One is the growth of business organizations themselves in a dynamic society, which produces both new demands for information and greater volumes of data processing. A second factor is the rapid improvement of information technology, which offers a potential competitive advantage to those firms that are among the first to innovate. Within the past two decades, both of these factors have operated to produce an atmosphere of hectic change for the information systems function in many organizations.

The concept of the system life cycle, introduced in Chapter 1, is a useful way of viewing the complex process of systems change. This process is diagramed in Fig. 11.1. The cycle may be perceived as beginning at the point of recognition that a new system is needed. This recognition may be sparked by new information requirements, by new technology, or simply by the inadequacies of an existing system to meet user needs. This is followed by the parallel processes of surveying the status of the existing information system and analyzing user requirements. These steps culminate in a synthesis phase in which a plan is developed for overcoming the deficiencies of the existing system. Next comes a more detailed design of the new system, followed by its

FIGURE 11.1
The system life cycle.

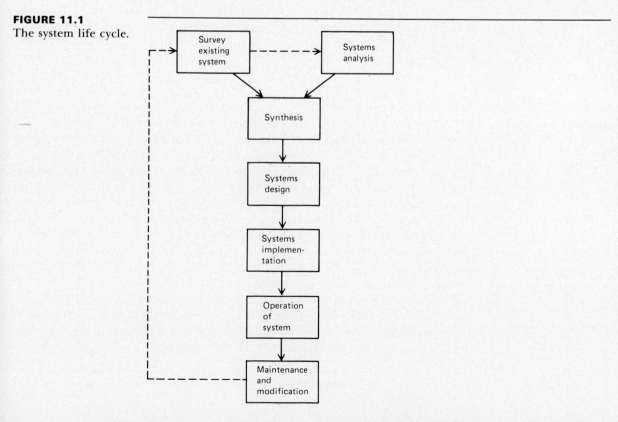

implementation and operation. During the operating stage of its life cycle, an information system normally undergoes maintenance and minor modification. Ultimately the system is found to be obsolete or inadequate, and the life cycle process begins anew.

The system life cycle concept is very general and may be applied to the entire information system or to any of its component parts, such as equipment, software, procedures, and application subsystems. Of course, the specific activities performed within each phase, and the time and resources required for each phase, will vary, depending on the type of project. In this chapter the first four steps in the life cycle are examined—survey, analysis, synthesis, and design. The implementation phase is covered in a subsequent chapter. Emphasis here is placed upon the objectives, policies, and techniques most commonly adopted at each step in the systems change process.

Systems Analysis

to establish objectives for the design of my system

As used in this section *systems analysis* refers to the process of examining user information requirements within an organization in order to establish objectives and specifications for the design of an information system. According to recent studies, the systems analysis phase of the systems life cycle is the phase that is perhaps most critical to the success or failure of a systems development effort.[1] This section focuses upon broad policies, objectives, and frameworks that contribute to a successful strategy of systems change. Many of the specific techniques often associated with systems analysis are discussed later in this chapter in the sections on survey and design.

Who performs systems analysis?

to develop the system in b system to satisfy user needs

According to the traditional view, the functions of systems analysis and design in an organization are performed by persons who are called *systems analysts*. They are responsible for the development of information systems that employ available systems technology to satisfy user information requirements in an optimal manner. This generally involves the design of computer applications and the preparation of specifications for computer programming. The position requires both experience with systems technology and familiarity with the operations of the organization, for this person must serve to bridge the gap between the user and the technology. The systems analyst is the central figure in the system life cycle, playing a leading role in systems survey, analysis, synthesis, design, and implementation. Therefore this chapter is written primarily from the perspective of the systems analyst.

Citing a lack of appreciation of managerial realities among systems analysts, some authorities have recently suggested a new job function called *information analyst*. This person has both the technical skills and the organizational knowledge to serve as a liaison between managers having little technical

---

[1] James D. McKeen, "Successful Development Strategies for Business Application Systems," *MIS Quarterly* (September 1983): 47–65.

knowledge and systems analysts who are generally more technology-oriented than management-oriented. The information analyst presumably has the expertise to effectively identify a manager's information requirements in a way that is satisfactory to both the manager and a systems designer. The information analyst may even be a member of the manager's staff, rather than a member of the computer department. Although the concept of the information analysis function is appealing, available evidence suggests that it has not yet been implemented on a widespread basis, and that the traditional systems analyst still plays a dominant role.[2]

The systems approach

The systems approach to systems change emphasizes a number of specific approaches and policies relating to the planning of systems investigations. One is an emphasis on viewing problems and alternatives from the standpoint of the entire organization, rather than from the standpoint of any single department or interest group. Another is the requirement of a careful step-by-step approach to each task, which necessitates the thorough exploration of all implications and alternatives at each step in the project. A third useful approach is an emphasis on defining the objectives of the system as a framework for analysis of problems and opportunities.

Still another essential aspect of the systems approach to systems change is the use of the "team approach," in which systems specialists, operating managers, and other groups that are significantly affected by a systems change participate together in a coordinated effort throughout the various stages of the project. Use of the team approach to systems investigation reflects formal recognition of the fact that problems of major importance in an organization cannot be approached from a limited perspective. For example, accountants alone cannot design a reporting system that is to provide useful information to marketing executives. Similarly, computer specialists alone cannot be expected to design a computerized data processing system to replace an already operating manual system. Responsibility for such major projects should be assigned to a team whose members represent all the diverse specializations relevant to the problem. Such an approach is not only likely to produce more effective results but also will facilitate the acceptance of the results by all parties concerned. Thus operating managers will feel more favorably disposed toward a system they helped to develop than toward one imposed upon them by what they consider "outside" forces.

In the context of computerized information systems, the most critical need for close cooperation arises between operating management and systems specialists. Operating managers often fail to recognize the potential benefits of computerization, whereas systems specialists often fail to understand the complexities of an operating system. If allowed to work in isolation from each

---

[2]Kate M. Kaiser and William R. King, "The Manager-Analyst Interface in Systems Development," *MIS Quarterly* (March 1982): 49–59.

other, these two groups may never feel compelled to respect each other's point of view. If obliged to work together on a project, the outcome of which will affect their own personal success, they are more likely to achieve a reconciliation of viewpoints sufficient to enable a working relationship to be established.

Perhaps the most important factor of all in successful planning for systems change is the involvement of top management. Such involvement begins with participation in the process of defining objectives for the information system. Top management must select the members of the project team, taking care to achieve a proper balance of operating managers and systems specialists. Top management must clearly define the responsibilities of the project team and demand from them a report containing a thorough analysis of the merits of all alternatives from the standpoint of the organization as a whole. Members of the project team must understand that they are responsible to top management for the eventual success or failure of the course of action they recommend.

Defining the objectives of the information system

The specific objectives of an information system are a function of the objectives of the organization that the system serves. Some authorities have suggested that every organization has a limited number of "key success factors" that must be identified to provide direction for systems planning.[3] By way of illustration, consider an automobile manufacturer, to whom the key success factors are product styling, manufacturing cost control, and an efficient dealer organization, according to Daniel. Identification of key success factors enables the systems planning and development group to focus on the elements of the information system that are most vital to the success of the organization.

Certain general objectives, important in all information systems, may be identified. A partial list of these would include the following.

1. *Usefulness.* The system should produce information that is timely and relevant for decision making by management and operating personnel within the organization.

2. *Economy.* All component parts of the system, including reports, controls, machines, etc., should contribute a benefit value at least as great as their cost.

3. *Reliability.* System output should possess a high degree of accuracy, and the system itself should be capable of operating effectively even while a human component is absent or while a machine component is temporarily inoperative.

---

[3]See, for example, D. Ronald Daniel, "Management Information Crisis," *Harvard Business Review* (September/October 1961): 111–121; William M. Zani, "Blueprint for MIS," *Harvard Business Review* (November/December 1970): 95–100; and John F. Rockart, "Chief Executives Define Their Own Data Needs," *Harvard Business Review* (March/April 1979): 81–93.

4. *Customer service.* The system should provide courteous and efficient customer service at points of interface with the organization's customers.

5. *Capacity.* The system should have sufficient capacity to handle periods of peak operation as well as periods of normal activity.

6. *Simplicity.* The system should be simple enough that its structure and operations can be easily understood and its procedures easily accomplished.

7. *Flexibility.* The system should be sufficiently flexible to accommodate changes of a reasonable magnitude in the conditions under which it operates or in the requirements imposed upon it by the organization.

Thinking about systems problems in terms of objectives such as these helps to clarify the true nature of such problems. For example, the problem of maintaining adequate internal control must be examined as a trade-off between the objectives of economy and reliability. Similarly, the problem of cutting clerical costs must be analyzed in terms of a trade-off between the objective of economy, on the one hand, and capacity, flexibility, and customer service, on the other. Once the objectives that are relevant to a particular problem are specified, a framework is provided for subsequent data collection and analysis. Of course, it is impossible for any system to completely satisfy all these objectives, but the objectives themselves do provide useful guidelines for systems planning.

Top-down vs. bottom-up approach

Two broad strategies of information systems analysis and design may be identified. The *bottom-up approach* seeks to develop an information system through an orderly process of transition, building upon transaction processing subsystems. As information needs are identified, these subsystems are modified and expanded to provide information for planning, control, and decision making as a by-product. The growth of the subsystems is planned and coordinated to achieve integration.

The *top-down approach* begins with a definition of both the organization's objectives and strategies and proceeds to an examination of the decision-making process. Information requirements are determined according to what is needed for decision making. The information system is viewed as a total system, fully integrated, rather than as a collection of loosely coordinated subsystems. Top management participates more directly in the analysis and design process.

The top-down approach is obviously more consistent with the systems approach described earlier. Its potential flaw is that an organization may attempt to apply the approach on a scale that is too broad, in search of the elusive "total information system." This could lead to a dramatic failure. The best procedure is probably a combination of the top-down and bottom-up approaches that incorporates the systems approach but focuses on one or a few subsystems at a time, taking into account the unique needs and capabilities of the particular organization.

Assessing the information needs of management

Because management decisions are based on information, it is axiomatic that the successful management of an organization is related to the effectiveness of its information system. In turn, the system's effectiveness depends upon the extent to which it satisfies the information needs of the managers and other users it serves. Therefore the formal study of management's information requirements is an important part of systems analysis.

In practice, however, there seem to be many pressures that result in neglect of a systematic approach to assessing management's information needs. For example, managers may feel that they are too busy to participate seriously in such a project. Furthermore, there is a natural tendency in information processing to restrict input collection to only those data that are provided as a by-product of accounting transactions and clerical procedures. Typically, those responsible for data processing are more interested in and knowledgeable about procedures and equipment rather than management decision making. They may interpret volume of output as being synonymous with quality of output. In the face of such pressures, positive steps must be taken to ensure that systems analysis and design give proper consideration to the information needs of management.

A proper analytical approach to assessing management's information needs should begin with an identification of the decisions for which management requires information. A useful framework for the study of management decisions is provided by Anthony,[4] who classifies management activities into three broad categories of strategic planning, management control, and operational control. He defines *strategic planning* as the process of deciding on the objectives of the organization, on the changes in these objectives, on the resources used to attain these objectives, and on the policies that are to govern the acquisition, use, and disposition of these resources. *Management control* is the process by which managers ensure that resources are obtained and used effectively and efficiently in the accomplishment of the organization's objectives. *Operational control* is the process of ensuring that specific tasks are carried out effectively and efficiently. To clarify these definitions, Anthony presents a table, reproduced in Fig. 11.2, listing several types of decision-making activities which fall under each heading.

Keen and Scott Morton[5] identify a second dimension by which management decisions may be characterized—that being the degree of structure they possess. At one extreme are *structured decisions,* which are repetitive and routine and well-enough understood to have been delegated to clerks or to have been automated on a computer. At the other extreme are *unstructured decisions,*

---

[4]Robert N. Anthony, *Planning and Control Systems, A Framework for Analysis* (Boston: Division of Research, Graduate School of Business Administration, Harvard University, 1965). Copyright © 1965 by the President and Fellows of Harvard College. The definitions in this paragraph are from pages 16–18.

[5]Peter G. W. Keen and Michael S. Scott Morton, *Decision Support Systems: An Organizational Perspective* (Reading, Mass.: Addison-Wesley, 1978), pp. 85–86.

Strategic Planning	Management Control	Operational Control
Choosing company objectives	Formulating budgets	
Planning the organization	Planning staff levels	Controlling hiring
Setting personnel policies	Formulating personnel practices	Implementing policies
Setting financial policies	Working capital planning	Controlling credit extension
Setting marketing policies	Formulating advertising programs	Controlling placement of advertisements
Setting research policies	Deciding on research projects	
Choosing new product lines	Choosing product improvements	
Acquiring a new division	Deciding on plant rearrangement	Scheduling production
Deciding on non-routine capital expenditures	Deciding on routine capital expenditures	
	Formulating decision rules for operational control	Controlling inventory
	Measuring, appraising, and improving management performance	Measuring, appraising, and improving workers' efficiency

FIGURE 11.2
Examples of activities in a business organization included in major framework headings. (Robert N. Anthony, *Planning and Control Systems, A Framework for Analysis.* Boston: Division of Research, Graduate School of Business Administration, Harvard University, 1965, p. 19. Copyright © 1965 by the President and Fellows of Harvard College. Reprinted by permission.)

which are nonrecurring and nonroutine to the extent that no framework or model exists for solving them, and the decision maker must rely primarily or exclusively on judgment and intuition. Between these extremes is a category of *semistructured decisions,* which are those which may be partially but not fully automated because they require subjective assessments and judgments in conjunction with formal data analysis and model building. Keen and Scott Morton propose that their three-way classification of decisions be merged with Anthony's framework to produce a two-dimensional taxonomy of decisions. They illustrate this taxonomy by means of a table, reproduced in Fig. 11.3, which contains an example of each of nine different categories of decisions.

There is a rough correspondence between a manager's level in the organization and the nature of his or her decision responsibilities. That is, top management executives generally face unstructured or semistructured decision problems that involve strategic planning issues. Managers in the middle levels of the organizational hierarchy generally must deal with semistructured de-

Type of Decision	MANAGEMENT ACTIVITY			Support Needed
	Operational Control	Management Control	Strategic Planning	
Structured	1 Inventory reordering	4 Linear programming for manufacturing	7 Plant location	Clerical, EDP or management science models
Semistructured	2 Bond trading	5 Setting market budgets for consumer projects	8 Capital acquisition analysis	Decision support systems
Unstructured	3 Selecting a cover for *Time* magazine	6 Hiring managers	9 R&D portfolio management	Human intuition

FIGURE 11.3
The Keen and Scott Morton decision taxonomy. (Peter G. W. Keen and Michael S. Scott Morton, *Decision Support Systems: An Organizational Perspective.* Reading, Massachusetts: Addison-Wesley Publishing Company, 1978, p. 87. Reprinted by permission.)

cision problems of a management control nature. Supervisors and employees at the lowest levels of the organization typically face semistructured or structured decision problems involving operational control. In any event, it is important to examine the types of decisions for which a manager is responsible as a first step in designing an information system to support that manager's activities, and the decision taxonomy presented above provides a useful framework for doing this.

To illustrate this point, consider a lower-level manager involved in operational control activities. The scope of authority of such a manager is typically limited to a particular department or a particular category of work. The decisions for which he or she is responsible are known, and these tend to be structured or semistructured decisions for which the required data and decision rules have been explicitly identified, perhaps in an operating manual. The information the manager needs must generally be detailed, accurate, short-term in perspective, provided frequently and regularly, and obtained from sources internal to the organization. If these needs for information are not being completely satisfied, the manager can probably identify what additional information should be available. As a result of these factors, the process of identifying the information requirements of lower-level managers does not usually present major problems.

At the other extreme is a top-level manager involved in strategic planning, whose scope of responsibilities encompasses the entire firm, and whose functions are defined according to such vague phrases as "setting objectives," "establishing policies," and "devising market strategies." To the extent that such a manager's decision problems can be explicitly identified, they tend to be unstructured or semistructured. The information required for this type of manager is primarily external information dealing with the product markets, the economy, the company's competitors, the availability of resources, and other environmental factors. Such information generally must also be highly summarized, encompass a broad time horizon, deal with a large number of variables, be future-oriented, and be available for demands that arise on an irregular and infrequent basis. Because of these factors, a top-level manager may find it difficult to specify information requirements. Thus a precise identification of the decision responsibilities and information requirements of top-level managers engaged in strategic planning is not a simple task.

Because most structured decision problems have already been successfully automated, and because most unstructured decision problems must be dealt with primarily by human intuition, Keen and Scott Morton suggest that the power of the computer can now be most effectively employed by developing systems to assist managers in semistructured decision situations. A system of this type is called a *decision support system,* which they define as "a conversational, interactive computer system with access through some form of terminal to the analytic power, models, and data base held in the machine."[6] Sprague and Watson state that "evidence suggests many firms are moving to develop systems such as these that have as their main focus the support of managerial decision making."[7] Figure 11.4 illustrates the elements of a decision support system and their relationship to one another.[8]

The key element of any decision support system is the decision maker whom the system is designed to support. The system designer must fully understand the decision process from both a quantitative and a behavioral perspective and must establish a combination of models, data bases, and software systems that can effectively supplement (rather than replace) the manager's judgment in making the decision. The key element of the software system is the user interface, which provides the user with a set of commands (verbs such as FIND, DISPLAY, GRAPH, etc.) that may be used to access and manipulate all the other elements of the system. The user interface must be human-oriented rather than system-oriented in order to accommodate managers who lack the knowledge or inclination to deal with standard computer languages.

One early attempt to develop a computer-based system to support strategic planning decisions of a semistructured nature is represented by the management planning model developed by Gershefski for the Sun Oil Company.[9] This model utilized computer simulation to enable managers to explore the

---

[6]*Ibid.,* p. 58.

[7]Ralph H. Sprague, Jr., and Hugh J. Watson, "Bit by Bit: Toward Decision Support Systems," *California Management Review* (Fall 1979): 61.

[8]This figure is adopted with minor modification from Sprague and Watson's fig. 1, p. 64.

[9]See George W. Gershefski, "Building a Corporate Financial Model," *Harvard Business Review* (July/August 1969): 61–72.

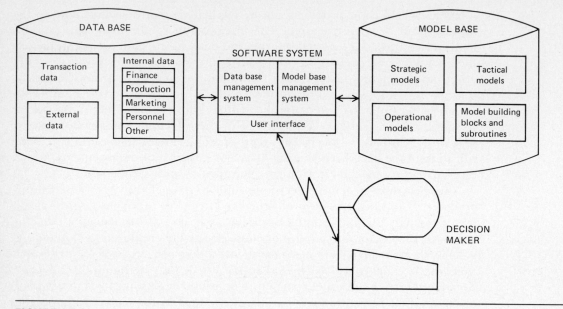

FIGURE 11.4
Components of a decision support system. (Adapted from fig. 1, p. 64, in Sprague and Watson's "Bit by Bit: Toward Decision Support Systems." © Copyright [1979] by the Regents of the University of California. Reprinted from *California Management Review*, volume xxii, no. 1, by permission of the Regents.)

potential impacts of various decisions or policies in terms of profits, market share, and other objectives. This experiment was widely heralded as a breakthrough at first but is now generally regarded to have been a failure. Keen and Scott Morton claim that a major reason for this failure was "the approach of defining the data base to be used and *then* finding the decisions it could support."[10] The point is that the systems analyst must first understand the decision process—and then build a system to support it.

Decision support systems should be viewed as a worthwhile extension of traditional data processing systems. Traditional systems capture transaction input, perform some structured tasks, and generate information useful to those who perform other structured tasks. Data base management systems enable a systematic integration of transaction data and other relevant internal and external data. Decision support systems appear to be the next logical extension of the use of computer technology in organizations. Viewed in this light, the concept of the decision support system provides a useful perspective the systems analyst can draw upon in preparing for and carrying out an assessment of management's information processing needs.

Systems Survey

Systems survey is the systematic gathering of facts relating to the existing state of an information system. It is generally done by a systems analyst. Its purpose

---

[10]Keen and Scott Morton, *Decision Support Systems*, p. 85.

is to obtain an accurate perspective on the existing system in order that areas of weakness causing problems can be identified, and that changes necessary to correct such weaknesses and resolve major problems can begin to be conceived. A systems survey may be carried out concurrently with systems analysis or may be conducted separately as part of a more limited systems investigation.

The systems survey generally focuses on the visible components of an information system. These components include (1) resources, such as hardware, software, and personnel; (2) data, such as the system input, files, output, and documentation; and (3) activities, such as procedures, functions, and decisions. In this section several approaches and techniques for the systems survey are reviewed and discussed.

Human factors in systems survey

One of the primary sources of information to the systems analyst regarding the operation of an existing system is the people who are involved in operating it and utilizing its output. Thus the systems analyst needs to work closely with the people in a system during the survey phase of a systems investigation. Although this may occasionally involve merely recording observations, it will much more frequently require the systems analyst to conduct interviews with operating people and managers. To fulfill this aspect of the role effectively, the systems analyst needs to be sensitive to the feelings of people generally and aware of some of the more common human problems that arise in an organization during a systems investigation.

The presence in their midst of a systems specialist, who is a staff person or perhaps even an outsider, can be disconcerting to operating managers and personnel. The fact of the sudden interest in their work is an indication that a possible change may be under consideration. Requests for information and interviews are disruptive of the normal routine. In such a situation the fear of uncertainty natural in people can generate mistrust and rumors and perhaps be damaging to morale and efficiency.

Proper planning of systems investigations recognizes that people do not fear change by itself but do have a fear of the uncertainty that accompanies change. Such uncertainty should be minimized to the greatest possible extent. This can be accomplished by a policy of open communication with employees for the purpose of clarifying the intentions of the company regarding the investigation in progress. Generally, the objective of such a policy should be to develop an attitude in employees that enables them to identify *with* the company and the system in its efforts toward improvement. The policy should prevent the formation of an employee attitude that perceives the company and the system as something having goals and plans separate from, or even opposed to, those of employees. Several more specific methods of accomplishing this objective are briefly discussed here.

As a first step in the survey phase of a systems investigation, the analyst should arrange to hold meetings with operating managers whose departments may be affected by the study. The scope of the study should be made clear as to whether a major change, such as automation, is being contemplated, or whether modifications of lesser magnitudes are the goal. The analyst should discuss the reasons for the study in positive terms, stressing the contribution that each department makes to the organization and the desire of company management to provide them with the best possible support. Stating objectives in negative terms, such as mentioning a need to correct existing problems, raise efficiency, or cut costs, should be avoided. The analyst should emphasize a personal need for the assistance of operating managers and their personnel in the project and encourage them to participate by offering their ideas and suggestions.

In cases in which the change being considered is very broad in scope, as in the case of a study to assess the feasibility of computerizing an existing manual or semiautomated system, the systems analyst must anticipate that many operating managers and their subordinates will fear the loss of their jobs, their seniority, or their status. Many personnel policies may be used to soften the impact of such major changes, and the analyst should make sure that management communicates its intentions in this regard to its employees. For example, existing employees may be given the first chance at new positions that become available and should be encouraged to test for such positions. Training programs may be offered by the company or by the firm from which equipment is being acquired. Communication with employees on this subject should stress the increased opportunities for advancement and more rewarding work that will result from the change.

In most medium-to-large-sized organizations, a policy of relocation of displaced employees in jobs of equal pay and status will be feasible. If hiring rates are temporarily reduced, the normal attrition of employees will enable such displaced personnel to be assimilated into the regular work force within a year or two. In the case of employees who are within a few years of retirement, it may be possible to arrange for an early retirement. In the case of persons whose employment is terminated, severance pay and assistance in obtaining new positions may be provided. Such policies may be expensive, but the decline in morale caused by the lack of such policies could be even more expensive. In any event, all such policies to be adopted should be communicated to employees, and the full backing and genuine interest of top management should be made clear.

The planning of a systems investigation should also take into account human factors and attitudes with respect to the top management personnel who are closely involved with the study. One factor of primary importance is the willingness of top management to involve itself in monitoring and providing direction for the systems effort. Of equal importance is the concern of top management in maintaining an atmosphere of good human relations and high morale among employees. Also important is a willingness to adjust to changes in organizational relationships and to become familiar with a new pattern of systemization or a completely new technology. To the extent that each of these factors is present in top management, the process of systems change will be much easier to plan for and carry out.

Review of system documentation

One important and useful source of facts about an information system is the documentation of the system. Ideally this should include complete procedures manuals, organization charts, job descriptions, training materials, sample copies of documents and reports, file descriptions, flowcharts of systems, programs and document flows, program listings, operating instructions for equipment, and so forth. One of the systems analyst's first tasks in the systems survey should be to gather all this material that is available. If such material is not available or not complete, the analyst will find it useful to develop it, at least in rough form.

It should be noted that such items of documentation as procedures manuals, job descriptions, and flowcharts describe how the system is intended to work, but this is not necessarily how it actually works. Throughout the systems survey, the analyst should be alert for differences between the intended operation of a system and its actual operation, for these often provide important insights into problems and weaknesses.

The systems analyst should also carefully review the content and design of documents and reports used in the information system. If a problem of lack of information exists at some point in the system, it could be that data from which to generate that information are not being collected, or perhaps, once collected, they are not being processed properly or completely. If the problem is one of failure to collect the necessary data, the need for redesign of input documents and procedures for recording input data is indicated. A review of documents and reports and the related data collection and processing procedures may also provide useful insights on other types of problems. For example, it may be that some data collection and processing steps are being duplicated, in which case a consolidation of documents or reports, or an integration of processing procedures might produce a cost savings. Similarly, a lack of control might be corrected by instituting a change in the procedures for data collection or processing or perhaps by prenumbering a document.

Document flowcharting

The preparation of document flowcharts is a useful technique of systems survey. A *document flowchart* is a diagram illustrating the flow of documents relating to a particular transaction through an organization. It provides the systems analyst with a broad view of the formal communications network in an organization.

Information obtained from the review of systems documentation forms the primary basis for preparation of a document flowchart. After gathering this material, the analyst must determine the departments, persons, and outside parties involved in the operation or transaction being analyzed. All the relevant documents and other significant forms of communication that are part of the process must be established. The place of origination of each document, its distribution, the purposes for which it is used, and its ultimate disposition should be determined.

Although there is very little standardization of document flowcharting symbols and their meanings, Fig. 11.5 illustrates symbols that are widely used. Note that several of these symbols are equivalent to those used in systems flowcharting (e.g., Fig. 5.17). In fact, many systems analysts incorporate some or all systems flowcharting symbols and conventions into their document flowcharts, in effect combining these two forms of flowcharting.

The first step in drafting a document flowchart is to segment a blank page into columns by means of vertical lines. One column must be reserved for each entity involved in the process, including departments, managers, clerks,

FIGURE 11.5
Symbols for document flowcharting.

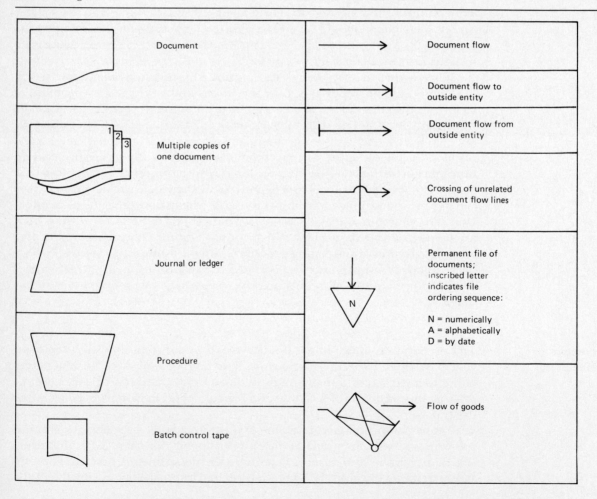

Symbol	Meaning	Symbol	Meaning
	Document		Document flow
			Document flow to outside entity
	Multiple copies of one document		Document flow from outside entity
			Crossing of unrelated document flow lines
	Journal or ledger	N	Permanent file of documents; inscribed letter indicates file ordering sequence: N = numerically A = alphabetically D = by date
	Procedure		
	Batch control tape		Flow of goods

and so forth. Each column is labeled at the top with the name of its respective entity. The origination of each document on a chart is done by the department or entity within which the document's flow begins. The name of each document or description of each procedure is inscribed within the respective symbol. The final disposition of a document, either by filing or by other means, takes place in the department in which its flow terminates.

The document flowchart is generally assumed to represent a batch mode of processing. Thus each document shown on a chart represents a batch of like documents. Several copies of a given document might be prepared, in which case each copy is numbered on the flowchart to facilitate tracing the subsequent flow of each separate copy. The procedure or file symbol is used to describe what is done to each document within each column. However, a more extensive description of the procedures and controls present in the system should be prepared separately as part of the documentation supporting the flowchart. A copy of each document shown on the flowchart should also be included in this supporting documentation.

As an illustration of how a document flowchart of an accounting procedure might be prepared, consider the following description of the processing of data relating to charges to patients by a hospital. When a patient enters the hospital, an admitting department prepares a record of admittance in four copies. It keeps one copy and sends one each to a medical records section, to the nurses' station on the floor on which the patient is located, and to the accounts receivable section. In accounts receivable, a ledger record is prepared for each patient. Requests for various services for patients originate at the nurses' station and are sent to various hospital departments, such as pharmacy, X-ray, or laboratories. All patient charges are originated in these departments, and a copy of each charge voucher is sent from the charging department to accounts receivable, where they are posted to the patient's ledger card. When the patient is released, the nurses' station prepares two copies of a notice of release. One is sent to the medical records section, where it is filed with the record of admittance. Another is sent to accounts receivable, where it is posted. The accounts receivable department then prepares three copies of a claim report, one of which it keeps, one of which is sent to the patient's insurance company, and one of which is sent to the medical records section to be filed with the record of admittance.

As indicated previously, the process of preparing a document flowchart is simplified if one begins by identifying all departments and other entities, and all documents involved in the process. From the description above, five entities can be identified as participants in the document flow process. These are (1) the admitting department; (2) the medical records section; (3) the nurses' station; (4) the accounts receivable department; and (5) the service departments, which are lumped into one category because their roles in the document flow process are identical. Five documents can also be identified: (1) the record of admittance, (2) the request for services for patients, (3) the patient charge voucher, (4) the notice of patient release, and (5) the claim report. Once the process is analyzed in this manner, preparation of the document flowchart is relatively straightforward. A complete document flowchart of this process is shown in Fig. 11.6.

By integrating much of the material obtained in the review of system documentation, the document flowchart provides the analyst with a basic understanding of the process being charted. It may be used in several ways to pinpoint weaknesses in a system. It is particularly useful in analyzing the adequacy of control procedures in a system, such as internal checks and separation of functions. The document flowchart might also reveal inefficiencies present in a system, such as absence of adequate communication flows, an unnecessary complexity in document flows, or procedures responsible for causing wasteful delays. Document flowcharts may also be prepared as part of the systems design process and should be included within the documentation of an information system.[11]

Because the document flowchart is an excellent vehicle for describing document flows and procedures within an information system, it is used extensively to describe accounting systems in Part 4 of this book, which deals with accounting applications. Accordingly, several additional examples of document flowcharts may be found in Chapters 16 through 20.

Volume analysis

Measures relating to the volume of processing are also important to the systems analyst at this stage. For each processing operation, an estimate of average volume should be obtained, as well as an assessment of the variability of volume, particularly with regard to the frequency and duration of periods of peak volume. Trends in the average and peak volume are also significant as indicators of future capacity requirements. Sometimes a relationship between processing volume and sales volume can be developed and used to generate predictions of future processing volume on the basis of available estimates of future sales volume. In addition to measures of volume, the analyst should obtain data on the percentage utilization of individual items of equipment and on the time required for, and time actually spent by, each employee in performing the tasks of which his or her job consists. All these data are useful to the analyst in assessing the degree to which available processing capacity is being utilized by the current system, and the extent to which the capacity of the current system is sufficient to meet future processing requirements.

Work measurement

One well-developed set of techniques for obtaining and making use of data on the time required for employees to perform their jobs goes by the title of *work measurement*. This set of techniques is primarily applicable to jobs con-

---

[11]For a more extensive treatment of the preparation of document flowcharts and their use in the evaluation of internal control, see Max Laudeman, "Document Flowcharts for Internal Control," *Journal of Systems Management* (March 1980): 22–30.

FIGURE 11.6

Document flowchart of hospital accounting for patient records.

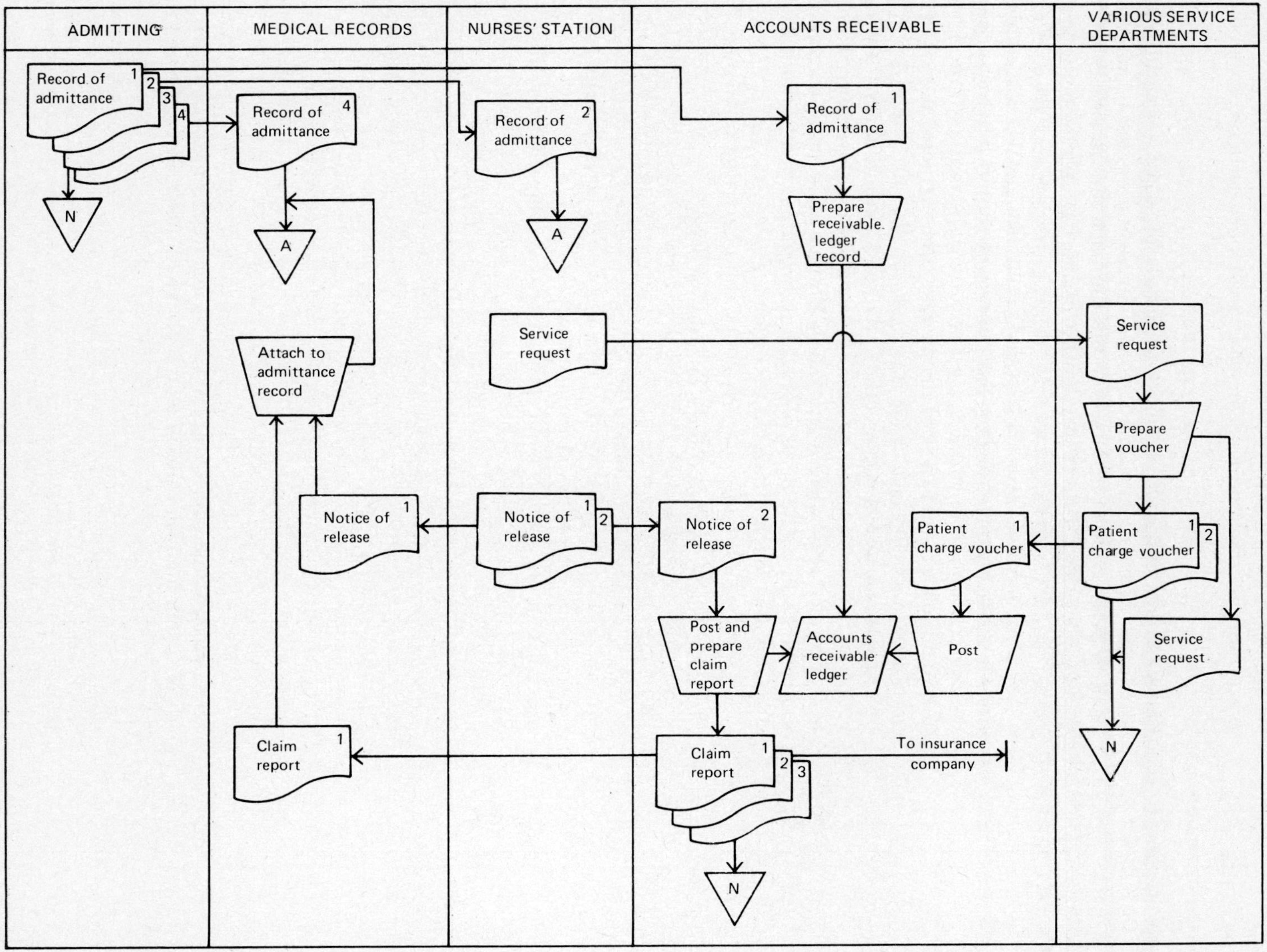

sisting of routine, repetitive clerical activities such as filing, typing, calculating, posting, sorting, and so forth, rather than to less structured functions such as management or creative work. To some extent, the applicability of work measurement techniques has declined in recent years, owing both to a tendency toward relaxation of rigid work standards as part of an increased emphasis on employee morale and to the increasing degree of automation of routine clerical functions. However, the approach can potentially be very useful in some cases and, as such, is worthy of at least a brief general description here.

A work measurement study begins by breaking down the routine functions in the department or process under investigation into the set of distinct tasks or activities of which each consists. A time and motion study of each task is made to obtain a measure of the average time for performance of a single unit of each activity, such as the typing of a single purchase order or posting of transactions to a single account. Time and motion study involves observation of the performance of a task by a skilled employee and maintenance of a record of time spent. Observations should be taken at several different times to obtain a sample of observations representative of the various conditions under which the task is performed.

Once a measure of average time per unit of activity is obtained, it should be adjusted for work delays such as interruptions, errors, machine breakdowns, and satisfaction of personal needs for rest or other relief. This adjustment is usually made in the form of a percentage of work time. For example, if ten percent of total work time is considered an adequate adjustment for work delays, then the average time per unit of activity is increased by ten percent to give an adjusted average time.

The next step is to multiply the adjusted average time per unit of activity by the average volume of units of activity in a processing cycle, which may be a day, a week, or a month, depending on the operation. This gives the total time required for each separate activity during the processing cycle. Once this is done for all activities in the process or operation, the sum of the total times for all activities provides a measure of the total work time required in the operation during a processing cycle. At the same time, a measure of the total time spent on the job by all employees in the operation during a processing cycle can be determined. Dividing the total time required by the total available working time (see Fig. 11.7) provides a rough measure of the percentage utilization of available capacity in the operation.[12]

A work measurement study potentially can contribute a great deal toward accomplishing the objectives of a systems investigation. It may provide a basis for resolving the major problems that initiated the study by utilizing the avail-

---

[12]For a more detailed discussion of the application of work measurement methods, see Donald S. Anderson, "Supervisors as Work Measurement Analysts," *Management Services* (January/February 1971): 20–26; and Robert I. Stevens and Walter J. Bieber, "Work Measurement Techniques," *Journal of Systems Management* (February 1977): 15–27.

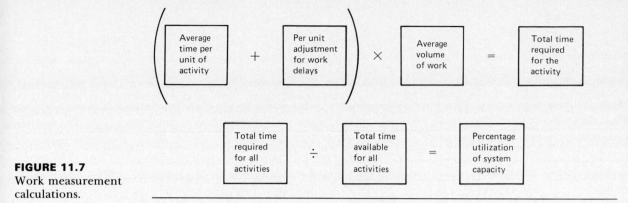

FIGURE 11.7
Work measurement
calculations.

able capacity of the current system rather than expanding that capacity, perhaps needlessly, through increased hiring or mechanization. It enables a judgment to be made of the extent to which the current system can accommodate expected increases in the volume of processing. As will be discussed in the section on systems design, it provides a basis for a more equitable and efficient redistribution of work in an operation, which may be accompanied by the elimination of some jobs at a considerable cost saving. Finally, after a work measurement study has been completed, it is quite useful to adopt a permanent program of maintaining and updating work measurement data to provide standards for evaluating the performance of clerical employees.

Reliability analysis   A technique drawn from the engineering field has been proposed to measure in probabilistic terms the reliability of a data processing system in executing a particular task or set of tasks.[13] This technique is intended to assess the effectiveness of procedures that incorporate control checks, such as the use of a control total in posting a batch of transactions to an account. Such procedures might be broken down into the initial process itself, the control check, and the error correction step, as illustrated in Fig. 11.8.

The system reliability measure is computed from a series of reliability measures for the individual components of the process. The individual reliability measures required are the following probability estimates.

P = the probability that the original process (such as posting) is correctly executed.

D = the probability that the control check (such as comparison of control totals) will detect and signal an error, given that one exists.

N = the probability that the control check will not signal an error if no error exists.

[13]Barry E. Cushing, "A Mathematical Approach to the Analysis and Design of Internal Control Systems," *The Accounting Review* (January 1974): 24–41.

FIGURE 11.8
Steps in a controlled process. (Barry E. Cushing, "A Mathematical Approach to the Analysis and Design of Internal Control Systems," *The Accounting Review* (January 1974): 24–41. Reprinted by permission.)

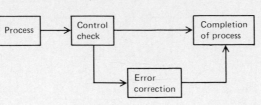

C = the probability that the error correction process will find and correct an error, given that one exists and has been signaled.

F = the probability that in the event that the control check signals an error when none exists this will be discovered and the original process results allowed to stand.

Note that each of the parameters represents the probability of a correct system action, and that for each one, there is a complementary probability of error. For example, $1 - P$ is the probability that the original process is incorrectly executed.

The *system reliability* is defined as the probability that the process will be completed with no errors. Completion of the process with no errors will occur when any two of the three steps preceding process completion (see Fig. 11.8) are correctly performed. Therefore reliability (indicated by R) is equal to the sum of (1) $P \times N$, the probability that the process is executed correctly and the control step does not signal an error; (2) $P \times (1 - N) \times F$, the probability that the process is executed correctly, the control check erroneously signals an error, but the control error is discovered and the process results are not changed; and (3) $(1 - P) \times D \times C$, the probability that an error in the process is made but that the control check signals an error and the proper correction is made. In terms of a formula, the system reliability is

$$R = [P \times N] + [P \times (1 - N) \times F] + [(1 - P) \times D \times C].$$

FIGURE 11.9
Illustrative reliability calculations.

Hypothetical Estimates	Calculations		
$P = 0.8$	(1) $P \times N$	= (0.8) (0.9)	= 0.7200
$D = 0.95$	(2) $P \times (1 - N) \times F$ =	(0.8) (0.1) (0.99)	= 0.0792
$N = 0.9$	(3) $(1 - P) \times D \times C$ =	(0.2) (0.95) (0.98)	= 0.1862
$C = 0.98$		R	= 0.9854
$F = 0.99$			

In Fig. 11.9 the calculation of system reliability is illustrated for a set of hypothetical component reliability estimates.

The reliability model can be extended to systems incorporating a series of control checks and to systems in which several types of errors having different probabilities may occur. It may also be extended to take into account the costs of control procedures and of undetected errors.

The reliability model provides a useful framework for collecting information about data processing activities and their associated controls and for evaluating the effectiveness of the controls. It may also be used in the systems design process to help decide whether new controls are needed. It may be applied to clerical procedures or to automated systems. Thus it is useful to the systems analyst in a variety of ways.

Interviews with personnel

An extremely useful source of facts and information during a systems survey is the interview. Interviews may be held with operating employees, supervisors, managers, or executives. The experience of such persons with the detailed workings of a system provides a valuable source of information for the analyst. Interviewees are likely to provide the analyst with some useful initial ideas about existing problems and possible solutions. Their familiarity with system operations enables them to provide valuable opinions regarding the feasibility of possible solutions suggested by the analyst.

A systems analyst should prepare for an interview by studying both the organization chart and the job description to learn the function of the interview subject and making a list of points to be covered. During the interview, the analyst must take care to make the subject feel at ease, by being friendly and tactful. He or she should let the subject know the purpose of the interview and the time that will be required. Questions should deal with what the person's job consists of, how it relates to other parts of the system, how the person likes the job, and how the job itself might be improved. The analyst should take notes during the interview and should augment these notes with detailed impressions shortly after the completion of the interview.

Use of checklists

Another common technique of systems survey and analysis is the use of *checklists,* or standardized questionnaires dealing with some particular aspect of the information system. These generally consist of a comprehensive list of questions dealing with such things as the steps in an investigation process or the control procedures appropriate for a particular operation. Responses are generally limited to a yes or no, or perhaps to choice of a point on a scale. If the checklist is being used to evaluate some aspect of the system, a weighting factor may be assigned to each question, reflecting its relative importance. Hence the checklist can be used to derive a "score" representing the effectiveness of the system. The checklist is useful to the analyst in studying and evaluating systems because it is standardized and comprehensive—considerable thought has been invested into its preparation and it is not likely that any important factors have been overlooked.[14]

Review of personnel

Another step in systems survey and analysis is a review of the capabilities of personnel in the performance of the functions for which they are responsible. A related step is the assessment of capabilities and aptitudes of personnel with respect to the adjustment necessary to implement and operate a more advanced system. As an aid in this step, the analyst should analyze the task content of each job in question, as well as the requirements for successful performance of the job. To provide a basis for evaluation, the analyst may observe employees at work, interview the employees and their supervisors, administer special tests, and review formal personnel evaluation records. Ultimately, the analyst must also apply his or her own judgment to arrive at evaluations that will be useful to the analysis process.

Problem analysis

Prior to completion of a systems survey it will be useful for the analyst to prepare a summary description of the problems that have been identified. Often the description of a systems problem will be suggestive both of the weaknesses that cause the problem and the corrective measures needed to resolve the problem. For example, a problem described as "lack of reliability of output" in a data processing system suggests a lack of certain internal check procedures, the initiation of which might well resolve the problem. Similarly, a problem of "lack of information by which to evaluate the performance of sales clerks" indicates that the identity of the salesperson is probably not being recorded on input documents at the point of sale. This suggests the solution of revising the design of sales documents and instituting a procedure whereby all sales clerks are required to enter their name or an identifying number on the sales document at the time of the sale. Some additional processing steps would also be required, including sorting all sales slips by sales clerk and accumulating a total number of sales and the total dollar amount of sales for each.

In other cases, however, the solution of a systems problem will be anything but obvious from its description. For example, a problem of "lack of current information on parts inventory balances" suggests the possible inadequacy of the entire materials inventory data processing system. Data collection procedures, documents, files, reports, processing methods, and use of equipment

---

[14]An example of a checklist relating to forms design appears in Fig. 3.7. For an example of an internal control questionnaire relating primarily to a manual system, see Howard F. Stettler, *Auditing Principles,* 4th ed. (Englewood Cliffs, N.J.: Prentice-Hall, 1977), pp. 608–621. A questionnaire used to evaluate EDP controls appears in W. Thomas Porter and William E. Perry, *EDP: Controls and Auditing,* 4th ed. (Boston: Kent Publishing Company, 1984), pp. 512–528.

should all be reviewed to assess whether a correction of existing weaknesses will resolve the problem, or whether it will not be possible to remedy the situation without automating the system. Furthermore, the scope of the problem is such that the benefits of resolving it will have to be carefully weighed against the cost of doing so. It is probably safe to say that most systems problems possess at least this degree of difficulty, perhaps because the simple ones have already been solved.

**Systems
Synthesis**

The synthesis phase of the system life cycle involves bringing together the results of the systems survey and of the analysis to devise recommendations for revision of the existing system and/or development of a new system. At the beginning of this stage, the systems analyst should have an evaluation of the information needs of managers and other system users, an account of perceived problems in the existing system, and a complete description of the system and how it operates. Using these as the basis for the analysis, the analyst must determine what weaknesses are present in the existing system that cause each of the indicated problems. Then he or she must decide how each of the weaknesses can be corrected in such a way that the problems are resolved and the needs for information are satisfied. In some cases, the main question will be whether the existing system can simply be modified to correct its weaknesses, or whether it must be completely replaced by a newly developed system based upon a higher level of automation.

An important step in the synthesis phase is an evaluation of the relative merits of the alternative solutions under consideration. Each alternative should be assessed with respect to the initially stated objectives of the organization and the information system. The pivotal objective is that of economy, to which all other objectives are related. The cost factor may limit the extent to which other objectives can be achieved. Therefore all cost factors relating to each alternative should be carefully measured, and the benefits of each alternative should be delineated. With respect to measurement of the benefits of the various alternatives, the participation of the users of the information systems is a necessary factor. The information developed from this analysis of alternatives forms the primary basis for management's final choice.

If one or more of the alternatives under consideration represents a major systems modification, or involves a large-scale acquisition of computer hardware, software, or services, then a major feasibility study incorporating many factors must be undertaken. This topic is explored in the next chapter.

The climax of the period of systems synthesis is the presentation of recommendations to management. Depending on the preferences of management and the nature of the problem, such recommendations may be in the form of a delineation of alternatives or the expression of a preference for a specific solution. In any event, management will be interested primarily in a summary of the major recommendations, the advantages and disadvantages of each, the estimated costs and cost savings generated by the changes, the data used as a basis for the recommendations, and the methods used in collecting the data. In addition to skills in analysis, design, and implementation of information systems, the systems analyst must possess a considerable measure of persuasive power and communicative skill to be successful in this stage of a systems investigation.

Systems Design

Systems design is the process of preparing detailed specifications for the development of a new system. The starting point of systems design is the development plan prepared during systems synthesis, as modified and/or approved by management. The design phase must fill in all the details of this development plan in order that the new system may be successfully implemented.

Systems design begins with specification of the required system outputs, which includes the content, format, volume, and frequency of reports and documents. Next is the determination of the content and format of system inputs and files. Following these steps comes the all-important design of processing steps, procedures, and controls. At the completion of the systems design process, a plan for implementation of the new system should be prepared.

This section reviews some of the techniques used during the systems design process. Some other tools and techniques of systems design have already been covered in previous chapters. These include forms design (Chapter 3), coding (Chapter 3), systems flowcharting (Chapter 5), program flowcharting (Chapter 6), decision tables (Chapter 6), and document flowcharting (earlier in this chapter). To obtain a more complete feel for the nature of systems design, the reader may wish to review these other topics in conjunction with study of this section.

Output design

The basic objectives and general content of output reports and documents will have been determined as part of the systems analysis and synthesis. During the design phase, the detailed content and format of system outputs must be established. At this point it is necessary to consult with the users of the system output to determine what specific pieces of data or information they require, how they use the data or information, and what format they would find best suited to their needs.

One useful tool for designing the format of computer output reports or forms is the *printer layout chart*. This chart, illustrated in Fig. 11.10, is a grid of empty spaces containing 50 rows and 150 columns, which represent the printing spaces available on one page of computer printout. The systems designer can use several of these to experiment with various possible formats for computer-printed documents or reports. Sample outputs written on these charts can be shown to the eventual users of the output to obtain their preferences. When a format is settled upon, its print layout becomes a useful input to the program coding process.

FIGURE 11.10

Printer layout chart. *(Courtesy of IBM Corporation.)*

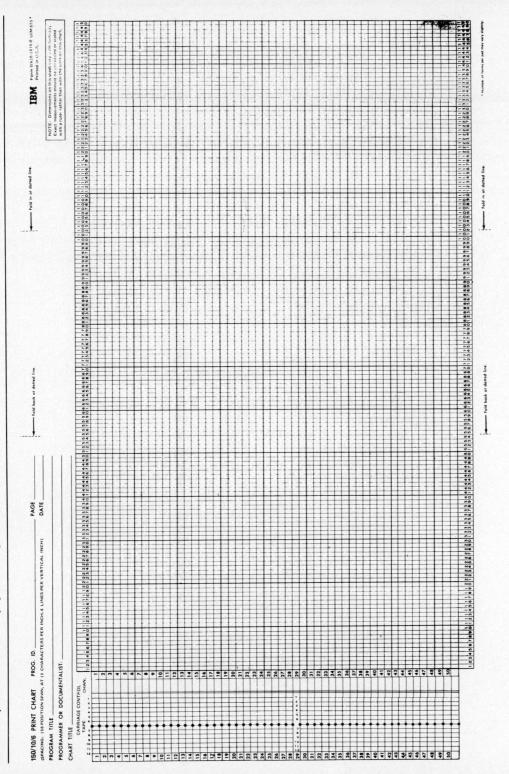

461

In addition to the conventional tabular format of management reports, modern computer technology enables the preparation of reports in graphic form. Large volumes of data may often be condensed into a few pages of graphic reports. Such reports generally may be interpreted more quickly and more meaningfully than tabular reports, thereby enabling managers to make faster and better decisions. Some of the most commonly used forms of computer graphic output are bar charts, trend lines, and pie charts. These and several other forms of computer graphics are illustrated in Fig. 11.11.

In addition to the content and format of reports and other system outputs, another important aspect of report design is their timing. In this respect, four categories of reports may be identified—(1) scheduled reports, (2) unscheduled special-purpose analyses, (3) triggered exception reports, and (4) demand reports. Scheduled reports have a prespecified content and format and are prepared on a regular basis; examples include monthly departmental performance reports, weekly sales analyses, and annual corporate financial state-

FIGURE 11.11
Examples of computer graphic output.

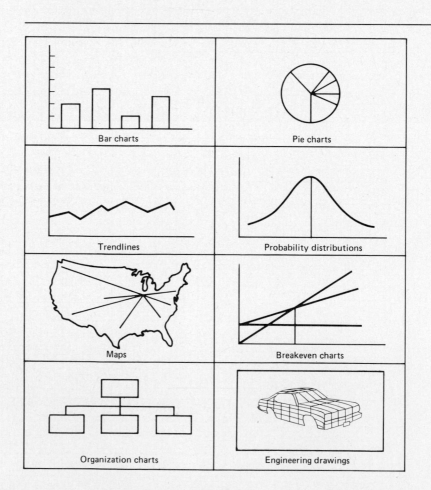

ments. Special-purpose analyses have no prespecified content or format and are not prepared according to any regular schedule; rather, they are generally prepared in response to a management request to investigate a specific problem or opportunity.

Triggered exception reports have a prespecified content and format but are prepared only in response to the presence of abnormal conditions that "trigger" the reporting process. Excessive absenteeism, cost overruns, inventory shortages, failures to meet sales quotas, and other situations that require immediate corrective action are the kinds of conditions that might trigger such reports. Demand reports also have a prespecified content and format but are prepared only in response to a request from a manager or other employee. Both triggered exception reports and demand reports exemplify how the power of modern computer systems can be effectively used to facilitate the management process.

Input and file design

As with the system output, the general content of system inputs and files is established during the systems analysis and synthesis. Thus the focus of systems design is primarily on the formats to be used. A useful tool for formatting computer input and file records is the *record layout sheet,* which is a blank form upon which may be entered the content, position, format, and other characteristics of the record. An illustration of a partially completed record layout appears in Fig. 11.12. Once these are completed for all input and file records in a system, they are used in the process of coding the computer program.

Prototyping

Prototyping is a systems design technique that involves the development of a simplified working model, or prototype, of an information system. Only the most basic user information requirements and functions are incorporated into

FIGURE 11.12
Record layout.

Field Name	Account Number	Customer Name	Customer Address
Characteristics	Numeric; Key	Alphanumeric	Alphanumeric
Position	01-08	09-32	33-104

Region Code	Type Code	Salesman Name	Credit Rating
Numeric	Numeric	Alphanumeric	Alphanumeric
105-107	108-110	111-122	123-125

Credit Limit	Date of Last Sale	Account Balance
Money	Date	Money
126-134	135-140	141-149

the prototype system, along with a small but representative data base. The goal is to implement the prototype system within a very short time period, perhaps days or weeks. The system is then demonstrated to the users, who are allowed to experiment with using it and to suggest modifications. The proposed modifications are incorporated into the prototype, and the experimentation process is repeated with the users until they are satisfied that the system effectively meets their requirements. That version of the prototype then becomes the basis for the final systems design and implementation.

Prototyping is an effective systems design technique because it involves the users intimately in the process of establishing information requirements. Accordingly, the risk that the system implemented will not be used is greatly reduced, if not eliminated. The technique is most commonly used in the development of information retrieval systems and decision support systems. It is generally not an economical approach for development of computer-based batch processing systems that involve complex processing requirements.[15]

Process design

Once the content and format of inputs, files, and outputs have been designed, the next step is to design the operations by which the inputs and files will be processed and the outputs prepared. The process design should ensure an efficient and well-coordinated series of operations. Flowcharts are the most commonly used process design technique. For the design of a manual system, a document flowchart is useful. For the design of a computer-based system, a systems flowchart provides a broad view of the process, whereas a program flowchart provides a more detailed view.

Another process design technique that has become increasingly more popular in recent years is the *structure chart,* or *HIPO chart.* The acronym HIPO stands for Hierarchy plus Input Process Output and is the name given by IBM to this technique. The technique is based upon a diagram of the functions performed in a process. Each block in the diagram represents a separate function. The individual blocks are linked by straight lines in a hierarchical structure very much like an organization chart. Lower-level blocks in the hierarchy represent more detailed breakdowns of the functions within the higher-level blocks. A simple example of a structure chart, representing the process of accounting for patient charges in a hospital, appears in Fig. 11.13.

There can be any number of levels within a structure chart, and some branches may have more levels than others. The block at the top level represents the overall process, whereas the blocks at the second level represent the major functions necessary to accomplish the process. Blocks at the third and lower levels represent specific processing steps at increasingly finer levels

---

[15]An extended discussion of prototyping is found in Justus D. Naumann and A. Milton Jenkins, "Prototyping: The New Paradigm for Systems Development," *MIS Quarterly* (September 1982): 29–44.

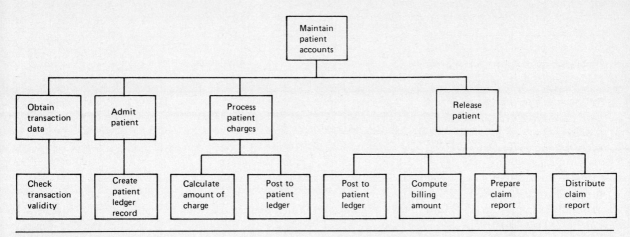

FIGURE 11.13
Structure chart of hospital patient accounting process.

of detail. Whereas the simplest structure chart may have only three levels, a more complex and detailed chart may have as many as seven levels.

The structure chart facilitates system design by providing a logical overview of the processing steps in the system. It provides a blueprint for the preparation of computer program code and may serve as a replacement for, or a supplement to, the program flowchart. Its primary disadvantage is that it does not show the exact sequence in which the process steps must be performed. Nonetheless, the structure chart is becoming more and more common as a tool of systems design.

Work distribution analysis

Another systems design technique is an extension of work measurement referred to as *work distribution analysis.* This technique uses the total time requirements for each activity in a processing cycle, which are determined by work measurement, as a basis for equitable allocation of tasks to employees in an operation. The primary tool is the work distribution table, an example of which is shown in Fig. 11.14. All activities in an operation and the total time each requires are listed line by line on the left side of the table, and each employee's name is listed at the top of a separate column on the right side. Each activity is then allocated to one or more employees in such a way that the total working time for all employees equals the total number of hours for which each is employed per day. Slack time should be incorporated into the individual activity time estimates.

Certain aspects of the example in Fig. 11.14 have been oversimplified for illustrative purposes. First, each of the individual activities listed in the table normally would be broken down in much greater detail for purposes of work measurement. However, for purposes of work distribution analysis alone, this degree of consolidation is acceptable.

Second, the basis for assigning an activity to a particular employee is not

WORK DISTRIBUTION TABLE					
Accounts Payable Department Activity	Hours per day	Employee			
		Smith	Jones	King	Evans
File purchase order copies	2				2
Match receiving reports with vendor invoices	1				1
Verify accuracy of vendor invoices	6	4	2		
Post receipts to filed purchase orders	5	4			1
Prepare vouchers and checks for payment	8		4	4	
File vouchers payable by due date	1		1		
Batch total day's vouchers to be paid	1		1		
File paid vouchers by vendor	4			4	
Total hours per day	28	8	8	8	4

FIGURE 11.14
Sample work
distribution table.

indicated. The primary basis for such allocation should be the relative efficiency of each employee in the performance of each task; in this way the total utilization of employee time is minimized. Other considerations include the need to separate the performance of specific tasks for control purposes or to provide variety in the job assignments to all employees.

Work scheduling

Another factor essential to consider in the development of alternative job assignment plans is the set of scheduling constraints particular to the operation. These include the necessity for completing some tasks before others can begin or for avoiding the simultaneous scheduling of conflicting tasks, such as those that utilize the same item of equipment. Work scheduling involves the assignment of a time dimension to task performance and machine utilization. While important in manual systems, scheduling is an even more critical factor in automated information systems.

Comprehensive approaches to systems design

In recent years, several comprehensive approaches to systems design have been developed and documented and made available to organizations engaged in the development of information systems. The common feature of these approaches is the use of a set of standardized forms that are filled out by the systems designer to facilitate some aspect of the systems development process.

One such category of design aids focuses on the development of a comprehensive and standardized set of documentation of an existing system or of a system under development. Examples include ADS (Accurately Defined System), developed by NCR; BSP (Business Systems Planning), offered by IBM; and BICS (Business Information Control Study), also provided by IBM. These require the system designer to prepare precise output specifications, input requirements, descriptions of resources, activities, computations, logic requirements, and so forth. The resulting forms provide a basis for subsequent design and programming efforts.

A second category of design aids focuses more on the process of systems design. This category includes Honeywell's BISAD (Business Information Systems Analysis and Design) and Philips' ARDI (Analysis, Requirements Determination, Design and Development, Implementation and Evaluation). These provide a comprehensive description of the process of systems design and analysis, broken down into detailed steps with a variety of techniques provided to assist in performing each step. The systems designer would use an approach of this "checklist" type as a sort of guide through the development process in a systematic manner.

A third category of systems design aids includes those that attempt to use the computer to automate the systems design process. These methods are still being developed and are not yet in widespread use. They include ISDOS (Information System Design and Optimization System), developed at the University of Michigan, and the Hoskyns System, developed by a data processing consulting organization. To use these techniques, the designer is required to complete a comprehensive description of system requirements and characteristics. These are coded on special input forms, which are processed through a system that generates a computer program, written in a language such as COBOL. Ideally, this program then becomes a part of the information system. In theory, this approach represents the highest possible level of systems development—automated systems design. In practice, although this technique has been successfully used on a limited scale, there is still some question as to whether it will ever be feasible for large-scale systems design projects.

Summary

Information systems undergo a predictable life cycle that includes several steps including an analysis of user information requirements, a survey of existing systems directed at evaluating their efficacy in meeting present and future requirements, and a synthesis or specific plan for developing a new or modified system. These steps are followed by detailed design and implementation of the new system and its operation, maintenance, and modification.

Systems analysis is the process of examining user information requirements within an organization in order to establish objectives and specifications for the design of a new information system. Systems analysis is the most critical phase of the system life cycle. Accordingly, management involvement in systems analysis activities is important to the successful development and implementation of information systems.

Systems survey is the systematic gathering of facts about an existing information system. In completing a systems survey, the systems analyst might utilize such techniques as document flowcharting, work measurement, reliability analysis, interviewing, and checklists. Careful attention to human factors is also important in this phase of the system life cycle.

Systems design is the process of preparing detailed specifications for the development of a new information system. Among the techniques used by systems analysts in the design phase are printer layout charts, graphical design, record layouts, prototyping, structure charts, and work scheduling.

Review Questions

1. Define the following terms.

systems analysis	systems survey
systems analyst	document flowchart
information analyst	work measurement
bottom-up approach	system reliability
top-down approach	checklist
strategic planning	systems design
management control	printer layout chart
operational control	record layout sheet
structured decisions	prototyping
unstructured decisions	structure chart
semistructured decisions	HIPO chart
decision support system	work distribution analysis

2. What are the primary factors that have made the present era a period of frequent change in the information systems of business organizations?

3. Identify and briefly describe the stages in the system life cycle.

4. Explain the role of the systems analyst and describe the characteristics and abilities a person should possess to fill this role successfully.

5. List several aspects of what might be called the "systems approach" to systems investigations.

6. Describe the philosophy of the team approach to the analysis of information systems.

7. List several ways in which an organization's top management should be involved in the planning and administration of major systems change.

8. What is meant by "key success factors" within a business organization, and what is their importance to systems planning?

9. List several general objectives important in the analysis and design of information systems.

10. Explain the relative merits of the "top-down" and "bottom-up" approaches to systems analysis and design.

11. List several types of decision-making activities within the three major categories of Anthony's management framework.

12. Describe the decision taxonomy proposed by Keen and Scott Morton. Identify an example of one decision in each of their nine decision categories.

13. What significant differences exist among top-, middle-, and lower-level managers with respect to decision responsibilities and information requirements?

14. How are decision support systems related to traditional data processing systems?

15. A systems survey generally focuses on the visible components of an information system. What are these?

16. Detail the steps that a systems analyst should take to minimize the possibility of human problems in an information system during the period of systems survey.

17. What attitudes of top management should be taken into consideration by a systems analyst in planning a systems investigation?

18. List several items of system documentation that are an important source of information to the systems analyst during a systems survey. Why should caution be exercised in interpreting this material?

19. What weaknesses in an information system may be revealed by a review of the content and design of documents and reports?

20. Identify the symbols used in document flowcharting and indicate the meanings of each.

21. Describe the process of preparing a document flowchart.

22. What weaknesses in an information system may be revealed by an analysis of document flowcharts?

23. Describe the information the systems analyst should collect on volume of processing during a systems survey.

24. What is work measurement? For what types of jobs is this technique most appropriate? Give some examples.

25. Describe the steps necessary in a work measurement study to obtain (a) a measure of the total time required for each activity in a system during a

processing cycle and (b) a measure of the percentage utilization of system capacity.

26. List several ways in which a work measurement study can be useful to a systems investigation.

27. Explain the computation of the system reliability measure. Describe how it may be useful in systems investigations.

28. Describe briefly how the systems analyst should prepare for and conduct interviews with personnel during a systems investigation.

29. Explain how the use of checklists may be helpful to the systems analyst during a systems investigation.

30. Explain the purpose of the synthesis phase of the system life cycle. What activities are typically involved in this phase?

31. What steps are included in the systems design phase of the system life cycle? Identify a number of techniques useful in systems design.

32. Explain how printer layout charts and record layout sheets are used in systems design.

33. Identify and describe four different categories of reports that may be prepared as output of an information system.

34. Describe the steps involved in designing an information system using prototyping. Why is this an effective systems design technique?

35. What are the advantages and disadvantages of structure charts as a tool of systems design?

36. What is work distribution analysis? Draw an example of a work distribution table.

37. In work distribution analysis, what criteria may be used for assigning activities to employees?

38. Briefly describe some of the kinds of comprehensive, standardized approaches to systems design that have been developed in recent years. Identify the names of several of these.

Discussion Questions

39. The discussion of systems investigations in this chapter has been oriented toward a business organization. What significant differences in objectives and approaches would you expect in a system investigation of (a) a public school system, (b) a university, (c) a hospital, (d) an agency of government?

40. Your friend and fellow systems analyst Joe Doakes has made the following statement to you:

"The systems analyst does not have to be a psychologist, or be concerned with people problems in his work. His function is to determine the proper facilities, computer or otherwise, for performing the data processing functions of an organization. When this is finished he will then establish job specifications for employees in the system. He can perform these functions with a minimum of contact with people in the organization."

Do you agree with this statement? If not, what line of argument would you use in response to your friend?

41. It was suggested in this chapter that during a systems investigation an organization should make special efforts to ease fears among its employees about potential loss of jobs or seniority. However, it is also felt that one of the primary advantages of the mechanization of a system is the reduction in clerical costs. Are these two concepts inconsistent? What policies should be adopted in an organization during a systems investigation that would be consistent with both concepts?

42. Describe some examples of decisions in systems analysis that involve a trade-off between each of the following pairs of objectives.

   a) economy and usefulness
   b) economy and reliability
   c) economy and customer service
   d) simplicity and usefulness
   e) simplicity and reliability
   f) economy and capacity
   g) economy and flexibility

43. In adopting a broad strategy for information systems analysis and design, would you favor a "top-down" approach, a "bottom-up" approach, or a compromise approach? Discuss.

Problems and Cases

44. From the description below of processing of casualty claims by an insurance company, prepare a document flowchart.

The process begins with the receipt by the claims department of a notice of loss from a claimant. The claims department sends the claimant four copies of a proof-of-loss form on which must be detailed the cause, amount, and other aspects of the loss. The claims department also initiates a record of the claim at this time, which it transmits to the data processing section, where it is filed by claim number. The claimant must fill out the proof-of-loss forms in conjunction with an adjustor, who must concur in the estimated amount of loss. The claimant and adjustor each keep a copy of these forms and send the other two copies to the claims department. The adjustor also submits a separate report at this point. On the basis of this information, the claims department authorizes a payment to the claimant and forwards a copy of the proof-of-loss form to data processing. The data processing department prepares checks in payment of claims and mails them to the customer, removes paid claims from its file, and prepares a list of disbursements, which it transmits to the accounting department.

45. Mr. Joe Grey, a senior consultant, and Mr. David Young, a junior consultant, were assigned by their firm to a systems analysis job for a client company. The objective of the study was to consider the feasibility of integrating and automating certain clerical functions. Mr. Grey had previously worked on jobs for this client, but Mr. Young had been hired only recently.

On the morning of their first day on the job, Mr. Grey directed Mr. Young to interview a departmental supervisor and learn as much as he could about the operations of the department. Mr. Young went to the supervisor's office, introduced himself, and made the following statement: "Your company has hired my firm to study the way your department works and to make recommendations as to how its efficiency could be improved and its cost lowered. I would like to interview you to determine what goes on in your department."

Mr. Young questioned the supervisor for about thirty minutes but found him to be uncooperative. He then gave Mr. Grey an oral report on how the interview had gone and what he had learned about the department.

REQUIRED

Describe several flaws in the approach taken to obtain information about the operation of the department under study. How should this task have been performed?

46. As a systems consultant of wide repute, you have been invited to the executive offices of Consolidated Flypaper Corporation for an interview with the controller. The controller has indicated to you that he is concerned about the operation of the company's payroll processing system. Recent expansion of the company has placed a strain on the system such that frequent overtime is necessary for regular processing to be completed.

The payroll and cost distribution sections of the company perform their functions almost entirely manually, with the only mechanical aids being typewriters and hand calculators. In addition to the problem of frequent overtime being necessary, the controller has indicated some additional problems with the system, including a lack of useful management reports that could be produced by the system and possible weaknesses in internal controls within the system. The controller has indicated that he is considering three possible alternatives, including hiring additional employees in the payroll and cost distribution sections, acquiring an electronic accounting machine for use in those sections, or installing a small business computer.

The controller has assured you that the president and other top executives of Consolidated Flypaper agree with the necessity of a systems study conducted by a qualified outsider. You have been introduced to the assistant controller, who performs internal auditing functions, and told that he is available to assist you full-time if necessary.

You have agreed to accept this assignment and have decided to send two of your assistants to complete the initial work while you finish another project. You direct your assistants to complete a preliminary evaluation of possible alternatives, which you will use in making a final decision and preparing recommendations.

REQUIRED Prepare a schedule of activities to guide your assistants in performing their assignment. Be fairly explicit regarding the kind of information they might expect to find in a payroll processing system, how they should go about collecting it, and how to proceed in analyzing it. Please note that you are not being asked to give a solution to the problem but only to describe, with reference to the particular situation, how a systems analyst would proceed with the initial phases of a systems investigation.

47. A partially completed charge sales systems flowchart appears in Fig. 11.15. The flowchart depicts the charge sales activities of the Bottom Manufacturing Corporation.

A customer's purchase order is received and a six-part sales order is prepared therefrom. The six copies are initially distributed as follows.

Copy No. 1—Billing copy, to billing department

Copy No. 2—Shipping copy, to shipping department

Copy No. 3—Credit copy, to credit department

Copy No. 4—Stock request copy, to credit department

Copy No. 5—Customer copy, to customer

Copy No. 6—Sales order copy, file in sales order department

When each copy of the sales order reaches the appropriate department or destination, it calls for specific internal control procedures and related documents. Some of the procedures and related documents are indicated on the flowchart. Other procedures and documents are labeled letters *a* to *r*.

REQUIRED List the procedures or the internal documents that are labeled letters *c* to *r* in the flowchart of Bottom Manufacturing Corporation's charge sales system.

Organize your answer as follows. (Note that explanations of the letters *a* and *b* that appear in the flowchart are entered as examples.) (CPA Examination)

FLOWCHART SYMBOL LETTER	PROCEDURES OR INTERNAL DOCUMENT
a	Prepare six-part sales order.
b	File by order number.

BOTTOM MANUFACTURING CORPORATION
Flowchart of Credit Sales Activities

Sales order	Credit	Finished goods

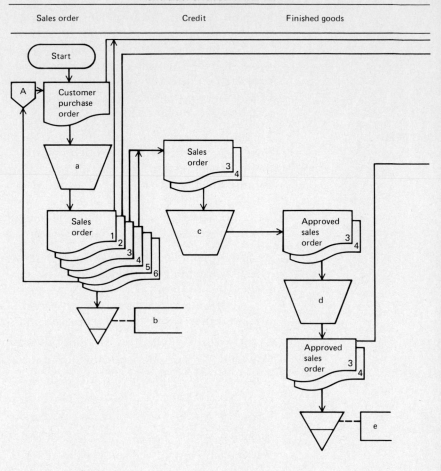

CODE:
A = Customer

FIGURE 11.15

474

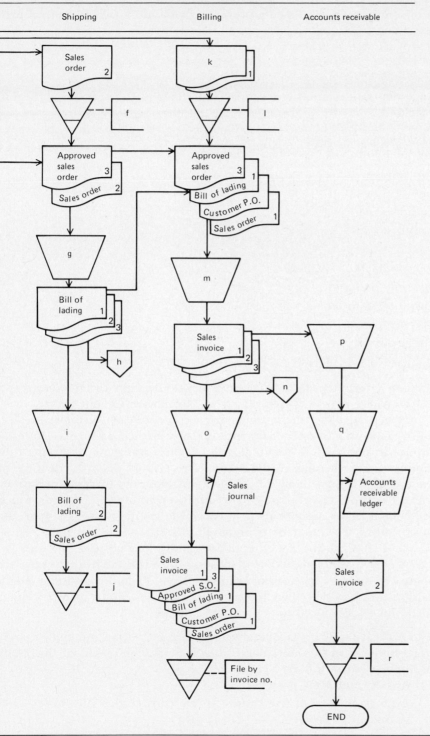

Shipping   Billing   Accounts receivable

48. A reliability analysis of a data processing task and a related control procedure obtained the following parameter estimates.

$P = 0.84$ $C = 0.98$

$D = 0.90$ $F = 0.80$

$N = 0.95$

REQUIRED

Compute the reliability measure for items processed through this system.

49. An inventory record contains the following data elements, each containing the number of characters indicated.

Part number	7
Description	20
Location code	4
Unit cost	8
Vendor code	5
Vendor name	20
Quantity on hand	5
Quantity on order	5
Reorder point	5
Order quantity	5

REQUIRED

Prepare a record layout for this record.

50. Prepare a document flowchart of the process described in the paragraph below. Where necessary, add narrative explanation to your chart.

The billing department prepares five copies of each customer invoice, and a batch total of the sale amount on each invoice. Two copies of each invoice in the batch are sent, along with the adding machine tape containing the batch total, to the accounts receivable department. One of these copies is then immediately filed alphabetically by customer name. The other copy is used to post to accounts receivable ledger cards, which are pulled from a numerically sequenced file. As the posting is done, another adding machine tape is prepared in which the ledger balances before and after posting are entered as negative and positive amounts, respectively. At the completion of posting, the two batch total tapes are compared to check the accuracy of the process. Then the customer ledger cards are returned to their original file, and the second invoice copy is filed numerically by customer account number.

51. The Walla Walla Widget Company has completed a time and motion study of its Billing and Accounts Receivable Section. The results of that study in summary form follow.

Activity and Time per Unit:

☐ Type an invoice in five copies from a copy of the sales order—196 seconds per invoice.

☐ Batch total the complete set of invoices for a day—three seconds per invoice.

☐ Separate copies of each invoice and send copies one and two to the mailroom—five seconds per invoice.

☐ File one invoice copy alphabetically—fifteen seconds per invoice.

☐ File one invoice copy numerically—one second per invoice.

☐ Post debits from another invoice copy to the accounts receivable ledger—thirty seconds per invoice.

☐ Post cash receipts to the accounts receivable ledger from remittance advices—thirty seconds per remittance advice.

☐ Total the balances of the accounts receivable ledger, and reconcile to sales, cash receipts, and yesterday's total—1000 seconds per day.

☐ Type customer statements from accounts receivable ledger—150 seconds per statement.

Information on daily volume:

☐ Invoices—200 per day.

☐ Remittances—100 per day.

☐ Customer statements—800 customer accounts. Statements are sent out in a monthly cycle such that about one twentieth of all customer statements are sent out daily.

Other information:

☐ A twenty percent allowance should be made for work delays and to provide sufficient slack time in the system to allow for periods of peak volume.

REQUIRED

a) What is the total work time required per day to perform all activities in this operation? Assuming three full-time workers (eight hours per day), what is the percentage utilization of capacity in this system?

b) Suppose the system employs two full-time workers (eight hours per day) and one part-time worker who works exactly the number of hours necessary to complete all work. Prepare a work distribution table showing how the various tasks might be allocated among these employees.

52. Ferraro Corporation's computer program to maintain its parts inventory records has five major modules, which operate as follows.

a) The "obtain transaction data" module updates a transaction summary log and checks the transaction's validity, either accepting it as valid or writing an error message.

b) The "process new item" module creates a new parts inventory master file record.

c) The "process issue transaction" module deducts the issue amount from the quantity on hand and computes the amount to be reordered, if any.

    d) The "process receipt transaction" module adds the receipt amount to the quantity on hand, deducts the receipt amount from the quantity on order, and updates the supplier record.

    e) The "prepare outputs" module writes the updated master record, prepares the stock status report, and prepares purchase orders.

REQUIRED

Prepare a structure chart of Ferraro Corporation's parts inventory file maintenance process.

53. Beccan Company is a discount tire dealer that operates twenty-five retail stores in the metropolitan area. Both private-brand and name-brand tires are sold by Beccan. The company operates a centralized purchasing and warehousing facility and employs a perpetual inventory system. All purchases of tires and related supplies are placed through the company's central purchasing department to take advantage of quantity discounts. The tires and supplies are received at the central warehouse and distributed to the retail stores as needed. The perpetual inventory system at the central facility maintains current inventory records, designated reorder points, optimum order quantities, and continuous stocktakings for each type of tire and size and other related supplies.

    The documents employed by Beccan in their inventory control system and their use are presented below.

☐ *Retail stores requisition.* This document is submitted by the retail stores to the central warehouse whenever tires or supplies are needed at the stores. The shipping clerks in the Warehouse Department fill the orders from inventory and have them delivered to the stores.

☐ *Purchase requisition.* The inventory control clerk in the Inventory Control Department prepares this document when the quantity on hand for an item falls below the designated reorder point. The document is forwarded to the Purchasing Department.

☐ *Purchase order.* The Purchasing Department prepares this document when items need to be ordered. The document is submitted to an authorized vendor.

☐ *Receiving report.* The Warehouse Department prepares this document when ordered items are received from vendors. The receiving clerk completes the document by indicating the vendor's name, the date the shipment is received, and the quantity of each item received.

☐ *Invoice.* An invoice is received from vendors, specifying the amounts owed by Beccan.

    The departments involved in Beccan's inventory control system are described below.

☐ *Inventory Control Department.* This department is responsible for the maintenance of all perpetual inventory records for all items carried in inventory. This includes current quantity on hand, reorder point, optimum order quantity, and quantity on order for each item carried.

□ *Warehouse Department.* This department maintains the physical inventory of all items carried in inventory. All orders from vendors are received (receiving clerk) and all distributions to retail stores are filled (shipping clerks) in this department.

□ *Purchasing Department.* The Purchasing Department places all orders for items needed by the company.

□ *Accounts Payable Department.* Accounts Payable maintains all open accounts with vendors and other creditors. All payments are processed in this department.

REQUIRED Prepare a flow diagram to show how these documents should be coordinated and used among the departments at the central facility of Beccan Company to provide adequate internal control over the receipt, issuance, replenishment, and payment of tires and supplies. You may assume that the documents have a sufficient number of copies to ensure that the perpetual inventory system has the necessary basic internal controls. (CMA Examination)

54. Citizens' Gas Company is a medium-size gas distribution company that provides natural gas service to approximately 200,000 customers. The customer base is divided into three revenue classes. Data by customer class are shown below.

CLASS	CUSTOMERS	SALES IN CUBIC FEET	REVENUES
Residential	160,000	80 billion	$160 million
Commercial	38,000	15 billion	25 million
Industrial	2,000	50 billion	65 million
		145 billion	$250 million

Residential customer gas usage is primarily for residential heating purposes and, consequently, is highly correlated to the weather, i.e., temperature. Commercial and industrial customers, on the other hand, may or may not use gas for heating purposes, and consumption is not necessarily correlated to the weather.

The largest twenty-five industrial customers of the total of 2000 account for $30 million of the industrial revenues. Each of these twenty-five customers uses gas for both heating and industrial purposes and has a consumption pattern which is governed almost entirely by business factors.

The company obtains its gas supply from ten major pipeline companies. The pipeline companies provide gas in amounts specified in contracts which extend over periods ranging from five to fifteen years. For some contracts the supply is in equal monthly increments, whereas for others the supply varies in accordance with the heating season. Supply over and above the contract amounts is not available, and some contracts contain take-or-pay clauses, i.e., the company must pay for the volumes specified in the contract, whether or not it can take the gas.

To assist in matching customer demand with supply, the company maintains a gas storage field. Gas can be pumped into the storage field when supply exceeds customer demand, and likewise gas can be obtained when demand exceeds supply. There are no restrictions on the use of the gas storage field except that the field must be filled to capacity at the beginning of each gas year (September 1). Consequently, whenever the contractual supply for gas for the remainder of the gas year is less than that required to satisfy projected demand and replenish the storage field, the company must curtail service to the industrial customers (except for quantities that are used for heating). The curtailments must be carefully controlled so that an oversupply does not occur at year end. Similarly, care must be taken to ensure that curtailments are adequate during the year to protect against the need to curtail commercial or residential customers in order to replenish the storage field at year end.

In recent years, the company's planning efforts have not provided a firm basis for the establishment of long-term contracts. The current year has been no different. Planning efforts have not been adequate to control the supply during the current gas year. Customer demand has been projected only as a function of the total number of customers. Commercial and industrial customers' demand for gas has been curtailed excessively. This has resulted in lost sales and caused an excess of supply at the end of the gas year.

In an attempt to correct the problems of Citizens' Gas, the president has hired a new director of corporate planning and has instructed the director to present him with a conceptual design of a system to assist in the analysis of the supply and demand of natural gas. The system should provide a monthly gas plan for each year for the next five years, with particular emphasis on the first year of the plan. The plan should provide a set of reports which assists in the decision-making process and which contains all necessary supporting schedules. The system must provide for the use of actual data during the course of the first year to project demand for the rest of the year and the year in total. The president has indicated to the director that he will base his decisions on the effect on operating income of alternative plans.

REQUIRED

a) Discuss the criteria which must be considered in specifying the basic structure and features of Citizens' Gas Company's new system to assist in planning its natural gas needs.

b) Identify the major data items that should be incorporated into Citizens' Gas Company's new system to provide adequate planning capability. For each item identified, explain why the data item is important and the level of detail that would be necessary to be useful. (CMA Examination)

55. The Darwin Company has performed a work measurement study on one of its clerical departments. Activities performed within that department, and the number of hours per day consumed by each activity after adjustments for rest time and slack time, are as follows.

Activity	A	B	C	D	E	F	G
Hours/day	2	3	6	3	6	5	3

The department employs four persons: Adams, Baker, Clark, and Dill. Adams, Baker, and Clark work eight hours each day, from 8 A.M. to noon and from 1 P.M. to 5 P.M. Dill works four hours each day, from 8 A.M. to noon.

The scheduling of these activities and their assignment to the employees must conform to the following conditions.

☐ A must be completed before B may begin.

☐ B must be completed before either C or D may begin.

☐ E must be completed before F may begin.

☐ A, B, D, and G may be performed by only one person at a time. The other three activities may be separated among several employees working simultaneously.

☐ Because of internal control considerations, activity F must be performed by a person or persons different from those who perform activity G.

☐ G and D utilize the same machine and thus cannot both be performed at the same time.

☐ No employee should spend over one half of his or her time on the job performing the same task.

REQUIRED

a) Prepare a work schedule containing four vertical columns, one for each employee, and eight horizontal rows, one for each hour between 8 A.M. and 5 P.M., excluding the noon hour. Assign each of the seven tasks to appropriate time periods within the work time of each employee. Be sure that your assignment is consistent with all the conditions specified above.

b) Prepare in good form a work distribution table for this department's operations.

56. Charting, Inc., a new audit client of yours, processes its sales and cash receipts documents in the following manner.

1. *Payment on account.* The mail is opened each morning by a mail clerk in the sales department. The mail clerk prepares a remittance advice (showing customer and amount paid) if one is not received. The checks and remittance advices are then forwarded to the sales department supervisor, who reviews each check and forwards the checks and remittance advices to the accounting department supervisor.

The accounting department supervisor, who also functions as credit manager in approving new credit and all credit limits, reviews all checks for payments on past-due accounts and then forwards the checks and remittance advices to the accounts receivable clerk, who arranges the advices in alphabetical order. The remittance advices are posted directly to the accounts receivable ledger cards. The checks are endorsed by stamp and totaled. The total is posted to the cash receipts journal. The remittance advices are filed chronologically. After receiving the cash from the previous day's cash sales, the accounts receivable clerk prepares the daily deposit slip in triplicate. The third copy of the deposit slip is filed by date, and the second copy and the original accompany the bank deposit.

2. *Sales.* Sales clerks prepare sales invoices in triplicate. The original and second copy are presented to the cashier. The third copy is retained by the sales clerk in the sales book. When the sale is for cash, the customer pays the sales clerk, who presents the money to the cashier with the invoice copies.

A credit sale is approved by the cashier from an approved credit list after the sales clerk prepares the three-part invoice. After receiving the cash or approving the invoice, the cashier validates the original copy of the sales invoice and gives it to the customer. At the end of each day, the cashier recaps the sales and cash received and forwards the cash and the second copy of the sales invoices to the accounts receivable clerk.

The accounts receivable clerk balances the cash received with cash sales invoices and prepares a daily sales summary. The credit sales invoices are posted to the accounts receivable ledger, and then all invoices are sent to the inventory control clerk in the sales department for posting to the inventory control cards. After posting, the inventory control clerk files all invoices numerically. The accounts receivable clerk posts the daily sales summary to the cash receipts journal and sales journal and files the sales summaries by date.

The cash from cash sales is combined with the cash received on account to comprise the daily bank deposit.

3. *Bank deposits.* The bank validates the deposit slip and returns the second copy to the accounting department, where it is filed by date by the accounts receivable clerk.

Monthly bank statements are reconciled promptly by the accounting department supervisor and filed by date.

REQUIRED

You recognize that there are weaknesses in the existing system and believe a chart of information and document flows would be beneficial in evaluating this client's internal control in preparing for your examination of the financial statements. Complete the flowchart, given in Fig. 11.16, for sales and cash receipts of Charting, Inc., by labeling the appropriate sym-

FIGURE 11.16

CHARTING, INC.

FLOWCHART FOR SALES AND CASH RECEIPTS

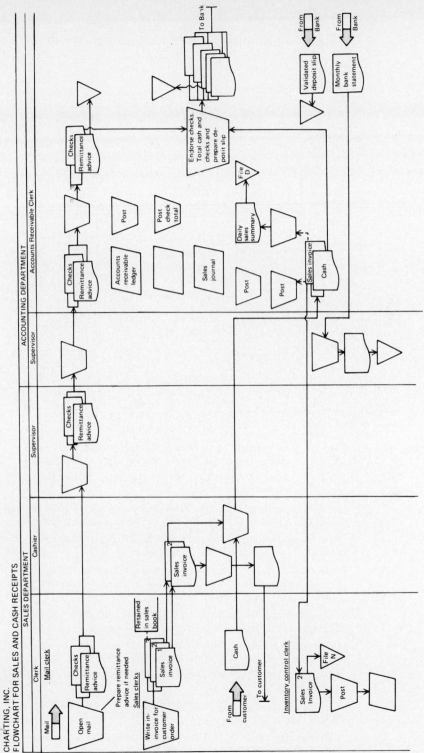

bols and indicating information flows. The chart is complete as to symbols and document flows. The following symbols are used. (CPA Examination)

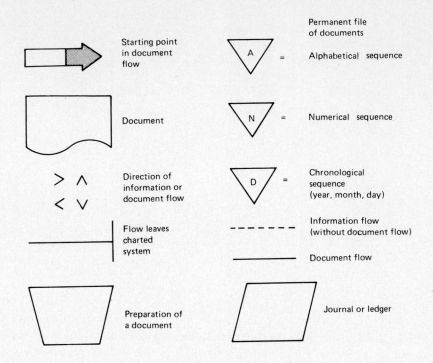

References

Ahituv, Niv; Michael Hadass; and Seev Neumann. "A Flexible Approach to Information System Development." *MIS Quarterly* (June 1984): 69–78.

Alloway, Robert M., and Judith A. Quillard. "User Managers' Systems Needs." *MIS Quarterly* (June 1983): 27–41.

Anderson, Anker. *Graphing Financial Information: How Accountants Can Use Graphs to Communicate.* New York: National Association of Accountants, 1983.

Anderson, Donald S. "Supervisors as Work Measurement Analysts." *Management Services* (January/February 1971): 20–26.

Anthony, Robert N. *Planning and Control Systems, A Framework for Analysis.* Boston: Division of Research, Graduate School of Business Administration, Harvard University, 1965.

Boar, Bernard. "Application Prototyping: A Life Cycle Perspective." *Journal of Systems Management* (February 1986): 25–31.

Boynton, Andrew C., and Robert W. Zmud. "An Assessment of Critical Success Factors." *Sloan Management Review* (Summer 1984): 17–27.

Canning, Richard G. "What Information Do Managers Need?" *EDP Analyzer* (June 1979): 1–12.

Cougar, J. Daniel, and Robert W. Knapp, eds. *System Analysis Techniques.* New York: Wiley, 1974.

Cushing, Barry E. "A Mathematical Approach to the Analysis and Design of Internal Control Systems." *The Accounting Review* (January 1974): 24–41.

Daniel, D. Ronald. "Management Information Crisis." *Harvard Business Review* (September/October 1961): 111–121.

Gane, Chris, and Trish Sarson. *Structured Systems Analysis: Tools and Techniques.* Englewood Cliffs, N.J.: Prentice-Hall, 1979.

Gershefski, George W. "Building a Corporate Financial Model." *Harvard Business Review* (July/August, 1969): 61–72.

Gremillion, Lee L., and Philip Pyburn. "Breaking the Systems Development Bottleneck." *Harvard Business Review* (March/April 1983): 130–137.

Ives, Blake. "Graphical User Interfaces for Business Information Systems." *MIS Quarterly* (Special Issue 1982): 15–47.

Kaiser, Kate M., and William R. King. "The Manager-Analyst Interface in Systems Development." *MIS Quarterly* (March 1982): 49–59.

Kauber, Peter G. "Prototyping: Not a Method But a Philosophy." *Journal of Systems Management* (September 1985): 28–33.

Keen, Peter G. W., and Michael S. Scott Morton. *Decision Support Systems: An Organizational Perspective.* Reading, Mass.: Addison-Wesley, 1978.

Kotter, John P., and Leonard A. Schlesinger. "Choosing Strategies for Change." *Harvard Business Review* (March/April 1979): 106–114.

Laudeman, Max. "Document Flowcharts for Internal Control." *Journal of Systems Management* (March 1980): 22–30.

McKeen, James D. "Successful Development Strategies for Business Application Systems." *MIS Quarterly* (September 1983): 47–65.

Meador, C. Lawrence; Martin J. Guyote; and Peter G. W. Keen. "Setting Priorities for DSS Development." *MIS Quarterly* (June 1984): 117–129.

Naumann, Justus D., and A. Milton Jenkins. "Prototyping: The New Paradigm for Systems Development." *MIS Quarterly* (September 1982): 29–44.

Rockart, John F. "Chief Executives Define Their Own Data Needs." *Harvard Business Review* (March/April 1979): 81–93.

Sprague, Ralph H., Jr., and Hugh J. Watson. "Bit by Bit: Toward Decision Support Systems." *California Management Review* (Fall 1979): 60–68.

Stevens, Robert I., and Walter J. Bieber. "Work Measurement Techniques." *Journal of Systems Management* (February 1977): 15–27.

Sumner, Mary, and Jerry Sitek. "Are Structured Methods for Systems Analysis and Design Being Used?" *Journal of Systems Management* (June 1986): 18–23.

Takeuchi, Hirotaka, and Allan H. Schmidt. "New Promise of Computer Graphics." *Harvard Business Review* (January/February 1980): 122–131.

Wilkinson, Joseph W. "Effective Reporting Structures." *Journal of Systems Management* (November 1976): 38–42.

Zani, William M. "Blueprint for MIS." *Harvard Business Review* (November/December 1970): 95–100.

C H A P T E R   1 2

Systems Evaluation and Selection

This chapter deals with the process of evaluating and selecting new systems and with the major factors that an organization should consider during this decision process. Note that the term new systems encompasses a variety of possible user situations. For example, it could refer to a potential computer user trying to decide whether to acquire its first computer system. Alternatively, it could refer to an established computer user who is considering replacement of a computer system. It could also apply to the acquisition of software packages, data communications services, time-sharing services, expanded equipment configurations, and so forth. Another possibility is that of an established computer user facing a choice among several applications for the computer.

There are many similarities among the several user situations cited, but there are also important differences. This chapter approaches the topic of systems evaluation and selection from the perspective of the potential first-time computer user. Many of the concepts and approaches discussed are also applicable to the other user situations; however, when this is not true, the chapter elaborates on those considerations relevant to other specific circumstances.

In all cases, the first step in systems evaluation and selection should be a *feasibility study,* which is an investigation of whether the acquisition or development of a new system is practical. For first-time users, the next step is the *applications study,* which involves the preparation of a detailed description of the tasks that the new system is intended to perform. For any system being acquired from an outside party, the next step is to receive presentations from selected vendors, evaluate their relative merits, and make a final selection. This chapter covers each of these three major steps in the systems evaluation and selection process.

The Feasibility Study

Prior to a system feasibility study, an organization typically faces several alternatives. One obvious alternative is to continue using its existing information system, perhaps with some limited modifications. The potential first-time computer user may consider a service bureau, a time-sharing service, a microcomputer, a minicomputer, or a small business computer system in addition to a full-scale system purchased or rented from a computer manufacturer or leased from a third party. Established computer users seeking to upgrade their facilities obviously face a more limited array of choices. With respect to software, the established computer user must first decide what type of programs are needed and then must decide whether to develop these internally or acquire them from software vendors—a classic "make-or-buy" decision.

One of the first steps in the feasibility study is to assign responsibility for carrying out the investigation. As with any systems study, one of the significant considerations here is that the group carrying out the study should include both persons with technical knowledge and persons with knowledge of and experience in the operation of the business. If the company has no previous experience with computers, persons with technical knowledge may not be available within the organization. In some such cases, it may be possible to utilize the services of a consulting firm, particularly one that has both technical competence and some familiarity with the company or the industry. In other cases, reliance may have to be placed upon representatives of a vendor. In companies in which a computer data processing function does exist, persons with technical competence can be obtained from within. To serve as a source of operating knowledge and experience, representatives should be obtained from top management, as well as from those operating areas that will be most involved in the utilization of a computer, such as accounting and production in a manufacturing company.

The initial phases of a feasibility study are very much similar to the initial phases of systems investigations generally. An emphasis should be placed upon defining objectives and delineating system requirements. The required system output includes management information, documents, files, and so forth. The existing system is subjected to a rigorous analysis to determine whether it can meet the current and future requirements in accordance with the objectives. If a long-range systems plan has been developed and put into effect, this process will be greatly facilitated.

Three dimensions of feasibility should be evaluated during a feasibility study. These are technical feasibility, economic feasibility, and operational feasibility.[1] *Technical feasibility* involves whether a proposed system is or is not attainable, given the existing state of technology. *Economic feasibility* involves whether a proposed system will or will not produce economic benefits that exceed its cost. *Operational feasibility* involves a determination of whether the system will be used and of how useful it will be within the operating environment of the organization.

The evaluation of technical feasibility can be left primarily to computer specialists and need not concern us here. Operational feasibility must be evaluated largely on a subjective basis, but its attainment obviously depends on the degree of involvement of top management and user groups in analysis and implementation and on management's regard for the human factors in systems change. These topics are covered in Chapters 10 and 11.

The evaluation of economic feasibility—the primary concern of this section—involves a careful investigation of cost and benefit factors associated with each proposed alternative. Because an accountant is familiar with cost concepts, he or she can make a significant contribution to this evaluation. The basic framework for the evaluation is the capital budgeting model. This model requires that, for each alternative under consideration, dollar estimates be made of (1) the amount of the initial outlay, (2) the amount of operating costs and other cash outflows associated with the system during each period over

---

[1]George Glaser, "Plain Talk about Computers," *Business Horizons* (Fall 1967): 33–38.

the life of the system, and (3) the amount of cost savings and other benefits during each period over the life of the system. The choice among alternatives is then based upon the alternative that provides the highest net present value after discounting net cash flows at the organization's opportunity cost of capital.

If it is decided that the organization's existing information system is likely to be inadequate to meet its objectives and requirements, an investigation of the possible alternatives is initiated. An early attempt should be made by the study group to narrow the range of alternatives to a small set, in order to provide a focal point for subsequent efforts at data collection and review. The stated objectives and requirements provide guidelines for this process. Some alternatives may be eliminated at this point by the technical feasibility criterion. Operational feasibility, including such factors as the competence of personnel and their attitudes toward the various options, may rule out some other possibilities.

Once the feasibility study group has completed the initial culling of alternatives, the primary basis for subsequent analysis becomes the relative economic merits of the remaining alternatives. Whereas it is not too difficult to develop estimates of the initial outlay and operating costs required for a computer system, making reliable estimates of the amount of expected cost savings and other benefits can be quite a formidable task. Each of these categories of cost is now discussed in turn.

Initial outlay costs

The initial outlay costs of a computer system include the costs of initial systems design and programming, personnel training, site preparation, equipment installation, system testing and conversion, software costs, and equipment costs. Actually, the equipment costs may either represent an initial outlay, if the system is purchased, or an operating cost, if the system is rented or leased. Approximately fifty percent of larger computer systems are purchased, whereas seventy percent of minicomputers and small business computer systems are purchased. Virtually all microcomputer systems are purchased. For comparative purposes, the presentation in this section assumes that the computer equipment is purchased. The relative merits of purchasing as opposed to renting or leasing a computer system are discussed in a later section of this chapter.

Equipment costs and capabilities vary over an extremely wide range. At the lower end of the scale are microcomputer or personal computer (PC) systems, for which purchase prices range between $2,500 and $10,000. A typical business-oriented PC system consists of a CRT display unit, a detachable keyboard, one or two floppy disk drives, a CPU with 64,000 to 512,000 bytes of main memory, and a printer. Software typically includes a simple operating system, a language processor such as BASIC, COBOL, or PASCAL, and such packages as a word processor, a spreadsheet program, a simple data base package, and a graphics processor.

At the next level up the scale are multiuser microcomputer systems. These consist of a central PC that controls a hard disk unit and from one to three printers, and that is linked to as many as thirty workstations, each of which is a PC with its own keyboard, display, floppy disk drive, and perhaps a printer. The central PC typically has from 0.5 to 4 megabytes of memory, and its attached hard disk unit may add up to 30 megabytes of additional memory. Software consists of the typical PC software described in the previous paragraph, plus a data communications package that manages the interaction between the central PC and the workstations. A system of this type costs between $10,000 and $25,000, plus $1,500 to $3,000 for each workstation.

At the next highest level are minicomputer systems, of which two categories may be distinguished—(1) small business computers and (2) general-purpose minicomputers. Small business computer systems are characterized by equipment and software designed specifically to handle conventional business data processing applications. The basic configuration of a small business computer includes a CPU with 64,000 to 512,000 bytes of main memory, a CRT terminal, a hard disk drive having a storage capacity of 10 to 100 megabytes, and a printer. Also included may be tape drives, a card reader, or a floppy disk drive. Many small business computers can operate with multiple workstations. Software generally includes one or more language processors such as COBOL or RPG (report program generator), plus a number of business and accounting application packages. The purchase cost of a small business computer system ranges from $25,000 to $100,000.

A general-purpose minicomputer system consists of a CPU with 0.5 to 16 megabytes of main memory, together with disk drives, tape drives, printers, and terminals. Available hard disk storage capacity ranges from 10 to 500 megabytes. Typical software includes a multiprogrammable operating system, one or more language processors, a data base management system, and numerous application packages. The price range for a configuration of this type is from $35,000 to $200,000.

At the upper end of the scale are the largest computer installations, which contain one or more CPUs with main memory capacity of from 8 to 64 megabytes. Such a system would incorporate a large number and variety of input, output, and storage units, perhaps including specialized devices such as optical character readers, voice response units, or computer output microfilm devices. A wide variety of general- and special-purpose software is available for such systems. A configuration in this category would cost from half a million to several million dollars.

In addition to equipment and software, initial outlay costs include the costs of hiring, training, and making organizational adjustments. If the organization is acquiring a computer for the first time, many people will have to be hired for both managerial and operating positions, and some relocation of existing personnel may be necessary. For any type of systems change, there will be costs associated with training of personnel. Steps should be taken to ensure that employee morale does not deteriorate as a result of a major systems change, and in some cases, these steps could be expensive.

Another portion of the initial outlay will be for preparation of the computer site. A small computer system requires little site preparation, but a larger general-purpose computer system often requires that considerable effort be devoted to the selection and development of a home for computer equipment and staff. Even if the site is to be part of an existing building, the cost of the remodeling necessary to accommodate a computer system is still likely to be substantial. The addition of electrical outlets, climate control, communications capacity, and raised floors will often be required. Space must also be provided to house systems analysts, programmers, data preparation personnel and equipment, supervisors, and so forth.

The initial systems analysis and programming is another element that adds to the initial outlay cost. The operating system, utility routines, compilers, and so forth, are obtained from the vendor. Some vendors charge for these separately, whereas others provide them as part of a package with the equipment. In addition to this software, however, much time and effort will be required to program the user's applications and to test and document them. Again, application programs may be obtained from the computer vendor or from other software suppliers, but such programs usually must be modified to fit the user's requirements, and this may consume a great deal of time. The development of a complete set of application systems documentation is also time-consuming. The cost of application systems development, documentation, and testing primarily takes the form of salaries paid to systems analysts and programmers but may also include rental of outside computer time for purposes of program testing.

Another portion of the initial outlay cost will be for the process of conversion itself. The cost of converting files to the storage media of the new system may be quite large if the old system is a manual one with files of printed documents. However, the main element of conversion cost arises from a period of parallel operation of the old and new systems prior to the final change-over. The major portion of conversion cost goes for wages and salaries of computer operators and other staff personnel. During the parallel operation period, these employees often must work long overtime hours, which adds even more to conversion costs.

The installation of hardware and software and the other activities requiring an initial outlay are part of the process of implementation, which is discussed in greater depth in the next chapter.

Operating costs

The costs of operating a computer system may be divided into three major categories—equipment costs, personnel costs, and other costs. From a cash flow standpoint, equipment costs are part of operating costs when the equipment is rented or leased; otherwise, they are part of the initial outlay. However, even if all equipment is purchased, there is likely to be a significant annual cash outflow for equipment replacement and expansion.

Personnel costs include the salaries of systems analysts, application programmers, and systems programmers. Skilled people for these positions are in short supply, and so their salaries tend to be high. Also included in personnel costs are the salaries of computer operators, data preparation personnel, supervisory personnel, and data processing management.

The remainder of the costs of operation in a computer system include such categories as software, supplies, and overhead. Software costs include the purchase or rental of program packages from manufacturers or independent software vendors. Supplies include paper, preprinted forms, diskettes, magnetic tapes, removable disk packs, and so forth. Overhead is composed of the cost of utilities, including power for the computer itself and for the air conditioning required by the computer, lighting, and telecommunications services. Equipment maintenance costs and insurance costs are other elements of overhead. Building occupancy costs should also be taken into consideration if there are cash flows or opportunity costs specifically identifiable with the occupancy of building space by the computer system.

According to a recent broad survey of data processing budgets, hardware costs average about forty-two percent of computer system operating costs, whereas personnel costs account for about thirty-two percent of the total, and other costs account for the remaining twenty-six percent.[2] This survey confirmed a recent sharp decline in the percentage of computer system operating costs represented by personnel costs; this percentage had averaged about fifty percent until 1980, according to a similar previous survey.[3] There are two major reasons for this trend. One is a significant decline in data entry operators, who are being replaced by user source data entry. The other is a decline in large-scale systems analysis and design work, as organizations make greater use of purchased software, program generators, and user-developed applications on personal computers. As the personnel cost percentage has declined, the operating cost percentages associated with hardware (especially personal computers), software, supplies, and overhead have increased significantly.

For most organizations the total data processing budget amounts to a relatively small percentage of gross revenues. According to the recent data processing budget survey cited above, this percentage averages six tenths of one percent, although it generally exceeds one percent for very large organizations and for organizations in the fields of banking, health care, and education.[4]

---

[2]John W. Verity, "1986 DP Budget Survey," *Datamation* (April 1, 1986): 74–78.
[3]Janet Crane, "Trends in DP Budgets," *Datamation* (May 1981): 140–150.
[4]Verity, "1986 DP Budget Survey," p. 78.

**Benefits of a
computer system**

The most difficult part of a feasibility study is to place a dollar value on the benefits that will come about as the result of computerization. Several different categories of cost savings and other benefits are usually cited as justification for computer acquisition, and some of the more significant of these are briefly discussed here.

Perhaps the most common expectation is that a new computer will result in cost savings because of reductions in clerical personnel. It is true that clerical cost savings are likely to represent one of the major benefits of computerization. However, from the standpoint of an analysis of cash flows, it is necessary to consider the pattern of these savings over time. For example, if a policy of relocation of displaced personnel together with the reduction of hiring rates necessary for their assimilation is adopted, the clerical cost savings will be realized gradually rather than suddenly. Furthermore, it is reasonable to expect that the computer will continue to take over clerical functions after its implementation and will thus effect a gradual increase in clerical cost savings over time. However, it is relevant to point out that much of the savings from reductions in clerical personnel may be offset by the personnel costs relating to the staffing of the computer system.

Whereas clerical cost savings usually represent the primary initial justification for computer acquisition, the primary long-term justification for the computer must be its contribution to better management. The production management function is one area in which this contribution is often expected. More accurate and comprehensive information should be made available by the computer to enable production planning to be more sensitive to market conditions and to the availability of raw materials. Tighter control over waste and inefficiency in production can be accomplished with faster and more accurate production control information. Cost savings from greater production efficiency are difficult to estimate accurately, but they can be substantial. Care should be taken to separate those savings attributable solely to computerization from those that could be achieved by improvements other than computerization.

Another form of cost savings arises from having fewer funds tied up in working capital. The computer can help to reduce inventory balances by keeping a more accurate and up-to-date record and by automatically reordering items that need to be replenished. Accounts receivable balances can be reduced by means of faster billing and closer monitoring of past-due accounts. Cash balances can be reduced because of more accurate forecasting of cash requirements. All the funds thus freed can be invested in income-producing projects, thereby contributing to cash inflow.

Computerization can also help an organization provide better service to its customers. Increased control over inventories means fewer stockouts. Increased efficiency in the handling of customer orders means fewer errors and faster order handling and delivery. Increased automation enables faster responses to inquiries from customers or potential customers concerning the status of their account or the availability of a product. Advantages of this type are quite difficult to quantify. Nevertheless, they are real and should not be overlooked, particularly if the company operates in a highly competitive market.

A significant benefit of the acquisition of personal computers is the improvement in productivity of office workers. The use of spreadsheet programs significantly improves the productivity of accountants and middle managers. Word processing applications of PCs improve the productivity of secretaries. Engineers, salespeople, bankers, stockbrokers, and numerous other office workers have found that PCs can significantly reduce the time required to perform routine analytical and clerical functions.

Finally, the computer benefits that are perhaps the most difficult to quantify are those relating to improvements in management decision making. The computer provides management with more timely, more comprehensive, and more reliable information. It will provide a basis for better management control by spotlighting the extremes of good performance and bad performance in the organization. It offers the potential for development of planning models and quantitative techniques designed to support the decision-making process for critical management decisions. Such improvements will probably be realized gradually rather than quickly. Therefore estimates of their contribution to cash flow should be conservative for the first few years after computerization.

An example of a comprehensive analysis of estimated cash flows relating to computer acquisition appears in Fig. 12.1. On the basis of these tentative estimates of cash flows, the feasibility study group must formulate a recommendation either (1) to discontinue further investigation of computer acquisition and maintain or modify the existing system or (2) to go ahead with the plan for the new system. This decision should be made primarily on an economic basis. The best framework for making this decision is the capital budgeting model, in which all estimated future cash flows are discounted back to the present, using a discount rate that reflects the time value of money to the organization. From the resulting amount is deducted the initial outlay cost to obtain the *net present value*. A positive net present value is an indication that the alternative is economically feasible.[5]

Even if a decision is made at this point to halt the investigation and go no further in considering a new system, it is likely that the feasibility study will have produced some benefits through the correction of inefficiencies or the initiation of other improvements in the system. However, if the decision is made to go ahead with the system selection and acquisition effort, then the study group enters a new phase at this point, which is the detailed study of applications for the new system.

---

[5]For an excellent treatise on capital budgeting, see Harold J. Bierman, Jr., and Seymour Smidt, *The Capital Budgeting Decision*, 5th ed. (New York: Macmillan, 1980).

	YEAR 1	YEAR 2	YEAR 3	YEAR 4	YEAR 5	YEAR 6
Initial outlay costs						
Hardware	$300,000					
Software	50,000					
Training	20,000					
Site preparation	40,000					
Initial systems design	150,000					
Conversion	30,000					
Recurring costs						
Hardware expansion	—	$ 20,000	$ 30,000	$ 30,000	$ 40,000	$ 40,000
Software	—	10,000	20,000	20,000	25,000	25,000
System maintenance	6,000	12,000	13,000	14,000	15,000	16,000
Personnel costs	50,000	80,000	90,000	100,000	120,000	140,000
Supplies	10,000	16,000	18,000	20,000	22,000	25,000
Overhead	30,000	45,000	50,000	55,000	60,000	64,000
Total outflows	$686,000	$183,000	$221,000	$239,000	$282,000	$310,000
Benefits						
Clerical cost savings	$ 60,000	$150,000	$160,000	$170,000	$180,000	$190,000
Working capital savings	40,000	100,000	100,000	100,000	100,000	100,000
Profits from sales increases	—	20,000	60,000	90,000	110,000	140,000
Production efficiences	—	30,000	60,000	90,000	110,000	140,000
Total inflows	$100,000	$300,000	$380,000	$450,000	$500,000	$570,000
Net inflow (outflow)	($586,000)	$117,000	$159,000	$211,000	$218,000	$260,000

FIGURE 12.1
Example of cash
flows associated with
computer system
acquisition.

The Applications Study

The applications study phase of the systems evaluation and selection process involves a detailed description of the work load that the new system will be required to perform. While the information developed in the feasibility study will be a useful starting point, the objectives of the applications study require a much finer degree of detail than is required to evaluate economic feasibility. The primary goal of the applications study is to produce a set of *specifications* that represent an itemized description of the data processing objectives and requirements of the organization. The specifications are provided to those equipment, service, or software vendors that the organization selects to submit proposals. The vendors who accept such invitations may then use the specifications as a basis for developing presentations geared to the specific requirements of the user organization.

Completion of the applications study and development of specifications are important steps for an organization that is preparing to procure systems or services from an external vendor. However, if the systems selection involves internal development and programming of information systems applications, with little or no impact on the organization's hardware or software configuration, then the applications study will be skipped and the study group will proceed directly to the design phase.

Content of specifications

A set of specifications typically includes certain general information, a detailed description of the user's applications, and an indication of the user's expectations of the vendors with respect to their presentations. Each of these categories of information is hereby examined in turn.

General information.   A set of specifications should first include general background information on the company. A concise outline of the company's facilities, products, financial circumstances, and organization serves as an appropriate introduction. This should be followed by a more extensive description of the company's present data processing system, including major applications and existing equipment. A brief indication of the more serious inadequacies or problems with the present system could be useful here. Other general information should include the company's expectations with respect to the dates of submission of proposals and the date that the final decision on selection of a vendor will be made.

Description of applications.   The heart of the specifications will be a description of proposed applications. Each application should be treated separately. One of the most important elements in the presentation of an application will be the system flowchart, showing the input to and output from the computer runs. Input to the application should be further described by its sources, the operations performed on it prior to conversion to computer input, and its average and peak volume.

A specification of the contents of the master file is also a useful part of the description of each application. Record layouts describing the length, format, and other characteristics of each type of master file record should be included. The frequency and method of file updating, as well as the urgency and frequency of inquiries to the file, should be included in the description. The number of records contained in the file should be given and an estimate of the rate of growth expected in this number made.

The output required of each application should also be described. The points important to be clarified are (1) the information to be contained in each report and its format; (2) the average size (length) of each report; (3) the frequency with which each report is to be prepared and the necessity for timeliness in its preparation and distribution; and (4) the persons or locations to which each report is to be distributed.

Requirements for vendor presentation. The third major category of information to be submitted in the specifications should be a list of major items the user company expects each vendor to cover in its proposal. Significant in this respect is first of all the hardware configuration proposed by the vendor, including a description of the central processor and its characteristics, the number and type of input and output units and a description of their speed and other vital characteristics, and the type of file media and related equipment. A topic important in the consideration of hardware will be its cost, which requires a description of alternative lease or purchase plans the vendor offers and other major terms of contract, such as length of lease and cancellation clauses. An indication of when installation could commence and an estimate of when it could be completed should also be included. Floor space required, electric power, and other aspects of the installation should be covered. Any user restrictions concerning cost, hardware characteristics, delivery date, or available floor space should be revealed.

The user will also expect the vendor to discuss system software in the proposal. Any user requirements regarding compiler languages are relevant. Any utility routines or application packages that the user feels are needed or desired should be discussed. The vendor should be expected to mention all compilers, assemblers, utility routines, and so forth, that are proposed for the system and indicate what usage is recommended for each.

The vendor should also be required to submit a proposed processing schedule for the user. This will provide some assurance that the proposed system is actually capable of meeting the user's data processing requirements. The vendor should be requested to give attention to the effects of peak processing periods on the schedule.

The user will be interested in several other types of services provided by the vendor, such as the facilities available for testing programs prior to installation, any training programs offered by the vendor for the user's employees, the amount of assistance available from the vendor during the preparation for installation and conversion, the arrangements for hardware maintenance, and the availability of backup facilities in the event of a system failure. Charges for any or all these services should be included in the description.

Most of the major topics that would be covered in a set of specifications have been mentioned. In addition to these, the user may indicate some special requirements or restrictions that he or she wishes the vendor to recognize in his or her case. After the specifications have been provided to the vendors, the next step in the process is to await receipt of their various proposals. This is followed by the difficult process of evaluating the proposals and selecting a vendor.

Vendor Selection   The term computer vendor generally is interpreted as a reference to the relatively few large computer manufacturers. However, the computer industry contains a variety of firms. In addition to the major computer manufacturers, other major segments of the industry include minicomputer and microcomputer manufacturers, turnkey systems suppliers, mainframe replacement vendors, supplies vendors, service bureaus, time-sharing vendors, computer-leasing companies, used-computer brokers, peripheral equipment manufacturers, facilities management vendors, EDP consultants, and software vendors. An organization considering computer acquisition may find it worthwhile to consider the services of firms in several of these industry segments in addition to, or as an alternative to, the major computer manufacturers. Certainly a restriction of consideration to the computer manufacturers alone is inappropriate. For one thing, many firms in other segments of the computer industry offer services or equipment equivalent to that of the manufacturers—but at a lower price. In addition, if more alternatives are considered, the likelihood that the resulting system will more closely meet the needs and objectives of the user organization is increased.

Accordingly, one of the first steps in the vendor selection process is the determination of which type or types of vendor the organization wishes to consider. This must be followed by a determination of which specific vendors will be invited to submit proposals. To assist in this determination, the organization may classify the features it desires in its system as either "mandatory" or "desirable." Any vendors whose systems do not satisfy the mandatory requirements are automatically eliminated from further consideration. The remainder are invited to submit proposals by providing them with a "request for proposal," or "RFP," that consists primarily of the specifications developed in the applications study.

This section begins by briefly describing the products and services offered by firms in each of the computer industry segments mentioned above. Following this is a discussion of the vendor evaluation process. The section then concludes by examining the alternative methods of financing the acquisition of a computer system.

The computer industry

In the following paragraphs, fourteen categories of firms in the computer industry are described.

Computer manufacturers. Each of the major computer manufacturers is involved in most or all of the industry segments listed above. The distinguishing feature of the firms in this group is their production for commercial sale of a wide range of general-purpose computer systems. The primary computer manufacturer is IBM, whose share of the general-purpose computer market has averaged sixty-five percent for the past several years. The policies and actions of IBM dominate the industry. Other computer manufacturers have had difficulty making a profit in this environment, and several have dropped out of the market completely, including RCA in September 1971 and Xerox Data Systems in July 1975.

Besides IBM, the other major computer manufacturers include Unisys (produced by the merger of the Burroughs and Sperry corporations in 1986), NCR Corporation, Honeywell Information Systems, Control Data Corporation, and Digital Equipment Corporation. For most of these firms, the only effective way to compete with IBM has been to specialize in a market area in which IBM is relatively weak. For example, Control Data concentrates primarily on very large and fast computers for scientific applications and thus sells many machines to research institutions and universities. Unisys and NCR have a sizable market share in the banking industry, and both have also concentrated heavily in the small business systems segment of the market.

Mainframe replacement vendors.   The dominance of IBM in the general-purpose computer market segment has spawned a unique group of companies known as mainframe replacement vendors. These are companies that build and sell central processing units (or "mainframes") that may be substituted for those offered by IBM. Because they are based upon more advanced technology, the mainframe replacements are generally faster, smaller, and less expensive than their IBM counterparts. They are designed to operate using IBM operating systems and other software, and therefore little or no conversion costs are associated with the replacement of an IBM mainframe by one of these units. Offsetting the advantages of greater performance and lower cost is the risk of receiving a lesser quantity and quality of service from the mainframe replacement vendors than from IBM's renowned customer service staff. As a result it is generally only the more experienced computer users, with less dependence on the vendor's service staff, who should consider a mainframe replacement.

In recent years IBM has responded to the competitive pressures created by mainframe replacements by upgrading its technology and lowering its prices. In turn, other major computer manufacturers have been forced to do the same. From the standpoint of computer users, this has certainly been a positive development. However, it has also reduced the economic advantages of mainframe replacements.

Service bureaus.   A data processing service bureau is an organization that provides data processing services, primarily batch processing, on its own equipment to users for a fee. For firms too small to afford the considerable investment of an "in-house" computer system, a service bureau may offer an attractive alternative. Because many users are sharing the computer facilities of the service bureau, the cost to each user is only a fraction of the total cost of a computer system.

Most data processing service bureaus charge a standard rate for time or perhaps for each item processed. They may add charges for materials, or perhaps a fixed fee to cover administrative costs. Service bureaus provide generalized programs for most standard applications or will write a specialized program for a single user for an extra fee. Utilization of service bureaus requires the physical transporting of source document input to the bureau and of processed output to the user.

In addition to the cost advantages to small users, the use of data processing service bureaus affords several other advantages. A firm that has its own computer system may arrange for backup facilities to be made available through a service bureau. Such backup facilities would be helpful during a major equipment malfunction or during a period of peak processing volume. In addition, a service bureau may offer specialized equipment, programs, or expertise that would not otherwise be available to a computer user. Service bureaus also offer to users who are awaiting installation of a new computer system an opportunity to test programs on a computer model like the one being acquired.

Use of a service bureau also has disadvantages. The most significant of these relates to data security. Because the user of a service bureau must relinquish control of vital business data to the bureau, the user should assure himself or herself that proper control procedures are being followed and that proper security provisions are in effect. Another disadvantage is that the generalized programs offered by the service bureau may not exactly meet the data processing requirements of the user. In addition, the scheduling of a user's data processing work by a service bureau may cause the user to wait significantly longer for the work to be completed than if the user owned a facility or did the work manually.

Time-sharing vendors. The time-sharing vendor is an organization that provides for a fee the usage of a central computer and online file storage to users who obtain access through remote terminals and telecommunications lines. As with the service bureau, the primary advantage is the cost savings achieved through the sharing of a central computer system by many users. The time-sharing service differs from that of the service bureau in that the former is an online processing service, whereas the latter is a batch processing service. The most significant disadvantage of time-sharing is the high cost of data transmission over long distances.

Three basic categories of time-sharing services are available. One is a problem-solving or scientifically oriented service. This type of time-sharing service is the most common and has several advantages. First, it provides computer availability to organizations that do not have access to private facilities at a relatively low cost that varies with usage. Second, it provides an interactive capability. This means that the user can obtain a problem solution quickly and then structure another problem based upon that solution, and so on. A third important advantage is that time-sharing vendors generally offer several specialized library programs, many of which a user might find helpful.

The second basic category of time-sharing service is business-oriented batch processing, in which the input consists of transaction data and the output consists of documents and reports. In addition to a terminal, the user of this service may also have a special printer or other specialized input-output equipment. Because business applications generally involve high volumes of data input and output and because the cost of data transmission is high, this type of service is often not economical relative to the service bureau. In addition, the problems of data security and control are perhaps even more serious than those in service bureaus because of shared file storage. The main advantage of this service is that it provides a real-time capability, which in some cases may improve the efficiency of the user's operations or provide the user with a significant competitive advantage.

The third type of service offered by time-sharing vendors is an information utility service. This service provides the user with access to a large centralized data base containing information relevant to specific needs of each user. One example related to accounting is a credit reference service. The centralized data base of such an organization contains credit information on all potential credit customers within a community. Subscribers may obtain access to this information via telephone whenever a customer applies for credit.

The cost of a time-sharing service generally includes a fixed monthly charge for the terminal and other equipment and variable charges for terminal hookup, central processor time, and file storage used. The cost of a terminal varies widely but generally ranges between $100 and $500 per month. The charge for terminal hookup time is usually between $5 and $30 per hour. The charges for central processor time and file storage are generally small relative to terminal and hookup costs. However, pricing patterns among time-sharing vendors are quite diverse, and so the potential user is well advised to shop around for a vendor whose pricing policies are most favorable relative to the expected usage pattern.

Minicomputer manufacturers.   These companies offer high-performance systems that are fast, reliable, inexpensive, and possessed of all the logical capabilities of large computers. The pioneer companies in this market placed little emphasis on peripheral equipment, high-level languages, and systems support, and targeted their products to scientists, engineers, and researchers who possessed sufficient technical skills to utilize them effectively despite these handicaps. More recently, the emphasis of several minicomputer manufacturers has shifted toward the business-oriented user, and today the so-called small business computer represents a major component of the minicomputer market. Another recent development in this industry segment is the erosion of sales of smaller minicomputer systems attributable to the growing popularity of personal computers. Minicomputer manufacturers have responded to this trend by placing greater emphasis on "superminis," which are the largest and most sophisticated minicomputer systems having a purchase price of $100,000 or more.

Turnkey systems suppliers.   Because minicomputer manufacturers have generally not been strong in providing software and services to first-time small business computer users, another group of companies has emerged to fill this void. These companies are called turnkey systems suppliers because their systems are (theoretically) delivered to customers ready to use by simply turning them on. A turnkey systems supplier does not manufacture computer equipment but instead buys equipment from a minicomputer manufacturer and then writes application software that is tailored both to that equipment and to the user needs of its customers. The most successful turnkey systems suppliers target their offerings to specific classes of customers, such as automobile distributors, medical clinics, or food wholesalers, in order to develop the specialized expertise necessary to provide high-quality service. As a result, turnkey systems suppliers are an option that should be given serious consideration by a first-time computer user.

Microcomputer manufacturers. In the late 1970s another wave of small computers entered the marketplace, creating still another industry segment. Because these computers are even smaller, faster, and less expensive than minicomputers, they have been tabbed microcomputers, but they are also called desktop computers or personal computers. These machines have proved to be popular among small businesspersons and independent professionals such as accountants, architects, physicians, and engineers, as well as among middle managers and professional staff within large organizations. They may be used for file processing applications that have a limited volume of input, output and storage; for financial modeling and spreadsheet analysis applications; for simple computational applications such as forecasting, discounted cash flow analysis, and engineering problem solving; for preparation of graphic output; and for word processing. Contemporary microcomputer software integrates these various capabilities into one software package, allowing users to easily perform a variety of operations on the same set of data. For small organizations, the microcomputer provides a viable means of automating routine clerical functions. Within large organizations, microcomputers have effectively tackled many functions that the central computer staff considered too small or too unimportant to deserve prompt attention. Owing to the remarkable versatility and low cost of the microcomputer, this segment of the computer industry should continue to show substantial growth over the next few years.

Computer-leasing companies. These companies usually offer a computer user an opportunity to lease a computer system at rates below the rental rates charged by the manufacturers. Offsetting this basic advantage is the basic disadvantage that these leasing contracts are for a long-term period with no options to cancel. Thus the flexibility and avoidance of risk present in rental contracts with the manufacturer is not present in contracts with leasing companies. These companies basically provide a financing alternative to purchasing or renting, and this option has proved attractive to many organizations. Approximately twenty-five percent of the general-purpose computer systems in use are financed in this manner.

Used-computer brokers. These organizations operate primarily as agents for sellers of used computers, assisting them in finding a buyer. Their fee is determined as a percentage, commonly ten percent, of the selling price. Used-equipment prices range from as low as ten percent for older equipment to as high as ninety percent for newer equipment. In addition to the cost advantage, the used-computer broker can often provide immediate delivery of equipment, whereas delivery of new equipment usually requires a delay of from three to twelve months. While first-time computer users may wish to consider the used-computer alternative, most buyers of used computers are well-established users who wish to upgrade their facilities and know exactly what equipment they want. Because the total number of computer systems in use continues to increase, the market for used computers has grown rapidly, passing the $1 billion mark in 1976 according to one estimate.

Peripheral equipment manufacturers. These firms manufacture a variety of input, output, and memory devices. Although the computer manufacturers are a major segment of this group, there are a large number of independents. Relative to central processor units, peripheral equipment represents sixty percent of the dollar value of all computer hardware sales. From the user's point of view, the most significant thing about this industry segment is that the independents may offer price and performance advantages over the computer manufacturers. Some may offer devices that are equivalent to those of IBM, for example, but at a lower cost. Others may offer devices technologically superior to those available from the computer manufacturers at equivalent prices.

Facilities-management vendors. A facilities-management vendor is an organization that contracts to manage the data processing facilities of a user for a fee. In most cases the hardware is owned or leased by the user and is located at the user's site. The facilities-management firm operates under guidelines and schedules established by the user. Banks, insurance companies, and hospitals are among the most significant users of facilities-management services.

Facilities management offers several advantages, the most significant of which is the reduction of staffing problems relating to the computer facility. Qualified EDP personnel are in short supply, and users of smaller systems have difficulty attracting qualified people and evaluating their work. Another advantage is the control of costs and efficiency that is provided by a contract that establishes a schedule and specifies a fee. Other advantages include availability of specialized knowledge and expertise, the ability to balance staff levels over periods of high and low volume, and the possibility of more effective security and control being implemented.

For the company contemplating acquisition of its first computer system, a facilities-management firm can provide useful assistance in vendor selection as well as manage the system through implementation and the early period of operation. Facilities-management personnel should be familiar with a wide range of equipment and software available on the market.

Facilities management does have significant disadvantages. A primary one is that a major segment of the user's operation is turned over to the control of outsiders. The personnel provided by a facilities-management vendor may not be as sensitive to the needs and objectives of the user organization as would be the user's own personnel. Facilities management is probably not an appropriate alternative to consider for an organization that has an effectively operating computer system staffed with experienced and qualified personnel.

EDP consultants. The two foremost types of firms that offer independent EDP consulting services are the major private consulting firms and the large public accounting firms. Both employ people who specialize in EDP consulting. A service of this type is often invaluable to the user considering computer acquisition for the first time. With little knowledge and no experience, first-time buyers are often taken advantage of by equipment salespeople whose primary objective is to make a sale. The experience and objective viewpoint of the EDP consultant helps to ensure that decisions are based upon facts and needs rather than emotions.

Software vendors. Firms in this industry segment specialize in the development and marketing of program packages. These include standardized applications packages, utility programs, data base management systems, report generators, data communications software, and operating systems. Prior to IBM's unbundling of hardware and software prices in 1969, most software development work by these vendors was done under contracts with users. The unbundling stimulated the development of a market for software products. Currently, the purchase of commercial software packages is more common than in-house software development in many organizations. As with peripheral equipment, the software products available from the independent software vendors may offer price or performance advantages over those available from the computer manufacturers.

Supplies vendors. This market segment consists of a large number of firms that sell magnetic tape, disk packs, diskettes, preprinted computer forms, and related computer media and accessories. Among these are the large computer vendors, but neither they nor any other firms have a dominating influence on this market. According to one estimate, spending on these products amounts to over six percent of all data processing expenditures. Significant price and product quality differences do exist in this market, and so computer users are well advised to shop carefully for their computer supplies.

Summary. The division of the computer industry into the fourteen segments described here does not represent a standardized or generally accepted method of classification. There are certainly some other less significant segments not described here, and there are other ways of subdividing these segments. Once again, the major purpose of this discussion was to point out the wide variety of options open to the computer user.

For the potential first-time computer user, minicomputer or microcomputer manufacturers, turnkey systems suppliers, service bureaus, time-sharing vendors, and used-computer brokers, in addition to the major computer manufacturers, may be considered as alternatives during the feasibility study. The advice of EDP consultants may be useful in carrying out the feasibility study. If the decision is made to acquire a computer system, either a facilities-management vendor or an EDP consultant may provide useful assistance in preparing specifications and evaluating vendor proposals.

Once the applications study has been completed, the specifications are provided to a number of computer vendors (generally three to five) who are invited to submit proposals. The time lapse between providing a vendor with the specifications and receiving the proposals averages about two months. During that period each of the different vendors may desire clarification of various aspects of the specifications, and the company should be prepared to provide such guidance. In the next section, the criteria for evaluating vendor proposals are discussed.

After a vendor for the main system has been selected, the user may wish to consider alternative sources of peripheral equipment, software, or supplies. Vendor selection must be followed by a decision of how to finance the computer acquisition. At this point, computer-leasing companies may be considered. A subsequent section of this chapter discusses purchasing and leasing as alternative means of financing.

Evaluation of vendor proposals

After the proposals of all vendors have been received, the difficult choice among equipment configurations and vendors must be made. The most important factors in the selection of an equipment configuration are hardware and software performance and cost. One popular means of comparing the hardware and software performance of computer systems is the *benchmark problem.* This is a data processing task typical of the jobs a new computer system will be required to perform, so it provides a useful means for making a comparison among proposed systems. A second approach is to develop a performance-cost ratio for each proposed system. The problem with this approach is that it is difficult to reduce all the various aspects of system performance to a formula that is to be solved to provide a number representing a comparable measure of performance. A third approach is the use of mathematical models to simulate the performance of each proposed system relative to the complete processing requirements of the user.

A thorough analysis of the proposed processing schedule of each vendor also provides an indication of the capability of the proposed hardware and software to accomplish the required data processing functions of the user company. Necessary for making a determination of whether the schedule allows enough time to complete each application is knowledge about rated speeds of each hardware item, including the average speed of the central processor in executing a typical mix of instructions. Because many business data processing applications are input/output bound, the speeds of input/output hardware may often determine the rate at which each application can be processed. The time required for each unit of activity multiplied by the volume of activity for each application provides a fair measure of the total time required for each in the schedule. The schedule should also make allowances for periods of peak volume.

Another significant factor in equipment selection is the compatibility of the proposed system with the user company's present data processing system. This is particularly important if the user company is already automated and is seeking to obtain more capacity. A closely related factor is the *modularity* of a proposed system, which is its capacity to be expanded with a minimum of difficulty to meet growth in the user company's needs. Modularity relates both to hardware and software. For example, the capacity of a system may be expanded by adding more primary storage, faster input/output equipment, or a faster central processor. Hardware changes, particularly a change in CPU, will require changes in software. The ease with which such changes can be made is what is referred to as modularity.

In some cases, there may be specific criteria of critical importance to the selection decision. For example, in the selection of an online system to support customer service activities or key operating functions, response time and equipment reliability are critical factors. For another example, if the system is to be used for storage and retrieval of sensitive data, the security features of the hardware and software become a critical factor.

Still another important element of the equipment selection decision is the choice among vendors. The reputation of each vendor and the support that each is able and willing to provide to the user are very significant. Support consists of such things as training for user personnel; use of equipment for testing purposes; contracts for maintenance; assistance in systems analysis and design, in implementation, and in eliminating bugs during the early stages of operation; and provision for system backup in the event of failure. The relationship between a computer vendor and a user company is complex and has many facets. During the period of implementation especially, this relationship will be a very close one. Throughout the period of their association, the user company will be placing reliance upon the vendor. The choice of vendor is thus a decision that must be carefully weighed.

Outside sources of information should not be overlooked during the vendor selection process. For example, other users of a vendor's systems may provide useful insights regarding system performance and vendor support. A somewhat more objective source of information is the user ratings of computer hardware and software systems regularly compiled and published by organizations such as the Datapro Research Corporation.[6] These ratings are

---

[6]Datapro Research Corporation, "User Ratings of Mainframes," in *Datapro 70: The EDP Buyer's Bible* (Delran, N.J.: Datapro Research Corporation, 1986).

based upon comprehensive surveys of large numbers of computer users and are widely regarded as a valuable source of information on user opinions.

Many authorities recommend the use of an objective procedure for evaluating the overall merits of vendor proposals, taking into account all the relevant criteria. One such approach is known as *point scoring*. Under this procedure, the various criteria are listed and a weighting factor is applied to each criterion according to its relative importance to the user. Then each vendor is assigned a score on each criterion according to how well its proposal measures up to the ideal for that criterion. Summation of the scores for the individual criteria then gives an overall score that may be used to compare the various vendors. A simple illustration of how this form of point scoring might work is provided in Fig. 12.2.

Point scoring provides a useful way of obtaining an overall view of the vendor proposals and how they compare. The process of selecting criteria and assigning weights and points tends to focus attention on the factors relevant to the decision process. However, care must be taken to avoid placing too much emphasis on the outcome of the point scoring technique. It should be kept in mind that both the weights and the points are assigned subjectively, and therefore a sizable margin for potential error should be provided in interpreting the results. For example, the results shown in Fig. 12.2 are too inconclusive to support a final decision that Vendor #3's proposal is best. It would be appropriate in this case to experiment with other possible values of weights and point assignments and study the impact of the alternative values on the result.

Another objective technique for evaluating the relative merits of proposed systems is known as *requirements costing*. Under this approach a list is made of all the required features for the new system. Then, if any feature is not present in a particular system, an estimate is made of the cost to purchase or develop that feature for that system. Therefore the total cost for each system is computed by adding its acquisition cost to the cost of purchasing or developing any additional required features not possessed by the system. The resulting sums represent the total costs for systems having all the required

FIGURE 12.2
The point scoring method of evaluating vendor proposals.

Criterion	Weight	Vendor #1	Vendor #2	Vendor #3
Hardware performance	60	40	60	50
Software capability	70	55	40	60
System reliability	40	25	30	35
Rental cost	60	60	35	50
Ease of use	40	30	25	35
Ease of conversion	20	15	20	15
Modularity	40	30	40	30
Vendor support	40	40	30	30
Documentation	30	25	20	20
TOTALS	400	320	300	325

features and thus provide an equitable basis for comparing the alternative systems.

Neither requirements costing nor point scoring is totally objective. The disadvantage of point scoring is that it does not incorporate dollar estimates of costs and benefits. Requirements costing partially overcomes this problem but generally overlooks intangible factors such as system reliability and vendor support. The ideal selection technique would be one that reduces all factors to dollar estimates of costs and benefits. While it is generally not possible to reduce factors such as those listed in Fig. 12.2 to precise dollar terms, an attempt to do so may be no more subjective than the point scoring approach. In any event the final choice among vendor proposals is not likely to be a clear-cut decision. In the final analysis, this decision cannot be based solely upon objective criteria but must rely to some extent on subjective factors.

Financing system acquisition

Closely related to the choice among vendor proposals is the selection of a method of financing the acquisition of major items of equipment or software. The three primary alternatives are purchasing the system, renting it from the vendor, or leasing it from either the vendor or a computer-leasing company.

The major difference between renting and leasing is in the length of the agreement. A rental contract may generally be terminated by giving ninety days prior notice, whereas a lease contract may be written to cover a fixed period of from two to ten years. Rental payments are higher than lease payments for the equivalent hardware. Rental contracts often include an extra charge for usage of the computer for more than 176 or 200 hours during a month. Lease contracts typically do not contain extra-use charges and usually provide the user (lessee) with an option to purchase the system at a specified price at the conclusion of the lease term. Under both rental and lease plans, the manufacturer provides maintenance of the equipment, and the charge for this service is included in the monthly payment.

The terms of equipment purchase from a computer manufacturer are relatively straightforward. Computer equipment prices generally average between twenty-five and fifty times the monthly rental charges for the same hardware. Equipment maintenance must be handled by separate contract payable on a monthly basis. For the protection of the user, a purchase contract may include provision for a penalty payment in the event of late delivery and a commitment to provide maintenance service during the first ninety days after installation.

The relative economic merits of purchasing a computer system as opposed to either renting or leasing it are highlighted in Fig. 12.3. This illustration shows the annual cash flows over an eight-year life for a computer system that could be purchased for $1,080,000 or rented for $25,000 per month ($300,000 per year). When purchasing a computer, an investment tax credit (ITC) can sometimes be taken. Congress has instituted and repealed the ITC several times. Prior to 1986 a 10% ITC could be taken at the time of purchase. However, the Tax Reform Act of 1986 repealed the ITC for years after 1985. For illustration purposes, Figure 12.3 shows the ITC included in the analysis.

Depreciation for tax purposes is computed according to the accelerated cost recovery system over a five-year period at rates of fifteen percent of the purchase price for the first year, twenty-two percent for year 2, and twenty-one percent for years 3 through 5.[1] The tax savings are computed as a percentage of tax-deductible expenses (depreciation and maintenance), assuming a marginal federal plus state income tax rate of fifty percent (i.e., fifty percent of $162,000 + $30,000 in year 1). The after-tax cash flow in years 1 through 5 is actually an inflow because the tax savings more than offset the maintenance payment during those years. The cumulative cash flow represents the net total of all current and prior years' cash flows as of the end of each period.

The patterns of cash flow under both rental and lease plans are similar, although the amounts would differ. The rental or lease payment is tax deductible, and so the after-tax cash flow is equal to the total payment to the vendor minus the tax savings. By comparing the cumulative cash flows for rental with those for purchase, it is evident that rental is significantly more expensive over the long run, although this effect takes about four to five years to be realized.

Two other cost factors not reflected in Fig. 12.3 also favor purchasing. One is that equipment owned by the user has a residual value on the used-computer market. A second is that a purchaser does not pay extra-use charges. However, the overall cost advantage of purchasing would be somewhat offset if the analysis were adjusted to take into account the time value of money, because the purchase requires an immediate outlay, whereas both rental and lease contracts call for deferred payments. Even taking this into account, however, purchasing still has a lower total cost, and this represents its primary advantage.

Despite its higher cost, renting a computer system does have significant advantages. One is the avoidance of the large initial outlay of cash. A second is the flexibility provided by the ability to cancel the rental arrangement after giving a ninety-day notice. The most important aspect of this flexibility is the avoidance of risks from being "locked in" to a particular system. Examples of such risks are the risk that the equipment configuration may become obsolete as more efficient and less costly equipment becomes available in the market; the risk that the equipment rented may not perform as expected; the risk that the user may outgrow the equipment configuration sooner than expected; and the risk that the level of support provided by the vendor may not be adequate.

In terms of cost and risk, lease contracts fall in between purchase and rental contracts. Lease payments are smaller than rental payments, but leasing is still not as economical as purchasing in the long run. The lessee does not own the equipment and so, to some extent, avoids the risks of ownership by the ability to terminate the lease arrangement once the contract runs out. The length of a lease can be negotiated, and longer-term contracts require smaller

---

[1]The federal income tax provisions illustrated here for both depreciation and the investment tax credit apply to assets purchased prior to 1987. For assets purchased after 1986, these tax rules have been modified by the Tax Reform Act of 1986.

FIGURE 12.3

Comparative cash flows: purchase vs. rental of a computer system.

					YEAR				
	0	1	2	3	4	5	6	7	8
Purchase:									
a. Purchase payment	$1,080,000	—	—	—	—	—	—	—	—
b. Depreciation	—	$162,000	$237,600	$226,800	$226,800	$226,800	—	—	—
c. Maintenance	—	30,000	30,000	30,000	30,000	30,000	30,000	30,000	30,000
d. Tax savings from investment tax credit [10% of a]	(108,000)	—	—	—	—	—	—	—	—
e. Tax savings from deductible expenses [50% of (b + c)]	—	(96,000)	(133,800)	(128,400)	(128,400)	(128,400)	(15,000)	(15,000)	(15,000)
f. After-tax cash outflow (inflow) [a + c − d − e]	972,000	(66,000)	(103,800)	(98,400)	(98,400)	(98,400)	15,000	15,000	15,000
g. Cumulative cash outflow [f + previous g]	972,000	906,000	802,200	703,800	605,400	507,000	522,000	537,000	552,000
Rental:									
h. Rental payment	—	$300,000	$300,000	$300,000	$300,000	$300,000	$300,000	$300,000	$300,000
i. Tax saving [50% of h]	—	(150,000)	(150,000)	(150,000)	(150,000)	(150,000)	(150,000)	(150,000)	(150,000)
j. After-tax cash outflow	—	150,000	150,000	150,000	150,000	150,000	150,000	150,000	150,000
k. Cumulative cash outflow [j + previous K]	—	150,000	300,000	450,000	600,000	750,000	900,000	1,050,000	1,200,000

(handwritten note next to row f, year 0: 1,080,000 − 108,000)

monthly payments. Other advantages of leasing are the avoidance of extra-use charges and the availability of the option to purchase.

Basically, then, the choice of a method of financing system acquisition involves a trade-off between the risks of a long-term commitment and cost factors as measured by cash flow analysis using present value methods. Each organization must decide for itself which option best fits its requirements.

Summary

The first step in systems evaluation and selection is generally a feasibility study that examines the estimated costs and benefits of the system. Economic feasibility should be evaluated by discounting estimated future cash flows to arrive at the net present value of a proposed system. However, the technical and operational feasibility of proposed new systems should also be considered.

The computer industry consists of vendors offering products and services in numerous categories. Among these categories are computer manufacturers, mainframe replacement vendors, service bureaus, time-sharing vendors, mini-computer manufacturers, turnkey systems suppliers, microcomputer manufacturers, computer-leasing companies, used-computer brokers, peripheral equipment manufacturers, facilities-management vendors, EDP consultants, software vendors, and supplies vendors. An organization considering the acquisition of computer products or services may find it worthwhile to consider vendors in several of these industry segments.

A commonly used technique for comparing alternative vendor proposals is point scoring. This method requires that evaluative criteria be identified and assigned numeric weights. Each vendor's proposed system is then assigned a numeric score for each criterion. These weights and scores are then multiplied and summed to obtain a total score for each vendor proposal. Care should be taken in applying this technique, because the assigned weights and scores are inherently subjective. However, there exists no totally objective technique for comparing alternative vendor proposals.

Review Questions

1. Define the following terms.

feasibility study	specifications
applications study	computer utility
technical feasibility	benchmark problem
economic feasibility	modularity
operational feasibility	point scoring
net present value	requirements costing

2. What are the three major steps in the systems evaluation and selection process?

3. What should be the qualifications of the persons who carry out a feasibility study?

4. Outline and briefly describe the steps in a feasibility study.

5. Identify three dimensions of system feasibility and explain how each should be evaluated.

6. What three categories of cash flow estimates should be made during a computer feasibility study? List several individual elements within each category. Once these estimates have been made, what basic framework should be used in evaluating the feasibility of alternatives?

7. Briefly describe a typical equipment configuration within each of the following categories of computer system: (a) microcomputer, (b) multiuser microcomputer system, (c) small business computer, (d) general-purpose minicomputer, and (e) large-scale computer. What would be a typical price range for each?

8. List several categories of personnel that are necessary in a computer system. How does the total operating cost expended for personnel generally compare with the total operating cost expended for equipment in a computer system?

9. Other than hardware and personnel costs, what are some of the categories of costs incurred by a data processing facility?

10. What percentage of a total organizational budget is generally consumed by expenditures on data processing?

11. What is the difference between a feasibility study and an applications study?

12. What is the goal of an applications study?

13. Outline and briefly describe the content of a set of specifications.

14. Describe in detail the information that should be contained in a description of input, files, and output for an application in a set of specifications.

15. Describe in detail the information that a company should request a vendor to include in its presentation of a proposed computer system for the company.

16. Briefly describe the steps in the vendor selection process.

17. List and briefly describe fourteen major segments of the computer industry. At what point in the computer acquisition process would the products or services of each segment be considered?

18. List several criteria that should be used by a company to select a computer vendor from among several that have presented proposals. What techniques might be used as a basis for the final selection?

19. Explain how the capability of a proposed computer system to meet a processing schedule might be evaluated.

20. Explain the characteristics of purchase, rental, and lease contracts as methods of financing computer system acquisition. What are the advantages of each to the user?

Discussion Questions

21. Discuss the role of the accountant in the computer acquisition process. Should the accountant play an active role, or should all the work done be left to computer experts? In what aspects of computer acquisition might the expertise of the accountant produce a useful contribution?

22. Computer manufacturers generally employ very competent personnel who will assist a customer in designing a system for no charge or for a relatively small fee. Being good businesspeople interested in repeat sales, representatives of a computer manufacturer will certainly consider very seriously the needs and objectives of the customer. Why, then, should a firm contemplating the acquisition of a computer system for the first time consider employing the relatively expensive services of an EDP consultant?

23. While reviewing a list of benefits from a computer vendor's proposal, you note an item that reads: "improvements in management decision making—$50,000 per year." How would you interpret this item? What influence should it have on the computer acquisition decision?

24. You are participating in a feasibility study for a company that is considering the acquisition of its first computer system. The company's management has decided that a warehouse adjoining the main plant should be used to house the computer system if it is acquired. This warehouse was built only five years ago, but the company has not used it since discontinuing a major product line three years ago. The warehouse was rented briefly to another firm but is not presently in use for any purpose.

You feel that the warehouse would make an excellent location for a new computer facility. How should a cost of space utilization for the computer facility be determined for inclusion in the feasibility study? Discuss.

Problems and Cases

25. The Schulte Corporation has recently decided to replace its computer system with a larger, more advanced model. Proposals have been received from three vendors. As chairman of the Evaluation Committee, you have prepared a list of nine criteria for comparing these proposals and have ranked each vendor on a scale of 1 to 10 on each criterion. The criteria and assigned ranks are as follows.

1. hardware performance: vendor A-9, vendor B-8, vendor C-6
2. software capability: A-8, B-6, C-7
3. system reliability: A-7, B-9, C-6
4. rental cost: A-7, B-6, C-9

    5. ease of use: A-7, B-8, C-7
    6. ease of conversion: A-8, B-9, C-6
    7. modularity: A-8, B-9, C-5
    8. vendor support: A-6, B-9, C-7
    9. documentation: A-8, B-7, C-6

You have prepared a tentative set of weightings for the nine criteria as follows: hardware performance—50, software capability—50, system reliability—30, rental cost—30, ease of use—50, ease of conversion—20, modularity—20, vendor support—50, documentation—20. Upon reviewing these with the manager of Information Systems, you receive the following reaction: "These weights are generally fine, except that vendor support isn't that critical to us anymore. We have an experienced and capable staff. I'd give that a weight of only about 20. On the other hand, software capability is extremely critical. How good is the operating system? What kind of utilities, data management packages, and compilers are they offering? I think that ought to rate a 70."

REQUIRED

    a) Prepare a point scoring analysis of the three vendor proposals using your tentative set of weights.
    b) Prepare a point scoring analysis using the weights as adjusted by the manager of Information Systems.
    c) What conclusions can you reach as a result of this analysis? Discuss.

26. The Valentine Company is acquiring a new computer system and must decide how the acquisition is to be financed. If the system is purchased, it will cost $550,000, and the separate maintenance contract will cost $2,000 per month. An investment tax credit of ten percent could be taken. The machine would be depreciated using the accelerated cost recovery system. Assume a marginal income tax rate of fifty percent. Trade-in value of the machine would be about $360,000 at the time of purchase and would decline at approximately $3,000 per month for each month thereafter. Assume that there is no salvage value.

    If the system is leased, the monthly payment will be $12,000 per month, which includes maintenance. There will be no extra-use charges. The lease contract could be canceled at the end of any one-year period at no penalty. An option to purchase is included in the lease contract that specifies that the customer may purchase the system at the end of any year at the following prices.

End of year	1	2	3	4	5	6–10
Purchase price	$500,000	$430,000	$360,000	$290,000	$220,000	$150,000

REQUIRED

    a) Prepare for both the purchase and the lease situation a schedule of annual and cumulative cash flows at the beginning of the first year and during each year for ten years afterward.

b) Management is interested in the impact of the trade-in value on the comparison of purchasing to leasing. Prepare a schedule showing the "net purchase cost," which is the cumulative cash outflow under purchasing minus the trade-in value, over the ten-year period.

c) Considering only the cash flow considerations and ignoring the effects of discounting of cash flows, which of the two choices is more attractive?

d) If the cash flows were discounted, how would this affect the relative attractiveness of leasing and purchasing?

e) Cite some factors in addition to those mentioned above that would have some bearing on the decision.

27. You are an accountant employed by the Argus Corporation. You are serving as an accounting consultant to a software evaluation and selection project. The choice has been narrowed down to three software packages (call them package #1, package #2, and package #3), and you have decided to use requirements costing to make the final choice.

You have gathered the following information.

☐ Argus has identified five features that it would like the system to have. Label them A, B, C, D, and E.

☐ Package #1 costs $100,000 and possesses all the desirable features except E. However, an optional routine that incorporates E can be purchased for an additional $20,000.

☐ Package #2 costs $80,000 and possesses all features except B and E. However, feature B could be developed at a cost of $25,000, and feature E can be developed for $10,000.

☐ Package #3 costs $80,000 and possesses all features except B and D. For this package, feature B could be constructed for $25,000, and feature D for $15,000.

REQUIRED

a) Determine the total cost required to buy each package and, where necessary, modify it to contain all desirable features. Which package looks best?

b) Suppose that you could develop feature E for package #1 for a cost of $10,000, which would mean that you wouldn't have to buy the optional subroutine associated with this feature. How would this change (if at all) your answer to part (a)?

c) Suppose that the project team decides that feature D is an unnecessary luxury that need not be developed. How would this change (if at all) your answer to part (a)? [Note: Ignore the changes in assumptions mentioned in part (b).]

d) List some factors other than package features and costs that might affect your choice among these three packages.

28. You are a systems consultant for Cooper, Price, and Arthur, CPAs. During your country club's annual match play tournament, your second-round

opponent is Mr. Frank Fender, owner of a large automobile dealership. During the course of the round, Fender describes to you a proposal he has recently received from Turnkey Systems Corporation to install a computer in his dealership. The computer would take over data processing for inventories, receivables, payroll, accounts payable, and general ledger accounting. Turnkey personnel would install the system and train Fender's employees. The proposed system is to cost $70,000.

Suppose that Fender asks your opinion of this proposal. Without going into too much detail, identify the major themes you would try to touch upon in responding to his inquiry.

29. **Note:** To complete this problem, it is necessary that your school's library subscribe to *Datapro 70: The EDP Buyer's Bible* or to a similar data processing library service.

Read the report entitled "All about Minicomputers" in Volume 1 of *Datapro 70*. Using the comparison charts at the back of the report, identify five minicomputer systems manufactured by five different companies.

REQUIRED

Prepare a table listing the following information for each of these computers.

Name of computer	Computer #1	Computer #2	Etc.
Internal storage:			
Capacity of basic system, bytes			
Maximum capacity, bytes			
Access time, microseconds			
Mass storage capabilities:			
Floppy disk drive (yes or no)			
Pack disk drive (yes or no)			
Input/output devices:			
Punched card reader-speed			
Punched card punch-speed			
Line printer-speed			
Reel-to-reel tape drive-speed			
CRT (yes or no)			
Software support:			
COBOL (yes or no)			
BASIC (yes or no)			
Multiprogramming (yes or no)			
General accounting packages (yes or no)			
Data base management (yes or no)			
Pricing:			
Purchase price of basic system, $			
Monthly rental of basic system, $			

30. XYZ Conglomerate Company has completed a feasibility study to upgrade their computer system. Management asked for a detailed schedule of the benefits of this new system. The following document was provided.

BENEFITS TO BE DERIVED FROM THE NEW SYSTEM

1. Production:
   a) Marketing forecasting is presently in dollars per product line. Calculation of units by product line takes an estimated two man days, a total of $80. This saving would be repeated each time the market forecast was updated, presumably monthly. The program to calculate the forecast in units would also be more accurate than the present method of applying factors to dollar value. $ 960
   b) More effective inventory control would permit an overall reduction in inventory. The ability to quickly establish total requirements would help to overcome parts "stock out" situations. For this calculation, we estimate a 10% inventory reduction. The cost of capital at XYZ Conglomerate Company approximates 20%, and the benefit then approximates 20% of $100,000. $20,000
   c) Evaluation of changes to plans will be possible in detail. This is not so under our manual system. Parts explosions are time-consuming and can only be done monthly. The impact here would be increased production flexibility and the reduction of sales losses due to Finished Goods stock outs. We estimate that this can be valued as the equivalent of hiring two clerks. $15,000 $35,960

2. Engineering:
   a) Use of the computer in filing and updating Bills of Material would save 40% of the Industrial Engineer's time. $ 4,000
   b) The improved updating of files, which includes the Bills of Material and Product Structure files which affect many areas, should save a minimum 25% of one clerk (if we took all areas, this would probably be closer to 50%). $ 1,500

c) Estimated clerical savings in labour calculations, rates, and bonus detail is two days per
week or 40% of one person. $ 2,000 $ 7,500

3. Sales:

a) Improved reporting will enable Sales Staff
and Sales Management to react more quickly
to prevailing conditions. The implied benefit would be sales increases, especially during
promotions, and a better sales/expense ratio.
We are assuming an improvement in sales of
only $1,000 per man for a total of $5,000. $ 5,000

4. Marketing:

a) Revised reports and an improved forecasting
system will help in establishing sales trends
and will help Production Department flexibility and inventory control.

5. Accounting:

a) Standard costing of all Bills of Material, and
in fact, the side effect of being able to cost
new products quickly, can be expressed as
the equivalent of saving 30–40% of the Plant
Accountant's time. $ 3,000

b) A revised incentive earnings and payroll system installed on the computer should reduce
the Payroll Department clerical labour from
roughly three days to one day—possible ben-
efit of 40% of one clerk. $ 2,400 $ 5,400

TOTAL $53,860

REQUIRED

As financial officer of the company, which of the above benefits would you
accept as relevant to the cost justification of the system? Defend your answer. (SMAC Examination)

31. In the fall of 1978, the President of the ABC Company was informed that
the introduction of a new product line and the demands imposed by a
recently introduced job costing system would mean a serious evaluation
of ABC's current manual operations should be made in order to determine their ability to cope with an expanding workload. The President
decided that a feasibility study should be conducted by a group of key

company personnel with the help of any outside organization whom his executive committee felt might provide some valuable insight to the problems being faced. He also directed that the study committee should carry out a thorough feasibility study and on the basis of their findings, report to him their evaluation of three alternatives:

1. Introduce a larger, general-purpose computer capable of processing an integrated management information system encompassing many company activities.
2. Evaluate the use of a minicomputer capable of handling only the order entry, inventory and job costing systems.
3. Continue with the present manual operations..

When questioned by various members of the study group regarding his own ranking concerning the relative importance of each of the various selection criteria, the President indicated that the ongoing cost of whatever system was selected would be his prime concern.

He also mentioned that he would consider the cost of new system development to be important, as would the payback period of each of the alternatives. The President also pointed out that any good system would provide timely and accurate information concerning the operations of the company and would provide the internal controls necessary to satisfy both the internal and external auditors. Since the Board of Directors had been actively pursuing new product opportunities through diversification and mergers, he felt that the ability of a system to handle an increasing workload would be of concern as well.

At other times, during discussions with various members of the study committee, the President indicated that some factors, although not of concern to the same degree as those above, should be studied and considered by the committee. Since the company was located in a smaller centre, about two hours driving time from the nearest major city, he felt the recommended system should provide a degree of reliability. Any hardware problems would mean the system would be down for at least two hours before a service technician would arrive from the city.

The recommended system should provide enough flexibility to eventually support new applications and should have sufficient storage capacity to meet current data storage requirements and provide the capacity to expand with the new applications.

Toward the end of the feasibility study, the committee developed the following alternative evaluation matrix.

The various evaluation criteria that the President had indicated should be analyzed are listed down the left-hand side of the matrix and numbered 1 through 10. The committee's findings concerning the relative ability of each alternative to meet these criteria are shown in Columns I, II, and III.

Alternative Evaluation Matrix

EVALUATION CRITERIA	ALTERNATIVE		
	I LARGER COMPUTER	II MINICOMPUTER	III MANUAL SYSTEM
Performance			
1. Accuracy	Very good	Very good	Fair
2. Control capability	Very good	Very good	Poor
3. Flexibility	Very good	Good	Fair
4. Growth potential	Very good	Limited to 3 years without degradation	Very poor
5. Reliability	Good	Good	Fair
6. Speed	Very good	Good	Can't meet schedules (poor)
7. Storage capacity	Good	Good	No problem
Costs			
8. System development	$60,000	$40,000	0
9. System operation	$10.00 to $1.50 per product	$8.50 to $1.30 per product	$19.00 per product
10. Payback	15 months	12 months	n.a.

REQUIRED

a) The President must choose a committee to conduct the feasibility study. Who should be represented on this committee?

b) Identify and explain the various steps which the study committee should follow in conducting the feasibility study.

c) i) On the basis of the information given, apply a weighting factor and explain why you chose that particular weighting factor for each of the evaluation criteria. Most important factor(s) should be given a weight factor of 10, important criteria a factor of 5 and less important a weight of 3.

ii) Rank each alternative on the basis of its ability to meet each criteria and assign a rating from 1 to 5. The ranks are as follows:

very poor —1
poor —2
fair —3
good —4
very good —5

For example, in considering the speed of each alternative, the manual system, being the slowest of the three, might be given a rating of 1, the minicomputer would be next at 4 and the larger computer, since it is the fastest, would be rated at 5.

Finally, by multiplying the weighting factor of each selection criteria times the rating of each alternative, establish the weighted rating for each component. Based upon the total rate for the system, recommend the system which best meets the overall needs of the company. (SMAC Examination)

32. The Jacob J. Cohen company avoided the use of computers for many years because J. J. disliked them. J. J. recently expired suddenly, and his successor (and daughter), Sheila J. Cohen, has an open mind with regard to computers. She has decided to conduct a cost/benefit analysis of various systems for a period of three years, and has established the following facts:

1. Four alternatives are to be considered:
   a) To keep on with the present manual system.
   b) To use the services of Sharecomp, the only computer service bureau providing local service.
   c) To purchase a mini-computer from the C.B.M. Corporation, and modify the software to suit Cohen Co.
   d) To contract with Advanced Data Products for the provision of a suitable in-house system.

2. The present manual system uses four accounting machines that rent for $300 per month each, and employs six clerks at an annual average salary of $12,000. The predicted expansion of the firm will require one extra accounting machine and one extra clerk in year three. The cost of the accounting machines, and the salaries of the clerks will increase by at least 10% each year. If the manual system is replaced, $5,000 per clerk will be needed for severance pay.

3. Sharecomp has simplified the Cohen business information needs down to a series of transactions. It is prepared to sign a three year contract to process all transactions at a fixed price of $1.35 per transaction. There will be around 40,000 transactions in the first year, increasing by 20% for each of the following two years. One clerk would be needed to provide the necessary interaction with Sharecomp.

4. C.B.M. (a very large firm) will sell a suitable system for $90,000 at the beginning of the first year. Maintenance for the first year will be $9,000, and is expected to increase by 12% per year. All initial software will be included in the purchase price.

   One programmer-operator at a salary of $25,000 per year, rising by 10% each year, will be needed, and two clerks. This system will accommodate the expected expansion of Cohen Co., and allow for some new developments.

5. Advanced Data Products (a small firm) will lease a suitable system to the company, and develop the software needed. It will agree to a three year contract at a fixed price of $40,000 per year, including software maintenance, and a development charge of $35,000 to be paid during the first year. The system will also accommodate the expected expansion, and would require two clerks, but no operator. It also would allow for some new developments.

a) What is the net cost of each alternative, discounted by a cost of capital of 20% to a present value? (For ease of calculation, assume that all costs are incurred at the beginning of each year. As a result, the costs for the first year will not be discounted. The costs for the second and third years will be discounted by factors of .83 and .69 respectively.)

b) What additional advantages might be offered by each alternative?

c) Considering the risks involved, which alternative would you select? Justify your selection. (SMAC Examination)

33. The Widget Manufacturing Company is a major producer of widgets with total sales of approximately $50 million annually. Their information systems department currently has an ABC Model 115 computer which operates twelve hours per day, five days per week, processing the usual applications of payroll, general accounting, inventory control and accounts receivable in batch mode. This equipment also supports an online order entry system with four cathode ray tube (CRT) terminals located in the sales department. This application processes an average of 240,000 transactions per year.

The company prepared a two year information systems plan. D. MacTavish, the Director of Information Systems for Widget, determined that the present computer could absorb any additional workload caused by rapidly increasing sales. This could be handled by scheduling a full second shift and possibly a third shift. The present computer would not have sufficient memory or be fast enough, however, to handle a new production scheduling system which was planned and which would require more terminals to be added in the production planning department and at several locations throughout the plant. This new system would increase the number of terminal transactions by approximately 720,000 per year but would require approximately one year to develop and implement following the availability of a new system.

After a presentation to the President and Executive Committee, MacTavish was authorized to prepare the hardware and software specifications for a system which would meet the needs of Widget for the next two years. Also, because the company was expanding so quickly, MacTavish was asked by the President to include the cost of renting space in a nearby office building in which the entire information systems department could be located. This would provide space in the Widget head office building for additional staff which were needed by other company departments. MacTavish was asked to prepare a financial summary showing the cost of the present system and any proposed systems for presentation to the company Board of Directors.

The Widget information systems department currently occupies approximately 3,300 square feet of space in the basement of the Widget head office building.

MacTavish prepared the specifications for the new systems and sent

them to the ABC Computer Company, the supplier of the present computer. He also invited the PQR Company to submit a proposal for their
equipment and software, and decided to ask the XYZ Service Bureau to
respond with the prices they would charge to process Widget's information systems. Included in the specifications were all processing volumes
and transaction rates for existing systems as well as those which were expected for the proposed application. Also included was the fact that
Widget currently used 75 reels of magnetic tape for storing master files
and for security backup of important disk files. This figure was expected
to increase to 100 reels with the implementation of the production scheduling system.

The important facts from each of the three proposals which were received are as follows.

The ABC Proposal. The ABC representative recommended a Model 138
computer which leased for $273,478 per year. This system would have
sufficient memory and be fast enough to handle all current applications
plus the new system. Since it is also a member of the same "family" of
computers as Widget's Model 115, it would use the same software as the
115 and, therefore, require the same amount of training as was needed
on the present equipment. He pointed out, however, that the larger 138
could use a new series of terminals which ABC had recently announced
and would enable Widget to acquire the additional terminals it needed
to replace its present terminals at a total cost of $14,100 per year for the
two years. This new system would require the same space as the present
Model 115.

The PQR Proposal. The PQR Company recommended a Model 906 system. The equipment which would be located in the Widget computer
centre would cost $213,660 per year and all of the necessary terminals
would be supplied at a cost of $9,468. PQR's marketing policy differed
from that of ABC in that all software and staff training costs were included
in the price of the equipment. They also were willing to provide a discount of $66,000 during the second year if Widget would sign a two year
lease for the equipment. The PQR proposal indicated that their equipment would fit into an area equivalent to that occupied by the present
computer.

The XYZ Proposal. The XYZ Service Bureau proposal involved the installation of a minicomputer at the Widget Company computer centre
which would be used for editing and balancing all batch input. The data
would be sent over a telephone line several times per day to a large computer located at the Service Bureau where it would be processed. Output
would be returned to Widget over the same communications line to the
minicomputer where it would be stored on a disk until it could be printed
out and distributed. The online order entry system and the new production scheduling system would use terminals connected to the large computer at the Service Bureau and any printed output from these systems
would be sent by telephone line to the minicomputer for printing and

distribution. The cost to Widget for leasing the minicomputer would be $32,724 per year and terminals would be leased for $11,000 annually. The cost of the communications line between the minicomputer at the Widget offices and the large system at the Service Bureau would be $21,420 each year with an installation charge the first year of $4,020.

On the basis of benchmark tests which XYZ had performed using existing Widget programs running on the large computer at the Service Bureau, XYZ estimated that the cost of running all batch programs would be $132,000 per year. The cost of storing the backup and master file tapes for Widget would be one dollar per tape per year.

XYZ used a price schedule for online applications based on the number of transactions entered through the terminals. Their price was quoted at ten cents per transaction. Software charges were included in the prices quoted. As an incentive to Widget, XYZ offered a volume discount of $109,800 during the second year and agreed to provide all necessary training of Widget staff during the first year of the agreement at no cost. Widget would have to pay for training during the second year. Since XYZ used an ABC computer at their Service Bureau, Widget staff could take the same courses and at the same cost as they would have required had the larger ABC machine been selected.

In the opinion of XYZ, the installation of a minicomputer by Widget would reduce the space requirements in their computer centre by 450 square feet.

Space Cost. During negotiations with the owner of a nearby office building, MacTavish was able to negotiate the lease of space for his department at a rate of $10 per square foot per year, the amount of space dependent on the alternative selected by the Widget Board of Directors.

Present Computer Costs. The following is a schedule of present computer costs:

Central site hardware (per month)	$16,764.00
Software (per month)	1,516.00
CRT terminals (per month)	1,292.50
Training costs (total annual cost)	7,000.00

NOTE: All hardware and software is leased. The company follows the policy of capitalizing lease payments for financial statement purposes.

REQUIRED   As MacTavish, write a report to the Board of Directors recommending which proposal to accept. Your report should include the quantitative and qualitative aspects of each proposal. Indicate what impact, if any, the decision regarding the development of the proposed production scheduling system would have on your recommendation. (SMAC Examination)

34. You are an administrative services specialist for the CPA firm of Xeron, York, and Zapata. The Avalon Electronics Company, one of your firm's clients, has asked you to study for them the feasibility of computer ac-

quisition. The company has a sales volume of $10,000,000 and has been having some problems with profit margins, making only a two percent return on sales as opposed to the industry average of ten percent.

The applications that Avalon would like to automate initially are payroll, accounts receivable and billing, parts inventory, finished goods inventory, and general ledger. A need for frequent inquiry into the parts inventory and finished goods inventory files exists. The firm also expects to grow by a factor of fifty percent in the next five years. You have determined that the required equipment configuration includes a central processor with a 512,000 character storage capacity, a disk drive unit with a 64 million character storage capacity, a flexible disk input/output unit, three CRT display/keyboard units, and a line printer that operates at 160 lines per minute. Monthly rental for a configuration of this sort would be $3,000.

You estimate costs of systems personnel as follows: one systems analyst-programmer at $2,400 per month, one operator at $1,600 per month, and one full-time and one half-time CRT operator at $1,000 and $500 per month, respectively.

Monthly rental of software would total $500 per month, and other miscellaneous overhead would total about $2,000 monthly.

Initial outlay costs for this system would include expenditures for site preparation, file conversion, hiring and training of personnel, and modification and testing of programs. You estimate that these costs will total $40,000.

You have estimated that the new computer system would generate cost savings in two primary areas, which are clerical costs and inventory carrying costs. Implementation of the new system would initially reduce the number of people in accounts receivable and billing from four to one, and in payroll, from two to one. Each of these employees makes $1,200 per month. Also, the number of people in the parts inventory section could be reduced from four to two. These people each make $1,000 per month.

If Avalon does not computerize, in five years six people will be needed in accounts receivable and billing instead of four, three will be needed in payroll instead of two, and six will be needed in parts inventory instead of four. If the firm does computerize, no new people would be required in these areas in five years, and in addition, the accounts payable and job order cost functions could be computerized by that time, saving a net of three additional employees. You estimate that the net impact of these factors will be that clerical cost savings will increase by thirty percent per year each year through the first five years following installation of the computer, if the computer is acquired.

You feel confident that the increased efficiency in reordering and control of parts inventory resulting from computerization would reduce the company's inventory balance of $1,600,000 by twenty percent. The

funds thus freed would generate savings at an annual rate of fifteen percent (the firm's cost of capital). You estimate that the amount of cost savings from inventory reduction will increase by ten percent per year over
the next five years if the computer is acquired.

Although you did not attempt to estimate the dollar amount, you feel
that significant intangible benefits would accrue to the firm if it acquired
a computer. These include improved production efficiency, better customer service, and better management reports and decision making.

You have estimated that after five years Avalon will require a CPU
with 1,024,000 characters of main memory, an additional disk drive, an
additional CRT terminal, and several additional programs. You project
that this represents an increase in hardware and software rental charges
of approximately twenty percent per year. In addition, another full-time
CRT operator will have to be hired, and the salaries of all computer personnel will have to be increased regularly; this translates into an average
annual increase in computer personnel costs of fifteen percent. Finally,
overhead costs will increase at an annual rate of ten percent.

REQUIRED

a) Calculate the total monthly operating costs required for the proposed
   system during the month immediately following its implementation.
   Determine the total monthly cost savings from personnel reductions
   and inventory reductions during that month.
b) To simplify your analysis, assume that monthly costs and cost savings
   remain constant from month to month within each year, and that the
   percentage increases described in the problem all take place at once
   as Avalon Electronics moves from one year into the next. Prepare a
   schedule showing total monthly operating costs (in each of the four
   major categories described in the problem) for years one through five,
   and showing total monthly cost savings (in each of the two major categories given) for years one through five.
c) Convert the monthly cost and cost savings totals computed in part (b)
   to annual figures. Then prepare a table with six columns and four
   rows as follows: columns for the initial outlay and each of the first
   five years; and rows for cost, cost savings, net inflow or outflow (cost
   savings minus cost), and cumulative inflow or outflow. Complete the
   table. What is the payback period for the computer acquisition?
d) (Optional for those students who have studied discounted cash flow
   analysis.) What is the net present value of the computer acquisition
   investment?
e) Identify some factors not reflected in the calculations outlined above
   that should also be considered in the feasibility decision. Considering
   all factors, would you recommend that Avalon Electronics acquire a
   computer at this time? Why or why not?

References

Bierman, Harold, Jr., and Seymour Smidt. *The Capital Budgeting Decision.* 5th ed. New York: Macmillan, 1980.

Buss, Martin J. D. "How to Rank Computer Projects." *Harvard Business Review* (January/February 1983): 118–125.

Caswell, Stephen A. "Computer Peripherals: A Revolution Is Coming." *Datamation* (May 25, 1979): 83–87.

Cortada, James W. *EDP Costs and Charges: Finance, Budgets, and Cost Control in Data Processing.* Englewood Cliffs, N.J.: Prentice-Hall, 1980.

Crane, Janet. "Trends in DP Budgets." *Datamation* (May 1981): 140–150.

Cunningham, Peter A., and Walter P. Smith. "Computer Services: A Menu of Options." *Datamation* (May 25, 1979): 89–91.

Datapro Research Corporation. *Datapro 70: The EDP Buyer's Bible.* Delran, N.J.: Datapro Research Corporation, 1986.

Geran, Michael J. "Mainframes: How Long the Mainstay for Their Vendors?" *Datamation* (May 25, 1979): 98–102.

King, John Leslie, and Edward L. Schrems. "Cost-Benefit Analysis in Information Systems Development and Operation." *Computing Surveys* (March 1978): 19–34.

King, Karl G., and Mark L. Hildebrand. "How to Help a Client Select a Data Processing System." *Practical Accountant* (September 1979): 43–53.

Miller, Frederick W. "Used Computers: A Lower Cost Alternative." *Infosystems* (March 1980): 66–70.

Milne, Bruce. "Staying Alive in the Turnkey Systems Business." *Mini-Micro Systems* (May 1979): 127–130.

Page, John R., and H. Paul Hooper. "How to Buy a Computer." *CPA Journal* (September 1979): 39–45.

Parker, M. M. "Enterprise Information Analysis: Cost-Benefit Analysis and the Data-Managed System." *IBM Systems Journal* **21** (1982): 108–123.

Porochnia, Leonard. *The Minicomputer: To Buy or Not to Buy?* New York: National Association of Accountants, 1982.

Radell, Nicholas J. "Optimizing the Management Consultant." *Data Management* (August 1977): 32–36.

Schmedel, Scott. "Taking on the Industry Giant: An Interview with Gene M. Amdahl." *Harvard Business Review* (March/April 1980): 82–93.

Smith, Robert D. "Measuring the Intangible Benefits of Computer-Based Information Systems." *Journal of Systems Management* (September 1983): 22–26.

Szatrowski, Ted. "Rent, Lease, or Buy?" *Datamation* (February 1976): 59–68.

Verity, John W. "1986 DP Budget Survey." *Datamation* (April 1, 1986): 74–78.

C H A P T E R 1 3

Systems Implementation

LEARNING OBJECTIVES

Careful study of this chapter should enable students to:

- [ ] Describe the steps in the systems implementation process.
- [ ] Utilize the Gantt chart and the PERT technique for planning and controlling complex projects such as systems implementation.

After the system analysis and design have been completed and management has approved the recommendations of the systems study group for system modification or choice of a vendor from whom to acquire equipment, the focus of the systems investigation is transformed dramatically from the realms of analysis, deliberation, and creative thinking to the realm of action. The plans and theories of the systems study group must be put into practice in the arena of the real world. This period of time, between the acceptance of recommendations by management and the acceptance of the new system as an operational success, is referred to as the period of systems implementation.

Depending on the size of an organization and the level of sophistication of its information system, a systems implementation project could involve either a major revision to a manual system, conversion from a manual to an automated system, or conversion from an automated system to a larger and/or more advanced automated system. Within a computer system, implementation often refers to the development of and conversion to a major software system. However, systems implementation generally involves the performance of a fairly well defined set of activities. The first section of this chapter will discuss the steps in the implementation process, using implementation of a computer system as the primary point of reference. The second and final section of the chapter provides an extensive discussion of *PERT* (Program Evaluation and Review Technique), which is a commonly used technique for the planning and scheduling of complex projects such as systems implementation.

The Implementation Process

Any major implementation project will involve the following activities: planning and scheduling of the implementation process, organizational planning and personnel administration, final systems design and testing, establishment of standards of performance and control procedures, site preparation, conversion from old to new system, and follow-up review and evaluation of results. This section discusses each of these activities in detail. Whereas most of the discussion relates directly to computer implementation, many of the concepts also apply to major revision of manual systems or major software development projects.

Planning and scheduling

During the implementation period, many varying activities will be proceeding simultaneously. A great deal of planning and coordination is necessary to ensure that these activities are accomplished smoothly and with dispatch. Responsibility for the performance of each function must be fixed, and a timetable for the completion of each task must be established. Estimates of the cost of each activity must be developed for purposes of preparing a financial budget. Provisions should be made for monitoring the performance of all activities and making adjustments where necessary to ensure continued progress. These activities are generally the responsibility of an implementation team composed of users, executives, and systems personnel.

Two techniques that provide an explicit framework for scheduling, co-ordinating, expediting, and monitoring the progress of the implementation effort are PERT (to be discussed later in the chapter) and the *Gantt chart.* The Gantt chart is a form of bar chart adapted to project planning and control. Project activities are listed on the left-hand side of the chart, and units of time in days or weeks are shown across the top. Corresponding to each activity, a bar is drawn showing the time period over which that activity is expected to be performed. A sample Gantt chart illustrating these concepts appears in Fig. 13.1.

As a project proceeds, a procedure should be adopted for recording the completion of each activity on the Gantt chart. In Fig. 13.1 the procedure used for this purpose is to fill in the open space within each bar in proportion to the percentage of completion of each activity. Then at any time, it is possible to determine quickly which activities are on schedule and which are behind schedule. This capacity to show in graphic form the entire schedule for a large, complex project, including progress to date and current status, is the primary advantage of the Gantt chart.

Rather than focus on implementation techniques, some authorities stress the importance of implementation strategies in planning for systems imple-mentation. For example, Alter describes a strategy he calls "implementation risk analysis."[1] This involves identifying in advance those conditions that de-crease the likelihood of successful implementation. These conditions, called "risk factors," include such things as nonexistent or unwilling users, large numbers of users, inability to specify usage patterns in advance, inability to predict and cushion impact on all parties, lack or loss of management support, and lack of experience with similar systems. Once the potential risk factors are identified for a particular system, implementation strategies are devised to cope with each risk factor. Among the possible implementation strategies are testing prototype systems, using an evolutionary approach, simplifying the system, obtaining user participation or commitment, obtaining management support, providing training, providing for ongoing user assistance, and tai-loring the system to the user's capabilities. Alter goes so far as to suggest that if adequate implementation strategies cannot be devised to deal with the iden-tified risk factors, then the project should be either abandoned or deferred.

Organizational planning and personnel administration

Any change in established routines of work in an organization requires atten-tion to the human factors involved in the change. As in systems analysis and design, the participation of employees in the process of implementation will tend to prevent serious problems of resistance to change. A policy of com-municating openly and honestly with employees during this period is advis-

---

[1]Steven L. Alter, *Decision Support Systems: Current Practice and Continuing Challenges* (Reading, Mass.: Addison-Wesley, 1980), chapter 7.

FIGURE 13.1
Sample Gantt chart.

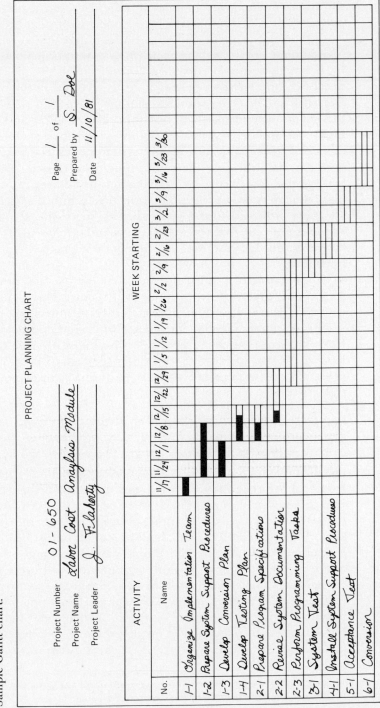

able. Management and the systems group should be alert to sense any deterioration in employee morale or other serious problems and should be prepared to take appropriate steps to deal with such problems.

According to many authorities, it is important to recognize that any organizational work system is made up of two interdependent systems—a technical system and a social system. The technical system consists of the tasks, processes, and technologies required to accomplish the organizational objective, such as converting inputs to outputs. The social system involves people—their skills, attitudes, values, and interrelationships, and the incentive structures and authority structures within which they work. Clearly, the performance of the organizational work system depends upon the performance of both the technical and social systems and upon the smooth interaction of these two systems. Many systems implementation failures can be attributed to systems designers who concentrated on the technical system without devoting adequate attention to the social system. Successful systems implementation requires not only that the effectiveness and efficiency of the technical system be improved, but also that the quality of working life among employees be improved.[2]

In a company acquiring a computer for the first time, the areas of personnel and organization planning will require much greater attention than will those areas in a company that is merely converting from one computer system to another. The latter company will experience many of the same problems, but on a much smaller scale. Examples of problems commonly confronted are communication with employees, adjustment of organization structure, selection of personnel, relocation of displaced personnel, and personnel training.

Communication with employees. The period prior to computer installation can be a very difficult one from the standpoint of an organization's relationship with its employees. Once the fact is known that a computer will soon be installed, the natural reaction of employees to the uncertainty of the situation is one of apprehension. If it remains unchecked, such apprehension could well degenerate into an attitude of resistance and distrust.

If proper employee relations policies are adhered to during the initial period of systems survey and analysis, communication with employees prior to computer installation will follow naturally. Employees should be made aware of the possibility that the organization will undergo a major systems change, and they should be informed of management's plans for personnel in the event of such a change. Management must now provide evidence that it fully intends to honor the reassurances made during the survey. Specific plans relating to relocation of displaced personnel, staffing of new positions from the existing employee group, training programs offered to employees,

---

[2]Robert P. Bostrom and J. Stephen Heinen, "MIS Problems and Failures: A Socio-Technical Perspective, Part I: The Causes," *MIS Quarterly* (September 1977): 17–32.

and so forth, should be announced. Even though such announcements may not placate everyone in the short run, their long-run effect will almost certainly be better than policies of silence or glib reassurance. Either of these latter policies is likely to generate resentment, resistance, and a loss of morale among employees and perhaps cause the company to lose employees who could otherwise be assigned to jobs in the new system.

Announcements to employees regarding computerization should always emphasize the positive aspects of the change—opportunities to devote more attention to the creative aspects of one's job while the computer performs the routine functions, opportunities for more rapid advancement and higher salaries, and so forth. The need for cooperation of employees at all levels of the organization to facilitate successful implementation should be stressed. Throughout the entire employee relations effort, the interest and concern of top management should be made clear.

Adjustment of organization structure.   A company's first venture into computerization of data processing will require significant adjustments to its organization structure. A new set of departments will have to be staffed. Major categories of jobs to be established and defined include analyst, programmer, computer operator, and various managers. The problem of the appropriate level in the organization structure for the head of data processing will have to be resolved. The structure of the data processing department itself will have to be established. Even a company converting from an existing computer system to a larger or more advanced system may be faced with problems of expansion of the data processing organization, or a major change in its status in the company organization.

Selection of personnel.   Once the personnel needs have been specified, the task of filling these needs must begin. Considerations relating to employee morale indicate that employees whose jobs may be replaced or significantly altered by computer acquisition should be given the first chance at testing for positions in the new system. It may even be easier to train these people in computer operations than to orient computer specialists to the company's operations and procedures. It is likely, however, that some positions will have to be filled by outsiders.

Once again, the problems faced by a company computerizing for the first time are much greater in the area of personnel selection than they are for other firms. Such a company should probably seek professional assistance for this purpose. Usually such assistance can be obtained from the vendor. Computer work demands a unique set of aptitudes and abilities, including logical thinking, attention to detail, problem-solving ability, and the capacity to tolerate frustration and hard work. Selection of supervisory personnel in this field requires even greater care. These problems are compounded by the existence of a shortage of qualified computer specialists in the labor market.

Relocation of displaced personnel.   Computerization will result in the elimination of a number of clerical and some supervisory positions. The manner in which this problem is approached will have a significant effect upon employee morale and loyalty. As stated above, some of these employees may be capable of obtaining positions in the new system. Others may be transferred to other departments within the organization. Since the period of preparation for installation will extend up to a year or more, the suspension of hiring when combined with the normal rate of attrition, which is generally high among clerical employees, may effect a partial solution to the problem of personnel displacement. For those employees who are nearing retirement age, the opportunity for early retirement can be provided. In those cases in which there appears to be no alternative to termination of an employee's services, the company should give a generous separation bonus and assistance in finding a comparable position in another organization.

A company's treatment of personnel displaced as a result of computer acquisition will affect the loyalty and morale not only of employees directly affected but of all employees throughout the organization. A company's actions in this regard will be interpreted as a reflection of its attitude toward its employees in general. The problem is even more serious as it relates to displaced supervisors, who may have given many years of loyal service to the company and will probably be most difficult to relocate in comparable positions. Careful planning and an attitude of social responsibility are requisites for the organization to resolve these problems successfully.

Personnel training.   During the implementation of a major information systems change, employees at all levels of the organization require training in order to perform their jobs in the new system effectively. Computer operators must be taught the operational procedures they are to follow. Training of programmers and analysts must not only emphasize the technical aspects of their jobs but must also provide an orientation to the organization's policies and operations. Employees who will supply input to the new system must be taught the correct way to do this. Managers and other users must be taught how to interact with the system to obtain the information they require. Even those employees who initially have no interaction with the new system should be given orientation sessions designed to develop their understanding of the new system and what it can accomplish for them.

Training programs may be given by vendor representatives, outside training specialists, and/or fellow employees. Most systems vendors provide some technical training at little or no additional charge to the customer organization. Employees within the organization who are among the first to receive training can often do a good job of training their fellow employees. It is becoming increasingly common for systems vendors to supply their customers with self-study manuals and/or special software modules that provide computer-assisted instruction. Although an effective training program may be time-consuming and expensive, it is also a key to the successful implementation of any new information system.

Final systems design

The core of the implementation process is the detailed design of the new system. The preliminary systems design developed during the survey and analysis stage, as modified to obtain management approval, provides the starting point for the final systems design. For each application of the computer, the content and format of input, output, and file records must be established, and the relationships of individual record types within the overall data base must be specified. The flow of documents and reports within the organization must be modified to incorporate the role of the computer. Detailed document flowcharts and systems flowcharts are the primary design tools for this purpose.

The programming process is a major part of the final systems design. As outlined in Chapter 6, the steps in the programming process include preparing program flowcharts and decision tables, coding the program modules, desk checking the code listings, compiling the program modules, and correcting the programs for diagnostic messages indicating errors in program code. If the programs are being developed for a new computer system that has not yet been installed, the compilation and correction process will require the use of outside equipment, generally provided by the vendor. Another important part of the programming process is the compilation of final systems documentation in the form of a system reference manual for users, analysts, and programmers. Closely related to this is the preparation of operating documentation in the form of run manuals to assist computer operators in running the programs on the computer.

Also during the final systems design process, plans must be developed for the conversion to the new system. Training programs must be prepared. Plans for testing the new systems and programs must be established. A detailed conversion plan and schedule should be prepared. A processing schedule for the new system should be established. The necessary forms and supplies for the new system should be procured. These steps help to ensure a smooth conversion from the old system to the new one.

Testing

Before a newly designed system is implemented, it must be subjected to extensive testing to establish its logical correctness and consistency with design specifications. Documents and reports, processing procedures, computer programs, and other elements of the system should all be given a trial run in circumstances as realistic as possible. Three commonly used forms of testing are walkthroughs, processing of test transactions, and acceptance testing.

A *walkthrough* is a meeting at which a detailed review of system procedures or program logic is carried out in a step-by-step manner. Such a meeting may take place at any point in the systems design process. Walkthroughs during the early stages of systems design are generally attended by systems analysts, managers, and other system users and deal with the contents of inputs, files, and outputs and with data and information flows through the organization. Walkthroughs during the later stages of systems design are generally attended by programmers and deal with the logic and structure of program code. To be most effective, walkthroughs should be scheduled to occur on a regular basis throughout the final systems design process.

The processing of test transactions is designed to check a program's response to all possible combinations of input and file data that it may encounter. Appropriate controls and routines for dealing with input errors and other unusual conditions should be incorporated into each program, and hypothetical test transactions and file records must be devised specifically to test their adequacy and completeness. For a large program consisting of several modules, each module is first tested independently, and then the program as a whole is tested. For each test transaction, the correct system response must be specified in advance in order to provide a basis for evaluation of the test results. Whenever the test results indicate that a significant change must be made in a program, the proposed change should be reviewed and approved by system users. As with program compilation, if the programs are being developed for a new computer system that has not yet been installed, then the program tests must be performed on outside equipment.[3]

An *acceptance test* is a systems test in which test transactions and test acceptance criteria are developed by the system users, who also review the test results and decide whether the system is acceptable to them. Acceptance testing generally follows the processing of test transactions by the systems development team and immediately precedes the conversion process. Rather than using hypothetical transaction and file records, an acceptance test generally uses copies of real transaction and file records. Users may actually participate in such steps as preparing records for computer input, reviewing computer outputs, and processing computer-generated documents. Any final decisions to accept the system or to require specific modifications are the responsibility of the users.

Establishment of standards and controls

An essential aspect of the final systems design phase of implementation is the establishment of job performance standards and control techniques and procedures for the new system. Often these factors are not considered until after the new system becomes operational, and this can lead to many unanticipated problems. Planning for assignment of job responsibilities must take internal control considerations into account. Job descriptions and work schedules should make provision for the execution of control procedures. Personnel

---

[3]For a more detailed discussion of the processing of test transaction data, see Chapter 15.

selection should be affected by the performance standards attached to each position to be filled. Documentation standards and data security provisions should be formulated. Error checks should be built into all computer software systems, and procedures must be developed to guide system operators or users in responding to various error conditions that may be identified by the system. A policy of continuous planning for and evaluation of the new system should be devised. The significance of these various factors is such that the next chapter is devoted entirely to an extensive treatment of them.

Site preparation

Once a specific equipment configuration has been selected, requirements for a site can be determined and work can begin on the selection and preparation of the site. A computer site should be located as centrally as possible to facilitate the frequent communication required between the computer activity and all other operations in the organization. Space will have to be provided not only for equipment and operators but also for storage of cards, tapes, and other supplies and for the offices of analysts, programmers, and supervisors. The site should be laid out to facilitate efficient operation. The possibility of future expansion of the system should also be considered in site selection and preparation.

Depending on the size of the equipment configuration being acquired, computer installation may require extensive physical changes in the location selected. A micro- or minicomputer may require very little in the way of physical site preparation, but a larger system may require additional electrical outlets, data communications facilities, lighting, and air conditioning. Security measures such as fire protection and emergency power supply may also be necessary. Some companies have constructed a separate building or an expansion of their existing building specifically to house their computer center. Thus site preparation can be quite costly, but it usually does not create major problems, such as those that may be encountered in connection with personnel adjustments and systems design. The vendor is usually able and willing to provide competent assistance in this task.

Conversion

One of the first major activities in the conversion phase of systems implementation is the conversion of master files from old to new system media. If the old system is a manual one, this process will be difficult and time-consuming. It will involve transcribing the data from each record on file to the new storage medium, which could be ledger cards, punched cards, magnetic tape, or magnetic disk. Care must be taken to ensure the reliability of the data converted. If the system conversion is from one computer system to another, the conversion of files from one computer data media to another generally will not be a significant problem.

If the program of preparation for installation has been adequately planned, the installation of the equipment should occur almost simultane-ously with the completion of program testing, conversion of files, employee training, and site preparation. The next major activity during the period of conversion is *parallel operation* of new system and old system to provide a final test of the new system. Both systems will be operated on a full-time basis, and their output compared. Differences must be analyzed to determine their cause, and the new system should be modified appropriately.

The period of parallel operations is one of the most costly and demanding in the entire computer acquisition process. Most employees connected with the project will be required to work long hours of overtime to operate both systems, compare results, and make necessary adjustments. These factors ar-gue for minimizing the length of this period. However, successful implemen-tation will require extensive testing of the reliability of the new system, and this fact argues for a longer period of parallel operations. Generally, three or four parallel runs of each application are sufficient to eliminate most of the major problems in a newly designed system. Since some applications will be run daily, others weekly, others monthly, and so forth, the period of parallel operations will be very hectic for a month or two and then gradually wind down to final conversion after three or four months.

Many small organizations do not have the staff, or cannot afford the ex-pense, for a full parallel operation. An alternative approach to final systems testing is called a *pilot operation*. This form of testing involves a sample of trans-actions. The sample may include historical records that have already been processed, or artificial transactions devised to test the system under various unusual conditions. The results of such tests would be compared with those previously generated by the manual system or with those predetermined for artificial transactions. Because the volume of sample transactions is much smaller than regular processing volume, a pilot operation is less expensive and less time-consuming than parallel operation.

Follow-up

After a new system has been in operation for a brief period, perhaps two to four months, the systems group should perform a follow-up analysis and ap-praisal of its performance. The analysis should be designed to reveal and cor-rect any weaknesses in the new system that have become evident. The extent to which the new system is meeting its planned objectives should be evaluated. The adequacy of standards and controls to keep the system operating as ex-pected should be assessed. Major differences between actual and expected per-formance should be brought to the attention of management, and necessary adjustments should be initiated. The system should be analyzed through ob-servation and interviews with employees to discover weaknesses, which should then be corrected. Even after the system review study is complete, continuous attention should be given to the possibility of correcting weaknesses and im-proving the system.

PERT: A Project Scheduling Technique

The Program Evaluation and Review Technique is a useful management tool for planning, coordinating, and controlling large, complex projects such as computer implementation. The development and initial application of PERT was done in connection with the development of the Polaris submarine-launched ballistic missile by the United States Navy in the late 1950s. PERT has since been used for many applications in business. An extensive discussion of PERT is presented here to develop an understanding of and appreciation for the usefulness of this analytical technique in systems implementation. According to one recent survey of systems management techniques, PERT was used in project planning in thirty-nine percent of the systems projects included in the survey.[4]

PERT concepts and definitions

The PERT technique involves the diagrammatical representation of the sequence of activities comprising a project by means of a network consisting of arrows and nodes (see Fig. 13.2). Arrows in a PERT network represent "tasks" or "activities," which are distinct segments of the project requiring an expenditure of time and resources. Nodes in a network symbolize "events," or milestone points in the project representing the completion of one or more activities and/or the initiation of one or more subsequent activities.[5] An event is thus a point in time and does not consume any time in itself, as does an activity.

The first step in applying PERT to project planning is to determine all the individual tasks in the project that are separate and distinct from all other tasks. Then all the immediate predecessor tasks must be established for each task. That is, if task A is the immediate predecessor of task B, then task A must be completed before task B is begun, and task B may be begun immediately upon completion of task A. Some tasks may have several immediate predecessors, and such a task may not be begun until all its immediate predecessors have been completed. Once all of the activities in a project have been determined and their precedence relationships established, the PERT network can be drawn.

One of the primary aspects of the PERT technique is the analysis of the network in terms of the time required to complete each activity and the project as a whole. For each separate activity an estimate of completion time in hours, days, weeks, or months must be made. Once this is completed, the next step is to determine the network's *critical path,* the path of activities from beginning event to ending event that requires the greatest total expenditure of time. The sum of the estimated activity times for all activities on the critical

---

[4]John H. Lehman, "How Software Projects Are Really Managed," *Datamation* (January 1979): 124.

[5]In a variation of these conventions used by some PERT analysts, nodes represent activities and arrows represent the time sequence of activities.

Activity	Time (days)	Predecessor activities
A	3	None
B	8	None
C	6	A
D	0	A
E	7	B,D
F	4	C

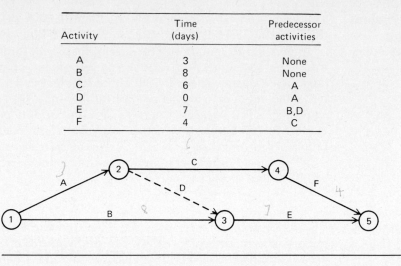

FIGURE 13.2
A simple PERT network.

path is the total time required to complete the project. These activities are "critical" because any delay in their completion will cause a delay in the project. Activities not on the critical path are not critical, since they will be worked on simultaneously with critical path activities and their completion could be delayed up to a point without delaying the project as a whole.

Consider the simple PERT network illustrated in Fig. 13.2. Note how the network itself is constructed from the precedence relationships shown in the figure. The example illustrates a common PERT convention—the labeling of activities with capital letters and of events with numbers. Also illustrated is a new concept, the "dummy activity," D, represented by the dashed arrow in the network. This activity is not really an activity at all in that it does not require any expenditure of time or resources. However, it is required in the network to show that activity A is an immediate predecessor of activity E. This relationship could not be represented by routing the arrow symbolizing activity A into the node preceding activity E because that would imply that activity B is an immediate predecessor of activity C, which is not true.

There is a total of only three paths through the network of Fig. 13.2. A comparison of the total time required for each of these paths reveals that the path consisting of activities B and E requires the greatest total expenditure of time, 15 days, and is therefore the critical path. The paths consisting of activities A, D, E, and of A, C, F require a total of 10 and 13 days, respectively. Activities not on the critical path can be delayed without delaying the project and are thus said to have a quantity of *slack time*. Because any delay in a critical path activity will delay the project as a whole (in this case beyond 15 days), critical path activities have zero slack time. A procedure for calculating the quantity of slack time for all activities not on the critical path will be presented shortly.

Most projects to which PERT is applied are sufficiently complex that the total number of paths through the network will be quite large. Thus a more efficient procedure for finding the critical path must be used than complete enumeration of all paths. The first step in such a procedure is to find the earliest start time, ES, and earliest finish time, EF, for each activity in the network, proceeding in sequence from the earlier activities to the later activities, or from left to right in the network diagram. ES represents the earliest possible time that the activity can begin. For all activities that have no predecessors, ES = 0. For those activities that have one or more predecessors, ES depends on the finish times of the predecessor activities. Because all its predecessor activities must be completed before the activity may start, ES is equal to the greater of the EFs of all immediate predecessor activities. To find EF for any activity, add the time required to complete the activity to the ES value for that activity. The value of EF for the final event in the network represents the total required project completion time.

In terms of the illustration of Fig. 13.2, ES = 0 for activities A and B. Because activity A requires 3 days, EF = 0 + 3, or 3 days for activity A. Because activities C and D may begin once A is finished, ES = 3 for both activities C and D. EF values for activities B, C, and D are therefore 8, 9, and 3, respectively. ES for activity F is equal to EF for its predecessor, activity C, or 9 days. For activity E, ES is equal to the larger of the EF values for its two predecessor activities, B and D, because both must be completed before E may begin. Therefore, ES for activity E is equal to EF for activity B, or 8 days. Finally, the EF values for activities E and F may be obtained by adding their activity times to their ES values; this yields EF values of 15 and 13 for activities E and F, respectively. Once both activities E and F are completed, the project as a whole is completed; accordingly, the total required project completion time is 15 days. Figure 13.3 summarizes ES and EF values for all the network activities.

The next step in the procedure for finding the critical path is to find the latest start time, LS, and latest finish time, LF, for each network activity. LF for an activity represents the latest time that activity could finish without causing the project as a whole to be delayed. LS for an activity is equal to its LF

FIGURE 13.3
Early start and early finish values for sample problem.

ACTIVITY	TIME (DAYS)	ES	EF
A	3	0	3
B	8	0	8
C	6	3	9
D	0	3	3
E	7	8	15
F	4	9	13

minus its activity time. To calculate LS and LF values for the activities in a network, we must begin with the activities at the end of the network and work backward.

For our sample network, LF for the two ending activities, E and F, is equal to 15 days, since any delay in their completion beyond 15 days would cause a delay in the entire project. To find LS for these activities, subtract their required completion times, 7 days and 4 days, respectively, from their LF values. This yields LS = 15 − 7 = 8 for activity E, and LS = 15 − 4 = 11 for activity F. Now, for immediate predecessor activities, LF equals LS of the successor activity. Because activity C is the immediate predecessor of activity F, and because LS for activity F is 11 days, LF for activity C is also 11 days. Similarly, LF for both activities B and D is equal to LS for activity E, or 8 days. Finally, LS for activities B, C, and D, obtained by subtracting their required completion times from their LF values, equals 0, 5, and 8 days, respectively.

LF for any activity that has two or more successor activities, such as activity A in our sample network, is equal to the smaller of the LSs of the various successor activities. Activity A has two successor activities, C and D, with LS values of 5 and 8, respectively. Therefore LF for activity A is equal to 5 days. Note that if activity A were to finish instead in 8 days, then the start of activity C would be delayed beyond its LS of 5 days, thereby causing a delay in completion of the entire project beyond the necessary 15 days. The value of LS for activity A is equal to 5 − 3, or 2 days. Figure 13.4 summarizes the values of LS and LF for all the activities in the sample project.

Continuing the procedure, the next step is to calculate the slack time for each activity. An activity's slack time will be equal to the difference between its LS and ES. Figure 13.5 illustrates the calculation of slack time by this method for each activity in our sample problem. Note that slack time could also be computed by finding the difference between LF and EF, which would yield identical results. To understand the logic of the slack time calculation, consider activity C. Its ES is 3 days. However, its LS value of 5 days indicates that its start could be delayed by up to 2 days without delaying the overall project (assuming that its predecessor and successor activities are not also delayed). Hence activity C is said to have slack time of 2 days.

FIGURE 13.4
Late start and late finish values for sample problem.

ACTIVITY	TIME (DAYS)	LS	LF
A	3	2	5
B	8	0	8
C	6	5	11
D	0	8	8
E	7	8	15
F	4	11	15

ACTIVITY	LS	ES	SLACK TIME
A	2	0	2
B	0	0	0
C	5	3	2
D	8	3	5
E	8	8	0
F	11	9	2

FIGURE 13.5
Calculation of activity slack times for sample problem.

Once slack time has been calculated for all activities, critical path activities are identified as those that have zero slack. In our sample problem, activities B and E have zero slack and therefore form the critical path. Note that it is possible for a network to have more than one critical path. For example, if the time required for activity A in this illustration had been 5 days instead of 3, the path containing activities A, C, and F would also have been a critical path.

Knowledge of which activities in a project are critical is extremely useful to management for planning and control purposes. There is usually ample reason for management to desire to complete a project as quickly as possible. A major reason is that while resources such as staff and equipment are at work at one job, they cannot be put to work on other jobs. Waste and inefficiency in resource utilization can be very expensive in terms of revenue lost (sometimes called opportunity cost). The faster one project can be completed, the faster the resources used on it can be transferred to other revenue-producing activities.

For planning and control purposes, a critical path activity is obviously one requiring a maximum of management attention if the total project completion time is to be minimized. Such activities should be monitored very closely to ensure that delays in their completion will be rendered unlikely. On the other hand, activities not on the critical path require less management attention and monitoring. The larger the slack time for an activity, the less closely it needs to be monitored.

The PERT technique is useful not only at the beginning of a project but also throughout the entire period during which the project is being worked on. As individual activities are completed, their estimated completion times can be replaced in the network by their actual completion times. This adjustment may cause the critical path itself to change, and so the slack time for all activities needs to be continually recalculated to provide a basis for dynamic project control. As work on the project proceeds, a measure should be maintained of how much ahead or behind schedule the project is. If the project is behind schedule, the network can be used to determine which activities are the best candidates for an effort at acceleration of completion times. Thus

PERT can be a useful management tool during the entire period of project execution.

PERT applied to computer implementation

Figure 13.6 provides an illustration of a PERT network representing the activities involved in implementing a computer system. The activity times shown in the illustration correspond to those required for a medium- to large-scale installation. A smaller-size installation might require less time, whereas a very large installation might require more time, but the activities and precedence relationships represented by the network itself are applicable to any computer implementation project.

For review purposes, the reader should verify that the critical path for this network consists of activities B, C, F, H, I, J, K, and M, that the total required project time is 83 weeks, and that the slack times for activities A, D, E, G, and L are 5, 5, 27, 13, and 21 weeks, respectively.

Other applications of PERT

PERT generally is useful to the administration of complex projects of a non-routine or nonrecurring nature. For an operation that is routine or repetitive, such as mass production, a great deal of past experience is generally available

FIGURE 13.6
PERT network of the computer implementation process.

Activity	Time (weeks)	Predecessor activities	Activity description
A	36	None	Physical preparation (including vendor lead time)
B	4	None	Organizational planning
C	2	B	Personnel selection
D	2	A	Equipment installation
E	10	C	Personnel training
F	15	C	Detailed systems design
G	9	F	File conversion
H	4	F	Establish standards and controls
I	9	H	Program preparation
J	9	I	Program testing
K	20	D,E,G,J	Parallel operations
L	8	I	Finalize system documentation
M	20	K,L	Follow-up

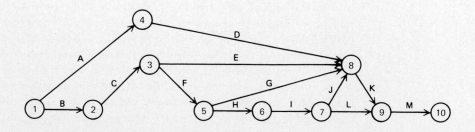

for planning and control purposes. PERT is of little use in such a situation. Some of the most common and successful applications of PERT have been to research and development activities, construction projects, and the marketing of new products.

PERT with uncertain time estimates

In a real-world application of PERT to a complex project the estimates of completion times for activities will seldom be certain. To cope with uncertainty in activity time estimates, the application of PERT in practice usually proceeds by estimating three possible duration times for each activity. These are a most optimistic estimate of required time (labeled a), a most likely estimate (m), and a most pessimistic estimate (b). A weighted average of these three time estimates is then calculated to establish the "expected completion time" for the activity. The weighted average formula applies a weight of one to both the most optimistic and the most pessimistic estimates and a weight of four to the most likely estimate. The formula is thus as follows.

$$\text{Expected time} = \frac{a + 4m + b}{6}.$$

The expected completion time may be looked upon as an average or mean figure. This formula is based upon a statistical frequency distribution known as the beta distribution, which the developers of PERT considered to be a reasonable approximation of the typical distribution of activity times. In practice it has been proved to provide time estimates accurate enough to be more useful than the single-valued estimate, which often turns out to be too low.

A measure of the relative dispersion of completion time around the expected completion time for an activity is the standard deviation. A formula for computing the standard deviation of completion time for an activity from the estimates of most optimistic and most pessimistic time follows.

$$\text{Standard deviation (activity)} = \frac{b - a}{6}.$$

This formula also represents an approximation and is based upon the practice often followed by statisticians of estimating the standard deviation of a unimodel distribution to be roughly one sixth of the range of the distribution. Again, this formula has been proved in practice to provide a reasonably accurate measure of dispersion.

When expected activity times and their standard deviations are computed in this manner, the PERT network is solved using the expected activity times. The total required project time obtained is thus an expected or mean time. Therefore the probability that the project will be completed within this expected total time is exactly 0.5, or one half. The standard deviation of total project time around this mean expected time is computed using the following formula.

$$\text{Standard deviation (project)} = \sqrt{\begin{array}{l}\text{the sum of the squares of}\\ \text{the standard deviations of}\\ \text{all critical path activities.}\end{array}}$$

Using this standard deviation and a table of areas under the normal curve, the probability of completing the project within any given time period can be determined.

PERT under uncertainty: an example

Consider the PERT network shown in Fig. 13.7. Estimates of most optimistic, most likely, and most pessimistic completion times in days for each activity are given. In addition, both the expected completion time and standard deviation for each activity have been computed according to the above formulas and are also included in the illustration. The reader should verify the accuracy of these calculations and should verify also that the critical path consists of activities A, D, and G with a total expected project completion time of 23 days.

Calculation of the standard deviation of completion time for the project as a whole according to the formula is as follows.

$$\begin{aligned}\text{Standard deviation (project)} &= \sqrt{2^2 + 2^2 + 1^2}\\ &= \sqrt{9}\\ &= 3.\end{aligned}$$

The usefulness of this approach stems from the determination of the probability of getting the project finished within some specified time period. For example, suppose we want to know the probability of completing the project in 27 days or less. The first step is to compute z, which is the number of stan-

FIGURE 13.7
Sample PERT
network with related
time data.

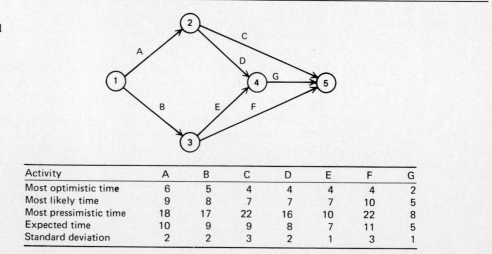

Activity	A	B	C	D	E	F	G
Most optimistic time	6	5	4	4	4	4	2
Most likely time	9	8	7	7	7	10	5
Most pressimistic time	18	17	22	16	10	22	8
Expected time	10	9	9	8	7	11	5
Standard deviation	2	2	3	2	1	3	1

dard deviations from the mean represented by our given time of 27 days. If we label the given time G.T., the mean expected time E.T., and the project standard deviation S.D., the formula for z is as follows.

$$z = \frac{\text{G.T.} - \text{E.T.}}{\text{S.D.}}$$

For 27 days, z is computed as follows in this example.

$$z = \frac{27 - 23}{3} = 1.3.$$

The next step in this analysis is to find the probability associated with the calculated value of z by referring to a table of areas under the normal curve such as that shown in Fig. 13.8. In the example, a z of 1.3 corresponds to a probability of 0.90320. This is interpreted to mean that the probability of completing the project within 27 days or less is 0.90320. For review purposes the reader may wish to verify that the probabilities of getting the project done within 17, 20, and 29 days are 0.02275, 0.15866, and 0.97725, respectively.

Knowledge of the probabilities associated with various possible values of

FIGURE 13.8
Probabilities associated with values of z or less under the normal curve.

z = Number of standard deviations from the mean

P = Probability that the actual value of the variable will be z or less.

z	P	z	P	z	P
−3.0	.00135			1.0	.84134
−2.9	.00187	−0.9	.18406	1.1	.86433
−2.8	.00256	−0.8	.21186	1.2	.88493
−2.7	.00347	−0.7	.24196	1.3	.90320
−2.6	.00466	−0.6	.27425	1.4	.91924
−2.5	.00621	−0.5	.30854	1.5	.93319
−2.4	.00820	−0.4	.34458	1.6	.94520
−2.3	.01072	−0.3	.38209	1.7	.95543
−2.2	.01390	−0.2	.42074	1.8	.96407
−2.1	.01786	−0.1	.46017	1.9	.97128
−2.0	.02275	0.0	.50000	2.0	.97725
−1.9	.02872	0.1	.53983	2.1	.98214
−1.8	.03593	0.2	.57926	2.2	.98610
−1.7	.04457	0.3	.61791	2.3	.98928
−1.6	.05480	0.4	.65542	2.4	.99180
−1.5	.06681	0.5	.69146	2.5	.99379
−1.4	.08076	0.6	.72575	2.6	.99534
−1.3	.09680	0.7	.75804	2.7	.99653
−1.2	.11507	0.8	.78814	2.8	.99744
−1.1	.13567	0.9	.81594	2.9	.99813
−1.0	.15866			3.0	.99865

project completion time may be very valuable to management for planning purposes. It allows management to judge the probable length of time for which the resources required for the project will be tied up at work on the project and therefore unavailable for other useful work. If management can also estimate the cost per day of utilization of the resources, the probability of various total costs for the project can be determined. For example, if the cost per day of the resources required for the sample problem of Fig. 13.5 is $1,000, then the probability that the total resource cost for the project will be $23,000 or less is 0.5; that it will be $27,000 or less is 0.90320; and so on. If the project represents something for which a contract price is being negotiated, information of this sort would obviously be very valuable to management.

The critical path method

It is also possible to introduce cost considerations into a PERT analysis in another way. For example, it may be possible to reduce the completion time of one or more activities by accelerating the work effort on the activity. However, it is likely that such accelerated effort will require an extra expenditure of cost, such as that required for overtime pay for employees. Thus the benefit from reducing the total completion time of a project by accelerated efforts on certain activities must be balanced against the extra cost of doing so. A related problem is to determine which activities must be accelerated to reduce the total project completion time. This form of analysis is referred to as the Critical Path Method (CPM). Although worthy of mention, CPM will not be illustrated here.[6]

Summary

Systems implementation is the process of converting the product of systems analysis and design into an effectively operating information system. Steps in the systems implementation process include planning and scheduling implementation tasks, communicating with employees, adjusting organizational structures, selecting and training personnel, relocating displaced personnel, developing and testing computer programs, preparing equipment sites, converting to the new system, and conducting follow-up appraisal.

Two techniques commonly used in systems implementation are the Gantt chart and the PERT technique. The Gantt chart is a form of bar chart in which scheduled and completed activities are displayed against a time line scaled in weeks or days. PERT involves a diagrammatical representation of the sequence of activities comprising a project by means of a network in which arrows represent activities and nodes represent events. Both techniques provide a framework for scheduling, coordinating, expediting, and monitoring the progress of the implementation effort.

[6]For a presentation of CPM, see Jerome D. Wiest and Ferdinand K. Levy, *A Management Guide to PERT/CPM*, 2d ed. (Englewood Cliffs, N.J.: Prentice-Hall, 1977), chapter 5.

Review Questions

1. Define the following terms.

PERT	parallel operation
Gantt chart	pilot operation
walkthrough	critical path
acceptance test	slack time

2. What basic change of emphasis takes place in a systems investigation when work on implementation begins?

3. List several categories of activities commonly performed as part of a systems implementation project.

4. Describe some of the planning and scheduling considerations important to systems implementation.

5. Explain the concept of implementation risk analysis.

6. Describe in detail the activities in the area of personnel and organizational adjustment that should be performed by a company preparing for computer installation.

7. What steps should a company take to cope with problems of employee morale that may arise when plans to acquire a computer become known to employees?

8. During a large systems implementation project, what types of training programs are required, and who may provide these training programs?

9. Describe in some detail the major activities in the final systems design phase of preparation for computer installation.

10. Identify and describe three commonly used forms of systems testing.

11. Describe several factors that should be taken into account during systems implementation with respect to the establishment of standards and controls for the new system.

12. Describe in some detail the process of preparing a site for the physical location of a computer system in a business organization.

13. Outline and describe the major activities in a company during the conversion phase of computer implementation.

14. What are the major considerations in the decision of how long the period of parallel operations should be? What is the usual length of this period?

15. Describe the process of the follow-up review to a systems investigation.

16. What do the arrows and nodes in a PERT network signify?

17. What is a "dummy activity" in a PERT network, and why is it sometimes necessary for networks to contain such activities?

18. Explain how PERT is useful to management planning and control of large complex projects.

19. List four common applications of PERT in business.

20. Explain how cost considerations might be introduced into an analysis using PERT.

Discussion Questions

21. Modeling techniques such as PERT are often based upon assumptions or estimates that are frequently inaccurate. Discuss the implications of this observation for the usefulness of such techniques.

22. Assume that you are a systems consultant advising a firm's management on implementation of a new computer system. Management has decided not to retain several employees after the system is implemented. Some of these employees have many years of service to the firm. How would you advise management to communicate this decision to its employees?

Problems and Cases

REQUIRED

23. Given in Fig. 13.9 are a set of activities, single-activity time estimates, and precedence relationships for a project.
    a) Construct a PERT network for this project.
    b) Determine the critical path and the total completion time for the project.
    c) For each activity, determine the earliest finish time, the latest finish time, and the slack time.

24. Shown in Fig. 13.10 is a list of project activities accompanied by the scheduled starting time and completion time of each activity.

REQUIRED

    a) Using a format similar to that illustrated in Fig. 13.1, prepare a Gantt chart for this project.
    b) Assume that it is February 16, and activities A and B have been completed, activity C is half completed, activity F is twenty-five percent completed, and the other activities have not yet commenced. Record this information on your Gantt chart. Is the project behind schedule, on schedule, or ahead of schedule? Explain.
    c) Note that the project parameters given for this problem are identical to those given in problem 23. Discuss the relative merits of the Gantt chart and the PERT technique as tools for project planning and control.

FIGURE 13.9

Activity	A	B	C	D	E	F	G	H
Activity time	6	3	5	4	3	7	4	6
Predecessors	none	none	B	A,C	A,C	B	D	E,F

Activity	Starting date, Monday, week of:	Ending date, Friday, week of:
A	Jan. 5	Feb. 9
B	Jan. 5	Jan. 19
C	Jan. 26	Feb. 23
D	Mar. 2	Mar. 23
E	Mar. 2	Mar. 16
F	Feb. 2	Mar. 16
G	Mar. 30	Apr. 20
H	Mar. 23	Apr. 27

FIGURE 13.10

25. A construction company has contracted to complete a new building and has asked for assistance in analyzing the project. Using the Program Evaluation and Review Technique (PERT), the network in Fig. 13.11 has been developed. All paths from the start point to the finish point, event 6, represent activities or processes that must be completed before the entire project, the building, will be completed. The numbers above the paths or line segments represent expected completion times for the activities or processes. The expected time is based upon the commonly used, 1–4–1, three-estimate method. For example, the three-estimate method gives an estimated time of 4.2 to complete event 1.

REQUIRED

a) The critical path (the path requiring the greatest amount of time) is

   1) 1–2–5–6
   2) 1–2–3–4–6
   3) 1–3–4–6
   4) 1–7–8–6
   5) 1–9–6

FIGURE 13.11

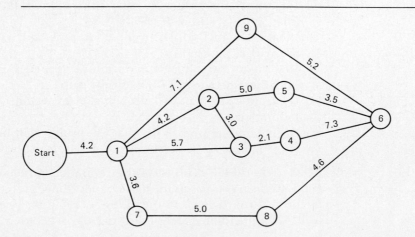

b) Slack time on path 1–9–6 equals
   1) 4.3
   2) 2.8
   3) .9
   4) .4
   5) 0

c) The latest time for reaching event 6 via path 1–2–5–6 is
   1) 20.8
   2) 19.3
   3) 17.4
   4) 16.5
   5) 12.7

d) The earliest time for reaching event 6 via path 1–2–5–6 is
   1) 20.8
   2) 16.9
   3) 16.5
   4) 12.7
   5) 3.5

e) If all other paths are operating on schedule but path segment 7–8 has unfavorable time variance of 1.9,
   1) the critical path will be shortened.
   2) the critical path will be eliminated.
   3) the critical path will be unaffected.
   4) another path will become the critical path.
   5) the critical path will have an increased time of 1.9. (CPA Examination)

26. Shown in Fig. 13.12 is a PERT network and a related set of activity time estimates, in weeks.

REQUIRED

  a) Determine the expected completion time of each activity.
  b) Determine the earliest expected finish time, latest expected finish time, and slack time of each activity.
  c) What is the total project completion time, and what activities are on the critical path?
  d) Determine the standard deviation of expected completion time for only those activities on the critical path.
  e) Determine the standard deviation of expected completion time for the project.
  f) Determine the probability that the project will be completed within (1) 41 weeks, (2) 47 weeks, (3) 50 weeks, (4) 59 weeks.

27. Refer to the PERT network of the computer implementation process in Fig. 13.6. Using *months* as the basic unit of time, prepare a Gantt chart for the project represented in the figure. Assume that each activity is scheduled to begin immediately following the scheduled completion of any

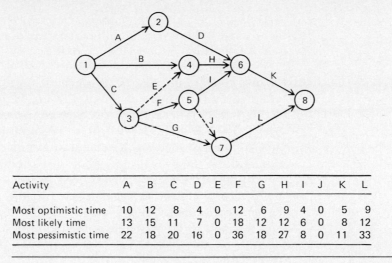

Activity	A	B	C	D	E	F	G	H	I	J	K	L
Most optimistic time	10	12	8	4	0	12	6	9	4	0	5	9
Most likely time	13	15	11	7	0	18	12	12	6	0	8	12
Most pessimistic time	22	18	20	16	0	36	18	27	8	0	11	33

FIGURE 13.12

predecessor activities. Also, to simplify your analysis, you may assume that four weeks equal one month.

28. Edward Jones is responsible for finding a suitable building and establishing a new convenience grocery store for ThriftMart, Inc. Jones enumerated the specific activities which had to be completed and the estimated time to establish each activity. In addition, he plans to prepare a network diagram to aid in the coordination of the activities. The list of activities to locate a building and establish a new store is as follows:

ACTIVITY NUMBER	DESCRIPTION OF ACTIVITY	ESTIMATED TIME REQUIRED
1–2	Find building	4 weeks
2–3	Negotiate rental terms	2 weeks
3–4	Draft lease	4 weeks
2–5	Prepare store plans	4 weeks
5–6	Select and order fixtures	1 week
6–4	Delivery of fixtures	6 weeks
4–8	Install fixtures	3 weeks
5–7	Hire staff	5 weeks
7–8	Train staff	4 weeks
8–9	Receive inventory	2 weeks
9–10	Stock shelves	1 week

Note: Activity number 1–2 represents an activity that begins at event 1 and ends at event 2.

REQUIRED

a) Prepare a PERT network diagram for this project.

b) Identify the critical path and the total time required for finding and establishing the new convenience store.

c) Prepare a Gantt chart for this project.

d) Edward Jones would like to finish the store two weeks earlier than indicated by the schedule, and as a result, he is considering several alternatives. One such alternative is to convince the fixture manufacturer to deliver the fixtures in four weeks rather than in six weeks. Should Jones arrange for the manufacturer to deliver the fixtures in four weeks if the sole advantage of this schedule change is to open the store two weeks early? Justify your answer.

e) A program, such as the one illustrated by the network diagram for the new convenience store, cannot be implemented unless the required resources are available at the required dates. What additional information does Jones need to administer the proposed project properly? (CMA Examination)

29. Whitson Company has just ordered a new computer for its financial information system. The present computer is fully utilized and no longer adequate for all of the financial applications Whitson would like to implement. The present financial system applications must all be modified before they can be run on the new computer. Additionally, new applications which Whitson would like to have developed and implemented have been identified and ranked according to priority.

Sally Rose, Manager of Data Processing, is responsible for implementing the new computer system. Rose listed the specific activities which had to be completed and determined the estimated time to complete each activity. In addition, she prepared a network diagram to aid in the coordination of the activities. The activity list and the network diagram are presented in Fig. 13.13.

REQUIRED

a) Determine the number of weeks which will be required to implement fully Whitson Company's financial information system (i.e., both existing and new applications) on its new computer and identify the activities which are critical to completing the project.

b) The term *slack time* is often used in conjunction with network analysis.

    1) Explain what is meant by *slack time.*

    2) Identify the activities that have slack time and indicate the amount of slack time available for each.

c) Whitson Company's top management would like to reduce the time necessary to begin operation of the entire system.

    1) Which activities should Sally Rose attempt to reduce in order to implement the system sooner? Explain your answer.

    2) Discuss how Sally Rose might proceed to reduce the time of these activities.

ACTIVITY	DESCRIPTION OF ACTIVITY	EXPECTED TIME REQUIRED TO COMPLETE (IN WEEKS)	VARIANCE IN EXPECTED TIME (IN WEEKS)
AB	Wait for delivery of computer from manufacturer	8	1.2
BC	Install computer	2	.6
CH	General test of computer	2	.2
AD	Complete an evaluation of manpower requirements	2	.8
DE	Hire additional programmers and operators	2	1.6
AG	Design modifications to existing applications	3	1.2
GH	Program modifications to existing applications	4	1.4
HI	Test modified applications on new computer	2	.4
IJ	Revise existing applications as needed	2	.6
JN	Revise and update documentation for existing applications as modified	2	.4
JK	Run existing applications in parallel on new and old computers	2	.4
KP	Implement existing applications as modified on the new computer	1	.6
AE	Design new applications	8	3.2
GE	Design interface between existing and new applications	3	1.8
EF	Program new applications	6	2.6
FI	Test new applications on new computer	2	.8
IL	Revise new applications as needed	3	1.4
LM	Conduct second test of new applications on new computer	2	.6
MN	Prepare documentation for the new applications	3	.8
NP	Implement new applications on the new computer	2	.8

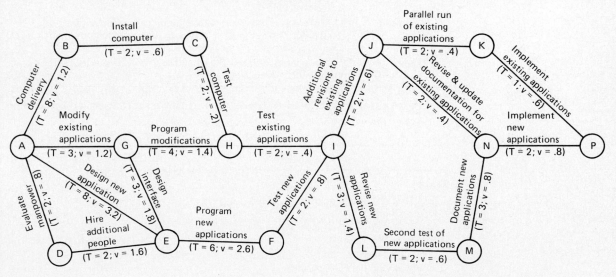

T = Expected time in weeks to complete activity

v = Variance in expected time in weeks

FIGURE 13.13

d) The General Accounting Manager would like the existing financial information system applications to be modified and operational in 22 weeks.

   1) Determine the number of weeks which will be required to modify the existing financial information system applications and make them operational.

   2) What is the probability of implementing the existing financial information system applications within 22 weeks? (CMA Examination)

30. Benjamin and Watson Enterprises has decided to acquire a new computer system and is presently entering a twelve-month implementation period. A schedule of activities for this period follows.

BEGINNING OF	ACTIVITY
Month 1	A data processing manager-programmer is hired. That person is responsible for final systems design and program flowcharting.
Month 5	A programmer is hired. The coding process is begun.
Month 6	A data entry operations supervisor is hired and immediately assumes responsibility for keying the programs.
Month 7	Program testing is begun, which requires rental of outside facilities. The rental contract with the company renting the building selected as the computer site is terminated. The remodeling of this site in preparation for installation is begun.
Month 10	Two data entry operators are hired. The file conversion process begins.
Month 11	Site remodeling, program testing, and file conversion are completed. The computer is installed, and two computer operators are hired. Parallel operation begins.
Month 13	Parallel operation is completed and final changeover to the new system is achieved.

The monthly costs attached to these various implementation activities include the following.

NATURE OF COST	COST PER MONTH
Salaries	
Data processing manager-programmer	$2500
Programmer	1700
Data entry operations supervisor	1200
Data entry operator	900
Computer operator	1200
Overtime during parallel operation	3000
Rental of time for program testing	600
Remodeling of site	2000
Computer rental	6000
Miscellaneous overhead after system is installed	$1000

In addition, the future site of the computer is presently being rented out at $1000 per month.

Prepare an implementation cost schedule for the twelve-month implementation period. Show each cost as a one-line item, and show the total cost incurred during each of the twelve months. Also show the total cumulative cost as of the end of each month.

31. Shaky Construction Company has an opportunity to submit a bid for the construction of a new apartment building. From specifications provided by the developer, a PERT network for the project has been developed and is shown in Fig. 13.14. Also shown for each activity arc estimates of most optimistic, most likely, and most pessimistic completion times in weeks (*a, m,* and *b,* respectively).

   a) Compute the expected completion time for all activities in the project.
   b) Determine the network critical path and the total expected completion time for the project.
   c) Determine the standard deviation of completion time for the project.
   d) Shaky's management policy with respect to submitting bids is to bid the minimum amount that will provide a ninety-two percent probability of at least breaking even. Materials for this project will cost $900,000, and all other costs will vary at a rate of $10,000 per week

FIGURE 13.14

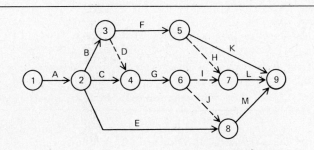

Activity	a	m	b	Activity description
A	5	8	17	Excavate basement
B	5	8	11	Build concrete elevator tower
C	3	5	7	Pour concrete foundation
D	0	0	0	Dummy activity
E	6	9	18	Excavate parking ramp area
F	5	8	17	Install temporary manual elevator
G	5	7	12	Erect main building
H	0	0	0	Dummy activity
I	0	0	0	Dummy activity
J	0	0	0	Dummy activity
K	4	7	10	Install automatic elevator
L	7	10	31	Complete interior work
M	4	6	11	Erect parking ramp

Activity	a	m	b
E	1	2	3
F	3	5	10
G	3	6	9

FIGURE 13.15

for every week spent working on the project. What amount should be bid under this policy.

e) Assume that Shaky's bid was accepted and that the project has been in progress for 20 weeks. Activities A, B, and C have been completed. Activities E, F, and G are in progress, with the estimates in Fig. 13.15 made of time required to complete them.

No change has been made in the time estimates for activities K, L, and M. Draw a revised PERT network representing the remainder of the project (excluding completed activities). Determine the critical path for the remainder of the project and the remaining project completion time.

References

Alter, Steven L. *Decision Support Systems: Current Practice and Continuing Challenges.* Reading, Mass.: Addison-Wesley, 1980.

Bostrom, Robert P., and J. Stephen Heinen. "MIS Problems and Failures: A Socio-Technical Perspective, Part I: The Causes." *MIS Quarterly* (September 1977): 17–32.

Bronsema, Gloria S., and Peter G. W. Keen. "Education Intervention and Implementation in MIS." *Sloan Management Review* (Summer 1983): 35–43.

Canning, Richard G. "Strategies for Introducing New Systems." *EDP Analyzer* (July 1985): 1–12.

Desanctis, Gerardine, and James F. Courtney. "Toward Friendly User MIS Implementation." *Communications of the ACM* (October 1983): 732–738.

Donaldson, Hamish. *A Guide to the Successful Management of Computer Projects.* New York: Halsted, 1978.

Keen, Peter G. W. "Information Systems and Organizational Change." *Communications of the ACM* (January 1981): 24–33.

Kotter, John P., and Leonard A. Schlesinger. "Choosing Strategies for Change." *Harvard Business Review* (March/April 1979): 106–114.

Lehman, John H. "How Software Projects Are Really Managed." *Datamation* (January 1979): 119–129.

Lucas, Henry C. "Unsuccessful Implementation: The Case of a Computer-Based Order Entry System." *Decision Sciences* (January 1978): 68–79.

Plasket, Richard L. "Project Management: New Technology Enhances Old Concepts." *Journal of Systems Management* (June 1986): 6–10.

Powers, Richard F., and Gary W. Dickson. "MIS Project Management: Myths, Opinions, and Reality." *California Management Review* (Spring 1973): 147–156.

Wiest, Jerome D., and Ferdinand K. Levy. *A Management Guide to PERT/CPM.* 2d ed. Englewood Cliffs, N.J.: Prentice-Hall, 1977.

C H A P T E R   1 4

Internal Control in Computer-Based Information Systems

LEARNING OBJECTIVES

Careful study of this chapter should enable students to:

☐ Discuss key issues relating to organization of the information systems function in business organizations.

☐ Evaluate the quality of management controls and security controls in an information systems department.

☐ Evaluate the quality of application controls within a computerized information systems application.

In Chapter 4 we discussed general concepts of internal control and illustrated their application to manual data processing operations. Now that we have developed a more complete understanding of computer data processing, and of the planning and development of computer-based information systems, it is appropriate to consider the application of internal control concepts in organizations using a computer-based information system. The importance of an understanding of internal control in computer-based information systems is underscored by the following conclusion from a recent survey of internal control in American corporations.

> The aspect of internal control that troubles executives most, and which we consider to be most serious, is the increasing dependence of companies on computers for operational effectiveness and for financial reporting. Technological progress in data processing has greatly increased a number of internal control risks, and these are compounded by a substantial shortage in adequately trained data processing and internal audit personnel.[1]

In short, the widespread use of computers to support operating functions and to process accounting data in modern corporations has led many authorities to question the adequacy of internal control systems in these corporations.

Although the general objectives of internal control remain the same regardless of the method of data processing, the specific control procedures used in a computer-based accounting information system are likely to differ from the control procedures employed in a manual accounting system. This is because there are certain fundamental differences between computer-based systems and manual systems. These differences are effectively described in the professional standards of the AICPA as follows.

> The methods an entity uses to process significant accounting applications may influence the control procedures designed to achieve the objectives of internal accounting control. Those characteristics that distinguish computer processing from manual processing include—
>
> a) *Transaction trails.* Some computer systems are designed so that a complete transaction trail that is useful for audit purposes might exist for only a short period of time or only in computer-readable form.
> b) *Uniform processing of transactions.* Computer processing uniformly subjects like transactions to the same processing instructions. Consequently, computer processing virtually eliminates the occurrence of clerical error normally associated with manual processing. Conversely, programming errors (or other similar systematic errors in either the computer hardware or software) will result in all like transactions being processed incorrectly when those transactions are processed under the same conditions.
> c) *Segregation of functions.* Many internal accounting control procedures once performed by separate individuals in manual systems may be concentrated

[1] Robert K. Mautz, Walter G. Kell, Michael W. Maher, Alan G. Merten, Raymond R. Reilly, Dennis G. Severance, and Bernard J. White, *Internal Control in U.S. Corporations: The State of the Art* (New York: Financial Executives Research Foundation, 1980), p. 8.

in systems that use computer processing. Therefore, an individual who has access to the computer may be in a position to perform incompatible functions. As a result, other control procedures may be necessary in computer systems to achieve the control objectives ordinarily accomplished by segregation of functions in manual systems. Other controls may include, for example, adequate segregation of incompatible functions within the computer processing activities, establishment of a control group to prevent or detect processing errors or irregularities, or use of password control procedures to prevent incompatible functions from being performed by individuals who have access to assets and access to records through an online terminal.

d) *Potential for errors and irregularities.* The potential for individuals, including those performing control procedures, to gain unauthorized access to data or alter data without visible evidence, as well as to gain access (direct or indirect) to assets, may be greater in computerized accounting systems than in manual systems. Decreased human involvement in handling transactions processed by computers can reduce the potential for observing errors and irregularities. Errors or irregularities occurring during the design or changing of application programs can remain undetected for long periods of time.

e) *Potential for increased management supervision.* Computer systems offer management a wide variety of analytical tools that may be used to review and supervise the operations of the company. The availability of these additional controls may serve to enhance the entire system of internal accounting control on which the auditor may wish to place reliance. For example, traditional comparisons of actual operating ratios with those budgeted, as well as reconciliations of accounts, are frequently available for management review on a more timely basis if such information is computerized. Additionally, some programmed applications provide statistics regarding computer operations that may be used to monitor the actual processing of transactions.

f) *Initiation or subsequent execution of transactions by computer.* Certain transactions may be automatically initiated or certain procedures required to execute a transaction may be automatically performed by a computer system. The authorization of these transactions or procedures may not be documented in the same way as those initiated in a manual accounting system, and management's authorization of those transactions may be implicit in its acceptance of the design of the computer system.

g) *Dependence of other controls on controls over computer processing.* Computer processing may produce reports and other output that are used in performing manual control procedures. The effectiveness of these manual control procedures can be dependent on the effectiveness of controls over the completeness and accuracy of computer processing. For example, the effectiveness of a control procedure that includes a manual review of a computer-produced exception listing is dependent on the controls over the production of the listing.[2]

---

[2]Statements on Auditing Standards (SAS) No. 1, AU Sec. 320.33, as amended by SAS No. 48 issued by the Auditing Standards Board in July 1984.

This chapter covers a variety of internal control policies, procedures, and techniques relating to computer-based information systems. However, the reader should note that these specific controls are invariably based upon general control concepts such as responsibility accounting, organizational independence, internal check, and numerous others.

The chapter is divided into four major sections. In the first are discussed both the internal organization of a typical computer data processing facility and the control considerations relevant to the design of this organization structure. In the second are discussed management control policies and procedures relating to computer personnel, computer operations activities, and the systems development process. The third section describes a variety of control standards and policies applicable to the operation of a computer facility. Control procedures and techniques involved in the actual processing of data on a computer system are explained in the fourth and last section.

Organization of the Information Systems Function

There are two basic subdivisions of the information systems function. One is the operations activity, which is concerned with the day-to-day processing of data on the computer system. The other is the systems activity, which involves the development and maintenance of the computer software, particularly application programs but also including utility routines, data management systems, and the operating system as well. Within these broad areas are found a number of more specific functions, typically allocated among several departments.

This section is divided into two parts. In the first are described the roles and responsibilities of the various departments or individuals within the information systems organization structure. The second focuses on the internal control considerations relevant to the allocation of those responsibilities.

Information systems responsibilities

Figure 14.1 provides an illustration of a typical organization structure for the information systems function in a larger company. Of course the exact allocation of responsibilities within the systems function will vary from one organization to another, depending on specific needs and circumstances. Therefore this chart is not intended to represent a prescription for systems organization in all companies but instead is merely an example consistent with organizational patterns found in many companies that can serve as a vehicle for discussion.

As discussed in Chapter 10, the top executive of the information systems function may or may not be a vice-president having equal status with other top-level executives in the organization. The position as a member of top management affords participation in setting objectives for the organization, in long-range planning to meet objectives, in establishing broad policies for the organization, and in making decisions at the top management level. One of the primary contributions to these activities is his or her ability to articulate

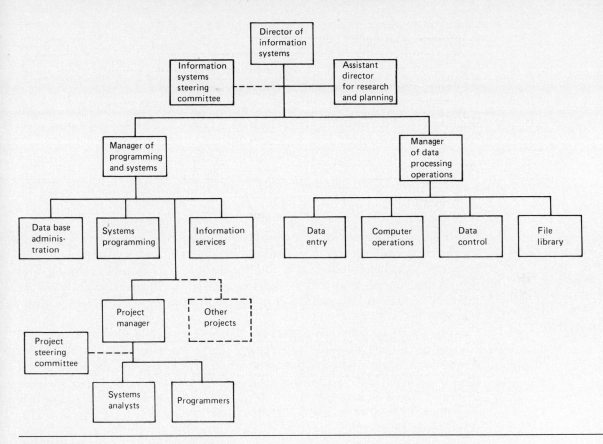

FIGURE 14.1

Organization of the information systems function.

the extent to which the information system can contribute to the achievement of plans and objectives and the execution of policies and decisions. The position also allows the encouragement of the profitable use of the information system in all other functional areas of the organization.

Regardless of whether the top computer executive has the status of vice-president, he or she must perform the role of manager of the systems activity, whose responsibilities include the development of profitable new applications and the efficient processing of existing applications. He or she is accountable for the costs associated with the equipment and personnel required for the system and is responsible for maintaining a modern, up-to-date facility that takes maximum advantage of new technological developments. Such responsibilities require a good combination of administrative skills and technical competence.

The top computer executive is assisted in carrying out these responsibilities by an executive-level information systems steering committee, the role of which has been discussed in Chapter 10, and by one or more administrative staff personnel. A key staff person here is the assistant director for research and planning, who is responsible for monitoring current developments in information technology, forecasting future technological developments, investigating ways of applying these new technologies within the organization, preparing the organization's long-range systems plans and budgets, and serving as a liaison to the organization's strategic long-range planning activity. In a large information processing facility, other staff officers at this level might include a quality control manager, a security officer, a personnel administrator, and/or a documentation standards officer.

The manager of programming and systems is responsible for managing the development of new information systems applications and for the maintenance and improvement of existing programs and data bases. He or she must establish and enforce standards for systems design, programming, and system documentation. The manager is responsible for planning and controlling the implementation of new systems applications and is accountable for the costs and progress of systems development efforts. Responsible to him or her are specialists in data base administration, systems programming, and information services, as well as systems analysts and programmers who are involved in various systems development and application program maintenance projects.

The data base administration function is responsible for the design and control of the organization's data bases. The data base administrator must establish the appropriate content and format of data records, the structure of data relationships, the appropriate data names and key fields. He or she controls and monitors data base usage through the assignment of user passwords and the collection of statistics on utilization of data and programs and also is concerned with efficient use of physical data storage equipment. The data base administrator must maintain a close liaison with system users, providing documentation and other aids to the effective use of data base systems.

The systems programming group is responsible for the effective functioning of the operating system, utility routines, compilers, data base management systems, and other software. They also provide technical support to the data base administrator and to applications programmers on matters relating to the systems software. Another systems programming responsibility is the implementation of enhancements to the systems software to improve the efficiency of operation of the computer system.

The information services function provides support for end-user applications of information technology. This includes assisting end-users in the acquisition, implementation, utilization, and maintenance of personal computers and related software packages. It may also involve training of end-users to effectively utilize decision support systems, query languages, and other user-oriented computer resources. As computer resources continue to evolve in the direction of greater user-friendliness, the information services function is taking on an increasingly important role within all well-managed systems departments.

Project managers direct a group of analysts and programmers in the process of designing and implementing new systems applications or performing program maintenance on existing applications. They are responsible for planning, administering, and controlling all phases of the development effort for a specific project. As discussed in Chapter 10, a project steering committee consisting of users, management representatives, and senior systems personnel should be appointed to provide guidance to the project manager during this process. As indicated on the chart, there will generally be more than one project under development in an organization at any given time.

The systems analysis function involves the design of computer applications to satisfy user needs in an organization. The position of systems analyst requires both experience in systems design and familiarity with the operations of the organization, for this person must serve to bridge the gap between the user and the technology of the computer system. The programming function involves converting the designs of the analyst into a set of computer instructions. Programming is generally regarded as a lower-level position than systems analysis because the position does not require the same degree of familiarity with the organization's operations. The specific steps involved in the programming process are described in Chapter 6.

The manager of data processing operations is responsible to the top computer executive for the day-to-day performance of data processing operations. Once new systems designs have been fully implemented, their successful execution becomes the responsibility of this department. As shown, a common pattern of division of responsibilities within this department involves separation among the functions of (1) data entry, (2) computer operations, (3) data control, and (4) file custodianship.

The data entry function involves the preparation and verification of source data for computer processing. Depending on the type of data input used, this may involve keypunching, key-to-tape encoding, key-to-disk equipment, or online data terminals. This function may also include the operation of peripheral equipment such as sorters, remote job entry devices, or data communications equipment.

The computer operations function actually runs the computer and its related input, output, and storage devices. Included are such activities as loading card decks, mounting tapes and disk packs, and monitoring and responding to console messages. In a multiprogramming environment in which several programs may be running simultaneously, the computer operator's job is dynamic and exacting.

The data control function maintains a record of all work in process, monitors the flow of work within and through the processing department, and distributes systems output upon completion of processing. The data control group is also responsible for checking the accuracy of input and output against preestablished control totals, for ensuring that established control procedures are adhered to during processing operations, and for following up on errors identified by computer editing and validation programs.

The file librarian function is responsible for maintaining a separate storage area—the file library—for control of files and programs stored on cards, magnetic tape, or disk packs. The file librarian should maintain an inventory of all files and programs in the library and should keep a record of files and program copies checked out for use by other systems personnel.

In many computer installations, there are additional functional specializations not mentioned here, such as data communications specialists, operations research personnel, scheduling personnel, and training specialists. On the other hand, in a small installation many of the functions shown in Fig. 14.1 might be combined. Some perspective on the relative proportions of employees in these various functional specialties is provided by a recent survey of 131 large computer sites. According to this survey, the typical large company employs about 250 people in its computer facility, including 17.1 percent in data entry, 23.1 percent in computer operations, 12 percent in systems analysis, 22.3 percent in programming, 6.7 percent in systems programming, 4.8 percent in management, and the remaining 14 percent in other support functions.[3] Furthermore, the basic separation of systems development and maintenance from data processing operations was found in virtually all the computer sites surveyed.

Organizational independence within the systems function

The effective achievement of organizational independence in a computer-based information system requires a clear division of authority and responsibility among the following functions: (1) application systems analysis and programming, (2) computer operations, (3) systems programming, (4) transaction authorization, (5) file library, and (6) data control. As pointed out in the AICPA's professional standards:

> In a computerized accounting system, functions that would be incompatible in a manual system are often performed by computer. Individuals who have access to computer operations may then be in a position to perpetrate or conceal errors or irregularities. This need not be a weakness if there are control procedures that prevent such an individual from performing incompatible functions within the accounting system. These control procedures might include (a) adequate segregation of incompatible functions within the data processing department, (b) segregation between data processing and user department personnel performing review procedures, and (c) adequate control over access to data and computer programs.[4]

The most important segregation of functions within the data processing department is that between application systems analysis and programming, on the one hand, and computer operations personnel, on the other. A programmer or systems analyst who is also permitted to operate the computer

---

[3]From a study conducted by International Data Corp., as reported in Bruce P. Hoard, "Division of 250 Employees Found Typical MIS Profile," *Computerworld* (August 25, 1980): 4.

[4]Statements on Auditing Standards (SAS) No. 1, AU Sec. 320.68, as amended by SAS No. 48 issued by the Auditing Standards Board in July 1984.

could easily make unauthorized changes in application programs. Alternatively, a computer operator who has unrestricted access to program copies and detailed documentation also could implement unauthorized program changes. Thus systems analysis and programming, and computer operations are incompatible functions in a data processing environment. Organizational independence accordingly requires that programmers and analysts not have access to the computer room, and that operators have access to programs and documentation only when authorized and supervised.

Separation of the analysis and programming function from other functions should be accompanied by a policy of formal authorization for necessary program changes. A written description of such changes and the reasons for them should be submitted to a data processing manager, chief analyst, or some other person in a position of authority, whose authorization should be required prior to testing such changes, and whose approval of test results should be required prior to final implementation of program changes. Complete documentation of all program changes should be retained.

The computer operations function is particularly sensitive from a control standpoint and thus requires additional controls. Close and effective supervision of the operations activity is one such control. Another is a policy of rotation of operations personnel among jobs and shifts in order to avoid having any single operator who always processes the same job. Still another useful control procedure is a requirement that a minimum of two qualified personnel be on duty in the computer room during all processing. In addition, a copy of the printout from the computer console should be maintained as a record of processing. This console log should be reviewed periodically for any evidence of irregularity in connection with manual intervention by the operator during regular processing.

Another point stressed in the professional standards, as quoted above, is "adequate control over access to data and computer programs." Separation of the file librarian function accomplishes this control by limiting all access to data files except by authorized personnel under authorized conditions. The file librarian also keeps a record of all such usage, and this record should be periodically reviewed for evidence of unusual circumstances.

For organizations large enough to afford a greater degree of specialization, the separate data control function provides an additional measure of organizational independence. The presence of data control personnel further inhibits the possibility of unauthorized access to the computer facility, provides an additional element of supervision of computer operations personnel, and contributes to more efficient data processing operations.

The systems programming function is also very sensitive from a control standpoint. With detailed knowledge of the operating system and other systems software, the systems programmer may have the opportunity to make unauthorized changes in application programs or data files. To minimize this risk, the systems programmer must not be permitted access to application programs and their documentation or to live files and data bases.

The function of transaction authorization properly resides outside the systems department. User departments responsible for submitting computer input should also submit a signed authorization form accompanying each batch of input. The signature verifies that the input has been properly prepared and reviewed, and that appropriate control totals have been compiled. Data control personnel should verify the presence of appropriate authorization signatures and control totals prior to submitting user-prepared input for processing.

In a micro- or minicomputer installation, adequate segregation of functions is often not possible because the computer may be physically located within the user department, and user department personnel may program and operate the computer. In this environment, other elements of internal control should be stressed in order to compensate for the potential control deficiencies. These compensating controls include restrictions on physical access to the equipment; the use of locks and keys on the machine itself; password controls over access to data files and programs; effective supervision on the part of user department managers; automatic preparation of a transaction log for review by management; careful review of processing logs and batch totals by supervisory personnel; and sound personnel practices, including bonding of key employees, enforced vacations, and periodic rotation of duties.[5]

Management Control of the Information Systems Function

The folklore of the computer industry includes numerous stories of poorly run computer facilities, systems projects whose completion time and cost requirements far exceed expectations, and even some projects that were never successfully implemented after consuming millions of dollars worth of developmental effort. To a great extent situations of this type represent failures of management control. The basic principles of responsibility accounting are directly relevant to the information systems function. The effective application of these principles, by means of documenting personnel activities and reporting on the performance of systems staff personnel and managers, greatly reduces the possibility of major cost overruns or spectacular project failures and substantially improves the efficiency and effectiveness of the information systems function.

Some key elements of management control of the systems function have been discussed in prior chapters. One is the long-range systems plan that, like all plans, provides a framework for management control and a standard

---

[5]For a look at this issue in greater depth, see Harry Zimmerman, "Minicomputers: The Challenge for Controls," *Journal of Accountancy* (June 1980): 28–35; or William G. Birtle, Barry D. Hawkins, and Walter D. Pugh, "How to Evaluate Accounting Controls in a Minicomputer Installation," *Practical Accountant* (August 1980): 47–53; or American Institute of Certified Public Accountants, *Audit and Control Considerations in a Minicomputer or Small Business Computer Environment* (New York: AICPA), 1981.

against which performance may be measured. A second such element is a system of charging user departments for computer services, which provides important feedback both to the users themselves and to top-level systems managers and their superiors on the overall performance of the systems function. A third is a project development plan for each major systems project, often accompanied by a Gantt chart or a PERT schedule, which provides a basis for control of the systems development effort.

This section describes three additional elements of management control over the systems function. First is the measurement and evaluation of the performance of programmers and systems analysts. Second is the control of systems projects under development by means of periodic progress reviews and post-implementation follow-up. Third is the measurement and evaluation of performance of the computer operations activity and its personnel.

Programmer/analyst performance evaluation

A key element of performance evaluation of systems personnel is the collection of information on the specific activities in which those personnel have been involved. This requires the use of a time-reporting system under which each analyst and programmer is required to account daily for how his or her time was spent, with activities classified according to the projects and programs worked on as well as the type of work performed. An example of a daily time sheet for this purpose is shown in Fig. 14.2. Note that the information collected on this form provides input not only for employee performance evaluation but also for project cost accumulation and reporting.

Because the analysis and programming effort involved in large systems development projects may span a long period of time, it is a mistake to wait until the project is completed to evaluate the performance of the analysts and programmers involved. Instead, each project should be broken down into a series of small parts, or modules, each of which may be assigned to a single individual. For each module certain objectives are established, such as test specifications for a section of program code, or documentation specifications for a portion of the systems design. Estimates incorporated in the project plan provide standards of quality, time, and cost against which the performance of the person assigned to the job may be evaluated. The evaluation itself is performed immediately upon completion of each module.

With respect to programming, it is possible to develop rough measures of accomplishment for comparative purposes. The number of instructions that a completed program module contains may be divided by the number of hours spent by the programmers in preparing the module to provide a measure of "instructions per hour." This measure may then be used to compare the relative efficiency of all programmers within the organization. Further provisions have to be made to take into account factors such as the differences in size and complexity of programs and the variations in experience levels of programmers. Nonetheless, this approach in its simplest form does at least furnish some objective information with which to control programming ac-

FIGURE 14.2

Daily time sheet for programmers and analysts. (This figure is reprinted with permission from Rudolph E. Hirsch, "Data Processing *Can* be Cost-Controlled," *Price Waterhouse Review*, Summer 1970.)

NAME _A.E. Neumann_   EMPLOYEE NO. _39070_   DATE _5/22/81_

| TIME CHARGED TO | | TYPE OF WORK | | | | | | | | | | |
PROJECT	PROGRAM	SYSTEM ANALYSIS	SYSTEM DESIGN	DETAIL DIAGRAMMING	PROGRAMMING	TESTING AND DEBUGGING	CONVERSION AND PARALLEL	DOCUMENTATION	TRAVEL	TRAINING	MEETING	OTHER*
1260	007				2							
8971	012			1								
6407	023			1								
6407	024				2							
0705	101					1		1				
TOTALS				2	4	1		1				

*For "Other" categories, use the project code indicated below.

  9000-1 Vacation
  9000-2 Holiday
  9000-3 Personal Time
  9000-4 Illness
  9000-5 Professional or Technical Societies

tivities, and it also provides a basis for estimating the time and cost requirements of future developmental projects.[6]

If a reasonably standard measure of "instructions per hour" can be developed, it becomes possible to budget programmer hours and then to prepare programmer performance reports that compare these estimates with actual performance and determine variances. An example of such a performance report is shown in Fig. 14.3.

With respect to systems analysis, measures of employee performance cannot be quite as precise. Time and cost standards are more difficult to develop in the absence of a unit of work such as number of instructions. However, the quality of documentation prepared may be evaluated, and over a period of time, a reasonably accurate subjective impression may be formed of how efficiently an analyst performs his or her assigned tasks. Since much of the analyst's job requires interaction with system users, on the one hand, and with programmers, on the other, skill in interpersonal relations is an important factor in the success of employees assigned this role.

Systems project controls

The systems development process should be subject to strict management control. One key element of this control is the assignment of responsibility for the success of each project to a project manager and a project team. Another is the project development plan that divides the project into phases, with time and cost estimates for each phase. The plan should specify *project milestones,* or significant points in the developmental effort at which a formal review of progress is made. An important element of such progress reviews is a comparison of actual completion times for each project phase with estimated completion times. Data on the actual completion times can be accumulated from the daily time sheets filled out by programmers and analysts. Figure 14.4 provides an illustration of a possible format for such a progress report.

In addition to the time and cost analysis, a project progress review should consider a number of other factors—for example, the adherence of the project team to quality standards for documentation, program testing, and system auditability. In addition, estimates of remaining project completion times, costs, and benefits should be reevaluated based upon the additional experience gained since the previous progress review. If this reassessment reveals a significant change in expectations, the entire project timetable should be revised, and it may even be necessary to consider whether the project should be completely halted.

Another important aspect of project control is the follow-up review subsequent to implementation of a new computer application. This should be done periodically for all applications for the purpose of evaluating whether each is generating economic benefits in excess of costs in an amount consis-

---

[6]Further discussion of programmer performance evaluation is provided by Trevor D. Crossman, "Taking the Measure of Programmer Productivity," *Datamation* (May 1979): 144–147.

FIGURE 14.3

Programmer performance analysis. (This figure is reprinted with permission from Rudolph E. Hirsch, "Data Processing *Can Be Cost-Controlled. Price Waterhouse Review,* Summer 1970.

NAME   NORMAN, A.E.   REPORTING PERIOD   7/16–31/81

PROJECT AND PROGRAM	*IF COMPLETE	DESCRIPTION	LANGUAGE	NO. OF INSTRUCTIONS	PROGRAMMING HOURS				COMPUTER TEST HOURS			
					PERIOD	TO DATE ACTUAL	TO DATE ESTIMATED	VARIANCE	PERIOD	TO DATE ACTUAL	TO DATE ESTIMATE	VARIANCE
0041/012	*	TRAVEL EXPENSE DISTB.	COBOL	425	–	13	15	–2	–	2	2	0
0702/009	*	UPDATE CUSTOMER FILE	COBOL	650	–	64	50	+14	–	19	7	+12
0705/101	*	PRINT MAIL LABELS	COBOL	40	2	6	5	+1	1	2	1	+1
1260/007		TIME CARD EDIT	COBOL	512	2	24	20	+4	–	4	5	–1
6407/023		STORES ISSUE REGISTER	COBOL	375	1	9	7	+2	–	–	–	–
6407/024		STORES ISSUE TOTALS	COBOL	185	2	5	5	0	–	–	–	–
8971/012		OPTIMIZE MAINTENC.	COBOL	94	1	12	10	+2	–	2	2	0
TOTALS				2,281	8	133	112	+21	1	29	17	+12

572

FIGURE 14.4

Systems project progress report. (This figure is reprinted with permission from Rudolph E. Hirsch, "Data Processing *Can Be Cost-Controlled*," *Price Waterhouse Review*, Summer 1970.)

PROJECT IDENTIFICATION 0702. CUSTOMER FILE PROCESSING

STATUS AS OF 7/31/81

PROGRAM	DESCRIPTION	TARGET DATE	SYSTEM ANALYSIS	SYSTEM DESIGN	DETAIL DIAGRAMMING	PROGRAMMING	TESTING AND DEBUGGING	CONVERSION AND PARALLEL	DOCUMENTATION	TRAVEL	TRAINING	MEETINGS	COMPUTER TIME	KEYPUNCH AND DATA PREP.	COST
0000	GEN. PROJECT	6/2/0								8	1	4	2		$ 177
0001	INPUT EDIT	7/9/0							5			2	4		330
0003	CREATE FILE	8/4/0	1			30	4	7	8				3	1	541
0004	SELECT 01	8/6/0		2	2	15	13	6	9				1	1	962
0007	SELECT 02	9/1/0				10	11	4	6				2	2	510
0009	UPDATE	9/1/0				12	13	1	7				1	2	638
0015	RESTARTS	9/1/0	1	2	7		4	9	2			1		3	453
	TOTAL THIS PERIOD		2	4	9	67	45	27	37	8	1	7	13	9	$3,611
	TOTAL TO DATE		46	35	42	128	105	44	69	16	16	21	39	15	$9,771
	ESTIMATE		50	30	40	135	120	40	70	18	10	5	25	20	$8,607
	VARIANCE		-4	+5	+2	-7	-15	+4	-1	-2	+6	+16	+14	-5	+$1,164

tent with the original project proposal and development plan. Any significant unfavorable variance should require an explanation from the persons responsible for the original estimates and should initiate efforts to correct the situation if possible. These follow-up reviews not only help to control project development activities but also help to encourage more accurate and objective initial estimates of project costs and benefits.

Control of computer operations

A basic element of computer operations control is the data processing schedule. The schedule is prepared at the beginning of each shift by a supervisor or scheduling clerk. It should assign each incoming job to an appropriate time period in a way that maximizes the productive utilization of all available equipment to the greatest possible extent. The schedule should also provide time for necessary preventive maintenance and should allow some slack time for the inevitable equipment malfunctions requiring corrective maintenance and for occasional reruns of incorrectly processed work.

Evaluation of the performance of all machine operators should be based upon a comparison of actual processing time with scheduled processing time for all jobs run by each operator. Of course, actual processing time must be adjusted for losses of productive time due to malfunctions or other factors not under the control of the operator. Furthermore, the scheduled processing time must be adjusted for variations in actual volume of processing from average volume to provide an equitable standard.

The performance of data entry personnel may be evaluated in two ways. One is by measuring their output in terms of keystrokes per hour or some similar measure and then comparing each individual operator's rate with an average or standard. A second is to measure the error rate of all data entry work in terms of the percentage of errors discovered by key verification or by editing routines built into the computer programs. Obviously, these two approaches complement each other because one is basically a measure of efficiency and the other is a measure of quality.

Also useful for computer operations control are data on machine utilization for the computer hardware. The simplest way to collect such data is to require each shift operator to fill out a daily computer log indicating the jobs processed or other events occurring during the time available. An example of a form for this purpose is illustrated in Fig. 14.5. In addition, whenever productive computer time is lost owing to equipment malfunction, operator error, or other problems, a separate form should be filled out specifying the amount of time lost and identifying the cause of the problem.

Data collected in this fashion provide useful input to a number of management reports and analyses. For example, computer time recorded for testing of systems under development can be charged to the specific project. Also, the lost-time data can be aggregated weekly or monthly to provide an analysis of the causes of lost time. Finally, the daily computer logs themselves can be aggregated to provide a breakdown of total available computer time for each

FIGURE 14.5

Daily computer log. (This figure is reprinted with permission from Rudolph E. Hirsch, "Data Processing *Can Be Cost-Controlled,*" *Price Waterhouse Review,* Summer 1970.)

SYSTEM TYPE AND NUMBER ___570/50-1___

DATE ___5/22/81___

PROJECT PROGRAM IDENTIFICATION	PROGRAMMER	OPERATION CODE	MODE	ELAPSED TIME START	STOP	TOTAL	COMPUTER TIME START	STOP	TOTAL	LOST TIME CODE	Trouble Report Number	OPERATOR	COMMENTS
0001/000		30		0801	0857	56	4625	4718	93			J.C.	
1214/004		10		0858	1004	66	4718	4828	110			J.C.	
0705/101	13	11		1005	1100	55	4828	4920	92			J.C.	
0041/012		10		1102	1240	98	4920	5083	163			J.C.	
1600/008		10		1241	1243	2	5083	5086	3	42	2-14	L.B.B.	
0705/101	13	12		1245	1314	29	5086	5134	48			L.B.B.	

OPERATION CODES:

10 – PRODUCTION	20 – IDLE	30 – PREVENTIVE MAINTENANCE
11 – DEBUGGING	21 – SPECIAL	31 – UNSCHEDULED MAINTENANCE
12 – ASSEMBLY	22 – POWER OFF	

LOST TIME CODES:

40 – LOST TIME-COMPUTER	43 – LOST TIME-PROGRAM
41 – LOST TIME-OPERATOR	49 – LOST TIME-OTHER
42 – LOST TIME-INPUT DATA	

575

week or month into categories such as (1) productive time, (2) idle time, (3) reruns, and (4) machine maintenance and downtime.[7] Reports of this type are extremely useful to systems management in evaluating the efficiency of the computer operations activity, scheduling future processing operations, estimating operating costs for new projects, and establishing management policies for the operations function.

There are a number of ways of using the computer itself to collect and report information on the effectiveness of computer usage. *Hardware monitors* are devices that may be connected to a computer to collect information on the percent utilization of various system resources (CPU, channels, etc.) and on the number of occurrences of particular events (disk accesses, print lines, etc.). *Software monitors* are programs that may be linked to the operating system for the same purpose. *Job accounting routines* are programs, also linked to the operating system, to measure and record resource utilization for each job processed in order to facilitate cost accounting and charging computer users for services. These tools also provide a source of useful information for systems management.

Procedural and Security Controls for the Computer Facility

Procedural controls (general)

The AICPA's professional standards suggest a two-way classification of controls in a computer-based accounting information system: "General controls are those controls that relate to all or many computerized accounting activities. . . . Application controls relate to individual computerized accounting applications."[8] Among the most critical general controls are those relating to the plan of organization of data processing activities and the separation of incompatible functions, discussed earlier in this chapter. This section covers the remaining general controls, including documentation standards, data security procedures, physical protection of computer facilities, insurance, provisions for backup, hardware controls, and computer security planning. The next section covers application controls.

Documentation standards

Good documentation is an important asset to the efficient operation and control of a computer-based information system. Data-processing management must establish and enforce standards that specify what documentation is required for projects under development and for fully implemented systems. An important part of the progress reviews of systems projects involves a management review of the adequacy of documentation. There is a natural ten-

---

[7]According to a 1971 survey conducted by the consulting firm of A. T. Kearney & Co., the breakdown of available time among twenty-two more efficient computer-using companies into these categories was (1) eighty-one percent, (2) ten percent, (3) six percent, and (4) three percent. See Walter Schroeder, "The EDP Manager—and the Computer Profit Drain," *Computers and Automation* (January 1971): 14–18.

[8]Statements on Auditing Standards (SAS) No. 1, AU Sec. 320.34, as amended by SAS No. 48 issued by the Auditing Standards Board in July 1984.

dency for many systems analysts and programmers to view documentation as a necessary evil at best, and so management must continually stress its importance as part of a professional approach to systems work.

Documentation may be classified into three basic categories—(1) administrative documentation, (2) systems documentation, and (3) operating documentation. *Administrative documentation* represents a description of overall standards and procedures for the data processing facility, including policies relating to justification and authorization of new systems or systems changes; standards for systems analysis, design, and programming; procedures for file handling and file library activities; and so forth. *Systems documentation* includes a complete description of all aspects of each systems application, including narrative material, charts, and program listings as described in Chapter 6. *Operating documentation* includes all information required by a computer operator to run the program, including the equipment configuration used, variable data to be entered on the computer console, descriptions of conditions leading to program halts and related corrective actions, and so forth.

The purposes served by well-planned and enforced documentation standards within an organization are many. Among the benefits resulting from good documentation are facilitation of communication among system users, analysts, and programmers during systems development; facilitation of regular progress reviews of systems development work; provision of a reference and training tool for systems users, machine operators, and newly hired employees within the systems function; and simplification of the program maintenance function.

Good documentation is particularly important in view of the high rate of turnover among systems analysts and programmers. If a programmer leaves an organization in the middle of a major project, much time may be wasted by colleagues attempting to continue the work if the programmer has not maintained up-to-date documentation. If a programmer responsible for developing some of the existing applications in a system leaves without having provided adequate documentation, the making of necessary changes in those applications may be extremely difficult, perhaps almost as difficult as developing completely new programs. These potential problems underscore the necessity of requiring analysts and programmers to adhere to documentation standards in their work.

Protection of facilities

An organization's investment in computer facilities often amounts to hundreds of thousands or millions of dollars. It follows that this equipment should receive adequate physical protection. Access to the computer system itself and to all online data terminals should be restricted at all times to authorized personnel only. The temptation to locate the computer facilities in a glass-encased "showcase" should be avoided, for this presents an inviting target for ill-intentioned persons. Contingency plans for protection of equipment during natural disasters or riots should be established.

Data security

Good internal control in a computer installation requires that provisions be made for protection of files and programs from unauthorized disclosure or accidental destruction. The requirements of authorization and supervision for the removal of tapes or disk packs from a file library represent an essential element of such control. Both the computer room and the file storage locations should be protected against fire, dust, excesses of heat or humidity, or other adverse conditions.

Tape rings and file labels are useful devices in protecting against accidental writing over or erasure of files. A *tape file protection ring* is a device that, when inserted on a reel of magnetic tape, permits writing on the tape. In the absence of the ring, the tape may not be written on, and the data on the reel are protected. Thus the tape ring is removed when any application is processed for which the tape file need only be read. File labels are both internal and external. An *external label* is merely a gummed paper label attached to a tape reel or disk pack, upon which may be written the file identification, date processed, and other information. *Internal labels* are written in machine-readable form on the data recording media and are of three different types. A *volume label* identifies the contents of each separate data recording medium, such as a tape reel, diskette, or disk pack. Each volume may contain one or more files. A *header label* appears at the beginning of each separate file and contains the file name, expiration date, and other file identification information. The header label is read by the computer prior to processing the file and is checked against the program to ensure that the file is the correct one for the program. A *trailer label* appears at the end of each file and serves as an indicator that the end of the file has been reached. The trailer label often contains file control totals, which are checked against those accumulated during processing.

In addition to protection against loss or destruction, an information systems control plan should also make provisions for reconstruction of records, should such loss actually occur. Duplicate tapes of programs and important files should be stored in a location away from the computer facility as a protection against a major disaster such as fire or flood. One data retention procedure used most commonly with magnetic tape files is known as the *grandfather-father-son concept*. Under this plan the three most recent master files are all retained, with the son file being the most recent. If the processing to produce the son file from the father file is accomplished with no errors or destruction of records, the grandfather file is then no longer needed and can be reused as the new son file at the next file update. If an error or loss of records does occur in the father and/or the son file during processing, the grandfather file can be used as a basis for reconstruction.

With respect to disk files, a file security program requires that the contents of the file be duplicated, generally by writing the file onto magnetic tape. If transactions are processed in batches, the duplicate serves as the father file in the event of errors or destruction of data in the updating process. If transactions are processed online, a log of all transactions may also be recorded on disk or tape, which, together with the most recent duplicate copy of the file, could be used to reconstruct the current disk file.

When a data base management system is used to maintain and process accounting data, additional data security is provided by the presence of a data base administrator, the use of a data dictionary, and concurrent update controls. The data base administrator establishes and enforces standard procedures for accessing and updating the data base. The data dictionary should ensure consistency in the way that data items are defined and used. Concurrent update controls protect individual records from potential errors that could occur if two users attempt to update the same record simultaneously; this is accomplished by "locking out" one user until the system has finished processing the update entered by the other user.[9]

With respect to highly confidential data, protection against unauthorized disclosure is provided by a paper shredder and by cryptographic protection. A shredder may be used to chop and mutilate confidential papers and printouts, such as customer listings, research data, and payroll registers, once they are no longer needed. *Cryptographic protection* involves the translation of data into a secret code for storage purposes or prior to data transmission. The data may then be translated back to meaningful form for authorized usage. Cryptographic protection is particularly important when confidential data are being transmitted from remote terminals because data transmission lines can be electronically monitored without the user's knowledge.

Hardware controls

Several control features are built into the hardware in a computer system. One example is *duplicate circuitry* in the arithmetic unit of the central processor that results in duplicate performance of computations and subsequent comparison of the two results. *Dual reading* is another hardware control in which records on cards, tape, or random access media are read twice by separate reading components, and the results of both read operations are compared. Still another hardware control is the *echo check,* in which the accuracy of data transmissions to an output device is checked by comparing a signal sent back to the computer from the output device with the data originally sent. Generally, when such comparisons reveal a discrepancy, the function is repeated.

Hardware controls may also be used to help control access to a computer system. Many computer systems may be switched off and on using a lock and key similar to an automobile ignition. Also, some computer terminals may be given an electronic identification number that enables the central processor to recognize whether or not it is being accessed from an authorized terminal.

The use of the parity bit to check the accuracy of data transfer within a computer system is one type of hardware control already discussed. (See Chap-

---

[9]For further discussion of control considerations in a data base environment, see *Report of the Joint Data Base Task Force,* Walter D. Pugh, Chairman (New York: American Institute of Certified Public Accountants, 1983).

ter 5.) Two-dimensional parity checking is an extension of parity checking commonly used for data transmission over telecommunications facilities. This involves use of a redundant column of check bits for each record in addition to a redundant row of check bits. The parity checking is thus done both vertically and horizontally. This form of control is important in telecommunications because noise bursts frequently cause two or more adjacent bits to be lost or picked up. A vertical parity check alone would not catch all such errors.

Two additional hardware controls that help to prevent processing errors are *preventive maintenance* and *uninterruptible power systems*. Preventive maintenance involves regular testing of all system components and replacement of those found to be in a weak condition. This greatly reduces the likelihood of a system failure during regular operations. An uninterruptible power system consists of an auxiliary power supply that operates as a buffer between the power input from the electric company and the power usage by the computer. Such systems smooth out the flow of power to the computer, eliminating loss of data that might be caused by momentary surges or dips in power flow. In the event of complete power failure, uninterruptible power systems provide a backup power supply to keep the computer operating without interruption until regular power is restored.[10]

Insurance

Recognizing that it is impossible to fully protect computer facilities and data from all possible harm, an insurance program should be a key part of an organization's control strategy. Major risks to be insured against include fire, flooding, severe weather, riots, and sabotage. The fidelity bond (see Chapter 4) provides insurance against the risk of loss from embezzlement. Fidelity bonds are particularly essential in small installations in which extensive separation of functions is not possible. In some installations that handle work for outsiders in addition to their own work, liability insurance for losses incurred owing to errors in performing the work may be necessary.

Backup systems and procedures

Another form of protection against risk consists of backup systems and procedures. With respect to disasters that could completely disable a computer facility, an organization should have a disaster recovery plan that will prepare it to recover its data processing capacity as smoothly and quickly as possible. This plan should establish priorities for the recovery process, such as by identifying those applications most critical in keeping the organization running. A key element of the plan is an arrangement with the vendor or a service bureau that permits usage of their facilities in the event of an emergency. Also essential for disaster recovery is the storage of duplicate copies of critical files

---

[10]The cost and benefits of uninterruptible power are discussed in greater depth in Neil D. Kelley, "The Economics of Uninterruptible Power," *Infosystems* (September 1980): 55–64.

and programs in a location away from the organization's main computer center.[11]

Backup procedures must also be established to deal with temporary hardware failures that inevitably occur. The capability of a system to continue performing its functions in the presence of hardware failure is known as *fault tolerance*. Within individual hardware devices, fault tolerance is provided by the use of redundant components, any one of which can take over for another in the event of failure. The same principle can be extended to systems that consist of several hardware devices. For example, in a real-time system for which maintaining a constant level of service is essential, hardware components such as terminals, multiplexors, disk files, or even CPUs may be duplicated so that the system can switch to the backup component if necessary.

Computer security planning

Many authorities in the systems field are now advocating a systematic approach to the management of data processing security that may be referred to as "computer security planning." Under this approach, an organization attempts to identify all possible threats or hazards associated with its data processing equipment and operations. Then it attempts to assess vulnerabilities—i.e., threats for which there is a lack of protection—and risks—i.e., the likelihoods that each threat will actually come to pass. Finally, it attempts to estimate the exposure for each threat, which is the harm or loss that will be suffered if the threat actually does come to pass.

Based upon the vulnerability and risk analysis outlined above, the organization then prepares a computer security plan that attempts (1) to minimize the likelihood of each threat, (2) to minimize the exposure if the threat is not avoided, and (3) to provide for recovery from the damage associated with any threats that are not avoided. The elements of such a computer security plan are the internal control policies and procedures described throughout this chapter; however, data security procedures, system access controls, and backup systems are generally emphasized. The advantage of the computer security planning approach is that it helps the organization to select that set of control policies and procedures that optimizes the level of computer security relative to cost.[12]

Application Controls

Application controls are those that relate to specific processing jobs as they are performed at the computer facility. They involve the data inputs, files, programs, and outputs of a specific computer application, rather than the

---

[11]For further discussion of disaster recovery plans and backup facilities, see Larry Lettieri, "Disaster Recovery: Picking Up the Pieces," *Computer Decisions* (March 1979): 16–22, 27; and Wayne L. Rhodes, Jr., "Second Site Protection," *Infosystems* (September 1980): 46–52.

[12]For further discussion of computer security planning, see K. S. Shankar, "The Total Computer Security Problem: An Overview," *Computer* (June 1977): 50–62; and Richard G. Canning, "The Security of Managers' Information," *EDP Analyzer* (July 1979): 1–13.

computer system in general. Their primary objective is to maintain the accuracy of the system's outputs, data files, and transaction records. They include batch totals, source data controls of various kinds, programmed input validation routines, control over the errors and exceptions revealed by other controls, checkpoint/restart recovery procedures, and online data entry controls.

Batch totals

Batch totals are as essential to computerized batch processing as they are to manual data processing. In a computerized batch processing application, batch totals are accumulated manually from source documents prior to input preparation. The original totals are then compared with machine-generated totals at each subsequent processing step. Any discrepancy may indicate a loss of records or errors in data transcription or processing.

Three forms of batch totals commonly used in computer systems are *financial totals, hash totals,* and *record counts.* A financial total is simply the total of a dollar field in a set of records, such as total sales or total cash receipts. A hash total is a total generated from a field that would usually not otherwise be added, such as a total of all customer account numbers or employee identification numbers. A record count is a total of the number of input documents to a process or of records processed in a run.

One special form of batch total is the *cross-footing balance test.* This can be performed only on a set of data that is additive horizontally (across several columns) as well as vertically (down each column). When the column that contains the horizontal sums of all the other columns is added downward, the resulting total should also equal the horizontal sum of all the other column totals. For example, the sum of the gross pay column in a payroll application should equal the sum of the net pay column plus all deductions columns.

For large volumes of data, the effective use of batch totals requires that they be accumulated for smaller subsets of the total set of records, such as for every fifty items. In this way any errors that are encountered will be isolated among a smaller group of records, making it easier to find the specific record or records that are in error.

Source data controls

These include a number of checks on the accuracy and completeness of computer input prior to processing. One form of checking the accuracy of input data is key verification, which may be done using a key-to-tape encoder or other key-operated data entry device. (See Chapter 5.) Where keyverification is not considered to be essential or is too expensive, a substitute source data control is the visual inspection of printed input listings prior to processing.

Another source data control is *check digit verification,* which may be performed by any data entry device having a processing capability, including a key-to-disk-to-tape system or an intelligent terminal. In check digit verification, all authorized identification numbers contain a redundant digit, called the check digit or *self-checking digit*. This digit is a numerical function of the other digits in the number. For example, in the number 90614, the last digit, 4, could be generated by subtracting the sum of the first four digits from the next highest number ending in zero $(20 - 16 = 4)$. The number 41365 would fail this test. To use check digit verification, the microprocessor within the data entry device must be programmed to perform the check digit test each time an identification number (such as a customer account number or employee number) is entered. If an error in the keying of an identification number occurs, check digit verification will probably (but not certainly) detect the error and signal the operator. As a result, most such errors may be corrected prior to submission of the input for computer processing.

As is the case in manual systems, sequentially prenumbered forms provide a useful form of control over source documents to computer systems. In a computer system, control of sequentially prenumbered forms is facilitated by using the computer to determine and report the numbers of forms that have not been processed. The forms containing these numbers can then be traced in order to ensure that all data that should be processed are eventually received by the system.

The turnaround document is defined in Chapter 5 and described as a means of reducing the data preparation work load. Since turnaround documents are automatically prepared as computer output, the data they contain are generally much more accurate than if they had been manually keyed. As a result, when they return to the system as computer input, their greater reliability provides better internal control.

Various activities of the data control function (described earlier in this chapter) contribute significantly to source data control. When source data are received for processing, data control personnel check for necessary user authorizations and record the name and source of the transactions, the record count, control totals, and other relevant information concerning the input in a control log. Data control personnel then monitor the progress of the source data through the data preparation process, expediting the process when necessary to meet the processing schedule, rechecking record counts and control totals after the data preparation process is completed, and initiating any necessary corrections to the data prior to submitting them for computer processing.

Input validation routines

Input validation routines are programs or routines therein that utilize the computer to check the validity and accuracy of input data. These are also called *edit programs*, and the specific types of accuracy checks they perform are called *edit checks*. In many cases input validation is performed by a separate program prior to regular processing, in which case any errors discovered may be corrected before the input is processed (see Fig. 14.6). In other cases input validation is performed as part of regular processing, in which case input records rejected as invalid must be resubmitted in the next regular processing run.

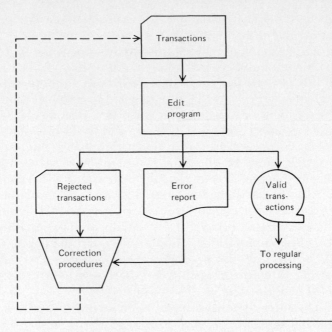

FIGURE 14.6
Edit program.

There are several different types of edit checks used in input validation routines. A *sequence check* is a check on whether a batch of input data is in the proper numerical or alphabetical sequence. A *field check* is a check on the characters in a field to ensure that they are of the class the field is supposed to contain. For example, a field check on a numeric field would indicate an error if it revealed that the field contained blanks or alphabetic characters. A *sign check* is a check to ensure that the data in a field are of the appropriate arithmetic sign. For example, data in a field such as inventory balance should never have a negative sign.

Other edit checks include the *validity check,* which tests identification numbers or transaction codes for validity by comparison with ones already known to be authorized. For example, in a sequential file updating process, any transaction for which the control field value does not match that of an existing file record, and that is not coded as a new record to be added to the file, should be flagged as invalid. Check digit verification may be performed in an input validation routine in the same way that it is performed when input is prepared. Still another common form of edit check is a *limit check,* which is a test to ensure that a numerical amount in a record does not exceed some acceptable limit that has been predetermined. For example, the hours-worked field in a payroll processing run may be checked to ensure that no input record contains hours worked in excess of sixty in a single week. A *reasonableness test* is a check of the logical correctness of relationships among the values of data items on an input record and its corresponding file record. For example, a

journal entry that debits inventory and credits wages payable is not reasonable. Similarly, the quantity received of inventory items might be tested for
reasonableness by checking whether it exceeds twice the value of the order
quantity of the item.

One other form of edit check is the *redundant data check*. This check requires that two identifiers be included for each input transaction record that
is to be updated in order to confirm that the correct match will be obtained
by cross-checking. For example, if both the customer account number and the
first five letters of the customer's name are included on the input record, the
system can check, after obtaining a match on account number, whether the
first five letters also match those on the file. This check has the purpose
of preventing the posting of transactions to the wrong master file records.

**Online access
controls**

Virtually all modern data processing systems may be accessed from terminals
located at a distance from the central computer site. This means that system
access controls must include not only restrictions on physical access to the
central computer but also controls over access to the system from online terminals. Restrictions on physical access to terminals are helpful but not always
effective. Therefore online access controls are primarily focused on the systems software that controls the interaction between terminal users and the
system.

One type of online access control mentioned previously is to provide each
terminal with an electronic identification number. The system is then programmed to accept commands and transactions only from terminals having
authorized identification numbers. Also, those online systems that need to be
operational only during business hours (such as a banking system) may be
programmed to enable a supervisor to deactivate the system by signing off
from a terminal at the end of each day. Then the system would accept no more
transactions until the supervisor activated it by signing on at the beginning
of the next day.

The most essential and universally used form of online access control is
a system of user codes and passwords. Under this system each authorized user
is assigned a unique user code number and password that must be keyed into
the system prior to using it. There have been a number of well-publicized cases
of persons who have gained unauthorized access to online systems by repeated
testing of user numbers until a valid one is discovered or by correctly guessing
a user's password. The risk of this type of unauthorized system access can be
all but eliminated by a well-designed online access control system that includes
the following features. First, the system should shut off service to the terminal
of any user who is unable to provide a valid user number or password within
three attempts. Second, passwords should be randomly assigned by the system
rather than selected by users, because users often choose a word or name that
may be easily guessed. Third, if a user who has supplied a valid user number
is unable to supply a valid password within five or six attempts, the user num-

ber itself should be invalidated. Fourth, in highly sensitive systems, repeated attempts to access the system utilizing invalid user numbers or passwords should cause security personnel to immediately investigate the terminal from which such attempts are being originated. Finally, the access control process should be performed by a device (i.e., a microcomputer) that is external to the mainframe computer so that no one can obtain access of any kind to the mainframe without first supplying a valid user number and password.

Once an authorized code number and password have been accepted by the system and the user is allowed to proceed, the system may apply a *compatibility test* to transactions or inquiries entered by the user. This checks whether the user having the code number given is authorized to initiate the type of transaction or inquiry being entered. For example, factory employees would not be authorized to make entries involving accounts payable. This helps to prevent both unintentional errors and deliberate attempts to manipulate the system.

To perform compatibility tests, the system must maintain an internal *access control matrix* consisting of (1) a list of all authorized user code numbers and passwords, (2) a list of all files and programs maintained on the system, and (3) a record of the type of access each user is entitled to have to each type of file and program. "Type of access" refers to the things that the user is authorized to do to the file or program; examples of possible types of access include (1) no access permitted, (2) access to summary information only, (3) read and display individual records, and (4) various combinations of types of changes, including modifying field values within a record, adding a new record, deleting an existing record, or redefining the record structure. An example of an access control matrix appears in Fig. 14.7. According to the access

FIGURE 14.7
Access control matrix.

USER IDENTIFICATION		FILES			PROGRAMS			
Code number	Password	A	B	C	1	2	3	4
12345	ABC	0	0	1	0	0	0	0
12346	DEF	0	2	0	0	0	0	0
12354	KLM	1	1	1	0	0	0	0
12359	NOP	3	0	0	0	0	0	0
12389	RST	0	1	0	0	3	0	0
12567	XYZ	1	1	1	1	1	1	1

Codes for type of access:
0 = No access permitted.
1 = Read and display only.
2 = Read, display, and update.
3 = Read, display, update, create, and delete.

codes assigned to the various users in this example, user 12345-ABC is permitted only to read and display file C and is permitted no access of any kind to any other file or program. User 12359-NOP may perform any and all operations on file A but may access no other file or program. User 12389-RST is apparently a programmer who is authorized to make any type of change in program 2 and also to read and display records in file B. User 12567-XYZ, probably a supervisor, is authorized to read and display the contents of any and all files and programs.

A system of online access controls based upon user code numbers and passwords is effective only as long as each user's code number and password remain a secret to everyone except the user. For this reason, the system should be programmed never to display or print a user code number or password, and users should be cautioned not to disclose theirs to other persons. In addition, all passwords should be modified frequently to reduce the likelihood that a current password will become known to someone other than its authorized user. One other procedure useful to the maintenance of system security is for the system to record all attempts to access it from an unauthorized terminal or using an unauthorized user code number or password. Periodic review of this record by a security officer should disclose attempts by unauthorized persons to access the system.

Online data entry controls

This category includes all controls over the accuracy and integrity of input data entered into the system from online data terminals. Most controls in this category are specialized forms of input validation routines that are unique to online systems. In addition, many of the edit checks described in the previous section are useful in online systems as well as in batch systems. These include field checks, validity checks, limit checks, reasonableness tests, and the redundant data check.

If the personnel assigned to enter data input are generally inexperienced in the use of systems or terminals, then the system may be programmed to control the data entry process using a technique known as *prompting*. Under this approach the system displays a request to the user for each required item of input data and then waits for an acceptable response before requesting the next required item. An alternative procedure for this purpose is called *preformatting*, which involves the display of a document format containing blanks for the data items that the user must fill in. If preformatting or other free-form methods of data entry are used, the system should also perform a *completeness test* on each input record to check whether all the data items required for a particular transaction have in fact been entered by the terminal operator.

Any errors or possible errors in online data entry detected by input validation routines should cause an error message to be displayed to the terminal operator. Because terminal operators are often inexperienced system users, the error message should be as clear as possible with respect to which item is in error, what the error is, and what the operator should do. The system should then recheck the operator's response to the error message prior to accepting any further transaction input.

After all data for a transaction have been entered by a terminal operator, another technique for checking their accuracy is to have the system send certain data back to the terminal for comparison with the data originally sent. This is called *closed loop verification*. For example, the terminal could count the number of bits sent for each message, and the system could count the number of bits received and transmit this bit count back to the terminal for comparison with the terminal's count. If the two counts are not equal, a data transmission error has occurred, and the terminal can retransmit the transaction. Closed loop verification may also involve participation on the part of the terminal operator. For example, if one of the data items being entered is an item number or account number, the system may retrieve the item description or account name, display it on the operator's terminal, and wait for confirmation from the operator that the description or name corresponds to the number the operator entered. This form of closed loop verification is an alternative to the redundant data check as a protection against entering a valid but incorrect identification number.

In online data entry systems in which large numbers of transactions are entered, the system should create a *transaction log*, or detailed record of every transaction. In addition to the transaction data, each log record should contain the date and time of entry, the terminal and operator identification, and an internal sequence number indicating the sequence in which the transaction was entered. If the current version of an online file is damaged, the transaction log is used to help reconstruct the file. If a system malfunction occurs that temporarily shuts down the system, the internal sequence number of the last transaction successfully processed by the system can be displayed on the operator's terminal once service is restored; this ensures that no transactions are lost, or inadvertently entered twice, as a result of a system malfunction.

Other programmed controls

In addition to batch totals, label checking, and input validation, there are other control procedures that may be incorporated into the application programs. *Overflow procedures* are one example. These are programmed routines for dealing with an arithmetic result that exceeds the capacity of the computer's numeric storage register. Since this could only happen with an abnormally large number, this condition invariably indicates an error of some kind. Thus a routine designed to react to this problem should print out and flag all the details of the transaction for manual review.

For large batch processing jobs requiring a run time of an hour or more, there is a danger that a hardware failure midway through the job could necessitate running the entire job a second time. Such hardware failures cannot be prevented, but their consequences to large jobs can be mitigated through the use of *recovery procedures*. One such procedure is the taking of *checkpoints* at periodic intervals during the processing of the program. A checkpoint is an exact copy of all the data values and status indicators relating to the program at some point in time. The checkpoint is generally written from primary memory onto a disk or tape file. If a hardware failure occurs between checkpoints, the job can be restarted after the hardware is repaired by reading in the last checkpoint, rather than going back to the beginning of the job.

A complementary recovery procedure for data files is called *rollback*. Under this procedure a log of the preupdate values is prepared for every record that is updated within a particular interval. Then if a hardware failure occurs that could have caused erroneous data to be written on the file, the log is processed to "roll back" the file, restoring all records updated since the beginning of the current interval to their correct values at that point. The file updating process then resumes from that point.

Output controls

Controls over reports, checks, documents, and other printed computer outputs represent another important category of application controls. Output controls are performed by data control personnel and by the users of the output. Data control personnel should review all output for reasonableness and proper format and should reconcile output control totals with corresponding input control totals. Data control personnel are also responsible for distributing each set of computer output to the appropriate user department. Special care should be taken in handling checks and other sensitive documents and reports. Users are also responsible for carefully reviewing the completeness and accuracy of all computer output that they receive.

Control of errors and exceptions

Output controls also include procedures for investigating and correcting errors identified by edit programs, batch total checks, source data controls, and other programmed controls. These procedures are usually the responsibility of the data control department. Procedures for correction and reentry of erroneous input should be prescribed, and data control personnel are responsible for making sure that such procedures are carried out accurately. Corrected input should again be submitted to validation routines, for the error rate on error corrections is perhaps higher than on any other type of transaction. Exceptions encountered during processing, such as transaction amounts or file balances that exceed prescribed limits, should be investigated to reveal their cause. User department personnel should be notified of those errors caused by incorrect input submitted by them.

A useful technique for controlling data processing errors and exceptions is maintenance of an error log. For every error, the information initially recorded in the log would include the type of record, the transaction identification number, the processing date, the specific field in error, and the error type. As errors are corrected and the corresponding data successfully resubmitted to the system, the status of the error record in the log would be changed from "open" to "closed," and a notation of the resubmission date and the cause of the error would be entered. The error log may be maintained manually by data control personnel, or it may be maintained by the computer. Periodically, the error log may be used to prepare management reports summarizing the number of errors by record type, by error type, and by cause. Also, reports listing all outstanding errors should be regularly provided to operations supervisors to enable them to follow up on uncorrected errors and make sure that all errors are corrected as quickly as possible.

Application controls: an example

To illustrate the use of many of the application controls described in this section, consider the example of a credit sales transaction. At a minimum the required input data will include (1) the customer's account number, (2) the inventory item number, (3) the quantity sold, (4) the sale price, and (5) the delivery date. If the customer purchased more than one type of inventory item, then the inventory item number, quantity sold, and price fields will occur more than once in the sales transaction record. To process this transaction, the system must access each inventory master record to subtract the quantity sold from the quantity on hand and access the master customer account record to add the total sale amount to the customer's account balance.

If these sales transactions are being processed in batches, then the following batch totals may be prepared manually (with the help of an adding machine) by the persons who assemble the batches of sales documents for submission to data processing: (1) a record count of the number of customer transactions, (2) a record count of the number of inventory transactions, (3) hash totals of the quantity sold and price fields, and (4) a financial total of the total dollar sales (price × quantity). If the data are then keyed onto a machine-readable medium using a "smart" data entry device, such as a shared processor key-to-disk-to-tape system, then these batch totals can be accumulated by that system during the keying process and checked against the original batch totals immediately upon completion of the keying process. In addition, such a system could perform check digit verification on the account numbers and item numbers, perform a limit check on the delivery dates, and perform a field check for numeric characters in the quantity, date, and price fields. As a result, a number of possible errors in the input data would be discovered (and corrected) prior to submitting the data for processing on the main computer.

Alternatively, if the data are keyed onto a machine-readable medium using a "dumb" data entry device, such as a conventional keypunch, then key-verification may be used to compensate for the device's inability to perform the functions of the "smart" machine. Furthermore, the records might subsequently be processed on the computer by an edit program (see Fig. 14.6), which would transcribe them to a faster input medium (i.e., cards to tape) and perform the various processing functions of the "smart" data entry device, including accumulating the batch totals and performing check digit verification, limit checks, and field checks. Transaction batches that pass the edit program's tests would be ready for submission to file update processing, whereas those batches in which the edit program identifies errors would be investigated, corrected, and resubmitted to the edit program.

Once the input records are ready for processing against the master files, care must be taken to ensure that the right copies of the master files are loaded on the system. The disk packs or tape reels containing the customer and inventory master files should have external labels containing their name and processing date, and the operator should check these labels carefully prior to loading the files. Both files should also have an internal header label containing this information, and the file update program should be designed to check these header labels prior to accepting any transactions for processing. Each master file may also include a trailer label containing a record count and one or more other file totals, and these would be checked and updated during the file update processing run.

Because the file update program accesses the customer and inventory master file records, it can perform additional tests on the accuracy of the input data. These include (1) validity checks on the customer account numbers and inventory item numbers, (2) sign checks on inventory balances on hand after subtracting sales quantities, (3) limit checks on the total amount sold to each customer relative to that customer's credit limit, (4) limit checks on the sale price of each item sold relative to the permissible range of prices for that item, and (5) reasonableness tests of the quantity sold of each item relative to normal sales quantities for that item. In addition, to prevent the possibility that valid but incorrect account numbers or item numbers might be entered, redundant data such as the customer name and item description could be included in each input record and cross-checked against the corresponding values in the respective master files. This would prevent the posting of the credit sale to the wrong customer account, or the posting of the inventory reduction to the wrong inventory master record.

Outputs of the file update processing run will include billing and/or shipping documents, and a control report. Data control personnel should be responsible for distributing all copies of the billing and shipping documents to the appropriate departments or persons within the organization. The control report will contain batch totals accumulated during the file update run and a listing of any transactions rejected by the input validation routines within the file update program. The batch totals should be reconciled to those prepared prior to the file update run, and any rejected transactions or discrepancies in batch totals should be investigated and corrected by data control personnel.

If the sales transactions are being entered using an online system rather than using batch processing, then all the data entry controls must be concentrated on the interaction between the terminal user and the system. The first step is for the system to check the validity of the terminal itself and of the user code number and password entered by the user when the system is first accessed. Personnel authorized to enter sales transactions should be provided with user code numbers and passwords that do not permit them to enter any other types of transactions or commands.

To assist authorized personnel in entering sales transactions, the system may be programmed to list a series of requests for the customer account number, item number, and other required data. After each request, the system would wait for a valid response from the terminal operator prior to making the next request. Alternatively, the system could display a blank sales transaction format and wait for the operator to complete it. As the data are entered, the system would perform validity checks, field checks, limit checks, sign checks, and reasonableness tests in the same manner as the batch processing system. However, a significant advantage of the online system for data entry is that if the system detects errors, it can notify the terminal operator immediately and thus initiate a real-time correction and reentry of the data in question.

To prevent entry of valid but incorrect account numbers or item numbers, redundant data could be entered and cross-checked, as in the batch processing system. Alternatively, a form of closed loop verification could be used in which the system receives only the account number and item number from the terminal, retrieves the customer name and item description corresponding to these numbers from the master files, and displays these on the terminal. The terminal operator would then visually examine the name and description, then either signal the system to proceed if these were correct or enter a corrected account number or item number if the system displays the wrong name or description.

It should be clear from this example that the design of a system of application controls requires ingenuity and care. Each significant item of input data should be checked by at least one method. However, cost-benefit relationships must also be considered in designing application control systems. Generally, tests performed by the computer, such as edit checks, are less costly and more effective than tests, such as keyverification and visual inspection, performed by people. Also, it is preferable to catch data entry errors as soon as possible after they are made, because this enables such errors to be corrected more easily.

Summary

Widespread use of computers to support operating functions and to process accounting data in modern corporations has caused concern among many executives about the quality of controls over their computer-based information systems. Although computerization of information processing does not change general control objectives and policies, it will change some important control procedures.

Among the important general controls in a computer-based information system are organizational separation of incompatible functions, performance evaluation standards for personnel, project scheduling and monitoring procedures, computer operations controls, documentation standards, data security controls, and backup procedures. These various control policies and procedures may be coordinated using a computer security planning process that identifies threats and risks and then designs a security plan that minimizes these.

Application controls are those that relate to specific data processing jobs as they are performed at the computer facility. Important application controls include batching and batch total checks, source data controls, programmed input validation, online access controls, and output controls. These must be coordinated in a way that optimally protects the security and integrity of the transaction and data flows associated with each information systems application.

Review Questions

1. Define the following terms.

project milestones	input validation routine
hardware monitors	edit program
software monitors	edit check
job accounting routines	sequence check
tape file protection ring	field check
volume label	sign check
header label	validity check
trailer label	limit check
grandfather-father-son concept	reasonableness test
duplicate circuitry	redundant data check
dual reading	compatibility test
echo check	access control matrix
preventive maintenance	prompting
uninterruptible power systems	preformatting
fault tolerance	completeness test
financial total	closed loop verification
hash total	transaction log
record count	overflow procedures
cross-footing balance test	recovery procedures
check digit verification	checkpoint
self-checking digit	rollback

2. What differences between computer data processing and manual processing influence the procedures used to achieve internal accounting control?

3. What are the two basic subdivisions of a typical information systems department?

4. Describe the nature of the roles played by a top computer executive who is also a member of the top management group in a business organization.

5. Describe the functions performed by a manager of programming and systems, a data base administrator, a systems programmer, an information services specialist, a project manager, and a systems analyst in a typical data processing department.

6. Describe the functions performed by a manager of data processing operations, an input preparation department, a computer operations department, a file librarian, and a data control group in a typical data processing department.

7. Which functions within an information systems department should be organizationally independent? Why?

8. What procedures should be utilized in a computer system to control program changes?

9. What elements of internal control should be stressed in a micro- or minicomputer installation that is too small for separation of functions to be practical?

10. Identify several key elements of management control of the systems function.

11. Explain how the performances of systems analysts and computer programmers should be evaluated.

12. Describe how management control of project development activities should be maintained.

13. Describe several elements of a program of management control of computer operations.

14. Explain the distinction between general controls and application controls in an EDP system.

15. Identify and describe three categories of systems documentation.

16. What reasons exist for maintaining up-to-date documentation in a computer system?

17. What provisions should be made in a computer system to protect files, programs, and equipment from loss or destruction? What provisions for reconstruction of records in the event of loss should be made?

18. Describe several types of computer hardware controls.

19. What forms of insurance should be maintained as part of the control plan for a computer installation?

20. Describe several approaches to the use of backup facilities or procedures for prevention of losses due to systems malfunctions or natural disasters.

21. Explain the concept of computer security planning. What is its primary advantage?

22. What types of errors are batch totals intended to reveal? Describe four types of batch totals and give an example of each.

23. Describe several types of source data controls that might be used in a computer installation.

24. Identify and describe several edit checks that might be included in an input validation routine. Give an example of each.

25. Explain the nature and purpose of online access controls. Describe several examples and explain how each might be utilized.

26. What are online data entry controls? Describe several examples and explain how each might be utilized.

27. List several edit checks that are equally useful in both batch and online processing systems.

28. Describe three categories of programmed controls over computer data processing and give an example of each.

29. Describe some output controls that should be utilized in a computer-based information system.

30. What procedures should be established for control over errors and exceptions in a computer-based system?

31. Describe an example of how various application controls might be applied to the processing of sales transactions.

Discussion Questions

32. Many persons believe that programming is basically a creative activity and should therefore not be subject to cost controls and other managerial regulation. Discuss this point of view.

33. A computer implementation project is often performed in a state of crisis, with the implementation group working feverishly to keep pace with the implementation schedule. In this atmosphere, corners are often cut with respect to documentation and programmed controls. What arguments do you feel would be effective to prevent such cutting of corners, even though doing so could delay implementation?

34. Theoretically a control procedure should be adopted if its benefit value exceeds its cost. Explain how the benefit value and cost of the following controls can be estimated.
    a) separation of functions
    b) data security provisions
    c) turnaround documents
    d) input validation routines

35. Discuss how reliability analysis (see Chapter 11) could be applied to the design and evaluation of internal controls in a computer-based information system. For which types of internal controls would it probably be most useful? Why?

36. The function of transaction authorization should be performed by responsible persons outside the systems department. However, computers are increasingly being programmed to initiate transactions, such as by issuing a purchase order when an inventory balance is low. Discuss whether such automatic transaction generation represents a violation of good internal control principles.

Problems and Cases

37. Prepare a segment of a program flowchart showing how a check of a header label by a program would work.

38. Prepare a systems flowchart illustrating the grandfather-father-son concept.

39. What control or controls would you recommend in a computer system to prevent the following situations from occurring?

    a) The "time worked" field for salaried employees is supposed to contain a "01" for one week. For one employee, this field contained the number 40, and a check for $6872.51 was accidentally prepared and mailed to this employee.

    b) A programmer obtained the master payroll file tape, mounted it on a tape drive, and changed his own monthly salary from $1400 to $2000 through the computer console.

    c) A bank programmer wrote a special routine, punched a set of cards for the routine, obtained the program that calculates interest on customer accounts, and processed the cards against the program to add the routine to the program tape. The routine adds the fraction of a cent of each customer's interest, which would otherwise be rounded off, to her own account.

    d) The master accounts receivable file on disk was inadvertently destroyed and could not be reconstructed after being substituted for the accounts payable file in a processing run.

    e) A company lost almost all its vital business data from a fire that destroyed the room in which it stored its magnetic tape files.

    f) A programmer quit the firm in the middle of a programming assignment. Because no other programmers could make sense of the work already completed, the project was begun over from scratch.

    g) During payroll processing, an error correction entry performed by the console operator resulted in the unintentional recording of data on the payroll master tape file, which destroyed several records on that file.

    h) During keypunching of customer payment records, the digit "0" in a payment of $123.40 was mistakenly punched as the letter "O." As a result, the transaction was not correctly processed and the customer received an incorrect statement of account.

i) After updating the inventory master file maintained on magnetic tape, the old master tape was removed for use in other applications. The updated master was then accidentally mislabeled and its contents subsequently erased. Considerable difficulty was encountered in reconstructing the master inventory file.

40. What control or controls would you recommend in an online computer system to prevent the following situations from occurring?

a) Unauthorized access to the system is gained by a teenager who programs a microcomputer to enter repeated user numbers until a correct one is found.

b) An employee gains unauthorized access to the system by observing her supervisor's user number and then correctly guessing the password after twelve attempts.

c) A salesperson keying in a customer order from a remote terminal entered an incorrect stock number. As a result, an order for fifty typewriters was placed for a customer who had intended to order fifty typewriter ribbons.

d) A salesperson provided with a terminal with which to enter customer orders used it to initiate a $500 increase in his own monthly salary.

e) A salesperson keying in a customer order from a remote terminal inadvertently omitted the delivery address from one order.

f) A company's research and development center utilized remote terminals tied into its computer center 100 miles away. By utilizing a wiretap, the company's largest competitor was able to steal secret plans for a major product innovation.

g) Because of failure in a $400 multiplexor serving terminals at eight drive-in windows, a bank was forced to shut down the windows for two hours during a busy Friday afternoon.

h) A twenty-minute power failure that shut down a firm's computer system resulted in loss of data for several transactions that were being entered into the system from remote terminals.

41. Consider the following set of numeric computer input data.

EMPLOYEE NUMBER COL. 1–3	PAY RATE COL. 4–6	HOURS WORKED COL. 7–8	GROSS PAY COL. 9–13	DEDUCTIONS COL. 14–18	NET PAY COL. 19–23
121	250	38	$9500	01050	08450
123	275	40	11000	01250	09750
125	200	90	16000	02000	12000
122	280	40	11200	11000	00200

REQUIRED

a) From the data above calculate one example of a hash total, a record count, and a financial total.

b) For each of the controls listed below, give a specific example from the four records above of an error or probable error that would be caught by the control.

field check   reasonableness test

sequence check   cross-footing balance test

limit check

42. Check digit verification schemes apply a series of mathematical operations to the first $n - 1$ digits of an n digit number to determine the correct value of the nth digit. Assume that check digit verification is to be applied to a five-digit number. One check digit scheme, called the "simple sum" method, would determine the sum of the first four digits and subtract that sum from the next highest multiple of ten to obtain the check digit. Another scheme, called the "2–1–2" method, would compute a weighted sum of the first four digits, with the first and third digits from the right (excluding the check digit) weighted by a factor of two, and the second and fourth digits from the right weighted by a factor of one. This sum is then subtracted from the next highest multiple of ten to obtain the check digit.

Listed below are two columns of five-digit numbers. All six of the numbers in the left-hand column are valid according to both check digit methods described above. (You might want to verify this.) The numbers in the right-hand column are erroneous versions of their column counterparts. The first two contain single transcription errors, in which one digit has been copied incorrectly. The second two contain transposition errors, in which two digits have been transposed. The third two are completely garbled.

14267	14567
23573	28573
32582	35282
43274	43724
50609	36609
92487	65937

REQUIRED

a) Determine which of the numbers in the right-hand column would fail check digit verification under (1) the simple sum method and (2) the "2–1–2" method.

b) Extrapolating from the results of part (a), can you form any general conclusions about the relative effectiveness of the two check digit methods with respect to the different types of errors?

43. Your company has procured a number of minicomputers for use in various locations and applications. One of these has been installed in the stores department which has the responsibility for disbursing stock items and for maintaining stores records. In your audit you find, among other

things, that a competent employee, trained in computer applications, receives the requisitions for stores, reviews them for completeness and for the propriety of approvals, disburses the stock, maintains the records, operates the computer, and authorizes adjustments to the total amounts of stock accumulated by the computer.

When you discuss the applicable controls with the department manager, you are told that the minicomputer is assigned exclusively to that department and that it therefore does not require the same types of controls applicable to the large computer systems.

REQUIRED Comment on the manager's contentions, discussing briefly five types of control that would apply to this minicomputer application. (CIA Examination)

44. Shown in Fig. 14.8 are data relating to the evaluation of programming job performance by four programmers employed in the Welfare Department.

REQUIRED
    a) Which programmer's performance is best? Explain.
    b) Which programmer's performance is worst? Explain.
    c) Can you rank the other two programmers in terms of performance? Why or why not?

45. You are the data security administrator for a small computer installation. This system uses two programs—a payroll processing system and an inventory processing system—and maintains three files—a payroll master file, an inventory master file, and a master transaction log. You are to establish an access control matrix that permits varying levels of access authority with respect to these systems and files to the following system users.
    a) salesperson—read and display records in the inventory master file.
    b) inventory control analyst—read, display, update, create, and delete records in the inventory master file.
    c) payroll analyst—read, display, and update records in the payroll master file.
    d) personnel manager—read, display, update, create, and delete records in the payroll master file.

FIGURE 14.8

Performance factor	Programmer			
	Adams	Baker	Cline	Davis
Instructions per hour	12	15	12	15
Program complexity	Low	Medium	Medium	Low
Years of experience	6	1	2	4

e) payroll programmer—perform any and all operations on the payroll system, plus read and display payroll master file records and transaction log records.

f) inventory programmer—perform any and all operations on the inventory system, plus read and display inventory master file records and transaction log records.

g) data processing manager—read and display any and all programs and files.

h) yourself—perform any and all operations on any and all programs and files.

You will assign each user a six-character user code and select access authority codes for each user based upon the following access authority coding system.

0 = no access permitted.

1 = read and display only.

2 = read, display, and update.

3 = read, display, update, create, and delete.

REQUIRED   Prepare the access control matrix.

46. The Foster Corporation recently fired its director of Information Systems after experiencing several years of budget overruns in systems development and computer operations. As an internal auditor with computer management experience, you have been appointed as interim director and charged to investigate the problems that the department has experienced.

A significant obstacle to your investigation has been a lack of written information about the activities of the department or the policies under which it was managed. The previous director apparently managed in an informal manner, communicating assignments, standards, and performance evaluations to his employees verbally. This style of management was apparently popular with many employees but unpopular with many others, some of whom have left the company.

The major systems project under development is a management information system. Objectives for this project are loosely defined, although a good deal of analysis, design, and programming has been completed. The project director estimates that this project is roughly half finished.

The computer operations department runs jobs on an "as received" basis. The operations supervisor suggests that a newer, faster, and more reliable system is needed to satisfy demand during peak periods and to cope with expected growth in processing requirements.

REQUIRED   Identify and briefly describe several elements of control that appear to be lacking in this situation and that you feel should be implemented in the Information Systems Department.

✓47. The Moose Wings Co-operative Flight Club owns a number of airplanes and gliders. It serves less than 2,000 members, who are numbered sequentially from the founder, Tom Eagle (0001), to the newest member, Jacques Noveau (1368). Members rent the flying machines by the hour, and all planes must be returned on the same day. The Club uses a C.R.T. terminal on its premises, and a dial-up line, to send the billing data to a computer utility. The utility bills all members for the cost of flights taken on a monthly basis.

For each flight taken, the following record is keyed in. A space is left between each data item.

Member number	0001-1368	4 digits
Date of flight start	Day: Month: Year	6 digits
Plane used	G, C, P, or L*	1 character
Time of take off	Hour Minute	4 digits
Time of landing	Hour Minute	4 digits

*Note: G = Glider
       C = Cessna
       P = Piper Cub
       L = Lear

The following six records were among those entered for the flights taken on November 1, 1981:

1234	311181	G	0625	0846
4111	011181	C	0849	1023
1210	011181	P	0342	0542
0023	011181	X	0159	1243
012A	011181	P	1229	1532
0999	011181	L	1551	1387

REQUIRED

a) For each of the five data fields, suggest editing controls that could be included in the program to detect possible errors.
b) Identify and describe any errors in the above records. (SMAC Examination)

48. You are performing an audit of the EDP function of a chemical company with about $150 million in annual sales. Your initial survey discloses the following points.

1. The EDP manager reports to the director of accounting who, in turn, reports to the controller. The controller reports to the treasurer who is one of several vice-presidents of the company. The EDP manager

has made several unsuccessful requests to the director of accounting for another printer.

2. There is no written charter for the EDP function, but the EDP manager tells you that the primary objective is to get the accounting reports out on time.

3. Transaction tapes are used daily to update the master file and are then retired to the scratch tape area.

4. A third-generation computer with large disk capacity was installed three years ago. The EDP activity previously used a second-generation computer, and many of the programs written for that computer are used on the present equipment by means of an emulator.

5. You observe that the output from the computer runs is written on tape for printing at a later time. Some output tapes from several days' runs are waiting to be printed.

6. The EDP manager states that the CPU could handle at least twice the work currently being processed.

REQUIRED

a) Identify the defect inherent in each of the six conditions shown above.

b) Briefly describe the probable effect if the condition is permitted to continue. (CIA Examination)

49. Talbert Corporation hired an independent computer programmer to develop a simplified payroll application for its newly purchased computer. The programmer developed an online, data-based micro-computer system that minimized the level of knowledge required by the operator. It was based upon typing answers to input cues that appeared on the terminal's viewing screen, examples of which follow:

a) Access routine:

   1) Operator access number to payroll file? — password.
   2) Are there new employees? — validity check, field check, Y or N.

b) New employees routine:

   1) Employee name? — alphabetic field check.
   2) Employee number? — numeric field check
   3) Social security number? — check digit verification
   4) Rate per hour? — limit check cannot be more than certain no
   5) Single or married? — validity check, alphabetic field check, valid codes S or M
   6) Number of dependents? — numeric field check
   7) Account distribution?

c) Current payroll routine:

   1) Employee number? — numeric field check
   2) Regular hours worked? — limit check, cannot be more than 40
   3) Overtime hours worked? —   "   "   "   "   "   20
   4) Total employees this payroll period? record count.

The independent auditor is attempting to verify that certain input validation (edit) checks exist to ensure that errors resulting from omissions, invalid entries, or other inaccuracies will be detected during the typing of answers to the input cues.

Identify the various types of input validation (edit) checks the independent auditor would expect to find in the EDP system. Describe the assurances provided by each identified validation check. Do not discuss the review and evaluation of these controls. (CPA Examination)

50. Babbington-Bowles is an advertising agency that employs 625 salespersons who travel and entertain extensively. Salespersons are paid both salary and commissions, and receive a check at the end of each month. The nature of their job is such that expenses of several hundred dollars a day might be incurred. In the past, these expenses were included in the monthly pay check. Salesmen were required to submit their expense reports, with supporting receipts, by the twentieth of each month. These would be reviewed suitably, and then sent to data entry in a batch. Suitable controls were incorporated on each batch during input, processing and output.

This system worked well from a company viewpoint, and the internal auditor was convinced that, while minor padding of expense accounts might occur, no major losses had been encountered.

With rising interest rates, the salespersons were unhappy. They pointed out that they were often forced to carry several thousand dollars for a month. If they were out of town around the twentieth, they might not be reimbursed for their expenses for two months. They requested that Babbington-Bowles provide a service whereby a salesperson or his or her representative could submit receipts and expense reports to the accounting department and receive a check almost immediately.

The data processing manager said this could be done. A CRT terminal would be set up in the accounting office, along with a small printer. The salesperson's name would be entered, along with the required expense amount broken down into the standard categories. A program would process these data to the proper accounts, and if everything checked out suitably, print the check on pre-signed check blank stock in the printer.

Identify five important controls and explain why they might be incorporated in the system. These controls may be physical, they may relate to jobs and responsibilities, or they may be part of the program. (SMAC Examination)

51. The Department of Taxation of one state is developing a new computer system for processing state income tax returns of individuals and corporations. The new system features direct data input and inquiry capabilities. Identification of taxpayers is provided by using the social security number for individuals and federal identification number for corporations. The new system should be fully implemented in time for the next tax season.

The new system will serve three primary purposes as described below.

☐ Data will be input into the system directly from tax returns through cathode ray tube (CRT) terminals located at the central headquarters of the Department of Taxation.

☐ The returns will be processed using the main computer facilities at central headquarters. The processing includes:

—verification of mathematical accuracy.

—auditing the reasonableness of deductions, tax due, etc., through the use of edit routines; these routines also include a comparison of the current year's data with the prior years' data.

—identification of returns which should be considered for audit by revenue agents of the department.

—issuing refund checks to taxpayers.

☐ Inquiry service will be provided taxpayers upon request through the assistance of Tax Department personnel at five regional offices. A total of 50 CRT terminals will be placed at the regional offices. A taxpayer will be allowed to determine the status of his/her return or get information from the last three years' returns by calling or visiting one of the Department's regional offices.

The State Commissioner of Taxation is concerned about data security during input and processing over and above protection against natural hazards such as fire, floods, etc. This includes protection against the loss or damage of data during data input or processing or the improper input or processing of data. In addition, the Tax Commissioner and the State Attorney General have discussed the general problem of data confidentiality which may arise from the nature and operation of the new system. Both individuals want to have all potential problems identified before the system is fully developed and implemented so that the proper controls can be incorporated into the new system.

REQUIRED

a) Describe the potential confidentiality problems that could arise in each of the following three areas of processing and recommend the corrective action(s) to solve the problem.

1) Data input.

2) Processing of returns.

3) Data inquiry.

b) The State Tax Commission wants to incorporate controls to provide data security against the loss, damage, or improper input or use of data during data input and processing. Identify the potential problems (outside of natural hazards such as fire, floods, etc.) for which the Department of Taxation should develop controls, and recommend the possible controls for each problem identified. (CMA Examination)

52. TuneFork, Inc. is a large wholesaler of sheet music, music books, musical instruments and other music related supplies. The company acquired a medium-sized, tape oriented computer system last year, and an inventory control system has been implemented already. Now the systems department is developing a new accounts receivable system.

The flow chart in Fig. 14.9 (shown on the next page) is a diagram of the proposed accounts receivable system as designed by the systems department. The objectives of the new system are to produce current and timely information that can be used to control bad debts, to provide information to the sales department regarding customers whose accounts are delinquent, to produce monthly statements for customers, and to produce notices to customers regarding a change in the status of their charge privileges.

Input data for the system are taken from four source documents—approved credit applications, sales invoices, cash payment remittances, credit memoranda. The accounts receivable (A/R) file is maintained on magnetic tape by customer account number. The record for each customer contains identification information, last month's balance, current month's transactions (detailed), and current balance. Some of the output items generated from the system are identified and described briefly below.

☐ Accounts receivable register (weekly)—a listing of all customers and account balances included on the accounts receivable file.

☐ Aging schedule (monthly)—a schedule of all customers with outstanding balances detailing the amount owed by age classifications—0–30 days, 30–60 days, 60–90 days, over 90 days old.

☐ Delinquency and write-off registers (monthly)—(1) a listing of those accounts which are delinquent and (2) a listing of customers accounts which have been closed and written off; related notices are prepared and sent to these customers.

REQUIRED

a) TuneFork Inc.'s systems department must develop the system controls for the new accounts receivable system. Identify and explain the systems controls which should be instituted with the new system. When appropriate describe the location in the flow chart where the control should be introduced.

b) The credit manager has indicated that the department receives frequent telephone inquiries from customers regarding their accounts. The manager has asked if the department could have a cathode ray tube (CRT) terminal connected to the main computer. Can a CRT terminal be used with the new accounts receivable system as proposed to satisfy the needs of the credit manager? Explain your answer. (CMA Examination)

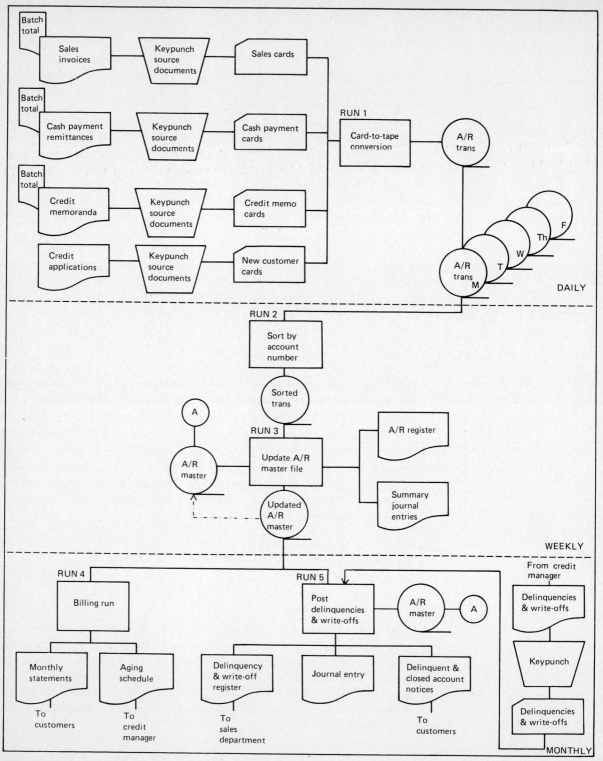

FIGURE 14.9

53. Prepare a flowchart of a program incorporating several control features as described below.

A file is read that contains an employee identification number, a department number, employee name, pay rate, hours worked, gross pay, net pay, and total deductions. The program performs various control checks and edits as follows.

a) Sequence check—the cards are checked to ensure that they are in numerical sequence by employee identification number.

b) Field check—the department number is checked to ensure that it contains numeric data.

c) Validity check—the employee identification number is checked to ensure that it is either less than 2500 or greater than 4300.

d) Limit checks—pay rate and hours worked are checked to ensure that they do not exceed $18.00 and 70, respectively.

e) Sign check—net pay is checked to ensure that it is positive.

f) Edit check—gross pay for each record is tested to ensure that it is equal to the product of pay rate and hours worked.

g) Cross-footing balance test—at the completion of processing, the total of gross pay is compared with the sum of the total of net pay and of deductions.

h) Control totals—a hash total of employee identification number, a record count, and financial totals of gross pay and total deductions are accumulated during processing and checked for accuracy against predetermined control totals read from the trailer label.

If an error is encountered by checks (a) through (f), the record data are printed out together with an error message. Each record should be checked for the existence of all these conditions, so some records may be printed out more than once with more than one error message. When processing is completed, messages should be printed out indicating whether or not conditions (g) and (h) are satisfied.

References

Allen, Brandt. "Embezzler's Guide to the Computer." *Harvrd Business Review* (July/August 1975): 79–89.

———. "The Biggest Computer Frauds: Lessons for CPAs." *Journal of Accountancy* (May 1977): 55–62.

American Institute of Certified Public Accountants. *Statements on Auditing Standards No. 1–49.* New York: American Institute of Certified Public Accountants, Inc., 1972–1984.

———. *Controls over Using and Changing Computer Programs.* New York: American Institute of Certified Public Accountants, Inc., 1979.

———. *Audit and Control Considerations in a Minicomputer or Small Business Computer Environment.* New York: American Institute of Certified Public Accountants, Inc., 1981.

———. *Audit and Control Considerations in an Online Environment.* New York: American Institute of Certified Public Accountants, Inc., 1983.

Birtle, William G.; Barry D. Hawkins; and Walter D. Pugh. "How to Evaluate Accounting Controls in a Minicomputer Installation." *Practical Accountant* (August 1980): 47–53.

Buss, Martin D. J., and Lynn M. Salerno. "Common Sense and Computer Security." *Harvard Business Review* (March/April 1984): 112–121.

Canning, Richard G. "Information Security and Privacy." *EDP Analyzer* (February 1986): 1–11.

———. "The Security of Managers' Information." *EDP Analyzer* (July 1979): 1–13.

Crossman, Trevor D. "Taking the Measure of Programmer Productivity." *Datamation* (May 1979): 144–147.

Dascher, Paul E., and W. Ken Harmon. "Assessing Microcomputer Risks and Controls for Clients." *CPA Journal* (May 1984): 36–41.

Goldstein, Andy. "Operating Systems Offer Security Features to Control Computer Access." *Computer Technology Review* (Winter 1985): 191–199.

Hansen, William A. "The Operator's Changing Status." *Datamation* (January 1979): 189–193.

Hirsch, Rudolph E. "Data Processing *Can* Be Cost-Controlled." *Price Waterhouse Review* (Summer 1970): 65–72.

Kelley, Neil D. "The Economics of Uninterruptible Power." *Infosystems* (September 1980): 55–64.

Lettieri, Larry. "Disaster Recovery: Picking Up the Pieces." *Computer Decisions* (March 1979): 16–22, 27.

Luke, Larry R. "Password Security Systems." *EDPACS* (October 1984): 1–6.

Lyons, Norman R. "Segregation of Functions in EFTS." *Journal of Accountancy* (October 1978): 89–92.

Martin, James. *Security, Accuracy, and Privacy in Computer Systems.* Englewood Cliffs, N.J.: Prentice-Hall, 1973.

Matthews, Joseph R. "A Survey of EDP Performance Measures." *Government Data Systems* (July/August 1978): 29–32.

Mautz, Robert K.; Walter G. Kell; Michael W. Maher; Alan G. Merten; Raymond R. Reilly; Dennis G. Severance; and Bernard J. White. *Internal Control in U.S. Corporations: The State of the Art.* New York: Financial Executives Research Foundation, 1980.

Meyer, Carl H., and Walter L. Tuchman. "Putting Data Encryption to Work." *Mini-Micro Systems* (October 1978): 46–52.

Murray, W. H. "Security Considerations for Personal Computers." *IBM Systems Journal* **23** (1984): 297–304.

Parker, Donn B. *Crime by Computer.* New York: Scribner's, 1976.

Porter, W. Thomas, and William E. Perry. *EDP Controls and Auditing.* 4th ed. Boston: Kent, 1984.

Price Waterhouse & Co. *Guide to Accounting Controls: EDP.* New York: Price Waterhouse & Co., 1979.

Report of the Joint Data Base Task Force. Walter D. Pugh, Chairman. New York: American Institute of Certified Public Accountants, 1983.

Rhodes, Wayne L., Jr. "Second Site Protection." *Infosystems* (September 1980): 46–52.

St. Clair, Linda. "Security for Small Computer Systems." *EDPACS* (November 1983): 1–10.

Schroeder, Walter, J. "The EDP Manager—and the Computer Profit Drain." *Computers and Automation* (January 1971): 14–18.

Shankar, K. S. "The Total Computer Security Problem: An Overview." *Computer* (June 1977): 50–62.

Sykes, David J. "Protecting Data by Encryption." *Datamation* (August 1976): 81–85.

Troy, Gene. "Thwarting the Hackers." *Datamation* (July 1984): 117–128.

Wood, C.; E. B. Fernandez; and R. C. Summers. "Data Base Security: Requirements, Policies, and Models." *IBM Systems Journal* **19** (1980): 229–252.

Zimmerman, Harry. "Minicomputers: The Challenge for Controls." *Journal of Accountancy* (June 1980): 28–35.

Zmud, Robert W. "Design Alternatives for Organizing Information Systems Activities." *MIS Quarterly* (June 1984): 79–93.

Auditing of Computer-Based Information Systems

Careful study of this chapter should enable students to:

☐ Describe the objectives of audits of computer-based information systems.

☐ Design a plan for the evaluation of internal control in a computer-based information system.

☐ Explain how computer audit software is used in the audit of computer-based information systems.

To complete this unit on the management of information systems, this chapter describes the concepts and techniques used in auditing computer-based systems. As discussed in Part 1, the internal audit function in an organization is a key element of management control, providing an independent appraisal of management performance as well as a review of the effectiveness of the internal control system. The rapid growth of the internal auditing profession in recent years reflects a growing recognition of the importance of the internal auditor on the management team.

Of course there are a number of other categories of auditors in addition to internal auditors. For example, the General Accounting Office of the United States Congress and various legislative audit agencies of state governments employ auditors to evaluate management performance and compliance with legislative intent in government departments and bureaus. The Defense Contract Audit Agency of the Department of Defense employs auditors to review the financial records of companies having defense contracts with the government. Public accountants, or "external auditors," provide an independent review of the financial statements of publicly held corporations. While this chapter is written primarily from the perspective of the internal auditor, many of the concepts and techniques discussed here are equally applicable to these other types of auditing.

The American Accounting Association has prepared the following general definition of *auditing*.

> Auditing is a systematic process of objectively obtaining and evaluating evidence regarding assertions about economic actions and events to ascertain the degree of correspondence between those assertions and established criteria and communicating the results to interested users.[1]

Certain aspects of this definition are of particular interest. For example, note that the auditor "objectively" obtains and evaluates evidence. Objectivity is critical to the credibility and usefulness of the auditor's findings, which is why the audit function should be organizationally independent of those functions it is assigned to review. Also, auditing is described as a "systematic process," which suggests a step-by-step approach characterized by careful planning and judicious selection and execution of appropriate techniques. A later section of this chapter reviews the steps in the auditing process. Furthermore, note that much of auditing involves the collection, review, and documentation of audit "evidence." Finally, in developing recommendations, the auditor uses "established criteria" as a basis for evaluation. With respect to audits of computer-based information systems, these established criteria are the principles of management and control of information systems described in the previous five chapters in Part 3.

---

[1]Committee on Basic Auditing Concepts, *A Statement of Basic Auditing Concepts* (Sarasota, Fla.: American Accounting Association, 1973), p. 2.

Electronic data processing has had a major effect upon auditing, owing primarily to the absence of a visible audit trail in computerized systems. More specifically, computerized data processing systems maintain files on media that are machine-readable, such as magnetic tape or disk. File content may be printed out infrequently or at irregular intervals. A history of the activity relating to each individual file may not be maintained. In online processing, even a printed record of input may not be produced.

The importance of internal control and the natural tendency toward elimination of visible audit trails in computerized information systems underscore the need to involve the auditor in the systems design process. In this role, the auditor may suggest the incorporation of necessary internal controls and audit trails into new systems while they are being developed, and while there is still time to implement such suggestions economically. This will not only minimize the need for expensive modifications of systems after implementation but should also reduce the extent of testing required during the regular audit process.

The first reaction of auditors to the use of computers in data processing was to attempt to perform their audits with the printed records and output provided by the system, ignoring the computer and its programs. This approach was referred to as auditing "around" the computer. The assumption underlying this approach was that if a sample of system output was correctly obtained from system input, then the processing itself must be reliable. This was a reasonable approach fifteen or twenty years ago when knowledge of electronic data processing among auditors was limited. However, both the increasing difficulty of applying this approach to a disappearing audit trail and the development of better methods of auditing computer systems have combined to discredit the old approach of auditing around the computer.

The alternative to auditing around is referred to as auditing "through" the computer. This approach uses the computer itself to check the adequacy of system controls and the accuracy of system output. Most of the auditing techniques discussed in this chapter involve auditing through the computer.

However, if auditors must work directly with the computer, they must possess some degree of computer expertise. According to one study, modern organizations have tried several approaches to the development of such expertise on their internal audit staffs, including (1) training data processing specialists in audit concepts and methods, (2) training internal auditors in data processing techniques and practices, and (3) supplementing the internal audit staff with a few data processing specialists.[2] That study concluded that a combination of the second and third approaches appears to be most effective at the present time. However, in the long run the acquisition of computer science expertise by accounting and auditing students during their professional education may offer the greatest promise of resolving this problem.

---

[2]Stanford Research Institute, *Systems Auditability & Control Study, Data Processing Audit Practices Report* (Altamonte Springs, Fla.: Institute of Internal Auditors, 1977), chapter 5.

The chapter is divided into five major sections. In the first section the scope and objectives of internal audit work are briefly described. The second section provides a brief overview of the steps in the auditing process. The third section deals with the process of evaluating internal controls in a computer-based information system and explains several techniques used for this purpose. In the fourth section, techniques for evaluating the reliability and integrity of financial and operating information maintained on the computer are described. The fifth section discusses the review of performance of systems management and operations in a computer-based information system.

Scope and Objectives of Audit Work

According to the *Standards for the Professional Practice of Internal Auditing* promulgated by the Institute of Internal Auditors in 1978,

> the scope of the internal audit encompasses the examination and evaluation of the adequacy and effectiveness of the organization's system of internal control and the quality of performance in carrying out assigned responsibilities.[3]

The institute further delineates five specific standards dealing with the following aspects of the scope of audit work.

1. Reliability and integrity of information.
2. Compliance with policies, plans, procedures, laws, and regulations.
3. Safeguarding of assets.
4. Economical and efficient use of resources.
5. Accomplishment of established objectives and goals for operations or programs.

This section describes each of these five standards and discusses their implications with respect to computer-based information systems.

The first internal audit scope standard states that

> internal audits should review the reliability and integrity of financial and operating information and the means used to identify, measure, classify, and report such information.[4]

In modern organizations, much of the information referred to in this standard is maintained on a computer system. Therefore the auditor must have a clear understanding of how this information is processed on the computer in order to meet this standard. Furthermore, the auditor will have to rely on the computer in order to access the information to be reviewed. To best fulfill the requirements of this standard, the auditor should actually use the computer itself as a primary tool for carrying out many of the necessary auditing procedures.

---

[3]Institute of Internal Auditors, *Standards for the Professional Practice of Internal Auditing* (Altamonte Springs, Fla.: Institute of Internal Auditors, Inc., 1978), p. 3.

[4]*Ibid.*, p. 3.

The second standard states that

> internal auditors should review the systems established to ensure compliance with those policies, plans, procedures, laws, and regulations which could have a significant impact on operations and reports and should determine whether the organization is in compliance.[5]

There are numerous examples of policies, plans, procedures, laws, and regulations relating to computer-based information processing: These include policies for hiring, assignment, evaluation and promotion of EDP personnel; three- or five-year plans for the information processing facility; operating procedures for data processing equipment; and laws and regulations dealing with corporate financial reporting, information privacy, and internal controls. Therefore reviewing compliance with matters such as these requires a considerable amount of review of the information processing facility itself.

According to the third scope standard,

> internal auditors should review the means of safeguarding assets and, as appropriate, verify the existence of such assets.[6]

Modern organizations generally use computers to account for and control such assets as inventories, plant and equipment, and receivables. Furthermore, many organizations use their computers to prepare checks. In such cases, a review of the means of safeguarding assets is to a great extent a review of computer processing of asset information. Furthermore, to verify the existence of recorded assets, the auditor must use the computer to obtain a listing of the assets to be verified.

The fourth standard is that

> internal auditors should appraise the economy and efficiency with which resources are employed.[7]

The standard is applicable to all operations, departments, and managers within the organization, including the systems department. Information processing resources include both data processing equipment and personnel such as systems analysts, programmers, and equipment operators. In Part 3 of this book a number of principles underlying the effective and efficient use of these resources have been discussed. It is the proper application of these principles that the auditor must review in order to comply with this standard.

According to the fifth scope standard,

> internal auditors should review operations or programs to ascertain whether results are consistent with established objectives and whether the operations or programs are being carried out as planned.[8]

---

[5]*Ibid.*, p. 4.

[6]*Ibid.*, p. 4.

[7]*Ibid.*, p. 4.

[8]*Ibid.*, p. 4.

Again, this is a standard that is applicable to all parts of an organization. In the systems management area, it applies to such things as feasibility studies for new systems, long-range information systems plans, and system project development activities.

In conclusion, the scope of internal auditing work can be divided into three major categories. The first of these is the *internal control audit,* the scope of which roughly corresponds to the second and third standards discussed above. The second major category is the *financial audit,* which correlates with the first of the five scope standards.[9] The third major category, corresponding to the fourth and fifth scope standards, is the *management audit,* often referred to as the *operational audit.* These three major categories are each described in turn in the three final sections of this chapter. A fourth category of lesser general importance, which is not discussed further in this chapter, is referred to as the *compliance audit.* This type of audit is a subset of the work referred to in the second scope standard and specifically deals with an organization's compliance with laws, contract provisions, government regulations, and other obligations to external parties.

An Overview of the Auditing Process

Whether performed by internal, external, or governmental auditors, and whether their scope involves internal controls, financial information, or management performance, all audits consist of a very similar sequence of activities. Generally, the auditing process may be divided into the following four steps.

1. Planning.
2. Evidence gathering.
3. Evidence evaluation.
4. Communication of results.

This section of the chapter discusses some of the major factors involved in each of these four steps.

Audit planning

The first step in audit planning is to establish the scope and objectives of the audit. These depend on who the audit is for and what type of audit is desired. For example, the independent audit of financial statements of publicly held corporations is directed at corporate stockholders and has the purpose of evaluating the fairness of presentation of corporate financial statements. The

---

[9]Note that since the first standard refers to both "financial and operating information," it would perhaps make better sense to use the term *information audit.* However, because of the traditional emphasis of internal auditors on financial information, the term *financial audit* has become generally accepted, even though the scope of such audits is expanding to encompass nonfinancial information.

scope and objectives of internal audits vary widely but are generally established either implicitly or explicitly by management.

Once the audit scope and objectives are defined, the auditor must develop (or reestablish) a general familiarity with the operations of the entity to be audited. Discussions with management personnel and a review of summary documentation and operating information are useful for this purpose. This should enable the auditor to identify any potential audit risks or problems to which he or she may be exposed.

To conclude the planning stage, the auditor prepares a preliminary audit program that delineates the nature, extent, and timing of specific audit tests and procedures that will achieve the desired audit objectives and minimize the audit risks. In conjunction with this step, a preliminary time budget for the audit is prepared, and audit staff members are assigned to perform specific portions of the audit work. This audit program is "preliminary" in the sense that it may be revised during the audit if necessary in view of the audit findings.

Collection of audit evidence

Audit evidence is gathered by means of a number of different kinds of tests and procedures. These include (1) observation of the operating activities of the audited organization and its employees; (2) physical examination of the quantity and/or condition of tangible assets such as equipment, inventory, or cash; (3) confirmation of information accuracy by means of written communication with independent third parties; (4) inquiry directed at employees of the audited organization, often facilitated by questionnaires or interview checklists; (5) recalculation of quantitative information on records and reports; (6) vouching, or examining the accuracy of documents and records, especially by means of tracing the information through the processing system to its source; and (7) analytical review of relationships and trends among financial and operating information in order to detect items that should be further investigated. A given audit will generally consist of several tests and procedures from most or all of these categories. It is also appropriate to point out that many audit tests and procedures cannot feasibly be performed on the entire population of activities, records, assets, or documents under review and so must be performed on a sample basis.

Evaluation of audit evidence

Three broad options available to the auditor at the evaluation stage are (1) to decide that the evidence supports a favorable conclusion with respect to the operations, controls, or information being audited, (2) to decide that the evidence supports an unfavorable or negative conclusion, or (3) to decide that the available evidence is inconclusive and that more evidence should be collected.

In making the evaluation decision, the auditor utilizes the concepts of *materiality* and *reasonable assurance*. That is, the auditor desires reasonable assurance that there is not a material error or deficiency in the information or process being audited. The concept of reasonable assurance implies that the auditor does not seek complete assurance because to do so would be prohibitively expensive; however, this also implies that the auditor is willing to accept some degree of risk that the audit conclusion will be incorrect. The concept of materiality recognizes that some errors or deficiencies are bound to exist in any system, and therefore the auditor should focus on detecting and reporting only those errors and deficiencies that could possibly have a significant impact on decisions. Determining what is and what is not material in a given set of circumstances is primarily a matter of judgment. It should be noted that consideration of materiality and reasonable assurance is important at the audit planning stage, when the auditor is deciding how much audit work is necessary, as well as at the evidence evaluation stage.

As the audit proceeds, it is important that the auditor carefully document his or her findings and conclusions in a set of audit working papers. Documentation should occur at all stages of the audit, but it becomes especially critical at the evaluation stage when final conclusions must be reached and supported.

Communication of audit results

Once the audit work is completed and final conclusions have been reached, the auditor prepares a report of his findings and recommendations. This report is provided to management, shareholders, the board of directors, or other appropriate parties. At some point following the communication of audit results, it may be desirable for the auditor to perform a follow-up study to ascertain whether his or her recommendations have been implemented.

Internal Control Audits of Computer-Based Information Systems

In performing a study and evaluation of internal control in a computer-based information system, the auditor should attempt to accomplish the following six objectives.

Objective 1. To ascertain that the design and implementation of application programs is performed in accordance with management's general and specific authorization.

Objective 2. To ascertain that any and all changes in application programs have the authorization and approval of management.

Objective 3. To ascertain that provisions exist to ensure the accuracy and integrity of computer processing of files, reports, and other computer-generated records.

Objective 4. To ascertain that application program source data that are inaccurate or not properly authorized are identified and dealt with in accordance with prescribed managerial policies.

Objective 5. To ascertain that computer operators and other persons with online access to the system cannot accomplish unauthorized modification of input, output, programs, or data files.

Objective 6. To ascertain that provisions exist to protect data files from unauthorized access, modification, or destruction.

This section discusses each of these objectives in turn, focusing on the auditing techniques and procedures available to accomplish them.

As a framework for the discussion of each objective, the "conceptually logical approach" to internal control evaluation advocated by the AICPA is used. This approach involves the following four steps.[10]

1. Consider the types of errors and irregularities that could occur.
2. Determine the accounting control procedures that should prevent or detect such errors and irregularities.
3. Determine whether the necessary procedures are prescribed and are being followed satisfactorily.
4. Evaluate any weaknesses, i.e., types of potential errors and irregularities not covered by existing control procedures, to determine their effect on (a) the nature, timing, or extent of auditing procedures to be applied and (b) suggestions to be made to the client.

The determination of "whether the necessary procedures are prescribed," mentioned in 3, is called the "system review," whereas the determination of whether these procedures "are being followed satisfactorily" is done via *tests of compliance*. Generally, the system review will consist of such audit procedures as review of system documentation and inquiry of personnel. Audit procedures most commonly associated with tests of compliance include observation of system operations, test checking of system inputs and outputs, tracing of transactions through the system, and confirmation of system data with third parties.

Generally, if the EDP control system does not appear to satisfy one or more of the six objectives, the auditor should consider whether or not compensating controls exist with respect to the particular errors or irregularities in question. It is not surprising that the control objectives are to some extent overlapping with respect to certain types of errors and irregularities, because the concept of redundancy is central to many kinds of control systems. Therefore control weaknesses in one area may be acceptable if they are compensated for by control strengths in other areas.

Once the auditor has completed the system review and tests of compliance with respect to each objective, and has considered the adequacy of compensating controls, he or she should have a clear understanding of the kinds of errors and irregularities that could occur. This provides a sound basis for developing recommendations to management and for determining the ap-

---

[10]Statement on Auditing Standards (SAS) Nos. 1 to 49, AU Sec. 320.69.

propriate extent of reliance on the EDP control system for financial auditing purposes.

Objective 1: program development

The focus of the first objective is on the program development process, particularly as it relates to accounting application programs. Essentially, two things could go wrong in this process. First, inadvertent errors could be introduced into the programs through misunderstanding of system specifications or simply careless programming. Second, unauthorized instructions could be deliberately included in the programs by persons whose motives are contrary to those of management.

The control procedures that should prevent these problems involve the quality and integrity of the process of systems analysis, design, and implementation. Generally, the specifications for application programs should have the authorization and approval of management, and in particular the approval of those functional departments and other system users whose operations are affected by the new system. A thorough process of testing and approval of test results for new systems should be in use. Finally, the system itself and all related authorizations and approvals should be well documented.

The auditor who actually participates in the systems design process as a member of the project development team is in a position to influence the project manager to follow these preferred practices. However, there is a danger in this situation that the auditor will lose the objectivity necessary to perform an independent evaluation function. Therefore the auditor's role should be limited to an independent review of, rather than participation in, systems development activities. Furthermore, there is no requirement that such a review take place after the systems development process is completed. Independent reviews by auditors during the systems development process will be much more effective in achieving audit objectives.

During the system review stage of the examination, the auditor should obtain copies of written policies and procedures pertaining to systems development. He or she should then review those standards that relate to the authorization and approval of new systems, the involvement of user departments and other appropriate personnel in the systems design process, the review and evaluation of programmer output, the documentation and the testing of new systems, and the review and approval of test results. The auditor should also discuss these prescribed policies and procedures with management, system users, and EDP personnel to obtain their understanding of how such policies and procedures are intended to be applied. Finally, the auditor should review in some detail the application systems documentation.

Tests of compliance with respect to systems development policies should include interviews with managers and system users that attempt to ascertain the extent of their actual involvement in the design and implementation of specific application systems. In addition, evidence of such involvement, in the form of participation in systems development groups and signed approvals at various stages of the development process, should be sought. In the former case, this involves review of minutes of meetings of systems teams. In the latter case, this requires review of system specifications, preliminary system design documentation, test data specifications, test results, and records of final conversion for signatures evidencing the necessary authorizations and approvals.

Among the most important controls over new system development is the processing of test data. The auditor should review thoroughly all available client documentation relating to the testing process and should ascertain that all program routines affecting accounting data were tested. This involves an examination of the test specifications, a review of the test data, and an evaluation of test results. When unexpected test results were obtained, the auditor should ascertain how the problem was resolved.

The review and evaluation of internal controls relating to EDP systems development should be performed for each significant application program. However, once the review has been completed for a particular application, it need not be done again in future years. Therefore the auditor should regularly perform such a review only for newly developed application programs. For ongoing applications after the initial review, the auditor's concern shifts to controls over program changes, which are the focus of the second of our six objectives.

If the auditor concludes that system development controls for a particular application program are inadequate, the inadequacy may be compensated for by the presence of strong processing controls (see Objective 3). However, such reliance on compensatory processing controls would require that the auditor obtain persuasive evidence of compliance with these controls through such techniques as independent processing of test data. If it is not possible to obtain such evidence of effective compensating controls, the auditor may have to conclude that a material weakness in internal control exists such that the risk of significant errors or irregularities in application programs is unacceptably high.

Objective 2:
program changes

The things that could go wrong with respect to program changes are essentially the same as with new program development. First, inadvertent errors could be introduced into programs undergoing an authorized change either because of a misunderstanding of change specifications or careless programming. Second, unauthorized instructions could be deliberately inserted into existing programs. These problems could potentially affect not only application programs but also systems programs, such as utilities and operating systems. Accordingly, the suggested internal controls and audit procedures discussed in this section apply to all types of programs used by the computer department.

Internal controls should exist that ensure the authorization, documentation, review, testing, and approval of all program changes. In addition, however, controls must exist to prevent deliberate and unauthorized program modification. These include separation of the programming, operations, and file librarian functions, and procedures to control access to computer equipment and program files.

With respect to authorized program changes, part of the auditor's system review should include the examination of written policies and standards, as well as discussions with EDP management concerning how these policies and standards are intended to be implemented. The auditor should also review organization charts and job descriptions and make related inquiries to ascertain the existence of separation of the functions of programming, computer operations, and file librarian. Written policies pertaining to control over access to computer equipment, program files, and program documentation should be examined. Discussions with EDP management, programmers, operations personnel, and the file librarian will help the auditor understand how the written policies and procedures are intended to be implemented.

An important part of the auditor's tests of compliance with respect to these controls is the observation of EDP operations. The auditor should attempt to ascertain that systems analysts, programmers, and other nonoperations personnel do not have unrestricted access to computer equipment or program files. The effectiveness of the supervision of computer operations should be evaluated. The auditor should observe whether application program usage records are consistently maintained by a file librarian and, if they are, should review those records for evidence of any unusual access to program files.

In many modern organizations, greater emphasis is being placed upon remote terminals and minicomputers located in centers of activity at a distance from the central computer site. In this situation the concept of "restricted access" takes on new dimensions because it is far more difficult to restrict access to a multitude of separate locations than to a single centralized location. In this type of environment, the auditor should attempt to ascertain that only a limited number of persons are authorized to operate each terminal or minicomputer, and that access is restricted by means of supervisory controls, password access controls built into the systems software, controls over equipment keys, and, wherever possible, by locating the equipment in a limited access area.

Tests of compliance relating to authorized program changes should begin with a review of the documentation of such changes and the related authorizations and approvals. Particular attention should be given to the authorization for the changes, evidence of review and approval of changes in program code, and the quality of testing of the modified program. Note that it is important to test the entire program rather than just the portion that was modified, in order to prevent a programmer from inserting an unauthorized routine into a separate part of the program during the process of making an authorized program change.

A powerful tool for testing for the presence of unauthorized program changes is a source code comparison program.[11] This program will perform a detailed match of the current version of the application program with a previous version. The auditor should have thoroughly tested the previous version or have other good reasons to have confidence in its integrity. The output of this process is a report identifying the differences between the two programs. The auditor must then review each difference to ascertain that it represents an authorized change.

Two additional techniques that involve using the computer to detect unauthorized program changes are *reprocessing* and *parallel simulation*. To use the reprocessing technique, the auditor must verify the integrity of a copy of the application program and then save that copy for future use. At subsequent intervals on a surprise basis, the auditor uses the previously verified version of the program to reprocess data that have been processed by the current version, and the output of the two runs is compared. Any discrepancies in the two sets of output are then investigated to ascertain their cause. Parallel simulation works in a similar fashion except that instead of using a previously verified copy of the application program, the auditor writes his or her own version of the program or of those parts of the program that are of audit interest. The auditor's version of the program is then used to reprocess the data, and the output is compared with the output from the current version of the program.

The auditor's review of program change controls should encompass each significant application program and should be repeated periodically. In fact, whenever the organization is implementing a major change in an application program, the auditor should be called in to observe the testing and implementation, to review related authorizations and documents, and if necessary, to perform independent tests. If this is not done, and the auditor's subsequent examination reveals inadequacies in the program change controls, it may not be possible to rely on the system with respect to the accuracy of program outputs subsequent to the change. In addition, the auditor should always perform some program tests on a surprise basis as a precaution against unauthorized program changes that may be inserted after the auditor's examination is completed, and then removed prior to the next scheduled audit.

If the auditor concludes that internal controls over program changes are deficient—and especially if this deficiency is caused by a lack of separation of functions or inadequate restrictions on access to equipment or program files—the possibility that the auditor can place any reliance on EDP controls is remote. If such controls are present but are only partially effective, then the presence of excellent processing controls together with the auditor's independent tests of such controls may compensate for such deficiencies.

---

[11]A specific program for this purpose is described by Donald L. Adams in "Alternatives to Computer Audit Software," *Journal of Accountancy* (November 1975): 56.

Objective 3: processing

At the stage of processing input data on the computer to update files or to generate documents and reports, several things could go wrong. Incorrect or unauthorized source data could fail to be detected. Attempts to correct inaccurate data could fail or could introduce additional errors. Correct input or file data could be inadvertently rendered incorrect through improper operating procedures,[12] system malfunctions, or program errors of either a deliberate or unintentional nature. Computer output could fail to be properly distributed or could become available to unauthorized persons. Our third objective is to ascertain that processing controls exist to prevent, or to detect and correct, these kinds of problems.

The processing controls that should be present in a well-managed data processing facility include file labeling techniques, reconciliation of output control totals, maintenance of a console log, incorporation of data edit routines and other programmed controls into application programs, effective supervision of computer operations, good operating documentation and run manuals, preparation of file change listings and summaries for user department review, the use of vendor-supplied hardware and system software controls, and the maintenance of proper levels of temperature, humidity, and other environmental conditions in the computer facility.

The auditor's system review with respect to processing controls should include an examination of written installation standards relating to file labeling, console logs, control totals, environmental controls, and output distribution. Copies of operator's run manuals should be reviewed. The nature of processing controls used in specific accounting applications should be ascertained by a review of application documentation. Vendor literature describing available hardware and system software controls should be examined. Finally, the auditor should interview computer operators, operations supervisors, EDP management, and other appropriate personnel to develop an understanding of how these various types of controls are intended to be applied in practice.

If the auditor suspects or uncovers evidence indicating that a particular application program may contain significant flaws, then a detailed review of some or all of the program logic may be necessary. This is a time-consuming procedure that requires the auditor to be proficient in the programming language. Therefore it would be used only when no alternative method is available to accomplish the auditor's objective. To perform such a review, the auditor would normally refer to systems flowcharts, program flowcharts, and other program documentation in addition to a listing of the program source code. There are several software packages the auditor may use to assist in this review, including (1) *automated flowcharting programs,* which interpret the program source code and generate a program flowchart corresponding to it; (2)

---

[12]Computer operators could also deliberately introduce unauthorized or erroneous data; this is covered by Objective 5.

automated decision table programs, which generate a decision table representing the program logic; (3) *scanning routines,* which search a program for occurrences of a specified variable name or other combinations of characters; and (4) *mapping programs,* which can be activated during regular processing of application programs to identify those portions of the application program that are not executed.

As a part of the tests of compliance with respect to processing controls, the auditor should evaluate the adequacy of controls prescribed by run manuals and other operating documentation and then observe computer operations for evidence that these prescribed controls are actually being followed. Specific things that the auditor should observe are the reconciliation of output control totals, handling of application program error listings, logging of console intervention by the computer operator, label checking and other file handling operations, and adherence to prescribed environmental controls. The auditor should also evaluate the organization's practices relating to the use of available hardware and system software controls and then observe the actual application of these practices.

The auditor's tests of compliance should also include a review of the console log for evidence that all operator intervention is in accordance with prescribed policies and procedures. The auditor should make an independent test of the reconciliation of a sample of output control totals with corresponding input totals, and follow up on any discrepancies. The auditor should also observe the distribution of outputs of accounting application programs and determine that all recipients of such outputs are properly authorized. Ideally, the output distribution function should be the responsibility of data control personnel rather than computer operators.

Certain types of accounting transactions are sensitive from the standpoint of internal control. Among these are changes in customer credit ratings, product prices, and employee pay rates. Also in this category are transactions generated automatically by the computer system as a by-product of routine processing. The auditor should obtain evidence that output listings of these kinds of transactions are regularly reviewed by appropriate user departments. The auditor may also wish to verify a sample of these transactions by comparing them with user department records or by confirmation.

The auditor should evaluate the adequacy of data edit routines incorporated into client application programs and then review the output of such programs for evidence that such edit tests have been applied. Client procedures for follow-up and correction of edit errors should be observed and evaluated. Additional assurance as to the adequacy of client data editing may be obtained by using computer audit software[13] to independently edit selected accounting files. As mentioned earlier, the use of test decks is an additional method of testing the data edit provisions that have been incorporated into

---

[13]The nature and application of computer audit software are explained in the following section of this chapter dealing with the financial audit of computer-based information systems.

application programs. Furthermore, live processing of test transactions without the knowledge of computer operators enables the auditor to test the client's operating procedures for dealing with unusual or erroneous transactions.

Generally, it will be necessary for the auditor to reevaluate the client's processing controls periodically in order to justify continuing confidence in them. If the auditor concludes that the organization's processing controls are not satisfactory with respect to some or all application programs, he or she may nonetheless decide that internal controls in the related user departments (user controls), and source data controls are strong enough to compensate for such deficiencies. However, if these alternative controls are not sufficient to compensate for the deficiencies in processing controls, the auditor must conclude that a material weakness exists in the organization's internal control system.

Several specialized techniques exist that enable the auditor to use the computer to perform compliance tests of data edit routines and other programmed controls in application programs. These include (1) processing of test data, (2) program tracing, and (3) embedded audit modules. In the following paragraphs, the nature and application of each of these techniques are explained.

Processing of test data.   Processing of test data involves the introduction of hypothetical transactions into a computer system to check the completeness and accuracy of the system's processing and control procedures. Previous chapters have referred to this technique as an important means of testing new computer programs before they become operational. It is sometimes referred to as the "test deck" approach because punched cards were once the primary medium for introducing the test transactions. This technique is designed to test system compliance with respect to processing controls associated with an application program.

Figure 15.1 contains a systems flowchart representing an overview of the test data process. As a first step in this process, the auditor reviews the system's documentation to develop a clear understanding of the nature and function of the program being tested. He or she should identify the edit routines, programmed controls, and alternative logic paths present and then prepare a set of hypothetical transactions containing both valid and invalid data designed to test all portions of the program having audit significance. Examples of the kinds of invalid data that might be included are records with missing data, fields containing unreasonably large amounts, unusual relationships among data in two or more fields, invalid account numbers or processing codes, nonnumeric data in numeric fields, records out of sequence, illogical accounting journal entries, and so forth. Some transactions should contain multiple errors. In addition, all the alternative logic paths should be checked for proper functioning by one or more of the test transactions.

To facilitate the preparation of test transactions, the auditor may obtain a listing of actual transactions, as well as of test transactions used by the pro-

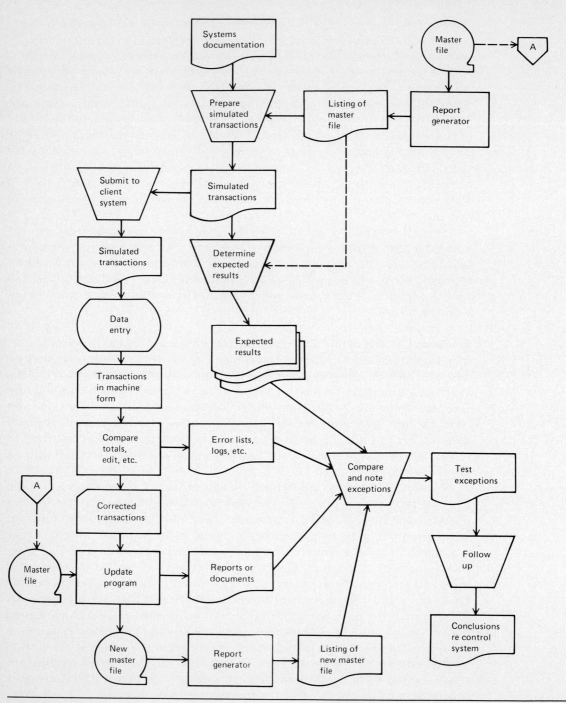

FIGURE 15.1
Overview of test
data process.

grammer. However, the availability of the programmer's test data may be useful for reference purposes but does not relieve the auditor of the responsibility to perform an independent test using independently prepared test data. If available, the auditor may use a *test data generator* program to automatically prepare a set of test data based upon specifications describing the logical characteristics of the program to be tested.

Once the hypothetical transactions have been prepared, the auditor should review a listing of the current version of the master file or files maintained by the application program and manually determine what the expected results of processing the test transactions should be. The test data are then introduced into the system, either as source documents (as shown in Fig. 15.1) or in machine-readable form at a subsequent processing step. Alternatively, the auditor may process the test data independently of the organization's data processing personnel.

After the test data are processed, the actual system output, including error reports or logs, documents, reports, and file update listings, is compared with the predetermined correct output. Any discrepancies indicate a potential lack of compliance with appropriate processing controls and should be thoroughly investigated to determine their cause.

Although the processing of test transactions is a very effective means of testing system compliance with processing controls, it does have some disadvantages. The auditor typically must spend considerable time developing an understanding of the system and preparing an adequate set of test transactions. Furthermore, care must be taken to ensure that the test transactions do not affect the company's actual master file records. This might involve procedures to reverse the effects of the test transactions, or perhaps a separate run in which the test transactions are processed against a copy of the master file rather than against the real file. However, the use of a separate run removes some of the reality that is obtained from processing the test transactions along with the regular transactions. A further problem is that these special procedures may reveal the existence and nature of the auditor's test to the employees of the computer facility. Thus these procedures may be less effective than a concealed test would be.

Program tracing. *Program tracing* is a technique that enables the auditor to obtain a detailed knowledge of the logic of an application program, as well as test the program's compliance with its control specifications. To use this technique, the auditor processes the application program either with regular or test transactions but activates a trace routine built into the system software. This routine will cause the computer to print out in sequential order a list of all the application program steps (line numbers or paragraph names) executed during the program run. This list is intermingled with the regular program output so that the auditor can observe the precise sequence of events that took place during program execution. The auditor then reviews a copy of the source program in conjunction with the trace output to confirm his or her expectations of the way the program works.

This technique may enable the auditor to detect the presence of unauthorized program instructions, incorrect logic paths, or unused program sections within application programs. Such conditions should be investigated further to ascertain their cause and effect. Program tracing can be a very effective computer auditing technique. However, it is also time-consuming and requires that the auditor be proficient in the programming language used by the application program.

Embedded audit modules. *Embedded audit modules* are special portions of an application program designed to perform functions of particular use to auditors. For example, such modules might be designed to monitor all transaction activity and notify the auditor of any transactions having special audit significance, such as unauthorized attempts to access the system or dollar amounts in excess of prescribed limits. In one variation of this approach known as *real-time notification,* the auditor is informed of such transactions immediately as they occur by means of a message printed on the auditor's terminal. A more common approach is for the system to write all relevant information concerning such transactions on a tape or disk file called the *audit log*.[14] The auditor then periodically requests a printout of the audit log and investigates the transactions on it.

Another variation of this technique is known as *tagging*. Under this approach, selected records are marked with a special code. As the application programs process these records, the audit modules will capture all data relating to the marked records on a file that can subsequently be reviewed by the auditor. This enables the auditor to observe in detail all aspects of the processing of particular transactions through the information system.

Objective 4: source data

The focal point of Objective 4 is the accuracy and integrity of the data input to application programs. The errors or irregularities that could occur are that inaccurate or unauthorized source data could be introduced into the system and posted to system files by the computer. Internal controls should exist that will prevent, detect, and correct inaccurate or unauthorized source data. Among the most important of such controls is the existence of an independent data control function assigned responsibility for source data accuracy and integrity. Specific control techniques include user authorization of source data; desk checking of input data listings; check digit verification during data encoding; keyverification of important data items; reconciliation of batch control totals; logging the receipt, movement, and disposition of data input; the use of turnaround documents where feasible; the use of edit programs to check source data accuracy prior to processing; and special handling of any input errors discovered by these other controls.

---

[14]A colorful acronym sometimes used to describe the audit log is SCARF, which stands for "System Control Audit Review File."

As part of the system review, the auditor should examine organization charts and job descriptions to ascertain the existence of a data control function that is organizationally independent of user departments or the computer operations function. Written descriptions of the general procedures used for control of source data should be reviewed. The documentation of significant accounting applications should be examined to develop an understanding of the flow of accounting data to and from the EDP function, and of the specific source data control procedures applied to such data. One tool the auditor may use to document the results of a review of source data controls for a particular application is the *input controls matrix* (see Fig. 15.2), which shows the control procedures applied to each field of an input record. The auditor should also obtain a copy of the signatures or other forms of authorization required for each significant type of input transaction. Finally, the auditor should interview system users, EDP management, and data control

FIGURE 15.2
Input controls matrix.

RECORD NAME: Employer Weekly Time Report / INPUT CONTROLS	Employee number	Last name	Department number	Transaction code	Week ending (date)	Regular hours	Overtime hours			Comments
Batch totals					✓	✓				
Hash totals	✓									
Record counts										Yes
Cross-footing balance										No
Key verification	✓				✓	✓				
Visual inspection										All fields
Check digit verification	✓									
Prenumbered forms										No
Turnaround document										No
Edit program										Yes
Sequence check	✓									
Field check	✓		✓		✓	✓				
Sign check										
Validity check	✓		✓	✓						
Limit check					✓	✓				
Reasonableness test					✓	✓				
Redundant data check	✓	✓	✓							
Completeness test			✓	✓	✓	✓				
Overflow procedure										
Other:										

personnel to develop an understanding of how the prescribed source data control procedures are intended to be applied.

In a small business data processing operation, or in a minicomputer installation located in a department or small division of a larger company, it is unlikely that an independent data control function will exist because it is simply not economically feasible. To compensate for this lack, other control procedures must be that much stronger. These include user department controls over data preparation, batch control totals, edit programs, system access restrictions, and error handling procedures. These controls should be the focus of the auditor's system review and compliance tests whenever there is no independent data control function in the installation being reviewed.

Tests of compliance with respect to source data controls should include observation of the operations of the data control function to ascertain its independence from other functions within the EDP department as well as from user departments. The degree of control exercised over the data control log should also be observed. To verify the fact that batch control totals are being properly applied, the auditor should trace a sample of control totals through the input process. Control totals provided by user departments should be compared with those recorded in the data control log and to those generated by the computer during the preparation of input listings or the running of data edit programs. Any exceptions to proper reconciliation of control totals should be investigated. Finally, the auditor should compare a sample of transactions from computer listings of edited transactions to the data on the original source documents and investigate any significant discrepancies.

Using the list of required source data authorizations obtained during system review, the auditor should examine samples of accounting source data for evidence that proper authorizations were present and were checked by data control personnel prior to acceptance of the data for computer processing. Any significant exceptions to proper source data authorization should be investigated by the auditor. Furthermore, the auditor should observe the performance of specific input verification procedures, such as checking for authorizations, review of input listings, logging, check digit verification, keyverification, reconciliation of input control totals, and processing of edit programs. Of particular importance here is observation of procedures used to control exceptions, such as transactions that fail check digit tests or edit program error listings.

A technique enabling comprehensive testing of both source data controls *and* processing controls is called the *mini-company test* or *integrated test facility* (ITF). This is an extension of the concept of test data processing that involves introducing a small set of records representing a fictitious entity into the master files of the system under review. The fictitious entity might be a dummy division, department, branch office, customer, etc. Test transactions may then be processed against these fictitious master records without affecting the real master records. Further, the test transactions may be processed along with the real transactions, and the employees of the computer facility need not be aware that the testing is being done. The integrated test facility therefore eliminates two of the primary disadvantages of processing test data, in that there is no need to reverse the effects of test transactions on the actual master file records, and the existence of the test can be concealed from the employees whose work is being checked. However, care must be taken in designing the integrated test facility to ensure that it does not cause real transactions to be initiated unnecessarily, and that its fictitious records are not aggregated with regular records during the preparation of summary reports for management.

Even though the prescribed source data controls may not change from year to year, the strictness with which they are applied may change. Therefore the auditor who intends to rely on EDP source data controls should perform compliance tests of them on a regular basis. If the auditor concludes that source data controls are not adequate with respect to a particular application system, other controls that may compensate are user department controls and computer processing controls. If these other controls do not compensate for the inadequacies in source data controls, the auditor may have to conclude that the EDP internal control system as a whole is unsatisfactory.

Objective 5: operations

The focus of Objective 5 is on persons who operate computer equipment. Specifically, it concerns the possibility that such persons may use the computer to deliberately introduce unauthorized transactions or program changes into the system. In this regard the term "computer operator" encompasses not only persons who run computer equipment at central data processing sites but also those who have online access to the system from remote terminals.

Effective internal control over computer operations requires that this function be organizationally independent of the programming, data control, and file librarian functions. Responsibility for supervision of computer operations should be assigned to a qualified employee. The access of computer operators to systems documentation and to program and data files should be controlled. There should be a data processing schedule indicating when each significant application is to be processed, and records of actual system utilization should be collected and compared with the schedule. The duties of computer operators should be periodically rotated, and vacations for them should be mandatory. In addition, such processing controls as data editing, control totals, and maintenance of a console log are also effective with respect to computer operations. Particularly important is that all these provisions should be applied not only to day-shift operations but also to evening and overnight shifts.

Access to the central computing facility and to remote terminals should be controlled both by sound personnel practices and by physical security measures such as door locks and alarms. Online access to the central computer and its files should be controlled by employing user passwords and related system software access controls. Transactions entered on an online basis should be recorded by the system in a transaction log for subsequent review and analysis.

To develop an understanding of management-prescribed internal controls relating to computer operations, the auditor should review organization charts, job descriptions, policy and procedure manuals, operator run manuals, system documentation, and related materials. This understanding should be supplemented by discussions with EDP management, operations supervisors, systems programmers, and other appropriate employees.

In a small business environment, separation of functions and restricted access to equipment may not be economically feasible. To compensate for lack of these controls in such situations, the auditor must ascertain that other operations controls are strong enough to compensate. In particular, a strong system of password access controls is especially critical. Authorization and supervision of equipment use and externally maintained control totals are also helpful.

The auditor's tests of compliance of operating controls should begin with observation of the computer operations function. Evidence should be obtained that access to computer equipment is controlled according to prescribed policies; that console logs, equipment utilization records, and error transaction logs are conscientiously maintained; that operators do not have unrestricted access to system documentation, program tapes, and data files; and that operations supervision is consistent and effective. As implied earlier, such observation should encompass evening and overnight shifts if significant application programs are processed at those times. The audit log concept described earlier in this chapter is a useful extension of the auditor's capacity to observe computer operations.

The auditor's tests of compliance should also include a review of operator work records for evidence of compliance with rotation and vacation policies. The auditor will wish to compare equipment utilization records with processing schedules for evidence of any unusual discrepancies between actual and scheduled processing times.[15] The auditor should also review the console log for evidence that it is complete, that it is periodically reviewed by appropriate persons outside the operations function, and that it contains no indications of unusual or unauthorized operator intervention. The auditor should probe any questionable console log entries to determine whether they were investigated by appropriate personnel and how they were resolved.

If erroneous transactions detected by source data or processing controls are recorded in an error log by operators or data control personnel, the auditor should examine the error log to determine that the disposition of errors is properly noted and that errors are not allowed to remain unresolved for an excessive period of time. The auditor may wish to test check the recording, investigation, and correction of a sample of errors. Any errors recorded in

---

[15]It should be noted that in advanced systems employing multiprocessing, it is more difficult to predict how long a particular job *should* take because that depends on the mix of other jobs that happen to be using the system's resources at the time.

the log that have not been resolved within a reasonable time period should be investigated by the auditor.

With respect to remote online access to the system, the auditor's tests of compliance should include observation and inquiry concerning access to and operation of computer terminals. The auditor should evaluate the adequacy of system software access control methods and of password assignment procedures. Processing of a sample of password assignment requests should be investigated for evidence of compliance with prescribed procedures. The auditor should examine a sample of assigned passwords and their associated access authority for evidence that password holders may have access authority incompatible with their other responsibilities. Online transaction logs should be examined for evidence that they are regularly reviewed by appropriate personnel, and that any unauthorized online access or attempts to initiate improper transactions are identified, investigated, and adequately resolved.

If the auditor concludes that computer operations personnel have the opportunity and ability to initiate unauthorized computer transactions, then the only other controls that could possibly compensate for this deficiency are excellent user department controls. Essentially, user personnel would have to be able to recognize anything unusual in the output they receive from the computer. Otherwise, the auditor should conclude that the EDP internal control system is seriously deficient.

Objective 6: data files

Objective 6 is concerned with the accuracy, integrity, and security of data stored in machine-readable files. In the absence of good controls, stored data could be modified in an unauthorized manner, inadvertently or intentionally destroyed, or made available to persons outside the organization against the wishes of management.

As part of the system review, the auditor should examine job descriptions, policy and procedure manuals, and related documentation to ascertain the existence of such controls as a separate file librarian function, restrictions on access to disk and tape files as well as to systems documentation, maintenance of a usage log for these materials, use of both internal and external file labels, maintenance of file control totals by persons independent of data processing, provisions for reconstruction of lost data or files, use of offsite locations for storage of duplicate copies of critical data, and special controls over master file conversions during system changeovers. The auditor should also discuss with EDP management and file librarians the way in which these controls are intended to be applied.

The auditor's tests of compliance with data controls should include observation of the file librarian's activities to ascertain that other systems personnel are not permitted unrestricted access to data files, that a usage record for such data files is maintained, and that the file librarian is not permitted to operate computer equipment. The auditor should determine that someone with appropriate authority is responsible for regular review of the librarian's usage records and follow up in cases of unauthorized or unscheduled usage. The auditor may also wish to investigate a selected number of cases of unusual access to data files.

When data control personnel regularly check data file control totals with corresponding user totals maintained outside the EDP function, the auditor should test check a number of these comparisons for accuracy. Simultaneously the auditor may wish to foot the data file using a computer audit software package to check the accuracy of the file totals maintained by the EDP function.

As part of the observation of computer operations, the auditor should ascertain that operating personnel are adhering to prescribed file security provisions, such as the checking of file labels, preparation of duplicate files, and prompt removal of duplicate file copies to offsite storage locations.

Whenever the implementation of a new EDP system requires that data files be changed from one storage medium to another (especially from a written medium to a machine-readable medium), the auditor should be concerned that this file conversion process is properly controlled. The auditor should evaluate the prescribed file conversion controls, and test the conversion of files by comparing selected records from the new file with their counterparts on the old. The auditor may wish to independently perform a series of edit checks on the new file using a computer audit software package. Ideally, EDP personnel will inform the auditor when important conversions of files are scheduled, in order that the auditor may be present to observe the process and accompanying control procedures.

The most significant deficiency in file security would be lack of proper separation of functions accompanied by failure to restrict access to sensitive data files. If such deficiencies are present, the auditor must conclude that there are material weaknesses in the EDP internal control system. Alternatively, such controls are only partially deficient, or if other file security controls are not satisfactory, strong controls over processing, operations, and user functions may compensate, and reliance on the EDP internal control system may be possible.

Conclusion

Application of the concept of auditing by objectives as explained above provides focus to the auditor's study and evaluation of EDP internal controls. The auditing by objectives approach may be implemented by means of an audit procedures checklist organized around the six objectives. Such a checklist should direct the auditor to reach a separate conclusion regarding the extent of achievement of each objective and suggest appropriate compensating controls when a particular objective is not fully achieved. When distinct application programs are being reviewed, separate versions of the checklist should be completed for each significant application. This approach represents a comprehensive, systematic, and effective means of evaluating internal controls in a computer-based information system.

One other conclusion may be formed based upon the nature of several of the auditing techniques reviewed in this section. Techniques such as real-time notification, the audit log, tagging of transactions, and the integrated test facility all should be incorporated into a system during the design process, rather than as an afterthought once the system has been implemented. Also, many of the application control techniques the auditor expects to find in a system are easier to design into the system in the first place than to attach later on. These points give added emphasis to the importance of involving the auditor in the systems design process while there is still time to adopt his or her suggestions for incorporating control techniques and audit features into new application systems.

Financial Audits and Computer Audit Software

As explained earlier in this chapter, the first of the five standards dealing with the scope of internal audit work is that

> internal auditors should review the reliability and integrity of financial and operating information and the means used to identify, measure, classify, and report such information.[16]

And of course the primary objective of the external auditor is to evaluate the information reported by management in annual financial statements. The *general* methodology for this type of audit work is discussed extensively in numerous standard textbooks on auditing[17] and so is not belabored here. Accordingly, this section deals with *specific* auditing procedures and techniques directed at auditing financial and operating information maintained on a computer system.

In those situations in which the computer plays a significant role in processing, storing, and reporting the information subject to audit, the auditor should generally audit *through* the computer if practical. This means that the auditor should use the computer to the maximum extent feasible in (1) gathering evidence about the reliability of internal controls in the systems that produced the information (using the methodology explained in the previous section), which will influence the auditor's preliminary judgments concerning the accuracy of the system outputs; and (2) performing a variety of auditing operations on the computer files used to store the information. These latter operations are performed using computer programs written especially for auditors called *Generalized Audit Software Packages* (GASP), or simply *computer audit software.* Several packages of this type are available from software vendors as well as from the larger public accounting firms. This section describes the nature of computer audit software and explains how it may be applied in the auditing process.

---

[16]Institute of Internal Auditors, *Standards for the Professional Practice of Internal Auditing,* p. 3.

[17]For example, see Alvin A. Arens and James K. Loebbecke, *Auditing: An Integrated Approach,* 3d ed. (Englewood Cliffs, N.J.: Prentice-Hall, 1984); or Jack C. Robertson and Frederick G. Davis, *Auditing,* 4th ed. (Dallas: Business Publications, 1985).

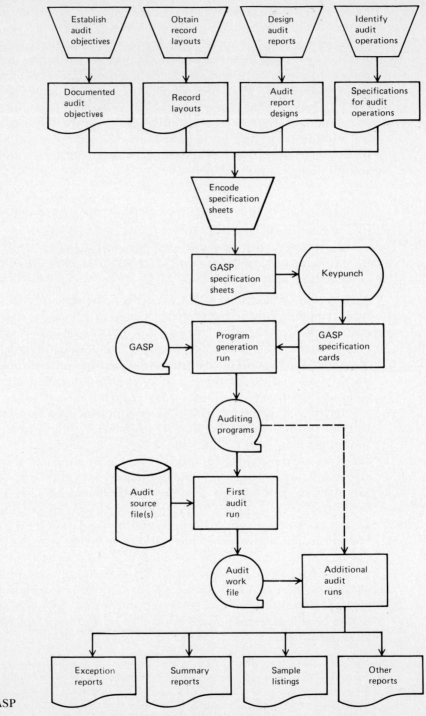

FIGURE 15.3
Overview of GASP
processing.

In Fig. 15.3 is a systems flowchart that provides an overview of the processing steps required to utilize a GASP. Once the auditor has established the audit objectives of the application, obtained knowledge of the format and content of the files to be audited, designed the format of the desired audit reports, and determined the operations necessary to accomplish the objectives and produce the reports, all these details concerning the application are encoded by the auditor on a set of preformatted specification sheets. The data on the specification sheets are keypunched onto a deck of cards, which is then processed as input to the GASP. This step generally results in a computer program, or set of programs, either in machine language or in a higher-level language such as COBOL. In the latter case the higher-level language program must then be compiled before being processed. In essence, the GASP is a computer program that generates other computer programs based upon the auditor's specifications, and it is these other computer programs that perform the audit functions.

In the next step, the source files containing the information subject to audit are processed as input to the audit program generated by the GASP. Usually, there are a series of such computer runs, each designed to perform selected auditing operations as necessary to produce one of the specified audit reports. A general list of the functions performed by computer audit software appears in Fig. 15.4. Frequently, the major objective of the first of these computer runs is to extract specific information of interest to the auditor

FIGURE 15.4
General functions of computer audit software.

FUNCTION	EXPLANATION
REFORMATTING	Audit software extracts relevant information from source files, rearranges it as required by the auditor, and creates audit work files from it.
CALCULATION	Audit software can perform the four basic arithmetic operations: add, subtract, multiply, and divide.
LOGICAL OPERATIONS	Audit software can perform logical operations such as comparing data values, selecting records based on specified criteria, and editing data for consistency and completeness.
DATA EDITING	Audit software can perform numerous edit checks on the data content of machine readable records.
FILE MANIPULATION	Audit software can perform basic file handling operations such as sorting and merging.
REPORT GENERATION	Audit software can generate standard audit documents and reports such as confirmations and aging schedules, and other reports in formats specifically designed by the auditor.
STATISTICS	Audit software can select random samples, compute means and variances, and perform other basic statistical functions.

ADVANTAGE	EXPLANATION
ACCESS	Audit software provides improved access to data stored in machine readable form.
SCOPE	Audit software enables the auditor to examine more records than would otherwise be possible.
COST	Audit software reduces the cost of auditing in large organizations which are extensively computerized.
INDEPENDENCE	Audit software is used under the auditor's control, thereby lessening the auditor's dependence on EDP personnel.
SIMPLICITY	Audit software is easy to learn about and to use, and requires only minimal knowledge of computer technology.
GENERALITY	Audit software performs a variety of auditing tasks, and can function in a variety of auditing environments.
UNDERSTANDING	A by-product of using audit software is that the auditor gains a better understanding of the information system.

FIGURE 15.5
Summary of audit
software advantages.

from the source file or files and reformat it into an audit work file. The desired audit reports are then generated by a subsequent series of computer runs that use the audit work file as input.

The primary purpose of the GASP is to assist the auditor in reviewing and retrieving information stored on computer files. Note, however, that the use of a GASP is normally one of the first steps in the financial audit. Once the auditor receives the reports prepared by the GASP application, most of the audit work still remains to be done. Items listed on exception reports must be investigated, file totals and subtotals must be verified against other sources of information such as the general ledger, and items selected for audit samples must be examined and evaluated. In summary, while the advantages to the auditor of using a GASP (summarized in Fig. 15.5) are numerous and compelling, a computer program cannot replace the auditor's judgment or free the auditor from significant participation in all phases of the audit.

An example of a GASP application

In this section the functions that can be performed using computer audit software are explained in greater detail using as an example the audit of accounts receivable information produced by a computerized order entry, billing, and customer accounting system.[18] Assume that this system maintains an accounts receivable master file and transaction detail files for sales on account, cash collections, and credit memos. The auditor has obtained copies of record layouts for these files, which are reproduced in Fig. 15.6. The following specific

---

[18]Systems of this kind are described more fully in the next chapter.

RECORD NAME: *Accounts Receivable Master*

FIELD NAME	Account Number	Name	Address				Credit Code	Credit Limit	Previous Balance	Current Balance
			Street	City	State	Zip				
POSITION	1-6	7-31	32-56	57-74	75-76	77-81	82-83	84-91	92-99	100-107

RECORD NAME: *Sales Detail*

FIELD NAME	Account Number	Transaction Code	Transaction Date	Reference Number	Amount
POSITION	1-6	7	8-13	14-18	19-26

RECORD NAME: *Cash Collections Detail*

FIELD NAME	Account Number	Transaction Code	Transaction Date	Reference Number	Amount
POSITION	1-6	7	8-13	14-18	19-26

RECORD NAME: *Credit Memo Detail*

FIELD NAME	Account Number	Transaction Code	Transaction Date	Credit Memo Number	Amount
POSITION	1-6	7	8-13	14-18	19-26

FIGURE 15.6
Record layouts for accounts receivable system.

objectives for the GASP application have been delineated by the auditor: (1) recalculate the current balance of every master record from the previous balance and the intervening transactions and identify all accounts having an incorrect current balance; (2) sum the current balance, credit sales, cash collections, and credit memo amounts for verification of their totals against other independently maintained information; (3) perform edit checks on selected fields in each file to confirm the reliability of data editing performed within the EDP function; (4) check the transaction files for any records that do not match with a master record; (5) prepare an aging schedule of the receivables and an analysis of accounts having current balances in excess of their credit limit, in order to evaluate the sufficiency of the allowance for uncollectible accounts and to assess the performance of the credit department; (6) select a sample of accounts for confirmation in order to verify the existence and accuracy of the receivables recorded on the master file; and (7) analyze cash collections and credit memos subsequent to the test date for those customers who do not respond to confirmation requests. In the following paragraphs, the steps necessary to accomplish these objectives using computer audit software are described. The reader should note that each of the general audit software functions delineated in Fig. 15.4 is utilized one or more times in the course of this application.

A systems flowchart showing the sequence of computer operations necessary to accomplish the first six objectives appears in Fig. 15.7. Input to the first computer run consists of all four of the source files, each sequenced by account number. If any of these files had originally been in some other sequence (for example, the transaction files might have been maintained in sequence by transaction date), then a previous run using the GASP to sort these records by account number would have been necessary.

One objective of this first pass is to merge the data from all four files into

FIGURE 15.7
Application of computer audit software to accounts receivable.

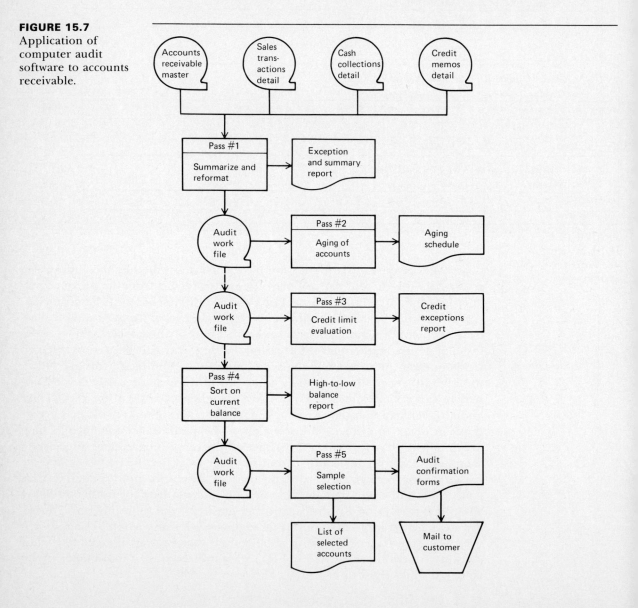

a single information set for each customer and then extract from this customer information set only that information necessary to perform the subsequent auditing operations. The information so extracted is recorded on an audit work file. In this case assume that the auditor elects to include the following items in his or her work file: (1) account number, (2) name, (3) address, (4) credit limit, (5) current balance, (6) last invoice (sale) date, (7) last invoice amount, (8) last credit (payment or credit memo) date, and (9) last credit amount. For each account record, an audit record containing these data is created, and these audit records are written in sequential order onto a separate file.

This first run also performs a variety of tests on the information recorded on each of the four input files and prints an exception report containing the results of these tests. For each customer information set, all sales on account are added to the previous balance, and all cash collections and credit memo amounts are subtracted; if the result is not equal to the current balance amount, data pertaining to the account are printed on the exception report. A series of edit checks could also be performed on selected data from each of the four types of records, with all erroneous records listed on the exception report. Among the edit checks that could be performed in this case are validity checks on the transaction codes and dates, a completeness test of each type of record, a sign test of the current balance, field checks of all numeric fields, and a sequence check of each file based on account number. Furthermore, any transaction detail records that lack an accounts receivable master record having the same account number would be listed on the exception report. All significant exceptions identified by these checks should be investigated by the auditor to ascertain their cause and evaluate their implications with respect to the overall reliability of the accounts receivable information.

Additional operations performed during this first pass are footing the amount fields for cash collections, sales on account, credit memos, and account balances and printing a summary report containing these file totals. These may then be compared with corresponding totals from the sales and cash receipts journals and the general ledger accounts for credit sales, sales returns and allowances, and accounts receivable. If these totals cannot be reconciled, there may be a serious deficiency in the quality of the information maintained by the system.

On the second pass, the audit work file is processed to generate an aging schedule for the receivables. Most audit software contains built-in logic specifically designed to perform aging operations. Immediately following this step, a third pass is made, during which the current balance for each customer is compared with the credit limit, and all accounts having balances in excess of the credit limit are printed on a report. During this third pass, the total of all such balances, as well as the total excess of such balances over the corresponding credit limit, can be accumulated and then printed at the bottom of the report. Both the aging schedule and the credit exceptions report could then be used by the auditor to appraise the adequacy of the allowance for uncollectible accounts and to provide a basis for evaluating the credit department's effectiveness in administering credit policies.

On the fourth pass, the records on the audit work file are re-sorted into sequence from high to low current balance. Each account is classified into a dollar range based upon its current balance; for example, over $20,000, $19,501 to $20,000, $19,001 to $19,500, and so on, down to $0 to $500. A summary report is printed that lists the number of accounts and the cumulative dollar amount within each range. This report is useful to the auditor in designing a sampling plan for selecting accounts to be confirmed. For example, the auditor may decide to select all accounts over $15,000, ten percent of the remaining accounts over $5,000, two percent of the remaining accounts over $1,000, and one percent of the accounts of $1,000 or less. This type of sampling plan, called *stratified sampling*, enables the auditor to include in the sample a relatively high percentage of the total number of *dollars* in the population, even though the sample may include a very low percentage of the total number of *accounts*. The high-to-low-balance summary report helps the auditor to decide how many strata to use and what strata boundaries to establish.

Once the sampling plan has been established, the re-sorted audit work file is input to a fifth pass that selects the specific accounts to be included in the sample. A list of these accounts is printed for the auditor. In addition, virtually all audit software packages have a built-in formatting capability for audit confirmations, and this pass results in the printing of these confirmations for the accounts in the sample. The auditor will then supervise the mailing of these confirmation forms to the customers.

Generally, there will be some customers who do not respond to confirmation requests. However, the auditor can obtain evidence concerning the validity of those accounts by examining subsequent collections from those customers. In this case, for example, the auditor might wait a month or so after sending out the confirmations and then write a program using the audit software package to scan the cash collections and credit memo files and identify and print records of all cash collections and credit memos for those customers in the sample who did not respond to the confirmation request.

Once the auditor has obtained and examined confirmation responses and other relevant evidence, the results of the sample must be evaluated. Some audit software packages have the capability of statistically evaluating sample results by computing means, variances, confidence intervals, sampling risks, and so forth. A common approach when the GASP does not possess this capability is to use a separate time-sharing program for the statistical evaluation.

In summary, the use of a GASP in this illustration provided the auditor with the ability to quickly and inexpensively review the accounts receivable information, identify questionable records that should be investigated further, prepare several summary reports, select a sample of accounts for confirmation, and automatically print the confirmation forms. Furthermore, it is quite significant that the auditor is able to do these things independently of EDP personnel. However, the results obtained from using the GASP generally represent only the first step in the audit. Once these results are made available to him or her, the auditor must still investigate exceptions, audit sample items, independently verify file totals, evaluate the significance of summary reports, and perform numerous other auditing procedures.

Management Audits of Computer-Based Information Systems

The steps involved in a management audit of a computer-based information system, and many of the techniques and procedures used, are very similar to those used in internal control audits or financial audits. The basic differences involve the scope and objectives of the management audit. Whereas the scope of the internal control audit is confined to internal controls, and the scope of the financial audit is confined to the output of information systems, the scope of the management audit is much broader, encompassing all aspects of the management of the information systems activity. Furthermore, the objectives of management audits involve evaluating such factors as effectiveness, efficiency, and the accomplishment of organizational objectives. This section briefly outlines some of the most significant aspects of the management of computer-based information systems, in order to provide a framework for understanding the scope of management audits of such systems. The section concludes with a brief discussion of the application of standard auditing procedures and techniques to the performance of management audits.

The principles of good systems management provide a standard against which the attributes of an actual system can be measured. Many of these principles have been described at length in the previous five chapters of Part 3. Accordingly, what is presented here is simply an outline of major topics intended to refresh the reader's memory.

Our outline divides systems management principles into six basic categories: (1) organizational arrangements, (2) systems planning, (3) personnel policies, (4) management of systems development projects, (5) financial controls, and (6) computer operations. Organizational arrangements include such matters as the role and responsibilities of the MIS director, the existence and effective functioning of an MIS steering committee, and the proper distribution of functions within the systems department. Systems planning encompasses the prioritization of potential systems development projects, the preparation of systems development plans, the projection of future hardware and personnel requirements, and the preparation of an overall long-range financial plan for the systems development activity that is integrated with the organization's long-range planning process. Personnel policies include standards for hiring, training, and assigning EDP personnel; establishing job descriptions and performance standards; evaluating employee performance; and effectively involving appropriate management personnel in activities such as systems planning, project selection, and development of new systems.

Good principles of management relating to systems development projects include the use of feasibility studies and other systematic project or vendor selection methods, the preparation of systems development schedules and budgets, the establishment of project milestones, the regular use of project progress reviews, and adherence to good documentation standards. Financial controls encompass the application of responsibility accounting and reporting standards to systems departments and projects, including the use of financial budgets and performance reports, and the use of a system of charging computer users for the cost or value of the computer services they consume. Computer operations management involves the use of a data processing schedule, the maintenance of activity logs, the existence and use of good operating documentation such as run manuals, the use of computer hardware and software performance monitors, adherence to a regular equipment maintenance schedule, and proper controls over equipment access.

The process of performing a management audit parallels the process of performing an internal control audit or a financial audit. The first step is planning, during which the audit scope and objectives are established, a preliminary review of the system performed, and a tentative audit program prepared. Evidence gathering includes such activities as review of operating policies and documentation, inquiry of management and operating personnel, perhaps aided by the use of questionnaires or checklists, observation of operating functions and activities, examination of financial and operating plans and reports, tests of accuracy of operating information, and tests of compliance with prescribed policies and procedures.

At the evidence evaluation stage, the auditor is basically measuring the actual system against an ideal system that would follow all the best principles of systems management. One important consideration here is that the *results* of management policies and practices are more significant than the policies and practices themselves. That is, if excellent results are being achieved through policies and practices that are theoretically deficient, then the auditor must carefully consider whether recommended improvements would substantially improve results. In any event, the auditor should thoroughly document the findings and conclusions and communicate the audit results to management in an effective manner.

To be a good management auditor probably requires some degree of management experience. Persons with excellent backgrounds in auditing but without management experience often lack the perspective necessary to understand the management process. Thus the ideal management auditor is probably a person with training and experience as an auditor but also with a few years' experience in a managerial position.

Summary

An audit is a systematic and objective process that involves planning audit procedures, gathering and evaluating evidence, and communicating results and conclusions. Audits of computer-based information systems involve evaluation of the effectiveness of these systems in meeting standards for (1) the reliability and integrity of information; (2) compliance with policies, plans, procedures, laws, and regulations; (3) safeguarding of assets; (4) economical and efficient use of resources; and (5) accomplishment of established objectives and goals for operations or programs.

Three major categories of audits of computer-based information systems are internal control audits, financial audits, and management audits. Internal control audits are designed to evaluate the quality of control policies and procedures relating to computer program development, program changes, computer processing, source data entry, the computer operations function, and computer data storage. Financial audits focus on the reliability and integrity of financial and operating information and make extensive use of computer audit software. Management audits involve evaluation of the effectiveness and efficiency of information systems management in accomplishing the objectives of the organization.

Review Questions

1. Define the following terms.

auditing	automated decision table program
internal control audit	scanning routine
financial audit	mapping program
management audit	test data generator
operational audit	program tracing
compliance audit	embedded audit module
confirmation	real-time notification
vouching	audit log
analytical review	tagging
materiality	input controls matrix
reasonable assurance	mini company test
tests of compliance	integrated test facility
reprocessing	generalized audit software package
parallel simulation	computer audit software
automated flowcharting program	stratified sampling

2. Why is it said that the audit trail has disappeared in computerized data processing systems?

3. Distinguish between auditing "around" and auditing "through" the computer.

4. Describe the five standards of internal auditing that deal with the scope of internal audit work. Briefly explain how each standard applies to the audit of computer-based information systems.

5. Describe the four major stages of the auditing process.

6. Identify several auditing tests and procedures used for purposes of collecting audit evidence.

7. In evaluating audit evidence, what are the auditor's options with respect to possible conclusions? What role do materiality and reasonable assurance play in forming these conclusions?

8. Identify six objectives of internal control audits of computer-based information systems.

9. List the four steps in the AICPA's "conceptually logical approach" to internal control evaluation. Where do "system review" and "tests of compliance" fit into this approach?

10. Explain the concept of compensating controls. How do they affect the auditor's study and evaluation of internal control?

11. With respect to the program development process, (a) what are the potential control problems, (b) what internal controls should be present, (c) what should the auditor examine during the system review, (d) what tests of compliance can the auditor perform, and (e) what compensating controls may exist in the event that program development controls are inadequate?

12. With respect to program changes, (a) what are the potential control problems, (b) what internal controls should be present, (c) what should the auditor examine during the system review, (d) what tests of compliance can the auditor perform, and (e) what compensating controls may exist in the event of inadequate program change controls?

13. Explain how a source code comparison program works. Why is this particularly valuable to the auditor?

14. With respect to computer processing of data, (a) what are the potential control problems, (b) what internal controls should be present, (c) what should the auditor examine during the system review, (d) what tests of compliance can the auditor perform, and (e) what compensating controls may exist in the event that processing controls are inadequate?

15. Explain why the auditor might decide to perform a review of program logic. What are some of the tools available to assist the auditor in this process?

16. Explain in detail the steps that an auditor would follow in processing test data to test the adequacy of computer processing controls.

17. What are some of the disadvantages to the auditor of processing test data?

18. Explain how the auditor would use the technique of program tracing.

19. With respect to computer source data controls, (a) what are the potential control problems, (b) what internal controls should be present, (c) what should the auditor examine during the system review, (d) what tests of

compliance can the auditor perform, and (e) what compensating controls may exist in the event that source data controls are inadequate?

20. In what ways does the minicompany test eliminate two of the disadvantages of processing test data?

21. With respect to the operation of computer equipment, (a) what are the potential control problems, (b) what internal controls should be present, (c) what should the auditor examine during system review, (d) what tests of compliance can the auditor perform, and (e) what compensating controls may exist in the event that operating controls are inadequate?

22. With respect to controls over computer data files, (a) what are the potential control problems, (b) what internal controls should be present, (c) what should the auditor examine during system review, (d) what tests of compliance can the auditor perform, and (e) what compensating controls may exist in the event that control over data files is inadequate?

23. Describe in general the steps that an auditor follows in using a generalized audit software package.

24. Describe in general the functions that can be performed by computer audit software.

25. Explain several of the advantages to the auditor of using computer audit software.

26. Explain why the use of computer audit software does not replace the need for the auditor's judgment.

27. Describe the steps followed in applying computer audit software to the audit of accounts receivable.

28. What are the similarities and differences between management audits and financial or internal control audits?

29. Briefly outline some of the primary aspects of management of computer-based information systems that are the potential objects of a management audit.

30. Outline the steps in the process of performing a management audit.

Discussion Questions

31. Discuss the extent to which the auditor should be a "computer expert" in order to effectively perform audits in an organization with a computer-based information system.

32. Should the internal auditor be extensively involved as a member of systems development teams that design and implement computer-based information systems? Why or why not? Discuss.

33. If an organization's internal audit department needs to develop an EDP auditing capability, do you feel that the best approach would be (a) to train computer specialists in auditing, (b) to train auditors in data processing, (c) to employ computer specialists on the audit staff who will work with regular auditors on EDP audit teams, or (d) some other approach? Discuss.

Problems and Cases

34. You are an internal auditor for the Quick Manufacturing Company. You are participating in the audit of the company's computer-based information system. The company uses the computer in most of its significant accounting applications. You have been reviewing the internal controls associated with these computer systems. You have studied the company's extensive documentation of its systems, and you have interviewed the EDP Manager, Operations Supervisor, and other employees in order to complete your standardized computer internal control questionnaire.

You report to your supervisor that the company has designed an excellent and comprehensive set of internal controls into its computer systems. The supervisor thanks you for your efforts and asks you to prepare a summary report of your findings for inclusion in a final overall report on accounting internal controls.

REQUIRED

Aren't you forgetting an important audit step? Explain. Then list five examples of specific audit procedures that you might recommend be performed before you reach a final conclusion.

35. As an internal auditor, you have been assigned to evaluate the controls and operation of a computer payroll system. The audit technique which you will be using is online testing of the computer systems and/or programs by submitting independently created test transactions with regular data in a normal production run.

REQUIRED

a) List four advantages of this technique.
b) List two disadvantages of this technique. (CIA Examination)

36. You are the director of internal auditing at a university. Recently, you met with the manager of administrative data processing and expressed the desire to establish a more effective interface between the two departments.

Subsequently, the manager of data processing requested your views and help on a new computerized accounts payable system being developed. The manager recommended that Internal Auditing assume line responsibility for auditing suppliers' invoices prior to payment. The manager also requested that Internal Auditing make suggestions during development of the system, assist in its installation, and approve the completed system after making a final review.

State how you would respond to the administrative data processing manager, giving the reason why you would accept or reject each of the following.

    a) The recommendation that your department be responsible for the preaudit of suppliers' invoices.

    b) The request that you make suggestions during development of the system.

    c) The request that you assist in the installation of the system and approve the system after making a final review. (CIA Examination)

37. You are involved in the internal audit of accounts receivable, which represent a significant portion of the assets of a large retail corporation. Your audit plan requires the use of the computer, but you encounter the reactions described below.

    a) The computer operations manager says that all time on the computer is scheduled for the foreseeable future and that it is not feasible to perform the work for the auditor.

    b) The computer scheduling manager suggests that your computer program be cataloged into the computer program library (on disk storage) to be run when computer time becomes available.

    c) You are refused admission to the computer room.

    d) The systems manager tells you that it will take too much time to adapt the computer audit program to the EDP operating system and that the computer installation programmers would write the programs needed for the audit.

For each of the four situations described, state the action the auditor should take to proceed with the accounts receivable audit. (CIA Examination)

38. You are auditing the financial statements of Aardvark Wholesalers, Inc. (AW), a wholesaler having operations in twelve western states and total revenues of around $75 million. AW uses a computer system in several of its major accounting applications. Accordingly, you are undertaking to study AW's internal control relating to its computer system.

    You have obtained a manual containing job descriptions for key personnel in AW's Information Systems Division. Excerpts from these include:

Director of Information Systems. Reports to Administrative Vice-President. Responsible for defining the mission of the Information Systems Division in the organization and for planning, staffing, and managing a department that optimally executes this mission.

Manager of Systems and Programming. Reports to Director of Information Systems. Responsible for managing a staff of systems analysts and programmers whose mission is to design, program, test, implement, and maintain cost-effective data processing systems. Also responsible for establishing and monitoring documentation standards.

Manager of Operations. Reports to Director of Information Systems. Responsible for cost-effective management of computer center operations, for enforcement of processing standards, and for systems programming, including implementation of vendor upgrades of operating systems.

Keypunch Shift Supervisor. Reports to Manager of Operations. Responsible for supervision of keypunch operators and monitoring of data preparation standards.

Operations Shift Supervisor. Reports to Manager of Operations. Responsible for supervision of computer operations staff and monitoring of processing standards.

Data Control Clerk. Reports to Manager of Operations. Responsible for logging and distribution of computer input and output, monitoring of source data control procedures, and custody of program and data files.

REQUIRED

   a) Prepare an organization chart for AW's Information Systems Division.

   b) Comment on the adequacy (from an internal control standpoint) of this organization structure; specifically,

     i) what, if anything, is good about it?

     ii) what, if anything, is bad about it?

     iii) what, if any, additional information would you require before you could make a final judgment on the adequacy of AW's separation of functions in the Information Systems Division?

39. You are a manager for the regional CPA firm of Dewey, Cheatem, and Howe. Upon reviewing working papers prepared by staff accountants working under you on the Welfare Department audit, you find that the test data concept was used to test the department's Welfare Accounting program. Specifically, a duplicate copy of the program and of the welfare accounting data file were obtained, and the test transaction deck used by the department's programmers in preparing the program was borrowed. These were processed on DC&H's home-office computer, and a copy of the edit summary report listing no errors was included in the working papers, along with a notation by the audit senior that the test indicates good application controls.

You note that the quality of the audit conclusions obtained from this test are flawed in several respects, and you decide to require your subordinates to perform the test over again.

REQUIRED

Identify three problems (or potential problems) with the way this test was performed. For each of the problems that you identify, suggest one or more procedures that may be performed during the revised test in order to avoid flaws in the audit conclusions obtained from it.

40. The Robinson's Plastic Pipe Corporation uses a computerized inventory data processing system. The basic input record to this system has the format shown in Fig. 15.8.

     You are performing an audit of source data controls for this system. You have decided to use an input control matrix for this purpose.

Prepare an input controls matrix using the same format, and listing the same input controls, as the one in Fig. 15.2, except replace the field names shown in the figure with those of the inventory transaction file shown in Fig. 15.8. Place checks in the cells of the matrix that represent input controls you might expect to find with respect to each field.

41. You are an internal auditor for the Military Industrial Company. You are presently involved in preparing test transactions for the company's weekly payroll processing program. Each input record to this program contains the following data items.

SPACES	DATA ITEM
1–9	Social security number
10	Pay code (1 = hourly; 2 = salaried)
11–16	Wage rate or salary
17–19	Hours worked, in tenths
20–21	Number of exemptions claimed
22–29	Year-to-date gross pay
30–80	Employee name and address

The program performs the following edit checks on each input record.

☐ field checks to identify any records not having numeric characters in the fields for wage rate/salary, hours, exemptions, and year-to-date gross pay.

☐ validity check of the pay code.

☐ limit check to identify any hourly employee records having a wage rate higher than $20.00.

FIGURE 15.8

PARTS INVENTORY TRANSACTION FILE		
Field name	Field type	Positions
Item number	Numeric	1–6
Description	Alphanumeric	7–31
Transaction date	Date	32–37
Transaction type	Alphanumeric	38
Document number	Alphanumeric	39–46
Quantity	Numeric	47–51
Unit cost	Monetary	52–58

☐ limit check to identify any hourly employee records having hours worked greater than 70.0.

☐ limit check to identify any salaried employee records having a salary greater than $2000.00 or a salary less than $100.00.

Those records that do not pass all of these edit checks are listed on an error report. For those records that do pass all of these edit checks, the program performs a series of calculations. First, the employee's gross pay is determined. Gross pay for a salaried employee is equal to the salary amount contained within spaces 11–16 of the input record. Gross pay for an hourly employee is equal to the wage rate times the number of hours up to 40, plus 1.5 times the wage rate times the number of hours in excess of 40.

The program computes federal withholding tax by multiplying gross pay times a tax rate determined for each employee based upon the table in Fig. 15.9. The program next computes state withholding tax by multiplying gross pay times a tax rate determined for each employee based upon the table in Fig. 15.10. The program then computes FICA tax withholdings by multiplying gross pay by six percent, except that no FICA taxes are withheld once year-to-date gross pay exceeds $25,000.

The program next computes the employee's pension contribution, which is three percent of gross pay for hourly employees and four percent of gross pay for salaried employees. Finally, the program computes the employee's net pay, which is gross pay minus tax withholdings and pension contribution. Once all these calculations have been completed for one employee record, the program prints that employee's paycheck and summary earnings statement and then proceeds to the next employee in-

FIGURE 15.9

Number of Exemptions	GROSS PAY RANGE			
	$0–99.99	$100–249.99	$250–499.99	Over $500
0–1	.06	.12	.18	.24
2–3	.04	.10	.16	.22
4–5	.02	.08	.14	.20
Over 5	.00	.06	.12	.18

FIGURE 15.10

Number of Exemptions	GROSS PAY RANGE	
	$0–249.99	Over $250
0–3	.03	.05
Over 3	.01	.03

put record to perform edit checks and payroll calculations, continuing this cycle until all input records have been processed.

For the moment, you are concerned only with preparing a set of test transactions containing one of each possible type of error, and another set of test transactions that will test each of the computational alternatives one at a time. Transactions to test for multiple errors in one record, or to test for multiple combinations of logic paths, are to be developed later.

Each test transaction you prepare need not include a social security number or an employee name and address (your assistant will add those after reviewing a file printout). Accordingly, each of your test transactions will consist of a series of twenty characters representing data in spaces 10–29 of an input record. For example, a test transaction for an hourly employee having a wage rate of $9.50, who worked 40.5 hours, who claims two exemptions, and who has year-to-date gross pay of exactly $12,000 would be 10009504050201200000.

REQUIRED

a) Prepare a set of test transactions, each of which contains one of the possible kinds of errors tested for by the edit checks. Determine the expected results of processing for each of these test transactions.

b) Prepare a set of test transactions, each of which tests one of the ways in which gross pay may be determined. Determine the expected gross pay for each of these transactions.

c) Prepare a set of test transactions, each of which tests one of the ways in which federal withholding tax may be computed. Determine the expected value of federal withholding tax for each of these test transactions.

d) Prepare a set of test transactions, each of which tests one of the ways in which state withholding tax may be computed. Determine the expected value of state withholding tax for each of these test transactions.

e) Prepare a set of test transactions, each of which tests one of the ways in which FICA withholding tax may be computed. Determine the expected value of FICA withholding tax for each of these test transactions.

f) Prepare a set of test transactions, each of which tests one of the ways in which the pension contribution may be computed. Determine the expected value of the pension contribution for each of these test transactions.

42. An auditor is conducting an examination of the financial statements of a wholesale cosmetics distributor with an inventory consisting of thousands of individual items. The distributor keeps its inventory in its own distribution center and in two public warehouses. An inventory computer file is maintained on a computer disk and at the end of each business day the file is updated. Each record of the inventory file contains the following data.

☐ Item number

☐ Location of item

☐ Description of item

☐ Quantity on hand

☐ Cost per item

☐ Date of last purchase

☐ Date of last sale

☐ Quantity sold during year

The auditor is planning to observe the distributor's physical count of inventories as of a given date. The auditor will have available a computer tape of the data on the inventory file on the date of the physical count and a general purpose computer software package.

REQUIRED

The auditor is planning to perform basic inventory auditing procedures. Identify the basic inventory auditing procedures and describe how the use of the general purpose software package and the tape of the inventory file data might be helpful to the auditor in performing such auditing procedures.

Organize your answer as follows. (CPA Examination)

Basic inventory auditing procedure	How general purpose computer software package and tape of the inventory file data might be helpful

43. The Thermo-Bond Manufacturing Company maintains its fixed asset records on its computer. Data content of the fixed asset master file includes the following items.

ITEM NUMBER	LOCATION	DESCRIPTION
1	1–6	Asset number
2	7–30	Description
3	31	Type code
4	32–34	Location code
5	35–40	Date of acquisition
6	41–50	Original cost
7	51–56	Date of retirement*
8	57	Depreciation method code
9	58–61	Depreciation rate
10	62–63	Useful life (years)
11	64–73	Accumulated depreciation at beginning of year
12	74–83	Year-to-date depreciation

*For assets still in service, retirement date is assigned the value 99/99/99.

Explain several ways in which a generalized computer audit software package could be used by an auditor to assist in achieving audit objectives relating to the audit of Thermo-Bond's fixed asset account.

44. You are auditing the financial statements of the Preston Manufacturing Company. At the beginning of the current fiscal year, the company converted its general ledger accounting from a manual to a computer-based system. The new system involves the use of two computer files, the contents of which are indicated in Fig. 15.11.

Each day, as detailed transactions are processed by Preston's other computerized accounting systems, summary journal entries are accumulated and at the end of the day are added to the general ledger file. At the end of each week, and also at the end of each month, the general journal file is processed against the general ledger control file to compute a new current balance for each account and to print a trial balance.

Your review and evaluation of internal controls with respect to this particular system has led to the conclusion that *no reliance* can be placed on those controls in performing the financial audit.

You have decided to use your firm's generalized computer audit software package to perform certain procedures and tests on these files. You have available to you

a) a complete copy of the general journal file for the entire year,

FIGURE 15.11

GENERAL JOURNAL		
Field name	Field type	Size
Account number	Numeric	6
Amount	Monetary	9.2
Debit/credit code	Alphameric	1
Date (MM/DD/YY)	Date	6
Reference document type	Alphameric	4
Reference document number	Numeric	6

GENERAL LEDGER CONTROL		
Field name	Field type	Size
Account number	Numeric	6
Account name	Alphameric	20
Beginning balance/year	Monetary	9.2
Beg-bal-debit/credit code	Alphameric	1
Current balance	Monetary	9.2
Cur-bal-debit/credit code	Alphameric	1

    b) a copy of the general ledger file as of the fiscal year end (i.e., current balance = year-end balance), and

    c) a printout of Preston's year-end trial balance listing the account number, account name, and balance of each account on the general ledger control file.

REQUIRED

Assume that you are using a Generalized Audit Software Package with a comprehensive set of capabilities. Prepare an application design for this problem, including

    a) a description of the data content of each output report, preferably in the form of a tabular layout chart of the report format.

    b) accompanying each report from part (a) a description of the auditing objectives of each report and how the report would be used in subsequent auditing procedures to achieve those objectives.

    c) a detailed system flowchart of the application.

References

Adams, Donald L. "Alternatives to Computer Audit Software." *Journal of Accountancy* (November 1975): 54–57.

Adams, Donald L., and John F. Mullarkey. "A Survey of Audit Software." *Journal of Accountancy* (September 1972): 39–66.

American Institute of Certified Public Accountants. *Statements on Auditing Standards No. 1–49.* New York: AICPA, 1972–1984.

————. *The Auditor's Study and Evaluation of Internal Control in EDP Systems.* New York: AICPA, 1977.

————. *Management, Control and Audit of Advanced EDP Systems.* New York: AICPA, 1977.

————. *Audit Considerations in Electronic Funds Transfer Systems.* New York: AICPA, 1978.

————. *Computer-Assisted Audit Techniques.* New York: AICPA, 1979.

————. *Audit Approaches for a Computerized Inventory System.* New York: AICPA, 1980.

————. *Audit and Control Considerations in a Minicomputer or Small Business Computer Environment.* New York: AICPA, 1981.

————. *Audit and Control Considerations in an On-Line Environment.* New York: AICPA, 1983.

Arens, Alvin, A., and James K. Loebbecke. *Auditing: An Integrated Approach.* 3d ed. Englewood Cliffs, N.J.: Prentice-Hall, 1984.

Borthick, A. Faye. "Audit Implications of Information Systems." *CPA Journal* (April 1986): 40–46.

Cerullo, Michael J., and John C. Corless. "Auditing Computer Systems." *CPA Journal* (September 1984): 18–33.

Committee on Basic Auditing Concepts, *A Statement of Basic Auditing Concepts.* Sarasota, Fla.: American Accounting Association, 1973.

Crouse, David W. "Risk Analysis in an EDP Audit Environment." *Internal Auditor* (December 1979): 69–77.

Gliezner, Shmuel. "The Dummy Entity, a Valuable Audit Tool." *EDPACS* (June 1985): 1–20.

Institute of Internal Auditors. *Standards for the Professional Practice of Internal Auditing.* Altamonte Springs, Fla.: Institute of Internal Auditors, 1978.

Jancura, Elise G. "Technical Proficiency for Auditing Computer-Processed Accounting Records." *Journal of Accountancy* (October 1975): 46–59.

Loebbecke, James K.; John F. Mullarkey; and George R. Zuber. "Auditing in a Computer Environment." *Journal of Accountancy* (January 1983): 68–78.

Mair, William C.; Donald R. Wood; and Keagle W. Davis. *Computer Control & Audit.* Altamonte Springs, Fla.: Institute of Internal Auditors, 1978.

Mastromano, Frank M. "The Changing Nature of the EDP Audit." *Management Accounting* (July 1980): 27–30, 34.

Nottingham, C. "Conceptual Framework for Improved Computer Audits." *Accounting and Business Research* (Spring 1976): 140–148.

Perry, William E., and Henry C. Warner. "Systems Auditability: Friend or Foe?" *Journal of Accountancy* (February 1978): 52–60.

Pound, G. D. "A Review of EDP Auditing." *Accounting and Business Research* (Spring 1978): 108–128.

Reneau, J. Hal. "Auditing in a Data Base Environment." *Journal of Accountancy* (December 1977): 59–65.

Richardson, Dana R. "Auditing EFTS." *Journal of Accountancy* (October 1978): 81–87.

Robertson, Jack C., and Frederick G. Davis. *Auditing.* 4th ed. Dallas: Business Publications, 1985.

Skudrna, Vincent J., and Frank J. Lackner. "The Implementation of Concurrent Audit Techniques in Advanced EDP Systems." *EDPACS* (April 1984): 1–9.

Stanford Research Institute. *Systems Auditability & Control Study, Data Processing Audit Practices Report.* Altamonte Springs, Fla.: Institute of Internal Auditors, 1977.

Vanecek, Michael T., and George Scott. "Data Bases—The Auditor's Dilemma." *CPA Journal* (January 1980): 26–35.

Vasarhelyi, Miklos A. "Audit Automation: Online Technology and Auditing." *CPA Journal* (April 1985): 10–17.

Weber, Ron. "An Audit Perspective of Operating System Security." *Journal of Accountancy* (September 1975): 97–100.

Wilkins, Barry J. *The Internal Auditor's Information Security Handbook.* Altamonte Springs, Fla.: Institute of Internal Auditors, 1979.

Yarberry, William A., "Auditing the Change Control System." *EDPACS* (June 1984): 1–5.

ACCOUNTING INFORMATION SYSTEMS APPLICATIONS

C H A P T E R 1 6

Accounting Information Systems for Marketing Management

LEARNING OBJECTIVES

Careful study of this chapter should enable students to:

☐ Describe the decision responsibilities and information requirements of marketing management.

☐ Describe the information provided to marketing management by the accounting information system.

☐ Prepare flowcharts describing data and information flows within a sales order processing system.

☐ Design and evaluate control policies and procedures for a sales order processing system.

CHAPTER OUTLINE

All business organizations must produce a product or provide a service for which a market demand exists. From this market demand must be generated a stream of revenue sufficient to cover the firm's costs and expenses, replace its assets, and provide its capital suppliers with a return on their investment. The accounting information system plays an important role in this revenue generation process because it is a primary source of information to the executives who manage the marketing function. The accounting system is also responsible for processing all customer transactions.

It is therefore evident that a close relationship must exist between the accounting and marketing functions in a business organization. This chapter explores the general nature of that relationship. The decision responsibilities and information requirements of the marketing function are described, and the role of the accounting information system in meeting these information requirements and in processing sales transactions is explained and illustrated. The discussion is intended to be general in nature rather than descriptive of the real system of a specific company.

The remaining chapters in Part Four examine the relationship of the accounting information system to other functional areas of management within a typical business organization. Chapter 17 covers the purchasing function, Chapter 18 covers production, and Chapters 19 and 20 cover the personnel and finance functions, respectively. The purpose of these chapters is to integrate and illustrate the application of the concepts, tools, and technology covered in the previous parts of this book. In particular, the concepts of control and organization, the tool of flowcharting, and the technology of computer-based information systems are stressed.

In Part Four the various subsystems of the accounting information system are discussed separately rather than as one total system. This is done primarily as a matter of convenience of presentation, however, and should not obscure the fact that the various functional areas are very much interdependent in terms of both operations and information. As the reader proceeds through Part Four, the interrelationships among the various information subsystems should be noted.

The Marketing Management Function

In Chapter 2 it is emphasized that knowledge of the organization structure of a company provides the systems analyst with important insights into the decision responsibilities and information requirements of the various managers and personnel within the organization. This and subsequent chapters apply this concept by illustrating typical forms of organization within each of the several functional areas of business firms. The illustrations provide a framework for discussion of decision responsibilities and information requirements within each functional area. Figure 16.1 provides an example of a typical marketing organization structure. Each of the executive positions shown in the chart is examined in this section.

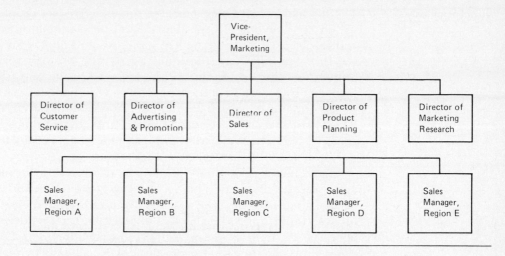

FIGURE 16.1
Marketing
organization
structure.

**The top marketing
executive**

The vice-president of marketing is responsible to the company president for the effective planning, coordination, and control of the marketing effort. The position requires participation in companywide planning, specifically as it relates to marketing activities, as well as participation with other top-level executives in the establishment of pricing policies, which encompasses not only setting base prices but also instituting discount policies, credit terms, and warranty policies. The marketing vice-president also may participate in forming the most significant policy decisions relating to the specific areas for which marketing staff executives are responsible, such as new product introduction or the planning of a major advertising campaign. The role requires review and evaluation of the performance of subordinate executives.

The marketing vice-president in a business organization may be looked upon as a strategist seeking an optimal allocation of "scarce resources" to achieve the maximum advantage for the firm in the environment of the marketplace. Scarce resources include personnel—staff specialists and sales force—and funds. The marketing vice-president must allocate these resources among such activities as selling effort, advertising and promotional campaigns, and marketing research studies. Environmental forces include customers, competitors, the economy, and government.

To fulfill the responsibilities of the position, the vice-president of marketing relies on extensive information obtained from various sources. The planning function requires environmental information on such matters as economic trends, competitors' plans, and customers' attitudes, as well as internally generated information such as sales forecasts and market research studies. The pricing decision requires all of the kinds of information above plus internal information on the cost of products and the cost of credit and warranty policies. The control function requires information as a basis for evaluating the performance of all subordinate executives.

Director of sales

The director of sales is responsible for the effectiveness of the selling effort within the firm and also participates in the planning of sales with the marketing vice-president to establish standards and quotas for the sales force. If the firm's products are consumer goods sold through wholesale and retail outlets, the director of sales will be involved in the selection of the most effective of such distribution channels. The regional sales managers who report to the director of sales have similar responsibilities on a smaller scale. The director of sales must review, evaluate, and control the performance of the regional sales managers, who, in turn, must review, evaluate, and control the performance of their respective sales forces.

Sales forecasts provide the director of sales and the regional sales managers with an information base for planning the sales effort. Similarly, reports of actual sales, or *sales analyses,* provide an information base for control. Sales analysis reports may classify sales in several ways. To the regional sales manager, classification by salesperson is most meaningful as a tool for evaluating salespeople. To the director of sales, a sales analysis by regions and perhaps by territories within regions is useful. To individual salespeople, sales analysis by customer is very useful.

Whereas a sales analysis reports only sales volume, a *profitability analysis* breaks down the marginal contribution to profit made by each territory, customer, distribution channel, or other unit. Profitability is a function of both the volume and profit margin of a product. Reports of this nature are even more useful to sales managers and the sales force for planning and control than sales analyses because they indicate directly the marginal contribution to profit of each individual selling activity. However, such reports are more difficult for an information system to generate because they require variable product cost data in addition to sales volume data.

Also useful in controlling the selling effort are analyses of the activities of individual salespeople, including customers called upon, time spent with each, literature distributed, demonstrations presented, and so forth. Individual salespersons require certain operational information for use in executing sales transactions such as information on the availability and location of inventories, the time required for delivery to a customer, and the credit standing of a customer. In addition, information on the incremental cost of various selling activities is useful to salespeople and sales managers for purposes of cost control. Important in this respect are analyses of the incremental costs of calling on a particular class of customer, of utilizing a particular type of distribution channel, or of serving a particular territory.

Director of advertising and promotion

The director of advertising and promotion is responsible for planning and control of promotional activities. Together with a staff, the director plans advertising campaigns and other promotional strategies, such as dealer incentives, contests, and trade show displays, and then must coordinate the execution of these strategies and evaluate their effectiveness as a basis for subsequent planning. The director must allocate a limited promotional budget among various product lines, territories, etc., to obtain maximum results.

Sales and profitability analysis information that provides breakdowns by territory, by product line, and perhaps by customer is relevant to the planning and control of advertising and promotion. Information on customer attitudes and plans is also useful for planning. Information on the cost of individual advertising and promotional campaigns is necessary for control purposes. Information that specifically relates sales and profit performance with advertising and promotional efforts is especially useful for planning and control.

Director of product planning

The director of product planning is responsible for planning the characteristics of the product line. This involves decisions relating to such factors as styling and packaging, as well as to the planning and introduction of new products. Also involved is the function of reviewing the performance of existing products—their sales, profitability, and potential—and deciding or recommending whether any such products should be removed from the product line.

Sales analyses and profitability analyses by product lines are vital to the product planning function. Information on present and future product costs is also useful to decisions on styling, packaging, and the deletion of products from the line. Information on customer attitudes is important to decisions on styling and new-product introduction. Projected cost and revenue information is essential for making recommendations on new-product introduction.

Director of customer service

The director of customer service is responsible for policies and decisions relating to the servicing of customer needs after the sale of the product. The director may administer a staff that responds to customer complaints or that reviews the adequacy of retail facilities, and may administer a maintenance organization if the product is a technical one. The basic objective is to ensure that customers achieve the level of satisfaction of needs or desires expected from the product.

The information used in the customer service function is for the most part obtained directly from customers and includes requests for information or technical assistance, complaints, requests for maintenance, and so forth. Information on the incremental cost of customer service activities and the performance of customer service personnel is useful for purposes of control.

Director of marketing research

The director of marketing research is responsible for planning and administering the data gathering and analysis activities of the marketing research staff. This staff carries out special studies of consumer behavior and other subjects of interest to marketing executives. The director must allocate scarce resources among alternative projects and interpret the results of such projects for other marketing executives and top management. Marketing research studies are often a primary basis for planning in such areas as new-product introduction, advertising, and pricing. For the most part the marketing research staff is not a user, but a producer, of information, which it generates from data collected by means of scanning the environment.

Sources of Marketing Information

In terms of volume of information, the accounting information system is the primary source of marketing information in most business organizations. However, a well-managed marketing activity cannot rely solely on financial information and must therefore exploit other sources of information, including its own salespeople and staff personnel, other departments within the firm, and the environment. This section discusses the nature of the data collected and the information generated from each of these sources.

The accounting information system

The accounting information system provides two basic types of information to marketing management: information generated from the processing of sales orders, and cost reports and analyses.

Sales order processing. The sales order processing cycle begins with the initiation of an order by a customer and ends with the delivery of goods to the customer. The basic data source is the sales invoice, an example of which is illustrated in Fig. 16.2. The invoice serves as a record of the sales transaction, and copies sent to the customer provide notice that shipment has been made and payment is due. In addition, items that were ordered but not shipped owing to insufficient supply are listed as *backordered,* which means that they will be shipped as soon as the stock is replenished. Note how much of the data collected on the sales invoice is coded to facilitate subsequent processing. For example, the salesperson's number, customer account number, and item code provide a basis for generating sales and profitability analyses by salesperson, by customer, and by product. In addition, the invoice itself is numbered to provide a basis for future reference and audit.

Data from the sales invoice represent one of the primary inputs to the marketing data base, which in turn is the major repository of information useful to marketing management. The marketing data base contains information relating to finished goods inventories, customers, and sales. The finished goods inventory information is used to check on inventory availability at the time of the sale. Customer records include accounts receivable and credit history information that may be used as a basis for evaluating the credit worthiness of a customer who has placed an order. The sales information is used to generate the various sales analysis reports that provide vital management information to marketing executives.

Sales analysis reports generally present dollar and/or unit sales for the most recent period (week or month) and for the year to date. In addition, for

			NEEDMORE MANUFACTURING COMPANY			

NEEDMORE MANUFACTURING COMPANY

987 Glendale Needmore, Tx 78799   Tel. 512/836-0107   Invoice No. 10001

INVOICE

Customer Order No. 45236	Order date 7/10/86	Salesperson Code 24 – 76	Customer Account No. 24 – 93106

Sold to:

Hardware Wholesalers
1006 East 61st
Austin, Texas 78744

Ship to:

Same

Shipper Austin Trkg. 24061	Date shipped 7/12/86	Invoice date 7/12/86	Terms of sale 2/10, net 30

Item code	Description	Quantity ordered	Back-ordered	Quantity shipped	Unit price	Item total
10562	Hammer	100		100	$1.00	$100.00
20651	Sickle	50	20	30	1.75	52.50
38214	Hoe	50		50	2.50	125.00
38526	Rake	80	30	50	3.25	162.50
	Freight					5.61
	Total					$445.61

FIGURE 16.2
Sales invoice.

comparison purposes it is useful if sales quotas and/or prior-year sales are reported along with actual sales for the current period. An example of a report analyzing sales by territory, and by salesperson within territory, is provided in Fig. 16.3. A report of this type would be useful to the sales manager of a territory for purposes of evaluating the territory's sales force. Similarly, a report analyzing sales by territory within a region would be useful to a regional sales manager in evaluating territorial sales managers, whereas a report of aggregate sales by region would be useful to the director of sales in evaluating regional sales managers.

Within a typical business organization, sales may be analyzed according to several detailed and aggregate classifications to provide useful information to various marketing executives at all levels of the organization. In addition to breakdowns by salesperson, territory, and region, sales may be analyzed by individual product, product class, major customers, type of customer, distribution channel, and so forth. Furthermore, reports may be prepared in which sales are detailed according to two or more classification categories. Examples would include a breakdown of sales by product for key customers or by type of customer for each territory. Sales analyses are useful not only because they

Period ending: March 31, 1987					Territory: East Texas	
Salesperson	Period	Actual sales	Prior year	% Change	Quota	% Variance from quota
Benjamin, H.L.	This month	$50,000	$40,000	+25%	$48,000	+4%
	Year to date	120,000	115,000	+ 4%	125,000	-4%
Carlton, J.C.	This month	$40,000	$38,000	+ 5%	$45,000	-11%
	Year to date	105,000	110,000	- 5%	130,000	-19%
Territory totals	This month	$300,000	$285,500	+ 5%	$350,000	-14%
	Year to date	850,000	840,000	+ 1%	950,000	-11%

FIGURE 16.3
Sales analysis by
salesperson and
territory.

provide a historical summary for control purposes but also because they provide information relevant to planning advertising and promotional campaigns, selling activities, price changes, composition of product lines, and other marketing activities.

Profitability analysis reports are generated from sales records together with product cost data. Such reports generally may be prepared using the same categories of classification as sales analyses. An example of a profitability analysis by product class and model for a customer is illustrated in Fig. 16.4. This sample report reveals that the contribution margin (excess of revenues over variable costs) for this customer exceeds the amount budgeted, primarily because unfavorable volume variances for low-margin products in each class are more than offset by favorable volume variances among high-margin products. This type of information is useful both to salespeople and to sales managers for purposes of allocating sales effort among products and customers. Similar product profitability breakdowns may be generated by distribution channel, by territory, or by salesperson. Aggregate product profitability information may also be generated for use by top-level marketing executives in product planning.

A third major category of information generated from the processing of sales orders includes various analyses of sales trends. For example, projections developed from sales trends are useful for purposes of forecasting sales; sales forecasts, in turn, can be utilized in the planning and control of marketing activities. Further, analyses of historical sales trends contribute to evaluating the success of various marketing actions, such as advertising campaigns, special promotions, or price changes.

ATLANTA WHOLESALE APPLIANCE COMPANY

Date: October 31, 1986

Account number: 16520

| Product | | Per unit gross margin | * – – – – – – – – – – – Year-to-date Totals – – – – – – – – – – – – | | | | | |
Class	Model		1985 actual	Unit sales 1986 actual	1986 budget	Actual contribution margin	Budgeted contribution margin	Variance
Refrigerator-Freezer	RF-10	$ 40	1,800	2,000	2,100	$ 80,000	$ 84,000	$ (4,000)
	RF-14	60	3,500	4,000	4,100	240,000	246,000	(6,000)
	RF-16	80	3,000	3,600	3,500	288,000	280,000	8,000
	RF-20	100	1,200	1,500	1,400	150,000	140,000	10,000
Freezer	F-16	75	1,100	1,280	1,300	96,000	97,500	(1,500)
	F-20	90	1,500	1,750	1,800	157,500	162,000	(4,500)
	F-24	130	600	750	700	97,500	91,000	6,500
Totals, all products						$1,109,000	$1,100,500	$ 8,500

FIGURE 16.4
Profitability analysis
by product for key
customer.

The procedures involved in processing sales order transactions, maintaining the marketing data base, and generating the various reports are described in detail in a later section of this chapter.

Cost reports and analyses. All cash disbursements made by an organization must be recorded by its accounting system. A good system will record enough information about the nature and purpose of each disbursement to enable useful reports to be generated. One significant example is information about product costs. This information is used in establishment of pricing policies, in product planning, and in various profitability analyses. Manufacturing companies generally maintain fairly elaborate cost accounting systems to generate accurate and useful product cost data.

To be most useful, product cost information should be segregated according to the fixed and variable components of manufacturing costs and selling expenses. For purposes of marketing cost control, each detailed element of selling expense should also be segregated into its fixed and variable elements. Ordering information in this way enables marketing management to evaluate the incremental cost of various alternative marketing actions under consideration.

Although incremental product cost information is very useful to marketing management, it is also very difficult for an accounting system to provide. The primary problem is that not all cost elements are either rigidly fixed or directly variable with unit sales volume. In addition, the accounting systems of many firms are designed to fulfill external reporting requirements, which dictate that the cost per unit of a manufactured product include all manufacturing costs, including both fixed and variable costs. Selling expenses are generally reported as one lump sum or according to functional classifications, with no recognition given to their fixed and variable components. Most data classification systems, such as charts of accounts, were originally designed primarily to facilitate external reporting. In order for accounting information systems to provide incremental cost information, each type of cost must first be separated into fixed and variable components, and then systems of data collection and classification must be redesigned to facilitate the necessary processing steps.

In addition to product cost information, a firm's accounting information system should provide cost reports by responsibility centers within the marketing department. These reports compare costs incurred with budgeted costs for each responsibility center. Such reports are useful to marketing executives for controlling the allocation of budgeted funds to their most profitable uses. In addition, project cost reports comparing and analyzing estimated and actual costs for significant marketing projects should be prepared. Examples of such projects would include market research studies, advertising campaigns, and other promotions and surveys.

The accounting information system must also participate in the preparation of revenue cost projections upon which decisions regarding new-product introduction are based. While records of sales of similar products provide one basis for revenue projections, per unit cost projections are developed using the estimates of labor and material requirements obtained from the engineering department. An estimate of the amount of the initial cash outlay for promotion and new equipment is also required. Once all cash flow projections have been made, the decision should be based upon a capital budgeting analysis that predicts the expected present value and risk factors involved in the decision. Accounting executives are generally familiar with capital budgeting techniques and should participate in the development of these analyses.

Several subsystems of the accounting information system contribute to the generation of cost information and reports of the type discussed in this section. The next four chapters discuss further the structure and operations of these subsystems.

The marketing department

A significant share of the information that the marketing department uses for marketing management is typically generated from within the department. One significant data source in this category is the salesperson's call report, an example of which is illustrated in Fig. 16.5. This report is intended to be filled out by each salesperson for each call he or she makes on a customer, whether or not the customer makes a purchase. All firms would not necessarily

SALESPERSON ACTIVITY REPORT		
Salesperson number Name	Date of call	Time spent

Account data		
Name _____	Acct. number _____	
Address _____ _____	Buyer's name _____	

Type of store		Account status		Order status	
	Furniture sales		Prospect		Order received
	Local dept. store		Old account		Will send later
	Dept. store chain		New account		Won't buy now
	Other		No interest		No interest

Comments

FIGURE 16.5
Salesperson's call report.

find it appropriate to collect and utilize data of this sort, but when the technique is employed, it yields a very useful source of information for evaluation of the sales force and of feedback from customers regarding their needs for, and opinions on, the firm's products.

2) The marketing research studies prepared by the marketing research department constitute a second significant source of marketing information within the marketing department. These studies may range from pilot studies of consumer reaction to the introduction of a new product or to a new advertising campaign in a limited market area, to general surveys of customer attitudes throughout the country. Such studies may be performed as needed by other marketing departments or on a regular basis. The primary source of data input for these studies is the external environment. The marketing research staff applies its expertise in statistical sampling and statistical inference techniques to "process" these data into information. Marketing research information is potentially useful to almost all marketing decisions involving the planning function.

3) A third important source of marketing information within the marketing department consists of sales forecasts. Estimates provided by the sales force

play a major role in developing such forecasts, although historical records of past sales are also important. Sales forecasts are used as a basis for planning the activities of the entire firm and are also very useful as standards for management control of the sales force. Statistical techniques such as exponential smoothing or regression and correlation analysis may be used to generate these forecasts.

Other internal sources

In addition to the accounting and marketing departments, other departments within a firm may contribute significantly to the flow of information to marketing personnel. For example, the production and/or engineering department may provide information relating to product quality or design useful to product planning or to salespeople. The economics department, if one exists, may provide useful analyses of the economy or of the particular industrial field within which the firm operates. The personnel department may provide information relating to potential marketing department employees. In many firms a smooth interface between the marketing department and a research and development department is essential to product planning. While information from all these sources may be important, it is generally neither as regular nor as voluminous as the information provided by the accounting department or that generated within the marketing department itself.

External information sources

Much useful marketing information may be obtained directly from scanning the external environment without the need for an intermediate data processing step. One type of information that fits within this category relates to the activities and plans of competitive firms. Information about the nature of the products, prices, and advertising of competitors is very useful to marketing planning. Information about the plans of competitors, while not easily obtained, is also extremely useful. Trade publications, the promotional literature of competitors, and communication with customers are potential sources of this information.

General information on economic and industry trends may also be obtained directly from the environment. Information on demographic characteristics of the market—rural vs. urban; population, education, and income levels; population in various age groups; etc.—falls in this category. The United States Bureau of the Census and other federal and state government agencies constitute one important source of such information. Trade associations that gather, analyze, and distribute information relating to a particular industry are another.

There are definite problems with respect to deciding what environmental information is needed and establishing a regular mechanism for its acquisition and analysis. Unlike accounting information, environmental information is not made available automatically as the by-product of some other essential business process. Marketing executives must accept the responsibility for becoming familiar with external information sources and obtaining the environmental information of most relevance to their particular functions.

The Sales Order Processing System

The general nature of the input to and output from the sales order processing system has already been discussed. This section will outline the accounting transactions involved in the process, examine the content and structure of the marketing data base, and then describe in detail an example of (1) a manual system, (2) a computer-based batch processing system, and (3) a real-time system for processing sales orders and generating marketing information.

The accounting transactions

The primary accounting journal entry reflecting sales order processing appears as follows.

Accounts Receivable	XXX	
Sales		XXX

Almost all sales of a manufacturing company, as well as a significant portion of the sales of retail companies, are recorded in this manner. For firms that maintain inventory on a perpetual basis, these sales entries are accompanied by the following entry.

Cost of Goods Sold	XXX	
Finished Goods Inventory		XXX

Certain variations from these basic entries may also occur. For example, when a customer returns merchandise, or asks for an adjustment in price because of damaged merchandise, the following entry is made.

Sales Returns and Allowances	XXX	
Accounts Receivable		XXX

These journal entries represent the most important transactions that are initiated as a result of sales order processing. Transactions involving the collection of accounts receivable are treated in Chapter 20.

In manual systems, journal entries are usually recorded either in a general journal or on a journal voucher. The manual systems described in Chapters 16 through 20 assume that journal vouchers (see Fig. 16.6) are used. In this way, illustrative document flowcharts of these systems (such as Fig. 16.8) show the exact point in the system at which journal vouchers are prepared for each of the important journal entries initiated by the process.

The marketing data base

An example of the data content and organization of a marketing data base appears in Fig. 16.7. This data base is essentially a network consisting of two interrelated families of records. One of these families includes finished goods inventory data, whereas the other includes customer data. In addition, trans-

JOURNAL VOUCHER				
Date 7/6/86			Voucher Number 3706	
Prepared by: J. Mitchell		Approved by: J. Hoover	Posted by: N. Richards	
Account Number	Account Title	Amount		
		Debit	Credit	
5 - 112	Accounts Receivable Control	$42,635 91		
5 - 113	Sales		$42,635 91	
EXPLANATION				
To record total daily billings.				

FIGURE 16.6
Journal voucher.

action records such as the production order, sales invoice, credit memo for sales returns and allowances, cash receipt, and salesperson's call report are associated with one or both of these families.

Each customer record in the system contains a single value for all the data fields listed under "Customer File." In addition, each customer record owns one or more "Customer Transaction" records; that is, Customer Transaction is a repeating group with respect to the Customer File. In turn, each Customer Transaction record is a summary of the data contained in a Sales Invoice, Credit Memo, Cash Receipt, or Salesperson's Call Report. The "Transaction Type Code" and "Document Number" in the Customer Transaction record enable the system to access a more detailed transaction record (for example, a complete sales invoice) when necessary. At any given time, only transactions from the current month or year will be stored in the marketing data base, although records of older transactions may be stored offline.

Basic inputs to the customer file portion of the marketing data base include routine sales and cash receipts transactions, credits for sales returns and allowances, salesperson's call reports, and nonroutine adjustments such as changes of address, addition of new credit customers, bad-debt write-offs, and corrections of errors. Basic outputs include statements of account that are mailed to customers each month, responses to requests for credit approval for individual customers, and various reports such as the accounts receivable aging schedule.

FIGURE 16.7
Marketing data base.

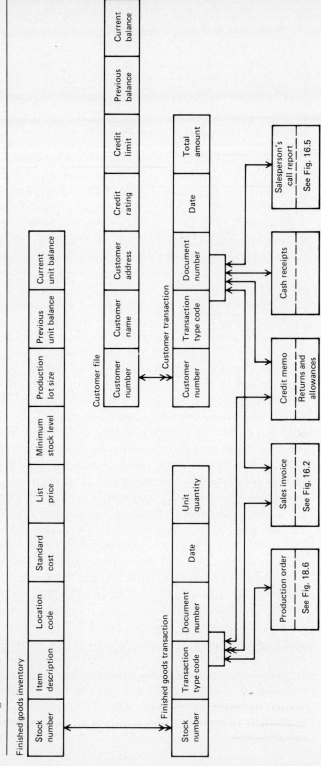

Each finished goods inventory record in the marketing data base contains a single value for each of the data fields listed under "Finished Goods Inventory" in Fig. 16.7. Furthermore, each finished goods inventory record owns one or more "Finished Goods Transaction" records, each of which is a summary of a production order, sale, or sales return transaction. When it is necessary to access the detailed transaction record (such as a complete production order) from the transaction summary record, the "Transaction Type Code" and "Document Number" fields provide the required reference data.

Basic inputs to the finished goods inventory portion of the marketing data base include records of sales transactions, production orders initiated, and production orders completed, as well as miscellaneous additions, corrections, and adjustments. The data stored here provide important reference information for production planning, warehouse and stockroom operations, and selling operations. Basic outputs that may be generated include a *stock status report,* which is a listing of data values for each inventory record; a report of items out of stock or below the prescribed minimum stock level; or an analysis of product turnover.

A marketing data base structured as outlined above contains most of the data necessary to generate a variety of sales analysis reports. These would include sales analysis by customer, by type of customer (if a subcode for type of customer is included in each customer's account number), by product, by product class (if a subcode for product class is included in each inventory stock number), by salesperson (coded on the invoice), by territory (if a subcode for territory is included in each salesperson number), or by any number of cross classifications of the categories above. Note, however, that the most useful form of sales analysis is one in which current sales data are compared with sales quotas and/or prior year's sales figures for comparable periods, and performance variances or percentage changes are highlighted. To enable this system to generate this type of report, it could be assumed that monthly quotas and prior year's monthly sales totals are simply an additional type of finished goods and customer transaction record that may be stored in the data base for this purpose.

In a manual data processing system or a conventional computer-based batch processing system, the marketing data base exists in the form of a series of separately maintained files. For example, there might be separate files for customer data, finished goods data, sales data, salesperson's call reports, and so on. Updating each of these files for input transactions requires a separate set of procedures. In addition, each file is separately processed to generate output reports, and such reports can reflect only that information that is contained on the specific file from which it was generated. Furthermore, output reports are generally prepared only at predetermined intervals (such as monthly) and must usually conform to a predesigned fixed format.

In contrast, if the marketing data base is maintained using a data base management system of the kind described in Chapter 9, it is possible to combine many of the separate updating procedures referred to above into an integrated data base maintenance process. For example, merely adding a new sales invoice to the data base automatically initiates the necessary update of inventory records for shipments *and* the update of the customer's record for the credit sale. The same would be true for any other type of transaction affecting the marketing data base. Also, the data base management system would enable users to generate at any time they desire a report in any format they wish to specify, and the content of such a report is not limited to that of a particular record but rather may include any of the data items contained in the marketing data base. Thus the marketing function provides ample demonstration of the advantages of the data base concepts and techniques.

A manual system

The document flowchart in Fig. 16.8 illustrates one example of a manual system for processing sales orders in a manufacturing company. Most such companies will differ in some ways from this example, but in most cases the general pattern of information flow will not vary a great deal from the illustration.

The illustration shows the sales order process beginning with the receipt of the customer's purchase order, which is used to prepare a sales order. Actually, the sales order may have been prepared prior to the receipt of the purchase order by a salesperson in the field or by a sales order clerk receiving telephone orders. Once they have received an order, most industrial firms will transmit some form of documentary acknowledgment to the customer. As shown in the illustration, this is commonly a duplicate copy of the customer's purchase order.

The sales order contains basically the same data as the invoice except for such things as item *extensions* (price times quantity calculations), shipping charges, taxes, invoice total, and credit terms. In cases in which the quantity delivered is less than the quantity ordered, the extra units are backordered. A notation is made in the finished goods file so that when the stock is replenished, the goods will be shipped automatically to the customer. Many firms, particularly those in which backordering is not common, do not use a separate sales order document. Instead, they begin to prepare the sales invoice immediately upon receipt of orders and use extra copies of the invoice in place of the several copies of the sales order.

One copy of the sales order is filed numerically in the sales order department. Three other copies are sent to the finished goods storeroom or warehouse. If the customer's credit is not established, the sales order may be routed through the credit department, where a credit check is performed before shipment is authorized. In the finished goods storeroom, the products ordered are retrieved from available stock. The sales order serves as an authorization to release the goods to the shipping department and is used as a source document to post shipments to the finished goods inventory file. If any goods ordered are backordered, a notation to that effect is made on the sales order, and one copy is filed by storeroom personnel for future reference.

Those goods in stock are assembled and transferred to the shipping de-

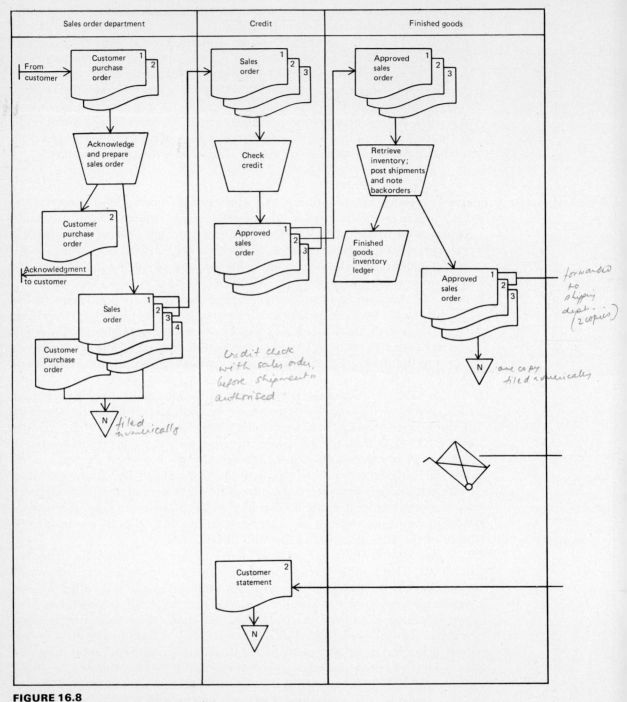

FIGURE 16.8
Document flow in a manual system for sales order processing.

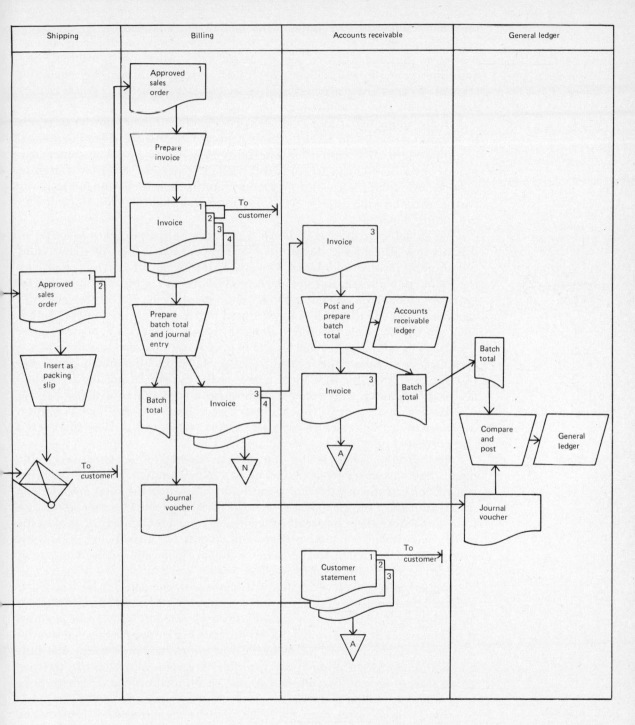

partment, along with two copies of the sales order. To acknowledge the transfer of responsibility for these goods from the storeroom to shipping, an employee of shipping will sign a copy of the sales order indicating the exact quantities to be shipped. This copy will then be sent to billing. The remaining copy of the sales order may be enclosed as a *packing slip* with the goods as they are shipped to the customer.

In the billing department the sales order evidencing the transfer of goods to shipping provides the basis for preparation of the invoice. After the invoice is prepared, the first (and often a second) copy is sent to the customer. Another copy is sent to the accounts receivable department, where it is used to post the billing to the customer's account and is then filed alphabetically by customer name. One other copy of the invoice is filed by invoice number in the billing department.

An example of the use of batch totals for control purposes is found in this process. The billing department compiles a batch total of the amount billed on all invoices in a batch. Once preparation of the batch is complete, the billing department uses the batch total to prepare a journal voucher. The journal voucher contains the summary entry debiting accounts receivable and crediting sales for the total amount billed and is sent to the general ledger clerk. In the accounts receivable department, as invoices are posted to the subsidiary ledger, another batch total is prepared. This second batch total is compiled by summing the individual ledger balances after posting and subtracting the sum of the individual ledger balances prior to posting. This total is also sent to the general ledger section where it is compared with the amount of the entry on the journal voucher. Any discrepancy between these two totals indicates the existence of one or more errors, which can then be discovered and corrected.

Periodically, usually at the end of each month, the accounts receivable department may prepare a statement of each customer's account, detailing transactions in the most recent period and indicating the total amount due on account from the customer. One copy of this statement is sent to the customer, another is kept by accounts receivable, and another may be sent to the credit department for their records. Statements of this sort are commonly prepared and utilized by retail businesses but are generally not used in regular dealings between industrial firms.

Organizational independence with respect to the sales order process is achieved by separation of the custodial functions performed by finished goods and shipping from the recording functions performed by billing and accounts receivable, and from the authorization functions performed by the sales order and credit departments. This separation of duties helps to ensure that only goods intended for shipment to customers are removed from the finished goods storeroom, and that all such goods are shipped only to authorized customers and are billed properly.

Special procedures must be established for handling sales returns and allowances. Each adjustment should be approved by a person in a position of responsibility, such as the credit manager. The basis for approval should be a letter from the customer. Issuance of a credit memo formally recognizing the adjustment should, in the case of sales returns, also require a receiving report as verification of the return of goods. A copy of the credit memo is sent to the customer, another is filed, and another is used as a source document for posting to the accounts receivable ledger. At the end of a day or week, the person authorizing these credits should prepare and send to the general ledger clerk a journal voucher containing a summary entry for all sales returns and allowances during the period.

In a manual system, the regular preparation of reports such as sales and profitability analyses may not be feasible. In very small companies, no such reports need be generated because the manager or owner probably knows enough about the customers and sales. Somewhat larger companies may obtain a limited analysis of sales by recording all sales in specially formulated journals in which, for example, separate rows are used for each product, separate columns for each time period, and separate pages for each salesperson. The data on such journals may then be aggregated across one or more of these dimensions to provide summary analyses of sales by product or by salesperson for particular periods of time.

A computer-based batch processing system

A document flowchart of the sales order and accounts receivable process for a typical manufacturing company that uses a computer-based system appears in Fig. 16.9. Once again, it must be emphasized that the illustration is not intended to demonstrate how the process should be accomplished but merely to show one example of how it might be done.

A comparison of Fig. 16.9 with its manual counterpart, Fig. 16.8, reveals that procedures relating to sales order preparation, credit checking, order assembly in finished goods, and shipping are the same. However, the functions of billing and accounts receivable have been assumed by the computer. When the shipping department is finished with a sales order, it sends a copy indicating which items were shipped and which were backordered to the computer department. This department inputs a record for each individual item shipped or backordered. These records become input to a series of computer runs that produce invoices, update the finished goods inventory master file, produce a list of inventory items that are out of stock or in short supply, update the master sales file, produce a sales analysis report at the end of each week or month, update the general ledger file, update the accounts receivable master file, produce customer statements of account at the end of each month, and produce an aged accounts receivable schedule at the end of each month. A systems flowchart of the computer operations necessary to accomplish these various processes appears in Fig. 16.10.

To simplify its interpretation, the systems flowchart is separated by dashed lines into three separate categories of operations. These are (1) input preparation and data control, (2) accounts receivable and inventory processing,

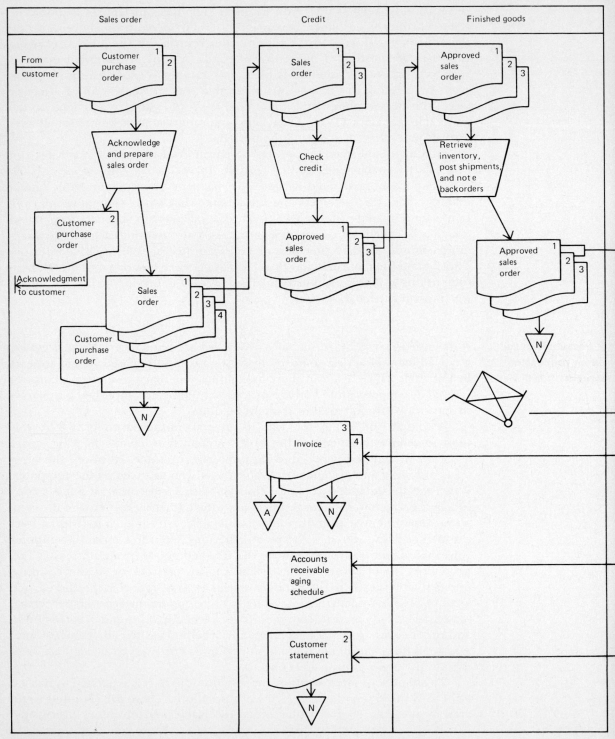

FIGURE 16.9   Document flow in computerized batch processing of sales orders.

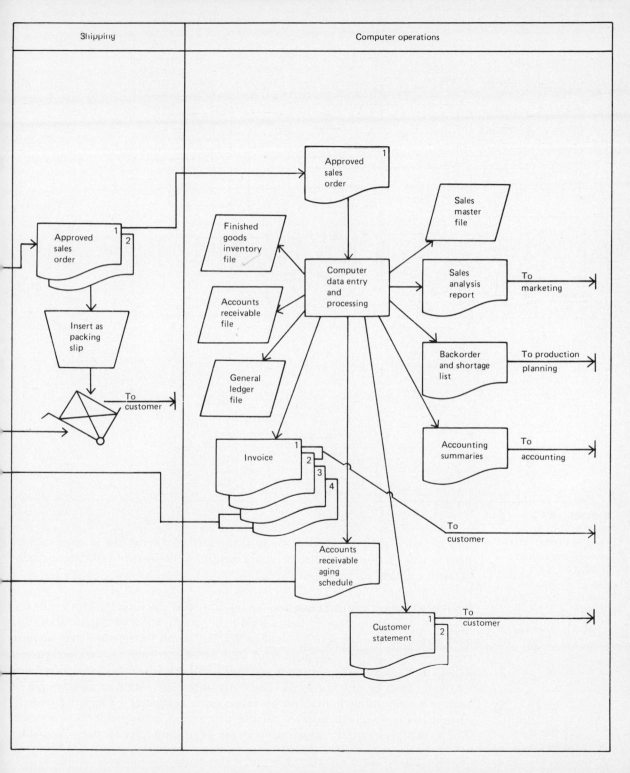

Shipping	Computer operations

Approved sales order 1

Approved sales order 1 2

Insert as packing slip

To customer

Finished goods inventory file

Accounts receivable file

General ledger file

Computer data entry and processing

Sales master file

Sales analysis report — To marketing

Backorder and shortage list — To production planning

Accounting summaries — To accounting

Invoice 1 2 3 4

To customer

Accounts receivable aging schedule

Customer statement 1 2 — To customer

System flow chart

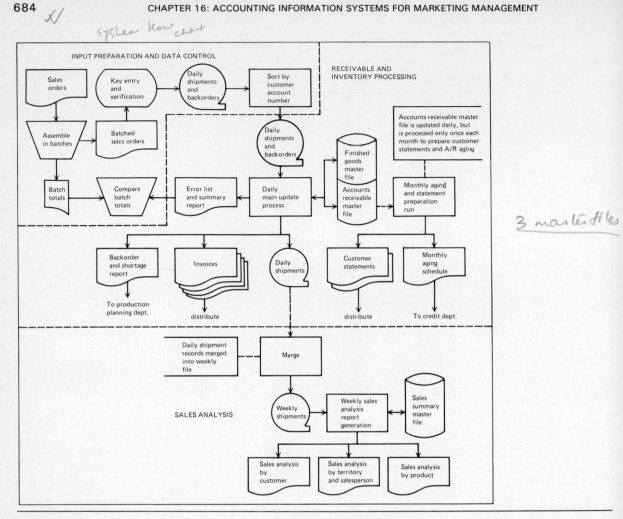

FIGURE 16.10
System flow in
computerized batch
processing of sales
orders.

and (3) sales analysis. Each of these three sets of operations is discussed in turn in this section. Also discussed are a number of control policies and procedures relating to these processes.

Input preparation and data control.   Each day, this operation begins with the assembly of sales orders in batches and the preparation of batch totals. For each batch of sales orders, control totals that could be accumulated include record counts of the total number of sales orders, shipments, and backorders as well as hash totals of customer account numbers, inventory stock numbers, or the number of units ordered. The batch totals are retained and compared with summary totals generated by subsequent computer processing to help ensure that no records are lost during processing or improperly processed. The next step in input preparation is the keying and verification of a shipment or backorder record for each item ordered. It is assumed that these records are keyed onto magnetic tape using a key-to-tape encoder or key-to-disk-to-tape system. The computer is then used to sort these magnetic tape records into sequential order according to the customer account number.

There are several alternative means by which these input preparation operations could have been accomplished. For example, the shipment and backorder records could have been keyed into punched cards and sorted on a card sorter. Alternatively, these records could be keyed onto a diskette and then transferred to magnetic tape or disk for sorting and processing. Another alternative used by many mail-order companies is to send the customer a preprinted order form on which items to be ordered may be marked; when returned, such forms can be read by optical character recognition equipment and recorded on magnetic tape or disk.

Accounts receivable and inventory processing.   The main step in this operation is the daily processing of shipment and backorder records to update the accounts receivable and inventory master files. In the manual system, these steps are performed by employees in the accounts receivable and finished goods inventory departments. Because the input records are sequenced by customer account number, the accounts receivable master file is accessed sequentially during this run. Therefore finished goods inventory records must be accessed randomly using the stock number as the key. The updating process results in the addition of the amount billed to each customer to that customer's accounts receivable balance, as well as the subtraction of the quantity shipped of each inventory item from that item's balance on hand. Furthermore, backorder records are posted to the appropriate inventory master in order that when the stock is replenished, the system can automatically initiate shipment of the backordered goods.

In addition to updating the accounts receivable and finished goods inventory master files, the daily main update run produces several outputs. One is a tape containing records of all shipments for the day, which becomes input to sales analysis processing. Another output is a report of backordered items and other inventory items for which the balance on hand is below the minimum stock level; this report is provided to the production planning department to aid in decisions regarding which items should be produced. Also generated are four copies of a customer invoice for each order, which are distributed as shown in Fig. 16.9. In the manual system, the invoice preparation function is performed by employees in the billing department.

A fourth output of this run is a listing of error transactions and summary information. Error transactions include any input records that failed an input validation test or other processing check in the program. This list should be provided to the data control clerk for follow-up and error correction. The summary report includes batch totals accumulated during the run that are compared with those calculated manually prior to keying. Also included on the summary report are (1) the summary journal entry debiting accounts receivable and crediting sales and (2) if a perpetual inventory system is used, the summary journal entry debiting cost of goods sold and crediting finished goods inventory. These summary journal entries may be posted to the general ledger either manually, by a separate computer run, or (if the general ledger is maintained online) by directly accessing the affected general ledger records at the conclusion of the main update run.

The other process illustrated in this section of the flowchart is a monthly run utilizing the accounts receivable master file as input. This run results in the preparation of statements of account, which are mailed to customers, and an aging schedule of accounts receivable, in which each customer's account is categorized according to whether and by how much it is past due. The aging schedule is submitted to the credit department to be used in customer credit checks and to initiate special collection procedures when necessary.

Sales analysis.   The illustration assumes that sales analysis operations are performed weekly, although a monthly cycle is also quite common. It is also assumed that a magnetic disk master file summarizing previous sales activity is maintained as a source of data for preparing sales analysis reports. Before these reports can be prepared, this sales summary master file must be updated for sales transactions of the most recent week. In turn, this requires that the daily shipment tape must be merged into a single weekly shipments tape, which is then processed against the sales summary master at the end of each week. This process is performed sequentially by customer account number, and therefore sales analysis reports by customer or by customer class may be prepared as a by-product of the update run.

Next, the sales summary master file may be sorted into sequence by salesperson number, and then subsequently by product stock number, in order to generate sales analysis reports by territory and salesperson,[1] and by product item and product class. Alternatively, the use of a direct access storage medium such as magnetic disk permits separate indexes to be maintained for the sales summary master file—one for salesperson numbers and one for product stock numbers. Because these indexes would be in sequential order (though the records are not), these various sales analysis reports could be produced without the need for intermediate sorting steps. Once the preparation of the various sales analysis reports is completed, they are distributed to the appropriate executives in the marketing department.

Control policies and procedures.   A number of control policies and procedures should be integrated into the computerized processing of sales orders. Two examples already mentioned are the keyverification of shipment and backorder records, and the preparation and checking of batch totals. Several other examples may be cited. In the area of data security, each of the tape

---

[1]This assumes that each salesperson serves within a single territory only, so that sales for a territory is simply the sum of the total sales for all salespersons assigned to that territory.

and disk files used in this system should have both internal and external labels to ensure that no file will be inadvertently processed by the wrong program. Backup copies of the three master files stored on magnetic disk should be periodically written onto magnetic tape and subsequent transaction tapes saved to permit reconstruction of any master file whose contents are destroyed. Tape file protection rings should be removed from the transaction and backup tapes saved for this purpose in order to prevent such tapes from being written on. Current copies of these tape and disk files, when not in use, should be stored in a tape library and removed only for authorized purposes. Backup copies of master files and transaction records should be stored in a secure off-site location.

In the area of processing controls, input validation routines should be included in each file maintenance program in the system. Examples of the edit checks that might be included in these routines are field checks on all numeric fields in the input data; sequence checks of the input records; validity checks on customer account number, inventory stock number, and salesperson number; and reasonableness tests of price and quantity data from the orders. The list of error transactions produced by each file maintenance run should be reviewed by data control or supervisory personnel, and each error transaction should be corrected and resubmitted into the system.

Variations from the basic transactions, such as new-customer accounts, sales returns and allowances, or corrections and adjustments of file records, would normally be included in the regular file processing runs. Data entry personnel should check for the appropriate approval on source documents for transactions of this type. Input records for these items would include a transaction code identifying the nature of each record for the program. Each updating program would then check for and report any records having invalid transaction codes.

A real-time system

A systems flowchart of a real-time sales order processing system is illustrated in Fig. 16.11. In this section the description of this system emphasizes the differences between real-time and batch processing systems and describes control procedures and techniques appropriate for the real-time system.

As shown in the flowchart, a salesperson using the real-time system may obtain access to the system from the field, either through a portable terminal or through regional centers. The salesperson may check the availability of inventory items for the customer, check the customer's credit and the status of the account, initiate a transaction, and confirm the transaction immediately to the customer. A shipping order is quickly transmitted to a terminal in the stockroom or a warehouse if prompt shipment is desired. The transaction is immediately posted to the appropriate records within the marketing data base and to the general ledger.

Multiple copies of the invoice for each transaction may be printed out immediately as the order is processed. Alternatively, in order to avoid tying

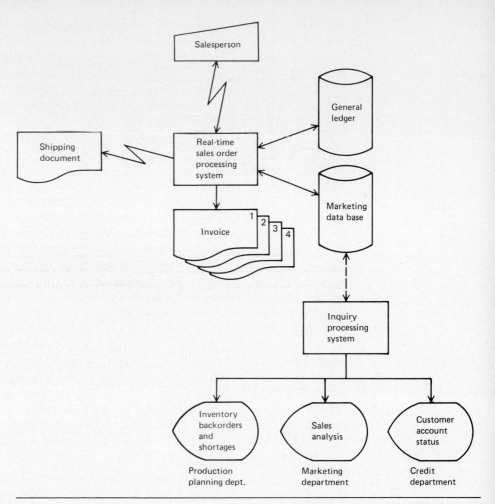

FIGURE 16.11
Real-time sales order
processing system.

up a printer permanently for this purpose, the invoice data could be spooled
onto a tape or disk file. Then all invoices could be printed out in a batch once
a day or at some other regular interval.

In a batch processing system such as the one described in the previous
section, management reports are printed at regular intervals. In a real-time
system that incorporates an inquiry processing capability, the need for regular
preparation of printed management reports is reduced or eliminated. Instead,
each manager uses a terminal to access the marketing data base and retrieve
relevant management information. For example, as illustrated in Fig. 16.11,
production planners can obtain on demand a list of inventory items backordered or in short supply to assist them in scheduling production. Similarly,
sales analysis reports in any desired format can be obtained by marketing
executives using a terminal. Credit managers can obtain a receivables aging

schedule at any time or inquire into the current status of a specific customer's account.

In addition to these differences in management reporting, this example illustrates several other major differences between batch processing and real-time systems. For example, in the batch processing system, entering data into the system requires several steps. First, the source document (the sales order) has to be prepared, approved by the credit department, used by the finished goods storeroom personnel in retrieving the goods for shipment, and finally used as a source document for keying and verifying shipment and backorder records. Once the data are recorded on machine-readable media (cards or tape), they must be sorted and read in separately for each separate file update. The existence of these several steps in the batch processing system means that (1) there are several possibilities for errors to occur and (2) the entire process consumes a sizable quantity of time.

In contrast, the real-time system replaces document preparation, keying, sorting, and reading with a single step—the keying of the relevant data into the system using a terminal. Credit checking is done automatically, and all the files are updated in one process, without reloading and re-sorting of tapes or disks. The general ledger is also updated in this process, with no separate procedures being required. Basically, the real-time system accomplishes, in a single automatic process, the same result that requires several different steps, all requiring manual intervention, in the batch processing system.

The real-time system does have a major disadvantage with respect to control of data accuracy: There is only one point in the system at which the accuracy of data can be controlled—the point of entry of data into the system. If the system accepts inaccurate data, the chance to discover and correct the error before it contaminates all files, documents, and reports is lost. However, in another sense this fact is an advantage; it means that control of data accuracy can be focused at a single point, the point of data entry, with the assurance that if all errors are prevented there, no subsequent errors are likely.

The first essential control feature of a real-time sales order processing system is the assignment of a unique user code to each salesperson. The user code number of each salesperson should be known only to that person. Each time the salesperson desires access to the system, the user code number is the first item of data to be entered. The system should check the validity of the user code number before accepting any further instructions or data from the salesperson. Furthermore, each salesperson's user code number should contain an internal code that defines the transactions he or she is authorized to initiate and the files to which he or she is authorized to have access. A salesperson should be restricted to initiating only sales orders and inquiring only into the marketing data base.

Another control feature over data entry into a real-time system is simplicity of operator data entry procedures. This might be effected by displaying an invoice format for the salesperson to fill in or by writing questions on the terminal that ask the salesperson for each required item of data. The system thereby guides the salesperson through the data entry process and will not accept the order until all the required data have been entered.

One major form of data control lost in a real-time system is the batch total. Since transactions are entered one at a time as they occur, there is no such thing as a batch of input records in a real-time system. Responsibility for controlling the accuracy of data input in a real-time system therefore shifts more heavily to data editing routines programmed into the system. With respect to sales order data, the first of these should be a validity check on the customer account number and on the inventory stock number of each item ordered. The system should accept orders from new customers to whom no account number has been assigned but should not initiate shipping papers until a credit check is performed.

To ensure that the salesperson does not enter a valid but incorrect account number or stock number, a redundant data check may be used. This would require that the salesperson also enter the first few letters of the customer name and the item description. The system could then check whether the number and letters provided by the salesperson match those in the customer account record and the inventory stock record. Alternatively, closed loop verification could be used for this purpose. Given only the account number and item numbers, the system could retrieve the customer name and item descriptions from the files and display these data back to the salesperson's terminal for verification.

Another type of edit routine in this system would be a field check to ensure that the quantity and price fields contain numeric data only. In addition, if the salesperson enters item prices, the accuracy of the prices entered may be tested by comparing them with the list prices on file in the marketing data base.

The various types of reasonableness tests constitute still another class of input validation checks that may be included in this system. First, the reasonableness of the product relative to the customer might be tested. For example, it would not be reasonable for a men's clothing store to order women's underwear. For another example, the reasonableness of the quantity ordered relative to the product might be tested. An order for a large quantity of a large product, such as 500 magnetic disk drive units, would not be reasonable. Conversely, an order for a very small quantity of a small product, such as ten punched cards, would not be reasonable.

If any of these editing routines detect a possible error, the salesperson is requested to reenter the item in question. After all data have been entered and have passed the various edit routines, the system may print or display critical data back to the salesperson, requesting verification of its accuracy. This step would detect data transmission errors in which the data were entered correctly but were incorrectly transmitted to the system.

The design of a system of editing routines requires ingenuity and care. All the techniques described above would not necessarily be appropriate for a given user. The system designed must balance cost and risk factors in a manner appropriate for the organization using the system.

Still another aspect of the overall control of the real-time sales order processing system involves the maintenance of a transaction log. Such a log is useful both for audit purposes and because it enables reconstruction of the marketing data base in the event of its accidental destruction. The transaction log could be maintained on a separate disk unit or on magnetic tape and would be printed out periodically. The marketing data base would also be periodically written onto magnetic tape. Therefore if any portion of the data base were destroyed, it could be reconstructed using the most recent tape listing and the transaction log.

Summary

The accounting information system plays a key role in providing information for marketing management. Accounting information is used by marketing executives in establishing pricing policies, in evaluating selling performance, in evaluating advertising and promotion strategies, and in planning the product mix.

Much of the accounting information provided to marketing management is generated as a by-product of the processing of customer sales orders. The focal point of this process is the maintenance of a marketing data base organized around customer and product inventory information. Sales order processing may be accomplished by using a manual data processing system or by using a computer-based system operating either in a batch processing mode or in a real-time mode. This system provides marketing management with much useful information on customers, products, sales, and inventories.

Review Questions

1. Define the following terms.

   sales analysis   stock status report

   profitability analysis   extensions

   backorder   packing slip

2. Describe or illustrate an example of a typical marketing organization structure. Why is an understanding of the marketing organization structure necessary to the analysis of marketing information systems?

3. Describe the decision responsibilities and information requirements of
   a) the top Marketing executive,
   b) the director of sales,
   c) the director of advertising and promotion,
   d) the director of product planning,
   e) the director of customer service, and
   f) the director of marketing research.

4. Describe the nature of the marketing information provided, and the related data sources used, by
   a) the accounting information system,
   b) the marketing department,
   c) other sources of information within the business organization, and
   d) external information sources.

5. Describe in detail the data recorded on a sales invoice.

6. Describe in detail the data recorded on a salesperson's call report.

7. What are the accounting journal entries that summarize the activities involved in the processing of sales transactions?

8. Describe the data content and organization of the marketing data base.

9. Describe the nature and purpose of a journal voucher.

10. What departments in a manufacturing company might be involved in the manual processing of sales and maintenance of accounts receivable? What documents might be involved and what information would each contain? Where would each originate and to whom would it be distributed?

11. What control procedures are involved in manual processing of sales orders and accounts receivable in a typical manufacturing company?

12. What procedures might be established for handling backordered goods in a manual data processing system? In a computerized data processing system?

13. How is organizational independence achieved with respect to sales order and accounts receivable processing?

14. Describe an appropriate set of procedures for processing sales returns and allowances.

15. Describe the similarities and differences in processing of sales order transactions in a typical manufacturing company using a computer rather than a manual data processing system. Emphasize documents, departments, and reports involved in the process.

16. What control procedures might be involved in batch processing of sales transactions by a typical manufacturing company that uses a computer data processing system?

17. Explain how the use of magnetic disk storage permits both the accounts receivable and finished goods inventory master files to be updated for sales activity in a single computer run. Would this be feasible if both of these master files were stored on magnetic tape?

18. Explain how a summary master file of sales data stored on a magnetic disk may be processed to generate sales analyses by customer, by sales-

person, and by product without the need for intermediate sorting operations.

19. Prepare a systems flowchart of a real-time system for processing sales orders.

20. Describe some of the major differences between a computerized batch processing system and a real-time system for processing sales orders.

21. Describe several control procedures and techniques appropriate for a real-time sales order processing system. What is the major difference in emphasis between these techniques and those in a batch processing system?

Discussion Questions

22. This chapter primarily emphasized the marketing information requirements of a manufacturing firm with a large sales force. Compare the organizational structure, information requirements, and data sources of this type of organization with those of
    a) a large retail organization,
    b) a firm that does all selling by direct mail,
    c) a large motel chain, and
    d) a hospital.

23. Some companies have created the post of product line manager within the marketing department. There may be several product line managers, each responsible for a related group of products. Discuss the effects on decision responsibilities and information requirements within the marketing department of this type of organization.

24. Create a definition for the term *marketing information system.* Discuss the conceptual and operational relationships between marketing information systems and accounting information systems.

Problems and Cases

25. As a systems analyst for the Dolphin Motor Company, you have been asked to design a computer report that will analyze product sales by dealers. The company sells three major lines of cars—the Dolphin, the Eagle, and the Flyer—and all dealers carry all three lines. Assume that space constraints limit the report such that a maximum of eight columns of data may be placed across the width of a page. Of course, there are no constraints regarding how many lines of data may be used for each dealer.

    In designing the report, you may make any reasonable assumptions about the availability of data. Make sure that you take into account the need for effective presentation of information, the need for standards of comparison, and the principle of management by exception.

26. Shown in Fig. 16.12 is a document flowchart of sales order, billing, and accounts receivable procedures (including everything except cash re-

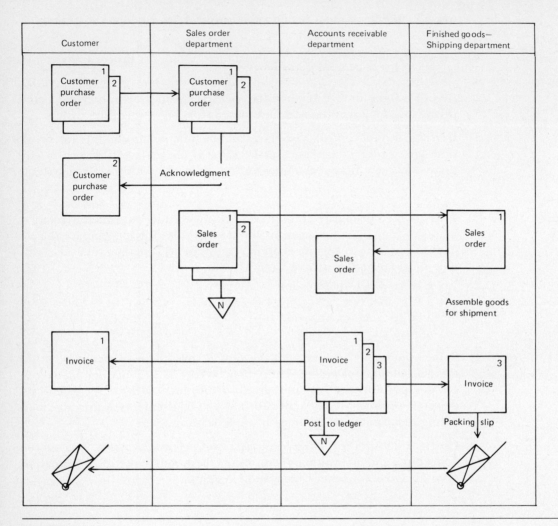

FIGURE 16.12

ceipts) for Tabco Manufacturing, Inc. What changes would you recommend to improve control and efficiency?

27. What controls in a sales order processing system are designed to provide the best protection against the following errors or manipulations?

a) Theft of goods by shipping department personnel, who claim that subsequent shortages are due to errors made by personnel in the finished goods storeroom.

b) An error in posting from a copy of an invoice to the accounts receivable ledger.

c) Sale to a customer who is four months behind in making payments on his account.

d) Failure to send a bill for goods ordered and shipped to a customer.

e) Sale and shipment of goods to a fictitious customer.

f) Authorization of a credit memo for a sales return when the goods were never actually returned.

g) Billing a customer without recording the account receivable, in order to conceal theft of subsequent collections.

h) Billing a customer for the quantity of raw materials ordered, when the quantity shipped was actually less than the quantity ordered owing to an out-of-stock condition.

28. Your company has just acquired a data base management system, and one of the first applications of it will be to marketing data. A sales invoice form identical to that in Fig. 16.2 is used. You are to diagram the data structure of the invoice as a first step in the application design. Use a format similar to that in Fig. 16.7. Note that the data base will contain only the variable data on the invoice, not the constant data.

29. Cragg and Company utilizes a real-time sales order processing system. Sales orders are entered into the system by salespeople utilizing portable data terminals from customer offices. For each sale, the salesperson enters his or her personal user code number, the customer's account number, and the item number, quantity ordered, and price of each item sold.

numeric check
validity check
reasonableness test
closed loop veri.
redundant data

REQUIRED

Describe several means by which the system should be programmed to check the accuracy and validity of the input data entered by salespeople. Relate your answer specifically to the data items mentioned.

30. The Rigby Company has twelve major product lines with twenty to thirty items in each product line. Product line managers have been selected to assume product planning responsibilities for each product line. As a systems analyst in charge of designing marketing information systems, you wish to show these product line managers the kind of information that can be made available to them.

REQUIRED

Design a computerized sales analysis report that analyzes sales by product item within each product line. Assume that space constraints limit the report such that a maximum of eight columns of data may be placed across the width of a page. In designing the report, you may make any reasonable assumptions about the availability of data. Make sure that you take into account the need for effective presentation of information, the need for standards of comparison, and the principle of management by exception.

31. Elite Publishing Company has established a subsidiary, Business Book Club, Inc. (BBC), that will operate as described below.

BBC's editors will select from among recently published books in the business area those it feels will be of most interest to businesspeople. These books can be purchased in large lots at approximately forty percent of list price. BBC plans to sell these books to its club members at approximately seventy-five percent of list price.

Solicitation of new customers will be done through advertising by direct mail and in selected publications. Such advertisements will offer four free books if one is purchased and if the purchaser agrees to become a member of the club. Each club member will be sent a list of new selections each month. Members are not required to buy any books. After purchase of four books a member is sent a list of selections from which he or she may choose a free book.

You have been called upon to design a computerized billing and book inventory system for BBC. Assume that you have asked various managers about their information needs and find that the advertising manager wants to know which advertising media are more effective, the credit manager wants to know which accounts are more than ninety days past due, and the editors want to know which books are best-sellers.

REQUIRED

a) Identify the master files you feel should be maintained in this system and list the data content of each.

b) Identify the input transactions that this system must process, and the output documents and reports that the system must be designed to produce.

c) Assume that transaction inputs will be recorded on magnetic tape, and that the master files will be stored on magnetic disk units. Prepare systems flowcharts of all computer runs necessary to process the inputs, maintain the master files, and generate the outputs for your system.

32. George Beemster, CPA, is examining the financial statements of the Louisville Sales Corporation, which recently installed an offline electronic computer. The following comments have been extracted from Mr. Beemster's notes on computer operations and the processing and control of shipping notices and customer invoices:

☐ To minimize inconvenience, Louisville converted without change its existing data processing system, which utilized tabulating equipment. The computer company supervised the conversion and has provided training to all computer department employees (except keypunch operators) in systems design, operations, and programming.

☐ Each computer run is assigned to a specific employee, who is responsible for making program changes, running the program, and answering questions. This procedure has the advantage of eliminating the need for records of computer operations because each employee has responsibility for his or her own computer runs.

☐ At least one computer department employee remains in the computer room during office hours, and only computer department employees have keys to the computer room.

☐ System documentation consists of those materials furnished by the computer company—a set of record formats and program listings. These and the tape library are kept in a corner of the computer department.

☐ The Company considered the desirability of programmed controls but decided to retain the manual controls from its existing system.

☐ Company products are shipped directly from public warehouses which forward shipping notices to general accounting. There a billing clerk enters the price of the item and accounts for the numerical sequence of shipping notices from each warehouse. The billing clerk also prepares daily adding machine tapes ("control tapes") of the units shipped and the unit prices.

☐ Shipping notices and control tapes are forwarded to the computer department for keypunching and processing. Extensions are made on the computer. Output consists of invoices (in six copies) and a daily sales register. The daily sales register shows the aggregate totals of units shipped and unit prices which the computer operator compares to the control tapes.

☐ All copies of the invoice are returned to the billing clerk. The clerk mails three copies to the customer, forwards one copy to the warehouse, maintains one copy in a numerical file, and retains one copy in an open invoice file that serves as a detailed accounts receivable record.

REQUIRED Describe weaknesses in internal control over information and data flows and the procedures for processing shipping notices and customer invoices and recommend improvements in these controls and processing procedures. Organize your answer sheet as follows. (CPA Examination)

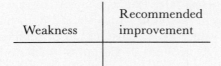

Weakness	Recommended improvement

33. When a shipment is made, the Shipping Department prepares a shipping order form. This form is in three copies. The first copy is sent out with the goods to the customer as a packing slip. The second copy is forwarded to the Billing Department. The third copy is sent to the Accountant. When the Billing Department receives the second copy of the shipping order, it uses the information thereon to prepare a two-part sales invoice. The second copy of the shipping order is then filed in the Billing Department. The first copy of the sales invoice is sent to the customer. The second copy of the sales invoice is forwarded to the Accountant. Periodically, the Accountant matches the copy of the shipping order with the copy of the

sales invoice and files them alphabetically by customer name. Before doing so, however, the Accountant uses the copy of the sales invoice to post the sales entry in the subsidiary accounts receivable ledger.

REQUIRED

    a) For use in appraising internal control, prepare a flowchart covering the flow of documents reflected in the above situation.

    b) List those deficiencies and/or omissions revealed by the flowchart which would lead you to question the internal control. (CIA Examination)

34. Value Clothing is a large distributor of all types of clothing acquired from buy-outs, overstocks and factory seconds. All sales are on account with terms of net 30 days from date of monthly statement. The number of delinquent accounts and uncollectible accounts have increased significantly during the last twelve months. Management has determined that the information generated from the present accounts receivable system is inadequate and untimely. In addition, customers frequently complain of errors in their accounts.

The current accounts receivable system has not been changed since Value Clothing started its operations. A new computer was acquired 18 months ago but no attempt has been made to revise the accounts receivable application because other applications were considered more important. The work schedule in the Systems Department has slackened slightly enabling the staff to design a new accounts receivable system. Top management has requested that the new system satisfy the following objectives.

1. Produce current and timely reports regarding customers which would provide useful information to:
   a) aid in controlling bad debts.
   b) notify the Sales Department of customer accounts which are delinquent (accounts which should lose charge privileges).
   c) notify the Sales Department of customers whose accounts are considered uncollectible (accounts which should be closed and written-off).

2. Produce timely notices to customers regarding:
   a) amounts owed to Value Clothing.
   b) a change of status of their accounts (loss of charge privileges, account closed).

3. Incorporate the necessary procedures and controls to minimize the chance for errors in customers' accounts.

Input data for the system would be taken from four source documents—credit applications, sales invoices, cash payment remittances, and credit memoranda. The accounts receivable master file will be maintained on a machine-readable file by customer account number. The preliminary design of the new accounts receivable system has been completed by the Systems Department. A brief description of the proposed reports and other output generated by the system are detailed below.

1. *Accounts Receivable Register*—a daily alphabetical listing of all customers' accounts which shows balance as of the last statement, activity since the last statement, and account balance.

2. *Customer Statements*—monthly statements for each customer showing activity since the last statement and account balance; the top portion of the statement is returned with the payment and serves as the cash payment remittance.

3. *Aging Schedule—All Customers*—a monthly schedule of all customers with outstanding balances displaying the total amount owed with the total classified into age groups—0–30 days, 30–60 days, 60–90 days, over 90 days; the schedule includes totals and percentages for each age category.

4. *Aging Schedule—Past Due Customers*—a schedule prepared monthly which includes only those customers whose accounts are past due, i.e., over 30 days outstanding, classified by age. The credit manager uses this schedule to decide which customers will receive delinquent notices, temporary suspension of charge privileges, or have their accounts closed.

5. *Activity Reports*—monthly reports which show:
   a) customers who have not purchased any merchandise for 90 days.
   b) customers whose account balance exceeds their credit limit.
   c) customers whose accounts are delinquent yet they have current sales on account.

6. *Delinquency and Write-off Register*—a monthly alphabetical listing of customers' accounts which are:
   a) delinquent.
   b) closed.

   These listings show name, account number, and balance. Related notices are prepared and sent to these customers.

7. *Summary Journal Entries*—entries are prepared monthly to record write-offs to the accounts receivable file.

REQUIRED

a) Identify the data which should be captured and stored in the computer-based file records for each customer.

b) Review the proposed reports to be generated by the new accounts receivable system.
   i) Discuss whether the proposed reports should be adequate to satisfy the objectives enumerated.
   ii) Recommend changes, if any, which should be made in the proposed reporting structure generated by the new accounts receivable system. (CMA Examination)

35. Company A is a small manufacturer of farm equipment and related parts. Their finished products can be shipped as a complete unit or in subassemblies which the end user would put together.

Orders are received by the company either by mail, or by telephone from their various distributors or the company's salesmen. These orders are processed, and a three-part shipping document is produced showing the complete units and/or parts. This document is then filed by territory. Periodic checks are made against this file and orders destined to be sent to certain territories are pulled and given to the Credit Department for approval. If the order is not approved, it is returned to the salesman. On approval of the order the three-part shipping document is sent to the Shipping Department where individual items are pulled out of stock and loaded on a truck. The goods being shipped are accompanied by one copy of the shipping document, while the other two are retained by the company. One copy is filed and the remaining copy is sent to the Invoicing Department where a check is made for any back-ordered items. Extensions are made on this copy of the shipping document and a four-part invoice is produced. Invoice totals are posted to the customer's accounts receivable file. The copy of the shipping document is then sent to the Inventory Department to update their records. Two copies of the invoice are sent to the customer. The third is filed by customer, and the fourth is filed by salesman.

Upon receipt of monies owing to the company, a credit is posted against the customer's accounts receivable file and the salesman's copy of the invoice is marked as paid. The salesman's paid invoices for a certain period will produce a commission report for input to the payroll.

Credits are issued to customers for damaged stock. These credits are again posted against the accounts receivable file and filed by customer and salesman.

REQUIRED

a) Draw the document flowchart for *the existing manual system.*
b) Assume you have acquired a minicomputer with online disk storage, CRT input, printer and disk back-up.

   i) Prepare a system flowchart showing how you would modify Part (a) above to computerize the system.

   ii) Specify the information contained in each file required. (SMAC Examination)

References

Arthur Andersen & Co. *A Guide for Studying and Evaluating Internal Accounting Controls.* Chicago: Arthur Andersen & Co., 1978.

Bentz, William F., and Robert F. Lusch. "Now You Can Control Your Product's Market Performance." *Management Accounting* (January 1980): 17–25.

Cash, James I., Jr., and Benn R. Konsynski. "IS Redraws Competitive Boundaries." *Harvard Business Review* (March/April 1985): 134–142.

Doppelt, Neil. "Down-to-Earth Marketing Information Systems." *Management Advisor* (September/October 1971): 19–26.

Flesher, Dale L. "An Operational Audit of Marketing." *Internal Auditor* (February 1983): 23–29.

Goodman, Sam R. "Sales Reports That Lead to Action." *Financial Executive* (June 1973): 20–29.

Goslar, Martin D. "Capability Criteria for Marketing Decision Support Systems." *Journal of Management Information Systems* (Summer 1986): 81–95.

Hughes, G. David. "Computerized Sales Management." *Harvard Business Review* (March/April 1983): 102–112.

Jackson, Barbara B., and Benson P. Shapiro. "New Way to Make Product Line Decisions." *Harvard Business Review* (May/June 1979): 139–149.

Price Waterhouse & Co. *Guide to Accounting Controls: Revenues and Receivables.* New York: Price Waterhouse & Co., 1979.

Savesky, Robert S. "How Good Is Your Company's Sales Forecast?" *Price Waterhouse Review* **22** (1977): 30–37.

Sterling, T. D. "Consumer Difficulties with Computerized Transactions: An Empirical Investigation." *Communications of the ACM* (May 1979): 283–289.

Accounting Information Systems for Purchasing Management

LEARNING OBJECTIVES

Careful study of this chapter should enable students to:

☐ Describe the decision responsibilities and information requirements of purchasing management.

☐ Describe the information provided to purchasing management by the accounting information system.

☐ Prepare flowcharts describing data and information flows within a purchasing and inventory data processing system.

☐ Design and evaluate control policies and procedures for a purchasing and inventory data processing system.

CHAPTER OUTLINE

Purchasing management involves planning and controlling the procurement of raw materials, goods, and supplies inventories. Inventory management involves planning and controlling the receipt, storage, and disposition of these inventories. The information requirements and data processing procedures associated with these two closely related management functions are the subject of this chapter.

In wholesale and retail firms, the purchasing and inventory management functions are directed at goods purchased for direct resale. In manufacturing companies, materials are purchased to serve as inputs to a production process. This chapter emphasizes the purchasing and inventory management activities of a typical manufacturing company. However, many of the concepts and techniques described are also applicable to the purchasing and inventory management problems of wholesale and retail firms.

In manufacturing firms the functions of purchasing management, inventory management, and production management are very closely related. The combination of these three functions is sometimes referred to as *logistics management*—planning and controlling the physical flow of materials through an organization. The interrelationship of these functions is reflected in typical organization structures for manufacturing firms, in which the purchasing department, the receiving department, and the inventory stores department are key components of the production organization (see Fig. 17.1). The information requirements and data processing procedures associated with the production management function are the subject of the following chapter.

The Purchasing and Inventory Management Function

The purchasing function is the primary management function in the purchasing and inventory management system. The basic decisions for which the purchasing department is responsible include (1) the quantity to be purchased, (2) the timing of purchases, and (3) the vendor from whom to purchase.

Deciding upon the quantity and timing of each item purchased is called the inventory control function and was discussed briefly in Chapter 4 as an example of a feedforward control system. The inventory control function has been the frequent subject of applications of mathematical modeling techniques. The basic objective is to determine for each inventory item the order quantity and reorder point that minimize the sum of the costs of ordering the item, carrying the item in inventory, and being out of stock. Application of the mathematical models requires that these three cost factors be quantified, that the future requirements for the item be known or estimated, and that an estimate of vendor lead time be prepared.[1]

---

[1]For an extensive coverage of mathematical modeling techniques of inventory control, see Harvey M. Wagner, *Principles of Operations Research*, 2d ed. (Englewood Cliffs, N.J.: Prentice-Hall, 1975), chapter 19.

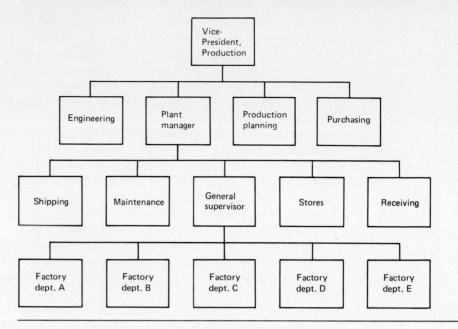

FIGURE 17.1
Production
department
organization.

The information required for estimating future requirements for an item and vendor lead time can be generated by formal information systems within an organization. In a retail organization, future demand can be estimated by applying forecasting techniques to historical records of past sales. In a manufacturing organization, future requirements can be accurately estimated if production planning is effectively integrated with sales forecasting. Vendor lead time can be estimated if formal records of past dealings with vendors are maintained.

Inventory costs are generally the most difficult elements of the model to estimate. Carrying costs include all costs that vary with the quantity of goods in inventory. The most significant element of carrying cost is the opportunity cost of the funds tied up in inventory. Stated another way, this cost represents the revenue lost from investing funds in inventory rather than in revenue-generating activities. Other elements of inventory carrying cost include the incremental costs of spoilage, breakage, pilferage, obsolescence, insurance, taxes, and space utilization. Ordering cost refers only to those costs that vary with the number of orders placed and generally involves the costs of processing the order and the fixed costs of shipping. Stockout cost, which involves lost goodwill or inefficiencies in operations, is practically impossible to measure and is therefore usually the subject of arbitrary estimates.

In general, mathematical modeling techniques are applied only to the high-cost, high-usage items of inventory. For low-cost, low-usage items, carrying and ordering costs are so insignificant that reorder point and order quantity can be set with the sole objective of eliminating stockouts. Once the order quantity and reorder points of an item are determined, they are stored along with other data pertaining to the item in the master inventory file. Clerks or machines then are responsible for applying these policies to determine the timing and size of individual orders.

An alternative to the mathematical modeling approach to inventory control in a manufacturing company is called *materials requirements planning* (MRP). Under this approach, the production planning department prepares a schedule of the quantities of each product to be manufactured during, for example, the next three months. Based upon this schedule, it may then be determined exactly what quantities of raw materials, parts, and supplies will be required—and at what points in time. This enables the purchasing department to purchase exactly those items that are needed for delivery when they are needed, thereby minimizing the need for safety stock as a hedge against the uncertainty of production requirements. Thus MRP enables the reduction of materials inventory levels but places much greater demands on the information system to maintain accurate inventory records.[2]

An extension of MRP is the *just-in-time* (JIT) *system* of inventory and production management. This system aims at minimizing or virtually eliminating manufacturing inventories by scheduling inventory deliveries at the precise times and locations needed. A factory utilizing a JIT system would establish multiple receiving docks, each assigned to accept deliveries of materials needed at work centers located nearby. This contrasts to the traditional approach of a single receiving facility located adjacent to a centralized factory stores department. Under JIT, materials are delivered in small lots at frequent intervals to the specific locations that require them, as opposed to infrequent bulk deliveries to a central receiving and storage facility. JIT systems are designed to reduce the cost of materials handling and storage. They require an information system that can effectively coordinate and monitor purchasing, delivery, and production activities on a real-time basis.

The other significant management decision made by the purchasing function is selection of vendors for inventory items. In a retail organization, there are buyers who specialize in related lines of merchandise. When the decision is made to carry a particular type of merchandise in the store, it becomes the buyer's responsibility to select a supplier. Examples of factors relevant to the decision are price, reliability, product styling, brand image, and quality. Information on prices and styles is provided by representatives of the various suppliers. Information on brand image and quality should be known to the buyer from his or her knowledge about the lines of merchandise in which he or she specializes. Information on reliability—the supplier's history of meet-

---

[2]For further discussion of MRP, see Jeffrey G. Miller and Linda G. Sprague, "Behind the Growth in Materials Requirements Planning," *Harvard Business Review* (September/October 1975): 83–91; and Daniel P. Keegan, "Some Second Reflections on MRP," *Price Waterhouse & Company 1975 Review* 3 (1977): 38–43.

ing quantity specifications and delivering goods promptly—should be maintained as part of a vendor history file within the purchasing department.

In a manufacturing organization, the selection of vendors for raw materials is made when the engineering department provides the specifications for a new part to the purchasing department. Purchasing then prepares requests for price quotations that are sent to potential suppliers. Once these price quotations are received, the purchasing department selects a vendor for the item. The decision is based not only on price but also on reliability, quality, and perhaps whether a given supplier is also a significant customer. Records of dealings with vendors should be maintained to provide information about reliability and product quality. The quality of a vendor's products can be measured in terms of how frequently products received from the vendor fail to pass inspection or testing performed by the receiving department.

Under a JIT system, the critical factors in selecting vendors are (1) their dependability to deliver the exact materials needed to the proper location at the specified time and (2) the quality of their products. A late delivery or a delivery of defective parts and materials would wreak havoc with a finely tuned JIT production schedule and so cannot be tolerated. As a result a key component of most JIT systems is the certification of suppliers. Only a small number of carefully chosen supplier companies are certified, based upon their commitment to reliability and quality control. This results in a very close relationship between a manufacturing company and its suppliers, in which the manufacturer may assist its suppliers in product design, production scheduling, and quality control.[3]

Once a vendor has been selected for a product, the identity of the vendor becomes a part of the master inventory record of that product. Vendor selection thus does not have to be performed each time the product is ordered. However, the identity of possible alternative vendors may also be included in the file in case the primary vendor is temporarily out of stock. Periodically, decisions may be made to change primary vendors for some products if a primary vendor does not provide satisfactory service or goes out of business.

The Purchasing and Inventory Data Processing System

The basic accounting journal entries that summarize the purchasing process vary depending on whether the firm uses a perpetual or a periodic inventory accounting system. In a perpetual system, one basic entry is used to record purchases.

The accounting transactions

Raw Materials Inventory	XXX	
Accounts Payable		XXX

Purchase returns and allowances are reflected as a reversal of that entry. If inventory counts reveal that actual quantity on hand is less than the quantity

---

[3]An excellent discussion of JIT is provided by Arjan T. Sadhwani, M. H. Sarhan, and Dayal Kiringoda, "Just-In-Time: An Inventory System Whose Time Has Come," *Management Accounting* (December 1985): 36–44.

recorded, the Raw Materials Inventory account is written down and the debit entered to Cost of Goods Sold or to a special loss account.

If a periodic inventory system is used, purchases are recorded by the following journal entry.

Purchases	XXX	
Accounts Payable		XXX

Purchase returns and allowances are recorded in a special contra-account as follows.

Accounts Payable	XXX	
Purchase Returns and Allowances		XXX

Periodically, a complete physical inventory is taken, and the following journal entry is made.

Inventory (Ending)	XXX	
Cost of Goods Sold	XXX	
Purchases		XXX
Inventory (Beginning)		XXX

This entry adjusts the inventory balance to its correct level and records Cost of Goods Sold for the period as the total of Purchases for the period plus the net reduction (or minus the net increase) in the Inventory account.

The purchasing data base

An example of the data content and organization of a purchasing and raw materials inventory data base appears in Fig. 17.2. This data base is structured as a network consisting of two interrelated families of records. One of these families contains raw materials inventory data, whereas the other contains data on raw materials vendors. Transaction records associated with one or both of these families include materials inventory requisitions, purchase requisitions, price quotations, purchase orders, inventory receipts, purchase returns and allowances, vouchers payable, and cash disbursements.

Each raw materials inventory record in the data base contains a single value for all the data fields listed under "Raw Materials Inventory," with the "Item Number" serving as the primary key. In addition, each raw materials inventory record owns one or more "Raw Materials Transaction" records. In turn, each Raw Materials Transaction record is a summary of the data contained in a Materials Requisition, Purchase Requisition, Price Quotation, Purchase Order, Receiving Report, or Purchase Return. The "Transaction Type Code" and "Document Number" in the Raw Materials Transaction record permit the system to access a more detailed transaction record (for example, a complete purchase order) whenever necessary.

In a manual data processing system, a materials ledger card (see Fig. 17.3) for each inventory item is commonly maintained by the accounting department or a production department. The data shown in the top portion of the materials ledger card are essentially equivalent to the data in the "Raw Ma-

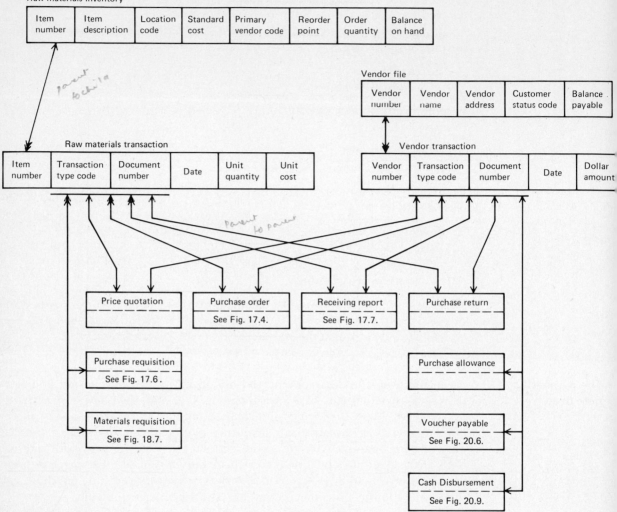

FIGURE 17.2
Purchasing and
inventory data base.

terials Inventory" record of the data base, whereas the data shown under "Transactions" in the lower-left portion of the card are similar to those contained in the "Raw Material Transaction" record in the data base. One significant difference is that the materials ledger card does not contain unit cost information for every transaction—a common limitation of manual systems for inventory record keeping. In an automated system, all inventory receipts would be recorded at their purchase cost, whereas all issues would be recorded on a FIFO (first in, first out), average, LIFO (last in, first out), or other cost basis. Also note that the materials ledger card maintains a record of the quan-

MATERIALS LEDGER CARD						Reorder point: 150		
Item number: 5216408			Description: bearing					

Location		Standard unit cost	Vendor			Order quantity		
Row 26	Bin 12	$1.40	Code 3621	Name Needmore Mfg.		500		

Transactions						Balances		
Date	Reference		Issued	Rec'd	Ordered	On hand	On order	Available
1/2/86	P.O.	1008			500	0	500	500
1/7/86	Rec.	1095		300		300	200	500
1/9/86	Req.	1056	200			100	200	300
1/14/86	Rec.	1208		200		300	0	300
2/4/86	Req.	1128	200			100	0	100
2/9/86	P.O.	1101			500	100	500	600
2/16/86	Rec.	1375		500		600	0	600

FIGURE 17.3
Sample materials ledger card.

tity available, which is the sum of the quantity on hand and the quantity on order. The quantity available is not stored separately on the data base but may be computed at any time for any inventory item using data available elsewhere in the data base.

Updating the raw materials inventory portion of the data base consists primarily of appending new transaction records to the data base, creating a new "Raw Material Transaction" summary record for each new transaction, and adjusting the appropriate fields within the "Raw Materials Inventory" master record. This should be done daily, because the inventory data serve as an important reference for personnel in production planning, purchasing, and production operations. In a manual system, this update is accomplished by posting the transaction data to the materials ledger card and recalculating the "On Hand," "On Order," and "Available" balances. Other inputs include nonroutine transactions such as error corrections or changes in location, standard cost, or primary vendor. Outputs from processing the inventory data base include stock status reports, exception reports on high- and low-activity items, and purchase requisitions or purchase orders to replenish the stock of low-balance items.

Each vendor record in the purchasing and raw materials inventory data base contains a single value for each of the data fields listed under "Vendor File" in Fig. 17.2, with the "Vendor Number" serving as the primary key. In addition, each vendor record owns one or more "Vendor Transaction" records; in turn, each Vendor Transaction record is a summary of data contained in a Price Quotation record, Purchase Order, Receiving Report, Purchase Return or Allowance record, Voucher Payable, or Cash Disbursement record. The "Transaction Type Code" and "Document Number" in the Vendor Transaction record enable the system to access one of these more detailed records whenever necessary.

In a manual data processing system, it is not uncommon that no master file dealing exclusively with vendors is maintained. Instead, records of dealings with particular vendors are scattered throughout files of disbursement vouchers, purchase orders, and receiving reports. In some manual systems a file of ledger cards summarizing financial transactions with each vendor may be maintained.

The vendor file portion of the purchasing and inventory data base may be updated daily or weekly. Basic inputs include orders, receipts, disbursement authorizations, and other transactions of the kind listed above and shown in Fig. 17.2. As these are added to the data base, new Vendor Transaction records are created, and when necessary the "Balance Payable" field in the Vendor File is updated. Other inputs include nonroutine transactions such as a change in a vendor's address or customer status, or an error correction.

The primary output documents generated from the data base are checks in payment of accounts payable. Useful output reports that may be produced include cash flow commitments schedules and vendor performance reports. A cash flow commitments schedule represents a summarization by expected payment date of cash payment commitments as reflected in disbursement vouchers and purchase orders and would be prepared weekly to assist financial executives in short-run budgeting of cash flows. A vendor performance report is a summary of past dealings with a particular vendor, including price quotations, orders placed, late shipments, early shipments, shipments rejected for poor quality, and shipments of the incorrect quantity. Virtually all records within the vendor file portion of the data base provide source data for this report. The vendor performance report enables purchasing management to continuously monitor vendor conduct and is an important input to the vendor selection decision. It may be generated weekly, monthly, or on demand, depending on how critical vendor performance is to the organization.

In a manual data processing system, a file of open purchase orders (that is, orders that have not yet been completely filled) plays a central role in purchasing operations. This file would consist simply of purchase order documents, such as the one shown in Fig. 17.4. Such a file is often maintained manually for reference purposes even when the purchasing function is automated. Basic inputs to the open purchase order file are new orders placed and receipts of goods on order. If partial shipment is received, a notation of the receipt may be posted to the appropriate purchase order record. Once a purchase order is completely filled, it should be removed from the open purchase order file. The file itself provides an important source of information for purchasing, accounting, and production personnel.

Purchase order records that are also maintained on a computer file would contain essentially the same data as shown in Fig. 17.4, with the purchase order number serving as the control field. However, automating the maintenance of purchase order records enables the preparation of such useful reports as a cash flow commitments schedule and a list of orders for which delivery is past due.

FIGURE 17.4
Sample purchase order.

NEEDMORE MANUFACTURING COMPANY				
PURCHASE ORDER	987 Glendale Needmore, Texas 78799		No. 12153	
TO	Avalon Electronics 401 Cherry Street Waco, Texas 78123		Show the above order number on all invoices and shipping papers	

Vendor number 8015	Order date 3/14/86	Req. number 27654	Buyer Dave Watson	Terms 2/10
F.O.B. Shipping point	Ship via express	Deliver on At once	Remarks	

Item number	Part number	Quantity	Description	Price
1	86402	20	Transistor	$1.44
2	78712	20	Diode	1.65
3	81296	10	Capacitor	2.40
		Buyer _____		

FIGURE 17.5

Document flow in a manual system for processing purchasing transactions.

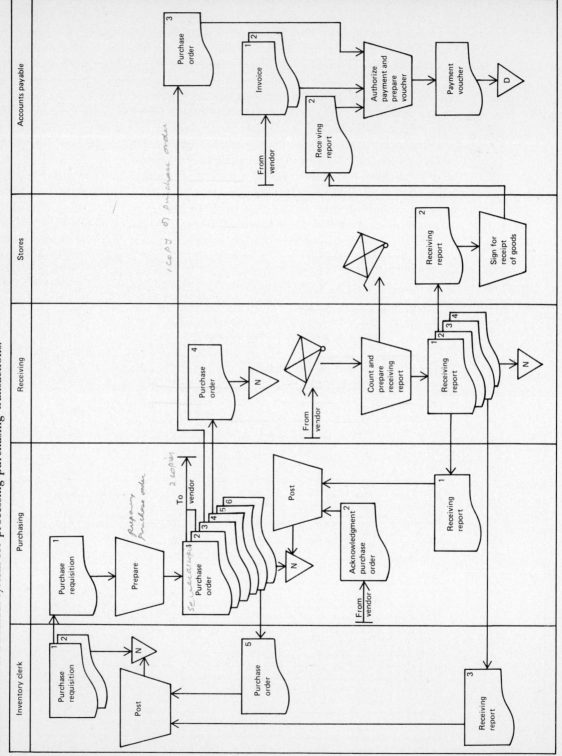

A manual system

The document flowchart of Fig. 17.5 illustrates one example of a manual system for processing purchase transactions in a manufacturing company. Most companies will differ in some respects from this example, but in most cases, the general pattern of information flow, even in nonmanufacturing organizations, will not vary a great deal from the illustration.

As the illustration shows, the purchasing process begins with the initiation of a *purchase requisition* by the inventory clerk. The purchase requisition, illustrated in Fig. 17.6, indicates that the supply of an item of inventory is low and a reorder is necessary. The quantity required and the number of the primary vendor are also indicated. One copy of each requisition prepared is sent to the purchasing department, and a second is filed by requisition number by the inventory clerk.

Using the purchase requisitions, the purchasing department prepares purchase orders. In some cases, the purchasing department may utilize a vendor other than the primary vendor or may change the order quantity to comply with the vendor's shipping quantity per package. Several copies of each purchase order are prepared. Two are generally sent to the vendor, with the request that one be returned as an acknowledgment. At least one copy is filed in the purchasing department, and other copies may be sent to the inventory clerk, accounts payable, and receiving.

The purchasing department records the receipt of acknowledgments from vendors, and also the receipts of items ordered, in the open purchase order file. Purchasing department personnel are responsible for following up on orders for which no acknowledgment has been received or for which delivery is overdue. In the event that goods received are damaged or do not pass quality inspection, the receiving report will so indicate, and the purchasing de-

FIGURE 17.6
Sample purchase requisition.

NEEDMORE MANUFACTURING COMPANY			Req. No. 1245		
PURCHASE REQUISITION			Date 2/10/86		
Date needed 2/15/86		Vendor code 3725	Prepared by J. Trimble		Department stores
Part number	Quantity	Description	Quantity on hand	Reorder point	Reorder quantity
72142	450	Shaft	40	100	400

partment must correspond with the vendor to arrange an appropriate adjustment.

Another copy of the purchase order is provided to the inventory clerk for posting to the "on order" field of the raw materials inventory records. Still another copy should be provided to the receiving department. This copy is filed by purchase order number and checked by receiving personnel when the goods are received to verify that the goods were actually ordered. For control purposes, the quantity ordered should not be included on this copy. This will encourage the receiving department personnel to carefully count the quantity of each item received.

When the goods are received by the receiving department, a document recording the receipt is prepared. An example of this document, called a receiving report, is illustrated in Fig. 17.7. Inspectors in the receiving department examine the goods for damage or poor quality, and an indication of acceptance or rejection of the goods is made on the receiving report. The receiving department files one copy of each receiving report by its document number. Another copy is routed to the purchasing department for posting to the open purchase order file. Still another copy is sent to the inventory clerk, where it is posted to the master inventory file. The receipt will increase the quantity on hand in the file and decrease the quantity on order. A final copy accompanies the goods to the storeroom and then is sent to the accounts payable department.

The transfer of custody of goods from the receiving department to the parts storeroom is a significant event for control purposes. The transfer of accounting control for the goods should be evidenced by the signature of stores

FIGURE 17.7
Sample receiving report.

RECEIVING REPORT			No. 6405
Prepared by	Date	"P.O." number	Vendor

Quantity	Units	Description

Delivered by	Inspected by _____
	Remarks:
Shipping weight	

personnel on the copy of the receiving report. Stores personnel must verify that the correct items have been received in the appropriate quantities prior to signing the receiving report because they are responsible for subsequent shortages. The signed copy of the receiving report is immediately routed to the accounts payable department. The signature ensures the accounts payable personnel that the goods for which they approve payment are safely in the custody of storeroom personnel.

The accounts payable department receives vendor invoices requesting payment for goods delivered. Before approving these invoices for payment, accounts payable clerks check each one against its corresponding receiving report and purchase order. The department maintains its own file of open purchase orders for this purpose. The purchase order is checked to ensure that the goods were ordered and that the quantities received and prices charged are consistent with the order. If the shipment is a partial shipment, the quantity received is posted to the purchase order. The receiving report is checked to ensure that the quantities received are equal to the quantities invoiced. The accuracy of the extensions on the vendor's invoice must be verified. Once all these steps have been completed, a voucher is prepared that authorizes the cash disbursement in payment of the invoice. These documents are then filed according to the due date of the invoice. Cash disbursement procedures are discussed in Chapter 20.

Organizational independence with respect to the purchasing function is achieved by separation of the operating function performed by the purchasing department from the custodial functions performed by the receiving and stores department. Furthermore, both of these functions are separated from the recording functions performed by the accounts payable department and the inventory clerk. This separation helps to ensure that only authorized orders are placed, and that all goods that are ordered are actually received and properly and accurately recorded.

Another significant control procedure with respect to raw materials inventories is the reconciliation of actual inventory quantities with the inventory records. This may be done on a periodic basis, with high-cost and high-usage items being reconciled more frequently than low-cost, low-usage items. In addition, this reconciliation should also be performed whenever it becomes obvious that there is a discrepancy; for example, when the inventory record shows a negative balance or when no parts are available even though the record shows a positive balance. These reconciliations should be performed by accounting department personnel who are independent of both inventory record keeping and stores.

The control policies exercised with respect to the purchasing operation and personnel are also important. Budgetary control over the cost of purchased raw materials might be achieved by a standard cost system in which the purchase price variance is the responsibility of the purchasing department head. Budgetary control over the purchase of supplies, or of merchandise in a retail organization, is often exercised over the department requesting the supplies or merchandise rather than over purchasing. To control the possibility that purchasing personnel might favor certain vendors who offer them gifts or kickbacks, a policy that no such gifts may be accepted by purchasing personnel should be enforced. Use of the purchase requisition as the basis for purchase order preparation also provides control in this sense in that the requisition evidences a definite need for the goods by the company. Finally, it may also be a good control policy to require that all purchasing employees involved in vendor selection make known any significant financial interest they may have in supplier companies.

A computer-based batch processing system

A document flowchart of the purchasing process for a typical manufacturing company that uses a computer-based system appears in Fig. 17.8. This illustration is merely an example rather than a description of the actual system of a real company. Much of the description is also applicable to nonmanufacturing organizations.

A comparison of Fig. 17.8 with its manual counterpart in Fig. 17.5 reveals that the computer has completely replaced the manual system's inventory clerk. However, the functions performed by purchasing, receiving, stores, and accounts payable are very similar in both systems. One minor difference is that the accounts payable department now prepares two copies of the voucher. One is filed in voucher number sequence, with the supporting invoice and receiving report documentation attached. The second copy is provided to the computer operations department as a source document for a computerized cash disbursements system (described in Chapter 20). Another difference is that the computer prepares purchase orders instead of the purchasing department. In addition, the computer generates two reports for the purchasing department and one for the controller, which may not have been available in the manual system.

A systems flowchart of the operations involved in the computerized purchasing system appears in Fig. 17.9. For purposes of simplification, the flowchart is separated by dashed lines into four major categories of operations: input preparation and data control, inventory processing, purchasing information processing, and vendor file processing and reporting. After coverage of each of these four areas of operation, this section concludes with a discussion of control policies and procedures in the system.

Input preparation and data control.   Each day, this operation begins with the assembly of inventory transaction source documents in batches and the preparation of batch totals. Note that inventory issues and other inventory transactions are processed along with receipts in one integrated process. The origination of issue documents is covered in Chapter 18.

Control totals that might be obtained for each batch of inventory transactions include record counts of the total number of transactions, the total number of issues, and the total number of receipts, as well as hash totals of

FIGURE 17.8
Document flow in computerized batch processing of purchase transactions.

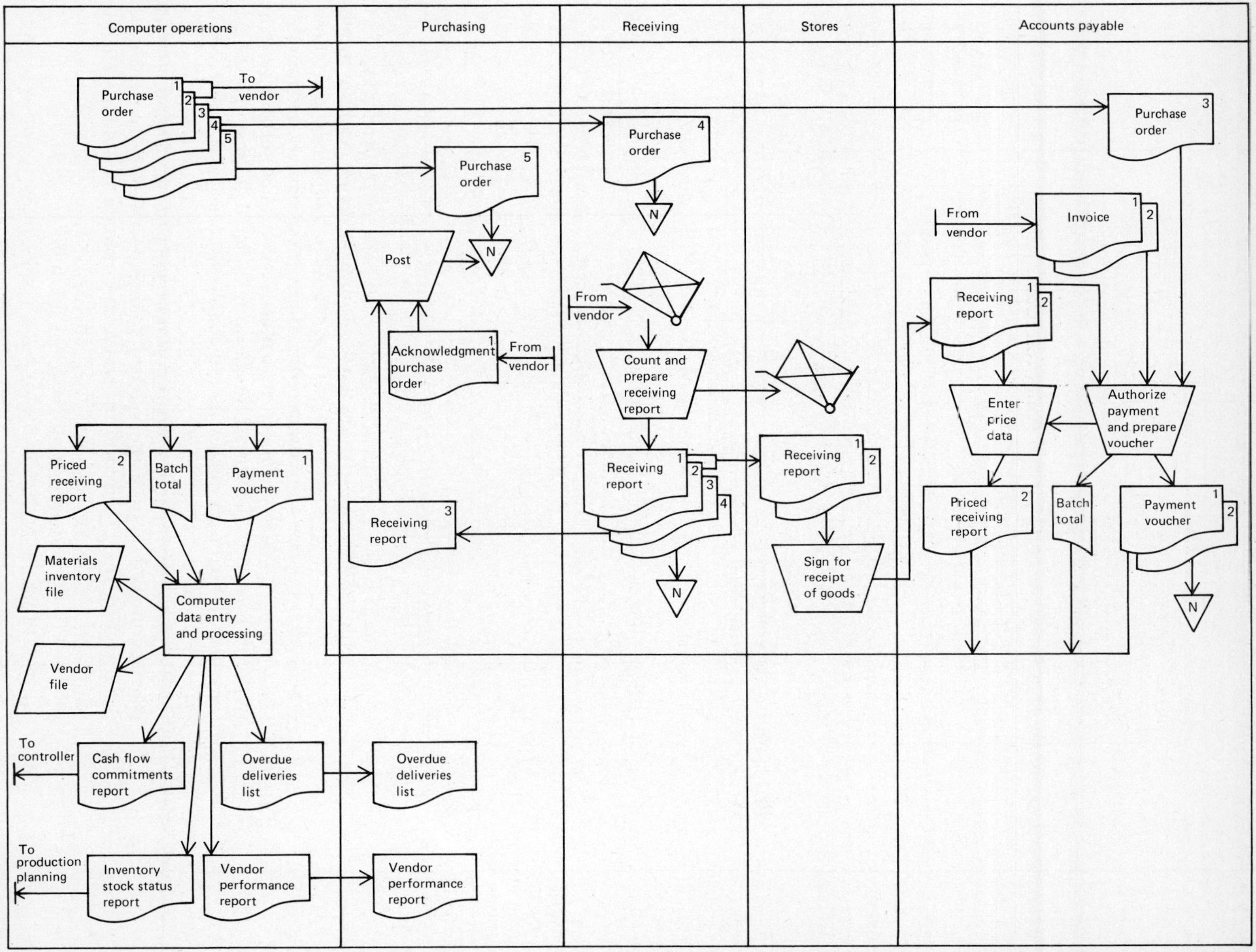

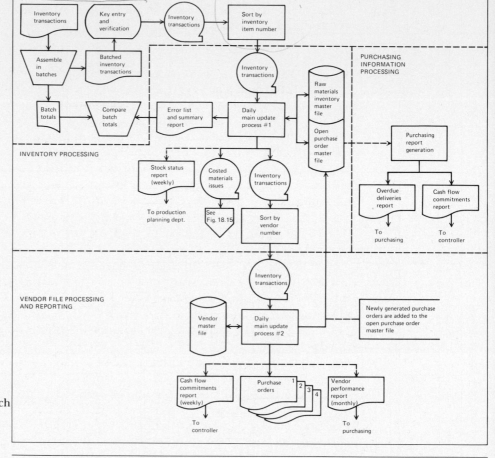

FIGURE 17.9
System flow in computer-based batch processing of purchasing and inventory transactions.

all inventory stock numbers, the number of units issued, and the number of units received. These batch totals are retained for comparison with those generated after the inventory update run. If any discrepancies are found in the comparison of batch totals, they may indicate that some records were lost or improperly processed. Subsequent checking in detail of those specific batches for which a discrepancy exists should enable discovery and correction of any errors.

The next step in input preparation is keying and verification of inventory transaction records from the batched source documents. It is assumed that these records are keyed onto magnetic tape using a key-to-tape encoder or key-to-disk-to-tape system. Alternative methods of input preparation include the use of punched cards or diskettes as an input medium.

Following the preparation of input records, the next step is to sort them into sequence by inventory item number. If the records are on magnetic tape as shown in Fig. 17.9, this step is performed on the computer using a tape sort program. The records are then ready for processing to update the raw materials inventory master file.

Inventory processing.   This step is performed daily and involves one main updating program. The inventory transaction records on magnetic tape are input to this program. The program sequentially accesses the raw materials inventory master file and updates the appropriate master file record for each transaction. This is the task performed by the inventory clerk in the manual system. Furthermore, for inventory receipt transactions, this program randomly accesses the appropriate purchase order master record, appends the quantity received to the appropriate line-item subrecord of the purchase order, subtracts the quantity received to determine a revised quantity on order, and then deletes from the file any purchase orders that have been completely filled. In the manual system, these steps are performed in the purchasing department.

This update run also generates a magnetic tape file containing costed materials issue records. Each record on this tape indicates the cost of an inventory item issued into production, determined on a FIFO, LIFO, or other basis from the cost data recorded on the inventory file. This tape is used in a computerized system of accounting for materials costs in production, as explained in Chapter 18.

Two output reports are also generated by the raw materials inventory updating program. One is a list of error transactions flagged by one or more input validation routines of the update program. This report also contains the batch totals mentioned above and summary journal entries for the inventory transactions, including the debit to raw materials inventory and the credit to accounts payable for inventory receipts. The second output report is a stock status report on the inventory file. The dashed line to this report indicates that this report is printed only once each week rather than every day. Copies of the stock status report might be provided to stores' personnel, for reference in stores-keeping operations, and to production planning personnel, for use in planning future production.

Another function of the materials inventory update program is to identify all inventory items for which the quantity available has fallen below the reorder point, so that an order for these items may be initiated. For such items a reorder record is created and added to the inventory transaction tape. When this program is finished, the inventory transaction tape is re-sorted by vendor number for subsequent processing to update the vendor master file.

Purchasing information processing.   Two reports may be generated using the data available in the open purchase order master file. One is an overdue deliveries report, which lists those orders for which the promised or expected delivery date has passed without the order having been received. This report is provided to the purchasing department for their use in following up on these orders and would probably be prepared weekly. The other report is a schedule of cash flow commitments as reflected in outstanding purchase orders. This report would be provided to the controller or treasurer for use in planning short-run cash flows and would also probably be generated on a weekly basis.

Vendor file processing and reporting. The vendor file processing program has two primary functions. One is to update the vendor master file for orders, receipts, returns, allowances, and any other transactions with each vendor. The other is to generate purchase order documents. Input to this program consists of the inventory transactions tape, which has been sorted into sequence by vendor number. The vendor master file may then be accessed sequentially to update the master record corresponding to each transaction.

If there are one or more purchase requisition or inventory reorder records for a particular vendor, a purchase order to that vendor is initiated. For each purchase order, the vendor's name and address, shipping arrangements, and credit terms are pulled from the vendor master file. The quantity to be ordered and other relevant inventory data are obtained from the input record. A purchase order number is assigned sequentially to each order according to the next highest number available on the open purchase order master file. An original and three copies of each new purchase order are then printed out, and the new purchase order record is also added to the open purchase order master file.

Two reports may be prepared as a by-product of the vendor file processing run. One is a short-run cash flow commitments schedule, based upon disbursement authorization records contained in the vendor master file. Like its counterpart generated from the open purchase order master, this report would probably be prepared once weekly and would be provided to the controller or treasurer for use in short-term cash management. The second report deals with vendor performance and represents a summary of past transactions with particular vendors, highlighting such matters as compliance with requested delivery dates, discrepancies between quantities ordered and quantities received, discrepancies between prices quoted and prices billed, and number of defective items received. This report would probably be generated monthly for each vendor or on a demand basis when requested for a specific vendor. The vendor performance report goes to the purchasing department for use in vendor selection.

Control policies and procedures. Among the control policies and procedures that might be used in this system for computerized batch processing of purchasing and inventory information are two that have already been mentioned—keyverification of inventory transaction records and batch totals. This section will discuss other examples in the areas of data security and input validation.

Data security in this operation primarily involves the master disk files of open purchase orders, raw materials inventory, and vendor records, as well as the tapes of inventory transactions and costed materials issues. Each of these files should have appropriate internal and external labels to prevent their being processed by the wrong program or on the wrong date. Tape file protection rings should be removed from the transaction tapes after they are written to prevent the data on them from being written over or erased during subsequent processing. Duplicate versions of the three disk master files should be periodically written onto magnetic tape, and subsequent transaction tapes should be saved to permit reconstruction of any master file whose contents are destroyed. Current copies of these tape and disk files should be stored in a file library when not in use and removed only when properly authorized. The backup copies of these files should be stored in a secure off-site location.

The inventory update program should contain an input validation routine that performs various edit checks on the inventory transactions. These would include a validity check on transaction codes, on the inventory item number, and on the vendor number. Check digit verification might be performed on stock numbers for all transactions adding new master records to the file. A field check should be performed on numeric fields in each record such as quantity and unit cost. The input records should be checked for correctness in sequence, and any records out of sequence should be rejected. A reasonableness test might also be performed on the quantity and unit cost on each input record relative to the corresponding values of those items on the inventory master file. Any issue transactions that reduce the balance on hand as recorded in the inventory master to a negative amount should be flagged for review. The list of error transactions containing items that fail to pass one or more of these tests should be reviewed by data control personnel, and each error should be corrected prior to resubmitting the transaction in the next day's run. Similar edit checks might also be included in the vendor file processing run.

A real-time system

In a manufacturing company, a real-time system for purchasing and inventory management maintains online files of open purchase orders, materials inventories, and vendor information. These files are updated immediately upon the occurrence of all order transactions, including initiation of purchase orders, receipt of order acknowledgments, receipt of deliveries, counts and inspections of items received, and transfer of items received to stores. Terminals providing online access to the system would be available to the purchasing, receiving, and stores departments, as well as to production planning and accounting personnel.

Based upon a master production schedule maintained as part of an MRP or JIT system, purchase orders would be automatically generated by the system at the time specified by the schedule. The system would also provide for generation of purchase orders based upon manual entry of purchase requisition data.

In the receiving department, deliveries are checked against open orders on the system prior to delivery acceptance. Discrepancies between orders and receipts with respect to quantities, prices, delivery dates, or other terms are highlighted by the system on the terminal display to facilitate the delivery acceptance process. The receiving department terminal is then used for online entry of the details of each receipt transaction.

The purchasing department utilizes this system to obtain real-time access to information useful in a variety of ways. The system can analyze the status of any open purchase order or orders to generate order status reports by inventory item, by vendor, or by purchase order. The system also generates reports of vendor quotations for any inventory item, and summary reports of vendor performance, to assist purchasing agents in vendor selection. The system also monitors delivery receipts relative to scheduled delivery dates and automatically generates reports of overdue deliveries.

Accounting personnel utilize the system to check receipts against invoices as part of the disbursement authorization process. Real-time reports of short-term cash flow commitments reflected in open purchase orders and unpaid disbursement vouchers may also be generated on demand to assist in financial planning.

Production planning personnel utilize the system to check the status of materials inventories on hand and on order. This information is essential for production scheduling. Further discussion of computer-based production planning and control is provided in the following chapter.

Real-time purchasing and inventory management systems are also commonly used in retail establishments having large sales volumes, such as grocery, clothing, and department stores. A key element of this system is a point-of-sale (POS) terminal from which retail sales transactions are entered as they occur. These transactions are immediately posted to perpetual inventory records maintained in an online file. At frequent intervals these records are automatically examined by the system, and orders are initiated as needed to replenish the stock.

Effective internal controls are essential to the operation of a real-time purchasing and inventory management system. Among the more critical controls are access controls, compatibility tests of transaction entries, editing and validation of input data, reasonableness testing of input data, flagging of unusual conditions such as negative inventory balances or receipts of unordered items, and maintenance of transaction logs and backup files.

Summary

The accounting information system plays a key role in providing information for purchasing and inventory management. The system maintains materials inventory and vendor master files and generates information useful for inventory ordering, vendor selection, financial forecasting, production planning, the monitoring of order status. Purchasing and inventory data processing may be accomplished by using a manual data processing system or by using a computer-based system operating either in a batch processing mode or in a real-time mode.

Although this chapter has emphasized the purchasing and inventory management problems of manufacturing companies, many of the concepts and procedures described here are equally applicable to wholesale and retail enterprises that purchase inventories for resale.

The purchasing function is closely interrelated with the finance and production planning functions. Financial planners utilize information in the purchasing data base to forecast short-term cash flows. Production planners utilize inventory and order status information to assist them in scheduling production.

Review Questions

1. Define the following terms.

   logistics management   just-in-time system

   materials requirements planning   purchase requisition

2. Describe or illustrate an example of a typical production organization structure.

3. What are three basic decisions for which the purchasing department is responsible? Describe the decision criteria and related information requirements for making these decisions.

4. Describe two alternative approaches to the inventory control function.

5. What accounting journal entries summarize the activities involved in the processing of purchase transactions?

6. Describe the data content and organization of the purchasing and raw materials inventory data base. Identify input transactions to this data base, and output reports generated from it.

7. What departments in a business organization might be involved in the manual processing of purchase transactions? What documents might be used and what data would each contain? In what department would each document originate, and where and for what purposes would each be distributed?

8. Describe the nature and purpose of the receiving report.

9. What control policies and procedures are involved in manual processing of purchase transactions in a typical business organization?

10. How is organizational independence achieved with respect to the processing of purchase transactions?

11. Describe possible similarities and differences in processing of purchase transactions using a computer rather than a manual system. Emphasize documents, departments, and reports involved in the process.

12. Explain how and by what department in an organization each of the following reports might be used:
    a) stock status report
    b) cash flow commitments summary
    c) overdue deliveries listing
    d) vendor performance report

13. Describe several control policies and procedures that might be used in batch processing of purchase transactions by a business organization using a computer.

14. Describe the nature and function of a real-time system applied to the purchasing function of a typical business organization.

Discussion Questions

15. The purchasing process described in this chapter related to a single plant or store. What differences would exist in the information system of a multiplant or multistore company in which the purchasing operation is centralized?

16. The computerized system described in this chapter prepared purchase orders as one of its outputs. A simplifying assumption was made that each item of inventory was purchased from only one vendor. Under what circumstances might it be more appropriate to select a vendor at the time of placing the purchase order? How would the design of the computerized system have to be revised to do this?

Problems and Cases

17. What internal controls relating to a purchasing procedure would provide the best protection against the following situations?
    a) A purchasing agent ordered unnecessary goods from a company of which he is one of the officers.
    b) A vendor overcharged for goods purchased.
    c) There was an error in the vendor's favor in calculating the total on an invoice.
    d) Inventory was stolen by stores personnel who claim to have never received the goods from the receiving department.
    e) A vendor invoiced the company for a greater quantity of goods than were received.
    f) A vendor delivered unordered goods and sent an invoice requesting payment for them.
    g) A vendor sent two copies of an invoice. The copies became separated and eventually two checks in payment of the two copies of the same invoice were prepared and mailed.

18. Long, CPA, has been engaged to examine and report on the financial statements of Maylou Corporation. During the review phase of the study of Maylou's system of internal accounting control over purchases, Long was given the document flowchart for purchases shown in Fig. 17.10.

   a) Identify the procedures, relating to purchase requisitions and purchase orders, that Long would expect to find if Maylou's system of internal accounting control over purchases is effective. For example, purchase orders are prepared only after giving proper consideration to the time to order, and quantity to order. Do not comment on the effectiveness of the flow of documents as presented in the flowchart or on separation of duties.

   b) What are the factors to consider in determining
      i) the time to order?
      ii) the quantity to order? (CPA Examination)

19. Lecimore Company has a centralized purchasing department which is managed by Joan Jones. Jones has established policies and procedures to guide the clerical staff and purchasing agents in the day-to-day operation of the department. She is satisfied that these policies and procedures are in conformity with company objectives and believes there are no major problems in the regular operations of the Purchasing Department.

   Lecimore's Internal Audit Department was assigned to perform an operational audit of the purchasing function. Their first task was to review the specific policies and procedures established by Jones. The policies and procedures are as follows:

   ☐ All significant purchases are made on a competitive bid basis. The probability of timely delivery, reliability of vendor, etc., are taken into consideration on a subjective basis.

FIGURE 17.10

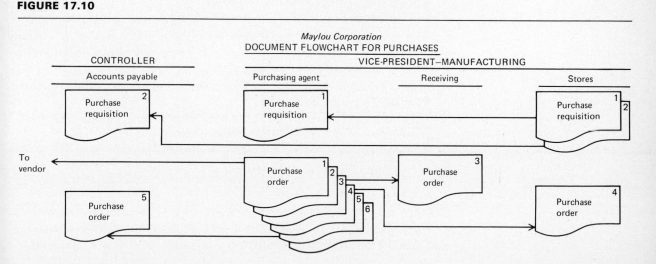

Maylou Corporation
DOCUMENT FLOWCHART FOR PURCHASES

☐ Detailed specifications of the minimum acceptable quality for all goods purchased are provided to vendors.

☐ Vendor's adherence to the quality specifications is the responsibility of the Materials Manager of the Inventory Control Department and not the Purchasing Department. The Materials Manager inspects the goods as they arrive to be sure the quality meets the minimum standards and then sees that the goods are transferred from the receiving dock to the storeroom.

☐ All purchase requests are prepared by the Materials Manager based upon the production schedule for a four-month period.

The internal audit staff then observed the operations of the purchasing function and gathered the following findings:

☐ One vendor provides 90 percent of the critical raw material. This vendor has a good delivery record and is very reliable. Furthermore, this vendor has been the low bidder over the past few years.

☐ As production plans change, rush and expedite orders are made by production directly to the Purchasing Department. Materials ordered for cancelled production runs are stored for future use. The costs of these special requests are borne by the Purchasing Department. Jones considers the additional costs associated with these special requests as "costs of being a good member of the corporate team."

☐ Materials to accomplish engineering changes are ordered by the Purchasing Department as soon as the changes are made by the Engineering Department. Jones is very proud of the quick response by the purchasing staff to product changes. Materials on hand are not reviewed before any orders are placed.

☐ Partial shipments and advance shipments (i.e., those received before the requested date of delivery) are accepted by the Materials Manager who notifies the Purchasing Department of the receipt. The Purchasing Department is responsible for follow-up on partial shipments. No action is taken to discourage advance shipments.

REQUIRED

Based upon the Purchasing Department's policies and procedures and the findings of Lecimore's internal audit staff:

1. identify weaknesses and/or inefficiencies in Lecimore Company's purchasing function, and
2. make recommendations for those weaknesses/inefficiencies which you identify.

Use the following format in preparing your response.

Weaknesses/Inefficiencies   *Recommendations*
1.   1.

(CMA Examination)

20. The accounting and internal control procedures relating to purchases of materials by the Branden Company, a medium-sized concern manufac-

turing special machinery to order, have been described by your junior accountant in the following terms:

After approval by manufacturing department supervisors, materials purchase requisitions are forwarded to the purchasing department supervisor who distributes such requisitions to the several employees under his control. The latter employees prepare prenumbered purchase orders in triplicate, account for all numbers, and send the original purchase order to the vendor. One copy of the purchase order is sent to the receiving department in which it is used as a receiving report. The other copy is filed in the purchasing department.

When the materials are received, they are moved directly to the storeroom and issued to the supervisors on informal requests. The receiving department sends a receiving report (with its copy of the purchase order attached) to the purchasing department and forwards copies of the receiving report to the storeroom and to the accounting department.

Vendors' invoices for material purchases, received in duplicate in the mailroom, are sent to the purchasing department and directed to the employee who placed the related order. The employee then compares the invoice with the copy of the purchase order on file in the purchasing department for price and terms and compares the invoice quantity received as reported by the shipping and receiving department on its copy of the purchase order. The purchasing department employees also check discounts, footings, and extensions after which they initial the invoice to indicate approval for payment. The invoice is then submitted to the voucher section of the accounting department where it is coded for account distribution, assigned a voucher number, entered in the voucher register, and filed according to payment due date.

REQUIRED

Discuss the weaknesses, if any, in the internal control of Branden's purchasing and subsequent procedures. Suggest supplementary or revised procedures for remedying each weakness with regard to (a) requisition of materials and (b) receipt and storage of materials. (CPA Examination)

21. You have been engaged by the management of Alden, Inc., to review its internal control over the purchase, receipt, storage, and issue of raw materials. You have prepared the following comments which describe Alden's procedures.

☐ Raw materials, which consist mainly of high-cost electronic components, are kept in a locked storeroom. Storeroom personnel include a supervisor and four clerks. All are well trained, competent, and adequately bonded. Raw materials are removed from the storeroom only upon written or oral authorization of one of the production foremen.

☐ There are no perpetual-inventory records; hence, the storeroom clerks do not keep records of goods received or issued. To compensate for the lack of perpetual records, a physical-inventory count is taken monthly by the storeroom clerks who are well supervised. Appropriate procedures are followed in making the inventory count.

☐ After the physical count, the storeroom supervisor matches quantities counted against a predetermined reorder level. If the count for a given part is below the reorder level, the supervisor enters the part number on a materials-requisition list and sends this list to the accounts-payable clerk. The accounts-payable clerk prepares a purchase order for a predetermined reorder quantity for each part and mails the purchase order to the vendor from whom the part was last purchased.

☐ When ordered materials arrive at Alden, they are received by the storeroom clerks. The clerks count the merchandise and check to see that the counts agree with the shipper's bill of lading. All vendors' bills of lading are initialed, dated, and filed in the storeroom to serve as receiving reports.

REQUIRED

Describe the weaknesses in internal control and recommend improvements of Alden's procedures for the purchase, receipt, storage, and issue of raw materials. Organize your answer sheet as follows. (CPA Examination)

Weaknesses	Recommended improvements

22. Figure 17.11 shows a document flowchart prepared by an accounting clerk to document purchasing and cash disbursement procedures for EBM, Inc. As a systems analyst, point out the weaknesses in the procedures and describe inefficiencies or manipulations that could occur as a result of these weaknesses.

23. Anthony, CPA, prepared the flowchart (Fig. 17.12) which portrays the raw materials purchasing function of one of Anthony's clients, a medium-sized manufacturing company, from the preparation of initial documents through the vouching of invoices for payment in accounts payable. The flowchart was a portion of the work performed on the audit engagement to evaluate internal control.

REQUIRED

Identify and explain the systems and control weaknesses evident from the flowchart. Include the internal control weaknesses resulting from activities performed or not performed. All documents are prenumbered. (CPA Examination)

24. Wooster Company is a beauty and barber supplies and equipment distributorship servicing a five state area. Management generally has been pleased with the overall operations of the company to-date. However, the

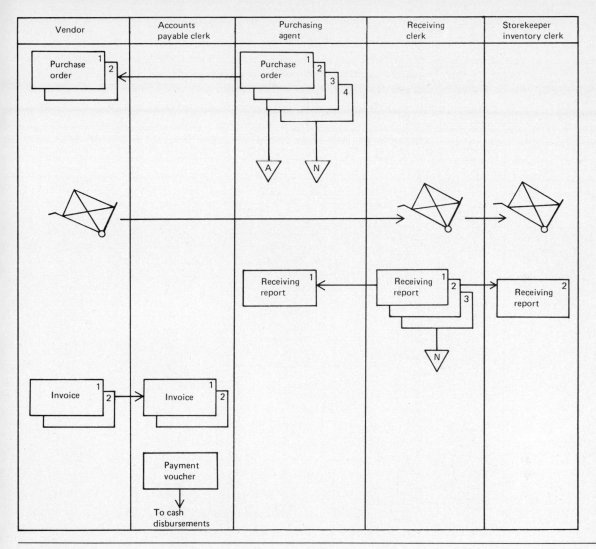

FIGURE 17.11

present purchasing system has evolved through practice rather than having been formally designed. Consequently, it is inadequate and needs to be redesigned.

A description of the present purchasing system is as follows. Whenever the quantity of an item is low, the inventory supervisor phones the purchasing department with the item description and quantity to be ordered. A purchase order is prepared in duplicate in the purchasing department. The original is sent to the vendor, and the copy is retained in the purchasing department filed in numerical order. When the shipment

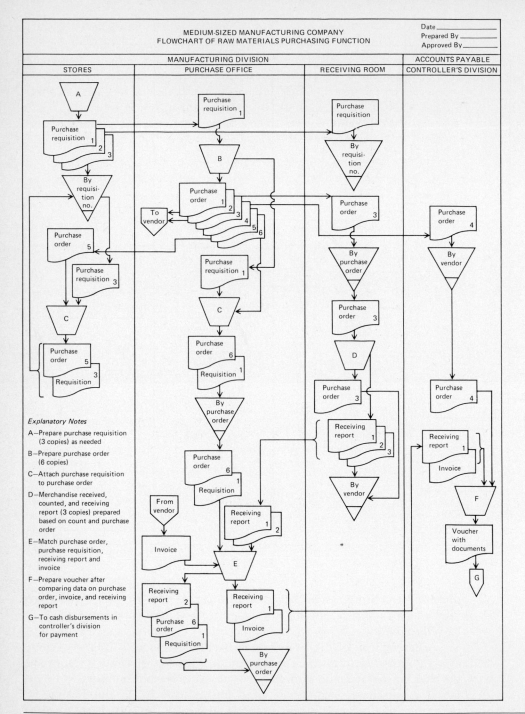

FIGURE 17.12

arrives, the inventory supervisor sees that each item received is checked off on the packing slip which accompanies the shipment. The packing slip is then forwarded to the accounts payable department. When the invoice arrives, the packing slip is compared with the invoice in the accounts payable department. Once any differences between the packing slip and the invoice are reconciled, a check is drawn for the appropriate amount and is mailed to the vendor with a copy of the invoice. The packing slip is attached to the invoice and filed alphabetically in the paid invoice file.

REQUIRED

Wooster Company intends to redesign its purchasing system from the point in time when an item needs to be ordered until payment is made. The system should be designed to ensure that all of the proper controls are incorporated into the system.

a) Identify the internally and externally generated documents that would be required to satisfy the minimum requirements of a basic system and indicate the number of copies of each document that would be needed.

b) Explain how all of these documents should interrelate and flow among Wooster's various departments including the final destination or file for each copy. (CMA Examination)

25. Tralor Corporation manufactures and sells several different lines of small electric components. Its Internal Audit Department completed an audit of the expenditure cycle for the company. Part of the audit involved a review of the internal accounting controls for payables including the controls over the authorization of transactions, the accounting for transactions, and the protection of assets. The following comments appear in the internal audit staff's working papers.

a) Routine purchases are initiated by user activities on authorized purchase requests. Such purchases are actually made by the Purchasing Department using prenumbered purchase orders approved by authorized purchasing agents. The original of the five-part purchase order goes to the vendor, a copy is retained in Purchasing, a copy is sent to the user department, a copy is sent to the Receiving Department to be used as a receiving report, and a copy is sent to the accounts payable section of the Accounting Department.

b) Because of complex technical and performance criteria, purchases of specialized goods and services are negotiated directly between the user department and the vendor. Established procedures require that the specialist-user and the Purchasing Department approve invoices for such purchases prior to recording and payment. Strict budgetary control of such purchases is maintained at the specialist-user level.

c) The accounts payable section maintains a list of persons in Purchasing authorized to approve purchase orders and of persons in operating departments authorized to approve invoices for specialized pur-

conlin not upto date

chases. The list was last updated two years ago and is seldom used by accounts payable clerks.

d) All vendor invoices are numbered upon receipt and recorded in a pre-voucher register. The register is annotated to indicate the dates invoices involving special purchases are forwarded to operating departments for approval, and the dates they are returned. Review of the register indicated that there were seven open invoices for special purchases which had been forwarded to operating departments for approval over thirty days ago and had not yet been returned.

e) Prior to making entries in accounting records, a transaction audit is performed by an accounts payable clerk. This involves matching the accounts payable copy of the purchase order with a copy of a properly authorized receiving report and the vendor's invoice, or obtaining departmental approval of invoices for special purchases. Other aspects of the transaction audit involve checking the mathematical accuracy of all documents and determining the appropriate accounting distribution.

f) After invoices are recorded in the approved voucher register, they are filed in alphabetical order. Unpaid invoices are processed for payment on the 5th and 20th of each month, and all cash discounts are taken whether or not earned.

g) Supporting documents are cancelled upon payment by an authorized person in the treasurer function who signs the checks. Payments are made based upon original documents only.

h) Pre-numbered blank checks are kept in a locked safe and access is limited to authorized persons. Other documents and records maintained by the accounts payable section are readily accessible to all persons assigned to the section and to others in the accounting function.

REQUIRED

Review the eight comments which appear in the internal audit staff's working papers. Determine whether the internal audit staff's findings indicate that a strength or weakness exists in the controls of the expenditure cycle.

a) For each internal control **strength** identified, explain how the described procedure contributes toward achieving good authorization, accounting, or asset protection controls.

b) For each internal control **weakness** identified, explain why it is a weakness and present a recommendation to correct the weakness. (CMA Examination)

Use the following format to present your answer.

Comment number	Strength(s) or weakness(es)	Explanation as to why finding is a strength or weakness	Recommendation to correct weakness

26. What internal controls in a computerized inventory update program should provide the best control over the following situations?

   a) Posting of an inventory receipt to the wrong file record owing to an incorrect item number.

   b) Failure to process several inventory transactions because the cards were lost while being brought to the computer center from the keypunch room.

   c) Processing of an issue transaction in which the quantity issued was erroneous, with the result that the on-hand balance in the inventory record fell below zero.

   d) Erasure of the only copy of the inventory master tape owing to inadvertent use of the tape as an output file in another program.

   e) Posting of an inventory receipt on which the item cost was erroneously keypunched as $20.00; the correct unit cost was $2.00.

   f) Owing to several miscellaneous errors occurring over a period of several years, a large discrepancy arose between the quantity on hand of an important subassembly and the balance on hand according to the inventory master.

27. Culp Electronics Company processes inventory receipts as they arrive at the receiving dock by means of online data terminals located in the Receiving Department. All of the six Receiving Department employees have been taught to operate the terminals. Each inventory receipt entered into the system is processed to update the appropriate records in both (1) an inventory master file and (2) a file of open purchase orders.

REQUIRED
   a) What items of data should be entered into the system each time an operator uses the terminal to report the receipt of a shipment?

   b) Describe several means by which the system could be programmed to check the accuracy and validity of the input data entered from the Receiving Department. Relate your answer specifically to the data items mentioned in part (a).

28. The Doyle Company processes its inventory transactions by computer. Data on inventory receipts, issues, and other file changes are keyed directly from source documents onto magnetic tape using key-to-tape encoders. The transaction tape is then sorted and processed to update an inventory file maintained on a magnetic disk unit. Outputs of this process include a list of items to be reordered on magnetic tape, a printed stock status report, and a summary printout listing error transactions and run totals.

REQUIRED
   a) Prepare a systems flowchart of all operations described above.

   b) Describe a comprehensive set of control policies and procedures for this computerized inventory processing system. Describe the nature and purpose of each policy or procedure. Be sure to relate each policy or procedure specifically to the data and operations of the system as described above.

29. Your company has just acquired a data base management system, and one of the first applications of it will be to purchasing data. A purchase order identical to that in Fig. 17.4 is used. You are to diagram the data structure of the purchase order as a first step in the application design. Use a format similar to that in Fig. 17.2. Note that the data base will contain only the variable data on the purchase order, not the constant data.

30. Prepare a systems flowchart of the real-time purchasing and inventory management information system for a manufacturing company described in this chapter.

31. You are to design an integrated system for processing purchase transactions using magnetic disk file storage. The system maintains an inventory master file, an open purchase order master file, and a vendor history file, all on the disk. System inputs are receipts and issues of inventory keyed in as they occur from receiving or stores. System outputs are batches of purchase orders, each in four copies, and periodically generated reports of cash flow commitments, overdue deliveries, and vendor performance.

    The system outputs are generated by programs that are separate from the main update program. The main program begins by updating the inventory master file. If the balance of the item falls below its reorder point, the item is written onto a reorder file on a separate disk. This file is processed at the end of each day to prepare the purchase orders.

    The main program then updates the open purchase order file for inventory receipts. If a receipt completes the purchase order, the purchase order is deleted from the file, and vendor performance data obtained from the completed purchase order is then processed to update the appropriate vendor history record.

    The purchase order preparation program operates on the reorder list after that list has been sequenced by vendor code number. This program accesses the vendor history file to obtain the name and address associated with each vendor number from the reorder file. It then generates the completed production order, adds it to the open purchase order file, and writes the purchase order.

REQUIRED
    a) Prepare a systems flowchart of this system.
    b) Prepare a macroflowchart of the main update program.
    c) Prepare a macroflowchart of the purchase order preparation program.

32. Electrophonics Ltd. assembles electronic equipment of a specialized nature from parts purchased from a number of different vendors. Three product lines (burglar alarms, automatic telephone answering systems, and telephone amplifiers) are handled by three separate product departments, which make use of a single, small purchasing department responsible for purchase orders, inventory control, and cash disbursements to vendors. All purchases of components are made on credit. This purchasing de-

partment consists of a manager who investigates and selects the vendors, a data entry clerk, and a stock control clerk who receives and issues inventory items.

The purchasing department has ordered a mini-computer to be dedicated to this function. All files will be stored on magnetic disk. The computer will support two main systems. The first is responsible for processing purchase orders, receiving invoices from vendors, and generating payment authorizations. The second is responsible for registering the receipt of items to inventory and the issue of items from inventory, and for producing lists of approved vendors and products, and current inventory levels. Because of the volatile nature of the business, re-order decisions are made by the three product-line departments. In this problem we are solely concerned with the first system. The following narrative describes the proposed operation of this system.

Purchase requisition forms (PRF) will be received from each of the three product-line departments. Once each day, the batch of requisitions will be keyed into the computer. A program called "Purchase Requisition Log" (PRLP) will check that each field on the purchase order is complete, and of the right data type, and enter the details on a file for unsorted purchase requisitions (UPRF). Once all orders are entered, a program called "Purchase Requisition Sort" (PRSP) will sort all requisitions by vendor number, creating a file for sorted purchase requisitions (SPRF). The completion of this program will trigger a third, called "Purchase Order Generate" (POGP) which will access data from a vendor file (VF) and print actual purchase orders (APO) for transmittal to the vendor. Each purchase order will contain all items to be ordered from the vendor in question, and will be assigned a purchase order number. This program will also add the new purchase orders to a file of "pending purchase orders" (PPOF), creating an updated file of pending purchase orders (UPPOF).

Towards the end of each day, all invoices received that day from vendors (VI) will be keyed in. A program called "Vendor Invoice Log" (VILP) will check that the invoice contains a purchase order number, and create an unsorted file for new vendor invoices (UVIF).

Finally, a program called "Match Orders to Invoices" (MOIP) will process the items in the unsorted vendor invoice file (UVIF), against the current inventory status file (CISF) (which contains details of receipts to inventory), and the pending purchase orders file. This program will use the updated pending purchase orders file (UPPOF) to create the new pending purchase order file (PPOF) by removing orders that have arrived, and print checks for vendor payments (VP) including vendor name, amount, and purchase order number. It will also print address labels (AL), containing vendor name and address.

REQUIRED

a) Using standard symbols, draw a systems flowchart for the operations described in the above narrative. Place the letter abbreviations used in the question in each box.

b) As described, the system is incomplete. Excluding possible controls, or additional reports that *might* be useful to management, identify three additional output files or reports that are essential for the operation of the system as described, and state which program would produce them.

c) Apart from the simple edit checks in the "Purchase Requisition Log" program, and the "Vendor Invoice Log" program, no controls are built into the system. Identify and describe three desirable manual or computer controls. (SMAC Examination)

References

Arthur Andersen & Co. *A Guide for Studying and Evaluating Internal Accounting Controls.* Chicago: Arthur Andersen & Co., 1978.

Bonczek, Robert H.; Clyde W. Holsapple; and Andrew B. Whinston. "Aiding Decision Makers with a Generalized Data Base Management System: An Application to Inventory Management." *Decision Sciences* (April 1978): 228–245.

Burton, Terence T. "Get Back to Basics with MRP." *Internal Auditor* (October 1979): 66–76.

Donelson, William S., II. "MRP—Who Needs It?" *Datamation* (May 1979): 185–194.

Hall, Robert W., and Thomas E. Vollmann. "Planning Your Material Requirements." *Harvard Business Review* (September/October 1978): 105–112.

Keegan, Daniel P. "Some Second Reflections on MRP." *Price Waterhouse & Company Review* (1977, No. 3): 38–43.

Kraljic, Peter. "Purchasing Must Become Supply Management." *Harvard Business Review* (September/October 1983): 109–117.

Miller, Jeffrey G., and Peter Gilmour. "Materials Managers: Who Needs Them?" *Harvard Business Review* (July/August 1979): 143–153.

Miller, Jeffrey G., and Linda G. Sprague. "Behind the Growth in Materials Requirements Planning." *Harvard Business Review* (September/October 1975): 83–91.

Nakano, Jinichiro, and Robert W. Hall. "Management Specs for Stockless Production." *Harvard Business Review* (May/June 1983): 84–91.

Price Waterhouse & Co. *Guide to Accounting Controls: Purchases & Payables.* New York: Price Waterhouse & Co., 1979.

Sadhwani, Arjan T., M. H. Sarhan, and Dayal Kiringoda. "Just-in-Time: An Inventory System Whose Time Has Come." *Management Accounting* (December 1985): 36–44.

Wagner, Harvey M. *Principles of Operations Research.* 2d ed. Englewood Cliffs, N.J.: Prentice-Hall, 1975.

C H A P T E R   1 8

Accounting Information Systems for Production Management

LEARNING OBJECTIVES

Careful study of this chapter should enable students to:

☐ Describe the decision responsibilities and information requirements of production management.

☐ Describe the information provided to production management by the accounting information system.

☐ Prepare flowcharts describing data and information flows within a production management information system.

☐ Design and evaluate control policies and procedures for a production data processing system.

Production management involves planning and controlling the process of manufacturing a product. It encompasses determining what should be produced, specifying how and when it should be produced, and monitoring the steps in the production process. The production management function must be closely coordinated with the purchasing and inventory management function described in the previous chapter. The nature of the production management function, and of the information systems that serve it, constitutes the subject of this chapter.

The Production Management Function

Referring to the organization chart in Fig. 17.1, we observe that the production management function is primarily the responsibility of the production planning department, the plant manager, the general supervisor, and the various production department supervisors. Generally the production planning department is responsible for planning and scheduling of production, whereas the plant manager, general supervisor, and departmental supervisors are responsible for the coordination and control of production operations. Important service functions to these activities are performed by the engineering, maintenance, and stores departments.

Production planning

The production planning function involves determining what should be produced and when it should be produced. Closely related to production planning is the engineering function of determining how a given product should be produced.

Deciding what should be produced consists basically of establishing the appropriate quantities of each product to be manufactured during a given time period. The decision process encompasses the specification of a suitable mix of styles, sizes, colors, and other features. For those firms that manufacture goods to customer orders, this aspect of production planning may be quite simple, especially if there is a large *backlog* of orders that have been received but not filled. However, those firms that manufacture goods for inventory must utilize information on both current inventory levels and forecasted sales by product for making these decisions.

The engineering function involves establishing, for each product or subassembly the firm manufactures, the standard quantity of each raw material or part required for the product, the precise labor operations required for each product, the standard amount of time each operation should consume, and the workstation or machine at which each operation should be performed. These specifications are developed for a product at the time when it is first introduced into the firm's product line and may be revised periodically thereafter. Materials specifications for a product are embodied in a document called a *bill of materials*, illustrated in Fig. 18.1. Labor operations, with their corresponding machine requirements and standard time requirements,

BILL OF MATERIALS				
Assembly No. 2742816	Assembly Name Miniature Calculator	Page 1 of 2	Approved by FDK	Date 1-9-86
Part Number	Description			Quantity per Assembly
7054396	Calculator Unit			1
4069136	Lower Casing			1
1954207	Screw			8
3099218	Battery			1
4069245	Upper Casing			1
1954209	Screw			6

FIGURE 18.1
Bill of materials.

are indicated on a document called an *operations list* or *routing sheet,* illustrated
in Fig. 18.2. Copies of both these documents are prepared and kept current
by the engineering department for every item produced and are used extensively in production planning and control. In a firm that uses a standard cost
system, the standard materials cost per unit and standard labor rate per operation might also be included on the bill of materials and operations list,
respectively.

Planning the specific time at which product items will be manufactured
is referred to as production scheduling. The scheduler must know what quantities of each product are to be produced, what resource requirements exist

FIGURE 18.2
Operations list.

OPERATIONS LIST					
Stock number	Description		Date prepared	By	
Dept. no.	Oper. no.	Operation description	Machine requirements	Stand. hours	Set-up hours

for each product, and what resources are available. Determination of the quantities to be produced is the stage in production planning that precedes scheduling. Resource requirements are then established by multiplying the quantity of each product to be produced by the standard per unit requirements specified in the bill of materials and operations list for the product. Three types of resources—materials, labor, and equipment—must be brought together at the same point in time for production to occur. The availability of these resources is made known to the scheduler by materials stock status reports, personnel reports, and machine availability and capacity reports. The scheduler must coordinate the work of all production employees and the use of all available machines and materials throughout the plant to achieve maximum production at a minimum expenditure of time and resources. His or her output is a production schedule for each factory production department—a schedule that indicates what jobs must be performed within that department during the period covered by the schedule.

Finally, the production scheduler must know the relative priorities of the various items in the process of production. Some items will have high priority because they are out of stock, backordered, rush ordered, or behind schedule for a promised delivery date. Such high-priority items must be given preference over lower-priority items in production scheduling and operations.

Operations control   The operations control function includes all activities related to expediting, coordinating, and controlling the operations of the various production departments. At least three basic standards—time standards, cost standards, and quality standards—must be met in this function. Time standards are embodied in the operations lists, which in turn are embodied in the production schedule. The control function with respect to time standards is carried out by production department supervisors, who must coordinate the operations of the workers and equipment under their direction to complete the scheduled production. The performance of the supervisors is evaluated by the general supervisor and plant manager on the basis of comparison of scheduled unit production with actual unit production. The supervisors must also observe the priorities attached to various production jobs; their success in this regard is also an important element of performance.

The control function with respect to cost standards is also carried out by production department supervisors; the results can be evaluated by the plant manager and general supervisor on the basis of reports generated by the cost accounting department. The decisions of the departmental supervisors regarding the assignment of workers to jobs are made in accordance with the experience, efficiency, and quality of each employee's work. The quality of those decisions and the quality of each supervisor's supervision are reflected in materials usage costs and labor costs. Other decisions of the departmental supervisors are reflected in overhead costs such as repairs and maintenance, supplies, small tools, power, and so forth. A good cost accounting system uses the standard material and labor requirements developed by the engineering department to provide a standard cost per unit for all production work performed. Cost accounting reports such as the one illustrated in Fig. 18.3 compare actual costs within each department with standard costs and thus provide important feedback to departmental supervisors on their performance. Similar reports are provided to the plant manager and the general supervisor for use in evaluating their own performance and that of the supervisors under their supervision.

The quality control function may be performed by the engineering department and/or by a separate inspection or quality control department. The function involves testing or inspecting completed items of production for defects in materials or workmanship. It is often performed on a sample basis, in which case the entire lot of completed items is not inspected unless a certain portion of the sample is found to be defective. All defective units are returned to the appropriate factory department for reworking. Costs of reworking are relevant to performance evaluations of department supervisors and the general supervisor and should therefore be charged to the department in which the defective work occurred.

One other important production control function is the *expediting* or *dispatching* function. This function involves monitoring the progress of production, particularly of high-priority items. The expediter must have knowledge of the current status of all work in process. He or she is frequently called upon to report such information in response to a customer request. The expediter is responsible for maintaining a smooth flow of production through the factory and may authorize deviations from the production schedule if necessary to accomplish this goal. The expediter must also report significant deviations

FIGURE 18.3
Labor cost efficiency report for a production department.

DAILY LABOR COST EFFICIENCY REPORT										
Dept. no. 473 Machining			Supervisor: Oscar Nagursky			Date: Feb. 28, 1986				
Employee		Order No.	Operation		Stand. Rate	Hours		% Efficiency	Total Cost	
No.	Name		No	Description		Actual	Stand.		Actual	Stand.
4099	Jones, Harold	1406	352	Drill	3 00	3 6	3 5	97	10 80	10 50
4099	Jones, Harold	1406	382	Burr	3 00	4 4	4 0	91	13 20	12 00
4166	Bond, Jim	1381	425	Grind	2 90	3 0	3 6	120	8 70	10 44
4166	Bond, Jim	1406	392	Bore	2 90	5 0	5 5	110	14 50	15 95
	Dept. Totals					128 0	125 4	98	362 20	356 20

from scheduled production to the plant manager, the general supervisor, and the production planning department.

Factory automation

Production management has been one of the primary areas for the application of computer technology in business organizations. This section briefly describes some of the principal applications of computer technology to the production function.

Computer-aided design (CAD) involves the use of a computer system featuring high-resolution graphics terminals and graphics software to assist engineers in the design and alteration of manufactured products. These systems enable product designers to create an image of a product design, rotate it on the screen for viewing from various perspectives, scale it up or down, create product specifications for a completed design, store them in memory, and prepare engineering drawings. Advanced CAD software can also assist in design evaluation by simulating product testing, by generating performance information, and by preparing cost estimates for proposed designs. The advantages of CAD are that it speeds product design and evaluation and facilitates the alteration of existing product designs.

Numerical control is the use of a computer system to automatically control the operation of a machine tool in the performance of standardized production operations. Numerical control substantially improves the precision and consistency of machine operations relative to manual control. The integration of numerical control with other factory operations, such as shop-floor control, is referred to as *computer-aided manufacturing* (CAM). *CAD/CAM systems* integrate CAD and CAM by utilizing the product specifications prepared by CAD to automatically generate operational specifications for manufacturing operations under CAM.

Manufacturing resource planning (labeled MRP-II to distinguish it from the original MRP, materials requirements planning) is a comprehensive computerized planning and control system for manufacturing operations. Whereas MRP focuses on materials inventories and the purchasing function, MRP-II enhances MRP by incorporating capacity planning for factory work centers and scheduling of production operations. Thus MRP-II integrates planning and control of the three key manufacturing resources—materials, labor, and equipment. It utilizes a master production schedule to simulate scheduled factory operations in order to forecast future resource requirements. An effective MRP-II system reduces the costs of (1) carrying excess inventories, (2) factory overtime, and (3) expediting; furthermore, it also enables quick adjustment of work loads, inventory deliveries, and equipment schedules whenever production plans are altered.

Robotics involves the utilization of programmable machines (robots) to manipulate tools, parts, or materials to perform a variety of specific production tasks. Among the more common production tasks performed by robots are parts handling, simple assembly, machining, spray painting, and welding. Robots are especially appropriate for moving heavy materials, for monotonous and repetitive tasks, and for hazardous work. Other advantages include their ability to work around the clock, the quality and consistency of their work, and their dependability.

Flexible manufacturing systems (FMSs) utilize a computer to automate and integrate the performance of all major production tasks within a factory, including production planning, stock control, materials handling, machine scheduling and operation, and quality control. An FMS enhances the numerical control and shop-floor control features of CAM by adding automated materials transport and the use of robotics. The "flexibility" of an FMS refers to the ability to switch rapidly from the production of one kind of product to another, albeit similar, product. An effectively operating FMS improves plant and equipment capacity utilization, reduces retooling and setup costs, improves product quality, reduces direct labor costs, reduces work-in-process inventories, and permits rapid adjustment of production in response to shifts in customer demand. The ultimate goal of an FMS is to fully automate the production process.

The Production Information System

Most manufacturing organizations have two primary information subsystems for production management. One concerns the physical operations and elements of production, whereas the second concerns the cost elements of production. In automated systems, these two subsystems tend to become integrated, and so this chapter covers both subsystems. This section reviews the accounting transactions arising from production operations, describes and illustrates the production data base, and then discusses examples of manual, computerized batch processing, and real-time information systems for production management.

The accounting transactions

All the accounting transactions pertaining to production operations within a company are internal transactions, which means that there is no outside party to these transactions. Two basic accounting journal entries summarize the activities of the production process. The first of these follows.

Work-in Process Inventory	XXX	
Raw Materials Inventory		XXX
Payroll		XXX
Manufacturing Overhead		XXX

This is a composite entry representing the charging of the three major categories of manufacturing cost to production in process. The raw materials inventory portion of the entry is generally made at the beginning of production of a batch of units, when materials are issued for production from the storeroom. The payroll portion of the entry is made every week or every other week, depending on how frequently production employees are paid. The overhead portion of the entry represents overhead applied to work in process rather than actual overhead incurred. It is necessary to make this distinction because manufacturing overhead costs, unlike materials and labor, cannot be traced directly to units of work in process. Therefore overhead is generally applied at a standard rate, using direct labor hours or machine hours as a base.

The actual overhead costs are recorded by the accounting department as they are incurred. Numerous factory overhead accounts, including supplies, indirect labor, small tools, overtime premium, power and other utilities, insurance, taxes, maintenance, and depreciation, are debited for these costs. These detailed overhead accounts are coded both by type of cost and by the department for which the cost is incurred. Credits are made to accounts payable, payroll (for indirect labor, overtime premium, etc.), and other accounts (accumulated depreciation, accrued taxes, etc.). At the end of each reporting period (generally monthly), all balances in these detailed overhead accounts are closed to the manufacturing overhead control account. The net balance remaining in the manufacturing overhead control account after the closing represents overapplied or underapplied overhead. In a standard cost system, this difference is broken down into standard overhead cost variances. The net difference is eventually written off to cost of goods sold.[1]

There are two alternative techniques of cost accounting for work-in-process inventories. These are called *job order costing* and *process costing*. In job order costing, manufacturing costs are accumulated by production jobs in process, and there is a single work-in-process control account representing the total amount charged to all jobs in process. In process costing, manufacturing costs are accumulated by departments, and there are separate work-in-process accounts for each department. Therefore in process costing the transfer of work in process from one department to another is accompanied by a journal entry transferring the accumulated manufacturing costs from one department's work-in-process account to the other's. Firms that produce goods to specific customer orders generally utilize job order costing, whereas firms that produce goods for inventory may use either job order or process costing. The systems described and illustrated in this chapter are based on the model of a firm that produces goods for inventory and uses a job order costing system.[2]

The second basic accounting journal entry relating to the production process follows.

Finished Goods Inventory XXX
    Work-in-Process Inventory XXX

---

[1] For a more extensive discussion of accounting for overhead costs, see Charles T. Horngren, *Cost Accounting: A Managerial Emphasis*, 5th ed. (Englewood Cliffs, N.J.: Prentice-Hall, 1982), chapters 4 and 7.

[2] For a more extensive coverage and comparison of job order and process costing, see *ibid.*, chapters 4 and 17.

This entry reflects the completion of production goods and their transfer from the final assembly department into the finished goods storeroom, or to the shipping department for shipment to warehouses or customers.

The production data base

Taking a broad view, the production data base in a manufacturing company may be looked upon as a set of closely related data bases, including the marketing data base (discussed in Chapter 16), the purchasing and materials inventory data base (discussed in Chapter 17), the product structure data base, and the production work-in-process data base, which is the heart of the system. This is illustrated in Fig. 18.4. The marketing data base indicates the demand rate and finished goods inventory level of all manufactured products, thereby enabling the preparation of a master production plan for the organization. The master production plan shows the quantity of each product to be manufactured each week for several weeks into the future.

The product structure data base details the engineering specifications for each product, including the quantities of various raw materials items required and the exact sequence of operations performed in the manufacturing process. Thus the product structure data base essentially consists of the bill of materials and operations list for each product.

The purchasing and materials inventory data base shows the quantities of each item of raw materials inventory that are on hand or on order. This information is essential to the determination of a detailed production schedule.

FIGURE 18.4
Overview of production data base.

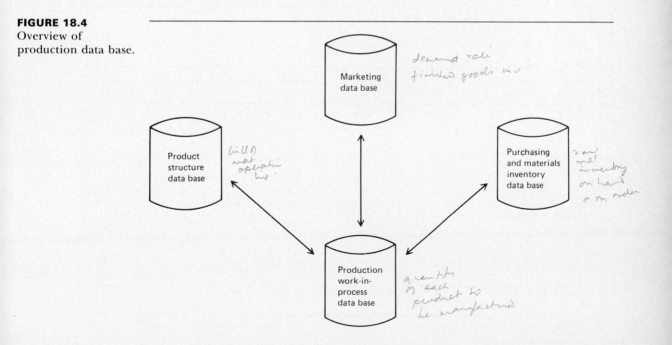

In turn, the master production plan, in conjunction with the bills of materials, indicates the quantities of various items of raw materials that need to be ordered. As materials are issued into production, the on-hand balances of the appropriate inventory accounts are reduced accordingly.

As shown in Fig. 18.4, the production work-in-process data base is the core of the production data base. Figure 18.5 provides an example of the data content and organization of a production work-in-process data base. This data base contains a series of records for each production order currently being processed in the factory. This includes a master work-in-process record, a set of materials requisition records for each type of material used in the product, and a set of operations records for each scheduled production operation required in manufacturing the product. These records are structured as a tree, with the master work-in-process record representing the parent and the materials requisition and production operations records representing the children. Production order number serves as the primary key for work-in-process records, each of which contains accumulated manufacturing cost data and an entry for the order quantity and scheduled completion date.

The primary inputs to the production work-in-process data base are newly initiated production orders and records of activities completed within the factory. The initiation of production orders is based upon the master production plan. Access to the product structure data base permits a complete set of material requisition records and production operations records to be generated. These are linked to a work-in-process master record to form a tree, which is then added to the data base. Next, as materials are issued into production in the factory, records of the actual quantity and cost are entered, and the req-

FIGURE 18.5
Production work-in-process data base.

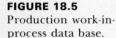

Work in process

Production order number	Finished goods stock number	Order quantity	Starting date	Completion date	Overhead base code	Overhead rate	Materials total cost	Labor total cost	Overhead total cost

Materials requisition

Production order number	Requisition number	Issue date	Department number	Inventory item number	Quantity	Unit cost	Status code

Production operations

Production order number	Operation number	Department number	Machine number	Operation description	Set-up time	Operation time	Starting date	Quantity completed

uisition "status code" is changed from "scheduled" to "issued." Records of quantity, time, and cost of completed labor operations are also entered into the data base, updating the appropriate production operations records and adding to the accumulated materials and overhead costs in the work-in-process master. Eventually the last product is transferred to the finished goods storeroom; this causes the removal of the complete tree of the production order record from the data base and initiates an increase in the on-hand quantity in the finished goods inventory section of the marketing data base.

Several output documents and reports may be generated from the production work-in-process data base. One is a production order, illustrated in Fig. 18.6, that provides the factory and the production planning department with a written reference document for each production order in process. Another is a materials requisition, illustrated in Fig. 18.7, that authorizes the transfer of raw materials from the storeroom to the appropriate factory department. Each day, the production operations records are processed sequentially by department number and machine number to prepare complete production schedules for each department. Daily reports on labor cost efficiency (see Fig. 18.3) and materials usage efficiency may be generated by comparing actual and planned quantities. As production orders are completed, summary cost reports may be prepared for the accounting department.

In a manual data processing system, two sets of records are generally maintained for each production order in process. First, the production planning department maintains records of open production orders, entering written notes of completed operations. Second, the cost accounting department maintains work-in-process cost records detailing the accumulated manufacturing costs for each production order in process. The open production order

FIGURE 18.6
Production order. (Reprinted by permission from *Primary Metals—Basic Production Planning and Control System,* Vol. 1. Copyright © 1971 by International Business Machines Corporation.)

MILL WORK TICKET

M.O. ITEM 123456 00	CUSTOMER FISM STEEL	SHIP-TO NO. 1240	CUSTOMER NO. 1011	CUSTOMER ORDER NO. 12C418-11	DATE PROM. 4-217	QUAL. CQ	SPEC NO. 1420	PROC NO. 711

PRODUCT GROUP HR F PKL SULF HVY OIL ME COIL	ORDERED WEIGHT 24.000	INGOT SPEC CODE 107 3412	HEAT NO. 27463	PRODUCT SIZE—IN. T—W—L .125 X 56.5 X COIL

OPER NO	FAC NO	OPERATION DESCRIPTION	T	SIZE W	L	PROC CODE	DATE SCHD	LIFTS SCHD	WEIGHT SCHED	SPECIAL INSTRUCTIONS	X O	SP NO
05	00	PROVIDE STEEL	4.0	X 54.0	X112.0		203	4	27200			
10	12	HR 1FIN COIL	.125	X 56.5	XCOIL	212	205	4	24800	CONTACT MET BI4 ROLLING		
15	22	PKL OIL ME				111	210	4	24300	CUT OUT WELDS		
20	81	PACKAGING				714	214	4	24300	USE CUST SKIDS		
25	91	SHIPPING	.125	X 56.5	XCOIL		217	4	24300	NO DELIV FRI PM		

MATERIALS REQUISITION				No. 14160		
Date	Department Issued to		Production order no.			
Item No.	Item description		Quantity	Cost/unit	Total cost	
Received by _____			Date _____			

FIGURE 18.7
Materials requisition.

file serves as an important reference regarding the status of orders in process and also serves as a production schedule by identifying those operations currently due to be performed.

The work-in-process cost records may consist simply of a cost summary sheet, as illustrated in Fig. 18.8. The cost accounting department records the data on these records from source documents evidencing material and labor usage in production. As explained earlier, overhead costs charged to work in process represent applied rather than actual costs. Once a production order is completed, the cost data on this record are summarized to determine total and per unit cost for the items produced.

When a manufacturing company converts from a manual to an automated data processing system for production data, the open production order file and the work-in-process cost file are prime candidates for integration. This is because both files are organized according to production orders in process. The combined master file would contain complete data on operations, quantities, and costs for each order. Ultimately, an integrated file of this type will evolve into a production work-in-process data base of the kind illustrated in Fig. 18.5. The data base approach is proving to be extremely effective in maintaining production records and scheduling and controlling production activities in many manufacturing companies.

A manual system

A document flowchart of a manual system for processing data relating to production operations appears in Fig. 18.9. Once again it must be emphasized that this and all subsequent illustrations are examples, rather than descriptions, of a real system. The production area is one in which the differences between firms are often quite significant. However, for most manufacturing firms the general pattern of information flows is likely to be similar to that shown.

PRODUCTION ORDER COST SUMMARY			

Order no.	Item no.	Item description	

Quantity started	Date started	Quantity completed	Date completed

Direct materials costs

Date	Dept. no.	Req. no.	Description	Total cost	

Direct labor costs

Date	Dept. no.	Oper. no.	Description	Total hrs.	Total cost	

Applied manufacturing overhead costs

Date	Dept. no.	Basis of application	Total cost	

FIGURE 18.8
Work-in-process cost summary sheet.

The illustration shows that production data processing begins in the production planning department. This department reviews current sales forecasts from the marketing department, finished goods stock status reports from the finished goods department, and raw materials stock status reports from the inventory clerk. On the basis of these inputs, the department decides the types and quantities of products that will be produced during the next period. The operations list is then used as a basis for generating production orders, and the materials specifications list is used to prepare materials requisitions for each production order.

One copy of each production order is sent to the cost accounting department, where it is used to establish a work-in-process record for the job. A second copy is sent to the production department in which the work is to begin. This copy will accompany the work in process on its way through the factory. A third copy is retained by production planning and filed in the open production order file.

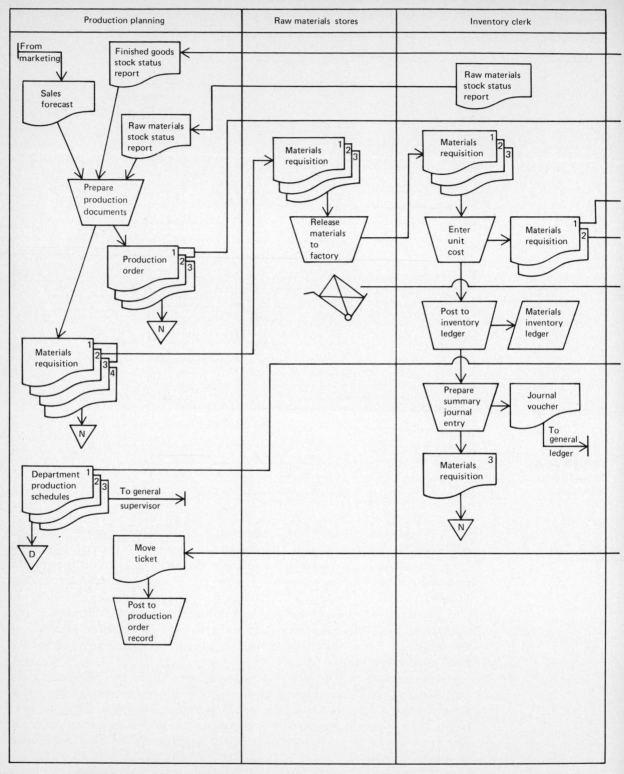

FIGURE 18.9 Document flow in a manual system for processing of production data.

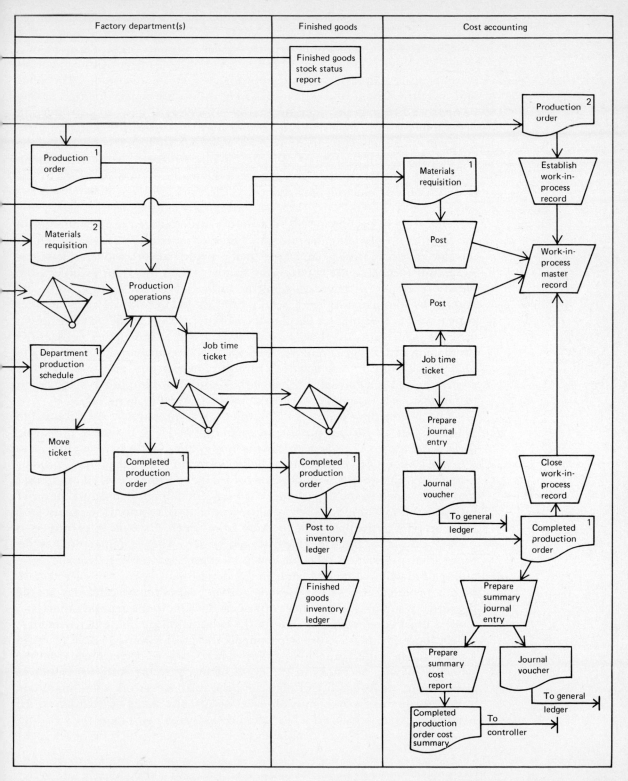

751

The production planning department also prepares several copies of a materials requisition (see Fig. 18.7) authorizing the transfer of raw materials from the stores department to the appropriate factory department. The items and quantities listed on the materials requisition are determined according to the specifications provided on the bill of materials. For each production order, one or more materials requisitions may be issued by production planning—one for each department to which materials are issued according to the bill of materials. In some cases, all materials may be issued to one department, whereas in other cases various portions of the materials may be issued to several different production departments as the work proceeds through the factory.

One copy of each materials requisition is filed by requisition number in the production planning department. Three other copies of each are sent to the raw materials storeroom, where they provide authorization to the stores supervisor to release the goods to the factory. When this transfer occurs, the person receiving the materials signs the form and has the cost per unit data entered by the inventory clerk, who retains one copy and transmits another copy to cost accounting for entry to the work-in-process master. The recipient of the goods retains the third copy to be attached to the factory copy of the production order. The inventory clerk posts each requisition to the issues and on-hand fields of the raw materials inventory master and, after each batch is posted, prepares a journal voucher of the debit to work in process and credit to raw materials inventory that is sent to the general ledger clerk.

The production planning department also prepares daily production schedules for all factory production departments. The basis for preparing these schedules is the open production order file, which is kept current to reflect all operations remaining to be performed on all outstanding production orders. The production schedule for each department lists all operations to be performed in the department each day, including the production order number, the machine number, quantity, total time required, start and stop time, priority of the order, the location from which the work in process is to arrive, and the location to which it must be sent when completed. Each departmental production schedule must, of course, properly reflect the availability of machine time and labor in the department. A copy of each department's production schedule is sent at the beginning of each day to the department supervisor. Another copy of each is sent to the general supervisor, while a third copy is filed by date in the production planning department.

In the individual factory departments the production schedule provides a guide to the supervisor in assigning workers to jobs. Departures from the schedule may be necessary in the event of machine breakdowns, employee absenteeism, unavailability of materials, the need to rework some materials, and so forth. Supervisors must observe the priority status of each job to the maximum extent possible if it becomes necessary to depart from the schedule. As each factory employee completes the operation to which he or she is as-

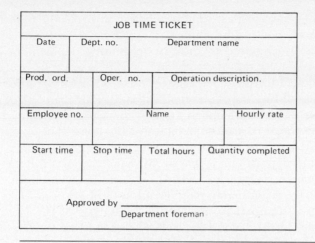

JOB TIME TICKET			
Date	Dept. no.	Department name	
Prod. ord.	Oper. no.	Operation description.	
Employee no.		Name	Hourly rate
Start time	Stop time	Total hours	Quantity completed

Approved by _____
Department foreman

FIGURE 18.10
Job-time ticket.

signed, a job time ticket (see Fig. 18.10) is prepared detailing the work performed. All job time tickets are approved and signed by the department supervisor and sent to the cost accounting department for posting to the work-
in-process cost summary sheets.

The transfer of work in process from one workstation or department to
another as operations are completed is recorded on a document called a move
ticket. Move tickets are provided to production planning as a source for updating the production order file. The final move ticket, signed by an employee
in finished goods, records the transfer of the product to the finished goods
storeroom. When this copy of the move ticket is received by production planning, the corresponding production order may be removed from the open
production order file.

The cost accounting department is responsible for maintaining the file
of work-in-process cost records. New records are added to this file upon receipt of new production orders initiated by production planning. Materials
costs are posted to this file from copies of materials requisitions. Direct labor
costs are posted from job time tickets. Overhead costs are often applied on
the basis of direct labor hours or direct labor costs and therefore are posted
at the same time as labor costs. The cost accounting department initiates a
journal voucher reflecting each batch of job time tickets posted that contains
a debit to work in process and credits to payroll and manufacturing overhead.
This journal voucher is transmitted to the general ledger clerk and posted to
the general ledger.

When the finished products are transmitted to the finished goods storeroom from the factory, the production order and attached materials requisitions accompany them. This completed production order is used by finished
goods personnel to post to the finished goods inventory file. The copy is then

transmitted to cost accounting, where it provides the basis for closing the work-in-process record of the job. After each batch of these is processed, a journal voucher is prepared by the cost accounting department indicating the debit to finished goods inventory and credit to work in process. The voucher is transmitted to the general ledger clerk for posting to the general ledger. The cost accounting department also prepares for the controller a completed production order cost summary, which contains an outline of all materials, labor, and overhead costs accumulated for the job.

The cost accounting department is responsible for the periodic preparation of departmental cost performance reports for the various production departments. Actual materials usage and labor costs for this purpose are accumulated from materials requisitions and job time tickets. Actual overhead costs are obtained from a summary analysis of the factory overhead ledger provided by the accounting clerk responsible for maintaining that ledger. This analysis indicates the total of each type of overhead cost incurred by each factory department. The cost accounting department maintains current standard costs for materials usage, labor, and overhead, and these standard costs are also used in preparing performance reports. As indicated in the report illustrated previously in Fig. 18.3, each departmental cost performance report is a summary and comparison of actual and standard costs for the most recent period, with cumulative totals encompassing several recent periods perhaps also provided. Copies of each of these reports are sent to the appropriate departmental supervisors, and duplicate copies of all reports may be provided to the general supervisor, the plant manager, the controller, and other executives.

Organizational independence with respect to production processing operations is achieved by separation of the authorization function performed by the production planning department from the recording functions performed by the inventory clerk, the cost accounting department, and the general ledger clerk, and from the operating and custodial functions of the various factory departments and the raw materials and finished goods storerooms. This separation of duties provides assurance that all movements of materials in the firm are properly authorized and accurately recorded.

The most significant control problems in the production area are prevention of loss of inventories and the maintenance of efficient production operations. Controls over loss of inventories, in addition to separation of duties, include effective supervision by factory supervisors and stores supervisors, limitations on access to the storerooms containing raw materials and finished goods, and physical security measures such as the placing of plant protection personnel at factory gates. Also important are the documentary controls on all transfers of materials within the factory. In the case of all such transfers, the recipient of the materials must sign a document acknowledging the receipt and verifying the accuracy of the amount recorded on the document. The document, which may be a materials requisition or a move ticket, is then immediately routed to a recording center, such as cost accounting or production planning. If materials shortages do occur, this system enables tracing the responsibility for the shortages to a specific department.

Control of production efficiency is provided by comparisons of actual production with scheduled production and by departmental cost performance reports. Comparisons of actual and scheduled production by the departmental supervisors, general supervisor, and production planning department establish a basis for daily control of operations. The expediting function, which closely monitors the progress of high-priority items through production and brings any delays to the attention of the appropriate managers, also contributes to the day-to-day control of production efficiency. Departmental cost performance reports measure production efficiency in financial terms, on a daily, weekly, or monthly basis. In the long run, departmental cost performance reports contribute to control of production efficiency by encouraging supervisors and managers to improve their decisions, policies, and procedures.

One other aspect of production control not reflected in the flowchart is quality control. The quality inspector's station is often the last factory department through which a product passes before it reaches the finished goods storeroom. If the product passes inspection, the inspector's report is attached to the move ticket that acknowledges receipt of the goods in the finished goods storeroom. These documents are routed to production planning. Any items that do not pass inspection are sent back to the appropriate factory department, and an inspector's report indicating the rejection is routed to production planning. The latter department must then include the necessary rework operations in preparation of subsequent production schedules. Periodically prepared summaries of work failing to pass inspection may be used by production management to pinpoint quality control problems within the factory.

The flowchart also does not indicate the special procedures that are necessary in the event that actual materials usage is greater than or less than the amount requisitioned. If the supervisor decides a larger quantity of materials is needed, he or she must inform the production planning department of the items and quantities required. The production planning department issues another materials requisition, which undergoes processing identical to the original version. To provide control over materials issued in this manner, the authority to initiate requests for additional materials must be restricted to supervisors only, since supervisors will eventually be held accountable for the excess materials costs.

If a quantity of raw materials is left over after production within a department is completed, the departmental supervisor must prepare two copies of a returned materials report. These copies are taken, together with the materials themselves, to the raw materials storeroom. There, the custodian signs one copy acknowledging receipt of the exact items and quantities indicated on the report, and this copy is sent to cost accounting for posting to the work-in-process master file. The other copy is provided to the inventory clerk for posting to the raw materials inventory file.

A computer-based batch processing system

A document flowchart of the production information system of a typical manufacturing company using computerized batch processing appears in Fig. 18.11. As in previous descriptions of batch processing systems, it is assumed that master files are maintained on magnetic disk storage, and that magnetic tape is used for data input.

A comparison of Fig. 18.11 with its manual counterpart, Fig. 18.9, reveals that the computer has replaced the inventory clerk and has assumed many of the clerical functions performed within the production planning and cost accounting departments. The production planning department decides what is to be produced on the basis of the same information—sales forecasts and inventory status reports—but this information is prepared by computer instead of by various other departments. Production planning prepares a set of manufacturing authorizations indicating the quantity of each product to be produced and the relative priorities of each product. This is provided to the input preparation department and becomes input to a computerized process that prepares production orders, materials requisitions, and production schedules. The open production order file, maintained by the production planning department in the manual system, and the work-in-process master file, maintained by the cost accounting department in the manual system, are instead maintained together as a single integrated file by computer.

The functions performed by raw materials stores, the various factory departments, the finished goods department, and the general ledger clerk are quite similar in the two systems. The factory departments must route the job time tickets and move tickets to input preparation instead of to cost accounting and production planning. Factory supervisors must still manually prepare requisitions for excess materials needed or reports for unnecessary materials returned in the event that actual usage varies from the amount originally requisitioned. The finished goods department is no longer responsible for maintaining the finished goods master file, which is instead maintained by computer. The general ledger clerk receives journal vouchers as computer printouts rather than as manually prepared documents. Actually, the general ledger function itself could easily be computerized, and a system incorporating this feature is described in Chapter 20.

Figures 18.12, 18.13, and 18.15 illustrate by means of systems flowcharts the computer operations involved in (1) production order and materials requisition preparation, (2) production scheduling, and (3) cost accounting. This section discusses each of these three areas of computer operations and describes control policies and procedures directly applicable to these operations.

An important feature of the computerized production information systems described and illustrated here is the integration of open production order and work-in-process data. The combined file resulting from the integration of these two files is referred to as the "production order cost and operations data base." The key field for this data base is production order number. The data base contains both physical and cost data for all operations and materials connected with the order. In addition, it is assumed that standard cost data are recorded on this data base. In each of the three areas of computer operations covered in this section, the production order cost and operations data base is the key master file in updating and reporting processes.

Preparation of production planning documents. The input preparation and computer processing operations necessary to prepare production orders and materials requisitions are illustrated in Fig. 18.12. These operations are initiated once each week by receipt of "authorization-to-manufacture" documents or lists from the production planning department. Batch totals prepared from these documents might include a record count and hash totals of product stock number and quantity to be produced. After keying and verification, the authorization-to-manufacture records are sorted into sequence by product stock number, which is the same sequence followed for the bill of materials file and operations list file. The sorting step is performed using a tape-sort program on the computer.

The next step in this process is the processing of the authorization-to-manufacture records on the computer together with the operations list file, the bill of materials file, and the production order cost and operations data base. This process is performed sequentially by product stock number. For each product to be manufactured, a production order is compiled from the authorization-to-manufacture record and corresponding operations list record. A production order number is assigned to this document according to the next highest number available on the production order cost and operations data base. Two or more copies of the production order are printed. For each product, a materials requisition is also compiled from data on the authorization-to-manufacture record and corresponding bill of materials record. Several copies of the materials requisition are then printed out. All the materials and operations data, including standard cost data, from the bill of materials and operations list are written into a new record on the production order cost and operations data base. The final output of this computer run is a printed listing of error transactions, batch totals, and other summary information that is compared with the manually generated batch totals as a means of data control.

Production scheduling. This activity is assumed to be performed daily in the computerized system, as in the manual system. A systems flowchart of the process appears in Fig. 18.13. The process begins with the updating of the production order cost and operations data base for move tickets evidencing the completion of an operation at one workstation and the transfer of the work to the next scheduled workstation. Move tickets are received during the shift from the factory and assembled into batches at the completion of the shift. Batch totals will include a record count as well as hash totals of production order number and quantity of units completed. The batched move tickets are then keyed onto tape and verified, after which they are sorted by

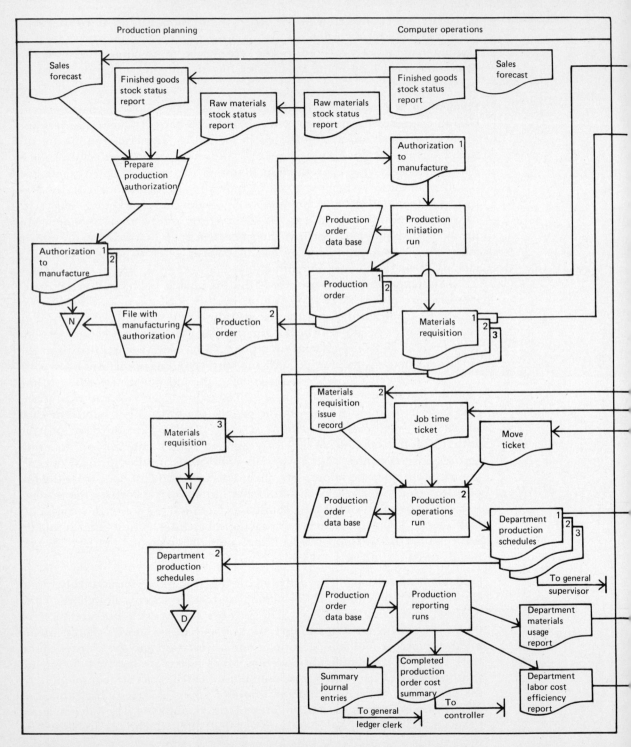

FIGURE 18.11 Document flow in computerized batch processing of production data.

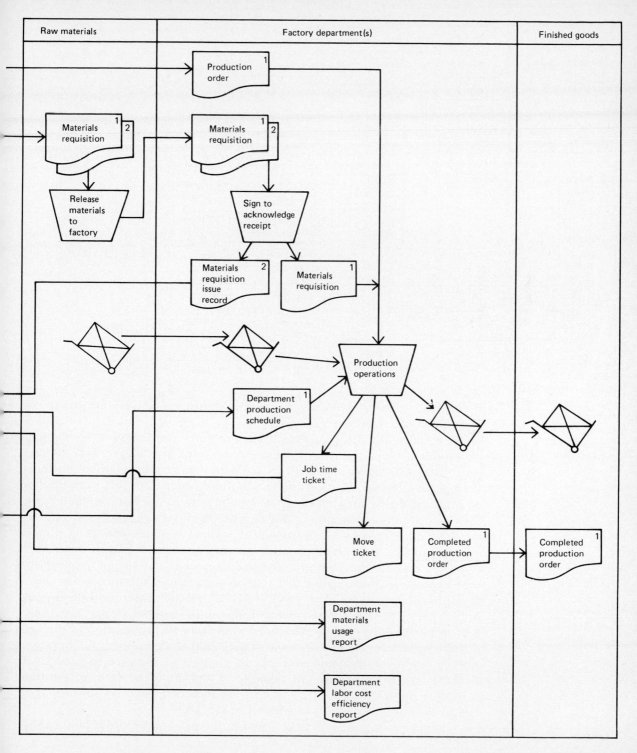

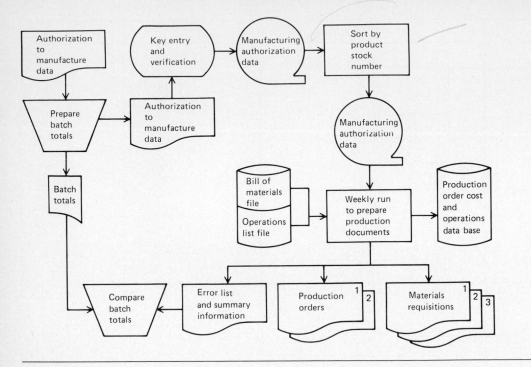

FIGURE 18.12
Computerized batch processing system for preparation of production orders and materials requisitions.

production order number for processing against the production order cost and operations data base.

The collection and preparation for computer processing of source data on production operations is a common application of source data automation. This observation applies to source data such as that recorded on move tickets and job-time tickets. Numerous portable data recorders exist that are designed primarily for collecting production data in machine-readable form. Also used are data collection terminals with which factory employees may enter production data by means of setting various switches indicating the operation number, start and stop time, quantity completed, and so forth. Such terminals may be directly online to the computer or connected to an offline tape drive or microcomputer that records data from all terminals for subsequent batch processing. Also common is the use of turnaround documents upon which production order number, operation number, department number, and related data may be precoded at the time of preparation of the production orders. As the operations are completed, the employee number, time worked, and quantity completed may be entered on the card in predefined fields for machine reading. An example of a prepunched card for job time recording upon which production data are recorded for mark sensing upon completion of operations is illustrated in Fig. 18.14.

The processing of move tickets against the production order cost and op-

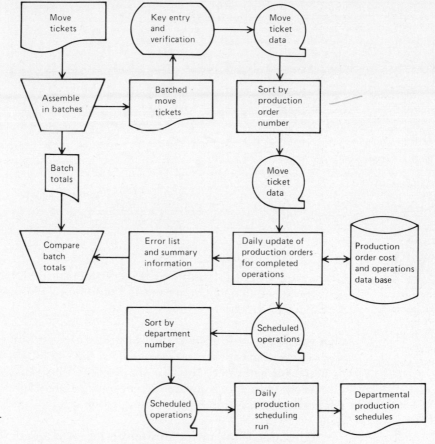

FIGURE 18.13
Computerized batch processing system for production scheduling.

erations data base updates the record of operations performed on that data base and therefore keeps current the records of operations still remaining to be performed for each production order. Two outputs are generated from this process. One is the familiar printed listing of error transactions and summary information. Batch totals on this printout are compared with those prepared manually prior to processing to check on the reliability of the processed input records. The other output is a tape listing of operations scheduled for performance during the forthcoming shift. Each record on this list includes the production order number, operation number, department number, workstation number, quantity to be completed, and standard time requirement for each operation, as well as an indication of the priority of each operation and the appropriate sequence of performance of operations. This tape is then sorted by department number and processed by a special program that prepares departmental production schedules for all production departments. This program contains data on the machine and labor capacity of each department.

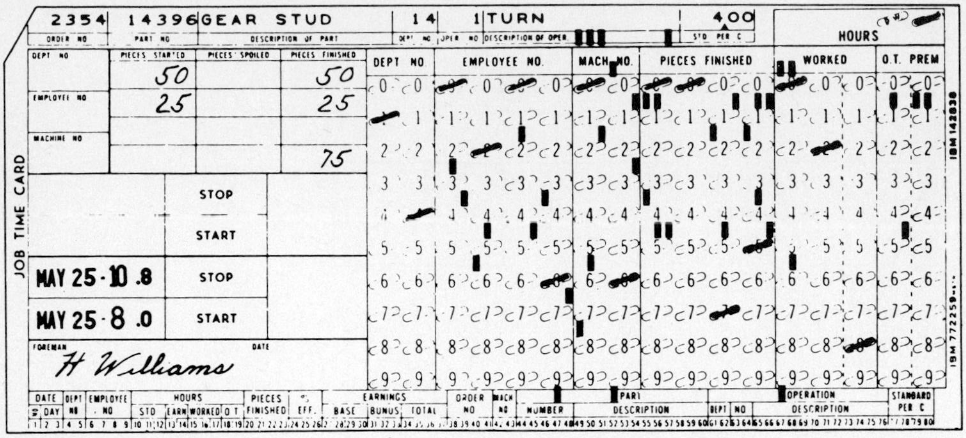

FIGURE 18.14
Turnaround document for collection of production data using mark sensing. (Reprinted by permission from *Basic Applications— System/360 Model 20.* Copyright © 1971 by International Business Machines Corporation.)

Often programs of this sort may be very sophisticated, having a capability to generate schedules that represent the optimum assignment of resources for maximum production.

Cost accounting. A systems flowchart of daily computerized operations for cost accounting appears in Fig. 18.15. All the operations shown are assumed to be performed once daily. To simplify the illustration and accompanying discussion, the chart is divided by means of dashed lines into three separate application areas—materials costing, labor costing, and finished goods update.

Materials costing operations utilize the costed materials issues tape generated as an output of updating the raw materials inventory file as illustrated in Fig. 17.9. Each record on this tape contains the requisition number, production order number, code number of the department to which the materials were issued, quantity issued, and unit cost from materials requisitions evidencing issues from stores into production. This tape must be sorted into sequence by production order number prior to processing against the production order cost and operations data base. The computer run updates the materials usage and cost records in this data base. As outputs of the run emerge (1) a printed list of error transactions and summary information, which includes the summary journal entry debiting work in process and crediting raw materials inventory, and (2) a tape of materials usage data, containing actual vs. standard usage and resulting cost variances for all completed operations. The latter tape is sorted by department number and processed to generate daily material usage reports for each production department.

Labor costing operations begin each day with the assembly of job time tickets into batches and computation of batch totals. Among the batch totals prepared might be a record count of the number of job time tickets and hash

FIGURE 18.15
Computerized batch processing system for cost accounting.

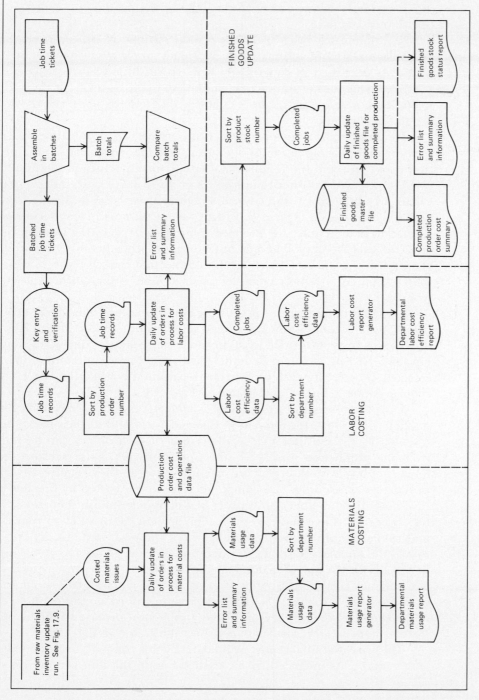

totals of employee number, pay rate, and hours worked. Job time records are then keyed onto magnetic tape, verified, and sorted into sequence by production order number for processing against the production order cost and operations data base.

Labor-intensive firms that have a high volume of job time records will generally use a more automated form of data preparation than the one illustrated. As described in conjunction with processing of move tickets, several possible techniques of source data automation may be used for this purpose, including portable data recorders, factory data collection terminals, or turnaround documents.

The next step in this operation is the processing of job time records to post the time of completion of operations and labor rate data to the production order cost and operations data base. If manufacturing overhead is applied on the basis of direct labor hours or direct labor cost, this process also calculates applied overhead costs and records these costs in the file. One output of this process is a printed listing of error transactions and summary information that includes the summary journal entry debiting work in process and crediting the payroll and manufacturing overhead control accounts. The report also contains the batch totals accumulated during the run, which are then compared with those compiled prior to input preparation as a data control check.

A second output of this processing run is a tape of labor cost efficiency data. This tape contains the actual and standard time and standard labor rate of all operations performed by all production employees during the day. The tape is sorted by department number and employee code and is then processed to generate for each production department a daily labor cost efficiency report similar to the one illustrated in Fig. 18.3.

The other output of this process is a tape listing of all cost data for production orders that are completely finished as a result of the operations represented by the job time cards. All records of such orders can be removed from the production order cost and operations data base because they no longer represent work-in-process inventory, nor do they require any further production scheduling. The completed jobs tape is sorted by finished goods inventory stock number and is processed to update the finished goods inventory master for the completed stock. The printed listing of error transactions and summary information generated from this run contains, among other things, the summary journal entry debiting finished goods and crediting work in process for the cost of manufacturing the items. The second printed report generated by this run is a series of completed production cost summaries for each product completed. Each of the summary reports on this printout details all production costs for the particular production order and might follow a format similar to the cost summary sheet illustrated in Fig. 18.8.

The third and final report printed out by this run is a finished goods stock status report. As indicated by the dashed line in the illustration, this report is assumed to be prepared once each week rather than once a day, although the latter frequency could certainly be adhered to if considered beneficial.

Control policies and procedures.   Batch totals, turnaround documents, and keyverification are methods of control over the computerized production information system that are discussed above. The topics of data security and input validation as they relate specifically to this system are now addressed.

The focal point of data security in this system must be the production order cost and operations data base. If this data base is destroyed, the basis for production scheduling and costing of work in process is lost. A duplicate copy of this data base should be prepared at the completion of each day's processing. This copy and all subsequent transaction tapes, including the manufacturing authorization data tape, the move ticket data tape, the costed materials issues tape, and the job time records tape, should be saved to permit reconstruction of the current version of the data base if necessary. Internal and external labels identifying the files and their dates of expiration should be used to help prevent the accidental destruction of one of these files. The tape file protection ring should be removed from all current versions of the tape files to protect against their being written on. The disk pack containing the current copy of the production order cost and operations data base should be stored in a file library when not in use and removed only for authorized purposes. The backup copy of the data base and the related transaction tapes should be stored in a secure off-site location.

Three other master files maintained on disk in this system are the bill of materials file, the operations list file, and the finished goods master file. Disk packs containing these files should also be stored in the file library when not in use and should be protected by the use of internal and external labels. Other tape files, including the scheduled operations tape, the materials usage data tape, the labor cost efficiency data tape, and the completed jobs tape, should be secured while in use by the removal of tape file protection rings and the use of internal and external labels.

Each of the five major file updating programs in the production information system should contain an input validation routine that performs several edit checks on each input transaction. Because each of these processes is performed in sequential order, a sequence check on the input records should always be performed. A validity check of the value in the control field of each input record must always be performed in a sequential file updating program. In addition, when updating the production order cost and operations data base for move tickets and job time tickets, the validity of the operation number, department number, and workstation or machine number should be checked. When this data base is updated for materials issues, the validity of inventory stock number and department number should be checked. These validity checks are accomplished by comparing the values of these items on the input records with the values of the same items in the master record.

Field checks and reasonableness tests should be performed on the values of all numeric items that are not validity checked. The fields involved are quantity to be produced on the authorization-to-manufacture records, quantity completed on move tickets, quantity and unit cost on materials issues, hours worked, pay rate and quantity completed on job time tickets, and quantity completed and unit cost on finished job records. The reasonableness of values for each of these items is tested by comparison with average or expected values recorded on the master files.

A final set of edit checks is necessary in all programs that update the production order cost and operations data base. In explanation, note that this data base includes records of scheduled operations and requisitioned materials that are updated as operations are completed and materials are issued. Because of this, the programs that update the file can be written to detect any unreported operations performed and materials issued. For example, if the completion of operation A has not been recorded, but the completion of operation B that follows A has been recorded, an error exists—either A has been completed but not recorded, or B has been improperly recorded as complete. Similarly, if an issue of materials has not been recorded, but the completion of an operation requiring those materials has been recorded, an error exists. All discrepancies of this type should be reported on the list of error transactions.

Further control over production information processing is accomplished by review and follow-up on the various error transaction reports. This function should be the responsibility of personnel other than operators or programmers, preferably data control personnel or a supervisor. The source of each error transaction should be traced as a means of ensuring the accuracy of error corrections and identifying potential weak areas of control. Error corrections should be prepared and submitted to the system as quickly as possible.

A real-time system

In a manual or computerized batch processing system for production information processing, the cycle of planning and control information flows is repeated primarily daily or weekly. Production scheduling is done daily. Most production orders are initiated at the beginning of each week. Production cost data may be reported daily, weekly, or even monthly. In small firms, an information flow cycle of this length may be acceptable. As firms grow larger, the production management function will employ expediters to monitor production work requiring closer attention than that provided by daily or weekly feedback. At some point in the growth of a manufacturing firm, the use of an online computer system to provide real-time scheduling and control of production operations becomes economically feasible.

Spurred by the increasing popularity of factory automation, real-time production information systems are rapidly displacing manual and computerized batch processing systems for production data processing. In higher-level automated factory systems such as FMS, production planning and scheduling, cost accounting, and related data processing functions are integrated with the systems that control factory machines and processes. In this section the data processing side of a real-time production information system is described without consideration of whether it is integrated with an automated factory system.

A system flowchart of a real-time production information system appears in Fig. 18.16. Data on factory operations may be automatically entered into the system as a by-product of the operations, or they may be entered via online terminals, badge readers, keyboards, or other online data collection devices. For each factory operation, the system collects the production order number, operation number, employee number, machine number, and materials quantity. Job start and stop time may be recorded automatically. Data on the movement of work in process from one workstation to another would also be collected by the system.

FIGURE 18.16
Real-time production
information system.

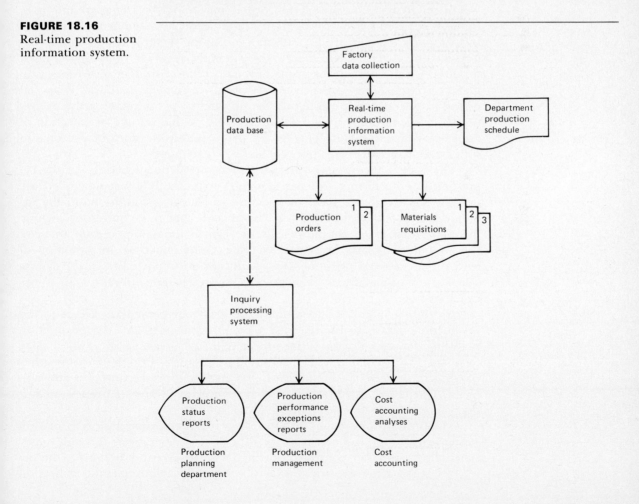

Data keyed into the system by factory workers should be checked for accuracy by input validation routines that examine the validity of data such as order numbers and employee numbers and evaluate the reasonableness of quantity and time data. If data of questionable accuracy are detected, the system asks the worker to recheck and reenter them.

Input data on all factory activities are entered into the system as they occur. Therefore the production data base contains current information on the status of all production orders, employees, machines, materials, costs, schedules, and so on. All these status records are updated in a single integrated process as inputs recording the completion of an operation or the movement of materials are received from the factory. Furthermore, as illustrated in Fig. 18.4, the production data base links this current status information on production work in process to the engineering specifications within the product structure data base and to raw materials and finished goods inventory information within the purchasing and marketing data bases.

In this system new production orders may either be triggered automatically or initiated by the production planning department. If the data base incorporates a master production plan indicating the quantity of each product scheduled for completion each week, then the system may be programmed to automatically initiate materials purchase orders, production orders, and materials requisitions at the necessary points in time. In addition, if special orders or rush orders are received, the production planning department may use its online terminal to enter the relevant data and initiate preparation of the necessary documents. The system prints multiple copies of production order and materials requisition documents as required.

The system also prepares departmental production schedules at the beginning of each factory shift but has the capability to adjust scheduled operations on a real-time basis in response to changing conditions in the dynamic factory environment. Examples of such changing conditions include machine breakdowns, employee absenteeism or illness, operations that are not completed within the scheduled time, faulty materials, introduction of rush orders, and so forth. As such conditions are reported to it, the system reacts quickly to adjust its status records and reschedule operations in an optimal fashion.

An online inquiry processing system provides immediate access to the production data base for the cost accounting department, the production planning department, and other production executives using online display terminals. This system may be used to make inquiries into the current status of work in process or to request reports analyzing production cost and efficiency. The content and format of such reports may either be predesigned or determined by the user at the time of the inquiry.

The primary advantages provided by a real-time production information system involve improvements in the efficiency of operations through better scheduling and faster control reporting. With respect to scheduling, the objectives are to achieve maximum factory throughput and machine utilization while minimizing both the value of work-in-process inventories and the completion time of all orders in accordance with their relative priorities. With respect to production control, a real-time system can provide online monitoring of critical situations. For example, the system can check the status of rush orders at periodic intervals and prepare a report on any rush orders falling behind schedule. Scheduled operations on which no operator has reported starting or completing can be reported to the appropriate supervisor. Data input of questionable accuracy can be reported for follow-up and possible subsequent correction. Significant cost overruns can be reported as they occur if desired. Raw materials inventory can be reordered immediately as materials usage lowers available quantities below the reorder point. Current information is always available on the status of work in process in response to inquiries from management or production personnel.

An effective real-time production information system changes the pattern of accounting and management control in a factory environment. Traditional control systems are based on periodic reporting of cost variances, schedule overruns, and quality control deviations. By providing immediate feedback on the status of the production process, a real-time system can flag control problems as they occur and initiate prompt corrective action. Periodic control reports are outmoded in this environment because problems are identified and corrected long before they are reflected in weekly or monthly summary reports.

Summary

In a modern manufacturing company, the accounting information system is integrated with the production planning and control system. The production information system maintains a data base of product specifications, production orders in process, and production schedules. This is augmented by inventory and cost data maintained by the accounting system. The information available from this system is useful to production management in the planning and control of factory operations.

The advent of factory automation is transforming the nature of information systems for production planning and control. Traditional manual and computerized batch processing systems that operate on weekly or monthly cycles are being displaced by real-time systems that monitor and regulate production processes as they occur. This has created a need to reevaluate the applicability of traditional concepts of accounting control in the modern factory environment.

Review Questions

1. Define the following terms.

   backlog   computer-aided manufacturing
   bill of materials   CAD/CAM systems
   operations list   manufacturing resource planning

routing sheet   robotics

expediting   flexible manufacturing systems

dispatching   job order costing

computer-aided design process costing

numerical control

2. Describe in general the decision responsibilities and information requirements of the production planning function.

3. What are three basic types of standards that must be met in the production operations control function? What information, from what sources, is required in controlling operations to achieve each standard?

4. Identify the two primary information subsystems in production planning and control.

5. Describe some of the principal applications of modern computer technology to the production function.

6. What are the accounting journal entries that summarize the activities involved in the production process?

7. Explain the distinction between applied and actual overhead costs. Why is it necessary to use applied overhead costs in production costing?

8. Identify the relationships that exist between the production work-in-process data base and other data bases in a manufacturing company.

9. Describe the data content and organization of the production work-in-process data base. Identify the primary inputs to and outputs from this data base.

10. What departments in a business organization might be involved in the manual processing of production information? What documents and reports might be used, and what information would each contain? In what department would each document or report originate, and where and for what purpose would each be distributed?

11. What functions must be separated to achieve organizational independence with respect to production information systems?

12. What control policies and procedures are important in a production information processing system?

13. What special control procedures are necessary in a production information system in the event that actual materials usage is greater than or less than the amount originally requisitioned?

14. Describe possible similarities and differences in processing of production information using a computer system rather than a manual one. Emphasize documents, departments, and reports involved in the process.

15. Describe or illustrate how production orders and materials requisitions might be prepared by computer.

16. Explain several ways in which source data automation might be applied to the collection of data on production operations.

17. Explain or illustrate how the computer might be used to prepare production schedules for factory departments.

18. Describe several control policies and procedures that might be used in batch processing of production information by a typical manufacturing company utilizing a computer system.

19. Describe the nature of a real-time information processing system for production planning and control.

20. Explain several advantages provided by a real-time production information system.

Discussion Questions

21. This and the preceding chapter primarily emphasized the logistics information requirements of a manufacturing firm. Discuss the basic similarities and differences in organization structure, information requirements, and data sources between the logistics system of a manufacturing firm and that of
    a) a transportation company, such as a railroad or airline,
    b) a construction company, or
    c) a professional service firm such as a public accounting partnership.

22. Advanced factory automation technology generally incorporates a real-time production information system that integrates production and accounting data to provide real-time control of manufacturing operations. Discuss the implications of this emerging technology for traditional management accounting control concepts.

Problems and Cases

23. What control policies and procedures in a production information system would provide the best control over the following situations?
    a) A production order was initiated for a product for which demand no longer exists.
    b) Items of in-process inventory were stolen by a production employee.
    c) The "rush order" tag on a partially completed production job became detached from the materials and lost, causing a costly delay in completing the job.
    d) A production employee prepared a materials requisition, used the document to obtain $300 worth of parts from the parts storeroom, and stole the parts.

     e) A supervisor's insistence that every worker in his department must learn to use every machine in his department resulted in an increase in the proportion of work done by the department that failed to pass quality control tests.

     f) A production worker entering job time data over a terminal mistakenly entered 3000 instead of 300 in the quantity completed field.

     g) A dishonest parts storeroom employee issued quantities of parts ten percent lower than indicated on several materials requisitions and stole the excess quantities.

     h) Incorrect keypunching of the production order number from a materials requisition caused a materials issue to be posted to the wrong production order.

24. Your company has just acquired a data base management system that will first be applied to production data. You are to design the product structure segment of the data base, which will include a bill of materials and operations list for each product. Currently, these specifications are maintained on documents identical in format to those in Figs. 18.1 and 18.2. Prepare a data base design diagram for the product structure, using a format similar to that of Fig. 18.5.

25. Assume that you are a management consultant for a large public accounting firm. One of your firm's clients is the Willard Corporation, a medium-sized manufacturing firm. Willard's controller has recently come to you for advice regarding the following problems.

     ☐ The proportion of customer orders filled by the promised delivery date has declined from ninety percent to fifty percent within the past year.

     ☐ Production costs have risen dramatically because of increased charges for overtime, rework, and idle time waiting for materials or machines.

     ☐ The company has doubled the number of expediters employed from three to six with no noticeable lessening of the problems.

What are some important questions you would ask the controller in attempting to gain insight into these problems? Relate your questions specifically to the company's production information system and its approach to production management.

26. Your company has just acquired a data base management system that will first be applied to cost accounting data. These data are presently accumulated manually on production order cost summary forms identical to that shown in Fig. 18.8. You are to diagram the data structure of the production order cost summary segment of the data base as a first step in the application design. Use a format similar to that of Fig. 18.5.

27. In Fig. 18.17 is a document flowchart prepared by a clerk to document data flows relating to production operations for the April Manufacturing Company.

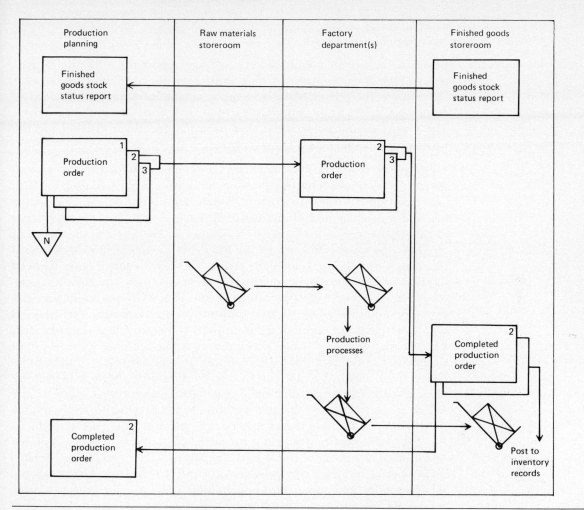

FIGURE 18.17

REQUIRED

a) Describe several deficiencies in internal control in the system shown in Fig. 18.17. For each deficiency, indicate an error, manipulation, or inefficiency that could result.

b) Indicate the best means of remedying each deficiency described in part (a).

28. The Caesar Manufacturing Company uses sheet metal and other uncut and unshaped raw materials in its production process. Accordingly, control of materials usage and spoilage is a significant management problem. The company utilizes a standard cost system that specifies standard materials usage for each operation performed in production. Each departmental supervisor is responsible for materials usage variances arising from operations performed by the employees under his or her supervision on the machines in the department. The primary means of control available

to supervisors are the assignment of employees to machines and supervision of employee work.

Design a format for a daily materials usage report for a factory department. Make any reasonable assumptions about the availability of data for inclusion in the report. Make sure that you take into account the need to relate the report to the supervisor's objectives and decision alternatives. The report should present the vital information effectively and use the principle of management by exception.

29. Valpaige Co. is an industrial machinery and equipment manufacturer with several production departments. The company employs automated and heavy equipment in its production departments. Consequently, Valpaige has a large Repair and Maintenance Department (R & M) for servicing this equipment.

The operating efficiency of the R & M Department has deteriorated over the past two years. Further, repair and maintenance costs seem to be climbing more rapidly than other department costs. The Assistant Controller has reviewed the operations of the R & M Department and has concluded that the administrative procedures used since the early days of the department are outmoded due in part to the growth of the company. The two major causes for the deterioration, in the opinion of the Assistant Controller, are an antiquated scheduling system for repair and maintenance work and the actual cost system to distribute the R & M Department's costs to the production departments. The actual costs of the R & M Department are allocated monthly to the production departments on the basis of the number of service calls made during each month.

The Assistant Controller has proposed that a formal work order system be implemented for the R & M Department. The production departments would submit a service request to the R & M Department for the repairs and/or maintenance to be completed including a suggested time for having the work done. The Supervisor of the R & M Department would prepare a cost estimate on the service request for the work required (labor and materials) and indicate a suggested time for completing the work on the service request. The R & M Supervisor would return the request to the production department which initiated the request. Once the production department okays the work by returning a copy of the service request, the R & M Supervisor would prepare a repair and maintenance work order and schedule the job. This work order provides the repair worker with the details of the work to be done and is used to record the actual repair/maintenance hours worked, and the materials and supplies used.

Producing departments would be charged for actual labor hours worked at a predetermined standard rate for the type of work required. The parts and supplies used would be charged to the production departments at cost.

The Assistant Controller believes that only two documents would be required in this new system—a *Repair/Maintenance Service Request* initiated by the production departments and the *Repair/Maintenance Work Order* initiated by the R & M Department.

REQUIRED

a) For the *Repair/Maintenance Work Order* document:

1) Identify the data items which would be important to the Repair and Maintenance Department and the production departments which should be incorporated into the *work order*.

2) Indicate how many copies of the *work order* would be required and explain how each copy would be distributed.

b) Prepare a document flow diagram to show how the *Repair/Maintenance Service Request* and the *Repair/Maintenance Work Order* should be coordinated and used among the departments of Valpaige Co. to request and complete the repair and maintenance work, to provide the basis for charging the production departments for the cost of the completed work, and to evaluate the performance of the Repair and Maintenance Department. Provide explanations to the flow diagram as appropriate. (CMA Examination)

30. The Miller Manufacturing Company maintains an online production work-in-process data base and updates it using a real-time factory data collection system. Upon completing a job, a factory employee enters (1) his or her employee number, (2) the machine number, (3) the production order number, (4) the operation number, and (5) the quantity completed. The system notes the time of each transaction, performs a variety of edit checks on the data input, and if the data are accepted, updates the appropriate records on the data base.

REQUIRED

Prepare a program flowchart of an input validation routine that checks the accuracy of each item of input data listed above. Note that it will be helpful for the system to access some data within the data base as a means of checking some or all of the input items. However, your flowchart should stop short of illustrating update procedures.

31. The Gibson Manufacturing Company utilizes an online production information system that has access to the following files stored on an online disk unit.

a) A production order file, which keeps track of the operations performed and still to be performed, the quantities in process, and the accumulated materials, labor, and overhead costs for all outstanding production orders.

b) A finished goods inventory file, which includes data on the quantity and production cost of all finished products in stock.

c) An employee data file, which is keyed by employee number and includes the employee's pay rate and all other essential payroll data.

One of the programs in this system processes data on completed operations entered by factory employees using terminals. For each operation completed, the following data are entered: production order number, operation number, employee number, quantity completed, start time, and stop time. The program performs various edit checks and validity checks on data entered. If the input is valid, the program updates the production order record for completion of the operation and corresponding labor cost data. If the operation represents the completion of the entire production order, the program updates the finished goods inventory file for the completed stock, writes a completed production order cost summary report on a separate disk file for subsequent processing by another program, and removes the completed production order record from the production order file.

REQUIRED

Prepare a macroflowchart of the program described above. Assume that the checking of whether the input data are valid represents one macrostep. Show all necessary input and output steps and each major decision and processing step, as required to complete the necessary processing.

32. Processing of production orders in the Monahan Manufacturing Company is performed as follows. At the end of each week, the production planning department prepares a list of products and quantities to be produced during the next week. Using this list as a source, data entry personnel key "authorization-to-manufacture" records onto magnetic tape. This tape is sorted by the computer into product stock number sequence and then processed together with an operations list file on magnetic tape to generate production orders. For each new production order, the program (1) prepares three copies of a production order document, (2) writes the production order onto a disk file of open production orders, and (3) punches an operations card for each operation to be performed on the production order.

The operations cards are used as turnaround documents. They are distributed to the factory departments where each operation is to be performed. After completing an operation, factory employees mark the elapsed time, quantity completed, etc., on the card and submit it to the data processing center. There a reproducer is used to mark sense and punch the data entered by the factory employees into the card. The cards are converted to magnetic tape using an offline converter. The magnetic tape records are then sorted by production order number and processed to update the open production order master. After the master has been updated for all completed operations, the program generates departmental production schedules for the next day.

REQUIRED

a) Prepare a systems flowchart of all operations described.
b) Describe several control policies and procedures that should be incorporated into this computerized system. Indicate the purpose of

each policy or procedure. Relate your answer specifically to the computer-related activities described in the case.

c) Explain how departmental production schedules may be generated from the updated production order master file without sorting that file by department number.

References

Aggarwal, Sumer C. "MRP, JIT, OPT, FMS?" *Harvard Business Review* (September/October 1985): 8–16.

Appleton, Dan. "A Manufacturing Systems Cookbook, Part I." *Datamation* (May 1979): 179–184.

Dilts, David M., and Grant W. Russell. "Accounting for the Factory of the Future." *Management Accounting* (April 1985): 34–40.

Ford, F. Nelson; William N. Ledbetter; and Brian S. Gaber. "The Evolving Factory of the Future: Integrating Manufacturing and Information Systems." *Information & Management* (February 1985): 75–80.

Gand, Harvey, and Milt E. Cook. "Choosing an MRP System." *Datamation* (January 1985): 84–98.

Gerwin, Donald. "Do's and Don'ts of Computerized Manufacturing." *Harvard Business Review* (March/April 1982): 107–116.

Gunn, Thomas. "The CIM Connection." *Datamation* (February 1986): 50–58.

Horngren, Charles T. *Cost Accounting: A Managerial Emphasis.* 5th ed. Englewood Cliffs, N.J.: Prentice-Hall, 1982.

Jelinek, Mariann, and Joel D. Goldhar. "The Strategic Implications of the Factory of the Future." *Sloan Management Review* (Summer 1984): 29–37.

Kaplan, Robert S. "Yesterday's Accounting Undermines Production." *Harvard Business Review* (July/August 1984): 95–101.

Karchner, Quentin L., Jr. "How One Plant Automated Its Collection of Data." *Management Accounting* (September 1980): 45–48.

Price Waterhouse & Co. *Guide to Accounting Controls: Production Costs & Inventories.* New York: Price Waterhouse & Co., 1979.

Severance, Jay, and Ronald R. Bottin. "Work-in-Process Inventory Control through Data Base Concepts." *Management Accounting* (January 1979): 37–41.

Vickery, Adrian R. "Design of a Manufacturing Data Base for Management Use." *Computers & Industrial Engineering* **7** (1983): 225–240.

Wetherbe, James C., and Scott Conrad. "What MIS Executives Need to Know About Robotics." *Journal of Systems Management* (May 1983): 38–42.

Accounting Information Systems for Personnel Management

LEARNING OBJECTIVES

Careful study of this chapter should enable students to:

☐ Describe the decision responsibilities and information requirements of personnel management.

☐ Describe the information provided to personnel management by the accounting information system.

☐ Prepare flowcharts describing data and information flows within a payroll data processing system.

☐ Design and evaluate control policies and procedures for a payroll data processing system.

CHAPTER OUTLINE

Personnel management involves planning, coordinating, and controlling the use of human resources within an organization. Information systems for personnel management are concerned with the processing of information about people within an organization—their recruitment, training, safety, and compensation. The accounting information system generates much information useful to personnel management through systems for processing employee payrolls. This chapter briefly reviews the personnel management function, discusses the nature and sources of personnel information, and explores in more detail the payroll processing system.

The Personnel Management Function

A typical organization structure for the personnel management function is illustrated in Fig. 19.1. However, the personnel management function in an organization does not take place entirely within the personnel organization. Every supervisor within an organization plays a major role in the management of the personnel under his or her supervision. In this sense the personnel management function is the most decentralized of all the management functions. The personnel organization is responsible for those personnel management activities that are most conveniently performed on a centralized basis. This section will review the personnel management responsibilities and related information requirements of the typical departmental supervisor, as well as of the top personnel executive and the various personnel staff functions.

The top personnel executive

The place of the top personnel executive in the organizational structure varies from company to company. In some companies he or she is a vice-president with status equal to that of the vice-presidents for production, marketing, and finance. In other companies the position is subordinate to the vice-president for production. In the latter case responsibilities of the top personnel executive would primarily involve production employees, and executives in other functional areas would hold primary responsibility for personnel management within their respective areas.

FIGURE 19.1
Personnel organization structure.

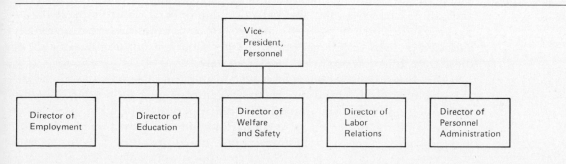

Because of the increasing recognition of the importance of human resources to the business organization, the top personnel executive is increasingly being accepted as a participant in top management planning for corporate resource allocation. In this role, he or she contributes a perspective on the personnel management implications of corporate plans for expansion or contraction of operations. The formal output of this process should be a staffing plan, which forecasts the organization's needs for personnel of various skills and levels of education and experience. In addition, the top personnel executive is responsible for developing recommendations to top management concerning companywide personnel policies. Examples of such policies include hiring practices, job performance standards, health and safety standards, and wage and salary plans.

The top personnel executive is also responsible for the administration of the various personnel staff functions. The staffing plan provides a basis for planning and controlling the activities of employment, and education and training. Major decisions in the areas of welfare and safety, labor relations, and personnel administration require the approval of the top personnel executive. The development of a personnel management organization, the delegation of authority to carry out personnel management activities, and the monitoring of performance of those activities are further administrative functions of the top personnel executive.

The information needs of the top personnel executive are broad. On the one hand, he or she requires quantitative information concerning the number of existing employees in various skill and experience categories, trends in hours worked, efficiency, accident rates, turnover and absenteeism, future staffing requirements, cost of alternative wage and salary proposals, existing labor market conditions, and so forth. Formal information systems are typically designed to fulfill many of these information requirements. On the other hand, the top personnel executive requires qualitative information involving such factors as employee motivation, morale, abilities, and interpersonal relationships. Factors of this sort are not as easily evaluated by formal information systems. However, information of this type is one of the primary products of informal information channels within an organization.

The personnel staff functions

The personnel staff functions of employment, education and training, welfare and safety, labor relations, and personnel administration are representative of the way in which personnel management responsibilities are functionally allocated in many large organizations. The primary responsibilities of each of these staff functions are briefly reviewed here.

The director of employment is responsible for such activities as the development of job specifications, recruiting, interviewing and testing of potential employees, and maintaining files of job applicants. The director is also in charge of hiring, placement, and counseling and may play a role in decision making with respect to promotions and terminations. Programs for recruitment, hiring, training, and advancement of members of minority and disadvantaged groups are an important aspect of this function. The information requirements of the director of employment are both internal and external. The primary internal information need concerns staffing requirements within the firm—both job specifications and quantity requirements. The primary external information need concerns sources of staffing, such as employment agencies, training schools, and college placement offices.

The director of education and training is responsible for developing the skills of personnel at all levels of the organization. At the lowest level, this involves the training of machine operators and clerks. At a higher level it encompasses the training of supervisors and staff personnel. At its highest level it concerns the development of executive skills and experience. Essential to the administration of training programs are such factors as organization and planning of the training program; development of training materials; selection of trainees, instructors, and training site; and evaluation of results. Administration of executive programs includes determination of desired executive capabilities, selection of candidates, choice of a program of development, and evaluation of results.

The director of welfare and safety is responsible for establishing and enforcing health and safety standards within the organization. With respect to health, this function involves maintaining employee medical records, administering physical examinations at the time of employment and periodically thereafter, and providing first-aid and other medical services. With respect to safety, such matters as the establishing of safety rules, planning for the use of protective clothing and mechanical safeguards, administering a program of safety education, and investigating the causes of accidents are involved.

In an organization that has a significant percentage of employees belonging to a union, the director of labor relations plays an important role. This individual has the primary responsibility to prepare for and conduct collective bargaining negotiations with union representatives. Other responsibilities include handling of grievances and arbitration with respect to the union contract and maintaining compliance with federal and state labor legislation.

The personnel administration function encompasses a variety of personnel services. These include wage and salary programs, profit sharing and incentive plans, pension plans, executive compensation packages, group insurance plans, employee credit unions, plant cafeterias, in-house publications, recreation programs, and employee suggestion plans. The function also includes the maintenance of up-to-date personnel records on all employees within the organization.

**The departmental
supervisor**

Each departmental supervisor within an organization is directly responsible for the day-to-day planning, coordination, and control of that department's employees and must organize the tasks to be performed, assign employees to jobs, coordinate their activities, motivate them, monitor their performance, evaluate their abilities, provide on-the-job training, and enforce company policies.

Much of the information required by the departmental supervisor to perform the personnel management function may be obtained simply from observation and experience. However, the formal information system provides useful supplementary information. This would include statistics concerning the productivity (output per work-hour) of each employee at each job within the department. Among other useful information regarding individual employees are rate of absenteeism and tardiness, quality of work performed, and level of skills. Qualitative assessments provided by other employees or supervisors concerning personality and character may also be useful.

Sources of Personnel Information

The primary sources of personnel information are the accounting information system and the personnel department. Personnel information is also obtained from other sources inside the business organization as well as from external sources. This section reviews the nature of the information available from each of these sources.

The accounting information system

The payroll processing system is the traditional channel within which personnel information is generated from accounting data. The human resource accounting system is a new channel for such information and is, in fact, used in only a very small number of companies, primarily on an experimental basis. Both these systems are discussed here; the payroll processing system is discussed in greater detail in a subsequent section. Cost estimation for wage negotiations is a third source of accounting information for personnel management discussed in this section.

The payroll processing system.   With respect to the processing of factory payrolls, the two basic input documents are the job time card and the employee clock card. The nature and use of the job time card as a source of data for labor cost distribution is described in Chapter 18, and two examples of job time cards are illustrated in Figs. 18.10 and 18.14. The employee clock card, illustrated in Fig. 19.2, indicates the total number of hours the employee spends at work each day. This document serves as the basic input to the payroll calculation and paycheck preparation function.

With respect to the processing of payrolls for clerical, sales, and salaried employees, the nature of data input is somewhat different. Because administrative and selling expenses are not charged to production in process, the job-time card is not used. However, a form similar to a job time card may be used if administrative expenses are charged to specific projects, such as a software development project, a sales promotion, or a research and development project (see Fig. 14.2). The employee clock card may be used for those clerical

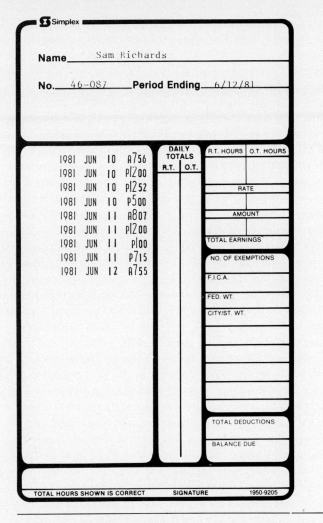

FIGURE 19.2
Employee clock card.
(Courtesy of Simplex
Time Recorder Co.,
Gardner,
Massachusetts.)

employees who are paid on an hourly basis but is not needed for those paid
a salary. The monthly gross pay of a salaried employee is a known constant
except in those cases in which some salaried employees are paid for overtime
work. For salespeople paid on a commission basis, sales data are required for
payroll processing.

Another basic class of inputs to the payroll processing system includes
additions, deletions, and adjustments of various kinds to employee payroll
records. The category of adjustments includes salary or wage rate changes,
address changes, departmental transfers, changes in tax exemptions, changes
in deduction authorizations, and so forth. The volume and variety of these
transactions are often quite large.

Among basic outputs of payroll processing are employee paychecks and earnings statements and various reports required by governmental authorities. However, a variety of useful personnel information may be generated as a by-product of payroll processing. Reports that measure employee efficiency or productivity are one example. From the job time cards, the average time spent by each production employee in performing each job operation can be determined. For each operation the average time spent by all employees in performing that operation can be derived. If a standard cost system or work measurement system is used, a comparison of average actual time to standard time provides a measure of the efficiency with which each operation is being performed. The relative efficiency of each employee can be generated by taking a weighted average of his or her efficiency in all the various operations performed by that person. Finally, the aggregation of these statistics by department provides a measure of departmental efficiency useful in evaluating the performance of departmental supervisors. If a standard cost system is employed, efficiency measures in the form of labor cost variances can also be provided. An example of a report containing information of this type is illustrated in Fig. 18.3.

Several other types of reports and analyses may be generated from payroll processing. These include reports of absenteeism and tardiness by employee; analyses of indirect labor by type of cost—supervision, materials handling, inspection, etc.—and by department; reports on actual and standard labor costs for completed production orders; analyses of overtime pay by department; analyses of fringe benefit costs; and reports on sales commission expenses. Also valuable in staff planning are certain aggregate statistics accumulated during payroll processing, such as total number of employees, total hours worked, total labor cost, average wage rate, rate of absenteeism, rate of turnover, and average and total fringe benefit costs. These statistics are most meaningful when trends in their values are analyzed and correlated with each other and with other factors. For example, useful management information may be obtained from correlating the rate of turnover with average hours worked per employee, or the rate of absenteeism with the number of units that fail to pass quality control inspection.

Human resource accounting.   The basic philosophy of human resource accounting is that human resources are assets, and that the investment in acquiring and developing these resources should be accounted for as an asset. Expenditures for hiring and training, which would be expensed in conventional accounting systems, are capitalized and allocated to individual employees. As with the cost of other assets, this cost is amortized over the expected useful life of the asset. The net investment in an employee who is terminated is written off as a loss.

Useful information for staff planning is provided by the human resource accounting system. The year-to-year change in the total balance of the human resources account (annual investment minus amortization and turnover losses) provides an indication of management's performance in maintaining and developing human assets. Adding the human resources account into the total asset base may provide more significant measures of return on investment. Information concerning the probable loss of human resources is useful to decisions regarding employee layoffs. Finally, capital investment information may be more meaningful if each investment proposed includes an analysis of the human resources that must be invested in the project and those that will be consumed by the project.

Human resource accounting is a new and unconventional technique. It is not recognized for tax purposes or for financial reporting under generally accepted accounting principles. Its use imposes additional requirements for data collection and processing, record keeping, and reporting upon accounting information systems. Despite these disadvantages, human resource accounting seems likely to become an important element of accounting information systems in an age during which human knowledge and ability is recognized as being of critical importance to the modern business organization.[1]

Cost estimation for wage negotiations. Contract negotiations with labor unions require management to make trade-offs between such factors as the wage rate, paid vacations, paid holidays, contributions to employee insurance and pension plans, and overtime premiums. Each of these factors has a cost, and management should be provided with estimates of the cost implications of various alternative contract proposals to use as a basis for bargaining. Cost accountants and payroll accountants are in the best position to develop such estimates and should therefore participate in this aspect of collective bargaining. Accounting systems should be designed to facilitate the preparation of whatever kinds of information management deems useful for this purpose.[2]

The personnel department

Much valuable information for personnel management is generated by and maintained within the personnel department. One of the best sources of information is the personnel data file, in which is maintained a complete record of each employee in the organization. This record includes such data as the physical characteristics of the employee, background of education and experience, basic payroll information, quantitative and qualitative evaluations

---

[1]For further discussion of human resource accounting, see R. Lee Brummet, Eric G. Flamholtz, and William C. Pyle, "Human Resource Accounting—A Challenge for Accountants," *Accounting Review* (April 1968): 217–224; and Mohammad A. Sangeladji, "Human Resource Accounting: A Refined Measurement Model," *Management Accounting* (December 1977): 48–52.

[2]For an extensive treatment of this topic, see Harry C. Fisher, *The Uses of Accounting in Collective Bargaining* (Los Angeles: Institute of Industrial Relations, University of California, 1969). Also see Walter A. Hazelton, "How to Cost Labor Settlements," *Management Accounting* (May 1979): 19–23.

of past performance, state of health and medical history, and results of tests of ability and aptitude. This data file provides a basic source of information for decisions regarding assignment of employees to positions, approval of raises and promotions, and selection of supervisory and management trainees. If properly organized to facilitate information retrieval and aggregation, the employee data base can also be a useful tool for companywide staff planning.

Other information developed and maintained by the personnel department includes job specifications, which detail the training and experience required to qualify for each job in the organization; aggregate safety and accident statistics; forecasts of staffing requirements by job category within the organization; and records and statistics concerning training programs, health services, employee credit unions, and other employee services.

Other internal sources

One of the primary sources of personnel information is the departmental supervisor, who is responsible for providing merit evaluations of the employees under his or her supervision. These are basically qualitative evaluations of such factors as personality, initiative, attitude, judgment, and character. Departmental supervisors also supply the personnel department with information concerning the staffing requirements of their department in terms of the number of employees required and the desired qualifications.

Other functional departments within the firm may also contribute worthwhile information for personnel management. For example, the engineering department may develop job time standards for use in evaluating employee performance. The legal department may provide advice concerning legal aspects of employee relations. The economics department may provide special studies of labor market conditions and their implications for hiring policies or wage negotiations.

External information sources

External sources of information for personnel management include employment agencies, labor unions, vocational and training schools, university placement offices, and various governmental agencies. Information regarding potential employees may be obtained from employment agencies, schools, personal references, and in some cases, labor unions. Labor unions also serve as a spokesperson for employees with respect to their satisfaction with the existing labor contract and the topics that will most concern them during negotiation of the next contract. Various agencies of state and federal government often make available research studies or statistical compilations concerning such factors as labor market conditions, prevailing wage rates, levels of unemployment, and industry accident rates. College placement offices provide statistics on expected number of graduates by area of specialization. Personnel managers must be familiar with all these various external sources of personnel information.

The Payroll Processing System

The general nature of the input to and output from payroll processing has already been reviewed. This section will outline the accounting transactions involved in the process, describe in detail the data maintained in the payroll master file, and then explore in some depth examples of a manual payroll system and a computer-based payroll system.

The accounting transactions

There are two basic accounting journal entries that reflect payroll processing. The first of these shows payroll cost distribution to various expense and inventory accounts.

Work-in-Process Inventory	XXX	
Manufacturing Overhead	XXX	
General and Administrative Expense	XXX	
Selling Expense	XXX	
Payroll		XXX

The debit portions of this entry are classified according to the type of cost and the department number of the employee and are accumulated for purposes of preparing departmental cost performance reports. The work-in-process portion of the entry is further classified and accumulated by production order as explained in Chapter 18.

The second of the two basic accounting journal entries in payroll processing reflects the payroll calculation and paycheck preparation process.

Payroll	XXX	
Federal Income Tax Withholdings Payable		XXX
FICA Tax Withholdings Payable		XXX
State Income Tax Withholdings Payable		XXX
Group Insurance Premiums Payable		XXX
Pension Fund Witholdings Payable		XXX
Savings Bond Deductions Payable		XXX
Union Dues Deductions Payable		XXX
Cash		XXX

The deduction accounts shown in the entry represent the most common payroll deductions. After the payroll preparation is completed, the total balance in each of these liability accounts is paid with a single check. The credit to cash represents the total of all employee paychecks issued. The debit to the payroll control account in this entry should be exactly equal to the total credit to this account in the previous entry.

The payroll data base

In manual data processing systems, a payroll master file is generally maintained by the accounting department, and a personnel master file is maintained by the personnel department. Since the entity—the employee—around which these files are organized is the same for both files, they are a prime candidate for integration when the organization converts to an automated system. Thus the payroll data base may be looked upon as a subset of the personnel data base.

An example of the data content and organization of a payroll data base is illustrated in Fig. 19.3. The figure indicates that there is a one-to-one relationship between an employee's personnel records and his or her payroll record. The payroll segment of the data base is in the form of a two-level tree in which a series of deduction records form a repeating group within the employee payroll record.

Several fields shown within the payroll data base require further explanation. The "pay basis" code indicates whether the employee is paid on an hourly, salaried, or other basis. The "debit code" indicates the account to which the employee's gross pay is charged—direct labor, indirect labor, sales commission, etc. The "number of exemptions" and "marital code" are required for computing federal income tax withholdings. For each employee, there will be a separate deduction record for each type of deduction from that employee's gross pay, including federal and state taxes, social security taxes, life and health insurance premiums, pension fund contributions, savings bond purchases, union dues, and so forth. Each deduction record contains codes identifying the type of deduction and the basis or rate of calculation. Quarterly and year-to-date totals of gross pay, net pay, and each type of deduction must be maintained for periodic reporting to the federal government.

The payroll data base is updated once at the end of each payroll period for all adjustments to employee records, new hires, terminations, and time-worked data for hourly employees. The output of this process includes employee paychecks and earnings statements and a *payroll register,* which is a listing of payroll data for each employee for the current payroll period. A separate *deduction register* may also be prepared detailing the miscellaneous deductions of each employee. These two reports are illustrated in Fig. 19.4. At intervals other than during payroll preparation, the payroll data base is used to prepare various reports for managers and the government.

The processing of payroll transactions affects not only the payroll data base but also numerous other data bases within a business organization. For example, new hires, terminations, job transfers, pay increases, and similar transactions must also be posted to the personnel data base. If payroll and personnel records are properly integrated, then only one updating process will be required to post these transactions to all affected records. For another

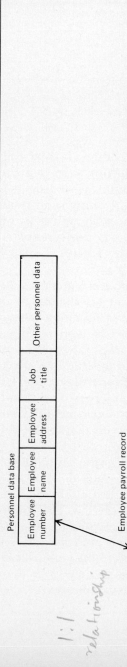

FIGURE 19.3
Payroll data base.

789

PAYROLL REGISTER   DATE _____

YEAR-TO-DATE EARNINGS	YEAR-TO-DATE WITH. TAX	DEPT	EMPLOYEE NUMBER	NAME OF EMPLOYEE	HOURS WORKED	BASE RATE	EARNINGS REGULAR	EARNINGS OT PREM	EARNINGS OTHER	EARNINGS TOTAL	DEDUCTIONS FICA	DEDUCTIONS WITH. TAX	DEDUCTIONS MISC.	NET PAY
3002|38	267|68	01	206	W V ASTOR	44|0	2|250	99|00	4|50		103|50	3|74	10|85	8|75	80|15
2684|30	361|44	01	342	A F DUFFY	50|0	2|250	112|50	11|25		123|75	4|49	11|87	3|25	104|14
2432|71	255|24	01	518	B H ENGLISH	40|0	2|150	86|00			86|00	3|12	6|58	4|50	71|80
1807|50	266|22	01	615	F L FARELY	42|0	1|500	63|00	1|60	4|00	68|60	2|49	7|78	3|50	54|83
2175|64	269|82	01	703	J E GENDER	42|0	1|350	77|70	1|99	6|00	85|69	3|10	8|36	2|50	71|73
2231|27	342|54	01	893	F A HARRIS	44|0	1|900	83|60	4|06	5|75	93|41	3|39	11|26	3|75	75|01
1945|78											4|04	16|40	7|42	106|76
1870|32											3|38	8|70	5|80	94|92
2461|11											3|20	14|70	2|20	86|70
875|82											4|16	20|10	18|40	95|91
2521|12											4|08	21|00	21|61	89|47
2434|61											3|28	16|10	7|60	82|36
2220|02											3|85	25|60	17|41	

TYPE
1—SINGLE PERIOD
2—SPECIFIC PERIOD
3—STANDING

WHEN MADE
1—FIRST WEEK   5—1ST AND 2ND WEEK
2—SECOND WEEK   6—2ND AND 4TH WEEK
3—THIRD WEEK   7—EACH WEEK
4—FOURTH WEEK

DEDUCTION REGISTER   DATE _____

DEPT	NUMBER	NAME OF EMPLOYEE	DED. CODE	TYPE CODE	WHEN MADE	TOTAL DEDUCTIONS	SAVINGS BOND	HOSPITAL INSURANCE	GROUP LIFE INS.	CREDIT UNION	RETIRE ANNUITY
01	206	W V ASTOR	4	3	4	8|75				8|75	
01	342	A F DUFFY	2	3	4	1|25		1|25			
01	342	A F DUFFY	4	3	4	2|00				2|00	
01	518	B H ENGLISH	1	3	6	2|00	2|00				
01	518	B H ENGLISH	5	3	4	2|50					2|50
01	615	F L FARELY	2	3	4	1|50		1|50			
01	615	F L	3	3	4	2|00			2|00		
01	703					2|50	2|50				

FIGURE 19.4
Payroll and deduction registers. (Reprinted by permission from *Basic Applications— System/360 Model 20.* Copyright © 1971 by International Business Machines Corporation.)

example, the debit distribution of the gross payroll must be posted to several data bases, including the production work-in-process data base (see Chapter 18), and numerous overhead and expense ledgers within the accounting data base (see Chapter 20). In a highly automated system, these operations could be integrated with payroll processing, but most business organizations have not yet achieved such a high level of integration.

A manual system

Figure 19.5 illustrates one example of a manual system for processing a factory payroll. Unless otherwise indicated in the discussion, the flowchart is also applicable to the processing of an office employee payroll. A payroll master file is maintained by the payroll department. Terminations, hirings of new employees, changes in employee wage rates, tax status, or deduction authorizations, and any other changes in this file that affect payroll preparation must be approved by the personnel department, which also maintains a record of these data for each employee in a personnel data file. Good internal control requires that the internal audit department periodically compare the payroll data in the payroll master file with that in the personnel file to prevent unauthorized changes in the payroll master.

Regular payroll processing begins with the collection of employee time-worked data. The flowchart illustrates this process with respect to factory employees. The job-time ticket is filled out by each employee for each job upon which he or she works during the day. For control purposes, each job-time ticket should be verified and signed by the departmental supervisor.

Each day, the job-time tickets are transmitted to the timekeeping department where they are reconciled to the employee clock cards. The clock cards are generally prepared by using a time clock upon which employees punch in and out of work. The reconciliation step is a check that the total time spent

FIGURE 19.5
Document flow in a manual system for payroll processing.

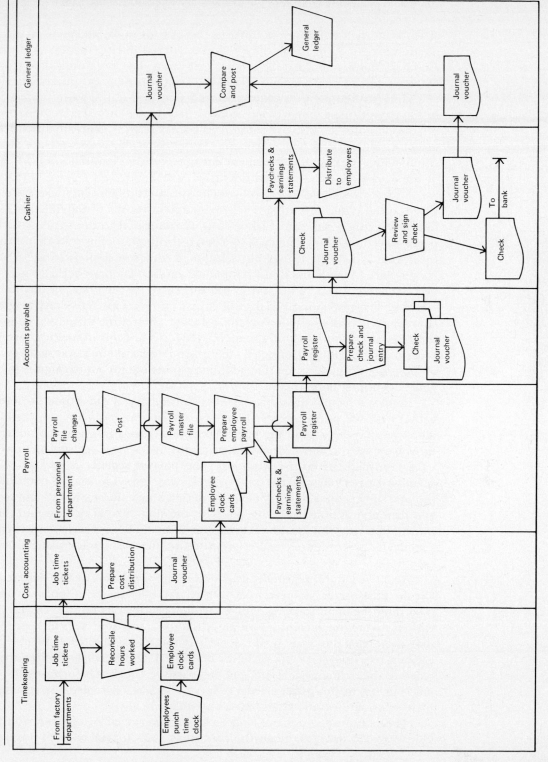

at work by each employee is equal to the sum of the time spent on all production orders upon which the employee worked during the day. This internal check helps to ensure the accuracy of input data regarding time worked
by factory employees prior to its use in various subsequent processing steps.

Time-worked data for salaried employees does not need to be provided
to the payroll department. Time-worked data for factory service department
or office employees who are paid on an hourly basis is generally provided by
use of a time clock or by departmental supervisors. If salespeople are paid by
commission, the payroll department must receive the required input from one
of the marketing or sales departments.

After reconciliation to employee clock cards, the job time tickets are provided to the cost accounting department for purposes of payroll cost distribution. At this point, direct labor costs are allocated to the various work-in-
process accounts, and a journal voucher recording a debit to work-in-process
inventory and credit to payroll is initiated and transmitted to the general
ledger clerk. As explained in Chapter 18, applied factory overhead may also
be calculated at this point and would therefore be included on this journal
voucher. The distribution of payroll costs to the various subsidiary ledger accounts of the manufacturing overhead ledger, the selling expense ledger, and
the general and administrative expense ledger is not shown on the chart. This
function is typically performed by the payroll department in a manual system,
and this department would then also be responsible for preparing the journal
voucher summarizing the distribution.

Employee clock cards are provided to the payroll department where, together with the payroll master file, they provide the basis for preparation of
employee paychecks and the payroll register. Once gross pay and all deductions have been computed and entered into the payroll register, net pay can
be determined. When preparation of the payroll register is completed, the
accuracy of net pay calculations is checked by cross-footing, or determining
the sum of the gross pay, net pay, and deductions columns for all employees,
and then comparing total gross pay with the sum of total net pay and deductions. Following this internal check, the individual paychecks and earnings
statements are prepared and transmitted to the cashier for distribution to
employees.

Next the payroll register is provided to the accounts payable department.
On the basis of the column totals of the payroll register, a journal voucher
recording the debit to the payroll control account and credit to cash and the
various deduction accounts is prepared. At the same time, a check is prepared
that authorizes the transfer of the net pay total from the firm's regular bank
account to its payroll bank account. This check and journal voucher are provided to the cashier, who signs and deposits the check and forwards the journal voucher to the general ledger clerk. The payroll register is retained to
provide an audit trail of the payroll process.

At this point the general ledger clerk has received two journal vouchers.
One records a debit to the payroll control account for the gross pay of factory

employees, and the other records a credit for the same item. The amount of these two entries to the payroll control account should be exactly equal. If the amounts are not equal, an error has occurred either in direct labor cost distribution or paycheck preparation, and the error must be discovered and corrected. This form of internal check is called a *zero balance check* because the balance of the payroll control account should be zero after these entries are made. Similar checks could be made on the payroll distribution to manufacturing overhead, selling expense, and general and administrative expense.

The use of a separate payroll bank account improves internal control because it facilitates the preparation of bank reconciliations. It is much easier to prepare two separate reconciliations, and to trace the source of any discrepancies, than to prepare one large reconciliation of a single account. Periodically, the internal audit department must prepare the reconciliation of the payroll bank account. The payroll bank statement, deposit tickets, and cancelled paychecks provide a basis for this function.

Organizational independence with respect to payroll processing is achieved by the multitude of functional separations that exist in the system. Perhaps the most significant of these is the separation of time keeping from payroll preparation, which tends to prevent errors or manipulations involving submission of time data for terminated or nonexistent employees. This type of error or manipulation is also inhibited by separation of payroll preparation from paycheck distribution, together with special procedures for handling unclaimed paychecks. Separation of the personnel function from the payroll preparation function, along with periodic comparison of the payroll records of both functions, tends to prevent errors or manipulations with respect to the payroll master file. Separation of the timekeeping function from the factory departments tends to prevent errors or manipulations involving input data for factory employees. Separation of the cost distribution and payroll preparation functions tends to prevent errors or manipulation in the distribution of payroll costs or the calculation of gross pay. Finally, the separate internal audit function provides an independent check on the operation of the entire payroll system.

Special control procedures are necessary in a payroll processing system for handling unclaimed paychecks. If paychecks are distributed by hand to employees, unclaimed paychecks for terminated or absent employees will be fairly common. Even if paychecks are distributed by mail, some may occasionally be returned for lack of a forwarding address. In any event, the unclaimed paycheck indicates the possibility of manipulation. The internal audit department should trace the preparation of such paychecks to the original timekeeping records and should check the payroll master file against the personnel master in all such cases. The internal audit department should make further attempts to distribute such checks to the proper persons and, if unsuccessful, should lock them up for safekeeping and eventually destroy them.

The internal audit department is also responsible for certain other internal control activities with respect to payroll processing. A sample of payroll calculations may be reviewed in detail for each payroll period. Payroll calculations of paychecks for employees of the payroll department should be reviewed frequently in detail. Periodically, internal audit personnel should take charge of the distribution of paychecks to employees to ensure that all paychecks prepared are being received by bona fide employees.

The payroll processing function is one of the most time-consuming clerical functions in many organizations. In a manual payroll processing system it may be difficult to both complete payroll preparation and cost distribution and generate useful reports concerning labor costs, production efficiency, and so forth. Several devices have therefore been developed to facilitate payroll processing. One device is the payroll board, which is a type of pegboard designed so that several records may be written simultaneously using carbon paper. An example is illustrated in Fig. 19.6. In the board shown in the illustration, data written onto the employee earnings statement are simultaneously written onto the employee payroll master record and the payroll register. These data would include the employee's name and number, the date, hours worked, gross pay, itemized withholdings, other deductions, and net pay. Certain other data, such as check number and year-to-date earnings totals, are simultaneously written onto the employee payroll master record and the payroll register. The payroll cost distribution is entered only in the payroll register.

FIGURE 19.6
Payroll board for
simultaneous writing
of payroll records.

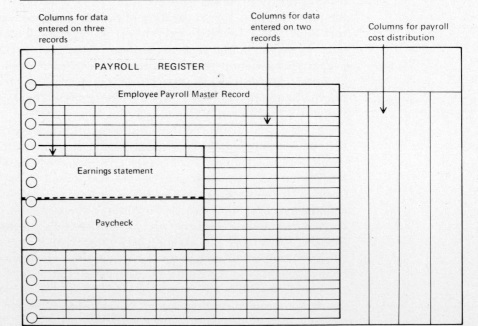

A computer-based batch processing system

Because of the volume and complexity of payroll processing, and the routine nature of payroll calculations and records, this operation has generally been one of the first to be computerized in most organizations. A document flowchart of a computer-based system for processing a factory payroll in a typical manufacturing company appears in Fig. 19.7. It is assumed that the payroll processing is performed in batch mode using magnetic tape input and magnetic disk file storage. A comparison of this system with its manual counterpart of Fig. 19.5 reveals that the computer has replaced the functions of cost distribution and payroll preparation but that many of the other functions remain unchanged.

The payroll master file is maintained by the computer operations department on magnetic disk. File changes must be authorized by the personnel department and are then transmitted to the input preparation department for keying onto magnetic tape. Job-time tickets and employee clock cards are prepared in the same manner as described for the manual system, but both of these input documents are also routed to input preparation for keying onto tape.

As in the manual system, employee checks and earnings statements are sent to the cashier for distribution to employees. At the same time, the payroll register is sent to the cashier, who prepares the check to authorize transfer of funds to the payroll bank account. The journal entry printouts are provided to the general ledger clerk for posting. As in the manual system, the internal audit section is responsible for preparing a reconciliation of the payroll bank account.

After the various input records have been keyed and verified, the input tape is taken to computer operations for processing. The computerized processing of job-time data to update records of cost and operations performed for production in process is discussed in Chapter 18 and illustrated in Fig. 18.15. The systems flowchart of Fig. 19.8 illustrates the computer processing of file changes and employee time card data to update the payroll master file and to prepare employee checks and earnings statements, the payroll register, and the summary payroll journal entry. The data preparation process generates batch totals and magnetic tape records sorted into sequence by employee number. The payroll register generated by the file update program is on magnetic tape and must be processed again to prepare a printed payroll register.

Some of the internal controls described for the manual payroll processing system are replaced in the computerized system by new sets of controls. For example, such batch totals as record counts of the number of employee time records and the number of file changes of each type, as well as hash totals of employee numbers and hours worked, should be prepared from source documents and compared with those accumulated during processing. Batch totals from the payroll master file itself, including the number of employees and a hash total of employee wage rates, should also be accumulated during processing and printed out for comparison with personnel department records.

FIGURE 19.7
Document flow in a computerized batch processing system for payroll processing.

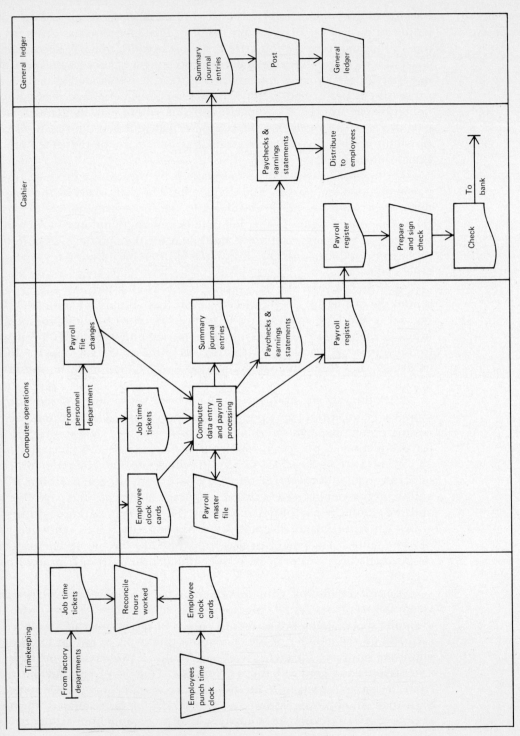

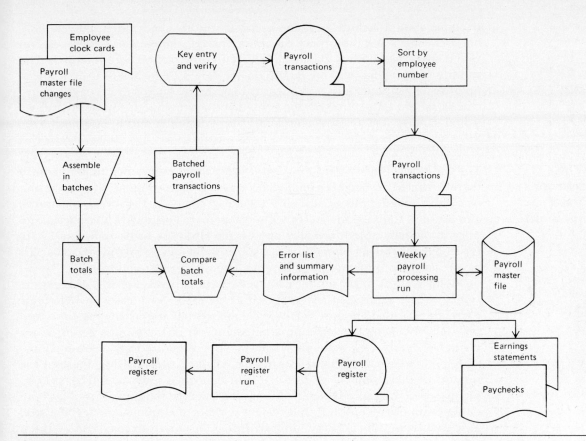

FIGURE 19.8
Systems flow in computerized batch processing of payrolls.

The keying step should be controlled by keyverification and the use of check digit verification on employee numbers. Furthermore, a printout of file change records might be prepared and sent to the personnel department for verification of the integrity of all file changes processed.

Other important areas of control with respect to computerized payroll processing include data security and input validation. For example, the payroll master file and the payroll transactions and payroll register tapes should make use of both internal and external labels to prevent accidental processing of these files by the wrong program. A backup copy of the payroll master file should be written onto magnetic tape at the completion of the file update process and stored in a secure off-site location. Tape file protection rings should be removed from the payroll transaction tape, the payroll register tape, and the backup master file tape to prevent them from being accidentally written on during processing. The disk pack containing the current copy of the payroll master file should be stored in the file library when not in use and removed only for authorized purposes. Edit checks within the main payroll program should include a sequence check, validity check on employee number, field check and limit check on hours worked, and reasonableness tests on rate increases and other file changes affecting the payroll computations. The validity of the computations might also be tested by means of a limit check on gross pay and net pay. Any records that violate one or more of these edit checks should be printed on the error list for subsequent follow-up and resubmission by someone independent of programming and operations.

Real-Time Systems for Personnel Management

The use of real-time systems for payroll processing is very uncommon because there is almost no need for immediate access to payroll data. The processing of payroll transactions occurs on a regular cycle, once each week or month, and all such transactions are processed together. This makes the payroll application ideally suited for batch processing. However, as described in Chapter 18, the processing of job time and job cost data on a real-time basis as part of a real-time production information system is fairly common.

With respect to personnel management in general, the use of real-time systems offers significant advantages in some cases. Such cases involve organizations in which employee skills are an extremely important resource, and decisions involving the selection and assignment of the human resource are made frequently. One example would be large organizations of professional people, such as management consultants, engineers, or lawyers, that sell the services of their employees for a fee, and that often must search for an employee whose specialized qualifications best meet the requirements of a client. Other examples include large placement services or employment agencies and military organizations. Large multidivisional corporations may also be interested in applying this approach to their top managerial and staff personnel.

A real-time personnel management system of this type would center around a personnel data base maintained on direct-access storage. The data base would be indexed according to classifications of skills, experience, and other qualifications possessed by employees. A software system would be designed to facilitate searching the data base for the names of employees possessing certain desired combinations of characteristics. For example, an employee may be sought who possesses an educational background in engineering and management, experience in industrial engineering, and the ability to speak a foreign language. If such an employee existed, that person's name could be retrieved by the system in a matter of seconds or minutes, and that person's qualifications listed or displayed for review by management. By means of the index of skills, the personnel data base becomes a *skills inventory file*.

Summary

The accounting information system provides much information useful to personnel management, primarily from the payroll data processing system. Other sources of information for personnel management include systems of cost estimation for wage negotiations, human resource accounting systems, personnel department records, and performance evaluations prepared by functional department supervisors.

Payroll data processing involves large volumes of data and computation but is quite routine. Thus it is a prime candidate for automation and is often one of the first computer applications to be implemented in an organization. Payroll processing by computer is generally accomplished in batch mode because there is little need for real-time access to payroll information. However, in organizations that employ large numbers of highly trained employees, a real-time personnel management information system may be very useful for the effective management of human resources.

Review Questions

1. Define the following terms.

   payroll register   zero balance check
   deduction register   skills inventory file

2. In very general terms, what is personnel management and what type of information is processed by an information system for personnel management?

3. Describe or illustrate an example of a typical personnel organization structure. Describe the responsibilities of each separate personnel function within the organization.

4. Describe the information requirements of the top personnel executive in an organization.

5. Describe the personnel management responsibilities and related information requirements of the typical departmental supervisor within an organization.

6. Describe the nature of the personnel information generated by
   a) the accounting information system,
   b) the personnel department,
   c) other sources of information within the business organization, and
   d) sources external to the business organization.

7. What input data are required for processing the payrolls of
   a) factory employees,
   b) salaried employees, and
   c) salespeople paid on a commission basis?

8. Identify several examples of nonroutine file maintenance transactions involving the payroll master file.

9. What is human resource accounting and how is it different from conventional accounting? Illustrate by means of sample journal entries.

10. What accounting journal entries summarize the activities involved in payroll processing?

11. Describe in detail the data content of a payroll data base.

12. What departments in a manufacturing company might be involved in the manual processing of payrolls? What documents might be processed and what data would each contain? Where would each originate, and where and for what purposes would it be distributed?

13. Describe several control procedures that might be used in a manual system for payroll processing.

14. How is organizational independence achieved with respect to payroll processing?

15. Explain some of the control procedures in payroll processing commonly performed by internal auditing personnel.

16. What is a payroll board and how might it be used?

17. Describe the similarities and differences in processing of payrolls in a typical business organization using a computer rather than a manual data processing system. Emphasize documents, departments, and reports involved in the process.

18. What internal controls might be used in computerized payroll processing?

19. Why is it uncommon for real-time systems to be applied to payroll processing?

20. What type of organization would utilize a real-time system for personnel management? Explain how such a system would be useful.

Discussion Questions

21. Do some research to discover how financial accounting theorists define the term *asset*. Are human resources considered as assets under this definition? Is it possible to record human resources as assets under generally accepted accounting principles? Should it be possible to do so? Discuss.

22. Do you expect that in the near future most large firms will utilize a real-time personnel management system? Discuss.

23. Does a good departmental supervisor really need quantitative information, such as measures of employee productivity, to adequately perform the personnel management function? Discuss.

Problems and Cases

24. You are engaged in auditing the financial statements of Henry Brown, a large independent contractor. All employees are paid in cash because Mr. Brown believes this arrangement reduces clerical expenses and is preferred by his employees.

During the audit you find in the petty cash fund approximately $200, of which $185 is stated to be unclaimed wages. Further investigation reveals that Mr. Brown has installed the procedure of putting any unclaimed wages in the petty cash fund so that the cash can be used for disbursements. When the claimant to the wages appears, he or she is paid from the petty cash fund. Mr. Brown contends that this procedure reduces the number of checks drawn to replenish the petty cash fund and centers the responsibility for all cash on hand in one person inasmuch as the petty cash custodian distributes the pay envelopes.

a) Does Mr. Brown's system provide proper internal control of unclaimed wages? Explain fully.

b) Because Mr. Brown insists on paying salaries in cash, what procedures would you recommend to provide better internal control over unclaimed wages? (CPA Examination)

25. What controls in a manual system for processing factory payrolls are designed to provide the best protection against the following errors or manipulations?

a) The carrying of names of former employees on the payroll after their termination in order to receive and cash their paychecks.

b) Incorrect recording of hours worked on a job.

c) A dishonest payroll employee overstating the pay rate or hours worked of friends in order that their paychecks are higher than they should be.

d) A factory employee punches a friend's clock card in at 1:00 and out at 5:00 while the friend spends the afternoon playing golf.

e) An arithmetic error in calculation of gross pay for a factory employee.

f) Incorrect calculation of federal income tax deduction such that gross pay does not equal the sum of all deductions plus net pay.

g) The cashier pocketing and cashing unclaimed paychecks of terminated employees.

h) An arithmetic error in the calculation of labor costs allocated to jobs in process.

26. Prepare a record layout for the following payroll transactions that are to be processed as input to a computerized payroll data base identical to that in Fig. 19.3.

a) Add an employee payroll record for a newly hired employee.

b) Change an existing employee's number of exemptions.

c) Add a deduction record for an employee who authorizes a monthly savings bond deduction.

d) Change an employee's regular pay rate.

27. The Kowal Manufacturing Company employs about 50 production workers and has the following payroll procedures.

The factory supervisor interviews applicants and on the basis of the

[handwritten margin notes: "eliminate → no wage documentation of wage some kind of negotiated before hired no segregation of duties"]

interview either hires or rejects the applicants. The applicant who is hired prepares a W-4 form (Employee's Withholding Exemption Certificate) and gives it to the supervisor. The supervisor writes the hourly rate of pay for the new employee in the corner of the W-4 form and then gives the form to a payroll clerk as notice that the worker has been employed. The supervisor verbally advises the payroll department of rate adjustments.

A supply of blank time cards is kept in a box near the entrance to the factory. All workers take a time card on Monday morning, fill in their names, and note in pencil on the time card their daily arrival and departure times. At the end of the week the workers drop the time cards in a box near the door to the factory. The completed time cards are taken from the box on Monday morning by a payroll clerk. Two payroll clerks divide the cards alphabetically between them, one taking the A to L section of the payroll and the other taking the M to Z section. Each clerk is fully responsible for a section of the payroll. The clerk computes the gross pay, deductions, and net pay, posts the details to the employee's earnings records, and prepares and numbers the payroll checks. Employees are automatically removed from the payroll when they fail to turn in a time card.

[handwritten margin note: "batch"]

The payroll checks are manually signed by the chief accountant and given to the supervisor. The supervisor distributes the checks to the workers in the factory and arranges for the delivery of the checks to the workers who are absent. The payroll bank account is reconciled by the chief accountant who also prepares the various quarterly and annual payroll tax reports.

[handwritten margin note: "Prenumbered cheques"]

List your suggestions for improving the Kowal Manufacturing Company's system of internal control for the factory hiring practices and payroll procedures. (CPA Examination)

28. The Karras Corporation is a large multidivisional enterprise. One of its divisions is located in Farmbelt, Iowa. In the spring of 1978 the personnel manager of the Farmbelt Division and an assistant went on a recruiting trip to several Midwest business schools. Four graduating business school students were hired as management trainees. The total cost of the recruiting trip was $4000.

In the summer of 1978 the four management trainees were sent to Chicago for a corporate training program. Travel and lodging for the trip cost $2400. Corporate headquarters charged the division $800 per trainee as the cost of the training session. Upon completion of the training program, each of the four new employees was assigned to an assistant manager position at the Farmbelt Division.

In late 1978 Karras Corporation's top management decided to institute an extreme cost-cutting campaign for the year 1979. The manager of the Farmbelt Division wondered whether to retain the services of the four new assistant managers. The manager had planned to assign them to permanent management positions in July 1979. If they were released, their salaries of $16,800 each for the first six months of 1979 could be saved. However, four new employees would eventually have to be recruited, trained, and allowed to gain some experience for the four management positions that would be open July 1979.

a) Show by means of journal entries how the recruiting, training, and travel expenditures would be treated using conventional accounting principles.

b) Show by means of journal entries how the recruiting, training, and travel expenditures would be treated using human resource accounting.

c) If the four new assistant managers are released, what journal entry would be made in a conventional accounting system? In a human resource accounting system?

d) Would the conventional or human resource accounting system provide more meaningful information in this case for purposes of deciding whether to release or retain the four assistant managers? Explain.

29. A CPA's audit working papers contain a narrative description of a **segment** of the Croyden Factory, Inc., payroll system and an accompanying flowchart (Fig. 19.9) as follows:

NARRATIVE

The internal control system with respect to the personnel department is well-functioning and is **not** included in the accompanying flowchart.

At the beginning of each work week payroll clerk No. 1 reviews the payroll department files to determine the employment status of factory employees and then prepares time cards and distributes them as each individual arrives at work. This payroll clerk, who is also responsible for custody of the signature stamp machine, verifies the identity of each payee before delivering signed checks to the foreman.

At the end of each work week the foreman distributes payroll checks for the preceding work week. Concurrent with this activity, the foreman reviews the current week's employee time cards, notes the regular and overtime hours worked on a summary form, and initials the aforementioned time cards. The foreman then delivers all time cards and unclaimed payroll checks to payroll clerk No. 2.

REQUIRED

a) Based upon the narrative and accompanying flowchart, what are the weaknesses in the system of internal control?

b) Based upon the narrative and accompanying flowchart, what inquiries should be made with respect to clarifying the existence of **possible additional weaknesses** in the system of internal control?

Note: Do not discuss the internal control system of the personnel department. (CPA Examination)

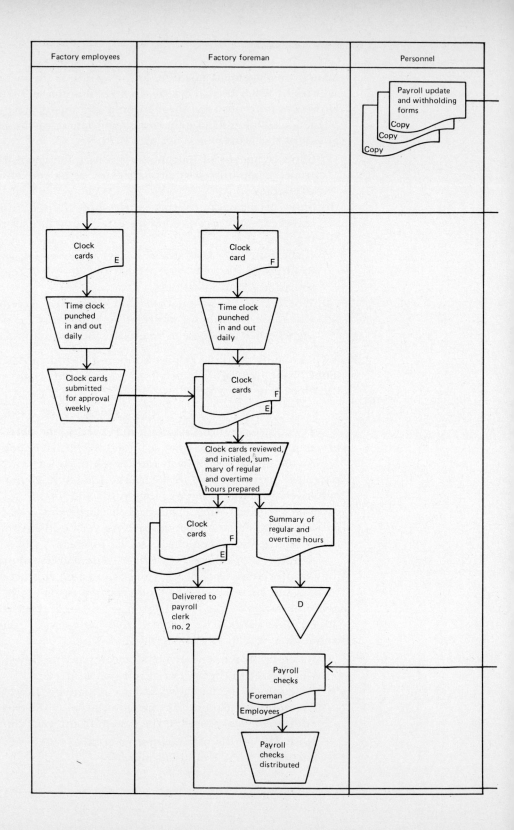

FIGURE 19.9
Croyden, Inc.,
factory payroll
system.

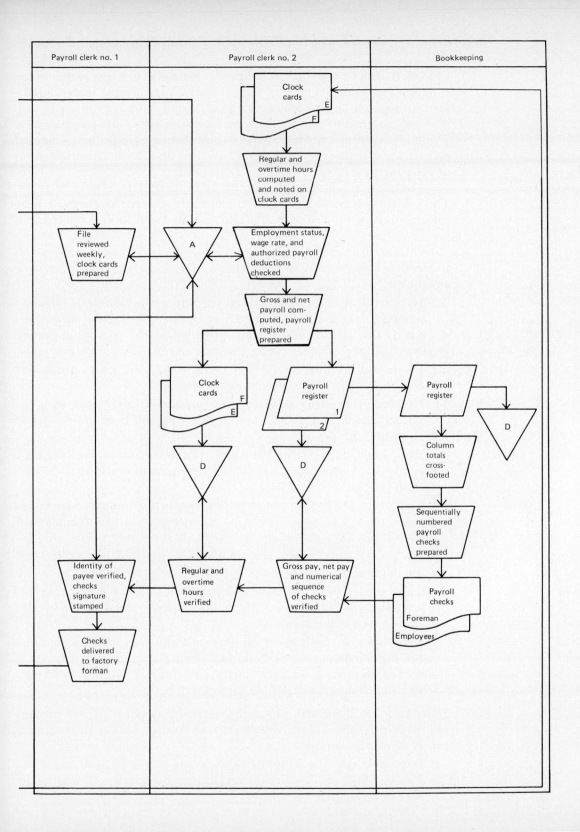

30. The internal audit department of Manor Company conducts audits in the company's several plants on a regular basis. The internal audit department is expected to perform operational audits. A team of internal auditors was assigned to review the payroll department of the Galena plant. The internal audit consisted of (1) various tests to verify the numerical accuracy of the payroll department's records and (2) the determination of the procedures used to process the payroll.

The internal audit team found that all numerical items were accurate. The proper hourly rates were used and the wages and deductions were calculated correctly. The payroll register was properly footed, totaled, and posted.

Various plant personnel were interviewed to ascertain the payroll procedures being used in the department. The audit team's findings were as follows:

☐ The payroll clerk receives the time cards from the various department supervisors at the end of each pay period, checks the employee's hourly rate against information provided by the personnel department, and records the regular and overtime hours for each employee.

☐ The payroll clerk sends the time cards to the plant's data processing department for compilation and processing.

☐ The data processing department returns the time cards with the printed checks and payroll register to the payroll clerk upon completion of the processing.

☐ The payroll clerk verifies the hourly rate and hours worked for each employee by comparing the detail in the payroll register to the time cards.

☐ If errors are found, the payroll clerk voids the computer-generated check, prepares another check for the correct amount and adjusts the payroll register accordingly.

☐ The payroll clerk obtains the plant signature plate from the accounting department and signs the payroll checks.

☐ An employee of the personnel department picks up the checks and holds them until they are delivered to the department supervisors for distribution to the employees.

REQUIRED

a) Based upon the findings of the internal audit team, identify the shortcomings in the payroll procedures used in the payroll department of the Galena plant and suggest corrective action the internal audit team should recommend. (CMA Examination)

31. Describe internal controls in a computerized system for payroll processing that are designed to provide the best protection against the following errors or manipulations.

a) Overstatement of an employee's wage rate on the payroll master file.

b) Placing the name of a fictitious employee on the payroll master file.

c) Entry of eighty as the value of hours worked on a particular date for an employee who only worked eight hours on that date.

d) A computer operator entering a payroll transaction card to increase the operator's own salary by fifty percent.

e) A programmer obtaining the payroll master file and entering an increase in his own salary.

f) Accidental erasure of a portion of the payroll master file tape by a computer operator making an error correction entry over the console.

g) Destruction of a large portion of the payroll master file when the disk pack containing the file was used as a scratch file for another application.

32. The Vane Corporation is a manufacturing concern which has been in business for the past eighteen years. During this period, the company has grown from a very small family-owned operation to a medium-sized manufacturing concern with several departments. Despite this growth, a substantial number of the procedures employed by Vane Corp. have been in effect since the business was started. Just recently Vane Corp. has computerized its payroll function.

The payroll function operates in the following manner. Each worker picks up a weekly time card on Monday morning and writes in his name and identification number. These blank cards are kept near the factory entrance. The workers write on the time card the time of their daily arrival and departure. On the following Monday the factory foremen collect the completed time cards for the previous week and send them to data processing.

In data processing the time cards are used to prepare the weekly time file. This file is processed with the master payroll file which is maintained on magnetic tape according to worker identification number. The checks are written by the computer on the regular checking account and imprinted with the treasurer's signature. After the payroll file is updated and the checks are prepared, the checks are sent to the factory foremen who distribute them to the workers or hold them for the workers to pick up later if they are absent.

The foremen notify data processing of new employees and terminations. Any changes in hourly pay rate or any other changes affecting payroll are usually communicated to data processing by the foremen.

The workers also complete a job time ticket for each individual job they work on each day. The job time tickets are collected daily and sent to cost accounting where they are used to prepare a cost distribution analysis.

Further analysis of the payroll function reveals the following:

a) A worker's gross wages never exceed $300 per week.

b) Raises never exceed $0.55 per hour for the factory workers.

c) No more than 20 hours of overtime is allowed each week.

d) The factory employs 150 workers in ten departments.

The payroll function has not been operating smoothly for some time, but even more problems have surfaced since the payroll was computerized. The foremen have indicated that they would like a weekly report indicating worker tardiness, absenteeism, and idle time, so they can determine the amount of productive time lost and the reason for the lost time. The following errors and inconsistencies have been encountered the past few pay periods:

a) A worker's paycheck was not processed properly, because he had transposed two numbers in his identification number when he filled out his time card.

b) A worker was issued a check for $1,531.80 when it should have been $153.81.

c) One worker's paycheck was not written, and this error was not detected until the paychecks for that department were distributed by the foreman.

d) Part of the master payroll file was destroyed when the tape reel was inadvertently mounted on the wrong tape drive and used as a scratch tape. Data processing attempted to reestablish the destroyed portion from original source documents and other records.

e) One worker received a paycheck for an amount considerably higher than he should have. Further investigation revealed that 84 had been punched instead of 48 for hours worked.

f) Several records on the master payroll file were skipped and not included on the updated master payroll file. This was not detected for several pay periods.

g) In processing nonroutine changes a computer operator included a pay rate increase for one of his friends in the factory. This was discovered by chance by another employee.

REQUIRED Identify the control weaknesses in the payroll procedure and in the computer processing as it is now conducted by the Vane Corp. Recommend the changes necessary to correct the system. Arrange your answer in the following columnar format:

Control Weaknesses   Recommendations

(CMA Examination)

33. The Sharpesville Insurance Company utilizes a computer-based system with disk file storage. Among the files it maintains on disk are a salesperson's payroll master sequenced by salesperson number, and a policyholder's master sequenced by policy number.

Each salesperson's monthly gross pay is equal to $500 plus commission. Each salesperson's commission is calculated as five percent of all premiums collected during the first year of the policy from policyholders who purchased from the salesperson and one percent of all premiums collected during the next four years from those policyholders.

Each day, the policyholders' master file is updated for new policies sold and premium payments received on outstanding policies. All premium payments are collected on a monthly basis. At the end of each month, the policyholders' master and salespersons' payroll master are processed to generate the salespersons' paychecks. Each salesperson's paycheck and payroll statement data are punched onto cards, which are subsequently processed on an interpreter and distributed to salespersons. Other outputs from this run include three printed reports—a payroll register, a listing of all policyholders who did not pay their premium for the month, and a summary report.

REQUIRED

a) What data must be contained in each policyholder master record in order for that file to be used as described above in generating salespersons' payroll data? (Do not mention policyholder master data that are not used in generating salespersons' payroll data.)

b) Prepare a systems flowchart of the monthly payroll processing run described above.

c) Assume that the processing illustrated in part (b) is done sequentially. What operation must then be performed on the policyholder's master file prior to the run?

d) What accounting journal entry would be accumulated in the run and printed out as part of the summary information? (Show accounts debited and accounts credited.)

e) Prepare a macroflowchart of the monthly payroll processing program. The flowchart should include (1) separate input and output symbols for each file processed in the run; (2) decision symbols necessary to accomplish sequential processing, to determine whether or not to include each policyholder on the listing of policyholders behind on premium payments and to determine the appropriate rate to be used in calculating the salesperson's commission; and (3) a single processing step representing calculation of net pay and all processing steps necessary to accumulate gross pay.

34. The Mayberry Corporation has acquired a tape-oriented computer system that will perform several clerical functions previously done manually. You have been called upon to design a computerized system for one of these functions—the processing of factory payrolls.

The computerized system will include a medium-sized central processor, several tape drive units, one card reader, one printer, and several keypunch and verifier units. No other hardware is available for use in payroll processing.

You have investigated the existing manual system and have discovered that it operates in the following manner. Employee clock cards are maintained in the timekeeping department, each of which contains an employee number and name and the time clocked in and out of work for each day of the week by the employee. All these cards are sent to the payroll department at the end of each week. The payroll department also receives data on new employees, employee terminations, changes in address or deductions, and other nonroutine payroll transactions from the personnel department. The payroll clerks perform all steps necessary to prepare employee paychecks and earnings statements, to prepare a payroll register (weekly listing of payroll data for each employee), and to maintain payroll records as required for producing quarterly and annual summary reports on employee earnings and withholdings as required by the government.

Your discussions with various system users have produced one major finding. Factory supervisors are unanimous in requesting a weekly report on employee tardiness and absenteeism, which would include such data as the average number of hours lost through lateness and absenteeism per week during the current year for each employee in the supervisor's department.

REQUIRED

a) Describe the data content of any master file or files necessary to perform the payroll processing by computer.
b) Prepare a systems flowchart representing a preliminary design of the computerized payroll processing system. Show all operations required, commencing with receipt of source documents and terminating with production of all necessary system outputs. For simplicity, do not include in this preliminary design any internal control operations.

35. The Darwin Department Store pays all its employees on a salaried basis. Payroll processing is done once monthly by computer. The payroll master file is maintained on a disk file. The only transaction inputs to the run are file changes on magnetic tape. Outputs include (1) a report listing error transactions and summary information, (2) employee checks and earnings statements on punched cards, and (3) a payroll register on magnetic tape. The processing is done sequentially. The check and earnings statement cards are subsequently processed on an offline device to print the appropriate data on the face of the cards. The payroll register tape is also processed by a utility routine to prepare a printed payroll register printout.

REQUIRED

a) Explain what is meant by "file changes" in the description above. Give four examples you would expect to find in this process.
b) Prepare a systems flowchart of the computer processes described above.
c) List the components of the hardware configuration necessary to ac-

complish all phases of the processing described in the case subsequent to data entry. Be sure to allow for necessary offline operations.

d) Describe a comprehensive set of control policies and procedures for this payroll processing application. For each policy or procedure, indicate its objective and exactly how it would operate. Be sure to relate each policy or procedure specifically to the payroll processing system described above.

36. You are reviewing audit work papers containing a narrative description of the Tenney Corporation's factory payroll system. A portion of that narrative is as follows.

Factory employees punch time clock cards each day when entering or leaving the shop. At the end of each week the timekeeping department collects the time cards and prepares duplicate batch-control slips by department showing total hours and number of employees. The time cards and original batch-control slips are sent to the payroll accounting section. The second copies of the batch-control slips are filed by date.

In the payroll accounting section payroll transaction cards are keypunched from the information on the time cards, and a batch total card for each batch is keypunched from the batch-control slip. The time cards and batch-control slips are then filed by batch for possible reference. The payroll transaction cards and batch total card are sent to data processing where they are sorted by employee number within batch. Each batch is edited by a computer program which checks the validity of employee number against a master employee tape file and the total hours and number of employees against the batch total card. A detail printout by batch and employee number is produced which indicates batches that do not balance and invalid employee numbers. This printout is returned to payroll accounting to resolve all differences.

In searching for documentation you found a flowchart (Fig. 19.10) of the payroll system which included all appropriate symbols (American National Standards Institute, Inc.) but was only partially labeled. The portion of this flowchart described by the above narrative appears in Fig. 19.10.

REQUIRED

a) Number your answer 1 through 17. Next to the corresponding number of your answer, supply the appropriate labeling (document name, process description, or file order) applicable to each numbered symbol on the flowchart.

b) Flowcharts are one of the aids an auditor may use to determine and evaluate a client's internal control system. List advantages of using flowcharts in this context. (CPA Examination)

37. In connection with an examination of the financial statements of the Olympia Manufacturing Company, a CPA is reviewing procedures for accumulating direct labor hours. The CPA learns that all production is by

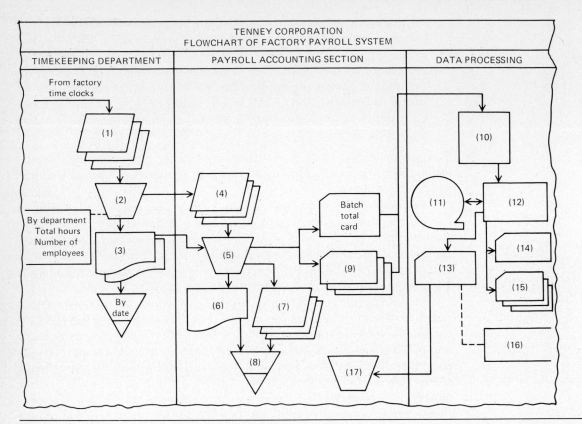

FIGURE 19.10

job order and that all employees are paid hourly wages, with time-and-one-half for overtime hours. Olympia's direct labor hour input process for payroll and job-cost determination is summarized in the flowchart shown in Fig. 19.11.

Steps A and C are performed in timekeeping, step B in the factory operating departments, step D in payroll audit and control, step E in data preparation (keypunch), and step F in computer operations.

REQUIRED

For each input processing step A through F
  a) list the possible errors or discrepancies that may occur, and
  b) cite the corresponding control procedure that should be in effect for each error or discrepancy.

Note: Your discussion of Olympia's procedures should be limited to the input process for direct labor hours, as shown in steps A through F in the flowchart. Do not discuss personnel procedures for hiring, promotion, termination, and pay rate authorization. In step F do not discuss equipment, computer program, and general computer operational controls.

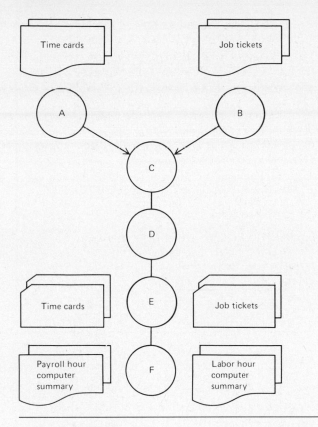

FIGURE 19.11

Organize your answer for each input-processing step as follows. (CPA Examination)

STEP	POSSIBLE ERRORS OR DISCREPANCIES	CONTROL PROCEDURES

References

Brummet, R. Lee; Eric G. Flamholtz; and William C. Pyle. "Human Resource Accounting—A Challenge for Accountants." *Accounting Review* (April 1968): 217–224.

Campion, William M., and Richard M. Peters. "How to Analyze Manpower Requirements Forecasts." *Management Accounting* (September 1979): 45–50.

Fahnline, R. H. "The Skills Inventory Put On." *Journal of Systems Management* (May 1974): 14–21.

Famularo, Joseph J., ed. *Handbook of Modern Personnel Administration.* New York: McGraw-Hill, 1972.

Fisher, Harry C. *The Uses of Accounting in Collective Bargaining.* Los Angeles: Institute of Industrial Relations, University of California, 1969.

Foulkes, Fred K. "The Expanding Role of the Personnel Function." *Harvard Business Review* (March/April 1975): 71–84.

Foulkes, Fred, K., and Henry M. Morgan. "Organizing and Staffing the Personnel Function." *Harvard Business Review* (May/June 1977): 142–154.

Hazelton, Walter A. "How to Cost Labor Settlements." *Management Accounting* (May 1979): 19–23.

Kaumeyer, Richard A. *Planning and Using Skills Inventory Systems.* New York: Van Nostrand Reinhold, 1979.

Price Waterhouse & Co. *Guide to Accounting Controls: Employee Compensation & Benefits.* New York: Price Waterhouse & Co., 1979.

Sangeladji, Mohammad A. "Human Resource Accounting: A Refined Measurement Model." *Management Accounting* (December 1977): 48–52.

Accounting Information Systems for Financial Management

Financial management involves decisions relating to sources of financing for, and uses of financial resources within, an organization. Financial information is any information concerning the flow of dollars through the organization. Virtually all activities and decisions within an organization are reflected in financial information. The financial management function and systems for providing financial information are thus vital to all business organizations, as well as to most other types of organizations. This chapter discusses the nature of the financial management function, and of systems for generating financial information, within the typical business organization.

The Financial Management Function

The financial management function encompasses both the role of *treasurership,* or administration of the finance function, and *controllership,* or administration of the accounting function. In many business organizations, the treasurership and controllership functions are combined organizationally under the authority of an executive vice-president for finance. An example of an organization structure of this type is illustrated in Fig. 20.1. The controllership function encompasses the collection and processing of transaction data and the reporting and interpretation of financial information. To the modern business organization attempting to generate an economic profit from scarce resources in a competitive environment, the availability of relevant, timely, and reliable financial information is essential. Because of the importance of

FIGURE 20.1
Organization structure for financial management.

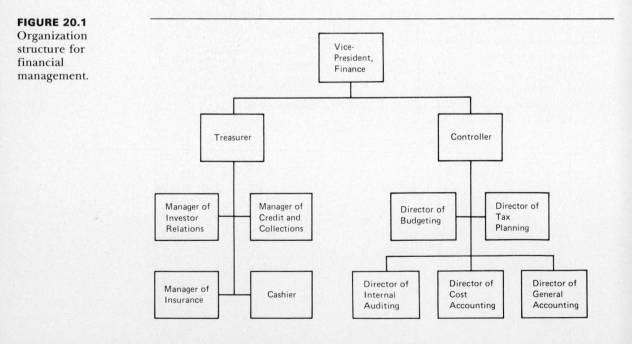

the financial reporting and interpretation activity, the controller has become an important participant in managerial decision making at the top level.

The controllership function and its subsidiary functions—budgeting, tax planning, internal auditing, cost accounting, and general accounting—are discussed in Chapter 2 and elsewhere throughout this book. Therefore the remainder of this section concentrates upon the functions of the top financial executive, the treasurer, and the various staff functions reporting to the treasurer. Each of these is discussed here in turn.

The Top Financial Executive

The top financial executive, often having the title of financial vice-president, is responsible both for administration of the functions under his or her authority and for making decisions and recommendations involving the most important aspects of the finance function. Into the latter category fall decisions concerning long-term financing, dividend policy, capital budgeting, short-term management of cash flows, and allocation of resources within the enterprise.

Decisions concerning long-term financing are generally made very infrequently in most business organizations, perhaps only once every few years. However, each major decision in this area will have a significant impact upon the firm's success and growth over an extended period of time. The two most crucial aspects of the long-term financing decision are timing and sources. The timing aspect involves determining the point in time at which entry into the capital markets can be achieved on terms most favorable to the firm. Selecting the sources of long-term financing involves choices among such alternatives as issuing bonds, common stock, or preferred stock. Dividend policy is also closely related to long-term financing because another source of long-term funds consists of retained earnings that are not paid out as dividends.

Much of the information required for decisions on long-term financing is external information concerning, for example, the state of the economy and its impact on stock and bond prices, interest rates, and the capital markets generally. Internally generated information useful to decision making in this area includes long-term past and future information regarding the firm's financial position and earnings performance. The basic financial statements generated by the accounting function—balance sheet, income statement, etc.—provide a perspective on past trends and present conditions in this regard. Major plans developed by top executives, and financial projections generated on the basis of such plans, are also an important source of information input.

Planning and control of capital expenditures are other areas of decision making in which the top financial executive is deeply involved. The planning of capital expenditures involves determining the total size of the capital expenditures budget for the firm each year or quarter and choosing among alternative fixed asset purchases. The control of capital expenditures deals with establishing policies for granting approval of expenditure requests and following up on the execution of the expenditure and the installation of the asset.

The information required for capital expenditure planning consists primarily of estimates of cash inflows and outflows and of risk factors associated with alternative fixed asset purchases. The discounting technique should be applied to cash flow estimates to derive a net present value for each alternative investment.[1] The availability of funds for capital expenditures may be estimated on the basis of sales forecasts and earnings projections. Information for control of capital expenditures begins with the formal request for authorization of the expenditure, which indicates the costs associated with the purchase, the expected benefits, and the projected revenues or cost savings. When the asset is purchased and received, a record of all vital data relating to the asset should be prepared and maintained for as long as the asset is owned and used. Other control information may be generated from follow-up studies that evaluate the accuracy of the original cost and revenue estimates.

Planning and control of operating expenditures are other areas of major concern to the top financial executive. These involve the preparation of annual operating budgets for departments and divisions within the organization, and the establishment of systems of control reporting that generate comparisons of actual performance of each department or division with the operating budget. Finally, planning and control of operating expenditures involve the interpretation of reported operating performance to provide a basis for managerial decisions and actions.

The treasurer

The treasurership function is primarily concerned with the management of short-term cash flows and with policymaking and administration with respect to various staff functions under the treasurer's authority. Cash management involves decisions relating to the investment of cash balances in excess of short-term cash requirements and decisions on timing and sources of short-term cash borrowing. Alternatives for short-term cash investment include United States Treasury bills, bank certificates of deposit, and commercial paper. Alternative sources of short-term borrowing include trade credit, commercial bank unsecured credit, and secured loans using inventories or accounts receivable as collateral.

The information requirements of short-term cash management involve both external and internal information. Decisions on investment of idle cash require information on the nature, yield, and maturity dates of various alter-

---

[1]For an extensive treatment of capital budgeting and cash flow discounting, see Harold Bierman, Jr., and Seymour Smidt, *The Capital Budgeting Decision*, 5th ed. (New York: Macmillan, 1980).

native investments. Decisions on short-term borrowing utilize information relating to sources of supply. The timing decision primarily depends on internal information concerning when excess cash balances will be available or when short-term borrowing will be required. Short-term cash budgets that project weekly or monthly cash flows for the immediate future are one source of such information. These budgets may be supplemented by revenue projections generated from accounts receivable data and by cash outflow projections generated from accounts payable and purchase commitments data.

Manager of investor relations

The manager of investor relations has the responsibility of developing and maintaining a satisfactory market for the firm's securities. This entails communications with stockholders; with security analysts, who advise investors; with stock exchanges, through which securities are traded; with investment bankers, through whom new securities are issued; and with the Securities and Exchange Commission, which regulates the securities markets. The information requirements of this position are primarily external. The stockholder record-keeping system provides some information of use to the investor relations manager, such as reports on the holdings and dealings of the company's largest shareholders. In addition, much company information is funneled through the investor relations manager and reported to stockholders, security analysts, and others interested in the company's activities.

Manager of credit and collections

The manager of credit and collections has the responsibility of developing and administering policies relating to the granting of credit and collection of accounts. Credit granting policies, credit limits, and collection procedures must be tight enough to avoid tying up funds in accounts receivable that could be profitably invested elsewhere. On the other hand, such policies and procedures must be loose enough to avoid the loss of sales and customers. The manager of credit and collections must find the optimum point of trade-off between these two objectives.

Some of the information requirements of the credit and collections function are external. For example, information on the credit worthiness of new customers is required to decide whether, and to what limit, to extend credit to them. Primary external sources of credit information include Dun & Bradstreet, which provides credit reports and ratings on business firms, and local credit bureaus, which provide credit reports on individuals. Much internal information should also be available to assist in credit decisions. Records of the payment history of a customer are useful to making decisions on whether to extend further credit. Records of current past-due balances are also relevant to the credit granting decision and necessary to the decision of whether to initiate special collection procedures. Reports analyzing customer accounts written off as uncollectible are constructive in the establishment of credit granting policies.

Manager of insurance

The manager of insurance is responsible for identifying and evaluating potential losses to the firm that are insurable, selecting the appropriate mix of insurance coverage and other methods for dealing with the potential losses, obtaining insurance coverage on terms favorable to the firm, and administering the firm's various insurance contracts. This responsibility requires the use of both external and internal information in decision making. External information requirements include knowledge of the characteristics and costs of various types of available insurance coverage. Examples of internal information requirements are measures of potential loss from physical damage to assets, disability or death of key employees, criminal action, and fraud or negligence on the part of employees. In the case of physical damage to assets, accounting records provide some useful information. However, in the case of the other types of losses mentioned, accurate measures of size and likelihood of potential loss may be hard to develop from available information. For administration of insurance programs, the insurance manager must receive information concerning payment of premiums, execution of new insurance contracts in accordance with established policies, maintenance and funding of reserves for self-insurance, and reporting and collection of claims.

Cashier

The function of cashier is primarily administrative rather than being a policymaking or decision-making function. The cashier is responsible for endorsing, depositing, and maintaining a record of cash receipts, and for reviewing disbursement authorizations, signing and distributing checks, and maintaining a record of cash disbursements. This function also encompasses the maintenance of banking arrangements for the organization.

The Financial Information System

This section reviews the basic accounting transactions reflecting the processing of information for financial management, describes the data content and organization of the financial accounting data base, and discusses and illustrates examples of manual and computer-based information systems for financial management. The systems illustrated are not those of any real organization but are intended to be representative of financial information systems in general.

The accounting transactions

Numerous accounting transactions summarize the processing of data from which accounting information for financial management is generated. The most significant of these are reviewed here.

Cash receipts and disbursements.   With respect to cash receipts, the primary accounting journal entry follows.

Cash	XXX	
Accounts Receivable		XXX

This summary entry is typically made daily for the complete batch of cash receipts processed during the day. Other miscellaneous accounts that reflect less regular sources of cash receipts include notes receivable, sales of fixed assets, and miscellaneous income from dividends, interest, or rentals.

The primary cash disbursement transactions are reflected by the following journal entry.

Accounts Payable	XXX	
Cash		XXX

This entry is also generally made each day to summarize the preparation and distribution of a batch of checks. Credits to accounts payable originate from purchases of inventory and fixed assets and from the incurrence of costs and expenses.

Another cash disbursement transaction reflecting a high volume of individual transactions appears thus.

Wages and Salaries Payable	XXX	
Cash		XXX

The liability account is originated weekly or monthly as payrolls are processed, and represents the difference between gross pay and all deductions. The entry itself reflects the distribution of paychecks to employees.

A third cash disbursement entry that represents the most regularly recurring transaction with stockholders follows.

Dividends Payable	XXX	
Cash		XXX

The liability account itself is originated by debiting the Retained Earnings account. This transaction is generally executed quarterly, and the entry summarizes the distribution of a batch of dividend checks to all stockholders. Most corporations utilize the services of a bank as transfer agent, which involves administering records of share transfers among stockholders. Many firms also have their transfer agent process dividend payments as well. Systems for administering capital stock records are not discussed further in this chapter.

Cost and expense distribution.   Various accounting processes culminate in the recording of costs and expenses. A composite entry reflecting several of the most significant of these processes follows.

Manufacturing Overhead	XXX	
Selling Expense	XXX	
General and Administrative Expense	XXX	
Accounts Payable		XXX
Payroll		XXX
Accumulated Depreciation		XXX
Supplies		XXX
Accrued Expenses Payable		XXX
Allowance for Bad Debts		XXX

The accounts debited in the above composite entry are control accounts, each of which encompasses a large number of subsidiary cost and expense accounts. Examples of the subsidiary accounts include wages and salaries expense, depreciation, insurance, taxes, utilities, advertising, supplies, travel, and bad debts. These debits arise from several processes. Perhaps the primary source is the debit distribution generated from the daily preparation of disbursement vouchers, which establish and authorize payment of accounts payable. The debit distribution summarizes the accounts to which the total amount payable is apportioned. The payroll entry is made as payrolls are processed weekly or monthly. The debit to supplies expense and credit to supplies inventory are made as supplies requisitions are processed but are subject to adjustment as periodic inventories of supplies are taken. The depreciation and accrual portions of the entry, including the estimate of bad debts expense, are generally made at the end of each month.

Fixed assets.   The recording of fixed asset acquisitions is reflected by the following journal entry.

Fixed Assets	XXX	
Accounts Payable		XXX

If the asset is a very large purchase, the credit portion of the entry may be partly recorded to a long-term liability account. Very small asset purchases may simply be expensed for the sake of convenience. This entry generally arises as part of the debit distribution of accounts payable, as described above. The volume of such transactions is usually minimal in relation to other debits arising from accounts payable processing.

Financial statement preparation.   Standard practice calls for most firms to prepare balance sheets and income statements monthly. Prior to this, a variety of *adjusting entries* must be made. These include accrual of expenses incurred but not yet paid, such as interest, wages and salaries, and utilities; expiration of prepaid expenses, such as depreciation, insurance, and supplies; accrual of revenue earned but not yet collected; recognition of the earned portion of revenues collected in advance; and other special entries such as adjustment of the inventory accounts to record the results of a physical inventory, or the elimination of profits and account balances arising from intercompany transactions. Following the preparation of financial statements, a series of *closing entries* are made. These reflect the zeroing out of all revenue and expense account balances and the transfer of the net credit or debit (net income or loss) to the retained earnings account.

The financial accounting data base

The overall structure of the financial accounting data base is illustrated in Fig. 20.2. The key master files in this data base are traditionally referred to as *ledgers;* this term is a carryover from manual systems in which these files are often maintained in bound ledger books. The *general ledger* is a master file in which a record is maintained for each and every account in the organization's accounting system. The key field for the general ledger consists of the account codes that compose the chart of accounts, illustrated in Figs. 3.8, 3.9, and 3.10. A *subsidiary ledger* is a master file of accounting records for a specific category of accounts. The most significant subsidiary ledgers are accounts receivable; inventory including raw materials, work-in-process, and finished goods; fixed assets; accounts payable; manufacturing overhead; selling expense; and general and administrative expense.

The basic format of all ledger accounts is identical, whether they are maintained manually or by computer. Each contains a key field (account number), an account name, an account balance as of the beginning of the current period, and a current account balance. In addition, each contains an itemization of all transactions affecting the account during the current period. Each transaction contains a notation referencing a source document or journal. The

FIGURE 20.2
Structure of the financial accounting data base.

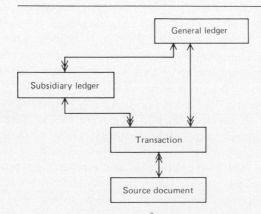

classic example of this format is the "T-account," which should be very familiar to all accounting students. In this format, the transaction record is a repeating group within the ledger record, as reflected by the double arrows pointing to the transaction record from the ledger records in Fig. 20.2. Also indicated by Fig. 20.2 is the fact that each source document record may support one or more transaction records.

The relationship between general ledger records and subsidiary ledger records requires that for each subsidiary ledger there will be a single general ledger control account. The balance of the control account represents the sum total of the balances of all the accounts in the subsidiary ledger. When a batch of transactions is recorded in a subsidiary ledger, the total amount of all those transactions is simultaneously recorded as a single transaction in the general ledger control account. For some general ledger accounts, such as cash, prepaid expenses, bonds payable, and retained earnings, there is no subsidiary ledger. Therefore, as implied by Fig. 20.2, transaction records affect these accounts directly rather than indirectly through a subsidiary ledger.

Several examples of subsidiary ledgers have been discussed and illustrated in previous chapters. For example, the finished goods inventory file and customer file discussed in Chapter 16 and illustrated in Fig. 16.7 are equivalent to a finished goods inventory ledger and accounts receivable ledger, respectively. Also, the raw materials inventory file and vendor file discussed in Chapter 17 and illustrated in Fig. 17.2 are equivalent to a raw materials inventory ledger and accounts payable ledger, respectively. Note that the data base structure corresponding to all four of those subsidiary ledgers is identical to the general structure shown in Fig. 20.2—that is, each subsidiary ledger record owns a series of transaction records, and each transaction record is related to a source document record. Also note, however, that each subsidiary ledger record format may go beyond the basic format described earlier to contain data fields unique to the particular entity, such as the customer credit rating or the inventory location code.

In manual accounting systems, all transactions are initially recorded in a *journal,* which lists the amounts debited or credited to each ledger account affected by each transaction. There are special journals for high-volume transactions such as cash receipts, cash disbursements, purchases, and sales, as well as a general journal for all other transactions. One of the most time-consuming of accounting operations is the posting of transactions from journals to ledgers. However, note that in a data base system the input of a source document record into the system automatically results in the creation of a transaction record, and that each transaction record is automatically linked (or "posted") to the appropriate ledger record by virtue of the fact that it contains the appropriate account number. Thus in a data base system the need for a separate posting operation is eliminated, and the system no longer maintains journals. However, if desired for auditing purposes, a journal can be prepared from the transaction records stored in this system. For example, a cash receipts journal for October 13, 1986, might be generated using a command such as "PRINT ALL TRANSACTION RECORDS HAVING TRANS-ACTION CODE = CR AND DATE = 101386."

In manual accounting systems, ledger records are often maintained on specially formatted cards such as the materials ledger card illustrated in Fig. 17.3. Another example is provided by the fixed asset ledger card shown in Fig. 20.3. Processing of fixed asset transactions in both manual and computer-based systems is discussed later in this chapter. The basic input transactions include the purchase of new fixed assets, additions to or major repairs on existing assets, and disposal through sale or scrapping of existing assets. Records of accumulated depreciation for each asset are also commonly maintained on the ledger card. The fixed asset ledger is used as a basic reference for general accounting, capital budgeting, insurance administration, and tax planning. Outputs that may be generated from the file of fixed asset ledger records include summary analyses of depreciation or asset cost by type of asset, by department, or by division.

The data content and organization of the manufacturing overhead ledger, the selling expense ledger, and the general and administrative expense ledger

FIGURE 20.3
Fixed asset ledger record.

PLANT AND EQUIPMENT HISTORY LEDGER

Kelly Manufacturing Corp.   1234 Fifth St.   Albany, NY 12205

Item No. 6648	Serial No. 613440736	Dept. No. 407

DESCRIPTION
IBM 4331 Processor, Model K2
Mainframe
Memory–2 megabytes

MANUFACTURER
IBM Corporation
Data Processing Division
1133 Westchester Ave.
White Plains, NY 10604

COST INFORMATION				RECORD OF IMPROVEMENTS		
Item	Date	Ref.	Amount	Date	Ref.	Amount
Acquisition	6/30/80	V-1089	$150,000 —			
Transportation In			—			
Installation Cost	6/30/80	V-1274	2,000 —			
Subtotal			$152,000 —			
Estimated Salvage Value			8,000 —			
Depreciable Cost			$144,000 —			

DEPRECIATION RECORD

Year	1980	1981	1982	1983	1984	1985	1986	1987	1988	19__
Rate	25%x½	25%								
Beginning Balance	$144,000	$126,000								
Annual Depreciation	18,000	31,500								
Adjustments to Depr.	—	—								
Reserve Balance	18,000	49,500								
Net Book Value	134,000	102,500								

correspond almost directly to the basic format of all ledger accounts as described above. The beginning balance of all accounts in these ledgers is always zero because they are closed to the profit and loss summary at the end of each period. Little descriptive information other than an account title is included in these account records. Each transaction subrecord within each subsidiary account contains the transaction date, amount, and disbursement voucher or other source document reference number. The only difference between these ledgers lies in the type of accounts included in each. Constituting the manufacturing overhead ledger are such accounts as inspection, supervision, maintenance and other indirect labor, small tools, factory utlities, and depreciation on plant and factory equipment. The selling expense ledger is composed of accounts for salaries and commissions of salespeople, salaries of sales supervisors and clerical staff, shipping expenses, depreciation of selling facilities and equipment, supplies, postage, advertising, travel, etc. The general and administrative expense ledger includes accounts for executive and clerical salaries, depreciation and rental of office facilities and equipment, supplies, postage, travel, contributions, and income taxes.

The cost and expense ledgers are updated for accounting transactions arising from accounts payable debit distribution; payroll processing; and depreciation, accruals, and other end-of-period adjustments. The most important reports generated from this file are departmental performance reports comparing the actual expenses incurred in each department, obtained from the ledger, with budgeted expenses, and perhaps also with expenses incurred for the same period in the previous year.

The data content and organization of the general ledger also corresponds to the universal ledger format described above. The inputs and outputs associated with the general ledger should be familiar to all accounting students. The inputs consist of debit and credit transactions recorded in journals or on journal vouchers (see Fig. 16.6). The primary outputs are the financial statements, including the balance sheet, income statement, and funds flow statement. For internal reporting purposes, financial statements for subsidiaries and divisions are also prepared, and these often include comparisons of current statement information with budgeted amounts.

Most modern organizations use budgeting in financial planning and control. This means that there must be a master file of budget information for each general ledger account, as well as for each cost and expense subsidiary account. There are several possible approaches. For example, budget data could be included within the general ledger records themselves, or they could be contained on a separate master budget file. Each budget record could contain an estimate of the monthly increases and decreases in the account over the budget horizon, or it could contain a formula by which such budget estimates could be computed. A commonly used formula for cost and expense accounts consists of an estimate of the fixed portion of the cost or expense for the period, plus the variable rate of the cost or expense, together with the base to which the rate is applied. For example, indirect labor for the assembly department might be budgeted at $1000 per month (the fixed portion) plus ten cents (the variable rate) per direct labor hour (the rate base). Therefore the budget record for the indirect labor account would contain separate fields for the monthly fixed cost, the variable cost rate, and a code indicating the base to which the variable cost rate is applied.

The master budget is updated periodically to reflect current information with respect to budget estimates. Many reports for control purposes are generated as output of the master budget. Reports comparing actual and budgeted expenses by department and division are essential for performance evaluation and feedback to managers. Such reports are prepared monthly, quarterly, and annually. The master budget may also be used to generate cash flow budgets on a monthly basis.

Manual systems

Manual data processing systems for processing cash receipts and cash disbursements are described in this section by means of document flowcharts. Brief descriptions of systems for maintaining the fixed asset ledger and the general ledger are also included. Emphasis is placed upon data flows and internal control provisions of these systems.

Cash receipts. Figure 20.4 illustrates the process of receiving payments on account for a typical manufacturing company. It is assumed that the company receives most such payments by check through the mail. These are opened in the mail room, where a list of all receipts in a batch is prepared, perhaps in the form of an adding machine tape. All checks are sent to the cashier's department for endorsement and deposit in the bank. The batch total accumulated in the mail room is used by the cashier's department as a check on the accuracy of the deposit. On the basis of the deposit, the cashier's department prepares a journal voucher debiting cash and crediting accounts receivable. This is sent to the general ledger section.

Enclosed with each customer's payment should be a *remittance advice,* which indicates the invoices, statement, or other items for which the payment is made. If most of its customers are small companies or individuals, a company should request that the customer return one copy of the invoice or statement with the payment, and this then serves as a remittance advice. Remittance advices are separated from checks in the mail room and sent in a batch to accounts receivable, where they are posted to individual accounts. At the completion of the posting process, a new balance of accounts receivable is calculated, and the total change in accounts receivable is determined. This total change is then compared by the general ledger section with the amount of the journal voucher from the cashier's department. If the two amounts do not agree, an error has occurred that must be discovered and corrected.

The accounts receivable clerk should periodically check the status of all open customer accounts. Any accounts for which payment is significantly past due should be brought to the attention of the manager of credit and collec-

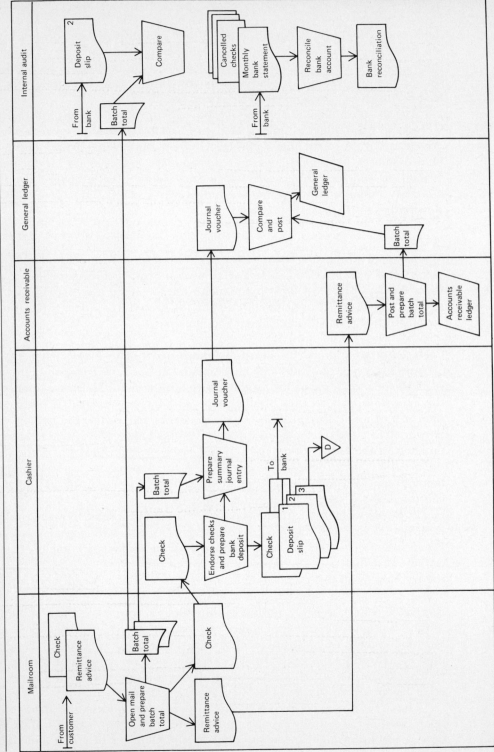

FIGURE 20.4 Document flow in a manual system for processing cash receipts.

tions. This information might be reported in the form of an aging schedule of all past-due accounts. On the basis of this feedback, the manager of credit and collections may decline to provide further credit to these customers and may also initiate special collection procedures. In the event that account write-offs become necessary, their initiation should occur in the credit department after all attempts to collect the account have proved unsuccessful. The credit department would prepare a journal voucher recording the debit to allowance for bad debts and the credit to accounts receivable for posting by the general ledger clerk. A copy of the write-off authorization would also be sent to the accounts receivable clerk for posting to the subsidiary ledger account.

The internal audit department plays an important role in the control of the cash receipts process. It receives a copy of the batch total of cash receipts from the mail room each day and a copy of each deposit slip. At the end of each month, it receives a bank statement, on the basis of which it prepares a bank reconciliation. Part of the work involved in preparing the bank reconciliation will be to compare each batch total with its corresponding deposit slip and bank statement entry. This check should reveal any errors or irregularities that occur after a proper batch total is accumulated in the mail room.

Organizational independence with respect to the cash receipts process is achieved by separation of the recording functions from the custodial function. Recording functions are performed by mail room personnel and by accounts receivable. The custodial function consists of the authority to endorse and deposit checks, which is the responsibility of the cashier. With respect to account write-offs, separation of their authorization from the maintenance of the account records and the handling of cash receipts is essential. The independently performed functions of the internal auditor also impose a control check on the process. The batch total procedure and preparation of the bank reconciliation provide further control.

The establishment of procedures to control sales of merchandise for cash is a major concern of retail enterprises. The most critical point in the process from a control standpoint is the point of the transaction itself. Once the transaction is properly recorded, a firm basis for control has been established. Two factors are most useful in securing control at the point of the transaction itself. One is the use of cash registers, whose control features include a display window in which the amount rung for a sale is shown, provision for issuing a receipt for each sale to the appropriate customer, and a locked-in paper tape record of each transaction. The second critical control factor is close supervision of personnel.

Many organizations use a form of internal check to control the cash sales process subsequent to the recording of the sale. Sales slips are prepared at the point of sale, and at the end of each day, they are processed in a batch to update sales records. A batch total of cash sales is obtained from this process. Also at the end of each day, cash from each register is collected and cash register tapes are used as a basis for preparing a deposit slip and a journal voucher to record the debit to cash and the credit to sales. The totals obtained

FIGURE 20.5 Document flow in a manual system for processing cash disbursements.

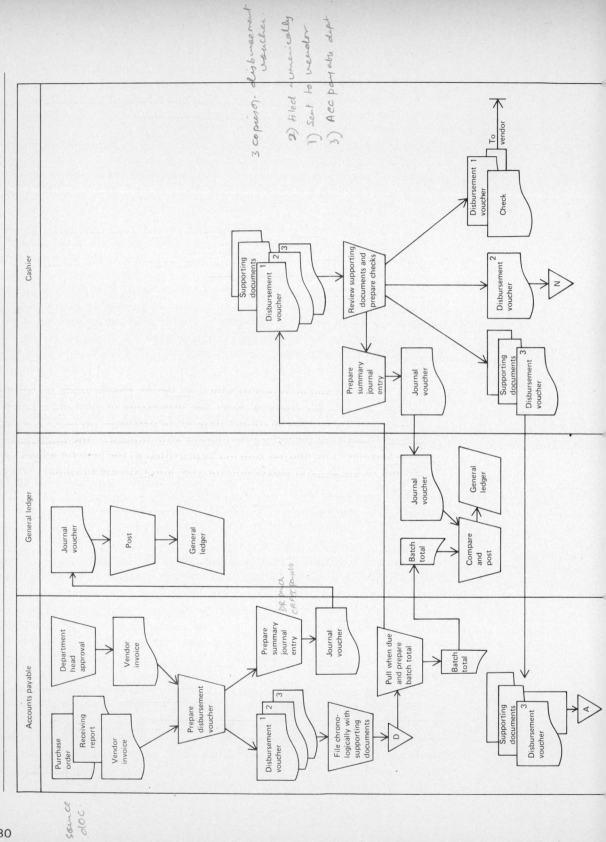

from these two processes are then reconciled, with adjustments made for credit sales, payments by check, sales returns, and like factors. If a discrepancy exists, steps can be taken to discover and correct the error.

Cash disbursements. A document flowchart of a manual system for processing cash disbursements is illustrated in Fig. 20.5. The accounts payable department maintains a file of invoices approved for payment by due date of the invoice. Approval of invoices for payment is made by the accounts payable department for inventory purchases on the basis of purchase orders and receiving reports. For costs and expenses and fixed asset purchases, payment authorization may be provided by the signature on the invoice of the department head to whose department the cost, expense, or asset is charged. For each invoice, or each set of invoices from one vendor, that has been approved for payment, a *disbursement voucher* is prepared. The disbursement voucher, illustrated in Fig. 20.6, is simply an authorization to pay a vendor for the invoices and amounts shown on the voucher.

Three copies of each disbursement voucher are prepared for each approved invoice and filed by due date together with all supporting documents. At the same time, the accounts payable department prepares the debit distribution; this details the accounts to which all debits arising from recognition of accounts payable are charged. After the processing of each day's batch of vouchers is completed, the accounts payable department prepares a journal voucher summarizing the debit distribution and indicating the total credit to accounts payable. The journal voucher is provided to the general ledger clerk for posting to the general ledger and the cost and expense subsidiary ledgers.

Each day the file of vouchers payable on that day is pulled. A batch total of the net amount to be remitted is prepared, and the disbursement vouchers and all supporting documents are provided to the cashier. The supporting

FIGURE 20.6
Disbursement voucher.

Voucher No. 1623	THE NEEDMORE MANUFACTURING COMPANY Needmore, Texas				
Remit to: Avalon Electronics 401 Cherry Street Waco, Texas 78123			Date entered: 5/14/87		

Your invoice Date	Number	Memo	Invoice Amount	Returns & allowances	Discount	Net remittance

documentation for each voucher is reviewed by the cashier, who then prepares and signs a check in payment of the voucher. For control purposes, a second person, perhaps the treasurer, may also review supporting documents and countersign each check. All supporting documents should be stamped paid or otherwise clearly marked to preclude their reuse to authorize disbursements. The checks are then mailed out together with a copy of the voucher, which serves as a remittance advice. A second copy of the disbursement voucher is filed by the voucher number. The supporting documents, including the vendor invoice and, where applicable, the receiving report and purchase order, are attached to the other copy of the disbursement voucher and returned to the accounts payable department for filing in the alphabetical vendor file. The cashier also prepares for each daily batch of checks a journal voucher that reflects the debit to accounts payable and the credit to cash, and that is transmitted to the general ledger clerk. This journal voucher is checked against the batch total prepared by the accounts payable department and is then posted to the general ledger.

The preparation of the bank reconciliation by the internal auditors provides a final control check on the cash disbursements process. All cancelled checks should be examined to ascertain the date of endorsement and name of endorser. All checks paid should be accounted for as either cancelled, outstanding, or voided. For this purpose, of course, checks must be sequentially prenumbered.

Organizational independence with respect to the cash disbursements process is obtained by separation of the recording and authorization functions performed by the accounts payable department and the general ledger clerk from the custodial function of the cashier, under whose authority checks are prepared, signed, and distributed. Other control procedures that reinforce the effectiveness of this separation include periodic reconciliation of the accounts payable control account balance with the total of the vouchers awaiting payment; the batch total of vouchers due for payment each day, prepared before the vouchers are transmitted to the cashier and checked after all checks have been prepared and mailed against the resulting journal entry; dual signing of the checks; and the preparation of the bank reconciliation.

In many firms it is convenient to be able to make some small cash disbursements in cash rather than by check. In such cases, a petty cash fund may be established from which such disbursements can be made. Use of the "imprest" system for maintaining such funds provides control over the cash disbursed in this manner. Under this system, the amount of the fund is set at some specified amount, such as $100. A petty cash fund custodian is made solely responsible for the fund, and this person should not have any other cash handling or recording functions. The appointed individual must prepare a petty cash voucher for all disbursements made from the fund and obtain the signature of the payee on each voucher. The fund custodian retains these vouchers so that at any given time the total amount of the vouchers plus the cash remaining in the fund should equal the total amount of the fund. The internal auditor may periodically make surprise counts of the fund to verify this condition.

When the amount of the petty cash fund is low, the fund custodian provides all petty cash vouchers to the accounts payable department. On the basis of these supporting documents, a disbursement voucher is prepared authorizing replenishment of the fund in the exact amount of the total of all the petty cash vouchers. The cashier then prepares and signs a check from this disbursement voucher to accomplish the replenishment. Petty cash vouchers must be marked paid at this time to prevent their reuse. Furthermore, the cashier should verify the unexpended balance of the fund at this time. The replenishment check should bring the fund balance up to its specified maximum level.

Fixed assets.   The primary procedures and controls in connection with accounting for fixed assets relate to the maintenance of the fixed asset ledger and the acquisition of new assets. In most firms this is a very small job requiring only a few minutes or hours each month. The paid disbursement vouchers and their supporting documentation provide source documents for the origination of asset records in the fixed asset ledger. This ledger is used for preparation and recording of depreciation. It may also be used to record appraisals for insurance purposes.

Control over the fixed assets themselves requires that the serial number and location of each asset be recorded in the fixed asset ledger. All transfers of an asset from one location to another should be authorized and documented, with the resulting documentation serving as a basis for recording such transfers in the fixed asset ledger. Periodically an inventory of fixed assets should be taken and the asset ledger adjusted if necessary. Reconciliation of the asset ledger to the fixed asset control account from time to time is also a necessary control procedure.

For control of fixed assets it is also essential that retirements of fixed assets be approved by a specified individual, and that a system exists to ensure prompt and accurate recording of such retirements. The journal voucher recording a sale or scrapping of an asset must be prepared with reference to the asset ledger to ensure proper recording of the gain or loss as well as removal of the cost and accumulated depreciation from the books.

Control procedures for fixed asset acquisition are also essential. Authorization for each asset purchase should be made by a designated manager on the basis of a request form that delineates the cost factors associated with the asset and the reasons for its purchase. Many firms utilize a system whereby asset purchases involving small amounts may be approved by lower-level managers, such as the general supervisor or director of sales, from their departmental capital expenditure budgets. Larger purchases require approval at higher levels, and very large purchases require the approval of the president and board of directors. Formal capital budgeting analysis, including cash flow projections and discounted present value calculations, should accompany these large proposals. Follow-up reports should be prepared on large projects to evaluate whether the expected results were actually achieved.

General ledger. This function primarily involves posting from journal vouchers, or from the general journal, to the general ledger accounts. Because the volume of work is typically quite small, this function is often combined with maintenance of the factory overhead ledger, the selling expense ledger, the general and administrative expense ledger, and the fixed asset ledger. Journal entries are generated from many different sources within the accounting department as by-products of almost all processing of accounting data. The general ledger clerk should check the equality of debits and credits for all journal entries prior to posting. At the end of each month, the general ledger clerk prepares and posts accrual and adjusting entries and prepares a postclosing trial balance to check the equality of debits and credits in the general ledger. All control accounts should be reconciled to the subsidiary ledgers at this time. Once any necessary corrections have been made, the closing entries are performed and the monthly financial statements are prepared.

Computer-based batch processing systems

This section describes and illustrates computer-based systems for batch processing of (1) cash receipts, (2) cash disbursements and accounts payable debit distribution, (3) fixed asset records, and (4) the general ledger. The systems described use magnetic tape input and maintain all master files on magnetic disk. System flows and controls are emphasized. The reader should find it interesting to examine the similarities and differences between these systems and their manual counterparts.

Cash receipts. Procedures for receipt of payments on account in a computer-based system would vary from those in a manual system only in that the data processing department would perform the function of posting payments to the accounts instead of the accounts receivable department. A systems flowchart of this process as performed by a data processing department appears in Fig. 20.7. Each day, the process begins with assembly of remittances in batches and preparation of batch totals for control purposes by personnel in the mail room. The documents are then transmitted to the input preparation department, where they are keyed onto magnetic tape. The key-to-tape encoder may also be used to keyverify the records at this time. As described in examples in earlier chapters, alternative forms of input that are often used include punched cards, diskettes, and online data entry.

In many organizations, the remittance advice is a turnaround document—a punched card or OCR document sent to the customer as a bill or statement with the request that it be returned with the customer's payment (and not folded, spindled, or mutilated!). When the turnaround document and payment are received from the customer, the payment must be checked for agreement to the amount billed. If the payment and the amount billed agree, the

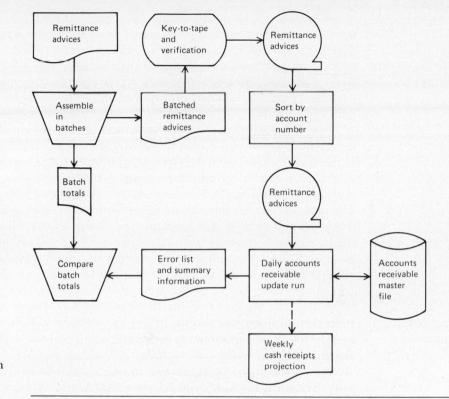

FIGURE 20.7
System flow in computerized batch processing of cash receipts.

turnaround document may be used as an input record with no additional keying of data. The use of turnaround documents not only speeds up the data entry process but also increases its accuracy because the data on the turnaround document are recorded automatically by the system as a by-product of computerized billing or statement preparation. In order to speed up the file updating process, turnaround document records are often transferred from OCR documents or punched cards (slow input media) to magnetic tape (much faster) prior to being processed against the master file.

The next step in the process is to sort the magnetic tape records into sequence by customer account number, the key field for the accounts receivable master file. Since the accounts receivable master is on magnetic disk, this step could conceivably be skipped and the input records processed randomly, making use of the direct access feature of the disk. However, the activity ratio for cash receipts transactions is generally high enough so that it is more efficient to sort the records first and then process them sequentially.

After sorting, the remittance records are processed to update the accounts receivable master file. Each remittance is posted to its corresponding master record, and the current account balance in the record is reduced by the amount of the remittance. In addition to the updated version of the accounts receivable master, this run produces a printout of error transactions and summary information, including batch totals and the summary journal entry debiting cash and crediting accounts receivable; and a printed report projecting short-term cash inflows resulting from customer payments on account balances due. The latter report, useful to short-term cash management by the treasurer, would probably be generated only once a week, as shown, rather than once a day.

Internal control procedures instituted in this system should include (1) keyverification of critical data on remittance records or, alternatively, the use of turnaround documents; (2) batch totals including a record count of remittances, a hash total of customer account numbers, and a financial total of remittance amounts; (3) data security provisions with respect to the transaction tape and master file disk pack, including the use of internal and external labels, off-site storage of a backup copy of the master file, and the use of a file library with controlled checkout procedures; and (4) an input validation routine in the main update program that performs such edit checks as a sequence check, field checks on all numeric data, validity check on account numbers, and a comparison of the amount remitted with the amount due. Furthermore, the batch totals on the error and summary printout must be compared with those generated prior to processing, and the error transactions themselves must be reviewed, corrected, and resubmitted as quickly as possible.

In retail firms, several techniques of source data automation may be applied to the recording of cash received over the counter. Some companies of this type attach to each inventory item a machine-readable tag containing stock number, cost, price, and other information. When a sale is made, the tag is removed and provided to data processing. Another possibility is the use of an online point-of-sale recorder equipped with a wand or scanner that can interpret the Universal Product Code imprinted on price tags.

Cash disbursements. The basic difference between a manual and computerized cash disbursements system is generally the automation of accounts payable record keeping and of check preparation. A systems flowchart of this process as performed by computer appears in Fig. 20.8. Each day this process begins with the assembly of those vouchers that have been approved for payment in batches for keying onto tape. Batch totals that might be prepared at this time include a record count of the number of vouchers, a hash total of vendor numbers, and a financial total of the amount to be added to the accounts payable master.

Each disbursement voucher in this system would contain, in addition to the data shown on the sample voucher illustrated in Fig. 20.6, an indication of the account or accounts to which the amount of each voucher is to be charged. For all purchases of inventory, the appropriate account number is the same—the raw materials inventory account. For purchase of fixed assets or incurrence of costs and expenses, the appropriate account number or num-

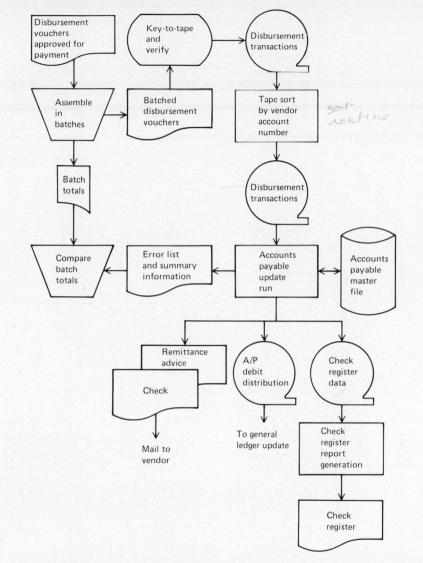

FIGURE 20.8
System flow in
computerized batch
processing of
accounts payable.

bers are entered on the vendor invoice in the department in which payment
of the invoice was authorized. These account numbers are then transcribed
from invoice to voucher as the voucher is prepared. Keyed onto tape from
each disbursement voucher are (1) a record of the payment authorization,
which will be added to the total amount payable to the vendor in the accounts
payable master file, and (2) one or more debit distribution records that indicate the ledger account or accounts to which each amount payable is to be
charged. Thus the debit distribution records form a repeating group within
each disbursement authorization record.

Once the disbursement transactions have been keyed onto magnetic tape, they must be sorted into sequential order by vendor account number prior to the main file update run. This step is performed by the computer under the control of a tape-sort program. Next, the sorted transaction tape is processed as input to the accounts payable update run. This run adds each disbursement record to the corresponding accounts payable master record and increases the total balance due in each master record by the amount of the authorized disbursement.

The accounts payable update run produces four outputs. First, the update program examines the due date of all items in the file and prepares a check and remittance advice in payment of all due invoices, while simultaneously deleting these paid invoices from the master file record. The program also prepares a cash disbursement register, or check register (see Fig. 20.9), that is simply a listing of the check number, amount, vendor, and other relevant data from each check written. The check register is a key element of the audit trail for cash disbursements. In this system the check register is shown to be recorded on magnetic tape for subsequent conversion to a printed report. The third output is a magnetic tape file containing all the debit distribution records; these will be processed as input to the general ledger in an operation described subsequently in this chapter. The other output of this run is a report listing error transactions and summary information. In addition to identifying disbursement transactions that do not pass field checks, validity checks, and other input validation tests, this report also lists any transactions for which the total of all debits in the debit distribution records is not equal to the total authorized disbursement according to the corresponding payment authorization record. The summary information includes an analysis of the accounts payable control account, including its beginning balance, total increases from newly authorized disbursements, total decreases from checks written, and ending balance.

In a fully integrated information system, the accounts payable master file would become part of a vendor master file, an example of which is shown in

FIGURE 20.9
Cash disbursements register.

CASH DISBURSEMENTS REGISTER

Date: Jan. 11, 1987

Chk. No.	Vendor No.	Vendor Name	Account Payable dr.		Discount cr.		Cash cr.	
1045	63218	National Supply	$ 512	67	$ 10	25	$ 502	42
1046	17641	Ross Mfg.	$ 95	07	$	95	$ 94	12
1047	41524	Northern Metal Prod.	$ 742	72	$ 14	85	$ 727	87
1048	36602	Webster Bros.	$ 4,208	18	$ 84	16	$ 4,124	02

Fig. 17.2. As explained in Chapter 17 and illustrated in Fig. 17.9, two additional reports could be generated from such a file. These are a summary of cash flow commitments by due date, which would be generated weekly to assist financial executives in short-term cash management, and a vendor performance report prepared monthly or on demand to assist purchasing agents in vendor selection.

Several control procedures relating to this system have already been mentioned, including keyverification of critical input data from the disbursement vouchers, the use of batch totals, and the incorporation of input validation routines into the accounts payable update program. Also important are data security provisions with respect to the accounts payable master file and the various transaction files. The specifics of application of all these control procedures should by now be familiar to the reader and are not elaborated on here.

Fixed assets.   A systems flowchart of monthly batch processing of fixed asset records by computer appears in Fig. 20.10. Fixed asset transactions are of several different types and may be recorded on various types of source documents. These transactions include new asset purchases, sales or scrappings of existing assets, location transfers, revisions to estimated useful life, major additions or write-downs, and several other kinds of adjustments. Even then, the monthly volume of these transactions is usually not great, and so it is assumed in the illustration that only one set of batch totals is prepared. Among the batch totals prepared would be a record count of the total number of transactions, record counts of the number of transactions of each type, a hash total of asset numbers, and a financial total of new asset purchases and other transactions affecting the dollar balance of the ledger records.

After batch totals are prepared, the fixed asset transactions are keyed onto tape and verified, and then they are sorted by asset number for processing to update the fixed asset ledger. This main updating program must be written to identify the transaction code of each record and to carry out the appropriate steps for each type of transaction. One output of this monthly run is simply a report listing the contents of the file for reference purposes. Another output is a tape listing of all depreciation charges and the overhead or expense account to which each is charged. This tape is sorted by account number and processed to update the general ledger in an operation described in the next section. The other output is a report listing error transactions and summary information, including batch totals and a summary journal entry. If new asset purchases are recorded in the accounts payable debit distribution, this summary entry will record only the effects of such asset transactions as sales, write-offs, or write-downs.

The batch totals on the summary printout must be compared with those accumulated prior to processing, and any errors revealed by this comparison or the error listing should be traced to their cause, corrected, and resubmitted to the system. Other internal control procedures in this system include keyverification of critical data on each transaction, data security provisions with

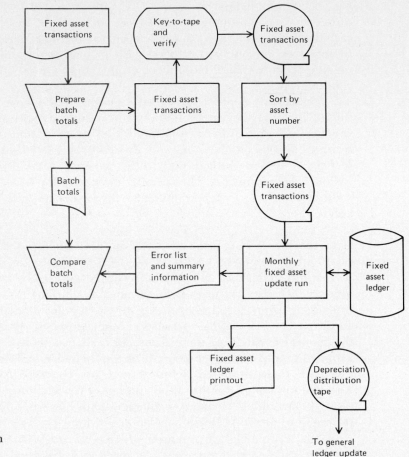

FIGURE 20.10
Computerized batch
processing of fixed
asset records.

respect to the fixed asset ledger file, and an input validation routine in the fixed asset update program. The input validation routine could be quite cumbersome in this program because a different set of edit checks must be used on each type of transaction, and there is a large variety of transaction types.

General ledger.   In the manual system described earlier in this chapter, it is assumed that subsidiary ledgers for manufacturing overhead, selling expenses, and general and administrative expenses are maintained separately from the general ledger. This is done primarily for convenience and to permit clerical specialization. However, in a computerized system, integration of these subsidiary ledgers with the general ledger provides greater advantages than does maintaining them separately. The system described in this section therefore assumes that the general ledger contains all the detailed cost and expense accounts.

The computerized general ledger may be updated several times during a month. The systems flow of this updating process, illustrated in Fig. 20.11, is actually a composite of updating processes that take place at different times and frequencies during a month. The accounts payable debit distribution tape, prepared as a by-product of daily input preparation for accounts payable processing (see Fig. 20.8), would be processed against the general ledger daily or weekly. The payroll distribution tape, a product of the processing of indirect factory labor and office payrolls, would be processed subsequent to each payroll operation; that might be weekly, biweekly, or monthly. The depreciation distribution tape, an output of fixed asset processing (see Fig. 20.10), would be processed once a month following the fixed asset update run. Other entries include summary entries from various daily or weekly batch processes, which should be posted as they occur, and end-of-month accrual, adjusting, and miscellaneous entries. Once each week a printout of the general ledger is obtained for reference purposes.

At the end of each month, the master budget is processed with the final monthly version of the general ledger to prepare various financial reports. It is assumed that both these files are sequenced by department number, which is the major key within the account number. This run generates departmental performance reports comparing actual and budgeted cost for all production departments, factory service departments, and selling and administrative units within the organization. An example of such a report is illustrated in Fig. 20.12. Reports aggregating these financial data for summarization of the performance of higher-level managers (see Fig. 2.5) cannot be printed in the same pass but may be recorded on tape for subsequent printing. As an example, the financial statements, which aggregate data from all departments according to account codes, are shown to be recorded on tape as an output of this run, after which this tape is processed to print a report comparing projected and actual financial results. In addition to generating these various reports, the run closes all revenue and expense account balances to the retained earnings account and prepares a beginning general ledger for the next period.

In a fully integrated accounting information system in which the general ledger is maintained online at all times, it is possible to post almost all accounting transactions automatically to the appropriate general ledger accounts as a by-product of other accounting operations. For example, as disbursement authorization transactions are being processed to update the vendor (accounts payable) master file, the system could access the appropriate general ledger accounts randomly to post the debit distribution for each transaction. The total credit to accounts payable would be posted to the general ledger control account at the completion of processing. Similar general ledger posting subroutines could be incorporated into payroll processing, inventory processing, fixed asset processing, accounts receivable processing, and all other computerized accounting systems. Under this approach, there would probably be a few transactions, such as capital transactions and month-end accruals, that would not originate from any other process and therefore would have to

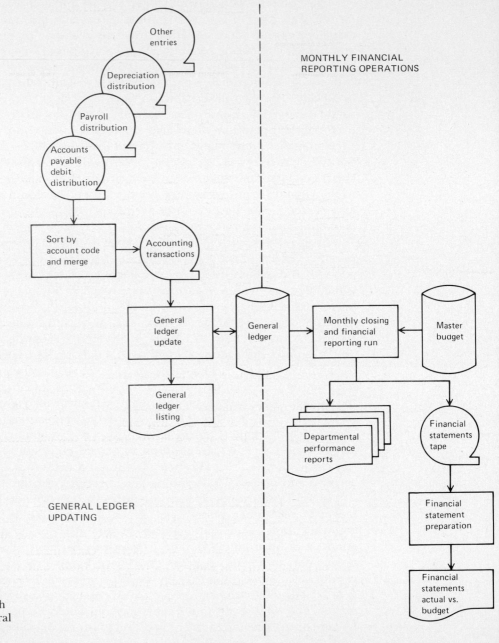

MONTHLY FINANCIAL
REPORTING OPERATIONS

GENERAL LEDGER
UPDATING

FIGURE 20.11
Computerized batch
processing of general
ledger updates and
financial reports.

OPERATING PERFORMANCE SUMMARY						
Department: # 473 Machining				Supervisor Oscar Nagursky		
Cost element	Month ending 2/28/87			Year to date		
	Budget	Actual	Over (under) budget	Budget	Actual	Over (under) budget
Controllable overhead						
Indirect labor	$4,750	$4,608	$(142)	$9,300	$9,248	$(52)
Idle time	250	304	54	480	502	22
Tools and supplies	880	856	(24)	1,720	1,702	(18)
Maintenance	750	802	52	1,450	1,638	188
Rework	120	70	(50)	230	180	(50)
Miscellaneous	200	230	30	380	370	(10)
Total controllable overhead	$6,950	$6,870	$(80)	$13,560	$13,640	$80
Direct labor	$13,200	$13,256	$56	$26,000	$26,384	$384

FIGURE 20.12
Cost performance report for a production department.

be prepared specifically for processing against the general ledger. Except for these few transactions, the need for frequent batch processing operations to update the general ledger would be eliminated by this technique. Furthermore, the general ledger account balances would be more current, which would make it more worthwhile for users to initiate online inquiries to the general ledger, or request reports from it on a demand basis.

Real-time systems

A real-time financial information system is organized around an online general ledger data base that is updated promptly as transactions occur. The general ledger data base is typically integrated with the accounts receivable, accounts payable, inventory, and payroll data bases in such a way that transactions posted to these data bases are immediately reflected in the appropriate general ledger records. The system may also provide for automatic generation and posting of adjusting and closing entries at the end of each month.

To be of maximum usefulness, a real-time financial information system should feature online data entry for all major classes of transactions, including sales, purchases, and cash receipts and disbursements. These transaction data are keyed into the system from online terminals, checked by input validation routines, and then posted both to the general ledger and to the appropriate subsidiary ledgers.

Inquiry processing is frequently used to extract management information from the real-time financial information system. Standard reports available on request from the system would include firm and divisional balance sheets and income statements; cost, revenue, and budget summaries by division, department, or project; and transaction registers and summaries for audit purposes. Most systems also permit users to create custom-tailored reports for special purposes.

The use of a decision support system in conjunction with a real-time financial information system is very common. A typical application involves the use of financial planning models that enable managers to simulate the financial effects of alternative decisions or policies. A related application involves the use of forecasting models to project future financial results under various assumptions regarding sales volumes, prices, costs, and other key variables. The use of such systems in a real-time, interactive mode is extremely beneficial because it enables the user to complete a series of analyses quickly, each one building upon the results previously obtained.

Another common use of the online financial data base involves downloading a subset of it to a microcomputer. This permits easy and rapid manipulation of the data base subset using spreadsheet packages, graphics software, or other user-friendly microcomputer programs.

Summary

Financial management, including both the treasurership and controllership functions, is the core application of an accounting information system. The primary subsystems involve the processing of cash receipts, cash disbursements, fixed asset transactions, and the general ledger. All major accounting files, including receivables, payables, and inventory master files, are actually subsidiary accounting ledgers whose summary balances each tie in with a general ledger control account.

This chapter describes manual and computer-based systems for processing cash receipts and cash disbursements and for maintaining fixed asset and general ledger files. Both manual and computerized accounting systems are commonly used, although manual systems are confined to small businesses and are being computerized at a rapid rate. Also expanding rapidly is the use of real-time financial information systems that integrate the general ledger with all the major subsidiary ledgers and maintain a continuously current financial data base for use in management planning and decision making.

Review Questions

1. Define the following terms.

treasurership	general ledger
controllership	subsidiary ledger
adjusting entries	journal
closing entries	remittance advice
ledger	disbursement voucher

2. Describe an example of an organization structure for the financial management function in a typical business organization. What are the primary decision responsibilities and information requirements of the financial management function?

3. What accounting journal entries summarize the data processing activities involved in
   a) cash receipts,
   b) cash disbursements,
   c) recording of overhead costs,
   d) recording of expenses,
   e) maintenance of fixed assets records, and
   f) financial statement preparation at the end of a month?

4. Describe the data content and organization of the financial accounting data base.

5. Describe the basic format of all accounting ledger records.

6. What should be the relationship between a general ledger control account and its corresponding subsidiary ledger? List some examples of accounts for which subsidiary ledgers are commonly maintained.

7. Explain how the use of a data base management system may eliminate the need for a separate posting operation in an accounting system.

8. What departments in a business organization might typically be involved in the manual processing (a) of cash receipts and (b) of cash disbursements? In both cases what documents might be used and what reports generated? What data or information would each document or report contain? In what department would each document or report originate, and where and for what purpose would each be distributed?

9. What control procedures might be used in manual processing of receipts of payments on account? How is organizational independence achieved with respect to this process?

10. What procedures might a retail organization establish to record and control cash sales?

11. What means of automating the recording of transactions are available to retail organizations?

12. What control procedures might be used in manual processing of cash disbursements in a typical business organization? How is organizational independence achieved with respect to this process?

13. Describe the imprest petty cash system. Indicate in your description the most significant control procedures in the system.

14. Describe procedures and controls in manual systems in a typical business organization for maintenance of (a) fixed asset records and (b) the general ledger.

15. Describe the similarities and differences in data flows and departmental functions between manual systems and computerized systems for processing of receipts of payments on account.

16. Describe and illustrate, using a systems flowchart, a computer-based batch processing system for processing of cash receipts. Describe several control policies and procedures appropriate for such a system.

17. Describe the similarities and differences in data flows and departmental functions between manual systems and computerized systems for processing cash disbursements.

18. Describe and illustrate, using a systems flowchart, a computer-based batch processing system for processing of cash disbursements. Describe several control policies and procedures appropriate for such a system.

19. Describe and illustrate, using a systems flowchart, a computer-based batch processing system for maintaining fixed asset records. Describe several control policies and procedures appropriate for such a system.

20. Describe and illustrate, using a systems flowchart, a computer-based batch processing system for maintaining general ledger records.

21. In a fully integrated accounting information system in which the general ledger is maintained online at all times, what advantages may be realized?

22. What data bases and input records are involved in a real-time financial information system?

23. Describe possible uses of real-time systems for processing of financial information in a typical business organization.

Discussion Questions

24. Discuss the similarities and differences between business organizations and nonprofit organizations with respect to the design of financial information systems.

25. Cite as many examples as you can of information processing interfaces (or interactions) between two or more of the marketing, logistics, personnel, and financial information subsystems of a typical business organization.

26. Discuss the similarities and differences in the functions of a treasurer and a controller. Is there a need for both these functional specializations to exist within a typical business organization, or could one executive effectively fill both roles?

27. Discuss the usefulness of incorporating a real-time capability into a mathematical modeling system used for financial planning.

Problems and Cases

28. Describe appropriate controls in a procedure for processing receipts of payments on account that would provide the best protection against the following contingencies.

    a) Theft of checks received through the mail by personnel in the mail room.

    b) An undetected error in posting from remittance advices to the accounts receivable ledger.

    c) Theft of funds by a cashier who, instead of endorsing checks received for deposit, cashes them and keeps the cash without recording its receipt.

    d) Covering up of embezzlement of checks received by adjustments of the accounts receivable ledger.

    e) Theft of cash by sales personnel in a retail organization, covered up by failure to record cash sales.

29. Describe appropriate controls in a procedure for maintaining fixed asset records that would provide the best protection against the following contingencies.

    a) Acquisition of a fixed asset for which no worthwhile use exists within the firm.

    b) A report by a department supervisor that an asset in the factory has been scrapped, when actually the supervisor has removed it and taken it home.

    c) A large overstatement of the fixed asset control account after several errors are made in updating the account over a period of years.

    d) Inaccurate charging of depreciation to departments because several items of equipment are no longer located in the departments for which they were originally acquired.

    e) Unauthorized sale of a fixed asset by an employee who retains the proceeds.

    f) Unauthorized use of a fixed asset by an employee for personal reasons unrelated to employment.

    g) Payment of insurance and property taxes on assets no longer owned by the company.

    h) Continued ownership of obsolete or otherwise nonproductive assets.

30. Describe appropriate internal controls in a cash disbursements procedure that would protect against the following contingencies.

    a) An employee writing a check payable to the employee or to a fictitious company.

    b) A large overstatement of the accounts payable control account owing to several errors made in posting to the account over a period of time.

    c) Payment of a fictitious invoice for goods that were never delivered.

    d) Issuance of two checks in payment of two copies of the same vendor invoice.

    e) Overpayment of a vendor owing to errors in the calculation of extensions on the vendor's invoice.

    f) Overpayment of a vendor owing to the use of inaccurate item prices on a vendor invoice.

    g) "Borrowing" of a portion of the petty cash fund for personal use by the fund custodian.

31. Cash receipts in the Whirlaway Company are processed in the following manner. The cashier opens all mail containing customer payments and prepares a batch control tape of the total amount received, which is sent to the general ledger clerk to support the appropriate journal entry. The cashier prepares two copies of a deposit slip, deposits the cash receipts in the bank, and files the bank-validated copy of the deposit slip by date. The cashier also sends the remittance advices to the accounts receivable clerk, where they are posted to customer accounts.

    Assume that no other operations or personnel are involved in the processing of cash receipts. Prepare a document flowchart of the processing described above. Then, identify several (at least three) deficiencies in internal control of the process; and for each deficiency, describe an error, manipulation, or inefficiency that could occur as a result.

32. Your company has just acquired a data base management system, and one of the first applications of it will be to accounts payable and cash disbursements processing. A disbursement voucher form identical to that in Fig. 20.6 is used, and in addition, the account number or numbers of the general ledger accounts to which the payment is distributed are printed on the face of each voucher. Diagram the data structure of the disbursement voucher as a first step in the application design. Use a format similar to those in Figs. 16.7 and 17.2. Note that the data base will contain only the variable data on the disbursement voucher, not the constant data.

33. You are auditing the Alaska Branch of Far Distributing Co. This branch has substantial annual sales which are billed and collected locally. As a part of your audit, you find that the procedures for handling cash receipts are as follows:

    Cash collections on over-the-counter sales and COD sales are received from the customer or delivery service by the cashier. Upon receipt of cash, the cashier stamps the sales ticket "paid" and files a copy for future reference. The only record of COD sales is a copy of the sales ticket which is given to the cashier to hold until the cash is received from the delivery service.

    Mail is opened by the secretary to the credit manager and remittances are given to the credit manager for review. The credit manager then places the remittances in a tray on the cashier's desk. At the daily deposit cut-off time the cashier delivers the checks and cash on hand to the assistant credit manager who prepares remittance lists and makes up the bank deposit that the manager also takes to the bank. The assistant credit manager also posts remittances to the accounts receivable ledger cards and verifies the cash discount allowable.

You also ascertain that the credit manager obtains approval from the executive office at Far Distributing Co., located in Chicago, to write off uncollectible accounts, and that the manager has retained in custody as of the end of the fiscal year some remittances that were received on various days during the last month.

REQUIRED

a) Describe the irregularities that might occur under the procedures now in effect for handling cash collections and remittances.
b) Give procedures that you would recommend to strengthen internal control over cash collections and remittances. (CPA Examination)

34. Superior Co. manufactures automobile parts for sale to the major U.S. automakers. Superior's internal audit staff is to review the internal controls over machinery and equipment and make recommendations for improvements where appropriate.

The internal auditors obtained the information presented below during the assignment.

☐ Requests for purchase of machinery and equipment are normally initiated by the supervisor in need of the asset. The supervisor discusses the proposed acquisition with the plant manager. A purchase requisition is submitted to the purchasing department when the plant manager is satisfied that the request is reasonable and if there is a remaining balance in the plant's share of the total corporate budget for capital acquisitions.

should be solid documentation for purchase justification

☐ Upon receiving a purchase requisition for machinery or equipment, the purchasing department manager looks through the records for an appropriate supplier. A formal purchase order is then completed and mailed. When the machine or equipment is received, it is immediately sent to the user department for installation. This allows the economic benefits from the acquisition to be realized at the earliest possible date.

maybe tenders

quality control for checking equipment

☐ The property, plant, and equipment ledger control accounts are supported by lapsing schedules organized by year of acquisition. These lapsing schedules are used to compute depreciation as a unit for all assets of a given type which are acquired in the same year. Standard rates, depreciation methods, and salvage values are used for each major type of fixed asset. These rates, methods, and salvage values were set ten years ago during the company's initial year of operation.

should be specific authorisation for return
proper documentation

☐ When machinery or equipment is retired, the plant manager notifies the accounting department so that the appropriate entries can be made in the accounting records.

periodic accounting

☐ There has been no reconciliation since the company began operations between the accounting records and the machinery and equipment on-hand.

REQUIRED   Identify the internal control weaknesses and recommend improvements which the internal audit staff of Superior Co. should include in its report regarding the internal controls employed for fixed assets. Use the following format in preparing your answer. (CMA Examination)

Weaknesses	*Recommendations*
1.	1.

35. The home office of GHP Insurance Company has a formal statement on policies and procedures for the expense reimbursement of agents. A description of these policies and procedures follows.

Agents are to obtain an expense report form at the beginning of each week. The completed forms are submitted to the Branch Manager at the end of each week. The Branch Manager looks over the expense report to determine if:

a) the expenses qualify for reimbursement under the company's expense reimbursement policy statement.
b) the amounts are reasonable.

Agents are asked to explain any questionable expense item and to show documentation supporting the amounts. Any single expenditure that is expected to exceed $100 should be approved by the Branch Manager in advance.

The Branch Manager approves each expense report by signing it and forwards the report to the Accounting Department at the home office. The Accounting Department makes the appropriate journal entries and posts to the general ledger accounts and agent subsidiary records. A check is prepared by the Cash Disbursements Office to each agent to whom an amount is owed. These expense reimbursement checks are sent to the Branch Manager, who then distributes them to the agents.

Agents may receive cash advances for expenses by completing a Cash Advance Approval form. The Branch Manager reviews these forms and gives approval by signing the forms. One copy of the form goes to the Accounting Department at the home office for recording in the general ledger accounts and agent subsidiary records. A second copy of the form is given to the agent who submits it to the Branch Office Cashier and obtains the cash.

At the end of the month, the Internal Auditing Department at the home office adds the total dollar amounts on the expense reports from each branch, subtracts the sum of the dollar totals on each branch's Cash Advance Approval form, and compares the net amount to the sum of the expense reimbursement checks issued to agents. Any differences are investigated.

The Foreign Corrupt Practices Act of 1977 has identified five general control objectives related to transactions or accounts—authorization, recording, safeguarding, reconciliation and valuation. To evaluate internal control effectively, these general objectives must be related to specific internal control procedures for each aspect of a system.

REQUIRED

a) Define and discuss each of the five general control objectives identified in the Foreign Corrupt Practices Act of 1977 (FCPA).

b) Discuss whether the internal control system of GHP Insurance Company for the reimbursement of agent expenses satisfies the first four general objectives—authorization, recording, safeguarding, and reconciliation—identified in FCPA of 1977. For each of the four objectives, use the following format in preparing your answer:

Control objective (for example, authorization)
    Strengths of system
        1.
        2.
        etc.
    Weaknesses of system
        1.
        2.
        etc.

(CMA Examination)

36. ConSport Corporation is a regional wholesaler of sporting goods. The systems flowchart in Fig. 20.13 and the following description present ConSport's cash distribution system.

a) The Accounts Payable Department approves for payment all Invoices (I) for the purchase of inventory. Invoices are matched with the Purchase Requisitions (PR), Purchase Orders (PO), and Receiving Reports (RR). The accounts payable clerks focus on vendor name and skim the documents when they are combined.

b) When all the documents for an invoice are assembled, a two-copy Disbursement Voucher (DV) is prepared and the transaction is recorded in the Voucher Register (VR). The Disbursement Voucher and supporting documents are then filed alphabetically by vendor.

c) A two-copy Journal Voucher (JV) that summarizes each day's entries in the Voucher Register is prepared daily. The first copy is sent to the General Ledger Department, and the second copy is filed in the Accounts Payable Department by date.

d) The vendor file is searched daily for the Disbursement Vouchers of invoices that are due to be paid. Both copies of Disbursement Vouchers that are due to be paid are sent to the Treasury Department along with the supporting documents. The cashier prepares a check for each vendor, signs the check, and records it in the Check Register (CR). Copy 1 of the Disbursement Voucher is attached to the check copy

FIGURE 20.13

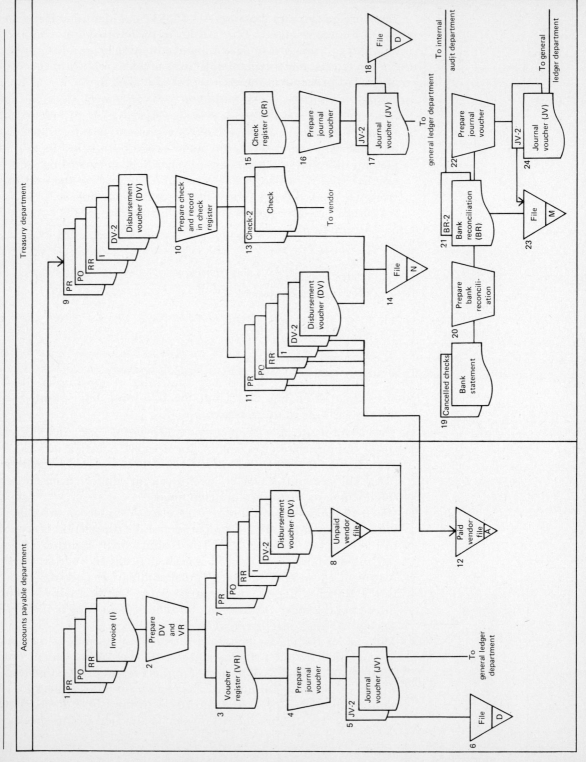

and filed in check number order in the Treasury Department. Copy 2 and the supporting documents are returned to the Accounts Payable Department and filed alphabetically by vendor.

e) A two-copy Journal Voucher that summarizes each day's checks is prepared. Copy 1 is sent to the General Ledger Department and Copy 2 is filed in the Treasury Department by date.

f) The cashier receives the monthly bank statement with cancelled checks and prepares the Bank Reconciliation (BR). If an adjustment is required as a consequence of the Bank Reconciliation, a two-copy Journal Voucher is prepared. Copy 1 is sent to the General Ledger Department. Copy 2 is attached to Copy 1 of the Bank Reconciliation and filed by month in the Treasury Department. Copy 2 of the Bank Reconciliation is sent to the Internal Audit Department.

REQUIRED

ConSport Corporation's cash disbursement system has some weaknesses. Review the cash disbursement system and for each weakness in the system:

1. identify where the weakness exists by using the reference number that appears to the left of each symbol.
2. describe the nature of the weakness.
3. make a recommendation on how to correct the weakness. (CMA Examination)

Use the following format in preparing your answer:

Reference number	Nature of weakness	Recommendation to correct weakness

37. The collection functions of the Robinson Company, a small paint manufacturer, are attended to by a receptionist, an accounts receivable clerk, and a cashier who also serves as a secretary. The company's paint products are sold to wholesalers and retail stores. The following describes all of the procedures performed by the employees of the Robinson Company pertaining to collections.

Since the Robinson Company is short of cash, the deposit of receipts is expedited. The receptionist turns over all mail receipts and related correspondence to the accounts receivable clerk who examines the checks and determines that the accompanying vouchers or correspondence contains enough detail to permit posting of the accounts. The accounts receivable clerk then endorses the checks and gives them to the cashier who prepares the daily deposit. No currency is received in the mail and no paint is sold over the counter at the factory.

The accounts receivable clerk uses the vouchers or correspondence that accompanied the checks to post the accounts receivable ledger cards. The bookkeeping machine prepares a cash receipts register as a carbon copy of the postings. Monthly the general ledger clerk summarizes the cash receipts register for posting to the general ledger accounts. The accounts receivable clerk also corresponds with customers about unauthorized deductions for discounts, freight or advertising allowances, returns, etc., and prepares the appropriate credit memos. Disputed items of large amount are turned over to the sales manager for settlement. Each month the accounts receivable clerk prepares a trial balance of the open accounts receivable and compares the resultant total with the general ledger control account for accounts receivable.

Discuss the internal control weaknesses in the Robinson Company's procedures related to customer remittances and the accounting for these transactions. In your discussion, in addition to identifying the weaknesses, explain what could happen as a result of each weakness. (CPA Examination)

38. The Rock Island Brewery has recently acquired a new disk memory device. Previously all files maintained by the company's computerized data processing center had been on magnetic tape. You are involved in designing a computer application that will process disbursement vouchers approved for payment and keyed onto magnetic tape. Following keyverification, these voucher records are then sorted by vendor account number and processed to update an accounts payable master file (maintained on magnetic tape) and a general ledger file (maintained on magnetic disk). Output of this processing run will include the updated versions of the two master files, a printed report containing error transactions and summary information, and a disbursements tape listing all voucher records for which payment is due. The disbursements tape is processed to generate (1) a remittance advice and check in payment of each voucher on the tape and (2) a disbursements register, which is simply a printed list of all checks paid.

    a) Prepare a systems flowchart of the operations described above.

    b) What is the minimum hardware configuration required to perform the processes above? (Assume no spooling.)

    c) What are the advantages of storing the general ledger file on the disk unit? What would be the advantages of storing the accounts payable file on the disk unit?

39. VBR Company has recently installed a new computer system which has online, real-time capability. Cathode ray tube terminals are used for data entry and inquiry. A new cash receipts and accounts receivable file maintenance system has been designed and implemented for use with this new equipment. All programs have been written, tested, and the new system is being run in parallel with the old system. After two weeks of parallel operation, no differences have been observed between the two systems other than keypunch errors on the old system.

     Al Brand, Data Processing Manager, is enthusiastic about the new equipment and system. He reveals that the system was designed, coded, compiled, debugged and tested by programmers utilizing an online CRT

terminal installed specifically for around-the-clock use by the programming staff; he claimed that this access to the computer saved one-third in
programming elapsed time. All files, including accounts receivable, are
online at all times as the firm moves toward a full data base mode. All
programs, new and old, are available at all times for recall into memory
for scheduled operating use or for program maintenance. Program documentation and actual tests confirm that data entry edits in the new system include all conventional data error and validity checks appropriate
to the system.

Inquiries have confirmed that the new system conforms precisely to
the flow charts, a portion of which are shown in Fig. 20.14. A turnaround
copy of the invoice is used as a remittance advice (R/A) by 99 percent of
the customers; if the R/A is missing the cashier applies the payment to a
selected invoice. Sales terms are net 60 days, but payment patterns are
sporadic. Statements are not mailed to customers. Late payments are com-
monplace and are not vigorously pursued. VBR does not have a bad debt
problem because bad debt losses average only 0.5% of sales.

Before authorizing the termination of the old system, Cal Darden,
Controller, has requested a review of the internal control features which
have been designed for the new system. Security against unauthorized access and fraudulent actions, assurance of the integrity of the files, and
protection of the firm's assets should be provided by the internal controls.

REQUIRED

a) Describe how fraud by lapping of accounts receivable could be committed in the new system and discuss how it could be prevented.

b) Based upon the description of VBR Company's new system and the
systems flowchart that has been presented:

1. Describe any other defects which exist in the system.
2. Suggest how each other defect you identified could be corrected.
(CMA Examination)

40. The Darwin Department Store maintains its customer accounts by computer. Once each day all receipts of payments on account are processed
to update an accounts receivable master file maintained on a disk storage
unit. All nonroutine file changes and other adjustments to the accounts
receivable master are also processed at the same time. All the input data
records are keypunched, after which the punched cards are processed by
a utility routine to transfer their contents to magnetic tape. The records
on tape are then sorted and processed sequentially to update the accounts
receivable master. The tape sort requires four tape drives. Output of the
updating run includes (1) a printed report listing error transactions and
summary information and (2) a printed report listing the records of all
past-due accounts.

REQUIRED

a) What data should be included on each cash receipt input record?
b) Give two specific examples of the "nonroutine file changes and other
adjustments" mentioned above.

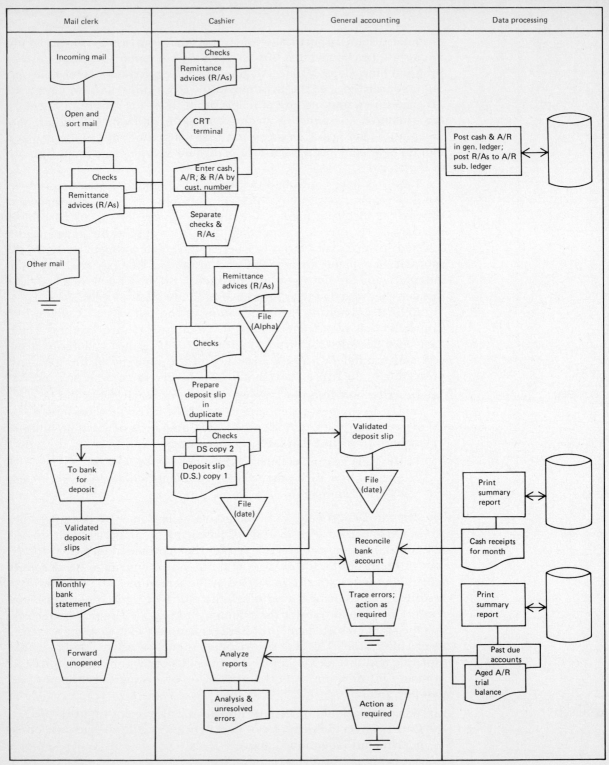

FIGURE 20.14

c) Prepare a systems flowchart of all computer processes described above.

d) List the components of the hardware configuration necessary to accomplish all phases of the processing described in the case subsequent to keypunching.

e) Describe a comprehensive set of control policies and procedures for this accounts receivable application. For each policy or procedure, indicate the objective and exact method of operation. Be sure to relate each policy or procedure specifically to the accounts receivable processing system described above.

41. The Able Manufacturing Company maintains a master budget file on magnetic tape. At the end of each month, this file is processed by computer together with a manufacturing overhead ledger, also maintained on magnetic tape, to generate performance reports for all production departments. The format of each such report is identical to that shown in Fig. 20.12 except that direct labor costs are not included in the report.

The budgeted amount of each cost element for the current month is computed as $(a + bx)$, where a is the fixed amount of that cost element per month, b is the variable rate of that cost element, and x is the value of the base to which the variable rate is applied. The rate base for each cost element is one of three different rate bases used, which are direct labor cost, direct labor hours, and machine hours. The value of each of these three bases for the current month is entered into the system at the beginning of processing.

REQUIRED

What specific data elements must be included in each overhead cost record of (a) the master budget and (b) the manufacturing overhead ledger in order for these files to be used as described above in generating performance reports for production departments?

42. Culp Electronics Company processes disbursement authorizations online as vendor invoices are matched with receiving reports, purchase orders, and other supporting documents in the accounting department. Each disbursement authorization is entered via a data terminal and processed to update the accounts payable master file. The debit portion of the entry is processed to update either (1) the inventory ledger, (2) the expense ledger, or (3) the fixed asset ledger, depending on what the disbursement is for.

For each disbursement authorization relating to an inventory purchase, the following data are entered: the vendor account number; amount due; discount rate; due date; and for each item purchased, the part number, price, and quantity.

REQUIRED

Consider only disbursement authorizations relating to inventory purchases as described. Describe several means by which the system could be programmed to check the accuracy and validity of the input data. Relate your answer specifically to the data items mentioned above.

References

Bierman, Harold, Jr., and Seymour Smidt. *The Capital Budgeting Decision.* 5th ed. New York: Macmillan, 1980.

Douglas, Patricia B., and Teresa K. Beed. *Presenting Accounting Information to Management.* Montvale, N.J.: National Association of Accountants, 1986.

Gulding, John F. "Redesigning Accounts Payable." *Management Accounting* (September 1983): 42–46.

Hill, Dan J., and Garold I. Rutherford. "Computerized Financial Data Reporting System." *Management Accounting* (July 1976): 57–60.

Lubas, Daniel P. "Developing a Computerized General Ledger System." *Management Accounting* (May 1976): 53–56.

Morley, James E., Jr. "Cash Management—Working for the Extra 1% or 2%." *Management Accounting* (October 1978): 17–22.

Page, John R., and H. Paul Hooper. *Accounting and Information Systems.* Reston, Va.: Reston, 1979.

Price Waterhouse & Co. *Guide to Accounting Controls—Financial Management.* New York: Price Waterhouse & Co., 1979.

———. *Guide to Accounting Controls— Financial Reporting.* New York: Price Waterhouse & Co., 1979.

———. *Guide to Accounting Controls—Productive Assets.* New York: Price Waterhouse & Co., 1979.

Schall, Lawrence D., and Charles W. Haley. *Introduction to Financial Management.* 2d ed. New York: McGraw-Hill, 1980.

Volk, Douglas A. "Managing Accounts Receivables—Systematically." *Management Accounting* (July 1980): 46–51.

Welsch, Glenn A., and Robert N. Anthony. *Fundamentals of Financial Accounting.* Rev. ed. Homewood, Ill.: Irwin, 1977.

Glossary

Acceptance test A test of a new system using specially developed transactions and acceptance criteria. The test results are evaluated to decide if the system is acceptable.

Access control matrix An internally maintained list that the computer uses to conduct a compatibility test to verify that the person attempting to access system resources is authorized. The matrix usually consists of a list of user codes, a list of all files and programs maintained on the system, and a list of the access each user is authorized to make.

Access method Any of the many techniques available to the computer user for moving data between the primary storage and input/output devices and secondary storage.

Access time The time required to transfer data to or from a storage device.

Accounting controls The plan of organization and the procedures and records concerned with the safeguarding of assets and the reliability of financial records.

Accounting cycle The activities corresponding to an organization's major accounting transactions. There are five major accounting cycles: acquisition and cash disbursements, payroll and personnel, sales and collection, capital acquisition and payment, and inventory and warehousing.

Accounting information system (AIS) The human and capital resources within an organization that are responsible for (1) the preparation of financial information, and (2) the information obtained from collecting and processing company transactions. The AIS is a subset of the management information system.

Acoustic coupler A device that allows a telephone handset to be hooked to data communications equipment. Digital data can then be translated into a sequence of tones that are then transmitted over regular telephone lines.

Action steps The rows in a decision table that indicate the specific actions taken in a computer program.

Activity ratio A measure of the proportion of master file records referenced during file processing.

Ad hoc queries Nonrepetitive requests for reports or answers to specific questions about the contents of the system's data files.

Ad hoc users Users who make unscheduled or as-needed inquiries of the data base.

Address The address that uniquely identifies each computer storage location.

Adjusting entries End-of-period entries designed to match revenues and expenses in the period they are earned or incurred. There are normally four types: the recognition of expenses incurred but not yet paid, the recognition of revenue earned but not yet received, the expiration of prepaid expenses, and the recognition of unearned (prepaid) revenues as revenue.

Administrative controls The plan of organization and all methods and procedures that are concerned with operational efficiency and adherence to managerial policies.

Administrative documentation A description of the overall standards and procedures for the data processing facility, including policies relating to justification and authorization of new systems or systems changes; standards for systems analysis, design, and programming; procedures for file handling and file library activities; and so forth.

ALGOL An acronym for *algo*rithmic *l*anguage, an international high-level language that is widely used in Europe. Like *FORTRAN,* it was designed mainly for scientific and mathematical applications.

Algorithm The sequence of rules or processes followed in solving a problem.

Allocation base A measure of the work performed by a computer system that is used in internal pricing of computer services. Three different allocation bases are commonly used: single factor, unit pricing, and multiple factor.

Alphanumeric The alphabetic, numeric, and special characters that can be processed by the computer.

Analog data Data transmitted from one location to another in the form of waves. For example, data are transmitted over telephone lines in analog form. Contrast with *digital data.*

Analysis and design phase A phase of the systems development life cycle that includes determining if an organization needs a new system or subsystem, surveying the existing system, and determining the user's needs.

859

Analytical review A review of relationships and trends among financial and operating information to detect items that should be investigated further.

APL An acronym for *a programming language*, which is a mathematically structured programming language developed by IBM. APL is often utilized on real-time and time-sharing computer systems.

Apple DOS The operating system used by Apple micro-computers.

Application The problem or data processing task to which a computer's processing power is applied.

Application controls Controls that relate to the data inputs, files, programs, and outputs of a specific computer application, rather than to the computer system in general. Contrast with *general controls*.

Application programmer A person who takes a logical model, or user view, of the data to be processed and then writes an application program using a programming language.

Applications software (or programs) The programs that perform the data or information processing tasks required by the user. Common accounting examples include accounts receivable and payable, inventory control, and payroll.

Applications study The preparation of a detailed description of the specific tasks that a new system is intended to perform.

Arithmetic processor A microprocessor that will complete arithmetic computations up to 200 times faster than a regular microprocessor.

Arithmetic-logic unit That portion of the CPU that executes arithmetic calculations and logic comparisons.

Artificial intelligence (AI) A field of study that is attempting to develop computers that have the ability to reason, think, and learn like a human being.

ASCII An acronym for *American Standard Code for Informational Interchange*, which is a standard seven-bit code that facilitates the interchange of data between data processing, data communications, and related equipment.

Assembler A computer program that converts assembly-level language to machine-level language.

Assembler language A programming language in which each machine-level instruction is represented by mnemonic characters that bear some relation to the instruction. It is also referred to as a *symbolic language*.

Asynchronous transmission Data transmission where each character is transmitted separately and is preceded by a start bit and followed by a stop bit, since the interval of time between characters can vary. Contrast with *synchronous transmission*.

Attribute A characteristic of interest in a file or data base; the different individual properties of an entity. Examples of attributes are employee number, pay rate, name, and address. Generally, the same attributes are maintained for all entities of the same type. However, the value of the attributes will be different for each entity.

Audio response unit A hardware device that converts computer output into a spoken output (i.e., telephone directory assistance).

Audit log A log, kept on magnetic tape or disk, of all computer system transactions that have audit significance.

Audit trail Media and procedures that allow transactions to be traced through all stages of data processing. This allows data to be followed from source document to output report or from output to the source documents from which they were derived.

Auditing A systematic process of objectively obtaining and evaluating evidence regarding assertions about economic actions and events to ascertain the degree of correspondence between those assertions and established criteria and communicating the results to interested users.

Automated decision table program A program that interprets the logic used in a computer program and displays the logic in the form of a decision table.

Automated flowcharting program A program that interprets the source code of a program and generates a flowchart of the logic used by the program.

Automated office A computerized system where all the hardware devices in an office are linked together, thereby allowing users to communicate electronically and to automate most business information processing tasks. Also called the *electronic office* and the *office of the future*.

Automated teller machine (ATM) A special-purpose intelligent terminal used by financial institutions to provide remote banking services.

Backlog Orders that have been received but not shipped.

Backordered items Items that were ordered but not shipped because of insufficient supply. They will be shipped as soon as the supply is replenished.

Backup (1) A copy of a program or file that is kept just in case the original is destroyed. The backup copy should be stored at a different physical location than the original copy. (2) Standby equipment for use in the event of damage to or failure of the equipment normally used in data processing.

Bandwidth The difference between the highest and the lowest frequency of a communications channel. This is usually expressed in cycles per second (hertz).

BASIC An acronym for *Beginner's All-purpose Symbolic Instruction Code*, a programming language that was designed specifically to be easy to learn and easy to use. It is most commonly used by small personal computers and by time-sharing devices.

Batch processing The accumulation of transaction records into groups or batches that are processed at some regular interval such as daily or weekly. The records are usually sorted into some sequence (such as numerically or alphabetically) before processing.

Batch total   A sum of a numerical item that is calculated from a batch of documents. This total is calculated prior to processing the batch, and the total is compared with machine-generated totals at each subsequent processing step to verify that the data were processed correctly. Any discrepancy may indicate a loss of records or errors in data transcription or processing. Common batch totals are financial totals, hash totals, and record counts.

Batching   The accumulation of similar input records so they can be processed together.

Baud rate   The speed with which data are electronically transferred from one location to another. In many data communications transmissions it is equal to one bit per second.

Benchmark problem   A data processing task that is executed by different computer systems. The results are used to measure systems performance and to make comparative evaluations between systems.

Bidirectional printer   A printer that prints the next line in reverse order when it gets to the end of a line.

Bill of materials   A document containing materials specifications for a particular product.

Binary   A selection or choice that has two possibilities. Also the number system that has a base of two rather than the base of ten, which is most commonly used.

Binary-coded decimal (BCD)   A six-bit coding system (or grouping of bits) used by some computers to represent data.

Bit   A binary digit, which is the smallest storage location in a computer. A bit may either be "on" or "off" or "magnetized" or "nonmagnetized." A combination of bits (usually eight) are used to represent a single character of data.

Bits per second (bps)   A unit of measurement for how many bits of data are transmitted electronically.

Block   A group of records that are stored together and handled as a unit. When stored on a magnetic medium, blocks of records are often separated by an interblock gap.

Block code   A coding system where blocks of sequential numbers are set aside for a specific category of items. For example, all asset accounts may be given a code between 100 and 199.

Block diagram   A program flowchart.

Bottom-up approach   An approach to developing an information system that proceeds from the lowest level in an organization (individual transactions) up through the highest level (top management needs). As information needs are identified, transaction processing subsystems are developed, modified, and expanded to provide the information needed. The growth of the subsystem is planned and coordinated to achieve integration. Contrast with *top-down approach*.

Broadband line   A communications channel that is capable of handling high-speed data transmissions, usually in the range of 20,000 to 500,000 bits per second. Their pri-

mary use is for high-speed data transmission between computer systems.

Bubble memory   Computer storage that consists of a chip covered with a thin magnetic film that forms a bubble when a magnetic field is applied. It has approximately ten times the storage capacity of a semiconductor chip.

Budget   A formal statement of the goals and plans of an organization expressed in financial terms.

Buffer   A temporary storage area that is used to balance the operating speed differences between a high-speed device like a computer and a lower-speed device like a printer. They are also often used between computers and data communications devices.

Bug   An error in a program or computer application, or a malfunction in a hardware component. Correcting the mistakes and malfuntions is referred to as debugging.

Bus   The path for moving data, instructions, or other signals between the various components of the CPU. The bus could be in the form of a cable or in the form of the connecting paths within a microcomputer chip.

Bus size   The number of bits that can be transmitted at one time from one location in the computer to another.

Byte   A group of adjacent bits that is treated as a single unit by the computer. The most common size for a byte is eight bits. An eight-bit byte can be used to represent an alphanumeric, numeric, or special character, or two numeric characters can be "packed" into a single eight-bit byte.

C   A popular high-level microcomputer language that is easy to use and highly efficient.

Calculation of data   Any form of mathematical manipulation of data.

Canned software   A software program that is written by computer manufacturers or software development companies for sale on the open market to a broad range of users with similar needs.

Capital budget   An estimate of funds to be appropriated for the acquisition of major capital assets and for investment in long-term projects.

Card   See *punched card*.

Card deck   A set of punched cards.

Card punch   An output device that stores data on punched cards by punching holes in the card.

Card reader   An input device that reads punched cards by interpreting the holes in the cards.

Carriage   The device on a printer or typewriter that feeds the paper past the printing mechanism and that automatically feeds, spaces, skips, or ejects paper forms.

Cash budget   A projection of an organization's cash inflows and outflows over the short run.

Cassette tape   A simple and inexpensive, but slow, secondary storage medium. Its most popular use is as a backup medium for hard disks.

Cathode-ray tube (CRT)   Another name for the monitor on a computer. Sometimes a terminal is referred to as a *CRT* as well.

Cell   (1) The intersection of a row and column in an electronic spreadsheet. (2) A small section of a larger metropolitan area in which cellular radio is used.

Cellular radio   A means of making greater use of radio frequencies. A large area is divided into smaller sections called cells, and each radio frequency is assigned to a different user in each cell. A powerful central computer controls transmission between cells.

Central processing unit (CPU)   The hardware that contains the circuits that control the interpretation and execution of instructions and that serves as the principal data processing device. Its major components are the arithmetic-logic unit, the memory, and the control unit. The CPU is also known as the central processor or the mainframe.

Centralized data processing network   A large, centralized computer system that handles a company's data processing needs. These systems require complex software and were designed to provide a company with an "economy of scale" advantage in their data processing operations.

Chain   A group of data records that are linked together by pointers. The chaining process allows records to be accessed in a particular order even though they may not be stored on the direct access device in that order.

Channel   (1) A path that electronic signals follow when traveling between electronic devices. (2) A hardware device that acts as a communications interface between the CPU and input/output devices.

Character   A letter, numeric digit, or other symbol used for representing data that are processed by a computer.

Charged-couple device   A slower sequential-access form of semiconductor memory.

Chart of accounts   A listing of all balance sheet and income statement account number codes for a particular company.

Check bit   See *parity bit*.

Check digit   A redundant digit in a data field that provides information about the other digits in the data field. It is used to check for errors or loss of characters in a data field as a result of data transfer operations. If data are lost or erroneously changed, the check digit algorithm will signal that an error has occurred because the check digit does not match the other data in the field.

Check digit verification   The edit check that recalculates a check digit to verify that an error has not been made. This calculation can only be made on a data item that has a check digit.

Checklist   A systems survey and analysis tool that is used to gather information about some particular aspect of the information system.

Checkpoint   A recovery procedure where an exact copy of all the data values and status indicators of a program are captured at periodic points during a long processing run.

Should a system failure occur, the system could be backed up to the checkpoint and processing could begin again at the checkpoint rather than at the beginning of the program.

Child   A record type, or node, in a tree structure that is associated with a record type at a higher level. Contrast with *parent*.

Chip   A small silicon chip with integrated circuits etched in the silicon.

Circuit   The communication path between two or more points that facilitates an orderly flow of electrons from one electronic component to another.

Circuit board   A specially designed board on which a variety of circuits have been inscribed or printed.

Classifying data   Assigning identification codes (account numbers, etc.) to data records based on a predetermined system, such as a chart of accounts.

Clock   The internal device within a computer that sends out periodic pulses that are designed to synchronize the timing of the internal components.

Closed loop verification   An input validation where data that have just been entered into the system are sent back to the sending device so the user can verify that the correct data have been entered.

Closing entries   Accounting entries that zero out all revenue and expense accounts at the end of a fiscal period.

Coaxial cable   A group of copper or aluminum wires that have been wrapped and shielded to reduce interference. The cables are used to transmit electronic messages between hardware devices.

COBOL   An acronym for *common business-oriented language*, a high-level programming language developed for business data processing applications. It is the most popular business-oriented language.

CODASYL   An acronym for the *Conference on Data Systems Languages*, the group of users and manufacturers who developed COBOL.

Coding   (1) The assignment of numbers, letters, or other symbols according to a systematic plan so that a user can determine the classifications to which a particular item belongs and distinguish items within a given classification from each other. (2) Developing the programming language instructions that direct a computer to perform a specific data processing task.

Collate   The combination of two or more groups of data into a single group that is sequenced in a specific order.

Collator   A device that collates data.

Collusion   The conspiracy of two or more people to commit fraud.

Color monitor   A monitor that can display data in a variety of colors.

Command   An instruction that tells a computer to accomplish a specific task.

Common carrier   A governmentally regulated private organization that provides telecommunications equipment and service for use by the public.

Communications channel   The line, or link, between the sender and the receiver in a data communications network.

Communications control program   A program that manages the computer's data communications activities and interacts with the various terminals. It allows a microcomputer to be used as an intelligent terminal and to communicate with other computers tied into a data communications network.

Communications interface device   A device in a data communications system that interfaces between the sending and receiving devices and the communications channel. Examples include modems, multiplexors, concentrators, and front-end processors.

Communications monitor   Programs that control and support data communications within a communications network.

Communications network   An information system consisting of one or more computers, a number of other hardware devices, and communications channels all linked together into a network.

Communications processor   See *front-end processor*.

Communications satellite   A satellite that is placed in stationary orbit over the equator with the intended purpose of providing communications relay services to locations on the earth.

Communications software   Software that controls the transmission of data electronically over communications lines.

Comparison of data   The simultaneous examination of two or more items of data.

Compatibility test   Testing a password to determine whether it is authorized to initiate the type of transaction or inquiry being entered. For example, factory employees would not be authorized to make entries involving accounts payable.

Compilation time   The amount of time it takes to convert source code into object code.

Compile   The process of converting source code (e.g., BASIC) into object code (e.g., machine language).

Compiler   A program that converts all high-level language commands into machine language commands before any commands are executed. Contrast with *interpreter*.

Completeness test   An online data entry control in which the computer checks to see if all the required data for a particular transaction have been entered by the user.

Complex network   A network in which some or all of the relationships are many-to-many.

Compliance audit   A review to determine how well a company is complying with laws, contract provisions, government regulations, and other obligations to external parties.

Computer address   See *address*.

Computer-assisted design/computer-assisted manufacturing (CAD/CAM)   The use of a computer system featuring high-resolution graphics terminals and graphics software to assist engineers in the design, alteration, and manufacturing of products.

Computer audit software   See *generalized audit software package*.

Computer console   A hardware device computer operators use to interact with large computer systems.

Computer operator   A person who operates the computer and its related peripheral devices.

Computer output microfilm (COM)   A hardware device that uses a photographic process to record computer output on photosensitive film in microscopic form.

Computer personnel   Those individuals who use, design, operate, control, and manage an EDP system.

Computer program   See *program*.

Computer programmer   See *programmer*.

Computer system   The input/output devices, data storage devices, CPU, and other peripheral devices that are connected together. The software necessary to operate the computer is also considered a part of the system.

Concentrator   A communications device that combines signals from several sources and sends them over a single line. The concentrator can also perform such tasks as data formatting, data validation, and data backup.

Conditional statement   A computer program statement that is executed only after a certain condition has been met.

Confirmation   A written request (usually from an auditor) that is sent to an outside party to verify the accuracy of information provided by a company regarding the transactions between the outside party and the company.

Connect time   The amount of time a person is connected to a computer, to a time-share system, or to a bulletin board service.

Constant data   The preprinted data on a form.

Contention control   An approach to controlling a shared communications line in which a terminal continues to listen to a line until it is free and then transmits its data.

Contingency theory   An organizational theory that states that the structure of an organization is contingent upon a number of factors such as size, diversity and complexity of products, and variability of business environment.

Control module   The main body of a structured program. Its purpose is to call upon the various program modules when they are needed.

Control total   See *batch total*.

Control unit   The CPU component that interprets program instructions and controls and coordinates the system's input, output, and storage devices.

Controllable costs   Costs over which managers, through the exercise of their delegated authority, have some influence. These are the costs that should be used to judge the performance of a manager.

Controller   (1) A hardware device that translates channel signals for input/output devices. (2) The chief accounting executive in an organization, usually ranked on the same level with or one level below a vice-president. The controller typically has responsibility for things such as budgeting, records management, tax planning, and internal audit.

Conversion   The process of converting data from one form to another (e.g., from punched card to magnetic tape) or of converting from an old system to a new one.

Coprocessor   A microprocessor that performs special processing functions.

Cost center   An organizational unit whose assigned objective is to accomplish its goals and operational functions by keeping costs at a minimum. Cost center reports should focus on how well costs were controlled within the center.

Counter   An electronic device that keeps track of the number of occurrences of a particular event. This is usually a certain memory storage location that increments each time the event occurs.

CP/M   An acronym for *Control Program/Monitor*, the eight-bit operating system that became an early de facto standard for microcomputers.

Critical path   The path of activities in a PERT network that requires the greatest total expenditure of time.

Cross talk   A phenomenon where one signal creates interference for another signal.

Cross-footing balance test   When worksheet data are totaled both across and down, the total of the horizontal totals can be compared against the total of the vertical totals to make sure the worksheet balances.

Cryptographic protection   The translation of data into a secret code for storage or data transmission purposes. Cryptographic protection is particularly important when confidential data are being transmitted from remote terminals because data transmission lines can be electronically monitored without the user's knowledge.

Cursor   A movable point of light that is displayed on a video terminal display to indicate where data should be entered.

Customized software   Programs that are written to meet the unique needs of a particular company.

Cybernetics   The theoretical study of feedback control systems.

Cylinder   The vertically aligned tracks on each surface of a hard disk.

Daisy wheel printer   A printer that rotates a print element that looks like a daisy and causes the print element to strike a ribbon when the desired character is in the proper location.

Data   A set of characters that is accepted as input to an information system for further storing and processing. After processing, the data become information.

Data base   A set of interrelated, centrally controlled data files that are stored with as little data redundancy as possible. A data base consolidates many records previously stored in separate files in a common pool of data records and serves a variety of users and data processing applications.

Data base administrator   The person responsible for coordinating, controlling, and managing the data in the data base.

Data base approach   The use of data bases as the primary data storage structure. Contrast with the *file-oriented approach.*

Data base control system   The software program that controls the various components of the data base management system.

Data base management system (DBMS)   The specialized computer program that manages and controls the data and interfaces between the data and the application programs.

Data base retrieval system (DBRS)   Public data bases, or electronic libraries, that contain millions of items of data that can be retrieved, reviewed, analyzed, etc., for a fee.

Data base system   The combination of the data base, the data base management system, and the application programs that access the data base through the data base management system.

Data bus   The path, or circuitry, the computer uses to move data and instructions between the different parts of the CPU, and to and from the input/output devices.

Data classification   The assignment of identification codes to data according to some predetermined system of classification.

Data collection   The observation or recording of data, generally in the form of either a written source document or some magnetic medium. The data are typically collected so that they can be input into the system.

Data communications   The transmission of data from a point of origin to a point of destination.

Data communications device   Any device that facilitates the transfer of data between two points.

Data control function   An organizational unit that maintains a record of work in process, monitors the flow of work in the data processing department, distributes systems output, checks the accuracy of input and output against preestablished control totals, ensures that established control procedures are adhered to, and follows up on errors identified by computer editing and validation programs.

Data conversion   See *conversion.*

Data definition language (DDL)   The data base management system language that ties the logical and physical views of the data together. It is used to create the data base, to describe the schema and subschematas, to describe the records and fields in the data base, and to specify any security limitations or constraints imposed upon the data base.

Data dictionary/directory An ordered collection of data elements that is essentially a centralized source of data about data. For each data element used in the organization, there is a record in the data dictionary that contains data about that data element.

Data independence A data organization approach where the data and the application programs that use the data are independent. This means that each may be changed without affecting the other.

Data item The smallest unit of data; it represents a single value.

Data maintenance The storage, updating, indexing, or protection of data that are required for future use.

Data manipulation language (DML) The data base management system language that is used to update, replace, store, retrieve, insert, delete, sort, and otherwise manipulate the records and data items in the data base.

Data preparation device A device that takes source documents and prepares them for entry into the computer (e.g., card-to-disk system).

Data processing A systematic sequence of operations performed on data.

Data processing center The room that houses a company's computer system (the hardware, software, and people who operate the system).

Data processing manager The person who is in charge of the data processing system of a company.

Data processor Any device that may perform processing operations on data.

Data protection A variety of procedures designed to prevent data destruction and unauthorized use of data.

Data query language (DQL) A high-level English-like command language that is used to interrogate a data base. Most contain a fairly powerful set of commands that are easy to use yet provide a great deal of flexibility.

Data redundancy Storing the same item of data in two or more files within an organization.

Data refinement The classifying, batching, verification, sorting, transmission, and/or transcription of data in order to facilitate the processing of data.

Data transmission The transfer of data between two or more locations.

Data value The actual data stored in a field. It is the value that describes a particular attribute of an entity.

Debugging The process of checking for errors in a computer program and correcting the errors that are discovered.

Decentralized system An information processing system that has an independent CPU and a data processing manager at each location.

Decision rule The vertical columns in a decision table that represent a combination of logical relationships and the actions that should be taken for each of those logic conditions.

Decision support systems (DSS) An interactive computer system designed to help with the decision-making process by providing access to a computerized data base and decision-making model.

Decision table A tabular representation of program logic that indicates the combination of logic conditions that are possible and the courses of action taken by the program for each condition.

Decode The process of determining the meaning of coded information.

Deduction register A detailed listing of the miscellaneous deductions for each employee.

Desk checking A visual and mental review of a newly coded program to discover keying or program errors.

Desk top computer See *microcomputer*.

Detailed systems design phase The systems development activity where the specific details of the system are designed. This phase includes the design of input and output documents, files and data bases, record layouts, processing procedures, etc.

Diagnostic messages Messages that inform the programmer of syntax errors.

Diagnostic routine A routine that is designed to detect a malfunction in the CPU or a peripheral unit.

Dial-up line See *switched line*.

Digital data The type of data stored within a computer; data in discrete form such as the presence or absence of electrical pulses. Contrast with *analog data*.

Direct access An access method that allows a particular record to be accessed without reading all the other records. Since each storage location on a direct-access storage device has a unique address, the computer can find the record needed as long as it has the record's address.

Direct-access storage device (DASD) A storage device (such as a disk drive) that can directly access its individual storage locations to store or retrieve data.

Direct addressing An addressing approach in which there is a direct relationship between record keys and machine addresses. For example, invoices 0001 to 9999 may be stored at machine addresses 0001 to 9999.

Directory A partition set up by the disk operating system that tells the location of all the files contained on the disk

Disbursement voucher An authorization to pay a vendor for the invoices and amounts shown on the voucher.

Disk See *hard disk*.

Disk drive The hardware device that reads from and writes to disk storage.

Disk operating system (DOS) An operating system that is disk-based (usually stored on a floppy disk, as with microcomputers).

Disk pack A set of magnetized disks that can be removed from the disk drive unit. Also called *removable disks*. Contrast with *fixed disk*.

Diskette A round piece of flexible magnetic film enclosed within a protective cover. It is a popular storage medium for microcomputers.

Dispatching See *expediting*.

Distributed data processing (DDP) A system where computers are set up at remote locations and then linked to a centralized mainframe computer.

Division remainder method A form of hashing in which record addresses are found by dividing the record key by a prime number approximately equal to the total number of storage addresses required for the file. The quotient is discarded and the remainder is used as the record address.

Divisional organization structure An organizational structure in which the company is divided into several divisions, each of which is relatively independent of the others and operates almost as a separate smaller company. Contrast with *functional organization structure*.

Document flowchart A diagram illustrating the flow of documents through the different departments and functions of an organization.

Documentation Written material consisting of instructions to operators, descriptions of procedures, and other descriptive material. Documentation may be classified into three basic categories: (1) administrative documentation, (2) systems documentation, and (3) operating documentation.

Domain A column in a relational data base.

Dot-matrix printers A printer that forms characters on paper using a series of small dots.

Downtime The amount of time that a computer system or a device within a computer system is inoperable due to a malfunction or power loss.

Dual reading A hardware control in which records on cards, tape, or random-access media are read twice by separate reading components and the results of the read operations are compared.

Dummy activity A PERT activity that is not really an activity at all in that it does not require any expenditure of time or resources. However, it is required in the network to show that one activity is an immediate predecessor of another activity.

Duplex system A centralized network that utilizes two central processors, one of which can back up the other. Contrast with *simplex system*.

Duplicate circuitry A hardware control in which two separate circuits in the arithmetic unit perform calculations and compare the results for accuracy.

Earliest finish time (EF) In a PERT network, the earliest start time for an activity plus the time required to complete the activity.

Earliest start time (ES) In a PERT network, the earliest possible time that an activity can begin.

Echo check A hardware control that verifies transmitted data by having the receiving device send the message received back to the sending device so that the message received can be compared with the message sent.

Economic feasibility The process of determining whether or not the benefits of a proposed system will exceed the costs.

Economic order quantity The order quantity that minimizes the sum of holding costs and ordering costs for a particular item.

Edit A process of checking the correctness of data and then correcting any mistakes found.

Edit check The accuracy checks performed by an edit program.

Edit program A computer program that verifies the validity and accuracy of input data.

Electronic data processing (EDP) The processing of data utilizing a computer system. Little or no human intervention is necessary while data are being processed. Contrast with *manual data processing system*.

Electronic funds transfer (EFT) The transfer of funds between two or more organizations or individuals using computers and other automated technology.

Electronic identification number A unique number assigned to a remote-access device. A system can be programmed to accept commands and transactions only from terminals having authorized identification numbers.

Electronic mail A system that allows a person to send a message to another person using the computer.

Electronic spreadsheet An applications program used for analysis, planning, modeling, and decision support. It is a worksheet, or matrix of rows and columns, containing blank cells into which numeric data, alphabetic data, or formulas can be entered.

Electrostatic discharge printer A dot-matrix printer that forms characters on aluminized paper by discharging a voltage that removes dots on the aluminized paper.

Embedded audit modules A special portion of an application program that keeps track of items that are of interest to auditors such as any unauthorized attempts to access the data files.

Embezzlement The fraudulent appropriation of business property by an employee. It is often accompanied by falsification of records.

Enable To turn a computer system or device on so it can operate.

Encode To take information and translate it into machine-readable code; to write program code.

End-of-file (EOF) A marker at the end of a group of data that indicates that the end of the data file has been reached.

End-user computing The ability of end-users to create, control, and implement their own information system.

End-users The people in an organization who use the information produced in the organization.

Enhanced graphics adapter (EGA) An adapter that allows better resolution in color graphics.

Entity The item about which information is stored in a record. Examples of an entity include an employee, an inventory item, or a customer account.

Erasable programmable read-only memory (EPROM) A read-only memory chip that can be erased and reprogrammed for further use.

Ergonomics The study of the effect of the work environment on workers. Some of the goals of ergonomics are to adapt machines to the convenience of operators, maximize efficiency, and make the workplace as safe and comfortable as possible.

Error A mistake or unintended result.

Error file An output file where the errors encountered during data processing are stored.

Error message A message from the computer indicating it has encountered a mistake or malfunction.

Error rate A measure of the number of errors encountered in an activity.

Even parity See *parity bit.*

Exception reporting Output from a system that includes only that information that might affect a user's decision or cause him or her to take action.

Execution time The time required to perform a computer instruction.

Expansion card See *multifunction board.*

Expansion slots Spaces on the motherboard of a microcomputer that will allow the user to expand the capacity and functions of the computer.

Expected completion time In a PERT network, the time that it is estimated that an activity will take to be completed. It is a weighted average of three estimates of the time required to complete an activity: (1) the most optimistic estimate of required time, (2) the most likely, and (3) the most pessimistic.

Expediting A production control function that involves monitoring the progress of production, used particularly with high-priority items.

Expert system (ES) A computerized information system that allows nonexperts to make decisions about a particular problem that are comparable with those of an expert in the area.

Exposure A measurement of risk where the potential magnitude of an error, in dollars, is multiplied by the error's estimated frequency (probability) of occurrence, to obtain a measure of the expected loss for a specified period of time.

Extended binary-coded decimal interchange code (EBCDIC) An eight-bit coding system (or grouping of bits) used by the computer to represent data.

Extension A price-times-quantity calculation.

External label A label on the outside of a magnetic storage medium (tape, disk, etc.) that identifies the data contained on the storage medium.

External transaction A transaction that takes place between a company and some external party such as a customer or supplier.

Facilities management vendor An organization that contracts to use guidelines and schedules established by the user to manage their data processing facilities for a fee. In most cases the hardware is owned or leased by the user and is located at the user's site.

Facsimile transmission The electronic transmission of pictures, contracts, signatures, etc., over data communications lines.

Fault tolerance The capability of a system to continue performing its functions in the presence of a hardware failure.

Feasibility study An investigation to determine if the development of a new application or system is practical. This is one of the first steps in the systems evaluation and selection process.

Feedback The informational output of a process that returns as input to the process, in the sense that it initiates the action necessary for process control.

Feedback control system A system that operates by measuring some aspect of the process being controlled and adjusting the process when the measure indicates that the process is deviating from plan.

Feedforward control system A control system that monitors both process operations and inputs in an attempt to predict potential deviations, in order that adjustments can be made to avert problems before they occur.

Femtosecond One quadrillionth of a second.

Fiber optics cable A data transmission cable consisting of thousands of tiny filaments of glass or plastic.

Fidelity bond A contract with an insurance company that provides a financial guarantee of the honesty of a named individual.

Field That part of a data record that contains the data value for a particular attribute. For each record, the fields are generally kept in the same order. For example, the first field in all accounts receivable records may be reserved for the customer account number.

Field check An edit check in which the characters in a field are examined to make sure they are of the correct field type (e.g., numeric data in numeric fields).

File   A set of logically related records, such as the payroll records of all employees.

File access   The way the computer finds, or retrieves, each record it has stored.

File maintenance   The periodic processing of transaction files against a master file. This maintenance, which is the most common task performed in virtually all data processing systems, includes record additions, deletions, updates, and changes. After file maintenance, the master file will contain all current information.

File maintenance programs   Programs that update master files.

File organization   The way data are stored on the physical storage media, either in sequential order or randomly (without sequential order). These are referred to as the sequential and direct (or random, nonsequential, or relative) file organization.

File-oriented approach   The use of separate files as the primary structure for storing data. Contrast with the *data base approach*.

File processing   See *file maintenance*.

Filtration of data   Screening out extraneous data from further processing.

Financial accounting   The subset of accounting concerned with providing accounting information to outside users. The primary outputs are the income statement and the balance sheet.

Financial audit   A review of the reliability and integrity of financial and operating information and the means used to identify, measure, classify, and report such information.

Financial total   The total of a dollar field, such as total sales, in a set of records. It is usually generated manually from source documents prior to input and compared with machine-generated totals at each subsequent processing step. Any discrepancy may indicate a loss of records or errors in data transcription or processing.

Firmware   Software that is permanently installed in the read-only memory of a computer.

Fixed costs   Costs that remain fixed even though the level of activity changes. As the level of activity increases, the per-unit fixed cost will decrease.

Fixed disk   A set of magnetic disks that are permanently attached to the disk drive unit and cannot be removed (as opposed to a *removable disk*).

Fixed-head disk   A disk drive unit in which there is a separate read/write head for each track. Contrast with *movable-head disk*.

Fixed-length record   A record that is fixed in length because it contains the same number of fields in each record. Contrast with *variable-length record*.

Flat file   A file structure where every record is identical to every other record in terms of attributes and field lengths.

Flexible budgeting   The process of adjusting the budgeted elements of performance for differences between the forecast level of activity and the actual level of activity. This allows performance reports to be adjusted for differences between planned and actual activity levels. This means that all cost and expense items must be classified as fixed or variable.

Flexible manufacturing systems   The use of a computer to automate and integrate the performance of all major production tasks within a factory, including production planning, stock control, materials handling, machine scheduling and operation, and quality control.

Floppy disk   A 5¼-inch diskette.

Flowchart   A diagrammatical representation of the flow of information and the sequence of operations in a process or system.

Flowcharting template   A rectangular piece of plastic that has had flowcharting symbols cut out of it. It is used to draw flowchart symbols.

Foreign Corrupt Practices Act of 1977   An act of Congress that, among other things, requires all publicly held corporations to maintain good systems of internal accounting control.

Form   A document preprinted with headings and other constant data, containing spaces for variable data to be inserted.

FORTH   A popular microcomputer language that makes use of reverse polish notation.

FORTRAN   An acronym for *formula trans*lator, a high-level computer language oriented toward scientific applications. Since FORTRAN lacks features that are often required for business and accounting applications, it is not a popular business-oriented language.

Fourth generation computer   A digital computer that uses large-scale integration (LSI) or very large scale integration (VLSI) circuitry.

Fourth generation languages   High-level, application, or user-oriented languages that are easy to learn and do not require the user to understand the details of the computer.

Friction-feed printers   A printer that uses the paper-feed mechanism commonly used by typewriters.

Front-end processor (FEP)   A dedicated communications computer that is connected to a host CPU. It handles the communications tasks so the CPU can spend its time processing data.

Full-duplex channel   A data transmission channel that allows data transmissions in both directions at the same time. Contrast with *half-duplex* and *simplex channels*.

Fully indexed file   An indexed file where there is an entry in the index file for every record in the data file. Contrast with *partially indexed file*.

Fully inverted file   An inverted file where there are inverted lists for every one of the file attributes. Contrast with *partially inverted file*.

Functional organization structure An organizational structure where employees with the same or similar duties are grouped together within the organizational subunits of a company. Contrast with *divisional organization structure*.

Gantt chart A bar graph adapted to project planning and control. Project activities are shown on the left, whereas units of time are shown across the top. The time period over which each activity is expected to be performed is shown with a horizontal bar on the graph.

Gateway A communications interface device that allows a local area network to be connected to external networks and to communicate with external mainframes and data bases.

General controls Controls that relate to all or many computerized accounting activities, such as those relating to the plan of organization of data processing activities and the separation of incompatible functions. Contrast with *administrative controls*.

General ledger A computerized master file or data base—or in a manual system, a book—that includes information on every one of the accounts in the organization's accounting system.

General-purpose ("generic") software Software that meets a wide variety of user needs, such as electronic spreadsheets, data base packages, and word processing.

Generality A basic principle of program design that states that programs should be designed for general applications and not just for a specific application.

Generalized Audit Software Package (GASP) A specially written software package that can be used to perform audit tests on the data files of a company.

Gigabyte A billion characters of data.

Goal conflict A situation where an action or decision relating to the achievement of a subgoal of an overall goal is counterproductive to another subgoal of the same overall goal.

Goal congruence A situation where an organization is able to divide their overall goal into subgoals in such a way that the people working to accomplish the subgoals are also contributing to the achievement of the overall goal without affecting anyone else's ability to achieve their subgoals.

Grandfather-father-son concept A process of maintaining backup copies of files on magnetic tape or disk. The three most current copies of the data are retained, with the son being the most recent.

Graphics software Software that presents numerical information in graphic or pictorial form.

Graphics terminal A hardware device that produces graphic images like bar graphs or line graphs.

Group code A coding scheme where there are two or more subgroups of digits within a code number, and each subgroup is used to identify an item.

Half-duplex channel A data transmission channel that allows two-direction transmissions but only one direction at a time. Contrast with *full-duplex* and *simplex channels*.

Hard copy A printed copy of computer output.

Hard disk A magnetic storage disk made of rigid material and enclosed in a sealed disk unit to cut down on the chance of the magnetic medium being damaged by foreign particles. A hard disk has a much faster access time and greater storage capacity than a floppy disk.

Hardware Physical equipment, or machinery, that is used in a computer system.

Hardware monitor A device that is connected to a computer to collect information on the percent utilization of various system resources. It also provides information on the number of occurrences of particular events, such as the number of disk accesses or the number of print lines.

Hash total A total generated from a field that is not usually totaled otherwise, such as a total of all customer account numbers. It is usually generated manually from source documents prior to input and compared with machine-generated totals at each subsequent processing step. Any discrepancy may indicate a loss of records or errors in data transcription or processing.

Hashing An addressing approach in which record keys are used to help determine where data are to be stored or retrieved. See *division remainder method*.

Head (1) The device that reads and/or writes data to a storage medium. (2) The first record in a linked list.

Header label or record A machine-readable label or record at the beginning of a file that contains the file name, expiration date, and other file identification information. The data in the label are used to identify and control the file.

Hexadecimal The number system that is base 16. It uses the digits 0 through 9 as well as the letters A through F.

Hierarchical network A variation of the star network; the configuration looks like a hierarchical organization chart.

Hierarchical organization structure A pattern of subdividing organizational goals and tasks into a graded series of lower-level goals and tasks.

Hierarchical program design The process of designing a program from the top level down to the detail level.

High-level language A language that is not restricted to only one computer or family of computers. It usually utilizes macroinstructions and statements that closely resemble human language.

HIPO chart An acronym for *H*ierarchy plus *I*nput *P*rocess *O*utput chart, a diagram that presents program functions and logic from the general to the detailed level.

History file Records of account balances and of past transactions that have already been processed to update appropriate master files. These records are retained for reference purposes.

Hybrid network A combination of both star and ring network configurations.

Impact printer A printer that operates by mechanically striking an embossed character against an inked ribbon positioned next to the paper.

Implementation The process of installing a computer. This includes selecting the equipment and installing it, training personnel, establishing operating policies, getting the software onto the system and functioning properly, etc.

Implementation phase The systems development life cycle phase where all implementation tasks are carried out.

Index file A file of record identifiers and their corresponding storage locations.

Indexed-sequential access method (ISAM) A file organization and access approach where records are stored in the sequential order of their primary key on a direct-access storage device. An index file is also created, which allows the file to be accessed, updated, etc., randomly.

Indexing Creating a catalog of reference information about a body of stored data to facilitate the retrieval of specific items of data upon request.

Information Data that have been processed and organized into output that is meaningful to the person who receives it.

Information analyst A person with the technical skills and the organizational knowledge to serve as a liaison between managers having little technical knowledge and systems analysts who are generally more technology-oriented than management-oriented.

Information graphics Graphic output that is typically produced by people for their own use or for the use of their colleagues in solving a particular problem. Contrast with *presentation graphics*.

Information systems steering committee An executive-level advisory board that oversees the information systems function.

Ink-jet printer Printers that spray ink through an electronic field to form a dot-matrix character.

Input Data entered into the computer system either from an external storage device or from the keyboard of the computer.

Input controls matrix A matrix that shows the control procedures applied to each field of an input record.

Input device Hardware used to enter data into the computer system.

Input/output bound A system that can process data faster than it can receive input and send output. Consequently, the processor has to wait on the I/O devices.

Input/output (I/O) port The connection where data enter or exit the computer system. The port provides the path for data communications between devices.

Input validation routine A program or routine that utilizes the computer to check the validity or accuracy of input data.

Inquiry A request for information from a computer system.

Inquiry processing Processing user information queries by searching master files for the desired information and then organizing the information into an appropriate response.

Installation The process of setting up (installing) a computer, its peripheral devices, and the software.

Integrated circuits Small silicon chips that contain the circuitry used by the computer.

Integrated software A software program that allows the user to easily switch back and forth between several general-purpose applications such as spreadsheet, data base, graphics, and word processing.

Integrated spreadsheet See *electronic spreadsheet*.

Integrated test facility A process by which a dummy company or division is introduced into the company's computer system. Test transactions may then be processed against these fictitious master records without affecting the real master records. Further, the test transactions may be processed along with the real transactions, and the employees of the computer facility need not be aware that the testing is being done.

Integration The combining of previously separated subsystems into a single system, thereby eliminating duplicate recording, storage, reporting, and other processing activities within the organization.

Intelligent terminal An input/output device that can also perform data processing and storage tasks. A recent trend is to combine microcomputer and terminal technology into one.

Interactive debugging A process where each program statement is interpreted and checked for syntax errors when it is entered into the system.

Interblock gap (IBG) A blank space on a magnetic tape that separates two blocks of data. The IBG allows the tape drive to stop and then to reach the correct speed before any records are read from the tape.

Interface The common boundary between two pieces of hardware or between two computer systems. It is the point at which the two systems communicate with each other.

Interference Unwanted signals that reduce the quality of the signals being transmitted or processed.

Internal check The process of verifying the accuracy and reliability of accounting data, often by utilizing the maxim of the double entry accounting system that debits must equal credits.

Internal control The plan of organization and all the coordinate methods and measures adopted within a business to safeguard its assets, check the accuracy and reliability of its accounting data, promote operational efficiency, and encourage adherence to prescribed managerial policies.

Internal control audit A review of company controls to see if they are in compliance with the policies, plans, procedures, laws, and regulations affecting the organization. The audit should also review the means of safeguarding assets and, as appropriate, verify the existence of such assets.

Internal pricing   A system for charging user departments for computer services.

Internal storage   See *memory unit.*

Internal transactions   Transactions that take place between different departments or divisions of the same business.

Interpreter   A program that, one statement at a time, translates the source language to machine code and then executes it. Contrast with *compiler.*

Interrupt   The suspension of data processing so some other program can be processed. Control is usually returned to the original program after the second program is through with its processing.

Inverted file   A file for which inverted lists are maintained for some (partially inverted) or all (fully inverted) of the attributes in the file.

Inverted list   A list of pointers stored within an index. The pointers are usually the addresses of all records in the file that have a particular characteristic or data value.

Investment center   An organizational unit whose assigned objective is to accomplish its goals by maximizing return on investment. Investment center reports should include costs, revenues, and assets associated with its operation.

Job accounting routines   Programs that may be linked to the operating system to measure and record resource utilization for each job that is processed. This facilitates cost accounting and charging users for the amount of computer time utilized.

Job-control language (JCL)   The language used to instruct the operating system.

Job-control program   That part of the operating system that reads and interprets instructions written in job-control language.

Job order costing   A costing process where manufacturing costs are accumulated by production jobs in process. A single work-in-process account is used to represent the total amount charged to all jobs in process.

Journal   (1) The accounting record of original entry. (2) The transaction file used in double entry accounting.

Joystick   A input device that consists of a stick that can be tilted in any direction to position the cursor on a graphics screen. A joystick is usually used in conjunction with a computer game.

Justify   To align the data in a field to either the far right or the far left. Data can also be centered in a field.

Just-in-time (JIT) system   A system that minimizes or virtually eliminates manufacturing inventories by scheduling inventory deliveries at the precise times and locations needed. Materials are delivered in small lots at frequent intervals to the specific locations that require them, as op-

posed to infrequent bulk deliveries to a central receiving and storage facility.

Key   A unique identification code assigned to each data record within a system.

Key transformation   See *hashing.*

Keyboard   The number, letter, and special character keys used to type data into a key-driven device.

Keypunch/keyverification machine   A keyboard-operated device used to punch holes in a card to represent data. The machine can also be used to rekey the data to verify that the data have been entered correctly.

Keypunching   The process of recording data on a punched card.

Key-to-disk-to-tape encoder   A device for keying in data from several stations and combining the data on disk before transferring the data to magnetic tape.

Key-to-tape encoder   A device for keying in data and recording them on magnetic tape.

Kilobyte (K)   1,024 bytes of memory capacity. K is usually expressed in terms of 1,000 characters of memory; that is, 64K represents approximately 64,000 characters of memory.

LAN interface   The hardware device that interfaces between the local area network (LAN) cable and the hardware devices (computers, printers, etc.) connected to the LAN.

Language translator   A software program that is used to convert instructions written in a programming language into machine language. There are three types: assemblers, compilers, and translators.

Lapping   Concealing a cash shortage by means of a series of delays in posting collections to accounts.

Laser   A tightly packed, narrow beam of light formed by the emission of high-speed molecules.

Laser disks   See *optical disk.*

Laser printer   A printer that uses a laser beam to form an electrostatic image.

Latest finish time (LF)   In a PERT network, the latest time that an activity can finish without causing the project as a whole to be delayed.

Latest start time (LS)   In a PERT network, the latest finish time minus the activity time.

Layout   The design or plan for such items as reports, file contents, input documents, etc.

Lead time   The time between ordering an item and receiving that item.

Leased line   A phone line devoted exclusively to the use of one customer. The cost is fixed and is determined by the length of the line.

Ledger   (1) The master files used in accounting. (2) A book of accounts in which data from transactions recorded in journals are posted and thereby classified and summarized.

Letter-quality printer A printer that produces a letter that looks like it has been typed on a typewriter.

Levels of supervision The number of ranks between the highest and lowest supervisory levels of an organization.

Librarian The person in charge of an organization's library of programs, program documentation, and data files.

Library manager That part of the operating system that keeps track of the storage location of all software used by the system.

Light pen A pencil-shaped device that uses photoelectric circuitry to enter data through the video display terminal of the computer system. Their principal use is in graphics applications.

Limit check An edit check to ensure that a numerical amount in a record does not exceed some acceptable predetermined limit.

Line printer A printer that prints one line at a time. Printer speed is measured in characters per second.

Line-sharing device A device that combines the data from several terminals or computers and sends the data over a single line to the host computer.

Linked lists A file organization and access approach in which each data record contains a pointer field containing the address of the next logical record in the list. Thus all logically related records are linked together by pointers.

List (1) A group of records "connected" by pointers. (2) To print or show on the screen any data that satisfy certain criteria.

Load To enter data into the working registers of a computer so that data may be processed.

Local area network (LAN) A network that links together microcomputers, disk drives, word processors, printers, etc., that are located within a limited geographical area, such as the same building.

Lock out A process whereby two users are unable to update a data record at the same time. In essence, one user is "locked out" so that the second update cannot be accomplished until the first is completed.

Log A record of some data processing activity.

Logic errors Errors that occur when the instructions given to the computer do not accomplish the desired objective. Contrast with *syntax errors*.

Logical view The manner in which users conceptually organize, view, and understand the relationships among data items. Contrast with *physical view*.

Logic-seeking printer A printer that is able to determine if it is faster to print a short line backward or forward.

Logistics management Planning and controlling the physical flow of materials through an organization, including the functions of purchasing management, inventory management, and production management.

LOGO A high-level interactive programming language designed for young students.

Low-level language Languages that are not very far removed from machine language. An example is an assembly-level language.

Machine dependent A program that can only be used on a certain make and model computer.

Machine independent The ability to execute a program on a number of different machines from different manufacturers.

Machine instruction An instruction that a computer can directly understand and execute.

Machine language Binary code that can be interpreted by the internal circuitry of the computer.

Macro In general-purpose software, (1) a series of commands that can be given a name, stored, and activated each time the keystrokes must be repeated, or (2) a programming command.

Macroflowchart A flowchart in which each flowchart symbol represents a set of related program steps. Contrast with *microflowchart*.

Macroinstructions Computer language instructions that translate into two or more machine-level instructions.

Magnetic bubble See *bubble memory*.

Magnetic card A card with a magnetic surface on which data can be stored.

Magnetic characters A set of characters printed in magnetic ink. The characters are read by a special device called a magnetic ink character recognition reader.

Magnetic core Widely used as the primary storage media in second and third generation computers. It consists of tiny iron oxide rings strung on wires that provide electrical current to magnetize the rings.

Magnetic disk A magnetic storage medium consisting of one or more flat round disks with a magnetic surface upon which data can be written.

Magnetic drum A secondary storage medium that stores data on a circular cylinder that has a magnetic surface.

Magnetic ink character recognition (MICR) The recognition of characters printed by a machine that uses a special magnetic ink. It is used widely in the banking industry to encode checks.

Magnetic tape A secondary storage medium that is about one-half inch in width and that has a magnetic surface on which data can be stored. The most popular types are seven-track and nine-track tapes.

Main circuit board See *motherboard*.

Main memory The internal memory directly controlled by the CPU. This usually consists of the ROM and RAM of the computer.

Mainframe computer (1) Same as CPU. (2) A large-size digital computer, typically with a separate, stand-alone CPU. It is larger than a minicomputer.

Maintainability A basic principle of program design that states that extra care should be taken in program design so that maintenance will be easier over the life of the program.

Management accounting The subset of accounting concerned with internal information needs and how such information should be put to use.

Management audit A review of how well management is utilizing company resources and how well company operations and programs follow established objectives and are being carried out as planned.

Management by exception A reporting procedure whereby management is only made aware of an exception if it is significant, such as actual costs being significantly greater than budgeted figures.

Management control Motivating, encouraging, and assisting officers and employees to (1) achieve corporate goals and objectives as effectively and efficiently as possible and (2) observe corporate policies.

Management information system The set of human and capital resources within an organization that is responsible for collecting and processing data so that useful information can be provided to all levels of management so they can plan and control the activities of the organization.

Management science A discipline that approaches management decision making by trying to construct a mathematical model of real problems. These models are then used to make actual decisions.

Manual data processing system A system in which the major share of the data processing load is performed by people. Contrast with *electronic data processing*.

Manufacturing resource planning A comprehensive computerized planning and control system for manufacturing operations. It is an enhancement of materials requirements planning that incorporates capacity planning for factory work centers and scheduling of production operations.

Many-to-many (M:M) A relationship where each child record may have many parent relationships and each parent record may have many associated child records. Contrast with *one-to-many*.

Mapping program A program that is activated during regular processing and provides information as to which portions of the application program were not executed.

Master file A permanent file of records that reflects the current status of relevant business items such as inventory, accounts receivable, etc. The master file is updated with the latest transactions from the current transaction file.

Materiality The concept that an auditor should focus on detecting and reporting only those errors, deficiencies, and omissions that could possibly have a significant impact on decisions.

Materials requirements planning An approach to controlling and minimizing the inventory of raw materials. The production planning department prepares a schedule of the quantities of each product to be manufactured during a given time period and then purchases raw materials, parts, and supplies when they are needed.

Matrix organization structure An organizational structure in which both functional departments and project/product groups exist. Employees will have responsibilities to both a functional department and a particular project or product line.

Media conversion program A program used to transfer data from one form of medium to another (e.g., tape to disk, card to tape).

Megabyte (M) A million characters of data.

Megahertz (MHz) A million computer cycles per second.

Memory manager That part of the operating system that assigns primary memory space to programs and data, maintains a record of available memory, and protects the areas reserved for one program from being used by other programs.

Memory unit The part of the CPU where data and instructions are stored internally.

Menu A list of computer commands, or options, that are displayed by a program. The user chooses the desired option to cause the desired action to take place.

Merge To combine two or more groups of data into a single group of data that are in a specified order.

Message The data transmitted over a data communications system.

Microcode Elementary computer operations and programs that are permanently stored in a computer's read-only memory.

Microcomputer A small computer system that ranges in size from a "computer on a chip" to a system that can cover a desktop. Often called a personal or desktop computer, they usually sell for less than $5000.

Microfloppy diskette A 3½-inch diskette.

Microflowchart A flowchart in which each program step is flowcharted in detail. Contrast with *macroflowchart*.

Microprocessor A large-scale or very large scale integrated circuit on a silicon chip. Some of the more common microprocessors in use are the 8088, 8086, 80286, 80386, Z80, 68000, and the 8080.

Microsecond One millionth of a second.

Micro-to-mainframe link Special software that allows data to be transferred back and forth between a microcomputer and a mainframe computer.

Millisecond One thousandth of a second.

Mini company test See *integrated test facility*.

Minicomputer A digital computer that is usually larger than a microcomputer but smaller than a mainframe computer. It has a higher performance, a more powerful instruction set, higher prices, more input/output capability, a greater variety of programming languages, and a more powerful operating system than a microcomputer. However, it has less of the above than a mainframe computer does.

Mnemonic code The use of symbols, such as abbreviations or contractions, to help computer users remember what a computer instruction stands for. For example, MPY for multiply, or SUB for subtract.

Modeling software Programs that have the capability to develop models of complex problems, ask what-if questions, perform simulations, and assist in setting goals.

Modem (From *Modulator/dem*odulator) A communication device that converts the computer's digital signals into analog signals that can be sent over phone lines. The modem can be internal (mounted on a board within the computer) or external (a free-standing unit).

Modified canned software Canned software that has been modified to meet the particular needs of the user.

Modular programming A process where the programmer divides a program into small segments called modules. The individual modules are developed and tested to make sure they work properly and are linked together to form the large program.

Modularity (1) The ability of a computer system to be expanded (both hardware and software) with a minimum amount of difficulty. The easier it is for a system to be expanded, the more modular it is considered. (2) A principle of program design that states that programs should be developed using modular programming.

Modules Small, relatively well defined segments or subroutines of a program that perform a separate logical function.

Monitor (1) A video display unit or CRT. (2) Software that controls how a system operates. See *hardware monitor* and *software monitor*.

Motherboard The main circuit board of a microcomputer. It usually contains the memory, the CPU, and the input/output circuitry.

Mouse A small device that is connected to a computer, usually by a cord. To issue a command, the user moves the mouse; that movement is translated into a movement of the screen's cursor.

Movable-Head Disk A disk drive unit where there are only one or a few read/write heads per surface. Contrast with *fixed-head disk*.

MS/DOS An acronym for *MicroSoft/Disk Operating System*, the operating system used by IBM and IBM-compatible microcomputers.

Multidrop line A communications channel configuration in which most terminals are linked together, with only one or a few terminals linked directly to the CPU.

Multifunction board An expansion board for a personal computer that can contain one or more of the following: additional memory, a parallel port, a serial port, a game port, a clock/calender, and various other functions, depending on the manufacturer.

Multifunction card machine A device that both reads and punches computer cards.

Multifunctional workstations High-powered microcomputers that share common resources and are capable of both word and data processing.

Multiplexor A communications device that combines signals from several sources and sends them out over a single line. Multiplexors can also split the signals back out into the individual messages.

Multiprocessing The simultaneous execution of two or more tasks, usually by two or more processing units that are part of the same system.

Multiprogramming The appearance of simultaneous execution of two or more programs by switching back and forth between the programs.

Nanosecond One billionth of a second.

Narrowband line A phone line designed to accept data transmissions up to 300 bits per second. They are not suitable for transmitting audible or voicelike signals.

Natural languages Fourth generation languages that closely resemble English.

Net present value A process of discounting all estimated future cash flows back to the present, using a discount rate that reflects the time value of money to the organization.

Network (1) A group of interconnected computers and terminals; a series of locations tied together by communications channels. (2) A data structure involving relationships among multiple record types such that each parent may have more than one child record type and each child may have more than one parent record type.

Network master controller A chip, expansion card, hard disk drive, or dedicated computer that is the intelligence of a local area network and acts as a traffic manager to route data between the hardware and to prevent and detect data collisions.

Network server A hard disk containing the software, or protocols, that run a local area network and the programs that are available for network users.

Network switching The routing of all data and messages through a central computer for forwarding to the correct location.

Node (1) A terminal point in a communications system. (2) A record type in a tree data base structure.

Nonimpact printer A printer that transfers images to paper without actually striking the paper.

Numerical control The use of a computer system to automatically control the operation of a machine tool in the performance of standardized production operations.

Object code The output of a compiler or assembler program. It can be executed by the computer without further processing.

Object program A compiled or assembled machine-level program that can be executed by the computer. The source program and the translator are inputs to the computer translation process, and the output is the machine-executable object program.

Odd parity   See *parity bit*.

Office automation system   See *automated office*.

Offline device   Any device that is not connected to or controlled by the main CPU. To disconnect a peripheral device from the host computer is referred to as taking the device offline. Offline devices are usually used to prepare data for entry into the computer system (e.g., key-to-tape encoder, keypunch/verification equipment). Contrast to *online device*.

One-to-many (1:M)   A relationship where each child record has only one parent record, but each parent record can have many associated child records. Contrast with *many-to-many*.

Online device   A hardware device that is connected directly to the CPU by cable or telephone line (e.g., CRT terminal, disk drive). Contrast with *offline device*.

Online processing   Processing individual transactions as they occur and from their point of origin rather than accumulating them to be processed in batches. This requires the use of online data entry terminals and direct-access file storage media so each master record can be accessed directly.

Online updating   File maintenance in which individual transactions are processed as they occur to update a master file. See *online processing*.

Operands   That part of a computer instruction upon which an operation is performed.

Operating budget   An estimate of an organization's revenues and expenses for a time period, usually a month or a year.

Operating documentation   All information required by a computer operator to run the program, including the equipment configuration used, variable data to be entered on the computer console, descriptions of conditions leading to program halts and related corrective actions, and so forth.

Operating system   A software program that controls the overall operation of a computer system. Its functions include controlling the execution of computer programs, scheduling, debugging, storage assignment, data management, and input/output control.

Operation phase   The last phase of the systems development life cycle, where the newly developed system is used and modified as required.

Operational audit   See *management audit*.

Operational control   The process of ensuring that specific tasks are carried out effectively and efficiently.

Operational document   A document that is generated as a result of transaction processing activities. Examples include purchase orders, customer statements, and employee paychecks. Contrast with *source document*.

Operational feasibility   The process of determining whether or not a proposed system will be used by the people in an organization. It also determines how useful the system will be within the operating environment of the organization.

Operations list   A document showing the labor operations, with their corresponding machine and standard time requirements, that are needed to produce a particular product.

Operations research   See *management science*.

Operator   See *computer operator*.

Optical character recognition (OCR)   The use of light-sensitive hardware devices to convert human-readable characters into computer input. Since OCR readers can only read certain items, a special machine-readable font is used.

Optical disk   A mass storage medium that uses lasers to write to and read from a special disk. The disks are capable of storing billions of bits.

Optical mark reader (OMR)   A hardware device that reads marks made in specific locations on preprinted forms. The marks are interpreted by the OMR and converted into machine input.

Organizational independence   See *separation of duties*.

Original equipment manufacturer (OEM)   A vendor who buys hardware, develops specialized software, and sells the two as a complete, integrated computer system. See *turnkey system*.

Output   The information produced by a system. Output is typically produced for the use of a particular individual or group of users.

Output device   A device that prints, displays, or stores data output.

Output media   The media on which computer output is displayed or stored, such as floppy disks, paper documents, and magnetic tape.

Overall system plan   A long-range plan summarizing an organization's future system resource requirements. It includes the personnel, hardware, and financial requirements; the projects giving rise to those requirements; and the time frame for which the projections are made.

Overflow procedures   Programmed routines for dealing with an arithmetic result that exceeds the capacity of the computer's numeric storage register.

Overlap   The execution of input/output operations by peripheral devices while the CPU continues processing data.

Packed decimal   The storage of two numbers into a single eight-bit byte.

Packets   A group of messages that are transmitted together over data communications lines.

Packing slip   A document that is sent with the goods shipped to the customer.

Page   A segment of a program or data. It is usually of fixed length.

Page printer A printer that prints one page at a time. Speed is measured in either pages per second or lines per second.

Paging A process that automatically and continually transfers blocks of memory (pages) between primary and direct-access secondary storage. In effect, it allows computers to appear to have an unlimited amount of internal memory. See *virtual memory*.

Paper tape A continuous strip of paper, approximately one inch wide, that is used to record data for computer processing. Holes punched in the tape are used to represent the data.

Parallel operation Performing two or more processing tasks simultaneously within a single CPU.

Parallel port A communications interface that allows data to be transmitted a whole character (eight bits) at a time. Contrast with *serial port*.

Parallel processing A process where both the new and old data processing systems are operating at the same time during conversion to the new system. The output of both systems are compared, and any discrepancies are examined further to find and correct the cause.

Parallel simulation An approach auditors use to detect unauthorized program changes and data processing accuracy. The auditor writes his or her own version of a program and then reprocesses data. The output of the auditor's program and the client's program are compared to verify that they are the same.

Parallel transmission The transmission of data in groups of two or more bits. Contrast with *serial transmission*.

Parent A record type, or node, in a tree structure that is associated with a record type at a lower level. Contrast with *child*.

Parity bit An extra bit added to a byte, character, or word. As is needed the parity bit is magnetized to make sure there is always an odd (or even) number of magnetized bits. The computer uses the odd (or even) parity scheme to check the accuracy of each item of data.

Partially indexed file An indexed file in which the index contains one entry for every *n*th key, where *n* is the number of records that fit in each storage location. Contrast with *fully indexed file*.

Partially inverted file An inverted file for which inverted lists are maintained for some but not all attributes. Contrast with *fully inverted file*.

PASCAL A high-level, general-purpose computer language that has become increasingly popular for both large and small computers. It offers powerful data structuring and data manipulation features.

Password A series of letters or numbers or both that allow users to access and use system resources. Their use helps prevent unauthorized tampering with hardware, software, and most especially, the organization's data.

Payroll register A listing of payroll data for each employee for the current payroll period.

Performance report A summary of actual, as opposed to planned, results achieved by a particular manager.

Peripherals The hardware devices (such as those used for input, output, processing, and data communications) that are connected to the CPU.

Peripherals manager That part of the operating system that controls the assignment of input and output devices to jobs in process.

Personal computer See *microcomputer*.

Personal identification number (PIN) A confidential code known only to an individual and a financial institution that allows the individual to conduct banking transactions at automated teller machines.

PERT An acronym for *Program Evaluation and Review Technique*, which is a commonly used technique for the planning, coordinating, controlling, and scheduling of complex projects such as systems implementation.

Physical view The way data are physically arranged and stored on disks, tapes, etc. EDP personnel use this view to make efficient use of storage and processing resources. Contrast with *logical view*.

Picosecond One trillionth of a second.

Pilot operation A systems test where sample transactions are processed by the new system. Usually, historical transactions are used and the results are compared with the results of the original processing.

Pin-feed printer A printer that uses pins in fixed positions to feed the paper through the printer. It only accepts paper of a certain width. Contrast with *tractor-feed printer*.

Pixel The smallest particle of information that appears on a monitor's screen. The greater the number of pixels, the better the monitor's resolution.

PL/I A high-level language designed for scientific and business applications. It is oriented toward applications that require a significant number of computations and the processing of large amounts of data records.

Plotter A hard-copy output device that produces drawings and other graphical output by moving an ink pen across a page.

Point-of-sale (POS) recorder (terminal) An electronic device that functions as both a terminal and a cash register. Its use is common in retail stores, and it is used to record sales information at the time of the sale and to perform other data processing functions.

Point scoring An objective procedure for evaluating the overall merits of vendor proposals. Selection criteria are determined and a weight is assigned to each criterion based upon its relative importance to the user. Each system is then evaluated on its individual merits, and each vendor is assigned a score for each criterion according to how well its proposal measures up to the ideal for that criterion. Summation of the scores for the individual criteria then gives an overall score that may be used to compare the various vendors.

Point-to-point line   A communications channel configuration that uses a separate line between each terminal and the central computer.

Pointer   A data item contained in an index, a record, or some other set of data that contains the address of a related record.

Polling control   An approach to controlling a shared communications line. The computer asks each remote terminal on the line if it needs to send any data and then allows each terminal, in turn, to transmit its data.

Portable computer   A microcomputer designed such that it can be carried from one location to another.

Posting   The process of updating accounting ledgers with the transactions recorded in journals.

Preformatting   An online data entry control that has the computer display a blank document on the screen, and the user then fills in the document as needed.

Presentation graphics   Graphic output that is produced for formal presentations. It is often presented on color transparencies or slides or some other high-resolution color medium. Contrast with *information graphics*.

Preventive control system   A control system that places restrictions on and requires documentation of employee activities in such a way that the occurrence of errors and deviations is retarded. Because preventive controls operate from "within" the process being controlled, they are perhaps the type of control most consistent with the original meaning of the term *internal control*.

Preventive maintenance   A program of regularly examining the hardware components of a computer and replacing any that are found to be weak.

Primary key   A unique identification code assigned to each record within a system. The primary, as opposed to secondary, key is usually the one that is most frequently used to distinguish, order, and reference the records. Records are usually kept in sequence according to their primary key.

Primary memory   See *memory unit*.

Printer   An output device that produces a hard copy of computer output.

Printer interface   The device that allows a computer to communicate with a printer. There are two kinds of printer interfaces: parallel and serial.

Problem-Solving Language   A high-level language that is designed to help the programmer solve specific types of problems. The programmer only needs to specify the input, the output, and the parameters of the problem. The procedures used to solve the problem are embedded within the language.

Procedure-Oriented Language   A high-level language in which the programmer must specify the logic necessary to accomplish a specific task. For example, COBOL and FORTRAN.

Process costing   A costing process where there are separate work-in-process accounts for each department, and manufacturing costs are accumulated by department and then transferred to the next department when the product is transferred to that department.

Processing   The manipulation of the data that are required to solve a particular problem or meet a specific need for information. This may involve one or more of the following: calculation, comparison, summarization, filtration, or retrieval of data.

Profit center   An organizational unit whose objective is to accomplish its goals and operational functions with the highest possible net profit. Profit center reports should include the costs and revenues for the profit center and should focus on net profit.

Profitability analysis   A sales report that reports the marginal contribution to profit for each territory, customer, or other unit.

Program   A set of instructions that can be executed by a computer.

Program flowchart   A diagrammatical representation of the logic and sequence of processes used in a computer program.

Program generators   Computer programs designed to speed up the process of writing programs. The user specifies certain information, such as what the screen layouts should look like and what processing procedures need to be performed, and the program generates program instructions.

Program maintenance   The revision of a computer program in order to meet new program instructions, satisfy system demands such as a new report, correct an error, or make changes in file content.

Program specifications   A document that specifies the data requirements; processing details; input, output, and storage requirements; and any other details needed to develop and code a computer program.

Program tracing   A technique that enables the user to obtain a detailed knowledge of the logic of an application program, as well as test the program's compliance with its control specifications. The user processes the application program with regular or test transactions and activates a trace routine built into the system software. This routine causes the computer to print out in sequential order a list of all the application program steps executed during the program run.

Programmable memory   Computer memory that can be changed, reused, and programmed for different purposes.

Programmer   A person who develops, codes, and tests computer programs.

Programming language   The language the programmer uses to write a computer program. Examples include COBOL, BASIC, PASCAL, and LOGO.

Project development plan   A proposal to develop a particular computer system application. It contains an analysis of the requirements and expectations of the proposed application.

Project milestones   Significant points in a development effort where a formal review of progress is made.

Prompting   An online data entry control that uses the computer to control the data entry process. The system displays a request to the user for each required item of input data and then waits for an acceptable response before requesting the next required item.

Protection of stored data   The procedures and techniques used to prevent the destruction or unauthorized disclosure of data.

Protocol   The set of rules governing the exchange of data between two systems or components of a system.

Prototyping   A systems design technique in which a simplified working model, or prototype, of an information system is developed. The prototype system is implemented and demonstrated to users. User suggestions are incorporated into the prototype, and the process is repeated until the users are satisfied that the system effectively meets their requirements.

Pseudocode   An informal design language oriented toward structured programming. It uses English language phrases to describe the processing logic of a computer program.

Public data network   Large, usually privately owned organizations that sell computing services and information to the public for a fee.

Punched card   A card, containing either eighty or ninety-six columns, that is used to store data. The pattern of the holes in each column represents a character of data.

Punched card system   The earliest form of automated data processing. It stored data on a card using holes punched in a certain sequence to represent data. The computer and magnetic storage devices have made punched card systems obsolete.

Purchase requisition   A document that indicates that the supply of an item of inventory is low and a reorder is necessary.

Quad-density storage medium   A magnetic medium that allows four times as much data storage as a single-density storage medium.

Query   A request for specific information from a computer. Queries are often used with a data base management system to extract data from the data base.

Query languages   Languages used to process data files and to obtain quick responses to questions about those files.

Random-access memory (RAM)   A temporary storage location for computer instructions and data. RAM may have data both written to it and read from it.

Randomizing   See *hashing*.

Range check   An edit check designed to verify that data fall within a certain predetermined range of acceptable values.

Rate variance   That portion of a total variance attributable to a deviation from a standard rate or price, such as a labor rate or a materials price.

Read head   The magnetic head designed to read information from a tape or disk. Usually, a single read/write head is used instead of two separate heads.

Read-only memory (ROM)   Internal CPU memory that can be read but usually may not be changed.

Real-time notification   A variation of the embedded audit module where the auditor is notified of each transaction as it occurs by means of a message printed on the auditor's terminal.

Real-time system   A system that is able to respond to an inquiry or provide data in sufficient time that it is meaningful to the user. These systems are usually designed for very fast response.

Reasonable assurance   The concept that an auditor cannot seek complete assurance that an item is correct since to do so would be prohibitively expensive. Instead, the auditor accepts a reasonable degree of risk that the audit conclusion is incorrect.

Reasonableness test   An edit check of the logical correctness of relationships among the values of data items on an input record and the corresponding file record. For example, a journal entry that debits inventory and credits wages payable is not reasonable.

Record   A set of logically related data items that describe specific attributes of an entity, such as all payroll data relating to a single employee.

Record count   A total of the number of input documents to a process or of records processed in a run. It is usually generated manually from source documents prior to input and compared with machine-generated totals at each subsequent processing step. Any discrepancies may indicate a loss of records or errors in data transcription or processing.

Record layout   A document that illustrates the arrangement of items of data in input, output, and file records.

Record layout sheet   A blank form used to enter the content, position, format, and other characteristics of a record. This is then used in writing code for a computer program.

Record length   The number of bytes in a record.

Records management   Planning and controlling the creation, deletion, processing, updating, storing, retrieving, and retention of data processing records.

Recoverable error   An error within a program that does not cause the program to stop processing. That is, it can be detected and corrected so that the program can continue operation.

Recovery procedures   A set of procedures that are followed if the computer quits in the middle of processing a batch of data. The procedures allow the user to recover from hardware or software failures.

Redundant data check An edit check that requires two identifiers to be included in each input record. An example might be the customer's account number and the first five letters of the customer's name. If these input values do not match, the record would not be updated.

Register A high-speed temporary storage location that is used in transferring instructions and data between memory and the control or the arithmetic-logic units.

Relational data base A data base model in which all data elements are logically viewed as being stored in the form of two-dimensional tables called relations. These tables are, in effect, flat files where each row represents a unique entity or record. Each column represents a field where the record's attributes are stored. The tables serve as the building blocks from which data relationships can be created.

Relationship The correspondence or association between entities in a data base.

Remittance advice An enclosure included with a customer's payment that indicates the invoices, statements, or other items paid.

Remote batch processing Accumulating transaction records in batches at some remote location and then transmitting them electronically to a central location for processing.

Remote job entry The process of entering data into a system from a remote location that is tied to the main computer by a communication link.

Remote terminal A device for communicating with a computer from sites that are physically separated from the computer. The remote terminal and the computer are tied together by communications links such as telephone lines.

Removable disk See *disk pack.*

Reorder point The level to which the inventory balance of an item must fall before an order to replenish the stock is initiated.

Repeating group The child record in a one-to-many relationship.

Report file A temporary file generated as an intermediate step in the preparation of a report.

Report generators Computer programs designed for making report writing easier and faster.

Report layout sheet A sheet of paper with a grid of empty spaces that is used to design the layout of a computer-generated report.

Report program generator (RPG) An easy-to-learn business-oriented programming language designed to help the user design reports. The program can also be used for other data processing tasks. Fairly simple RPG programs can perform rather sophisticated data processing tasks.

Reprocessing An approach auditors use to detect unauthorized program changes. The auditor verifies the integrity of an application program and then saves it for future use. At subsequent intervals, and on a surprise basis, the auditor uses the previously verified version of the program to reprocess data that have been processed by the version

used by the company. The output of the two runs is compared and discrepancies investigated.

Requirements costing In evaluating and selecting a system, a list is made of all the required features of the desired system. If a proposed system does not have a desired feature, the cost to develop or purchase that feature is added to the basic cost of the system. This allows different systems to be evaluated based upon the costs to provide the required features.

Resolution A term used to describe the density and overall quality of the display on a video terminal.

Response time The amount of time that elapses between making a query and receiving a response.

Responsibility accounting The reporting of financial results in accordance with the assignment of managerial responsibilities within an organization. There are three major factors in a responsibility accounting system: (1) assignment of managerial responsibility, (2) translation of responsibilities into a formal set of financial goals, and (3) a comparison of actual performance versus the established goals.

RGB monitor A color monitor. *RGB* stands for red, green, and blue.

Rigidity The tendency within an organization to resist change.

Ring network A configuration where the data communications channels form a loop or circular pattern when the local processors are linked together. Contrast with *star network.*

Robotics The utilization of programmable machines (robots) to manipulate tools, parts, or materials to perform a variety of production or other tasks.

Rollback A process whereby a log of all preupdate values is prepared for each record that is updated within a particular interval. Then if there is a system failure, the records can be restored to the preupdate values and the processing started over.

Root The upper-most record type in a tree or hierarchical data base structure.

Routing sheet See *operations list.*

RPG See *report program generator.*

RS-232 A name for the industry standard for serial communications between a computer and peripheral devices. One of the most common uses of RS-232 is for data communications.

Run manual A manual that contains the program logic, controls, operating instructions, and other information and documentation necessary to run a particular program.

Run time The time required for data to be retrieved and processed by a computer.

Sales analysis A report of actual sales that provides an information base for control and planning. Sales figures can be classified and reported in several different ways to meet the needs of different users.

Satellite microwave   A microwave data transmission system that transmits data between earth stations and satellites and back to earth again.

Scanning routine   A software routine that searches a program for the occurrence of a particular variable name or other combinations of characters.

Scheduling program   That part of the operating system that establishes priorities for all jobs and schedules and directs the flow of jobs through the system.

Schema   A description of the types of data elements that are in the data base, the relationships between the data elements, and the structure or overall logical model used to organize and describe the data.

Screen   The surface upon which information is displayed on a video display unit.

Scrolling   The movement of information on a video terminal up or down a row (or column) at a time. As the top row disappears the bottom row appears, and vice versa.

Secondary key   A field that can be used to identify records in a file. Unlike the primary key, it does not provide unique identification.

Secondary storage   Storage media like magnetic disks or magnetic tape where data that are not currently needed by the computer can be stored. Also referred to as *auxiliary storage.*

Self-checking digit   See *check digit.*

Semiconductor   A tiny silicon chip upon which a number of miniature circuits have been inscribed.

Semistructured decisions   Decisions that may be partially but not fully automated because they require subjective assessments and judgments in conjunction with formal data analysis and model building.

Separation of duties   The separation of assigned duties and responsibilities in such a way that no single employee can both perpetrate and conceal errors or irregularities.

Sequence check   An edit check that determines whether a batch of input data is in the proper numerical or alphabetical sequence.

Sequence code   A method of uniquely identifying items by assigning them a unique code in a specified (usually consecutively numbered) sequence.

Sequential-access method (SAM)   An access method that requires data items to be accessed in the same sequential order that they were written.

Serial port   A communications interface that only allows data to be sent one bit at a time. Contrast with *parallel port.*

Serial transmission   The transmission of data one bit at a time. Contrast with *parallel transmission.*

Service bureau   An organization that provides data processing services on its own equipment to users for a fee. Because many users are sharing the computer facilities of the service bureau, the cost to each user is only a fraction of the total cost of a computer system.

Sign check   An edit check that verifies that the data in a field are of the appropriate arithmetic sign.

Simple network   A network in which all the data relationships are one-to-many.

Simplex channel   A data transmission channel that allows data transmissions in only one direction. Contrast with *half-duplex* and *full-duplex channels.*

Simplex system   A centralized network with only one central processor. Contrast with *duplex system.*

Skills inventory file   A personnel data base that includes an index of the skills possessed by the company's employees.

Slack time   The amount of time that noncritical path activities in a PERT network may be delayed without extending the total project time. Critical path activities may not be delayed without delaying the total project completion time.

Small business computer   A stand-alone computer system that is designed to perform standard business applications such as order entry, inventory, payroll, or accounts receivable.

Software   A computer program that gives instructions to the CPU. The term *software* is also used to refer to programming languages and computer system documentation.

Software house   A company that specializes in software development, sales, and support.

Software license   A contract between the company who developed the software and the person who buys the software. It usually states that the user will only make archival backup copies of the software.

Software monitors   Programs that may be linked to the operating system in order to keep track of the utilization of various system resources.

Software package   A software program and related documentation that is available commercially.

Sort/merge programs   A computer program, often referred to as a utility program, that can either sort a file in a certain order or merge two or more sorted files into one file, or both.

Sorting of data   Arranging batches of input data into a desired numerical or alphabetical order.

Source code or program   A computer program written in a source language such as BASIC, COBOL, or assembly language. The source project is translated into the object (machine language) program by a translation program such as a compiler or assembler.

Source data automation (SDA)   The collection of transaction data in machine-readable form at the time and place of its origin. Examples of SDA devices are optical scanners and automated teller machines.

Source document   A document containing the initial record of a transaction that takes place. Examples of source documents, which are usually recorded on preprinted forms, include sales invoices, purchase orders, and employee time cards. Contrast with *operational document.*

Span of control   The number of subordinates reporting to a superior.

Specifications   An itemized description of an organization's data processing objectives and requirements. They are given to equipment, service, and software vendors to assist them in providing bids to the organization. Detailed specifications are the primary goal of an applications study. Also see *program specifications*.

Spooling   (1) The simultaneous operation of two or more input/output devices by the system. (2) Temporarily storing data on disk or tape files until another part of the system is ready to process it.

Spreadsheet package   See *electronic spreadsheet*.

Stand-alone system   A computer system that will operate without any help from other computers or peripheral devices.

Standard costs   The cost that should be incurred in producing a unit of product under efficient operating conditions.

Standard network architecture   A proposed system of standardized hardware, software, and communications channel interfaces.

Star network   A configuration in which there is a centralized real-time computer system to which all other computer systems are linked. Contrast with *ring network*.

Start bit   A bit used in asynchronous data transmission to signal the start of a character or set of data that is being transmitted. Compare with *stop bit*.

Stewardship function   The responsibility of providing accounting information to the owners (stockholders) of a company.

Stock status report   A report on each inventory item sold by the company, including information about items out of stock, items below minimum stock level, item turnover analysis, etc.

Stop bit   A bit used in asynchronous data transmission to signal the end of a character or set of data that is being transmitted. Compare with *start bit*.

Storage   Placing data in internal memory or on a medium such as magnetic disk, magnetic tape, or punched cards from which it can later be retrieved and used.

Storage capacity   The number of bytes or characters of data that a device can store.

Storage protection   Preventing stored data from being accidentally erased or destroyed. This is often a hardware protection like the write-protect tab on a floppy disk or the file protection ring on a magnetic tape.

Strategic planning   The process of deciding on an organization's objectives, on changes in these objectives, on the resources used to attain these objectives, and on the policies that are to govern the acquisition, use, and disposition of these resources.

Stratified sampling   A sampling approach where a population is divided into two or more groups to which different selection criteria can be applied.

Structured chart   See *HIPO chart*.

Structured decisions   Repetitive and routine decisions that are well enough understood to have been delegated to clerks or to have been automated on a computer. Contrast with *unstructured decisions*.

Structured programming   A modular approach to programming in which each module performs a specific function, stands alone, and is coordinated by a control module. It is also referred to as "GOTOless" programming because the modular design makes GOTO statements unnecessary.

Structured walk-through   A formal review process in program design in which one or more programmers walk through the logic and code of another programmer to detect weaknesses and errors in program design.

Suboptimization   A problem that occurs when an organizational subunit, by attempting to optimize its assigned subgoals, makes it harder for the organization as a whole to optimally accomplish its collective goal. This is generally caused by the inefficient breakdown of goals into subgoals.

Subroutine   A small program module within a program that is called as it is needed by the main program.

Subschema   A subset of the schema that includes only those data items used in a particular application program or by a particular user. It is also the way the user defines the data and the data relationships.

Subsidiary ledger   A computerized master file or, in a manual system, a book of accounting records for a specific category of accounts. For example, an accounts receivable subsidiary ledger.

Subvoice grade line   See *narrowband line*.

Summarization of data   A processing activity that aggregates pieces of data into meaningful totals or condensations.

Supercomputer   A very large high-speed computer used by businesses and organizations that have high-volume needs.

Supervisor program   The "chief executive officer" program of the operating system. It directs the operations of all other programs and is called upon to resolve conflicts between other components of the operating system.

Suspense file   A file containing records that have been identified as erroneous or that are of uncertain status.

Swapping   The process of bringing in a page of information from auxiliary storage to replace the information currently in memory.

Switched line   A regular dial-up telephone line. The charges for line usage are usually based upon the amount of time used and the length of line used.

Symbolic language   A language in which each machine instruction is represented by symbols that bear some relation to the instruction. For example, the symbol A might represent the ADD command.

Synchronous transmission   Data transmission where start and stop bits are required only at the beginning and end of a block of characters. Contrast with *asynchronous transmission*.

Synonym   A word having the same, or nearly the same, meaning as another in the language. A word or expression accepted as another name for something.

Syntax   The rules of grammar and structure that govern the use of a programming language.

Syntax errors   Errors that result from improper use of the programming language or from incorrectly typing the source program. Contrast with *logic errors*.

Synthesis   The system's development process that brings together the results of the systems survey and the systems analysis in order to recommend revisions to the existing system and/or to develop a new system. If the recommendations are accepted by management, work can proceed on a detailed system design.

System   (1) An entity consisting of two or more components or subsystems that interact to achieve a goal. (2) The equipment and programs that make up a complete computer installation. (3) The programs and related procedures that perform a single task on a computer.

Systems flowchart   A diagrammatical representation that shows the flow of data through a series of operations in an automated data processing system. It shows how data are captured and input into the system, the processes that operate on the data, and system outputs.

System reliability   The probability that a certain process will be completed without any errors.

System review   A determination as to whether necessary procedures are prescribed.

Systems analysis   (1) A rigorous and systematic approach to decision making, characterized by a comprehensive definition of available alternatives and an exhaustive analysis of the merits of each alternative as a basis for choosing the best alternative. (2) Examining user information requirements within an organization in order to establish objectives and specifications for the design of an information system.

Systems analysts   The people within an organization who are responsible for the development of the company's information system. The analyst's job generally involves the design of computer applications and the preparation of specifications for computer programming.

Systems concept   The choices among alternative courses of action within a system that must be evaluated from the standpoint of the system as a whole rather than any single subsystem or set of subsystems.

Systems design   The process of preparing detailed specifications for the development of a new information system.

Systems documentation   A complete description of all aspects of each systems application, including narrative material, charts, and program listings.

Systems software   Software that interfaces between the hardware and the application program. Systems software can be classified as operating systems, data base management systems, utility programs, language translators, and communications software.

Systems survey   The systematic gathering of facts relating to the existing information system. This is generally carried out by a systems analyst.

Table file   A file of reference data (generally numeric) that is retrieved during data processing to facilitate calculations or other processing tasks.

Tagging   An audit procedure where certain records are marked with a special code before processing. During processing, all data relating to the marked records are captured and saved so that they can be verified later by the auditors.

Tape drive   The device that controls the movement of the magnetic tape and that reads and writes the tape.

Tape file protection ring   A circular plastic ring that determines when a tape file can be written upon. When the ring is inserted on a reel of magnetic tape, data can be written on the tape. If the ring is removed, the data on the tape cannot be overwritten with new information.

Technical feasibility   The process of deciding whether or not a proposed system is feasible, given the available technology.

Telecommunications   See *data communications*.

Telecommunications system   An information system making use of data communications technology.

Teleconferencing   The ability to have a conference involving a number of different people in different locations by linking them together electronically so they can communicate.

Teleprinter   An automatic printing device that provides a typed copy of the input or output.

Teleprocessing system   A system where remote users are connected to the company's central computer by data communications lines.

Template   A general-purpose spreadsheet application, with appropriate headings, formulas, functions, and other logic, that is saved so it can be reused at a later date.

Terabytes   A trillion characters of memory.

Terminal   An input/output device for entering or receiving data directly from the computer. Also referred to as *cathode-ray tube* (CRT) or *visual display terminal* (VDT).

Terminal emulator   A microcomputer that uses communications software to emulate a dedicated terminal.

Terrestrial microwave system   A microwave data transmission system that utilizes transmission facilities located on the earth instead of using satellites.

Test data   Data that have been specially developed to test the accuracy and completeness of a computer program. The results from the test data are compared with hand-calculated results to verify that the program operates properly.

Test data generator   A program that, based upon specifications describing the logic characteristics of the program to be tested, automatically generates a set of test data that can be used to check the logic of the program.

Tests of compliance   A test performed by the auditor to determine the effectiveness of the internal controls.

Thermal printer   A printer that uses heat to transfer characters to heat-sensitive paper.

Thimble printer   A printer that operates like a daisy wheel printer except that the print element looks like a thimble.

Throughput   The total amount of useful work performed by a computer system during a given period of time.

Time-sharing   A concept where small slices of CPU time from a large mainframe computer are sold to a number of small users.

Time-sharing vendors   An organization that for a fee allows users to access a central computer and online file storage using remote terminals or computers and telecommunications lines.

Top-down approach   An approach to developing an information system that develops a definition of the organization's objectives and strategies and then develops a system based upon what is needed for decision making.

Touch-sensitive screens   A screen that allows users to enter data or select menu items by touching the surface of a sensitized video display screen with their finger or with a special pointer.

Track   The horizontal rows on magnetic tape. A typical tape will have nine tracks, eight for data characters and one for the parity bit.

Tractor-feed printer   A printer that uses pins to pull the paper through the printer. Since the pin assemblies are movable, more than one paper width can be used. Contrast with *pin-feed printer*.

Trailer label or record   A record at the end of a file containing data about the file such as control totals.

Transaction   An agreement between two entities to exchange goods or services having some measurable economic value.

Transaction code   A code that identifies what kind of transaction is contained within the record.

Transaction file   A relatively temporary data file containing transaction data that is typically used to update a master file.

Transaction log   A detailed record of every transaction entered in a system with data entry.

Transaction processing cycle   See *accounting cycle*.

Transaction trail   See *audit trail*.

Transcription of data   Transferring data from one form to another, such as from a paper document to a magnetic medium.

Translator   See *language translator*.

Transmssion of data   Sending data from one location to another.

Transposition error   An error that results when the numbers in two adjacent columns are inadvertently exchanged (for example, 64 rather than 46).

Tree   A data structure, or logical data model, in which relationships among data items are expressed in the form of an hierarchical structure.

TRS-DOS   The operating system used by Tandy (Radio Shack) computers.

Tuple   A row in a relational data base.

Turnaround document   A humanly readable document that is prepared by the computer as output, sent outside the system, and then returned as input into the computer. An example is a utility bill.

Turnkey system   A system that is delivered to customers and is (theoretically) ready to use by simply turning it on. A turnkey system supplier buys hardware, writes application software that is tailored both to that equipment and to the specific needs of its customers, and then markets the entire system.

Uninterruptible power systems   An alternative power supply device that protects against loss of power and fluctuations in the power level.

Universal Product Code (UPC)   A machine-readable code that is read by optical scanners. The code consists of a series of bar codes and is printed on most products sold in grocery stores.

UNIX   A flexible and widely used operating system for sixteen-bit machines.

Unstructured decisions   A type of management decision characterized by nonrecurring and nonroutine decisions. The decision maker must rely primarily on judgment and intuition to make the decision. Contrast with *structured decisions*.

Updating   Changing stored data to reflect more recent events. For example, changing the accounts receivable balance because of a recent sale or collection. See *file maintenance*.

Upward compatible   A phrase used to describe a hardware device that can perform anything a previous model could do. A company can upgrade to a new model and still process the software and data files used on the old model.

Usage variance   That portion of a total variance attributable to a deviation from some standard amount of usage. For example, labor hours or material quantities.

User schema or view   See *subschema*.

Users group   A group of people who get together and share information and programs for a certain kind of computer.

Utility program   A set of prewritten programs that perform a variety of file and data handling tasks and other housekeeping chores. Examples include sorting files, merging files, and transferring data from one file to another.

Validity check An edit test in which an identification number or transaction code is validated by comparing it against a table of valid identification numbers or codes maintained in computer memory.

Variable costs Costs that rise or fall in proportion to increases or decreases in the level of activity.

Variable data Data that must be inserted on a preprinted form.

Variable-length record A record whose length (size) can vary depending on how many fields are included in a record or on the size of the fields. They are used when the amount of data to be stored per record differs. Compare with *fixed-length record*.

Variance The difference between actual and budgeted dollar amounts for each item on a budget.

Verification of data Using a variety of procedures to check the accuracy of data prior to submitting them for processing.

Very large scale integration (VLSI) A process where a large number (1000 or more) of integrated circuits are placed on one chip.

Videotex A data communications service utilizing a telephone, a television, and a special decoder to provide access to a public data base. Possible uses include electronic shopping, electronic banking, and electronic newspaper delivery.

Virtual memory (storage) A process where online secondary storage is considered an extension of primary memory, thus giving the appearance of a larger, "virtually unlimited" amount of internal memory. Pages of data or program instructions are swapped back and forth between secondary and primary storage as needed. See *paging*.

Visual display terminal (VDT) See *terminal*.

Voice input A data input unit that recognizes human voices and converts spoken messages into machine-readable input.

Voice mail A service that converts voice messages into computer data and stores them so that they can be retrieved later by the person for whom the message was intended.

Voice response unit See *audio response unit*.

Voiceband line A phone line designed to accept data transmissions between 300 and 9600 bits per second. They can be used for transmitting voice or data communications.

Volatility The relative frequency of additions, deletions, and other transactions requiring reference to a particular master file during a specified time period. That is, the total number of transactions relating to a file divided by a standard unit of time.

Volume label An internal label that identifies the contents of each separate data recording medium, such as a tape, diskette, or disk pack.

Voucher A document that summarizes the data relating to a disbursement and represents final authorization of payment.

Vouching Examining the accuracy of documents and records, especially by tracing the information through the processing system to its source.

Walk-through A meeting attended by those associated with a project, in which a detailed review of systems procedures and/or program logic is carried out in a step-by-step manner.

WATS line An acronym for Wide-Area Telephone Service line, a phone line where the customer pays a fixed charge to use the line and then pays an additional charge that varies directly with the amount of extra usage.

Wideband line See *broadband line*.

Window A portion of the CRT screen that is dedicated to a specific purpose.

Word A group of bytes moved and processed by a computer. The most common size for large computers is thirty-two bits, and for smaller computers, it is sixteen bits.

Word length The number of bits, characters, or bytes in a computer word.

Word processing A program that facilitates the creation, processing, editing, formatting, and printing of text data.

Work distribution analysis A systems design technique that uses the total time requirements of all processing cycle activities to equitably allocate system tasks to workers in an organization.

Work measurement Gathering and utilizing data on the amount of time required for an employee to perform a certain job.

Wraparound The ability to have information that is being displayed on the video screen move to the beginning of the next line after it reaches the end of the previous line.

Write The process of recording data on some storage medium.

Write head The magnetic head designed to write information to a tape or disk. Usually, a single read/write head is used instead of two separate heads.

Write-protect notch The notch on a floppy disk that must be uncovered before information can be written to the disk. If the notch is covered, information can only be read from the disk.

XENIX An operating system designed to allow multiple uses and to allow a user to run several programs at the same time.

Xerographic printer A printer that uses dry ink to form characters on electrically charged paper.

Zero-balance check An internal check that requires the balance of the payroll control account to be zero after all entries to it are made.

Index